Harry Tatone 5.⁶⁰

5/85

THE EPISTLE TO THE HEBREWS

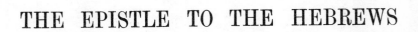

THE
EPISTLE TO THE HEBREWS

THE GREEK TEXT

WITH NOTES AND ESSAYS

BY THE LATE

BROOKE FOSS WESTCOTT, D.D., D.C.L.

LORD BISHOP OF DURHAM

SOMETIME REGIUS PROFESSOR OF DIVINITY
IN THE UNIVERSITY OF CAMBRIDGE

WM. B. EERDMANS PUBLISHING COMPANY
GRAND RAPIDS   MICHIGAN

Βλεπετε μὴ παραιτήcηcθε τὸν λαλοῦντα· εἰ γὰρ ἐκεῖνοι οὐκ
ἐξέφυγον ἐπὶ γῆc παραιτηcάμενοι τὸν χρηματίζοντα, πολὺ μᾶλλον
ἡμεῖc οἱ τὸν ἀπ οὐρανῶν ἀποcτρεφόμενοι.

Hebr. xii. 25.

Cήμερον ἐὰν τῆc φωνῆc αὐτοῦ ἀκούcητε,
μὴ cκληρύνητε τὰc καρδίαc ὑμῶν.

Ps. xcv. 7 ; *Hebr.* iii. iv.

This edition is published
by special arrangement with
THE MACMILLAN COMPANY

Reprinted, January 1984

ISBN 0-8028-3289-X

PHOTOLITHOPRINTED BY EERDMANS PRINTING COMPANY
GRAND RAPIDS, MICHIGAN, UNITED STATES OF AMERICA

EVERY student of the Epistle to the Hebrews must feel that it deals in a peculiar degree with the thoughts and trials of our own time. The situation of Jewish converts on the eve of the destruction of Jerusalem was necessarily marked by the sorest distress. They had looked with unhesitating confidence for the redemption of Israel and for the restoration of the Kingdom to the people of God; and in proportion as their hope had been bright, their disappointment was overwhelming when these expectations, as they had fashioned them, were finally dispelled.

They were deprived of the consolations of their ancestral ritual: they were excluded from the fellowship of their countrymen: the letter of Scripture had failed them: the Christ remained outwardly unvindicated from the judgment of high-priests and scribes; and a storm was gathering round the Holy City which to calm eyes boded utter desolation without any prospect of relief. The writer of the Epistle enters with the tenderest sympathy into every cause of the grief and dejection which troubled his countrymen, and transfigures each sorrow into an occasion for a larger hope through a new revelation of the glory of Christ. So it will be still, I cannot doubt, in this day of our own visitation if we look, as he directs us, to the Ascended Lord. The difficulties which come to us through physical facts and theories, through criticism, through wider views of human history, correspond with those which came to Jewish Christians at the close of the Apostolic age, and they will find their solution also in fuller views of the Person and Work of Christ. The promise of the Lord awaits fulfilment for us in this present day, as it found fulfilment for them: *In your patience ye shall win your souls.*

This conviction has been constantly present to me in commenting on the Epistle. I have endeavoured to suggest in the notes lines of thought which I have found to open light upon problems which we are required to face. In doing this it has throughout been my desire to induce my readers to become my fellow-students, and I have aimed at encouraging sustained reflection rather than at entering on the field of controversy. No conclusion is of real value to us till we have made it our own by serious work; and controversy tends no less to narrow our vision than to give to forms of language or conception that rigidity of outline which is fatal to the presentation of life.

Some perhaps will think that in the interpretation of the text undue stress is laid upon details of expression; that it is unreasonable to insist upon points of order, upon variations of tenses and words, upon subtleties of composition, upon indications of meaning conveyed by minute variations of language in a book written for popular use in a dialect largely affected by foreign elements. The work of forty years has brought to me the surest conviction that such criticism is wholly at fault. Every day's study of the Apostolic writings confirms me in the belief that we do not commonly attend with sufficient care to their exact meaning. The Greek of the New Testament is not indeed the Greek of the Classical writers, but it is not less precise or less powerful. I should not of course maintain that the fulness of meaning which can be recognised in the phrases of a book like the Epistle to the Hebrews was consciously apprehended by the author, though he seems to have used the resources of literary art with more distinct design than any other of the Apostles; but clearness of spiritual vision brings with it a corresponding precision and force of expression through which the patient interpreter can attain little by little to that which the prophet saw. No one would limit the teaching of a poet's words to that which was definitely present to his mind. Still less can we suppose that he who is inspired to give a message of GOD to all ages sees himself the completeness of the truth which all life serves to illuminate.

I have not attempted to summarise in the notes the opinions of modern commentators. This has been done fairly and in detail by Lünemann. Where I feel real doubt, I have given the various views which seem to me to claim consideration: in other cases I have, for the most part, simply stated the conclusions which I have gained. I have however freely quoted patristic comments, and that in the original texts. Every quotation which I have given has, I believe, some feature of interest; and the trouble of mastering the writer's own words will be more than compensated by a sense of their force and beauty.

It did not appear to fall within my scope to discuss the authorship of the Commentary which I have quoted under the name of Primasius (Migne, *P. L.* lxviii). The Commentary is printed also under the name of Haymo (Migne, *P. L.* cxvii) with some variations, and in this text the lacuna in the notes on c. iv. is filled up.

As far as I have observed the Commentary of Herveius Burgidolensis ('of Bourg-Dieu or Bourg-Deols in Berry' † 1149, Migne, *P. L.* clxxxi) has not been used before. The passages which I have given will shew that for vigour and independence and sobriety and depth he is second to no mediæval expositor. I regret that I have not given notes from Atto of Vercelli († c. 960, Migne, *P. L.* cxxxiv). His commentary also will repay examination[1].

[1] The following summary enumeration of the chief patristic Commentaries may be of some use:

i. GREEK.

ORIGEN. Of his xviii Homilies and Books (τόμοι) on the Epistle only meagre fragments remain; but it is not unlikely that many of his thoughts have been incorporated by other writers. An investigation into the sources of the Latin Commentaries is greatly to be desired.

THEODORE OF MOPSUESTIA. The Greek fragments have been printed by Migne, *P. G.* lxvi, pp. 651 ff.

CHRYSOSTOM. xxxiv Homilies. These were translated into Latin by Mutianus Scholasticus at the request of Cassiodorus (c. 500), and this translation was largely used by Western writers.

It would be impossible for me to estimate or even to determine my debts to other writers. I cannot however but acknowledge gratefully how much I owe both to Delitzsch and to Riehm. The latter writer appears to me to have seized more truly than any one the general character and teaching of the Epistle.

For illustrations from Philo I am largely indebted to the *Exercitationes* of J. B. Carpzov (1750), who has left few parallels unnoticed. But I have always seemed to learn most from Trommius and Bruder. If to these Concordances—till the former is superseded by the promised Oxford Concordance—the student adds Dr Moulton's edition of Winer's Grammar and Dr Thayer's edition of Grimm's Lexicon, he will find that he has at his command a fruitful field of investigation which yields to every effort fresh signs of the inexhaustible wealth of the Written Word[1].

THEODORET. Migne, *P. G.* lxxxii.
JOHN OF DAMASCUS. Migne, *P. G.* xcv.
ŒCUMENIUS. Migne, *P. G.* cxix.
EUTHYMIUS ZIGABENUS, ed. N. Calogeras, Athens 1887.
THEOPHYLACT. Migne, *P. G.* cxxv.

ii. LATIN.

PRIMASIUS. Migne, *P. L.* lxviii. Also under the name of HAYMO. Migne, *P. L.* cxvii.
CASSIODORUS (a few notes). Migne, *P. L.* lxx.
ALULFUS. Migne, *P. L.* lxxix. (a collection of passages from Gregory the Great).
ALCUIN. Migne, *P. L.* c. (on cc. i—x. chiefly from Chrysostom [Primasius]).
SEDULIUS SCOTUS. Migne, *P. L.* ciii.
RABANUS MAURUS. Migne, *P.L.* cxii. (chiefly extracts from Chrysostom).
WALAFRID STRABO. Migne, *P. L.* cxiv. (*Glossa Ordinaria*).

FLORUS DIACONUS. Migne, *P. L.* cxix. (a collection of passages from Augustine). Assigned also to Bede and Robertus de Torreneio (Migne, *P. L.* ccii).
ATTO OF VERCELLI. Migne, *P. L.* cxxxiv. Old materials are used with independence and thought.
BRUNO. Migne, *P. L.* cliii.
LANFRANC. Migne, *P. L.* cl.
HUGO DE S. VICTORE. Migne, *P.L.* clxxv. (Interesting discussions on special points.)
HERVEIUS BURGIDOLENSIS. Migne, *P. L.* clxxxi. (of the highest interest).
PETER LOMBARD. Migne, *P. L.* cxcii. (*Collectanea*).
THOMAS AQUINAS. It would be of considerable interest to compare the Latin translation of Chrysostom with the notes of Primasius (Haymo), Alcuin and Atto.

[1] For the Index I am indebted to my son, the Rev. G. H. Westcott, M.A., now of the S.P.G. Mission, Cawnpore.

No work in which I have ever been allowed to spend many years of continuous labour has had for me the same intense human interest as the study of the Epistle to the Hebrews. If this feeling, which must shew itself in what I have written, moves others to work upon the book with frank and confident reverence, to listen to the voice which speaks to us 'to-day' from its pages, to bring to the doubts, the controversies, the apparent losses, which distress us, the spirit of absolute self-surrender to our King-priest, the living and glorified Christ, which it inspires, my end will be fully gained. Such students will join with me in offering a devout thanksgiving to GOD that He has made a little plainer to us, through lessons which have seemed to be a stern discipline, words which express the manifold experience of life and its final interpretation:

πολυμερῶς καὶ πολυτρόπως πάλαι ὁ Θεὸς λαλήσας τοῖς πατράσιν ἐν τοῖς προφήταις ἐπ᾽ ἐσχάτου τῶν ἡμερῶν τούτων ἐλάλησεν ἡμῖν ἐν υἱῷ.

B. F. W.

WESTMINSTER,
August 26, 1889.

NOTICE TO SECOND EDITION.

THE present Edition is essentially a reprint of the former one. I have indeed endeavoured to make one or two notes clearer, and I have noticed one or two new facts. The kindness of friends, among whom I may again mention Dr C. J. Beard and the Rev. H. A. Brooksbank, has enabled me to correct many misprints in references. To the former I am also indebted for additions to the Index.

The engrossing cares of new work have made it impossible for me to consider afresh conclusions which I formed when I was able to study all the materials which I thought likely to contribute to a right decision; but indeed in any case I should have been unwilling to do more than remove unquestionable errors in the revision of a Commentary which, however imperfect, was the best I was able to make when I was wholly occupied by the subject.

The more I study the tendencies of the time in some of the busiest centres of English life, the more deeply I feel that the Spirit of GOD warns us of our most urgent civil and spiritual dangers through the prophecies of Jeremiah and the Epistle to the Hebrews. May our Nation and our Church be enabled to learn the lessons which they teach while there is still time to use them.

B. F. D.

ROBIN HOOD'S BAY,
Sept. 12*th*, 1892.

CONTENTS

INTRODUCTION TO THE EPISTLE

I. TEXT.

THE original authorities for determining the text of the Epistle Original authorities. are, as in the case of the other books of the New Testament, numerous and varied. There are however, from the circumstances of the history of the Epistle, comparatively few patristic quotations from it, and these within a narrow range, during the first three centuries.

The Epistle is contained in whole or in part in the following sources :

1. GREEK MSS. 1 GREEK MSS.
i Primary Uncials.

    (i) *Primary uncials :*

        ℵ, Cod. Sin. sæc. IV. Complete.

        A, Cod. Alex. sæc. V. Complete.

        B, Cod. Vatic. sæc. IV. The MS. is defective after ix. 14 καθα[ριεῖ]. ['Manus multo recentior supplevit.' This text is sometimes quoted by Tischendorf as *b, e. g.* ix. 18; x. 4, 23; xi. 15; xii. 24.]

        C, Cod. Ephr. sæc. V. Contains ii. 4 μερισμοῖς—vii. 26 ἄκακος. ix. 15 ἐστίν—x. 24 ἀγά[πης]. xii. 16 μή τις —xiii. 25 Ἀμήν.

        D₂, Cod. Clarom. sæc. VI. Complete. (E₃ is a copy of D₂ after it had been thrice corrected.)

        H₂, Cod. Coislin. sæc. VI. Contains i. 3 ῥήματι—8 εἰς τόν. ii. 11 δι᾽ ἥν—16 Ἀβραάμ. iii. 13 ἄχρις—18 μὴ εἰσε. iv. 12 ζῶν—15 ἡμῶν. x. 1 τῶν [μελλό]ντων—7 θέλημά σου. x. 32 [ὑπε]μείνατε—38 ἡ ψυχή μου. xii. 10 οἱ μέν—15 πολλοί (with some gaps). The scattered fragments have been edited by H. Omont, Paris 1859. Fa (sæc. VII) contains only x. 26.

(ii) *Secondary uncials :*

K$_2$, Cod. Mosqu. sæc. IX. Complete.

L$_2$, Cod. Angel. sæc. IX. Complete to xiii. 10 οὐκ ἔχουσιν.

M$_2$, (Hamb. Lond.) sæc. IX, x. Contains i. 1 πολυμερῶς— iv. 3 εἰς τήν. xii. 20 [λιθο]βολισθήσεται—xiii. 25 Ἀμήν.

N$_2$, (St Petersburg) sæc. IX. Contains v. 8 [ἔ]παθεν—vi. 10 ἐπιλαθέσ[θαι].

P$_2$, Cod. Porphyr. sæc. IX. Complete (xii. 9, 10 illegible).

To these must be added MSS., as yet imperfectly known, which have been described by Dr C. R. Gregory.

Ψ Cod. Athous Lauræ sæc. VIII, IX. Complete with the exception of one leaf containing viii. 11 καὶ οὐ μή—ix. 19 Μωυσέως.

Ɔ Cod. Rom. Vat. sæc. V. Contains xi. 32—xiii. 4.

The Epistle is not contained in the Greek-Latin MSS. F$_2$ (Cod. Aug. sæc. IX) and G$_3$ (Cod. Boern. sæc. IX). The last verses of Philemon (21—25) are wanting in the Greek text of both MSS. F$_2$ gives the Latin (Vulgate) version of the Epistle. G$_3$ |has after Philemon 20 in Christo

ἐν. $\overline{χρω}$

ad   laudicenses   incipit   epistola

Προς λαουδακησας. αρχεται ἐπιστολη (sic Matthæi).

The archetype of the MSS. was evidently mutilated before either of the copies was written, so that there is no reason to suppose that this note was derived from it.

The following unique readings of the chief MSS. offer instructive illustrations of their character. Readings which are supported by some late MS. evidence are enclosed in ( ).

Unique readings :

(*a*) Of ℵ.

i. 5 *om.* αὐτῷ.

ii. 18 *om.* πειρασθείς.

iii. 8 πιρασμῷ (for παραπικρασμῷ).

iv. 6 ἀπιστίαν.

    7 ὁρ. τινα.

    9 *om. vers.* add. A.

    11 *om.* τις add. C.

vii. 21 *om.* εἰς τὸν αἰῶνα.

viii. 3 *om.* καί 2⁰.

ix. 5 ἔνεστιν (ἔστιν).

x. 7 *om.* ἥκω.

    12 ἐκ δεξία.

    18 ἀφεις (ἄφεσις), *om.* τούτων.

    26 τῆς ἐπιγνωσίαν τῆς.

    32 τὰς πρ. ἁμαρτίας.

    36 χρείαν (χρι-) ἔχετε   κομίσασθαι.

    39 ἀπωλίας.

xi. 31 ἡ + ἐπιλεγομένη΄ π.

xii. 1 τηλικοῦτον (τοσοῦτον).

    2 *om.* τοῦ θεοῦ.

    10 ὁ μὲν γάρ.   *om.* εἰς τό.

None of these readings have the least plausibility. Most of them are obvious blunders, and many have been corrected by later hands.

(*b*) Of A.

ii. 15 ἀποκαταλλάξῃ (ἀπαλλάξῃ).

iii. 9 οἱ π. ἡμῶν.

    17 τίσιν δὲ + καί.

iv. 3 *om.* ὡς ?   *om.* εἰ.

    4 *om.* ἐν τ. ἡ. τ. ἑβδ.

viii. 1 ἐν τ. λεγ.

x. 29 *om.* ἐν ᾧ ἡγιάσθη.

xi. 1 βουλομένων (βλεπομένων).

    13 προσδεξάμενοι.

    23 δόγμα ?

    39 τὰς ἐπαγγελίας (-είας).

xii. 8 νόθροι.

    22 οὐ γάρ (ἀλλά)   ἐπουρανίων.

    27 *om.* ἵνα μ. τὰ μὴ σαλ.

xiii. 11 *om.* περὶ ἁμαρτίας.

    21 παντὶ + ἔργῳ καὶ λόγῳ ΄ἀγ.

Of these again no one possesses any intrinsic probability, and several are transcriptional errors.

(*c*) Of B.

i. 3 φανερῶν.

    4 *om.* τῶν.

    (8 *om.* τοῦ αἰῶνος.)

    14 διακονίας.

ii. 4 συνμαρτυροῦντος.

    8 *om.* αὐτῷ (1).

iv. (7 προείρηκεν.)

    8 οὐκ ἄρα.

    9 ἀπόλειται (ἀπολείπεται).

    12 ἐναργής.

    16 *om.* εὔρωμεν.

vii. 2 παντός.

    12 *om.* καὶ νόμου.

    15 *om.* τήν.

viii. 7 ἑτέρας (δευτέρας).

    (9 ἡμέραις.)

ix. 2 + τὰ´ ἄγια.

Even though no one of these readings may give the original text, few are mere blunders.

(*d*) Of C.

iv. 8 μετ᾽ αὐτά (comp. v. 3).

    12 ζῶ (zω for zω̂).

(ix. 20 διέθετο (ἐντείλατο).)

xiii. 7 ἀναθεωρήσαντες.

(*e*) The peculiar readings of D₂ are far too numerous, especially in chapters x.—xiii. to be given in detail. A few examples must suffice :

ii. 4 τοῦ θεοῦ (αὐτοῦ).

    14 τῶν αὐ. + παθημάτων. θανάτου + θάνατον.

iii. 13 ἁμαρτίαις (τῆς ἁμ.).

iv. 11 εἰσ. + ἀδελφοί. ἀληθείας (ἀπειθείας).

vi. 18 μετά (διά).

vii. 27 ὁ ἀρχιερεύς.

ix. 9 ἥτις + πρώτη.

    18 ἡ πρ. + διαθήκη.

    23 καθαρίζεται.

x. 1 καθαρίσαι (τελειῶσαι).

    10 αἵματος (σώματος).

    26 περιλείπεται θυσίαν περὶ ἁμαρτίας προσενενκῖν.

    33 ὀνιδιζόμενοι (θεατριζόμενοι).

    35 ἀπολύητε (ἀποβάλητε).

xi. 23 Add. πίστι μέγας γενόμενος Μωυσῆς ἀνῖλεν τὸν Αἰγύπτιον κατανοῶν τὴν ταπίνωσιν τῶν ἀδελφῶν αὐτοῦ.

xii. 23 τεθεμελιωμένων (τετελειωμένων).

    (28 εὐχαρίστως (εὐαρέστως).)

    29 κύριος γάρ (καὶ γάρ).

xiii. 11 καταναλίσκονται (κατακαίεται).

    17 ἀποδώσονται περὶ ὑμῶν (ἀποδώσοντες).

    25 τῶν ἁγίων (ὑμῶν).

These variations it will be seen are wholly different in character, and have more the character of glosses than true variants.

Compare also i. 7, 9; iii. 1; iv. 1, 5, 12, 13, 16; v. 2, 7, 11, 12, 13; vi. 2, 6, 10, 12, 19, 20; vii. 6, 13, 18, 19, 20, 24; viii. 9; ix. 1, 5, 13, 14, 26, 28; x. 3, 7, 20, 25, 28, 32, 37; xi. 1, 4, 9, 11, 12, 14, 15, 32, 33, 36; xii. 2, 7, 10, 11, 17, 22, 25; xiii. 3, 6, 7, 8, 16, 21, 22.

The dual combinations of the primary uncials are all of interest:

$\aleph$B   i. 8; vi. 3; vii. 23; viii. 10, 12; ix. 2, 3, 10.

BC   vii. 21.

BD$_2$ iv. 3; v. 3; vi. 2; vii. 4, 5; viii. 6; ix. 11.

$\aleph$A   i. 9; vii. 27; ix. 24; x. (34), 38; xi. 12, 38.

AC   iii. 13; iv. 3; vi. 7; vii. (6), 13; x. 11; xiii. 21.

AD$_2$ ix. 14; x. 34; xi. 8.

$\aleph$C   v. 12; vii. 26; xiii. 6.

$\aleph$D$_2$ i. 12; x. 30; xii. 3, 21; xiii. 21.

CD$_2$ iv. 12; vii. 9.

Compare also

$\aleph$ vg ii. 1; iv. 6; $\aleph$ syrr vi. 9; $\aleph$ ægg. ix. 25; D$_2$ vg x. 23.

A vg iii. 14.

B vg viii. 10; B d vi. 2; B ægg. iii. 2; B æth iii. 6; B verss ix. 1, 4.

C vg ii. 5 (6).

The selection of readings given below the text will indicate fairly, I believe, the extent of early variations, but it will not supersede the use of a full critical apparatus.

(iii)   *Cursives :*

iii *Cursives.*

Nearly three hundred (Scrivener, *Introd.* 264 ff.) are known more or less completely, including 17 (Cod. Colb. sæc. XI, = 33 Gosp.), 37 (Cod. Leicestr. sæc. XIV), 47 (Cod. Bodl. sæc. XI), which have been collated by Dr Tregelles for his edition of the Greek Testament.

The MS. 11 (Acts 9 Stephens $\iota\gamma'$) of the Cambridge University Library MS. 11. (Kk. VI. 4) contains some remarkable and unique readings (compare Addit. Note on 1 John ii. 20).

ii.   8 ὑπὸ τοὺς πόδας αὐτοῦ.

    10 τὸν ἀρχηγὸν τῆς σωτηρίας αὐτόν.

    18 ἐν ᾧ (add. γὰρ 1ª m. ?) πέπονθεν αὐτὸς τοῖς πειραζομένοις δύναται βοηθῆσαι.

iii.   13 ἐξ ὑμῶν τις.

iv.   4 *om.* ἐν.

v.   12 λόγων (given by Stephens).

The MS. is at present defective from vii. 20 γεγονότες to xi. 10 τοὺς θεμ.

ἔχουσαν, and again from xi. 23 ὑπὸ τῶν to the end.   This mutilation is
later than the time of Stephens, who quotes from it on :

    ix. 3 τὰ ἅγια τῶν ἁγίων.

        15 λάβωσιν οἱ κληρονόμοι.

    x. 6 ἐζήτησας.

        34 ἔχειν ἑαυτοῖς.

    xii. 28 λατρεύομεν.

    xiii. 15 ἀναφέρομεν.

MS. 67**.   The surprising coincidences of the corrections in 67 (67**) with M_2 give
a peculiar value to its readings of 67** where M_2 is defective.   It agrees
with M_2 in two readings which are not found in any other Greek MS :

    i. 3 om. αὐτοῦ.

    ii. 9 χωρίς.

See also, i. 2 ἐσχάτου.   3 om. ἡμῶν.   11 διαμενεῖς.   iii. 1 om. Χριστόν.   4
om. τά.   6 ὅς (?).   10 ταύτῃ.   xii. 25 οὐρανοῦ.   26 σείσω.   xiii. 18 πειθόμεθα.
On the other hand it is quoted as giving i. 7 πνεῦμα.   iii. 14 πίστεως.
17 om. τεσσ. ἔτη.   It would be interesting to learn whether all these
corrections are in the same hand.

The following readings are remarkable :

    v. 12 om. τίνα (unique).

    vii. 4 om. οὗτος (D_2*).

    ix. 14 ἁγίου (D_2* Latt.).

        23 καθαρίζεται (D_2* me).

    xi. 4 om. εἶναι (unique).

        37 ἐν μηλ. καὶ αἰγείοις.

    xii. 18 om. καὶ (κεκαυμ.) D_2*.

See also iv. 12 ; vi. 10 ; vii. 17 ; viii. 4 ; ix. 9 ; x. 12, 15 ; xi. 5, 26 ; xii. 15.
The corrections appear to shew the eclectic judgment of one or more
scholars ; and suggest some interesting questions as to the texts of later
MSS.

2 VER-
SIONS.
i Latin.   2. VERSIONS.

    i. *Latin :*

        The Epistle is preserved entire in two Latin Texts.

(a) The
Old Latin.   (a) *The Old Latin.*

        d (Cod. Clarom.), the Latin Version of D_2 ; of which
          e (Cod. Sangerm.) is a copy with a few corrections.

The Greek text represented by d corresponds for the most part
with D_2 (*e.g.* i. 7 ; ii. 14 ; iv. 11, 16 ; vi. 10, 20 ; vii. 1 f., 20 ; ix.
(5), 9, 10, 11, 18 ; x. 1, 3, 6, 7, 26, (33,) 38 ; xi. 23 ; xii. 22, 23, 26,
29 ; xiii. 17)); but in many places it differs from it (*e.g.* i. 9 ; ii. 4,

6, 8; iii. 1, 13; iv. 12, 13; v. 6, 7, 11; vi. 1, 2, 18, 19; vii. 11, 13, 27; viii. 9; ix. 23; xi. 13, 32; xiii. 2, 20). In some of these cases the difference may be due to errors in the transcription of D_2 (*e.g.* i. 9; iii. 1, (13); iv. 12, 13; vi. 1, (18); viii. 9, &c.); but elsewhere the difference points to a variation in a Greek text anterior to the archetype of D_2 (*e.g.* ii. 4, 6, 8; v. 6, (7,) 11; vi. 2; vii. 11, 27; ix. 23; xi. 13) and even to a misreading of it (vi. 10; xiii. 2).

The text of *d* has been given by Delarue [under Sabatier's name] in *Bibl. Lat. Vers. Ant.* III. (but far less accurately than by Tischendorf in his edition of *Cod. Clarom.*, 1852) with the variations of *e*, and a large collection of Patristic quotations; but the genealogy of the early Latin texts has still to be determined with the help of a fuller apparatus.

Where it differs from the Vulgate *d* most frequently witnesses to an older Greek text (*e.g.* i. 12; ii. 4, 8; iii. 9, 13; vi. 2, 7; viii. 2, 11; ix. 11; x. 9; xi. 3), yet not always (*e.g.* i. 7; iii. 17; vii. 23; viii. 12; ix. 2; xi. 4). See also vi. 17; vii. 20; viii. 10; ix. 10; x. 28, 38; xi. 18, 32; xii. 3, 26.

The Latin versions of the Epistle offer a subject for most instructive Latin quotations. study, which has not yet been adequately dealt with. The earliest specimen is found in the quotation of vi. 4—8 given by Tertullian (*de Pudic.* 20). This is equally distinct from the Old Latin of *d* and *e* and from the Vulgate text (*e.g.* v. 4 participaverunt spiritum sanctum. *v.* 5 verbum Dei dulce, occidente jam ævo. *v.* 6 cum exciderint, refigentes cruci in semetipsos, dedecorantes. *v.* 7 humorem, peperit herbam. *v.* 8 exustionem). The next important specimen of the Old Latin is a quotation of iii. 5—iv. 13 in Lucifer of Cagliari († 371 A.D.) which agrees substantially with the texts of *d* and *e*, the variations not being more than might be found in secondary copies of the same writing (*de non convers. c. hæret.* 10). The quotations of Jerome, Augustine, Ambrose, Hilary &c. indicate the currency of a variety of texts in the 4th and 5th centuries, but these have not been classified.

The text of *d* and *e* in this Epistle is singularly corrupt. The scribe of The text *d* was evidently ignorant of Latin forms and words (i. 4 facto, 7 angelus; of *d*; ii. 10 dicebat, per quo; iv. 15 habet; v. 9 operantibus; vi. 5 uirtutis futuri sæcula, 15 petitus, 17 inmobilem nobilatis suæ; vii. 25 accendentes, 26 cælestis; x. 2 purgari [mundati], 27 horribis quidam execratio iudici, 30 vindicas; xi. 5 inveniebamur, 28 ne que subastabat; xii. 3 pectoribus; xiii. 10 herere [edere], 11 alium [animalium]). His deficiency becomes conspicuously manifest because he had to transcribe in this book a text which had already been corrected, and in many cases he has confused together two readings so as to produce an unintelligible result (*e.g.* ii. 14 similiter et ipse participes factus est eorumdem passione ut per mortem mortem destrueret qui imperium... iv. 2 sed non fuit prode illis verbum auditus illos non temperatos fidem auditorum; 12 scrutatur animi et cogitationis et cogitationis cordis; v. 11 et laboriosa quæ interprætatio est; vi. 16 et omnique controversia eorum novissimum in observationem; viii. 12 malitiæ eorum et peccati illorum et injustis eorum; ix. 1 prior eius justitia constitutionis cultura; x. 2 nam necessansent offerri. See also ii. 3, 6; iv. 16; v. 7; vi. 1, 7, 10; vii. 19, 20; viii. 3; ix. 9; x. 2, 27, 33, 39; xi. 6, 31; xii. 1, 25).

of e;   The scribe of *e* seems to have known a little Latin (he was ignorant of Greek) and he has corrected rightly some obvious blunders (ii. 12 pro (per) quo; iii. 18 introituros (-rus); v. 14 exercitatas (-tus); vi. 16 et omni (*om.* que); vii. 25 accedentes (accend-): 26 cælis (cælestis); 28 jurisjurandi (-ndo); viii. 7 secundus inquireretur (-das, -rere); x. 33 taliter (et aliter) &c.). Sometimes however his corrections are inadequate (*e.g.* ix. 24 apparuit *per se* for *per sæ*) and sometimes they are wrong (*e.g.* viii. 1 *sedet* for *sedit*); and he has left untouched the gravest corruptions (iv. 2, 13; vi. 5, 17; ix. 1, 8 f. &c.), and many simple mistakes (ii. 9; iii. 10; v. 1; x. 2 &c.). It is evident that in this Epistle he had no other text to guide his work.

In spite of the wretched form in which the version has come down to us, it shews traces of freedom and vigour, and in particular it has often preserved the absolute participial constructions which are characteristic of the Epistle (*e.g.* i. 2 etiam fecit, 3 purificatione peccatorum facta, 14 qui mittuntur propter possessuros... ii. 8 subjiciendo autem... ii. 18; v. 7 lacrimis oblatis; vi. 11 relicto igitur initii Christi verbum (-o); x. 12 oblata hostia, 14 nos sanctificans; xi. 31 exceptis exploratoribus; xii. 28 regno immobili suscepto).

of Harl.   The important Harleian MS. (B.M. *Harl.* 1772) contains many traces of
1772;   another early version, especially in the later chapters, as Griesbach (*Symb. Crit.* i. 327) and Bentley before him noticed. Other MSS. also contain numerous old renderings. Among these one of the most interesting is
of Bent-   Bentley's S (comp. Dict. of Bible, *Vulgate*, p. 1713), in the Library of Trinity
ley's S.   College, Cambridge (B. 10. 5, sæc. IX.). This gives in agreement with *d* and *e*

   i.   7 ignem urentem.
   ii.   3 in nobis.
         18 *om.* et (bis).
  iii.   16 omnes.
 viii.   10 in sensibus eorum.
 xiii.   17 *om.* non.

   It has also many (apparently) unique renderings :
   ii.   1 audimus.
         11 et ex uno.
   vi.   16 majorem sibi.

vi. 17 immotabilitatem ['i.e. *immutabilitatem* more Saxonico' R. B.].
vii. 25 ad dnm.
viii. 5 monstratum.
ix. 7 offerebat.
x. 13 de cætero, fratres, exspectans [H$_3$ has in the mg. of iv. 14 ἀδελφοί, and so Col. iii. 4. D$_2$ adds ἀδελφοί in iv. 11, and 37 in xii. 14].
xi. 12 quæ in ora est.
28 primogenita.
xii. 5 filii mei nolite.
26 mouebat.
xiii. 10 deservierunt.
19 ut celerius (*Harl.* ut quo).
It agrees with *Harl.* in
i. 12 amictum inuoluens eos (*Harl.* inuolues).
x. 14 emundauit...uestram (se Bentl.).
xii. 16 primitias suas.
xiii. 18 habeamus.

(*b*) The translation incorporated in the Vulgate appears to have been based upon a rendering originally distinct from that given by *d*, from which it differs markedly in its general style no less than in particular renderings. It was in all probability not made by the author of the translation of St Paul's Epistles; but this question requires a more complete examination than I have been able to give to it. The Greek text which it represents is much mixed. In very many cases it gives the oldest readings (*e.g.* i. 3; iii. 1, 10; iv. 7; vi. 10; vii. 21; viii. 4, 12; ix. 9; x. 30, 34, 38; xi. 11; xii. 18), but not unfrequently those which are later (*e.g.* i. 12; v. 4; viii. 2, 11; ix. 10, 11; xi. 3; xii. 28), and the best MSS. are often divided (*e.g.* ii. 5, 14, 18).

(*b*) The Vulgate.

ii. *Syriac.*

ii *Syriac.*

(*a*) The version in the *Syriac Vulgate* (the *Peshito*) is held to be the work of a distinct translator (Wichelhaus, *De vers. simpl.* 86), but the question requires to be examined in detail. The position which the Epistle occupies in the version (see § III.) is favourable to the belief that it was a separate work. The text of the Peshito in this Epistle is mixed. It contains many early readings (*e.g.* i. 2; v. 3, 9; vi. 7, 10; vii. 17, 23; viii. 12; ix. 11; x. 30, 34; xi. 4, 32, 37; xii. 3, 7, 18), and many late readings (*e.g.* i. 1, 3, 12;

(*a*) The Peshito.

ii. 14 ; iii. 1, 9 f.; vii. 14, 21 ; viii. 2, 4 ; x. 34, 38 ; xi. 3, 4 f.; xii. 8 ; xiii. 4).

Many of the renderings are of interest (*e.g.* ii. 9 ; iii. 8 ; iv. 7 ; v. 7 f.; vi. 2, 4 ; vii. 19, 26 ; x. 29, 33 ; xi. 17, 19, 20 ; xii. 1 ; xiii. 16).

Compare also the following passages : ii. 13 ; iv. 8, 16 ; vii. 2, 11, 20 ; viii. 9 ; x. 5, 11, 17 ; xi. 11[1].

(*b*) The Harclean.

(*b*) The *Harclean (Philoxenian) Syriac* Version has now been made complete, the missing portion, xi. 28 to the end, being found in the Cambridge MS. Though the text represented by the Harclean version is generally of a later type than that represented by the Peshito where the two versions differ (*e.g.* i. 2, 3 ; viii. 4, 12 ; ix. 10, 13, 28 ; x. 8, 30 ; xii. 3, 18), it preserves some earlier readings (*e.g.* i. 5, 8 ; ii. 14 ; v. 4 ; x. 2, 9, 28, 30). In some doubtful cases the two versions represent different ancient readings (*e.g.* iii. 13 ; iv. 2 ; vii. 4 ; ix. 10, 14 ; x. 11 ; xiii. 15)[2].

The text of the missing portion has been printed by Prof. Bensly (*The Harklean Version of the Epistle to the Hebrews*, chap. xi. 28—xiii. 25, *now edited for the first time with Introduction and Notes on the version of the Epistle....*Cambridge, 1889). It contains the following variations from the text which I have printed :

xi. 29 (διέβησαν)+οἱ υἱοὶ Ἰσραήλ.

31 ἡ+ἐπιλεγομένη΄ πόρνη.

32 om. καὶ 1°.

ἐπιλ. γάρ με.

B. τε (or καὶ B.) καὶ Σ. καὶ Ἰ.

τῶν+ἄλλων΄ πρ.

34 στόμα.

xii. 3 ἑαυτόν or αὐτόν.

8 νόθοι ἐστὲ καὶ οὐχ υἱοί.

11 πᾶσα δέ.

18 ὄρει ψηλ.

21 Μωυσῆς+γάρ.

24 παρὰ τὸ τοῦ ᾽Α.

25 παραιτ. τὸν ἐπὶ γῆς χρημ.

28 ἔχομεν...λατρεύομεν.

αἰδοῦς καὶ εὐλαβείας.

[1] I have not thought it necessary to quote all the renderings in the notes.

[2] The readings referred to here and in the next page are not always given expressly in the inner margin.

xiii. 4 πόρν. δέ.
    6 +καὶ οὐ φοβ.
    9 περιπατήσαντες (probably).
   15 δι' αὐτοῦ + οὖν.
   18 πεποίθαμεν.
    ἔχομεν ἐν πᾶσιν (so connected).
   20 Ἰησοῦν + Χριστόν.
   21 om. ἀγαθῷ.
    ἐν ὑμῖν.
    om. τῶν αἰώνων.
   25 +Ἀμήν.

iii. *Egyptian.*

(a) *Memphitic (Coptic).* The Epistle is contained entire in this early and important version.

The Greek text which the version represents is of great excellence (*e.g.* i. 2, 3, 8; ii. 14; iii. 1, 2, 9; iv. 12; v. 1; vii. 4, 23; viii. 4, 11; ix. 2, 10, 11; x. 8, 15, 30, 34; xi. 3, 5, 11; xii. 18, 20; xiii. 4); but it has an admixture of later readings (*e.g.* i. 12; v. 10; vi. 10, 16; vii. 21; viii. 2, 12; x. 16, 38); and some readings which, though early, are certainly wrong (*e.g.* ii. 6; ix. 14; x. 32; xiii. 20).

(b) *Thebaic (Sahidic).* Of this version the following fragments have been published :

   vii. 11 εἰ—21 αἰῶνα.
   ix. 2 σκηνή—10 ἐπικείμενα.
   ix. 24 οὐ γάρ—28 σωτηρίαν.
   x. 5 διό—10 ἐφάπαξ.
   xi. 11 πίστει—22 ἐνετείλατο.
   xii. 1 τοιγαροῦν—9 ἐνετρεπόμεθα.
     18 οὐ γάρ—27 σαλευόμενα.

The value of the version may be seen by its renderings in the following passages : ix. 10, 25, 26; xi. 11; xii. 7, 18.

(c) *Bashmuric.* The fragments of this version (quoted as *Æg.*), which was derived from the Thebaic, are

   v. 4 Ἀαρών—9 ἐγένετο.
    13 λόγου—vi. 3 ποιήσομεν.
   vi. 8—11; 15—vii. 5 ἐντολήν (more or less mutilated).

Marginal notes:

iii *Egyptian.*

(a) *Memphitic.*

(b) *Thebaic.*

(c) *Bashmuric.*

vii. 8 ἀποθνήσκοντες—13 ταῦτα.

16 ἀκαταλύτου—x. 23 καθαρῷ.

The dependence of this version upon the Thebaic and the close agreement of the present text with that version in the passages which are found in both (yet see ix. 2, 4, 10) gives great value to its evidence where the Thebaic is defective (*e.g.* vii. 4, 22, 23 ; viii. 1, 4, 11, 12 ; ix. 11, 13, 14 ; x. 4). Its agreement with B and *Æth.* in ix. 2, 4 is specially worthy of notice.

The text of the Egyptian versions offers a singularly interesting field of study. It would be instructive to tabulate in detail their coincidences even in this single epistle with B, A and C.

Later versions. The Epistle is found entire in the later versions, *Armenian, Æthiopic, Slavonic.* It does not, however, seem to have been included in the *Gothic ;* for the Epistle to Philemon is followed immediately by the Kalendar in the Ambrosian MS. A of the Epistles (E. Bernhardt, *Vulfila oder die Gothische Bibel,* s. xxiv. 1875).

General character of the text. The text of the Epistle is on the whole well preserved, but there are some passages in which it is not unlikely that primitive errors have passed into all our existing copies ; *e.g.* iv. 2 (Addit. note) ; xi. 4 (Addit. note), 37 ; xii. 11 ; xiii. 21 ; see also x. 1 (Addit. note). Some primitive errors have been corrected in later MSS. : vii. 1 ; xi. 35.

The following passages offer variations of considerable interest, and serve as instructive exercises on the principles of textual criticism : i. 2, 8 ; ii. 9 (Addit. note) ; iv. 2 (Addit. note); vi. 2, 3 ; ix. 11 ; x. 34 ; xi. 13 ; xii. 7.

The general contrast between the early and later texts is well seen by an examination of the readings in : i. 2, 3, 12 ; ii. 1, 14 ; iii. 1, 9 ; v. 4 ; vi. 10 ; vii. 11, 16 ; viii. 4, 11 ; ix. 1, 9, 10 ; xi. 3, 13 ; xii. 15, 18, 20 ; xiii. 9.

II. TITLE.

In the oldest MSS. (אAB : C is defective but it has the sub- The Title in the oldest MSS.
scription προc εβραιογc) the title of the Epistle, like that of the other
Epistles to Churches, is simply προc εβραιογc, 'to Hebrews.' There
is no title or colophon to the Epistle in D₂, but it has a running
heading προc εβραιογc.

The absence of title in D₂ is contrary to the usage of the MS.; and it is
also to be noticed that the colophon to the Epistle to Philemon (πρὸς
Φιλήμονα ἐπληρώθη) gives no notice that any other Epistle is to follow, as is
done in other cases (e.g. πρὸς Τίτον ἐπληρώθη, ἄρχεται πρὸς Φιλήμονα). In
fact the Epistle to Philemon is followed by the *Stichometry* (*Hist. of
Canon of N. T.* p. 563), and the Epistle to the Hebrews has been
added by the Scribe as an appendix to the archetype of the other
Epistles.

The Egyptian versions (*Memph. Theb.*) have the same simple
title : *to the Hebrews.*

This title, as in other cases, was gradually enlarged. The Later enlarge-ments.
Peshito Syriac and the New College MS. of the *Harclean* give
the Epistle to the Hebrews : the Cambridge MS. of the *Harclean
Syriac* gives in its title *the Epistle to the Hebrews of Paul the
Apostle,* but in the subscription the Epistle is called simply *the
Epistle to the Hebrews.*

Later Greek MSS. give Παύλου ἐπιστολὴ πρὸς Ἑβραίους, as in the
Epistle to the Romans &c., (P₂), and, at greater length, τοῦ ἁγίου καὶ
πανευφήμου ἀποστόλου Παύλου ἐπιστολὴ πρὸς Ἑβραίους (L₂). Some-
times historical statements are inwoven in the title : ἐγράφη ἀπὸ
Ἰταλίας διὰ Τιμοθέου ἡ πρὸς Ἑβραίους ἐπιστολὴ ἐκτεθεῖσα ὡς ἐν πίνακι
(M₂); Παῦλος ἀπόστολος Ἑβραίοις τάδε συγγενέσιν (f Scr).

The title forms no part of the original document; but it The Title added at an early date.
must have been given to the book at a very early date, when
it first passed into public use as part of a collection of Apostolic
letters. And it was rightly given in regard to the permanent
relation which the book occupies to the whole message of the
Gospel. For while the treatment of the subjects with which it

deals and the subjects themselves are of universal interest, the
discussion is directed by special circumstances. The arguments
and reflections in their whole form and spirit, even more than in
special details, are addressed to 'Hebrews,' men, that is, whose
hearts were filled with the thoughts, the hopes, the consolations,
of the Old Covenant, such perhaps as, under another aspect, are
described as οἱ ἐκ περιτομῆς (Acts x. 45 ; xi. 2 ; Gal. ii. 12 ; Col.
iv. 11 ; Tit. i. 10).

Tertullian has preserved an interesting notice of another name,
which was given to the Epistle in North Africa, and which apparently
dates from a time earlier than the formation of the collection of
Apostolic Epistles. He quotes it definitely as *Barnabæ titulus ad
Hebræos* (*de Pudic.* 20) ; and there can be no reasonable doubt that
the Epistle of Barnabas which is included in the African (Latin)
Stichometry contained in the *Cod. Clarom.* (D_2) refers to this book.
There is not however the least evidence that it was ever called 'the
Epistle to the Laodicenes' (not in Philastr. *Hær.* 89 or *Cod. Boern.*
G_3), or 'the Epistle to the Alexandrines' (*Can. Murat.* fertur
etiam ad Laudicenses [epistola], alia ad Alexandrinos, Pauli nomine
finctæ ad hæresem Marcionis, et alia plura quæ in Catholicam
ecclesiam recipi non potest) although it might be described as
'directed to meet (πρὸς τὴν αἵρεσιν) the teaching of Marcion.'
(Comp. *Hist. of N. T. Canon*, p. 537.)

Identified
with 'the
Epistle of
Barnabas'
in the *Cla-
romontane
Sticho-
metry.*

The identification of *the Epistle of Barnabas* of the Claromontane
Stichometry with *the Epistle to the Hebrews* was first suggested by
Martianay (Jerome, *Bibl. Div.* Proleg. iv : Migne *P. L.* xxviii. 124), and
maintained by Credner. Two books only can come into consideration, the
Apocryphal Letter of Barnabas and the Epistle to the Hebrews. These
are so different in length that when the question is one of measurement it
is practically impossible to confuse them. In *Cod. Sin.* ℵ, which contains
both, *the Epistle to the Hebrews* occupies 40½ columns and *the Epistle of
Barnabas* 53½ columns; and, to take another equivalent of the Epistle to
the Hebrews, the Epistle to the Galatians, the Ephesians, and Titus
together occupy 41 columns. It may then be fairly concluded that in
any scheme of reckoning the Epistle to the Hebrews will give a number of
lines (στίχοι) approximately equal to the combined numbers of the lines in
these three Epistles, and that the 'lines' in the Letter of Barnabas will be
about a third more. Thus in the Greek numeration given by Martianay

(*l.c.*), which is found in several MSS., the three Epistles give a total of 702 (293 + 312 + 97) and the number assigned to Hebrews is 703. The numeration in the Claromontane list is different, but it leads to the same result: the three Epistles have a total sum of 865 (350 + 375 + 140), and the number assigned to 'the Epistle of Barnabas' is 850. It would be difficult to add anything to the force of this correspondence.

There is however another independent testimony to the relative length of the (apocryphal) Letter of Barnabas in the Stichometry of Nicephorus. In this the lines of the fourteen Epistles of St Paul are given only in a total sum: then the lines of Barnabas are reckoned as 1360, and the lines of the Apocalypse at 1400. In other words, according to this calculation, which represents a different numeration from that given in the Claromontane Stichometry, the length in lines of the Epistle of Barnabas is a little less than that of the Apocalypse. Now in the Claromontane list the lines of the Apocalypse are reckoned as 1200, and the lines of 'the Epistle of Barnabas' are 850. Taking then the proportion of the Hebrews to the apocryphal Barnabas in *Cod. Sin.*, and assuming that the Claromontane Barnabas is the Epistle to the Hebrews, the lines of the apocryphal Barnabas on this scale would be 1150. Again the coincidence is practically complete.

The position of the Book in the Stichometry, after the Catholic Epistles and before the Revelation, the Acts of the Apostles and the Shepherd, points to the same conclusion; nor would it be necessary in the case of the single letter of the supposed author to identify it further by the addition of the address.

Little stress however can be laid on these details. The length of the apocryphal Barnabas absolutely excludes it; and the exact agreement of the length of the book named with the Epistle to the Hebrews leaves no room for doubt as to their identification.

Wherever the nature of the book is defined by early writers it is called an 'Epistle.' The description is substantially correct, though the construction of the writing is irregular. It opens without any address or salutation (comp. 1 John i. 1), but it closes with salutations (xiii. 24 f.). There are indeed personal references throughout, and in the course of the book there is a gradual transition from the form of an 'essay' to that of a 'letter': ii. 1; iii. 1, 12; iv. 1, 14; v. 11; vi. 9; x. 19; xiii. 7, 22 ff.

The writer himself characterises his composition as λόγος παρακλήσεως (xiii. 22 note); and the verb which he uses of his communication (διὰ βραχέων ἐπέστειλα *l.c.*), while it does not necessarily describe a letter (in Acts xxi. 25 the true reading is ἀπεστείλαμεν, and ἐπιστεῖλαι in Acts xv. 20 is probably to *enjoin*), yet presupposes a direct personal address (ἐπιστέλλειν is used of the Epistle by Clem. Alex. *ap.* Euseb. *H. E.* vi. 14; comp. Clem. R. 1 *Cor.* 7, 47, [62]), though personal relationships are kept in the background till the end.

The conjecture that the salutation at the opening of the Epistle has been removed cannot be regarded as worthy of serious discussion. An 'editor' who had mutilated the beginning of the book (to say no more) would not have left c. xiii. as it stands.

It is of interest to notice the delicate shades of feeling marked by the transition from 'we' to 'ye' as the writer speaks of the hopes and trials and duties of Christians, *e.g.* iii. 12, 13, 14; x. 22 ff., 25 f.; 36, 39; xii. 1, 2, 3; 8—12; 25, 28 f.; xiii. 5, 6; 9, 10; 15, 16.

For the most part he identifies himself with those to whom he writes, unless there is some special point in the direct address: i. 2; ii. 1, 3; 8 f.; iii. 19; iv. 1 ff.; 11, 13 ff.; vi. 1; 18 ff.; vii. 26; viii. 1; ix. 24; x. 10; xi. 3, 40.

III. POSITION.

The places occupied by the Epistle in different authorities indicate the variety of opinions which were entertained in early times as to its authorship.

The place of the Epistle in

In the oldest Greek MSS. (אABC) it comes immediately before the Pastoral Epistles following 2 Thess.; and this is the position which it generally occupies in MSS. of the Memphitic Version (Woide, *App. Cod. Alex. N.T.* p. 19; Lightfoot *ap.* Scrivener, *Introd.* 386 f., 390). This order is followed also by many later MSS. ($H_2P_2$17 &c.), and by many Greek Fathers.

the oldest Greek MSS.,

In *Cod. Vat.* B there is important evidence that it occupied a different position in an early collection of Pauline Epistles. In this MS. there is a marginal numeration which shews that the whole collection of Pauline Epistles was divided, either in its archetype or in some earlier copy, into a series of sections numbered consecutively. In this collection the Epistle to the Hebrews came between the Epistles to the Galatians and to the Ephesians.

in the marginal numeration of B,

The paragraphs in B, so far as they come under consideration here, begin:

NH′ Gal. v. 16.
NΘ′ Hebr. i. 1.
Ξ′ — iii. 1.
ΞA′ — iv. 14.
ΞB′ — vi. 9.
ΞΓ′ — vii. 19.
ΞΔ′ — ix. 11.

The remainder of the Epistle accounts for sections ΞE′—ΞΘ′. Then follows

O′ Eph. i. 1.

This arrangement preserved by B approximates to that of the Thebaic and Bashmuric versions, in which the Epistle comes between 2 Corinthians and Galatians (Zoega, *Cat. Codd. in Mus. Borg.* pp. 186, 140; comp. Lightfoot *ap.* Scrivener *l.c.* pp. 339, 404). Cassiodorus (*Instit.* 14) gives another arrangement of the same type, placing the epistle between Colossians and 1 Thessalonians.

The order of the Books in a Latin MS. of St Paul's Epistles (glossed) in the Chapter Library at Westminster is worth quoting: Romans; 1, 2 Corinth.; 1, 2 Thess.; 1, 2 Tim.; Gal., Eph., Col., Phil., Hebr., Philm., Titus. The order is marked in the colophons, *e.g.* Explicit epistola ad Philippenses. Præfatio epistolæ ad Hebræos; Explicit epistola ad Hebræos. Incipit epistola ad Philemonem.

In the Syriac versions the Epistle comes after the Pastoral in the Syriac and later Greek MSS. (K₂ L₂ &c.), probably under Syrian influence, has passed into the 'Received text.' Compare Epiph. *Hær.* xlii. p. 373.

The same order is found in Latin MSS. For in the West the in Latin MSS. Epistle did not originally form part of the collection of the writings of St Paul; and other clear traces remain of the absence of the book from the Apostolic collection. Thus in *Cod. Clarom.* D₂ the Epistle, as has been seen, appears as an appendix to the Pauline Epistles, being separated from the Epistle to Philemon by the Stichometry. The archetype of this MS. and the original text from which the Gothic version was made, evidently contained only thirteen Epistles of St Paul.

Another testimony to the collection of thirteen Epistles of St Paul is given by the remarkable Stichometry printed by Mommsen from a MS. belonging to the Library of Sir T. Phillipps (*Hermes*, 1886, p. 146).

Item indiculum novi testamenti

   evangelia $\overline{\text{IIII}}$. Matheum $\overline{\text{vr}}$ $\overline{\text{II}}$ DCC

        Marcus $\overline{\text{ver}}$ ∞ DCC

        Johannem $\overline{\text{vr}}$ ∞ DCCC

        Luca $\overline{\text{vr}}$ $\overline{\text{III}}$ CCC

  fiunt omnes versus $\overline{\text{x}}$

  eplae Pauli $\overline{\text{n}}$ XIII

  actus aplorum $\overline{\text{ver}}$ $\overline{\text{III}}$ DC

  apocalipsis $\overline{\text{ver}}$ ∞ DCCC

  eplae Iohannis $\overline{\text{III}}$. ur CCCCL
  una sola.

  eplae Petri II. $\overline{\text{ver}}$. CCC
  una sola.

Thus at the earliest date at which we find a collection of St Paul's Epistles in circulation in the Church, the Epistle to the Hebrews was by some definitely included in his writings, occupying a place either among or at the close of the Epistles to Churches: by others it was treated as an appendix to them, being set after the private letters: with others again it found no place at all among the Apostolic writings.

IV. ORIGINAL LANGUAGE.

The statement of Clement of Alex. that the Epistle was written in Hebrew.

The earliest direct notice of the Epistle, quoted by Eusebius (*H. E.* vi. 14) from Clement of Alexandria, states that it 'was written (by Paul) to Hebrews in the Hebrew language (*i.e.* the Aramaic dialect current in Palestine at the time, Acts xxii. 2) and translated (into Greek) by Luke.' (See § XI.) This statement was repeated from Eusebius (and Jerome who depended on him), as it appears, and not from Clement himself, by a series of later writers both in the East and West (Theodoret, Euthalius, John of Damascus, Œcumenius, Theophylact, Primasius, Rabanus Maurus, Thomas Aquinas: see Bleek, 8 f.; Credner, *Einl.* 533), but there is not the least trace of any independent evidence in favour of the tradition, nor is it said that any one had ever seen the original Hebrew document. The unsupported statement of Clement, which Origen discredits by his silence, is thus the whole historical foundation for the belief that the Epistle was written in Hebrew. The opinion however was incorporated in the *Glossa Ordinaria*, and became the traditional opinion of the mediæval Western Church. When Widmanstadt first published the Syriac text of the New Testament, he even argued that the text of the Epistle to the Hebrews was the original of St Paul. The belief in a Hebrew original was maintained by one or two scholars in the last century (J. Hallet, J. D. Michaelis); and lately it has found a vigorous advocate in J. H. R. Biesenthal (*Das Trostschreiben d. Ap. Paulus an d. Hebräer*, 1878; comp. Panek, *Comm. in Ep. Prolegg.* § 2 ; 1882), who thinks that the Epistle was written in 'the dialect of the Mishna, the language of the schools' in the apostolic age, into which he has again rendered the Greek.

The words of Widmanstadt are : Ex quibus omnibus coniecturam non levē capi posse arbitror, et Mathæū Euāgelium suū, et Paulū ad Hebræos Epistolam sermone Syro, Hebraici populi vulgari usu trito, ut a Iudeis passim omnibus intelligerentur, scripsisse, eaq; in Syrorum Ecclesiis iam usq; a temporibus Apostolorum cōservata fuisse (Nov. Test. Syr. *Præf.* a xxxxxx. 3, 1555). There is a small commentary based on the Syriac, published not many years afterwards, in which it is argued that : in Syro Paulo multa sunt quæ non tantum lucem adferunt obscurioribus sed etiam interpretum discussiones bellissime componunt, ex græcanicarum vocum ambiguitate prognatas (*Enarratio Ep. ad Hebr. B. Pauli Apost.* a Syro sermone in Latinum conversæ, ex M. Galeni Vestcappellii prælectionibus concinnata opera ac studio Fr. Andreæ Crocquetii...Duaci, 1578).

The words of the *Glossa Ordinaria* are instructive as shewing how a statement grows precise by lapse of time: Hanc...epistolam ad Hebræos conscriptam Hebraica lingua fertur apostolus misisse; cujus sensum et ordinem retinens Lucas evangelista post excessum beati apostoli Pauli Græco sermone composuit (Migne, *P. L.* cxiv. p. 643).

Card. Caietan, writing in 1529, says that one of the two preliminary points which he must discuss is : 'an hæc epistola fuerit condita Hebraico sermone ut communiter supponitur.' He decides without hesitation against the common opinion.

Not to dwell on the insufficiency of the statement of Clement, in the absence of all collateral external testimony, to justify the belief

The statement untrustworthy and opposed to clear internal evidence of language, and

that the Epistle was written in Hebrew, internal evidence appears to establish absolutely beyond question that the Greek text is original and not a translation from any form of Aramaic. The vocabulary, the style, the rhetorical characteristics of the work all lead to the same conclusion. It is (for example) impossible to imagine any Aramaic phrase which could have suggested to a translator the opening clause of the Epistle, πολυμερῶς καὶ πολυτρόπως; and similar difficulties offer themselves throughout the book in the free and masterly use of compound words which have no Aramaic equivalents (e.g. μετριοπαθεῖν v. 2; εὐπερίστατος xii. 1). The structure of the periods is bold and complicated, and the arrangement of the words is often singularly expressive (e.g. ii. 9). Paronomasias (e.g. i. 1; ii. 10; v. 8; vii. 23 f.; ix. 28; x. 34, 38 f.) are at least more likely to have been due to the writer than to have been introduced or imitated by a translator. But on the other hand stress must not be laid on a (falsely) assumed change in the meaning of διαθήκη in ix. 15 ff., or the obviously fortuitous hexameter in the common text of xii. 13.

of the quotations from O. T.

A still more decisive proof that the Greek text is original lies in the fact that the quotations from the O. T. are all (except x. 30 ‖ Deut. xxxii. 35) taken from the LXX, even when the LXX differs from the Hebrew (é.g. ii. 7 παρ᾽ ἀγγέλους; x. 38 καὶ ἐὰν ὑποστείληται; xii. 5 f. μαστιγοῖ). And arguments are based on peculiarities of the LXX, so that the quotations cannot have been first introduced in the translation from Aramaic to Greek (e.g. x. 5 ff. σῶμα κατηρτίσω; xii. 26 f. ἅπαξ).

No difficulties of interpretation removed by the hypothesis.

It may also be added that the passages in which difficulties in the Greek text are supposed to be removed by the hypothesis of a false rendering of the original offer no solid support to the theory. Scholars who allege them shew little agreement as to the difficulties or as to the solutions of them. Thus in the two lists given by Michaelis and Biesenthal, of eighteen and nineteen passages respectively, only four are identical (i. 2; vi. 19; ix. 17; x. 1), and in these four the solutions are different.

The passages alleged by Michaelis (Bleek, i. p. 23 anm.) are i. 2; ii. 1, 9;

iii. 3 f.; v. 13; vi. 14, 19; vii. 14; ix. 2—4, 14—17; x. 1; xi. 11, 35; xii. 15, 18, 25; xiii. 9, 15. Those alleged by Biesenthal are: i. 2; ii. 3; iii. 13; iv. 12, 13; vi. 19; vii. 4, 5, 15, 27; viii. 2; ix. 16 f.; x. 1, 11; xi. 26, 27; xii. 18.

V. DESTINATION.

The letter is described in all existing copies as addressed 'to Hebrews'; and Tertullian, who assigned the authorship to Barnabas, gave it the same destination (*de Pudic.* 20 Barnabæ titulus ad Hebræos). There is, as has been already seen (§ III.), no evidence that it ever bore any other address. Though there is no reason to suppose that the title is original, it expresses at least the belief of those by whom the Epistle was placed among the apostolic Scriptures, and describes truly the character of those for whom it was written, so far as their character can be determined from its general scope, as men who by birth and life were devoted to the institutions of Israel.

According to the earliest evidence the Epistle was addressed to 'Hebrews.'

The argument of von Soden (*Jahrb. f. Protest. Theol.* 1884), who endeavours to shew that it was written to Gentiles, cannot be regarded as more than an ingenious paradox by any one who regards the general teaching of the Epistle in connexion with the forms of thought in the apostolic age.

The term Ἑβραῖος (or rather Ἐβραῖος) occurs in the N. T. in two senses

Use in the N. T. of 'Hebrew,'

(a) of language :
    Acts vi. 1 τῶν Ἑλληνιστῶν πρὸς τοὺς Ἑβραίους.

(b) of descent :
2 Cor. xi. 22 Ἐβραῖοί εἰσιν;...Ἰσραηλεῖταί εἰσιν;...σπέρμα Ἀβραάμ εἰσιν;...
    Phil. iii. 5 Ἑβρ. ἐξ Ἑβραίων.

The title properly describes 'the people from beyond the river Euphrates'; and is the national name of the race having regard to the divine call. In this widest sense Eusebius speaks of Philo as Ἑβραῖος: *H. E.* ii. 4 τὸ γένος ἀνέκαθεν Ἑβραῖος ἦν. Comp. *H. E.* iii. 4.

The two other names by which Jews are styled in the N. T., Ἰουδαῖος and Ἰσραηλείτης, have each their distinct meaning.

Ἰουδαῖος is the name of the people as forming a religious commonwealth; 'Jew,' and is used of the people especially after the Return (1 Cor. i. 22 ff.; Apoc. ii. 9).

Hence in the Gospel of St John 'the Jews' (οἱ Ἰουδαῖοι) is the common title for those who stood apart from Christ and represented the nation from the side of unbelief.

'*Israelite.*' Ἰσραηλείτης is the name of special privilege.

John i. 48 (47); Acts ii. 22; iii. 12; v. 35; xiii. 16; xxi. 28; Rom. ix. 4; xi. 1; 2 Cor. xi. 22.

In connexion with Ἰσραηλείτης the phrases οἱ υἱοὶ Ἰσραήλ (c. xi. 22 note), ὁ λαὸς Ἰσραήλ, Ἰσραήλ (Rom. ix. 6), ὁ Ἰσραήλ (John i. 31 note), ὁ Ἰσραήλ τοῦ θεοῦ (Gal. vi. 16), must be studied. See also σπέρμα Ἀβραάμ ii. 16 (note).

In itself the title 'Hebrew' is not local but national. It describes a quality of race and not of dwelling. We have to inquire therefore whether the Epistle enables us to define this wide term more exactly.

Traits of the Society addressed.

At once we find that the book contains numerous indications of the circumstances and character of those to whom it was written.

There is no trace of any admixture of heathen converts among them; nor does the letter touch on any of the topics of heathen controversy (not xiii. 9, see note). It is therefore scarcely possible that it could have been written to a mixed Church generally, or to the Jewish section of a mixed Church. In either case allusions to the relations of Jew and Gentile could scarcely have been avoided.

They were a small body (v. 12), and they were addressed separately from 'their leaders' (xiii. 24). At the same time they were in a position to be generous, and for this trait they were and had been distinguished (vi. 10).

Their special trials came through disappointment of their first expectations. They had failed to grow under the discipline of experience, and so had degenerated: v. 11 f. (νωθροὶ γεγόνατε); vi. 1; x. 25.

The widening breach between the Church and the Synagogue rendered it necessary at last to make choice between them, and 'the Hebrews' were in danger of apostasy: ii. 1, 3; iii. 6, 12 ff.; iv. 1, 3, 11; vi. 6; x. 25, 29, 39. They had need therefore of effort and patience: iv. 14; vi. 11 f.; x. 23, 36; xii. 1, 3 ff., 12 ff.

In earlier days they had borne reproach and hardships: x. 32 ff.; still they 'had not yet resisted unto blood': xii. 3 ff.; though some at least 'in bonds' claimed their sympathy and help: xiii. 3; and perhaps their former 'leaders' had suffered even to martyrdom: xiii. 7.

From these individual traits it is clear that the letter is addressed to a definite Society and not to 'Hebrew' Christians generally. This is proved yet more directly by the fact that the writer hoped to visit them (xiii. 23) as he had been with them before (xiii. 19). At the same time, though he spoke of them as 'brethren' (iii. 1 note) and 'beloved' (vi. 9, note), he does not speak of them as 'children' (τέκνα). *General result. A shadow over the close of the First Age.*

The living picture of the character and position of this definite and marked Society will repay careful study (v. 11 ff.; vi. 9 ff.; x. 32 ff.; xii. 3 ff.); and whatever obscurity may hang over its local position, its spiritual features stand out with vivid clearness. We have in the Epistle to the Hebrews a picture of early Christian life such as is drawn in detail nowhere else (compare 3 John), and which still, as we must see, represents a necessary phase in the growth of the Church. The first enthusiasm and the first hope had, as we shall notice later, passed away. Believers began to reckon loss and gain. Some were inclined to overrate the loss; and we learn elsewhere that dark clouds hung over the close of the apostolic age. Compare 2 Tim. i. 15; Apoc. ii. iii.; 2 Pet. iii. 1 ff.; 1 John ii. 18 ff.

We might have expected it to be otherwise, and we do in fact unconsciously clothe the first centuries in light. But in this Letter the reality of imperfection meets us; and in the very sadness of the portraiture we feel with fresh force that Christianity is historical, entering into life and subject to the common influences of life.

And more than this: we learn from this Epistle that the early difficulties of Churches were not dealt with tentatively, as if the truth were the result of the free conflict of thought. The false view was met at once by the corresponding lesson. Error called out the decisive teaching but it had no part in creating it.

The phase of feeling traced in the Epistle has been spoken of as a necessary one in the development of Christian life. It is not difficult to see how this was so. Those who suffered in the trial were Jews; and the narrative of the Acts shews plainly with what loyal *The trial implied was inevitable.*

devotion the first believers from among the Jews observed the Law. Even at a later date St Paul before the Sanhedrin claimed to be a true Jew. For a time this fellowship of the Church and Synagogue was allowed on both sides. Little by little the growth of the Gentile element in the Church excited the active hostility of the Jews against the whole body of Christians, as it troubled the Jewish converts themselves. This hostility could not fail to be intensified in Palestine by the spread of aggressive nationalism there shortly before the outbreak of the Jewish war (comp. Jos. *de B. J.* ii. 23, 29 ff. ; iv. 11 ff.) ; and it is not unlikely that the solemn cursing of the heretics (*Minîm*) in the Synagogues, which became an established custom after the fall of Jerusalem (Weber *Altsynag. Theol.* 147 f.), may have begun from that time (comp. Just. M. *Dial.* 16 and Otto's note; Epiph. *Hær.* xxix. 9, i. p. 124).

The time of decision slowly reached.

Meanwhile the Jewish converts had had ample time for realising the true relations of Christianity and Judaism. Devotion to Levitical ritual was no longer innocent, if it obscured the characteristic teaching of the Gospel. The position which rightly belonged to young and immature Christians was unsuited to those who ought to have reached the fulness of truth (v. 11 ff.). Men who won praise for their faith and constancy at the beginning of a generation which was emphatically a period of transition, might well deserve blame and stand in peril of apostasy, if at the end of it they simply remained where they had been at first. When as yet the national unbelief of the Jews was undeclared, it was not possible to foresee that the coming of Christ would bring the overthrow of the old order. The approaching catastrophe was not realised in the earlier apostolic writings. In the Epistle to the Hebrews it is shewn to be imminent. In the Gospel and Epistles of St John it is, as it were, lost in the fulness of the life of the Church.

The very remarkable account which Hegesippus has given of the death of James the Just (c. 63 A.D.), the brother of the Lord, preserved by Eusebius (*H. E.* ii. 23), supplies, with all its strange and exaggerated details, a commentary both on the Jewish feeling towards Christians and on the Christian feeling towards Jews in Jerusalem about this time.

We can see then generally what was the character of the body to whom the letter was addressed. Where can we look for such a body? Some have found it in the 'Hebrew' Christians of Asia Minor generally, or in some special congregation of Syria, Asia Minor, Greece, Italy or Africa, and more particularly at Antioch or Rome or Alexandria. Lately the opinion that the letter was addressed to the Roman Church has found considerable favour. But the dominant conception of the Old Testament Institutions as centering in sacrificial and priestly ordinances seems to be fatal to all these theories which are not supported by any direct evidence, for no conclusion can be fairly drawn as to the original destination of the Epistle from the fact that Clement of Rome was acquainted with it. Such a view, unlike that of the observance of special days or meats, must be generally dependent in a large measure upon local circumstances of a narrow range. It is possible indeed that special circumstances with which we are unacquainted may have influenced the feelings of a small society, and there was in fact a 'Synagogue of Hebrews' at Rome (Schürer *Gesch. d. Jüd. Volkes....*ii. 517 συναγωγὴ Αἰβρέων), but we naturally look, if there is nothing to determine our search otherwise, to some place where Judaism would present itself with practical force under this aspect.

Such a Society naturally looked for where the priestly aspect of Judaism was dominant,

In this way our choice is limited to Egypt, with the Temple at Leontopolis, and to Palestine, with the Temple at Jerusalem. Nowhere else would the images of sacrifice and intercession be constantly before the eye of a Jew.

There is very little evidence to shew that the Temple at Leontopolis exercised the same power over the Alexandrian Jews as that at Jerusalem exercised over the Palestinian Jews and the Jews generally. Even in Egypt the Temple at Jerusalem was recognised as the true centre of worship. Nor is there the least ground for thinking that any of the divergences in the Epistle from the details of the Temple ceremonial coincide with peculiarities in the service at Leontopolis. On the contrary, the furniture of the Temple at Jerusalem was more like that of the Tabernacle, which is described in the Epistle, than was that of the Egyptian Temple. But on the

not in Egypt, but

in Palestine.

other hand it is certain that the kind of feeling which the Epistle is designed to meet must have been powerful at Jerusalem and in its neighbourhood. The close connexion of the early Church with the Temple, the splendour and venerable majesty of the ritual, could not fail to make the thought of severance from Judaism most grievous to those who had hitherto been able to share in its noblest services according to the custom of their youth.

The Temple worship the authoritative embodiment of the Mosaic system,

Nor is it a serious objection to this conclusion that the Temple is nowhere mentioned in the Epistle and that the ritual details are those of the Tabernacle and not those of the second Temple. The readers were influenced by the actual form in which the Mosaic ordinances were embodied. The writer, perhaps from his external circumstances or more probably in order to lay his reasoning on its deepest foundation, goes back to the first institution of the system. He shews how the original design of the priestly ritual of the Law, and therefore of necessity of all partial and specific embodiments of it, was satisfied by Christ. The Temple service, with all its peculiarities, finally drew its sanction from the Law. The ritual of the Tabernacle was the divine type of which the ritual of the Temple was the authoritative representation. And according to the popular tradition it was believed that 'the tabernacle' and its furniture, which had been removed by Jeremiah from the first Temple before its destruction, would in due time be restored (2 Macc. ii. 4 ff. and Grimm's notes).

though it was a religious declension.

And further it must be added that the Temple, like the Kingdom with which it was coordinate, was spiritually a sign of retrogression. It was an endeavour to give fixity to that which was essentially provisional. And thus the writer of the Epistle, by going back to the fundamental legislation, significantly indicates that the Mosaic Law first found accomplishment in Christ and not in that outward Levitical system in which it seemed superficially to receive its perfect embodiment.

The Society of 'Hebrews' to be fixed probably

It is then most reasonable from general considerations to find the Society to whom the letter was addressed in Jerusalem, or in the neighbourhood of Jerusalem.

In accordance with this view it may be added that Eusebius at or near Jeru-salem. speaks on another authority (ἐξ ἐγγράφων) of the Church of Jerusalem up to the time of the revolt under Hadrian as having 'been wholly composed of Hebrews' (συνεστάναι τὴν πᾶσαν ἐκκλησίαν ἐξ Ἑβραίων πιστῶν *H.E.* iv. 5; comp. vi. 14). Up to the same date all the bishops were 'of the circumcision' (*l.c.*).

So also in the Clementine Homilies (xi. 35) 'James that is called brother of the Lord' is said to be 'entrusted with the administration of the Church of the Hebrews in Jerusalem' (πεπιστευμένος ἐν Ἰερουσαλὴμ τὴν Ἑβραίων διέπειν ἐκκλησίαν), and 'the letter of Clement' prefixed to the same work is addressed to 'James the Lord and bishop of bishops, who administers the holy Church of Hebrews in Jerusalem' (διέποντι τὴν ἐν Ἰερουσαλὴμ ἁγίαν Ἑβραίων ἐκκλησίαν).

It may therefore be fairly concluded that when the title πρὸς Ἑβραίους was added to the Epistle, it was an expression of the belief that the letter was addressed to the Church of Jerusalem or some sister Church in Palestine dependent upon it.

In this restricted sense the title might perhaps be original, though this supposition is, as has been seen, otherwise unlikely. Compare the title τὸ καθ᾽ Ἑβραίους εὐαγγέλιον.

The conclusion which has been reached is not beyond doubt, The conclusion must remain uncertain. but it satisfies the conditions of the problem most simply. It is indeed possible that exceptional circumstances, which it is impossible for us now to determine, may have given occasion to the letter. It is, for example, quite conceivable, as has been already admitted, that a society of 'Hebrews' at Rome may have been led to develop the sacrificial theory of Judaism and to insist upon it and so to call out 'the word of exhortation.' Such conjectures, however, need not detain us. It is well to recognise how little we can determine by the help of the data at present available. That which is beyond doubt, that which indeed alone concerns us, is the spiritual character of the readers of the Epistle. This we can definitely grasp wherever it may have been developed. And it is unquestionable that it would be likely—most likely—to be developed in Palestine.

W. Grimm has discussed in considerable detail (*Zeitschrift f. wissensch. Theol.* 1870, 19 ff.) the claims of Rome, Jerusalem, and Alexandria to be considered as the place to which the Epistle was directed. He decides against all, and suggests Jamnia. It is better however to acquiesce in simply recognising the conditions which the place must satisfy.

VI. DATE.

The Epistle written just before the outbreak of the Jewish war. The date of the Epistle is fixed within narrow limits by its contents. A generation of Christians had already passed away (xiii. 7; ii. 3). There had been space for great changes in religious feeling (x. 32), and for religious growth (v. 11 f.).

On the other hand the Levitical service is spoken of as still continued (viii. 4 f.; ix. 6, 9; x. 1 ff.; xiii. 10 ff.); and, even if the references to its present continuance could be explained away (comp. Just. *Decl.* 117; Orig. *c. Cels.* v. 25), it is inconceivable that such a national calamity as the Jewish war should be unnoticed if it had already broken out, and still more, if it had been decided. Indeed the prospect of exclusion from the privileges of the old service is the very essence of the trial of 'the Hebrews'; and the severity of the trial is in itself a decisive proof of the influence which the Temple ritual exercised at the time.

The letter may then be placed in the critical interval between A.D. 64, the government of Gessius Florus, and 67, the commencement of the Jewish War, and most probably just before the breaking of the storm in the latter year, as the writer speaks of the visible signs of the approach of 'the day' (x. 25; comp. viii. 13 ἐγγὺς ἀφανισμοῦ); and indicates the likelihood of severer trials for the Church (xii. 4 οὔπω, xiii. 13 f.).

In order to place the Epistle in its historical setting it may be added that Nero was in Greece at the time, endeavouring to enter into the old spirit of Greek art; Apollonius of Tyana was teaching at Rome. The fire at Rome, which first brought the Christians into popular notice, took place in A. D. 64, and St Paul was martyred in the next year.

This general conclusion can hardly be questioned if the significance of the Fall of Jerusalem is realised. That catastrophe was not relieved, as the Babylonian overthrow had been, by any promise of restoration. To the Christians it was the fulfilment of the Lord's final judgment, the sign of His coming. No event in such a connexion could mark more distinctly the close of the old Dispensation; and no one who sympathised with the best hopes of Israel could have failed to leave some trace of the effect of the visitation in his argument, when the tragic event was not only fresh in his memory but also had a close connexion with his theme.

The theories which assign the Epistle to a later date, after the persecution of Domitian, or in the time of Trajan, seem to be utterly irreconcilable with the conditions and scope of the writing.

VII. THE PLACE OF WRITING.

Tradition is silent as to the place from which the Epistle was written. No independent authority can be given to the subscription which is found in A ἐγράφη ἀπὸ Ῥώμης. This, as in the case of similar subscriptions to the other Epistles, appears to have been a deduction from words in the Epistle itself (xiii. 23 f.). And so it is given in the words of the text and enlarged in later MSS.: e.g. P$_2$, ἐγράφη ἀπὸ Ἰταλίας. K$_2$, ἐγράφη ἀπὸ Ἰταλίας διὰ Τιμοθέου. H$_3$, Παύλου ἀποστόλου ἐπιστολὴ πρὸς Ἑβραίους ἐγράφη ἀπὸ Ἰταλίας διὰ Τιμοθέου. Nor again is there anything in the Epistle itself which leads to a definite conclusion. No argument can be drawn from the mention of the release of Timothy (xiii. 23), for nothing is known of the event to which reference is made; and the phrase ἀσπάζονται ὑμᾶς οἱ ἀπὸ τῆς Ἰταλίας (xiii. 24), which seems at first sight to promise more, gives no certain result. For the words admit grammatically of two opposite renderings. They may describe Italian Christians in their own country, or Italian Christians in a foreign land. The first sense is given by the translation (which is certainly possible), 'those in Italy send salutations from Italy,' where the preposition is conformed to the idea of the verb (comp. Luke xi. 13 ὁ πατὴρ ὁ ἐξ οὐρανοῦ δώσει. Math. xxiv. 17 ἆραι τὰ ἐκ τῆς οἰκίας. Col. iv. 16 τὴν ἐκ Λαοδικείας [ἐπιστολήν] with Bp Lightfoot's note); and more simply by the translation 'those who belong to Italy,' the Italian Christians (comp. Acts x. 23 τῶν ἀπὸ τῆς Ἰόππης. xii. 1 τῶν ἀπὸ τῆς ἐκκλησίας. xvii. 13 οἱ ἀπὸ τῆς Θεσσαλονίκης Ἰουδαῖοι); and in this sense a close parallel has been pointed out in Pseud.-Ign. ad Her. 8 ἀσπάζονταί σε οἱ ἐπίσκοποι...καὶ πάντες οἱ ἀπὸ Φιλίππων ἐν Χριστῷ ὅθεν καὶ ἐπέστειλά σοι. But it is difficult to understand how any one could give the salutations of the Italian Christians generally (as distinguished from οἱ ἀπὸ Ῥώμης, or the like); so that it appears on the whole to be more natural to adopt the second rendering ('the Christians from Italy'), and to suppose that the writer is speaking of a small group of friends from Italy, who were with him at the time. So far the words seem to favour a place of writing in Asia, Syria, or Egypt. In any case, however, it is impossible to lay stress upon a clause which evidently had a particular and special sense for those to whom the message was sent.

The place of writing must then be left in complete uncertainty. Plausible conjectures unsupported by evidence cannot remove our ignorance even if they satisfy our curiosity.

VIII. STYLE AND LANGUAGE.

The language of the Epistle is both in vocabulary and style purer and more vigorous than that of any other book of the N.T.

i. Vocabulary of the Epistle.

i. The vocabulary is singularly copious. It includes a large number of words which are not found elsewhere in the apostolic writings, very many which occur in this book only among the Greek Scriptures, and some which are not quoted from any other independent source. Even when allowance is made for the requirements of the peculiar topics with which the writer deals, the number of peculiar words is still remarkable. In the Pastoral Epistles however the proportion is still greater.

Dr Thayer reckons the same number of peculiar words (168) in the Pastoral Epistles and the Epistle to the Hebrews, but the latter is the longer in about the proportion of 21 to 15.

The following words are not quoted from any source independent of the Epistle: ἀγενεαλόγητος (vii. 3); αἱματεκχυσία (ix. 22); ἔκτρομος (xii. 21 marg.); εὐπερίστατος (xii. 1); θεατρίζειν (x. 33; ἐκθεατρίζειν in Polyb.); μισθαποδότης (xi. 6) and μισθαποδοσία (ii. 2; x. 35; xi. 26) for the Classical μισθοδότης and μισθοδοσία; πρόσχυσις (xi. 28); συγκακουχεῖν (xi. 25); τελειωτής (xii. 2). *(a) Peculiar words.*

The list of classical words which are found in the Epistle and in no other part of the Greek Scriptures is large: ἀκλινής (x. 23); ἀκροθίνιον (vii. 4); ἀλυσιτελής (xiii. 17); ἀμήτωρ, ἀπάτωρ (vii. 3); ἀναλογίζεσθαι (xii. 3); ἀνασταυροῦν (vi. 6); ἀνταγωνίζεσθαι (xii. 4); διόρθωσις (ix. 10); ἐκδοχή (x. 27); ἐκλανθάνειν (xii. 5); ἐνυβρίζειν (x. 29); ἐπεισαγωγή (vii. 19); εὐαρέστως (xii. 28); κατάδηλος (vii. 15); κατασκιάζειν (ix. 5); ὄγκος (xii. 1); παραπλησίως (ii. 14); συμπαθεῖν (iv. 15; x. 34); συνεπιμαρτυρεῖν (ii. 4); τομώτερος (iv. 12); ὑπείκειν (xiii. 17). *(b) Words found in this book only of the Greek Scriptures.*

Other words peculiar to the Epistle among Biblical writings belong to the later stage of Greek Literature: ἀθέτησις (vii. 18; ix. 26); ἄθλησις (x. 32); ἀκατάλυτος (vii. 16); ἀμετάθετος (vi. 17 f.); ἀπαράβατος (vii. 24); ἀφορᾶν (xii. 2); δυσερμήνευτος (v. 11); εὐποιΐα (xiii. 16); καταγωνίζεσθαι (xi. 33); Λευιτικός (vii. 11); μεσιτεύειν (vi. 17); μετριοπαθεῖν (v. 2); πολυμερῶς, πολυτρόπως (i. 1); σαββατισμός (iv. 9); τραχηλίζειν (iv. 13); τυμπανίζειν (xi. 35); ὑποστολή (x. 39).

A very large number of words used by good Greek authors and found also in the LXX. are found in this Epistle only in the New Testament: αἴγεος (-ειος,) αἰσθητήριον, αἴτιος, ἀνακαινίζειν, ἀναρίθμητος, ἀντικαταστῆναι, ἄπειρος, ἀποβλέπειν, ἁρμός (Apocr.), ἀφανής, ἀφανισμός, ἀφομοιοῦν (Apocr.), βοτάνη, γενεαλογεῖν, γεωργεῖν (Apocr.), γνόφος, δάμαλις, δεκάτη, δέος (Apocr.), δέρμα, δημιουργός (Apocr.), διάταγμα (Apocr.), διηνεκής, διϊκνεῖσθαι, δοκιμασία, ἔγγυος (Apocr.), ἐκβαίνειν, ἔλεγχος, ἕξις (Apocr.), ἐπιλείπειν, ἐπισκοπεῖν, ἔπος, εὐαρεστεῖν, εὐλάβεια, εὐλαβεῖσθαι, θεράπων, θύελλα, θυμιατήριον, ἱερωσύνη, ἱκετήριος, κακουχεῖν, καρτερεῖν, καταναλίσκειν, κατάσκοπος, καῦσις, μερισμός, μετάθεσις, μετέπειτα (Apocr.), μυελός, νέφος, νόθος (Apocr.), νομοθετεῖν, νωθρός (Apocr.), ὁμοιότης, πανήγυρις, παραδειγματίζειν, παραπίπτειν, παραρρεῖν, πεῖρα, πηγνύναι, πρίζειν (πρίειν), προβλέπειν, πρόδρομος (Apocr.), προσαγορεύειν (Apocr.), πρόσφατος, στάμνος, συναπολλύναι, συνδεῖν, τιμωρία, τράγος, τρίμηνος, φαντάζειν, φοβερός, χαρακτήρ (Apocr.). *(c) Words found in the LXX. used in this Book only of N. T.*

The non-classical words found in the LXX. which are found only in this Epistle in the N. T. are comparatively few: ἀγνόημα, αἴνεσις, ἀπαύγασμα (Apocr.), δεκατοῦν, ἐγκαινίζειν, ἐμπαιγμός, θέλησις, λειτουργικός, μηλωτή, ὀλεθρεύειν, ὁρκωμοσία, παραπικραίνειν, πρωτοτόκια.

A study of the lists of words in these three different classes will illustrate the freedom and power with which the author of the

Epistle dealt with the resources of the Greek language. His love for compound words is characteristic of the period at which he wrote, but their number is largely in excess of the average of their occurrence in the N. T.

Seyffarth has calculated that there are in the Epistle to the Romans 478 'vocabula composita et decomposita' and in the Epistle to the Hebrews 534 (*De ep. ad Hebr. indole*, § 40, 1821. This Essay contains good materials, but they require careful sifting).

Words with a peculiar Biblical sense.

The number of words found in the Epistle which have a peculiar Biblical sense is comparatively small. Some are derived from the Greek translation of the books of the Hebrew Canon (*e.g.* ἀγάπη, ἄγγελος, ἀδελφός, αἰών, ἀναφέρειν, ὁ διάβολος, ἱλαστήριον, καθαρίζειν, κληρονομεῖν &c., λειτουργεῖν &c., μακροθυμία, ὁμολογεῖν, παιδεία, πειράζειν, πίστις, πρωτότοκος, σάρκινος, φωτίζειν, χάρις), some from the Apocrypha (*e.g.* ἔκβασις, κοινός, κόσμος, κτίσις), some owe their characteristic force to Christian influences (ἀπόστολος, κοσμικός).

The absence of some words (*e.g.* πληροῦν, εὐαγγέλιον, οἰκοδομεῖν, μυστήριον, σύν) is remarkable.

ii. Style.

ii. The style is even more characteristic of a practised scholar than the vocabulary. It would be difficult to find anywhere passages more exact and pregnant in expression than i. 1—4; ii. 14—18; vii. 26—28; xii. 18—24. The language, the order, the rhythm, the parenthetical involutions, all contribute to the total effect. The writing shews everywhere traces of effort and care. In many respects it is not unlike that of the Book of Wisdom, but it is nowhere marred by the restless striving after effect which not unfrequently injures the beauty of that masterpiece of Alexandrine Greek. The calculated force of the periods is sharply distinguished from the impetuous eloquence of St Paul. The author is never carried away by his thoughts. He has seen and measured all that he desires to convey to his readers before he begins to write. In writing he has, like an artist, simply to give life to the model which he has already completely fashioned. This is true even of the noblest rhetorical passages, such as c. xi. Each element, which seems at first sight to offer itself spontaneously, will be found to

have been carefully adjusted to its place, and to offer in subtle
details results of deep thought, so expressed as to leave the
simplicity and freshness of the whole perfectly unimpaired. For
this reason there is perhaps no Book of Scripture in which the
student may hope more confidently to enter into the mind of the
author if he yields himself with absolute trust to his words. No
Book represents with equal clearness the mature conclusions of
human reflection.

The contrast of the Style of the Epistle to that of St Paul may be *Contrast*
noticed in the passages which are quoted as echoes of St Paul's language: *with the style of St Paul.*

 ii. 10. Comp. Rom. xi. 36.

 iii. 6. —— v. 2.

 xi. 12. —— iv. 19.

The richer fulness of expression is seen in corresponding phrases : e. g.
Col. iii. 1, compared with c. xii. 2 (note).

The writer does not use St Paul's rhetorical forms τί οὖν; τί γάρ; ἀλλ᾽
ἐρεῖ τις..., μὴ γένοιτο, ἄρα οὖν, οὐκ οἴδατε (Credner *Einl.* s. 547). On the
other hand we notice the peculiar phrases, ὡς ἔπος εἰπεῖν, εἰς τὸ διηνεκές,
ἔλαθον ξενίσαντες, and the particle ὅθεν.

Seyffarth has rightly called attention to the relative frequency of the
use of participial constructions in the Epistle : Octogies atque quater in...
epistola habes participia activa, centies et septies participia passiva et
media, atque septies genitivos absolutos...In epistola...ad Romanos multum
prolixiori nonagies reperi constructionem quam dicunt participialem activam,
duodequadragesies tantum constructionem participialem passivam atque
mediam, nec tamen ullibi genitivos absolutos. Decies tantum Paulus
apostolus, quantum vidi, in omnibus epistolis suis utitur genitivis absolutis
plerumque contra regulas a grammaticis scriptas...(*de ep. ad Hebr. indole*
§ 36).

Some correspondences with the Epistles of St Paul to the Romans (in
addition to those given above) and Corinthians (1) which have been
collected (Holtzmann *Einl.* 315 f.) deserve to be quoted, if only to shew the
difference of style in the Epistle to the Hebrews : vi. 12 f. (Rom. iv. 13, 20);
x. 38 (Rom. i. 17); xii. 14 (Rom. xii. 18; xiv. 19); xiii. 1 (Rom. xii. 10);
id. 2 (Rom. xii. 13); *id.* 9 (Rom. xiv. 3 f.); ii. 4 (1 Cor. xii. 4, 7—11); *id.* 8
(1 Cor. xv. 27); *id.* 10 (1 Cor. viii. 6); *id.* 14 (1 Cor. xv. 26); iii. 7—19 ;
xii. 18—25 (1 Cor. x. 1—11); v. 12 (1 Cor. iii. 2); v. 14 (1 Cor. ii. 6); vi. 3
(1 Cor. xvi. 7); ix. 26 (1 Cor. x. 11); x. 33 (1 Cor. iv. 9); xiii. 10 (1 Cor. x.
14—21); *id.* 20 (1 Cor. vii. 15; xiv. 33).

The close resemblance of the language of the Epistle to that of St Luke *Resem-blance of the language to that of St Luke.*
was noticed by Clement of Alexandria (*ap.* Euseb. *H. E.* vi. 14...Λουκᾶν
[φησίν]...μεθερμηνεύσαντα ἐκδοῦναι τοῖς Ἕλλησιν· ὅθεν τὸν αὐτὸν χρῶτα
εὑρίσκεσθαι κατὰ τὴν ἑρμηνείαν ταύτης τε τῆς ἐπιστολῆς καὶ τῶν πράξεων—the

form of expression is remarkable), and his criticism was repeated by later writers. The significance of the coincidences may have been overrated, but no impartial student can fail to be struck by the frequent use of words characteristic of St Luke among the writers of the N.T. *e.g.* διαμαρτύρεσθαι (ii. 6), ἀρχηγός (ii. 10), ὅθεν (ii. 17), ἱλάσκεσθαι (ii. 17), μέτοχος (iii. 1), περικεῖσθαι accus. (v. 2), εὔθετος (vi. 7), καταφεύγειν (vi. 18), πατριάρχης (vii. 4) εἰς τὸ παντελές (vii. 25), σχεδόν (ix. 22), ἀνώτερον (x. 8), ·παροξυσμός (x. 24), ὕπαρξις (x. 34), ἀναστάσεως τυγχάνειν (xi. 35), ἔντρομος (xii. 21), ἀσάλευτος (xii. 28), οἱ ἡγούμενοι (xiii. 7), ἀναθεωρεῖν (xiii. 7).

Imagery of the Epistle.

The imagery of the Epistle is drawn from many sources. Some of the figures which are touched more or less in detail are singularly vivid and expressive: iv. 12 (the word a sword); vi. 7 f. (the land fruitful for good or evil); vi. 19 (hope the anchor); xi. 13 (the vision of the distant shore); xii. 1 (the amphitheatre); 8 ff. (the discipline of life). A whole picture often lies in single words: ii. 1 (παραρυῶμεν); iv. 2 (συνκεκερασμένος -ους); 9 (σαββατισμός); 13 (τετραχηλισμένα); v. 2 (περίκειται ἀσθένειαν, comp. x. 11 περιελεῖν); vi. 1 φερώμεθα); 6 (ἀνασταυροῦντες); viii. 5 (σκιά, comp. ix. 23 f.; x. 1, 11); 13 (γηράσκον); x. 20 (ὁδὸς ζῶσα); 33 (θεατριζόμενοι); xii. 23 (πανήγυρις). Compare also i. 3; ii. 9, 15; iii. 2; v. 12 f.; x. 22, 27; xii. 13.

IX. THE PLAN.

The general progress of thought in the Epistle is clear; but, at the same time, in a writing so many-sided, where subjects are naturally foreshadowed and recalled, differences of opinion must arise as to the exact divisions of the argument. The following arrangement gives at least an intelligible view of the main relations of the different parts of the Book.

THE THEME OF THE EPISTLE; THE FINALITY OF CHRISTIANITY : i. 1—4.

I. THE SUPERIORITY OF THE SON, THE MEDIATOR OF THE NEW REVELATION, TO ANGELS : i. 5—ii. 18.

II. MOSES, JOSHUA, JESUS, THE FOUNDERS OF THE OLD ECONOMY AND OF THE NEW : iii., iv.

III. THE HIGH-PRIESTHOOD OF CHRIST, UNIVERSAL AND SOVE-
REIGN (MELCHIZEDEK): v.—vii.

IV. THE FULFILMENT OF CHRIST'S PRIESTLY WORK: viii. 1—
x. 18.

V. THE APPROPRIATION AND VITAL APPLICATION OF THE
TRUTHS LAID DOWN: x. 19—xii.
A PERSONAL EPILOGUE: xiii.

These chief divisions can be followed a little more in detail:

THE THEME OF THE EPISTLE: THE FINALITY OF CHRISTIANITY:
i. 1—4.

   i. *The contrast of the Old Revelation and the New in method,
time, persons (vv. 1, 2).*

   ii. *The nature and the work of the Son, in regard to His
Divine Personality and to the Incarnation (v. 3).*

   iii. *Transition to the detailed development of the argument (v. 4).*

I. THE SUPERIORITY OF THE SON, THE MEDIATOR OF THE
NEW REVELATION, TO ANGELS: i. 5—ii. 18.

   i. *The testimony of Scripture (i. 5—14).*

   ii. *The peril of neglecting the new revelation through the Son
(ii. 1—4).*

   iii. *The fulfilment of the divine destiny of man in the Son of
man (Jesus) through suffering (ii. 5—18).*

II. MOSES, JOSHUA, JESUS, THE FOUNDERS OF THE OLD
ECONOMY AND OF THE NEW: iii., iv.

   i. *Moses and Jesus: the servant and the Son (iii. 1—6).*

     (1) A general view of the dignity of Jesus (1, 2).

     (2) Moses represents a house: Jesus the framer of
it (3, 4).

     (3) Moses a servant: Jesus a son (5, 6).

   ii. *The promise and the people under the Old and the New
Dispensations (iii. 7—iv. 13).*

     (1) Faith the condition of blessing (iii. 7—19).

     (2) The promise remaining (iv. 1—13).

One feature in this plan will strike the student. The central portion of each of the first three divisions is mainly occupied with solemn warnings ; while the last division is a most grave and earnest exposition of the duties which follow from the confession of Christ's Priestly work. The writer is unwilling, even in the development of the Truth, to allow the loftiest conception of the Gospel to appear to be a theory only. It is for him intensely practical ; and the note of entire and reverential awe closes his description of the privileges of Christians (xii. 28 f.).

X. CHARACTERISTICS.

The Epistle to the Hebrews is one of three Books in the N. T. specially addressed to those who were Jews by descent, the other two being the Gospel according to St Matthew and the Epistle of St James (James i. 1 ταῖς δώδεκα φυλαῖς). To these however 1 Peter, probably addressed to those who had passed through Judaism to Christianity, may be added (1 Pet. i. 1 ἐκλεκτοῖς παρεπιδήμοις διασπορᾶς Πόντου...).

Each of these books is marked by a characteristic view of the Faith. St Matthew, according to general consent, gives the lineaments of the Davidic King. In St James we have the power of ' a perfect law ' (James i. 25 ; ii. 8): in St Peter the accomplishment of prophecy (1 Peter i. 10—12): in the Epistle to the Hebrews the efficacy of an eternal priesthood (Hebr. vii. 23 ff.).

This general connexion indicates the true position of the Epistle, which is that of a final development of the teaching of 'the three,' and not of a special application of the teaching of St Paul. It is, so to speak, most truly intelligible as the last voice of the apostles of the circumcision and not as a peculiar utterance of the apostle of the Gentiles (Gal. ii. 9 f.). The apostles of the circumcision regarded Judaism naturally with sympathy and even with affection, for it was that through which they had been led little by little to see the meaning of the Gospel. The Apostle of the Gentiles, with all his

Side notes:

Books of the N. T. addressed to Jewish Christians.

The Epistle to the Hebrews the final expression of the teaching of 'the Three.'

love for his countrymen and all his reverence for the work wrought through the old Covenant, no less naturally regarded Judaism, as it was, as a system which had made him a persecutor of the Faith. For St Paul the Law is a code of moral ordinances : for the writer of the Epistle to the Hebrews it is a scheme of typical provisions for atonement.   For the one it is a crushing burden : for the other it is a welcome if imperfect source of consolation.   And it is in virtue of this general interpretation of the spirit of the Levitical system that the unknown apostle to whom we owe the Epistle to the Hebrews was fitted to fulfil for the Church the part which was providentially committed to him.

Two comple- mentary aspects of the Law.
We must indeed regard the Law under these two distinct aspects, in order that we may fully appreciate its character and its office. We must, that is, regard it on the one side as a body of command- ments imposed upon man's obedience ; and we must regard it on the other side as a system of ritual provided by God's mercy.   The one view is, as has been remarked, characteristic of St Paul, and the other of the author of the Epistle.   Each when carefully studied reveals the failure of the Law to satisfy man's needs, and so shews its necessary transitoriness.   As a legal code it tended to bondage, and was in- capable of fulfilment, and so brought a deep knowledge of sin (Rom. iii. 20 ἐπίγνωσις ἁμαρτίας).   As an institution for the removal of sin, it was designed only to deal with ceremonial defilement, and was therefore essentially insufficient (Hebr. x. 3 f.).   Thus the Epistle to the Hebrews completes the teaching of St Paul on the imperfection of the Law.   St Paul from the subjective side shews that the individual can be brought near to God only by personal faith and not by any outward works : the author of the Epistle from the objective side shews that purification cannot be gained by any sacrifices 'of bulls and goats' but only through the offering of the Blood of Christ.

General differences between St Paul and the Epistle.
The difference between St Paul and the writer of the Epistle in their view of the Law may be presented in another light.   St Paul regards the Law mainly in relation to the requirements of man's discipline : his fellow-apostle in relation to the fulfilment of God's

counsel. For St Paul the Law was an episode, intercalated, as it were, in the course of revelation (Rom. v. 20 παρεισῆλθεν) : for the writer of the Epistle it was a shadow of the realities to which the promise pointed. It is closely connected with this fundamental distinctness of the point of vision of the two teachers that St Paul dwells with dominant interest on the individual aspect of the Gospel, the writer of the Epistle on its social aspect : for the one the supreme contrast is between flesh and spirit, for the other between the image and the reality, the imperfect and the perfect : for the one Christ is the direct object of personal faith, for the other the fulfiller of the destiny of man.

But this difference, however real and intelligible, does not issue in any opposition between the two writers. Both views are completely satisfied by the Incarnation ; and each writer recognises the truth which the other develops. In the Epistle to the Ephesians St Paul gives the widest possible expression to the social lessons of the Faith ; and the writer to the Hebrews emphasises with the most touching solemnity the significance of personal responsibility (e.g. c. vi.). At the same time the writer to the Hebrews suggests the unity, the harmonious unfolding, of the divine plan, in a way which is foreign to the mode of thought of him who was suddenly changed from a persecutor to an apostle. His eyes rest on one heavenly archetype made known to men as they could bear the sight in various degrees. He presupposes a divine ideal of the phenomenal world and of outward worship. This, he argues, was shadowed forth in the Mosaic system ; and found its perfect embodiment under the conditions of earth in the Christian Church. He looks therefore with deep sympathy upon the devotion with which the Hebrews had regarded the provisions made by the Law for dealing with the power and guilt of sin. He enters into their feelings, and points out how Christ satisfied them by His Person and His work.

It is not difficult to see how the circumstances in which the **The writer of the Epistle deals with the double dis-** 'Hebrews' were placed gave a peculiar importance to the thought of priestly atonement with which they had been familiar. The Hebrews were necessarily distressed by two main trials. They had met with a double disappointment. They were disappointed at the nature of Christianity. They were disappointed specially as to the attitude of Israel towards it.

1. The early expectations of a triumphant Return of Christ had not been fulfilled. His sufferings were not (as some at least had hoped) a mere transient phase of His work, quickly forgotten in the glory which followed. The difficulties therefore which the apostles met at the first preaching recorded in the Acts had to be met in a new form. The apostles had shewn that the Death of Christ was no obstacle to His Messiahship in view of His Resurrection and implied Return (Acts ii., iii., v.). It had to be shewn now that suffering was essential to His work. A suffering Messiah had to be accepted in His earthly reproach (xiii. 13; comp. 1 Cor. i. 23), while the prospect of visible triumph was withdrawn from view.

2. This was one trial. There was another also not less grievous. It became more and more clear that the Jews as a people would not receive Jesus as the Christ. Their national unbelief, apart from all direct persecution, brought with it a growing alienation of the Synagogue from the Church. It was more and more difficult to hold to both. The right of participation in the ministrations of the Temple was in process of time necessarily withdrawn from Christians if they held their faith, and they were forced to look elsewhere for that which might supply their place.

These trials from the point of sight of a Jewish Christian were most real. He could not but ask, Was there to be no Kingdom for Israel? Had God cast away His people? Were Christians to be deprived of the manifold consolations of sacrificial worship and priestly atonement? And we must at least in some degree understand their bearing before we can enter into the spirit of the Epistle.

To this end it is necessary to realise distinctly the sharp contrast between the early popular expectations of what Christianity should be, especially among Jewish converts, and what it proved to be. And it is necessary also to realise the incompleteness with which the significance of the Lord's sufferings was at first apprehended. When these points are placed in proper relief then the importance and the power of the argument in the Epistle to the Hebrews become evident. For the writer shews that the difficulty which arises from the sufferings of the Son of man (Jesus) includes the answer to the difficulty which was felt in exclusion from the Temple. The humiliation of Christ a little below the angels, over whom in essence He is supreme, gives efficacy to His continuous intercession based upon the atonement, and is for men a pledge of His unfailing sympathy. Faith in Him therefore made the outward consolations of the Temple wholly superfluous. At the same time this apprehension of Christ's redemptive and priestly work made it evident that those who clung to an external system, such as that of the Law, could not truly embrace the Gospel. The Judaism which was not in due time taken up and transfigured by the Gospel of necessity became antagonistic to it. He who remained a Jew outwardly could not but miss in the end the message of Christ, just as the Christian, who understands his position, is essentially independent of every support of the old Covenant.

By emphasising these thoughts the writer of the Epistle shews the essential transitoriness of the Law. But he recognises no less clearly its positive teachings. This also belonged to his office. *The essential work of Judaism* For Judaism proclaimed most impressively three fundamental facts with which it dealt provisionally; and a sympathetic intelligence of that to which it witnessed and of that which it offered leads to the true understanding of Christianity as the divine accomplishment of the education of the world.

Judaism affirmed that the destiny of humanity is the attainment of likeness to God, an end to be reached under the actual conditions of life only through restrictions and painful effort. The holiness of God, to which man has to be conformed, is on the one side love and on the other side righteousness.

Judaism again affirmed that man as he is cannot at his own pleasure or in his own right draw near to God. The ceremonial law in all its parts deepened the consciousness of sin.

And yet again Judaism affirmed that it was the good pleasure of God to enter into Covenant with man, of which external institutions were the abiding sign and seal, a testimony at once and a promise.

fulfilled in Christ.

The writer of the Epistle shews from the position of the believing Jew how the revelation of the Son of God deals with these facts finally. 'Jesus, the Son of God' (iv. 14; comp. Acts ix. 20), fulfilled the destiny of man, Himself true man, by bringing humanity to the throne of heaven. He fulfilled this destiny through suffering and death, bearing Himself the last consequences of sin and overcoming death through death. And yet more, He communicates through all time the virtue of His life to those who come to God through and in Him.

The place of præ-Judaic Revelation.

Under this aspect the significant emphasis which the writer lays upon the præ-Judaic form of Revelation becomes fully intelligible. The Gospel, as he presents it, is the fulfilment of the purpose of creation and not only of the Mosaic system. Melchizedek is a more prominent figure in his treatment of the O. T. than Abraham. Thus the work of Judaism is made to appear as a stage in the advance towards a wider work which could not be achieved without a preparatory discipline. So regarded the provisions of the Law can be seen in their full meaning, and by the help of their typical teaching a suffering Messiah can be acknowledged in His Majesty by the true Jew.

The God of Abraham and the God of Moses is, in other words, 'a living God.' His revelation of Himself answers to the progress of life (iii. 12). His worship is realised in a personal revelation (ix. 14). His action corresponds with an individual judgment (x. 31). His reward lies in the manifestation of His Presence (xii. 22 ff.).

The universal teaching of the Epistle comes from its special relations.

We can now see more clearly than before how the general aim of the writer to present Christianity as the absolute revelation of God, the absolute satisfaction of man's needs, was furthered by his desire to deal with the peculiar trials of the Hebrews who felt keenly not only the shame and sufferings of the Messiah, but their own shame and sufferings from national hostility. These trials in fact served as an occasion for developing the new thoughts which the Book adds to the apostolic presentation of the Truth. They placed in a clear light the need which men have for a continuous assurance of present help in the actual difficulties of life. And so the opportunity was given in the order of Providence for developing the truth of Christ's High-priestly work, towards which the aboriginal religion, represented by Melchizedek, and the Mosaic system, had both pointed. For while the writer labours to establish the absolute Majesty of the new dispensation in comparison with the old, he does so especially by connecting its power with the self-sacrifice of Christ. That which seemed to be the weakness of the Gospel is revealed upon a closer vision to be its strength. In proportion as men can feel what Christ is (such is the writer's argument) they can feel also how His death and His advocacy more than supply the place of all sacrifices and priestly intercessions, how they lay open the victory of humanity in the Son of man over sin and death. In other words, under this light the Death of Christ becomes intelligible in itself without regard to the thought of a Return. The sense of His present priestly action gains a new force. The paradox of a suffering Messiah is disclosed in its own glory.

Through such a view of Christ's work, illuminated in the fuller view of His Person, the Hebrew believer, in short, found his dis-appointments unexpectedly transformed. He recognised the majesty of Christ's spiritual triumph. He perceived the divine significance of Christ's sufferings, and through that he perceived also the interpre-tation of the sufferings of men. Thus the immediate purpose of the writer was fulfilled; and that which was an answer to the difficulties of the Hebrew Christian has been made the endowment of the whole Church. For in this Epistle we have what is found in no other Book of the N. T., that which may be called a philosophy of religion, of worship, of priesthood, centred in the Person of Christ. The form of the doctrine is determined by the O. T. foundations, but the doctrine itself is essentially new. In the light of the Gospel the whole teaching of the O. T. is seen to be a prophecy, unquestionable in the breadth and fulness of its scope.

But while the thoughts of the absolute value of Christ's sufferings Diffi-
and of the application of their virtue to men are brought out with culties which

remain
can be
borne.

prevailing force, it is not argued that all difficulty is removed from
the present prospect of Christianity.   There are still, the writer
implies, difficulties in the state of things which we see.   We cannot
escape from them.   But enough can be discerned to enable men to
wait patiently for the appointed end.   There is a triumph to come;
and, in looking forward to this, Christians occupy the position which
the Saints have always occupied, the position of faith, of faith
under trials.   The heroic records of c. xi. lead up to the practical
charge of c. xii. 1 ff.

Meanwhile the writer calls upon his readers to make their choice
boldly.   Judaism was becoming, if it had not already become,
anti-Christian.   It must be given up (xiii. 13).   It was 'near
vanishing away' (viii. 13).   It was no longer debated whether
a Gentile Church could stand beside the Jewish Church, as in the
first period of conflict in the apostolic age; or whether a Jewish
Church should stand beside the Gentile Church, as in the next period.
The Christian Church must be one and independent.   And thus the
Epistle is a monument of the last crisis of conflict out of which the
Catholic Church rose.

The Old
ennobled
not dis-
paraged.

This view is the more impressive from the prominence which is
assigned in the Epistle to the Old Testament, both to the writings
and to the institutions which it hallows.   There is not the least
tendency towards disparagement of the one or the other.

From first to last it is maintained that God *spoke to the fathers in
the prophets*.   The message through the Son takes up and crowns all
that had gone before.   In each respect the New is the consummation of the Old.   It offers a more perfect and absolute Revelation,
carrying with it a more perfect and absolute Mediation, and establishing a more perfect and absolute Covenant, embodying finally the
connexion of God and man.   There is nothing in the Old which is
not taken up and transfigured in the New.

For it is assumed throughout the Epistle that all visible
theocratic institutions answer to a divine antitype (archetype).   They
are (so to speak) a translation into a particular dialect of eternal
truths : a representation under special conditions of an absolute ideal.

In some sense, which we can feel rather than define, the eternal is declared to lie beneath the temporal (xii. 27). In virtue of this truth the work of Christ and the hope of the Christian are both described under Jewish imagery, without the least admixture of the millenarian extravagances which gained currency in the second century. There is for the believer a priestly consecration (x. 22 note), an altar (xiii. 10 note), a sabbath-rest (iv. 9).

It follows therefore that in studying the Levitical ritual we must recognise that there is a true correspondence of the seen with the unseen, a correspondence which extends to the fulness of life, and not simply a correspondence of a world of ideas (κόσμος νοητός), as Philo supposed, to a world of phenomena.

The same principle holds still under the Christian dispensation. We see the reality but only in figures (e.g. Apoc. xxi. 16). Judaism was the shadow, and Christianity is the substance; yet both are regarded under the conditions of earth. But the figures have an abiding significance. There is a heavenly city in the spiritual world, an organised body of rational beings; ' a congregation ' (ἐκκλησία) which answers to the full enjoyment of the privileges of social life: xi. 10 (ἡ τοὺς θεμ. ἔχ. πόλις); xi. 16; xii. 22 f. (comp. viii. 11; xiii. 14; and Addit. Note on xi. 10). There is also a heavenly sanctuary there, which was the pattern of the earthly, to confirm the eternal duty and joy of worship: viii. 2, 5.

In this aspect the Epistle fulfils a universal work. It is addressed to Hebrews, and meets, as we have seen, their peculiar difficulties, but at the same time it deals with the largest views of the Faith. This it does not by digression or contrast. It discloses the catholicity of the Gospel by the simple interpretation of its scope. It does not insist on the fact as anything new or strange. It does not dwell on 'the breaking down of the middle wall of partition' (Eph. ii. 14), or on 'the mystery which in other ages was not made known...that the Gentiles are...fellow-partakers of the promise in Christ Jesus' (Eph. iii. 4 ff.; Rom. xvi. 25 f.). The equality of men as men in the sight of God is implied in the declaration which is made of the Person and the Work of Christ.

Faith is the condition of a divine fellowship, and that is essentially universal. The truth that there is no difference between Jew and Gentile has passed beyond the stage of keen controversy. It is acknowledged in the conception which has been gained of the Incarnation.

Relation of the Epistle to the Gospel of St John.

Viewed in this light, the Epistle to the Hebrews forms a complement to the Gospel of St John. Both Books assume the universality of Christianity as the one religion of humanity, without special argument (comp. John i. 12). Both regard 'the Jews'—the men who clung to that which was transitory as if it were absolute and eternal—as enemies of Christ. Both recognise completely the provisional office of the Old Dispensation (John iv. 22 ff.). But they do this from different sides. The Epistle to the Hebrews enables us to see how Christianity is the absolute fulfilment of the idea of the positive institutions of the Law through which it was the good pleasure of God to discipline men, while the Fourth Gospel shews us in the *Word become flesh* the absolute fulfilment of the idea of creation which underlies the whole of the Old Testament.

It is also not without interest that the foundation of the characteristic teaching of the Epistle to the Hebrews on the High-priesthood of Christ is found in the Lord's words preserved by St John more distinctly than in the other Gospels, though the Evangelist himself does not develop the truth. Thus, in the discourse which defines the nature of the new Society in relation to its Head (John x. 1—21), the Lord reveals His victory through death : He shews Himself in a figure as Victim at once and Priest (*vv.* 17 f.). Elsewhere He proclaims that He will draw all men to Himself when He is lifted up from the earth (xii. 32 ἐκ τῆς γῆς), that His removal from the limitations of our present bodily existence is the condition of His spiritual gift (xvi. 7), that He hallows His people in Himself (c. xvii.). Compare Matt. xx. 28 ; Luke xxii. 37.

In these revelations we have the thoughts which are wrought into a concrete whole in the Epistle to the Hebrews under the imagery of the Levitical system. But it will be noticed that the teaching which St John has preserved offers the final form of the

Truth. St John's theory (if we may so speak) of the work of Christ is less developed in detail than that which is found in the Epistles of St Paul and in the Epistle to the Hebrews; but his revelation of Christ's Person is more complete. He concentrates our attention, as it were, upon Him, Son of God and Son of man, and leaves us in the contemplation of facts which we can only understand in part.

One further observation must still be made. The style of the Book is characteristically Hellenistic, perhaps we may say, as far as our scanty evidence goes, Alexandrine; but the teaching itself is, like that of St John, characteristically Palestinian. This is shewn not only by the teaching on details, on the heavenly Jerusalem, and the heavenly Sanctuary, on Satan as the king of death, on angels, on the two ages (comp. Riehm, *Lehrbegriff* ss. 248, 652 ff.), but still more by its whole form. The writer holds firmly to the true historical sense of the ancient history and the ancient legislation. Jewish ordinances are not for him, as for Philo, symbols of transcendental ideas, but elements in a preparatory discipline for a divine manifestation upon earth. Christ is High-priest not as the eternal Word, but as the Incarnate Son who has lived and suffered and conquered as true man. At the same time the Apostle teaches us to recognise the divine method in the education of the world. He shews how God has used (and, as we are led to conclude, how He uses still) transitory institutions to awaken, to develop, to chasten, our thoughts of spiritual things. The Epistle is, to sum up all most briefly, the seal of the divine significance of all life. The interpretation, given in its salient points, of the record of the O. T., and of the training of Israel, is a prophetic light for the interpretation of the history of mankind.

The Epistle Hellenistic in style, but Palestinian in teaching.

XI. HISTORY AND AUTHORSHIP OF THE EPISTLE.

The earliest traces of the Epistle in Clement of Rome.

In discussing the history of any one of the writings of the New Testament it is necessary to bear in mind the narrow range of the scanty remains of the earliest Christian literature, and the little scope which they offer for definite references to particular Books. It might perhaps have been expected that the arguments of the Epistle to the Hebrews would have given it prominence in the first controversies of the Church, but this does not appear to have been the case. Traces of its use occur indeed in the oldest Christian writing outside the Canon, the letter written by Clement of Rome to the Corinthians, but it is not referred to by name till the second half of the second century. There can be no doubt that Clement was familiar with its contents. He not only uses its language (*ad Cor.* 17, 36), but imitates its form in such a way (*ad Cor.* 9, 12, 45) as to shew that he had the text before him; but the adaptations of words and thoughts are made silently, without any mark of quotation or any indication of the author from whom they are borrowed (comp. Euseb. *H. E.* iii. 38; Hier. *de vir. ill.* 15). The fact that the Book was known at Rome at this early date is of importance, because it was at Rome that the Pauline authorship was most consistently denied and for the longest period. In this connexion it is of interest that there are several coincidences of expression with the Epistle in the Shepherd of Hermas, which seem to be sufficient to shew that Hermas also was acquainted with it.

A comparison of the parallel passages leaves no doubt that Clement imitated the earlier text of the Epistle. This seems to be clear if (*e.g.*) Clement's references to Noah and Rahab are set by the side of Hebr. xi. 7, 31.

ad Cor. 9 Νῶε πιστὸς εὑρεθεὶς διὰ τῆς λειτουργίας αὐτοῦ παλιγγενεσίαν κόσμῳ ἐκήρυξε, καὶ διέσωσε δι᾽ αὐτοῦ ὁ δεσπότης τὰ εἰσελθόντα ἐν ὁμονοίᾳ ζῷα εἰς τὴν κιβωτόν.

ad Cor. 12 διὰ πίστιν καὶ φιλοξενίαν ἐσώθη ʻΡαὰβ ἡ πόρνη......
The parallel with Hebr. i. 3 f. makes it impossible to suppose that both
writers are borrowing illustrations from some common source:

    ad Cor. 36 ὅς ὢν ἀπαύγασμα τῆς μεγαλωσύνης αὐτοῦ τοσούτῳ μείζων ἐστὶν
ἀγγέλων ὅσῳ διαφορώτερον ὄνομα κεκληρονόμηκεν· γέγραπται γὰρ οὕτως· ὁ
ποιῶν τοὺς ἀγγέλους αὐτοῦ πνεύματα...
The most striking parallels with Hermas are *Vis.* ii. 3, 2 : Hebr. iii. 12 ;
Sim. i. 1 f.: Hebr. xi. 13 ff.; xiii. 14.

    The other evidence which can be alleged to shew that the Epistle Supposed
references
was known by the earliest Christian writers is less clear. Polycarp in Poly-
gives the Lord the title of 'High-priest' (c. 12 *pontifex*), a title carp and
Justin.
which is peculiar to the Epistle among the apostolic writings, but it
is not possible to conclude certainly that he derived it directly from
the Book. So again when Justin Martyr speaks of Christ as
'apostle' (*Apol.* i. 12, 63 : Hebr. iii. 1) and applies Ps. cx. to Him
(*Dial.* 96, 113), he may be using thoughts which had become current
among Christians, though these correspondences with characteristic
features of the Epistle are more worthy of consideration because
Justin has also several coincidences with its language (viii. 7 f., *Dial.*
34; ix. 13 f., *Dial.* 13; xii. 18 f., *Dial.* 67).

    On the other hand the Epistle was not included among the Not
reckoned
apostolic writings received by Marcion; nor does it find any place as St
Paul's by
in the Muratorian Canon (comp. p. xxviii.), while by this catalogue Marcion
it is distinctly excluded from the Epistles of St Paul (*septem* scribit or *Can.*
Murat.
ecclesiis).

    Hier. *Præf. in Ep. ad Tit.* Licet non sint digni fide qui fidem primam
irritam fecerunt, Marcionem loquor et Basilidem et omnes hæreticos qui
Vetus laniant Testamentum : tamen eos aliqua ex parte ferremus si saltem
in Novo continerent manus suas...Ut enim de ceteris epistolis taceam, de
quibus quidquid contrarium suo dogmati viderant eraserunt, nennullas
integras repudiandas crediderunt, ad Timotheum videlicet utramque, ad
Hebræos, et ad Titum. The last clause evidently refers to Marcion
personally. Tertullian charges Marcion with the arbitrary rejection of the
Pastoral Epistles, but he is naturally silent on his rejection of the Epistle
to the Hebrews on which he agreed with him (*adv. Marc.* v. 21).

    Towards the close of the second century there is evidence of a Opinions
as to the
knowledge of the Epistle in Alexandria, North Africa, Italy and the Epistle at
West of Europe. From the time of Pantænus it was held at the end of

the
Second
Century.
Alex-
andria.

Alexandria to be, at least indirectly, the work of St Paul and of canonical authority; and this opinion, supported in different forms by Clement and Origen, came to be generally received among the Eastern Greek Churches in the third century.

The Epistle is quoted as St Paul's by Dionysius of Alexandria (Euseb. *H.E.* vi. 41), by Theognostus, head of the Catechetical School (Routh, *Rell. Sacr.* iii. 409: Hebr. vi. 4; Athan. *Ep. ad Serap.* iv. 9 ff. [Migne, *P.G.* xxvi. 650 f.]), by Peter of Alexandria (Routh, *Rell. Sacr.* iv. 35) and by the Synod of Antioch c. 264 A.D. (Routh, *Rell. Sacr.* iii. 299). It seems to have been used by Pinytus, Bp of Gnossus in Crete (Euseb. *H.E.* iv. 23: Hebr. v. 12—14), and by Theophilus of Antioch (*ad Autol.* ii. 25: Hebr. v. 12; xii. 9). Methodius also was certainly acquainted with the Epistle (*Conv.* iv. 1, Hebr. i. 1; id. v. 7, Hebr. xi. 10; *de Resurr.* 5, Hebr. xii. 5), though he does not quote it as St Paul's (the supposed reference to Hebr. xi. in *Conv.* v. 7 κατὰ τὸν ἀπόστολον is doubtful). It is quoted as Scripture in the first of the Letters to Virgins which bear the name of Clement (*Ep. ad Virg.* i. 6: Migne, *P.G.* i. 391); and it is referred to in the Testaments of the xii. Patriarchs (*Test. Levi* § 18: Hebr. vii. 22 ff.).

North
Africa.

About the same time a Latin translation of the Epistle found a limited public recognition in North Africa, but not as a work of St Paul. So Tertullian speaks of it as being 'more widely received among the Churches than the Shepherd' (*de Pudic.* 20 utique receptior apud ecclesias illo apocrypho Pastore mœchorum). Cyprian however never quotes it and, by repeating the statement peculiar to Western writers that St Paul 'wrote to seven churches' (*de exhort. mart.* 11), he also implicitly denies its Pauline authorship.

Italy.

In Italy and Western Europe the Epistle was not held to be St Paul's and by consequence, as it seems, it was not held to be canonical. Hippolytus (Lagarde pp. 64, 89, 118, 149) and Irenæus (Euseb. *H. E.* v. 26) were acquainted with it, but they held that it 'was not Paul's' (Steph. Gobar *ap.* Phot. *Cod.* 232); and if Irenæus had held it to be authoritative Scripture, he could hardly have failed to use it freely in his Book 'against heresies.' Caius also reckoned only thirteen Epistles of St Paul (Euseb. *H. E.* vi. 20; Hier. *de vir. ill.* 59); and Eusebius, where he mentions the fact, adds that the opinion was 'still held by some Romans.'

Phot. *Cod.* 232 (Migne, *P. G.* ciii. 1103); Stephen Gobar (vi. cent.) states ὅτι Ἱππόλυτος καὶ Εἰρηναῖος τὴν πρὸς Ἑβραίους ἐπιστολὴν Παύλου οὐκ ἐκείνου εἰναί φασιν...The statement as to Hippolytus is confirmed by a reference which Photius elsewhere makes to Hippolytus himself: *Cod.* 121 (*P. G.* ciii. 403) λέγει δὲ ἄλλα τέ τινα τῆς ἀκριβείας λειπόμενα καὶ ὅτι ἡ πρὸς Ἑβραίους ἐπιστολὴ οὐκ ἔστι τοῦ ἀποστόλου Παύλου. With regard to Irenæus there is no direct confirmation. Eusebius (*l.c.*) simply says that he quoted 'phrases from the Epistle to the Hebrews and the so-called Wisdom of Solomon' in his Book of 'Various Discussions.' The connexion shews that, if he had quoted it as St Paul's, Eusebius would have noted the fact. Stephen Gobar may have interpreted the silence of Irenæus in his quotations, or something in the form of it, as a practical denial of the Pauline authorship. So Jerome paraphrases the words of Eusebius as to Caius (*l.c.*) τὴν πρὸς Ἑβραίους μὴ συναριθμήσας ταῖς λοιπαῖς by *decimam quartam quae fertur ad Hebraeos dicit non eius esse.*

The coincidences with the language of the Epistle, which are quoted from Irenæus, would at the most prove no more than that he was acquainted with the Book, which is established by other evidence (ii. 30, 9: Hebr. i. 3).

The Epistle is not quoted by Novatian, or Arnobius (yet see ii. 65: Hebr. ix. 6), or Lactantius, who however seems to have been acquainted with it (*Inst.* iv. 20: Hebr. viii. 7 ff.; iv. 14: Hebr. iii. 3 ff.; v. 5 f.; vii. 21; comp. Lardner, *Credibility*, lxv. § 6, 4, 14 ff.). They did not therefore, we may conclude, recognise its canonical authority.

Victorinus of Pettau repeats the familiar Western clause that 'Paul recognises seven churches' (Routh, *Rell. Sacr.* iii. 459).

It is impossible to decide certainly whether the Epistle formed a *Syria.* part of the earliest Syriac Version. The position which it holds in the Peshito at present shews at least that it was not regarded strictly as one of St Paul's Epistles but as an appendix to the collection. In accordance with this view it is called simply the 'Epistle to the Hebrews,' and not, after the usage in the other Epistles, 'the Epistle of Paul to the Hebrews.'

It is instructive to notice that in the Cambridge MS. of the (later) Harclean Version the title given is 'The Epistle to the Hebrews, of Paul the Apostle.' The Oxford (New Coll.) MS. of the same Version, which White published, has only 'The Epistle to the Hebrews,' comp. p. xxvii.

This meagre account indicates all the independent external Three opinions evidence which has been preserved by tradition as to the origin of as to the Epistle the Epistle. Later writers simply combine and repeat in various current. ways the views which it represents. To speak summarily, when the book first appears in general circulation three distinct opinions about it had already obtained local currency. At Alexandria the Greek Epistle was held to be not directly but mediately St Paul's, as either a free translation of his words or a reproduction of his thoughts. In North Africa it was known to some extent as the work of Barnabas and acknowledged as a secondary authority. At Rome and in Western Europe it was not included in the collection of the Epistles of St Paul and had no apostolic weight.

In order to decide between these conflicting judgments, and to account for their partial acceptance, it is necessary to examine the evidence more in detail.

The testimony of Alexandria. CLEMENT.The testimony of Alexandria is the earliest and the most explicit. It has been preserved by Eusebius from lost writings of Clement and Origen. Clement, he writes (*H. E.* vi. 14), says in his outlines (Ὑποτυπώσεις) 'that the Epistle is Paul's, and that it was written to Hebrews in the Hebrew language, and that Luke translated it with zealous care and published it to the Greeks; whence it is that the same complexion of style is found in the translation of this Epistle and in the Acts. [Further] that the [ordinary] phrase 'Paul an Apostle' was not placed at the head of the Epistle for good reason; for, he says, in writing to Hebrews who had formed a prejudice against him and viewed him with suspicion, he was wise not to repel them at the beginning by setting his name there.' The last clause only is quoted in Clement's own words, but there can be no doubt that Eusebius has given correctly the substance of what he said, as far as it goes, but much is left undetermined which it would be important to know. There is nothing to indicate the source of Clement's statement, or how far it was the common opinion of the Alexandrine Church at the time, or whether the hypothesis of a Hebrew original was framed to explain the peculiarities of the un-Pauline style. In part this deficiency may be supplied by another quotation from Clement in regard to the Epistle which Eusebius makes in the same place. 'The blessed PANTÆ- NUS.presbyter [Pantænus?] used to say: since the Lord was sent to the Hebrews, as being the Apostle of the Almighty, Paul through modesty, as was natural since he had been sent to the Gentiles, does not style himself apostle of the Hebrews, both for the sake of the honour due to the Lord, and because it was a work of supererogation for him to write to the Hebrews, since he was herald and apostle of the Gentiles.' It appears then that the exceptional character of the Epistle had attracted attention at Alexandria in the generation before Clement, and that an explanation was offered of one at least of its peculiarities. It is possible therefore, though not likely, that Clement derived from his master the idea of a Hebrew original. At any rate the idea was compatible with what he had learnt from Pantænus as to the authorship of the Greek text.

The whole passage of Eusebius (*H. E.* vi. 14) deserves to be quoted at length: τὴν πρὸς Ἑβραίους δὲ ἐπιστολὴν Παύλου μὲν εἶναί φησιν [ἐν ταῖς Ὑποτυπώσεσι] γεγράφθαι δὲ Ἑβραίοις Ἑβραϊκῇ φωνῇ· Λουκᾶν δὲ φιλοτίμως αὐτὴν μεθερμηνεύσαντα ἐκδοῦναι τοῖς Ἕλλησιν· ὅθεν τὸν αὐτὸν χρῶτα εὑρίσκεσθαι κατὰ τὴν ἑρμηνείαν ταύτης τε τῆς ἐπιστολῆς καὶ τῶν Πράξεων· μὴ προγεγράφθαι δὲ τό 'Παῦλος ἀπόστολος' εἰκότως· ''Ἑβραίοις γάρ,' φησιν, 'ἐπιστέλλων, πρόληψιν εἰληφόσι κατ' αὐτοῦ καὶ ὑποπτεύουσιν αὐτόν, συνετῶς πάνυ οὐκ ἐν ἀρχῇ ἀπέστρεφεν αὐτοὺς τὸ ὄνομα θείς.' Εἶτα ὑποβὰς ἐπιλέγει '"Ἤδη δέ, ὡς ὁ μακάριος ἔλεγε πρεσβύτερος, ἐπεὶ ὁ κύριος ἀπόστολος ὢν τοῦ παντοκράτορος ἀπεστάλη πρὸς Ἑβραίους, διὰ μετριότητα ὁ Παῦλος, ὡς ἂν εἰς τὰ ἔθνη ἀπεσταλμένος, οὐκ ἐγγράφει ἑαυτὸν Ἑβραίων ἀπόστολον διά τε τὴν πρὸς τὸν κύριον τιμήν, διά τε τὸ ἐκ περιουσίας καὶ τοῖς Ἑβραίοις ἐπιστέλλειν ἐθνῶν κήρυκα ὄντα καὶ ἀπόστολον.'

There is no direct evidence to identify Pantænus with 'the blessed elder,' for Clement appears to have derived his information from more than one of his generation (comp. Euseb. *H. E.* v. 11), but the identification appears to be natural from the position which Pantænus occupied (comp. *H. E.* v. 11; vi. 13).

The use of ἤδη in the second (verbal) quotation from Clement seems to imply that Clement is meeting a difficulty which was freshly urged in his own time. It had been, he seems to say, adequately met before.

If Pantænus had spoken of a Hebrew original it is most likely that Clement would have noticed the fact. The argument from style may naturally mark a second stage in the controversy as to the authorship of the Epistle.

The judgment of Origen is quoted by Eusebius (*H. E.* vi. 25) in Origen his own words. After remarking that every one competent to judge of language must admit that the style of the Epistle to the Hebrews is not that of St Paul, and also that every one conversant with the apostle's teaching must agree that the thoughts are marvellous and in no way inferior to his acknowledged writings, Origen, he tells us, after a while continued, 'If I were to express my own opinion I 'should say that the thoughts are the thoughts of the apostle, but 'the language and the composition that of one who recalled from 'memory and, as it were, made notes of what was said by his 'master. If therefore any Church holds this Epistle as Paul's, let 'it be approved for this also [as for holding unquestioned truths], for 'it was not without reason that the men of old time have handed 'it down as Paul's [that is, as substantially expressing his thoughts]. 'But who wrote the Epistle God only knows certainly. The account 'that has reached us is twofold: some say that Clement, who 'became bishop of the Romans, wrote the Epistle, others that Luke 'wrote it, who wrote the Gospel and the Acts. But on this I will 'say no more.'

The relation of the testimony of Origen to that of Clement.   This testimony is of the highest value as supplementary to and in part explaining that of Clement. Origen does not refer to any 'Hebrew' original. It is not possible then that this hypothesis formed part of the ancient tradition. It was a suggestion which Origen did not think it worth while to discuss. He was aware that some Churches did not receive the Epistle as St Paul's. In the strictest sense of authorship he agreed with them. At the same time he held that in a true sense it could be regarded as St Paul's, as embodying thoughts in every way worthy of him.

The result of the testimony of Alexandria.   Thus Clement and Origen, both familiar with the details of the tradition of 'the men of old time' to whom they refer, agree in regarding the Greek Epistle as St Paul's only in a secondary sense. Clement regards it as a free translation of a 'Hebrew' original, so made by St Luke as to shew the characteristics of his style: Origen regards it as a scholar's reproduction of his master's teaching. Each view must have been consistent with what was generally received; and this can only have been that the Epistle rightly had a place among the apostolic letters though its immediate authorship was uncertain. The practice of Clement and Origen is an application of this judgment. Both use the Epistle as St Paul's without any qualification because it was naturally connected with the collection of his letters; and Origen goes so far as to say that he was prepared to shew that 'the Epistle was Paul's' in reply to those 'who rejected it as not written by Paul' (*Ep. ad Afric.* 9); and in another passage, preserved indeed only in a Latin translation, he speaks of 'fourteen Epistles of St Paul' (*Hom. in Jos.* vii.).

The judgment of Origen must be given in the original (Euseb. *H. E.* vi. 25).

ὅτι ὁ χαρακτὴρ τῆς λέξεως τῆς πρὸς Ἑβραίους ἐπιστολῆς οὐκ ἔχει τὸ ἐν λόγῳ ἰδιωτικὸν τοῦ ἀποστόλου, ὁμολογήσαντος ἑαυτὸν ἰδιώτην εἶναι τῷ λόγῳ, τουτέστι τῇ φράσει, ἀλλ' ἔστιν ἡ ἐπιστολὴ συνθέσει τῆς λέξεως ἑλληνικωτέρα, πᾶς ὁ ἐπιστάμενος κρίνειν φράσεων (al. φράσεως) διαφορὰς ὁμολογήσαι ἄν. πάλιν τε αὖ ὅτι τὰ νοήματα τῆς ἐπιστολῆς θαυμάσιά ἐστι καὶ οὐ δεύτερα τῶν ἀποστολικῶν γραμμάτων, καὶ τοῦτο ἂν συμφήσαι εἶναι ἀληθὲς πᾶς ὁ προσέχων τῇ ἀναγνώσει τῇ ἀποστολικῇ.

τούτοις μεθ' ἕτερα ἐπιφέρει λέγων

ἐγὼ δὲ ἀποφαινόμενος εἴποιμ' ἂν ὅτι τὰ μὲν νοήματα τοῦ ἀποστόλου ἐστὶν ἡ δὲ φράσις καὶ ἡ σύνθεσις ἀπομνημονεύσαντός τινος [τὰ ἀποστολικὰ καὶ ὡσπερεὶ σχολιογραφήσαντός τινος] τὰ εἰρημένα ὑπὸ τοῦ διδασκάλου. εἴ τις οὖν ἐκκλησία ἔχει ταύτην τὴν ἐπιστολὴν ὡς Παύλου, αὕτη εὐδοκιμείτω καὶ ἐπὶ τούτῳ. οὐ γὰρ εἰκῇ οἱ ἀρχαῖοι ἄνδρες ὡς Παύλου αὐτὴν παραδεδώκασι. τίς δὲ ὁ γράψας τὴν ἐπιστολήν, τὸ μὲν ἀληθὲς θεὸς οἶδεν, ἡ δὲ εἰς ἡμᾶς φθάσασα ἱστορία ὑπό τινων μὲν λεγόντων ὅτι Κλήμης ὁ γενόμενος ἐπίσκοπος Ῥωμαίων ἔγραψε τὴν ἐπιστολήν, ὑπό τινων δὲ ὅτι Λουκᾶς ὁ γράψας τὸ εὐαγγέλιον καὶ τὰς Πράξεις.

ἀλλὰ ταῦτα μὲν ὧδε ἐχέτω.

The sense of the ambiguous phrase τίς ὁ γράψας τὴν ἐπιστολήν (Rom. xvi. 22) is fixed by the context beyond all reasonable doubt. The 'writing' included all that is described under 'expression' (φράσις) and 'composition' (σύνθεσις). In this sense, on the ground that the Epistle shewed correspondences of style with their acknowledged compositions, some held that Clement and some that St Luke 'wrote' it.

The Homily from which this passage was taken was written after A.D. 245. The Epistle to Africanus was written A.D. 240. We may therefore rightly conclude that we have in the quotation Origen's mature and final judgment from a critical point of sight. Practically he might still use it as St Paul's in the sense which he explains.

Looking back over the records of the fir : three centuries Eusebius expressed the judgment to which the facts pointed plainly with all their apparent discrepancies. In different places he ranks the Epistle among 'the acknowledged' (iii. 25), and the 'controverted' Books (vi. 13). He held himself that it was originally written in 'Hebrew,' and that Clement of Rome (rather than St Luke) had

The judgment of EUSEBIUS.

translated it, on the ground of its likeness to Clement's own Letter both in style and subject-matter (iii. 38). He used the Greek text as St Paul's habitually ; and reckoned his Epistles as fourteen (*H. E.* iii. 3), though he noticed that 'some rejected the Epistle to the Hebrews on the ground that it was controverted (ἀντιλέγεσθαι) by the Roman Church as not being Paul's.' At the same time he justified his own decision by the plea that it was reasonable 'on the ground of its antiquity that it should be reckoned with the other writings of the Apostle' (*H. E.* iii. 38). Such a statement would be inconsistent with the idea that he held it to be St Paul's in the same sense as the other Epistles. He held it to be canonical Scripture and Pauline, so to speak, for ecclesiastical use. Eusebius in other words, like Origen, was chiefly concerned to maintain the canonicity of the Epistle, and he upheld its ultimate Pauline authorship as connected with its apostolic authority.

The following are the passages in which Eusebius states the facts as to the Epistle in his own words.

H. E. iii. 3 τοῦ δὲ Παύλου πρόδηλοι καὶ σαφεῖς αἱ δεκατέσσαρες ἐπιστολαί. ὅτι γε μὴν τινες ἠθετήκασι τὴν πρὸς Ἑβραίους, πρὸς τῆς Ῥωμαίων ἐκκλησίας ὡς μὴ Παύλου οὖσαν αὐτὴν ἀντιλέγεσθαι φήσαντες, οὐ δίκαιον ἀγνοεῖν. καὶ τὰ περὶ ταύτης δὲ τοῖς πρὸ ἡμῶν εἰμημένα κατὰ καιρὸν παραθήσομαι.

H. E. iii. 37 [Κλήμης] σαφέστατα παρίστησιν ὅτι μὴ νέον ὑπάρχει τὸ σύγγραμμα. ἔνθεν εἰκότως ἔδοξεν αὐτὸ τοῖς λοιποῖς ἐγκαταλεχθῆναι γράμμασι τοῦ ἀποστόλου· Ἑβραίοις γὰρ διὰ τῆς πατρίου γλώττης ἐγγράφως ὡμιληκότος τοῦ Παύλου, οἱ μὲν τὸν εὐαγγελιστὴν Λουκᾶν οἱ δὲ τὸν Κλήμεντα τοῦτον αὐτὸν ἑρμηνεῦσαι λέγουσι τὴν γραφήν. ὃ καὶ μᾶλλον εἴη ἂν ἀληθές, τῷ τὸν ὅμοιον τῆς φράσεως χαρακτῆρα τήν τε τοῦ Κλήμεντος ἐπιστολὴν καὶ τὴν πρὸς Ἑβραίους ἀποσώζειν, καὶ τῷ μὴ πόρρω τὰ ἐν ἑκατέροις τοῖς συγγράμμασι νοήματα καθεστάναι.

Theodoret (*Præf. in Ep. ad Hebr.*) exaggerates, when he says of Eusebius, οὗτος τοῦ θειοτάτου Παύλου τήνδε τὴν ἐπιστολὴν ὡμολόγησεν εἶναι καὶ τοὺς παλαιοὺς ἅπαντας ταύτην περὶ αὐτῆς ἔφησεν ἐσχηκέναι τὴν δόξαν.

No evidence for the Pauline authorship of the Greek text.

It will be evident from the facts which have been given how slender is the historical evidence for the Pauline authorship of the Epistle when it is traced to the source. The unqualified statements of later writers simply reproduce the testimony of Clement or Origen as interpreted by their practice. But it is not clear that any one among the earliest witnesses attributed the Greek text to St Paul. It is certain that neither Clement nor Origen did so, though they used the Epistle as his without reserve. What they were concerned to affirm for the book was Pauline, or, we may say more correctly, apostolic authority.

Viewed in this light the testimony of Alexandria is not irreconcilable with the testimony of the West. The difference between the two springs from the different estimate which they made of the two elements of the problem, canonicity (apostolicity) and authorship. The Alexandrines emphasised the thought of canonicity and, assured of the canonicity of the Epistle, placed it in connexion with St Paul. The Western fathers emphasised the thought of authorship and, believing that the Epistle was not properly St Paul's, denied its canonical authority. The former were wrong in affirming Pauline authorship as the condition of canonicity. The latter were wrong in denying the canonicity of a book of which St Paul was not recognised as the author. Experience has shewn us how to unite the positive conclusions on both sides. We have been enabled to acknowledge that the canonical authority of the Epistle is independent of its Pauline authorship. The spiritual insight of the East can be joined with the historical witness of the West. And if we hold that the judgment of the Spirit makes itself felt through the consciousness of the Christian Society, no Book of the Bible is more completely recognised by universal consent as giving a divine view of the facts of the Gospel, full of lessons for all time, than the Epistle to the Hebrews.

The East and West press unduly partial truths.

In deciding the question of the authorship of the Epistle the uniform testimony of the Roman Church, in which the Epistle was known from the earliest times, is of decisive importance. If St Paul had written it, it is difficult to understand how Clement could have been unacquainted with the fact, and how it should have been persistently denied or disregarded by all the later writers of the Church, so far as we know, for more than two centuries. On the other hand, if the Epistle was added as an appendix to St Paul's Epistles in an Eastern collection of apostolic writings made about the same time as Marcion's, it is easy to see, from the example of the Syriac Versions, how naturally St Paul's name would be extended to it, and then how various explanations would offer themselves to account for its peculiarities. For the distinct theories of Clement and Origen shew that these were no part of an original tradition.

The judg-
ment of
ATHANA-
SIUS, and

The practical judgment of Alexandria found formal expression in a Festal Epistle of Athanasius (A.D. 367). Among the books of the Old and New Testaments which he reckons as 'held canonical and divine,' he enumerates 'fourteen Epistles of the Apostle Paul' in the order of the oldest MSS. ('... 2 Thess., Hebrews, 1 Timothy...'). And from his time this reckoning of the 'fourteen Epistles' became universal among Greek writers; but there is no reason to suppose that either he or the other fathers who followed him wished to go beyond the testimony of Clement and Origen and Eusebius.

of the
later Greek
Fathers.

The Epistle is used without reserve as a writing of St Paul's by Alexander of Alexandria in writing to Arius (Theodor. *H. E.* i. 4; Socr. *H. E.* i. 6), and there is no reason for thinking that on this point Arius differed from the other teachers of Alexandria. At a later time some Arians denied the Pauline authorship of the Book while still they used it (Epiph. *Hær.* lxix. 14; comp. Theodoret, *Præf. ad Epist.*). The Epistle is also quoted as St Paul's (not to mention lesser names) by Didymus (*de Trin.* i. p. 23; Migne, *P. G.* xxxix. 307), Isidore of Pelusium (*Epp. Lib.* i. 7 ; 94, Hebr. iv. 13), Cyril of Alexandria (*de ador. in spir. et ver.* ii. p. 58; Migne, *P. G.* lxviii. 226) and other Alexandrine fathers; by Cyril of Jerusalem (*Cat.* iv. 36 τὰς Παύλου δεκατέσσαρας ἐπιστολάς, by Jacob of Nisibis and Ephrem Syrus (Bleek, *Einl.* § 39); by the Cappadocian fathers Basil (*adv. Eunom.* i. 14; iv. 2) and the two Gregories, Gregory of Nyssa (*In Christi Resurr.* ii.; Migne, *P. G.* xlvi. 639) and Gregory of Nazianzus (δέκα δὲ Παύλου τέσσαρές τ' ἐπιστολαί, Migne, *P. G.* xxxvii. 474); by Epiphanius (*Hær.* lxxvi. p. 941 ἐν τεσσαρεσκαίδεκα ἐπιστολαῖς τοῦ ἁγίου ἀποστόλου Παύλου. Comp. *Hær.* xlii. p. 373), and by the representatives of the Church of Antioch, Theodore of Mopsuestia (Kihn *Theodor v. Mopsuestia* 61 ff.) and Chrysostom (*Præf. in Com.*).

The later
judgment
of the
Western
Church,
JEROME,
AUGUS-
TINE.

From the fourth century the canonical authority of the Epistle came to be recognised in the West, and in part, as a consequence, its Pauline authorship. Fathers, like Hilary, who were familiar with Greek writers naturally adopted little by little their mode of speaking of it. Still the influence of the old belief remained; and Jerome shews that the judgment which Eusebius notes in his time still survived unchanged : 'The custom of the Latins' he says 'does not receive it among the canonical Scriptures as St Paul's' (*Ep. ad Dard.* 129). And while he himself rightly maintained its canonical authority and used it freely, he was ever scrupulously careful to indicate in his quotations that he did not by so doing decide the question of its authorship. Augustine adopted the same general view as Jerome, and under his influence lists of Books for use in Church were authorised at three African Councils, at Hippo in 393, and at Carthage in 397 and 419. In all of these the Epistle to the Hebrews was included ; and henceforward, while the doubts as to the authorship of the Epistle were noticed from time to time, the canonical authority of the Book was not again called in question in the West till the time of the Reformation. The Catalogue of the second Council of Carthage was transcribed in a letter of Innocent I to Exsuperius, and became part of the Law of the Roman Church.

The language of the decrees of the African Councils preserves a significant trace of the transition from the earlier view in the West to that which finally prevailed. In the Council of Hippo and the first Council of Carthage the enumeration runs : *Pauli Ap. Epistolæ xiii.: eiusdem ad Hebræos una.* In the second Council of Carthage the two clauses are combined : *Epist. Pauli Ap. numero xiv.*

The Epistle is used as St Paul's among others by Hilary (*De Trin.* iv. 11), Lucifer (*De non conv. c. hær.*, Migne, *P.L.* xiii. 782), Victorinus Afer (*c. Ar.* ii. 3), Pacianus (*Ep.* iii. 13), Faustinus (*De Trin.* ii. 13), Ambrose (*De Sp. S.* iii. 8, 51), Pelagius (*Comm. in Rom.* i. 17), Rufinus (*Comm. in Symb. Apost.* 36, Pauli apostoli epistolæ quatuordecim).

On the other hand it is not used by Phæbadius, Optatus, Zeno, Vincent of Lerins, Orosius. Philastrius notices that it was not read in Churches (*Hær.* 88), or, at least, only sometimes (*Hær.* 89, interdum).

The language of Jerome is full of interest, and in several places it is easy to see the influence of the Greek or Latin work which he has before him. He repeats the familiar Western saying that 'St Paul wrote to seven Churches,' adding that 'very many rejected the Epistle to the Hebrews,' which would have given an eighth (*Ep. ad Paul.* 53 (103) § 8; *de virr. ill.* 5). He notices the Western custom and tradition which questioned its authority and denied its Pauline authorship (*Ep. ad Evang.* 73 (126) § 4; *ad Dard.* 129 § 3; *Comm. in Matt.* xxvi. 8, 9; *in Is.* vi. 2; viii. 16 f.). He discusses the common objections to the Pauline authorship (*de virr. ill.* c. 5; *Comm. in Gal.* i. 1), and notices one which he probably owed to Origen (*Ep. ad Afri.* 9), that the Epistle contained references to Apocryphal Books (*Comm. in Is.* vi. 9 ff.). In many places he uses the Epistle as St Paul's without any reserve (*Comm. in Is.* v. 24; vii. 14); and again he speaks of 'the writer of the Epistle whoever he was,' 'the Apostle Paul or whoever wrote the Epistle' (*Comm. in Amos* viii. 7, 8; *in Jerem.* xxxi. 31 f.).

The language of Augustine is equally uncertain. At one time he leaves the question of the canonicity of the Epistle uncertain (*Inchoat. Expos. Ep. ad Rom.* § 11). At another time he inclines to accept it on the authority of 'the Eastern Churches' (*de pecc. mer. et remiss.* i. 27, 50). And in common use he quotes it in the same way as the other Epistles of St Paul, though less frequently (*Serm.* lv. 5 &c.).

It is needless to follow in detail the statements of later writers. A few interesting traces of old doubts survive. The Epistle was wanting in the archetype of D_2 and probably in the archetype of F_2 and G_3 (see pp. xvi., xxvii.). Some Commentators deal only with thirteen Epistles of St Paul (Hilary of Rome, Migne *P. L.* xvii. pp. 45 ff.; Pelagius, *P. L.* xxx. pp. 645 ff.; comp. Cassiod. *de inst. div. litt.* iv. 8), though Hilary and Pelagius speak of the Epistle to the Hebrews elsewhere as a book of the Apostle. But the notices as to the authorship of the Book are for the most part simple repetitions of sentences of Jerome. Here and there a writer of exceptional power uses his materials with independence, but without real knowledge. Thomas Aquinas, for example, marshals the objections to the Pauline authorship and the answers to them in a true scholastic form, and decides in favour of the Pauline authorship on the ground of ancient authority and because 'Jerome receives it among the Epistles of Paul.'

As the contrary has been lately stated, it may be well to say that Leo the Great quotes the Epistle as St Paul's (*Serm.* xliv. § 2; comp. *Serm.* iii. (ii.) 1; xxiv. (xxiii.) 6; lxviii. (lxvi.) 3; lxix. (lxvii.) 2; [*Ep.* lxv. § 11]). He quotes it indeed, as Bleek justly observed, comparatively rarely.

Various opinions at the Renaissance and in later times.

At the revival of Greek learning in Europe, when 'the Grammarians' ventured to reopen questions of Biblical criticism, the authorship and, in part, the authority of the Epistle was called in question. On this, as on other similar subjects, Card. Caietan [Th. de Vio] spoke with unusual freedom. Erasmus, with fuller knowledge, expressed his doubts 'not as to the authority but as to the author of the Epistle, doubts' he adds characteristically 'which would remain till he saw a distinct judgment of the Church upon the point.' Luther denied the Pauline authorship of the Book without hesitation, and, referring to the earlier traditions, conjectured that it was more likely to have been written by Apollos

(comp. Bleek, 249 *n.*).   Calvin, while maintaining the full apostolical authority of the Epistle, professed that he 'could not be
brought to think that it was St Paul's.'   He thought that it might
be a work of St Luke or of Clement.   Beza also held that it was
written by a disciple of St Paul.   At first he inclined to adopt
Luther's conjecture as to the authorship, but this opinion he afterwards withdrew silently.

The judgment of Card. Caietan is worth noticing more in detail, for
even Bleek had not seen his Commentary.   He first quotes the statements
of Jerome at some length, and concludes from these that St Paul cannot
be confidently held to be the author of the Epistle.   He then goes on to
argue that doubt as to the authorship of the Book involves doubt as to its
authority.   This doubt as to the authority of the Epistle he justifies by
reference to what he regards as false arguments in i. 5 b, ix. 15 ff.   He
regards ii. 3 as inconsistent with a belief in the Pauline authorship, but
adds, that following common custom he, like Jerome, will call it St Paul's.

He explains the stress which he lays on the evidence of Jerome by a
significant sentence: quos [libros] ille canonicos tradidit, canonicos
habemus ; et quos ille a canonicis discreuit, extra canonem habemus.

The Colophon of the Commentary is interesting.   Caietæ die 1 Junii
M.D.XXIX.   Commentariorum Thomæ de Vio, Caietani Cardinalis sancti
Xisti in omnes genuinas epistolas Pauli et eam quæ ad Hebræos inscribi-
tur, Finis.

The review of the historical evidence as to the authorship of the Internal
Epistle will have shewn sufficiently that there was no clear or evidence;
uniform tradition on the subject in the early Church.   Obvious
circumstances are adequate to explain why the names of St Paul,
and St Luke, of Barnabas, and Clement were connected with it ;
and in no case is the external testimony of such a character as to
justify the belief that it was derived from a tradition contemporary
in origin with the Book.   It remains therefore to consider how far
internal testimony helps towards the solution of the question.

The direct evidence furnished by the Epistle is slight, though direct,
there is not the least indication that the author wished to conceal
his personality.   He was intimately acquainted with those to whom
he writes: vi. 9 f.; x. 34 (τοῖς δεσμίοις συνεπαθήσατε) ; xiii. 7 ; xiii.
19 (ἵνα τάχειον ἀποκατασταθῶ ὑμῖν), but the last clause does not
necessarily imply that he belonged to their society, or that he was

in confinement. He speaks of Timothy as a common friend : xiii. 23 (γινώσκετε τὸν ἀδελφὸν ἡμῶν T. ἀπολελυμένον...compare note on the passage), and there is no reason to question the identity of this Timothy with the companion of St Paul. He places himself in the second generation of believers, as one who had received the Gospel from those who heard the Lord (ii. 3).

This last statement has been justly held to be a most grave (or indeed fatal) objection to the Pauline authorship. It is not possible to reconcile it without unnatural violence with St Paul's jealous assertion of his immediate discipleship to Christ (contrast Gal. i. 1; 11 f.). On the other hand these few notices might all apply equally well to St Luke or Barnabas or Clement.

indirect.   The language and the teaching of the Epistle offer materials for comparison with writings of the four authors suggested by tradition. With St Luke the comparison is practically confined to the language : with Barnabas, if we assume that his letter is authentic, Clement and St Paul, it embraces both language and teaching.

Comparison with St Luke,   It has been already seen that the earliest scholars who speak of the Epistle notice its likeness in style to the writings of St Luke ; and when every allowance has been made for coincidences which consist in forms of expression which are found also in the LXX. or in other writers of the N. T., or in late Greek generally, the likeness is unquestionably remarkable. No one can work independently at the Epistle without observing it (comp. p. xlvii.). But it is not possible to establish any sure conclusion on such a resemblance. The author of the Epistle may have been familiar with the writings of St Luke themselves, or he may have been in close connexion with the Evangelist or with those whose language was moulded by his influence. In any case the likeness of vocabulary and expression is not greater than that which exists between 1 Peter and the Epistles of St Paul. If indeed it were credible that the Epistle was originally written in ' Hebrew,' then the external and internal evidence combined would justify the belief that the Greek text is due to St Luke. If that opinion is out of the question, the historical evidence for St Luke's connexion with the Epistle is either destroyed or greatly weakened, and the internal evidence gives no valid result.

The superficial resemblances between the Epistle and the Letter with CLEMENT of Clement, both in vocabulary and form, are very striking. It would be easy to draw up a list of parallelisms in words and manner sufficient to justify the judgment of Eusebius (comp. pp. lxii., lxx.). But these parallelisms are more than counterbalanced by differences in both respects. Clement has an unusually large number of peculiar words; and his heaping together of coordinate clauses (as 1, 3, 20, 35, 36, 45, 55), his frequent doxologies (20, 38, 43, 45, 50, 58, 59), and to a certain extent (comp. p. 476) his method of quotation, sharply distinguish his writing from the Epistle to the Hebrews. Moreover a closer examination of the parallelisms with the Epistle makes it clear that they are due to a use of it, like the use which is made of Epistles of St Paul (*e.g.* c. 49). And, what is of far greater moment, the wide difference between the two works in range of thought, in dogmatic depth, in prophetic insight, makes it impossible to suppose that the Epistle to the Corinthians could have been written after the Epistle to the Hebrews by the same writer. Clement is essentially receptive and imitative. He combines but he does not create. Even if the external evidence for connecting him with the Epistle were greater than it is, the internal evidence would be incompatible with any other connexion than that of a simple translator (comp. Lightfoot, *Clement* i. 101 f.).

Some differences in style between the Epistle and the writings with ST PAUL, of St Paul have been already noticed. A more detailed inquiry shews that these cannot be adequately explained by differences of subject or of circumstances. They characterise two men, and not only two moods or two discussions. The student will feel the subtle force of the contrast if he compares the Epistle to the Hebrews with the Epistle to the Ephesians, to which it has the closest affinity. But it is as difficult to represent the contrast by an enumeration of details as it is to analyse an effect. It must be felt for a right appreciation of its force. So it is also with the dogmatic differences between the writer and St Paul.

There is unquestionably a sense in which Origen is right in saying that 'the thoughts' of the Epistle are the thoughts of St Paul. The writer shews the same broad conception of the universality of the Gospel as the Apostle of the Gentiles, the same grasp of the age-long purpose of God wrought out through Israel, the same trust in the atoning work of Christ, and in His present sovereignty. He speaks with the same conscious mastery of the Divine Counsel. But he approaches each topic from a different side. He looks at all as from within Israel, and not as from without. He speaks as one who step by step had read the fulfilment of the Old Covenant in the New without any rude crisis of awakening or any sharp struggle with traditional errors. His Judaism has been all along the Judaism of the prophets and not of the Pharisees, of the O. T. and not of the schools (comp. § x.).

with BARNABAS.   The differences between the Epistle and the Epistle which bears the name of Barnabas involve a contrast of principles and will be considered separately (see § xii.).

We are left then with a negative conclusion. The Epistle cannot be the work of St Paul, and still less the work of Clement. It may have been written by St Luke. It may have been written by Barnabas, if the 'Epistle of Barnabas' is apocryphal. The scanty evidence which is accessible to us supports no more definite judgment.

Luther's conjecture that the Epistle was written by APOLLOS.   One conjecture, however, remains to be noticed, not indeed for its own intrinsic worth, but because it has found favour with many scholars. Luther, as we have seen, with characteristic originality conjectured that it was the work of Apollos. The sole ground for the conjecture is the brief description of Apollos which is found in the N. T. (Acts xviii. 24 ff.; 1 Cor. i. 12; iii. 4 ff.). But the utmost which can be deduced from these notices is that Apollos, so far as we know, might have written the Epistle; just as what we know of Silas is consistent with the belief that he wrote it, and has even suggested it. But on the other hand it is to be remembered that there is not the least evidence that Apollos wrote anything, or that he was the only man or the only Alexandrian in the Apostolic age who was 'learned...and mighty in the Scriptures,' or that he possessed these qualifications more than others among his contemporaries, or that, in the connexion in which they are noticed, they suggest the presence of the peculiar power which is shewn in the Epistle. The wide acceptance of the conjecture as a fact is only explicable by our natural unwillingness to frankly confess our ignorance on a matter which excites our interest.

And yet in this case the confession of ignorance is really the confirmation of an inspiriting faith. We acknowledge the divine authority of the Epistle, self-attested and ratified by the illuminated consciousness of the Christian Society : we measure what would have been our loss if it had not been included in our Bible ; and we confess that the wealth of spiritual power was so great in the early Church that he who was empowered to commit to writing this view of the fulness of the Truth has not by that conspicuous service even left his name for the grateful reverence of later ages. It was enough that the faith and the love were there to minister to the Lord (Matt. xxvi. 13).

The anonymous Epistle a witness to the spiritual wealth of the Apostolic age.

In the course of the last century the authorship of the Epistle has been debated with exhaustive thoroughness. Bleek's Introduction to his Commentary is a treasury of materials, arranged and used with scrupulous fairness. It would be difficult to make any important additions to his view of the external facts. All the recent Commentaries discuss the question more or less fully. It will be enough to refer to some representative writers who advocate the claims of particular men to the authorship. The case for St Paul is maintained, with various modifications, by Ebrard, Hofmann, Biesenthal, Kay : for St Luke, by Delitzsch : for Apollos by Alford, Kurtz, Farrar : for Barnabas by Grau, Renan, Zahn : for St Mark by E. S. Lowndes (comp. Holtzmann, *Einl.* 318 f.).

XII. THE EPISTLE TO THE HEBREWS AND
THE EPISTLE OF BARNABAS.

Two
letters
bore the
name of
Barnabas
in the
third
century.

Two Epistles, as has been already noticed, were circulated in the third century under the name of Barnabas. Both were for some time on the verge of the Canon of the N. T., and at last, a century later, one was by common consent included in it and the other excluded. Both deal with a question which was of momentous importance at the close of the apostolic age, and the manner in which they respectively deal with it illuminates the idea of inspiration, and reveals a little of the divine action in the life of the Church.

Both
answer a
question
of urgent
import-
ance in
the first
age.

The question arose of necessity from the progress of the Faith. As the Gentile churches grew in importance, Christians could not but ask how they were to regard the Scriptures and the institutions of Judaism?

The destruction of Jerusalem forced this inquiry upon believers with a fresh power. There was an apparent chasm opened in the line of divine revelation. All that had been held sacred for centuries was swept away, and yet the books of the Old Testament, which appeared to find an outward embodiment in the Jewish services, were still the authoritative Bible of Christians.

What was
the
relation of
Christ-
ianity to
the Old
Testa-
ment?

Could the Old Testament be thus kept? And if so, how were Christians to explain the contradiction between the hallowing of the writings, and the apparent neglect of their contents? The ordinances of the Law had not been formally abrogated: what then were the limits of their obligation? In what sense could writings, in which the ordinances were laid down, still be regarded as inspired by the Spirit of God, if the ordinances themselves were set aside?

A little reflection will shew that the difficulties, involved in these questions which the early Christians had to face, were very real and very urgent. The pregnant thoughts of the Epistle to the Hebrews— all that is contained in the words πολυμερῶς καὶ πολυτρόπως πάλαι ὁ θεὸς λαλήσας τοῖς πατράσιν ἐν τοῖς προφήταις—have indeed passed so completely into our estimate of the method of the divine education of 'the nations' and of 'the people,' that some effort is required now in order that we may feel the elements of the problem with which they deal. But we can realise the situation by removing this book from the New Testament, and substituting in imagination the Epistle of Barnabas for it.

Two opposite solutions of the difficulties obtained partial currency. It was said on the one side that the Old Testament must be surrendered: that Judaism and Christianity were essentially antagonistic: that Christ really came to abolish the work of an opposing power: that the separation of the Gospel from the Law and the Prophets must be final and complete. This view, represented in its most formidable shape by Marcion, was opposed to the whole spirit of the apostolic teaching and to the instinct of the Christian Society. It isolated Christianity from the fulness of human life, and it is needless to dwell upon it.

Two extreme solutions represented by Marcion, and

On the other side it was said, as in the Epistle of Barnabas, that God had spoken only one message and made one Covenant, and that message, that Covenant, was the Gospel; but that the message had been misunderstood from the first by the Jews to whom it was addressed, and that the Covenant in consequence had not been carried into effect till Christ came (Barn. iv. 6).

Barnabas.

This view is not in its essence less unhistorical than the other, or less fatal to a right apprehension of the conditions and course of the divine revelation. But it had a certain attractiveness from the symbolic interpretation of Scripture which it involved, and it seemed to guard in some sense the continuity of God's dealing with men. So it was that, if the Epistle to the Hebrews had not already provided help before the crisis of the trial came, and silently directed the current of Christian thought into the true channel, it would be hard to say how great the peril and loss would have been for later time.

For the Epistle to the Hebrews and the Epistle of Barnabas present a complete and instructive contrast in their treatment of the

Contrast between Barnabas

Old Testament Scriptures and of the Mosaic institutions. Both agree in regarding these as ordained by God, and instinct with spiritual truth, but their agreement extends no farther either in principles or in method.

(a) Barnabas sets forth what he holds to be the spiritual meaning of the Old Testament without principle or self-restraint. He is satisfied if he can give an edifying meaning to the letter in any way. He offers his explanations to all; and in the main deals with trivial details (*e.g.* c. ix., the explanation of IHT).

The writer of the Epistle to the Hebrews on the other hand exercises a careful reserve. He recognises a due relation between the scholar and his lesson; and the examples by which he illustrates his leading thoughts are all of representative force: the idea of rest (the Sabbath-rest, the rest of Canaan, the rest of Christ): the idea of priesthood (the priest of men, the priest of the chosen people): the idea of access to God (the High-priest in the Holy of holies, Christ seated on the right-hand of God).

The one example which the two Epistles have in common, the rest of God after creation, offers a characteristic contrast. In the Epistle to the Hebrews it suggests the thought of the spiritual destiny of man: in Barnabas it supplies a chronological measure of the duration of the world (Heb. iv.; Barn. xv.).

(b) Barnabas again treats the Mosaic legislation as having only a symbolic meaning. It had no historical, no disciplinary value whatever. The outward embodiment of the enigmatic ordinances was a pernicious delusion. As a mere fleshly observance circumcision was the work of an evil power (Barn. ix. 4) But the evil power apparently gave a wrong interpretation to the command on which it was based and did not originate the command (comp. Just. M. *Dial.* 16).

In the Epistle to the Hebrews on the other hand the Mosaic system is treated as a salutary discipline, suited for the training of those to whom it was given, fashioned after a heavenly pattern (vii. 5; x. 1), preparatory and not final, and yet possessing throughout an educational value. The Levitical sacrifices, for example, were fitted to keep alive in the Jews a sense of sin and to lead thought forward to some true deliverance from its power. The priesthood, again, and high-priesthood suggested thoughts which they did not satisfy, and exactly in proportion as they were felt to be divine institutions, they sustained the hope of some complete satisfaction. The purpose of God is indeed fulfilled from the first, though to us the fulfilment is shewn in fragments. Hence the writer of the Epistle to the Hebrews goes beyond the Law, and in the gentile Melchizedek finds the fullest type of the King-priest to come.

(c) There is another point of resemblance and contrast between the Epistle of Barnabas and the Epistle to the Hebrews which specially deserves to be noticed. Barnabas (c. xvi.) dwells on the perils and the failures of the external Law fashioned under the later Temple into a shape which affected permanence. In this he marks a real declension in the development of Judaism. The Temple, like the Kingdom, was a falling away from the divine ideal. The writer of the Epistle to the Hebrews recognises the same fact, but he places the original divine order apart from the results of man's weakness. He goes back to the Tabernacle for all his illustrations, in which the transitoriness of the whole system was clearly signified. (c) The Temple.

In a word, in the Epistle of Barnabas there is no sense of the continuity of the divine discipline of men, of an education of the world corresponding to the growth of humanity: no recognition of the importance of outward circumstances, of rules and observances, as factors in religious life: no acknowledgment of a relation of proportion between spiritual lessons and a people's capacity. It is an illustration of the same fundamental fault that we find in the Epistle not only a complete rejection of the letter of the Levitical system, but also an imperfect and inadequate view of Christian institutions. Summary.

On the other hand we have in Hebr. i. 1—4 a view of the unfolding and infolding of the divine counsel in creation of infinite fulness. The end is there seen to be the true consummation of the beginning. We discern that one message is conveyed by the different modes of God's communication to His people: that one

Voice speaks through many envoys: that at last the spoken word is gathered up and fulfilled in the present Son.

We have not yet mastered all the teaching of the pregnant words; yet even now we can perceive how the thoughts which they convey characterise the whole Epistle : how they arose naturally out of the circumstances of the early Church ; and, by comparison with the Epistle of Barnabas, how far they transcended the common judgment of the time. Under this aspect the Epistle to the Hebrews, by its composition and its history, throws light upon the ideas of Inspiration and a Canon of Scripture. On the one side we see how the Spirit of God uses special powers, tendencies and conditions, things personal and things social, for the expression of a particular aspect of the Truth ; and on the other side we see how the enlightened consciousness of the Church was in due time led to recognise that teaching as authoritative which was at first least in harmony with prevailing forms of thought.

ΠΡΟΣ ΕΒΡΑΙΟΥΣ

ΠΡΟΣ ΕΒΡΑΙΟΥΣ

ΠΟΛΥΜΕΡѠC ΚΑΙ ΠΟΛΥΤΡΟΠѠC πάλαι ὁ
θεὸς λαλήσας τοῖς πατράσιν ἐν τοῖς προφήταις ²ἐπ᾽

προcεβραιογc ℵAB me.   ηπροcεβραιογcεπιcτολη M₂.

ηπροcεβραιογcεπιcτοληπαγλογ 5.

INTRODUCTION (i. 1—4). The first
paragraph of the Epistle gives a summary view of its main subject, the
finality of the absolute Revelation
in Christ as contrasted with the preparatory revelation under the Old
Covenant.

The whole is bound together in one
unbroken grammatical construction,
but the subject is changed in its
course. In the first two verses God is
the subject : in the last two the Son ;
and the fourth verse introduces a
special thought which is treated in
detail in the remainder of the chapter.
Thus for purposes of interpretation
the paragraph may be divided into
three parts.

i. *The contrast of the Old Revelation and the New: vv.* 1, 2.

ii. *The nature and the work of
the Son: v.* 3.

iii. *Transition to the detailed
development of the argument: v.* 4.

It will be noticed that the Lord is
regarded even in this brief introductory statement in His threefold office
as Prophet (*God spake in His Son*),
Priest (*having made purification of
sins*), and King (*He sat down*).

i. *The contrast of the Old Revelation and the New* (1, 2).

The contrast between the Old Revelation and the New is marked in three
particulars. There is a contrast (*a*) in
the method, and (*b*) in the time, and
(*c*) in the agents of the two revelations.

(*a*) The earlier teaching was conveyed in successive portions and in
varying fashions according to the
needs and capacities of those who
received it : on the other hand the
revelation in Him who was Son was
necessarily complete in itself (comp.
John i. 14, 18).

(*b*) The former revelation was given
of old time, in the infancy and growth
of the world: the Christian revelation
at the end of these days, on the very
verge of the new order which of necessity it ushered in.

(*c*) The messengers in whom God
spoke before, were the long line of
prophets raised up from age to age
since the world began (Luke i. 70 ;
Acts iii. 21): the Messenger of the
new dispensation was God's own Son.

The first contrast is left formally
incomplete (*having...spoken in many
parts and in many modes...spake*).
The two latter are expressed definitely
(*of old time to the fathers, at the end
of these days to us—in the prophets, in
Him Who is Son*); and in the original,

after the first clause, word answers to word with emphatic correspondence : πολυμερῶς καὶ πολυτρόπως (1) πάλαι (2) ὁ θεὸς λαλήσας (3) τοῖς πατράσιν (4) ἐν τοῖς προφήταις (5): no corresponding clause (1′) ἐπ᾽ ἐσχάτου τῶν ἡμερῶν τούτων (2′) ἐλάλησεν (3′) ἡμῖν (4′) ἐν υἱῷ (5′).

The consideration of these contrasts places the relation of Christianity to all that had gone before in a clear light. That which is communicated in parts, sections, fragments, must of necessity be imperfect ; and so also a representation which is made in many modes cannot be other than provisional. The supreme element of unity is wanting in each case. But the Revelation in Christ, the Son, is perfect both in substance and in form. The Incarnation and the Ascension include absolutely all that is wrought out slowly and appropriated little by little in the experience of later life. The characteristics which before marked the revelation itself now mark the human apprehension of the final revelation.

The Incarnation, in other words, is the central point of all Life ; and just as all previous discipline led up to it πολυμερῶς καὶ πολυτρόπως, so all later experience is the appointed method by which its teaching is progressively mastered πολυμερῶς καὶ πολυτρόπως. All that we can learn of the constitution of man, of the constitution of nature, of the 'laws' of history must, from the nature of the case, illustrate its meaning for us (comp. 1 Cor. xiii. 9 ff.).

These thoughts find their complete justification in the two clauses which describe the relation to the order of the world of Him in Whom God spoke to us. God *appointed Him heir of all things*, and through Him *He made the world*. The Son as Heir and Creator speaks with perfect knowledge and absolute sympathy.

But while the revelations of the Old and the New Covenants are thus sharply distinguished, God is the One Author of both. He spoke in old time, and He spoke in the last time. In the former case His speaking was *upon earth* and in the latter case *from heaven* (c. xii. 25 note), but in both cases the words are alike His words. Not one word therefore can *pass away*, though such as were fragmentary, prospective, typical, required to be fulfilled by Christ's Presence (Matt. v. 18). In revelation and in the record of revelation all parts have a divine work but not the same work nor (as we speak) an equal work.

[1] *God having of old time spoken to the fathers in the prophets in many parts and in many modes* [2]*spake to us at the end of these days in* His Son, *whom He appointed heir of all things, through whom He also made the world.*

1. The order of the first words in the original text, by which the two adverbs (πολυμερῶς καὶ πολυτρόπως) come first, to which nothing afterwards directly answers (*Having in many parts and in many modes of old time spoken...*), serves at once to fix attention on the variety and therefore on the imperfection of the earlier revelations, and also to keep a perfect correspondence in the members which follow (πάλαι, ἐπ᾽ ἐσχάτου τῶν ἡμερῶν τούτων—λαλήσας, ἐλάλησεν—τοῖς πατράσιν, ἡμῖν—ἐν τοῖς προφήταις, ἐν υἱῷ).

At the same time the two main divisions of the revelation are connected as forming one great whole : *God having spoken...spake...*(ὁ θεὸς λαλήσας...ἐλάλησεν). It is not simply that the Author of the earlier revelation is affirmed to have been also the Author of the later (*God who spake... spake...*ὁ τοῖς πατράσιν λαλήσας θεὸς ἐλάλησεν or *God spake...and spake...*); but the earlier revelation is treated as the preparation for, the foundation of, the latter (*God having spoken... spake...*).

πολυμερῶς καὶ πολυτρόπως] *in many parts and in many manners*, Vulg.

multifariam multisque modis. Syr. Psh. *in all parts and in all manners* (Syr. Hcl. *in many parts...*).

The variety of the former revelation extended both to its substance and to its form. The great drama of Israel's discipline was divided into separate acts ; and in each act different modes were employed by God for bringing home to His people various aspects of truth. Thus the 'many parts' of the preparatory training for Christianity may be symbolised (though they are not absolutely coincident with them) by the periods of the patriarchs, of Moses, of the theocracy, of the kingdom, of the captivity, of the hierarchy, as Israel was enabled to assimilate the lessons provided providentially in the national life of Egypt, Canaan, Persia, Greece. And the many 'modes' of revelation are shadowed forth in the enactment of typical ordinances, in declarations of 'the word of the Lord,' in symbolic actions, in interpretations of the circumstances of national prosperity and distress. And further it must be noticed that the modes in which God spoke in the prophets to the people were largely influenced by the modes in which God spoke to the prophets themselves 'face to face,' by visions, by Urim and Thummim (comp. Num. xii. 6, 8). These corresponded in the divine order with the characters of the messengers themselves which became part of their message.

The general sense is well given by Theodoret : τὸ μέντοι πολυμερῶς τὰς παντοδαπὰς οἰκονομίας σημαίνει, τὸ δὲ πολυτρόπως τῶν θείων ὀπτασιῶν τὸ διάφορον, ἄλλως γὰρ ὤφθη τῷ 'Αβραὰμ καὶ ἄλλως τῷ Μωϋσῇ...τὸ μέντοι πολυμερῶς καὶ ἕτερον αἰνίττεται ὅτι τῶν προφητῶν ἕκαστος μερικήν τινα οἰκονομίαν ἐνεχειρίζετο, ὁ δὲ τούτων θεός, ὁ δεσπότης λέγω Χριστός, οὐ μίαν τινὰ ᾠκονόμησε χρείαν, ἀλλὰ τὸ πᾶν ἐνανθρωπήσας κατώρθωσε.

The adverbs are not rare in late

Greek : for πολυμερῶς see Plut. ii. 537 D ; Jos. *Antt.* viii. 3, 9 ; and for πολυτρόπως Philo, ii. 512M.; Max. Tyr. vii. 2. Πολυμερής is used of Wisdom in Wisd. vii. 22. The two corresponding adjectives occur together in Max. Tyr. xvii. 7 : There are, he says, two instruments for understanding, τοῦ μὲν ἁπλοῦ ὂν καλοῦμεν νοῦν, τοῦ δὲ ποικίλου καὶ πολυμεροῦς καὶ πολυτρόπου ἃς αἰσθήσεις καλοῦμεν. For similar combinations see Philo *de vit. Mos.* i. § 20 (ii. 99 M.) (πολυτρόπῳ καὶ πολυσχιδεῖ); *de decal.* § 17 (ii. 194 M.) (πολύτροποι καὶ πολυειδεῖς) ; *quis rer. div. hær.* § 58 (i. 514 M.) (πολλοὺς καὶ πολυτρόπους).

Clement of Alexandria in a remarkable passage (*Strom.* vi. 7, § 58, p. 769) uses the phrase of the action of the Word, Wisdom, the firstborn Son : οὗτός ἐστιν ὁ τῶν γενητῶν ἁπάντων διδάσκαλος, ὁ σύμβουλος τοῦ θεοῦ τοῦ τὰ πάντα προεγνωκότος· ὁ δὲ ἄνωθεν ἐκ πρώτης καταβολῆς κόσμου πολυτρόπως καὶ πολυμερῶς πεπαίδευκέν τε καὶ τελειοῖ. Comp. *Strom.* i. 4, 27, p. 331 εἰκότως τοίνυν ὁ ἀπόστολος πολυποίκιλον εἴρηκεν τὴν σοφίαν τοῦ θεοῦ, πολυμερῶς καὶ πολυτρόπως, διὰ τέχνης, διὰ ἐπιστήμης, διὰ πίστεως, διὰ προφητείας, τὴν ἑαυτῆς ἐνδεικνυμένην δύναμιν εἰς τὴν ἡμετέραν εὐεργεσίαν...

πάλαι] *of old time* (Vulg. *olim*) and not simply *formerly* (πρότερον c. iv. 6 ; x. 32). The word is rare in N.T. and always describes something completed in the past. Here the thought is of the ancient teachings now long since sealed.

ὁ θεὸς λαλήσας...ἐλάλησεν...] There is but one final Source of all Truth. The unity of the Revealer is the pledge and ground of the unity of the Revelation, however it may be communicated ; and His revelation of Himself is spontaneous. He 'speaks' in familiar intercourse. The word λαλεῖν is frequently used in the Epistle of divine communications: ii. 2, 3 ; iii. 5 ; iv. 8 ; v. 5 ; xi. 18 ; xii. 25. Compare John ix. 29 ; xvi. 13. This usage is not found in St Paul (yet

ἐσχάτου τῶν ἡμερῶν τούτων ἐλάλησεν ἡμῖν ἐν υἱῷ,

2 ἐσχάτου ℵABD₂M₂ (vg) me: ἐσχάτων ς syrr.

see Rom. iii. 19 ; 2 Cor. xiii. 3), but it is common in St Luke (Acts). The *Vulgate* rendering *loquens* (Old Lat. *locutus*)...*locutus est* exhibits a characteristic defect of the version in the rendering of participles (compare *v.* 3 *purgationem faciens; v.* 14 *missi*).

τοῖς πατράσιν] This absolute title the *fathers* occurs again John vii. 22 ; Rom. ix. 5 ; xv. 8 (in Acts iii. 22 it is a false reading). Compare Ecclus. xliv. Πατέρων ὕμνος.

More commonly we find '*our (your) fathers*': Acts iii. 13, 25 ; v. 30; vii. 11 &c.; 1 Cor. x. 1. The absolute term marks the relation of 'the fathers' to the whole Church.

ἐν τοῖς πρ.] *in the prophets* (Vulg. *in prophetis*), not simply *through them* using them as His instruments (c. ii. 2, 3), but *in them* (c. iv. 7) as the quickening power of their life. In whatever way God made Himself known to them, they were His messengers, inspired by His Spirit, not in their words only but as men; and however the divine will was communicated to them they interpreted it to the people : compare Matt. x. 20 ; 2 Cor. xiii. 3. (Ipse in cordibus eorum dixit quidquid illi foras vel dictis vel factis locuti sunt hominibus. *Herv.*) Conversely the prophet speaks 'in Christ' as united vitally with Him : 2 Cor. ii. 17 ; xii. 19.

Cf. Philo *de præm. et pœn.* 9 (ii. 417 M.) ἑρμηνεὺς γάρ ἐστιν ὁ προφήτης ἔνδοθεν ὑπηχοῦντος τὰ λεκτέα τοῦ θεοῦ.

The title 'prophet' is used in the widest sense as it is applied to Abraham (Gen. xx. 7), to Moses (Deut. xxxiv. 10; comp. xviii. 18), to David (Acts ii. 30), and generally to those inspired by God : Ps. cv. 15. Compare Acts iii. 21 τῶν ἁγίων ἀπ᾽ αἰῶνος αὐτοῦ προφητῶν. Luke i. 70. The prophets, according to a familiar Rabbinic saying, prophesied only of the

days of the Messiah (*Sabb.* 63 a ; Wünsche, *Altsyn. Theol.* s. 355). Comp. Philo *quis rer. div. hær.* § 52 (i. 510 f. M.).

2. ἐπ᾽ ἐσχάτου τῶν ἡμ. τ.] *at the end of these days:* Vulg. *novissime diebus istis*, O.L. *in novissimis diebus his*.

The phrase is moulded on a LXX rendering of the O. T. phrase בְּאַחֲרִית הַיָּמִים '*in the latter days*,' ἐπ᾽ ἐσχάτου τῶν ἡμερῶν (Gen. xlix. 1 : Num. xxiv. 14; Jer. xxiii. 20 v. l. ἐσχάτων ; xlix. 39 [xxv. 18]; comp. Deut. iv. 30 ; xxxi. 29), which is used generally of the times of Messiah (Is. ii. 2 ; Dan. x. 14 and notes).

Starting from this general conception Jewish teachers distinguished 'a present age,' 'this age' (עוֹלָם הַזֶּה, ὁ αἰὼν οὗτος, ὁ νῦν καιρός) from 'that age,' 'the age to come' (עוֹלָם הַבָּא, ὁ μέλλων αἰών, ὁ αἰὼν ἐκεῖνος, ὁ αἰὼν ὁ ἐρχόμενος).

Between 'the present age' of imperfection and conflict and trial and 'the age to come' of the perfect reign of God they placed 'the days of Messiah,' which they sometimes reckoned in the former, sometimes in the latter, and sometimes as distinct from both. They were however commonly agreed that the passage from one age to the other would be through a period of intense sorrow and anguish, 'the travail-pains' of the new birth (חֶבְלֵי הַמָּשִׁיחַ, ὠδῖνες Matt. xxiv. 8).

The apostolic writers, fully conscious of the spiritual crisis through which they were passing, speak of their own time as the 'last days' (Acts ii. 17; James v. 3: comp. 2 Tim. iii. 1); the 'last hour' (1 John ii. 18); 'the end of the times' (1 Pet. i. 20 ἐπ᾽ ἐσχάτου τῶν χρόνων : in 2 Pet. iii. 3 the true reading is ἐπ᾽ ἐσχάτων τῶν ἡμ.); 'the last time' (Jude 18 ἐπ᾽ ἐσχάτου χρόνου).

ὃν ἔθηκεν κληρονόμον πάντων, δι' οὗ καὶ ἐποίησεν τοὺς

ἐποί. τ. αἰῶνας ℵABD₂*M₂ (vg) syr vg: τ. αἰ. ἐποί. ϛ syr hl.

Thus the full phrase in this place emphasises two distinct thoughts, the thought of the coming close of the existing order (ἐπ' ἐσχάτου *at the end*), and also the thought of the contrast between the present and the future order (τῶν ἡμερῶν τούτων *of these days* as contrasted with 'those days').

ἐλάλησεν ἡμῖν] *spake to us*—the members of the Christian Church: x. 26; xiii. 1 (so Theophylact: ἐνοποιεῖ καὶ ἐξισοῖ τοῖς μαθηταῖς καὶ αὐτοὺς καὶ ἑαυτόν). The word was not directly addressed to the writer: ii. 3. The mission of Christ is here regarded as complete. It is true in one sense that He told His disciples the full message which He had received (John xv. 15), if in another sense He had, when He left them, *yet many things to say* (xvi. 12). This contrast between the divine, absolute, aspect of Christ's work, and its progressive appropriation by men, occurs throughout Scripture. Compare Col. iii. 1 ff., 5.

ἐν υἱῷ] The absence of the article fixes attention upon the nature and not upon the personality of the Mediator of the new revelation. God spake to us in one who has this character that He is Son. The sense might be given by the rendering *in a Son*, if the phrase could be limited to this meaning ('One who is Son'); but 'a Son' is ambiguous. See *v.* 5; iii. 6; v. 8; vii. 28. Compare John v. 27 note; x. 12; Rom. i. 4.

The absence of the article is made more conspicuous by its occurrence in the corresponding phrase. 'The prophets' are spoken of as a definite, known, body, fulfilling a particular office. The sense would lose as much by the omission of the article in this case (ἐν προφήταις 'in men who were prophets') as it would lose here by the insertion (ἐν τῷ υἱῷ *in the Son* c. vi. 6).

It is instructive to notice how com-

pletely the exact force of the original was missed by the later Greek Fathers. Even Chrysostom says: τὸ ἐν υἱῷ διὰ τοῦ υἱοῦ φησί, and Œcumenius repeats the words.

The new revelation is a continuation of the old so far as God is the author of both. It is wholly new and separate in character so far as Christ is the Mediator of it.

Herveius notices the difference between the Presence of God in the prophets and in His Son: In prophetis fuit Deus secundum inhabitationem gratiæ et revelationem voluntatis sapientiæ suæ, in Filio autem omnino totus manebat...utpote cui sapientia Dei personaliter erat unita.

ὃν ἔθηκεν...δι' οὗ καὶ ἐποίησεν...] The office of the Son as the final revealer of the will of God is illustrated by His relation to God in regard to the world, in and through which the revelation comes to men. He is at once Creator and Heir of all things. The end answers to the beginning. Through Him God called into being the temporal order of things, and He is heir of their last issue. All things were created 'in Him' and 'unto Him' (Col. i. 15, 16, ἐν αὐτῷ ἐκτίσθη, εἰς αὐτὸν ἔκτισται). The universal heirship of Christ is illustrated by, if not based upon, His creative activity.

ἔθηκεν κληρονόμον π.] Vulg. *quem constituit* (O. L. *posuit*) *heredem universorum*. Even that which under one aspect appears as a necessary consequence is referred to the immediate will of God (ἔθηκεν). For the use of τίθημι see Rom. iv. 17 (Gen. xvii. 5); 1 Tim. ii. 7; 2 Tim. i. 11. There is nothing to determine the 'time' of this divine appointment. It belongs to the eternal order. Yet see Ps. ii. 8; Matt. xxviii. 18 (ἐδόθη). We 'who see but part' may fix our attention on inceptive fulfilments.

κληρονόμον] The thought of son-ship passes naturally into that of heir-ship : Gal. iv. 7 ; compare Rom. viii. 17.

The word *heir* marks the original purpose of Creation. The dominion originally promised to Adam (Gen. i. 28; compare Ps. viii.) was gained by Christ. And so, in regard to the divine economy, the promise made to Abra-ham (compare Rom. iv. 13 ; Gal. iii. 29) and renewed to the divine King (Ps. ii. 8), which was symbolised by the 'in-heritance' of Canaan (Ex. xxiii. 30), became absolutely fulfilled in Christ.

The image of 'heirship' which is based apparently on the second Psalm (Ps. ii. 8) is recognised in the Gospels (Matt. xxi. 38 and parallels) where the contrast between 'the servants' (prophets) and 'the Son' is also marked.

At the same time, it must be care-fully noticed that the usage cannot be pressed in all directions. The term is used in relation to the possession, as marking the fulness of right, resting upon a personal connexion, and not, as implying a passing away and a suc-cession, in relation to a present pos-sessor (comp. Gal. iv. 1 ὁ κληρονόμος... κύριος πάντων ὤν). The heir as such vindicates his title to what he holds. Compare Additional Note on vi. 12.

The heirship of 'the Son' was realised by the Son Incarnate (*v.* 4) through His humanity : κληρονόμος γὰρ πάντων ὁ δεσπότης Χριστὸς οὐχ ὡς θεὸς ἀλλ' ὡς ἄνθρωπος (Theod.) ; but the writer speaks of 'the Son' simply as Son as being heir. In such lan-guage we can see the indication of the truth which is expressed by the statement that the Incarnation is in essence independent of the Fall, though conditioned by it as to its circumstances.

πάντων] The purpose of God ex-tended far beyond the hope of Israel; οὐκέτι γὰρ μερὶς κυρίου ὁ Ἰακώβ (Deut. xxxii. 9), ἀλλὰ πάντες (Theophlct.). Non

jam portio Domini tantum Jacob et portio ejus Israel, sed omnes omnino nationes (Atto Verc.).

δι' οὗ καὶ ἐποίησεν τ. αἰ.] This order, which is certainly correct, throws the emphasis on the fact of creation, which answers to the appointment of the Son as heir (καὶ ἐποίησεν, compare vi. 7; vii. 25). The creation does in-deed involve the consummation of things. The 'Protevangelium' is Gen. i. 26 f.

τοὺς αἰῶνας] the world, Vulg. sæcula. The phrase οἱ αἰῶνες has been inter-preted to mean

(1) 'Periods of time,' and especially 'this age' and 'the age to come,' as though the sense were that God created through the Son—Who is supra-temporal—all time and times.

(2) The successive emanations from the divine Being, as in the Gnostic theologies ; or the orders of finite being. Comp. *Const. Apost.* viii. 12 ὁ δι' αὐτοῦ [τοῦ υἱοῦ] ποιήσας τὰ χερου-βὶμ καὶ τὰ σεραφίμ, αἰῶνάς τε καὶ στρατιάς...

(3) The sum of the 'periods of time' including all that is manifested in and through them. This sense appears first in Eccles. iii. 11, an-swering to the corresponding use of עוֹלָם which is first found there. The plural עוֹלָמִים is found with this mean-ing in later Jewish writers, *e.g.* בּוֹרֵא עוֹלָמִים. Comp. Wisd. xiii. 9.

There can be little doubt that this is the right sense here (comp. xi. 3 note). The universe may be regarded either in its actual constitu-tion as a whole (ὁ κόσμος), or as an order which exists through time de-veloped in successive stages. There are obvious reasons why the latter mode of representation should be adopted here.

The difference between ὁ αἰών—the age—one part of the whole develop-ment, and οἱ αἰῶνες—the ages—the sum of all the parts, is well illustrated by the divine title 'the King of the ages' 1 Tim. i. 17 (ὁ βασιλεὺς τῶν αἰώνων; Tobit xiii. 6, 10; Henoch p. 86 Dillm. ὁ β. πάντων τῶν αἰ.; Ecclus. xxxvi. 22 (19) ὁ θεὸς τῶν αἰώνων; Henoch p. 83). In this aspect 'the King of the ages' is contrasted with 'the rulers of this age' (οἱ ἄρχοντες τοῦ αἰῶνος τούτου 1 Cor. ii. 6, 8). Compare παντοκράτωρ (Apoc. i. 8 &c.) with κοσμοκράτωρ (Eph. vi. 12).

The Rabbinic use of עוֹלָם is very wide. Thus they speak of the 'Macrocosm,' the universe, as עוֹלָם הגדול, and of the 'Microcosm,' man, as עוֹלם הקטון.

There is a very fine saying in *Aboth* iv. 'R. Jacob said This world is like a vestibule before the world to come: prepare thyself in the vestibule that thou mayest enter into the festival-chamber' (לטרקלין).

ἐπ. τοὺς αἰῶνας] The order of finite being even when it is regarded under the form of gradual development is spoken of as 'made' by a supra-temporal act. 'All creation is one act at once.'

πάντων...τοὺς αἰῶνας] *all things... the world*...all single things regarded in their separate being: the cycles of universal life.

For the fact of creation through the Son see John i. 3, 10; 1 Cor. viii. 6 (διά); Col. i. 16 (ἐν).

Philo speaks of the *Logos* as 'the instrument through which the world was made: εὑρήσεις αἴτιον μὲν αὐτοῦ (sc. τοῦ κόσμου) τὸν θεὸν ὑφ' οὗ γέγονεν· ὕλην δὲ τὰ τέσσαρα στοιχεῖα ἐξ ὧν συνεκράθη· ὄργανον δὲ λόγον θεοῦ δι' οὗ κατεσκευάσθη· τῆς δὲ κατασκευῆς αἰτίαν τὴν ἀγαθότητα τοῦ δημιουργοῦ (de Cher. 35; i. 162 M.). Comp. *de monarch.* ii. § 5 (ii. 225 M.); *leg. alleg.* iii. § 31 (i. 106 M.).

The first passage is singularly instructive as bringing out the difference between the Christian and Philonic conception of the divine action. Comp. Rom. xi. 36 (ἐκ, διά, εἰς); 1 Cor. viii. 6 (ἐξ, εἰς, διά). The preposition ὑπό

is not, I believe, used in connexion with creation in the N.T.

ii. *The Nature and work of the Son* (3).

The Nature and work of the Son is presented in regard to (1) His divine Personality and (2) the Incarnation.

(1) In Himself the Son is presented in His essential Nature, as the manifestation of the divine attributes (ἀπαύγασμα τῆς δόξης), and He embodies personally the divine essence (χαρακτὴρ τῆς ὑποστάσεως). In connexion with this view of His Nature, His work is to bear all things to their true end (φέρων τὰ πάντα).

(2) This general view of His work leads to the view of His work as Incarnate in a world marred by sin. In regard to this He is the One absolute Redeemer (καθαρ. τῶν ἁμ. ποιησάμενος) and the Sovereign representative of glorified humanity (ἐκάθ. ἐν δεξιᾷ τῆς μεγ. ἐν ὑψ.).

3 *Who, being the effulgence of His glory and the expression of His essence, and so bearing all things by the word of His power, after He had Himself made purification of sins, sat down on the right hand of the Majesty on high.*

3. The description of the Nature and Work of the Son of God in relation to the Father (*spake in, appointed, made*) given in the second verse is completed by a description of His Nature and Work in regard to Himself.

The description begins with that which is eternal. The participles 'being,' 'bearing' describe the absolute and not simply the present essence and action of the Son. Compare John i. 18; (iii. 13); Col. i. 15, 17. The ὤν in particular guards against the idea of mere 'adoption' in the Sonship, and affirms the permanence of the divine essence of the Son during His historic work.

At the same time the divine being of the Son can be represented to men

αἰῶνας· ³ὃς ὢν ἀπαύγασμα τῆς δόξης καὶ χαρακτὴρ τῆς

only under human figures. Since this is so, the infinite truth must be suggested by a combination of complementary images such as are given here in ἀπαύγασμα and χαρακτήρ. The first image (ἀπαύγασμα) brings out the conception of the source (πηγή) of the Son's Being, and of His unbroken connexion with the Father, as revealing to man the fulness of His attributes.

The second image (χαρακτήρ) emphasises the true Personality of the Son as offering in Himself the perfect representation of the divine essence of the Father (John xiv. 9).

Taken together the images suggest the thoughts presented by the theological terms 'coessential' (ὁμοούσιος) and 'only-begotten' (μονογενής).

The 'glory' of God finds expression in the Son as its 'effulgence': the 'essence' of God finds expression in Him as its 'type.' Neither figure can be pressed to conclusions. The luminous image may be said to have no substantive existence (τὸ γὰρ ἀπαύγασμα, φασίν (the followers of Sabellius, Marcellus, Photinus), ἐνυπόστατον οὐκ ἔστιν ἀλλ᾽ ἐν ἑτέρῳ ἔχει τὸ εἶναι Chrysost. Hom. ii. 1). The express image may be offered in a different substance. So it is that the first figure leaves unnoticed the Personality of the Son, and the second figure the essential equality of the Son with the Father. But that which the one figure lacks the other supplies. We cannot conceive of the luminous body apart from the luminous image; and we cannot identify the archetype and its expression.

Under another aspect we observe that the Divine Manifestation is placed side by side with the Divine Essence. It is in Christ that the Revelation is seen (ἀπαύγασμα). It is in Christ that the Essence is made intelligibly distinct for man (χαρακτήρ).

The two truths are implied by the

words of the Lord recorded in St John's Gospel v. 19, 30; xiv. 9. For the pre-existence of the Son compare c. vii. 3; x. 5.

It must farther be noticed that in the description of the Being of the Son language is used which points to a certain congruity in the Incarnation. This is the 'propriety' of His Nature to perfectly reveal God. Through Him God reveals Himself outwardly.

Under this aspect the clause which describes the action of the Son—φέρων τὰ πάντα τῷ ῥήματι τῆς δυνάμεως αὐτοῦ —gives in its most general form the truth expressed in the divine acts ὃν ἔθηκεν κληρονόμον πάντων, δι᾽ οὗ καὶ ἐποίησεν τοὺς αἰῶνας.

ἀπαύγασμα τῆς δόξης] the effulgence of His glory, Vulg. splendor gloriæ (and so Latt. uniformly).

ἀπαύγασμα] The verb ἀπαυγάζω has two distinct meanings:

1. To flash forth: radiate.
2. To flash back: reflect.

The noun ἀπαύγασμα, which is a characteristically Alexandrine word occurring in Wisdom (vii. 25), and in Philo, may therefore mean either

1. The effulgence; or
2. The reflection (refulgence).

The use of the word by Philo is not decisive as to the sense to be chosen. In one passage the sense 'effulgence' appears to be most natural: De concupisc. § 11 (ii. 356 M.) τὸ δ᾽ ἐμφυσώμενον (Gen. ii. 7) δῆλον ὡς αἰθέριον ἦν πνεῦμα καὶ εἰ δή τι αἰθερίου πνεύματος κρεῖττον, ἅτε τῆς μακαρίας καὶ τρισμακαρίας φύσεως ἀπαύγασμα.

In two others the sense 'reflection' is more appropriate: De opif. mundi § 51 (i. 35 M.) πᾶς ἄνθρωπος κατὰ μὲν τὴν διάνοιαν οἰκείωται θείῳ λόγῳ, τῆς μακαρίας φύσεως ἐκμαγεῖον ἢ ἀπόσπασμα ἢ ἀπαύγασμα γεγονώς, κατὰ δὲ τὴν τοῦ σώματος κατασκευὴν ἅπαντι τῷ κόσμῳ.

De plantatione Noæ § 12 (i. 337 M.) τὸ δὲ ἁγίασμα (Ex. xv. 17) οἷον ἁγίων ἀπαύγασμα, μίμημα ἀρχετύπου, ἐπεὶ τὰ αἰσθήσει καλὰ καὶ νοήσει καλῶν εἰκόνες.

The passage in Wisdom (vii. 25 f.) is capable of bearing either meaning. The threefold succession ἀπαύγασμα, ἔσοπτρον, εἰκών,—*effulgence, mirror, image*, no less than v. 25, appears to favour the sense of 'effulgence.' Otherwise ἔσοπτρον interrupts the order of thought.

In this passage the sense *reflection* is quite possible, but it appears to be less appropriate, as introducing a third undefined notion of 'that which reflects.' Moreover the truth suggested by 'reflection' is contained in χαρακτήρ, to which 'effulgence' offers a more expressive complement; and the Greek Fathers with unanimity have adopted the sense *effulgence* according to the idea expressed in the Nicene Creed, *Light of Light.* Several of their comments are of interest as bringing out different sides of the image: Orig. *in Joh.* xxxii. 18 ὅλης μὲν οὖν οἶμαι τῆς δόξης τοῦ θεοῦ αὐτοῦ ἀπαύγασμα εἶναι τὸν υἱόν... φθάνειν μέντοι γε ἀπὸ τοῦ ἀπαυγάσματος τούτου τῆς ὅλης δόξης μερικὰ ἀπαυγάσματα ἐπὶ τὴν λοιπὴν λογικὴν κτίσιν. Comp. *c. Cels.* v. 18; *de princ.* 1, 2, 4 (and Redepenning's note); *Hom. in Jer.* ix. 4 οὐχὶ ἐγέννησεν ὁ πατὴρ τὸν υἱὸν καὶ ἀπέλυσεν αὐτὸν ἀπὸ τῆς γενέσεως αὐτοῦ, ἀλλ' ἀεὶ γεννᾷ αὐτὸν ὅσον ἐστὶ τὸ φῶς ποιητικὸν τοῦ ἀπαυγάσματος. Greg. Nyss. *de perfecta Christ. forma*, Migne *Patr. Gr.* xlvi. p. 265 δόξαν καὶ ὑπόστασιν ὠνόμασε τὸ ὑπερκείμενον παντὸς ἀγαθοῦ...τὸ δὲ συναφές τε καὶ ἀδιάστατον τοῦ υἱοῦ πρὸς τὸν πατέρα διερμηνεύων...ἀπαύγασμα δόξης καὶ χαρακτῆρα ὑποστάσεως προσαγορεύει ...ἀλλὰ καὶ ὁ τὴν ἀπαυγάζουσαν φύσιν νοήσας καὶ τὸ ἀπαύγασμα ταύτης πάντως κατενόησε, καὶ ὁ τὸ μέγεθος τῆς ὑποστάσεως ἐν νῷ λαβὼν τῷ ἐπιφαινομένῳ χαρακτῆρι πάντως ἐμμετρεῖ τὴν ὑπόστασιν. Chrysostom (*Hom.* ii. 2) ἀπαύγασμα εἶπεν...ἵνα δείξῃ ὅτι κἀκεῖ (John viii.

12) οὕτως εἴρηται· δῆλον δὲ ὡς φῶς ἐκ φωτός. Theodoret *ad loc.* τὸ ἀπαύγασμα καὶ ἐκ τοῦ πυρός ἐστι καὶ σὺν τῷ πυρί ἐστι... ἀεὶ δὲ ἡ δόξα, ἀεὶ τοίνυν καὶ τὸ ἀπαύγασμα. Œcumenius *ad loc.* διὰ τοῦ 'ἀπαύγασμα' τὴν κατὰ φύσιν ἐκ τοῦ πατρὸς πρόοδον τοῦ υἱοῦ δηλοῖ· οὐδὲν γὰρ ὅλως οὐδαμοῦ κατὰ χάριν καὶ εἰσποίησιν πρόεισιν ἀπαύγασμά τινος, οὐκ ἀπὸ τοῦ ἡλίου, οὐκ ἀπὸ τοῦ πυρός, οὐκ ἀφ' ἑτέρου τινός, ἀφ' οὗ πέφυκεν ἀπαύγασμα προιέναι.

It is indeed true that the sense of 'effulgence' passes into that of 'reflection' so far as both present the truth that it is through Christ that God becomes visible to man. But in the one case the nature of Christ is emphasised and in the other His office. The 'effulgence' is the necessary manifestation of the luminous body: the 'reflection' is the manifestation through some medium as it takes place in fact.

It is however necessary to observe that 'effulgence' is not any isolated ray, but the whole bright image which brings before us the source of light. Comp. Greg. Nyss. *c. Eunom.* viii., Migne *Patr. Gr.* xlv. p. 773 ὡς ἐκ παντὸς τοῦ ἡλιακοῦ κύκλου τῇ τοῦ φωτὸς λαμπηδόνι ἀπαυγάζεται, τοῦ δὲ μέν τι λάμπει τὸ δὲ ἀλαμπές ἐστι τοῦ κύκλου· οὕτως ὅλη ἡ δόξα ἥτις ἐστὶν ὁ πατὴρ τῷ ἐξ ἑαυτῆς ἀπαυγάσματι, τουτέστι τῷ ἀληθινῷ φωτὶ πανταχόθεν περιαυγάζεται. And again, while the general figure guards the conception of the permanence of the relation between the source and the light, the 'effulgence' is regarded in its completeness (ἀπαύγασμα)—the light flashed forth, and not the light in the continuity of the stream.

τῆς δόξης αὐτοῦ] The 'glory of God' is the full manifestation of His attributes according to man's power of apprehending them, 'all His goodness' (Ex. xxxiii. 19 ff.). This 'glory' was the subject of His crowning revelation as contemplated by the prophets

ὑποστάσεως αὐτοῦ, φέρων τε τὰ πάντα τῷ ῥήματι τῆς

3 φανερῶν Β* (rell φέρων).

(Is. xl. 5 *the glory of the Lord shall be
revealed;* xlvi. 13 *in Zion salvation,
unto Israel my glory;* lx.1f.) and made
known in Christ (2 Cor. iv. 4, 6: comp.
Rom. ix. 23; 1 Tim. i. 11; John xi.
40; i. 14); compare *Introduction to
the Gospel of St John* xlvii. ff. It
is the final light (Apoc. xxi. 23) for
which we look (Tit. ii. 13; Rom. v. 2).
Under the Old Dispensation the
Shekinah was the symbol of it: Ex.
xxiv. 16; Ps. lxxxv. 9. Comp. Rom. ix.
4; (2 Pet. i. 17).

For illustrations see Rom. vi. 4; ix.
4; Col. i. 11; Eph. iii. 16; compare
2 Thess. i. 9; 1 Cor. xi. 7; Rom.
iii. 23.

Clement (1 *Cor.* c. xxxvi.) writes ὃς
ὢν ἀπαύγασμα τῆς μεγαλωσύνης αὐτοῦ,
taking the word μεγαλωσύνη from the
later clause and greatly obscuring the
fulness of the thought.

χαρακτὴρ τῆς ὑποστάσεως] *the expression of His essence,* Vulg. *figura* (O. L. *imago,* v. *character*) *substantiæ.* Syr. *image of His essence*

(ܨܠܡܳܐ ܕܟܝܳܢܶܗ).

The word χαρακτήρ is used from
the time of Herodotus (i. 116) of the
distinguishing features, material or
spiritual, borne by any object or
person; of the traits by which we
recognise it as being what it is.

It is specially used for the mark
upon a coin (Eurip. *El.* 558 f.; Arist.
Pol. i. 9) which determines the nature
and value of the piece. Comp. Ign.
ad Magn. 5 ὥσπερ γάρ ἐστιν νομίσματα
δύο, ὃ μὲν θεοῦ ὃ δὲ κόσμου, καὶ ἕκαστον
αὐτῶν ἴδιον χαρακτῆρα ἐπικείμενον ἔχει,
οἱ ἄπιστοι τοῦ κόσμου τούτου, οἱ δὲ πιστοὶ
ἐν ἀγάπῃ χαρακτῆρα θεοῦ πατρὸς διὰ
Ἰησοῦ Χριστοῦ.

In this connexion χαρακτήρ is applied to the impression of the en-
graving on a die or seal which is conveyed to other substances. Philo, *de*

Mund. opif. § 4 (i. 4 M.) ὥσπερ ἐν κηρῷ
τινι τῇ ἑαυτοῦ ψυχῇ...τοὺς χαρακτῆρας
ἐνσφραγίζεσθαι. *id.* § 53 (i. 36 M.) τῆς ἑκατέρας φύσεως
ἀπεμάττετο τῇ ψυχῇ τοὺς χαρακτῆρας;
de mundo § 4 (ii. 606 M.).
De plant. Noœ § 5 (i. 332 M.) ὁ Μωϋσῆς [τὴν λογικὴν ψυχὴν] ὠνόμασεν...τοῦ
θείου καὶ ἀοράτου εἰκόνα, δόκιμον εἶναι
νομίσας οὐσιωθεῖσαν καὶ τυπωθεῖσαν
σφραγῖδι θεοῦ, ἧς ὁ χαρακτήρ ἐστιν ὁ
ἀΐδιος λόγος.

By a natural transition from this
use, χαρακτήρ is applied to that in
which the distinguishing traits of the
object to which it is referred are
found. So Philo describes 'the spirit,'
the essence of the rational part of
man, as 'a figure and impress of
divine power': ἡ μὲν οὖν κοινὴ πρὸς τὰ
ἄλογα δύναμις οὐσίαν ἔλαχεν αἷμα, ἡ δὲ
ἐκ τῆς λογικῆς ἀπορρυεῖσα πηγῆς, τὸ
πνεῦμα, οὐκ ἀέρα κινούμενον ἀλλὰ τύπον
τινὰ καὶ χαρακτῆρα θείας δυνάμεως, ἣν
ὀνοματικυρίῳ Μωϋσῆς εἰκόνα καλεῖ, δηλῶν
ὅτι ἀρχέτυπον μὲν φύσεως λογικῆς ὁ θεός
ἐστι, μίμημα δὲ καὶ ἀπεικόνισμα ἄνθρωπος (*quod det. pot. insid.* § 23; i.
207 M.). And Clement of Rome speaks
of man as 'an impress of the image
of God': ἐπὶ πᾶσιν τὸ ἐξοχώτατον...
ἄνθρωπον...ἔπλασεν [ὁ δημιουργὸς καὶ
δεσπότης τῶν ἁπάντων] τῆς ἑαυτοῦ εἰκό-
νος χαρακτῆρα (Gen. i. 26 f.) (*ad Cor.*
i. 33).

Generally χαρακτήρ may be said to
be that by which anything is directly recognised through corresponding
signs under a particular aspect, though
it may include only a few features of
the object. It is so far a primary and
not a secondary source of knowledge.
Χαρακτήρ conveys representative traits
only, and therefore it is distinguished
from εἰκών (2 Cor. iv. 4; Col. i. 15;
1 Cor. xi. 7; Col. iii. 10) which gives a
complete representation under the
condition of earth of that which it

figures; and from μορφή (Phil. ii. 6 f.) which marks the essential form. There is no word in English which exactly renders it. If there were a sense of 'express' (*i.e.* expressed image) answering to 'impress,' this would be the best equivalent.

ὑπόστασις] The word properly means 'that which stands beneath' as a sediment (Arist. *de hist. an.* v. 19 and often), or foundation (Ezek. xliii. 11, LXX.), or ground of support (Ps. lxviii. (lxix.) 2; Jer. xxiii. 22, LXX.). From this general sense come the special senses of firmness, confidence (compare c. iii. 14 note; 2 Cor. ix. 4; xi. 17); reality ([Arist.] *de mundo* 4 τὰ μὲν κατ' ἔμφασιν, τὰ δὲ καθ' ὑπόστασιν, κατ' ἔμφασιν μὲν ἴριδες...καθ' ὑπόστασιν δέ...κομῆται...), that in virtue of which a thing is what it is, the essence of any being (Ps. xxxviii. (xxxix.) 6; Ps. lxxxviii. (lxxxix.) 48; Wisd. xvi. 21: compare Jerem. x. 17; Ezek. xxvi. 11).

When this meaning of 'essence' was applied to the Divine Being two distinct usages arose in the course of debate. If men looked at the Holy Trinity under the aspect of the one Godhead there was only one ὑπόστασις, one divine essence. If, on the other hand, they looked at each Person in the Holy Trinity, then that by which each Person is what He is, His ὑπόστασις, was necessarily regarded as distinct, and there were three ὑποστάσεις. In the first case ὑπόστασις as applied to the One Godhead was treated as equivalent to οὐσία: in the other case it was treated as equivalent to πρόσωπον.

As a general rule the Eastern (Alexandrine) Fathers adopted the second mode of speech affirming the existence of three ὑποστάσεις (real Persons) in the Godhead; while the Western Fathers affirmed the unity of one ὑπόστασις (essence) in the Holy Trinity (compare the letter of Dionysius of Alexandria to Dionysius of Rome, Routh, *Rell. sacræ*, iii. 390 ff.

and notes). Hence many mediæval and modern writers have taken ὑπόστασις in the sense of 'person' here. But this use of the word is much later than the apostolic age; and it is distinctly inappropriate in this connexion. The Son is not the image, the expression of the 'Person' of God. On the other hand, He is the expression of the 'essence' of God. He brings the Divine before us at once perfectly and definitely according to the measure of our powers.

The exact form of the expression, ἀπαύγ. τῆς δ. καὶ χαρ. τῆς ὑποστ. and not τὸ ἀπαύγ. τ. δ. καὶ ὁ χαρ. τῆς ὑποστ. or ἀπαύγ. δ. καὶ χαρ. ὑποστ., will be noticed (comp. *v.* 2 ἐν υἱῷ).

φέρων τε] *and so bearing*...We now pass from the thought of the absolute Being of the Son to His action in the finite creation under the conditions of time and space. The particle τε indicates the new relation of the statement which it introduces. It is obvious that the familiar distinction holds true here: '*καί* conjungit, *τε* adjungit.' The providential action of the Son is a special manifestation of His Nature and is not described in a coordinate statement: what He does flows from what He is.

The particle τε is rarely used as an independent conjunction in the N.T. It is so used again c. vi. 5; ix. 1; xii. 2; and in St Paul only Rom. ii. 19; xvi. 26; 1 Cor. iv. 21; Eph. iii. 19.

φέρων...] *bearing* or *guiding*, Vulg. *portans*, O. L. *ferens* v. *gerens*. This present and continuous support and carrying forward to their end of all created things was attributed by Jewish writers to God no less than their creation. 'God, blessed be He, bears (סובל) the world' (*Shem. R.* § 36 referring to Is. xlvi. 4; compare Num. xi. 14; Deut. i. 9). The action of God is here referred to the Son (comp. Col. i. 17).

The word φέρειν is not to be understood simply of the passive support of a burden (yet notice c. xiii. 13; xii.

δυνάμεως αὐτοῦ, καθαρισμὸν τῶν ἁμαρτιῶν ποιησάμενος

καθαρισμόν ℵAB vg: + δι' αὐτοῦ' καθ. D₂*: + δι' ἑαυτοῦ' καθ. ৎ syrr.   τ. ἁμαρτιῶν
ℵ*ABD₂*M₂ vg syr vg me: τ. ἁμ. + ἡμῶν ৎ syr hl: + ὑμῶν ℵᶜ.   τ. ἁμ. ποιησ. ἐκάθ.
ℵABD₂M₂ vg: ποιησ. τ. ἁμ. ἡμ. ἐκάθ. ৎ.

20); "for the Son is not an Atlas sustaining the dead weight of the world." It rather expresses that 'bearing' which includes movement, progress, towards an end. The Son in the words of Œcumenius περιάγει καὶ συνέχει καὶ πηδαλιουχεῖ...τὰ ἀόρατα καὶ τὰ ὁρατὰ περιφέρων καὶ κυβερνῶν. The same general sense is given by Chrysostom: φέρων...τουτέστι, κυβερνῶν, τὰ διαπίπτοντα συγκρατῶν. τοῦ γὰρ ποιῆσαι τὸν κόσμον οὐχ ἧττόν ἐστι τὸ συγκροτεῖν ἀλλ', εἰ δεῖ τι καὶ θαυμαστὸν εἰπεῖν, καὶ μεῖζον (Hom. ii. 3). And so Primasius: verbo jussionis suæ omnia gubernat et regit, non enim minus est gubernare mundum quam creasse...in gubernando vero ea quæ facta sunt ne ad nihilum redeant continentur.

Gregory of Nyssa goes yet further, and understands φέρων of the action by which the Son brings things into existence: τὰ σύμπαντα τῷ ῥήματι τῆς δυνάμεως αὐτοῦ φέρει ὁ Λόγος ἐκ τοῦ μὴ ὄντος εἰς γένεσιν· πάντα γὰρ ὅσα τὴν ἄϋλον εἴληχε φύσιν μίαν αἰτίαν ἔχει τῆς ὑποστάσεως τὸ ῥῆμα τῆς ἀφράστου δυνάμεως (de perf. Christ. forma, Migne Patr. Gr. xlvi. p. 265). For this sense of φέρειν compare Philo quis rer. div. hær. § 7 (i. 477 M.); de mut. nom. § 44 (i. 6, 7 M.). Philo expresses a similar idea to that of the text when he speaks of ὁ πηδαλιοῦχος καὶ κυβερνήτης τοῦ παντὸς λόγος θεῖος (De Cherub. § 11; i. 145 M.). And Hermas gives the passive side of it Sim. ix. 14, 5 τὸ ὄνομα τοῦ υἱοῦ τοῦ θεοῦ μέγα ἐστὶ καὶ ἀχώρητον καὶ τὸν κόσμον ὅλον βαστάζει· εἰ οὖν πᾶσα ἡ κτίσις διὰ τοῦ υἱοῦ τοῦ θεοῦ βαστάζεται...

τὰ πάντα] as contrasted with πάντα (John i. 2). All things in their unity: c. ii. 8, 10 (not iii. 4); Rom. viii. 32; xi. 36; 1 Cor. viii. 6; xv. 27 f.; 2 Cor.

iv. 15; v. 18; Eph. i. 10 f.; iii. 9; iv. 10, 15; Phil. iii. 21; Col. i. 16 f., 20; 1 Tim. vi. 13.

See also 1 Cor. xi. 12; xii. 6; Gal. iii. 22; Phil. iii. 8; Eph. i. 23; v. 13. The reading in 1 Cor. ix. 22, and perhaps in xii. 19, is wrong.

τῷ ῥ. τῆς δυν.] by the word—the expression—of His (Christ's) power, the word in which His power finds its manifestation (compare Rev. iii. 10 τὸν λόγον τῆς ὑπομονῆς μου). As the world was called into being by an utterance (ῥῆμα) of God (c. xi. 3), so it is sustained by a like expression of the divine will. The choice of the term as distinguished from λόγος marks, so to speak, the particular action of Providence. Gen. i. 3 εἶπεν ὁ θεός.

δυν. αὐτοῦ] The pronoun naturally refers to the Son, not to the Father, in spite of the preceding clauses, from the character of the thought.

καθ. ποιησάμενος] having made—when He had made—purification of sins. This clause introduces a new aspect of the Son. He has been regarded in His absolute Nature (ὤν), and in His general relation to finite being (φέρων): now He is seen as He entered into the conditions of life in a world disordered by sin.

The completed atonement wrought by Christ (having made) is distinguished from His eternal being and His work through all time in the support of created things (being, bearing); and it is connected with His assumption of sovereign power in His double Nature at the right hand of God (having made...He sat...). Thus the phrase prepares for the main thought of the Epistle, the High-priestly work of Christ, which is first distinctly introduced in c. ii. 17.

ποιησάμενος] The Vulgate, from the

ἐκάθισεν ἐν δεξιᾷ τῆς μεγαλωσύνης ἐν ὑψηλοῖς, ⁴τοσούτῳ

defectiveness of Latin participles, fails to give the sense: *purgationem peccatorum faciens* (compare *v.* 1 *loquens*). In *v.* 14 (*missi*) there is the converse error. The Old Latin had avoided this error but left the thought indefinite, *purificatione* (*purgatione*) *peccatorum facta*.

The use of the middle (ποιησάμενος) suggests the thought which the late gloss δι᾽ ἑαυτοῦ made more distinct. Christ Himself, in His own Person, made the purification: He did not make it as something distinct from Himself, simply provided by His power. Compare μνείαν ποιεῖσθαι Rom. i. 9; Eph. i. 16, &c.; ποιεῖσθαι δεήσεις 1 Tim. ii. 1; Luke v. 33; John xiv. 23, &c.

καθ. τῶν ἁμαρτιῶν] 2 Pet. i. 9 (personally applied). Compare Exod. xxx. 10 (LXX.); Job vii. 21 (LXX.). Elsewhere the word καθαρισμός is used only of legal purification (Luke ii. 22; Mk. i. 44 ‖ Luke v. 14; John ii. 6; iii. 25). The verb καθαρίζειν is also used but rarely of sin: c. x. 2 (ix. 14); 1 John i. 7, 9. Comp. Acts xv. 9; Eph. v. 26; Tit. ii. 14 (2 Cor. vii. 1; James iv. 8).

There is perhaps a reference to the imperfection of the Aaronic purifications (compare Lev. xvi. 30) which is dwelt upon afterwards, c. x. 1 ff.

The genitive (καθ. ἁμαρτιῶν) may express either

(1) the cleansing *of* sins, *i.e.* the removal of the sins. Compare Matt. viii. 3; Job vii. 21 (Ex. xxx. 10),

or (2) the cleansing (of the person) *from* sins. Comp. c. ix. 15.

The former appears to be the right meaning. See Additional Note.

τῶν ἁμαρτιῶν] *of sins* generally. Comp. Col. i. 14; Eph. i. 7. Elsewhere ἡμῶν (or αὐτῶν) is added: Matt. i. 21; Gal. i. 4; 1 Cor. xv. 3; 1 John iv. 10; Apoc. i. 5. Contrast John i. 29 (τὴν ἁμαρτίαν). For the contrast of the sing. and pl. see c. ix. 26, 28; x. 18, 26.

The result of this 'purification' is the foundation of a 'Holy' Church (comp. John xiii. 10 n.). The hindrance to the approach to God is removed.

ἐκάθισεν] c. viii. 1; x. 12; xii. 2. Comp. Eph. i. 20 (καθίσας); Apoc. iii. 21. Καθίσαι (intrans.) expresses the solemn taking of the seat of authority, and not merely the act of sitting. Comp. Matt. v. 1; xix. 28; xxv. 31. The phrase marks the fulfilment of Ps. cx. 1; Matt. xxii. 44 and parallels; Acts ii. 34; and so it applies only to the risen Christ. Angels are always represented as 'standing' (Is. vi. 2; 1 K. xxii. 19) or falling on their faces: and so the priests ministered, comp. c. x. 11. Only princes of the house of David could sit in the court (עזרה) of the Temple (Biesenthal). Hence 'the man of sin' so asserts himself: 2 Thess. ii. 4. Bernard says in commenting on the title 'thrones' (Col. i. 16): nec vacat Sessio: tranquillitatis insigne est (*de consid.* v. 4, 10).

ἐν δεξιᾷ] *v.* 13. The idea is of course of dignity and not of place ('dextra Dei ubique est'). All local association must be excluded: οὐχ ὅτι τόπῳ περικλείεται ὁ θεὸς ἀλλ᾽ ἵνα τὸ ὁμότιμον αὐτοῦ δειχθῇ τὸ πρὸς τὸν πατέρα (Theophlct.). Non est putandum quod omnipotens Pater qui spiritus est incircumscriptus omnia replens dexteram aut sinistram habeat…Quid est ergo 'sedit ad dexteram majestatis' nisi ut dicatur, habitat in plenitudine paternæ majestatis? (Primas.) Comp. Eph. iv. 10. We, as we at present are, are forced to think in terms of space, but it does not follow that this limitation belongs to the perfection of humanity.

Herveius (on *v.* 13) notices the double contrast between the Son and the Angels: Seraphin stant ut ministri, Filius sedet ut Dominus: Seraphin in circuitu, Filius ad dexteram.

τῆς μεγαλ.] c. viii. 1; Jude 25. The word is not unfrequent in the LXX. : *e.g.* 1 Chron. xxix. 11 ; Wisd. xviii. 24. 'The Majesty' expresses the idea of God in His greatness. Comp. Buxtorf *Lex. s. v.* גבורה. 1 Clem. xvi. τὸ σκῆπτρον τῆς μεγαλ., c. xxxvi. ἀπαύγασμα τῆς μεγαλ.

ἐν ὑψηλοῖς] Ps. xciii. (xcii.) 4 (LXX.). Here only in N.T. Comp. ἐν ὑψίστοις Luke ii. 14; Matt. xxi. 9 and parallels ; and ἐν τοῖς ἐπουρανίοις Eph. i. 3, 20; ii. 6; iii. 10; vi. 12.

The term marks the sphere of the higher life. Local imagery is necessarily used for that which is in itself unlimited by place (compare iv. 14 ; vii. 26). Τί ἐστιν Ἐν ὑψηλοῖς; Chrysostom asks, εἰς τόπον περικλείει τὸν θεόν; ἄπαγε (Hom. ii. 3). In excelsis dicens non eum loco concludit, sed ostendit omnibus altiorem et evidentiorem, hoc est quia usque ad ipsum pervenit solium paternæ claritatis (Atto Verc.).

The clause belongs to ἐκάθισεν and not to τῆς μεγαλωσύνης. The latter connexion would be grammatically irregular though not unparalleled, and τῆς μεγαλωσύνης is complete in itself.

This Session of Christ at the right hand of God,—the figure is only used of the Incarnate Son—is connected with His manifold activity as King (Acts ii. 33 ff.; Eph. i. 21 ff.; Col. iii. 1; c. x. 12) and Priest (1 Pet. iii. 22; c. viii. 1 ; c. xii. 2) and Intercessor (Rom. viii. 34). Comp. Acts vii. 55 f. (ἑστῶτα ἐκ δ.).

iii. *Transition to the detailed development of the argument* (4).

The fourth verse forms a transition to the special development of the argument of the Epistle. The general contrast between 'the Son' as the mediator of the new revelation and 'the prophets' as mediators of the old, is offered in the extreme case. According to Jewish belief the Law was ministered by angels (c. ii. 2; Gal. iii. 19; comp. Acts vii. 53), but even

the dignity of these, the highest representatives of the Dispensation, was as far below that of Christ as the title of minister is below that of the incommunicable title of divine Majesty. This thought is developed i. 5—ii. 18.

The abrupt introduction of the reference to the angels becomes intelligible both from the function which was popularly assigned to angels in regard to the Law, and from the description of the exaltation of the Incarnate Son. Moses alone was admitted in some sense to direct intercourse with God (Num. xii. 8 ; Deut. xxxiv. 10): otherwise 'the Angel of the Lord' was the highest messenger of revelation under the Old Covenant. And again the thought of the Session of the Son on the Father's throne calls up at once the image of the attendant Seraphim (Is. vi. 1 ff.; John xii. 41; iv. 2 ff.).

The superiority of Messiah to the angels is recognised in Rabbinic writings.

Jalkut Sim. 2, fol. 53, 3 on Is. lii. 13, *Behold my servant shall (deal wisely) prosper.* This is King Messiah. *He shall be exalted and extolled and be very high.* He shall be exalted beyond Abraham, and extolled beyond Moses, and raised high above the ministering angels (מלאכי השרת).

Jalkut Chadash f. 144, 2. Messiah is greater than the fathers, and than Moses, and than the ministering angels (Schoettgen, i. p. 905).

⁴ *having become so much better than the angels as He hath inherited a more excellent name than they.*

4. The thought of the exaltation of the Incarnate Son fixes attention on His Manhood. Under this aspect He was shewn to have become superior to angels in His historic work. And the glory of ' the name ' which He has 'inherited' is the measure of His excellence. Comp. Eph. i. 20 f.

τοσούτῳ...ὅσῳ] c. x. 25; vii. 20 ff. Comp. viii. 6. The combination is found in Philo (*de mund. opif.* § 50

κρείττων γενόμενος τῶν ἀγγέλων ὅσῳ διαφορώτερον
παρ᾽ αὐτοὺς κεκληρονόμηκεν ὄνομα.   ⁵ Τίνι γὰρ εἶπέν

4 om. τῶν᾽ (ἀγγ.) B.

(i. 33 M.); *Leg. ad Cai.* § 36) but not in
St Paul.

κρείττων] The word is characteristic
of the epistle (13 times). Elsewhere
it is found only in the neuter (κρεῖττον
4 times; 1 Cor. xii. 31 is a false
reading). The idea is that of
superiority in dignity or worth or
advantage, the fundamental idea being
power and not goodness (ἀμείνων and
ἄριστος are not found in the N. T.).

γενόμενος] The word stands in
significant connexion with ὤν (v. 3).
The essential Nature of the Son is
contrasted with the consequences of
the Incarnation in regard to His divine-
human Person (comp. c. v. 9). His assumption of humanity, which for a time
' made Him lower than angels,' issued
in His royal exaltation. Comp. Matt.
xxvi. 64; Luke xxii. 69 (ὁ υἱὸς τοῦ
ἀνθρώπου).

The Greek fathers lay stress upon
κρείττων as marking a difference in
kind and not in degree. Athan. *c.
Ar.* i. § 59 τὸ ἄρα 'κρείττων' καὶ νῦν
καὶ δι᾽ ὅλων τῷ Κυρίῳ ἀνατίθησι, τῷ
κρείττονι καὶ ἄλλῳ παρὰ τὰ γενητὰ
τυγχάνοντι. Κρείττων γὰρ ἡ δι᾽ αὐτοῦ
θυσία, κρείττων ἡ ἐν αὐτῷ ἐλπίς, καὶ
αἱ δι᾽ αὐτοῦ ἐπαγγελίαι, οὐχ ὡς πρὸς
μικρὰ μεγάλαι συγκρινόμεναι ἀλλ᾽ ὡς
ἄλλαι πρὸς ἄλλα τὴν φύσιν τυγχάνουσαι·
ἐπεὶ καὶ ὁ πάντα οἰκονομήσας κρείττων
τῶν γενητῶν ἐστί.

They also rightly point out that
γενόμενος is used of the Lord's Human
Nature and not of His divine Personality: τοῦτο κατὰ τὸ ἀνθρώπειον εἴρηκεν,
ὡς γὰρ θεὸς ποιητὴς ἀγγέλων καὶ δεσπότης ἀγγέλων, ὡς δὲ ἄνθρωπος μετὰ
τὴν ἀνάστασιν καὶ τὴν εἰς οὐρανοὺς
ἀνάβασιν κρείττων ἀγγέλων ἐγένετο.

For κρείττων, διαφορώτερος, see c.
viii. 6 note.

τῶν ἀγγέλων] The class as a definite whole (vv. 5,7,13),and not beings
of such a nature (ii. 2, 5, 7, 9, 16).

διαφ. παρ᾽ αὐτούς... ὄνομα] The
'name' of angels is 'excellent' (διάφορον, different, distinguished, for good
from others; comp. Matt. xii. 12
διαφέρει), but that inherited by the
Son is 'more excellent' (Vulg. *dif-
ferentius præ illis.* O.L. *procellentius
(excellentius) his (ab his)*). For the use
of παρά see iii. 3, ix. 23, xi. 4, xii. 24.

By the 'name' we are to understand
probably not the name of 'Son' simply,
though this as applied to Christ in
His humanity is part of it, but the
Name which gathered up all that
Christ was found to be by believers,
Son, Sovereign and Creator, the Lord
of the Old Covenant, as is shewn in
the remainder of the chapter. Comp.
Phil. ii. 9 (Eph. i. 21).

For the position of διαφορώτερον
compare xi. 25 (iii. 14).

κεκληρ.] The perfect lays stress
upon the present possession of the
'name' which was 'inherited' by the
ascended Christ. That which had
been proposed in the eternal counsel
(v. 2 ἔθηκεν) was realised when the
work of redemption was completed
(John xix. 30 τετέλεσται). The possession of the 'name'—His own
eternally—was, in our human mode of
speech, consequent on the Incarnation, and the permanent issue of it.

In looking back over the view of
the Lord's Person and Work given in
vv. 1—4 we notice

  1. *The threefold aspect in which
it is regarded.*

  (a) The Eternal Being of the
Son (ὤν, φέρων).

  (β) The temporal work of the
Incarnate Son (καθαρισμὸν ποιησάμενος, κρείττων γενόμενος).

(γ) The work of the Exalted Christ in its historical foundation and in its abiding issues (ἐκάθισεν, κεκληρονόμηκεν).

2. *The unity of Christ's Person.*

The continuity of the Person of the Son throughout is distinctly affirmed. He is One before the work of creation and after the work of redemption. Traits which we regard as characteristic severally of His divine and of His human nature are referred to the same Person. This unity is clearly marked :

God spake in His Son,
Whom He appointed heir of all things,
through Whom He made the world,
Who being...and bearing...
having made purification...
sat down,
having become...

Even during His dwelling on earth, under the limitations of manhood, the activity of His divine Being (φέρων τὰ πάντα) was not interrupted ; and His redemptive work must be referred to the fulness of His One Person.

3. *The unity of Christ's work.*

The Creation, Redemption, Consummation of all things are indissolubly connected. The heirship of Christ is placed side by side with His creative work. The exaltation of humanity in Him is in no way dependent on the Fall. The Fall made Redemption necessary, and altered the mode in which the divine counsel of love, the consummation of creation, was fulfilled, but it did not alter the counsel itself.

A mysterious question has been raised whether the terms 'Son' and 'Father' are used of the absolute relations of the divine Persons apart from all reference to the Incarnation. In regard to this it may be observed that Scripture tells us very little of God apart from His relation to man and the world. At the same time the description of God as essentially 'love' helps us to see that the terms 'Father'

and 'Son' are peculiarly fitted to describe, though under a figure, an essential relation between the Persons of the Godhead. This essential relation found expression for us in the Incarnation ; and we are led to see that the 'economic' Trinity is a true image, under the conditions of earth, of the 'essential' Trinity.

Comp. *v.* 2 ἐν υἱῷ ; vii. 3. John iii. 16, 17.

It is remarkable that the title 'Father' is not applied to God in this Epistle except in the quotation i. 5 ; yet see xii. 9.

See Additional Note on the Divine Names in the Epistle.

I. THE SUPERIORITY OF THE SON, THE MEDIATOR OF THE NEW REVELATION, TO ANGELS (i. 5—ii. 18).

This first main thought of the Epistle, which has been announced in *v.* 4, is unfolded in three parts. It is established first (i) in regard to the Nature and Work of the Son, as the Mediator of the New Covenant, by detailed references to the testimony of Scripture (i. 5—14). It is then (ii) enforced practically by a consideration of the consequences of neglect (ii. 1—4). And lastly it is shewn (iii) that the glorious destiny of humanity, loftier than that of angels, in spite of the fall, has been fulfilled by the Son of Man (ii. 5—18).

i. *The testimony of Scripture to the preeminence of the Son over angels* (i. 5—14).

The series of seven quotations which follows the general statement of the subject of the Epistle shews that the truths which have been affirmed are a fulfilment of the teaching of the Old Testament. The quotations illustrate in succession the superiority of the Son, the Mediator of the new Revelation and Covenant, over the angels, and therefore far more over the prophets, (1) as Son, (*vv.* 5, 6) and then in two main aspects, (2) as 'heir of all things' (*vv.* 7—9), and (3) as 'creator of the world' (*vv.* 10—12).

The last quotation (*vv.* 13, 14) presents (4) the contrast between the Son and the angels in regard to the present dispensation. The issue of the Son's Incarnation is the welcome to sit at God's right hand (κρείττων γενόμενος) in certain expectation of absolute victory, while the angels are busy with their ministries.

(1) 5, 6. *The essential dignity of the Son.*

The dignity of the Son as Son is asserted in three connexions, in its foundation (σήμερον γεγέννηκά σε); in its continuance (ἔσομαι αὐτῷ εἰς πατέρα); and in its final manifestation (ὅταν πάλιν εἰσαγάγῃ).

⁵ *For to which of the angels said He at any time,*
　My Son art Thou :
　I have today begotten Thee ?
and again,
　I will be to Him a Father,
　And He shall be to Me a Son ?
⁶ *And when He again bringeth* (or *when on the other hand He bringeth*) *in the Firstborn into the world He saith,*
　And let all the Angels of God worship Him.

The first two quotations are taken from Ps. ii. 7 and 2 Sam. vii. 14 (∥ 1 Chron. xvii. 13). Both quotations verbally agree with the LXX., which agrees with the Hebr.

The words of the Psalm are quoted again c. v. 5 and by St Paul, Acts xiii. 33. And they occur in some authorities (D a b c &c.) in Luke iii. 22. See also the reading of the Ebionitic Gospel on Matt. iii. 17.

The same Psalm is quoted Acts iv. 25 ff. Comp. Apoc. ii. 27; xii. 5; xiv. 1; xix. 15.

The passage from 2 Sam. vii. 14 is quoted again in 2 Cor. vi. 18 with important variations (ἔσομαι ὑμῖν... ὑμεῖς ἔσεσθέ μοι εἰς υἱοὺς καὶ θυγατέρας), and Apoc. xxi. 7.

Both passages bring out the rela-tion of 'the Son of David' to the ful-filment of the divine purpose. The promise in 2 Sam. vii. 14 is the historical starting point. It was spoken by Nathan to David in answer to the king's expressed purpose to build a Temple for the Lord. This work the prophet said should be not for him but for his seed. The whole passage, with its reference to 'iniquity' and chastening, can only refer to an earthly king; and still experience shewed that no earthly king could satisfy its terms. The kingdom passed away from the line of David. The Temple was destroyed. It was necessary therefore to look for an-other 'seed' (Is. xi. 1 ; Jer. xxiii. 5 ; Zech. vi. 12): another founder of the everlasting Kingdom and of the true Temple (compare Luke i. 32 f.; John ii. 19).

The passage from the Second Psalm represents the divine King under another aspect. He is not the builder of the Temple of the Lord but the representative of the Lord's triumph over banded enemies. The conquest of the nations was not achieved by the successors of David. It remained therefore for Another. The partial external fulfilment of the divine prophecy directed hope to the future. So it was that the idea of the theo-cratic kingdom was itself apprehended as essentially Messianic; and the application of these two representa-tive passages to Christ depends upon the prophetic significance of the critical facts of Jewish history.

The third quotation is beset by difficulty. Doubt has been felt as to the source from which it is derived. Words closely resembling the quotation are found in Ps. xcvii. (xcvi.) 7 προσκυνήσατε αὐτῷ πάντες οἱ ἄγγελοι αὐτοῦ (LXX.). But the exact phrase is found in the Vatican text of an addition made to the Hebrew in Deut. xxxii. 43 by the LXX. version which reads

εὐφράνθητε οὐρανοὶ ἅμα αὐτῷ,

ποτε τῶν ἀγγέλων

Υἱός μογ εἶ cý, ἐγὼ cήμερον γεγέννηκά ce,

5 τῶν ἀγγ. ποτε D₂* syr vg.

καὶ προσκυνησάτωσαν αὐτῷ πάντες υἱοὶ
θεοῦ·
εὐφράνθητε ἔθνη μετὰ τοῦ λαοῦ αὐτοῦ,
καὶ ἐνισχυσάτωσαν αὐτῷ πάντες ἄγγελοι
θεοῦ.
This gloss is quoted also by Justin
M. *Dial.* c. 130. It was probably derived from the Psalm (comp. Is. xliv.
23), and may easily have gained
currency from the liturgical use of
the original hymn. If (as seems
certain) the gloss was found in the
current text of the LXX. in the
apostolic age, it is most natural to
suppose that the writer of the Epistle
took the words directly from the
version of Deuteronomy.

The quotation of words not found
in the Hebrew text is to be explained
by the general character of Deut.
xxxii. which gives a prophetic history
of the Course of Israel, issuing in the
final and decisive revelation of Jehovah
in judgment. When this revelation
is made all powers shall recognise His
dominion, exercised, as the writer of
the Epistle explains, through Christ.
The coming of Christ is thus identified
with the coming of Jehovah. Comp.
Luke i. 76; Acts ii. 20, 21.

In the Targum on Deut. xxxii. 44
which bears the name of Jonathan ben
Uzziel there is the remarkable clause:
'He by His Word (במימריה) shall
atone for His people and for His
land.'

It may be added that the thought
both in Deuteronomy and in the
Psalm is essentially the same. The
Hymn and the Psalm both look forward to the time when the subordinate spiritual powers, idolised by the
nations, shall recognise the absolute
sovereignty of Jehovah.

Part of the same verse (Deut. xxxii.
43) is quoted by St Paul in Rom. xv.
10.

5. *τίνι γὰρ εἶπέν ποτε*] *For to
which...said He at any time?* The
use of the rhetorical question is
characteristic of the style of the
Epistle. Compare *v.* 14; ii. 2 ff.;
iii. 16 ff.; vii. 11; xii. 7.

The subject of the verb is taken
from the context. God is the Speaker
in all revelation (*v.* 1). It has been
objected that the title 'Son' is not
limited to the Messiah in the Old
Testament, but the objection rests
upon a misunderstanding. The title
which is characteristic of Messiah is
never used of Angels or men in the
Old Scriptures. Angels as a body
are sometimes called 'sons of God'
(Ps. xxix. 1, lxxxix. 6) but to no one
(τίνι) is the title 'Son of God' given
individually in all the long line of
revelation. The τίνι and the ποτέ are
both significant.

In like manner the title 'Son' was
given to Israel as the chosen nation:
Hos. xi. 1; Ex. iv. 22; but to no single
Jew, except in the passage quoted,
which in the original refers to Solomon
as the type of Him who should come
after.

Nor is it without the deepest significance that in these fundamental
passages, Ps. ii. 7, 2 Sam. vii. 14, the
speaker is 'the LORD' and not 'GOD.'
The unique title of Christ is thus
connected with God as He is the God
of the Covenant (*Jehovah, the* LORD),
the God of Revelation, and not as He
is the God of Nature (*Elohim,* GOD).

υἱός μου] The order is full of meaning. By the emphasis which is laid
upon υἱός the relation is marked as
peculiar and not shared by others.
My son art thou, and no less than
this; and not *Thou* too, as well as
others, *art my son.* Compare Ps.
lxxxviii. (lxxxix.) 27 πατήρ μου εἶ σύ.
At the same time the σύ is brought

καὶ πάλιν

    Ἐγὼ ἔϲομαι αὐτῷ εἰϲ πατέρα, καὶ αὐτὸϲ ἔϲται μοι εἰϲ γιόν ;
⁶ὅταν δὲ πάλιν εἰσαγάγῃ τὸν πρωτότοκον εἰς τὴν οἰκουμένην, λέγει

om. αὐτῷ אּ*.

into significant connexion with ἐγώ in
the next clause, where the emphasis
is laid on ἐγώ ('I in my sovereign
majesty') and not on σήμερον.

σήμερον] The word both in its
primary and in its secondary meaning
naturally marks some definite crisis,
as the inauguration of the theocratic
king, and that which would correspond
with such an event in the historic
manifestation of the divine King. So
the passage was applied to the Resurrection by St Paul (Acts xiii. 33 ;
comp. Rom. i. 4); and by a very early
and widespread tradition it was connected with the Baptism (Luke iii. 22
Cod. D; Just. M. *Dial.* c. 88, and
Otto's note).

Many however have supposed that
'*today*' in this connexion is the expression for that which is eternal,
timeless.

This view is very well expressed by
Primasius : Notandum quia non dixit :
Ante omnia secula genui te, vel in
præterito tempore; sed, *hodie*, inquit,
genui te, quod adverbium est præsentis temporis. In Deo enim nec
præterita transeunt nec futura succe-
dunt ; sed omnia tempora simul ei
conjuncta sunt, quia omnia præsentia
habet. Et est sensus : Sicut ego
semper æternus sum neque initium
neque finem habeo, ita te semper
habeo coæternum mihi.

Philo recognises the same idea :
σήμερον δέ ἐστιν ὁ ἀπέραντος καὶ ἀδιεξί-
τητος αἰών. μηνῶν γὰρ καὶ ἐνιαυτῶν
καὶ συνόλως χρόνων περίοδοι δόγματα
ἀνθρώπων εἰσὶν ἀριθμὸν ἐκτετιμηκότων·
τὸ δὲ ἀψευδὲς ὄνομα αἰῶνος ἡ σήμερον
(*de Prof.* § 11 ; i. 554 M.); and the idea
was widely current. Comp. Schöttgen,
ad loc. and c. iii. 13 note.

Such an interpretation, however,
though it includes an important truth,
summed up by Origen in the doctrine
of the eternal generation of the Son,
appears to be foreign to the context.

γεγέννηκα] The term marks the
communication of a new and abiding
life, represented in the case of the
earthly king by the royal dignity,
and in the case of Christ by the
divine sovereignty established by the
Resurrection of the Incarnate Son in
which His Ascension was included
(Acts xiii. 33; Rom. i. 4; vi. 4;
Col. i. 8; Apoc. i. 5).

For the use of γεννᾶν compare
1 Cor. iv. 15; and especially St John's
use: 1 John iii. 1 Add. Note.

ἐγὼ ἔσομαι...εἰς] The relation once
established is to be realised in a
continuous fulfilment. The future
points to the coming Messiah from
the position of the O. T. prophet.

The title πατήρ is applied to GOD
here only in the Epistle.

εἶναι εἰς] Comp. c. viii. 10; 2 Cor.
vi. 18. And in a somewhat different
sense, Matt. xix. 5; Acts xiii. 47;
1 Cor. xiv. 22; vi. 16; Eph. i. 12;
Luke iii. 5 &c.

6. ὅταν δέ] This third quotation is
not a mere continuation (καὶ πάλιν)
but a contrast (δέ). It marks the
relation of angels to the Son and not
of the Son to God; and again it points
forward to an end not yet reached.

ὅταν δὲ π. εἰσ.] The πάλιν has been
taken (1) as a particle of connexion
and also (2) as qualifying εἰσαγάγῃ.

In the first case it has received two
interpretations.

(*a*) *again*, as simply giving a new
quotation as in the former clause, ii.
13; iv. 5; x. 30 &c. But it is fatal

to this view, which is given by *Old Lat.* (*deinde iterum cum inducit*) and *Syr.*, that such a transposition of πάλιν is without parallel (yet see Wisdom xiv. 1). The ease with which we can introduce the word 'again' parenthetically hides this difficulty.

(*b*) *on the other hand, in contrast.* In this way πάλιν would serve to emphasise the contrast suggested by δέ. Comp. Luke vi. 43; Matt. iv. 7; 1 John ii. 8.

Such a use is not without parallels, Philo, *Leg. Alleg.* iii. § 9 (i. 93 M.) ὁ δὲ πάλιν ἀποδιδράσκων θεόν...ἡ δὲ πάλιν θεὸν ἀποδοκιμάζουσα..., and the sense is perfectly consistent with the scope of the passage. It would leave the interpretation of 'the bringing in of the Son' undefined.

(2) But it appears to be more natural to connect πάλιν with εἰσαγάγῃ (Vulg. *et cum iterum introducit*) and so to refer the words definitely to the second coming of the Lord. This interpretation is well given by Gregory of Nyssa: ἡ τοῦ 'πάλιν' προσθήκη τὸ μὴ πρώτως γίνεσθαι τοῦτο διὰ τῆς κατὰ τὴν λέξιν ταύτην σημασίας ἐνδείκνυται. ἐπὶ γὰρ τῆς ἐπαναλήψεως τῶν ἅπαξ γεγονότων τῇ λέξει ταύτῃ κεχρήμεθα. οὐκοῦν τὴν ἐπὶ τῷ τέλει τῶν αἰώνων φοβερὰν αὐτοῦ ἐπιφάνειαν σημαίνει τῷ λόγῳ ὅτε οὐκέτι ἐντῇ τοῦ δούλου καθορᾶται μορφῇ, ἀλλ' ἐπὶ τοῦ θρόνου τῆς βασιλείας μεγαλοπρεπῶς προκαθήμενος καὶ ὑπὸ τῶν ἀγγέλων πάντων περὶ αὐτὸν προσκυνούμενος. (*c. Eunom.* iv., Migne, *Patr. Gr.* xlv. p. 634; comp. *c. Eunom.* ii., *id.* p. 504.)

The advantage of taking πάλιν as 'on the other hand' is that the words then bring into one category the many preparatory introductions of the 'firstborn' into the world together with the final one. But one main object of the Epistle is to meet a feeling of present disappointment. The first introduction of the Son into the world, described in *v.* 2, had not issued in an open triumph and satisfied men's desires, so that there was good reason

why the writer should point forward specially to the Return in which Messiah's work was to be consummated. On the whole therefore the connexion of πάλιν with εἰσαγάγῃ seems to be the more likely construction. In any case the ὅταν εἰσαγάγῃ must refer to this.

ὅταν...εἰσαγάγῃ] The Latin rendering *cum introducit* (*inducit*), which has deeply coloured the Western interpretation of the phrase, is wholly untenable. In other places the construction is rightly rendered by the *fut. exact.*, *e.g.* Matt. v. 11 *cum male dixerint ;* xix. 28 *cum sederit* &c., and so in 1 Cor. xv. 26 many authorities read *cum dixerit.*

The construction of ὅταν with *aor. subj.* admits of two senses. It may describe a series of events reaching into an indefinite future, each occurrence being seen in its completeness (Matt. v. 11; x. 19; Mark iv. 15; Luke vi. 22; James i. 2); or it may describe the indefiniteness of a single event in the future seen also in its completeness (John xvi. 4; Acts xxiv. 22; 1 Cor. xv. 28). (The difference between the *pres. subj.* and the *aor. subj.* with ὅταν is well seen in John vii. 27, 31; xvi. 21.)

In other words ὅταν...εἰσαγάγῃ must look forward to an event (or events) in the future regarded as fulfilled at a time (or times) as yet undetermined. It cannot describe an event or a series of events, already completed in the past. We may, that is, when we render the phrase exactly 'whenever he shall have introduced,' contemplate each partial and successive introduction of the Son into the world leading up to and crowned by the one final revelation of His glory, or this final manifestation alone (comp. Col. iii. 4; 2 Thess. i. 10).

If, as seems most likely, the πάλιν is joined with εἰσαγάγῃ, then the second interpretation must be taken.

It follows that all interpretations which refer this second introduction

of the Son into the world to the Incarnation are untenable, as, for example, that of Primasius : Ipsam assumptionem carnis appellat alterum
introitum ; dum enim qui invisibilis
erat humanis aspectibus (John i. 10)
assumpta carne visibilem se probavit
quasi iterum introductus est.
Nor indeed was the Incarnation in
this connexion the first introduction
of Christ into the world. We must
look for that rather in the Resurrection
when for a brief space He was revealed in the fulness of His Manhood
triumphant over death and free from
the limitations of earth, having victoriously fulfilled the destiny of humanity. For the present He has
been withdrawn from ἡ οἰκουμένη, the
limited scene of man's present labours ;
but at the Return He will enter it
once more with sovereign triumph
(Acts i. 11).

τὸν πρωτότοκον] Vulg. primogenitum. The word is used absolutely of
Christ here only (comp. Ps. lxxxix.
(lxxxviii.) 28, LXX.). Its usage in other
passages,
Rom. viii. 29 πρ. ἐν πολλοῖς ἀδελφοῖς,
comp. Col. i. 15 πρ. πάσης κτίσεως,
Apoc. i. 5 ὁ πρ. τῶν νεκρῶν,
Col. i. 18 πρ. ἐκ τῶν νεκρῶν,
brings out the special force of the
term here, as distinguished from υἱός.
It represents the Son in His relation
to the whole family, the whole order,
which is united with Him. His triumph, His new birth (γεγέννηκα), is
theirs also (comp. 1 Pet. i. 3). The
thought lies deep in the foundations
of social life. The privileges and
responsibilities of the firstborn son
were distinctly recognised in the Old
Testament (Deut. xxi. 15 ff. [inheritance]; 2 Chron. xxi. 3 [kingdom]); as
they form a most important element
in the primitive conception of the
family, the true unit of society (Maine,
Ancient Law, 233 ff.). The eldest
son, according to early ideas, was the
representative of his generation, by
whom the property and offices of the

father, after his death, were administered for the good of the family.
The title 'firstborn' (בכור) was applied by Rabbinic writers even to God
(Schöttgen ad loc.) and to Messiah on
the authority of Ps. lxxxix. 27 (Shemoth R. § 19, pp. 150 f. Wünsche).
In Philo the Logos is spoken of as
πρωτόγονος or πρεσβύτατος υἱός, De
confus. ling. § 14 (i. 414 M.) τοῦτον
πρεσβύτατον υἱὸν ὁ τῶν ὄντων ἀνέτειλε
(Zech. vi. 12) πατήρ, ὃν ἑτέρωθι πρωτό
γονον ὠνόμασε..., id. § 28 (i. 427 M.) καὶ
ἂν μηδέπω μέντοι τυγχάνῃ τις ἀξιόχρεως
ὢν υἱὸς θεοῦ προσαγορεύεσθαι, σπουδα
ζέτω κοσμεῖσθαι κατὰ τὸν πρωτόγονον
αὐτοῦ λόγον, τὸν ἄγγελον πρεσβύτατον
ὡς ἀρχάγγελον πολυώνυμον ὑπάρχοντα.
Comp. de agricult. § 12 (i. 308 M.).
The wider sense of the term is
suggested by its application to Israel:
Ex. iv. 22; comp. Jer. xxxi. 9.
The patristic commentators rightly
dwell on the difference between μονο
γενής, which describes the absolutely
unique relation of the Son to the
Father in His divine Nature, and
πρωτότοκος, which describes the relation of the Risen Christ in His
glorified humanity to man : e.g. Theodoret: οὗτω καὶ μονογενής ἐστιν ὡς θεὸς
καὶ πρωτότοκος ὡς ἄνθρωπος ἐν πολλοῖς
ἀδελφοῖς. Compare Bp Lightfoot on
Coloss. i. 15.

εἰς τὴν οἰκουμ.] Vulg. in orbem
terræ. Comp. c. ii. 5 note; Acts xvii.
31.

λέγει] he saith, not he will say.
The words already written find their
accomplishment at that supreme crisis.
The different tenses used of the divine
voice in this chapter are singularly
instructive. The aor. in v. 5 (εἶπεν)
marks a word spoken at a definite
moment. The perf. in v. 13 (εἴρηκεν)
marks a word which having been
spoken of old is now finding fulfilment. Here the pres. regards the
future as already realised.
The contrast of λέγω and εἴρηκα is
seen clearly in John xv. 15 (comp.
xii. 50).

Καὶ προσκγνηcάτωcαν αγτῷ πάντεc ἄγγελοι θεογ.

⁷καὶ πρὸς μὲν τοὺς ἀγγέλους λέγει

καὶ προσκυν.] *And let...*The conjunction suggests others who join in
this adoration, or in some corresponding service of honour.

πάντες ἄγγ.] Biesenthal quotes a
passage from the Jerus. Talmud
(*Avod. Zar.* § 7) in which it is said
that when Messiah comes the demons
who had been worshipped among the
Gentiles shall do him homage, and
idolatry shall cease.

(2) 7—9. *The superior dignity
of the Son as anointed King* ('heir
of all things').

In the quotations already given the
author of the Epistle has shewn that
the language of the Old Testament
pointed to a divine Son, a King of an
everlasting Kingdom, a Conqueror, a
Builder of an abiding Temple, such
as was only figured by the earthly
kings of the chosen people. One truly
man was spoken of in terms applied
to no angel. In Jesus, the Messiah,
the Son of God, such language was
fulfilled.

He now shews the abiding royal
glory of the Son in contrast with the
ministerial and transitory offices of
angels. Angels fulfil their work through
physical forces and 'natural' laws
(*v.* 7): the Son exercises a moral and
eternal sovereignty (*v.* 8); and in
virtue of His own Character He receives the fulness of blessing (*v.* 9).
So He becomes 'heir of all things'.

The lesson is given in two quotations
from the Psalms. The first quotation
from Ps. civ. (ciii.) 4 agrees verbally
with the Alexandrine text of the
LXX. and with the Hebrew, save that
καί is inserted, an insertion which is
not uncommon. The second quotation
from Ps. xlv. (xliv.) 7, 8 differs from the
LXX. by the insertion of καί, by the
transposition of the article (ἡ ῥ. τ. εὐθ.
ῥ. for ῥ. εὐ. ἡ ῥ.), and probably by the
substitution of αὐτοῦ for σου after
βασιλείας, which is also against the

Hebrew. For ἀνομίαν some LXX. texts
give ἀδικίαν.

The use of these two Psalms is of
marked significance. Ps. civ. is a
Psalm of Creation : Ps. xlv. is a Psalm
of the Theocratic Kingdom, the Marriage Song of the King.

Neither Psalm is quoted again in
the N. T. The second passage is
quoted by Justin M. *Dial.* 56, 63,
86.

Both quotations are introduced in
the same manner by a preposition
marking a general reference (πρὸς μέν
...πρὸς δέ...: contrast τίνι εἶπεν *v.* 5).

⁷ *And of the angels He saith,*
   Who maketh His angels winds,
      And His ministers a flame of
fire;
   ⁸ *but of the Son He saith,*
   God is Thy throne for ever and
ever,
      And the sceptre of uprightness
is the sceptre of His kingdom.
[*or Thy throne, O God, is for ever
and ever,*
      And the sceptre of uprightness
is the sceptre of Thy kingdom.]
   ⁹ *Thou lovedst righteousness and
hatedst iniquity;*
   *Therefore God, Thy God, an-
ointed Thee with the oil of gladness
above Thy fellows.*

7. πρὸς μέν...] *of...in reference to...*
Rom. x. 21; Luke xii. 41; xx. 19 (c.
xi. 18). The contrast between 'the
angels' and 'the Son' is accentuated
(μέν--δέ iii. 5 f.). The rendering of
the original text of Ps. civ. 4 has
been disputed, but the construction
adopted by the LXX., the Targum
(comp. *Shemoth R.* § 25, p. 189 Wünsche) and A. V. seems to be certainly
correct. The words admit equally to
be taken 'making winds his messengers (angels)' ('making his messengers out of winds'), and 'making his
messengers (angels) winds'; but the
order of the words and, on a closer

'Ο ποιῶν τοὺς ἀγγέλους αὐτοῦ πνεύματα,
καὶ τοὺς λειτουργοὺς αὐτοῦ πυρὸς φλόγα·
⁸πρὸς δὲ τὸν υἱόν

7 ἀγγέλους + αὐτοῦ· D₂*.   πνεῦμα D₂.

view, the tenor of the Psalm are in favour of the second translation. The thought is that where men at first see only material objects and forms of nature there God is present, fulfilling His will through His servants under the forms of elemental action. So Philo views the world as full of invisible life; *de gig.* § 2 (i. 263 M.). In any case the LXX. rendering is adopted by the writer of the Epistle, and this is quite unambiguous. The Greek words describe the mutability, the materiality, and transitoriness of angelic service (comp. Weber, *Altsynag. Theologie*, § 34), which is placed in contrast with the personal and eternal sovereignty of the Son communicated to Him by the Father.

ὁ ποιῶν] The Greek Fathers lay stress on the word as marking the angels as created beings in contrast with the Son: ἰδοὺ ἡ μεγίστη διαφορά, ὅτι οἱ μὲν κτιστοὶ ὁ δὲ ἄκτιστος (Chrys.).

πνεύματα] *winds*, not *spirits*. The context imperatively requires this rendering. And the word πνεῦμα is appropriate here; for as distinguished from the commoner term ἄνεμος it expresses a special exertion of the elemental force: Gen. viii. 1; Ex. xv. 10; 1 K. xviii. 45; xix. 11; 2 K. iii. 17; Job i. 19; Ps. xi. (x.) 6, &c.

λειτουργούς] The word seems always to retain something of its original force as expressing a public, social service. Comp. Rom. xiii. 6; xv. 16; ch. viii. 2; and even Phil. ii. 25 (*v.* 30). See also 2 Cor. ix. 12.

The reference to the 'winds' and the 'flame of fire' could not fail to suggest to the Hebrew reader the accompaniments of the giving of the Law (c. xii. 18 ff.). That awful scene was a revelation of the ministry of angels.

The variableness of the angelic nature was dwelt upon by Jewish theologians. Angels were supposed to live only as they ministered. In a remarkable passage of *Shemoth R.* (§ 15, p. 107 Wünsche) the angels are represented as 'new every morning.' 'The angels are renewed every morning and after they have praised God they return to the stream of fire out of which they came (Lam. iii. 23).' The same idea is repeated in many places, as, for example, at length in *Bereshith R.* § 78, pp. 378 f. (Wünsche).

8. πρὸς δέ...] *in reference to...* The words in the Psalm are not addressed directly to the Son, though they point to Him.

ὁ θρόνος σου ὁ θεός...διὰ τοῦτο...ὁ θεός, ὁ θεός σου...] It is not necessary to discuss here in detail the construction of the original words of the Psalm. The LXX. admits of two renderings: ὁ θεός can be taken as a vocative in both cases (*Thy throne, O God,... therefore, O God, Thy God...*) or it can be taken as the subject (or the predicate) in the first case (*God is Thy throne*, or *Thy throne is God...*), and in apposition to ὁ θεός σου in the second case (*Therefore God, even Thy God...*). The only important variation noted in the other Greek versions is that of Aquila, who gave the vocative θεέ in the first clause (Hieron. *Ep.* lxv. *ad Princ.* § 13) and, as it appears, also in the second (Field, *Hexapla ad loc.*). It is scarcely possible that אלהים in the original can be addressed to the king. The presumption therefore is against the belief that ὁ θεός is a vocative in the LXX. Thus on the whole it seems best to adopt in the first clause the rendering: *God is Thy throne* (or, *Thy throne is God*), that is 'Thy kingdom is founded upon

'Ο θρόνοc ⌈coγ ὁ θεόc εἰc τὸν αἰῶνα [τοῦ αἰῶνοc],
καὶ ἡ ῥάβδοc τῆc εὐθύτητοc ῥάβδοc τῆc Βαcιλείαc αὐτοῦ⌉.
9ἨΓάπΗcαc Δικαιοcύ́νΗν καὶ ἐμίcΗcαc ἀνομίαν·

8 or σου, ὁ θεός, εἰς...βασιλείας σου.

8 om. τοῦ αἰῶνος B.   καὶ ἡ ῥ. ℵABD₂*M₂ me: om. καὶ ⌐ syrr.   ἡ ῥ. τῆς εὐθ...ῥ.
ℵᵃABM₂: ῥ. εὐθ...ἡ. ῥ. ⌐ D₂.   om. τῆς εὐθ. ῥ. ℵ*.   αὐτοῦ ℵB: σου AD₂ vg syrr.
9 ἀνομίαν BM₂ syr hl: ἀνομίας D₂*: ἀδικίαν ℵA.

God, the immovable Rock'; and to take ὁ θεός as in apposition in the second clause.

The phrase 'God is Thy throne' is not indeed found elsewhere, but it is in no way more strange than Ps. lxxi. 3 [Lord] be Thou to me a rock of habitation...Thou art my rock and my fortress. Is. xxvi. 4 (R.V.) In the LORD JEHOVAH is an everlasting rock. Ps. xc. 1 Lord, Thou hast been our dwelling-place. Ps. xci. 1 He that dwelleth in the secret place of the Most High... v. 2 I will say of the Lord, He is my refuge and my fortress, v. 9; Deut. xxxiii. 27 The eternal God is thy dwelling-place. Comp. Is. xxii. 23.

For the general thought compare Zech. xii. 8. This interpretation is required if we adopt the reading αὐτοῦ for σου.

It is commonly supposed that the force of the quotation lies in the divine title (ὁ θεός) which, as it is held, is applied to the Son. It seems however from the whole form of the argument to lie rather in the description which is given of the Son's office and endowment. The angels are subject to constant change, He has a dominion for ever and ever ; they work through material powers, He—the Incarnate Son—fulfils a moral sovereignty and is crowned with unique joy. Nor could the reader forget the later teaching of the Psalm on the Royal Bride and the Royal Race. In whatever way then ὁ θεός be taken, the quotation establishes the conclusion which the writer wishes to draw as to the essential difference of the Son and the angels. Indeed it might

appear to many that the direct application of the divine Name to the Son would obscure the thought.

εἰς τὸν αἰ. τοῦ αἰ.] The phrase ὁ αἰὼν τοῦ αἰῶνος is unique in the N. T. It is not unfrequent in the LXX. version of the Psalms together with εἰς αἰῶνα αἰῶνος and εἰς τὸν αἰῶνα καὶ εἰς τὸν αἰῶνα τοῦ αἰῶνος for וָעֶד לְעוֹלָם, עוֹלָם וָעֶד, לָעַד.

The phrase ὁ αἰὼν τῶν αἰώνων occurs in Eph. iii. 21, αἰῶνες αἰώνων in Apoc. xiv. 11, and οἱ αἰῶνες τῶν αἰώνων (εἰς τοὺς αἰ. τῶν αἰ.) not unfrequently (c. xiii. 21).

καὶ ἡ ῥάβδος εὐθύτητος] The καί, which is not found in the LXX. or the Hebr., is probably added by the apostle to mark the two thoughts of the divine eternity of Messiah's kingdom and of the essential uprightness with which it is administered.

The word εὐθύτης is found here only in the N.T. It occurs not very unfrequently in the LXX. for derivatives of יָשַׁר, and so Wisd. ix. 3 &c. It is not quoted from Classical writers in a moral sense.

For ῥάβδος compare Apoc. ii. 27, xii. 5, xix. 15. It is used in the LXX. as a rendering of מַטֶּה, שֵׁבֶט, שַׁרְבִּים. In classical Greek it is used rarely and only poetically (Pind. Ol. ix. 51) for the rod of authority. Virga 'justos regit, impios percutit'; sed hæc virga fortitudo est invicta, æquitas rectissima, inflexibilis disciplina (Atto Verc.).

9. ἠγάπησας...] Thou lovedst... The aorist of the LXX. gives a distinct application to the present of the Hebr. The Son in His Work on earth fulfilled the ideal of righteous-

Διὰ τοῦτο ἔχρισέν σε ὁ θεός, ὁ θεός coy, ἔλαιον ἀγαλλιάσεως
παρὰ τοὺς μετόχους coy·

ἔλεον B*: ἔλεος D₂*.

ness; and the writer of the Epistle looks back upon that completed work now seen in its glorious issue.

διὰ τοῦτο...] *For this cause...* *Therefore...* The words express the ground ('because thou lovedst') and not the end ('that thou mightest love'). Comp. ii. 1; ix. 15 (not elsewhere in ep.). For the thought see c. ii. 9; Phil. ii. 9 (διό); John x. 17.

ἔχρισεν] Comp. Luke iv. 18 (Is. lxi. 1); Acts iv. 27; x. 38. This unction has been referred (1) to the communication of royal dignity: 1 Sam. x. 1; xvi. 12 f.; and (2) to the crowning of the sovereign with joy, as at the royal banquet: Is. lxi. 3; comp. Acts ii. 36. The second interpretation is to be preferred. The thought is of the consummation of the royal glory of the Ascended Son of man rather than of the beginning of it. Primasius gives a striking turn to the words: Oleo autem exsultationis seu lætitiæ dicit illum unctum quia Christus nunquam peccavit, nunquam tristitiam habuit ex recordatione peccati. Quid est enim oleo lætitiæ ungi nisi maculam non habere peccati?

ὁ θεός, ὁ θεός σου] There can be no reason for taking the first ὁ θεός as a vocative, contrary to the certain meaning of the original, except that it may correspond with an interpretation of the first clause which has been set aside. The repetition of the divine Name has singular force: 'God, who has made Himself known as thy God by the fulness of blessings which He has given.'

παρὰ τοὺς μετόχους] *above thy fellows*, Vulg. *præ participibus tuis*, above all who share the privilege of ministering to the fulfilment of God's will by His appointment. There is no limitation to any sphere of being or class of ministers; but of men it is specially declared that Christ has

made believers 'a kingdom and priests' (Apoc. i. 6; comp. Matt. xxv. 34). They too have received 'an unction' (1 John ii. 20). Comp. 2 Cor. i. 21; Rom. viii. 17; 2 Tim. ii. 12.

ἔλ. ἀγαλλ.] Comp. xii. 2 χαρά. The same original phrase (שָׂשׂוֹן שֶׁמֶן) occurs again in Is. lxi. 3 (ἄλειμμα εὐφροσύνης) in opposition to 'mourning' (אֵבֶל). It refers not to the solemn anointing to royal dignity but to the festive anointing on occasions of rejoicing.

(3) 10—12. *The superior dignity of the Son as Creator in contrast with creation* ('through whom He made the world').

A new quotation adds a fresh thought. The exalted king, who is truly man, is also above all finite beings.

The words are taken from Ps. cii. (ci.) 26, 27, according to the LXX. text with some variations. The σύ is brought forward for emphasis, and ὡς ἱμάτιον is repeated by the best authorities; the Κύριε is added to the original text by the LXX. from the earlier part of the Psalm; and the present text of the LXX. followed by the Epistle has ἑλίξεις αὐτούς when ἀλλάξεις αὐτούς, a variant found in some copies, would have been the natural rendering in correspondence with ἀλλαγήσονται which follows. The introduction of Κύριε is of importance for the application made of the words. It is of the greater significance because in *v.* 24 אֵל is introduced (though the LXX. renders differently), while in every other case the sacred Name in the Psalm is (יָהּ) יהוה. The insertion of Κύριε therefore emphasises the thought that the majestic picture of divine unchangeableness belongs to God as He has entered into Covenant with man.

¹⁰καί

Σὺ κατ᾽ ἀρχάς, κύριε, τὴν γῆν ἐθεμελίωσας,
καὶ ἔργα τῶν χειρῶν σού εἰσιν οἱ οὐρανοί·
¹¹αὐτοὶ ἀπολοῦνται, σὺ δὲ διαμένεις·
καὶ πάντες ὡς ἱμάτιον παλαιωθήσονται,

The Psalm itself is the appeal of an exile to the LORD, in which out of the depth of distress he confidently looks for the personal intervention of Jehovah for the restoration of Zion. The application to the Incarnate Son of words addressed to Jehovah (see v. 6) rests on the essential conception of the relation of Jehovah to His people. The Covenant leads up to the Incarnation. And historically it was through the identification of the coming of Christ with the coming of 'the LORD' that the Apostles were led to the perception of His true Divinity. Compare Acts ii. 16 ff., 21, 36; iv. 10, 12; ix. 20; c. iii. 7, Addit. Note. It is not however to be supposed that Jehovah was personally identified with Christ. Rather the conception of the God of Israel was enlarged; and the revelation of God as Jehovah, the God of the Covenant, the God Who enters into fellowship with man, was found to receive its consummation in the mission of the Son.

¹⁰And [again of the Son He saith] *Thou, Lord, in the beginning didst lay the foundation of the earth, And the heavens are works of Thy hands.* ¹¹*They shall perish, but Thou continuest; And they all shall wax old as doth a garment;* ¹²*And as a mantle shalt Thou roll them up, As a garment, and they shall be changed: But Thou art the same, and Thy years shall not fail.*

10. καί...] The connexion of this passage with the former is very close although it introduces a new idea.

Comp. Acts i. 20. The conjunction carries with it the λέγει πρὸς τὸν υἱόν of vv. 8, 9. God through His Spirit so speaks in the Psalmist that words not directly addressed to Christ find their fulfilment in Him.

Σὺ...Κύριε...] It has been already noticed that the Σύ is brought forward by the writer of the Epistle, and the Κύριε added to the original text in the LXX. The addition corresponds with the omission of the divine Name (אֵל) in v. 24 owing to a false rendering, but it is significant as definitely connecting the thought of divine immutability with the thought of the divine revelation consummated in the Incarnation.

κατ᾽ ἀρχάς] Vulg. *in principio*, O. L. *initiis*. The phrase is a wrong rendering of לְפָנִים (ἔμπροσθεν Jud. i. 10, 11, 23, &c.). It occurs again Ps. cxix. (cxviii.) 152 as the rendering of קֶדֶם; and is found in Philo and classical writers.

11. αὐτοί] The heavens are taken as representing the whole visible universe.

ἀπολοῦνται] The idea, as it is afterwards developed (xii. 26 ff.), is of change, transfiguration, and not of annihilation: Is. li. 6, 16; lxv. 17; lxvi. 22; 2 Pet. iii. 13; Apoc. xx. 11. Thus Theophylact: μεῖζόν τι τῆς δημιουργίας ᾐνίξατο, τὴν μετασχημάτισιν τοῦ κόσμου, ἀλλαγήσονται γὰρ πάντα ἀπὸ τῆς φθορᾶς εἰς ἀφθαρσίαν.

διαμένεις] Latt. *permanebis* (διαμενεῖς). The present is more expressive. The compound marks continuance throughout some period or crisis suggested by the context: Luke i.

¹²καὶ ὡϲεὶ περιβόλαιον ἑλίξειϲ αϒτοϒϲ,
ὡς ἱμάτιον καὶ ἀλλαγήϲονται·
cϒ Δὲ ὁ αϒτὸϲ εἶ, καὶ τὰ ἔτη coϒ οϒκ ἐκλείψοϒϲιν.
¹³πρὸς τίνα δὲ τῶν ἀγγέλων εἴρηκέν ποτε
Κάθοϒ ἐκ Δεἔιῶν μοϒ
ἕωc ἂν θῶ τοϒϲ ἐχθροϒϲ coϒ ϒποπόΔιον τῶν ποΔῶν coϒ;

12 ὡς D₂*.   ἑλίξεις ABM₂ (latt) syrr me: εἰλίξεις א°: ἀλλάξεις א*D₂ (vg).   αὐ. ὡς
ἱμάτιον אABD₂*: om. ὡς ἱμ. ς vg syrr me.

22; xxii. 28; 2 Pet. iii. 4; Gal. ii. 5.
πάντες] The thought appears to be
of sphere succeeding sphere in increasing purity and therefore in increasing permanence: but all alike
are subject to time and to decay.
παλαιωθήσονται] c. viii. 13; Luke
xii. 33; Is. l. 9; li. 6; Ecclus. xiv. 17.
12. περιβόλαιον] a mantle. The
word suggests a costly robe: Jud.
viii. 26 (A) τῶν περιβολαίων τῶν πορ-
φυρῶν τῶν ἐπὶ τοῖς βασιλεῦσι Μαδιάμ.
Ezech. xxvii. 7. Comp. 1 Cor. xi. 15.
ἑλίξεις] The substitution of this
word for the natural rendering ἀλλάξεις
may have been due to a reference to
Is. xxxiv. 4 ἑλιγήσεται ὁ οὐρανὸς ὡς
βιβλίον. In the original the verb is
repeated (תַּחֲלִיפֵם וְיַחֲלֹפוּ).
ὁ αὐτός] The original is simply
'Thou art He.' Comp. Is. xli. 4; xliii.
10; xlvi. 4; xlviii. 12; Deut. xxxii. 39
(ἐγώ εἰμι).
See ch. xiii. 8 note.
(4) 13, 14. The superior dignity of
the Son as seated in Royal Majesty
assured of triumph ('having made
purification...He sat down...').
The comparison of the Son with
angels is completed by the development of the idea contained in the
fact of the Session of the Son at the
right hand of the Father. This idea
is conveyed by the opening words of
Ps. cx. and is spread throughout the
New Testament: Matt. xxii. 23 ff. and
parallels; Acts ii. 34 f. See also c. x.
13; 1 Cor. xv. 25; 1 Pet. iii. 22. The

Psalm (cx.) is quoted again cc. v. 6;
vii. 17, 21.
¹³But of which of the angels hath
He said at any time
Sit on My right hand,
Until I make Thine enemies
the footstool of Thy feet?
¹⁴Are they not all ministering
spirits sent forth unto service for
the sake of them that shall inherit
salvation?
13. πρὸς τίνα δέ...] But of which...
The writer appears to turn aside from
the contemplation of the unchangeableness of God seen in the Person of
Christ to the thought of the conflict
between good and evil wrought out in
time. Here also the supreme eminence
of the Son is conspicuous. The
language used of Him has been used
of no angel. He serenely waits for a
sure and absolute victory while they
are busied with ministerial offices.
For πρός see v. 7 note. The contrast
between τίνι εἶπέν ποτε (v. 5) and
πρὸς τίνα εἴρηκέν ποτε is full of meaning.
εἴρηκεν] See c. iv. 3; x. 9 notes.
κάθου...] The verb marks the continuance of the Session as distinguished from the assumption of the
place (v. 3 ἐκάθισεν). Comp. Luke
xxii. 69. For the image see Zech. vi.
13; Schöttgen on Matt. xxii. 44.
ἐκ δεξιῶν] This phrase, which is
with one exception (Mk. xvi. 5 ἐν
τοῖς δεξ.) the uniform phrase in the
Synoptists, is used twice only in this
Epistle. Elsewhere v. 3; viii. 1 (note);

¹⁴ οὐχὶ πάντες εἰσὶν λειτουργικὰ πνεύματα εἰς διακονίαν
ἀποστελλόμενα διὰ τοὺς μέλλοντας κληρονομεῖν σωτηρίαν;

14 διακονίας B.

x. 12; xii. 2 ἐν δεξιᾷ is written by the
author himself.

ἕως ἂν θῶ] Compare 1 Cor. xv. 28.
Our powers are inadequate to realise
that end.

ὑποπόδιον τῶν π.] Compare Josh.
x. 24 f.

14. οὐχί] c. iii. 17. For the interrogative form see v. 5 note.

πάντες] Whatever differences of
rank and dignity there may be among
them, all are alike in this.

λειτουργικὰ πν.] Vulg. administra-
torii spiritus, מַלְאָכֵי הַשָּׁרֵת (Ber. R.
8). The word occurs here only in
N.T. Comp. Philo, de carit. § 3 (ii.
387 M.) ἄγγελοι λειτουργοί. de gig. § 3
(i. 264 M.).

εἰς διακ. ἀποστ.] sent forth for
ministry as each occasion arises (Old
Lat. qui mittuntur. Vulg. missi).
Contrast 1 Pet. i. 12 (ἀποσταλέντι).
The difference between the general
office of the angels as spirits charged
with a social ministry (v. 7 λειτουργούς),
and the particular services (c. vi. 10
διακονοῦντες) in which it is fulfilled, is
clearly marked.

Herveius (and so Primasius) shews
how the angels, even on their missions,
remain in the presence of God:

Mittuntur igitur et assistunt, quia

etsi circumscriptus sit angelicus
spiritus, summus tamen spiritus ipse
qui Deus est circumscriptus non est.
Angeli itaque et missi ante ipsum
sunt quia quolibet missi veniant intra
ipsum currunt.

διὰ τοὺς μ. κλ. σ.] The service is
rendered to God for the sake of
believers. The use of διά (accus.) instead of ὑπέρ indicates a wider relation. Compare c. vi. 7 and contrast
vi. 20. The difference of idea is seen
in Col. iv. 3 compared with Eph. vi. 20.

κλῆρον. σωτηρ.] Compare c. vi. 12
(Additional Note); xii. 17; (1 Pet. iii.
9). See also Matt. xix. 29 (eternal
life); Luke x. 25; xviii. 18; Matt. xxv.
34; 1 Cor. vi. 9 f.; Gal. v. 21 (the
kingdom); 1 Cor. xv. 50 (incorruption).
'Salvation,' like 'eternal life,' is at
once present and future: c. v. 9; ix.
28.

σωτηρίαν] Salvation is contemplated in its essential character, and
not in the concrete form of the
expected and promised Salvation (ἡ
σωτηρία Acts iv. 12; John iv. 22).

Primasius refers the words to the
belief ('as the doctors say') that to
each of the faithful a guardian angel
is assigned 'from his birth or rather
from his baptism.'

Additional Note on i. 3. *The teaching upon Sin in the Epistle.*

There is no direct statement in the Epistle as to the origin of sin or the Univer-
universal sinfulness of men. It is however implied that all men are sality of
sinners. This thought lies in the description of the characteristics of the sin.
High-priest who is fitted to satisfy our needs (ἡμῖν ἔπρεπεν). He is
'separated from sinners' (vii. 26 κεχωρισμένος τῶν ἁμαρτωλῶν), where the
definite phrase οἱ ἁμαρτωλοί appears to describe a body commensurate with
humanity. The same idea is expressed still more forcibly in iv. 15, if the
interpretation given in the note upon the passage is correct. For while the
fact of sin is for us a fruitful source of temptation it is laid down that, when
Christ was in all other points tempted as we are, this one feature must
necessarily be excepted (πεπειρασμένον κατὰ πάντα καθ᾽ ὁμοιότητα χωρὶς
ἁμαρτίας). The common interpretation also suggests, though less distinctly,
the uniqueness of Christ's sinlessness.

Sin then is treated as universal, and men are held justly responsible for Responsi-
its consequences. They are conscious of sins (x. 2 συνείδησιν ἔχειν ἁμαρτιῶν), bility of
as hindering them from attaining their true destiny. In themselves they are, man.
so to speak, 'clothed in weakness' (v. 2 περίκειται ἀσθένειαν: comp. vii. 28
ἔχοντας ἀσθένειαν) which is shewn in many forms (iv. 15 ταῖς ἀσθενείαις).
They 'go astray and are ignorant' (v. 2). Their works as they stand alone
are 'dead works' (vi. 1 ; ix. 14 νεκρὰ ἔργα).

Meanwhile 'through fear of death'—which is assumed to be the end of
sin—'they are all their lifetime subject to bondage' (ii. 15). And probably
the reference to 'the devil,' 'who hath the power of death' (ii. 14 τὸν τὸ
κράτος ἔχοντα τοῦ θανάτου), points to the primal temptation and fall of man.

The writer of the Epistle, as the other apostolic writers, distinguishes
clearly between 'sin,' the principle, and 'sins,' the specific acts in which the
principle is embodied and manifested. The passages which deal with these
two conceptions must be noticed separately (comp. ix. 26 note).

1. Sin (ἡ ἁμαρτία, ἁμαρτία).   1. Sin.

The ritual of the O.T. recognised 'sin' no less than 'sins.' There were
sacrifices 'for (in the matter of) sin' (x. 6, 8 ; xiii. 11 περὶ ἁμαρτίας). The
burden of 'sins and iniquities' made such a general sacrifice necessary. But
'where remission of these is, there is no more offering for sin' (x. 18 οὐκέτι
προσφορὰ περὶ ἁμαρτίας). The power of sin lies in its transitory pleasures.
Sin offers enjoyment though it is but 'for a season' (xi. 25 πρόσκαιρον ἔχειν
ἁμαρτίας ἀπόλαυσιν). Even Christians are exposed to the peril of fatal
insensibility from its insidious assaults (iii. 13 ἵνα μὴ σκληρυνθῇ τις ἐξ ὑμῶν
ἀπάτῃ τῆς ἁμαρτίας). As in old time, unbelief still leads to disobedience to
God, and disobedience is sin (iii. 15—19). So it is that under different
figures sin is an encumbrance which tends to check the freedom of our
movements, and an adversary whom we find in our path. We must 'lay it
aside' that we may run our race (xii. 1 ἀποθέμενοι...τὴν εὐπερίστατον
ἁμαρτίαν) ; and we must 'strive against it' even unto blood (xii. 4 πρὸς τὴν
ἁμαρτίαν ἀνταγωνιζόμενοι). Such an effort, such a conflict, is possible, for

Christ 'hath been manifested to disannul sin through the sacrifice of
Himself' (ix. 26 εἰς ἀθέτησιν ἁμαρτίας). He has shewn it to us prostrate and
powerless through His work, and we can use the fruits of His victory.

2. Sins.   2. Sins (αἱ ἁμαρτίαι, ἁμαρτίαι).
'Sin' issues in a variety of 'sins.' The High-priesthood was instituted
to deal with these, 'to offer gifts and sacrifices for (in behalf of) sins' (v. 1
ὑπὲρ ἁμαρτιῶν: comp. vii. 27), or, as it is expressed more generally, 'to offer
for (in the matter of) sins' (v. 3 περὶ ἁμαρτιῶν). But the conscience of man
witnessed (x. 2) that such sacrifices as the Levitical Law prescribed were
powerless to 'take away' sins, when the sinner from time to time
acknowledged his guilt (x. 4 ἀφαιρεῖν ἁμαρτίας), or once for all to strip from
him the bands which they had formed (x. 11 περιελεῖν ἁμαρτίας). They
served indeed only to call to mind that which they could not remove (x. 3
ἀνάμνησις ἁμαρτιῶν). But a divine promise held out the hope of a new
Covenant when sins should be no more remembered (viii. 12; x. 17 τῶν
ἁμαρτιῶν οὐ μὴ μνησθῶ ἔτι); and this hope was fulfilled through the work of
Christ. He 'offered one sacrifice for (in behalf of) sins for ever' (x. 12 μίαν
ὑπὲρ ἁμαρτιῶν προσενέγκας θυσίαν εἰς τὸ διηνεκές). By this He 'Himself made
purification of sins' (i. 3 καθαρισμὸν τῶν ἁμαρτιῶν ποιησάμενος), and in virtue
of this He is able, having entered into the heavenly sanctuary, 'to make
propitiation for the sins of the people' (ii. 17 ἱλάσκεσθαι τὰς ἁμαρτίας τοῦ
λαοῦ). But for those who 'sin wilfully after that they have received the
knowledge (τὴν ἐπίγνωσιν) of the truth' 'there is no longer left a sacrifice
for (in the matter of) sins' (x. 26 οὐκέτι περὶ ἁμαρτιῶν ἀπολείπεται θυσία);
and there are cases when it is impossible for the Christian teacher 'to
renew to repentance' (vi. 6) such as have fallen away.

Thus Christ's work is now available for believers to overcome sin and
do away sins; but one crowning scene still remains to be realised. 'Christ
having been once offered (προσενεχθείς)'—the passive form seems to
express His willing submission to a divine law—'to bear (ἀνενεγκεῖν)
the sins of many'—to carry them up to the altar of the Cross (1 Pet.
ii. 24)—'shall appear a second time without sin (χωρὶς ἁμαρτίας)'—untouched and untroubled by the sin which He has overcome—'to them
that wait for Him unto salvation' (ix. 28).

Περί and   It will be observed that in all the passages quoted the prepositions περί
ὑπέρ.   and ὑπέρ retain their distinctive force: περί marks the object of the action,
'in the matter of,' while ὑπέρ adds the thought of the beneficial effect designed
in the action, 'in behalf of.' Compare for the use of περί Rom. viii. 3 (περὶ
ἁμαρτίας); 1 Pet. iii. 18 (π. ἁμαρτιῶν); 1 John ii. 2; iv. 10 (περὶ τῶν ἁμ.
ἡμῶν); and in a different connexion John viii. 46; xvi. 8 f.; xv. 22; and for
the use of ὑπέρ 1 Cor. xv. 3 (ὑπὲρ τῶν ἁμ. ἡμῶν); Gal. i. 4 (all. περί).

Words for   The vocabulary connected with sin is not large. Παράπτωμα and ἁμάρ-
sin.   τημα are not found (yet see παραπεσεῖν vi. 6). Ἀνομία (i. 9; x. 17) and
ἀδικία (viii. 12) occur only in quotations from the LXX. Παράβασις occurs
ii. 2; ix. 15; and παρακοή ii. 2. The word ἀγνόημα (ix. 7; comp. v. 2) is
unique in the N.T.

Additional Note on i. 4.   *The Divine Names in the Epistle.*

The Names by which the Lord is spoken of in the Epistle throw light
upon its characteristic teaching.   Speaking generally we may say that
Jesus directs our thoughts to His human Nature, *Christ* to His Work as
the Fulfiller of the old Dispensation, *Son* to His divine Nature, *Lord* itself
to His sovereignty over the Church.

The
Names
of the
Lord.

1.   Of these Names that which is distinctive of the Epistle is the human
Name, *Jesus*.   This occurs nine times, and in every case it furnishes the
key to the argument of the passage where it is found:

1.   *Jesus.*

ii. 9 τὸν βραχύ τι παρ᾽ ἀγγέλους ἠλαττωμένον βλέπομεν Ἰησοῦν...Although
humanity has not yet attained its end we see that the Son of Man—true
man—has fulfilled through suffering the destiny of the race.

iii. 1 κατανοήσατε τὸν ἀπόστολον καὶ ἀρχιερέα τῆς ὁμολογίας ἡμῶν Ἰησοῦν
(*text. rec.* Χριστὸν Ἰησοῦν).   In His manhood, our Lawgiver and Priest is
seen to rise immeasurably above Moses and Aaron, who occupied severally
the same offices under the Old Covenant.

vi. 20 ὅπου πρόδρομος ὑπὲρ ἡμῶν εἰσῆλθεν Ἰησοῦς...Our High-priest, even
when He enters into the immediate presence of God, to take His seat at
God's right hand, preserves no less a true humanity than the Jewish High-
priest who entered into the typical sanctuary.

vii. 22 κρείττονος διαθήκης γέγονεν ἔγγυος Ἰησοῦς.   The eternal priesthood,
answering to the better Covenant, is still the priesthood of One who is true
man.

x. 19 ἔχοντες παρρησίαν εἰς τὴν εἴσοδον τῶν ἁγίων ἐν τῷ αἵματι Ἰησοῦ.   The
virtue of the offered life of Him Who shares our nature is that wherein we
can draw near to God.   Contrast ix. 14.

xii. 2 ἀφορῶντες εἰς τὸν τῆς πίστεως ἀρχηγὸν καὶ τελειωτὴν Ἰησοῦν.   Our
strength in Christian effort is to fix our eyes upon Him Who in His
Manhood won for us the perfect victory of faith.

xii. 24 (προσεληλύθατε) διαθήκης νέας μεσίτῃ Ἰησοῦ.   Comp. vii. 22.

xiii. 12 Ἰησοῦς...ἔξω τῆς πύλης ἔπαθεν.

xiii. 20 ὁ ἀναγαγὼν ἐκ νεκρῶν...ἐν αἵματι διαθήκης αἰωνίου τὸν κύριον ἡμῶν
Ἰησοῦν.   This single reference in the Epistle to the Resurrection, combined
with the declaration of the twofold office of Christ as Shepherd and Lord,
is pointed by the use of His human Name.

It will be noticed that in every case but xiii. 12, which is a simple
historic statement, the name 'Jesus' occupies an emphatic position at the
end of the clause.

2.   The Name of *Christ* (*the Christ*) occurs just as many times as *Jesus*.
It is desirable to notice separately the two forms in which it is used.   The
definite form 'the Christ' (ὁ χριστός) appears always to retain more or less
distinctly the idea of the office as the crown of the old Covenant: the
anarthrous form 'Christ' (Χριστός) is rather a proper name.

2.   *Christ,*
the Christ.

The
Christ.

iii. 14 μέτοχοι τοῦ χριστοῦ γεγόναμεν...we have become partakers in Him Who has fulfilled the hope of the fathers.

v. 5 ὁ χριστὸς οὐχ ἑαυτὸν ἐδόξασεν γενηθῆναι ἀρχιερέα though the High-priesthood might have seemed to be necessarily included in the office to which He was sent.

vi. 1 τὸν τῆς ἀρχῆς τοῦ χριστοῦ λόγον, the elementary exposition of the Gospel as the true accomplishment of all that was promised to Israel.

ix. 14 τὸ αἷμα τοῦ χριστοῦ, the blood of Him to Whom every sacrificial ordinance of the Levitical ritual pointed. Contrast x. 19.

ix. 28 ὁ χριστὸς ἅπαξ προσενεχθείς...ὀφθήσεται. That which seemed to be disappointment in the Death of Him to Whom the people had looked shall hereafter be turned to glory.

xi. 26 τὸν ὀνειδισμὸν τοῦ χριστοῦ. Each hero of faith realised a little of that which is the part of the Messenger of God.

Christ.

The anarthrous form is less frequent:

iii. 6 (Μωυσῆς μέν)...Χριστὸς δὲ ὡς υἱός...

ix. 11 Χριστὸς δὲ παραγενόμενος ἀρχιερεύς...

ix. 24 οὐ γὰρ εἰς χειροποίητα εἰσῆλθεν ἅγια Χριστός (text. rec. ὁ χριστός).

The force of this Name will be felt if the student substitutes for it the human Name. Throughout c. ix. the thought is of the typical teaching of the Law.

3. Son, the Son.

3. The title Son is with one exception (i. 8) always anarthrous. The writer, that is, fixes the attention of his readers upon the nature implied by it:

i. 2 ἐλάλησεν ἐν υἱῷ as contrasted with ἐν τοῖς προφήταις.

i. 5 υἱός μου εἶ σύ (LXX.). So v. 5.

iii. 6 Χριστὸς δὲ ὡς υἱός as contrasted with Μωυσῆς...ὡς θεράπων.

v. 8 καίπερ ὢν υἱός, and therefore having personally right of access to the Father.

vii. 28 υἱόν, εἰς τὸν αἰῶνα τετελειωμένον as contrasted with ἀνθρώπους... ἔχοντας ἀσθένειαν.

4. The Lord.

4. The title Lord is comparatively rare.

ii. 3 (σωτηρία) ἀρχὴν λαβοῦσα λαλεῖσθαι διὰ τοῦ κυρίου.

vii. 14 ἐξ Ἰούδα ἀνατέταλκεν ὁ κύριος ἡμῶν. The title here is perhaps suggested by the royal tribe.

Compare also i. 10; xii. 14; xiii. 20.

5. Jesus Christ.

5. Of compound Names that which is elsewhere most common (more than thirty times in the Epistle to the Romans, eleven times in 1 Peter), Jesus Christ, is comparatively very rare:

x. 10 διὰ τῆς προσφορᾶς τοῦ σώματος Ἰησοῦ Χριστοῦ.

xiii. 8 Ἰησοῦς Χριστὸς ἐχθὲς καὶ σήμερον ὁ αὐτός...

xiii. 21 διὰ Ἰησοῦ Χριστοῦ, ᾧ ἡ δόξα εἰς τοὺς αἰῶνας τῶν αἰώνων.

The force of the full Name, which is an implicit Creed, will be obvious in each place.

The characteristic Pauline Name Christ Jesus does not occur in the Epistle (not iii. 1).

6. The Son of God.

6. The title the Son of God speaks for itself in the places where it is used:

vi. 6 ἀνασταυροῦντας ἑαυτοῖς τὸν υἱὸν τοῦ θεοῦ.

vii. 3 ἀφωμοιωμένος τῷ υἱῷ τοῦ θεοῦ, not υἱῷ θεοῦ. The Incarnate Son was the archetype of Melchizedek.

x. 29 πόσῳ χείρονος ἀξιωθήσεται τιμωρίας ὁ τὸν υἱὸν τοῦ θεοῦ καταπατήσας.

7. The complete affirmation of the divine and human natures of our High-priest is found in the phrase which occurs once, *Jesus, the Son of God:*

7. Jesus, the Son of the Son of God.

iv. 14 ἔχοντες ἀρχιερέα...Ἰησοῦν τὸν υἱὸν τοῦ θεοῦ.

Compare also the descriptive titles : ii. 10; iii. 1; xii. 2 ; xiii. 20.

It may be noticed that the title σωτήρ does not occur in the Epistle, though σωτηρία is not uncommon. The idea which it expresses finds a special embodiment in Christ's priestly office.

Sometimes the Lord, though unnamed, is assumed as the subject of the teaching of the prophets: ii. 14; x. 5 ff.; 37.

II.   ¹ Διὰ τοῦτο δεῖ περισσοτέρως προσέχειν ἡμᾶς τοῖς ἀκουσθεῖσιν, μή ποτε παραρυῶμεν.   ² εἰ γὰρ ὁ δι᾽

1 περισσ. δεῖ ℵ vg.   M₂ om. v. 1.

ii. *The peril of neglecting the new revelation through the Son* (ii. 1—4).

After establishing the superior dignity of the Son in comparison with that of angels, the writer of the Epistle pauses for a moment to enforce the practical consequences which follow from the truth before he sets forth the work of the Son for humanity. It is obvious that a revelation given through such a Mediator carries with it more solemn obligations on those who receive it and heavier penalties for neglect than a revelation made through angelic ministry.

Similar hortatory passages are introduced in the argument iii. 7—19, v. 11 ff.

Contrast Gal. i. 6—9.

The line of thought is direct and simple. There is always in men a tendency to forgetfulness of a past message under the influence of new forces. The authority of the message is a measure of the danger of such neglect (1, 2); and the Gospel comes to us with the highest possible attestation in regard to its Author and its messengers (3), and the manifold witness of God by which it was confirmed (4).

¹ *Therefore we must give the more earnest heed to the things that were heard lest haply we drift away from them.* ² *For if the word spoken through angels proved stedfast, and every transgression and disobedience received a just requital;* ³ *how shall we escape if we neglect so great salvation? which, having at the first been spoken through the Lord, was confirmed unto us by them that heard;* ⁴ *God bearing witness to it with them by signs and wonders, and by manifold powers, and by various gifts of the Holy Spirit according to His will.*

προσέχειν ἡμᾶς ℵABD₂ vg : ἡμ. προσ. ϛ.

1. διὰ τοῦτο] *For this cause...There-fore...*, because of the superiority of the Son over the angels, through whom the Law was given.

δεῖ] The word marks a logical necessity and not a moral obligation: *we must* rather than *we ought.* Compare xi. 6, ix. 26, and contrast ὀφείλειν v. 17, v. 3, 12. See 1 John ii. 6 note.

περισσ. προσ.] Vulg. *abundantius observare.* The adverb expresses, so to speak, an absolute excess (xiii. 19, c. vi. 17, vii. 15), and not simply a relative excess (μᾶλλον ix. 14, x. 25, xii. 9, 25). The connexion of περισσοτέρως with δεῖ is unnatural. The force of the comparative is 'more exceedingly than if there had been no such marked preeminence of the Son.' The form in -ως is not found in the LXX. or Philo.

προσέχειν] The full phrase προσ. τ. νοῦν does not occur in the N.T. (but see Job vii. 17 LXX.). The word is used of things Acts viii. 6; xvi. 14; 1 Tim. i. 4; Tit. i. 14; 2 Pet. i. 19; and of persons Acts viii. 10 f. ; 1 Tim. iv. 1. The absolute use occurs as early as Demosthenes. Compare vii. 13 n.

ἡμᾶς] *we* Christians. The obligation is a special one.

τοῖς ἀκουσθ.] *to the things that were heard*, to the message received by the apostles (οἱ ἀκούσαντες) when 'God spake in His Son' ; or, more simply, *to the things we heard* (as κατηχούμενοι) when first the Gospel was preached to us (ὁ λόγος τῆς ἀκοῆς c. iv. 2 ; 1 Thess. ii. 13. Comp. Rom. x. 17).

It is to be noticed that the writer of the Epistle does not use εὐαγγέλιον (the verb occurs iv. 2, 6). In the writings of St John it is found only in Apoc. xiv. 6.

μή ποτε] *lest haply*, Vulg. *ne forte*

ἀγγέλων λαληθεὶς λόγος ἐγένετο βέβαιος, καὶ πᾶσα

(O. L. *ne casu*) and not *lest ever.* Compare iv. 1.

παραρνῶμεν] The word παραρρεῖν is of considerable interest. It is constantly used of things which slip away, as a ring from the finger (Plut. *Amat.* p. 754 A), or take a wrong course, as a crumb of food passing into the windpipe (Arist. *de part. an.* iii. 3), or an inopportune subject intruding upon a company (Ælian, *V. H.* iii. 30). It occurs twice in the Greek translations of the Book of Proverbs. It is found in the sense of 'slipping away' in Symmachus' rendering of Prov. iv. 21 μὴ παραρρυησάτωσαν ἐξ ὀφθαλμῶν σου for the Hebr. אַל־יַלִּיזוּ מֵעֵינֶיךָ : Vulg. *ne recedant ab oculis tuis :* E. V. *Let them not depart from thine eyes.* And again it occurs of the person in Prov. iii. 21 (LXX.) υἱὲ μὴ παραρυῇς, τήρησον δὲ ἐμὴν βουλὴν καὶ ἔννοιαν, for the similar Hebrew בְּנִי אַל־יָלֻזוּ מֵעֵינֶיךָ : Vulg. *Fili mi, ne effluant hæc ab oculis tuis :* E. V. *Let them not depart from thine eyes.*

This latter usage is identical with the usage in the present passage: 'Do not be carried away from my teaching.'

The idea is not that of simple forgetfulness, but of being swept along past the sure anchorage which is within reach. (Compare Hesychius: παραρυῇς, μετεωρισθῇς, παραπέσῃς.) The image is singularly expressive. We are all continuously exposed to the action of currents of opinion, habit, action, which tend to carry us away insensibly from the position which we ought to maintain. The versions are very vague. The Syriac gives *fall* ܢܦܠ as in iv. 11 (μή τις πέσῃ). There are many Latin renderings: Vulg. *pereffluamus,* O. L. *labamur* (lebemur) or *labemus;* and in patristic quotations: *supereffluamus* (Hier.), *defluamus* (Aug.), *effluamus*

(Sedul.). Primasius was evidently perplexed by the phrase: *ne forte pereffluamus;* id est, ne forte pereamus et a salute excidamus; vel ne forte evanescamus, transeuntes in perditionem more fluminis currentis in mare...

The Greek Christian writers use the word in the same sense as it has here, and perhaps they derived the usage from the Epistle: e.g. Clem. Alex. *Pæd.* iii. § 58 p. 288 P. διὸ καὶ συστέλλειν χρὴ τὰς γυναῖκας κοσμίως καὶ περισφίγγειν αἰδοῖ σώφρονι, μὴ παραρρυῶσι τῆς ἀληθείας διὰ χαυνότητα. Orig. *c. Cels.* viii. 23 'The great mass of simple believers, who cannot keep every day as a divine festival, need sensible patterns in fixed holy days that they may not wholly drift away (ἵνα μὴ τέλεον παραρρυῇ) under popular influences from the observance of regular religious duties.'

2, 3 a. εἰ γάρ...] The necessity of heedful care is grounded on the certainty of retribution. This certainty is proportional to the authority of the revelation. Comp. 1 Clem. xli. 4 ὅσῳ πλείονος κατηξιώθημεν γνώσεως τοσούτῳ μᾶλλον ὑποκείμεθα κινδύνῳ.

ὁ δι' ἀγγ. λαλ. λόγος] the word—the revelation—*spoken through angels,* as the organs of the Divine communication, that is the Law. Vulg. *qui per angelos dictus est sermo.* The title λόγος (not νόμος) is given to the Law in order to characterise it as the central part of the Old Revelation round which all later words were gathered. So throughout the Epistle the Law is regarded as a gracious manifestation of the divine will, and not as a code of stern discipline. The connexion of the angels with the giving of the Law is recognised elsewhere in the N. T., Gal. iii. 19 διαταγεὶς δι' ἀγγέλων ; Acts vii. 53 (comp. *r.* 38) εἰς διαταγὰς ἀγγέλων. So also Josephus represents Herod as saying that the Jews 'learnt τὰ ὁσιώτατα τῶν ἐν τοῖς νόμοις δι' ἀγγέλων παρὰ τοῦ θεοῦ' (*Antt.*

παράβασις καὶ παρακοὴ ἔλαβεν ἔνδικον μισθαποδοσίαν,
³πῶς ἡμεῖς ἐκφευξόμεθα τηλικαύτης ἀμελήσαντες σωτη-

xv. 5, 3). By a natural process of interpretation the attendance of the angels at the revelation on Sinai (Deut. xxxiii. 2; Ps. lxviii. 17) was taken to indicate their ministration. The presence of angels is not noticed in Ex. xix., and Philo seems purposely to avoid referring the phenomena at the Lawgiving to their action (*de Decal.* § 9 (ii. 185 M.) κελεύσας...δημιουργηθῆναι...ψυχὴν λογικήν...).

ἐγέν. βέβαιος] *proved sure*, not only *was assured, confirmed* (ἐβεβαιώθη *v.* 3) by some external authority; but, as it were, vindicated its own claims. There is in the divine Law a self-executing power. It confirms itself. Compare the significant variation in the construction in Rom. ii. 6 ff. ἀποδώσει...τοῖς καθ᾽ ὑπομονὴν ἔργου ἀγαθοῦ δόξαν...τοῖς δὲ ἐξ ἐριθίας...ὀργὴ καὶ θυμός...together with Origen's note *in Rom.* Lib. ii. § 6.

The verb always retains its force in these periphrastic forms c. iii. 14; v. 5, 12; vi. 4; vii. 12, 18, 20, 23; x. 33; xi. 6 f.; xii. 8; 1 Cor. iii. 13; xi. 19.

παράβ. καὶ παρακ.] Vulg. *prævaricatio et inobedientia.* Παράβασις describes the actual transgression, a positive offence (the overt act); παρακοή describes properly the disobedience which fails to fulfil an injunction, and so includes negative offences (the spirit). Comp. 2 Cor. x. 6; Rom. v. 19 (Matt. xviii. 17 παρακούειν). The word παρακοή is not found in the LXX. (παρακούειν Esth. iii. 3, 8 [iv. 13]; Is. lxv. 12). *Prævaricatio* est vetita facere, *inobedientia* vero jussa non facere (Herv.).

In Rom. v. the sin of Adam is described successively as παράβασις *v.* 14 (the simple fact); παράπτωμα *v.* 17, 18 (contrasted with the δικαίωμα of Christ: the fact in its relation to the divine order); παρακοή *v.* 19 (con-

trasted with the ὑπακοή of Christ: the manifestation of the spiritual character).

παράβ....ἔλαβεν] The punishment meets the transgression, not the transgressor. There is an absolute correspondence. Compare Col. iii. 25 (Eph. vi. 8).

ἔνδικον] The word occurs again in Rom. iii. 8 : it is not found in the LXX. As distinguished from δίκαιος it describes that which conforms to, and not that which embodies, a rule. The word δίκαιος is used almost exclusively of persons as possessing the positive quality of righteousness. It is used also of judgment as being not only *right*, but *righteous :* John v. 30; vii. 24; Apoc. xvi. 7; xix. 2; 2 Thess. ii. 1. Comp. Luke xii. 57; and of the 'commandment' (Rom. vii. 12) and the 'ways' of God (Apoc. xv. 3).

μισθαποδοσίαν] Vulg. *mercedis retributionem,* O. L. *remunerationem,* and so Vulg. elsewhere. The word is found again in the Greek Scriptures only in c. x. 35, xi. 26, and the corresponding personal noun μισθαποδότης in c. xi. 6 for the classical μισθοδοσία, μισθοδότης. As compared with the corresponding words ἀνταπόδοσις (Col. iii. 24), ἀνταπόδομα (Lk. xiv. 12; Rom. xi. 9), the word appears to emphasise the idea of an exact requital of good or evil by a sovereign Judge. The discipline and punishment of the wilderness (c. iii. 16 ff.; 1 Cor. x. 6 ff.) furnished the typical illustration of this teaching which extends to the whole Jewish life: c. xii. 25, x. 28 f.

3. πῶς...;] The interrogative form is characteristic of the style of the Epistle (c. i. 5 note). Compare 1 Tim. iii. 5; 1 John iii. 17. *How shall we escape after neglecting...?* The neglect is assumed.

ἐκφευξόμεθα] The word is again used absolutely Acts xvi. 27; 1 Thess. v. 3.

ρίας, ἥτις, ἀρχὴν λαβοῦσα λαλεῖσθαι διὰ τοῦ κυρίου,
ὑπὸ τῶν ἀκουσάντων εἰς ἡμᾶς ἐβεβαιώθη, ⁴συνεπιμαρ-

4 συνεπιμ.: συνμαρτ. B.

τηλικ.] *so great* as has been seen from the nature of the Mediator. Comp. 2 Cor. i. 10. ᾿Αμελ. Matt. xxii. 5.

σωτηρίας] The character of the new dispensation is placed in contrast with the Law: 'salvation' (i. 14 note) with 'the word.' Comp. Jude 3; Acts xiii. 26. So Theodoret : ὁ μὲν νόμος λόγος ἦν τὸ πρακτέον ὑποδεικνύς, ἡ δὲ τοῦ κυρίου διδασκαλία τῆς αἰωνίου πρόξενος σωτηρίας. And Primasius : Lex promittebat terram...Evangelium regnum cælorum...Illa præstabat vindictam de terrenis hostibus : istud præstat de spiritualibus...Illa promittebat longævam vitam temporalem; Evangelium concedit vitam sine fine mansuram.

3 b, 4. The superior authority of the Gospel is shewn in three points, in its original announcement, in its convincing proclamation, and in the manifold divine attestation to its truth.

ἥτις] The pronoun preserves its full force : *Seeing that it...was confirmed...*῞Οστις as distinguished from ὅς is rightly described as 'qualitative and generic,' *a man (a thing) such as..., a class who...*, hence very commonly *whoever (whatever)...*Compare cc. viii. 56; ix. 2, 9; x. 35, 8, 11; xii. 5; xiii. 7, and Moulton on Winer, p. 209 n.

ἀρχὴν λαβοῦσα λαλ.] Vulg. *cum initium accepisset enarrari.* This singular mode of expression suggests somewhat more than the simple fact *having first been spoken*, and implies that the teaching of the Lord was the true origin of the Gospel. The phrase is not found elsewhere in the N. T. or in the LXX., but is frequent in late Greek writers (τὴν ἀρχὴν λ.): e.g. Philo, *de vita Mos.* i. § 14; (ii. 93 M.) [σημεῖον] τὴν ἀρχὴν τοῦ γενέσθαι λαβὸν ἐν Αἰγύπτῳ.

λαλεῖσθαι] i. 1 f.; iii. 5; xii. 25. The addition of the verb calls attention to the present preaching, and to the fact that this is based on the original preaching of Christ.

διὰ τοῦ κ.] *through the Lord* as the Messenger of the Father (c. i. 2). Vulg. *per dominum.* Comp. *v.* 2 ὁ δι᾿ ἀγγ. λαλ. λ. Contrast λαλεῖσθαι ὑπό Luke ii. 18; Acts xiii. 45; xvi. 14; xvii. 19; and λαλεῖσθαι παρά Luke i. 45.

τοῦ κυρίου] not τοῦ κυρίου ἡμῶν. Compare c. xii. 14. The idea is of the Sovereign Majesty of Christ in Himself. Contrast vii. 14, xiii. 20, viii. 2.

ὑπὸ τῶν ἀκ.] by the immediate hearers : Luke i. 2. Contrast 1 John i. 1.

Though St Paul was not a hearer of Christ in the flesh, yet it is scarcely conceivable that he should have placed himself thus in contrast with those who were : Gal. i. 12; and if the writer was a disciple of St Paul he must refer to other teachers also.

εἰς ἡμ. ἐβεβ.] was brought unto us—into our midst—and confirmed to us. Vulg. *in nos confirmata est.* The use of the preposition suggests an interval between the first preaching and the writer's reception of the message. It is to be noticed that the 'salvation' and not merely the message of it (Acts xiii. 26) was 'confirmed': the 'salvation' was shewn to be real in the experience of those who received it.

εἰς ἡμᾶς] Gal. iii. 14; John viii. 26; Rom. viii. 18; Acts ii. 22; 1 Pet. i. 4, 25. Compare Moulton's Winer, p. 776. ἐβεβαιώθη] Compare (Mk.) xvi. 20; Rom. xv. 8.

4. The divine witness to the 'salvation' of the Gospel is both continuous and manifold. The writer appeals to a succession of forms in which it was manifested in his ex-

τυροῦντος τοῦ θεοῦ σημείοις τε καὶ τέρασιν καὶ ποικίλαις
δυνάμεσιν καὶ πνεύματος ἁγίου μερισμοῖς κατὰ τὴν αὐτοῦ

om. τε M₂ vg syrr.　　　　αὐτοῦ: τοῦ θεοῦ D₂*.

perience and in that of those whom
he addressed.

1. Miracles (σημεῖα, τέρατα).
2. Powers, outwardly shewn in action
(ποικίλαι δυνάμεις).
3. Endowments, which might be
purely personal and unobserved (πν.
ἁγ. μερισμοῖς).
There is a progress from that which
is most striking outwardly to that
which is most decisive inwardly. The
outward phenomenon and the inward
experience are both in different ways
capable of various interpretations;
but they are complementary. The
one supplies that element of conviction
which the other wants.

The passage is of deep interest as
shewing the unquestioned reality of
miraculous gifts in the early Church:
and the way in which they were regarded as coordinate with other ex-
hibitions of divine power.

Compare 2 Cor. xii. 12; Gal. iii. 5;
Rom. xv. 19; c. vi. 4 f.

συνεπιμαρτυροῦντος] God also bearing witness with them to the truth of
the word. This witness is present and
not past. Vulg. contestante [O. L.
adseverante] Deo. The word is found
here only in the Greek Scriptures.
ἐπιμαρτυρεῖν occurs 1 Pet. v. 12; συμ-
μαρτυρεῖν Rom. ii. 15; viii. 16; ix. 1.
The word is not uncommon in late
writers: Clem. R. 1 Cor. 23, 43.

σημ. τε καὶ τέρ....] The τε, which is
not used in the common phrase σημ.
καὶ τέρ., shews that all the forms
of witness are probably regarded
singly, Acts xiii. 1; 1 Cor. i. 30; c. ix.
2; xi. 32. Comp. Acts ii. 22; 2 Thess.
ii. 9.

σημεῖα καὶ τέρατα] The combination
is found in the Synoptic Gospels
(Matt. xxiv. 24; Mk. xiii. 22), St John
(iv. 48), in St Paul's Epistles (Rom.

xv. 9; 2 Cor. xii. 12; 2 Thess. ii. 9),
and most frequently in the Acts (8
times cc. i.—xv.). It is not found in
the Catholic Epistles or the Apocalypse. In the Synoptic passages and
2 Thess. ii. 9 the phrase is used of the
manifestation of evil powers.

Τέρας is nowhere used by itself in
the N. T., though it is so used in the
LXX. (comp. Acts ii. 19; Joel iii. 3).
Σημεῖον and σημεῖα are common alone,
and especially in St John in reference
to Christ's works.

ποικ. δυν.] by manifold powers (Lat.
variis virtutibus) shewing themselves
in their characteristic results. Δύναμις
expresses here the power itself and
not the manifestation of the power.
See Mk. vi. 14; 1 Cor. xii. 10; Matt.
xi. 20 ff.; c. vi. 4 ff.

πν. ἁγ. μερισμοῖς] Vulg. sp. s. dis-
tributionibus (O. L. divisionibus).
Comp. 1 Cor. xii. 4, 11 (Acts ii. 3
διαμεριζόμεναι). The Holy Spirit is in
one sense the gift and in another the
Giver. Here there can be no doubt
that the thought is of the divine gift
(πν. ἁγ. not τὸ πν. τὸ ἁγ.) as imparted in
several measures by God. Compare
John iii. 34; 2 Cor. x. 13.

κατὰ τὴν αὐτ. θ.] according to His,
God's, not the Spirit's, will [willing].
Vulg. secundum suam [O. L. ipsius]
voluntatem. The clause refers to all
that has gone before. Comp. Eph.
iv. 7.

θέλησις] The word, which occurs
several times in the LXX., is found
here only in the N.T. As distinguished
from θέλημα (x. 7, 9, 36; xiii. 21), the
definite expression of will, it describes
the active exercise of will.

The use of these active verbal nouns
is characteristic of the style of the
Epistle. Among many others which
occur the following are found in the

θέλησιν; ⁵Οὐ γὰρ ἀγγέλοις ὑπέταξεν τὴν οἰκουμένην

5 ὑπέτ. +ὁ θεός C (vg).

N. T. only in this Book: μετάθεσις
(vii. 12; xi. 5; xii. 27); ἀθέτησις (vii.
18; ix. 26); ἄθλησις (x. 32); πρόσχυσις
(xi. 28); αἴνεσις (xiii. 15).

iii. *The fulfilment of the divine
destiny of man in the Son of man
through suffering* (ii. 5—18).

Two main thoughts are brought out
in this section.

(1) The promise of sovereignty to
man was fulfilled in Jesus ('the Son
of man'): 5—9.

(2) The fulfilment of man's destiny,
owing to the intrusion of sin, could
only be brought about through suffering, made possible for Christ and
effective for man through the Incarnation (10—18).

Throughout the section there is a
tacit reference to the objections which
were raised against the Lord's claims
to Messiahship on the ground of the
actual facts of His life and sufferings.

(1) *The promise of man's sovereignty and its potential fulfilment*
(5—9).

The writer of the Epistle has already assumed the establishment of
a new order corresponding with the
fulfilment of the purpose of creation.
The sovereignty of this order was not
prepared for angels (*v.* 5). It was
promised to man (6—8 a); and the
promise was fulfilled in 'Jesus' (8b—9).

5 *For not unto angels did He subject the world to come, whereof we
speak.*

6 *But one testified as we know
(somewhere) saying
What is man, that Thou art mind-
ful of him?
Or the son of man, that Thou visi-
test him?*

7 *Thou madest him a little lower
than angels;
With glory and honour Thou
crownedst him;*

*And didst set him over the works
of Thy hands:*
8 *Thou didst put all things in
subjection under his feet.*

5. οὐ γάρ...] *For not unto angels
did He subject*...The manifestations
of the Divine Presence which have
been shewn to attend the proclamation of the Gospel (*v.* 4) are intelligible
both from the Nature of the Son and
from the scope of His work. For the
greatness of the Son as the Revealer
of the New Dispensation and of its
preachers, His envoys, is revealed by
the fact that (*a*) the future dispensation,
which is, as has been already implied,
the fulfilment of the Creator's will,
was committed to man; and that (*b*)
man's sovereignty has been gained
for him, even after his failure, through
the Incarnation of Jesus 'the Son of
Man.'

γάρ] *For*...The particle refers directly to the signs of divine power
among believers which were a prelude
to the complete sovereignty. The
subject (God) is not expressed but
naturally supplied from the former
sentence.

οὐκ...ἀγγέλοις...] *not to angels*, to
beings of this class, but (as is shewn
in the next verses) to man...(comp.
c. i. 4 τῶν ἀγγέλων note). It is not
said that 'the present world' was subject to angels; but at the same time
the writer of the Epistle may well
have recalled the belief which found
expression in the LXX. Version of
Deut. xxxii. 8 that God assigned the
nations to the care of angels while
Israel was His own portion.

Compare Ecclus. xvii. 17 (14); Daniel
xii. 1; x. 13, 20. So too in later Jewish
literature, e.g. in the Book of Henoch,
angels are represented as having
charge over different elements.

ὑπέταξεν] *did He subject* in the

τὴν μέλλουσαν, περὶ ἧς λαλοῦμεν· ⁶διεμαρτύρατο δέ πού
τις λέγων

eternal counsel (comp. i. 2 ἔθηκεν)
made known through the Psalmist.
The word is borrowed by anticipation
from the Psalm.

τὴν οἰκ. τὴν μέλλ.] Vulg. *orbem terræ
futurum*, O. L. *sæculum futurum*,
Syr. ܥܳܬܺܝܕ݂ ܠܰܡܗܘܳܐ.

The phrase is not to be understood
simply of 'the future life' or, more
generally, of 'heaven.' It describes,
in relation to that which we may call
its constitution, the state of things
which, in relation to its development
in time, is called 'the age to come'
(ὁ μέλλων αἰών), and, in relation to its
supreme Ruler and characteristics, 'the
Kingdom of God,' or 'the Kingdom
of heaven,' even the order which
corresponds with the completed work
of Christ. Compare vi. 5 (μέλλων
αἰών), xiii. 14 (ἡ μέλλουσα [πόλις])
notes. Is. ix. 6.

ἡ οἰκουμένη] The word is used for
the world so far as it is 'a seat of settled government,' 'the civilised world.'
Thus in Greek writers it is used
characteristically for the countries occupied by Greeks, as distinguished
from those occupied by 'barbarians'
(Herod. iv. 110; Dem. *de Cor.* p. 242;
[*de Halonn.*] p. 85 f.), and at a later
time for the Roman empire (Philo,
Leg. ad Cai. § 45; ii. 598 M.).

Hence it came to be used even of a
limited district defined, as we should
say, by a specific civilisation (Jos. *Antt.*
viii. 13, 4 περιπέμψας κατὰ πᾶσαν τὴν
οἰκουμένην τοὺς ζητήσοντας τὸν προφήτην Ἠλείαν). Comp. Luke ii. 1;
Ex. xvi. 35 ἕως ἦλθον εἰς τὴν οἰκουμένην
[Alex. γῆν οἰκ.] 'to the borders of the
land of Canaan': compare Euseb.
H. E. vii. 31, 2 ἐκ τῆς Περσῶν ἐπὶ τὴν
καθ᾽ ἡμᾶς οἰκουμένην…And on the other
hand it was used to describe the whole
world as occupied by man (Luke iv. 5
[D τοῦ κόσμου]; Matt. xxiv. 14; Apoc.

xvi. 14); and men as occupants of the
world (Acts xvii. 31; xix. 27; Apoc.
iii. 10; xii. 9). Comp. Wisd. i. 7
πνεῦμα κυρίου πεπλήρωκε τὴν οἰκουμένην.
It was therefore perfectly fitted to
describe the Christian order under the
aspect of a moral, organised system :
comp. c. i. 6.

The word is found in St Paul only
Rom. x. 18 (Ps. xix. 5).

περὶ ἧς λαλ.] which is the subject of
the whole writing. The thought has
been already announced in i. 2 κληρονόμον πάντων.

6—8 a. *The promise.* The promise
of universal sovereignty was confirmed
to man in a passage of Scripture (Ps.
viii. 5—7) which fully recognises his infirmity. His weakness is first confessed
(*v.* 6); and then his triple divine endowment of nature, honour, dominion
(*v.* 7, 8 a).

The viiith Psalm is referred to by
the Lord Matt. xxi. 16 (comp. Matt.
xi. 25; 1 Cor. i. 27), and by St
Paul 1 Cor. xv. 27. Comp. Eph. i. 22.

It is not, and has never been accounted by the Jews to be, directly
Messianic; but as expressing the true
destiny of man it finds its accomplishment in the Son of Man and only
through Him in man. It offers the
ideal (Gen. i. 27—30) which was lost
by Adam and then regained and
realised by Christ.

Clement speaks of the application
of the words of the Psalm to man by
some: οὐ γὰρ ἐπὶ τοῦ κυρίου ἐκδέχονται
τὴν γραφὴν καίτοι κἀκεῖνος σάρκα ἔφε-
ρεν· ἐπὶ δὲ τοῦ τελείου καὶ γνωστικοῦ,
τῷ χρόνῳ καὶ τῷ ἐνδύματι ἐλαττουμένου
παρὰ τοὺς ἀγγέλους (*Strom.* iv. 3 § 8,
p. 566).

And so Chrysostom: ταῦτα εἰ καὶ
εἰς τὴν κοινὴν ἀνθρωπότητα εἴρηται, ἀλλ᾽
ὅμως κυριώτερον ἁρμόσειεν ἂν τῷ Χριστῷ
κατὰ σάρκα (*Hom.* iv. § 2).

And Theodoret: τὸ δὲ 'τί ἐστιν

Τί ἐϲτιν ἄνθρωποϲ ὅτι μιμνήϲκΗ ἀγτογ,
ἢ γίοϲ ἀνθρώπογ ὅτι ἐπιϲκέπτΗ ἀγτόν ;

6 τί ℵABD₂ vg syrr: τίϲ C* (latt.) me (so LXX A).

ἄνθρωπος;’ εἴρηται μὲν περὶ τῆς κοινῆς
φύσεως, ἁρμόττει δὲ τῇ ἐξ ἡμῶν ἀπαρχῇ,
ὡς οἰκειουμένης τὰ πάσης τῆς φύσεως·
τὰ δὲ ἡμέτερα οἰκειούμενος στόμα τῆς
φύσεως γέγονεν. αὐτὸς γὰρ τὰς ἁμαρτίας
ἡμῶν ἔλαβε καὶ τὰς νόσους ἐβάστασε
(ad loc.).

One peculiar difficulty meets us in
the use made of the Psalm by the
writer of the Epistle. The thought
expressed in the original by the words
rendered in the LXX. ἠλάττωσας αὐτὸν βραχύ τι παρ’ ἀγγέλους is that of
the nobility of man's nature which
falls but little short of the divine.
The words on the contrary as applied
to Christ describe a humiliation. This
application is facilitated by the LXX.
rendering, but does not depend upon
it. The essential idea is that the true
destiny of man described by the
Psalmist, which experience teaches us
that man himself has missed, was fulfilled otherwise than had been expected. Words which were used of
man in himself became first true of
One Who being more than man took
man's nature upon Him. In such a
case the description of dignity was
of necessity converted initially into a
description of condescension.

6. The thought of man's frailty
comes first. According to a remarkable Jewish tradition the words were
addressed by the ministering angels
to God when 'Moses went up to receive the Law.' 'O Lord of the
world,' they said, 'wilt Thou give to
flesh and blood that precious thing
which Thou hast kept for 974 generations? (Ps. viii. 5). Give Thy glory
rather to heaven' (Sabb. 88, 1).

5, 6. οὐ γὰρ ἀγγ....διεμαρτ. δέ...]
The form of the construction is expressive. The sovereignty was not
indeed designed for angels; but provision was made for it. When there

is a direct and sharp opposition, ἀλλά
follows a negative not...but. When
the negative marks a sentence which
is complete in itself, and another
statement is added as a fresh thought,
this, though it does in fact oppose the
former, is introduced by δέ. Comp.
vv. 8, 9 οὔπω—δέ; iv. 13; vi. 12;
Acts xii. 9, 14.

διεμ. δ. πού τις] In this quotation
only in this epistle (iv. 7 is not a case
in point) is there a reference to the
human author of the words; and here
God is addressed directly. At the
same time the reference is as general
as possible. The form of reference
is found in Philo, de temul. § 14 (i.
365 M.) εἶπε γάρ πού τις (Gen. xx. 12).
For πού see c. iv. 4 note.

Διαμαρτύρομαι is used absolutely
Luke xvi. 28; Acts ii. 40 (viii. 25);
1 Thess. iv. 6.

τί ἐστιν] i.e. how little outwardly,
and at first sight, compared with the
stately magnificence of Nature.

Comp. Ps. cxliv. 3; Job vii. 17.
The interpretation 'how great is man,'
i.e. in consequence of God's love shewn
to him, is quite foreign to the course
of thought. Nor again is there any
reference to the fact of the Fall.

ἄνθρωπος] אֱנוֹשׁ, man, with the
secondary idea of weakness.

υἱὸς ἀνθρώπου] בֶּן־אָדָם not ὁ υἱὸς
τοῦ ἀνθρώπου (בֶּן־הָאָדָם).

μιμνήσκῃ...ἐπισκέπτῃ] The twofold
regard of thought and action. Ἐπισκέπτεσθαι is used almost exclusively
in the LXX., as in the N. T., of a visitation for good. Luke i. 68, 78; vii. 16;
Acts xv. 14. The word was especially
used of the 'visits' of a physician.
Comp. Matt. xxv. 36; James i. 27.

7, 8 a. In spite of his frailty man
recognises his divine affinity. He is
more glorious than the world which

7ἨΛΆΤΤΩϹΑϹ ΑΥ̓ΤΌΝ ΒΡΑΧΎ ΤΙ ΠΑΡ᾽ ἈΓΓΈΛΟΥϹ,
ΔΌΞῌ ΚΑῚ ΤΙΜῌ ἘϹΤΕΦΆΝΩϹΑϹ ΑΥ̓ΤΌΝ,
[ΚΑῚ ΚΑΤΈϹΤΗϹΑϹ ΑΥ̓ΤΌΝ ἘΠῚ ΤᾺ ἜΡΓΑ ΤῶΝ ΧΕΙΡῶΝ ϹΟΥ,]
8ΠΆΝΤΑ ῬΠΈΤΑΞΑϹ ῬΠΟΚΆΤΩ ΤῶΝ ΠΟΔῶΝ ΑΥ̓ΤΟΥ̂·

ἐν τῷ γὰρ ῥ̔ποτάξαι [αὐτῷ] τὰ πάντα οὐδὲν ἀφῆκεν αὐτῷ

7 ἐστεφ. αὐτόν, +καὶ κατέστησας αὐτὸν ἐπὶ τὰ ἔργα τῶν χειρῶν σου ℵACD₂*M₂ vg (syrr) me (so lxx): om. B (syrr).   8 ἐν τῷ γὰρ ℵBD₂M₂: ἐν γὰρ τῷ ϛAC. αὐτῷ (1) om. B.   τὰ πάντα ὑποτάξαι αὐ. D₂ syrr me.

seems to crush him, in nature, endowment, destiny.

7. *ἤλαττ. βρ. τι...*] *Thou madest him a little lower...*Vulg. *Minuisti* (Old Lat.*minorasti*) *eum paulo minus ab angelis.* Βραχύ τι is used here of degree (compare 2 Sam. xvi. 1), and not of time (Is. lvii. 17 LXX. 'for a little while'). The Hebrew is unambiguous; and there is no reason to depart from the meaning of the original either in this place or in *v.* 9.

παρ᾽ ἀγγέλους] The original מֵאֱלֹהִים, rendered literally by Jerome *a deo*, is thus interpreted by the Targum and Syr. and by the Jewish Commentators (Rashi, Kimchi, Aben-Ezra), as well as by the LXX.

The original meaning is probably less definite than either 'a little less than angels' or 'a little less than God.' It would more nearly correspond to 'a little less than one who has a divine nature.' 'Thou hast made him to fall little short of being a God' (comp. 1 Sam. xxviii. 13). To our ears 'than God' would be equivalent to 'than the Eternal,' which would have been wholly out of place in the Psalm. And on the other hand 'than angels' obscures the notion of the 'divine nature' which lies in the phrase.

For the wider sense of אֱלֹהִים, see Ps. lxxxii. 1, 6 (John x. 34 f.); xxix. 1 (not Ex. xxi. 6).

δόξῃ καὶ τιμῇ] with the essential dignity and with the outward splendour which signalises it: Rom. ii. 7, 10; 1 Pet. i. 7; Apoc. iv. 9. The words occur in opposite order, 1 Tim. i. 17;

2 Pet. i. 17; Apoc. v. 12 f. The combination is common in LXX. *e.g.* Ex. xxviii. 2 (ת. καὶ δ. לִכְבוֹד וּלְתִפְאָרֶת).

ἐστεφάνωσας] *crownedst* as a conqueror; 2 Tim. ii. 5.

8. πάντα...αὐτοῦ] Man's sovereignty is exercised over a worthy domain. This clause completes the view of man's eminence in nature, glory, dominion. See Additional Note.

8 b, 9. *The divine fulfilment of the promise in the Son of man.* The promise to man has not however yet been realised. It assured to him a dominion absolute and universal; and as yet he has no such dominion (*v.* 8 b). But the words of the Psalm have received a new fulfilment. The Son of God has assumed the nature in which man was created. In that nature—bearing its last sorrows—He has been crowned with glory. The fruit of His work is universal. In 'the Son of man' (*Jesus*) then there is the assurance that man's sovereignty shall be gained (*v.* 9). Thus the fact of man's obvious failure is contrasted with the accomplishment of Christ's work which is the potential fulfilment of man's destiny (Humiliation, Exaltation, Redemption).

8b *For in that He subjected all things unto him, He left nothing that is not subject to him. But now we see not yet all things subjected to him.* 9 *But we behold Him who hath been made a little lower than angels, even Jesus, because of the suffering of death crowned with glory and honour, that by the grace of God He should taste of death for every man.*

ἀνυπότακτον. νῦν δὲ οὔπω ὁρῶμεν αὐτῷ τὰ πάντα ὑ̓ποτε-
ταγμένα· ⁹τὸν δὲ βραχύ τι παρ᾽ ἀγγέλουc ἠλαττωμένον βλέπομεν
Ἰησοῦν διὰ τὸ πάθημα τοῦ θανάτου δόξῃ καὶ τιμῇ ἐϲτεφα-

8. ἐν τῷ γὰρ ὑπ.] The 'for,' which
is directly connected with the preceding clause, points back to v. 5, so
that the connexion is: God did not
subject the future world to angels,
for He promised man an absolute
sovereignty which has still to be assured in that coming order. The τὰ
πάντα takes up the πάντα of the
Psalm.

νῦν δέ...] but at present, as the world
is....

αὐτῷ] i.e. to man.

9. τὸν δέ...] *But* in spite of the
obvious fact of man's failure the
promise has not failed : *we behold
Him that hath been made a little
lower than angels,* even *Jesus,...
crowned with glory and honour....*
The words of the Psalm have an
unexpected accomplishment. The
man thus spoken of as little less than
angels (so great is he) is represented
by Jesus, the Son of GOD become
flesh, and so made little less than
angels (so full of condescension was
He), and in that humanity which He
has taken to Himself crowned with
glory.

Jesus is not the 'man' of the
Psalmist, but He through whom the
promise to man has been fulfilled and
is in fulfilment; while the revelation of
the complete fulfilment belongs to
'the world to come.'

The definite article (τὸν δὲ βρ. τι
ἠλ.) does not refer to the Psalm as
fixing the original meaning of it, but
to the known personality of Christ in
whom the promise of the Psalm was
fulfilled.

βραχύ τι...] Vulg. *qui modico quam
angeli minoratus est....O. L. paulo
quam angelos minoratum...*See *v.* 7.

ἠλαττωμένον] not ἐλαττωθέντα. The
human nature which Christ assumed

He still retains. Comp. *v.* 18 πέπονθεν.
βλέπομεν] The change of the verb
from ὁρῶμεν in *v.* 8 cannot be without
meaning. Βλέπειν apparently expresses the particular exercise of the
faculty of sight (comp. John i. 29;
v. 19 ; ix. 7 ff.), while ὁρᾶν describes
a continuous exercise of it (c. xi. 27).
The difference is not marked by the
Latt. (*videmus...videmus...*).

Ἰησοῦν] The name comes in emphatically as marking Him who, being
truly man, fulfilled the conception of
the Psalmist of 'one made a little
lower than angels.'

The personal name *Jesus*, which
always fixes attention on the Lord's
humanity, occurs frequently in the
Epistle : iii. 1 ; vi. 20; vii. 22; x. 19;
xii. 2, 24; xiii. 12 (iv. 14; xiii. 20).
See Additional Note on c. i. 4.

For the separation of the Name
(*Him that hath been made...even
Jesus*) compare c. iii. 1 ; xii. 2, 24;
xiii. 20 (*our Lord even Jesus;* comp.
vi. 20; vii. 22;) 1 Thess. ii. 15; iii. 13.

διὰ τὸ πάθ. τοῦ θ.] Vulg. (Latt.)
propter passionem mortis. The suffering of death—the endurance of
the uttermost penalty of sin—was the
ground of the Lord's exaltation in
His humanity. Comp. Phil. ii. 9 (Rom.
viii. 17).

The words are not to be joined
with ἠλαττωμένον either in the sense
(1) that in this lay His humiliation,
or (2) that this was the aim of His
humiliation, that death might be possible, 'owing to the fact that death
has to be borne by men.' The main
thought of the passage is that man's
promised supremacy, owing to the
fall, could only be gained by sacrifice.
Stress is laid not upon the single
historic fact that the Lord suffered
death (διὰ τὸ παθεῖν θ.), but on the

ΝϹΩΜΕΝΟΝ, ὅπως χάριτι θεοῦ ὑπὲρ παντὸς γεύσηται θανάτου.

9 χάριτι: χωρίς.　See Additional note.

nature of the suffering itself (διὰ τὸ πάθημα).

ἐστεφανωμένον] As in the case of the Lord's humiliation so also in this of His exaltation the writer brings out the permanent effect (not στεφανωθέντα as ἐστεφάνωσας in v. 7).

ὅπως...] The particle is not strictly connected with ἐστεφανωμένον alone, but refers to all that precedes—to the Passion crowned by the Ascension. The glory which followed the death marked its universal efficacy. Thus Christ was made lower than angels that He might accomplish this complete redemption. The particle, which is much less frequent in the Epistles than ἵνα, occurs again c. ix. 15.

Under this aspect the words are illustrated by St John's view of the Passion as including potentially the glorification of Christ (John xiii. 31), a double 'lifting up' (xii. 32). So Œcumenius here says boldly δόξαν καὶ τιμὴν τὸν σταυρὸν καλεῖ.

χάριτι θεοῦ] Comp. 1 John iv. 10; John iii. 17; Rom. v. 8. Chrysostom: διὰ τὴν χάριν τοῦ θεοῦ τὴν εἰς ἡμᾶς ταῦτα πέπονθεν. For the anarthrous form (as contrasted with ἡ χάρις τοῦ θεοῦ xii. 15), 'by grace, and that grace of Him Whose Nature is the pledge of its efficacy,' see c. iii. 4 note. Comp. Lk. ii. 40; 1 Cor. xv. 10; 2 Cor. i. 12.

The reading χωρὶς θεοῦ is capable of being explained in several ways.

(1) Christ died 'apart from His divinity.' His divine Nature had no share in His death.

(2) Christ died 'apart from God,' being left by God, and feeling the completeness of the separation as the penalty of sin. Comp. Matt. xxvii. 46.

(3) Christ died for all, God only excepted. Compare 1 Cor. xv. 27.

(4) Christ died to gain all, to bring all under His power, God only excepted.

But all these thoughts seem to be foreign to the context, while it is natural to bring out the greatness of God's grace in fulfilling His original counsel of love in spite of man's sin. The reference to 'the grace of God' seems to be the necessary starting point of the argument in the next section: For it became...

ὑπὲρ παντός] Vulg. pro omnibus. Syr. for every man. Comp. Mark ix. 49; Luke xvi. 16. The singular points to the effect of Christ's work on the last element of personality. Christ tasted death not only for all but for each. The thought throughout the passage (v. 16) is directed to personal objects; and in such a connexion the phrase could hardly mean 'for everything' (neut.). This thought however is included in the masculine. Creation is redeemed in man (Rom. viii. 19 ff.). Comp. v. 11 ἐξ ἑνός.

The notes of the Greek commentators are of considerable interest.

ORIGEN: μέγας ἐστὶν ἀρχιερεὺς οὐχ ὑπὲρ ἀνθρώπων μόνον ἀλλὰ καὶ παντὸς λογικοῦ...καὶ γὰρ ἄτοπον ὑπὲρ ἀνθρωπίνων μὲν αὐτὸν φάσκειν ἁμαρτημάτων γεγεῦσθαι θανάτου, οὐκέτι δὲ καὶ ὑπὲρ ἄλλου τινὸς παρὰ τὸν ἄνθρωπον ἐν ἁμαρτήμασι γεγεννημένου, οἷον ὑπὲρ ἄστρων (Job xxv. 5) (In Joh. Tom. i. § 40).

THEODORET: τὸ μέντοι πάθος ὑπὲρ ἁπάντων ὑπέμεινε. πάντα γὰρ ὅσα κτίστην ἔχει τὴν φύσιν ταύτης ἐδεῖτο τῆς θεραπείας...He then refers to Rom. viii. 19 ff., and supposes that the angels will be gladdened by man's salvation: ὑπὲρ ἁπάντων τοίνυν τὸ σωτήριον ὑπέμεινε πάθος· μόνη γὰρ ἡ θεία φύσις τῆς ἐντεῦθεν γινομένης θεραπείας ἀνενδεής (ad loc.).

CHRYSOSTOM: οὐχὶ [ὑπὲρ] τῶν πιστῶν μόνον, ἀλλὰ καὶ τῆς οἰκουμένης

ἀπάσης· αὐτὸς μὲν γὰρ ὑπὲρ πάντων
ἀπέθανεν. *Hom.* iv. 2.

ŒCUMENIUS : οὐ μόνον ὑπὲρ ἀνθρώπων ἀλλὰ καὶ ὑπὲρ τῶν ἄνω δυνάμεων
ἀπέθανεν, ἵνα λύσῃ τὸ μεσότυχον [μεσό-
τοιχον] τοῦ φραγμοῦ καὶ ἑνώσῃ τὰ κάτω
τοῖς ἄνω (Eph. ii. 14).

Comp. 1 John ii. 2.

ὑπέρ] not *in place of*, but *in behalf
of*. Comp. v. 1; vi. 20; vii. 25; ix. 24.

γεύσηται θανάτου] Comp. Matt. xvi.
28; John viii. 52 note. Arist. *Apol.*
p. 110, l. 19.

The phrase, which is not found in
the Old Testament, expresses not only
the fact of death, but the conscious
experience, the tasting the bitterness,
of death. Man, as he is, cannot feel
the full significance of death, the
consequence of sin, though he is subject to the fear of it (*v.* 15); but
Christ, in His sinlessness, perfectly
realised its awfulness. In this fact
lies the immeasurable difference between the death of Christ, simply as
death, and that of the holiest martyr.
Chrysostom (Theodoret, Primasius)
less rightly understands the phrase of
the brief duration of Christ's experience of death : Non dixit Apostolus 'Subjacuit morti,' sed proprie
gustavit mortem, per quod velocitatem
resurrectionis voluit ostendere (Primasius).

Chrysostom (*Hom.* iv. 2) likens
Christ to the physician who, to encourage his patients, tastes that which
is prepared for them.

(2) *Man's destiny, owing to the
intrusion of sin, could only be fulfilled through suffering, made possible
for Christ and effective for man
through the Incarnation* (10—18).

The thought of death, and the fact
of Christ's death, lead the apostle to
develope more in detail the conditions
under which man's destiny and God's
promise were fulfilled in spite of sin.
The reality of the connexion between
the Son and the sons is first traced
back to their common source and
shewn to be recognised in the records

of the Old Testament (10—13). This
connexion was completed by the Incarnation with a twofold object, to
overcome the prince of death, and to
establish man's freedom (14, 15). And
such a completion was necessary from
the sphere, the scope, the application
of Christ's work (16—18).

The course of thought will appear
most plainly if it is set in a tabular
form :

Sovereignty for man fallen was won
through suffering (10—18).

(1) *The Son and the sons* (10—13).

The connexion lies in a common
source (11 a).

This is shewn in the Old Testament :

The suffering King (12),

The representative Prophet (13).

(2) *The connexion of the Son and the
sons completed by the Incarnation*
(14, 15),

with a twofold object :

To overcome the prince of death
(14 b),

To establish man's freedom (15).

(3) *The Incarnation necessary* (16—
18), from

The sphere of Christ's work (16),

The scope of Christ's work (17),

The application of Christ's work
(18).

10—13. *The Son and the sons.*
The difficulties which at first sight
beset the conception of a suffering
Messiah vanish upon closer thought.
For when we consider what is the
relation between the Son of man and
men—the Son and the sons—what
man's condition is, and how he can
be redeemed only through divine
fellowship, we ourselves can discern
the 'fitness' of the divine method of
redemption. So far therefore from
the Death of Christ being an objection
to His claims, it really falls in with
what deeper reflection suggests.

The connexion of the Son and the
sons is first referred to their common
source (*v.* 11 ἐξ ἑνός) and then shewn
to be recognised in the divine dealings

¹⁰᾿Ἔπρεπεν γὰρ αὐτῷ, δι᾿ ὃν τὰ πάντα καὶ δι᾿ οὗ τὰ πάντα, πολλοὺς υἱοὺς εἰς δόξαν ἀγαγόντα τὸν ἀρχηγὸν

with representative men under the Old Covenant, the suffering king, the typical prophet (12, 13).

There is throughout the section a reference to the Jewish expectation that Messiah should 'abide for ever' (John xii. 34).

¹⁰*For it became Him, for Whom are all things and through Whom are all things, in bringing many sons unto glory, to make the author (captain) of their salvation perfect through sufferings.* ¹¹*For both He that sanctifieth and they that are sanctified are all of One; for which cause He is not ashamed to call them brethren,* ¹²*saying*

I will declare Thy Name to my brethren.

In the midst of the congregation will I sing Thy praise.

¹³*And again: I will put my trust in Him. And again: Behold, I and the children which God gave me.*

10.　ἔπρεπεν γάρ...] For it became ...'Yes,' the apostle seems to say, '"taste of death by the grace of God," for we, with our poor powers, can say that in this there is supreme fitness.' The suffering of Christ in the fulfilment of His work corresponds with the truest conception which man can form of the Divine Nature.

ἔπρεπεν] Latt. *decebat*. Comp. c. vii. 26; Matt. iii. 15. The word as applied to God appears perhaps startling but it is not unfrequent in Philo, *e.g. Leg. Alleg.* i. 15 (i. 53 M.). The standard lies in what man (made in the image of God) can recognise as conformable to the divine attributes. For man still has a power of moral judgment which can help him to the interpretation of the action of God, and also of his own need (c. vii. 26).

The 'fitness' in this case lies in the condition of man. His life is attended by inevitable sorrows ; or,

to regard the fact in another light, suffering is a necessary part of his discipline as well as a necessary consequence of his state. It was 'fitting' then, in our language, that God should perfect Christ the 'One' Son by that suffering through which the 'many sons' are trained (xii. 5 ff.) because He, in His infinite love, took humanity to Himself. In Christ we can see the divine end of suffering: suffering consummated in glory. Chrysostom: ὁρᾷς τὸ παθεῖν κακῶς οὐκ ἔστιν ἐγκαταλελειμμένων.

This argument from 'fitness' is distinct from that of logical necessity (δεῖ *v.* 1), and of obligation from a position which has been assumed (ὤφειλε *v.* 17).

δι᾿ ὄν...δι᾿ οὗ...] This description of God, as being the final Cause and the efficient Cause of all things, takes the place of the simple title because the fitness of Christ's perfection through suffering appears from the consideration of the divine end and method of life.

δι᾿ οὗ] Compare Rom. xi. 36; 1 Cor. i. 9 (Gal. iv. 7 διὰ θεοῦ ; Rom. vi. 4 διὰ τῆς δόξης τοῦ πατρός).

The phrase is commonly used of the work of the Son : c. i. 2; 1 Cor. viii. 6 ; Col. i. 16; (1 John iv. 9); John i. 3, 10; but it cannot be referred to Him here, though Athanasius so uses the whole clause (*Ep. ad Episc. Æg. et Lyb.* § 15); and Chrysostom rightly calls attention to this application of δι᾿ οὗ to the Father as shewing that the characteristic use is no derogation from the divine nature of the Son: οὐκ ἂν τοῦτο ἐποίησεν εἴ γε ἐλαττώσεως ἦν καὶ τῷ υἱῷ μόνον προσῆκον (*ad loc.*).

πολλοὺς υἱούς] Christ has been spoken of as 'the Son.' Men now are made to share His title (comp. xii. 5). Chrysostom : καὶ αὐτὸς υἱὸς καὶ ἡμεῖς υἱοί· ἀλλ᾿ ὁ μὲν σώζει ἡμεῖς δὲ σωζόμεθα.

τῆς σωτηρίας αὐτῶν διὰ παθημάτων τελειῶσαι. ¹¹ ὅ τε
γὰρ ἀγιάζων καὶ οἱ ἀγιαζόμενοι ἐξ ἑνὸς πάντες· δι᾽ ἣν

The use of πολλούς brings no limitation to the scope of Christ's work (comp. ix. 28) which has just been described in its universal aspect (ὑπὲρ παντός). It simply emphasises the truth that the pattern of Christ's Life was in this aspect of wide application. Comp. Matt. xx. 28.

εἰς δόξαν ἀγαγόντα...τελειῶσαι] O. L. multis filiis in gloriam adductis, Vulg. qui multos filios in gloriam adduxerat. These Latin renderings suggest a wrong sense. Though the objects of ἀγαγόντα and τελειῶσαι are different the two acts which they describe are regarded as synchronous, or rather as absolute without reference to the succession of time. The perfecting of Christ included the triumph of those who are sons in Him. At the same time the work of God and the work of Christ are set side by side. God 'brings' (ἀγαγεῖν) the many sons and Christ is their 'leader' (ἀρχηγός).

The order, no less than the stress which is laid on the completed work of Christ, is fatal to the proposed connexion of ἀγαγόντα with Christ, who had 'brought many sons to glory' during His ministry, even if Christians, who are called His 'brethren' (v. 11), could in this place be spoken of as His 'sons' (in v. 13 the case is different). And so again the use of δόξα is decisive against the idea that God is spoken of as 'having brought many sons to glory' in earlier times.

For a similar combination of aorists see Matt. xxvi. 44; xxviii. 19 (βαπτίσαντες); Acts xxiii. 35 (κελεύσας); Rom. iv. 20; (Eph. v. 26); Col. ii. 13; 1 Tim. i. 12; c. ix. 12.

τὸν ἀρχηγὸν τῆς σωτ.] The author (or captain) of their salvation, O. L. ducem v. principem (Vulg. auctorem salutis). Neither word gives the fulness of sense. The ἀρχηγός himself first takes part in that which he

establishes. Comp. xii. 2; Acts iii. 15; v. 31; Mic. i. 13 (LXX.); 1 Macc. ix. 61. Comp. Iren. ii. 22. 4 prior omnium et praecedens omnes.

The word, which is common in the LXX., occurs in Clem. R. 1 Cor. c. xiv. ἀρχ. ζήλους, c. li. ἀρχ. τῆς στάσεως, and often elsewhere; e.g. 2 Clem. xx. 5 ὁ σ. καὶ ἀρχηγὸς τῆς ἀφθαρσίας; Jos. B. J. iv. 5. 2 ὁ ἀρχηγὸς καὶ ἡγεμὼν τῆς ἰδίας σωτηρίας; Ep. Vienn. 17 (Euseb. H. E. v. 1). See also classical examples in Wetstein on c. xii. 2. Compare αἴτιος c. v. 9.

διὰ παθ. τελειῶσαι] Latt. per passionem consummare. For consummare some Fathers read and explain consummari (Ruff. Sedul. Vigil.).

The conception of τελειῶσαι is that of bringing Christ to the full moral perfection of His humanity (cf. Luke xiii. 32), which carries with it the completeness of power and dignity. Comp. c. x. 1, 14; xi. 40; xii. 23; Phil. iii. 12 (v. 6).

This 'perfection' was not reached till after Death: v. 9; vii. 28. It lay, indeed, in part in the triumph over death by the Resurrection. Comp. Cyril Alex. ap. Cram. Cat. pp. 396, 399.

The sense of 'bringing to His highest honour,' or 'to the close of His earthly destiny,' is far too narrow. See Additional Note.

διὰ παθημάτων] See c. xiii. 12 note.

Theodoret supposes that 'the Word' perfected the human nature, the source of our salvation: τὸν θεὸν λόγον ἔδειξεν ἣν ἀνέλαβεν τελειώσαντα φύσιν. ἀρχηγὸς τῆς ἡμετέρας σωτηρίας ἡ ληφθεῖσα φύσις.

11—13. The title of 'sons' can be rightly applied to Christians as well as to Christ, for, though in different senses, they depend on one Father (v. 11); and this fact is recognised in the Scriptures of the old Covenant (vv. 12, 13).

11. ὅ τε γὰρ ἀγιάζων] The disci-

αἰτίαν οὐκ ἐπαισχύνεται ἀδελφοὺς αὐτοὺς καλεῖν, ¹²λέγων

11 αὐτοὺς ἀδ. M₂ syrr.

pline through which Christ reached perfection is that through which He brings His people. That which is appointed for them He also accepts (John xvii. 19), for both He and they are of One Father.

The present participles (ἁγιάζων, ἁγιαζόμενοι) mark the continuous, personal application of Christ's work. Comp. John xvii. 17 ff. For ἁγιάζειν see c. ix. 13 note.

οἱ ἁγιαζόμενοι] Vulg. qui sanctificantur. The thought is of the continual process at once in the individual soul and in the whole body of the Church (c. x. 14).

Comp. x. 10 (ἡγιασμένοι), 14; xiii. 12 (ἵνα ἁγιάσῃ). Christians are 'holy' ('saints'): c. vi. 10; xiii. 24; (iii. 1); and the end of their discipline is that they may 'partake in the holiness of God' (c. xii. 10). That which is true ideally has to be realised actually.

ἐξ ἑνός] of One, i.e. God. Comp. Ex. xxxi. 13; 1 Cor. i. 30 (viii. 6 quoted by Chrys.); Lk. iii. 38 τοῦ Ἀδάμ, τοῦ θεοῦ. The reference to Adam or to Abraham is partly inadequate and partly inappropriate.

πάντες] The writer regards the whole company of Christ and His people as forming one body, and does not distinguish specially the two constituent parts (ἀμφότεροι).

Some think that the statement in respect of Christ is to be confined to His Humanity. Others extend it to His whole Person. In the latter case, Theodoret (and other Greek Fathers) adds that we must remember that ὁ μέν ἐστι φύσει υἱὸς ἡμεῖς δὲ χάριτι (Œcum. ὁ μὲν γνήσιος ἡμεῖς δὲ θετοί).

It will appear that much is lost by any precise limitation of the words. The Lord both as Son of God and as

Son of Man can be spoken of as ἐκ Πατρός, and so men also both in their creation and in their re-creation. At the same time the language used (ὁ ἁγιάζων καὶ οἱ ἁγιαζόμενοι) naturally fixes attention on Christ and Christians in relation to the work of redemption and sanctification wrought out on earth.

δι' ἣν αἰτίαν] for which cause, that is, because they spring from the same source, though in different ways. Both in their being and in the consummation of their being the Son and the sons are 'of One.' For the phrase see 2 Tim. i. 6, 12; Tit. i. 13; (Luke viii. 47; Acts xxiii. 28).

With this specific form of the 'subjective' reason (comp. c. v. 3) compare the general form (διό iii. 7, 10 &c.), and the general form of the 'objective' ground (ὅθεν v. 17 note).

οὐκ ἐπαισχ....καλεῖν] He is not a-shamed to call (Vulg. non confunditur ...vocare...) in spite of the Fall, and of the essential difference of the sonship of men from His own Sonship. Comp. c. xi. 16.

ἀδελφούς] Comp. Rom. viii. 29.

Christians are 'brethren' of Christ (John xx. 17; Matt. xxviii. 10) and yet children (v. 13; John xiii. 33 τεκνία).

12, 13. The quotations in these verses develope the main idea of the section, that of Christ fulfilling the destiny of men through suffering, by recalling typical utterances of representative men: (1) of the suffering, innocent king; (2) of the representative prophet.

The ground of the application in the first case lies in the fact that the language used goes beyond the actual experience of David, or of any righteous sufferer.

In the second case the prophet

ἈπαΓΓελῶ τὸ ὄνομά coy τοῖc ἀδελφοῖc μογ,

ἐν μέcῳ ἐκκληcίαc γ́μνήcω ce·

¹³καὶ πάλιν

Ἐγὼ ἔcομαι πεποιθὼc ἐπ' αγ̓τῷ·

καὶ πάλιν

Ἰδογ̓ ἐγὼ καὶ τὰ παιδία ἅ μοι ἔδωκεν ὁ θεόc.

occupies a typical position at a critical period of national history. Ruler and prophet both identify themselves with their people. The one applies to them the express term 'brethren': the other takes his place among them as symbolising their true hope.

12. The quotation is taken from Ps. xxii. 22 and agrees with the LXX. except by the substitution of ἀπαγγελῶ for διηγήσομαι.

The Psalm itself, which probably dates from the time of David's persecution by Saul, describes the course by which 'the Anointed of the Lord' made his way to the throne, or more generally the establishment of the righteous kingdom of God through suffering. In *vv.* 21 ff. sorrow is turned into joy, and the words of the Psalmist become a kind of Gospel. Hence the phrase quoted here has a peculiar force. The typical king and the true King attain their sovereignty under the same conditions, and both alike in their triumph recognise their kinship with the people whom they raise (τοῖς ἀδελφοῖς).

The Psalm is quoted not unfrequently: Matt. xxvii. 46; Mk. xv. 34 (*v.* 1); Matt. xxvii. 39, 43 (*vv.* 7, 8); Matt. xxvii. 35; John xix. 24 (*v.* 18); comp. c. v. 7 (*v.* 24).

τὸ ὄνομά σου] *I will declare Thy Name*, for Thou hast proved to be what I have called Thee, 'my hope and my fortress, my castle and deliverer, my defender...who subdueth my people under me.' These many titles are summed up in the revelation of the Name of the Father: *nomen*

tuum quod est *Pater*, ut cognoscant Te Patrem, qui eos paterno affectu ad hæreditatem supernæ beatitudinis ut filios vocas (Herv.).

ἐν μέσῳ ἐκκλησίας] *in the midst of the congregation* when the people are assembled to exercise their privilege as citizens of the divine commonwealth.

13. The thought of 'brotherhood' is extended in the two following quotations and placed in its essential connexion with the thoughts of 'fatherhood' and 'sonship.' Brothers are supported by the trust in which they repose on one above them and by the love which meets the trust.

καὶ πάλιν Ἐγὼ ἔσομαι...] Words nearly identical (πεποιθὼς ἔσομαι ἐπ' αὐτῷ) occur in the LXX. in Is. viii. 17; xii. 2; 2 Sam. xxii. 3. The reference is certainly, as it appears, to Is. viii. 17, where the words immediately precede the following quotation. The two sentences of Isaiah are separated because they represent two aspects of the typical prophet in his relation to Christ. In the first the prophet declares his personal faith on God in the midst of judgments. In the second he stands forth with his children as representing 'the remnant,' the seed of the Church, in Israel. The representative of God rests in his heavenly Father, and he is not alone: his children are already with him to continue the divine relation.

καὶ πάλιν Ἰδοὺ ἐγώ...] Isaiah with his children were 'signs' to the unbelieving people. In them was seen the pledge of the fulfilment of God's

¹⁴ἐπεὶ οὖν τὰ παιδία κεκοινώνηκεν αἵματος καὶ σαρκός, καὶ
αὐτὸς παραπλησίως μετέσχεν τῶν αὐτῶν, ἵνα διὰ τοῦ

14 αἷμ. καὶ σ. אABCD₂M₂ (vg) syr hl me: σαρκ. καὶ αἷμ. ς (vg) syr vg.   τῶν
αὐτῶν + παθημάτων D₂*.

purposes. Thus, the prophet was a sign of Christ. What he indicated Christ completely fulfilled ; for under this aspect Christ is the 'father' no less than the 'brother' of His people. The words are not referred directly to Christ by a misunderstanding of the LXX.

The emphatic ἐγώ in both cases is to be noticed. Comp. i. 5 ; v. 5 ; x. 30; xii. 26.

καὶ πάλιν] Contiguous quotations from Deut. xxxii. 35 f. are separated by καὶ πάλιν in c. x. 30.

ἅ μοι ἔδωκεν] which God gave me in the crisis of national suffering as a pledge of hope. The prophet looks back on the moment when light broke through the darkness.

14, 15. The object of the Incarnation (the completed fellowship of the Son with the sons). The full connexion of 'the Son' and 'the sons' was realised in the Incarnation with a twofold object :

(1) To overcome the prince of death (v. 14), and

(2) To establish man's freedom, destroyed by the fear of death (v. 15).

That which has been shewn before to be 'fitting' (10—13) is now revealed in its inner relation to man's redemption. Christ assumed mortality that He might by dying conquer the prince of death and set man free from his tyranny.

Compare Athanas. de decr. Syn. Nic. § 14 ; c. Apollin. ii. 8 ; Greg. Nyss. c. Eunom. viii. p. 797 Migne.

In this paragraph man is regarded in his nature, while in the next (16—18) he is regarded in his life.

¹⁴Since therefore the children are sharers in blood and flesh, He also Himself in like manner partook of the same, that through death He

might (may) bring to nought him that had (hath) the power of death, that is the devil, ¹⁵and might (may) deliver all them, who through fear of death were all their lifetime subject to bondage.

14. ἐπεὶ οὖν...] Since therefore... Christ connects Himself with 'the children whom God had given Him.' These children were men. To complete His fellowship with them therefore it was necessary that He should assume their nature under its present conditions (αἷμα καὶ σάρξ).

For ἐπεί see c. v. 11 note.

τὰ παιδία] The phrase is taken up from the quotation just made. Isaiah and his children foreshadowed Christ and His children.

κεκοινώνηκεν......μετέσχεν......] are sharers in...He partook of... Vulg. communicaverunt (pueri)...participavit... O. L. participes sunt...particips factus. The Syr. makes no difference between the words which describe the participation in humanity on the part of men and of the Son of man. Yet they present different ideas. Κεκοινώνηκε marks the common nature ever shared among men as long as the race lasts : μετέσχεν expresses the unique fact of the Incarnation as a voluntary acceptance of humanity. And under the aspect of humiliation and transitoriness (αἷμα καὶ σάρξ) this was past (μετέσχεν).

For a similar contrast of tenses see 1 Cor. xv. 4 ; 1 John i. 1 ; Col. i. 16 ; John xx. 23, 29 ; and for the difference between κοινωνεῖν and μετέχειν see 1 Cor. x. 17—21 ; 2 Cor. vi. 14 ; Prov. i. 11, 18. Comp. c. iii. 1.

αἷμ. καὶ σ.] The same order occurs in Eph. vi. 12. Stress is laid on that element which is the symbol of life as subject to corruption (contrast Luke

θανάτου καταργήσῃ τὸν τὸ κράτος ἔχοντα τοῦ θανάτου,
τοῦτ' ἔστι τὸν διάβολον, ¹⁵καὶ ἀπαλλάξῃ τούτους, ὅσοι

θανάτου (1°) + θάνατον D₂*.   15 ἀπαλλ.: ἀποκαταλλάξῃ Α.

xxiv. 39). The common order (σὰρξ καὶ αἷμα) is undisturbed in Matt. xvi. 17; 1 Cor. xv. 50; Gal. i. 16. παραπλησίως] Vulg. similiter (which is also used for ὁμοίως c. ix. 21). The word occurs here only in the N. T. (cf. Phil. ii. 27); and it is not found in the LXX. Ὁμοίως seems to express conformity to a common type: παραπλησίως the direct comparison between the two objects. In ὁμοίως the resemblance is qualitative (similiter): in παραπλησίως both qualitative and quantitative (pariter). The two words are not unfrequently joined together: e.g. Dem. Ol. iii. 27 (p. 36 A). The Fathers insist on the word as marking the reality of the Lord's manhood: σφόδρα δὲ ἀναγκαίως καὶ τὸ παραπλησίως τέθεικεν ἵνα τὴν τῆς φαντασίας διελέγξῃ συκοφαντίαν (Theod.); οὐ φαντασίᾳ οὐδὲ εἰκόνι ἀλλ' ἀληθείᾳ (Chrys.). Comp. Phil. ii. 7 ἐν ὁμοιώματι ἀνθρώπων γενόμενος. Rom. viii. 3 ἐν ὁμοιώματι σαρκὸς ἁμαρτίας.

μετέσχεν] Contrast vii. 13 φυλῆς ἑτέρας μετέσχηκεν. The connexion with humanity remains: the connexion with humanity under the condition of transitoriness (αἷμα) was historical.

διὰ τοῦ θανάτου] by death, not by His death, though this application is necessarily included. Death that is truly death (1 John iii. 14), which was the utmost effect of Satan's power, became the instrument of his defeat: non quæsivit alia arma quibus pugnaret contra mortis auctorem, nisi ipsam mortem (Herv.). Christ by the offering of Himself (c. ix. 15, 28) made a perfect atonement for sin and so brought to nought the power of the devil. Comp. John xii. 31; Col. ii. 15.

It is not said here that he 'brought to nought death' (yet see 2 Tim. i. 10). That end in the full sense is

still to come (1 Cor. xv. 26); and it is reached by the power of the life of Christ (1 Cor. xv. 54 ff.).

καταργήσῃ] The word is found in the N. T. elsewhere only in St Paul (twenty-five times and in each group of his epistles) and in Luke xiii. 7. Comp. 2 Tim. i. 10; 1 Cor. xv. 26; Barn. v. 6).

Chrysost. ἐνταῦθα τὸ θαυμαστὸν δείκνυσιν, ὅτι δι' οὗ ἐκράτησεν ὁ διάβολος διὰ τούτου ἡττήθη.

τὸν τὸ κρ. ἔχ. τ. θ.] Latt. qui habebat mortis imperium. The phrase may mean that had or that hath. In one sense the power is past: in another it continues. Comp. Wisd. ii. 24.

The devil, as the author of sin, has the power over death its consequence (Rom. v. 12), not as though he could inflict it at his pleasure; but death is his realm: he makes it subservient to his end. Comp. John viii. 44; 1 John iii. 12; John xvi. 11; xiv. 30 (prince of the world). Death as death is no part of the divine order.

Œcum. πῶς ἄρχει θανάτου; ὅτι τῆς ἁμαρτίας ἄρχων ἐξ ἧς ὁ θάνατος, καὶ τοῦ θανάτου ἄρχει, ἤγουν κράτος θανάτου ἡ ἁμαρτία.

τὸν διάβολον] The title is found in St Paul only in Eph. and Past. Epp. The title ὁ Σατανᾶς is not found in this Epistle.

15. The overthrow of the devil involved the deliverance of men from his power.

ἀπαλλάξῃ] Latt. liberaret. The word is used absolutely ('set free'), and is not to be connected with δουλείας.

τούτους ὅσοι...] all men who had, as we see, come to a perception of their position as men. The unusual phrase vividly presents the picture of human misery as realised by the readers of the Epistle.

φόβῳ θανάτου διὰ παντὸς τοῦ ζῆν ἔνοχοι ἦσαν δουλείας.
¹⁶οὐ γὰρ δή που ἀγγέλων ἐπιλαμβάνεται, ἀλλὰ σπέρ-

διὰ παντὸς τοῦ ζῆν] O. L. semper vivendo. Vulg. per totam vitam. The verbal phrase expresses the activity of life and not only the abstract idea of life.

ἔνοχοι δουλείας] Vulg. obnoxii servituti. Comp. Mk. xiv. 64. This bondage was to the fear of death. To death itself men are still subject, but Christ has removed its terrors. Comp. Rom. viii. 15, 21. This is the only place in the Epistle in which the familiar image of bondage (δοῦλος, δουλόω, δουλεύω, δουλεία) is used.

In considering the Scriptural view of death it is important to keep the idea of a transition to a new form of being distinct from that of the circumstances under which the transition actually takes place. The passage from one form of life to another, which is involved in the essential transitoriness of man's constitution, might have been joyful. As it is death brings to our apprehension the sense of an unnatural break in personal being, and of separation from God. This pain comes from sin. The Transfiguration is a revelation of the passage of sinless humanity to the spiritual order.

16—18. *The necessity of the Incarnation.* The Incarnation is further shewn to be necessary from the consideration of

(1) The sphere of Christ's work, man (*v.* 16);

(2) The scope of Christ's work, the redemption of fallen man (*v.* 17); and (3) The application of Christ's work to individual men in the conflict of life (*v.* 18).

¹⁶*For He doth not, as we know, take hold of angels, but He taketh hold of Abraham's seed.* ¹⁷*Wherefore he was bound in all things to be made like unto His brethren that He might (may) be a merciful and*

faithful high-priest in the things that pertain to God, to make propitiation for the sins of the people.* ¹⁸*For wherein He Himself hath suffered being tempted, He is able to succour them that are tempted.*

16. The necessity of the Incarnation follows from a consideration of the sphere of Christ's work. His purpose is, as is confessedly admitted, to assist men and not primarily other beings, as angels, though in fact they are helped through men. He lays hold of 'a faithful seed' to support and guide them to the end which He has Himself reached.

οὐ γὰρ δή που...] O. L. *Nec enim statim...* Vulg. *nusquam enim...* The γάρ gives the explanation of the end of the Incarnation which has been stated in *v.* 14 *b.* The combination δή που (not in LXX.) is found here only in the N. T. It implies that the statement made is a familiar truth: 'For He doth not, as we well know...' The Versions fail to give the sense; and Primasius explains the *nusquam* of the Vulgate: id est nullo loco, neque in caelo neque in terra, angelicam naturam assumpsit.

ἐπιλαμβάνεται] The verb ἐπιλαμβάνεσθαι in the middle form has the general sense of *laying hold of* with the gen. of that which is taken hold of: Matt. xiv. 31; Luke ix. 47; Acts xxi. 30, &c.

In a particular case this may be with the additional notion of 'helping' suggested by the context: Jer. xxxviii. (xxxi *Hebr.*) 32 (quoted c. viii. 9).

Hence the verb is used absolutely in the sense of 'helping': Ecclus. iv. 11 ἡ σοφία υἱοὺς ἑαυτῇ ἀνύψωσε καὶ ἐπιλαμβάνεται τῶν ζητούντων αὐτήν. Is. xli. 8, 9 (R. V.). Comp. *Const. Apost.* vii. 38, 1 ἐν ταῖς ἡμέραις ἡμῶν ἀντελάβου ἡμῶν διὰ τοῦ μεγάλου σου ἀρχιερέως Ἰησοῦ Χριστοῦ.

The versions generally give the sense of 'take hold of' in the sense of appropriating : Syr. *he took not from angels* (ܐ ܡܠ)... *i.e.* he did not appropriate their nature; O. L. *adsumpsit,* or *suscepit.* Vulg. *apprehendit.*

This sense is given, I believe, uniformly by the Fathers both Greek and Latin who understand the phrase of the fact and not of the purpose of the Incarnation:

τί ἐστιν ὃ φησιν; οὐκ ἀγγέλου φύσιν ἀνεδέξατο ἀλλ᾽ ἀνθρώπου (Chrys.).

ἐπειδὴ ἀνθρώπειον ἦν ὁ ἀνέλαβε διὰ μὲν τοῦ πάθους τὸ τῶν ἀνθρώπων ἀπέδωκε χρέος, διὰ δὲ τῆς τοῦ πεπονθότος σώματος ἀναστάσεως τὴν οἰκείαν ἀπέδειξε δύναμιν (Theodoret).

οὐκ ἀγγέλων φύσεως ἐδράξατο οὐδὲ ἀνέλαβεν ἀλλ᾽ ἀνθρωπίνης (Œcum.).

But at the same time they recognise a secondary thought of 'laying hold of that which endeavours to escape' :

ἀπὸ μεταφορᾶς τῶν διωκόντων τοὺς ἀποστρεφομένους αὐτοὺς καὶ πάντα ποιούντων ὥστε καταλαβεῖν φεύγοντας καὶ ἐπιλαβέσθαι ἀποπηδώντων (Chrysost.).

τὸ ἐπιλαμβάνεται δηλοῖ ὅτι ἡμεῖς μὲν αὐτὸν ἐφεύγομεν οἱ ἄνθρωποι, ὁ δὲ Χριστὸς ἐδίωκε καὶ διώκων ἔφθασε καὶ φθάσας ἐπελάβετο (Œcum.).

Quare dixit *apprehendit,* quod pertinet ad fugientem ? Quia nos quasi recedentes a se et longe fugientes insecutus apprehendit (Primasius).

This sense however is inconsistent with the γάρ, and the plural ἀγγέλων, and would be a mere repetition of *v.* 14 *a*; while the sense 'taketh hold of to help,' is both more in accordance with the usage of the word and falls in perfectly with the argument. This being so, it is remarkable that this interpretation was not given by any one, as far as I know, before Chatillon in his Latin Version; and it then called out the severe condemnation of Beza: "...exsecranda...est Castellionis audacia qui ἐπιλαμβάνεται con-

vertit *opitulatur*" (*ad loc.*). But, in spite of these hard words, this sense soon came to be adopted universally. The present tense brings out the continuous efficacy of the help (*v.* 18, *v.* 11 ὁ ἁγιάζων).

σπέρματος Ἀβραάμ] Christ took hold of *a seed of Abraham,* that is a true seed, those who are children of faith, and not of 'the seed of Abraham,' the race descended from the patriarch. Comp. Lk. i. 55; John viii. 33, 37; Gal. iii. 16, 29; Rom. ix. 7 ff.; xi. 1; 2 Cor. xi. 22 (compare τέκνα Ἀ. Matt. iii. 9 ‖ Lk. iii. 8; John viii. 39; υἱοὶ Ἀ. Gal. iii. 7; Acts xiii. 26). The absence of the article shews that a character and not a concrete people ('the Jews') is described. At the same time the phrase marks both the breadth and the particularity of the divine promise which was fulfilled by Christ. Those of whom Christ takes hold have a spiritual character (faith), and they find their spiritual ancestor in one who answered a personal call (Abraham). Sive igitur de Judæis, sive de gentibus fideles, *semen Abrahæ* sunt quod Christus *apprehendit* (Herv.).

Nothing is said of the effect of the Incarnation on angels, or other beings than man. Man's fall necessarily affected all creation, and so also did man's restoration. But here the writer is simply explaining the fitness of the Incarnation.

Many however have endeavoured to determine why fallen man should have been redeemed and not fallen angels. Primasius, for example, suggests the following reasons:

1. Man was tempted by the devil: the devil had no tempter.

2. Man yielded to an appetite for eating which naturally required satisfaction. The devil as spirit was inexcusable.

3. Man had not yet reached the presence of God, but was waiting to be transferred thither. The devil was already in heaven.

ματος 'Αβραὰμ ἐπιλαμβάνεται. ¹⁷ ὅθεν ὤφειλεν κατὰ
πάντα τοῖς ἀδελφοῖς ὁμοιωθῆναι, ἵνα ἐλεήμων γένηται καὶ

It is evident that we have no powers to discuss such a subject. In this connexion too it may be noticed that the writer says nothing distinctly of the calling of the Gentiles. He regards the whole divine work of Christ under the aspect of typical foreshadowing. Comp. v. 11 note.

17. The necessity of the Incarnation is shewn further from a consideration of the scope of Christ's work. His purpose to help man involved the redemption of fallen man; and He who helps must have sympathy with those whom He helps. *Wherefore He was bound to be made like to His brethren in all things, that He might be a merciful and faithful High-priest...* For men are not only beset by temptations in the fierce conflicts of duty: they are also burdened with sins; and Christ had to deal with both evils.

Thus we are introduced to the idea which underlies the institution of Priesthood, the provision for a fellow-ship between God and man, for bringing God to man and man to God. See Additional Note.

ὅθεν] *Whence, wherefore...*since it was His pleasure to help fallen man. The word ὅθεν is not found in St Paul's Epistles. It is comparatively frequent in this Epistle, iii. 1; vii. 25; viii. 3; ix. 18. It occurs also (nine times in all) in St Matt., St Luke, Acts, 1 John. It marks a result which flows naturally (so to speak) from what has gone before.

ὤφειλεν] *he was bound...*Latt. *debuit* ...The requirement lay in the personal character of the relation itself. Comp. c. v. 3, 12; 1 John ii. 6 note.

Δεῖ (ἔδει) describes a necessity in the general order of things (*oportet*): ii. 1; ix. 26; xi. 6.

κατὰ πάντα] Vulg. *per omnia similari.* The 'likeness' which has

been shewn in nature before (14) is now shewn to extend to the circumstances of life: ἐτέχθη, φησίν, ἐτράφη, ηὐξήθη, ἔπαθε πάντα ἅπερ ἐχρῆν, τέλος ἀπέθανεν (Chrysost.). Id est educatus crevit, esuriit, passus est ac mortuus (Primas.).

ὁμοιωθῆναι] Comp. c. iv. 15 πεπειρασμένος κατὰ πάντα καθ' ὁμοιότητα (vii. 15 κατὰ τὴν ὁμοιότητα Μελχισεδέκ). Phil. ii. 7 ἐν ὁμοιώματι ἀνθρώπων γενόμενος. Rom. viii. 3; (Matt. vi. 8; Acts xiv. 11). The use of τοῖς ἀδελφοῖς calls up the argument of the former verses (v. 11).

ἵνα...εἰς τό...] Ἵνα expresses the immediate definite end: εἰς τό (which is characteristic of St Paul) the object reached after or reached. Εἰς τό... occurs vii. 25; viii. 3; ix. 14; xi. 3; xii. 10; xiii. 21.

ἵνα...γένηται] *that He might (may) become, shew Himself...* Latt. *ut fieret* ... The discharge of this function is made dependent on the fulfilment of the conditions of human life. Comp. v. 1 ff. The verb γίγνεσθαι suggests the notion of a result reached through the action of that which we regard as a law. Comp. i. 4; ii. 2; iii. 14; v. 9; vi. 4, 12; vii. 18, 26 &c.

ἐλεήμων...καὶ πιστός] It seems to be far more natural to take both these words as qualifying ἀρχιερεύς than to take ἐλ. separately: 'that He might become merciful, and a faithful high-priest.' Our High-priest is 'merciful' in considering the needs of each sinful man, and 'faithful' ('one in whom the believer can trust') in applying the means which He administers. It has been supposed that the one epithet expresses mainly the relation towards men and the other the relation towards God (c. iii. 2, 5); but here the relation towards men is alone in question, so that the faithfulness of Christ expresses that wherein

πιστὸς ἀρχιερεὺς τὰ πρὸς τὸν θεόν, εἰς τὸ ἱλάσκεσθαι

men can trust with absolute confidence.

The word πιστός admits two senses according as the character to which it is applied is regarded from within or from without.

A person is said to be 'faithful' in the discharge of his duties where the trait is looked at from within outwards; and at the same time he is 'trustworthy' in virtue of that faithfulness in the judgment of those who are able to rely upon him. The one sense passes into the other. See c. iii. 2, 5; x. 23; xi. 11.

πιστός] "Ιδιον τοῦ ὄντως καὶ ἀληθῶς ἀρχιερέως τοὺς ὧν ἐστὶν ἀρχιερεὺς ἀπαλλάξαι τῶν ἁμαρτιῶν (Œcumen., Chrysost.). Ministerium sacerdotis...est fidelem esse ut possit eos quorum sacerdos est liberare a peccatis (Primas.). Man gains confidence by the sight of Christ's love.

ἀρχιερεύς] The writer introduces quite abruptly this title which is the key-word of his teaching, and which is applied to the Lord in this Epistle only among the writings of the N. T. So also the title ἱερεύς is used of Christ only in this Epistle: x. 21 (ἱερέα μέγαν). Comp. v. 6, &c. (Ps. cx. 4). Yet see also Apoc. i. 13. The title is adopted by Clement: ad Cor. i. c. 36 εὔρομεν...Ἰησοῦν Χριστὸν τὸν ἀρχιερέα τῶν προσφορῶν ἡμῶν, c. 58 διὰ τοῦ ἀρχιερέως καὶ προστάτου ἡμῶν Ἰησοῦ Χριστοῦ. (See Lightfoot ad loc.) Comp. Ign. ad Philad. 9.

The rendering of the sing. in the Vulg. is uniformly pontifex (iii. 1; iv. 14 f.; v. 5, 10; vi. 20; viii. 1; ix. 11); the plur. in vii. 27, 28 is rendered sacerdotes (as O. L.). In the Old Latin pontifex does not appear except in Vigil. Taps. (iv. 15) though there is considerable variety of rendering: sacerdos, summus sacerdos, princeps sacerdos, princeps sacerdotum, princeps (iii. 1). On coins and in inscriptions pontifex generally corresponds with ἀρχιερεύς, while pontifex

maximus is represented by ἀρχιερεὺς μέγας or μέγιστος. Comp. Boeckh Inscrr. Gr. 3834, 3878, 3949, 4283 &c.; 2741 (ἀρχιερεὺς) note; 5899 (ἀρχ. Ἀλεξανδρείας καὶ πάσης Αἰγύπτου).

τὰ πρὸς τὸν θεόν] in the things (in all things) that pertain to God. Latt. ad Deum. The phrase expresses more than πρὸς τὸν θεόν and points to 'all man's relations towards God,' all the elements of the divine life (in his quæ sunt ad Deum in some old Lat. texts). Comp. c. v. 1; Ex. iv. 16; xviii. 19; Rom. xv. 17. (Lk. xiv. 32; xix. 42; Acts xxviii. 10.) Jos. Antt. ix. 11. 2 εὐσεβὴς...τὰ πρὸς τὸν θεόν. The phrase is not uncommon in classical writers: e.g. Arist. Pol. iii. 14 τὰ πρὸς τοὺς θεοὺς ἀποδέδοται τοῖς βασιλεῦσιν [ἐν τῇ Λακωνικῇ πολιτείᾳ]; Plut. Consol. ad Apoll. init.

εἰς τὸ ἱλάσκ. τὰς ἁμ.] O. L. ut expiaret peccata, and ad deprecandum (propitiandum) pro delictis. Vulg. ut repropitiaret delicta. For the construction of ἱλάσκεσθαι (ἐξιλάσκεσθαι) in biblical and classical Greek see Additional Note on 1 John ii. 2. The use of the accus. of the things cleansed occurs Lev. xvi. 16, 20, 33; Ezek. xliii. 20; 22, 26; xlv. 18, 20 (τὸ ἅγιον, τὸ θυσιαστήριον, τὸν οἶκον), and Dan. ix. 24 (ἀδικίας); Ps. lxiv. (lxv.) 4 (ἀσεβείας): Ecclus. iii. 30 (ἁμαρτίας). The essential conception is that of altering that in the character of an object which necessarily excludes the action of the grace of God, so that God, being what He is, cannot (as we speak) look on it with favour. The 'propitiation' acts on that which alienates God and not on God whose love is unchanged throughout.

So Chrysostom expresses the thought here: ἵνα προσενέγκῃ θυσίαν δυναμένην ἡμᾶς καθαρίσαι, διὰ τοῦτο γέγονεν ἄνθρωπος; and Œcumenius: διὰ τοῦτο γέγονεν (ἄνθρωπος) εἰς τὸ ἐξιλεώσασθαι ἡμᾶς καὶ καθαρίσαι τῶν ἁμαρτιῶν ἡμῶν. And Primasius:

τὰς ἁμαρτίας τοῦ λαοῦ· ¹⁸ἐν ᾧ γὰρ πέπονθεν αὐτὸς
πειρασθείς, δύναται τοῖς πειραζομένοις βοηθῆσαι.

17 τὰς ἁμαρτ.: ταῖς ἁμαρτίαις A (80 Ps. lxxvii. 38; lxxviii. 9; xxiv. 11).   18 πέπ.
αὐτ.: αὐτὸς πέπ. D₂.

misertus est [generis humani] sicut
fidelis pontifex, reconcilians nos Deo
Patri, et reconciliando purgans.
The present infin. ἱλάσκεσθαι must
be noticed. The one (eternal) act of
Christ (c. x. 12—14) is here regarded
in its continuous present application
to men (comp. c. v. 1, 2).

τὰς ἁμ. τοῦ λαοῦ] *the sins of the
people*, of all who under the new dispensation occupy the position of
Israel. The 'seed of Abraham' now
receives its fuller title. Comp. Matt.
i. 21; Luke ii. 10; and c. iv. 9; xiii.
12; (viii. 10; x. 30; xi. 25). For the
original use of the word for the old
'people' see v. 3; vii. 5, 11, 27; ix.
7, 19.

The use of the phrase suggests the
thought of the privileges of the Jew,
and at the same time indicates that
that which was before limited has
now become universal, the privilege
of faith and not of descent.

18. Christ's High-priestly work,
which has been considered in the last
clause of *v.* 17 in relation to God, is
now considered in relation to man.
In this respect the efficacy of His
High-priesthood, of His mercy and
faithfulness, is shewn in the power of
its application to suffering men. Propitiation must not only be made for
them but also applied to them. He
who propitiates must enter into the
experience of the sinner to support
him in temptation. And this Christ
can do; *for wherein He Himself
hath suffered...He is able to succour...*
He removes the barrier of sin which
checks the outflow of God's love to
the sinner, and at once brings help
to the tempted (contrast ἱλάσκεσθαι,
βοηθῆσαι) by restoring in them the
full sense of filial dependence. The
whole work of our High-priest de-

pends for its efficacy (γάρ) on the
perfect sympathy of Christ with
humanity and His perfect human
experience.

ἐν ᾧ γάρ] O. L. *in quo enim ipse
expertus passus est.* The ἐν ᾧ may
be resolved either into ἐν τούτῳ ὅτι
whereas (Rom. viii. 3?), or into ἐν
τούτῳ ὅ *wherein* (Rom. xiᵛ. 22; comp.
c. v. 8; Gal. i. 8; 2 Cor. v. 10; 1 Pet.
ii. 12). The latter construction is the
simpler and more natural (Vulg. *in eo
enim in quo passus est ipse et tentatus*).

Taking this construction therefore
we have two main interpretations:
1. 'For Himself having been tempted
in that which He hath suffered...'
(So Vigilius: in eo enim quo passus
est ille tentatus est.)
2. 'For in that in which He hath
suffered being tempted...'

According to the first view the
thought is that the sympathy of
Christ is grounded on the fact that
He felt temptation when exposed to
suffering.

According to the second view the
thought is that the range of Christ's
sympathy is as wide as His experience.

The second view seems to fall in
best with the context. The region
of Christ's suffering through temptation includes the whole area of human
life, and His sympathy is no less absolute. The αὐτός is not to be taken
exclusively either with πέπονθεν or
with πειρασθείς. Though Son Christ
Himself knew both suffering and
temptation.

Primasius (Atto) interprets very
strangely: in eo, id est homine.

ἐν ᾧ πέπονθεν] *wherein he hath
suffered.* The tense fixes attention
upon the permanent effect and not on

the historic fact. Comp. *v.* 9 ἠλαττωμένον, ἐστεφανωμένον, and iv. 15; xii.
3 notes. For πάσχειν see c. xiii. 12.
The suffering which was coincident
with the temptation remained as the
ground of compassion. For the
general thought compare Ex. xxiii.
9; Deut. x. 19.

πειρασθείς......πειραζομένοις] The
temptation of Christ is regarded in
its past completeness (cf. μετέσχεν
v. 14). The temptation of men is
not future only but present and continuous.

βοηθῆσαι] Vulg. *auxiliari:* Mark ix.
22, 24. c. iv. 16. The aor. expresses
the single, momentary, act of coming
to help. Compare the use of the
pres. inf. v. 7; vii. 25; and contrast
iv. 15 μὴ δυνάμενον συμπαθῆσαι with
v. 2 μετριοπαθεῖν δυνάμενος.

δύναται...βοηθῆσαι] The phrase
expresses more than the simple fact
(βοηθεῖ). Only one who has learnt by
suffering *can* rightly feel with another
in his sufferings. The perfect humanity of Christ is the ground of His
sympathy. Comp. c. iv. 15; John v.
27 (υἱὸς ἀνθρώπου).

Chrysostom rightly dwells on this
point: περὶ τοῦ σαρκωθέντος, ἐνταῦθα
φησίν,...οὐ γὰρ ὡς θεὸς οἶδεν μόνον,
ἀλλὰ καὶ ὡς ἄνθρωπος ἔγνω διὰ τῆς
πείρας ἧς ἐπειράθη· ἔπαθε πολλά, οἶδε
συμπάσχειν· and again: ὁ παθὼν οἶδε τί
πάσχει ἡ ἀνθρωπίνη φύσις.
So also Theodoret: ταῦτα κατὰ τὸ
ἀνθρώπειον εἴρηται. οὔτε γὰρ ἀρχιερεὺς
ἡμῶν ὡς θεὸς ἀλλ᾽ ὡς ἄνθρωπος, οὔτε ὡς
θεὸς πέπονθεν ἀλλ᾽ ὡς ἄνθρωπος, οὔτε
ὡς θεὸς διὰ τῆς πείρας μεμάθηκεν, ἀλλ᾽
ὡς θεὸς καὶ δημιουργὸς γινώσκει τὰ
πάντα σαφῶς.
The power of sympathy lies not in
the mere capacity for feeling, but in
the lessons of experience. And again,

sympathy with the sinner in his trial
does not depend on the experience of
sin but on the experience of the
strength of the temptation to sin
which only the sinless can know in
its full intensity. He who falls
yields before the last strain. Comp.
c. v. 8; vii. 26 notes. Sin indeed
dulls sympathy by obscuring the idea
of evil.

Under this aspect we can understand how Christ's experience of the
power of sin in others (as in the
instruments of the Passion) intensified,
if we may so speak, His sympathy.

In looking back over the whole
section it is important to notice the
stress which the writer lays upon the
historic work of Christ. Christ is not
simply a Teacher but a Redeemer, a
Saviour. The Redemption of man
and the fulfilment of his destiny is
not wrought by a moral or spiritual
union with God laid open by Christ,
or established in Christ, but by a
union of humanity with God extending to the whole of man's nature and
maintained through death. While the
writer insists with the greatest force
upon the transcendental action of
Christ, he rests the foundation of this
union upon Christ's earthly experience.
Christ 'shared in blood and flesh'
(*v.* 14), and 'was in all things made
like to His brethren' (*v.* 17). He took
to Himself all that belongs to the perfection of man's being. He lived according to the conditions of man's life
and died under the circumstances of
man's mortality. So His work extends to the totality of human powers
and existence, and brings all into
fellowship with the divine. Compare
Clem. R. *ad Cor.* i. 49; Iren. v. 1. 1;
ii. 22. 4; iii. 16. 6. The passages of
Irenæus will repay careful study.

Additional Note on ii. 8. Man's destiny and position.

The view of man's dignity a preparation for the Incarnation.

The view which is given in the quotation from Ps. viii. of the splendour of man's destiny according to the divine idea is necessary for the argument of the Epistle. It suggests the thought of 'the Gospel of Creation,' and indicates an essential relation between the Son of God and men. At the same time it prepares the way for the full acceptance of the great mystery of a redemption through suffering. The promise of dominion given in the first chapter of Genesis is renewed and raised to a higher form. Even as man was destined to rule 'the present world,' so is it the pleasure of God that he should rule 'the world to come.' His dominion may be delayed, misinterpreted, obscured, but the divine counsel goes forward to accomplishment through the sorrows which seem to mar it.

Contradictions in man's position.

For man, as we have seen (Addit. Note on i. 3), has missed his true end. He is involved in sin and in an inheritance of the fruit of sins. Born for God he has no right of access to God (c. ix. 8). For him, till the Incarnation, God was represented by the darkness of a veiled sanctuary. The highest acts of worship served only to remind him of his position and not to ameliorate it (x. 4, 11). He was held by fear (ii. 15). Yet the primal promise was not recalled. He stood therefore in the face of a destiny unattained and unrevoked: a destiny which experience had shewn that he could not himself reach, and which yet he could not abandon as beyond hope.

His moral prerogatives.

For man, as he is, still retains the lineaments of the divine image in which he was made. He is still able to pronounce an authoritative moral judgment: he is still able to recognise that which corresponds with the Nature of God (ii. 10 ἔπρεπεν αὐτῷ), and with the needs of humanity (vii. 26 ἔπρεπεν ἡμῖν). And in the face of every sorrow and every disappointment he sees a continuity in the divine action, and guards a sure confidence in the divine righteousness (vi. 10).

The moral 'fitness' of the Incarnation.

It follows therefore that there is still in humanity a capacity for receiving that for which it was first created. The Son could become true man without change in His Divine Person, and without any violation of the completeness of the Nature which he assumed. The prospect is opened of 'consummation through suffering.'

Additional Note on the reading of ii. 9.

The reading of the text χάριτι θεοῦ (*by the grace of God*) is given with two exceptions by all Greek MSS., including ℵABCD₂, by all Latin MSS., by Syr hl and me. For these words M₂ and 67** (which has remarkable coincidences with M₂, *e.g.* i. 3; iii. 6) give χωρὶς θεοῦ (*apart from God*) with later MSS. of Syr vg.

The MSS. of the Syriac Vulgate (Peshito) present a remarkable variety of readings. The text of Widmanstadt, followed by Schaaf, gives : *for God Himself* (literally *for He God*) *in His goodness tasted death for every man*. (So B. M. Rich 7160 A.D. 1203; Rich 7162 sæc. xiv.) The important MS. of Buchanan in the University Library, Cambridge, reads : *for He in His goodness, God, tasted death for every man ;* and this was evidently the original reading of B. M. Rich 7157 (finished A.D. 768). The MSS. in the Brit. Mus. Rich 7158 (sæc. xi) and Rich 7159 (sæc. xii) both give: *for He, apart from God, for every man tasted death ;* and this is the reading of the very late corrector of Rich 7157.

Tremellius gives from a Heidelberg MS.: *for He, apart from God, in His goodness tasted death for every man,* which combines both readings.

It appears therefore that, as far as known, no text of Syr vg exactly corresponds with either Greek reading. The connecting particle presupposes γάρ for ὅπως, which has no other authority ; and on the whole it is likely that the rendering of χωρίς was introduced after that of χάριτι, and that the earliest reading, which represents χάριτι θεός, is due to a primitive corruption of the Greek or Syrian text which was corrected in two directions[1].

Both readings were known to Origen; and the treatment of the variants by the writers who were acquainted with them offers remarkable illustrations of the indifference of the early Fathers to important points of textual criticism, and of their unhistorical method of dealing with them.

Origen refers to the two readings several times, but he makes no attempt to decide between them. The MS. which he used when he was writing the first part of his commentary on St John appears to have read χωρὶς θεοῦ. He notices χάριτι θεοῦ as read in some copies : χωρὶς γὰρ θεοῦ ὑπὲρ παντὸς ἐγεύσατο θανάτου, ὅπερ (H. and R. by conj. ἢ ὅπερ wrongly) ἔν τισι κεῖται τῆς πρὸς Ἑβραίους ἀντιγράφοις 'χάριτι θεοῦ' (*In Joh.* Tom. i. § 40); and in a passage written at a later time he uses the phrase χωρὶς θεοῦ in a connexion which seems to indicate that he took it from the text of this passage : μόνου 'Ιησοῦ τὸ πάντων τῆς ἁμαρτίας φορτίον ἐν τῷ ὑπὲρ τῶν ὅλων χωρὶς θεοῦ σταυρῷ ἀναλαβεῖν εἰς ἑαυτὸν καὶ βαστάσαι τῇ μεγάλῃ αὐτοῦ ἰσχύϊ δεδυνημένου (*In Joh.* Tom. xxviii. § 41 ; he has said just before: συγχρήσεται τῷ 'ὅπως χάριτι' ἢ 'χωρὶς θεοῦ'...καὶ ἐπιστήσει τῷ 'ὑπὲρ παντὸς' καὶ τῷ 'χωρὶς θεοῦ ὑπὲρ παντός'). Both readings seemed to him to give good sense, and he was unwilling to sacrifice either[2].

Eusebius, Athanasius and Cyril of Alexandria read χάριτι θεοῦ, and do not notice the variation χωρὶς θεοῦ.

Ambrose twice quotes *sine Deo* without any notice of another reading : *de Fide* ii. § 63; *id.* v. § 106; and explains the phrase in the latter place : id est, quod creatura omnis, sine passione aliqua divinitatis, dominici sanguinis redimenda sit pretio (Rom. viii. 21). The same reading is given by Fulgentius *ad Tras.* iii. 20 with the

---

[1] The Syriac translation of Cyril of Alexandria (*in Joh.* iii. pp. 432, 513 ed. Pusey) gives *by the grace of God.*

[2] It is not possible to lay stress on the *sine Deo*, which is found twice

in Rufinus' translation of the Commentary on Romans (iii. § 8; v. § 7), but it is most likely that this was taken from Origen's text.

comment: *sine Deo* igitur homo ille gustavit mortem quantum ad conditionem attinet carnis, non autem *sine Deo* quantum ad susceptionem pertinet deitatis, quia impassibilis atque immortalis illa divinitas...; and by Vigilius Taps. *c. Eut.* ii. § 5 (p. 17).

Jerome mentions both readings (*In Ep. ad Gal.* c. iii. 10) *Christus gratia Dei*, sive, ut in quibusdam exemplaribus legitur, *absque Deo pro omnibus mortuus est.* Perhaps the use of *absque* for *sine* indicates that his reference is to Greek and not to Latin copies, and it may have been derived from Origen.

Theodore of Mopsuestia (*ad loc.*) condemns severely χάριτι θεοῦ as foreign to the argument: γελοιότατον δή τι πάσχουσιν ἐνταῦθα τὸ 'χωρὶς θεοῦ' ἐναλλάττοντες καὶ ποιοῦντες 'χάριτι θεοῦ' οὐ προσέχοντες τῇ ἀκολουθίᾳ τῆς γραφῆς: while he maintains that it was necessary to insist on the impassibility of the Godhead (χωρὶς θεοῦ).

Chrysostom explains χάριτι θεοῦ without any notice of the variety of reading: ὅπως, φησί, χάριτι θεοῦ, κἀκεῖνος μὲν γὰρ διὰ τὴν χάριν τοῦ θεοῦ τὴν εἰς ἡμᾶς ταῦτα πέπονθεν (Rom. viii. 32).

Theodoret, on the other hand, explains χωρὶς θεοῦ and takes no notice of any variation: μόνη, φησίν, ἡ θεία φύσις ἀνενδεής, τἆλλα δὲ πάντα τοῦ τῆς ἐνανθρωπήσεως ἐδεῖτο φαρμάκου.

Theophylact (*ad loc.*) ascribes the reading χωρὶς θεοῦ to the Nestorians: (οἱ δὲ Νεστοριανοὶ παραποιοῦντες τὴν γραφήν φασι 'χωρὶς θεοῦ ὑπὲρ παντὸς γεύσηται,' ἵνα συστήσωσιν ὅτι ἐσταυρωμένῳ τῷ Χριστῷ οὐ συνῆν ἡ θεότης, ἅτε μὴ καθ' ὑπόστασιν αὐτῷ ἡνωμένη ἀλλὰ κατὰ σχέσιν), but quotes an orthodox writer as answering their arguments for it by giving the interpretation 'for all beings except God, even for the angels themselves.'

Œcumenius (*ad loc.*) writes to the same effect (ἰστέον ὅτι οἱ Νεστοριανοὶ παραποιοῦσι τὴν γραφήν...).

From a review of the evidence it may be fairly concluded that the original reading was χάριτι, but that χωρίς found a place in some Greek copies early in the third century, if not before, which had however only a limited circulation, and mainly in Syria. The influence of Theodore and the Nestorian controversy gave a greater importance to the variant, and the common Syriac text was modified in two directions, in accordance with Eutychian and Nestorian views. The appearance of χωρίς in a group of Latin quotations is a noteworthy phenomenon.

The variant may be due to simple error of transcription, but it seems to be more reasonably explained by the supposition that χωρὶς θεοῦ was added as a gloss to ὑπὲρ παντός or οὐδὲν ἀφῆκεν αὐτῷ ἀνυπότακτον from 1 Cor. xv. 27 ἐκτὸς τοῦ ὑποτάξαντος αὐτῷ τὰ πάντα, and then substituted for χάριτι θεοῦ. Χωρὶς Χριστοῦ is found Eph. ii. 12. It is scarcely possible that χάριτι θεοῦ can have been substituted for χωρὶς θεοῦ, though it is really required to lead on to the fuller development of the thought in *v.* 10.

Additional Note on ii. 10.　*The idea of* τελείωσις.

The idea of _τελείωσις_—consummation, bringing to perfection—is Use of characteristic of the Epistle. The whole family of words connected with τελειοῦν τέλειος is found in it: τέλειος (v. 14; ix. 11), τελειότης vi. 1 (elsewhere only &c. Col. iii. 14), τελειοῦν both of Christ (ii. 10; v. 9; vii. 28) and of men (x. 14 ; xi. 40; xii. 23; elsewhere in the N. T. of the Lord only in Luke xiii. 32 (τῇ τρίτῃ τελειοῦμαι) in His own declaration of the course of His work), τελειωτής (xii. 2 unique), τελείωσις (vii. 11, elsewhere only Lk. i. 45).

1. The words were already in use in the LXX. The adj. τέλειος is there 1. In the applied to that which is perfect and complete, possessing all that belongs LXX. to the 'idea' of the object, as victims (Ex. xii. 5), men (Gen. vi. 2); the heart (1 K. viii. 61 &c.). Compare Jer. xiii. 19 ἀποικίαν τελείαν (a complete removal); Ps. cxxxix. (cxxxviii.) 22 τέλειον μῖσος. Hence the word is used of mature Israelites, teachers: 1 Chron. xxv. 8 τελείων (מֵבִין) καὶ μανθανόντων (v. 7 כָּל־הַמֵּבִין πᾶς συνιών).

The noun τελειότης has corresponding senses. Jud. ix. 16, 19 ; Prov. xi. 3 (A); Wisd. vi. 15; xii. 17.

The verb τελειοῦν is employed to render several Hebrew words: Ezek. xxvii. 11 (τὸ κάλλος כְּלָל); 2 Chron. viii. 16 (τὸν οἶκον שְׁלֵם); 1 K. vii. 22 (τὸ ἔργον תָּמָם); Neh. vi. 16 (עָשָׂה). Comp. Ecclus. l. 19 (τὴν λειτουργίαν). And in the later books the word is used for men who have reached their full development: Wisd. iv. 13 τελειωθεὶς ἐν ὀλίγῳ ἐπλήρωσε χρόνους μακρούς. Ecclus. xxxiv. (xxxi.) 10 τίς ἐδοκιμάσθη καὶ ἐτελειώθη;

One peculiar use requires special attention. It is employed several times in the rendering of יָד מִלֵּא, τελειοῦν τὰς χεῖρας, 'filling the hands,' which describes the installation of the priests in the actual exercise of their office (the making their hands perfect by the material of their work), and not simply their consecration to it: Ex. xxix. 9 (10) τελειώσεις 'Ααρὼν τὰς χεῖρας αὐτοῦ; id. v. 29 τελειῶσαι ('Α. πληρῶσαι, Σ. τελειωθῆναι), 33; 35. Lev. viii. 33 τελειώσεως ; xvi. 32 ὃν ἂν τελειώσωσι τὰς χεῖρας αὐτοῦ ἱερατεύειν (ἄλλος· οὗ ἐπληρώθη ὁ τόπος ἱερατεύειν); Num. iii. 3 : and it is found absolutely in this connexion in Lev. xxi. 10 (some add τὰς χεῖρας αὐτοῦ). The Hebrew phrase is elsewhere rendered by ἐμπλῆσαι (πληροῦν) τὰς χεῖρας (τὴν χεῖρα): Ex. xxviii. 37 (41); Jud. xvii. 5 (Σ. ἐτελείωσαν τ. χ.). The installation (τελείωσις) of the priest was a type of that which Christ attained to absolutely. The priest required to be furnished in symbol with all that was required for the fulfilment of his office. Christ perfectly gained all in Himself.

The usage of the verbal τελείωσις corresponds with that of the verb : Judith x. 9; Ecclus. xxxi (xxxiv.) 8. It is applied to 'Thummim' (Neh. vii. 65 some copies; comp. Aqu. and Theodot. on Lev. viii. 8 and Field ad loc.); espousals (Jer. ii. 2); the inauguration of the temple (2 Macc. ii. 9; comp. Athanas. Ep. ad Const. § 14); and specially to 'the ram of installation' (אֵיל הַמִּלֻּאִים κριὸς τελειώσεως): Ex. xxix. 22, 26, 27, 31, 34; Lev. vii. 37 (27); viii. 21, 27, 28, 31, 33.

Comp. Philo, *Vit. Mos.* iii. § 17 (ii. 157 M.), ὃν (κριὸν) ἐτύμως τελειώσεως ἐκάλεσεν ἐπειδὴ τὰς ἁρμοττούσας θεραπευταῖς καὶ λειτουργοῖς θεοῦ τελετὰς ἔμελλον ἱεροφαντεῖσθαι.

The noun τελειωτής is not found in the LXX.

2. In the N. T.

2. In the Books of the N. T. (if we omit for the present the Epistle to the Hebrews) the adj. τέλειος is used to describe that which has reached the highest perfection in the sphere which is contemplated, as contrasted with that which is partial (1 Cor. xiii. 10), or imperfect (James i. 4), or provisional (James i. 25), or incomplete (Rom. xii. 2; James i. 17; 1 John iv. 18), and specially of Christians who have reached full growth in contrast with those who are immature or undeveloped (Eph. iv. 13; Col. i. 28; iv. 12), either generally (Matt. v. 48; xix. 21; 1 Cor. ii. 6; Phil. iii. 15; James iii. 2), or in some particular aspect (1 Cor. xiv. 20).

The noun τελειότης is found in Col. iii. 14, where love is said to be σύνδεσμος τῆς τελειότητος, a bond by which the many elements contributing to Christian perfectness are held together in harmonious unity.

The verb τελειοῦν is not unfrequent in the Gospel and first Epistle of St John. It is used in the discourses of the Lord of the work (works) which had been given to Him to do (iv. 34; v. 36; xvii. 4), and of the consummation of believers in one fellowship (xvii. 23 τετελειωμένοι εἰς ἕν).

The Evangelist himself uses it of the last 'accomplishment' of Scripture (xix. 28); and in his Epistle of love in (with) the believer (ii. 5; iv. 12; 17 μεθ' ἡμῶν), and of the believer in love (iv. 18). Elsewhere it is used of an appointed space of time (Luke ii. 43), of the course of life (Acts xx. 24), of faith crowned by works (James ii. 22), of the consummation of the Christian (Phil. iii. 12). Once it is used by the Lord of Himself: Luke xiii. 32 Behold I cast out devils and perform (ἀποτελῶ) cures to-day and to-morrow, and the third day I am perfected (τελειοῦμαι).

The verbal τελείωσις is once used (Luke i. 45) of the accomplishment of the message brought to the Mother of the Lord.

3. In ecclesiastical writers.

3. In ecclesiastical writers the baptized believer, admitted to the full privileges of the Christian life, was spoken of as τέλειος (comp. Clem. Al. Strom. vi. § 60). Hence τελειοῦν (and perficere) was used of the administration of Baptism (Athan. c. Ar. i. 34 οὕτω γὰρ τελειούμενοι καὶ ἡμεῖς...) and τελείωσις of the Baptism itself (Athan. c. Ar. ii. 42 εἰ γὰρ εἰς τὸ ὄνομα πατρὸς καὶ υἱοῦ δίδοται ἡ τελείωσις, c. 41 ἐν τῇ τελειώσει τοῦ βαπτίσματος. Comp. Cæsar. Dial. i. 12 ἐν τῇ σφραγῖδι τῆς μυστικῆς τελειότητος). So too the person who administered the Sacrament was called τελειωτής (Greg. Naz. Orat. xl. In bapt. § 44 ἀναστῶμεν ἐπὶ τὸ βάπτισμα· σφύζει τὸ πνεῦμα, πρόθυμος ὁ τελειωτής· τὸ δῶρον ἕτοιμον, comp. § 18). This usage is very well illustrated by a passage in writing falsely attributed to Athanasius: εἰ μή εἰσι τέλειοι χριστιανοὶ οἱ κατηχούμενοι πρὶν ἢ βαπτισθῶσι, βαπτισθέντες δὲ τελειοῦνται, τὸ βάπτισμα ἄρα μεῖζόν ἐστι τῆς προσκυνήσεως ὃ τὴν τελειότητα παρέχει (Ps.-Ath. Dial. i. c. Maced. 6). Comp. Clem. Al. Pæd. i. 6.

In a more general sense τελειοῦσθαι and τελείωσις were used of the death of the Christian, and specially of the death by martyrdom, in which the effort of life was completed (Euseb. H. E. iii. 35; vii. 15 ἀπαχθεὶς τὴν ἐπὶ θανάτῳ τελειοῦται, and Heinichen's note).

/The word τέλειος came naturally to be used of themselves by those who claimed to possess the highest knowledge of the truth, as initiated into its mysteries (Iren. i. 6 τελείους ἑαυτοὺς ἀναγορεύουσι, comp. c. 3 οἱ τελειότατοι. Valent. *ap.* Epiph. *Hær.* xxxi., § 5); and at the same time the associations of τελεῖσθαι ('to be initiated') were transferred to τέλειος and τελειοῦσθαι (comp. Dion. Ar. *de cœl. hier.* vi. § 3; Method. *de Sim. et Anna* 5 [ὁ θεὸς] ὁ τῶν τελουμένων τελειωτής; and 2 Cor. xii. 9 *v. l.*).

Throughout these various applications of the word one general thought is preserved. He who is τέλειος has reached the end which is in each case set before him, maturity of growth, complete development of powers, full enjoyment of privileges, perfect possession of knowledge.

The sense of the word in the Epistle to the Hebrews exactly conforms to this usage. The τέλειος—the matured Christian—is contrasted with the νήπιος the undeveloped babe (v. 14): the provisional and transitory tabernacle with that which was 'more perfect' (ix. 11). The ripe perfectness (τελειότης) of Christian knowledge is set against the first elementary teaching of the Gospel (vi. 1). Christ, as He leads faith, so to speak, to the conflict, carries it to its absolute triumph (xii. 2 τελειωτής). The aim of a religious system is τελείωσις (vii. 11), to bring men to their true end, when all the fulness of humanity in power and development is brought into fellowship with God. And in this sense God was pleased to 'make' the Incarnate Son 'perfect through suffering' (ii. 10; v. 9; vii. 28), and the Son, by His one offering, to 'make perfect them that are sanctified' (x. 14; xi. 40; xii. 23).

Additional Note on ii. 10.   The τελείωσις of Christ.

In connexion with the Person and Work of Christ the idea of τελείωσις finds three distinct applications.

(*a*) He is Himself 'made perfect': ii. 10 ff.; v. 7 ff.; vii. 28.

(*b*) He 'perfects' others through fellowship with Himself: x. 14; xi. 39 f.; xii. 23.

(*c*) His 'perfection through suffering' is the ground of absolute sympathy with men in their weakness, and failure, and efforts: ii. 17 f.; iv. 15; xii. 2.

A general view of the distinctive thoughts in these passages will illustrate the breadth and fulness of the teaching of the Epistle. The notes on the several passages will suggest in detail thoughts for further study.

(*a*) *The personal consummation of Christ in His humanity:* ii. 10 ff.; v. 7 ff.; vii. 28.

(*a*) Christ is 'made perfect.'

These three passages present the fact under three different aspects.

(*a*) The first passage (ii. 10 ff.) declares the general method by which the consummation was reached in regard to the divine counsel: God perfected His Incarnate Son through sufferings; and Man is able to recognise the fitness (ἔπρεπεν) of this method from the consideration of his own position and needs (πολλοὺς υἱοὺς εἰς δόξαν ἀγαγόντα).

(β) In the second passage (v. 7 ff.) we are allowed to see the action of the divine discipline upon the Son of man during His earthly life, in its course and in its end (ἔμαθεν ἀφ᾽ ὧν ἔπαθεν τὴν ὑπακοήν). He realised to the uttermost the absolute dependence of humanity upon God in the fulness of personal communion with Him, even through the last issues of sin in death.

(γ) In the third passage (vii. 28) there is a revelation of the abiding work of the Son for men as their eternal High Priest (υἱὸν εἰς τὸν αἰῶνα τετελειωμένον).

In studying this τελείωσις of Christ, account must be taken both (1) of His life as man (John viii. 40; 1 Tim. ii. 5 (ἄνθρωπος); Acts ii. 22; xvii. 31 ἀνήρ), so far as He fulfilled in a true human life the destiny of man personally; and (2) of His life as the Son of man, so far as He fulfilled in His life, as Head of the race, the destiny of humanity by redemption and consummation. The two lives indeed are only separable in thought, but the effort to give clearness to them reveals a little more of the meaning of the Gospel.

And yet again: these three passages are of great importance as emphasising the reality of the Lord's human life from step to step. It is at each moment perfect with the ideal of human perfection according to the circumstances.

It is unscriptural, though the practice is supported by strong patristic authority, to regard the Lord during His historic life as acting now by His human and now by His Divine Nature only. The two Natures were inseparably combined in the unity of His Person. In all things He acts Personally; and, as far as it is revealed to us, His greatest works during His earthly life are wrought by the help of the Father through the energy of a humanity enabled to do all things in fellowship with God (comp. John xi. 41 f.).

(b) Christ makes His people perfect.

(b) From the revelation of the τελείωσις of the Lord we pass to the second group of passages (x. 14; xi. 39 f.; xii. 23) in which men are shewn to receive from Him the virtue of that perfection which He has reached. Those who are 'in Christ,' according to the phrase of St Paul (which is not found in this Epistle; yet see x. 10, 19), share the privileges of their Head. These three passages also present the truth which they express in different lights.

(a) The first passage (x. 14) gives the one sufficient and abiding ground of man's attainment to perfection in the fact of Christ's work. Man has simply to take to himself what Christ has already done for him (τετελείωκεν εἰς τὸ διηνεκές).

(β) The second passage (xi. 39 f.) enables us to understand the unexpected slowness of the fulfilment of our hopes. There is a great counsel of Providence which we can trust (κρεῖττόν τι προβλεψαμένου).

(γ) And in the third passage a glimpse is opened of the righteous who have obtained the abiding possession of that which Christ has won (τετελειωμένων).

(c) Christ's perfection through suffering the pledge of His perfect sympathy.

(c) In the third group of passages which deal with Christ's 'perfection' in His humanity (ii. 17 f.; iv. 15; xii. 2) we are led to observe how His 'perfection through sufferings' becomes the ground and pledge of His unfailing sympathy with men. The experience of His earthly life (as we speak) remains in His glory.

Thus we see in succession (a) that Christ's assumption of true and perfect humanity (κατὰ πάντα τοῖς ἀδελφοῖς ὁμοιωθῆναι) becomes the spring of His High-priestly work in making propitiation for sins and rendering help to men answering to the universality (ἐν ᾧ πέπονθεν) of His own suffering and temptation (ii. 17 f.).

And next (β) that the assurance of sympathy based on the fellowship of Nature and experience (πεπειρασμένον κατὰ πάντα καθ' ὁμοιότητα) brings confidence to men in their approach to God for pardon and strength (iv. 14—16).

And yet again (γ) that Christ Himself in the fulfilment of His work proved from first to last (ἀρχηγὸν καὶ τελειωτήν) the power of that faith by which we also walk (xii. 1 f.).

No one can regard even summarily these nine passages without feeling their far-reaching significance. And it is of especial importance to dwell on the view which is given to us in the Epistle of the τελείωσις of Christ from its direct practical importance.

1. It gives a vivid and natural distinctness to our historic conception of the Lord's life on earth.

2. It enables us to apprehend, according to our power, the complete harmony of the Divine and Human Natures in One Person, each finding fulfilment, as we speak, according to its proper law in the fulness of One Life.

3. It reveals the completeness of the work of the Incarnation which brings to each human power and each part of human life its true perfection.

4. It brings the universal truth home to each man individually in his little life, a fragment of human life, and presents to us at each moment the necessity of effort, and assures us of corresponding help.

5. It teaches us to see the perfect correspondence between the completeness of the divine work (χάριτί ἐστε σεσωσμένοι), and the progressive realisation of it by man (δι' οὗ καὶ σώζεσθε).

Additional Note on ii. 13. Quotations from the Old Testament in cc. i., ii.

The passages of the O.T. which are quoted in the first two chapters of the Epistle offer a representative study of the interpretation of Scripture. The main principles which they suggest will appear from the simple recital of the points which they are used to illustrate.

1. *The Divine Son.*

   (a) His work for man. Ps. ii. 7 (i. 5 ; comp. v. 5).

    My Son art Thou;

    I have to-day begotten Thee.

The words are quoted also Acts xiii. 33 (of the Resurrection). Compare also the various readings of D in Luke iii. 22 ; and the reading of the Ebionite Gospel in Matt. iii. 17.

1. The Divine Son. (a) His work for man.

For the unique force of the address see note on the passage.

The thought implied is that the universal dominion of the Divine King is founded on His Divine Nature. The outward conquests of Israel can therefore only be earnests and types of something immeasurably higher.

If account be taken of the second reference to the passage (v. 5), it will appear that the foundation and assurance of Christ's work for men, His sovereignty and His priesthood, are laid in His divine character declared by the Father.

(β) His work for God.

(β) His work for God. 2 Sam. vii. 14 (i. 5).

I will be to Him a Father ;
And He shall be to Me a Son.

Comp. 2 Cor. vi. 18; Apoc. xxi. 7.

The words are taken from the answer of Nathan to David's desire to build a Temple for the Lord. The whole passage ('iniquity') can only refer to an earthly king ; yet no earthly king could satisfy the hope which the promise created. The kingdom was destroyed, and the vision of a new stock of Jesse was opened (Is. xi. 1; Jer. xxiii. 5; Zech. vi. 11 f.; Luke i. 32 f.). The Temple was destroyed and the vision of a new Temple was opened, a Temple raised by the Resurrection (John ii. 19).

In both these passages it will be observed that the Lord is the speaker, the God of the Covenant, the God of Revelation (Ps. ii. 7 *The Lord hath said...* ; 2 Sam. vii. 4 *the word of the Lord came to Nathan...* ; *v.* 8 *thus saith the Lord...*).

(γ) His final conquest.

(γ) His final conquest.

Deut. xxxii. 43 (LXX.) (i. 6).

Comp. Ps. xcvii. (xcvi.) 7 ; Rom. xv. 10.

The sovereignty of the Son is at last recognised by all created beings.

2. The Davidic King.

2. *The Davidic King.*

Ps. xlv. 6 f. (i. 8 f.).

The Psalm is the Marriage Song of the Sovereign of the theocratic kingdom. The King, the royal Bride, the children, offer a living picture of the permanence of the Divine Son with His Church, in contrast with the transitory ministry of Angels.

3. The Creator.

3. *The Creator ; the manifestation of God* (the Lord).

Ps. cii. 25 ff. (i. 10 ff.).

The Psalm is an appeal of an exile. The idea of the God of Israel is enlarged. He who enters into fellowship with man, takes man to Himself. The Covenant leads up to the Incarnation. The Creator is the Saviour. See Additional Note c. iii. 7.

4. The King-Priest.

4. *The King-Priest.*

Ps. cx. 1 (i. 13 ; comp. x. 12 f.).

Sit Thou at My right hand,
Till I make Thine enemies the footstool of Thy feet.

The Psalm, which probably describes the bringing of the Ark to Jerusalem by David, the new Melchizedek, king at once and fulfiller of priestly offices, describes the Divine King under three aspects as King (1—3), Priest (4), Conqueror (5—7). The opening words of the Psalm necessarily called up the whole portraiture; and one part of it (Ps. cx. 4) is afterwards dwelt upon at length (v. 6, 10; vi. 20; vii. 11 ff.).

5. *The Son of man,* as true man fulfilling the destiny of man, and the destiny of fallen man through suffering ('the servant of the Lord').

5. The Son of man.

(*a*) Man's destiny.

(*a*) Man's Destiny.

Ps. viii. 5 ff. (ii. 6 ff.).

Comp. Matt. xxi. 16; 1 Cor. xv. 27.

The Psalm, which was never reckoned as Messianic, presents the ideal of man (Gen. i. 27—30), a destiny unfulfilled and unrepealed.

(β). The suffering King.

(β) The suffering King.

Ps. xxii. 22 (ii. 11 f.).

The Psalm, which is frequently quoted in the Gospels to illustrate the desertion, the mockery, the spoiling of Christ, gives the description of the progress of the innocent, suffering King, who identifies himself with his people, to the throne. After uttermost trials sorrow is turned into joy, and the deliverance of the sufferer is the ground of national joy. Comp. Prof. Cheyne *On the Christian element in Isaiah,* § 2.

(γ) The representative prophet.

(γ) The representative prophet.

Is. viii. 17 f. (ii. 13).

The prophecy belongs to a crisis in the national history. In a period of the deepest distress the prophet teaches in his own person two lessons. He declares unshaken faith in God in the midst of judgments. He shews in himself and his children the remnant which shall preserve the chosen people.

To these passages one other must be added, Ps. xl. 6 ff. (x. 5 ff.), in order to complete the portraiture of the Christ. By perfect obedience the Son of man fulfils for men the will of God.

Several reflections at once offer themselves to the student who considers these quotations as a whole. (1) It is assumed that a divine counsel was wrought out in the course of the life of Israel. We are allowed to see in 'the people of God' signs of the purpose of God for humanity. The whole history is prophetic. It is not enough to recognise that the O. T. contains prophecies: the O. T. is one vast prophecy.

General conclusions.

(2) The application of prophetic words in each case has regard to the ideal indicated by them, and is not limited by the historical fact with which they are connected. But the history is not set aside. The history forces the reader to look beyond.

(3) The passages are not merely isolated phrases. They represent ruling ideas. They answer to broad conceptions of the methods of the divine discipline for the nation, the King, the prophet, man.

(4) The words had a perfect meaning when they were first used. This meaning is at once the germ and the vehicle of the later and fuller meaning. As we determine the relations, intellectual, social, spiritual, between the time of the prophecy and our own time, we have the key to its present interpretation. In Christ we have the ideal fulfilment.

So it is that when we look at the succession of passages, just as they stand, we can see how they connect the Gospel with the central teaching of the O. T. The theocratic Sovereign addressed as 'Son' failed to subdue

Summary review of the passages.

the nations and rear an eternal Temple, but none the less he gave definite form to a faith which still in one sense wants its satisfaction. The Marriage Song of the Jewish monarch laid open thoughts which could only be realised in the relation of the Divine King to His Church. The confidence with which the exile looked for the deliverance of Zion by the personal intervention of Jehovah, who had entered into covenant with man, led believers to see the Saviour in the Creator. The promise of the Session of Him who is King and Priest and Conqueror at the right hand of God, is still sufficient to bring strength to all who are charged to gather the fruits of the victory of the Son.

In this way the Majesty of the Christ, the Son of God, can be read in the O. T.; and no less the Christian can perceive there the sufferings of ' Jesus,' the Son of man, who won His promised dominion for man through death. The path of sorrow which He hallowed had been marked in old time by David, who proclaimed to his 'brethren' the 'Name' of his Deliverer, when he saw in the retrospect of the vicissitudes of his own life that which transcended them; and by Isaiah, who at the crisis of trial identified his 'children'—types of a spiritual remnant—with himself in absolute trust on God.

On the one side we see how the majestic description of the Mediator of the New Covenant given in the opening verses of the Epistle, is justified by a series of passages in which He is pointed to in the records of the Old Covenant as Son and Lord and Creator and Sharer of the throne of God; and on the other side even we can discern, as we look back, how it was 'becoming' that He should fulfil the destiny of fallen men by taking to Himself, like King and Prophet, the sorrows of those whom He relieved. The greatest words of God come, as we speak, naturally and intelligibly through the occasions of life. In the history of Israel, of the Christ, and of the Church, disappointment is made the door of hope, and suffering is the condition of glory.

Additional Note to ii. 17.   *Passages on the High-priesthood of Christ.*

The student will find it a most instructive inquiry to trace the development of the thought of Christ's High-priesthood, which is the ruling thought of the Epistle, through the successive passages in which the writer specially deals with it.

The thought is indicated in the opening verses. The crowning trait of the Son is that, *when He had made purification of sins*, He *sat down on the right hand of the Majesty on high* (i. 3). So the priestly and royal works of Christ are placed together in the closest connexion.

The remaining passages prepare for, expound, and apply the doctrine.

(1) *Preparatory.*

ii. 17, 18.   The Incarnation the foundation of Christ's High-priesthood.

iii. 1, 2.   The subject such as to require careful consideration.

iv. 14—16. Recapitulation of points already marked as a transition to the detailed treatment of the truth. Christ is a High-priest who has fulfilled the conditions of His office, who can feel with men, and who is alike able and ready to succour them.

(2) *The characteristics of Christ's High-priesthood.*

v. 1—10. The characteristics of the Levitical High-priesthood realised by Christ.

vi. 20; vii. 14—19. The priesthood of Christ after the order of Melchizedek.

vii. 26—28. The characteristics of Christ as absolute and eternal High-priest.

(3) *The work of Christ as High-priest.*

viii. 1—6. The scene of Christ's work a heavenly and not an earthly sanctuary.

ix. 11—28. Christ's atoning work contrasted with that of the Levitical High-priest on the Day of Atonement.

x. 1—18. The abiding efficacy of Christ's One Sacrifice.

(4) *Application of the fruits of Christ's High-priesthood to believers.*

x. 19—25. Personal use.

xiii. 10—16. Privileges and duties of the Christian Society.

These passages should be studied in their broad features, especially in regard to the new traits which they successively introduce. The following out of the inquiry is more than an exercise in Biblical Theology. Nothing conveys a more vivid impression of the power of the Apostolic writings than to watch the unfolding of a special idea in the course of an Epistle without any trace of conscious design on the part of the writer, as of a single part in some great harmony.

III. ^{1} Ὅθεν, ἀδελφοὶ ἅγιοι, κλήσεως ἐπουρανίου

II. Moses, Joshua, Jesus, the founders of the Old Economy and of the New (cc. iii., iv.).

The writer of the Epistle after stating the main thought of Christ's High-priesthood, which contained the answer to the chief difficulties of the Hebrews, pauses for a while before developing it in detail (cc. v.—vii.), in order to establish the superiority of the New Dispensation over the Old from another point of view. He has already shewn that Christ (the Son) is superior to the angels, the spiritual agents in the giving of the Law; he now goes on to shew that He is superior to the Human Lawgiver.

In doing this he goes back to the phrase which he had used in ii. 5. The conceptio ἱκουμένη ἡ μέλλουσα leads naturally to a comparison of those who were appointed to found on earth the Jewish Theocracy and the new Kingdom of God.

This comparison is an essential part of the argument; for though the superiority of Christ to Moses might have seemed to be necessarily implied in the superiority of Christ to angels, yet the position of Moses in regard to the actual Jewish system made it necessary, in view of the difficulties of Hebrew Christians, to develop the truth independently.

And further the exact comparison is not between Moses and *Christ*, but between Moses and *Jesus*. Moses occupied a position which no other man occupied (Num. xii. 6 ff.). He was charged to found a Theocracy, a Kingdom of God. In this respect it became necessary to regard him side by side with Christ in His humanity, with the Son, who was Son of man no less than the Son of God. In the Apocalypse the victorious believers 'sing the song of Moses and *the Lamb*' (Apoc. xv. 3). (Compare generally John v. 45 ff.)

And yet again the work of Joshua, the actual issue of the Law, cast an important light upon the work of Moses of which the Christian was bound to take account.

Thus the section falls into three parts.

i.   *Moses and Jesus: the servant and the Son* (iii. 1—6).
ii.   *The promise and the people under the Old and the New Dispensations* (iii. 7—iv. 13).
iii. *Transition to the doctrine of the High-priesthood, resuming* ii. 17 f. (iv. 14—16).

i.   *Moses and Jesus: the servant and the Son* (1—6).

The paragraph begins with an assumption of the dignity of the Christian calling, and of 'Jesus' through whom it comes (*vv.* 1, 2); and then the writer establishes the superiority of Christ by two considerations:

(1) Moses represents a 'house,' an economy: Christ represents 'the framer of the house,' God Himself (*vv.* 3, 4).

(2) Moses held the position of a servant, witnessing to the future: Christ holds the position of a Son, and the blessings which He brings are realised now (*vv.* 5, 6).

Perhaps we may see, as has been suggested, in the form in which the truth is presented—the Father, the faithful servant, the Son—some remembrance of Abraham, and Eliezer, and Isaac.

^{1} *Wherefore, holy brethren, partakers of a heavenly calling, consider the Apostle and High-priest of our confession, even Jesus,* ^{2} *faithful to Him that appointed Him, as also was Moses in all His* (God's) *house.* ^{3} *For He hath been counted worthy of more glory than Moses, by so much as He hath more glory than the house who established it.* ^{4} *For every house is established by some one; but He that established all*

μέτοχοι, κατανοήσατε τὸν ἀπόστολον καὶ ἀρχιερέα τῆς

1 κατανοήσατε: κατανοήσετε D₂*.

things is God. ⁵ *And while Moses was faithful in all His* (God's) *house as a servant, for a testimony of the things which should be spoken,* ⁶ *Christ is faithful as Son over His* (God's) *house; whose house are we, if we hold fast our boldness and the boast of our hope firm unto the end.*

vv. 1, 2. The thought of the majesty and sympathy of Christ, the Son, and the glorified Son of man, glorified through sufferings, which bring Him near to fallen man as Redeemer and High-priest, imposes upon Christians the duty of considering His Person heedfully, in His humanity as well as in His divinity.

1. ὅθεν] *Wherefore,* because Christ has taken our nature to Himself, and knows our needs and is able to satisfy them.

ἀδελφοὶ ἅγιοι] *holy brethren.* The phrase occurs only here, and perhaps in 1 Thess. v. 27. It follows naturally from the view of Christ's office which has just been given. This reveals the destiny of believers.

The epithet ἅγιοι is social and not personal, marking the ideal character not necessarily realised individually. (Compare John xiii. 10.)

In this sense St Paul speaks of Christians generally as ἅγιοι (*e.g.* Eph. ii. 19). Compare 1 Pet. ii. 5 ἱεράτευμα ἅγιον, *id.* ii. 9 ἔθνος ἅγιον.

Here the epithet characterises the nature of the fellowship of Christians which is further defined in the following clause.

The title ἀδελφοί occurs again in the Epistle *v.* 12; x. 19; xiii. 22. The sense of brotherhood springs from the common relation to Christ, and the use of the title here first may have been suggested by ii. 11 ff., to which however there is no direct reference. Contrast iv. 1. Filii unius cælestis Patris et unius Ecclesiæ matris (Herv.).

Primasius says: Fratres eos vocat tam carne quam spiritu, qui ex eodem genere erant, eandemque fidem habebant. This is true in itself, but perhaps does not lie in the writer's thoughts.

κλήσεως ἐπουρανίου] Comp. Phil. iii. 14 τῆς ἄνω κλήσεως.

The Christian's 'calling' is heavenly not simply in the sense that it is addressed to man from God in heaven, though this is true (comp. c. xii. 25), but as being a calling to a life fulfilled in heaven, in the spiritual realm. The voice from heaven to Moses was an earthly calling, a calling to the fulfilment of an earthly life.

Theophylact's words are too narrow when he says, treating heaven as a place not a state: ἐκεῖ ἐκλήθημεν, μηδὲν ἐνταῦθα ζητῶμεν. ἐκεῖ ὁ μισθός, ἐκεῖ ἡ ἀνταπόδοσις.

The word κλῆσις is found elsewhere in the N. T. only in St Paul and 2 Pet. i. 10. Comp. Clem. 1 *Cor.* vii; xlvi.

ἐπουρανίου] c. vi. 4; viii. 5; ix. 23; xi. 16; xii. 22. Comp. Eph. i. 3; Phil. ii. 10; John iii. 12 note; and, for the LXX., Ps. lxvii. 15; (Dan. iv. 23); 2 Macc. iii. 39.

μέτοχοι] Vulg. *participes.* The word occurs again *v.* 14 (τοῦ Χριστοῦ); vi. 4 (πνεύματος ἁγίου); xii. 8 (παιδείας) (elsewhere in N. T. Luke v. 7); Clem. 1 *Cor.* xxxiv. Comp. ii. 14 μετέσχεν (note).

As distinguished from κοινωνός, which suggests the idea of personal fellowship (comp. c. x. 33 note), μέτοχος describes participation in some common blessing or privilege, or the like. The bond of union lies in that which is shared and not in the persons themselves.

κατανοήσατε...πιστὸν ὄντα] O. L. intuimini...fidelem esse (fidelem existentem). Vulg. considerate......qui fidelis est.

όμολογίας ήμῶν ᾿Ιησοῦν, ²πιϲτὸν ὄντα τῷ ποιήσαντι αὐτὸν

᾿Ιησοῦν ΝΑΒC*D₂*M₂ vg me the: ᾿Ι. Χριστόν syrr: Χριστὸν ᾿Ι. ϛ.

The sense is not simply: 'Regard Jesus...who was...'; but 'Regard Jesus...as being....' Attention is fixed upon the perfect fidelity with which He fulfilled His work, and that essentially, both now and always (ὄντα not γενόμενον). Comp. i. 3 ὤν.

For the verb κατανοεῖν, which expresses attention and continuous observation and regard, see c. x. 24; James i. 23 f.; Luke xii. 24, 27. Philo, Leg. Alleg. iii. § 32 διὰ τῶν ἔργων τὸν τεχνίτην κατανοοῦντες. 1 Clem. xxxvii. 2.

The use of the second person (κατανοήσατε) is rare in the Epistle in such a connexion (comp. vii. 4 θεωρεῖτε). The writer generally identifies himself with those to whom he gives counsel (iv. 1, 11, 14, 16; vi. 1; x. 22 ff.: xii. 28; xiii. 13, 15).

τὸν ἀπόστολον καὶ ἀρχιερέα] 'Him who occupies the double position of legislator—envoy from God—and Priest.' In Christ the functions of Moses and Aaron are combined, each in an infinitely loftier form. The compound description (ὁ ἀπόστ. καὶ ἀρχ.) gathers up what has been already established as to Christ as the last revealer of God's will and the fulfiller of man's destiny. Comp. c. viii. 6 note.

Here the double office of Christ underlies the description of Christians which has been given already. ᾿Απόστολος gives the authority of the κλῆσις ἐπουράνιος and ἀρχιερεύς the source of the title ἅγιοι.

Bengel says admirably of Christ: qui Dei causam apud nos agit, causam nostram apud Deum agit.

ἀπόστολον] Comp. John xvii. 3 &c. Theodoret, referring to Gal. iv. 4, calls attention to the fact that the Father is said to have sent forth the Son γενόμενον ἐκ γυναικός and not γενέσθαι ἐκ γυναικός. He is ἀπόστολος

in respect of His perfect manhood. For the idea of .ἀπόστολος compare Just. M. Dial. 75. Lightfoot Galatians pp. 89 ff.

ἀρχ. τῆς ὁμολογίας ἡμῶν] Old Lat. principem constitutionis nostrae. The apostle and high-priest who belongs to, who is characteristic of our confession. In Christ our 'confession,' the faith which we hold and openly acknowledge, finds its authoritative promulgation and its priestly application.

The sense 'whom we confess' or 'who is the subject and sum of our confession' falls short of the meaning.

ὁμολ.] c. iv. 14; x. 23; 1 Tim. vi. 12 f. Comp. 2 Cor. ix. 13 (Rom. x. 9). Comp. Philo de Somn. i. § 38 (i.654 M.) ὁ μέγας ἀρχιερεὺς [τῆς ὁμολογίας] Clem. 1 Cor. xxxvi. ᾿Ιησοῦν Χριστόν, τὸν ἀρχιερέα τῶν προσφορῶν ἡμῶν...id. lxi. διὰ τοῦ ἀρχιερέως καὶ προστάτου τῶν ψυχῶν ἡμῶν ᾿Ιησοῦ Χριστοῦ...id. lxiv. διὰ τοῦ ἀρχιερέως καὶ προστάτου ᾿Ιησοῦ Χριστοῦ.

The word is objective here like πίστις. Theod. ὁμολ. δὲ ἡμῶν τὴν πίστιν ἐκάλεσεν (so Theophlct., Prim., Œcum.).

᾿Ιησοῦν] The human name of the Lord is chosen as presenting in brief the thoughts developed at the end of c. ii. The name Christ appears first in v. 6.

The use of the name is characteristic of the Epistle; see ii. 9 note, and Addit. Note on i. 4. It is of interest to notice that the usage in the Epistle of Barnabas is similar (Rendall on Barn. Ep. ii. 6). The difficulty of the Hebrews and their consolation turned on the Lord's humanity.

2. πιστὸν ὄντα τῷ ποιήσ. αὐ.] faithful in His perfect humanity to Him who appointed Him to His authori-

ὡς καὶ Μωϋσῆς ἐν [ὅλῳ] τῷ οἴκῳ ἀϒτοϒ. ³πλείονος γὰρ οὗτος

2 om. ὅλῳ B me the.   3 οὗτος δόξης ℵABCD₂: δ. οὗτ. ς M₂ vg.

tative and mediatorial office. Comp.
1 Cor. iv. 2.

τῷ ποιήσαντι] Old Lat. *creatori suo*
(*qui creavit eum*). Vulg. *ei qui fecit
illum*. The phrase is capable of two
distinct interpretations. It may be
understood (1) of the Lord's humanity,
or (2) of the Lord's office.

The language of i. 3 absolutely excludes the idea that the writer speaks
of Christ Himself personally as ποίημα,
or κτίσμα.

In favour of the first view it is
urged that the phrase is commonly
used of the Creator in reference to
men: *e.g.* Is. xvii. 7 (τῷ π. αὐτόν); Ps.
xciv. (xcv.) 6; Ps. cxlix. 2.

And the fathers constantly speak
of the Lord's humanity in these terms,
as, for example, Athanasius *de sent.
Dion.* (i. p. 496 Migne), though he
appears to interpret this passage
of the Lord's office as well as of His
humanity: *c. Ar.* ii. 7.

In itself this interpretation is admissible, but such a reference to the
Lord's human nature apart from His
office seems to be out of place.

It is better therefore to adopt
the second interpretation and refer
the 'making' to the Lord's office:
' who invested Him with His office,
who appointed Him, who made Him
Apostle and High Priest' comp.
Acts ii. 36). This sense is perfectly
natural (comp. 1 Sam. xii. 6; Mark
iii. 14).

So Theodoret: τῷ ποιήσαντι αὐτόν,
τουτέστιν ἀπόστολον καὶ ἀρχιερέα·...
ποίησιν δὲ οὐ τὴν δημιουργίαν ἀλλὰ τὴν
χειροτονίαν κέκληκεν. And Chrysostom: οὐδὲν ἐνταῦθα περὶ οὐσίας φησίν,
οὐδὲ περὶ τῆς θεότητος, ἀλλὰ τέως περὶ
ἀξιωμάτων ἀνθρωπίνων.

Primasius refers the word to the
Lord's humanity, being led astray by
the Latin rendering of Rom. i. 3: *qui
fecit illum*, juxta quod alibi dicitur

*qui factus est ei ex semine David
secundum carnem.*

ὡς καὶ Μωϋσῆς] The former discussion has prepared the way for this
comparison of 'Jesus' with the founder
of the Old Theocracy.

ἐν ὅλῳ τῷ οἴκῳ] The point of comparison lies in the fact that Moses
and Christ were both engaged, not as
other divine messengers with a part,
but with the whole of the divine
economy. The prophets dealt severally with this or that aspect of Truth,
the Kings with another region of life,
the Priests with another. But Moses
and Christ dealt with 'the whole
house of God.'

The words, taken from Num. xii. 7,
may go either with 'Moses' or with
' Jesus.' In either case the sense is
the same. Perhaps the reference of
αὐτοῦ to God, and the emphasis which
is naturally laid on the fact that the
office of Christ was as wide as that of
Moses, favours the connexion of the
words with 'Jesus.'

In their original reference to Moses
the words were much discussed by
Rabbinical writers, who found various
deeper meanings in נאמן (*faithful*),
as one who could speak with authority,
to whom the secrets of the Lord were
entrusted. Comp. Philo, *Leg. Alleg.*
iii. § 72 (i. 128 M.); § 81 (i. 132 M.).

For the perfect faithfulness of
Moses in his work see Ex. xl. 16.
The nobility of his service is recognised when that of Christ is set above
it. Comp. 1 Clem. xvii. 5.

τῷ οἴκῳ αὐτοῦ] His *house, i.e.* the
house of God, not of Christ or of
Moses. This is decided in the original
context: *The Lord...said...My servant Moses...is faithful in all Mine
house*, where the Targums give the
sense rightly 'in all My people.' The
familiarity of the words left no room
for misunderstanding to a Jew.

δόξης παρὰ Μωυσῆν ἠξίωται καθ᾽ ὅσον πλείονα τιμὴν

The 'house of God' is the organised society in which He dwells. Israel was the type of redeemed mankind. Compare 1 Tim. iii. 15; 1 Pet. iv. 17; Eph. ii. 21 f.; Hos. viii. 1.

This 'house' in relation to God is essentially one, but in relation to the two agents, Moses and 'Jesus,' through whom it is administered, it is twofold in form.

Compare Philo *de Somn.* i. § 32 (i. 648 M.) ὁ αἰσθητὸς οὑτοσὶ κόσμος οὐδὲν ἄρα ἄλλο ἐστὶν ἢ οἶκος θεοῦ, μιᾶς τῶν τοῦ ὄντως θεοῦ δυνάμεων καθ᾽ ἣν ἀγαθὸς ἦν (the reference is to Gen. xxviii. 17).

3, 4. The general affirmation of the dignity of Christ which has been included in the two preceding verses is enforced by a view of His superiority over Moses. Moses was, so to speak, lost in the economy which was given through him: Christ was the author of that which He instituted. ῞Οση, φησί, ποιήματος πρὸς ποιητὴν διαφορὰ τοσαύτη Μωϋσέως πρὸς τὸν Χριστόν (Theodt.).

πλείονος γάρ...] The duty of careful regard is pressed by the consideration of Christ's preeminence : *Regard... Jesus...for He hath been counted worthy of more glory than Moses...* The fidelity of Christ in dealing with the whole house of God was as complete as that of the Lawgiver who was raised above all other men, and His authority was greater.

For the use of πλείων compare c. xi. 4 (not in St Paul in this usage).

πλείονος...καθ᾽ ὅσον...] *He hath been counted worthy of more...by so much as...* Old Lat. *ampliorem gloriam ...consecutus est, quanto majorem honorem habet domûs qui præparavit ipsam...* Vulg. *amplioris gloriæ... dignus est habitus, quanto ampliorem h. h. d. qui fabricavit illam.*

οὗτος] He, who is the one present object of our thoughts. Compare c. x. 12 (vii. 1, 4). The usage is very

common in St John (*e.g.* i. 2; 1 John v. 6).

ἠξίωται] The thought is of the abiding glory of Christ, and not of the historic fact of His exaltation (ἠξιώθη). Comp. ii. 9 note. It is implied that that which was merited was also given. For ἀξιοῦσθαι see c. x. 29; 1 Tim. v. 17.

δόξης...τιμήν] *glory...honour.* The term is changed in the second case to cover more naturally the application to 'the house.' 'Glory' is internal, as light flashed forth from an object : 'honour' is external, as light shed upon it. Comp. ii. 7, 9; and for δόξα, 2 Cor. iii. 7 ff.

καθ᾽ ὅσον...] The remark is quite general. Here the force of the argument lies in the fact that Moses is identified with the system which was entrusted to him. He was himself a part of it. He did not originate it. He received it and administered it with absolute loyalty. But its author was God. And Christ is the Son of God. Hence the relation of Moses to Christ is that of a system to its author. The argument is indicated but not worked out in the next verse. Καὶ αὐτός, φησί, τῆς οἰκίας ἦν. καὶ οὐκ εἶπεν οὗτος μὲν γὰρ δοῦλος ἐκεῖνος δὲ δεσπότης, ἀλλὰ τοῦτο λανθανόντως ἐνέφηνεν (Chrys.).

Some have referred ὁ κατασκευάσας to Christ, as the real Founder of that Kingdom of God of which the Jewish economy was a shadow. This thought is completely in harmony with the argument of the Epistle, but it is not directly expressed elsewhere. And on this interpretation *v.* 4 must be taken as a parenthetical remark designed to guard the sovereign authorship of God in all things and His part in the ordering of the Law, a view which appears to be unsatisfactory. The compressed suggestiveness of the argument is not unlike John viii. 31— 36.

ἔχει τοῦ οἴκου ὁ κατασκευάσας αὐτόν· ⁴πᾶς γὰρ οἶκος
κατασκευάζεται ὑπό τινος, ὁ δὲ πάντα κατασκευάσας
θεός. ⁵καὶ Μωϋσῆς μὲν πιστὸς ἐν ὅλῳ τῷ οἴκῳ αὐτοῦ ὡς θεράπων
εἰς μαρτύριον τῶν λαληθησομένων, ⁶Χριστὸς δὲ ὡς υἱὸς

4 πάντα ℵABC*D₂*M₂: +τὰ π. ς.

ὁ κατασκευάσας] he that established,
Vulg. qui fabricavit. The word
(κατασκευάζειν) expresses more than
the mere construction of the house.
It includes the supply of all necessary
furniture and equipment. Comp. c.
ix. 2, 6; xi. 7; Num. xxi. 27.

4. πᾶς γάρ...] The general principle,
that the framer is superior to the
thing framed, admits of application in
the case of the Law. Even here we
must not rest on the system; for
every system, and this highest of all,
has its framer; and finally every
system is carried up to God as its
Author, and 'Jesus' our 'Apostle and
High-priest' is the Son of God.

Nothing is said here expressly of
the unique relation in which Christ,
as the Son, stands to God. That is
assumed, as having been already laid
down in the opening of the Epistle.

πάντα] all things taken severally,
and not the sum of all things (τὰ
πάντα). Comp. ii. 10.

θεός] For the difference of θεός and
ὁ θεός see Additional Note on 1 John
iv. 12. The anarthrous form (θεός)
wherever it is used in the Epistle
suggests the thought of the character
of God as God: i. 6; ii. 9 (note);
v. 12 (θεὸς ζῶν note); vi. 1, 5, 18; viii.
10; xi. 3, 16; xii. 23. The force of
it will be felt by comparing vi. 1, 5
with vi. 3; vi. 17 with vi. 18; xi. 3
with xi. 4.

5, 6. The superiority of Christ over
Moses is shewn also by another argument. Moses and Christ are not only
distinguished as standing to one another in the relation of an economy to
its author; but also in regard to the
respective economies which they administered. The position of Moses was,

by a necessary consequence, that of a
servant acting in a certain sphere, the
position of Christ that of a Son over
a certain sphere. And yet again, the
Mosaic order pointed forward as preparatory to that which should come
after: the Christian order includes
the blessings which it proclaims.

5. ἐν ὅλῳ τῷ οἴκῳ αὐτοῦ] in all
God's house, as before. The phrase
which marks the inferiority of Moses
to Christ marks at the same time
his superiority to all the other prophets.

ὡς θεράπων] Vulg. tanquam famulus
(O. L. servus). Here only in N. T.
Num. xii. 7 LXX. (עֶבֶד); Jos. i. 2;
viii. 31, 33; Wisd. x. 16. Comp. Clem.
1 Cor. c. 43 (see also cc. 17, 51) ὁ
μακάριος πιστὸς θεράπων ἐν ὅλῳ τῷ οἴκῳ
Μωνσῆς. Θεράπων suggests a personal
service freely rendered. Δοῦλος expresses a permanent social condition.
The same person may be described
by both words under different aspects.
Comp. Ps. cv. (civ.) 26; Apoc. xv. 3
(δοῦλος of Moses).

εἰς μαρτ. τῶν λαληθησομένων] for a
testimony of the things which should
be spoken by God through the prophets
and finally through Christ (i. 1). Old
Lat. in testimonio loquendorum.
Vulg. in testimonium eorum quæ
dicenda erant. The position of Moses
and of the Mosaic Dispensation was
provisional. Moses not only witnessed
to the truths which his legislation
plainly declared, but also to the truths
which were to be made plain afterwards. The O. T. in all its parts
pointed forward to a spiritual antitype.
Comp. Deut. xviii. 15 ff.

The rendering, 'to be spoken by
him' (Pesh.) or 'by the prophets of

ἐπὶ τὸν οἶκον ᴀᵧτοᵧ· οὗ οἶκός ἐσμεν ἡμεῖς, ἐὰν τὴν παρρησίαν καὶ τὸ καύχημα τῆς ἐλπίδος [μέχρι τέλους βεβαίαν]

6 οὗ οἶκος ℵABC: ὃς οἶκος D₂*M₂ vg.
ℵᶜAC (not disturbed in v. 14; vi. 3).

ἐάν (ℵ*) BD₂*M₂ vg: ἐάνπερ ϛ
om. μέχρι τ. βεβ. B (no omission in v. 14).

the O. T.' wholly obscures the contrast of the Old and New.
On the rarity of the future participle in the N. T. see Winer-Moulton,
p. 428.

6. Χριστὸς δέ] The name is changed.
The human title (v. 1 'Ιησοῦν) is replaced by the 'prophetic' title after
the full description of the relation of
the Incarnate Son to Moses. Χριστός
occurs again as a proper name without
the article ix. 11, 24.

ὡς υἱός...] Moses and Christ were
alike 'faithful' (v. 2), but their perfect
fidelity was exercised in different respects. Moses was faithful as a servant in the administration of God's
house : Christ was faithful as a Son as
sovereign over God's house (i. 2).
Comp. c. x. 21; Matt. xxi. 37 ff.
The form of the sentence requires
the extension of πιστὸς to Christ no
less than in v. 2 ; and probably of the
whole phrase πιστὸς ἐν ὅλῳ τῷ οἴκῳ,
so that ὡς υἱὸς ἐπὶ τὸν οἶκον corresponds with ὡς θεράπων εἰς μαρτ. τῶν
λαληθησομένων.

ἐπὶ τὸν οἶκον αὐτοῦ] over His, that is
God's, house. The phrase necessarily
retains one meaning throughout. The
Vulg. not unnaturally gives in domo
sua (Old Lat. ejus), making a contrast
apparently between 'in domo ejus' and
'in domo sua.'
For ἐπί (the force of which is missed
by the Latin version) compare c. x. 21.

οὗ οἶκος...] The writer might have
said, taking up the words of the quotation, οὗ ὁ οἶκος..., but he wishes to
insist on the character (οἶκος) and not
upon the concrete uniqueness (ὁ οἶκος)
of the Christian society. Comp. i. 2
ἐν υἱῷ.
Christians are 'the house of God,'
and no longer the Jews. They have
the fulness of blessing in their grasp

even if it is not yet manifested. On
the reference of the relative to a remote antecedent (θεός v. 4), see c. v. 7
note.

ἐάν...] The spiritual privileges of
Christians depend upon their firm
hold upon that glorious hope which
the Hebrews were on the point of
losing.
τὴν παρρησίαν] O. L. libertatem,
Vulg. fiduciam, c. x. 35, 19 ; iv. 16 ;
Eph. iii. 12.
Παρρησία always conveys the idea
of boldness which finds expression in
word or act.
τὸ καύχημα τῆς ἐλπ.] Old Lat. ex-
sultationem spei, Vulg. gloriam spei.
The Christian hope is one of courageous exultation. Comp. vi. 18 ff.
This exultation is here regarded in
its definite concrete form (καύχημα
boast) and not as finding personal expression (καύχησις boasting). Contrast
2 Cor. i. 14 with 1 Cor. i. 12 ; Rom.
iii. 27 with Rom. iv. 2.
μέχρι τέλ. βεβ.] If this clause is
genuine, and not an interpolation
from v. 14, then τῆς ἐλπίδος must be
taken with παρρ. as well as καύχημα,
the gender of βεβαίαν being determined by the former noun. This
connexion is unlikely, and so far the
internal evidence is against the au-
thenticity of the clause.
μέχρι τέλους] till hope passes into
sight. Comp. c. vi. 11 ; Apoc. ii. 26 ;
Matt. x. 22 ; 1 Cor. i. 8.
The conception of 'hope' occupies
an important place in the Epistle
(vi. 11, 18 ; vii. 19 ; x. 23, note).
'Hope' is related to 'Faith' as the
energetic activity of life is related to
life. Through hope the power of
faith is seen in regard to the future.
Hope gives distinctness to the objects
of faith.

ii. *The promise and the people
under the Old and the New Dispensations* (iii. 7—iv. 13).

The comparison of Christ with
Moses leads naturally to a comparison
of those who respectively received
their teaching. The faithlessness of
the Jews in the desert becomes an
eloquent warning to Christians who
are in danger of unbelief. Even the
date (about 'forty years' from the
Passion) seemed to give additional
force to the parallel. At the same
time the history of the past was fitted
to prepare 'the remnant' of Jewish
believers for the general faithlessness
of their countrymen. The Old Testament is in fact a record of successive
judgments of Israel out of which a
few only were saved.

The argument turns upon the
Psalmist's interpretation of the discipline of the wilderness (Ps. xcv.).
(1) Faith is first laid down as the condition of the enjoyment of the divine
blessing (iii. 7—19); and then (2) it is
shewn that the promise still remains
to be realised by Christians (iv. 1—
13).

(1) *Faith is the condition of the
enjoyment of the divine blessing* (iii.
7—19).

The condition of Faith is established by (a) the experience of the
wilderness (7—11), which (b) is applied generally (12—15), and then
(c) interpreted in detail (16—19).

The construction of the paragraph
is by no means clear. It is uncertain
whether *vv.* 12, 15 are to be connected
with the verses which precede or with
those which follow. On the whole it
seems to be simplest to take βλέπετε
(*v.* 12) as the sequel of διό (*v.* 7), treating *vv.* 7 b—11 as structurally parenthetical; and to join *v.* 15 with *v.* 13,
treating *v.* 14 also as parenthetical.
In any case the whole scope of the
passage remains the same.

(a) The example of the wilderness
(7—11).

The xcvth Psalm serves perfectly to
point the lesson which the Apostle
desires to draw. It contains an invitation to the people of God to worship, and a divine warning against
disobedience.

The Psalm has been used from the
earliest times in the Synagogue service for the Sabbath, and as "the
Invitatory Psalm" at Matins in the
Western Church.

It is assigned in the LXX. (not in
the Hebrew) to David (comp. c. iv. 7),
but this popular attribution cannot be
right.

The words which immediately precede the quotation (8—11) justify the
application to Christians:

*We are the people of His pasture,
and the sheep of His hand* (Lk. xii.
32 ποίμνιον).

The particular interpretation of
this claim gives also the particular
interpretation of 'today.' The voice
of God comes still to those who claim
to be His.

The quotation agrees with the
LXX. text except by the insertion of
διό and by the substitution of ταύτῃ
for ἐκείνῃ and of αὐτοὶ δέ for καὶ αὐτοί
in *v.* 10; [πειρασμοῦ is the true reading of LXX.] and of ἐν δοκιμασίᾳ for
ἐδοκίμασαν (*v.* 9).

7 *Wherefore—even as the Holy
Ghost saith,*
Today, if ye shall hear His voice,
8 *Harden not your hearts, as in
the Provocation,*
*At the day of the Temptation in
the wilderness,*
9 *Where your fathers tempted by
proving,*
And saw my works forty years.
10 *Wherefore I was displeased with
this generation,*
*And said They do always err in
their heart;*
But they did not know my ways,
11 *As I sware in my wrath,*
*They shall not enter into my
rest—*

7. διό] *Wherefore,* because it is
only by holding fast our hope that we

κατάσχωμεν. ⁷Διό—καθὼς λέγει τὸ πνεῦμα τὸ ⌈ἅγιον,
Σήμερον ἐὰν τῆc φωνῆc ἀγτοῆ ἀκογchτε,
⁸μὴ cκληργνητε τὰc καρδίαc γμῶν ὡc ἐν τῷ παραπικραcμῷ,

7...11 ἅγιον,...μου.
8 παραπικρασμῷ: πιρασμῷ ℵ.

can secure the privilege of the divine
society.
The point of transition lies in *v*. 6.
The condition of resolute fidelity suggests the consideration of the consequences of failure.
The construction of the clauses
which follow is uncertain. It may
be complete or incomplete. In the
former case two modes of construction
are possible. The quotation from Ps.
xcv. may be appropriated by the writer
of the Epistle and made part of his own
appeal, so that the words μὴ σκληρύνητε
... become the immediate sequel (διό
...μὴ σκληρ.). Or the whole quotation
may be parenthetical, and διό be
connected immediately with βλέπετε
in *v*. 12.
It is a serious objection to the
former view that the words μὴ σκληρύνητε... in the Psalm are spoken by
God, and it is unlikely that the writer
should so appropriate them, while
long parentheses are not alien from
his style; and further it may be urged
that βλέπετε by itself is abrupt as a
beginning.
If then the construction is complete
we must connect *v*. 7 directly with *v*.
12; but it is possible that the sentence
begun in *v*. 7 is left formally unfinished,
so that *v*. 12 takes up again the main
thought. Such a broken construction
may be compared with x. 16.
κ. λέγει τὸ πν. τὸ ἅγ.] Comp. ix. 8;
x. 15; Acts xxviii. 25. See also Mk.
xiii. 11; Acts xiii. 2; xx. 23; xxi. 11;
1 Clem. xiii. 1; xvi. 2. The same
words are afterwards referred to
'God': iv. 4 f.
It is characteristic of the Epistle
that the words of Holy Scripture are
referred to the Divine Author and

not to the human instrument. The
phrase τὸ πνεῦμα τὸ ἅγιον occurs again
c. ix. 8; x. 15: in clear contrast with
πνεῦμα ἅγιον ii. 4; vi. 4. Comp. c. x.
29 τὸ πνεῦμα τῆς χάριτος. The forms
τὸ πνεῦμα and τὸ ἅγιον πνεῦμα, which
are both used by St Paul, are not
found in this Epistle. It is however
to be noticed that the form τὸ ἅγιον
πνεῦμα is comparatively very rare. It
occurs Matt. xxviii. 19; Lk. xii. 10,
12; Acts i. 8; ii. 38; ix. 31; xiii. 4;
xvi. 6 (not ii. 33; x. 45; xv. 28);
1 Cor. (vi. 19;) xiii. 13.
σήμερον] *Today.* Comp. 2 Cor. vi.
2. The word emphasises the immediate
necessity of vigilance and effort. In
old times the people fell away when
the divine voice was still sounding in
their ears.
ἐὰν τῆς φ.] The original may be
rendered as a wish 'O that today ye
would...'; but the structure of the
Psalm favours the rendering of the
LXX. followed here, though, indeed,
ἐάν is used to represent a wish (Ps.
cxxxix. 19).
τῆς φωνῆς αὐτοῦ] *His voice*, that is,
the voice of God spoken through
Christ as the Apostle applies the
words. The application to Christ of
that which is said of the Lord in the
Old Testament was of the highest
moment for the apprehension of the
doctrine of His Person. Comp. Acts
ii. 21. See Additional Note.
8. μὴ σκληρύνητε...] *Harden not...*
Unbelief, like faith, finds one element
in man's self-determination. The
issue of unbelief is his act. On the
other hand he is subject to adverse
influences. It is alike true that he
'hardens his heart' and also that 'he
is hardened' (*v*. 13). Scripture recog-

κατὰ τὴν ἡμέραν τοῦ πειραςμοῦ ἐν τῇ ἐρήμῳ,
9οῦ ἐπείραςαν οἱ πατέρες ὑμῶν ἐν δοκιμαςίᾳ
καὶ εἶδον τὰ ἔργα μου τεσσεράκοντα ἔτη·
10διὸ προςώχθιςα τῇ γενεᾷ ταύτῃ

9 ὅπου D₂*.　　ἐπείρασαν (א*)ABCD₂*: ἐπ. + με ς M₂ vg syrr me (so LXX.).
ὑμῶν: ἡμῶν A.　ἐν δοκιμασίᾳ א*(A)BCD₂*M₂ me: ἐδοκίμασάν με ς (vg) (syrr) (so LXX.).
10 ταύτῃ אABD₂*M₂ vg: ἐκείνῃ ς C syrr me (so LXX.).

nises man's responsibility and no less the inexorable law of moral consequence by the working of which God hardens the heart of the disobedient and self-willed. In this respect the variations in the narrative of the Exodus are most instructive. Pharaoh 'hardened his heart' (Ex. viii. 15, 32; ix. 34). 'The Lord hardened' Pharaoh's heart (iv. 21; ix. 12; x. 1, 20, 27; xi. 10; xiv. 4, 8). Pharaoh's heart 'was hardened' (vii. 14, 22; ix. 7, 35).

The word σκληρύνειν, except in this context (vv. 13, 15; iv. 7), is found in the N. T. only in Acts xix. 9; Rom. ix. 18. It is used in the LXX. of 'the heart,' 'the spirit' (Deut. ii. 30), 'the back,' 'the neck.'

παραπικρασμῷ......πειρασμοῦ] The original text gives the two proper names: *As at Meribah, as in the day of Massah in the wilderness;* and perhaps the LXX., which elsewhere gives equivalents for proper names, may have intended Παραπικρασμός and Πειρασμός to be so taken.

The two acts of faithlessness referred to cover the whole period of the forty years (Num. xx. 1 ff.; Ex. xvii. 1 ff.; comp. Deut. xxxiii. 8). The rendering κατὰ τ. ἡ. (כיום) obscures the distinctness of the second (first) event, but does not destroy it.

The preposition κατά is probably to be understood in a temporal sense (*at the day*...iii. 13) and not of comparison, *like as on...secundum diem tentationis* (Vulg.), id est, sequentes et imitantes diem et tempus in quo patres vestri me tentaverunt (Herv.).

πειρασμοῦ] when the people 'tempted' God: comp. Ps. lxxviii. 17 ff.

9. οὗ] *where*, Vulg. *ubi*, and not 'in which' by attraction for ᾧ.

ἐπείρ. ἐν δοκιμασίᾳ] The absence of a direct object in this clause according to the true reading points to the connexion of ἐπείρ. as well as εἶδον with τὰ ἔργα μου (Vulg. *probaverunt et viderunt opera mea*). This rendering departs considerably from the Hebrew and from the LXX., but places in a more vivid light the character of unbelief. The faithless people tried and tested not the invisible God but His visible works. They found reason to question where they should have rested in faith.

τὰ ἔργα μου] The Hebrew is singular. The many works of God in the wilderness were all one work, one in essence and aim, whether they were works of deliverance or works of chastisement. Under this aspect acts of righteous judgment and of mercy were parts of the same counsel of loving discipline.

τεσσερ. ἔτη] In the original these words go with the following clause (and so in v. 17). Here they are transposed to draw attention to the duration of God's discipline. The period had a significant coincidence with the interval which had elapsed since the Passion at the time when the Epistle was written.

Jewish writers connected the 'forty years' in the wilderness with the time of Messiah. For example: R. Eliezer said: The days of the Messiah are forty years, as it is said: Ps. xcv. 10 (Sanh. 99. 1, quoted by Bleek).

10. διό...] *Wherefore...* The particle is inserted by the writer, who separates

καὶ εῖπον Ἀεὶ πλανῶνται τῇ καρδίᾳ·
αὐτοὶ δὲ οὐκ ἔγνωσαν τὰς ὁδούς μου·
¹¹ὡς ὤμοσα ἐν τῇ ὀργῇ μου
Εἰ εἰσελεύσονται εἰς τὴν κατάπαυσίν μου—⌐

the period of discipline from the sentence of rejection.

προσώχθισα] *I was wroth, vehemently displeased.* The original term (קוט) expresses loathing.

τῇ καρδίᾳ] *in their heart,* the seat of man's personal character, of his moral life. See Additional Note on c. iv. 12.

αὐτοὶ δέ...] *But they...*The particle seems to involve a silent reference to the constant warnings and teachings of God: 'I ever shewed them my purpose, but they on their part recognised not my ways.' Comp. viii. 9.

11. ὡς ὤμοσα] *according as I sware,* Vulg. *sicut juravi,* in that time of disobedience. Loqui Dei magnum est: jurare vero nimis metuendum (Primas.).

The rendering *so that* is not required by the original Hebrew, and is (apparently) unexampled in Greek. Comp. Winer p. 578 (Moulton's note). εἰ εἰσελεύσονται] *They shall not enter...* Compare Mark viii. 12 (εἰ δοθήσεται); Gen. xiv. 23; Num. xiv. 30; 1 Sam. iii. 17. See Winer-Moulton p. 627.

εἰς τὴν κατάπαυσιν] The rest was primarily Canaan (Deut. xii. 9 f.), and then that divine kingdom and order of which the earthly Canaan was an imperfect type. At the first the occupation of the promised Land was treated as being ideally the fulfilment of the highest destiny of Israel in perfect fellowship with God (Lev. xxvi. 11 f.). But the partial outward accomplishment of the national hope necessarily fixed attention upon the spiritual realities with which the imperfect earthly blessings corresponded. The unsatisfying character of the temporal inheritance quickened the aspiration after a truer inheritance which the prophets cherished and deepened.

The writer of the Epistle afterwards identifies the true rest with the rest of God after Creation (iv. 4). The rest which God had proposed for His people was no other than that into which He Himself had entered.

Primasius (translating Chrysostom) distinguishes these three rests: Notandum tres requies ab apostolo in hac epistola commemorari, unam sabbati, quo requievit Deus ab operibus suis; secundam Palæstinæ, in quam ingressi Israelitæ requieturi erant a miseria et laboribus multis; tertiam quoque, quæ vera est requies, regnum videlicet cælorum, ad quam quos pervenire contigerit planissime requiescent a laboribus et ærumnis hujus sæculi.

κατάπαυσις] In classical Greek the word means 'a stopping,' 'a causing to cease,' literally or figuratively: in the LXX. 'a rest' or 'rest.' Comp. Deut. xii. 9; Is. lxvi. 1 (Acts vii. 49); 2 Macc. xv. 1. It is found in the N. T. only in this context besides the quotation in the Acts.

(*b*) The general application of the lesson of the wilderness (12—15).

The words of the Psalm which have been quoted at length are now applied generally to Christians. The reality of the blessings which they have received depends upon the faith with which they receive the present voice of God while it is still addressed to them.

[Wherefore, I repeat,] ¹² *take heed, brethren, lest haply there shall be in any one of you an evil heart of unbelief, in falling away from Him who is a living God;* ¹³*but exhort your own selves day by day so long*

¹²βλέπετε, ἀδελφοί, μή ποτε ἔσται ἔν τινι ὑμῶν καρδία
πονηρὰ ἀπιστίας ἐν τῷ ἀποστῆναι ἀπὸ θεοῦ ζῶντος,

as it is called Today, that no one of
you be hardened by the deceitfulness
of sin—¹⁴for we are become partakers of Christ, if at least we hold
the beginning of our confidence firm
unto the end—¹⁵while it is said
Today, if ye shall hear His voice,
Harden not your hearts, as in the
Provocation.

12. βλέπετε, ἀδελφοί, μή...] The
words take up the διό of v. 7, enforced and illustrated by the teachings
of the Psalm. This use of βλέπειν μή
(for ὁρᾶν μή) is unclassical. It is not
unfrequent in the N. T.: c. xii. 25;
Matt. xxiv. 4; Acts xiii. 40, &c. For
ἀδελφοί see v. 1. The argument
which the title includes is written out
in v. 14.

μή ποτε ἔσται] The construction, as
distinguished from μὴ γένηται, marks
the reality and the urgency of the
danger. Comp. Mk. xiv. 2; Col. ii.
8; Gal. iv. 11 (μή πως κεκοπίακα).

ἔν τινι ὑμ.] in any one of you. A
single unbelieving soul might corrupt
the whole body.

καρδ. π. ἀπιστίας] The phrase is
remarkable. Καρδία πονηρά go closely
together, and ἀπιστίας characterises
the 'evil-heart'; as σῶμα τῆς ἁμαρτίας
Rom. vi. 6; σῶμα τῆς σαρκός Col. i.
22. Comp. Clem. 1 Cor. iii. 4.
This thought of 'unbelief,' 'unfaithfulness,' stands in contrast with the
'faithfulness' which was the glory of
Moses and of Christ (v. 2 πιστὸς ἐν
ὅλῳ τῷ οἴκῳ).

'Unbelief' (ἀπιστία) finds its practical issue in 'disobedience' (ἀπείθεια).
Comp. v. 19 (δι᾿ ἀπιστίαν); c. iv. 6 (δι᾿
ἀπείθειαν). See v. 19 note.

ἐν τῷ ἀποστῆναι] in falling away
from...shewn in this apostasy (Acts
iii. 26 ἐν τῷ ἀποστρέφειν). Unbelief
might prevail at last even after a
temporary victory of faith. The Vul-

gate rendering is expressive, cor....
discedendi.

For ἀποστῆναι compare Lk. viii. 13.
It is construed commonly with ἀπό
(Acts xv. 38), but also with the simple
genitive (1 Tim. iv. 1).

ἀπὸ θεοῦ ζῶντος] from Him Who
is a living God. The anarthrous
title (θεὸς ζῶν), which is far more
common than ὁ θ. ὁ ζῶν (comp. cc. ix.
14; x. 31; xii. 22), always fixes attention upon the character as distinguished from the 'Person' of God
(ὁ θεὸς ὁ ζῶν Matt. xvi. 16; xxvi. 63;
Apoc. xv. 7). In every case it suggests a ground for corresponding
thought or action (e.g. Acts xiv. 15
ἐπὶ θεὸν ζῶντα not τὸν θ. τὸν ζ.; 1 Thess.
i. 9; Rom. ix. 26 LXX.). The title is
generally used of God, as the Creator
and Preserver and Governor of the
world (Deut. v. 26; Josh. iii. 10;
1 Sam. xvii. 26 (A); 2 K. xix. 4, 16;
(Jer. xxiii. 36); Dan. vi. 20, 26;
(Ps. lxxxiv. 2), in contrast with the
idols ('vanities,' 'nothings,' θεοὶ νεκροί
Didache vi. 3) of heathendom. Here
it suggests, among other thoughts, the
certainty of retribution on unfaithfulness. The title is not found in the
Gospel or Epistles of St John (but
notice John vi. 57 ὁ ζῶν πατήρ).

In old times the glory of Israel was
the knowledge of 'the living God';
but now to fall back from Christianity
to Judaism was really to revolt from
Him (comp. vi. 5 ff.), for as God is
living so the revelation which He
gives of Himself is progressive. On
the one side He spake in His Son (i. 2
ἐλάλησεν), and on the other side He
is speaking still (xii. 25 τὸν λαλοῦντα).

The phrase reappears in Herm.
Vis. ii. 3, 2 σώζει σε τὸ μὴ ἀποστῆναί
σε ἀπὸ θεοῦ ζῶντος...Comp. 1 Clem. iii.
4 ἐν τῷ ἀπολιπεῖν ἕκαστον τὸν φόβον
τοῦ θεοῦ.

¹³ἀλλὰ παρακαλεῖτε ἑαυτοὺς καθ' ἑκάστην ἡμέραν, ἄχρις
οὖ τό Σήμερον καλεῖται, ἵνα μὴ σκληρυνθῇ ⌜τις ἐξ ὑμῶν⌝¹
ἀπάτῃ τῆς ἁμαρτίας· ¹⁴μέτοχοι γὰρ τοῦ χριστοῦ γεγό-

13 ἐξ ὑμῶν τις.

13 καλεῖται : καλεῖτε AC.   σκλ. τις ἐξ ὑ. ℵACHM₂ vg syrvg me: σκλ. ἐξ ὑ. τις BD₂
syr hl.   τῆς ἁμ.: ἁμαρτίαις D₂*.   14 τοῦ χρ. γεγόν. ℵABCD₂HM₂ vg : γεγ. τοῦ χρ. 𝕾.

13. ἀλλὰ παρακαλεῖτε ἑαυτούς...]
But in place of undue confidence, of
blindly reposing in the past, help,
encourage, *exhort your own selves.*
The virtual negative of the former
clause ('do not neglect the fresh
voices of God...') is naturally followed
by ἀλλά. The use of ἑαυτούς for the
more simple ἀλλήλους (*quisque se ipsum et alterum* Bengel) suggests the
close unity of the Christian body.
The similar usage of the pronoun in
other places will repay study: 1 Pet.
iv. 8, 10; Eph. iv. 32 εἰς ἀλλήλους,
ἑαυτοῖς; Col. iii. 13 ἀλλήλων, ἑαυτοῖς;
id. iii. 16; 1 Thess. v. 13.

For παρακαλεῖν see c. x. 25; Acts
xiv. 22; Jude 3; Rom. xii. 1. Chrysostom says ὅρα τὸ ἥμερον καὶ προσηνές.
οὐκ εἶπεν ἐπιτιμᾶτε, ἀλλὰ παρακαλεῖτε.
οὕτως ἡμᾶς χρὴ τοῖς ἀπὸ θλίψεως στενο-
χωρουμένοις προσφέρεσθαι.

καθ' ἑκάστην ἡμέραν] *day by day.*
There is continuous, daily need.

ἄχρις οὖ τό Σήμερον καλεῖται] Vulg.
donec hodie cognominatur. So long
as the term 'Today' (τὸ Σήμερον, not
ἡ σήμερον) is still used: so long as, in
the language of the Psalm, the voice
of God is still addressed to you in its
appointed time.

In various connexions the term
'Today' will have various interpretations. For the Church it is the whole
time till Christ's coming. For the
believer the period of his own life.
Thus Theodoret says : σήμερον τὸν
παρόντα κέκληκεν βίον, and Chrysostom : ἕως ἂν συνεστήκῃ ὁ κόσμος.
Primasius gives various interpretations in detail:

Hodie, id est in die Novi Testamenti;

vel omni tempore, quamdiu dicitur
hodie, nolite obdurare corda vestra :
hodie namque pro sempiterno ponitur,
donec mundus et vita præsens manet.
Comp. Clem. Alex. *Prot.* 9 § 84
μέχρι δὲ συντελείας καὶ ἡ σήμερον καὶ
ἡ μάθησις διαμένει, καὶ τότε ἡ ὄντως
σήμερον, ἡ ἀνελλιπὴς τοῦ θεοῦ ἡμέρα,
τοῖς αἰῶσι συνεκτείνεται. See also
c. i. 5 note.

ἵνα μὴ σκληρυνθῇ τις...*that no one...
be hardened.* The effect is here
attributed to sin while man is passive.
In the Psalm the activity of man's
opposition is marked : μὴ σκληρύνητε,
v. 8 note. The order of the words τις
ἐξ ὑμῶν, ἐξ ὑμῶν τις, is doubtful, and
involves a difference of emphasis not
without interest.

ἀπάτῃ τῆς ἁμαρτίας] Sin is represented as an active, aggressive, power :
c. xii. 4. Comp. Rom. vii. 8, 11; (v.
21; vi. 12; vii. 17, 20): 2 Thess. ii.
10 ἀπ. ἀδικίας; James i. 15.

The readers of the Epistle were in
danger of entertaining false views of
the nature of the promised salvation.
It was in this form that sin assailed
them, cloking itself under the dress of
faithfulness to the past.

Theophylact gives a more general
sense : ἀπάτην δὲ ἁμαρτίας καλεῖ ἢ τὴν
ἀπάτην τοῦ διαβόλου, τουτέστι τὸ μὴ
ἐλπίζειν ὅτι ἔσται ἀνταπόδοσις, ἢ, τὴν
ἀναλγησίαν, τὸ γὰρ λέγειν ὅτι λοιπὸν
ἅπαξ ἥμαρτον (*leg.* ἅπ. ἥμ. λοιπὸν) οὐκ
ἔχω ἐλπίδας, ἀπάτη ὄντως ἐστὶν ἁμαρτίας.

For the singular ἡ ἁμαρτία see c.
xii. 4 note. Additional Note on i. 3.

14. μέτοχοι γάρ...] Such an exhortation has a solid ground to rest
upon, *for we are become partakers in*

ναμεν, ἐάνπερ τὴν ἀρχὴν τῆς ὑποστάσεως μέχρι τέλους

14 ὑποστ.: + αὐτοῦ A vg.

Christ, or, more strictly, *in the Christ*, the hope of our fathers. We have been united with Him and so we have been made now to partake in the fulness of His life (Vulg. *participes Christi effecti sumus*). The old promises have found for us a complete fulfilment, though unbelief destroys it or hides it from us. The phrase can also be rendered *partakers with Christ*, *i.e.* Christ's fellows (c. i. 9; Luke v. 7); but this sense is far less natural here, and, as far as it is applicable, it is included in the more comprehensive idea.

In either case the thought is of a blessing conferred (γεγόναμεν), and not simply of a blessing enjoyed (ἐσμέν). For the form μετ. γεγόναμεν as contrasted with μετεσχήκαμεν (vii. 13), see c. ii. 2 note.

The form ὁ χριστός occurs again v. 5; vi. 1; ix. 14, 28; xi. 26. See Additional Note on i. 4.

For μέτοχοι see *v.* 1 note. Chrysostom thus paraphrases the words: μετέχομεν αὐτοῦ, φησίν, ἐν ἐγενόμεθα ἡμεῖς καὶ αὐτός, εἴπερ, αὐτὸς μὲν κεφαλὴ σῶμα δὲ ἡμεῖς, συγκληρονόμοι καὶ σύσσωμοι. And Primasius more fully: Christo participamur et jungimur, utpote unum et in illo existentes; siquidem hoc participamur illi quia ipse caput nostrum et nos membra illius, cohæredes et concorporales illi secundum spiritalem hominem, qui creatus est in ipso. In eo etiam participamur, quia corpus et sanguinem ejus sumimus ad redemptionem nostram.

ἐάνπερ...] *if at least...* The particle is not found in the LXX, and occurs again in N.T. in c. vi. 3 (not *v.* 6) only. That which has been stated as a fact (γεγόναμεν) is now made conditional in its permanence on the maintenance of faith. This is the ever-present antithesis of religion. That which

God has done is absolute; but man's appropriation of the gift must be by continuous effort. Comp. Col. iii. 3, 5 (ἀπεθάνετε..., νεκρώσατε οὖν).

ἐάνπερ τὴν ἀρχήν...] *if we hold fast the beginning of our confidence firm unto the end.* Vulg. *si initium substantiæ ejus usque ad finem firmum retineamus*. The beginning of our confidence is more than our first confidence. It describes that which is capable (so to speak) of a natural growth; a principle which is active at first, and continues to be progressively energetic. Comp. x. 32 ff.

There can be no doubt that ὑπόστασις is here used to express that resolute confidence, which opposes a strong resistance to all assaults. It is used in late Greek writers for firmness of endurance under torture (Diod. Sic. ii. 557 ἡ ἐν ταῖς βασάνοις ὑπόστασις τῆς ψυχῆς); and generally for courageous firmness of character (Polyb. vi. 55, 2): and so for resolution (Diod. Sic. ii. 57 κατὰ τὴν ἰδίαν ὑπόστασιν). The word occurs in a similar sense in 2 Cor. ix. 4; xi. 17. Compare cc. i. 3; xi. 1 and notes.

The Fathers give an objective sense to ὑπόστασις, as expressing that in virtue of which we are what we are, believers united with Christ, and this is expressed by the Vulgate (*substantiæ ejus*). Thus Chrysostom: τί ἐστὶν ἀρχὴ τῆς ὑποστάσεως; τὴν πίστιν λέγει, δι' ἧς ὑπέστημεν καὶ γεγενήμεθα καὶ συνουσιώθημεν, ὡς ἄν τις εἴποι. And Theodoret: τὴν ἀρχὴν τῆς ὑποστάσεως [τὴν πίστιν] κέκληκεν· δι' ἐκείνης γὰρ ἐνεουργήθημεν καὶ συνήφθημεν τῷ δεσπότῃ χριστῷ καὶ τῆς τοῦ παναγίου πνεύματος μετειλήφαμεν χάριτος. And Theophylact: τουτέστιν τὴν πίστιν, δι' αὐτῆς γὰρ ὑπέστημεν καὶ οὐσιώθημεν τὴν θείαν καὶ πνευματικὴν οὐσίωσιν καὶ ἀναγέννησιν. And so Primasius more in detail:

βεβαίαν ⌜κατάσχωμεν·⌝ ¹⁵ἐν τῷ λέγεσθαι

ϹΗΜΕΡΟΝ ἐὰΝ ΤΗ͂Ϲ ΦωΝΗ͂Ϲ ΑΥ̓ΤΟΥ͂ ἀΚΟΎϹΗΤΕ,

ΜῊ ϹΚΛΗΡΎΝΗΤΕ ΤᾺϹ ΚΑΡΔΊΑϹ ὙΜΩ͂Ν ὡϹ ἐΝ Τῷ ΠΑΡΑΠΙΚΡΑϹΜῷ.

κατάσχωμεν,

15 om. ὡς M₂.

Initium substantiæ dicit fidem Christi, per quam subsistimus et renati sumus, quia ipse est fundamentum omnium virtutum. Et bene substantiam eam vocat, quia sicut corpus anima subsistit et vivificatur, ita anima fide subsistit in Deo et vivit hac fide. Substantia autem Christi appellatur fides vel quia ab illo datur, vel certe quia ipse per eam habitat in cordibus fidelium.

According to this interpretation ἡ ἀρχὴ τῆς ὑποστάσεως has the same general sense as has been already given to ὑπόστασις alone.

μέχρι τέλους] *until the end.* The 'end' is not exactly defined. The writer leaves it undetermined whether the close of trial is the close of the individual life or of 'the age' itself. Comp. vi. 11.

15. ἐν τῷ λέγεσθαι] The connexion of the quotation is uncertain. It has been taken closely with *v.* 16. But the question τίνες γάρ, which marks a beginning, is fatal to this view.

Again it has been taken with *v.* 14, or, more particularly, with the conditional clause of it ἐάνπερ....This connexion gives a good sense, and brings the necessity of effort into close relation with obedience to every voice of God.

Chrysostom, followed by the later Greek commentators, supposed that the whole passage *vv.* 15—19 is an irregular parenthesis, and that the sequel of *v.* 14 is in c. iv. 1. But the abrupt ἐν τῷ λέγεσθαι without any particle, followed by τίνες γάρ...;, is strongly against this view, and also against the view that a new paragraph is begun in *v.* 15, which is not formally completed.

It is on the whole most natural to connect the quotation with *v.* 13. Ac-

cording to this view *v.* 14 is parenthetical, and brings out the real nature of the Christian privilege—a participation in the Messiah—and the condition on which it is kept.

If this connexion be adopted the sense is: 'exhort one another so long as it is called today...while the voice of God is still addressed to you, and still claims loyal obedience.'

(*c*) Detailed interpretation of the lesson of the Psalm (16—19).

The general application of the warning of the Psalm to Christians is confirmed by a closer interpretation of the circumstances. Those who incurred the displeasure of God and who were excluded from the promised rest, were the people who had been delivered from Egypt. Unbelief and disobedience finally cut off from their goal men who had entered on the way. So it may be with those who have been joined to Christ.

¹⁶ *For who when they heard did provoke? Nay, did not all they that came out of Egypt by Moses?* ¹⁷ *And with whom was He displeased forty years? Was it not with them that sinned, whose carcases fell in the wilderness?* ¹⁸ *And to whom did He swear that they should not enter into His rest, but to them that were disobedient?* ¹⁹ *And we see that they could not enter in because of unbelief.*

16—19. The succession of thought is significant. The very people whom God had rescued provoked Him (*v.* 16). They sinned and met with the fatal consequences of sin (*v.* 17). They disobeyed and received the sentence of rejection (*v.* 18). Unbelief (comp. *v.* 12) made them incapable of that rest towards which they had started by faith (*v.* 19).

¹⁶τίνες γὰρ ἀκούσαντες παρεπίκραναν; ἀλλ' οὐ πάντες οἱ ἐξελθόντες ἐξ Αἰγύπτου διὰ Μωυσέως; ¹⁷τίσιν δὲ προσώχθισεν τεσσεράκοντα ἔτη; οὐχὶ τοῖς ἁμαρτήσασιν, ὧν τὰ κῶλα ἔπεσεν ἐν τῇ ἐρήμῳ; ¹⁸τίσιν δὲ ὤμοσεν μὴ εἰσελεύσεσθαι εἰς τὴν κατάπαυσιν αὐτοῦ εἰ μὴ τοῖς ἀπειθήσασιν; ¹⁹καὶ βλέπομεν ὅτι οὐκ ἠδυνήθησαν εἰσελθεῖν δι' ἀπιστίαν.

17 τίσιν δέ: +καί A.   ἁμαρτ.: ἀπειθήσασιν A.   ἔπεσεν: ἔπεσαν D₂.

16. τίνες γάρ...] The warning is necessary. Christians have need of anxious care. For who were they who so provoked God in old times? Even those whom He had already brought from bondage.

τίνες...ἀλλ' οὐ πάντες...] For who...? Nay, did not...? Vulg. Quidam cum (τινὲς γάρ)...sed non universi...For some when they had heard did provoke (A.V.). This rendering is quite alien from the context. The vast mass who came out of Egypt could not be described as 'some.' On the other hand the interrogative completely corresponds with the two interrogatives which follow (τίνες...τίσιν ...τίσιν...); and the three questions point to the three stages of the divine displeasure. Nor does the faith of Joshua and Caleb invalidate the general statement.

παρεπίκραναν] The verb occurs here only in N.T., but it is not unfrequent in LXX. and Philo. It is used generally with acc. of object: Ps. lxxvii. (lxxviii.) 17 παρεπίκραναν τὸν ὕψιστον, but also absolutely: Ps. lxxvii. 8, γενεὰ σκολιὰ καὶ παραπικραίνουσα; Ezek. ii. 5, 7, 8 &c.

ἀλλ' οὐ...] Nay, such a question cannot be asked as if the answer were doubtful: was it not...?
For the use of ἀλλά compare Lk. xvii. 8 (ἀλλ' οὐχί...); Mk. xiv. 36; John xii. 27.

οἱ ἐξελθόντες] The word marks the act of the people, the manifestation of faith on their part, as well as the act of Moses. They 'came out' and not only 'were led out' (Acts vii. 36 ἐξήγαγεν; c. viii. 9).

διὰ Μωυσέως] The fact that Moses had been the instrument of their deliverance should have kept them from 'chiding with him' (Ex. xvii. 2).

17. The unbelief of the people shewed itself in open sin from first to last (v. 8).

τίσιν δὲ προσ.] And with whom...? In this place the writer gives the connexion of τεσσ. ἔτη which is found in the Hebrew. From the beginning of the wanderings to the end (Ex. xvii. 7; Num. xx. 13), the people sinned in like ways. In this verse and in the next (ἀπειθήσασιν) the reference is not to the general character of the people, but to the critical acts which revealed it.

ἁμαρτήσασιν] This is the only form of the aor. partic. in N. T. In the moods the form of ἥμαρτον is always used except Matt. xviii. 15 || Lk. xvii. 4 (ἁμαρτήσῃ); Rom. vi. 15.

τὰ κῶλα] The word is borrowed from the LXX. (Num. xiv. 29).
It seems best to take the clause ὧν ...ἐρήμῳ, as a subsidiary element in the description and not as an independent statement.

18. τίσιν δὲ ὤμοσεν μὴ εἰσελ.] The change of subject is unusual ('He sware that they...' and not 'He sware that He...').

τοῖς ἀπειθήσασιν] to them that disobeyed, that were disobedient. Vulg. qui increduli (O. L. contumaces) fuerunt. Unbelief passed into action. Comp. xi. 31; iv. 6, 11; Rom. xi. 30, 32, contrast vv. 20, 23.

19. καὶ βλέπομεν...] And we see... The conjunction introduces the gene-

ral conclusion: 'And so on a review of the record (or of the argument) we see...' Βλέπομεν may mean 'We see in the familiar record of the Pentateuch,' or, 'We see in the details just set forth.' The two interpretations really pass one into the other.

οὐκ ἠδυνήθησαν] Their exclusion from Canaan was not only a fact (οὐκ εἰσῆλθον), but a moral necessity.

δι' ἀπιστίαν] The failure of the first generation of redeemed Jews, who corresponded in position with the first generation of Christians, is traced back to its source. The faith which they had at the beginning failed them. They fell into unbelief; and unbelief issued in its practical consequences, disobedience, open sin. For the general relation of 'unbelief' and 'disobedience' see Rom. ii. 8 (τοῖς ἀπειθοῦσιν); iii. 3 (ἡ ἀπιστία); Acts xiv. 2 (οἱ ἀπειθήσαντες Ἰουδαῖοι); xix. 9 (ἠπείθουν); xxviii. 24 (ἠπίστουν). Compare John iii. 36 (ὁ πιστεύων, ὁ ἀπειθῶν).

Additional Note on iii. 7. *The application to Christ of words spoken in the O. T. of the Lord.*

We have already seen that words originally applied to 'the Lord' in the O. T. are used of Christ by the writer of the Epistle (i. 6; 10 f. note). The principle involved in this application of scriptural language was of great importance in the historical development of the doctrine of the Person of Christ. *The importance of the application to Christ of words*

Three main types of national expectation appear to have prevailed among the Jews at the time of the Advent, the expectation of 'a Davidic King,' of 'a day of the Lord,' of 'a Divine King and Judge.' Each expectation was connected with the thought of a passage from 'this age' of trial and suffering to 'the future age' of triumph and joy, through a crisis of travail-pains (see c. i. 2 note). The ground of the different hopes lay in the Scriptures, and it does not seem that they were united in any one of the consistent view. We read the O. T. in the light of the N. T., and it becomes difficult for us to appreciate the manifoldness of the aspects of the Divine Redemption which were offered separately in the prophets. But this manifoldness, this apparent vagueness or inconsistency, as we might think, must be realised before we can form a right estimate of the revelation of Christ. *spoken of the Lord. Three chief types of Messianic expectation at the time of the Advent.*

1. The first and most familiar portraiture of the expected Deliverer is as a King of the line of David (Is. xi. 1; lv. 3 f.; Jer. xxiii. 5; xxx. 9; Ezek. xxxiv. 23 f.; xxxvii. 24). At first the prophetic imagery suggests a line of kings who shall fulfil the counsels of God. 'The tabernacle of David' is to be restored (Amos ix. 11 f.; comp. Acts xv. 16 f.); and 'shepherds' are to be set over the regathered flock (Jer. xxiii. 4; comp. xxxiii. 17, 20 f., 26; 14—26 is not in LXX.). But in this royal line one King stands out in glory, in whom all the promises are concentrated, a King who shall 'execute judgment and justice on the earth' (Jer. xxiii. 5 ff.; comp. xxxiii. 15 ff.), and realise in peace and safety the will of the Lord (*id.*), through the gift of His Spirit (Is. xi. 2 ff.). He is to come from the city of David (Mic. v. 2), and to bring peace to the divided kingdom (Zech. ix. 10) and to the heathen (*id.*); and His throne is to be everlasting (Is. ix. 6 f.). *1. The Davidic King.*

After the Captivity the thought of the Davidic King falls again into the background. Zechariah alone touches upon it (iii. 8; vi. 12 f. with reference to Jer. xxiii. 5 f.). The people and not the royal line is the centre of hope. And it must be added that in the second part of Isaiah the name of David is only once mentioned, and that in a passage (lv. 3) which appears to indicate that the royal prerogatives of the ideal monarch are extended to the ideal people.

2. Meanwhile another view of the divine interposition in favour of Israel had been powerfully drawn. The prophets had said much of 'a day of the Lord.' The phrase extends through their writings from first to last, *2. The Day of the Lord.*

from Joel (i. 15; ii. 1, 11; iii. 14) to Malachi (iv. 5 [iii. 23]). On this 'great and terrible' day it is said that Jehovah Himself will execute judgment, bringing victory to His own people and ruin on His enemies and theirs (Joel iii. 14 ff.; comp. Is. ii. 12 ff.). The crisis is painted as full of gloom and anguish (Amos v. 18, 20), and fierce conflict (Ezek. xiii. 5). The people confident in their privileges desire the coming of the day: the prophet, who knows that the Presence of the Lord is a moral judgment, turns them to the thought of its terrors. The revelation of deliverance is a revelation of righteousness (Amos *l. c.*). In this conception therefore the idea of retribution for evil, of vengeance on the wicked, who are typically identified with the oppressors of Israel, prevails over every other (Is. xiii. 6, 9; Obad. 15; Zeph. i. 7 ff., 14 ff.). The Lord Himself carries out His will. The thought of deliverance is connected directly with His action. No human agent is singled out for the accomplishment of His counsel.

3. *The Divine King.* 3. These two conceptions of the Davidic king and of the judgment of Jehovah were united in the apocalyptic writings. In these the Saviour King is clothed with a supernatural character. Whatever may be the date of the Book of Daniel, there can be no doubt that it marks an epoch in the growth of the Messianic hopes of Israel. Henceforward the looked-for King appears under a new aspect, as the heavenly Fulfiller of the purpose of God. The image is mysterious and obscure in Daniel (vii. 13, 18); but it gains clearness in the later works which follow out the same line of thought, the Sibylline fragments, the book of Henoch, and the Psalms of Solomon. In these the figure of the Divine King is presented with ever-increasing glory; and it was probably in the latest period of the development of Jewish hope, to which they belong, that the title of 'the Christ,' 'the Anointed King,' which is used characteristically in the O. T. of the theocratic monarch, came to be appropriated to the expected Saviour.

The influence of the thought of the Lord's coming on Apostolic thought. We are able to see now how these various hopes were harmonised and fulfilled by Him whom we acknowledge as the Son of David, the Son of man, and the Son of God. And in the first age they contributed to guide the apostles naturally, if the word may be used, to the apprehension of the depths of His Being. In this respect it will be evident that the expectation of the coming of the Lord was of critical significance. The work of the Baptist was recognised as preparatory to this Divine Advent (Mk. i. 2; Lk. i. 76; Matt. xi. 10 [Mal. iii. 1]; Matt. xi. 14; xvii. 11; Mk. ix. 12; Lk. i. 16 f. [Mal. iv. 5 f.]; and the remarkable change of pronoun in the first quotation from Malachi (*before thee* for *before me*) seems designed to point to the coming of the Lord in One Who is His true Representative. The herald of the Lord was indeed the herald of Christ. This, St John tells us, was the Baptist's own view of his mission. He was sent to 'make straight the way of the Lord' (Is. xl. 3; John i. 23; comp. Matt. iii. 3; Mk. i. 2 f.; Lk. iii. 4 ff.). And after the Resurrection and the descent of the Spirit, the apostles proclaimed that in Christ the promise of the Lord's coming was indeed fulfilled (Acts ii. 16 ff., 21, 36, 38; iv. 12; Joel ii. 28 ff.), and looked forward to His revelation in glory (Zech. xiv. 5; Matt. xvi. 27; xxv. 31; Mk. viii. 38; 1 Thess. iii. 13; 2 Thess. i. 10), when He should exercise the divine office of judgment (Acts xvii. 31; Ps. ix. 8; 2 Thess. i. 7 f.; Is. lxvi. 15).

So it was that the apostolic writers applied to Christ the prerogatives of the Lord (Jer. xvii. 10, Apoc. ii. 23; comp. Num. xiv. 21, Apoc. i. 18; Ps. x. 16, Apoc. xi. 15), and His Sovereign Name (Deut. x. 17, Apoc. xix. 16; comp. Ps. xxiv. 10, 1 Cor. ii. 8), and the accomplishment of His promises (Is. lvii. 19, Eph. ii. 13 ff.; comp. Is. lx. 3 ff., 19, Apoc. xxi. 24 ff.). St Peter distinctly applies to Christ what was said of 'the Lord of hosts' (1 Pet. iii. 14, Is. viii. 12, 13). And St John in especial, looking back from the bosom of a Christian Church, found deeper meanings in His Master's words (John xiii. 19, Is. xliii. 10), and discerned that the divine vision of Isaiah was a vision of Christ (John xii. 39 ff.; Is. vi. 1 ff.). The very phrase in which he expresses the Gospel includes implicitly the declaration of the fulfilment of the promise of the Lord's dwelling with His people (John i. 14; Lev. xxvi. 11 f.; Ezek. xxxvii. 27).

From the study of such passages it is not difficult to see how, as has been briefly said, the fact of the Covenant leads to the fact of the Incarnation. The personal intercourse of God with man is a prophecy of the fulfilment of man's destiny: ἐν ἀρχῇ ἦν ὁ λόγος, καὶ ὁ λόγος ἦν πρὸς τὸν θεόν, καὶ θεὸς ἦν ὁ λόγος...καὶ ὁ λόγος σὰρξ ἐγένετο καὶ ἐσκήνωσεν ἐν ἡμῖν.

IV. ¹Φοβηθῶμεν οὖν μή ποτε καταλειπομένης ἐπαγ-

1 καταλειπ. ABCM₂: καταλιπ. ℵD₂* + τῆς' ἐπαγγ. D₂.

(2) iv. 1—13. *The promise remaining.*

It follows from the consideration of the history of Israel that the promise of God to His people was not fulfilled by the entrance into Canaan.

There is, therefore, (*a*) a rest, a divine rest, a rest from earthly labour, promised still and not enjoyed (1—10). And (*b*) towards this rest Christians must strive, filled with the feeling of their responsibility (11—13).

(*a*) The rest of God is prepared for believers in Christ (1—10).

The development of this main thought is somewhat perplexed and formally incomplete. The promise of the entrance into the divine rest is first assumed to apply to Christians (1, 2); the present reality of the rest is then established by the record of creation (3—5); and by the repetition of the promise to those who had entered into Canaan (6, 7); for that first rest could not satisfy the divine purpose (8—10). The writer takes for granted throughout that whatever God in His love has ever designed for man is brought within man's reach by Christ, 'the heir of all things,' the fulfiller of human destiny.

1, 2. The fate of those who were rescued from Egypt had a direct meaning for those to whom the Epistle was addressed. The people that were delivered did not 'enter into the rest of God,' but perished in the wilderness. And the next generation who occupied Canaan still found the promise unaccomplished, and so it remained till the time when Christ again proclaimed it for the vital appropriation of believers by faith. Thus, in other words, under one aspect the Israelites in the wilderness and the first Christians were in the same position. Both had a message of glad tidings to make their own; and the end of the message

in both cases was the same. But in the order of the Divine Providence Christians were placed in a more advantageous position (viii. 6 ff.) than Israel. Belief and obedience were more easily within their reach when the former discipline had done its work.

¹ *Let us fear, therefore, lest haply a promise being left of entering into His rest, any one of you should seem to have come short of it.* ² *For indeed we have had good tidings preached to us, even as also they; but the word of the message did not profit them, because it was not incorporated by faith in them that heard.*

1. φοβηθῶμεν οὖν...] *Let us fear therefore,* since Israel, redeemed from bondage, never entered into the rest which was prepared for them, *for we have had good tidings preached to us even as they.* Our position, like theirs, is one of trial. The position of privilege is the discipline of faith. To have been brought to Christ is a beginning and not an end. In such a case 'fear' is a motive for strenuous exertion.

The writer uses the first person (contrast ἐξ ὑμῶν) in sympathy with the whole Christian society.

καταλειπομένης...] *as there is still now left* (*v.* 6) *a promise* (Vulg. *pollicitatione*) *to enter* (*that one should enter*)... The promise was left because no purpose of God can fall to the ground; and this was unfulfilled in the case of those to whom it was first given. Outwardly the promise was fulfilled afterwards, for the next generation did enter Canaan; but that fulfilment did not exhaust the meaning of the promise (*v.* 8); and so in fact the promise was repeated.

The tense of the participle (καταλειπομένης) marks the present fact. There is a slight difference between

γελίας εἰcελθεῖν εἰc τὴν κατάπαυcιν αὐτοῦ δοκῇ τις ἐξ ὑμῶν
ὑστερηκέναι· ²καὶ γάρ ἐσμεν εὐηγγελισμένοι καθάπερ
κἀκεῖνοι, ἀλλ᾽ οὐκ ὠφέλησεν ὁ λόγος τῆς ἀκοῆς ἐκείνους,

δοκεῖ M₂.　　　　2 καὶ πάρεσμεν C*.

καταλείπεσθαι and ἀπολείπεσθαι (vv. 6, 9). ᾽Απολείπεσθαι is used from the point of sight of those who have gone away; καταλείπεσθαι of that which retains its original position.

μή...δοκῇ τις...] lest any one should seem... Vulg. ne existimetur aliquis... The phrase is less stern in expression than the simple ὑστερῇ (Œcum. ἀνεπαχθῆ τὸν λόγον ποιῶν οὐκ εἶπεν ὑστερήσει (-η) ἀλλὰ δοκῇ ὑστερίζειν), and yet it is more comprehensive in warning. It suggests that the mere appearance or suspicion of failure, even though it may not be fully justified, for man's judgment is necessarily fallible, is a thing to be earnestly dreaded. Other renderings, 'lest any should be shewn to...' or 'be judged to...,' or 'think that he has...,' are less natural and less forcible.

ὑστερηκέναι] to have come short, Vulg. deesse, to have failed to attain the promised rest in spiritual possession. The tense marks not only a present (Rom. iii. 23 ὑστεροῦνται) or past defeat (2 Cor. xii. 11 ὑστέρησα) but an abiding failure.

2. καὶ γάρ...] For indeed... Comp. v. 12; x. 34; xii. 29; xiii. 22. The omission of the pronoun (ἡμεῖς) throws the emphasis upon ἐσμὲν εὐηγ. (comp. xiii. 10). 'For indeed we have received a message of good tidings—a promise of rest—even as also they (v. 6). For ἐσμ. εὐηγγ. see vii. 20; x. 20 notes.

For the construction see Matt. xi. 5 || Lk. vii. 22; 2 Sam. xviii. 31; Joel iii. 32; and compare viii. 5 κεχρημάτισται Μωυσῆς : the perfect (ἐσμ. εὐηγγ.) marks the present continuance of the message, which was not simply one past announcement (v. 6 οἱ πρ. εὐαγγελισθέντες).

The Vulg. renders the phrase very inadequately: etenim et nobis nunti-

atum est. It may be added that the noun εὐαγγέλιον, which is found in all St Paul's Epistles except that to Titus, does not occur in the Epistle. καθάπερ] Elsewhere in the N.T. (not v. 4) only in St Paul's Epistles (about 15 times).

ἀλλά...τοῖς ἀκούσασιν] It is possible that there is here some primitive corruption of the text (see Additional Note). At the same time the general drift of the passage is clear, and both the readings which have found acceptance on adequate authority, (1) συνκεκερασμένους [-κεκραμένους], and (2) συνκεκερασμένος [-κεκραμένος], can be brought into agreement with it.

(1) If the former (συνκεκερασμένους) be adopted, the sense must be : 'But the mere hearing did not profit them because they were not united by faith with them that truly heard,' 'with the body of the faithful,' or, perhaps, 'with them that first heard,' 'with those to whom the message was given' (comp. ii. 3), that is, Moses and Joshua and Caleb. The verb συγκεράννυσθαι is used of the intimate association of familiar friendship in classical and late Greek; but this pregnant sense of οἱ ἀκούσαντες after ὁ λόγος τῆς ἀκοῆς and ἐὰν ἀκούσητε of the Psalm appears to be unnatural.

(2) If on the other hand we read συνκεκερασμένος there is a choice of two constructions. We may either (a) take τῇ πίστει as the dative of the instrument joining τοῖς ἀκούσασιν closely with συνκεκερασμένος : 'the word did not profit them because it was not incorporated by faith in them that heard,' 'because they were not vitally inspired with the divine message though they outwardly received it.' Or again (b) we may connect τῇ πίστει with συνκεκερασμένος, and regard τοῖς

μὴ ⌜συνκεκερασμένος⌝ τῇ πίστει τοῖς ἀκούσασιν. ³Εἰcεp-

2 συνκεκερασμένους

συνκεκερασμένος [-κεκραμένος]: συνκεκερασμένους [-κεκραμένους]: τῶν ἀκουσάντων
D₂* syr hl mg : see Additional Note.

ἀκούσασιν as a dative of reference:
'the word did not profit them *because
it was not united with faith for them
that heard*, 'because the word itself
was not quickened by the power of
faith so as to effect its vital work.'
Of these two interpretations the
former seems to be the simpler and
more expressive; but both are open
to the serious objection that it is
strange that ἐκείνους and τοῖς ἀκούσασιν should be applied to the same
persons.

On the whole however, if it be
supposed that the true reading has
been preserved by our existing authorities, the former of these two
renderings of the reading συνκεκερασμένος appears to offer the least difficulty; and it may be urged that
the addition of τοῖς ἀκούσασιν is required to bring out the reference to
the Psalm, while ἐκείνους points the
contrast with Christians.

οὐκ ὠφέλησεν] The familiar facts
carry the thought of the reader beyond this negative result. The word
heard and not welcomed involved
those to whom it was addressed in a
tragic fate.

ὁ λόγος τῆς ἀκοῆς] Vulg. *sermo
auditûs*. Syr. *the word which they
heard.* The phrase admits of two
renderings. It may mean (1) 'the
word of the message heard,' the
simple proclamation of the divine
tidings; or (2) ' the word of hearing,'
that is, the word as heard only,
according as ἀκοή is taken passively
or actively. The second sense which
falls in perfectly with the context is
justified by Ecclus. xli. 23 (xlii. 17)
λόγος ἀκοῆς 'a simple rumour'; but
the former sense is more in accordance
with the general (passive) usage of
ἀκοή itself for a message spoken and

heard: Is. liii. 1 (Rom. x. 16; John
xii. 38); Jer. x. 22 φωνὴ ἀκοῆς (and in
1 Thess. ii. 13 λόγος ἀκοῆς) seems to
mean 'a message of hearing,' that is, a
message not commended by any more
authoritative form of delivery.

The argument remains the same
in both cases whether the apostle
speaks of 'the simple delivery of the
message' or of 'the message which
was simply heard.'

μὴ συνκεκ.] The subjective negative
is naturally used with the participle
which gives the suggested reason
('since they were not...'); comp. *v.* 15
note.

συνκεκερασμένος] The compounds
of κεράννυσθαι are constantly used from
early times of the moral (and spiritual)
union of persons. So (συγκεκρ.) Xen.
Cyr. i. 4, 1 τοῖς ἡλικιώταις συνεκέκρατο
ὥστε οἰκείως διακεῖσθαι, (ἐγκεκρ.) Ign.
Eph. 5 τοὺς ἐγκεκραμένους αὐτῷ (τῷ
ἐπισκόπῳ), (ἀνακεκρ.) Plut. *Rom.* p.
36 D καιναῖς ἀνακραθέντων ἐπιγαμίαις
τῶν γενῶν. They are used also of the
union of things or qualities: 1 Cor. xii.
24 ὁ θεὸς συνεκέρασεν τὸ σῶμα. Plat.
Legg. xii. c. 10, p. 961 E τὰς αἰσθήσεις
τῷ κυβερνητικῷ νῷ συγκερασάμενοι...
Menander, ap. Stob. *Anthol.* 45, 8,
speaks of λόγου δύναμις ἤθει χρηστῷ
συγκεκραμένη. Plut. *Non posse suav.
vivi sec. Epic.* ii. p. 1101, B βέλτιον
ἐνυπάρχειν τι καὶ συγκεκρᾶσθαι τῇ περὶ
θεῶν δόξῃ κοινὸν αἰδοῦς καὶ φόβου
πάθος ... Comp. Ign. *ad Smyrn.* 3
κραθέντες τῇ σαρκὶ αὐτοῦ καὶ τῷ αἵματι
(al. πνεύματι), and Lightfoot *ad loc.*

3—7. The present experience of
Christians confirms the privilege of
faith (3); The fact that the rest itself
is already realised is witnessed by the
record of creation (4); The fact that
the promise of the rest still remains
is implied by the exclusion of the un-

χόμεθα ⌜γὰρ⌝ εἰς [τὴν] κατάπαγcιν οἱ πιστεύσαντες, καθὼς εἴρηκεν

Ὡc ὤμοcα ἐν τῇ ὀργῇ μογ
Εἰ εἰcελεγcονται εἰc τὴν κατάπαγcίν μογ,

καίτοι τῶν ἔργων ἀπὸ καταβολῆς κόσμου γενηθέντων,

οὖν

3 εἰσερχόμεθα אBD₂M₂: εἰσερχώμεθα A(ἰσερχ.)C (comp. vi. 3; Rom. v. 1; 1 Cor. xv. 49). γάρ BD₂ vg syr hl : οὖν אACM₂ me.   τήν (1°) אACM: om. BD₂*. εἰ om. A: ἢ C*.   κατ. μου: om. μου C*.

faithful from it (5); And a fresh word of God points to the end not yet reached (6, 7).

³ *For we that believe enter into the rest* of God; *even as He hath said,*
As I sware in my wrath,
They shall not enter into my rest; although the works were finished from the foundation of the world.
⁴ *For He hath said as we know (somewhere) of the seventh day on this wise:*
And God rested on the seventh day from all His works;
⁵ *And in this place again:*
⁶ *They shall not enter into my rest.*

Seeing therefore it remaineth that some should enter into it, and they to whom the good tidings were before preached entered not in because of disobedience, ⁷ *He again defineth a certain day, Today, saying in David, after so long a time as hath been said before,*
Today, if ye shall hear His voice, Harden not your hearts.

3. εἰσερχόμεθα γάρ...] The apostle assumes that actual experience establishes the reality of the promise and the condition of its fulfilment. 'I speak without hesitation' he seems to say 'of a promise left to us, *for we enter*, we are entering now, *into the rest* of God, *we that believed...*.' The verb εἰσερχόμεθα is not to be taken as a future (Vulg. *ingrediemur*), but as the expression of a present fact: John xiv. 3, 18; Matt. xvii. 11; 1 Cor. iii. 13; Col. iii. 6. Moreover the

efficacy of faith is regarded in its critical action (πιστεύσαντες) and not, as might have been expected, in its continuous exercise (πιστεύοντες). Comp. Acts iv. 32; 2 Thess. i. 10; 1 Cor. xv. 2. At the same time he does not say simply 'we enter in having believed' (πιστεύσαντες); but he regards 'believers' as a definite class who embraced the divine revelation when it was offered (οἱ πιστεύσαντες). Comp. c. vi. 18 οἱ καταφυγόντες.

εἰς τὴν κατάπαυσιν] not simply 'into rest' but *into the rest* of which the Psalmist spoke, 'into the rest of God.'

καθὼς εἴρηκεν, Ὡς ὤμοσα...] The words of the Psalm, as used here, prove that there is a rest and that it has not been attained. It follows therefore, this the writer assumes, that Christ has brought the rest within the reach of His people, as indeed Christians know. This interpretation of the quotation seems to be more natural than to suppose that the reference is designed to contrast the faith of Christians with the want of faith which caused the rejection of the Jews of the Exodus.

εἴρηκεν] Comp. *v.* 4; i. 13; x. 9 note; xiii. 5; Acts xiii. 34. The subject is simply, 'God,' or 'the Spirit,' and not 'the Scripture.'

καίτοι τῶν ἔργων...] *although the works* (of God) *were finished (done) from the foundation of the world.* Vulg. *et quidem operibus ab institutione mundi perfectis;* Syr. *although*

⁴εἴρηκεν γάρ που περὶ τῆς ἑβδόμης οὕτως Καὶ κατέπαυσεν ὁ
θεὸς ἐν τῇ ἡμέρᾳ τῇ ἑβδόμῃ ἀπὸ πάντων τῶν ἔργων αὐτοῦ, ⁵καὶ ἐν
τούτῳ πάλιν Εἰ εἰσελεύσονται εἰς τὴν κατάπαυσίν μου. ⁶ἐπεὶ
οὖν ἀπολείπεται τινὰς εἰσελθεῖν εἰς αὐτήν, καὶ οἱ πρότερον

4 ἐν τῇ...ἐβδ. om. A.   5 εἰ om. D₂*.

the works of God... There was therefore no failure on the part of God.
The divine rest was prepared. God
Himself had entered into it, though
it still remained that His people
should share it according to His
purpose. Thus the rest was at once
in the past and in the future.

καίτοι] In the N.T. Acts xiv. 17 only;
καίτοιγε John iv. 2. The word is used
with a participle in all periods of
Greek literature : Simon. ap. Plat.
Protag. 26 p. 339 C καίτοι εἰρημένον.
Epict. *Diss.* i. 8, 5.

ἀπὸ καταβολῆς κ.] c. ix. 26. See
Matt. xiii. 35 [Ps. lxxvii. (lxxviii.) 2
ἀπ᾽ ἀρχῆς LXX.]; xxv. 34; Lk. xi. 50;
Apoc. xiii. 8; xvii. 8. The phrase
is not found in the LXX. Compare
πρὸ καταβολῆς κ. John xvii. 24; Eph.
i. 4.

The writer of the Epistle by this reference completes the conception of
the promised rest. 'The rest of God,'
the rest which He had provided for
His people, is no other in its last
form than the rest which He Himself
enjoyed. Of this the earthly inheritance was only a symbol.

4, 5. The quotations in these verses
establish in detail the two conclusions
found in the words quoted in *v.* 3,
that there is a rest already prepared
(*v.* 4); and that Israel did not enter
into it (*v.* 5).

4. εἴρηκεν] Comp. *v.* 3 note.

που] Comp. ii. 6 note. This indefinite form of quotation is found
nowhere else in the N.T. It occurs
in other writers : Philo, *Quod Deus
immut.* § 16, i. p. 284 M.; *De prof.*
§ 36, i. 575; *De congr. er. gr.* § 31, i.
544; Clem. R. *ad Cor.* i. 15. The sense
of the particle is probably not local

(*somewhere*) but general ('as we know,'
'to quote familiar words').

περὶ τῆς ἐβδ.] It has been remarked
that 'the six days' are defined in the
record of creation by 'the evening and
the morning,' but to the seventh no
such limits are given. See *v.* 9 note.

κατέπαυσεν] The verb is used in an
intransitive sense (though rarely) in
classical Greek; and in the LXX.:
Ecclus. v. 6; 1 Macc. ix. 73 &c. It is
used in the commoner transitive sense
below *v.* 8.

5. ἐν τούτῳ πάλιν] sc. εἴρηκεν ὁ
θεός. The τούτῳ is neuter: *in this*
place, or phrase.

πάλιν] *again*, on the other side.
The failure of those to whom the
promise was originally made to attain
it, is a second element in the argument. There is a rest; and yet further
it has not been realised by men.

6. But when we recognise failure
it is not that we acquiesce in it. The
promise once made will have a fulfilment. *Some* must enter into the
rest: those who were formerly called
did not enter through disobedience;
therefore another time was afterwards
fixed when believers might gain by
ready self-surrender that which God
still offered. The conditional terms
are thus two and not one; for the
second clause (καὶ οἱ πρότ. εὐαγγελ.)
cannot be considered to be only explanatory of the first.

ἐπεὶ οὖν] See c. v. 11 note.

ἀπολείπεται] *v.* 9; x. 26. This certainty is left as a consequence of the
unrepealed (though unfulfilled) promise.

οἱ πρότερον εὐαγγ.] *they to whom the
good tidings were before preached...*
Vulg. *quibus prioribus annunciatum*

εὐαγγελισθέντες οὐκ εἰϲΗλθον δι' ἀπείθειαν, ⁷πάλιν τινὰ
ὁρίζει ἡμέραν, ϹΗΜΕΡΟΝ, ἐν Δαυεὶδ λέγων μετὰ τοσοῦτον
χρόνον, καθὼς ⌜προείρηται⌝,

ϹΗΜΕΡΟΝ ἐὰΝ ΤΗϹ φωΝΗϹ ΑΥΤΟΥ ἀΚΟΥϹΗΤΕ,
ΜΗ ϹΚΛΗΡΥΝΗΤΕ ΤᾺϹ ΚΑΡΔΙΑϹ ΥΜῶΝ·

⁸ εἰ γὰρ αὐτοὺς Ἰησοῦς κατέπαυσεν, οὐκ ἂν περὶ ἄλλης

προείρηκεν

6 ἀπείθειαν : ἀπιστίαν ℵ* vg.   7 τινὰ ὁρίζει ℵᶜ. προείρηται ℵACD₂* vg syrhl
me : προείρηκεν B : εἴρηται ϛ.   8 ἂν : ἄρα B.

est. Only two generations are contemplated, that of Moses and that of
Christ. The second generation of
Israel who entered into Canaan are
not considered to have received or
enjoyed the fulness of the original
promise.

δι' ἀπείθειαν] O. L. *propter con-
tumaciam.* The Vulgate rendering
propter incredulitatem (and so *v.* 11;
Rom. xi. 30, 32; Col. iii. 6 [O. L. *dis-
sidentia*]; Eph. ii. 2; v. 6: in iii. 12,
19 ἀπιστία is so rendered) obscures the
important difference between the state
of mind and the active expression of
it. Unbelief is manifested in disobedience (contrast iii. 19). The two
are placed in close connexion Rom.
xi. 20 ff., 30 ff.; comp. John iii. 36.

7. ὁρίζει] O. L. *præfinivit...* Vulg.
terminat... The Holy Spirit through
the writer of the Psalm (c. iii. 7) *defineth a certain day,* '*Today,*' *saying...* It seems more natural to take
'Today' as the explanation of 'a
certain day,' than to connect it with
'saying' as part of the quotation.

ἐν Δ. λέγων] *saying in the person
of David,* who was regarded as the
author of the whole Psalter; and not
'in the book of David' (the phrases
ἐν Ἠλίᾳ Rom. xi. 2, ἐν τῷ Ὡσηέ Rom.
ix. 25, are not exactly parallel). The
expression, which follows the common
mode of speaking, is not to be regarded by itself as decisive of the
authorship of the Psalm.

προείρηται] c. iii. 7, 15.

8—10. The words of the Psalmist
convey also another lesson. In one
sense it might be said that in the
second generation those who were
rescued from Egypt did enter into
the rest which was refused to their
fathers. But Canaan was not the
rest of God. The rest of God is a
Sabbath rest which man also is destined
to share, a rest after finished labour.
Therefore the Psalmist, in the troubled
rest of Canaan, still points his hearers
to an end unattained.

⁸ *For if Joshua had given them
rest, He would not have spoken after
this of another day.* ⁹ *There remaineth then a sabbath rest for the people
of God.* ¹⁰ *For he that is entered
into His rest hath himself also rested
from his works as God did from His
own.*

8. εἰ γὰρ...Ἰησοῦς] *For if Joshua...*
The Peshito defines the ambiguous
name (*Jesus*): *Jesus the son of
Nun...* (but not in Acts vii. 45).

αὐτούς] The antecedent is mentally
supplied: 'those in whom Christians
find their counterpart.' Comp. viii.
8, xi. 28. See Winer p. 183.

κατέπαυσεν] transitive (otherwise *vv.*
4 note, 10) as in Ex. xxxiii. 14; Deut.
iii. 20 &c.

οὐκ ἂν περὶ ἄλλης ἐλάλει...] *He would
not have continued to speak after
this,* after so long a time (*v.* 7), *of
another day.* O. L. *non de alio* (?)

ἐλάλει μετὰ ταῦτα ἡμέρας.   ⁹ ἄρα ἀπολείπεται σαββα-

μετὰ ταῦτα : μετ᾽ αὐτά C.   9 om. vers. ℵ* (suppl. A).   ἀπολείπεται : ἀπολειται B.

(Lcf. *de aliis*) *dixisset postera die.* Vulg. *nunquam de alia loqueretur posthac die.* For the unusual and expressive combination εἰ κατέπαυσεν οὐκ ἂν...ἐλάλει, see Additional Note.

It is assumed that if Joshua did not gain an entrance into the rest of God, no later leader did up to the time of Christ. No earthly rest indeed can be the rest of God (xi. 9 f.).

9. ἄρα ἀπολ....] c. xii. 8. This unclassical use of ἄρα in the first place of a sentence as defining a conclusion from the previous words is found in the Synoptists (Matt. xii. 28 ; Luke xi. 48) and in St Paul (Rom. x. 17; 1 Cor. xv. 18 &c.), especially in the form ἄρα οὖν (Rom. v. 18 &c.), but it is not found in St John or in the Catholic Epistles.

σαββατισμός] a sabbath rest (O. L. *requies,* Vulg. *sabbatismus,* Syr. *to keep a Sabbath-rest*)—a rest which closes the manifold forms of earthly preparation and work (the Hexaemeron of human toil): not an isolated sabbath but a sabbath-life. The change of term from κατάπαυσις is significant. The word is not quoted as used by any earlier writer. Σαββατίζω occurs not unfrequently in the LXX., and σαββατισμός itself is used in an enumeration of superstitious observances by Plutarch: *De superst.* 3; ii. p. 166 A.

The Sabbath rest answers to the Creation as its proper consummation. Such is the thought of Augustine at the end of his *Confessions* (xiii. 35 f.): Domine Deus, pacem da nobis, omnia enim præstitisti, pacem quietis, pacem sabbati, sabbati sine vespera. Omnis quippe iste ordo pulcherrimus rerum valde bonarum modis suis peractis transitorius est; et *mane* quippe in eis *factum est et vespera.* Dies autem septimus sine vespera est nec habet occasum, quia sanctificasti eum ad permansionem sempiternam ; ut id

quod tu post opera tua bona valde, quamvis ea quiete feceris, requievisti septimo die, hoc præloquatur nobis vox libri tui, quod et nos post opera nostra, ideo bona valde quia tu nobis ea donasti, sabbato vitæ æternæ requiescamus in te.

And again after giving a brief parallel of the six days of Creation with the ages of the world, he closes his *De civitate* (xxii. 30, 5) with the striking conception of the 'seventh day,' the 'Sabbath,' passing into an eternal 'Lord's day': De istis porro ætatibus singulis nunc diligenter longum est disputare. Hæc tamen septima erit sabbatum nostrum, cujus finis non erit vespera sed dominicus dies, velut octavus æternus, qui Christi resurrectione sacratus est, æternam non solum spiritus verum etiam corporis requiem præfigurans. Ibi vacabimus et videbimus; videbimus et amabimus; amabimus et laudabimus. Ecce quod erit in fine sine fine. Nam quis alius noster est finis nisi pervenire ad regnum cujus nullus est finis?

The remarks of the Greek fathers are less suggestive: σαββατισμὸν ὠνόμασε τὴν τῶν σωματικῶν ἔργων ἀπαλλαγήν (Theodoret). And Chrysostom : ὥσπερ γὰρ ἐν τῷ σαββάτῳ πάντων μὲν τῶν πονηρῶν ἀπέχεσθαι κελεύει, ἐκεῖνα δὲ μόνα γίνεσθαι τὰ πρὸς λατρείαν τοῦ θεοῦ, ἅπερ οἱ ἱερεῖς ἐπετέλουν, καὶ ὅσα ψυχὴν ὠφελεῖ καὶ μηδὲν ἕτερον, οὕτω καὶ τότε.

The Jewish teachers dwelt much upon the symbolical meaning of the Sabbath as prefiguring 'the world to come.' One passage quoted by Schoettgen and others may be given : 'The people of Israel said: Lord of the whole world, shew us the world to come. God, blessed be He, answered : Such a pattern is the Sabbath' (*Jalk. Rub.* p. 95, 4). In this connexion the double ground

τισμὸς τῷ λαῷ τοῦ θεοῦ· ¹⁰ ὁ γὰρ εἰсελθὼν εἰс τὴν κατά-
παυсιν ἀγτοῦ καὶ αὐτὸς κατέπαυсεν ἀπὸ τῶν ἔργων ἀγτοῦ ὥσπερ
ἀπὸ τῶν ἰδίων ὁ θεός. ¹¹ Сπογδάсωμεν οὖν εἰсελθεῖν εἰс ἐκείνην

11 εἰσελθεῖν : +ἀδελφοί D₂*.

which is given for the observance of
the Sabbath, the rest of God (Ex. xx.
11) and the deliverance from Egypt
(Deut. v. 15), finds its spiritual confirmation. The final rest of man answers to the idea of Creation realised
after the Fall by Redemption. Comp.
Schoettgen *ad loc.* and on *v.* 3.
τῷ λαῷ τοῦ θεοῦ] c. xi. 25. Comp.
1 Pet. ii. 10 (λαὸς θεοῦ). The phrase
often occurs by implication (Rom. ix.
25 f.; xi. 1 f. &c.). Comp. Gal. vi. 16
(ἐπὶ τὸν Ἰσραὴλ τοῦ θεοῦ); and contrast
c. ii. 17 (τοῦ λαοῦ); xiii. 12 (note);
Apoc. xviii. 4. Israel was the type of
the divine commonwealth. Sabbatismus non paucis reservatur sed *populo*,
id est magnæ multitudini; nec tamen
cuilibet populo, sed *populo Dei* (Herv.).
10.   ὁ γὰρ εἰσ.] *for he that is en-*
tered (enters), whoever has once entered, *into His rest,* the rest of God
(iii. 18; iv. 1)... The general statement gives the reason for the remarkable title which has been now given
to the rest (σαββατισμός) by reference
to *v.* 4.
The words may also be understood
(though this seems to be less likely)
as unfolding the nature of the promised rest.
The form of construction ⟨εἰσελθών,
κατέπαυσεν⟩ marks the perfectness of
the issue. The entrance and the rest
are coincident and complete. Comp.
Matt. xxv. 21, 23.
κατ. ἀπὸ τῶν ἔργων] Comp. Apoc.
xiv. 13.
ὥσπερ ἀπὸ τῶν ἰδίων ὁ θ.] *as God did*
from His own works, from the works
which, as far as man can conceive,
correspond with His Nature, and
which are spoken of as works, though
wrought without toil. Comp. 1 Cor.
iii. 8 κατὰ τὸν ἴδιον κόπον.

(*b*) The responsibility of such as
have received the promise of the rest
of God (11—13).
11—13. Since the promise remains
for Christians they must also heed
the warning (*v.* 11). The Gospel must
be received with a devotion which
answers to the character of the Power
by which it is offered (*vv.* 12, 13).
¹¹ *Let us therefore give diligence to*
enter into that rest, that no one fall
after the same example of disobe-
dience. ¹² *For the word of God is*
living, and active, and sharper than
any two-edged sword, and piercing
even to the dividing of soul and spirit,
and of joints and marrow, and quick
to judge the feelings and thoughts of
the heart. ¹³ *And there is no creature*
that is not manifest in His sight, but
all things are naked and laid open
to the eyes of Him to whom we have
to give account.
11.   σπουδάσωμεν οὖν...] *Let us*
give diligence (Latt. *Festinemus*),
strive earnestly...because 'the prize
is noble and the peril is great.' There
is need of active exertion that we may
secure what God has promised. So
Chrysostom: μέγα μὲν ἡ πίστις καὶ
σωτήριον καὶ ταύτης ἄνευ οὐκ ἔνι σωθῆναί
τινα. ἀλλ᾽ οὐκ ἀρκεῖ καθ᾽ ἑαυτὴν τοῦτο
ἐργάσασθαι ἀλλὰ δεῖ καὶ πολιτείας ὀρθῆς.
And Primasius, following him: Festinemus inquit quoniam non sufficit
sola fides sed debet addi et vita fidei
condigna... Herveius marks the situation of the Hebrews more exactly:
Festinemus ingredi nec in his terrenis
quæ nos impediunt immoremur. Festinemus fide et bonis operibus, quod
illi non faciunt qui carnaliter adhuc
legem observant et erga fidem et
spiritualem conversationem negli-
gentes existunt.

τὴν κατάπαυσιν, ἵνα μὴ ἐν τῷ αὐτῷ τις ὑποδείγματι πέσῃ
τῆς ἀπειθείας. ¹²Ζῶν γὰρ ὁ λόγος τοῦ θεοῦ καὶ ἐνεργὴς

om. τις א*.   ἀπειθείας: ἀληθείας D₂*.   12 ἐνεργής: ἐναργής B.

For σπουδάζειν see Eph. iv. 3; 2 Tim.
ii. 15; 2 Pet. i. 10; iii. 14.

εἰς ἐκείνην τὴν κατ.] *into that rest,*
that rest of God which is characterised
by such absolute blessedness (comp.
Matt. vii. 22 *ἐν ἐκείνῃ τῇ ἡμέρᾳ*; John
xi. 49 note).

ἵνα μὴ ἐν τῷ αὐτῷ...πέσῃ...] O. L. *ne
aliquis eodem exemplo cadat a veritate.* Lcf. *ne aliqui in idem ex.
contumaciæ cadant.* Vulg. *ne in
id ipsum quis incidat incredulitatis
exemplum.* Syr. *that we may not
fall in the manner of those who did
not believe.* These two forms of
rendering (Lcf., Vulg.; O. L., Syr.;)
represent two possible interpretations
of the words represented roughly by
'falling into' and 'falling after' the
same example. According to the first
interpretation πίπτειν ἐν ὑποδ. is a
compressed expression for 'falling into
the same type of disobedience and
thus exhibiting it.' But πίπτειν εἰς
ὑπόδειγμα, which is involved in this
explanation, is, under any circumstances, an extremely strange expression.

Hence it is better to follow the
second view, in which πίπτειν is taken
absolutely in the sense of 'falling'
'perishing' as opposed to 'standing'
(comp. 1 Cor. x. 12; Rom. xi. 11), and
ἐν ὑποδ. describes the lesson presented
by the fall.

Those who so fall become, in their
punishment, an example like that
offered by the Jews in the Wilderness,
an example, that is, of the fatal consequences of disobedience fitted to
alarm others. Unbelief (iii. 12) is
here seen in its practical issue (*v.* 6
note). The word ὑπόδειγμα occurs
2 Pet. ii. 6 with gen. pers. ('an example
to deter them'). See also John xiii.
15; and for a different use of the word
c. viii. 5 note.

The words τῆς ἀπειθείας are placed
at the end and isolated, so that attention is fixed and rests upon them
(comp. ix. 15; xii. 11).

The parallel suggested by the words
was the more impressive when the
Apostle wrote, because the generation
of the Exodus had borne much, like
the Hebrew Christians, before they
fell at last. And the spiritual trial of
Jews and Christians was essentially
the same: illi non crediderunt Deum
sufficere ad dandam requiem terræ
promissionis, et isti similiter Christum
ad dandam requiem perpetuam sufficere non credebant sine carnalibus
observantiis (Herv.).

12. The necessity of earnest effort
lies in the character of the divine
revelation. It is not 'a vain thing
for us: it is our life.'

The main thought in the description
of 'the word of God' is not that of
punishment, as it is taken by Chrysostom, but of its essential nature as it
enters into, permeates, transforms,
every element in man. There is no
question of an external rest apart
from the harmony of the believer with
God or, in the figure of *v.* 2, apart from
the vital union of the hearer with the
word. The rest is the consummation
of that divine fellowship of which the
life in Canaan was a type.

Thus Philo also saw in the 'perfect
light' of the seventh day a symbol of
'the light of virtue' in which the soul
finds true rest: ἐν ταύτῃ τῇ φύσει
παύεται ἡ τῶν θνητῶν σύστασις· καὶ
γὰρ οὕτως ἔχει· ὅταν ἀνατείλῃ φέγγος
τῆς ἀρετῆς, τὸ λαμπρὸν καὶ θεῖον ὄντως,
ἐπέχεται (is checked) τῆς ἐναντίας
φύσεως ἡ γένεσις (*Leg. Alleg.* i. § 8; i.
46).

The five successive epithets (ζῶν...
ἐνεργής...τομώτερος...διικνούμενος...κρι-
τικός...) applied to 'the word' mark

with increasing clearness its power to deal with the individual soul. There is a passage step by step from that which is most general to that which is most personal. Life is characterised by activity: the activity takes the special form of an internal examination, which reaches to the very foundations of our organization; and this is not physical only but inspired by a moral force, all-pervading, all-discerning, for it is indeed the force of God.

By 'the word of God' (ὁ λόγος τοῦ θεοῦ) we must understand the word which He speaks through His messengers or immediately in the heart of each man. Here the thought is in the first instance necessarily of the word spoken by the Son Who has again offered to man the rest of God. Comp. John xii. 48 (Deut. xviii. 18 f.). This sense is required by the whole course of the argument (iii. 7 λέγει, v. 15 ἐν τῷ λέγεσθαι, iv. 2 ἐσμὲν εὐηγγελισμένοι...ὁ λόγος τῆς ἀκοῆς, v. 4 εἴρηκεν, v. 7 ἐν Δαυεὶδ λέγων, v. 8 ἐλάλει).

The language is not directly applicable to the Personal Word Himself. He cannot properly be likened to the sword. The sword 'issues from his mouth' (Apoc. i. 16); and it may be concluded yet further that the author of the Epistle did not directly identify the divine Λόγος with the Son (i. 2). At the same time the truth that Christ is the Gospel which He brings is present to the writer's mind and influences his form of expression. Thus the passage shews how naturally the transition was made from the revelation of God to Him Who was at once the Revelation and the Revealer. Comp. 1 John i. 1 f. note.

It is not however surprising that the passage was commonly understood of the Personal Word by the Fathers: e.g. Eusebius *Theoph.* Cram. *Cat.* p. 460; Athanasius *c. Ar.* ii. §§ 35, 72; Isidore, *Cat.* p. 459; Œcumenius; Theophylact; Primasius; Herveius. The transition to this sense is given in Apoc. xix. 13.

The passage offers an instructive parallel with Philo. Philo speaks at length (*Quis rerum div. hær.* §§ 26 ff.; i. 491 ff. M.) of the Logos as 'the divider' (τομεύς) of things, basing his teaching on an interpretation of Gen. xv. 10. So the Logos divides material things into their indivisible atoms, the soul into rational and irrational, speech into true and false, formless matter into the elements, and so on. Two things only are left undivided: 'the nature of reason (τοῦ λογισμοῦ) in man and that of the Divine Logos above us, and these being indivisible (ἄτμητοι) divide other things innumerable. For the Divine Logos divides and distributes all things in nature, and our intellect (νοῦς) divides into infinitely infinite parts whatsoever matters and bodies it receives intellectually, and never ceases cutting them...' (i. p. 506 M.).

So elsewhere the virtuous man is said to remove the sores of vice by λόγος τομεύς, the knife of reason (*Quod det. pot. insid.* § 29, i. 212 M.). Compare *De Cher.* § 9 (i. p. 144 M.), where the flaming sword of the Cherubim is explained of the Logos used by the individual.

Thus as far as the 'cutting,' 'dividing' power of the Divine Logos is concerned, it is, according to Philo, exercised simply in the realm of being. It has no moral qualities. The moral divider is the human reason. Under other aspects however the Philonic Logos has a moral power (*Quod Deus sit immut.* § 28; i. p. 292 M.).

There is a yet more fundamental difference between the writer of the Epistle and Philo in the conception of the Divine Logos. With Philo it is characteristically the divine thought (the λόγος ἐνδιάθετος): with the writer of the Epistle the divine word (the λόγος προφορικός), as it is with St John.

The action of the word is regarded in relation to (1) man (v. 12), and (2) to all created things. It deals with man in respect (a) to his constitution,

καὶ τομώτερος ὑπὲρ πᾶσαν μάχαιραν δίστομον καὶ διϊκ-

διικνούμενος: δεικνύμενος D₂.*

both immaterial and material, and
(b) to his activity, in feeling and
reason.

12. ζῶν...καὶ ἐνεργὴς καὶ τομώτερος...]
The Word—the revelation—of God is
living (ζῶν), not simply as 'enduring
for ever,' but as having in itself
energies of action. It partakes in
some measure of the character of
God Himself (iii. 12 θεὸς ζῶν note;
x. 31). Comp. Acts vii. 38 λόγια
ζῶντα. John vi. 63 τὰ ῥήματα ἃ ἐγὼ
λελάληκα ὑμῖν πνεῦμά ἐστιν καὶ ζωή
ἐστιν taken up by St Peter v. 68 ῥήματα
ζωῆς αἰωνίου ἔχεις.
With this 'living word' believers
are incorporated.
Compare Orig. *de Princ.* i. 2, 3
Unde et recte mihi dictus videtur
sermo ille qui in Actibus Pauli scrip-
tus est quia *Hic* (?) *est verbum animal vivens* (cf. Lipsius, *Apokr. Apos-
telgesch.* ii. 1, 70 f.).
Comp. Philo, *Leg. Alleg.* iii. §§ 59,
61 (i. 120, 122 M.) ὁρᾷς τῆς ψυχῆς
τροφὴν οἵα ἐστί. λόγος θεοῦ (Ex. xvi.
15)...τὸ δὲ ῥῆμα μέρος αὐτοῦ· τρέφεται
δὲ τῶν μὲν τελειοτέρων ἡ ψυχὴ ὅλῳ τῷ
λόγῳ, ἀγαπήσαιμεν δ' ἂν ἡμεῖς εἰ καὶ
μέρει τραφείημεν αὐτοῦ.
The life of the Word is not only
present, but it is also vigorously
manifested. The Word is *active*
(ἐνεργής, O.L. *validum*, Vulg. *efficax*).
For ἐνεργής see 1 Cor. xvi. 9 θύρα...
ἐνεργής. Philem. 6 ὅπως ἡ κοινωνία...
ἐνεργὴς γένηται. The variant ἐναργής
(B, Hier. *in Isai.* lxvi. *evidens*) represents a very common confusion of
forms.
The activity of the Word is not
intellectual only but moral: it deals
with conduct as well as with knowledge. It is shewn in the power of
the Word to lay open the innermost
depths of human nature. The Word
has unrivalled keenness: it pierces
in fact to the most secret parts of
man; and that not as an instrument

merely but as a judge of moral issues.
It is sharper than the most formidable
weapon of earthly warfare: it finds
its way through every element of
our earthly frame: it scrutinises the
affections and thoughts of which our
bodily members are the present
organs.
The image of the sharp cutting
power (τομώτερος, Vulg. *penetrabilior*)
of the Word finds a striking parallel
in a line of Phocylides (*v.* 118),
ὅπλον τοι λόγος ἀνδρὶ τομώτερόν ἐστι
σιδήρου.
In this respect the word is compared with the sharpest of material arms, 'the two-edged sword.'
Comp. Apoc. i. 16 ἐκ τοῦ στόματος
αὐτοῦ ῥομφαία δίστομος ὀξεῖα ἐκπορευο-
μένη, ii. 12. Is. xlix. 2; (xi. 4; li. 16;
Hos. vi. 5). Schoettgen quotes a Jewish
saying to the effect that 'he who
utters the Shema is as if he held a
two-edged sword.'
The phrase is common in classical
writers, *e.g.* Eurip. *Hel.* 989.
Other examples are given by Wetstein.
For μάχαιρα see Eph. vi. 17 δέξασθε
...τὴν μάχαιραν τοῦ πνεύματος ὅ ἐστιν
ῥῆμα θεοῦ (ξίφος is not found in N.T.);
and for τομώτερος ὑπέρ Luke xvi.
8; Jud. xi. 25; c. iii. 3; ix. 23 (παρά).
καὶ διικνούμενος ἄχρι μερισμοῦ...]
The 'dividing' operation of 'the Word
of God' has been understood as
reaching to the separation of soul
from spirit, and of joints *from* marrow,
or to the separation, in themselves, of
soul and spirit, and of joints and
marrow. The latter interpretation
seems to be unquestionably right.
The Word of God analyses, lays bare,
reveals in their true nature, reduces
to their final elements, all the powers
of man. Chrysostom mentions both
views: τί ἐστι τοῦτο; φοβερόν τι ἠνίξατο.
ἢ γὰρ ὅτι τὸ πνεῦμα διαιρεῖ ἀπὸ τῆς
ψυχῆς, λέγει· ἢ ὅτι καὶ αὐτῶν (*leg.* δι'

νούμενος ἄχρι μερισμοῦ ψυχῆς καὶ πνεύματος, ἁρμῶν τε
καὶ μυελῶν, καὶ κριτικὸς ἐνθυμήσεων καὶ ἐννοιῶν καρδίας·

ψυχῆς καὶ ℵABCH vg syrr me: ψ.+τε′ καὶ ς D₂.   ἐνθυμήσεων : -σεως C*D₂*.
καὶ ἐνν.: ἐνν. τε D₂*.

αὐτῶν)τῶν ἀσωμάτων διικνεῖται, οὐ καθὼς
ἡ μάχαιρα μόνον τῶν σωμάτων. δείκνυσιν
...ὅτι...ὅλον δι′ ὅλου διικνεῖται τὸν ἄνθρωπον.(leg. τοῦ ἀνθρώπου) (ad l.).
The omission of the τε in the first
of the two double clauses (ψ. καὶ πν.
ἁρ. τε καὶ μ.) causes some difficulty as
to the construction. It has been
supposed that the first clause (ψ. καὶ
πν.) depends on the second 'unto the
division both of the joints and marrow
of soul and spirit'; and again that
the second clause, understood metaphorically, explains the extent of the
penetrative power of the Word 'unto
the division of soul and spirit, yea, of
both spiritual joints and marrow in
that internal frame.'

The first of these interpretations
presupposes a most unnatural construction; and the second is harsh and
forced, though Euripides (Hipp. 255)
speaks of the ἄκρος μυελὸς ψυχῆς.

It is more simple, and free from
objection, to regard the two compound
clauses as coupled by the τε, so that
the first two terms taken together
represent the immaterial elements
in man; while the two which follow
represent the material elements. Thus
the four in combination offer a general
view of the sum of man's powers in
his present organization. The divine
revelation penetrates through all. No
part of human nature is untouched by
it.

For this use of τε compare Acts
xxvi. 30; Luke xxiv. 20.

ψυχῆς καὶ πνεύματος] Vulg. animœ
ac spiritus. Compare 1 Cor. xv. 45;
1 Thess. v. 23. The broad distinction
between the two is given forcibly by
Primasius: Anima vivimus, spiritu
rationabiliter intelligimus: vita nobis
carnalis cum bestiis communis est,

ratio spiritalis cum angelis... Comp.
Additional Note.

ἁρμῶν τε καὶ μυελῶν] Vulg. com-
pagum quoque ac medullarum. Syr.
of joints and of marrow and bones,
the most critical parts of the physical
framework of man, and the inmost
media of his physical force. The
words are not found elsewhere in the
N.T. Œcumenius notices their relation to what goes before: εἰπὼν τὰ
ἀσώματα εἶπε καὶ τὰ σωματικά. The
plural μυελῶν expresses the idea of
the separate members in which the
'marrow' is found. The rendering of
the Peshito is a remarkable example
of an interpretative gloss.

κριτικὸς ἐνθυμήσεων καὶ ἐννοιῶν κ.]
Vulg. discretor (O. L. scrutator) cogi-
tationum et intentionum cordis. The
enumeration of the constituent elements of man is followed by a notice
of his rational activity as a moral
being. Over this, over the feelings
and thoughts of his heart, the Word
of God is fitted to exercise judgment.
The first word (ἐνθυμήσεων) refers to
the action of the affections, the second
(ἐννοιῶν) to the action of the reason.
Clement has a remarkable parallel:
ἐρευνητὴς γάρ ἐστιν (ὁ θεὸς) ἐννοιῶν καὶ
ἐνθυμήσεων (1 Cor. xxi. 9).

For ἐνθύμησις see Matt. ix. 4; xii.
25; Acts xvii. 29; and for ἔννοια,
1 Pet. iv. 1.

Both 'feelings' and 'thoughts' are
referred to 'the heart,' which represents the seat of personal, moral life.
It is of interest to trace the use of
the word through the Epistle: iii. 8
(iii. 15, iv. 7); iii. 10, 12; viii. 10
(x. 16); x. 22; xiii. 9.

13. The thought of the pervading
energy of the revelation of God in
regard to man is now extended to

¹³καὶ οὐκ ἔστιν κτίσις ἀφανὴς ἐνώπιον αὐτοῦ, πάντα δὲ
γυμνὰ καὶ τετραχηλισμένα τοῖς ὀφθαλμοῖς αὐτοῦ, πρὸς

13 κτίσις : κρίσις D₂*.

that of the universal Providence of God with regard to all created beings. Τί λέγω περὶ ἀνθρώπων, φησίν, κἂν γὰρ ἀγγέλους κἂν ἀρχαγγέλους κἂν τὰ Χερουβὶμ καὶ τὰ Σεραφὶμ κἂν οἰανδήποτε κτίσιν, πάντα ἐκκεκάλυπται τῷ ὀφθαλμῷ ἐκείνῳ; (Chrys.). Comp. Philo Leg. Alleg. iii. 60 (i. 121 M.). Timeamus ejus præsentiam cujus scientiam nullatenus effugere valeamus (Primas. Atto).

There is some difficulty as to the antecedent of the two pronouns (ἐνώπιον αὐτοῦ, τοῖς ὀφθαλμοῖς αὐτοῦ). They must evidently refer to the same subject; and since the subject in the second case is unequivocally personal ('Him to Whom we must render account'), there can be little doubt that we must understand 'God' in both places, suggested by the compound subject of the former sentence, 'the Word of God.' Nor is there anything unnatural in the transition from the manifestation of God through His Word to His Person.

For κτίσις (creature) see Rom. i. 25; viii. 39; 2 Cor. v. 17. Ἀφανής does not occur again in N. T.

The negative statement that nothing is hidden from the sight of God is supplemented by a positive statement that all things are stripped of every disguise which might conceal their true nature (γυμνά) and brought by an overmastering power into full view before His eyes (τετραχηλισμένα).

The general sense of τετραχηλισμένα (Latt. aperta, Syrr. revealed, made manifest) is clear, as it is given in the old versions (Hesych. τετραχηλισμένα· πεφανερωμένα), but it is by no means certain from what image the meaning is derived. The word τραχηλίζειν is not found in the LXX. It is fre-

quently used by Philo in the sense of prostrating, overthrowing ; e.g. Quis rer. div. hær. § 55 (i. p. 512 M.) ἀνὴρ ὄντως τραχηλίζων ἢ (lege ᾖ) τραχηλίζεσθαι δύναται : de vit. Mos. § 54 (ii. p. 127 M.) τραχηλιζόμενοι ταῖς ἐπιθυμίαις πάνθ᾽ ὑπομενοῦσι δρᾶν τε καὶ πάσχειν ('obtorto collo pertracti'); and, with a more general application, de exsecr. § 7 (ii. 433 M.) ἄρξεταί ποτε διαπνεῖν καὶ ἀνακύπτειν ἡ πολλὰ γυμνασθεῖσα καὶ τραχηλισθεῖσα γῆ. So Jos. B. Jud. iv. 6, 2. Comp. Plut. de Curios. ii. p. 521 B ὁρᾶτε τὸν ἀθλητὴν ὑπὸ παιδισκαρίου τραχηλιζόμενον (where the idea is of the head turned round to gaze, παρεπιστρεφόμενον, and so, in the next sentence, τραχηλιζομένους καὶ περιαγομένους).

The Greek Fathers were evidently perplexed by the word. Chrysostom appears to understand it of victims hung up (by the neck) and flayed : τὸ τετραχηλισμένα εἴρηται ἀπὸ μεταφορᾶς τῶν δερμάτων τῶν ἀπὸ τῶν ἱερείων ἐξελκομένων. ὥσπερ γὰρ ἐκεῖνα, ἐπειδάν τις σφάξας ἀπὸ τῆς σαρκὸς παρελκύσῃ τὸ δέρμα, πάντα τὰ ἔνδον ἀποκαλύπτεται καὶ δῆλα γίνεται τοῖς ἡμετέροις ὀφθαλμοῖς, οὕτω καὶ τῷ θεῷ δῆλα πρόκειται πάντα.

Theodoret interprets the word of victims prostrate and lifeless : τὸ δὲ τετραχηλισμένα τοῖς ὀφθαλμοῖς αὐτοῦ ἐκ μεταφορᾶς τέθεικε τῶν θυομένων ζώων, ἃ παντελῶς ἄφωνα κεῖται, τῆς σφαγῆς τὴν φωνὴν ἀφελομένης.

Œcumenius gives Chrysostom's meaning and another without deciding between them : τετραχηλισμένα δέ φησι τὰ γυμνὰ ἀπὸ μεταφορᾶς τῶν προβάτων τῶν ἐκ τραχήλου ἠρτημένων καὶ γεγυμνωμένων τῆς δορᾶς. ἢ τὸ τετραχηλισμένα ἀντὶ τοῦ κάτω κύπτοντα, καὶ τὸν τράχηλον ἐπικλίνοντα διὰ τὸ μὴ ἰσχύειν ἀτενίσαι τῇ δόξῃ ἐκείνῃ τοῦ Χριστοῦ καὶ θεοῦ

ὃν ἡμῖν ὁ λόγος.   ¹⁴"Ἔχοντες οὖν ἀρχιερέα
μέγαν διεληλυθότα τοὺς οὐρανούς, Ἰησοῦν τὸν υἱὸν τοῦ

ὑμῶν (leg. ἡμῶν) Ἰησοῦ. Theophylact prefers the interpretation of Chrysostom.

The word has been popularly explained as used of a wrestler who seizes the neck and thrusts back the head of his adversary (resupinare) so as to expose it fully to sight; but there is no direct evidence of the use of τραχηλίζω in this sense; and the words of Œcumenius point to the sense of pressing down the head, which agrees with the general idea of prostration.

πρὸς ὃν ἡμῖν ὁ λόγος] to whom₁we have to give account. (So Syr.) O. L. ante quem nobis oratio est. Vulg. ad quem (Hier. de quo) nobis sermo. Comp. Ign. ad Magn. 3. Compare Chrysostom Orat. ad illumin. 1 (ii. 274 ed. Gaume) οὐ γὰρ πρὸς τοὺς συνδούλους ἡμῖν ἀλλὰ πρὸς τὸν Δεσπότην ὁ λόγος ἐστί, καὶ τούτῳ τὰς εὐθύνας δώσομεν τῶν βεβιωμένων ἁπάντων. So he rightly gives the sense here: ᾧ μέλλομεν δοῦναι εὐθύνας τῶν πεπραγμένων. Primasius lays open the ground of the truth in impressive words: nec mirum si totus ubique totam suam agnoscat creaturam.

iii. *Transition to the doctrine of the High-priesthood of Christ, resuming* ii. 17 f. (14—16).

Having dealt with the relation of the Son of Man (iii. 1 *Jesus*) to Moses and Joshua; and with the relation of the promise which declares man's destiny to the people of God under the Old and New Dispensations, the writer now returns to the central thought of the High-priesthood, from which he has turned aside, and prepares for the full discussion of it in the following chapters (v.—x. 18). Briefly, he shews, we have a High-priest who has Himself entered the rest of God (v. 14); who can perfectly sympathise with us (v. 15); so that we

can ourselves draw near to God, with whom He is (v. 16).

¹⁴*Having therefore a great High-priest, Who hath passed through the heavens, Jesus the Son of God, let us cling to our confession;* ¹⁵*for we have not a High-priest that cannot be touched with the feeling of our infirmities, but one that hath been tempted in all points like as we are, apart from sin.* ¹⁶*Let us therefore come with boldness unto the throne of grace, that we may receive mercy and find grace to help us in time of need.*

14. ἔχοντες οὖν ἀρχ....] Comp. x. 19; xii. 1. The words point back to ii. 17; iii. 1. The fear of final failure, the consciousness of weakness and partial failure, turn the thoughts again to the Mediator.

Our High-priest, our Apostle, has done more than Aaron or Moses prefigured. He has entered into the rest which He foreshewed, so that He can also bring His people into it. He is seated at the right hand of God. But meanwhile man has his part to do; and as we strive to secure the promised rest we must cling firmly to the confession in which lies the assurance of success.

The simple fact that we have a High-priest is stated first (*Having therefore a High-priest*), and then His character and position are described: *Having therefore a High-priest, great* in His essential Nature (i. 1 ff.), and One *Who hath passed through the heavens*, and so come before the very Presence of God. The epithet μέγας does not go to complete the notion of High-priest, but characterises his dignity. Comp. x. 21; (xiii. 20). Philo *de somn.* i. § 38 (i. p. 654 M.) ὁ μέγας ἀρχιερεὺς [τῆς ὁμολογίας]; *de Abr.* § 40 (ii. 34 M.) ὁ μέγας ἀρχιερεὺς τοῦ μεγίστου θεοῦ.

διελ. τ. οὐρ.] *who hath passed*

θεοῦ, κρατῶμεν τῆς ὁμολογίας· ¹⁵οὐ γὰρ ἔχομεν ἀρχιερέα

through the heavens. O. L. *egressum*
cœlos. Vulg. *qui penetravit cœlos.*
Comp. Eph. iv. 10 (c. vii. 26 note).
Christ not merely ascended up to
heaven in the language of space, but
transcended the limitations of space.
Thus we say that He 'entered into
heaven' and yet is 'above the heavens.'
The phrase points out the superiority of Christ over the Jewish high-
priest and over the Jewish mediator.
He has passed not through the veil
only but through the heavens up to
the very throne of God (comp. ix.
24; i. 3), and entered into the royal
rest of God.

Theophylact well compares Christ
and Moses: οὐ τοιοῦτος οἷος Μωυσῆς,
ἐκεῖνος μὲν γὰρ οὔτε αὐτὸς εἰσῆλθεν εἰς
τὴν κατάπαυσιν οὔτε τὸν λαὸν εἰσήγαγεν·
οὗτος δὲ διεληλυθὼς τοὺς οὐρανοὺς συν-
εδριάζει τῷ Πατρὶ καὶ δύναται ἡμῖν τὴν εἰς
οὐρανοὺς εἴσοδον δοῦναι καὶ τῆς ἐν ἐπαγγελίαις καταπαύσεως κληρονόμους ποιῆσαι. And Primasius brings out aspects of μέγας: *Magnum pontificem*
eum appellat qui habet æternum sacerdotium, *semper vivens, ad interpellandum* pro nobis (c. vii. 25). Sic
enim dixit de illo angelus ad Mariam:
*Hic erit magnus et Filius altissimi
vocabitur* (Lk. i. 32).

Ἰησοῦν τὸν υἱὸν τοῦ θεοῦ] The two
titles are placed side by side in order
to suggest the two natures of the
Lord which include the assurance of
sympathy and power. For the use of
Jesus see ii. 9 note; and for *the Son
of God* see vi. 6; vii. 3; x. 29; and
Additional Note on i. 4. And for the
combination of the two see Acts ix. 20;
1 Thess. i. 10; 1 John i. 7; iv. 15; v. 5.

κρατῶμεν τῆς ὁμολ.] *Let us cling
to* our faith in Him, Whom we openly
confess, as truly human, truly divine
(Latt. *teneamus confessionem*). Οὐ τὸ
πᾶν τῷ ἱερεῖ δίδωσιν, ἀλλὰ καὶ τὰ παρ'
ἡμῶν ζητεῖ, λέγε δὴ τὴν ὁμολογίαν
(Theophlct.).

The phrase κρατεῖν τῆς ὁμολογίας, as
contrasted with κατέχωμεν τὴν ὁμολογίαν (c. x. 23), seems to mark the act of
grasping and clinging to that to which
we attach ourselves, as distinguished
from the act of holding firmly that
which is already completely in our
possession. Comp. vi. 18. Thus the
words imply danger and incite to
effort.

For ὁμολογία compare c. iii. 1; x.
23 note; 1 Tim. vi. 12 f.

The writer everywhere insists on
the duty of the public confession of
the faith. The crisis claimed not
simply private conviction but a clear
declaration of belief openly in the
face of men. Comp. 1 John iv. 2
note.

15. οὐ γάρ] The apostle calls for
effort, and he encourages it. By the
negative form of the sentence he recognises the presence of an objection
which he meets by anticipation. The
divine glory of Christ might have
seemed to interpose a barrier between
Him and His people. But on the
contrary, the perfectness of His sympathy is the ground for clinging to
the faith which answers to our needs.
He is as near to us as the human
high-priests (nay, nearer than they)
whose humanity inspired the Jewish
worshippers with confidence. *For we
have not a High-priest such as cannot be touched...but one that hath
been tempted...*

μὴ δυνάμενον...πεπειρασμένον δέ] The
power of Christ's sympathy is expressed negatively and positively. He
is not such as to be unable to sympathise: nay rather He has been tried
in all respects after our likeness, and
therefore He must sympathise from
His own experience.

μὴ δυνάμενον] *such that he cannot...*
For μή with participles in this Epistle
see iv. 2; vii. 3, 6; ix. 9; xi. 8, 13,
27; xii. 27; (vi. 1; x. 25; xiii. 17 are

μὴ δυνάμενον συνπαθῆσαι ταῖς ἀσθενείαις ἡμῶν, πεπει-

different); for οὐ xi. 1 (contrast 2 Cor. iv. 18), 35. For other examples of participles with οὐ see 2 Cor. iv. 8 f.; Gal. iv. 8, 27; Col. ii. 19; 1 Pet. i. 8; ii. 10 (not Eph. v. 4; Phil. iii. 3); Winer, pp. 606 ff.

συνπαθῆσαι] *to be touched with the feeling of.* Vulg. *compati*... c. x. 34 (συμπαθής 1 Pet. iii. 8. Vulg. *compatiens*). The verb occurs in Symmachus Job ii. 11, and in classical writers from Isocrates downwards. It expresses not simply the compassion of one who regards suffering from without, but the feeling of one who enters into the suffering and makes it his own. So Christ is *touched with the feeling of our weaknesses*, which are for us the occasions of sins, as knowing them, though not with the feeling of the sins themselves. Such weaknesses can be characterised by the circumstances of the Lord's life, natural weariness, disappointment, the feeling of desertion, shrinking from pain (contrast the sing. ἀσθένεια c. vii. 28 note). From temptations through such weaknesses the Hebrew Christians were suffering. Comp. v. 2; vii. 28; xi. 34. Clement also combines the thought of Christ's High-priesthood with that of His help to man's weakness: *ad Cor.* i. c. 36 αὕτη ἡ ὁδός, ἀγαπητοί, ἐν ᾗ εὕρομεν τὸ σωτήριον ἡμῶν, Ἰησοῦν Χριστόν, τὸν ἀρχιερέα τῶν προσφορῶν ἡμῶν, τὸν προστάτην καὶ βοηθὸν τῆς ἀσθενείας ἡμῶν. Compare Orig. *in Matt.* xiii. 2 Ἰησοῦς γοῦν φησίν Διὰ τοὺς ἀσθενοῦντας ἠσθένουν καὶ διὰ τοὺς πεινῶντας ἐπείνων καὶ διὰ τοὺς διψῶντας ἐδίψων, and Resch *Agrapha* p. 244.

πεπειρασμένον δέ...χ. ἁμαρτίας] O. L. *expertum in omnibus (omnia) secundum similitudinem sine peccato.* Vulg. *tentatum autem per omnia pro similitudine absque peccato.* Syr. Pesh. *tempted in everything as we (are), sin excepted.*

The words are capable of two distinct interpretations. They may (1) simply describe the issue of the Lord's temptation, so far as He endured all without the least stain of sin (c. vii. 26). Or they may (2) describe a limitation of His temptation. Man's temptations come in many cases from previous sin. Such temptations had necessarily no place in Christ. He was tempted as we are, sharing our nature, yet with this exception, that there was no sin in Him to become the spring of trial. The first of these thoughts is not excluded from the expression, which is most comprehensive in form, but the latter appears to be the dominant idea. In this sense there is a reference to the phrase in the Chalcedonic definition: Ἰησοῦν Χριστόν...ἐκδιδάσκομεν... κατὰ πάντα ὅμοιον ἡμῖν χωρὶς ἁμαρτίας. Comp. c. ix. 28.

We may represent the truth to ourselves best by saying that Christ assumed humanity under the conditions of life belonging to man fallen, though not with sinful promptings from within. Comp. c. ii. 18 note.

Comp. Greg. Nyss. *c. Eunom.* ii. p. 545 Migne: οὐδὲν ἀφῆκε τῆς φύσεως ἡμῶν ὃ οὐκ ἀνέλαβεν ὁ κατὰ πάντα πεπειραμένος καθ᾽ ὁμοιότητα χωρὶς ἁμαρτίας. ἡ δὲ ψυχὴ ἁμαρτία οὐκ ἐστὶν ἀλλὰ δεκτικὴ ἁμαρτίας ἐξ ἀβουλίας ἐγένετο... *c. Apoll.* xi. *id.* p. 1144 ὥσπερ γὰρ τὰ τοῦ χοϊκοῦ ἰδιώματα τοῖς ἐξ ἐκείνου ἐνθεωρεῖται, οὕτως ἐπάναγκες, κατὰ τὴν τοῦ ἀποστόλου ἀπόφασιν, τὸν κατὰ πάντα πεπειραμένον τοῦ ἡμετέρου βίου καθ᾽ ὁμοιότητα χωρὶς ἁμαρτίας. ὁ δὲ νοῦς ἁμαρτία οὐκ ἐστί, πρὸς πᾶσαν ἡμῶν οἰκείως ἔχειν τὴν φύσιν. *c. Eunom.* vi. *id.* p. 721.

Atto, pursuing the thought of Primasius, says well: Venit per viam humanæ conditionis per omnia sine peccato, nihil secum afferens unde morti debitor esset, sicut ipse in Evangelio testatur (St John xiv. 30).

ρασμένον δὲ κατὰ πάντα καθ᾽ ὁμοιότητα χωρὶς ἁμαρτίας.
¹⁶προσερχώμεθα οὖν μετὰ παρρησίας τῷ θρόνῳ τῆς χάρι-

The Greek Fathers generally interpret the words χωρὶς ἁμαρτίας in relation to the facts of Christ's life: ἐνταῦθα καὶ ἄλλο τι αἰνίττεται, ὅτι δυνατὸν χωρὶς ἁμαρτίας καὶ ἐν θλίψεσιν ὄντα διενεγκεῖν. ὥστε καὶ ὅταν λέγῃ ἐν ὁμοιώματι σαρκὸς οὐ τοῦτό φησιν ὅτι ὁμοίωμα σαρκὸς ἀλλ᾽ ὅτι σάρκα ἀνέλαβε. διὰ τί οὖν εἶπεν ἐν ὁμοιώματι; περὶ ἁμαρτωλοῦ σαρκὸς ἔλεγεν· ὁμοία γὰρ ἦν τῇ σαρκὶ τῇ ἡμετέρᾳ· τῇ μὲν γὰρ φύσει ἡ αὐτὴ ἦν ἡμῖν, τῇ δὲ ἁμαρτίᾳ οὐκέτι ἡ αὐτή (Chrys.).

ὡς ἄνθρωπος πεῖραν τῶν ἡμετέρων ἔλαβε παθημάτων μόνης τῆς ἁμαρτίας διαμείνας ἀμύητος (Theod.).

οὔτε γὰρ ἁπλῶς ἁμαρτίαν εἰργάσατο, οὔτε ὅτε ταῦτα ἔπασχεν ἁμαρτητικόν τι ἢ εἶπεν ἢ ἔδρασεν. ὥστε δύνασθε καὶ ὑμεῖς ἐν ταῖς θλίψεσιν χωρὶς ἁμαρτίας διαγενέσθαι (Theophlct.).

πεπειρασμένον] For the perfect, see ii. 18; xii. 3 notes.

κατὰ πάντα] in all things, as in nature so in life. Comp. ii. 17.

καθ᾽ ὁμοι.] c. vii. 15. Comp. Gen. i. 11 f. The words may mean 'according to the likeness of our temptations,' i.e. like as we are tempted (secundum similitudinem O. L.); or 'in virtue of His likeness to us,' i.e. ὁμοιωθεὶς ἡμῖν (ii. 17; pro similitudine Vulg.).

Primasius (compare Chrysostom quoted above) interprets the words as if they were καθ᾽ ὁμοιότητα σαρκὸς [ἁμαρτίας] (Rom. viii. 3): Pro similitudine carnis peccati absque peccato ... In hoc enim quia homo factus est, veram carnem habuit: in hoc vero quia carnem peccati non habuit sed absque peccato, similitudinem nostrae carnis habuit, quae est caro peccati, nam peccatum non habuit... Illius caro non fuit peccati sed munditiae et castitatis atque innocentiæ; quapropter non est tentatus in carne peccati ut peccatum faceret sed in similitudine carnis peccati ut absque

peccato maneret; and again on c. v. 2; tentari potuit per omnia similitudine carnis peccati absque peccato.

16. προσερχώμεθα οὖν...] The vision of the High-priest Who is not Priest only but King, Who is not only Son of God but Son of man, suggests the conclusion that believers, clinging to their confession, can and must use the infinite privileges which their Lord has gained for them. The minds of writer and readers are full of the imagery of the Levitical system, and of the ceremonial of the High-priestly atonement; and the form of the exhortation suggests the grandeur of the position in which the Christian is placed as compared with that of the Jew: 'Let us therefore, trusting the divine power and the human sympathy of 'Jesus the Son of God,' draw near, as priests ourselves in fellowship with our High-priest,—and not remain standing afar off as the congregation of Israel,—to the throne of grace, no symbolic mercy-seat, but the very centre of divine sovereignty and love...'

προσερχώμεθα] The word occurs here for the first time in the Epistle (comp. vii. 25 note; x. 1, 22; xi. 6). It is used in the LXX. for the priestly approach to God in service: e.g. Lev. xxi. 17, 21; xxii. 3, though it has also a wider application. That right of priestly approach is now extended to all Christians. Comp. Apoc. i. 6; v. 10; (xx. 6); 1 Pet. ii. 5, 9. See also ἐγγίζομεν, vii. 19, note.

The power of sympathy in our High Priest is made effective by the power of help: per hoc enim quod similia passus est potest compati; et per hoc quod Deus est in utraque substantia potest misereri (Primas. ad c. v.).

μετὰ παρρησίας] Latt. cum fiducia. (The Syr. Pesh. gives, as elsewhere,

τος, ἵνα λάβωμεν ἔλεος καὶ χάριν εὔρωμεν εἰς εὔκαιρον
βοήθειαν.

16 εὔρωμεν : om. B.　　　　　　om. εἰς D₂*.

'*with eye (face) open.*') So Acts ii.
29; iv. 29, 31; xxviii. 31. St Paul
uses ἐν παρρησίᾳ Eph. vi. 19; Phil. i.
20; Col. ii. 15; St John παρρησίᾳ
vii. 13 &c.; ἢ μηδὲν πρὸς τὴν πίστιν
διστάζοντες, ἢ ὅτι νενίκηκε τὸν κόσμον
(John xvi. 33), δῆλον οὖν ὅτι νικήσει
καὶ τοὺς νῦν ἡμᾶς θλίβοντας (Œcum.).
The phrase is perhaps used here in
the primary sense, 'giving utterance
to every thought and feeling and wish,'
though the word παρρησία is used
more generally elsewhere in the epistle:
iii. 6; x. 19, 35.

τῷ θρόνῳ τῆς χάριτος] The phrase is
to be compared with θρόνος δόξης
(Matt. xix. 28; xxv. 31; 1 Sam. ii. 8;
Jer. xiv. 21; xvii. 12; Ecclus. xlvii. 11);
ὁ θρόνος τῆς μεγαλωσύνης (c. viii. 1),
θρόνος ἀνομίας (Ps. xciii. (xciv.) 20),
θρόνος αἰσθήσεως (Prov. xii. 23). The
gen. in each case seems to express
that which is shewn in a position of
sovereign power. Thus the 'throne
of grace' is that revelation of God's
Presence in which His grace is shewn
in royal majesty. Of this revelation
the glory over the mercy-seat was a
faint symbol.

Philo speaks also of ὁ ἐλέου βωμός
de exsecr. § 7 (ii. 434 M.); and Clement
describes Christians as having come
ὑπὸ τὸν ζυγὸν τῆς χάριτος [τοῦ κυρίου]
(1 *Cor.* 16).

Θρόνος χάριτός ἐστιν (Ps. cx. 1) οὐ
θρόνος κρίσεως νῦν...θρόνος χάριτός
ἐστιν ἕως κάθηται χαριζόμενος ὁ βασιλεύς, ὅταν δὲ ἡ συντέλεια γένηται, τότε
ἐγείρεται εἰς κρίσιν (Chrys.).

On this 'throne of grace' Christ
Himself is seated: ἵνα μὴ ἀκούσας
αὐτὸν ἀρχιερέα νομίσῃς ἑστάναι εὐθέως
αὐτὸν ἐπὶ τὸν θρόνον ἄγει, ὁ δὲ ἱερεὺς οὐ
κάθηται ἀλλ' ἔστηκεν (Chrys.).

ἵνα λάβωμεν ἔ. καὶ χ. εὔρωμεν] *that we
may receive mercy and find grace.*

The twofold aim corresponds with the
twofold necessity of life. Man needs
mercy for past failure, and grace for
present and future work. There is
also a difference as to the mode of
attainment in each case. Mercy is to
be 'taken' as it is extended to man
in his weakness; grace is to be
'sought' by man according to his necessity. Ut misericordiam consequa-
mur, id est, remissionem peccatorum,
et gratiam donorum Spiritus Sancti
(Primas.).

For χάρις compare ii. 9; x. 29; xii.
15, 28; xiii. 9, 25.

For λαβεῖν compare John i. 16; xx.
22; Rom. viii. 15; 1 Pet. iv. 10; and
for εἰρεῖν Luke i. 30; Acts vii. 46;
2 Tim. i. 18.

εἰς εὔκαιρον βοήθειαν] Vulg. *gratiam
inveniamus in auxilio opportuno.*
The help comes when it is needed
and not till then (ii. 18 τοῖς πειραζομένοις βοηθῆσαι). Comp. Philo *de
migr. Abr.* § 10 (i. p. 445 M.) οὐκοῦν
ὅτι καὶ πρὸς βοήθειαν δύναμις ἀρωγὸς
εὐτρεπὴς ἐφεδρεύει παρὰ θεῷ καὶ αὐτὸς
ὁ ἡγεμὼν ἐγγυτέρω πρόσεισιν ἐπ' ὠφε-
λείᾳ τῶν ἀξίων ὠφελεῖσθαι δεδήλωται.
The clause goes with all that precedes:
'mercy' and 'grace' are always ready
at the present moment. Αν νῦν προσέλθης, φησί, λήψῃ καὶ χάριν καὶ ἔλεον·
εὐκαίρως γὰρ προσέρχῃ· ἂν δὲ τότε
προσέλθης, οὐκέτι· ἄκαιρος γὰρ τότε ἡ
πρόσοδος (Chrys. followed by the later
commentators).

Comp. Gen. xxxv. 3. One of the
names of Ahura Mazda is 'the One of
whom questions are asked' (*Zenda-
vesta* S.B.E. ii. p. 24 and note). Philo's
description of 'the Divine Word' as
High-priest in the soul of man is
worthy of study: *de prof.* §§ 20, 21
(i. pp. 562 f. M.).

Additional Note on the reading of iv. 2.

There is evidence of a twofold difference in the earliest authorities as to the reading of this verse. The difference in the forms συνκεκερασμ-, συνκεκραμ- may be neglected. The substantial differences which affect the interpretation of the passage lie in (1) -μένος, -μένους, and (2) τοῖς ἀκούσασιν, τῶν ἀκουσάντων, (τοῖς ἀκουσθεῖσι).

(1) (a) The *nom. sing.* (συνκεκερασμένος) is read by א (vg *non admistus*) d (*non temperatus*) syr vg (*because it was not mixed*) Cyr. Alex., Lcfr. (*non temperatus*), (Primas.).

(b) The *accus. plur.* (συνκεκερασμένους) is read by ABCD₂*M₂, the great mass of later MSS., some Lat. MSS. (am. *non admixtis*), syr hl (text *for they were not mixed*), me (*quia non confusi sunt*, Wilkins), Theod. Mops., Aug., Chrys., Theodt., Theophct.

(2) (a) τοῖς ἀκούσασιν is the reading of all the Greek MSS. with the exception of D₂* and 71.

(b) τῶν ἀκουσάντων is read by D₂* (and this may be the original of *auditorum* in d e Lcfr.), and by syr hl mg.

(c) τοῖς ἀκουσθεῖσι which appears to have been a conjecture of Theodore of Mopsuestia is read by 71, but the sense is given by the vg *ex his quæ audierunt.*

Thus four combinations which have early authority require to be considered.

(a) μὴ συνκεκερασμένος τῇ πίστει τοῖς ἀκούσασιν.

(β) μὴ συνκεκερασμένος τῇ πίστει τῶν ἀκουσάντων.

(γ) μὴ συνκεκερασμένους τῇ πίστει τοῖς ἀκούσασιν.

(δ) μὴ συνκεκερασμένους τῇ πίστει τοῖς [ἀκουσθεῖσιν v. ἀκούσμασιν].

Of these (β) may be set aside without hesitation. The variant τῶν ἀκουσάντων is not unlike one of the mechanical changes of D₂ (see vv. 1, 12, 16), and it gives no tolerable sense.

The other readings ((a), (γ), (δ)) give severally a good sense, though there are difficulties in each case (see Notes).

The external authority for (δ) is relatively so slight[1] that this reading can hardly be accepted unless the better attested readings are inadmissible. Moreover it simply gives in another form the thought which is conveyed by συνκεκερασμένος τῇ πίστει τοῖς ἀκούσασιν.

Our choice then lies between (a) and (γ). The authorities for (a) though few in number cover a very wide field, and reach in each case to the earliest accessible date. And further, while the change from -μένος to -μένους is natural both as a mechanical alteration and as the intentional correction of a scribe, the change from -μένους to -μένος is more difficult to account for. It would scarcely be made mechanically; and it is not obvious as a correction.

On the whole therefore it seems best to accept the reading συνκεκερασμένος τῇ πίστει τοῖς ἀκούσασιν as attested by varied ancient authority, adequately explaining the other readings, and giving a satisfactory sense.

---

[1] Comp. Iren. iii. 19, 1 nondum commixti verbo Dei Patris.

Some of the patristic explanations are worth quoting :

THEODORUS MOPS. (Cram. *Cat.* p. 177) : οὐ γὰρ ἦσαν κατὰ τὴν πίστιν τοῖς ἐπαγγελθεῖσι συνημμένοι, ὅθεν οὕτως ἀναγνωστέον, 'μὴ συγκεκερασμένους τῇ πίστει τοῖς ἀκουσθεῖσιν,' ἵνα εἴπῃ ταῖς πρὸς αὐτοὺς γεγενημέναις ἐπαγγελίαις τοῦ θεοῦ διὰ Μωυσέως.

THEODORET : τί γὰρ ὤνησεν ἡ τοῦ θεοῦ ἐπαγγελία τοὺς ταύτην δεξαμένους, μὴ πιστῶς δεξαμένους καὶ τῇ τοῦ θεοῦ δυνάμει τεθαρρηκότας καὶ οἷον τοῖς θεοῦ λόγοις ἀνακραθέντας;

CHRYSOSTOM : εἶτα ἐπάγει 'ἀλλ' οὐκ ὠφέλησεν ὁ λόγος τῆς ἀκοῆς ἐκείνους μὴ συγκεκραμένους (so MSS. ; edd. -μένης) τῇ πίστει τοῖς ἀκούσασιν,' δεικνὺς πῶς ὁ λόγος οὐκ ὠφέλησεν, ἐκ γὰρ τοῦ μὴ συγκραθῆναι οὐκ ὠφελήθησαν. Then afterwards he goes on to say, οἱ οὖν περὶ Χάλεβ καὶ Ἰησοῦν, ἐπειδὴ μὴ συνεκράθησαν τοῖς ἀπιστήσασι, τουτέστιν οὐ συνεφώνησαν, διέφυγον τὴν κατ' ἐκείνων ἐξενεχθεῖσαν τιμωρίαν. καὶ ὅρα γέ τι θαυμαστόν. οὐκ εἶπεν, οὐ συνεφώνησαν ἀλλ' οὐ συνεκράθησαν, τουτέστιν, ἀστασιάστως διέστησαν, ἐκείνων πάντων μίαν καὶ τὴν αὐτὴν γνώμην ἐσχηκότων.

This latter is the opinion which THEOPHYLACT quotes and criticises as Chrysostom's.

AUGUSTINE, in commenting upon Ps. lxxvii. (lxxviii.) 8 *non est creditus cum Deo spiritus ejus*, writes: ut autem cor cum illo sit et per hoc rectum esse possit, acceditur ad eum non pede sed fide. Ideo dicitur etiam in epistola ad Hebræos de illa ipsa generatione prava et amaricante, Non profuit sermo auditus illis non contemperatis (so MSS.) fidei eorum qui obaudierunt (*In Ps.* lxxvii. § 10); and again: erant illic etiam electi quorum fidei non contemperabatur generatio prava et amaricans (*id.* § 18)[1].

The note of PRIMASIUS is : non profuit illis, quia non fuit admistus et conjunctus fidei, et contemperatus fidei ex his promissionibus quas audierunt. Tunc enim prodesset iis sermo auditus si credidissent quoniam tunc esset contemperatus fide (? fidei). Quoniam vero non crediderunt, non fuit conjunctus fidei, ideoque nihil eis profuit quod audierunt...

Additional Note on iv. 8. *On some hypothetical sentences.*

It is worth while for the sake of some young students to illustrate a little in detail from the writings of the N. T. the various forms of the sentence which expresses the hypothetical consequence of an unfulfilled condition.

Two main cases arise. In one (I) the protasis expressed by εἰ with the indicative is followed by the imperfect indicative with ἄν. The thought here is of a present or continuous result which would have been seen now if the unfulfilled supposition had been realised. In the other (II), the protasis expressed by εἰ with the indicative is followed by the aorist indicative with ἄν. The thought here is of a past and completed result which would have ensued if the unfulfilled condition had been realised.

[1] This reference I owe to my very old friend the late Rev. A. A. Ellis, sometime Fellow of Trinity College.

No uniform rendering in English is able to give the exact force of these two different forms of expression. It has become common to translate (I) by *if (he) had...(he) would...*; and (II) by *if (he) had...(he) would have...* But if this rendering is adopted, the definite negation of the fact in the apodosis of (I) is commonly lost or obscured, and the statement appears to be simply hypothetical and to suggest a possible fulfilment in the future. On the other hand if (I) and (II) are translated in the same manner, the suggestion of the present or continuous fact in (I) is obliterated.

Each case therefore must be considered by itself in order that the translator may convey the truest impression of the original with regard to the context.

If we look at the two main cases more closely we shall see that each has two divisions according as εἰ is joined with the imperfect or with the aorist in the protasis. Thus four types of expression must be distinguished.

I.   (1) Εἰ imp. indic.......imp. with ἄν.
     (2) Εἰ aor. indic.......imp. with ἄν.

II. (1) Εἰ imp. indic.......aor. with ἄν.
     (2) Εἰ aor. indic.......aor. with ἄν.

I.   (1) Εἰ with *imp.* ind. in protasis followed by *imp.* in apodosis.

In this case the hypothetic unfulfilled condition and the consequence of its non-fulfilment are both regarded (*a*) generally as present, or (*b*), if not as present, as continuous and not definitely complete in a specific incident.

(*a*) Hebr. viii. 4 εἰ ἦν...οὐδ᾽ ἂν ἦν... (if he had been now invested with such an office...he would not be as he now is...).

Hebr. viii. 7 εἰ ἦν...οὐκ ἂν ἐζητεῖτο...
John v. 46 εἰ ἐπιστεύετε...ἐπιστεύετε ἄν.
— viii. 42 εἰ...ἦν...ἠγαπᾶτε ἄν...
— ix. 41 εἰ ἦτε...οὐκ ἂν εἴχετε.
— xiv. 7 εἰ ἐγνώκειτε...ἂν ἤδειτε.
— xv. 19 εἰ ἦτε...ἂν ἐφίλει.
— xviii. 36 εἰ ἦν...ἠγωνίζοντο ἄν...
Luke vii. 39 εἰ ἦν...ἐγίνωσκεν ἄν...
1 Cor. xi. 31 εἰ διεκρίνομεν...οὐκ ἂν ἐκρινόμεθα.
Gal. i. 10 εἰ ἤρεσκον...οὐκ ἂν ἤμην.

With these examples must be ranged also John viii. 19 εἰ ἤδειτε...αν ἤδειτε...

(*b*) Hebr. xi. 15 εἰ ἐμνημόνευον...εἶχον ἄν... (if they had continued to remember...they would all that time have had...).
Matt. xxiii. 30 εἰ ἤμεθα...οὐκ ἂν ἤμεθα...

In this connexion may be noticed

1 John ii. 19 εἰ ἦσαν...μεμενήκεισαν ἄν... where the pluperfect suggests a continuous state limited at a point in the past.

Sometimes an interrogation takes the place of the apodosis.

Heb. vii. 11 εἰ...τελείωσις ..ἦν...τίς ἔτι χρεία...;
1 Cor. xii. 19 εἰ δὲ ἦν...ποῦ τὸ σῶμα;

Sometimes the ἄν of the apodosis is omitted (as *indic.* in Latin : Hor. Od. ii. 17, 27.

John ix. 33 εἰ μὴ ἦν...οὐκ ἠδύνατο...

— xix. 11 οὐκ εἶχες...εἰ μὴ ἦν...

The unconditioned apodosis seems to emphasise what is implied in the protasis.

(2) Εἰ with the *aor.* indic. in protasis followed by *imp.* in apodosis. The hypothetic unfulfilled condition is placed as a definite incident in the past, while the result of the non-fulfilment is regarded as continuous in the present.

Hebr. iv. 8 εἰ κατέπαυσεν...οὐκ ἂν ἐλάλει... (if rest had been given at the entrance into Canaan, God would not have continued to speak as He does now...).

Gal. iii. 21 εἰ ἐδόθη...ἐν νόμῳ ἂν ἦν...

So LXX. Jer. xxiii. 22 εἰ ἔστησαν...καὶ εἰ ἤκουσαν...ἂν ἀπέστρεφον.

In this case also the ἂν of the apodosis is omitted :

John xv. 22 εἰ μὴ ἦλθον...οὐκ εἴχοσαν...

Matt. xxvi. 24 καλὸν ἦν...εἰ οὐκ ἐγεννήθη...

II. (1) Εἰ with the *imp.* indic. in protasis followed by *aor.* in apodosis.

The hypothetic unfulfilled condition is regarded as continuous and not definitely complete in the past, while the consequence of its non-fulfilment is specific and past:

John xiv. 28 εἰ ἠγαπᾶτε...ἐχάρητε ἄν (if ye had now been loving me...ye would at the moment of my saying...).

John iv. 10 εἰ ᾔδεις...σὺ ἂν ᾔτησας.

— xi. 21, 32 εἰ ἦς...οὐκ ἂν ἀπέθανεν.

— xviii. 30 εἰ μὴ ἦν...οὐκ ἂν παρεδώκαμεν.

Acts xviii. 14 εἰ ἦν...ἂν ἀνεσχόμην.

And here also we must place :

Matt. xii. 7 εἰ ἐγνώκειτε (real imp.)...οὐκ ἂν κατεδικάσατε.

— xxiv. 43 || Lk. xii. 39 εἰ ᾔδει (real imp.)...ἐγρηγόρησεν ἄν...

Sometimes the ἄν of the apodosis is omitted: Gal. iv. 15 εἰ δυνατόν... ἐδώκατε...

(2) Εἰ with the *aor.* indic. in protasis followed by *aor.* in apodosis. The hypothetic unfulfilled condition and the result of its non-fulfilment are regarded as definite incidents wholly in the past.

1 Cor. ii. 8 εἰ ἔγνωσαν...οὐκ ἂν ἐσταύρωσαν (if at the crisis of their trial they had known...they would not have crucified).

Matt. xi. 21 εἰ ἐγένοντο...πάλαι ἂν μετενόησαν || Lk. x. 13.

— xxiv. 22 || Mk. xiii. 20 εἰ μὴ ἐκολόβωσεν...οὐκ ἂν ἐσώθη...

So in LXX. Is. i. 9 εἰ μὴ...ἐγκατέλιπεν...ἂν ἐγενήθημεν. Rom. ix. 29.

Compare also :

Matt. xxv. 27 || Lk. xix. 23 διὰ τί οὐκ ἔδωκας...κἀγὼ ἐλθὼν...ἄν...ἔπραξα...

John xiv. 2 εἰ δὲ μή, εἶπον ἂν ὑμῖν...

Hebr. x. 2 ἐπεὶ οὐκ ἂν ἐπαύσαντο

In some passages there appears to be a combination of two forms of expression:

Luke xvii. 6 εἰ ἔχετε...ἐλέγετε ἄν..., as if the sentence would naturally have continued λέγετε, but then the ἔχετε was mentally corrected to εἴχετε to meet the actual case. Comp. Winer p. 383 with Dr Moulton's note.

John viii. 39 εἰ...ἔστε...ἐποιεῖτε (if this reading be adopted).

It may be added that the construction is relatively more frequent in St John's Gospel than in any other Book of the N. T.

Additional Note on iv. 12.   The origin and constitution of man.

I. *Theories of the origin of man.* The great mystery of the origin of man is touched in two passages of the Epistle which severally suggest the two complementary theories which have been fashioned in a one-sided manner as Traducianism and Creationism: c. vii. 10; xii. 9.

1. *Traducianism.* In c. vii. 10 (comp. *v.* 5) the force of the argument lies in the assumption that the descendants are included in the ancestor, in such a sense that his acts have force for them. So far as we keep within the region of physical existence the connexion is indisputable. Up to this limit 'the dead' do indeed 'rule the living.' And their sovereignty witnesses to an essential truth which lies at the foundation of society. The individual man is not a complete self-centred being. He is literally a member in a body. The connexions of the family, the nation, the race, belong to the idea of man, and to the very existence of man.

2. *Creationism.* But at the same time it is obvious that if this view gives the whole account of man's being, he is a mere result. He is made as it were a mere layer—*tradux*—of a parent stock, and owes to that his entire vital force. He is bound in a system of material sequences, and so he is necessarily deprived of all responsibility. Thus another aspect of his being is given in c. xii. 9. Here a distinction is drawn between 'the fathers of our flesh,' of our whole physical organisation, with its 'life,' and 'the Father of spirits,' among which man's spirit is of necessity included. There is then an element in man which is not directly derived by descent, though it may follow upon birth. And in the recognition of this reality of individuality, of a personally divine kinsmanship, lies the truth of Creationism. We are not indeed to suppose that separate and successive creative acts call into existence the 'spirits' of single men. It is enough to hold that man was so made that in his children this higher element should naturally find a place on their entrance into the world. That such an issue should ensue when the child begins his separate life is neither more nor less marvellous than that the power of vision should attend the adequate preparation of an organ of vision. So also, to continue the same illustration, the power of vision and the power of self-determination are modified by the organisms through which they act, but they are not created by them. The physical life and the spiritual life spring alike from the one act of the living God when He made man in His own image; through whatever steps, in the

unfolding of time, the decisive point was reached when the organism, duly prepared, was fitted to receive the divine breath.

But without attempting to develop a theory of Generationism, as it may Recogni-be called, as distinguished from Traducianism and Creationism, it is enough tion of the for us to notice that the writer of the Epistle affirms the two antithetic comple-mentary facts which represent the social unity of the race and the personal responsi- truths. bility of the individual, the influence of common thoughts and the power of great men, the foundation of hope and the condition of judgment.

The analysis of man's constitution given by implication in the Epistle II. *Consti-* corresponds with the fundamental division of St Paul (1 Thess. v. 23 *body, tution of soul, spirit*). *man.*

The *body* is noticed both in its completeness (x. 5) and in respect of the 1. *Body:* conditions of its present manifestation (*flesh,* v. 7, x. 20, xii. 9; *blood and flesh.* *flesh,* ii. 14). It is unnecessary to repeat what has been said in the notes on these passages. A comparison of c. v. 7 with c. x. 5 will place in a clear light the difference between 'the body,' which represents the whole organisation through which the growth and fulness of human life is represented according to the conditions under which it is realised (notice 1 Cor. xv. 44 σῶμα ψυχικόν, σῶμα πνευματικόν), and the 'flesh,' which represents what is characteristic of our earthly existence under the aspect of its weakness and transitoriness and affinity with the material world. The moral sense of 'flesh,' which is prominent in St Paul, does not occur in the Epistle.

The soul, the life (ψυχή), is an element in man which from the 2. *Soul.* complexity of his nature may be very differently conceived of. His 'life' extends to two orders, the seen and the unseen, the temporal and the eternal, the material and the spiritual. And according as one or the other is predominant in the thought of the speaker ψυχή may represent the energy of life as it is manifested under the present conditions of sense, or the energy of life which is potentially eternal. This manifoldness of the ψυχή is recognised in c. iv. 12. 'The Word of God' analyses its constituent parts and brings them before our consciousness. So it is that we have 'to gain our life,' 'our soul' in the education of experience inspired by faith (x. 39 ἡμεῖς...πίστεως εἰς περιποίησιν ψυχῆς· comp. Matt. x. 39; xi. 29; xvi. 25 f. || Mk. viii. 35 f. || Lk. ix. 24, xvii. 33; xxi. 19 κτήσεσθε). In the sadnesses and disappointments and failures of effort (c. xii. 3 ταῖς ψυχαῖς ἐκλυόμενοι) we have 'hope as anchor of the soul, entering into that which is within the veil' (vi. 19). And it is for the preservation of this harmonious sum of man's vital powers that Christian teachers watch unweariedly (c. xiii. 17 ἀγρυπνοῦσιν ὑπὲρ τῶν ψυχῶν).

Little is said in the Epistle on the 'spirit' (πνεῦμα) by which man holds 3. *Spirit.* converse with the unseen. Just as he has affinity by 'the flesh' with the animal world, so he has by 'the spirit' affinity with God. God is indeed 'the Father of spirits' (c. xii. 9), and in His presence we draw near to 'spirits of just men made perfect' (xii. 23).

These three elements have in themselves no moral character. They are 4. *Heart.* of the nature of powers to be used, disciplined, coordinated, harmonised. The expression of the moral character lies in 'the heart.' Men in a mere enumeration can be spoken of as 'souls,' but 'the heart' is the typical

8

centre of personal life. It is the 'heart' which receives its strong assurance by grace (c. xiii. 9). 'Unbelief' has its seat in 'the heart' (c. iii. 12 καρδία πονηρὰ ἀπιστίας). In Christ we can approach God 'with a true heart' (c. x. 22 μετὰ ἀληθινῆς καρδίας), offering Him the fulness of our individual being which we have realised for His service, having severally 'had our hearts sprinkled from an evil conscience' (id. ῥεραντισμένοι τὰς καρδίας ἀπὸ συνειδήσεως πονηρᾶς). See also c. iii. 8, 10, 15; iv. 7 (Ps. xcv. 8, 10); iv. 12 (note); viii. 10 (note); x. 16 (Jer. xxxi. 33).

5. Conscience.

For man has a sovereign power throned within him through which the divine law finds a voice. He has a 'conscience' (συνείδησις) whose judgments he can recognise as having final authority. He has 'conscience of sins' (c. x. 2). He knows that certain acts are evil and that he is responsible for them. In such a state he has an 'evil conscience' (c. x. 22; contrast c. xiii. 18 καλὴ συνείδησις). The conscience feels the defilement of 'dead works,' which counterfeit the fruits of its righteous claims on man's activity (c. ix. 14); and it furnishes the standard of that perfection towards which man aspires (c. ix. 9 κατὰ συνείδησιν τελειῶσαι. Additional Note).

Of the words which describe man's intellectual faculties διάνοια ('understanding') is found in a quotation in viii. 10; x. 16 (Jer. xxxi. 33); but νοῦς, which occurs in each group of St Paul's Epistles, is not found in this Book.

V.   ¹ Πᾶς γὰρ ἀρχιερεὺς ἐξ ἀνθρώπων λαμβανόμενος

III. The High-priesthood of Christ universal and sovereign (cc. v.—vii.).

In the last two chapters the writer of the Epistle has shewn the general superiority of 'Jesus,' the Founder of the New Covenant, over Moses and Joshua ; and, further, that the divine promise partially fulfilled by the occupation of Canaan still awaits its complete and absolute fulfilment. He is thus brought back to the thought of Christ's High-priesthood, in virtue of which humanity finds access to the Presence of God, 'His rest,' pursuing in detail the line of argument suggested in ii. 17, 18 and resumed in iv. 14—16.

In this section the Apostle deals with the general conception of Christ's High-priesthood. He treats of the accomplishment of Christ's High-priestly work in the next section.

The section consists of three parts. The writer first briefly characterises the work and the qualifications of a High-priest; and shews that the qualifications are possessed by Christ in ideal perfection, and that He completes the (theocratic) type of the Aaronic High-priest by adding to it the features of the (natural) type of the High-priesthood of Melchizedek (v. 1—10). Then follows a hortatory passage in which the duty of continuous and patient effort is enforced as the condition of right knowledge of the Christian revelation (v. 11—vi.). Having thus prepared the way for a fuller exposition of the truth with which he is engaged, the writer unfolds through the image of Melchizedek a view of the absolute High-priesthood of Christ (vii.).

Thus we have shortly :

i.   *The characteristics of a High-priest fulfilled in Christ* (v. 1—10).

ii.   *Progress through patient effort the condition of the knowledge of Christian mysteries* (v. 11—vi.).

iii.   *The characteristics of Christ as absolute High-priest shadowed forth by Melchizedek* (vii.).

i.   *The characteristics of a High-priest are fulfilled in Christ* (v. 1—10).

This paragraph falls naturally into two parts. (1) The characteristics of a High-priest are first laid down (v. 1—4); and then (2) it is shewn that these were perfectly satisfied by Christ (5—10).

(1)   The characteristics of a High-priest are drawn from a consideration of his office (v. 1); and from the qualifications which its fulfilment requires in regard to men and to God (2—4).

¹*For every High-priest, being taken from among men, is appointed for men in the things that pertain to God, that he may offer both gifts and sacrifices for sins;* ²*being able to bear gently with the ignorant and erring, since he also himself is compassed with infirmity,* ³*and by reason thereof is bound, as for the people so also for himself, to offer for sins.* ⁴*And no one taketh the honour to himself, but being called of God, even as was Aaron.*

1.   The general purpose of the institution of the High-priesthood.

πᾶς γάρ...] This section follows naturally from that which precedes. The perfect sympathy of our High-priest (iv. 15) satisfies one of the conditions which are necessarily attached to the office universally. On the ground of this fundamental correspondence between Christ's Nature and the High-priesthood, the writer proceeds to develop the idea of the High-priesthood before he applies it to Christ. The γάρ is explanatory and not directly argumentative ; and the Mosaic system is treated as embodying the general conception (πᾶς) ; but even so the type of Melchizedek's priesthood is not to

ὑπὲρ ἀνθρώπων καθίσταται τὰ πρὸς τὸν θεόν, ἵνα προσφέρῃ δῶρά [τε] καὶ θυσίας ὑπὲρ ἁμαρτιῶν, ²μετριοπαθεῖν

1 δῶρά τε ℵAC syr hl: om. τε B vg syr vg me: τε δῶρα D₂*.

be forgotten. The words recur c.
viii. 3.

ἐξ ἀνθ. λαμβ. ὑπὲρ ἀνθρ. καθ....] *being
taken from among men*...The human
origin of the High-priest is marked
as a ground of the fitness of his
appointment. A High-priest being
himself man can act for men : comp.
Ex. xxviii. 1 (*from among the children of Israel*). He is 'of men' and
'on behalf of men' (for their service),
and in the original these two phrases
correspond emphatically. Κἂν τῷ νόμῳ
οὐκ ἄγγελος ὑπὲρ ἀνθρώπων ἱερατεύειν
ἐτάχθη ἀλλ' ἄνθρωπος ὑπὲρ ἀνθρώπων
(Theod.). Chrysostom (followed by
later Fathers) remarks : τοῦτο κοινὸν
τῷ Χριστῷ. The present participle
(λαμβανόμενος, Vulg. *assumptus*, inadequately) suggests the continuity
of the relation (v. 4 καλούμενος, Vulg.
[ὁ καλ.] *qui vocatur*).

It is unnatural and injurious to the
argument to take ἐξ ἀνθρ. λαμβανόμενος
as part of the subject (Syr. *every
high-priest that is from men*).

καθίσταται] *is appointed*, Vulg.
constituitur. Καθίστασθαι is the ordinary word for authoritative appointment to an office : c. vii. 28 ; viii. 3 ;
(Tit. i. 5); Luke xii. 14; Philo, *de vit.
Mos.* ii. 11 (ii. 151 M.).

τὰ πρὸς τὸν θεόν] c. ii. 17 note ; Deut.
xxxi. 27 (LXX.).

ἵνα προσφ.] Comp. viii. 3 εἰς τὸ
προσφέρειν. In a considerable number
of passages ἵνα and εἰς τό occur in close
connexion : c. ii. 17 note ; 1 Thess.
ii. 16 ; 2 Thess. ii. 11 f.; iii. 9 ; 1 Cor.
ix. 18 ; 2 Cor. viii. 6 ; Rom. i. 11 ;
iv. 16 ; vii. 4 ; xi. 11 ; xv. 16 ; Phil.
i. 10 ; Eph. i. 17 f. Ἵνα appears to
mark in each case the direct and immediate end, while εἰς τό indicates
the more remote result aimed at or
reached.

προσφέρῃ] The word προσφέρειν is

commonly used in the LXX. for the
' offering' of sacrifices and gifts, and
it is so used very frequently in this
Epistle (19 times). It never occurs
in the Epistles of St Paul, and rarely
in the other books of N. T. Matt. v.
23 f. (comp. ii. 11); viii. 4 and parallels ; John xvi. 2 ; Acts vii. 42 ; xxi.
26. Compare ἀναφέρειν c. vii. 27 note.

This usage of προσφέρειν appears
to be Hellenistic and not Classical.

δῶρά τε καὶ θυσίας] O. L. *munera
et hostias*, Vulg. *dona et sacrificia*.
Δῶρον can be used comprehensively
to describe offerings of all kinds,
bloody and unbloody : viii. 4 (comp.
xi. 4). The same offering indeed
could be called, under different aspects,
a 'gift' and a 'sacrifice.' But when
'gifts' and 'sacrifices' are distinguished the former mark the 'meal-
offering' (מִנְחָה) and the latter the
bloody offerings. Comp. viii. 3 ;
ix. 9.

In this narrower sense the 'sacrifice' naturally precedes the 'offering'
(comp. Ps. xl. (6), c. x. 5). It is possible
that the transposition is made in order
to emphasise the thought that man
needs an appointed Mediator even to
bring his gifts to God. The particular reference is to the offerings of the
High-priest on the Day of Atonement,
'the Day' (*Joma*) as it is called in
the Talmud, which concentrated all
the ideas of sacrifice and worship, as
the High-priest concentrated all the
ideas of personal service (Lev. xvi. ;
Num. xxix.).

The clause ὑπὲρ ἁμαρτιῶν is to be
joined with θυσίας (*sacrifices for
sins*) and not with προσφέρῃ as referring to both nouns. The two ideas
of eucharistic and expiatory offerings
are distinctly marked.

For ὑπέρ see c. vii. 27 ; x. 12 ; (ix.

δυνάμενος τοῖς ἀγνοοῦσι καὶ πλανωμένοις, ἐπεὶ καὶ αὐτὸς

2 ἐπεὶ καί : καὶ γάρ D₂*.

7); 1 Cor. xv. 3 (Gal. i. 4). More commonly περί is used : v. 3; c. x. 6, 8, 18; xiii. 11; 1 Pet. iii. 18; 1 John ii. 2; iv. 10; Rom. viii. 3.

2—4. From the office of the Highpriest the writer passes on to his qualifications in regard to man and God. He must have sympathy with man (2, 3) and receive his appointment from God (4).

2. The capacity for calm and gentle judgment fits him for the fulfilment of his office in behalf of his fellow men. He offers sacrifices as one 'able to bear gently' with the ignorant and erring.

μετριοπαθεῖν] to feel gently towards, to bear gently with. Vulg. condolere. Ambr. affici pro... Syr. to make himself humble and suffer with. The proper idea of μετριοπαθεῖν (μετριοπαθής, μετριοπάθεια) is that of a temperate feeling (of sorrow and pain and anger) as contrasted with the impassibility (ἀπάθεια) of the Stoics (Diog. Laert. § 31 Aristoteles : ἔφη δὲ τὸν σοφὸν μὴ εἶναι μὲν ἀπαθῆ μετριοπαθῆ δέ). The word is frequently used by Philo : de Abrah. § 44 (ii. 37 M.) μήτε πλείω τοῦ μετρίου σφαδάζειν... μήτε ἀπαθείᾳ...χρῆσθαι, τὸ δὲ μέσον πρὸ τῶν ἄκρων ἑλόμενον μετριοπαθεῖν πειρᾶσθαι. de Jos. § 5 (ii. p. 45 M.) μυρία αὐτὸς ἔπαθον τῶν ἀνηκέστων ἐφ' οἷς, παιδευθεὶς μετριοπαθεῖν, οὐκ ἐγνάμφθην. de spec. legg. § 17 (ii. 315 M., joined with ἐπιεικής). id. de nobil. § 2 (ii. p. 439 M., opposed to ἡ ἀμετρία τῶν παθῶν).

Comp. Jos. Antt. xii. 3, 2, Plut. de frat. am. p. 489 c ἡ φύσις ἔδωκεν ἡμῖν πραότητα καὶ μετριοπαθείας ἔκγονον ἀνεξικακίαν. Clem. Alex. Strom. ii. 8, § 39 (p. 450 P.); iv. 17, § 100 (p. 611 P.).

In the Law no special moral qualifications are prescribed for the priests. Here the essential qualification which lies in their humanity is brought out.

Their work was not and could not be purely external and mechanical even if it seemed to be so superficially. Within certain limits they had to decide upon the character of the facts in regard to which offerings were made.

τοῖς ἀγνοοῦσι καὶ πλανωμένοις] Vulg. iis qui ignorant et errant. The compound description may either indicate the source (ignorance) and the issue (going astray) of sin; or it may describe sinners, so far as they come into consideration here, under two main aspects. Wilful, deliberate sin does not fall within the writer's scope, nor indeed within the scope of the Levitical Law. Such sin required in the first instance the manifestation of a sterner judgment. Comp. Num. xv. 22—31 (sins of ignorance and sins of presumption).

For the use of ἀγνοεῖν in LXX. (שָׁנָה, שָׁגַג) see 1 Sam. xxvi. 21; Ezek. xlv. 20 (Alex.); Lev. iv. 13; v. 18; Lev. iv. 2 (חָטָא בִשְׁגָגָה, LXX. ἁμάρτῃ ἀκουσίως, Aqu., Symm. ἀγνοίᾳ). Ecclus. v. 15. Compare ἄγνοια, Gen. xxvi. 10; Ecclus. xxviii. 7; xxx. 11; xxiii. 3; ἀγνόημα c. ix. 7 note. True knowledge implies corresponding action. Comp. 1 John ii. 3 note.

For πλανᾶσθαι, which is comparatively rare in the general sense of 'going astray' (sinning), see c. iii. 10; Tit. iii. 3; (James v. 19; 2 Tim. iii. 13; Apoc. xviii. 23). The full image is given Matt. xviii. 12; 1 Pet. ii. 25 (Is. liii. 6).

In iv. 15 our High-priest is described as one δυνάμενος συμπαθῆσαι ταῖς ἀσθενείαις, while here he generally is required μετριοπαθεῖν τοῖς ἀγνοοῦσιν καὶ πλανωμένοις. The one phrase describes his relation to the source of transgression, the other his relation to the transgressor. It is necessary that the true High-priest should be able

περίκειται ἀσθένειαν, ³καὶ δι' αὐτὴν ὀφείλει, καθὼς περὶ
τοῦ λαοῦ, οὕτως καὶ περὶ ἑαυτοῦ προσφέρειν περὶ ἁμαρτιῶν. ⁴καὶ οὐχ ἑαυτῷ τις λαμβάνει τὴν τιμήν, ἀλλὰ

3 δι' αὐτήν ℵABC*D₂*: διὰ ταύτην ς syr hl mg.   ἑαυτοῦ ℵAC: αὐτοῦ
(αὐτοῦ) BD₂*.   περὶ ἀμ. ℵABC*D₂*: ὑπὲρ ἀμ. ς.   4 λαμβάνει τις D₂.

to sympathise with the manifold forms
of weakness from which sins spring, as
himself conscious of the nature of sin,
but it is not necessary that he should
actually share the feelings of sinners, as
having himself sinned. Towards sinners he must have that calm, just feeling which neither exaggerates nor ex-
tenuates the offence. It may further
be noticed that Christ, as High-priest,
has no weakness, though He sym-
pathises with weaknesses (vii. 28;
iv. 15).

ἐπεί] The particle is unusually frequent (9 times) in this Epistle (10
times in St Paul), while ὅτι causal
only occurs in quotations (c. viii. 9 ff.).
See v. 11 note.

περίκειται ἀσθ.] V. L. gestat infirmitatem. Vulg. circumdatus est infir-
mitate. Syr. clothed with infirmity.
For the use of περίκειμαι, compare
(c. xii. 1); Acts xxviii. 20 τὴν ἅλυσιν
ταύτην περίκειμαι. Clem. 2 Cor. 1
ἀμαύρωσιν περικείμενοι. Ign. ad Trall.
12; and for the general thought see
c. vii. 28 ἔχοντας ἀσθένειαν. The image
is common in Greek literature from
the time of Homer: Il. xviii. 157 ἐπι-
ειμένοι ἀλκήν. Comp. Lk. xxiv. 49;
Col. iii. 12. Εἰδὼς τὸ μέτρον τῆς ἀνθρωπίνης ἀσθενείας ἐφ' ἑαυτῷ ἐπιμετρεῖ
καὶ τὴν συγγνώμην (Theoph.).
The exact opposite to περικεῖσθαι is
περιελεῖν (c. x. 11). With the sing.
(ἀσθένεια) contrast the plural c. iv. 15.

3. καὶ δι' αὐτήν] and by reason
thereof, i.e. of the weakness. This
clause may be an independent statement, or depend upon ἐπεί. On the
whole the form (καὶ δι' αὐτήν instead
of δι' ἥν) is in favour of the former
view; which is further supported by
the fact that weakness does not absolutely involve sin, so that the weak-

ness and the sin even in the case of
man, as he is, are two separate
elements.

In the case of the human High-
priest weakness actually issued in sin.
In this respect the parallel with
Christ fails. But it has been seen
(iv. 15) that a sense of the power of
the temptation and not the being
overpowered by it is the true ground
of sympathy. Comp. vii. 27.

ὀφείλει] he is bound in the very
nature of things, in virtue of his
constitution and of his office. He
must obtain purity for himself before
he can intercede for others. Comp.
c. ii. 17 note.

περὶ ἑαυτοῦ] The ceremonies of the
Day of Atonement are still foremost
in the writer's thoughts (Lev. xvi.).
Philo (Quis rer. div. hær. § 36,
i. 497 M.) regards the daily meal-
offering as the offering for the priest
(Lev. vi. 20), as the lamb was the
offering for the people.

προσφ. περὶ ἁμαρτιῶν] The constant
use of the singular in the sense of
'sin-offering' (x. 6, 8; xiii. 11 περὶ
ἁμαρτίας and LXX.) seems to shew
that here περὶ ἀμ. is to be taken
generally 'for sins,' while προσφ. is
absolute as in Luke v. 14, though not
elsewhere in this Epistle. See also
Num. vii. 18.

4. A second qualification for the
High-priesthood lies in the divine
call. He must be man, and he must
be called by God. The fact of human
sinfulness naturally leads to this complementary thought. Of himself a
man could not presume to take upon
him such an office. He could not
draw near to God being himself sinful: still less could he draw near to
God to intercede for others. At the

καλούμενος ὑπὸ τοῦ θεοῦ, καθώσπερ καὶ ᾽Ααρών. ⁵Οὕτως

καλούμενος ℵABC*D₂ syr hl : +ὁ′ καλ. ς vg syr vg.   καθώσπερ ℵ*ABD₂*:
καθάπερ ς ℵᶜ.   om. καὶ D₂* vg syr vg.   ᾽Ααρών ℵABCD₂: +ὁ′ ᾽Α. ς.

most he could only indicate in action the desire for fellowship with God.

ἑαυτῷ λαμβάνει] The idea of bold presumption does not lie in the phrase itself (Luke xix. 12), but in the context. The unusual form οὐχ ἑαυτῷ τις corresponds with οὐχ ἑαυτόν which follows.

τὴν τιμήν] Latt. *honorem*, the office. So ἡ τιμή is used of the High-priesthood by Josephus : *e.g. Antt.* iii. 8, 1.

ἀλλὰ καλούμ.] *but being called* (as called) he taketh it (λαμβάνει is to be supplied from the preceding λαμβάνει ἑαυτῷ).

The word καλεῖσθαι (comp. c. xi. 8) is specially used for the ' call' to the Christian Faith: c. ix. 15 (especially by St Paul and St Peter).

καθώσπερ καὶ ᾽Ααρών] Ex. xxviii. 1; Num. xvi.—xviii. Even Aaron himself, though specially marked out before (Ex. xvi. 33), did not assume the office without a definite call.

Aaron is the divine type of the High-priest, as the Tabernacle is of ritual service. He is mentioned in the N. T. besides only cc. vii. 11 ; ix. 4; (Lk. i. 5; Acts vii. 40).

From the time of Herod the succession to the High-priesthood became irregular and arbitrary and not confined to the line of Aaron (Jos. *Antt.* xv. 2, 4; xx. 9). Therefore the writer goes back to the divine ideal. The notoriousness of the High-priestly corruption at the time could not fail to give point to the language of the Epistle.

Schoettgen quotes from *Bammidbar R.* c. xviii.: Moses said [to Korah and his companions]: If Aaron my brother had taken the priesthood to himself ye would have done well to rise against him ; but in truth God gave it to him, whose is the greatness and the power and the glory. Whosoever

therefore rises against Aaron, does he not rise against God ? (Wünsche, p. 441).

(2) Having characterised the office and qualifications of a High-priest generally, the writer now goes on to shew that Christ satisfied the qualifications (5—8), and fulfils the office (9, 10).

The proof is given in an inverted form. The divine appointment of Christ is established first (5, 6); and then His power of sympathy (7, 8); and lastly His office is described (9, 10).

This inversion, in an elaborate parallelism, is perfectly natural, and removes the appearance of formality.

⁵*So Christ also glorified not Himself to become High-priest, but He that spake unto Him,*

Thou art My Son,
I have today begotten Thee:—
⁶*Even as He saith also in another place*

Thou art a priest for ever,
After the order of Melchizedek:—
⁷ *Who, in His days of flesh (or in the days of His flesh) having offered up, with strong crying and tears, prayers and supplications unto Him that was able to save Him out of death, and having been heard for His godly fear,* ⁸*though He was Son yet learned obedience by the things which He suffered;* ⁹*and having been made perfect He became to all that obey Him the cause of eternal salvation,* ¹⁰*being addressed by God as High-priest after the order of Melchizedek.*

5—8. The qualifications of Christ for the High-priesthood are established by His divine appointment (5, 6), and by His human discipline which became the ground of perfect sympathy (7, 8).

καὶ ὁ χριστὸς οὐχ ἑαυτὸν ἐδόξασεν γενηθῆναι ἀρχιερέα,
ἀλλ᾽ ὁ λαλήσας πρὸς αὐτόν

Υἱός ΜΟΥ εἶ ϲΎ, ἐγὼ ϲΉΜΕΡΟΝ ΓΕΓΈΝΝΗΚΆ ϲΕ ⁙

⁶καθὼς καὶ ἐν ἑτέρῳ λέγει

5 γεννηθῆναι D₂* : γενέσθαι A.   6 ἑτέρῳ + πάλιν D₂*.

5, 6. The divine appointment of Christ is exhibited in two passages of the Psalms in which the Lord who declares Him to be His Son declares Him also to be 'High-priest after the order of Melchizedek.' These two quotations from Ps. ii. 7; Ps. cx. 4 establish the source of the Lord's sovereign dignity as 'Son,' and mark the particular form in which this dignity has been realised. They correspond in fact to the two ideas ἐδόξασεν and γενηθῆναι ἀρχιερέα. The first passage which has been already quoted (i. 5) refers the glory of the Risen Christ, the exalted Son of man, to the Father. This glory is not exactly defined, but the position of sonship includes every special honour, kingly or priestly. He to whom this had been given could not be said to 'glorify himself.' The second quotation (Ps. cx. 4) defines the particular application of the first. The kingly priesthood of Melchizedek was promised to Christ. Such a priesthood naturally belongs to the exalted Son.

5. οὕτως καὶ ὁ χριστός] So Christ (the Christ) also... The title of the office emphasises the idea of the perfect obedience of the Lord even in the fulness of His appointed work. It is not said that 'Jesus' glorified not Himself, but 'the Christ,' the appointed Redeemer, glorified not Himself. Comp. iii. 14; vi. 1; ix. 14, 28; xi. 26 (ὁ χριστός); and iii. 6; ix. 11, 24 (χριστός).

οὐχ ἑαυ. ἐδόξ. γεν.] Vulg. non semetipsum clarificavit ut pontifex fieret. This fuller phrase, in place of the simple repetition of the words used before, 'took not to Himself the honour,' gives a distinct prominence

to the general character of Christ's work. 'He glorified not Himself so as (in the assertion of this dignity) to become High-priest.' Christ, as sinless man, could approach God for Himself; but He waited for His Father's appointment that He might approach God as Son of man for sinful humanity. Comp. John viii. 54, 42 ; Acts iii. 13.

The High-priesthood, the right of mediation for humanity, was a 'glory' to 'the Son of man.' Comp. John xvii. 5.

ἀλλ᾽ ὁ λαλ. πρὸς αὐτόν] but His Father glorified Him, that He should be made High-priest, even He that spake unto Him...(Ps. ii. 7 Κύριος εἶπεν πρός με).

σήμερον γεγέννηκά σε] Comp. i. 5 note. Hoc est dicere Ego semper et æternaliter manens semper te habeo filium coæternum mihi. Hodie namque adverbium est præsentis temporis quod proprie Deo competit (Prim., Herv.).

In connexion with the quotation from Ps. ii. 7 it must be observed that the LXX. translation of Ps. cix. (cx.) 3 gives a thought closely akin to it : ἐκ γαστρὸς πρὸ ἑωσφόρου ἐγέννησά σε, which was constantly cited by the Greek fathers as a true parallel.

6. καθὼς καί...] The absolute declaration of the Sonship of Christ found a special application in these words of another Psalm. The definite office of Priesthood is a partial interpretation of the glory of the Son. 'The Father glorified the Son to become High-priest, even as in fact (καί) He expressly declares.' This glorifying was not a matter of general deduction only but definitely foreshewn.

Σὺ ἱερεὺς εἰς τὸν αἰῶνα κατὰ τὴν τάξιν Μελχισεδέκ.

σὺ + εἶ′ vg syr hl me.

καθως καί] 1 Thess. v. 11; Eph. iv. 4. ἐν ἑτέρῳ] probably neuter, *in another place* (Ps. cx. 4). Comp. iv. 5; 1 Clem. viii. 4 ἐν ἑτέρῳ τόπῳ λέγει.

Psalm cx. describes the Divine Saviour under three aspects as King (1—3); Priest (4); Conqueror (5—7).

It is quoted in the N. T. to illustrate three distinct points in the Lord's Person.

(1) His Lordship and victory: Matt. xxii. 43 ff. and parallels (εἶπεν κύριος τῷ κυρίῳ μου...Εἰ οὖν Δαυεὶδ καλεῖ αὐτὸν κύριον...); 1 Cor. xv. 25; c. x. 12 f.

(2) His Exaltation at the right hand of God (κάθου ἐκ δεξιῶν μου...): Acts ii. 34 f.; c. i. 13.

And this phrase underlies the many references to Christ's 'sitting' (Matt. xxvi. 64) and taking His seat (Mark xvi. 19 ἐκάθισεν) at the right hand of God.

(3) His Priesthood (Σὺ ἱερεὺς εἰς τὸν αἰῶνα): v. 10 and in cc. vi. vii.

κατὰ τὴν τάξιν M.] Vulg. *secundum ordinem.* Syr. *after the likeness* (cf. vii. 15 κατὰ τὴν ὁμοιότητα)—*after the order*, to occupy the same position, as priest at once and king (Hebr. עַל־דִּבְרָתִי). For τάξις see 2 Macc. ix.

18; the word is used very widely in classical Greek for the 'position,' 'station' of a slave, an enemy &c. Comp. Philo, *de vit. Mos.* iii. § 21 (ii. p. 161 M.) οὐ μία τάξις τῶν ἱερωμένων.

It is worth while to summarise the characteristic note in which Primasius enumerates three main points in which the High-priesthood of Christ was, like that of Melchizedek, contrasted with the High-priesthood of Aaron:

(1) It was not for the fulfilment of legal sacrifices, sacrifices of bulls and goats; but for the offering of bread and wine, answering to Christ's Body and Blood. Animal offerings have ceased: these remain.

(2) Melchizedek combined the kingly with the priestly dignity: he was anointed not with oil but with the Holy Spirit.

(3) Melchizedek appeared once: so Christ offered Himself once.

Œcumenius, in almost the same form, marks the following points of resemblance in Melchizedek to Christ: ὅτι οὐ δι' ἐλαίου εἰς ἱερωσύνην ἐχρίσθη ὁ Μελχισεδὲκ ὡς 'Ααρών, καὶ ὅτι οὐ τὰς δι' αἵματος προσήγαγε θυσίας, καὶ ὅτι τῶν ἐθνῶν ἦν ἀρχιερεύς, καὶ ὅτι δι' ἄρτου καὶ οἴνου ηὐλόγησεν τὸν 'Αβραάμ.

Two features in Melchizedek's priesthood appear to be specially present to the mind of the writer, (1) that it was connected with the kingly office, and (2) that it was not made dependent on any fleshly descent, or limited by conditions of time. Melchizedek had no recorded ancestry and no privileged line of descendants. He represented a non-Jewish, a universal priesthood. In relation to the Priesthood he occupies the position which Abraham occupies in relation to the Covenant. Comp. Zech. vi. 13.

No early Jewish writer applies this promise of the priesthood to Messiah. Justin (*Dial.* cc. 33, 83) and Tertullian (*adv. Marc.* v. 9) mention that the Psalm was referred to by the Jews to Hezekiah. Compare Schoettgen, ii. 645. The *Aboth R. Nathan* from which he quotes an application of the words to Messiah is in its present form probably of post-Talmudical date (Zunz *Gottesd. Vort.* 108 f.; Steinschneider *Jewish Literature,* 40).

The Chaldee paraphrase of the verse (referring it to David) is remarkable: 'The Lord has determined that thou shalt be set Prince (לְרַבָּא) over the world to come, for thy desert, because thou art an innocent king.'

εἰς τὸν αἰῶνα] Christ is a Priest for ever, because He has no successor, nor any need of a successor. His High-

⁷ὃς ἐν ταῖς ἡμέραις τῆς σαρκὸς αὐτοῦ, δεήσεις τε καὶ

7 ὃς + ὢν D₂*.   om. τε vg (syr vg) me.

priestly Sacrifice, His High-priestly Entrance 'with His own blood' into heaven, to the presence of God, are 'eternal' acts, raised beyond all limits of time. Comp. ix. 12, 14; xiii. 20.

Here therefore there is no possibility of repetition, as in the Levitical sacrifices. All is 'one act at once,' while for men the virtue of Christ's sacrifice is applied in time.

Œcumenius understands the phrase of the perpetual memory of Christ's offering: οὐ γὰρ τὴν πρὸς ἅπαξ γενομένην ὑπὸ θεοῦ θυσίαν καὶ προσφορὰν εἶπεν ἂν εἰς τὸν αἰῶνα, ἀλλ᾽ ἀφορῶν εἰς τοὺς νῦν ἱερουργοὺς δι᾽ ὧν μέσων Χριστὸς ἱερουργεῖ καὶ ἱερουργεῖται, ὁ καὶ παραδοὺς αὐτοῖς ἐν τῷ μυστικῷ δείπνῳ τὸν τρόπον τῆς τοιαύτης ἱερουργίας.

Theophylact in much more careful language says: πῶς εἶπε τὸ εἰς τὸν αἰῶνα; ὅτι καὶ νῦν μετὰ τοῦ σώματος ὁ ὑπὲρ ἡμῶν ἔθυσεν ἐντυγχάνει ὑπὲρ ἡμῶν τῷ θεῷ καὶ πατρί...ἢ ὅτι ἡ καθ᾽ ἑκάστην γινομένη καὶ γενησομένη εἰς τὸν αἰῶνα προσφορὰ διὰ τῶν τοῦ θεοῦ λειτουργῶν αὐτὸν ἔχει ἀρχιερέα καὶ ἱερέα τὸν κύριον, καὶ ἱερεῖον ἑαυτὸν ὑπὲρ ἡμῶν ἁγιάζοντα καὶ κλώμενον καὶ διδόμενον. ὁσάκις γὰρ ταῦτα γίνεται ὁ θάνατος τοῦ κυρίου καταγγέλλεται.

7—10. The complicated sentence is divided into two main propositions by the two finite verbs (1) ὅς... προσενέγκας καὶ εἰσακουσθείς...ἔμαθεν... (2) καὶ τελειωθεὶς ἐγένετο. The first sentence describes the divine discipline through which Christ was perfected in His human nature: the second, the efficacy of the work which He was fitted to accomplish in His perfected humanity.

The great statement of the first sentence (ὃς ἐν ταῖς ἡμέραις τῆς σαρκὸς αὐτοῦ...ἔμαθεν ἀφ᾽ ὧν ἔπαθεν τὴν ὑπακοήν) is enlarged by two subordinate statements which illustrate the char-

acter of the divine discipline (δεήσεις τε καὶ ἱκετ....εὐλαβείας), and Christ's unique nature (καίπερ ὢν υἱός). Of these the first is again elaborated in detail. The character (δεή. καὶ ἱκετ.), the object (πρὸς τὸν δ. σ. αὐ. ἐκ θ.), and the manner (μ. κρ. ἱ. κ. δ.) of Christ's prayers are vividly given; and the answer to them is referred to its moral cause (ἀπὸ τῆς εὐλ.).

If the words are arranged in a tabular form their symmetrical structure is at once evident:

Who,

⁷ *in His days of flesh,*
  having offered up,
    with strong crying and tears,
    prayers and supplications
  unto Him that was able to save
    Him out of death,
  and having been heard
    for His godly fear,
⁸ *though He was Son, yet*
(1) *learned obedience*
  by the things which He suffered;
⁹ *and,*
  having been made perfect,
(2) *He became to all them that obey Him, the cause of eternal salvation,*
¹⁰ *being addressed by God, as High-priest after the order of Melchizedek.*

7, 8. Christ—the Son, the priest after the order of Melchizedek—has been shewn to have fulfilled one condition of true High-priesthood by His divine appointment: He is now shewn to have fulfilled the other, as having learnt through actual experience the uttermost needs of human weakness.

7. ὅς] The relative goes back to the main subject of *v.* 5, Christ, who has been more fully described in the two intervening verses. Here there is no difficulty. Comp. 2 Thess. ii. 9; 1 Pet. iv. 11. In c. iii. 6 the ambiguity is greater, but there οὗ is to be re-

ἱκετηρίας πρὸς τὸν δυνάμενον σώζειν αὐτὸν ἐκ θανάτου μετὰ κραυγῆς ἰσχυρᾶς καὶ δακρύων προσενέγκας καὶ

ferred to God and not to Χριστός. Comp. v. 11 note.

ἐν ταῖς ἡμ. τ. σ. a.] Vulg. *in diebus carnis suæ*, Syr. *when He was clothed with flesh*. The pronoun may be taken either with τῆς σαρκός or with the compound phrase, *in the days of His flesh*, or *in His days of flesh*. The general meaning of the phrase is well given by Theodoret as describing 'the time when He had a mortal body' (ἡμέρας δὲ σαρκὸς τὸν τῆς θνητότητος ἔφη καιρόν, τουτέστιν ἡνίκα θνητὸν εἶχε τὸ σῶμα. Quamdiu habitavit in corpore mortali. Primas.).

'Flesh' here describes not that which is essential to true humanity (Luke xxiv. 39), but the general conditions of humanity in the present life: Gal. ii. 20; Phil. i. 22, 24: 1 Pet. iv. 2. Comp. 1 Cor. xv. 50; and (perhaps) c. x. 20.

οὐκ εἶπεν ἡμέρας σαρκός......ὡς νῦν ἀποθεμένου αὐτοῦ τὴν σάρκα. ἄπαγε· ἔχει γὰρ αὐτὴν εἰ καὶ ἄφθαρτον· ἀλλ' ἡμέρας φησὶ σαρκὸς οἷον τὰς ἐν τῇ σαρκικῇ ζωῇ αὐτοῦ ἡμέρας (Œcum.). Comp. 2 Clem. v. 5 ἡ ἐπιδημία ἡ ἐν τῷ κόσμῳ τούτῳ τῆς σαρκὸς ταύτης μικρά ἐστιν καὶ ὀλιγοχρόνιος.

We can indeed form no clear conception of 'immortal,' 'incorruptible' flesh ; but the phrase represents to us the continuance under new conditions of all that belongs to the perfection of our nature.

The words ἐν τ. ἡμ. τ. σ. stand in contrast with τελειωθείς. It is not said or implied that the conflict of Christ continued in the same form throughout His earthly life. A contrast is drawn between the period of His preparation for the fulness of His Priestly work, and the period of His accomplishment of it after His 'consummation.'

ταῖς ἡμέραις] The use of the term 'days' for 'time' or 'season' seems to suggest the thought of the changing

circumstances of life (comp. Matt. xxviii. 20).

Compare also c. x. 32 ; i. 2.

For the plural see c. i. 2; x. 32; Eph. v. 16; 2 Tim. iii. 1 (ἔσχαται ἡμ.); James v. 3 (ἔσχ. ἡμ.); 1 Pet. iii. 20; 2 Pet. iii. 3; Apoc. ii. 13 &c.

προσ. καὶ εἰσακουσθείς] These participles have been interpreted as preparatory to ἔμαθεν ('after He had offered...He learnt'), or as explanatory and confirmatory of it ('in that He offered...He learnt'). Usage and the gradual development of the thought favour the first view. The 'obedience' of Christ was slowly fashioned through prayer, which was answered for His reverent devotion.

δεήσεις τε καὶ ἱκετ.] Vulg. *preces supplicationesque*. The first word δέησις is the general term for a definite request (*e.g.* James v. 16). The second ἱκετηρία (here only in N. T. in which no other word of its group is used) describes the supplication of one in need of protection or help in some overwhelming calamity. The one (δέησις) is expressed completely in words : the other (ἱκετηρία, properly an olive branch entwined with wool borne by suppliants) suggests the posture and external form and emblems of entreaty (comp. Mark xiv. 35).

The two words are combined Job xl. 22 (LXX.) (xli. 3); comp. Philo *de Cher.* § 13 (i. p. 147 M.). The difference between them is shewn strikingly in a letter of Agrippa given by Philo, *Leg. ad Caium* § 36 (ii. p. 586 M.) γραφὴ δὲ μηνύσει μου τὴν δέησιν ἣν ἀνθ' ἱκετηρίας προτείνω. Comp. 2 Macc. ix. 18.

πρὸς τὸν δυν.] The clause has been taken with δεήσεις καὶ ἱκετηρίας, but the general structure of the sentence, which appears to mark each element in the supplication separately, points to the connexion with the participle (προσενί'νκας); and the unusual constructio. of προσφ. πρός (for *dat.*) may be compared with γνωριζέσθω πρός (Phil. iv. 6 with Lightfoot's note). The prayers of the Son were directed Godward, each thought was laid open in the sight of Him *who was able to save out of death*.

σώζειν ἐκ θαν.] *to save out of death*, Vulg. *salvum facere a morte*. Syr. *to quicken him from death*. The phrase covers two distinct ideas, 'to save from physical death so that it should be escaped,' 'to bring safe out of death into a new life.' In the first sense the prayer recorded in John xii. 27 was not granted, that it might be granted in the second.

Σώζειν ἐκ does not necessarily imply that that is actually realised out of which deliverance is granted (comp. 2 Cor. i. 10), though it does so commonly (John xii. 27; and exx. in Bleek).

In σώζειν ἐκ (James v. 20; Jude 5) the dominant thought is of the peril *in* which the sufferer is immersed (contrast σώζειν εἰς 2 Tim. iv. 18); in σώζειν ἀπό (Matt. i. 21; Acts ii. 40; Rom. v. 9), of the peril *from* which he is rescued. Compare λυτροῦσθαι ἐκ 1 Pet. i. 18; λυτρ. ἀπό Tit. ii. 14; and ῥύσασθαι ἐκ Luke i. 74; Rom. vii. 24; 2 Cor. i. 10; Col. i. 13; 1 Thess. i. 10; 2 Tim. iii. 11; 2 Pet. ii. 9; ῥύσασθαι ἀπό Matt. vi. 13; Rom. xv. 31; 2 Thess. iii. 2; both constructions are found together 2 Tim. iv. 17, 18.

The force of the present σώζειν will be seen in contrast with σῶσαι Luke xix. 10.

μετὰ κραυγῆς ἰσχ.] Vulg. *cum clamore valido*. The passage finds a striking illustration in a Jewish saying: 'There are three kinds of prayers each loftier than the preceding: prayer, crying, and tears. Prayer is made in silence: crying with raised voice; but tears overcome all things ['there is no door through which tears do not pass']' Synopsis Sohar ap. Schoettgen *ad loc.*

There can be little doubt that the writer refers to the scene at Gethsemane; but the mention of these details of 'the loud cry' 'and tears' (John xi. 35 ἐδάκρυσεν; Luke xix. 41 ἔκλαυσεν), no less than the general scope of the passage, suggests the application of the words to other prayers and times of peculiar trial in the Lord's life. Compare John xi. 33 ff.; xii. 27 f.; (Matt. xxvii. 46, 50).

There is a tradition that originally the High-priest on the Day of Atonement, when he offered the prayer for forgiveness in the Holy of Holies, uttered the name of God with a loud voice so that it could be heard far off. Comp. Maimon. ap. Delitzsch, *Hebr.* ii. p. 471 (E. Tr.).

κραυγή] The loud cry of deeply-stirred feeling of joyful surprise: Lc. i. 42; Mt. xxv. 6; of partisan applause: Acts xxiii. 9; of grief: Apoc. xxi. 4 (not Apoc. xiv. 18); of anger: Eph. iv. 31. Compare Ps. xxii. 24 (LXX.); and see also κράζω in Gal. iv. 6; Rom. viii. 15.

μετὰ...δακρύων] c. xii. 17; Acts xx. 31 (not Mk. ix. 24). Compare Hos. xii. 4.

Epiphanius (*Ancor.* 31) seems to use ἔκλαυσε as a general periphrasis of the passage in St Luke (xxii. 43): οὐ μόνον γὰρ τὰ ἡμῶν βάρη ἀνεδέξατο ὑπὲρ ἡμῶν ἐλθὼν ὁ ἅγιος Λόγος ἀλλὰ καὶ ὑπὸ ἀφὴν ἐγένετο καὶ σάρκα ἔλαβε... ἀλλὰ καὶ ἔκλαυσε· κεῖται ἐν τῷ κατὰ Λούκαν εὐαγγελίῳ ἐν τοῖς ἀδιορθώτοις ἀντιγράφοις...καὶ γενόμενος ἐν ἀγωνίᾳ... καὶ ὤφθη ἄγγελος ἐνισχύων αὐτόν.

The question has been asked for what did Christ pray? (περὶ τίνων ἐδεήθη; περὶ τῶν πιστευσάντων εἰς αὐτόν Chrys.). Perhaps it is best to answer generally, for the victory over death the fruit of sin. This was the end of His work, and to this end every part of it contributed. Under this aspect the conditional prayers for His own deliverance (Matt. xxvi. 39 and parallels; John xii. 27) become intelligible. And the due connexion is established between the prayer at

εἰσακουσθεὶς ἀπὸ τῆς εὐλαβείας, ⁸καίπερ ὢν υἱός, ἔμαθεν

ἀκουσθείς D₂*.

the Agony, and the High-priestly prayer which preceded it. The general truth is admirably expressed by the Latin commentators: Omnia autem quae ipse egit in carne preces supplicationesque fuerunt pro peccatis humani generis. Sacra vero sanguinis ejus effusio clamor fuit validus in quo exauditus est a deo patre pro sua reverentia, hoc est, voluntaria obedientia et perfectissima caritate (Prim., Herv.).

προσενέγκας] Comp v. 1, note. Perhaps the use of the ritual word (προσενέγκας) of the Lord's prayers on earth points to the true sacrificial character of spiritual service: c. xiii. 15. The combination προσφέρειν δέησιν occurs in late Greek writers. See Lexx.

εἰσακουσθεὶς ἀπὸ τῆς εὐλαβείας] having been heard for His godly fear, O. L. exauditus a metu (all. ab illo metu v. propter timorem), Vulg. exauditus est pro sua reverentia. The Syr. transfers the words ἀπὸ τῆς εὐλ. from this clause to the next, learnt obedience from fear and the sufferings which He bore. True prayer— the prayer which must be answered— is the personal recognition and acceptance of the divine will (John xiv. 7: comp. Mark vi. 24 ἐλάβετε). It follows that the hearing of prayer, which teaches obedience, is not so much the granting of a specific petition, which is assumed by the petitioner to be the way to the end desired, but the assurance that what is granted does most effectively lead to the end. Thus we are taught that Christ learnt that every detail of His Life and Passion contributed to the accomplishment of the work which He came to fulfil, and so He was most perfectly 'heard.' In this sense He was 'heard for His godly fear' (εὐλάβεια).

The word εὐλάβεια occurs again in c. xii. 28 (only in N.T.) and the verb

in c. xi. 7. It is very rare in the LXX. Josh. xxii. 24 (דְּאָגָה); Prov. xxviii. 14; Wisd. xvii. 8. The adj. εὐλαβής is found Lev. xv. 31; Mic. vii. 2, v. l. The verb εὐλαβεῖσθαι is more frequent and represents no less than a dozen Hebrew words. Εὐλάβεια marks that careful and watchful reverence which pays regard to every circumstance in that with which it has to deal. It may therefore degenerate into a timid and unworthy anxiety (Jos. Antt. vi. 2, 179); but more commonly it expresses reverent and thoughtful shrinking from over-boldness, which is compatible with true courage: Philo, Quis rer. div. hær. § 6 (i. 476 M.) σκόπει πάλιν ὅτι εὐλαβείᾳ τὸ θαρρεῖν ἀνακέκραται. id. p. 477 μήτε ἄνευ εὐλαβείας παρρησιάζεσθαι μήτε ἀπαρρησιάστως εὐλαβεῖσθαι. Here the word in its noblest sense is singularly appropriate. Prayer is heard as it is 'according to God's will' (1 John v. 14 f.), and Christ by His εὐλάβεια perfectly realised that submission which is obedience on one side and fellowship on the other.

Primasius has an interesting note: pro sua reverentia: hoc est propter voluntariam obedientiam et perfectissimam caritatem...Notandum autem quia reverentia, secundum sententiam Cassiodori, accipitur aliquando pro amore, aliquando pro timore: hic vero pro summa ponitur caritate qua Filius Dei nos dilexit et pro summa obedientia qua fuit obediens Patri usque ad mortem.

The Greek Fathers take a less wide view. E.g. πλὴν μὴ τὸ ἐμὸν θέλημα ἀλλὰ τὸ σόν...ἦν ὡς ἀληθῶς πολλῆς εὐλαβείας...εἰσηκούσθη τοίνυν ὁ Χριστὸς οὐκ ἀπὸ τῆς παραιτήσεως ἀλλ' ἀπὸ τῆς εὐλαβείας (Œcum.).

The sense 'heard and set free from His fear' or 'from the object of His fear' is wholly untenable. For the

ἀφ᾽ ὧν ἔπαθεν τὴν ὑπακοήν, ⁹καὶ τελειωθεὶς ἐγένετο

use of ἀπό see Luke xix. 3; xxiv. 41;
Acts xii. 14; xxii. 11; John xxi. 6.

8. καίπερ ὢν υἱός...] *though He was
Son*...The clause has been taken with
the words which precede ('being heard
not as Son but for His godly fear'),
and with those which follow ('though
Son went through the discipline of
suffering to obedience'). The latter
connexion is most in accordance with
the whole scope of the passage.
Though Son and therefore endowed
with right of access for Himself to
the Father, being of one essence with
the Father, for man's sake as man
He won the right of access for humanity. In one sense it is true that
the idea of Sonship suggests that of
obedience; but the nature of Christ's
Sonship at first sight seems to exclude
the thought that He should learn
obedience through suffering.

For καίπερ see c. vii. 5; xii. 17;
Phil. iii. 4; 2 Pet. i. 12.

In *v.* 5 the title 'Son' has been
used of the Sonship of the exalted
Christ in His twofold nature. Here
it is used of the eternal, divine relation of the Son to the Father.
There is a similar transition from one
aspect to the other of the unchanged
Personality of the Lord in i. 1—4.
The Incarnation itself corresponds with
and implies (if we may so speak) an
immanent Sonship in the Divine
Nature. Thus, though it may be true
that the title Son is used of the Lord
predominantly (at least) in connexion
with the Incarnation, that of necessity
carries our thoughts further. Comp.
John v. 19 ff.

Chrysostom gives a personal application to the lesson: εἰ ἐκεῖνος υἱὸς ὢν
ἐκέρδανεν ἀπὸ τῶν παθημάτων τὴν ὑπα-
κοὴν πολλῷ μᾶλλον ἡμεῖς.

ἔμαθεν...τὴν ὑπακ.] *learned obedience*... The spirit of obedience is realised through trials, seen at least to
minister to good. Sufferings in this
sense may be said to teach obedience

as they confirm it and call it out
actively. The Lord 'learned obedience
through the things which He suffered,'
not as if the lesson were forced upon
Him by the necessity of suffering, for
the learning of obedience does not
imply the conquest of disobedience
as actual, but as making His own
perfectly, through insight into the
Father's will, that self-surrender which
was required, even to death upon the
cross (comp. Phil. ii. 8).

The Lord's manhood was (negatively) sinless and (positively) perfect,
that is perfect relatively at every
stage; and therefore He truly advanced by 'learning' (Luke ii. 52;
40 πληρούμενον), while the powers of
His human Nature grew step by step
in a perfect union with the divine in
His one Person.

τὴν ὑπακοήν] obedience in all its
completeness, the obedience which
answers to the idea. It is not said
that the Lord 'learned to obey.' For
the difference between ἔμαθεν τὴν
ὑπακ. and ἔμ. ὑπακ. see 1 John iii. 10
note; and contrast 2 Cor. x. 5 εἰς τὴν
ὑπακ. τ. χρ. with Rom. i. 5 εἰς ὑπακ.
πιστ. The word 'obedience' contains
a reference to the occasion of sin.
Man's fall was due to disobedience:
his restoration comes through o-
bedience. Comp. Rom. v. 19.

The alliteration in the phrase ἔμαθεν
ἀφ᾽ ὧν ἔπαθεν is common in Greek
literature from the time of Herodotus
downwards: Hdt. i. 207 τὰ δέ μοι παθήματα ἐόντα ἀχάριστα μαθήματα γέγονεν. Æsch. *Agam.* v. 177 πάθει μάθος
(comp. v. 250); Philo, *de Somn.* ii.
§ 15 (i. 673 M.) ἀναφθέγξεται ὁ (so
read, not ὁ) παθὼν ἀκριβῶς ἔμαθεν. *de
spec. leg.* 6 (ii. 340 M.) ἵνα ἐκ τοῦ παθεῖν
μάθῃ. Wetstein has collected many
examples.

9, 10. Christ, it has been seen,
satisfies the conditions of High-priesthood. He has received divine appointment: He is inspired with the

πᾶσιν τοῖς ὑπακούουσιν αὐτῷ αἴτιος σωτηρίας αἰωνίου,

9 πᾶσιν τ. ὑπ. αὐτῷ ℵABCD₂ vg syrr me : τ. ὑπ. αὐ. πᾶσιν Ϛ.

completest sympathy. But His High-priesthood goes immeasurably beyond that of the Levitical system in its efficacy. As He is in His humanity superior to Moses (c. iii. 1 ff. note), so He is superior to Aaron. The one fact has been affirmed directly (iii. 5 f.): the other fact is shewn in a type (Melchizedek). And this superiority is further shewn in the action of Christ as High-priest. The Levitical High-priest entered into the Holy of Holies *through the blood of goats and calves,* but Christ *through His own blood* to the presence of God Himself (comp. c. ix. 11 ff.). Yet further, the reference to Ps. cx. necessarily includes the thought of the Royal priesthood which is developed afterwards.

9. καὶ τελειωθείς...] *and having been made perfect...* Vulg. *et consummatus...* Syr. *and thus was perfected and...* Comp. ii. 10 note.

This perfection was seen on the one side in the complete fulfilment of man's destiny by Christ through absolute self-sacrifice, and on the other in His exaltation to the right hand of God, which was in the divine order its due consequence. Comp. c. ii. 9 διὰ τὸ πάθημα. Phil. ii. 9. Thus the word, which carries with it the conception of Christ's complete preparation for the execution of His priestly office, suggests the contrast between His priestly action and that of Aaron.

ἐγένετο] *became* in the fulfilment of what we conceive of as a natural law. It is said 'became' and not 'becomes' or 'is,' because on the divine side and in the eternal order the issue of Christ's work is complete. For γενέσθαι see *v.* 5; i. 4; ii. 17; vi. 20; vii. 22, 26.

Comp. Rom. viii. 29 f.; Col. iii. 1 ff.

πᾶσιν τοῖς ὑπακούουσιν] *to all that obey Him,* Gentiles as well as Jews. Comp. John i. 7. In this connexion

continuous active obedience is the sign of real faith (contrast iv. 3 οἱ πιστεύσαντες). The obedience of the believer to Christ answers to the obedience of the Son to the Father. By obedience fellowship is made complete. Si obedientia Filii causa est salutis humanæ, quanta nobis necessitas est obedire Deo, ut digni inveniamur ejus salutis quam nobis per Filium proprium donavit (Atto).

αἴτιος σωτ. αἰών.] *the cause of eternal salvation,* Latt. *causa salutis æternæ.* In ii. 10 the word corresponding to αἴτιος is ἀρχηγός. There the thought was of Christ going before the 'many sons' with whom He unites Himself. Here the thought is of that which He alone does for them. In the former passage He is the great Leader who identifies Himself with His people: in this He is the High-priest who offers Himself as an effectual sacrifice on their behalf.

The word αἴτιος does not occur elsewhere in N.T. Comp. 1 Sam. xxii. 22; 2 Macc. xiii. 4; Bel 42.

The phrase αἴτιος σωτηρίας is used by Philo of the brazen serpent (*De agric.* § 22, i. 315), and of Noah in relation to his sons (*De nobil.* § 3, ii. 440). Comp. *De vit. cont.* § 11 (ii. 485 M.). It is found not unfrequently in classical writers : *e.g.* Demosth. *De Rhod. libert.* § 4 (p. 191) μόνοι τῶν πάντων τῆς σωτηρίας αὐτοῖς αἴτιοι.

σωτ. αἰών.] This spiritual, eternal, divine deliverance answers to the external and temporal deliverance which Moses wrought. The phrase is not found elsewhere in N. T.

Comp. Is. xlv. 17 Ἰσραὴλ σώζεται ὑπὸ κυρίου σωτηρίαν αἰώνιον (תְּשׁוּעַת עוֹלָמִים).

The phrase corresponds with ζωὴ αἰώνιος (comp. 1 John v. 20, Addit. Note). Compare also c. vi. 2 κρίμα

¹⁰προσαγορευθεὶς ὑπὸ τοῦ θεοῦ ἀρχιερεὺς κατὰ τὴν τάξιν Μελχισεδέκ.

10 ἀρχ. + εἰς τὸν αἰῶνα´ (syr hl) me.

αἰώνιον. ix. 12 αἰωνία λύτρωσις. 15 ἡ αἰώνιος κληρονομία. xiii. 20 διαθήκη αἰώνιος. The words with which αἰώνιος is used in other books of the N. T. throw light upon its meaning : πῦρ Matt. xviii. 8; xxv. 41 (τὸ π. τὸ αἰ.); Jude 7 (π. αἰ.); κόλασις Matt. xxv. 46; σκηνή Luke xvi. 9 (αἱ αἰ. σκ.); βασιλεία 2 Pet. i. 11 (ἡ αἰ. β.); ὄλεθρος 2 Thess. i. 9; παράκλησις 2 Thess. ii. 16; χρόνοι Rom. xvi. 25; 2 Tim. i. 9; Tit. i. 2; θεός Rom. xvi. 20 (ὁ αἰ. θ.); κράτος 1 Tim. vi. 16; δόξα 2 Tim. ii. 10; 1 Pet. v. 10 (ἡ αἰ. δ.); εὐαγγέλιον Apoc. xiv. 6. The double correspondence of σώζειν, ὑπακοήν (vv. 7, 8) with ὑπακούουσιν, σωτηρίας is to be noticed. Three brief notes of Greek commentators deserve to be quoted :

τελείωσιν τὴν ἀνάστασιν καὶ τὴν ἀθανασίαν ἐκάλεσε· τοῦτο γὰρ τῆς οἰκονομίας τὸ πέρας (Theod.).

ἄρα οὖν τελείωσις διὰ τῶν παθημάτων γίνεται· πῶς οὖν ὑμεῖς δυσχεραίνετε ἐπὶ ταῖς τελειοποιοῖς θλίψεσιν; (Theoph.).

ὁρᾷς ὅσα περὶ ὑπακοῆς διαλέγεται ὥστε πείθεσθαι αὐτούς; δοκοῦσι γάρ μοι συνεχῶς ἀφηνιάζειν καὶ τοῖς λεγομένοις μὴ παρακολουθεῖν (Chrys.).

10. προσαγορευθεὶς...ἀρχ.] being addressed by God as High-priest.... O. L. vocatus (pronunciatus) sacerdos (princeps sacerdotum). Vulg. vocatus pontifex. The title (High-priest) is involved in the words of Ps. cx. v. 4 and v. 1 taken together ; comp. vi. 20. A royal priesthood is there combined with admission to the immediate Presence of God (sit... at my right hand), which was the peculiar privilege of the High-priest. At the same time the peculiar character of this priesthood (after the order of Melchizedek) includes the pledge of its eternal efficacy (eternal salvation). Comp. c. vii. 16 f. The

word προσαγορεύειν (here only in N.T.) expresses the formal and solemn ascription of the title to Him to whom it belongs ('addressed as,' 'styled'). Comp. 1 Macc. xiv. 40; 2 Macc. iv. 7; x. 9; xiv. 37; 1 Clem. 10, 17. Philo, de migr. Abr. § 24 (ii. 19 M.) πατὴρ μὲν τῶν ὅλων ὁ μέσος, ὃς ἐν ταῖς ἱεραῖς γραφαῖς κυρίῳ ὀνόματι καλεῖται ὁ Ὤν, αἱ δὲ παρ' ἑκάτερα πρεσβύταται καὶ ἐγγύταται τοῦ ὄντος δυνάμεις, ὧν ἡ μὲν ποιητικὴ ἡ δ' αὖ βασιλικὴ προσαγορεύεται· καὶ ἡ μὲν ποιητικὴ θεός...ἡ δὲ βασιλικὴ κύριος...

ii. Progress in patient effort (v. 11—vi. 20).

The general view which has been given of the Divine High-priest, of His office and of His qualifications, of His power of sympathy and of His direct appointment by God, leads naturally to a consideration of the obligations which this revelation imposes upon those to whom it is made. The highest truth is not to be mastered at once, nor without serious and continuous effort. It can only be grasped in virtue of a corresponding growth in those to whom it is addressed. There is always, in the case of those who have learnt somewhat, the danger of resting in their attainment, which is a fatal relapse. Yet we are encouraged by past experience to hold our hope firmly; and the promise of God remains sure beyond the possibility of failure.

These general thoughts are unfolded in four sections. (1) The mention of Melchizedek calls up the difficulties connected with his priesthood which the Hebrews were not prepared to meet. They had become stationary and therefore had lost the power of receiving higher teaching (v. 11—14). (2) Such a condition illustrates the paramount duty of Christian progress, and the perils of relapse (vi. 1—8). (3)

¹¹ Περὶ οὗ πολὺς ἡμῖν ὁ λόγος καὶ δυσερμήνευτος

11 +καὶ (περὶ) D₂*.　　　　om. ὁ (λόγος) D₂*.

At the same time the frank recognition of danger does not exclude the consolation of hope (vi. 9—12). And (4) though God requires patience from men, His promise can never fail (13—20).

It is of deep interest to observe that here for the second time the writer pauses when the subject of Christ's priestly work rises before him. He announced this subject in ii. 17, and directly turned aside from it to enforce the lessons of Israel's failure. He returned to the subject in iv. 14, and, after a fuller exposition of its outlines, he now again interrupts his argument to insist on the strenuous labour which believers must undertake that they may rightly enter into it.

Chrysostom says justly: ὅρα γοῦν αὐτὸν συνεχῶς ὠδίνοντα τὸν περὶ τοῦ ἀρχιερέως εἰσαγαγεῖν λόγον καὶ ἀεὶ ἀναβαλλόμενον...ἐπεὶ οὖν τοσαυτάκις ἐξεκρούσθη, ὡσανεὶ ἀπολογούμενός φησιν ἡ αἰτία παρ᾽ ὑμᾶς.

(1) *Stationariness in religious life and its consequences* (v. 11—14).

The life of faith is like the natural life. It has appropriate support in its different stages. Healthy growth enables us to appropriate that which we could not have received at an earlier stage. But this general law carries with it grave consequences. (a) The period of first discipleship may be misused, as by the Hebrews, so that we remain still mere 'babes' when it is past (11, 12). And so (b) when the time comes for maturer instruction we may be unprepared to apprehend it (13, 14).

¹¹*Of whom (which) we have many things to say and hard of interpretation since ye are become dull in your hearing.* ¹²*For when ye ought to be teachers by reason of the time, ye again have need that some one*

teach you the elements of the first principles of the oracles of God; and ye are become in need of milk, (and) not of solid food. ¹³For every one that partaketh of milk is without experience in the word of righteousness, for he is a babe. ¹⁴But solid food is for full-grown men, even those who in virtue of their state have their senses exercised to discern good and evil.

(a) The Hebrews have failed to grow with years (11, 12).

11 f. The difficulty of unfolding the truth of Christ's High-priestly office typified in Melchizedek is due to the spiritual state of the Hebrews. They are still babes when they ought to have advanced to ripe intelligence.

The character of the complaint seems to indicate clearly that the Epistle could not have been addressed to a large body as a whole, but to some section of it (comp. xiii. 17) consisting, as it appears, of men in the same general circumstances of age, position and opinion.

11. περὶ οὗ πολὺς ἡμῖν ὁ λόγος...] *Of whom (which).* Vulg. *De quo grandis nobis sermo*...The relative is ambiguous. It may mean *concerning which, i.e.* the High-priestly dignity of Christ, or *concerning whom.* In the latter case the antecedent may be *Christ* (περὶ οὗ χριστοῦ Œcum.) or *Melchizedek* (Pesh. *about this Melchizedek*) or (as a complex subject) *Christ a High-priest after the order of Melchizedek* (vi. 20; comp. ὅς v. 7).

The reference to Melchizedek simply appears to be too limited. Although Melchizedek is afterwards spoken of in detail (vii. 1 ff.), the mysteries to which the apostle refers do not lie properly in his person, but in Him whom he foreshadowed; and, again, the reference to Christ gene-

λέγειν, ἐπεὶ νωθροὶ γεγόνατε ταῖς ἀκοαῖς· ¹²καὶ γὰρ

rally is too vague. Hence it seems best to interpret the οὗ of Christ as typified by Melchizedek, or of Melchizedek as a type of Christ. Christ's Priesthood and Sacrifice is the main and most difficult subject of the Epistle; and this is foreshadowed in Melchizedek, whose significance was overlooked by the Jewish interpreters (*e.g.* Bereshith R.). In regard to the general sense it makes no difference whether the οὗ be neuter or masculine (with this reference), but the neuter is less in the style of the Epistle.

It will be observed that, while the writer of the Epistle recognises the difficulty of his theme, he declares no less plainly that he must deal with it. He speaks of *the* discourse, the teaching (ὁ λόγος), which (he implies) it is his duty and his purpose to deliver. There is no indication that the fulfilment of his design is contingent on those whom he addresses. His part must be done, however hard it may be to do it. In this respect he identifies himself with the society which he represents (ἡμῖν).

δυσερμήνευτος] *hard of interpretation:* Vulg. *ininterpretabilis ad dicendum:* hard for a writer to express, so that it will be fully understood. The difficulty of the interpreter lies in the small capacity of his audience. The addition of λέγειν, which corresponds with the image in ταῖς ἀκοαῖς, shews decisively, as is otherwise most natural, that the difficulty is considered with regard to him who has to make the exposition and not to those who have to receive it.

The sense is rightly given by the early commentators: ὅταν τις πρὸς ἀνθρώπους ἔχῃ (*l.* λέγῃ) μὴ παρακολουθοῦντας μηδὲ τὰ λεγόμενα νοοῦντας ἑρμηνεῦσαι καλῶς αὐτοῖς οὐ δύναται (Chrys.).

Difficultas interpretandi...non fuit

in ejus ignorantia cui revelata sunt mysteria a seculis abscondita sed potius in illorum tarditate qui imbecilles, *i.e.* infirmi in fide...(Primas., Herv.).

Philo speaks of seeing the unchanging beauty of the ideal world, ἀλέκτῳ τινὶ καὶ δυσερμηνεύτῳ θέᾳ (*De Somn.* i. § 32; i. 649 M.).

ἐπεὶ νωθροὶ γεγόνατε...] *since ye are become dull of hearing,* Vulg. *quoniam imbecilles facti estis ad audiendum...* The difficulty of which the apostle has spoken came from the fault of the Hebrews. They had become with years less quick in understanding and not more quick according to a natural and healthy development. Compare Chrysostom: τὸ εἰπεῖν ἐπεὶ νωθροὶ γεγόνατε ταῖς ἀκοαῖς δηλοῦντος ἦν ὅτι πάλαι ὑγίαινον καὶ ἦσαν ἰσχυροί, τῇ προθυμίᾳ ζέοντες (c. x. 32), καὶ ὕστερον αὐτοὺς τοῦτο παθεῖν μαρτυρεῖ.

As yet however this dulness had not extended to action though such an issue was not far off (c. vi. 12; comp. 2 Pet. ii. 20). Ὅρα δέ, writes Chrysostom, πῶς μέχρις ἀκοῆς τὴν νωθρότητα ἔστησε.

For νωθροί see c. vi. 12. The word is found in LXX., Prov. xxii. 29; Ecclus. iv. 29; xi. 12. The plural αἱ ἀκοαί expresses the powers of hearing. Comp. Mk. vii. 35.

ἐπεί] *since, seeing.* The conjunction is of frequent use in the Epistle, in which the strengthened form ἐπειδή is not found. See ii. 14; iv. 6; v. 2; vi. 13; ix. 17, 26; x. 2; xi. 11. It expresses a fact which influences a result, yet not so that the result is the direct and necessary consequence of it (ὅτι).

12. The fault of the Hebrews is clearly defined. When by reason of the time—because they had been Christians so long,—they ought to have been teachers, they were themselves in need of elementary teaching. For καὶ γάρ see iv. 2 note; for ὀφείλοντες,

ὀφείλοντες εἶναι διδάσκαλοι διὰ τὸν χρόνον, πάλιν
χρείαν ἔχετε τοῦ διδάσκειν ὑμᾶς τινὰ τὰ στοιχεῖα τῆς
ἀρχῆς τῶν λογίων τοῦ θεοῦ, καὶ γεγόνατε χρείαν ἔχοντες

12 λογίων : λόγων D₂* (vg syrr me).

ii. 17; v. 3 notes; and for διὰ τὸν
χρόνον compare v. 14 διὰ τὴν ἕξιν.
On διδάσκαλος Bengel says 'vocabu-
lum non muneris sed facultatis.'

π. χρείαν ἔχετε τοῦ διδ. ὑμᾶς τινὰ τὰ
στ.] ye have need again that some one
teach you the elements... The τινα is
ambiguous. It may be treated as
an interrogative (τίνα): 'that one
teach you what are the rudiments...'
(so Vulg. Syr. Orig. Cyr.), or as the
indefinite pronoun (τινά). In spite of
the ancient authority for the first
rendering, the second seems to be
preferable (comp. 1 Thess. iv. 9). It
gives a sharper antithesis to διδάσκαλοι εἶναι. And it could hardly be
said the Hebrews required to learn
what the elements of the Faith were.
They knew what they were though
they did not know them.
The constructions of χρείαν ἔχειν are
singularly varied. The phrase is used
absolutely (Mk. ii. 25; Acts ii. 45;
1 Cor. xii. 24; Eph. iv. 28; 1 John
iii. 17); with an object in the genitive
(γάλακτος, c. x. 36 &c.); with the
simple infinitive (1 Thess. i. 8; v. 1;
Matt. iii. 14 &c.); with ἵνα (John ii. 25;
xvi. 30; 1 John ii. 27); and here only
with the infinitive and article.
The phrase τὰ στοιχεῖα τῆς ἀρχῆς
τῶν λογίων τοῦ θεοῦ (Vulg. elementa
exordii sermonum Dei) is very remarkable. Even 'the beginning,' the
simplest fruitful presentation of the
Gospel, is complex. The divine message includes from the first distinct
elements which require to grow together. It is one, not as monotonous,
but in virtue of a vital unity.
'The beginning of the oracles of
God' corresponds with 'the beginning
of Christ' (vi. 1). Τῆς ἀρχῆς is not in
either place to be separated from the

genitive which follows as if it could
have one adjectival sense, 'the first
elements,' 'the first teaching.'
τὰ στοιχεῖα] the rudiments, the first,
simplest, elements of which anything
consists: 'the alphabet' of a subject.
The word occurs elsewhere in the
N.T. of the material elements of the
universe: 2 Pet. iii. 10, 12; and
metaphorically: Gal. iv. 3, 9; Col. ii.
8, 20.
τῶν λογίων τοῦ θεοῦ] Rom. iii.2. Comp.
1 Pet. iv. 11; Acts vii. 38. The phrase
might refer to the new revelation
given by Christ to His apostles (comp.
c. i. 2); but it seems more natural to
refer it to the collected writings of the
O. T. which the Hebrew Christians
failed to understand and so, through
mistaken loyalty to the past, were in
danger of apostasy.
For the patristic use of λόγιον,
which is common in LXX., see Euseb.
H. E. iii. 39; 1 Clem. 19, 53; Polyc.
ad Phil. 8.
γεγόνατε χρείαν ἔχοντες] Vulg. facti
estis quibus lacte opus sit. The change
of expression from χρείαν ἔχετε is most
significant. Χρείαν ἔχετε describes
the simple fact: this phrase points
out a fact which is the result of degeneracy. The Hebrews had through
their own neglect become young children again. So Chrysostom: οὐκ εἶπε
χρείαν ἔχετε ἀλλὰ γεγόνατε χρείαν
ἔχοντες..., τουτέστιν, ὑμεῖς ἠθελήσατε,
ὑμεῖς ἑαυτοὺς εἰς τοῦτο κατεστήσατε, εἰς
ταύτην τὴν χρείαν.
γάλα...στερεὰ τροφή] milk...solid
food...There has been much discussion
as to what should be understood by
these terms respectively. The early
commentators generally supposed that
'milk,' the food of young converts,
was the teaching on 'the Lord's

γάλακτος, ᵀ οὐ στερεᾶς τροφῆς. ¹³πᾶς γὰρ ὁ μετέχων
γάλακτος ἄπειρος λόγου δικαιοσύνης, νήπιος γάρ ἐστιν·

12 καὶ

καὶ οὐ א°AB*D₂ syrr : om. καὶ א*C vg me.   13 δικ. + ἐστίν D₂*.   νηπ. γ. + ἀκμήν D₂*.

humanity,' and His Resurrection and
Ascension, while 'the solid food' was
the more mysterious teaching on His
Godhead. Thus, for example, Primasius : Lac simplicis doctrinæ est in-
carnatio filii Dei, passio, resurrectio
illius, ascensio ad cælum : solidus
vero cibus perfecti sermonis est mysterium trinitatis, quomodo tres sunt in
personis et unum in substantia deitatis.
The true explanation lies in vi. 1
ff.
The respective topics of the two
stages of teaching are not spoken of
as more or less essential or important.
That which corresponds with the
'milk' is in fact 'the foundation.'
The 'milk' and 'solid food' are appropriate to different periods of
growth. The older Christian ought
to be able to assimilate fresh and
harder truths.
γάλακτος...] In Rabbinic language
young students were called 'sucklings'
(תינוקות). See Schoettgen on 1 Pet.
ii. 2. Comp. 1 Cor. iii. 2, Is. xxviii.
9.
The image occurs in Philo : De
agric. § 2 (i. 301 M.) νηπίοις μέν ἐστι
γάλα τροφή, τελείοις δὲ τὰ ἐκ πυρῶν
πέμματα. De leg. Spec. § 36 (ii. 332 M.).
Compare also a remarkable parallel in
Arrian : οὐ θέλεις ἤδη ὡς τὰ παιδία
ἀπογαλακτισθῆναι καὶ ἅπτεσθαι στερεᾶς
τροφῆς (Dissert. ii. 16, 39).
(b) Each age has its appropriate
support (13, 14).
13 f. The consequences of the fault
of the Hebrews are indicated by the
statement of a general law. Each
age has its proper food. But spiritual
maturity comes through discipline and
not through years only.
13. πᾶς γὰρ ὁ μετ. γάλ.] The argu-

ment would have been clearer if the
terms of the sentence had been inverted : ' For every one that is inex-
perienced...—as you shew yourselves
to be—is fed with milk...' But the
writer prefers to suggest the fact
that his readers are actually living in
the most rudimentary stage of faith,
' partaking of milk,' and so condemn-
ing themselves of unfitness for deeper
instruction. For every one that partaketh of milk, and the Hebrews had
brought themselves to this diet, is
according to the figure a mere infant,
and necessarily ignorant of the teachings and the problems of life. Such a
one therefore could not but be *without
experience of the word of righteousness* (Vulg. *expers sermonis justitiæ*),
unprepared by past training to enter
upon the discussion of the larger
problems of Christian thought.
The absence of the definite articles
(λόγος δικαιοσύνης not ὁ λ. τῆς δικ.)
shews that the main conception of
the phrase lies in the character and
not in the concrete realisation of the
' word.' It is not 'the word of righteousness,' the full exposition of the
Christian Faith (2 Cor. iii. 9), but
teaching such as belongs to it, ' teaching of righteousness,' teaching which
deals at once with the one source of
righteousness in Christ, and the
means by which man is enabled to be
made partaker of it. The doctrine of
Christ's priestly work is based upon
these conceptions, which belong to
the 'solid food' of the mature believer.
Chrysostom offers two interpretations of the phrase : ὁ ἄπειρος λόγου δικαιοσύνης, τουτέστι, τῆς ἄνω φιλοσοφίας
ἄπειρος, οὐ δύναται παραδέξασθαι βίον
ἄκρον καὶ ἠκριβωμένον· ἢ δικαιοσύνην

¹⁴τελείων δέ ἐστιν ἡ στερεὰ τροφή, τῶν διὰ τὴν ἕξιν τὰ
αἰσθητήρια γεγυμνασμένα ἐχόντων πρὸς διάκρισιν καλοῦ
τε καὶ κακοῦ.

ἐνταῦθα τὸν Χριστόν φησι καὶ τὸν ὑψηλὸν
περὶ αὐτοῦ λόγον.
The word ἄπειρος does not occur
again in the N. T.

14. Milk is the food of babes; and
he who is fed on milk—whether it be
in the due order of nature or by
lack of reasonable growth—is a babe.
But *solid food is for full-grown
men*.

The contrast between *babes* and
full-grown men occurs again Eph. iv.
13 f. μέχρι καταντήσωμεν...εἰς ἄνδρα
τέλειον, εἰς μέτρον ἡλικίας τοῦ πληρώ-
ματος τοῦ Χριστοῦ· ἵνα μηκέτι ὦμεν νήπιοι
...1 Cor. xiv. 20 τῇ κακίᾳ νηπιάζετε,
ταῖς δὲ φρεσὶν τέλειοι γίνεσθε. 1 Cor.
ii. 6, iii. 1. Comp. Philo, *Leg. Alleg.*
i. § 30 (i. 62 M.) τῷ τελείῳ κατ᾽ εἰκόνα
προστάττειν ἢ ἀπαγορεύειν ἢ παραινεῖν
οὐχὶ δεῖ...τῷ δὲ νηπίῳ παραινέσεως καὶ
διδασκαλίας [χρεία].

A man is said to be τέλειος who has
reached the full maturity of his
powers, the full possession of his
rights, his τέλος, his ' end.' This maturity, completeness, perfection, may
be regarded generally or in some
particular aspect. As compared with
the child, the full-grown man is τέλειος physically, intellectually, socially
(comp. 1 Cor. xiii. 10 f.; Gal. iv. 3); as
compared with the fresh uninstruct-
ed convert, the disciplined and experienced Christian is τέλειος (1 Cor.
xiv. 20; ii. 6; Eph. iv. 13; Phil. iii.
15; Col. i. 28; iv. 12; James i. 4).
There is also an ideal completeness
answering to man's constitution in his
power of self-control (James iii. 2), in
his love for his fellows (Matt. v. 48;
comp. xix. 21).

He is absolutely τέλειος in whom
each human faculty and gift has found
a harmonious development and use,
who has fulfilled the destiny of man by

attaining the likeness of God (Gen. i.
26).

In the same manner any object is
τέλειος which completely satisfies its
ideal, so that all the constituent
elements are found in it in perfect
efficiency (1 John iv. 18 ἡ τελεία ἀγάπη.
James i. 4, 17; comp. Rom. xii. 2).
Law is framed for the guidance of
man in the attainment of his proper
end: the perfect law therefore is 'the
law of freedom,' which completely
corresponds with the unhindered fulfilment of his duty (James i. 25). The
Levitical Tabernacle was designed to
represent under the conditions of
earth the dwelling of God among
men, offering a revelation of God and
a way of approach to God: the
heavenly Tabernacle through which
Christ's work is accomplished is 'the
greater and more perfect Tabernacle'
(ix. 11), the divine archetype of the
transitory copy.

Compare ii. 10 τελειῶσαι note.

The spiritual maturity of which the
apostle speaks is the result of careful
exercise. It belongs to those who
have their senses — their different
organs of spiritual perception—trained, in virtue of their moral state gained
by long experience.

διὰ τὴν ἕξιν] *by reason of, on account
of, habit*. Old Lat. *per (propter) habi-
tum*. Vulg. *pro consuetudine*. The
state in which they are is the ground
and pledge of the discipline of their
powers (διὰ τὴν ἕξιν not διὰ τῆς ἕξεως).

Ἕξις (here only in N.T.) expresses
not the process but the result, the
condition which has been produced
by past exercise and not the separate
acts following one on another (firma
quædam facilitas quae apud Græ-
cos ἕξις vocatur Quint. x. 1, 1). Comp.
Ecclus. *Prol.* ἱκανὴν ἕξιν περιποιησά-

μενος (having acquired sufficient experience), *id.* xxx. 14, Jud. xiv. 9 (Alex.): I Sam. xvi. 7.

τὰ αἰσθητήρια] Vulg. *sensus.* Here only in N.T. Comp. Jer. iv. 19 (LXX.) τὰ αἰσθ. τῆς καρδίας μου.

γεγυμνασμένα] Comp. c. xii. 11 ; 1 Tim. v. 7; 2 Pet. ii. 14.

For γεγυμν. ἔχοντες compare xii. 1, ἔχοντες περικείμενον.

πρὸς διάκρισιν κ. τε καὶ κ.] The phrase recalls the language of the O. T. *e.g.* Gen. iii. 5; Deut. i. 39; Is. vii. 16.

The discernment of ' good and evil '

is here regarded in relation to the proper food of the soul, the discrimination of that which contributes to its due strengthening. The mature Christian has already gained the power which he can at once apply, as the occasion arises. This power comes through the discipline of use which shapes a stable character.

Philo *De migr. Abr.* § 9 (i. 443 M.) ἕτερος νηπίων καὶ ἕτερος τελείων χῶρός ἐστιν, ὁ μὲν ὀνομαζόμενος ἄσκησις, ὁ δὲ καλούμενος σοφία.

Additional Note on v. 1.   *The præ-Christian Priesthood*[1].

I. THE IDEA OF PRIESTHOOD.

Man is born religious: born to recognise the action of unseen powers The idea about him and to seek for a harmonious relation with them, conceived of of priest- personally[2]. hood in

This thought is conveyed in the Mosaic record of Creation, by the the nature, statement that it was the purpose of God to 'make man in His image and after His likeness' (Gen. i. 27); that is to endow man with faculties by which he might attain to a divine fellowship, and finally share in the divine rest (Heb. iv. 9).

Even if man had not sinned he would have needed the discipline of life, supported by divine help, to reach this destiny[3].

As it is, the consciousness of sin, variously realised, hinders the present approach to God (the unseen power). However the unseen is realised, there is in men a shrinking from it.

Some means of approach to the unseen power therefore must be provided that a harmony may be established; and man naturally looks for some one through whom this access shall be gained. The provision of this access is the work of the priest.

It is then briefly the part of the priest to establish a connexion of man with God, and secondarily of man with man.

The priest brings man to God (the unseen power); and he brings God to man.

So it is that the conception which we form of priesthood shapes our whole view of religion (Hebr. vii. 12).

These thoughts are of universal application, and find manifold embodiments in the experience of mankind.

Of these manifold embodiments we must take account in our endeavour to grasp the full meaning of the Christian Dispensation.

The special training of the Jewish people is one part, the most history of intelligible part indeed, but yet only one part, of the universal training man. of humanity for the accomplishment of the divine purpose of creation.

---

[1] It had been my hope to write an Essay on the præ-Christian priesthood. This has been impossible; and I venture to give a few notes which indicate some of the main points in the inquiry.

J. Lippert's *Allg. Gesch. d. Priesterthums*, Berlin 1883—4, contains the most ample collection of materials with which I am acquainted. Tylor's *Primitive Culture*, London, 1871, and Spencer's *Ecclesiastical Institutions*, London, 1885, contain much that is of interest. The Jewish priesthood as a positive institution is well treated by Œhler; but it is desirable to place it in detailed comparison and contrast with ethnic priesthoods.

[2] No non-religious tribe is actually found or known to have existed. Tylor, *Primitive Culture*, i. 378.

[3] The Essay of Bp Bull *On the state of man before the Fall*, contains many most suggestive thoughts on this subject.

In considering the conception of the præ-Christian priesthood we must therefore notice the priesthood of the Nations (the natural priesthood), and the priesthood of the People (the theocratic priesthood).

II. THE PRIESTHOOD OF THE NATIONS. (THE NATURAL PRIESTHOOD.)

The conception of priesthood in its most general form is recognised universally: it belongs to the constitution of man. The facts of ethnic religions enable us to see the elements which were taken up and purified in Judaism.

i. Types of natural priest-hood.

i. *Types of natural priesthood.*

In many cases the idea of priesthood is most rude, imperfect and unworthy—perhaps by degradation—but it exists.

It may be that the agent seeks to coerce or to propitiate hostile powers; or to honour friendly powers.

But the essential idea is the same: he seeks to establish a harmony between those whom he represents and the unseen.

The mediating person is marked out variously according to circumstances, either (1) by superior station, or (2) by superior knowledge.

(1) By position.

(1) The chief types of priest in the former case are

(*a*) the head of the family: the father;

(*b*) the head of the race: the king.

(2) By knowledge.

(2) The second class is represented by the 'medicine-man': the sorcerer: the guardian of an oracular shrine.

(1) Priest-hood by position.

(1) (*a*) The family priesthood was very widely spread. Examples occur in all early history.

(*b*) The kingly priesthood was recognised in the great early civilised states: Egypt; Assyria; Greece; Rome.

The form of this royal priesthood was retained even when the royal government was overthrown (ἄρχων βασιλεύς, *rex sacrificulus*).

(2) Priest-hood by knowledge.

(2) The 'oracular' type of priesthood was dominant among the Arabian tribes, who had no central government. Notice Balaam (Num. xxii.).

Gradually the office was delegated to a caste or a class, which exercised more or less power. In classical Greece the power of the priesthood was exceptionally small.

ii. Examples of Natural Priesthood in O.T. (1) Before the Law.

ii. *Examples of natural priesthood in the O. T.*

There are many traces of this 'natural' priesthood in the O. T., both before and (2) after 'the Law.'

(1) *Natural priesthood in the O. T. before the Law.*

(*a*) The Patriarchs.

Gen. viii. 20 ff. (Noah).
— xiii. 4 (Abraham).
— xxvi. 25 (Isaac).
— xxxv. 1 (Jacob).
Comp. Job i. 5.

(*b*) Melchizedek.
> Gen. xiv. 18 ff.

(*c*) Jethro.
> Ex. xviii. 1, 12.
> Comp. Ex. xix. 22.

(2) *Natural priesthood in the O. T. after the Law.*

> (*a*) The Judges.
>> Jud. vi. 19 ff. (Gideon).
>> — xiii. 19 (Manoah).
>> — xvii. 5 (Micah).
>> [1 Sam. vii. 9 f. (Samuel); comp. vii. 1 (Eleazar).
>> — ix. 13 (Samuel).]

> (*b*) The Kings.
>> Saul : 1 Sam. xiii. 9 f.
>> — xiv. 34, 35.
>> David : 2 Sam. vi. 13 f.
>> — xxiv. 25 (1 Chron. xxi. 26).
>> Comp. xxiii. 16.
>> Solomon : 1 K. ix. 25 (2 Chron. viii. 12 f.).
>> Ahaz : 2 K. xvi. 12 f. (comp. 2 Chron. xxvi. 16 ff.).
>> Comp. Jer. xxx. 21.

(2) After
the Law.

III. THE PRIESTHOOD OF THE PEOPLE. (THE THEOCRATIC
PRIESTHOOD.)

i. *Jewish Monotheism.*

All monotheistic religions derive their origin from Abraham.
The Jews alone in the Old World made the belief in one God the foundation of life.

In the Scriptures of the O. T. no stress is laid upon abstract opinion as to the being of God in Himself. The character of God and the relation of man to God is made known through action.

The essential element of belief in one God is brought out in the history of Abraham. It lies in personal trust in Him, and not in thought about Him.

So again Moses enforces the belief in one God not as a new truth, but as the inspiration and support of personal and social duty.

Conduct, character, is the one end of the Mosaic system.

The heathen—the Canaanite nations specially—are punished not for false belief but for vile actions : Deut. xii. 31 ; Lev. xviii. 24 ff.

The fact of monotheistic belief is recognised in others (cf. Gen. xx. 2 f.); and if God took Israel for His peculiar people, it was not as 'a national God' (of limited sovereignty), but as the God of the whole earth : Ex. xix. 4 ff.; Deut. x. 14 f.

The legislation of Israel has then this moral purpose. God moves among His people to guide them to their end. So it came to pass that the

i. Charac-
teristics of
Jewish
monothe-
ism.

religious development of the Jews was against their nature; while the religious development of the Gentiles was an expression of their nature[1].

In the fulfilment of this discipline God manifested Himself to the people in different ways, by prophets, kings, priests[2].

The prophet spoke in the name of God: the king became the representative of the divine action: the priest expressed the idea of the fellowship of God and man.

The work of the priesthood was specially directed to the thoughts of sin: consecration: holiness.

ii. Stages in the organization of the Priesthood.

ii. *Organization of the Jewish priesthood.*

We notice stages in the organization of the priesthood.

(1) The whole people: Ex. xix. 6. See also Num. xvi. 3 (Korah: sons of Reuben): Ex. xxx 11—16 (atonement for each). Compare Apoc. i. 6; v. 10; xx. 6; 1 Pet. ii. 5, 9.

(2) Then Levi.

(a) Representatives: Num. iii. 9, 12 (*instead of all the firstborn*): ambiguity of the term. Comp. Deut. x. 8.

(b) Their consecration: Num. viii. 5 ff.

Notice (a) sprinkling (contrast Lev. viii. 6 of priests); cleansing (comp. Lev. xiv. 8 of the leper; Deut. xxi. 12 of woman captive).

(β) sacrifices: bullock for burnt-offering (comp. Lev. i. 3); for sin-offering (comp. Lev. iv. 3, 14).

(γ) their dedication to God: 'children of Israel' lay their hands upon them (comp. Lev. i. 4).

(δ) their resignation by God to the priest's service, as 'waved' before the Lord (of a gift resigned by God to priests): comp. Num. xviii. 6 f.

(ε) offering of victims: the Levites laying hands upon them.

(3) The separation of Aaron and his sons.

Their consecration: Lev. viii.; Ex. xxix.

(a) Washing. Comp. Ex. xl. 12; Lev. xvi. 4; and contrast Ex. xxx. 19 f.; xl. 31 f.

(β) Robing. Comp. Ex. xxviii. 40.

(γ) Anointing of Aaron. Comp. v. 30; Ex. xxviii. 41; xxx. 30; xl. 15; Lev. x. 7.

(δ) A threefold sacrifice: a bullock and two rams.

(ε) Personal application of the blood to Aaron and his sons: ear, hand, foot. Comp. Lev. xiv. 14.

---

[1] Compare Kurtz, *Hist. of Old Covenant* i. 126 ff. (E. Tr.).

[2] The derivation of כֹהֵן (*priest*) is keenly debated. Two derivations seem to deserve notice, (1) that the word is formed from כוּן and describes either 'one who presents an offering,' or 'one who stands to represent another'; and, (2) that it corresponds with Arab. *kahin*, 'soothsayer,' the earliest type of Shemitic priest in Arabia.

(ζ) Investment of Aaron and his sons with the elements of sacrifice.

(η) Sprinkling of the anointing oil and blood on Aaron and his sons and upon their garments. Ex. xxix. 21.

In each case people, tribe, family, as representatives, were taken by the free choice of God, and not in virtue of any natural privilege of position; Num. xvi. 7; xviii. 7; Ex. xxviii. 1; 1 Sam. ii. 28.

(4) The High-priest: Ex. xxix. 5—7; Num. xx. 26—28.

iii. *The priestly duties.*

General description : Deut. xxxiii. 8 ff.; 1 Sam. ii. 28.

iii. Priest-ly duties, general

(1) Teaching and administering the Law: Deut. xvii. 8 f. (a 'judge' and also recognised); Lev. x. 10 f.; Ezek. xliv. 23 f.; Mal. ii. 7. Comp. Hos. iv. 6 ff.; Amos ii. 6—8.

and special.

Notice the use of the 'lot': Lev. xvi. 8; comp. Num. xxvi. 55; Josh. vii. 14 ff.; 1 Sam. x. 17; xiv. 41; Prov. xvi. 33.

(2) Ministering the ceremonial.

(a) To prepare the shew-bread : Lev. xxiv. 5 ff.

(b) To burn incense: Ex. xxx. 7 f.; 2 Chron. xxvi. 16 ff.; Num. xvi. 40.

(c) To offer sacrifice: specially to sprinkle the blood; Lev. i. 5; v. 16.

(3) Blessing: Num. vi. 22 ff. Comp. Lev. ix. 22.

No necessity for laborious study, but for scrupulous care.

iv. *Political position of priests.*

The priests occupied a subordinate political position till the time of the Maccabees, with rare exceptions (2 Kings xi. 1 ff.). Eli was the only Judge from among them; and there were few priest-prophets. They were the ordinary ministers of the divine blessing with 'a self-denying ordinance.'

iv. Sub-ordinate political position of priests.

The Levites are commonly classed with 'the poor': a body without inheritance in an agricultural state: Deut. x. 8 f.; xii. 12, 18 f.; xiv. 29; xvi. 11, 14; xxvi. 11. Compare Gen. xlix. 5 ff.

Jerusalem not one of the forty-eight Levitical cities (Josh. xxi. 41); so that priests were strangers in the place of their service.

Contrast the position of the Brahmins; Magians (Hdt. i. 101, 132); Chaldæans (Diod. ii. 29); Egyptian priests (Hdt. ii. 35 ff.).

v. *The idea of the Theocracy embodied in the High-priest.*

The High-priest was the representative of the whole people: he took their names upon his shoulders and upon his heart : Ex. xxviii. 12, 29.

The same offering was made for his sins of ignorance as for the sins of the congregation: Lev. iv. 3, 13.

He bore upon his head the words which marked the consecration of the nation, and that in relation to their failures : Ex. xxviii. 36 ff.; comp. Num. xviii. 1.

In his person once in the year the people entered into the Presence of God.

VI.   ¹Διὸ ἀφέντες τὸν τῆς ἀρχῆς τοῦ χριστοῦ λόγον

(2) *The duty of Christian progress:
the perils of relapse* (vi. 1—8).

The apostle bases a general exhortation on the view which he has given
of the spiritual degeneracy of the
Hebrews. He first (*a*) enforces the
duty of progress, both positively and
negatively, and accepts the obligation
for himself (1—3); and then (*b*) por-
trays the perils of relapse, pointing
out the impossibility (from the human
side) of repeating the past, and appealing to the stern teaching of nature
(4—8).

(*a*) *The duty of progress* (1—3).
The succession of thoughts is simple
and natural. The general principle is
first stated, with a clear enunciation
of what must (1 *a*), and what must
not be done (1 *b*, 2); and then the
writer accepts the consequence as
decisive for his own teaching (3).

1—3. A question has been raised
whether these verses contain an exhortation to the Hebrews or a declaration of the writer's own purpose. The
two ideas seem to be inseparable. If
the readers are to strain forward to a
higher knowledge the writer must
lead them. If the writer is to aim at
the exposition of deeper truth it must
be with the conviction that his readers
will endeavour to follow him. Thus
he first identifies himself with those
whom he addresses (φερώμεθα) and
afterwards he indicates his own purpose definitely (ποιήσομεν). The words
ἀφέντες and τελειότης take their appropriate meanings in each case.

¹ *Wherefore leaving the word of the
beginning of Christ* (or *the Christ, the
Messiah*), *let us be borne on to perfection, not laying again a foundation
of repentance from dead works and
of faith upon God,* ²*of teaching* (or *a
teaching*) *of baptisms and laying on
of hands, of resurrection of the dead
and of eternal judgment.* ³*And this
will we do if God permit.*

διὸ ἀφέντες τὸν τ. ἀρχῆς τοῦ χ. λ....]

Vulg. *Quapropter intermittentes inchoationis Christi sermonem...* It
is characteristic of the tone of the
Epistle that the exhortation to progress is based directly on the stern
criticism which precedes (διό). At
first sight an adversative particle
would have seemed more natural.
But it is assumed that the position of
inferiority occupied by the readers of
the Epistle is not to be acquiesced in.
The fact that they do for the moment
hold it is an overwhelming reason for
effort. *Quia exercitatos sensus decet
nos habere in lege domini...ad pro-
funda et alta mysteria...ducamur*
(Primasius).

The necessary condition of progress
is a 'giving up.' We hold what we
have as a preparation for something
more. At the same time all that is surrendered is incorporated in that which
is afterwards gained. In relation to
the Hebrews the word ἀφέντες has
the sense of 'leaving' as applied to
those who advance to a deeper knowledge: in relation to the writer, as
applied to those who pass to a new
subject. Both senses are perfectly
natural, and there is no confusion in
the double application of the word.
For the thought compare Phil. iii. 14.

In the remarkable phrase ὁ τῆς
ἀρχῆς τοῦ Χριστοῦ λόγος, *the word*,
the exposition, *of the beginning*, the
elementary view *of the Christ*, there
can be little doubt that ἡ ἀρχὴ τοῦ
Χριστοῦ go together, and that ὁ
τῆς ἀρχῆς λόγος does not form a compound noun. On this point the order
seems to be decisive. 'The beginning
of Christ' (or 'the Christ') is 'the
fundamental explanation of the fulfilment of the Messianic promises in
Jesus of Nazareth.' Ἡ ἀρχὴ τοῦ
Χριστοῦ corresponds with ἡ ἀρχὴ τῶν
λογίων τοῦ θεοῦ (v. 12): the former
phrase concentrates attention upon
the personal Messiah, the latter on the
records in which He was foreshewn.

ἐπὶ τὴν τελειότητα φερώμεθα, μὴ πάλιν θεμέλιον κατα-
βαλλόμενοι μετανοίας ἀπὸ νεκρῶν ἔργων, καὶ πίστεως

1 φερώμεθα: φερόμεθα D₂* syr hl.

Sermonem inchoationis Christi vocat initium fidei, instructionem videlicet de nativitate Christi humana, de passione, de resurrectione, atque ascensione ejus et gratia baptismatis (Primas.).

ἐπὶ τὴν τελειότητα φερώμεθα] *let us be borne on to perfection.* Vulg. *ad perfectionem feramur.* The form of this positive charge is remarkable. The thought is not primarily of personal effort, 'let us go on,' 'let us press' (Old Lat. *tendamus;* Aug. *respiciamus*), but of personal surrender to an active influence. The power is working (comp. i. 3 φέρων τὰ πάντα): we have only to yield ourselves to it (comp. Acts xxvii. 15, 17). At the same time the influence and the surrender are continuous (φερώμεθα), and not (under this aspect) concentrated in one momentary crisis. The goal of this forward movement is 'perfection,' that is for the readers the full maturity of spiritual growth, opposed to νηπιότης (v. 13); and for the writer the teaching which corresponds with maturity. Philo (*De agric.* § 37; i. 324) distinguishes three classes ἀρχόμενοι, προκόπτοντες, τελειωμένοι. Compare John iii. 12 f. Additional Note on ii. 10.

The patristic interpreters understand τελειότης of practical life. So Chrysostom : πρὸς αὐτὴν χωρῶμεν λοιπόν, φησί, τὴν ὀροφήν, τουτέστι, βίου ἄριστον ἔχωμεν.

μὴ πάλιν θεμέλιον καταβαλλόμενοι] The emphasis lies upon the noun. The tense of the participle marks the effort. Jos. *Antt.* viii. 5, 1 οἰκοδομίαν κατεβάλετο.

The writer does not (of course) mean to say that his readers must build higher without having secured their foundation. He assumes that the recognition of the paramount duty of progress will constrain them to do this at once in order that they may duly advance.

The sense given by the Old Latin *fundamentum diruentes* (d) (not Augustine) is contrary to the usage of the middle.

For πάλιν see v. 6; and for θεμέλιον c. xi. 10 note.

θεμέλιον...μετανοίας...] The different elements in the 'foundation' appear to be distinguished in three groups, Repentance and Faith, Baptism and Laying on of hands, Resurrection and Judgment. Of these the first two are the fundamental characteristics of the Christian's temper, while the two pairs which follow give typical representatives of outward ordinances, and specific beliefs. Under another aspect the three groups deal with our personal character, our social relations, our connexion with the unseen world. The three pairs are not however strictly coordinate : μετ...καὶ π...., βαπτ...ἐπιθ. τε χ., ἀναστ. ν. καὶ κρ. αἱ. The centre pair are regarded as forming one great subject of teaching in two parts. For the use of τε compare ix. 1 note.

The history of the Acts shews how intimately each of these six articles was involved in the first teaching of the Apostles: ii. 38; iv. 2, 33; viii. 16 f.

For θεμέλ. καταβ. compare Philo, *de Gig.* § 7 (i. 266 M.) θεμέλιος...ὑποβέβληται...

θεμ. μετανοίας...καὶ πίστεως...] The genitive in each case describes an element of the foundation: a foundation consisting in repentance...and faith...   Comp. c. xii. 11 ; Rom. iv. 11 (?) ; 1 Cor. v. 8 ; Eph. vi. 14, 16 f. Comp. Winer, iii. 59, 8 (a).

μετανοίας...καὶ πίστεως...] Repentance and Faith are not treated as abstract subjects of debate, but as personal attributes.   Each has its supreme object in human life (repentance *from dead works*, faith *towards God*).   So it is that they are combined together in the first pro-

THE EPISTLE TO THE HEBREWS. [VI. 2

ἐπὶ θεόν, ²βαπτισμῶν ⌜διδαχῆς⌝ ἐπιθέσεώς τε χειρῶν,

2 διδαχὴν

2 βαπτισμόν D₂*.　　διδαχῆς אACD₂ vg : διδαχήν Bd.

clamation of the Gospel by Christ, Mark i. 15, and practically in the first proclamation of the Gospel by the Apostles, Acts ii. 38. Comp. Acts xx. 21.

'Repentance from dead works' gives the negative, 'faith towards God' gives the positive side of the Christian mind. The old must be abandoned, the new must be grasped.

μετανοίας ἀπὸ νεκρῶν ἔργων] The force of this unique expression depends upon the sense of 'dead works' (νεκρὰ ἔργα, Vulg. *opera mortua*), a phrase which occurs in the N. T. only here and c. ix. 14 καθαριεῖ τὴν συνείδησιν ἀπὸ νεκρῶν ἔργων, nor is there any parallel phrase. Faith is spoken of as 'dead' when it is unfruitful in deed (James ii. 17, 26). Sin again is said to be 'dead' when it is not called into activity (Rom. vii. 8). And the body is already 'dead' as carrying in it the doom of death : it has lost the power of abiding continuance (Rom. viii. 10 δι' ἁμαρτίαν). Once more, men are said to be 'dead' in relation to sin in three ways, (1) 'dead unto sin' (τῇ ἁμαρτίᾳ Rom. vi. 11) when their connexion with the principle of sin is broken *de facto* (v. 2 ἀπεθάνετε) and they use *de jure* the power of the new life (ζῶντας δέ....), (2) 'dead by transgressions and sins' as deprived of true life through the manifold instrumentality of sin (τοῖς παραπτώμασιν καὶ ταῖς ἁμαρτίαις Eph. ii. 1, 5), and (3) 'dead in transgressions' as abiding in them and devoid of the capacity for real action (ἐν παραπτώμασιν Col. ii. 13, but the ἐν is doubtful).

Compare also Matt. viii. 22; Luke ix. 60; xv. 24, 32 ; John v. 25; Eph. v. 14.

From the analogy of these usages it is possible to give a precise sense to the phrase 'dead works.' Dead works are not vaguely sins which lead to death, but works devoid of that

element which makes them truly works. They have the form but not the vital power of works. There is but one spring of life, and all which does not flow from it is 'dead.' All acts of a man in himself, separated from God, are 'dead works' (comp. John xv. 4 ff.). The first step in faith is to give up the selfish life which they represent.

Here the phrase has necessarily a special application. The writer of the Epistle is thinking, as it seems, of all the works corresponding with the Levitical system not in their original institution but in their actual relation to the Gospel as established in the Christian society. By the work of Christ, who fulfilled, and by fulfilling annulled, the Law, the element of life was withdrawn from these which had (so to speak) a provisional, and only a provisional, vitality. They became 'dead works.' Comp. Herm. *Sim.* ix. 21, 2 τὰ ῥήματα αὐτῶν μόνα ζῶσι, τὰ δὲ ἔργα αὐτῶν νεκρά ἐστι.

The contrast between πίστις and νεκρὰ ἔργα corresponds with and yet is distinct from that between πίστις and ἔργα νόμου in St Paul. 'Dead works' present the essential character of the works in themselves : 'works of law' present them in relation to an ideal, unattainable, standard.

It follows therefore that 'Repentance *from* dead works' expresses that complete change of mind—of spiritual attitude—which leads the believer to abandon these works and seek some other support for life.

For the construction μετάνοια ἀπό compare Acts viii. 22 μετανόησον ἀπὸ τῆς κακίας, and the characteristic phrase of the Apocalypse μετανοεῖν ἐκ : Apoc. ii. 21 f.; ix. 20 f.; xvi. 11.

The patristic interpretations of the phrase are vague : *e.g.* Primasius : Poenitentiam ab operibus mortuis agere est ipsa opera mala per pœnitentiam delere, qua animam mortificabant. Opera namque mortis sunt peccata.

πίστεως ἐπὶ θεόν] *of faith toward God*, Vulg. *fidei ad Deum*. This phrase also is unique.

πίστις is used (1) with gen. in each group of the writings of the N. T.: Mark xi. 22; Acts iii. 16; Rom. iii. 22; Apoc. xiv. 12; James ii. 1, &c.

(2) with εἰς, Acts xx. 21; xxiv. 24; xxvi. 18; Col. ii. 5; comp. 1 Pet. i. 21; Philem. 5.

(3) with ἐν, Eph. i. 15; 1 Tim. iii. 13; 2 Tim. iii. 15.

(4) with πρός, 1 Thess. i. 8.

Πιστεύειν ἐπί τινα occurs not unfrequently: Matt. xxvii. 42; Acts ix. 42; xi. 17; xvi. 31; xxii. 19; Rom. iv. 5, 24.

As distinguished from πιστεύειν εἰς perhaps πιστεύειν ἐπί (acc.) suggests the idea of being directed towards, and πιστ. ἐπί (dat.) resting upon some solid foundation (the Rock). The relation in ἐπί is external, in εἰς, internal.

2.   βαπτισμῶν διδαχῆς (διδαχήν)] Vulg. *baptismatum doctrinæ, impositionis quoque manuum*. The construction of διδαχῆς, if this reading be adopted, has been variously explained. It has been taken either (1) absolutely: *baptisms, teachings, and laying on of hands;* or, (2) in connexion with βαπτισμῶν, either as (a) depending on it and qualifying it; *baptisms of teaching*, baptisms involving teaching and not mere ceremonial lustrations; or as (β) governing βαπτισμῶν: *teaching of baptisms*.

The construction and sense of the whole passage are decidedly in favour of the last view. The order is decisive against taking the word διδαχῆς absolutely. There is no special propriety in speaking of Christian baptism as 'a baptism of teaching'; and on the other hand 'baptisms,' 'laying on of hands,' 'resurrection,' 'judgment,' form characteristic subjects of teaching. This construction is also supported by the

variant διδαχήν; and it makes but little difference whether we read διδαχῆς as parallel with θεμέλιον, or διδαχήν as explanatory of it; yet, on the whole, it seems simpler to take the genitive.

The unusual order is probably to be explained by the emphasis gained for the characteristic contents of the teaching by placing βαπτισμῶν first. If διδαχῆς were placed first, this would appear to be coordinate with μετανοίας and πίστεως rather than the elements which it includes.

The progress in the subjects of teaching is significant. It reaches from the first scene of the Christian life to the last, as it is made known to us. The two types of divine ordinances (*baptism, laying on of hands*) correspond broadly to the two characteristics of the Christian's temper already noticed. The first marks the passage from an old state to a new (the gift of life by the action of the Holy Spirit); the second, the arming for the fulfilment of the new service (the endowment for the work of life by the gift of the Holy Spirit). It appears to be of great importance to keep in close connexion the 'ordination' of the Christian layman and the 'ordination' of the Christian priest, as corresponding provisions for the impartment of strength required for the fulfilment of the two essential forms of service.

The simple *gen.* in place of περί with *gen.* is remarkable. Elsewhere in the N. T. the gen. is used only of the author: Acts ii. 42, τῇ διδαχῇ τῶν ἀποστόλων; 2 John 9; Apoc. ii. 14 f. It seems to express more completely the contents, the substance, of the teaching than the preposition which would give merely the subject.

βαπτισμῶν] Vulg. *baptismatum*. For the form see c. ix. 10; Mk. vii. 4; Col. ii. 12 *v. l.*

The plural and the peculiar form seem to be used to include Christian Baptism with other lustral rites. The 'teaching' would naturally be

ἀναστάσεως ᵀ νεκρῶν καὶ κρίματος αἰωνίου.   ³καὶ τοῦτο

2 τε

ἀναστ. τε ℵAC vg syrr me: om. τε BD₂*.   νεκρῶν: χειρῶν D₂*.

directed to shew their essential difference. Comp. Acts xix. 3, 4; John iii. 25 περὶ καθαρισμοῦ. Primasius explains the plural strangely: Quod dixit plurali numero...pro varietate accipientium posuit.

ἐπιθέσεώς τε χειρῶν] 'The laying on of hands' is the expressive symbol of a solemn blessing (Matt. xix. 13), of the restoration or communication of strength for a definite work. The significance of the act is clearly marked in healings in the Gospels: Mk. vi. 5 (comp. xvi. 18); viii. 23; Luke iv. 40; xiii. 13. It was regarded as natural by those who sought for help: Matt. ix. 18 (comp. Mk. v. 23); Mk. vii. 32. Compare also Acts xxviii. 8. In the record of the Acts 'laying on of hands' appears as (1) the complement of Baptism, the outward rite through which the gift of the Holy Spirit was normally made (Acts viii. 17 f.; xix. 6, 'Confirmation'); (2) the form of the appointment of 'the Seven' (Acts vi. 6, 'Ordination'); (3) the mode of separation for a special work (Acts xiii. 3). In the first two cases it is the act of Apostles. In the Epistles to Timothy it is used of 'ordination' and attributed to 'the presbytery' (1 Tim. iv. 14; comp. 2 Tim. i. 6); to Timothy himself (1 Tim. v. 22); to St Paul (2 Tim. i. 6; comp. 1 Tim. iv. 14).

Primasius (Atto), not unnaturally, limits the phrase to Confirmation: Impositionem manuum appellat per quam plenissime creditur accipi Spiritus sanctus, donum quod post baptismum ad confirmationem unitatis in ecclesia a pontificibus fieri solet (kindred texts vary); and the close connexion of ἐπιθ. χειρῶν with βαπτ. (βαπτ. ἐπιθ. τε χ.) may be urged in favour of this view.

ἀναστάσεως νεκρῶν καὶ κρίματος αἰωνίου] This last pair of truths taken together represents the permanence of our present actions, the significance of earthly life in the eternal order. Comp. Apoc. xiv. 13 (κόποι, ἔργα).

The genitives appear to depend on διδαχῆς (or διδαχήν) and not directly upon θεμέλιον. The teaching on these subjects made part of the foundation.

In connexion with the Resurrection three phrases must be studied:

(1) ἀνάστασις νεκρῶν Acts xvii. 32; xxiii. 6; xxiv. 21 (comp. v. 15); 1 Cor. xv. 12 ff.

(2) ἡ ἀνάστασις ἡ ἐκ νεκρῶν Luke xx. 35; Acts iv. 2. Comp. Acts x. 41; 1 Pet. i. 3; Col. i. 18, &c.

(3) ἡ ἐξανάστασις ἡ ἐκ νεκρῶν Phil. iii. 11.

The phrase 'eternal judgment' may be compared with 'eternal sin' (Mark iii. 29 αἰώνιον ἁμάρτημα).

Κρίμα describes the sentence and not the process. Compare John ix. 39 note; Matt. vii. 2; Acts xxiv. 25; and contrast c. ix. 27; x. 27 (κρίσις).

For αἰώνιος see c. v. 9 note.

3. καὶ τοῦτο ποιήσομεν] The fulfilment of the Apostle's purpose is not made in any way to depend on the condition of those whom he addresses. His message has to be delivered. Compare Ezek. ii. 5; and contrast φερώμεθα v. 1.

Hoc faciemus, hoc est, ad majora vos ducemus et de his omnibus quæ enumeravimus plenissime docebimus vos, ut non sit iterum necesse ex toto et a capite ponere fundamentum (Primas.).

ἐάνπερ ἐπιτρέπῃ ὁ θεός] Compare 1 Cor. xvi. 7. εἴωθε ὁ ἀπόστολος πάντα ἐξαρτᾶν τῆς θείας προμηθείας (Theod.). James iv. 15.

(b) The perils of apostasy (4—8).

The Apostle has given expression to a general charge in which he has joined his readers with himself (φε-

ποιήσομεν ἐάνπερ ἐπιτρέπῃ ὁ θεός. ⁴ Ἀδύνατον γὰρ τοὺς

3 ποιήσομεν אB vg: ποιήσωμεν ACD₂ (comp. v. 19; iv. 3).

ῥώμεθα), but he makes one limitation
to the efficacy of the work which he
proposes. He cannot do again what
has been done once for all. He cannot
offer a fresh Gospel able to change the
whole aspect of life and thought, if
the one Gospel has been received and
afterwards rejected (4—6). Nature
itself teaches that the divine gifts must
be used fruitfully: they carry with
them an inevitable responsibility (7, 8).

⁴ *For in the case of those who were
once for all enlightened, having both
tasted of the heavenly gift and been
made partakers of the Holy Spirit,
⁵ and who tasted the good word of God
and the powers of a world to come,
⁶ and fell away, it is impossible again
to renew them to repentance, seeing
they crucify to themselves the Son of
God afresh, and put Him to an open
shame.*

4—6. The necessity of progress lies
in the very nature of things. There
can be no repetition of the beginning.
The preacher cannot again renew to
'repentance' (μετάνοια), a complete
change of the intellectual, moral,
spiritual state. He must go on to
the completion of his work. Those
who fall away from the Faith, of which
they have felt the power, are as men
who crucify 'the Son of God.'

This description of apostates is
closely parallel with that given in the
Apostolical Constitutions (vi. 18, 2) of
'godless, impenitent leaders of heresy':
οὗτοί εἰσιν οἱ βλασφημήσαντες τὸ πνεῦμα
τῆς χάριτος (c. x. 29) καὶ ἀποπτύσαντες
τὴν παρ' αὐτοῦ δωρεὰν μετὰ τὴν χάριν,
οἷς οὐκ ἀφεθήσεται οὔτε ἐν τῷ αἰῶνι
τούτῳ οὔτε ἐν τῷ μέλλοντι.

The correlation of the four participles (φωτισθέντας, γευσαμένους, γενηθέντας, γευσαμένους) is by no means
clear, nor are the conjunctions decisive
(γευσαμένους τε...καὶ μετόχους γεν...καὶ
καλὸν γευσαμένους...). The τε may (1)
introduce a new and distinct clause

closely connected with φωτισθέντας
and in a sense subordinate to it (*who
were once enlightened and so tasted...,
and were made...*); or (2) it may be
taken in connexion with the καί...καί...
which follow, so that the three clauses
γευσαμένους τε..., καὶ μετόχους γενηθέντας...καὶ καλὸν γευσαμένους..., are coordinate with φωτισθέντας and explanatory of it (*who were once illuminated, having both tasted...and
been made partakers...and tasted...*);
or (3) it may be taken with the καί
which immediately follows, so that γευσαμένους τε...καὶ μετόχους...γενηθέντας
form the twofold explanation of φωτισθέντας while καὶ καλὸν γευσαμένους
is an independent clause (*who were
once illuminated—having both tasted
...and been made partakers...—and
who tasted...*). Both uses of τε are
fully justified. It occurs as a retrospective and additive conjunction both
simply (c. i. 3 note), and followed by
καί (Acts ii. 40; xxi. 30; xxii. 7;
xxiv. 23; xxvi. 30); and most commonly as a prospective and combina-
tive conjunction both with a single
clause following (c. ix. 19; Luke xxi.
11; Acts ii. 10), and with two or more
clauses following (Acts i. 8; xiii. 1;
1 Cor. i. 30).

The choice between the three constructions will be decided by individual
feeling as to the symmetry of expression and thought. On the whole
the third arrangement seems to bring
out most distinctly two fundamental
aspects of the reception of the Christian Faith, illumination in respect to
the divine action, and experience in
respect to the human appropriation.
The Christian is illuminated by the
conscious sense of the gift of life,
and by participation in the Spirit;
and he gains an individual sense of
the beauty (the intellectual grandeur)
of revelation, and of the powers of the
new Order.

ἅπαξ φωτισθέντας, γευσαμένους τε τῆς δωρεᾶς τῆς
ἐπουρανίου καὶ μετόχους γενηθέντας πνεύματος ἁγίου,

4 γενηθέντας: γεννηθέντας A.

The course of thought will be seen clearly if it is marked in a tabular form. The Christian has been
(1) Illuminated (in regard of the divine action) in two respects,
(a) By the consciousness of the reception of the gift of life (γευσ. τῆς δ. τῆς ἐπ.),
(β) By participation in the power of a wider life (μετ. γεν. πν. ἁγ.).
(2) And he has tasted (in regard of the individual experience)
(a) The beauty (intellectual grandeur) of revelation (καλ. θ. ρ.),
(β) The spiritual powers of the new order (δυν. μέλλ. αἰ.).

4. ἀδύνατον γὰρ τοὺς ἅπαξ φ....ἀνακαινίζειν...] For as touching those who were once enlightened...it is impossible to renew them... It is indeed necessary, the Apostle seems to say, that I should add this reserve 'if God will,' for there is only one fatal obstacle to the fulfilment of my work. It is impossible for man to renew to μετάνοια those who have fallen from the Faith. The ἀδύνατον at the head of the sentence is singularly impressive. So Chrysostom: οὐκ εἶπεν οὐ πρέπει οὐδὲ συμφέρει οὐδὲ ἔξεστιν ἀλλ' ἀδύνατον, ὥστε εἰς ἀπόγνωσιν ἐμβάλλειν.

τοὺς ἅπαξ φωτισθέντας] Vulg. eos qui semel illuminati sunt. The object is placed before the verb in order to fix attention upon the variety and greatness of the gifts which have been received and cast away. The enumeration of these abandoned blessings prepares for the statement of the impossibility of restoring them.

The word φωτίζεσθαι occurs again c. x. 32. The illumination both here and there (φωτισθέντες) is referred to the decisive moment when the light was apprehended in its glory (contrast Eph. i. 18 πεφωτισμένους). For the

image compare John i. 9; 2 Tim. i. 10; Eph. iii. 9; (Apoc. xxi. 23); 2 Cor. iv. 4, 6 (φωτισμός). See also Ecclus. xlv. 17; 4 (2) K. xii. 2. Inwardly this crisis of illumination was marked by a reception of the knowledge of the truth (c. x. 26); and outwardly by the admission to Christian fellowship. Hence φωτίζειν and φωτισμός were commonly applied to Baptism from the time of Justin (Apol. i. 61, 65; comp. Dial. c. 122) downwards. And the Syriac versions give this sense here: Pesh. who have once descended to baptism. Hcl. who have once been baptized. The addition of ἅπαξ (once for all) marks the completeness and sufficiency of the single act. The word is characteristic of the Epistle; ix. 7, 26 ff.; x. 2; (xii. 26 f.). Compare 1 Pet. iii. 18; Jude 3, 5; and ἐφάπαξ c. vii. 27 note; ix. 12; x. 10; 1 Cor. xv. 6; Rom. vi. 10.

The force of the tense is carried on through γευσαμένους, γενηθέντας, καλὸν γευσαμένους, in contrast with πάλιν v. 6.

γευσαμένους τε...καὶ μετόχους γεν....] This twofold blessing—the substance of illumination—describes first the conscious possession of the principle of life and then the sense of fellowship in a vaster life. The first element is that which the believer has personally in himself: the second that which he has by partaking in something which has a far wider action.

γευσ. τῆς δωρεᾶς τῆς ἐπουρανίου] who tasted of the gift, the heavenly gift, the gift of the divine life brought by Christ and in Him: John iv. 10 note. Compare Rom. v. 15, 17; viii. 32; 2 Cor. ix. 15. Any special interpretation, such as the Eucharist or more generally forgiveness, peace and the like, falls short of the general idea which is required here.

The gift is described as 'heavenly'

⁵καὶ καλὸν γευσαμένους θεοῦ ῥῆμα δυνάμεις τε μέλλοντος

5 δυν. τε μέλλ. αἰ.: Tert. occidente jam ævo.

(ἐπουράνιος) not in the sense that it comes from heaven, or has the character of heaven, but that it is realised in heaven. It belongs to a higher sphere of existence than earth.

For δωρεά see John iv. 10 note. The word is used in the N. T. only of spiritual gifts (? Rom. v. 17), and especially of the gift of the Holy Spirit. For ἐπουράνιος see c. iii. 1 note.

Γεύσασθαι expresses a real and conscious enjoyment of the blessing apprehended in its true character (comp. John vi. 56 ff. τρώγειν). Philo de Abr. § 19 (ii. 14 M.) τὸ δὲ μέγεθος αὐτῶν οὐ παντὶ δῆλον ἀλλὰ μόνον τοῖς γευσαμένοις ἀρετῆς. But at the same time the enjoyment as here described (γευσ. δωρεᾶς) is only partial and inchoative. To feast, to live upon the fulness of the divine blessing belongs to another order.

Compare γ. θανάτου Matt. xvi. 28; John viii. 52; c. ii. 9; γ. ὅτι χρηστὸς ὁ κύριος 1 Pet. ii. 3. See also Ps. xxxiii. (xxxiv.) 9.

The use of the gen. (γευσ. δωρεᾶς) here stands in sharp contrast with the use of the acc. in the following clause (καλὸν γευσ. θ. ῥῆμα). It is difficult to suppose that this repetition of the verb with a changed construction is without design and force. The difference which is inherent in the two cases ('a part of,' 'something of,' and 'the thing as a simple object') falls in perfectly with the scope of the passage. The divine life is apprehended little by little to the end : the divine word is apprehended in its character as a whole, and so each separate manifestation of spiritual power (δυνάμεις not τῶν δυνάμεων).

μετόχους γενηθ. πν. ἁγ.] The compound expression (μετόχ. γεν.), as distinguished from μετασχόντας (c. ii. 14), marks more than the simple fact of participation (c. vii. 13; 1 Cor. x. 17). It brings out the fact of a personal

character gained; and that gained in a vital development. Compare xii. 8; iii. 14; x. 33; xi. 6, 7.

For μέτοχος see c. iii. 1 note; and for πνεῦμα ἅγιον see ii. 4 note. The gift, the operation (πν. ἁγ.), is distinguished from the Person (iii. 7; ix. 8; x. 15, 29).

Comp. Orig. ap. Athan. Ep. ad Serap. iv. § 10.

5. The fact of illumination including the two elements of the communication of the divine (personal) life and of the participation in the divine (social) life, is followed by the fact of individual apprehension of the beauty of the message of God and of the manifestations of the higher life. The Christian life has been realised not only in its essential beginnings but in the fulness of its power. Both the blessings which are now put forward have become the objects of direct experience in their essential completeness (γευσαμένους...ῥῆμα...δυνάμεις).

καὶ καλὸν γευσ. θεοῦ ῥῆμα] Vulg. gustaverunt nihilominus bonum Dei verbum. The order of the original gives the sense 'tasted the goodness—beauty—of the Word of God.' For καλόν (Tert. dulce) compare c. x. 24 καλὰ ἔργα note; 1 Pet. ii. 12. That of which experience was made was not the whole message of the Gospel (ὁ λόγος τοῦ θεοῦ), but some special utterance (θεοῦ ῥῆμα), such as that which marks the confession of faith, apprehended in its true character as an utterance of God: Rom. x. 8; Eph. v. 26; comp. c. i. 3 n.; John vi. 68. Philo, de Prof. § 25 (i. 566 M.) ζητήσαντες καὶ τί τὸ τρέφον ἐστὶ τὴν ψυχὴν (Ex. xvi. 15) εὗρον μαθόντες ῥῆμα θεοῦ καὶ λόγον θεοῦ, ἀφ' οὗ πᾶσαι παιδεῖαι καὶ σοφίαι ῥέουσιν ἀέννασι. Comp. Leg. Alleg. iii. §§ 59, 61 quoted on c. iv. 12.

δυνάμεις μέλλοντος αἰῶνος] powers of a future age, powers, so to speak, of

αἰῶνος, ⁶καὶ παραπεσόντας, πάλιν ἀνακαινίζειν εἰς μετάνοιαν, ἀνασταυροῦντας ἑαυτοῖς τὸν υἱὸν τοῦ θεοῦ καὶ

6 παραπεσόντος D₂*.

another world. The indefinite expression suggests the idea of the
manifoldness of the energies of the
spiritual order of which each believer
feels some one or other (c. ii. 4). The
anarthrous αἰὼν μέλλων, which is not
found elsewhere, serves also to fix
attention on the character of the 'age'
as one hitherto unrealised, as distinguished from the conception of any
particular future order (comp. Eph. ii.
7: c. ii. 5 ἡ οἰκουμένη ἡ μέλλουσα). A
strangely similar phrase is quoted
from Philo, *Leg. Alleg.* i. § 12 (i. 50 M.),
ὁ θεὸς ἐπένευσεν αὐτῷ (Adam) δύναμιν
ἀληθινῆς ζωῆς.

It is significant that in the enumeration of the divine gifts received by
those who are conceived as afterwards
falling away there is no one which
passes out of the individual. All are
gifts of power, of personal endowment.
There is no gift of love. Under this
aspect light falls upon the passage
from Matt. vii. 22 f.; 1 Cor. xiii. 1 f.

In this connexion it will be noticed
that it was the presence of love
among the Hebrews which inspired
the Apostle with confidence (*v.* 10).
Hæc est margarita pretiosa caritas,
sine qua nihil tibi prodest quodcun-
que habueris; quam si solam habeas
sufficit tibi (Aug. *in* 1 *Joh. Tract.* v. §7).

6. καὶ παραπεσόντας] Vulg. *et pro-
lapsi sunt* (Tert. *cum exciderint*).
The catalogue of privileges is closed
by the statement of apostasy: *those
who were once for all enlightened...
and fell away...* Each part of the
picture is presented in its past completeness. Compare 1 John ii. 19.

The verb παραπίπτειν does not occur
elsewhere in the N. T. though the
noun παράπτωμα is common. The
verb and the noun occur together
Ezek. xiv. 13; xv. 8 (מַעַל).

The idea is that of falling aside from
the right path, as the idea of ἁμαρτάνειν is that of missing the right mark.

πάλιν ἀνακαινίζειν εἰς μετάνοιαν] *again
to renew them to repentance*, Vulg.
renovari rursum ad pœnitentiam
(so also Tert., Ambr., Hier.; d e alone
iterum renovare). The use of the
active voice limits the strict application of the words to human agency.
This is all that comes within the range
of the writer's argument. And further
the present (ἀνακαινίζειν) suggests continual effort. Some divine work then
may be equivalent to this renewing
though not identical with it (Matt.
xix. 26). The change in such a case
would not be a new birth, but a raising
from the dead.

'Ανακαινίζειν is found here only in
the N. T. It occurs five times in the
later books of the LXX., and in Herm.
Sim. viii. 6, 3; ix. 14, 3. Compare
ἀνακαινοῦν 2 Cor. iv. 16; Col. iii. 10;
ἀνακαίνωσις Rom. xii. 2; Tit. iii. 5,
where the idea is simply that of 'making new,' not of 'making again new.'

τὸ καινοὺς ποιῆσαι, Chrysostom says
from one point of sight, τοῦ λουτροῦ
μόνον ἐστί. Comp. Herm. *Sim.* viii. 6;
ix. 14.

The end of this renewal is μετάνοια,
a complete change of mind consequent
upon the apprehension of the true
moral nature of things. It follows
necessarily that in this large sense
there can be no second μετάνοια (comp.
v. 1). There may be, through the
gift of GOD, a corresponding change,
a regaining of the lost view with the
consequent restoration of the fulness
of life, but this is different from the
freshness of the vision through which
the life is first realised. The popular
idea of repentance, by which it is
limited to sorrow for the past, has
tended to obscure the thought here.

παραδειγματίζοντας. ⁷Γῆ γὰρ ἡ πιοῦσα τὸν ἐπ' αὐτῆς

παραδειγματίζοντες D₂.

ἀνασταυροῦντας...καὶ παραδειγματί-
ζοντας]Vulg. rursum crucifigentes (d e
recruciantes, Tert. refigentes cruci) et
ostentui habentes. The present participles (contrast παραπεσόντας of the
definite past act of apostasy) bring
out the moral cause of the impossibility which has been affirmed. There
is an active, continuous hostility to
Christ in the souls of such men as
have been imagined.

The two words express the main
idea under different aspects. The
first (ἀνασταυροῦντας) marks specially
the wrong done to Christ: the second
(παραδειγματίζοντας) the effect which is
produced upon others in deterring
them from the Faith.

ἀνασταυροῦντας] seeing they crucify
again. Τί δέ ἐστὶν ἀνασταυροῦντας;
ἄνωθεν πάλιν σταυροῦντας (Chrys.),
and so the other ancient interpreters
with the versions (comp. Hier. ad Gal.
v. 24 ἀνασταυροῦντες...quod nos inter-
pretari possumus recrucifigentes). In
classical Greek however the word has
the sense of 'raising on the cross,'
crucifying with the additional notion
of exposure: e.g. Herod. vii. 194, 238
(ἐκέλευσε ἀποταμόντας τὴν κεφαλὴν
ἀνασταυρῶσαι). There is the same
double meaning in other similar compounds: e.g. ἀναβλέπω. The word
is illustrated by the phrase attributed
to the Lord which is quoted by Origen
(In Joh. xx. 12) from 'the Acts of
Paul': ἄνωθεν μέλλω σταυρωθῆναι. Compare Resch, Agrapha, p. 430.

It was through faithlessness, by
clinging to selfish prepossessions instead of yielding to divine guidance,
that the Jews first crucified Christ.
Those who fall away practically repeat
the act as often as their unbelief is
shewn, and by the notoriety of their
apostasy put Him to open shame.

Perhaps there is the further thought
in the image of crucifixion that Christ
dwells in the believer. To fall away

from the faith is therefore to slay
Him. Contrast Gal. vi. 14.

This new crucifixion of Christ is
said to be ἑαυτοῖς, that is to their own
loss and condemnation (Tert. in se-
metipsis, Vulg. sibimetipsis). Compare Rom. xiii. 2; Matt. xxiii. 31;
Gal. vi. 14. The Fathers present the
impossibility as the impossibility of
repeating Baptism. So, for example,
Chrysostom: ὁ τοίνυν δεύτερον ἑαυτὸν
βαπτίζων πάλιν αὐτὸν σταυροῖ. And
Primasius: Quiiterumbaptizari volunt
quantum in se est Christum quoque
iterum crucifigere volunt et derisui
habere...quoniam sicut Christus semel
mortuus est in carne in cruce, ita et
nos semel mori possumus in baptismate peccato.

τὸν υἱὸν τοῦ θεοῦ] The use of the
title indicates the greatness of the
offence. Compare x. 29; iv. 14 note.

παραδειγματίζοντας] The verb occurs
as a variant in Matt. i. 19 (δειγματίσαι).
Comp. Num. xxv. 4 (LXX.).

7, 8. The law of human life, the
condemnation which follows from the
neglect of blessings, is illustrated by
an example from nature. The Parables
of the Lord and the usage of the
prophets suggest this method of enforcing truth. We spontaneously at-
tribute will, responsibility (πιοῦσα, τίκτουσα, εὐλογίας μεταλαμβάνει), even to
the earth. We look for certain results
from certain general conditions; and
not only so but we regard certain
results as naturally appropriate to
certain objects. Comp. Mark iv. 28
(αὐτομάτη): Rom. viii. 19 ff. The comparison between processes of agricul-
ture and moral training is common in
all literature. Comp. Philo de Agric.
§§ 1 ff. (i. 300 ff. M.).

The illustration here apparently is
not taken from the familiar image of
the field and the seed and the sower.
The case is rather that of the natural
produce of the land. No mention is

152

THE EPISTLE TO THE HEBREWS. [VI. 7

ἐρχόμενον πολλάκις ὑετόν, καὶ τίκτουσα ΒοτάΝΗΝ εὔθετον
ἐκείνοις δι' οὓς καὶ γεωργεῖται, μεταλαμβάνει εὐλογίας

7 ἐρχ. πολλ. אBD₂ syrr me : πολλ. ἐρχ. AC vg.
vg syr vg me.

καὶ γεωργ.: om. καὶ D₂*

made of human activity as contributing to the production of the 'herb'; though the land is such as is cultivated. From the land and from man it is reasonable to look for fruitful use of divine gifts. The human ministry of tiller and teacher falls into the background.

The primal record of Genesis furnishes the example of fruitful fertility (Gen. i. 11 βοτάνη) and the example of noxious growth (Gen. iii. 18 ἄκανθαι καὶ τρίβολοι), followed in the one case by blessing (i. 13), and connected in the other with a curse (iii. 17).

⁷*For land that drinketh the rain that cometh oft upon it and then bringeth forth herb meet for them for whose sake it is also tilled, receiveth blessing from God; ⁸but if it beareth thorns and thistles it is rejected and nigh unto a curse; whose end is for burning.*

7. γῆ γὰρ ἡ πιοῦσα] For land—to borrow an image from another form of GOD's works—land that in the season drank the rain of His gift... For the tense compare c. ix. 2; Rom. ix. 30; Phil. iii. 12 and Lightfoot *ad loc.*

πιοῦσα...τίκτουσα] The complete appropriation of the gift at the time when it comes precedes the production of the fruit. Here the Latin (as commonly with such participles) fails to express the full thought: *bibens...et generans...*(Tert. *quæ bibit...et peperit...*).

For πιοῦσα compare Deut. xi. 11. ('Sat prata biberunt.') The gift had not been rejected. So the parallel is established with those who had believed the Gospel.

τὸν ἐπ' αὐτῆς ἐρχόμενον πολλ. ὑ.] The harvest is prepared not by one gift of heaven but by many. The *gen.*

in ἐπ' αὐτῆς gives not only the idea of 'reaching to' but adds also that of extending over. Comp. James v. 17; Mk. iv. 26; Apoc. iii. 10. Chrysostom sees in ὑετόν a pointed reference to the human parallel, τὴν διδασκαλίαν φησίν. Compare Is. v. 6; Amos viii. 11.

καὶ τίκτουσα] *and then bringeth forth,* as the natural and proper fruit. The personal word gives force and vividness to the application of the image. Comp. James i. 15.

The more complete form of expression would have been τίκτουσα μέν...ἐκφέρουσα δέ..., but the first case is taken by itself as giving the true normal issue.

βοτάνην] the simplest natural produce: Gen. i. 11 ff. Hence the word is used in a bad sense for wild plants, weeds. Comp. Lightfoot on Ign. *Eph.* 10.

εὔθετον] Vulg. *opportunam* (Old Lat. *utilem, aptam*); Luke ix. 62; xiv. 35. The word probably is not to be taken absolutely but joined with ἐκείνοις.

δι' οὓς καὶ γεωργεῖται] *for whose sake it is also tilled.* For the use of καί compare c. vii. 26; 2 Cor. iii. 6; Col. iii. 15.

The laborious culture of the soil seems to be contrasted with its spontaneous fruitfulness. In its truest state, as fulfilling the divine purpose, it meets (so to speak) man's efforts for the service of man. Those 'for whom' it is cultivated are not the tillers themselves only (Vulg. *a quibus,* Old Lat. *propter quos*), nor yet the owners, but men at large.

It is easy to see an allusion to the human field tilled for God's glory: 1 Cor. iii. 9.

μεταλαμβάνει εὐλογίας] shares in

ἀπὸ τοῦ θεοῦ· ⁸ἐκφέρογϲα δὲ ἀκάνθαϲ καὶ τριβόλογϲ ἀδόκιμοϲ
καὶ κατάραϲ ἐγγύϲ, ἧϲ τὸ τέλοϲ εἰϲ καῦϲιν.　　⁹Πεπεἰϲ-

τοῦ θεοῦ : om. τοῦ D₂*.

blessing which is of wider range.
This blessing may best be supposed
to lie in increased fruitfulness: John
xv. 2.

For μεταλαμβάνει see c. xii. 10; 2
Tim. ii. 6.

8. ἐκφέρουσα δέ] *but if it bear*,
breaking the law of fruitfulness. The
word ἐκφέρουσα stands in contrast with
τίκτουσα, though in Gen. i. 12 ἐξήνεγκεν
is used of the productiveness of the
earth in answer to the divine command.
Usage hardly justifies the remark of
the Greek Fathers: οὐκέτι εἶπε τίκτουσα ἀλλ' ἐκφέρουσα, τὸ παρὰ φύσιν
τῆς ἐκβολῆς αἰνιττόμενος (Œcum.).

ἀδόκιμος...καῦσιν] The judgment on
the land, fruitful only for ill, is given
in three stages. It is *rejected*: such
land cannot any longer be reckoned
as land for fruitful service. It is *nigh
unto a curse*: it presents the outward features of the curse (Gen. iii.
17 f.), whence the near presence of
the curse is inferred. Its end is
burning. 'Αδόκιμος (Lat. *reproba*) is
found elsewhere in the N. T. only in
St Paul: *e.g.* 1 Cor. ix. 27; 2 Cor.
xiii. 5 ff.

For κατάρας ἐγγύς compare c. viii. 13
ἐγγὺς ἀφανισμοῦ. Primasius remarks
upon the phrase; Notandum quia non
dixit *maledicta est* sed *maledictioni
proxima* (φοβῶν ἅμα καὶ παραμυθού-
μενος Euth. Zig.); and Œcumenius
(following Chrysostom) ὁ δὲ ἐγγὺς
κατάρας γενόμενος καὶ μακρὰν γενέσθαι
δύναται διὰ μετανοίας.

ἧς τὸ τέλος εἰς καῦσιν] *whose end (i.e.*
the end of the land) *is for burning*,
Vulg. *cujus consummatio in com-
bustionem*. The rhythm of the whole
sentence shews that the relative looks
back to the main and not to the last
(κατάρα) antecedent.

So Œcumenius (after Chrysostom):
ἐὰν μέχρι τέλους ἐπιμείνῃ, φησί, καὶ

μέχρι τελευτῆς ἀκάνθας ἐκφέρων τότε
καυθήσεται. For εἰς compare Rom. x.
10; 1 Cor. xi. 17; and for καῦσις 2
Pet. iii. 10, 12; c. x. 27.

The image here appears to represent utter desolation as of a land
destroyed by volcanic forces (ἡ κατα-
κεκαυμένη). Compare Deut. xxix. 23.
The thought of purification by fire,
true in itself, is foreign to the context;
nor does the image of the burning of
the noxious growth of the land (Virg.
Georg. i. 84 ff.) seem to be sufficiently
expressive. Compare c. x. 26 f.; John
xv. 6.

The warning found a typical fulfilment in the overthrow of Jerusalem
and the old Theocracy.

(3) *Words of hope and encouragement* (9—12).

The spiritual dulness and sluggish-
ness of the Hebrews had not yet
checked their active exercise of Christian love. In this the Apostle found
the assurance of better things (9, 10).
And he grounded upon it his desire
for a corresponding development of
hope through long-suffering faith (11,
12). Thus in this brief section we
have a view of (*a*) the Apostle's confidence; and (*b*) the Apostle's wish.

⁹ *But we are persuaded of you,
beloved, better things and things that
accompany salvation, though we thus
speak;* ¹⁰ *for God is not unrighteous
to forget your work and your love,
which ye shewed toward His name in
that ye ministered to he saints and
still do minister.* ¹¹ *And we desire
that each one of you may shew the
same zeal that ye may attain unto the
fulness of hope even to the end;* ¹² *in
order that ye may not become sluggish,
but imitators of them that through
faith and long-suffering inherit the
promises.*

(*a*) The Apostle's confidence (9, 10).

μεθα δὲ περὶ ὑμῶν, ἀγαπητοί, τὰ κρείσσονα καὶ ἐχόμενα
σωτηρίας, εἰ καὶ οὕτως λαλοῦμεν· ¹⁰οὐ γὰρ ἄδικος ὁ

9 ἀγαπητοί: ἀδελφοί א* syrr.

9, 10. The Apostle guards himself against the supposition that he
classes the Hebrews among those who
had 'fallen away.' The presence of
active love among them was a sure
sign that God had not left them.

9. πεπείσμεθα δέ...σωτηρίας] *But
we are persuaded of you, beloved....*
The order of the words is most significant. First comes πεπείσμεθα, which
suggests a past conflict of feeling
issuing in a settled judgment. Then
follows the pronoun (περὶ ὑμῶν), which
at once separates the Hebrews from
the apostates who had been just
described. Then a unique title of
deep affection.

πεπείσμεθα] Compare Rom. xv.
14; and contrast c. xiii. 18 (πειθόμεθα); Gal. v. 10 (πέποιθα). The form
implies that the writer had felt misgivings and had overcome them. Chrysostom notices both the word and the
plural : οὐκ εἶπε νομίζομεν, οὐδὲ στοχα-
ζόμεθα, οὐδὲ προσδοκῶμεν, οὐδὲ ἐλπίζο-
μεν· ἀλλὰ τί; πεπείσμεθα, καὶ οὐ περὶ
ἑαυτοῦ τοῦτο μόνον φησὶν ἀλλὰ περὶ
πάντων, οὐ γὰρ εἶπε πέπεισμαι ἀλλὰ
πεπείσμεθα.

ἀγαπητοί] Vulg. *dilectissimi* (d
carissimi). The word occurs nowhere
else in the Epistle. The use of it in
this connexion emphasises the affection which the stern language of the
former paragraphs might seem to have
obscured or negatived. The title
generally suggests an argument : 1
Cor. x. 14; xv. 58; 2 Cor. vii. 1; xii.
19. Compare 1 John ii. 7 note.

τὰ κρείσσονα καὶ ἐχ. σωτ.] There
are but two issues : a better and a
worse. The comparative is not used
for the positive, but plainly suggests
the contrast (cf. c. vii. 7; xi. 40). For
the word (κρείσσονα), which is characteristic of the Epistle, see i. 4 note.
The exact meaning of ἐχόμενα σω-

τηρίας (Vulg. *viciniora* [d *proximiora.*
Aug. *adv. Cres.* iii. 74 *hærentia*]
saluti) is somewhat uncertain. The
phrase is parallel with and yet distinct
from (κατάρας) ἐγγύς (*v.* 8). The construction ἔχεσθαί τινος is used of local
contiguity (Mk. i. 38), and also of temporal connexion (Lk. xiii. 33 ; Acts xx.
15; xxi. 26). Hence ἐχ. σωτηρίας may
here mean either 'which issue in
salvation as immediately following,'
or 'which issue from salvation as immediately preceding.' Probably there
is no exact definition of the relation :
which accompany salvation, which
are closely connected with it, and so,
in some sense, bring it with them.
Comp. Luc. *Hermog.* 69 ἐλπίδος οὐ
μικρᾶς ἐχόμενα.

εἰ καί] *though,* Vulg. *tametsi* (d e
nam et sic, corruption of *tametsi ?*);
Luke xi. 8; xviii. 4; 2 Cor. xii. 11;
vii. 8 ; 1 Pet. iii. 14.

The circumstance thus introduced
may be either distinctly acknowledged
or simply admitted for the sake of
argument. In each case the καί emphasises the word which it precedes
by suggesting some limit which is
over-passed. Comp. Winer, p. 544.

10. οὐ γὰρ ἄδικος...ἀγάπης] The
active exercise of love, which is itself
a sign of the divine presence, carries
with it the assurance of a divine reward.
The deed and the result are regarded
from the human side as cause and
effect, service and reward, while essentially the one includes the other. The
thought is of character shewn in life,
and not of any special works which
have a merit of their own. The 'reward' is the power of more perfect
service (*v.* 7).

The claim (so to speak) on God's
righteousness (comp. Rom. iii. 5) is
not an assertion of merit. Its ground
lies in a perfect trust in His Nature

θεὸς ἐπιλαθέσθαι τοῦ ἔργου ὑμῶν καὶ τῆς ἀγάπης ἧς
ἐνεδείξασθε εἰς τὸ ὄνομα αὐτοῦ, διακονήσαντες τοῖς

10 τῆς ἀγάπης אABCD₂* vg syrr : +τοῦ κόπου' τῆς ἀγ. ς me (1 Thess. i. 3).

and Will as revealed to men within
and without. He is alike righteous
when He rewards and when He
punishes. Compare Chrys. on Col. i.
Hom. ii. § 4 εἰ κρίσις οὐκ ἔστιν, οὐκ ἔστι
δίκαιος ὁ θεός· κατὰ ἄνθρωπον λέγω.
εἰ δίκαιος οὐκ ἐστιν ὁ θεός, οὐδὲ θεὸς
ἐστίν. εἰ θεὸς οὐκ ἔστιν, ἁπλῶς ἅπαντα
φέρεται, οὐδὲν ἀρετή, οὐδὲν κακία.
The reward of God is the inherent
issue of action (1 John i. 9; Mark ix.
41); and without Himself it is value-
less (Matt. xx. 14 ὕπαγε). Compare
1 John i. 9 note.

For other forms of trust based
upon the essential character of God,
see 1 Cor. x. 13; 1 Thess. v. 24; 2 Tim.
i. 12.

The sense of God's righteousness
is indeed a necessary condition of
faith: c. xi. 6.

ἐπιλαθέσθαι] Compare Lk. xii. 6.
The thought is perfectly general, and
must not be limited either to the past
or to the future. We necessarily
present the relation of God to men in
terms of man's experience.

τοῦ ἔργου ὑμῶν καὶ τ. ἀγ.] the energy
of life in its unity (contrast c. x. 24),
of which love was the inspiration.

For the use of the singular see
Rom. ii. 7; Gal. vi. 4; 1 Thess. i. 3;
and also John iv. 34; vi. 29 (ἔργα *v.*
28); xvii. 4 and notes.

The nature of 'the work' of the
Hebrews is described in c. x. 32 ff.

Bengel notices the prominence
given to love, hope and faith successively in *vv.* 10—12.

ἧς ἐνεδ. εἰς τὸ ὄνομα αὐτοῦ] The
love was directed to God's name, to
God as He was made known in Christ,
and so found its objects in those who
were His children (οὐχ ἁπλῶς εἰς τοὺς
ἁγίους ἀλλ' εἰς τὸν θεόν, Chrys.). The
tense seems to point to some well-
known occasion.

For the construction with εἰς see
2 Cor. viii. 24.

The tense of ἐνεδείξασθε is accommodated to the first participle (διακονήσαντες). A present ἐνδείκνυσθε is
spontaneously supplied with διακονοῦντες. The 'name' (compare c. xiii. 15)
is specially mentioned (rather than
'towards Him') because the sonship
of believers is included in it; and the
Hebrews had satisfied the claim on
Christian love which lay in that
common tie.

The false translation of εἰς τὸ ὄνομα
of the Latin (*in nomine*), which obscures, if it does not wholly alter, the
sense, is the uniform Latin translation of εἰς τὸ ὄνομα. In some places
it leads (as here) to very serious misunderstanding; and it commonly influenced the A.V., as in the rendering
of the most important phrases :

(1) βαπτίζειν εἰς τὸ ὄνομα, Matt.
xxviii. 19; Acts viii. 16; xix. 5; 1 Cor.
i. 13, 15.

(2) συνάγεσθαι εἰς τὸ ὄνομα, Matt.
xviii. 20 (so R. V.).

(3) πιστεύειν εἰς τὸ ὄν., John i. 12;
ii. 23; iii. 18; 1 John v. 13. Compare
Matt. x. 41 f.

διακονήσαντες τοῖς ἁγίοις] See c.
x. 32 ff. Compare Rom. xv. 25. The
thought is of service to Christians as
Christians, c. xiii. 24 (iii. 1); and not
to Christians as men. Love of the
brethren (c. xiii. 1) is crowned at last
by love (2 Pet. i. 7).

There is nothing in such passages
as Rom. xv. 26; 1 Cor. xvi. 1; 2 Cor.
viii. 4; ix. 1 to show that the Christians
at Jerusalem had the title οἱ ἅγιοι
specially. Comp. Rom. xii. 13.

The title is used again of Christians
in the Epistle: xiii. 24, who are elsewhere addressed as ἀδελφοί (iii. 12;
x. 19; xiii. 22), ἀγαπητοί (*v.* 9 , ἀδελφοὶ ἅγιοι (iii. 1).

ἀγίοις καὶ διακονοῦντες. ¹¹ἐπιθυμοῦμεν δὲ ἕκαστον ὑμῶν
τὴν αὐτὴν ἐνδείκνυσθαι σπουδὴν πρὸς τὴν πληροφορίαν
τῆς ἐλπίδος ἄχρι τέλους, ¹²ἵνα μὴ νωθροὶ γένησθε,

διακονοῦντες : διακόνοντες D₂*.

(b) The Apostle's wish.

11, 12. The activity of practical
love among the Hebrews fills the
Apostle with the desire that the spirit
from which this springs may find a
wider work among them in the
strengthening of hope and faith,
through which alone the divine promises can be realised.

11. ἐπιθυμοῦμεν δέ...] Action alone
is not sufficient, nor can it be sustained without the inspiration of
hope.

The word of strong personal—even
passionate—desire, coveting (ἐπιθυμοῦμεν), is expressive of the intense
longing of the writer. There is no
exact parallel. Compare 1 Pet. i. 12;
(1 Tim. iii. 1). Chrysostom dwells on
the expression : ἐπιθυμοῦμεν φησίν
οὐκ ἄρα μέχρι ῥημάτων τοῦτο βουλόμεθα
μόνον; and again οὐκ εἶπε θέλω ὅπερ
ἦν διδασκαλικῆς αὐθεντίας, ἀλλ᾽ ὃ πατ-
ρικῆς ἦν φιλοστοργίας καὶ πλέον τοῦ
θέλειν ; and so later Fathers.

ἕκαστον ὑμῶν] The desire is individual, while the expression of confidence is general (v. 9). In this way
the force of ἐπιθυμοῦμεν is strengthened. The writer's wish goes beyond
the general character of the body, or
the perfection of some of the members
of it. Καὶ μεγάλων καὶ μικρῶν ὁμοίως
κήδεται (Chrys.).

τὴν αὐτὴν ἐνδ. σπ....τέλους] The
desire of the writer is that the
Hebrews should shew the same zeal
in other directions as they shewed in
works of love. Their hope was chilled.
It was essential that this should be
rekindled 'in regard to,' 'with a view
to securing' the fulness of hope even
to the end (Vulg. ad expletionem [d e
confirmationem] spei).

For the phrase ἡ πληροφορία τῆς
ἐλπίδος compare c. x. 22 πληροφορία

πίστεως. Col. ii. 2 ἡ πληροφορία τῆς
συνέσεως. It describes the fulness,
the full measure, of hope. The word
πληροφορία (not found in classical
writers) is always taken passively in
N. T. ('fulness' not 'fulfilling'); and
it seems better to understand it here
of the full development of hope than
of the full assurance of hope (1 Thess.
i. 5).

Such zeal issuing in such growing
hope must be exercised until the end
of the present period of trial and
discipline: compare c. iii. 6 note μέχρι
τέλους. The interpretation 'till it is
consummated' is contrary to the usage
of the phrase. On the Christian function of hope see c. iii. 6; x. 23 notes.

12. ἵνα μὴ νωθροὶ γέν., μιμ. δέ...]
that ye become not sluggish, but imitators..., Vulg. ut non segnes efficia-
mini (d ne sitis ægri) verum imi-
tatores... The object of the Apostle's
desire was that the Hebrews might
avoid an imminent peril, and strive
after a great ideal. If hope failed to
have her perfect work the dulness
which had already come over their
powers of spiritual intelligence would
extend to the whole of life (v. 11
νωθροὶ ταῖς ἀκοαῖς). In this one definite respect they had 'become' dull
(v. 11, γεγόνατε) : the danger was lest
they should 'become' dull absolutely
(ἵνα μὴ γένησθε ν.). On the other hand
if hope were kindled they would be
enabled to imitate the heroes of
faith.

The word μιμητής (which should
be rendered closely imitator and not
follower) is found here only in the
Epistle. Elsewhere in the N. T. it is
peculiar to St Paul (five times). The
word occurs as a false reading in
1 Pet. iii. 13.

τῶν διὰ π. καὶ μακρ...ἐπαγγ.] The

μιμηταὶ δὲ τῶν διὰ πίστεως καὶ μακροθυμίας κληρονο-

12 διὰ + τῆς π. D₂*.　　καὶ μακροθυμοῦντας D₂*.

model of Christian effort is offered by those who through the ex⬤⬤se of the characteristic graces of faith and long-suffering are even now realising in a true sense the promises of God. 'Faith' is the essential principle through which the blessing is gained, and 'long-suffering' marks the circumstance under which faith has to be maintained. The two graces of patience (ὑπομονή) and faith are combined in Apoc. xiii. 10 (xiv. 12); James i. 3; 2 Thess. i. 4.

The word μακροθυμία and its cognates are very rarely found except in Biblical Greek (Plutarch). Some form of the class occurs in each group of the writings of the N. T. except the writings of St John. It is important to distinguish μακροθυμία from ὑπομονή, with which it is often confounded by the Latin Versions. Ὑπομονή (c. x. 36; xii. 1) suggests the pressure of distinct trials which have to be borne. Μακροθυμία expresses the trial of unsatisfied desire. So God bears with men who fail to fulfil His will (Rom. ii. 4; ix. 22; 1 Tim. i. 16; 1 Pet. iii. 20; 2 Pet. iii. 15 τοῦ κυρίου); and in their place men seek to imitate His long-suffering: 1 Thess. v. 14; Gal. v. 22; Eph. iv. 2; Col. iii. 12; 2 Tim. iv. 2; James v. 7 f.

Μακροθυμία and ὑπομονή occur together in 2 Cor. vi. 4, 6 ἐν ὑπομονῇ πολλῇ, ἐν θλίψεσιν...ἐν γνώσει, ἐν μακροθυμίᾳ, ἐν χρηστότητι...Col. i. 11 εἰς πᾶσαν ὑπομονὴν καὶ μακροθυμίαν. 2 Tim. iii. 10 τῇ πίστει, τῇ μακροθυμίᾳ, τῇ ἀγάπῃ, τῇ ὑπομονῇ. James v. 10 f. The contrast lies in 1 Cor. xiii. 4, 7 ἡ ἀγάπη μακροθυμεῖ...πάντα ὑπομένει.

κληρονομούντων] who......inherit, Vulg. hereditabunt, d e potiuntur.

The participle is a strict present. Believers even now enter on their inheritance (c. iv. 3), and with them the saints of old time enjoy the fulfilment of that for which they looked

(c. xii. 22 ff.).

Compare 1 Cor. xv. 50 κληρονομεῖ; and contrast the perfect, c. i. 4; and the aorist, c. xii. 17.

For the image comp. i. 4, 14; ix. 15 and Additional Note.

There is an evident distinction between οἱ κληρονομοῦντες (τὰς ἐπαγγελίας) and οἱ κληρονόμοι (τῆς ἐπαγγελίας v. 17). The first phrase marks the direct realisation of the blessings of heirship, and the second simply the position.

The plural (αἱ ἐπαγγελίαι) represents the various promises made in old time in many parts (i. 1). Compare c. vii. 6; xi. 13; Rom. ix. 4; xv. 8; Gal. iii. 16. Clem. 1 Cor. 10 'Αβραάμ... ἐξῆλθεν...ὅπως...κληρονομήσῃ τὰς ἐπαγγελίας τοῦ θεοῦ. Ps. Sol. xii. 8 ὅσιοι Κυρίου κληρονομήσαιεν ἐπαγγελίας Κυρίου, and Ryle and James ad loc.

These many promises are gathered up in the one promise of that salvation which Christ wrought and which awaits its complete accomplishment: v. 17; ix. 15; x. 36; xi. 39.

(4)　The certainty of the divine promises (13—20).

The reference to the divine promises in v. 12 suggests the consideration that long-suffering (patience is necessary and reasonable. Though their fulfilment may be delayed it is certain. This certainty of fulfilment after long waiting is illustrated by (a) the fundamental promise to Abraham, which by its very form—pointing to a distant future—implied the exercise of patience (13—15). And (b) this promise partially, typically, yet not exhaustively fulfilled, has been handed down to us, doubly confirmed, so that we cannot doubt as to its uttermost accomplishment (16—18); (c) an accomplishment which is presented to us in the exaltation of the Son, Whom hope can follow now within the veil (19, 20).

μούντων τὰς ἐπαγγελίας.   ¹³ Τῷ γὰρ Ἀβραὰμ ἐπαγγειλάμενος ὁ θεός, ἐπεὶ κατ᾽ οὐδενὸς εἶχεν μείζονος ὀμόσαι,

¹³ For when God had made promise to Abraham, since He could
swear by no one greater, He sware
by Himself, saying, ¹⁴ Surely blessing
I will bless thee, and multiplying
I will multiply thee. ¹⁵ And thus,
having patiently endured, he obtained the promise.
¹⁶ For men swear by the greater,
and the oath is an end of all gainsaying in their case for confirmation.
¹⁷ Wherein God being minded to
shew more abundantly to the heirs
of salvation the immutability of His
counsel interposed by an oath, ¹⁸ that
by two immutable things, in which
it is impossible for God to lie, we
may have strong encouragement, who
fled for refuge to lay hold of the hope
set before us.
¹⁹ Which we have as an anchor of
the soul, a hope both sure and stead-
fast and entering within the veil;
²⁰ whither, as forerunner, Jesus
entered on our behalf, having become,
after the order of Melchizedek, a
High-priest for ever.

(a) The promise to Abraham (13—
15).

13—15. The example of Abraham
establishes two things, the certainty
of the hope which rests on a promise
of God, and the need of patience in
order to receive its fulfilment. God
promised with an oath: Abraham
endured to wait and that not in vain.
He is thus a perfect representative
of all 'who through faith and long-
suffering inherit the promises.'
By fixing the attention of his
readers on the promise to Abraham
the writer carries their thoughts beyond the Law. The Law appears as
a stage only in the fulfilment of the
promise. Comp. Gal. iv. 21 ff.

13. τῷ γὰρ Ἀ. ἐπαγγειλάμενος...καθ᾽
ἑαυτοῦ] For God having made
promise to Abraham...sware...Vulg.
promittens (Old Lat. cum repromi-

sisset)..juravit.... The promise was
given, and then the promise was confirmed by an oath (Gen. xii. 3, 7;
xiii. 14; xv. 5 ff.; xvii. 5 ff.; compared
with Gen. xxii. 16 ff.). The student
will do well to consider very carefully
the exact differences of form under
which the promise was given to Abraham at different times and afterwards
to Isaac (Gen. xxvi. 2 ff.) and to Jacob
(Gen. xxviii. 13 ff.).
This interpretation, which is directly suggested by the history, seems
to be better than that which regards
ἐπαγγειλάμενος and ὤμοσεν as contem-
poraneous, a construction which is in
itself perfectly admissible. (Comp. c.
ii. 10.)
It may be further added that the
interposition of an oath implied delay
in the fulfilment of the promise. No
oath would have been required if the
blessing had been about to follow
immediately. But in the nature of
the case the promise to Abraham
pointed to a remote future. Thus
his example was fitted to encourage
the Hebrews to trust in the unseen.
At the same time the promise was
absolute and not conditional (as 1 K.
ii. 4).

ἐπεὶ κατ᾽ οὐδενὸς εἶχεν μ. ὀ.] since
He could swear by no greater one
(according to usage). Vulg. quoniam
neminem habuit per quem juraret
majorem. Comp. Philo, Leg. Alleg.
iii. § 72 (i. 127 M.) ὁρᾷς ὅτι οὐ καθ᾽ ἑτέρου
ὀμνύει θεός, οὐδὲν γὰρ αὐτοῦ κρεῖττον,
ἀλλὰ καθ᾽ ἑαυτοῦ ὅς ἐστι πάντων ἄριστος
(in reference to Gen. xxii. 16).

ὤμοσεν καθ᾽ ἑαυτοῦ] The oath to
Abraham was the foundation of the
hope of Israel (Ps. cv. 6 ff.; Luke i.
73) and the support of all positive
religious faith. In this respect it is
important to notice that it is the
first explicit mention of the divine
oath, which however was implied in
the promise to Noah (Is. liv. 9; Gen.

ὤμοϲεν καθ᾽ ἑαυτοῦ, ¹⁴λέγων Εἰ μην εγλογῶν εγλογήϲω ϲε καὶ
πληθγνων πληθγνῶ ϲε· ¹⁵καὶ οὕτως μακροθυμήσας ἐπέτυχεν

14 εἰ μήν אABD₂*: εἰ μή C vg: ἦ μήν ϛ.

viii. 21 f.; ix. 11 ff.). Compare also
Gen. xv. 8 ff. Jewish scholars dwelt
on the thought of God's oath 'by
Himself': *Shemoth R.* 44 (on Ex.
xxxii. 13), What means *By Thyself?*
R. Eliezer replied : Moses spake thus
to the Lord (Blessed be He). If Thou
hadst sworn by heaven and earth, I
should say, since heaven and earth
shall perish, so too Thine oath. Now
Thou hast sworn to them by Thy
great name: as Thy great name lives
and lasts for ever and ever, Thy oath
also shall last for ever and ever.

The phrase ὀμν. κατά τινος does not
occur again in the N. T. (comp. Matt.
xxvi. 63). It is found in the LXX.:
Jer. xxix. 14 (xlix. 13); xxviii. (li.) 14;
Amos vi. 8 ; and in later Greek. The
classical construction (with the simple
acc.) is found in James v. 12.

14. εἰ μὴν εὐλογῶν...] Gen. xxii.
17. The writer of the Epistle substitutes σέ for τὸ σπέρμα σου in the last
clause. He concentrates his attention
on Abraham alone. Comp. Gen. xii. 3
with Gen. xxii. 18.

The promise which is quoted is
simply that of outward prosperity, of
which in part Abraham lived to see
the fulfilment. But the Messianic
promise, with which the readers were
familiar, was given under the same
circumstances.

εὐλογῶν εὐλογήσω] Old Lat. *bene-
dicendo benedixero.* Vulg. *benedi-
cens benedicam.* This construction
in imitation of Hebr. *inf. abs.* with the
finite verb is found in the N. T. only
in quotations from the LXX. in which
it is extremely frequent. Comp. John
iii. 29 χαρᾷ χαίρει note.

The form εἰ μήν both here and in
the text of the LXX. is attested by
overwhelming authority against the
common form ἦ μήν. The form εἰ is
recognised in *Etymol. Magn.* as an

alternative form for ἦ as ἐπίρρημα
ὁρκικόν with a reference to this passage.
It may be a dialectic peculiarity.

15. καὶ οὕτως...] *and thus,* confident in a promise solemnly ratified,
*having patiently endured...*The οὕτως
is to be taken separately and not in
close connexion with μακρ. ('having
thus patiently endured'). Comp.
Acts vii. 8; xxviii. 14; 1 Cor. xiv. 25.

According to the history twenty-
five years elapsed from the call of
Abraham to the birth of Isaac (Gen.
xii. 4; xxi. 5).

For μακροθυμήσας see *v.* 12 note.

ἐπέτυχεν τῆς ἐπαγγ.] *obtained the
promise,* Vulg. *adeptus est repromissionem.* The phrase following after
ἐπαγγειλάμενος and separated from it
by μακροθυμήσας cannot mean simply
'obtained from God the assurance of
a future blessing.' It affirms that in
some sense Abraham gained that for
which he looked. And in fact Abraham obtained the fulfilment of the
promise in its beginning in Isaac,
born past hope and given to him,
as it were a second time, and also
afterwards in Isaac's sons. In part
however the promise necessarily remained to be fulfilled in after time
(πληθύνων πληθυνῶ...καὶ ἐν σοὶ...), so
that through Christ Christians inherit
it. Compare c. xi. 33; Rom. xi. 7 ;
James iv. 2 ; and c. x. 36; xi. 15, 39
(κομίσασθαι).

In c. xi. 39 it is said of the faithful
fathers οὐκ ἐκομίσαντο τὴν ἐπαγγελίαν
(comp. xi. 15). Chrysostom calls
attention to the apparent contradiction and solves it : οὐ περὶ τῶν αὐτῶν
ἐνταῦθά φησι κἀκεῖ, ἀλλὰ καὶ διπλὴν
ποιεῖται τὴν παράκλησιν. ἐπηγγείλατο
τῷ Ἀβραάμ, καὶ τὰ μὲν ἐνταῦθα μετὰ
μακρὸν χρόνον ἔδωκε, τὰ δὲ ἐκεῖ οὐδέπω.

(*b*) The fulfilment of the promise
is doubly assured to us (16—18).

τῆς ἐπαγγελίας. ¹⁶ἄνθρωποι γὰρ κατὰ τοῦ μείζονος
ὀμνύουσιν, καὶ πάσης αὐτοῖς ἀντιλογίας πέρας εἰς βε-
βαίωσιν ὁ ὅρκος· ¹⁷ἐν ᾧ περισσότερον βουλόμενος ὁ

16 ἄνθρωποι אABD₂* vg syrr: ἄνθρ.+μέν C me.　π. αὐτ. ἀντιλ.: π. ἀντιλ. αὐτ.
D₂* syrr.　17 ἐν ᾧ: ἐν τῷ D₂*.　περισσότερον: -τέρως B.　β. ὁ θ.: ὁ θ. β. D₂.

16—18. The promise which Abraham received still awaits its complete accomplishment, and it is our inheritance, doubly confirmed to us as to him, being a promise, and a promise confirmed by an oath.

In this respect the character and purpose of a human oath illustrate the divine oath. An oath is a decisive appeal to the highest power to close all controversy. Therefore in condescension God interposed an oath to give to His promise this additional pledge of immutability for our encouragement.

The argument assumes the religious propriety of oaths.

16. ἄνθρωποι γάρ...] *For men,* being men, as men, not οἱ ἄνθρ. (c. ix. 27)—*swear by the greater...* Here the main thought is the fact of the oath. The character of the oath (κατὰ τ. μ.) follows from the nature of man. There can be no doubt from the context that τοῦ μείζονος is masculine (Vulg. *per majorem sui*), and not, as it might be (Matt. xii. 6 μεῖζον) neuter.

For the use of ἄνθρωποι, marking the nature and not the class, see John v. 41 compared with 2 Tim. iii. 2; Tit. iii. 8. Compare Philo, *de sacr. Ab. et Cain* § 28 (i. 181 M.) τοῦ πιστευθῆναι χάριν ἀπιστούμενοι καταφεύγουσιν ἐφ᾽ ὅρκον ἄνθρωποι. Cic. *de Offic.* iii. 31, 111.

πάσης...ἀντιλ. πέρας εἰς βεβ.] Vulg. *omnis controversiæ eorum finis ad confirmationem.* The oath has two results, negative and positive: it finally stops all contradiction; and it establishes that which it attests. It is on the one side *an end to all gainsaying* in the relation of man to man (αὐτοῖς).

By an appeal to a higher authority it stays the human denial of the statement which it affirms: ἐκ τούτου λύεται πάσης ἀντιλογίας ἀμφισβήτησις (Chrys.). And on the other side it issues in confirmation. The oath which silences contradiction confirms that in favour of which it is taken (βεβαίωσις, Phil. i. 7; Wisd. vi. 19). For the sense of ἀντιλ. see c. vii. 7 (xii. 3; Jude 11). The sense of 'controversy' (Ex. xviii. 16; LXX.) is too vague. The issue raised is simple and direct. (Comp. Prov. xviii. 18.)

Compare Philo, *de Somn.* i. § 2, τὰ ἐνδοιαζόμενα τῶν πραγμάτων ὅρκῳ διακρίνεται καὶ τὰ ἀβέβαια βεβαιοῦται καὶ τὰ ἄπιστα πίστιν λαμβάνει.

17. ἐν ᾧ...] *wherein, i.e.* in this method of appeal to remove all doubt and gainsaying, *God being minded to shew more abundantly* to man's apprehension than by a simple promise.... Περισσότερον is to be taken with ἐπιδεῖξαι (Acts xviii. 28). The oath was given to bring home to men the certainty of the divine promise. Compare Philo, *de Abr.* 46 (ii. 39 M.) φησί, κατ᾽ ἐμαυτοῦ ὤμοσα, παρ᾽ ᾧ ὁ λόγος ὅρκος ἐστί, ἕνεκα τοῦ τὴν διάνοιαν ἀκλινῶς καὶ παγίως ἔτι μᾶλλον ἢ πρότερον ἐρηρεῖσθαι.

βουλόμενος] As distinguished from θέλειν, βούλεσθαι regards a purpose with respect to something else, while θέλειν regards the feeling in respect of the person himself. Βούλεσθαι is used of the divine purpose: Matt. xi. 27 (Luke x. 22); 1 Cor. xii. 11; James i. 18; 2 Pet. iii. 9. For θέλειν see Mk. xiv. 36; Acts xviii. 21; Rom. ix. 22; 1 Cor. iv. 19; xv. 38; Col. i. 27; 1 Tim. ii. 4; James iv. 15; 1 Pet. iii. 17; Matt. xii. 7 (LXX.); Hebr. x. 5, 8 (LXX.).

τοῖς κληρ. τῆς ἐπαγγ.] The oath to

θεὸς ἐπιδεῖξαι τοῖς κληρονόμοις τῆς ἐπαγγελίας τὸ
ἀμετάθετον τῆς βουλῆς αὐτοῦ ἐμεσίτευσεν ὅρκῳ, ¹⁸ἵνα
διὰ δύο πραγμάτων ἀμεταθέτων, ἐν οἷς ἀδύνατον ψεύ-

ἐπιδεῖξαι: ἐπιδείξασθαι A.

Abraham was not for himself alone
even as the promise was not for himself
alone. It was for him and his seed :
for the father of the faithful and all
faithful sons (c. ii. 16). Thus the
phrase (*the heirs of the promise*)
includes all who under different circumstances and different degrees suc-
ceeded to the promise, the Patriarchs
(xi. 9), the præ-Christian Jews, Christians. The immediate application is
(ἔχωμεν) to the generation of believers
represented by the Hebrews who had
need of the assurance.

τὸ ἀμετ. τῆς βουλῆς] Vulg. *immo-
bilitatem consilii* (Old Lat. *voluntatis)
sui.*

The counsel was that of bringing
universal blessing through the seed of
Abraham (comp. Acts iii. 25). This
part of the promise has not been
directly quoted, but the reference to
it is perfectly intelligible from *v.* 14.

For the use of the adj. (τὸ ἀμετ.) see
Rom. ii. 4; viii. 3; 1 Cor. i. 25;
2 Cor. iv. 17 ; Phil. iii. 8.

The word βουλή is used of God
Luke vii. 30; Acts ii. 23; iv. 28;
xiii. 36; xx. 27; Eph. i. 11 κατὰ τὴν
β. τοῦ θελήματος αὐτοῦ.

ἐμεσίτευσεν ὅρκῳ] Latt. *interposuit
jusjurandum,* interposed, as it were,
between Himself and Abraham with
an oath : took the position of one
invoking a higher power.

The oath directly referred to is
that to Abraham; but the mention of
the oath carries the mind of the
reader to the oath by which Christ's
Priesthood was confirmed (c. vii. 20f.).
The promise to Abraham confirmed
by an oath is parallel to the promise
to Christ—and through Him to Christians—confirmed by an oath. The
latter oath shews how the first oath
was to attain fulfilment.

18 διὰ δ. πρ.: μετὰ δ. πρ. D₂*.

Delitzsch observes that a similar
thought lies in the prayer of Hezekiah
Is. xxxviii. 14 (Lord) be Thou surety
for me (עָרְבֵנִי).

The word μεσιτεύειν occurs here only
in N.T. It occurs both in Philo and
Josephus for that which interposes
between conflicting powers or persons:
Philo *de plant. Noæ* § 2 (i. 331) τοῦ
θείου νόμου...τὰς τῶν ἐναντίων (elements) ἀπειλάς...μεσιτεύοντος καὶ διαι-
τῶντος. Jos. *Antt.* vii. 8, 5; xvi. 4, 3.
For μεσίτης, see c. viii. 6 n.

18. ἵνα...ἰσχ. παράκ. ἔχ. οἱ καταφ....]
that...*we may have strong encouragement who fled...*Latt. *ut fortissi-
mum solacium habeamus qui con-
fugimus...*The whole context shews
that παράκλησιν is to be understood as
encouragement to maintain with boldness a position beset by difficulties,
and not simply passive *consolation.*
The word occurs again in the Epistle
c. xii. 5; xiii. 22.

The epithet (ἰσχυράν) is unusual
(comp. v. 7 κραυγὴ ἰσχ. [xi. 34]). It
describes that which possesses absolute might, and not simply strength
sufficient for a particular task. Compare 2 Cor. x. 10; Apoc. xviii. 2, 10;
xix. 6; Lk. xv. 14 (not Matt. xiv. 30).
For the order see ix. 12; and
distinguish the predicative use in
vii. 24.

On ἔχωμεν Chrysostom says with
true feeling : ὁρᾷς ὅτι οὐ τὴν ἀξίαν τὴν
ἑαυτοῦ σκοπεῖ ἀλλ᾽ ὅπως τοὺς ἀνθρώπους πείσῃ. Comp. 1 John ii. 1 note.

διὰ δύο πραγμ. ἀμ.] *by two immutable things,* the promise and the oath
(*vv.* 13, 17). Πρᾶγμα may mean either
object (c. x. 1; xi. 1) or *fact, action*
(Acts v. 4; Luke i. 1).

ἐν οἷς ἀδύν. ψεύσ.] That the promise
of God should fail is as inconceivable
as that His oath should fail. He must

σασθαι ᵀ θεόν, ἰσχυρὰν παράκλησιν ἔχωμεν οἱ καταφυ-

18 τὸν

τὸν θ. א*AC : om. τόν אᶜBD₂.

(as we speak) fulfil His promise: He must fulfil His oath. Comp. Philo, *de Sacr. Ab. et Cain* § 28 (i. 181 M.) οὐ δι᾽ ὅρκον πιστὸς ὁ θεὸς ἀλλὰ δι᾽ αὐτὸν καὶ ὁ ὅρκος βέβαιος. For ἀδύνατον comp. vi. 4 ; x. 4 ; xi. 6 ; and for ἀδύν. ψεύσ. see Tit. i. 2 ; Clem. R. i. c. 27 οὐδὲν ἀδύνατον παρὰ τῷ θεῷ εἰ μὴ τὸ ψεύσασθαι. For illustrations of the 'divine impossibility' see John v. 19 note. Aug. *de civ.* v. 10 Recte quippe [Deus] omnipotens dicitur qui tamen mori et falli non potest. Dicitur enim omnipotens faciendo quod vult, non patiendo quod non vult; quod ei si accideret nequaquam esset omnipotens. Unde propterea quædam non potest quia omnipotens est.

The use of ὁ θεός (*v.* 17) and θεόν is instructive. In the second case the idea is rather that of the nature of God than of His Personality: 'impossible for Him who is God....'

οἱ καταφυγόντες κρατῆσαι...] *we who* at the decisive moment *fled for refuge to lay hold of....* Comp iv. 3 οἱ πιστεύσαντες. Every other support was abandoned. The word occurs again Acts xiv. 6. Delitzsch refers to two striking passages of Philo : *Leg. All.* iii. § 12 (i. 95) ὁ δὲ ἐναντίος τούτῳ (who is destitute of feeling for the noble) φεύγει μὲν ἀφ᾽ ἑαυτοῦ καταφεύγει δ᾽ ἐπὶ τὸν τῶν ὄντων θεόν. *de prof.* § 18 (i. 560) μήποτ᾽ οὖν ἡ πρεσβυτάτη...μητρόπολις (among the cities of refuge) ὁ θεῖός ἐστι λόγος ἐφ᾽ ὃν πρῶτον καταφεύγειν ὠφελιμώτατον. So Clement speaks of Christians as τοὺς προσπεφευγότας τοῖς οἰκτιρμοῖς αὐτοῦ [τοῦ μεγάλου δημιουργοῦ καὶ δεσπότου τῶν ἁπάντων] διὰ τοῦ κυρίου ἡμῶν Ἰησοῦ Χριστοῦ (1 *Cor.* 20).

The words κρατῆσαι τ. προκ. ἐλπ. appear to be connected in different ways both with καταφυγόντες and with παράκλησιν. The position of the words

makes it difficult to separate κρατῆσαι from καταφυγόντες ; and under any circumstances οἱ καταφυγόντες would be most harsh if taken absolutely. At the same time the exact sense of κρατῆσαι carries back the thought of κρατ. τῆς προκ. ἐλπ. to παράκλησιν : 'that we who fled for refuge to seize the hope may have encouragement to keep hold on it.'

The idea of κρατῆσαι is ' to lay hold on and cling to that which has been so taken.' See iv. 14 note. By the choice of this word in place of λαβεῖν or the like, the writer emphasises the special duty of the Hebrews to keep their own by a fresh effort that which they had originally felt to be the one spring of safety, even the hope based on the efficacy of Christ's work, and specially of His Priestly intercession, whereby the promise of universal blessing through Abraham's seed is fulfilled.

This 'hope' is described as 'lying before us' (comp. c. xii. 1, 2), the prize of victory (Philo, *de mut. nom.* § 14 ; i. 591 M.), open and obvious, as soon as we embrace the Faith. It is treated as being at once God's gift and man's own feeling. It is both an 'objective' hope and a 'subjective' hope. For the power of hope see Rom. viii. 24. Philo makes hope the characteristic of a true man *Quod det. pot. ins.* § 38 (i. 218 M.) ἐγγράφεται γὰρ τῇ θεοῦ βίβλῳ ὅτι μόνος εὔελπις (*leg.* ὁ εὔελπις) ἄνθρωπος· ὥστε κατὰ τὰ ἐναντία ὁ δύσελπις οὐκ ἄνθρωπος. ὅρος οὖν...τοῦ... κατὰ Μωυσῆν ἀνθρώπου διάθεσις ψυχῆς ἐπὶ τὸν ὄντως ὄντα θεὸν ἐλπίζουσα.

(*c*) The promise fulfilled in the exaltation of the Son of man (19, 20).

19, 20. The promise has been fulfilled for humanity in the Son of man. Hope therefore can now enter into the very Presence of God where 'Jesus'

γόντες κρατῆσαι τῆς προκειμένης ἐλπίδος· ¹⁹ἢν ὡς ἄγκυραν
ἔχομεν τῆς ψυχῆς, ἀσφαλῆ τε καὶ βεβαίαν καὶ εἰcεργο-

19 ἔχομεν : ἔχωμεν D₂.

is, a High-priest for ever.

19. ἢν ὡς ἄγκ. ἔχ.] The hope created
and sustained by the promise keeps
the soul secure in all storms (1 Tim.
i. 19). The Anchor, which is not
mentioned in the O. T., is the familiar
symbol of hope. Clement of Alexandria mentions it as a device on Christian rings (*Pæd*. iii. § 59). It occurs
commonly with the ἰχθύς on epitaphs.
And names of hope (Elpis, [Helpis,]
Elpidius) are very frequent.

ἀσφ. τε καὶ βεβ. καὶ εἰσερχ.] These
words may refer, as far as the structure of the sentence is concerned,
either to 'hope,' the main subject, or
to the 'anchor,' with which it is compared. Patristic interpreters, following Chrysostom, connect them with
the anchor, and endeavour to lessen
the harshness of the last predicate
(εἰσερχομένην εἰς τὸ ἐσ. τ. καταπ.) by
drawing an ingenious contrast between
the earthly anchor which sinks to the
depths of the sea, and the spiritual
anchor which rises to the heights of
heaven (δείκνυσιν ὅτι καινή τις αὕτη τῆς
ἀγκύρας ἡ φύσις, οὐ κάτω πιέζουσα
ἀλλ' ἄνω κουφίζουσα τὴν διάνοιαν
Chrys. *ap*. Cram. *Cat*. vii. 522¹). But
no explanation of the kind can remove the strangeness of the image or
adapt the tense of εἰσερχομένην directly
to the action of the anchor. It seems
certain then that this clause at least
must refer to 'hope.' But there are
still two possible combinations. The
three predicates may be taken together referring to 'hope' or the two
first may be closely joined (τε...καί...
comp. *v*. 4) and referred to 'the
anchor,' while the third may give
a second characteristic of hope (ὡς
ἄγκυραν...καὶ εἰσερχομένην). In favour
of this view, which appears to be taken
by Œcumenius and Theophylact, it

may be urged that it gives distinctness to two aspects of hope, its immovable stability, and its penetrative
vigour. Perhaps however such a
division is artificial, so that it is best
to connect the whole description with
the principal subject (hope).

The stability of hope is twofold. It
is undisturbed by outward influences
(ἀσφαλής), and it is firm in its inherent
character (βεβαία). Comp. ii. 2 note.
Spes in nobis similitudinem exercet
anchoræ, quæ navem ne ad scopulos
frangatur retinet, et tutam facit ut non
timeat submergi, atque firmam ne
vel titubare possit (Herv.).

The participle εἰσερχομένην presents
hope as ever entering afresh into the
Divine Presence encouraged by past
experience.

εἰς τὸ ἐσώτ. τοῦ καταπ.] Hope enters
to the innermost Sanctuary, the true
Holy of Holies, that Presence of God,
where Christ is (comp. vii. 19). The
καταπέτασμα was the inner veil separating the Holy from the Most Holy
place (פָּרֹכֶת Matt. xxvii. 51; c. x.
20) as distinguished from the outer
veil (מָסָךְ κάλυμμα). The distinction
of the two is not strictly preserved in
the LXX.; see also c. ix. 3 μετὰ τὸ δεύτερον καταπέτασμα. Comp. Ex. xl. 5, 19.

Compare Philo *de vit. M.* iii. § 5
(ii. 148 M.) ἐκ τῶν αὐτῶν τό τε καταπέτασμα καὶ τὸ λεγόμενον κάλυμμα
κατεσκευάζετο. τὸ μὲν εἴσω κατὰ τοὺς
τέσσαρας κίονας ἵν' ἐπικρύπτηται τὸ
ἄδυτον, τὸ δὲ ἔξω κατὰ τοὺς πέντε...:
and so § 9. See also *de gig*. § 12 (i.
270 M.) for a spiritual interpretation.

Hope, like the anchor, is fixed on
the unseen: Nautis arenæ quibus
anchora figitur et hæret sunt tectæ
nec videri possunt, et tamen nautæ
sunt in securitate, licet illa videre non

¹ The printed text of the Homily is manifestly imperfect.

ΜΈΝΗΝ εἰς τὸ ἐcώτεροΝ τοῦ κατατετάϲματος, ²⁰ὅπου πρόδρομος
ὑπὲρ ἡμῶν εἰσῆλθεν Ἰησοῦς, κατὰ τὴν τάξιν Μελχιϲεδὲκ
ἀρχιερεὺς γενόμενος εἰς τὸν αἰῶνα.

20 Ἰησοῦς: +χριστός D₂*.

possint quibus anchoræ brachia fir-
miter adhæsere. Sic et nos in hujus
sæculi fluctibus positi cælestia non
videmus, et tamen illis ita per spem
conjuncti sumus ut nullo timoris in-
cursu moveri possimus (Herv.). Compare Primasius: Spes interiora vela-
minis penetrat dum per mentis con-
templationem futura bona conspicit,
dum cælestia præmia absque ulla
dubitatione credit sibi provenire,
sperat, amat, operibusque ostendit
quid credat et quid speret.

20. Hope enters where 'Jesus'—the
Son of man—has entered as the forerunner of redeemed humanity, *on our
behalf* (ὑπὲρ ἡμῶν), to make atonement
and intercession for us, and, yet more,
to prepare an entrance and a place
for us also. Comp. John xiv. 2.

Thus to the fulfilment of the type of
the High-priest's work another work
is added. The High-priest entered
the Holy of Holies on behalf of the
people, but they never followed him.
Christ enters heaven as forerunner of
believers. Comp. x. 19 ff. Προέδρα-
μεν ἵνα τοὺς ἑπομένους εἰσαγάγῃ (Euth.
Zig.).

The word πρόδρομος was used
especially of the men or troops which
were sent to explore before the advance of an army. Comp. Wisd. xii. 8
(Ex. xxiii. 28). In Num. xiii. 21 (22) it
is used, in a different connexion, of the
earliest fruits.

The use of the word εἰσῆλθεν fixes
attention on the fact of Christ's entrance into the Holiest—the transi-

tion from the seen to the unseen—and
not on His continuance as our High-
priest within the Veil (c. ix. 28).

For ὑπὲρ ἡμῶν compare ix. 24; ii.
9 (ὑπὲρ παντός).

Ἰησοῦς...ἀρχ. γενόμενος] The human
name of the Lord, placed emphatically
at the end of the sentence (see c. ii.
9 note), is here used (contrast ὁ χριστός
c. v. 5) in regard to His High-priesthood, in order to connect it definitely
with the fulfilment of His work on
earth, whereupon He *became* a High-
priest for ever.

The order of words in the last
clause, κατὰ τὴν τάξ. Μ. ἀρχ. γεν., is
emphatic. Stress is laid upon the
fact that Christ is High-priest after a
new and higher order. He does therefore all that the High-priest did and
more. Comp. vii. 11, 15; and contrast
v. 10 (v. 6; vii. 17).

From this passage it is clear that
the eternal High-priesthood of the
Lord 'after the order of Melchizedek,'
King and Priest, followed on His
exaltation to the throne of God in His
glorified humanity (comp. v. 9 f.; vii.
28). At the same time this view does
not exclude the recognition of the
Lord's Death as a priestly act whereby
He once for all offered Himself (vii.
27).

εἰς τὸν αἰῶνα] Etiam in futuro [sæ-
culo] pontificis agit opus, non tunc
pro peccatis nostris offerens, quæ
nulla erunt, sed ut bonum quod in
nobis operatus est indeficiens et stabile
permaneat (Herv.).

Additional Note on vi. 1—8.

In considering this passage several points must be kept in mind.

1. The apostasy described is marked not only by a decisive act (παραπεσόντας), but also by a continuous present attitude, a hostile relation to Christ himself and to belief in Christ (ἀνασταυροῦντας, παραδειγματίζοντας).

2. Thus there is no question of the abstract efficacy of the means of grace provided through the ordinances of the Church. The state of the men themselves is such as to exclude their application.

3. The case is hypothetical. There is nothing to shew that the conditions of fatal apostasy had been fulfilled, still less that they had been fulfilled in the case of any of those addressed. Indeed the contrary is assumed : *vv.* 9 ff.

4. But though the case is only supposed it is one which must be taken into account. It is possible for us to see how it can arise. The state of a man may become such as to make the application to him of the appointed help towards the divine life not only difficult but impossible.

5. Such a condition is noticed elsewhere c. x. 26 f.; comp. c. iii. 12; 1 John v. 16 (note).

And the frame of mind is recognised not only in relation to apostasy, but in relation to the first reception of the Gospel : Matt. xii. 31 (ἡ τοῦ πνεύματος βλασφημία), when the spirit, through which man has the power of approach to the Divine, becomes itself rebellious and defiant.

6. Compare also Gal. v. 4 (κατηργήθητε ἀπὸ Χριστοῦ); Rom. xi. 21 (τῶν κατὰ φύσιν κλάδων οὐκ ἐφείσατο); 1 Tim. iv. 1 (ἀποστήσονταί τινες τῆς πίστεως) ; 1 Tim. vi. 10 (ἀπεπλανήθησαν ἀπὸ τῆς πίστεως); 2 Pet. ii. 20; John xv. 1 ff., 6 (ἐβλήθη ἔξω, ἐξηράνθη, καίεται). In these passages various aspects of the sin and its consequences are indicated, which answer to the responsible action of man and the fulfilment of the divine law of retribution.

7. The analogy of human life furnishes an illustration of the general idea. A second birth is inconceivable : but a restoration to life is not so. This however does not come within the ordinary view. So it is in the spiritual life. A re-birth is impossible, yet even here a restoration to life may be accomplished.

The passage was variously interpreted in early times. TERTULLIAN, representing the sterner (Montanist) view, held that it declared that all who had fallen away from the faith, either by temporary apostasy or by gross sin, were cut off from it for their whole life, without possibility of readmission on repentance : *de Pudic.* xx. Hoc qui ab apostolis didicit et cum apostolis docuit, nunquam moecho et fornicatori secundam poenitentiam promissam ab apostolis norat.

In the earliest stage of the Novatianist controversy the words do not seem to have been quoted. Novatian himself does not refer to the epistle.

In the fourth century and onwards however it was pressed by those who held his views (comp. Theodoret *ad loc.*; Athanas. *Ep. ad Serap.* iv. § 13; Hieron. *adv. Jovin.* ii. 3; Ambros. *de Pœn.* ii. 2 §§ 6 ff.). But this opinion and this use of these words found no favour in the Catholic Church. On the contrary the Catholic writers limited the meaning of the passage to the denial of a second baptism. So among the Greek Fathers.

ATHANASIUS (*l. c.*) μίαν εἶναι τὴν ἀνακαίνισιν διὰ τοῦ βαπτίσματος καὶ μὴ δευτέραν ἀποφαίνεται.

EPIPHANIUS (*Hær.* lix. 2, p. 494) τῷ μὲν ὄντι τοὺς ἅπαξ ἀνακαινισθέντας καὶ παραπεσόντας ἀνακαινίζειν ἀδύνατον. οὔτε γὰρ ἔτι γεννηθήσεται Χριστὸς ἵνα σταυρωθῇ ὑπὲρ ἡμῶν· οὔτε ἀνασταυροῦν δύναταί τις τὸν υἱὸν τοῦ θεοῦ τὸν μηκέτι σταυρούμενον· οὔτε δύναταί τις λουτρὸν δεύτερον λαμβάνειν· ἐν γάρ ἐστι τὸ βάπτισμα καὶ εἷς ὁ ἐγκαινισμός.

CHRYSOSTOM (*ad loc.*) τί οὖν; ἐκβέβληται ἡ μετάνοια; οὐχ ἡ μετάνοια· μὴ γένοιτο· ἀλλ' ὁ διὰ λουτροῦ πάλιν ἀνακαινισμός. οὐ γὰρ εἶπεν ἀδύνατον ἀνακαινισθῆναι εἰς μετάνοιαν καὶ ἐσίγησεν, ἀλλ' εἰπὼν 'ἀδύνατον' ἐπήγαγεν 'ἀνασταυροῦντας'...ὁ δὲ λέγει τοῦτό ἐστι· τὸ βάπτισμα σταυρός ἐστι· συνεσταυρώθη γὰρ ὁ παλαιὸς ἡμῶν ἄνθρωπος....

THEODORET: τῶν ἄγαν ἀδυνάτων, φησίν, τοὺς τῷ παναγίῳ προσεληλυ-θότας βαπτίσματι...αὖθις προσελθεῖν καὶ τυχεῖν ἑτέρου βαπτίσματος· τοῦτο γὰρ οὐδέν ἐστιν ἕτερον ἢ πάλιν τὸν υἱὸν τοῦ θεοῦ τῷ σταυρῷ προσηλῶσαι.

ŒCUMENIUS: τί οὖν; ἐξέβαλε τὴν μετάνοιαν; μὴ γένοιτο...ἀλλὰ τὴν διὰ βαπτίσματος μετάνοιαν...ὅθεν καὶ εἶπεν 'ἀνακαινίζειν' ὅπερ ἴδιον βαπτίσματος.

EUTHYMIUS ZIG.: τί οὖν; ἐκβέβληται ἡ μετάνοια; μὴ γένοιτο· εἰπὼν γὰρ 'εἰς μετάνοιαν' οὐκ ἔστη μέχρι τούτου ἀλλ' ἐπήγαγεν 'ἀνασταυροῦντας ἑαυτοῖς τὸν υἱὸν τοῦ θεοῦ,' διὰ μετανοίας, φησίν, ἀνασταυρούσης τὸν Χριστόν...τὸ [γὰρ] βάπτισμα σταυρός ἐστιν...ὥσπερ οὖν ἅπαξ ἀλλ' οὐ δεύτερον ἐσταυρώθη ὁ Χριστὸς οὕτως ἅπαξ ἀλλ' οὐ δεύτερον χρὴ βαπτίζεσθαι.

And among the Latin fathers:

AMBROSE (*de Pœnit.* ii. 3): De baptismate autem dictum verba ipsa declarant quibus significavit impossibile esse lapsos renovari in pœnitentiam, per lavacrum enim renovamur...eo spectat ut de baptismo dictum credamus in quo crucifigimus filium Dei in nobis....

Possum quidem etiam illud dicere ei qui hoc de pœnitentia dictum putat, quia quæ impossibilia sunt apud homines possibilia sunt apud Deum....

Sed tamen de baptismo dictum, ne quis iteret, vera ratio persuadet.

PRIMASIUS: Quid ergo? exclusa est pœnitentia post baptismum et venia delictorum? Absit. Duo siquidem genera sunt pœnitentiæ, unum quidem ante baptismum, quod et præparatio baptismi potest appellari... alterum autem genus pœnitentiæ quo post baptismum delentur peccata quam beatus Apostolus minime excludit.

This specific and outward interpretation of the words is foreign to the scope of the passage, and indeed to the thought of the apostolic age; but none the less it presents in a concrete shape the thought of the Apostle. It brings out plainly that there can be no repetition of the beginning.

The forces which in the order of divine providence are fitted to call out faith in the first instance, and to communicate life, are not fitted to recreate it when it has been lost. There can be no second spiritual birth. The powers which are entrusted to the Christian society are inadequate to deal with this last result of sin; but the power of God is not limited. Compare Additional Note on 1 John v. 16.

HERVEIUS (reading *renovari*) emphasises the moral impossibility from the human side with singular power and freshness : Non...Montani vel Novati hæresim hic approbamus qui contendunt non posse renovari per pœnitentiam eos qui crucifixere sibimet filium Dei. Sed ideo impossibile esse dicimus ut tales renoventur quia nolunt renovari. Nam si vellent, esset utique possibile. Quod ergo renovari nequeunt non est excusatio infirmitatis eorum sed culpa voluntatis ipsorum qui malunt veteres perdurare quam renovari...sicque fit ut ad pœnitentiam redire non valeant....Quales et in monasteriis hodie sunt nonnulli, habentes quidem speciem pietatis virtutem autem ejus abnegantes, et ideo pœnitentiam agere non possunt, quia de solo exteriori habitu gloriantur et sanctos se esse putant quia sanctitatis indumentum portant.

Additional Note on vi. 12 :   The Biblical idea of 'inheritance' (κληρονομία).

The group of words κληρονόμος (i. 2 ; vi. 17 ; xi. 7), κληρονομεῖν (i. 4, 14; vi. 12 ; xii. 17), and κληρονομία (xi. 8) is characteristic of the Epistle. The idea of 'inheritance' which they convey is in some important respects different from that which we associate with the word. This idea finds a clear expression in the LXX. from which it was naturally transferred to the N. T. *Use in the LXX. of κληρονομία.*

The word κληρονόμος is rare in the LXX. It occurs only in Jud. xviii. 7; 2 Sam. xiv. 7; Jer. viii. 10; Mic. i. 15 (Jer. xlix. 1 Symm.) as the rendering of יוֹרֵשׁ, and in Ecclus. xxiii. 22. *κληρονόμος.*

Κληρονομεῖν and κληρονομία are very frequent. The former word occurs about 140 times and 100 times as the rendering of יָרַשׁ, and 18 times as the rendering of נָחַל. *κληρονομεῖν and κληρονομία.*

The latter word occurs more than 180 times and about 145 times as the representative of נַחֲלָה and about 17 times as the rendering of derivatives of יָרַשׁ.

The fundamental passage which determines the idea is the promise to Abraham Gen. xv. 7, 8 δοῦναί σοι τὴν γῆν ταύτην κληρονομῆσαι (following on *κληρονομεῖν.* vv. 3, 4 κληρονομήσει με); xxii. 17 κληρονομήσει τὸ σπέρμα σου τὰς πόλεις τῶν ὑπεναντίων. Comp. xxiv. 60 ; xxviii. 4.

Hence the phrase κληρονομεῖν τὴν γῆν is used constantly of the occupation of Canaan by the Israelites : Lev. xx. 24 ὑμεῖς κληρονομήσετε τὴν γῆν αὐτῶν καὶ ἐγὼ δώσω ὑμῖν αὐτὴν ἐν κτήσει: Deut. iv. 1, 5, 14 &c.; xxx. 5 ; Jos. i. 15; Jud. xviii. 9 ; Neh. ix. 15, 22 ff.; Obad. 20 ; and that also with a distinct reference to the destruction of the nations in possession of it : Num. xxi. 35 ;

Deut. ii. 24, 31; ix. 1; xxxi. 3. The land belonged to the Lord and He gave it to Israel (Ps. civ. (cv.) 44). In the Psalms this 'inheritance of the land' assumes a spiritual colouring as the privilege of the righteous : Ps. xxiv. (xxv.) 13; xxxvi. (xxxvii.) 9, 11 (Matt. v. 5), &c.; and in the second part of Isaiah the idea finds its complete fulfilment in the Messianic age : Is. liv. 3; lvii. 13; lx. 21; lxi. 7 (ἐκ δευτέρας κλ. τ. γ.); lxiii. 18; lxv. 9.

The word κληρονομεῖν is used even where the absolute claim urged by violence is unjust: 1 K. xx. (xxi.) 15 ff. (comp. 2 K. xvii. 24; Ps. lxxxii. (lxxxiii.) 13; Is. xiv. 21; Ezek. [vii. 24; xxxiii. 25]); and also where it expresses a rightful mastery used for a necessary destruction (Hos. ix. 6; Ezek. xxxvi. 12; Zech. ix. 4).

In all these cases κληρονομεῖν answers to יָרַשׁ. As the rendering of נָחַל it is used of the possession of Canaan (Ex. xxiii. 30), of inheritance generally (Jud. xi. 2), and metaphorically (Ps. cxviii. (cxix.) 111; Prov. iii. 35; xiii. 22 ἀγαθὸς ἀνὴρ κληρονομήσει υἱοὺς υἱῶν).

Comp. Ecclus. iv. 13; vi. 1; x. 11; xix. 3; xx. 25; xxxvii. 26; 2 Macc. ii. 4.

κληρο-
νομία.
The senses of κληρονομία correspond with those of κληρονομεῖν. It is used for an allotted portion, a possession, an inheritance (Num. xxiv. 18; xxvii. 7; xxxvi. 2 ff.; Deut. iii. 20; Ps. ii. 8; cxxvi. (cxxvii.) 3 ἡ κληρονομία Κυρίου υἱοί). The land itself is 'a possession' of the Lord : Jer. ii. 7 (comp. iii. 19). Two particular uses of the word require to be noticed : God is the κληρονομία of His people, and His people are His κληρονομία. The former usage is rare. In a peculiar sense God is spoken of as the 'inheritance'—'portion'—of the Levites: Num. xviii. 20; Josh. xiii. 14; Ezek. xliv. 28; but the same privilege is extended also to Israel: Jer. x. 16; xxviii. (li.) 19. On the other hand the thought of Israel as the 'inheritance' —'portion'—of God extends throughout the Old Testament: Deut. xxxii. 9; 1 Sam. x. 2; xxvi. 19; 2 Sam. xiv. 16; xx. 19; xxi. 3; 1 K. viii. 51, 53; Ps. xxvii. (xxviii.) 9; xxxii. (xxxiii.) 12; lxxiii. (lxxiv.) 2 &c.; Is. xix. 25; xlvii. 6; lxiii. 17; Jer. xii. 7 ff.; Joel ii. 17; Mic. vii. 14.

In all these cases κληρονομία represents נַחֲלָה which is much less frequently rendered by κλῆρος and μέρις. In Deuteronomy however God is spoken of as the κλῆρος of Levi (x. 9); and Israel as the κλῆρος (c. ix. 29; xviii. 2) and μέρις (c. ix. 26) of God. Comp. Ecclus. xxiv. 12; xlv. 22 (?).

Biblical idea of 'in-heritance.'
From these examples it will appear that the dominant Biblical sense of 'inheritance' is the enjoyment by a rightful title of that which is not the fruit of personal exertion. The heir being what he is in relation to others enters upon a possession which corresponds with his position; but there is no necessary thought of succession to one who has passed away (yet see Matt. xxi. 38 and parallels; Lk. xii. 13). An inheritance, in other words, answers to a position of privilege and describes a blessing conferred with absolute validity; and an heir (κληρονόμος) is one who has authority to deal with, to administer, a portion, a possession (κλῆρος).

The principle that 'inheritance is by birth and not by gift' (Arist. Pol. v. 8) has a spiritual fulfilment. When God 'gives' an inheritance (Acts vii. 5; xx. 32) it is because those to whom it is given stand by His grace in that filial relation which in this sense carries the gift.

In the N. T. the words are commonly used in connexion with the blessing (1 Pet. iii. 9) which belongs to divine sonship, the spiritual correlative to the promise to Abraham (Rom. iv. 13 f.; viii. 17; Gal. iii. 18, 29; iv. 1, 7; comp. c. vi. 12, 17; xi. 8). The son of God as son enjoys that which answers to his new birth (comp. Matt. v. 5; Eph. i. 14, 18; Col. iii. 24). This is described as 'eternal life' (Matt. xix. 29; Tit. iii. 7; comp. Mk. x. 17; Lk. x. 25; xviii. 18), or 'the kingdom of God' (1 Cor. vi. 9 f.; xv. 50; Gal. v. 21; comp. Matt. xxv. 34; Eph. v. 5; James ii. 5), or 'salvation' (c. i. 14), 'an inheritance incorruptible' (1 Pet. i. 4; comp. 1 Cor. xv. 50), 'the eternal inheritance' (c. ix. 15). Under one aspect it is realised through conflict (Apoc. xxi. 7).

This ruling sense illustrates the use of the word in the other connexions in which it is found. Esau vainly sought to 'inherit the blessing' (c. xii. 17): he had lost the character to which it belonged. Noah in virtue of his faith 'became heir of the righteousness which is according to faith' (c. xi. 7): faith produced in him its proper fruit. The Son as Creator was naturally appointed 'heir of all things' (c. i. 2); and in virtue of His work 'He hath inherited' in His glorified humanity 'a name more excellent than angels' (c. i. 4).

VII. ¹Οὗτος γὰρ ὁ Μελχισεδέκ, βασιλεὺς Σαλήμ, ἱερεὺς τοῦ θεοῦ

1 ὁ (συναντ.) C*: ὃς (συναντ.) אABD₂ (appy. a primitive error).

III. THE CHARACTERISTICS OF CHRIST AS ABSOLUTE HIGH-PRIEST SHADOWED FORTH BY MELCHIZEDEK (c. vii.).

The last words of the sixth chapter offered a twofold thought, which the writer of the Epistle now works out in detail, going back, after the solemn digression of c. vi., to the subject announced in c. v. 10. The priestly office of Christ is after the order of Melchizedek (1); and after this order He is High-priest for ever (2).

The main object of the section is to shew that there were in the O. T. from the first indications of a higher order of Divine Service than that which was established by the Mosaic Law; and that these found a perfect realisation in Christ, *a Son, perfected for evermore.*

(1) *The office of Christ after the order of Melchizedek* (vii. 1—25).

In these verses no mention is made of the High-priesthood. The writer deals with the general conception of priesthood as exhibited in Scripture. He marks (*a*) the characteristics of Melchizedek (1—3); and then (*b*) determines the relation of Melchizedek to the Levitical priesthood (4—10); and lastly (*c*) compares the Levitical priesthood with that of Christ (11—25).

(*a*) Characteristics of Melchizedek (1—3).

The Apostle (*a*) notices the positive facts related of Melchizedek; the description of his person; of his meeting with Abraham; of Abraham's offering (1, 2*a*); and then (β) indicates the significance of his character from the interpretation of his titles, King of Righteousness, King of Peace, and from the features in his portraiture which can be deduced from the silence of Scripture (2*b*, 3).

¹ *For this Melchizedek, king of Salem, priest of God Most High, who*

met Abraham as he was returning from the slaughter of the kings and blessed him, ²*to whom also Abraham divided a tithe of all—being first by interpretation king of Righteousness and then also king of Salem, which is king of Peace,* ³*without father, without mother, without genealogy, having neither beginning of days nor end of life, but made like to the Son of God,—abideth a priest perpetually.*

1, 2*a*. The historical facts as to Melchizedek.

1. οὗτος γάρ] The particle is explanatory and not strictly argumentative. The writer purposes to lay open how much is included in the phrase κατὰ τάξιν Μελχισεδέκ, to which he has again returned.

The connexion is obvious if the sentence is at once completed: οὗτος (c. vi. 20) γὰρ M......μένει ἱερεὺς εἰς τὸ διηνεκές. Christ is spoken of as High-priest for ever after the order of Melchizedek, for Melchizedek offers a figure of such an abiding office, inasmuch as *he abides a priest* without successor. The antitype however goes beyond the type (ἀρχιερεύς, εἰς τὸν αἰῶνα, as compared with ἱερεύς, εἰς τὸ διηνεκές). See *Additional Note.*

βασιλεὺς Σαλήμ] שָׁלֵם, like שָׁלוֹם, is properly an adj. *sound, at peace,* but is used (as שָׁלוֹם) here as a subst., *peace.* (So Philo *Leg. Alleg.* iii. 25; i. p. 102 M.)

The locality of the place does not in any way enter into the writer's argument. The Jewish tradition of the Apostolic age appears to have identified it with Jerusalem (Jos. *Antt.* i. 10, 2; *B. J.* vi. 10; and so *Targ. Onk.*; comp. Ps. lxxvi. 2).

In the time of Jerome Salem was identified with Salem, near Scythopolis, where the remains of Melchizedek's palace were shewn.

τοῦ ἱψίστου, †ό† cγναντήςαc Ἀβραὰμ ὑποστρέφοντι ἀπὸ τῆς κοπῆς
τῶν Βαcιλέων καὶ εὐλογήςαc αὐτόν, ²ᾧ καὶ Δεκάτην ἀπὸ πάντων
ἐμέρισεν Ἀβραάμ, πρῶτον μὲν ἑρμηνευόμενος Βαcιλεὺς

1, 2 αὐτόν...Ἀβραάμ : D₂* αὐτὸν καὶ Ἀβραὰμ εὐλογηθεὶς ὑπ' αὐτοῦ ὁ (sic) καὶ δεκ.
πάντων ἐμ. [αὐτῷ?].
2 ἀπὸ πάντων ἐμέρισεν : ἐμέρισεν ἀπὸ πάντων ℵ.   πάντων : παντός B.   Ἀβρ.:
+πατριάρχης syr hl.

(ἱερεὺς) τοῦ θεοῦ τοῦ ὑψίστου] Gen.
xiv. 18 (עֶלְיוֹן אֵל), identified with Jehovah v. 22. The epithet does not mark
a relation to inferior deities, but the
absolute elevation of the Lord. It
occurs again Num. xxiv. 16 (Balaam);
Deut. xxxii. 8 (Song of Moses); and in
the Psalms. It is found also in
Phœnician inscriptions, and (with the
corresponding fem.) in the Pœnulus
of Plautus (v. I. 1 Alonim valunoth).
The title occurs elsewhere in the N. T.
Mk. v. 7 (‖ Lk. viii. 28); Acts xvi. 17.
Comp. Lk. i. 32, 35; Acts vii. 48.

It is to be remarked that there are
elsewhere traces of a primitive (monotheistic) worship of El in Phœnicia
side by side with that of Baal, the
centre of Phœnician polytheism.
Comp. Œhler, Theol. of O. T. i.
90 f. (Eng. Tr.).

ὁ συναντήσας...ὑποστρέφοντι]...who
met...as he was returning, Latt. qui
obviavit...regresso (Gen. xiv. 17, LXX.
μετὰ τὸ ὑποστρέψαι as in Hebr.).
The time was that of the fulness
of Abraham's disinterested victory.
Probably the pres. part. is chosen
to mark this thought, which is less
clear in the original phrase. Compare
Philo, θεασάμενος ἐπανιόντα καὶ τρο-
παιοφοροῦντα (de Abr. § 40).
In Gen. xiv. 17 f. it is said 'The
king of Sodom went out to meet him
...and Melchizedek, king of Salem,
brought forth bread and wine....'
Since the latter detail is omitted here,
the former, which is included in it, is
rightly applied to Melchizedek. For
συναντᾶν see Lk. ix. 37; xxii. 10;
Acts x. 25.

ἀπὸ τῆς κοπῆς] Gen. xiv. 17; Deut.

xxviii. 25; Josh. x. 20. Κοπή (not
elsewhere in N. T.) and the original
phrase (מַכָּבוֹת) may mean only 'the
smiting,' 'the defeat.'

εὐλογήσας] By the act of blessing,
Melchizedek at once assumed the
position of a superior. And Abraham
on his part freely acknowledged Melchizedek's implied claim to superiority,
and divided to him a tithe from all
the spoil which he had taken (v. 4).

2b, 3. The historical details as to
Melchizedek having been given, the
writer of the Epistle goes on to interpret the Scriptural narrative so far
as it affects the view of Melchizedek's
character and person absolutely. He
points out its bearing on his position
in relation to Abraham and the Levitical priests in the next section.

Melchizedek's typical character is
shewn to be indicated positively by
what is said of him, and negatively by
what is not said.

Thus three distinct features are noted
in which Melchizedek points to Christ.
(1) His name and title: King of Righteousness and King of Peace. (2) His
isolation from all priestly descent, as
holding his priesthood himself alone.
(3) The absence of all record of his
birth and death.

In other words the record of Melchizedek points to Christ in character,
in office, in person (nature).

The clauses are not simply in apposition with the subject but are predicative: 'Melchizedek...as being,
first by interpretation...as being presented to us...remaineth.'

2b. πρῶτον μέν...ἔπειτα δέ] being

Δικαιοσύνης ἔπειτα δὲ καὶ Βασιλεὺς Σαλήμ, ὅ ἐστιν Βασιλεὺς Εἰρήνης, ³ἀπάτωρ, ἀμήτωρ, ἀγενεαλόγητος, μήτε

δὲ καί: om. καί me.

first by the *interpretation* of his name King *of* Righteousness, *and then also* (by his dominion) King *of* Salem, *which is,* King *of Peace.* His personal name and the name of his city are taken to correspond with the actual traits of his character.

ἑρμηνευόμενος] The simple form (commonly μεθερμην.) occurs elsewhere in N. T. John i. 44 (43) (ὁ ἑρμην.); ix. 7.

βασιλεὺς δικαιοσύνης] Jos. B. J. vi. 10 Μελχ. ὁ τῇ πατρίᾳ γλώσσῃ κληθεὶς βασιλεὺς δίκαιος.

δικαιοσύνης...εἰρήνης] The order in which the words occur is significant. Righteousness must come first. Compare Rom. v. 1; xiv. 17; Ps. lxxii. 3 (Hebr.); lxxxv. 10; Is. xxxii. 17; James iii. 18; c. xii. 11. Both are characteristic of the Messianic times (Is.ix.1—7). The one aspect is given in Ps. xlv. 4 ff.: Jer. xxiii. 6; xxxiii. 15 f.; Dan. ix. 24; Mal. iv. 2; and the other in 1 Chron. xxii. 8 ff.; Mic. v. 5. Theodoret (and others) notice how both graces perfectly meet in Christ for the blessing of humanity: αὐτὸς γὰρ [ὁ χριστός] ἐστι κατὰ τὸν ἀπόστολον ἡ εἰρήνη ἡμῶν (Eph. ii. 14), αὐτὸς κέκληται κατὰ τὸν προφήτην δικαιοσύνη ἡμῶν (Jer. xxiii. 6).

Compare Bernard, Serm. de div. xix. 4, Tu, homo, noli prius rapere quod tuum est, et justitiam quam Deo et pacem quam proximo debes contemnere (the reference is to Rom. xiv. 17).

The genitive in each case (βασ. δικ., βασ. εἰρ.) expresses the characteristic of the sovereign: he is a 'righteousness-king,' a 'peace-king,' one in whom and through whom righteousness and peace are realised. Compare Jer. xxxiii. 15; Is. ix. 6.

ἔπειτα δέ...] The personal character

of the priest-king leads to the notice (ἔπειτα δὲ καί) of the kingdom which he administered: being righteous in himself he kept peace under his sway.

ὅ ἐστιν] Mk. vii. 34; and with μεθερμηνευόμενον Mk. v. 41; xv. 22, 34. Comp. Lk. xii. 1; Gal. iv. 24 f.

There is no exact parallel in Scripture to this kind of use of names, which is common in Philo (comp. Siegfried, ss. 190 ff.). The nearest approach to it is perhaps in John ix. 7 Σιλωάμ (ὁ ἑρμηνεύεται Ἀπεσταλμένος). But the importance attached to names in the O. T. sufficiently explains it. Comp. Is. viii. 1, 18; ix. 6. Œhler, *O. T. Theology,* § 88.

3. The delineation of Melchizedek is expressive also negatively. The silence of Scripture, the characteristic form, that is, in which the narrative is presented, is treated as having a prophetic force. Melchizedek stands unique and isolated both in his person and in his history. He is not connected with any known line: his life has no recorded beginning or close.

Philo not unfrequently draws arguments from omissions in the Biblical narrative. Examples are given by Siegfried, *Philo von Alexandrien,* 179 : *e.g. Quod det. pot. insid.* § 48 (i. 224 M.).

ἀπ. ἀμ. ἀγεν.] Vulg. *sine patre, sine matre, sine genealogia.* The Pesh. renders these words by a paraphrase : 'whose father and mother are not written in genealogies.'

The words (ἀπάτωρ, ἀμήτωρ) were used constantly in Greek mythology (*e.g.* of Athene and Hephæstus); and so passed into the loftier conceptions of the Deity, as in that of Trismegistus quoted by Lactantius (iv. 13): ipse

ἀρχὴν ἡμερῶν μήτε ζωῆς τέλος ἔχων, ἀφωμοιωμένος δὲ

enim pater Deus et origo et princi-
pium rerum quoniam parentibus caret
ἀπάτωρ atque ἀμήτωρ a Trismegisto
verissime nominatur, quod ex nullo sit
procreatus. This familiar usage was
suited to suggest to the readers of
the Epistle the nature of the divine
priest shadowed out in the type. The
word ἀμήτωρ is used by Philo of Sarah,
De ebriet. § 14 (i. 365 M.); and in
Euripides Ion speaks of himself as
ἀμήτωρ ἀπάτωρ τε γεγώς (*Ion* 109).
Philo in a striking passage (*De
Prof.* § 20; i. 562 M.) describes the
Levites as being in some sense 'exiles
who to do God's pleasure had left
parents and children and brethren and
all their mortal kindred': ὁ γοῦν ἀρχη-
γέτης τοῦ θιάσου τούτου, he continues,
λέγων εἰσάγεται τῷ πατρὶ καὶ τῇ μητρί
Οὐχ ἑώρακα ὑμᾶς καὶ τοὺς ἀδελφοὺς οὐ
γινώσκω καὶ τοῖς υἱοῖς ἀπογινώσκω
ὑπὲρ τοῦ δίχα μεθολκῆς θεραπεύειν τὸ
ὄν. The words throw light on Lk.
xiv. 26.

In the case of the Jewish priests
a Levitical (Aaronic, Num. xvi. xvii.)
descent was required on the father's
side, an Israelitish, on the mother's.
(Comp. Ezra ii. 61 f.)

ἀγενεαλόγητος] *without genealogy,*
without any recorded line of ancestors.
He did not trace back his claims to
the priesthood to any forefather (comp.
v. 6). Perhaps the word (which is not
found elsewhere) suggests, though it
does not express, the thought that he
had no known descendants, and was
not the author of a priestly line.
Compare: Subito introducitur sicut
et Elias (Primas.).

μήτε ἀρχ. ἡμ. μήτε ζ. τ. ἔχων] Scripture records nothing of his birth or of
his death, of the beginning of a life of
manifold activity (ἀρ. ἡμερῶν, comp.
v. 7), nor of the close of his earthly
existence. Nothing in the phrase
indicates a miraculous translation or
the like. The silence may perhaps
seem to be more significant, since the

death of Aaron is described in detail:
Num. xx. 22 ff.

ἀφωμοιωμένος τ. υἱ. τ. θ.] Non dicitur
Filius Dei assimilatus Melchisedeko,
sed contra, nam Filius Dei est anti-
quior et archetypus (Bengel). So Theodoret : ἐκεῖνος τούτου τύπος, οὗτος δὲ
τοῦ τύπου ἡ ἀλήθεια. The truth is of
general application. The physical,
the historical, is the limited representation of the spiritual, the eternal.
    The choice of the participle in
place of ὅμοιος shews that the resemblance lies in the Biblical representation and not primarily in Melchizedek
himself. The comparison is not between Christ and Melchizedek, but
between Christ and the isolated portraiture of Melchizedek; and that in
regard to the divine Nature of the
Incarnate Son (τῷ υἱῷ τοῦ θεοῦ), and
not to His human Nature in which He
both was born and died, nor even to His
official dignity (τῷ χριστῷ). It is not
however implied that the record in
Genesis was purposely designed to
convey the meaning which is found in
it, but that the history sketched by
prophetic power has the meaning.
    Perhaps the remarkable variation
in the language, which cannot be
mere rhetorical ornament (μήτε ἀρχ.
ἡμ. μήτε ζωῆς τέλος, not μήτε ἀρχὴν μήτε
τέλος ζωῆς), may point to the fact that
the Son of God was (in His Divine
Nature) beyond time, while the human
life which He assumed was to be
without end. Compare Theophlct:
ὁ χριστὸς...ἅτε θεὸς...ἄναρχος κατὰ τὴν
τοῦ χρόνου ἀρχὴν εἰ καὶ τὸν πατέρα ἔχει
ἀρχὴν καὶ αἴτιον.

ἀφωμ.] Latt. *assimilatus* (*similatus*)
made like to. The word, which is
found in the best authors, does not
occur elsewhere in N. T. *Ep. Jerem.*
4, 62, 70.

On the likeness Primasius remarks
(following Chrysostom): In hoc est
similitudo quod nec illius (Melch.)
nec istius (Christi) initium legitur vel

τῷ υἱῷ τοῦ θεοῦ, μένει ἱερεὺς εἰς τὸ διηνεκές.   ⁴ Θεω-

finis : illius quia non est scriptum ;
istius autem quia omnino non est.

τῷ υἱῷ τοῦ θεοῦ] The choice of this
name here emphasises that aspect of
the Lord's person which was typified
by the absence of all notice of the
birth or death of Melchizedek. See
iv. 14; vi. 6; x. 29.

μένει ἱερεὺς εἰς τὸ διηνεκές] remaineth a priest perpetually, Latt.
manet sacerdos in perpetuum. The
use of the phrase εἰς τὸ διην. for εἰς τὸν
αἰῶνα marks his priesthood as continued to the end in his person without break. He had no successors
(so Theodoret rightly explains the
words: ἐπειδήπερ τὴν ἱερωσύνην οὐ παρ-
έπεμψεν εἰς παῖδας), and no provision
for a successor to him is recorded in
Scripture. He therefore abides a
priest 'perpetually,' 'for ever,' not
literally but in the Scriptural portraiture. This is one of the points in
which 'he was made like to the Son
of God.'

The idea that the perpetuity of his
priesthood lay in the fact that it was
continued in Christ (manet...non in se
sed in Christo. Primas.) destroys the
parallel; and the structure of the
whole paragraph absolutely forbids
the application of this clause to any
other than the Melchizedek of the
record in Genesis.

εἰς τὸ διην.] See c. x. 1 note. The
phrase does not describe absolute perpetuity, duration without end, but
duration continued under the conditions implied or expressed in the particular case. Thus it is said App. B. C.
i. § 4, δικτάτωρ εἰς τὸ διηνεκὲς ᾑρέθη.
Cf. Pun. viii. § 136. Heliodor. Æth.
i. § 14 φυγῇ εἰς τὸ διηνεκὲς ἐζημίωσαν.
Here no limit is marked negatively or
positively, and the phrase simply excludes interruption in Melchizedek's
tenure of his office. No one takes it
from him (comp. v. 8). Such a condition is equally satisfied by his actual
continuance for ever, a supposition

excluded by the circumstances; or by
the typical interpretation of the silence
of the record.

(b) The relation of Melchizedek to
the Levitical priesthood (4—10).

Having discussed the historical notice of Melchizedek in itself, the writer
goes on to consider his priesthood in
relation to that of the Law. In doing
this he first notices

(a) the general position of Melchizedek (4); and then gives in detail his
points of superiority

(β) in respect of Abraham, whom
he both tithed (5, 6a), and blessed
(6b, 7); and

(γ) in respect of the Levitical
priests, who exercised their functions
as dying men (8), and in Levi their
head implicitly paid tithes to Melchizedek (9, 10).

⁴ Now consider how great this man
was to whom Abraham gave a tithe
taken out of the chief spoils, Abraham
the patriarch. ⁵ And while those (the
priests) sprung from the sons of Levi,
on receiving the priest's office, have
commandment to take tithes from the
people according to the Law, that is
from their brethren, though they have
come out of the loins of Abraham, ⁶ he
whose genealogy is not counted from
them tithed Abraham, and blessed him
that hath the promises. ⁷ But without any gainsaying the less is blessed
by the greater. ⁸ And while here
dying men receive tithes, there one of
whom it is witnessed that he liveth.
⁹ And, so to say, through Abraham,
Levi also who receiveth tithes is
tithed ; ¹⁰ for he was yet in the loins
of his father when Melchizedek met
him.

4. The general superiority of Melchizedek over Abraham, the great
father of Israel, is stated summarily.
The artificial order of the words emphasises the idea which they convey,
the last phrases taking up in a more
striking form what has been said

ρεῖτε δὲ πηλίκος οὗτος ᾧ ^τ ΔΕΚΆΤΗΝ 'ΑΒΡΑΆΜ ἔΔωΚΕΝ ἐκ τῶν
ἀκροθινίων ὁ πατριάρχης.   ⁵καὶ οἱ μὲν ἐκ τῶν υἱῶν Λευεὶ

4 καὶ

4 πηλ. οὗτος : ἡλίκος D₂*.   δεκάτην BD₂* syr vg me :+καί' δεκ. ৬ℵAC vg syr hl.
'Αβρ. ἔδ.: ἔδ. 'Αβρ. A syr hl.

before (δεκάτην 'Αβραάμ...ἐκ τῶν ἀκροθινίων, ὁ πατριάρχης).

It is assumed throughout that the
receiver of tithe is greater than the
giver of tithe : in the case of the less
familiar blessing this superiority is
affirmed (v. 7).

θεωρεῖτε δέ] Now consider...Vulg.
intuemini (O.L. videtis, videte) autem.
The structure of the whole passage
shews that the verb is an imperative
and not an indicative. The word itself,
which expresses the regard of attentive contemplation, is frequent in the
historical books of the N.T. but is not
found elsewhere in the Epistles except
1 John iii. 17. The particle δέ marks
a fresh beginning. The general picture claims detailed study.   Comp.
viii. 1 ; xi. 1.

δεκάτην...ἔδωκεν] The offering appears as the spontaneous recognition
of the dignity of Melchizedek.

ἐκ τῶν ἀκροθ.] Vulg. de præcipuis.
O. L. de primitivis (primitiis)...,
Syr. the tithes and firstfruits. The
tithe was of the whole (ἀπὸ πάντων
v. 2), and it was taken from the
choicest of the spoil. The ἀκροθίνια
were specially the part of the spoil
which was offered as a thank-offering
to the gods : Herod. viii. 121 f.

πηλίκος] Latt. quantus (Aug. qua-
lis). The word is used properly of
magnitude in dimension : Gal. vi. 11 ;
Zech. ii. 2 (6) (LXX.). Comp. 4 Macc.
xv. 21 πηλίκαις καὶ πόσαις βασάνοις.

'Consider how great was this priest-
king, to whom...' The οὗτος looks
back to vv. 1—4; and the greatness of
Melchizedek is not first inferred from
Abraham's gift.

ὁ πατριάρχης] Abraham...Abraham
the patriarch. The title of honour
stands emphatically at the end of the

sentence. It is used again Acts ii. 29
(of David) and Acts vii. 8 f. (of the sons
of Jacob) and several times in the
Books of Chronicles of 'the chiefs of
the fathers' (1 Chron. ix. 9 Compl. ;
xxiv. 31, &c.) and 'captains' (2 Chron.
xxiii. 20), but not elsewhere in LXX.
The first thought is of Abraham as
the father of Israel ; but beyond this
he is the father of the whole family of
faith : Rom. iv. 11 f.

Quasi diceret, Quem vos excellen-
tiorem omnibus hominibus æstimatis,
hic decimas obtulit Melchisedech qui
in figura Christi præcessit (Primas.).

5, 6a. This is the first of the special
marks of superiority by which the
priesthood of Melchizedek was distinguished. The Levitical priests
tithed their brethren : Melchizedek, a
priest of another race, tithed Abraham
their common father. His priesthood
was absolute and not a priority in the
same family.

5. καὶ οἱ μὲν ἐκ τ. υἱ. Λ....λαμβ.]
'And to come to particulars (vv. 8, 9),
while the descendants of Levi on receiving (or, as receiving) the priesthood...' The phrase is capable of several interpretations. The whole may
form a compound subject, 'they ἐκ τῶν
υἱ. Λ. that receive the priest's office';
or the second part may be predicative, 'they ἐκ τῶν υἱ. Λ., as (on) receiving the priest's office.' And again,
the preposition ἐκ may be derivative ('those who traced their descent
from'), or partitive ('those from a-
mong'). The parallel clause ὁ μὴ ἐξ
αὐτῶν γεν. appears to be decisive in
favour of the 'derivative' sense of ἐκ,
and to favour the predicative interpretations of ἱερατ. λαμβ.

At the same time the description of
the priests as descended 'from the

τὴν ἱερατίαν λαμβάνοντες ἐντολὴν ἔχουσιν ἀποδεκατοῖν
τὸν λαὸν κατὰ τὸν νόμον, τοῦτ᾽ ἔστιν τοὺς ἀδελφοὺς
αὐτῶν, καίπερ ἐξεληλυθότας ἐκ τῆς ὀσφύος Ἀβραάμ·

5 ἀποδεκατοῖν BD₂*: -τοῦν 5⁸AC.   ὀσφρύος D₂*.

sons of Levi' and not 'from Levi' or 'from Aaron' is remarkable. By the use of this phrase the writer probably wishes to carry back the thought of the Mosaic priesthood to its fundamental idea. Levi and his descendants represented the dedication of Israel to God with all the consequent duties and privileges which were afterwards concentrated in priests and High-priest. Thus the phrase will mean 'those who tracing their descent from a dedicated tribe witnessed to the original destiny of Israel.'

The same thought appears to underlie the titles characteristic of Deuteronomy 'the priests, the Levites' (xvii. 9, 18; xviii. 1; xxiv. 8; xxvii. 9), 'the priests, the sons of Levi' (xxi. 5; xxxi. 9). Comp. Josh. iii. 3; viii. 33.

τὴν ἱερ. λαμβ.] Vulg. *sacerdotium accipientes*. This phrase (as distinct from ἱερατεύοντες) brings out the thought that the office was specifically committed to them. It was of appointment and not by nature. Comp. Ecclus. xlv. 7.

Ἱερατία (-εία) occurs in N.T. only here and in Luke i. 9. In relation to ἱερωσύνη (c. vii. 11 n., 12, 24) it expresses the actual service of the priest and not the office of priesthood. The tithes were given to the 'children of Levi' 'for their service,' Num. xviii. 21. Comp. Ecclus. xlv. 7, 20: ἱερατείειν, Luke i. 8 ('to perform the priest's office'), ἱεράτευμα, 1 Pet. ii. 5, 9 ('a body of ministering priests').

ἐντ. ἔχουσιν] In this case the claim to the tithe rested on a specific ordinance (κατὰ τὸν νόμον). Abraham spontaneously recognised Melchizedek's claim.

ἀποδεκατοῖν τὸν λ.] The Levites tithed the people (Num. xviii. 21 ff.) and

paid a tithe of this tithe to the priests (*id. vv.* 26 ff.). The priests can thus be said to tithe the people as claiming the tithe of the whole offering (comp. Tob. i. 7 ff.). They represented the right in its highest form, just as they represented in its highest form the conception of a body consecrated to the divine service.

The word ἀποδεκατόω (δεκατόω), which seems to be confined to Biblical and ecclesiastical writers, is used both of

(1) The person claiming the tithe from another (ἀποδεκ. τινα). 1 Sam. viii. 15, 17; Neh. x. 37; and of

(2) The person paying the tithe (ἀποδ. τι). Gen. xxviii. 22; Deut. xiv. 21; xxvi. 12; Matt. xxiii. 23; Luke xi. 42.

Ἀποδεκατεύω is found Lk. xviii. 12. Δεκατεύω is a classical word.

The peculiar form ἀποδεκατοῖν, which is given by BD₂*, is supported by κατασκηνοῖν Matt. xiii. 32; Mk. iv. 32; φιμοῖν 1 Pet. ii. 15; and similar forms which occur in inscriptions *e.g.* στεφανοῖν, ζηλοῖν.

This form, it may be observed, goes to confirm the writing ι *subscr.* in the contracted infinitives ἀγαπᾶν &c. ζῆν.

κατὰ τὸν νόμον] The right which the Levitical priests exercised was in virtue of a special injunction. They had no claim beyond that which the Law gave them.

τοὺς ἀδελφοὺς...καίπερ ἐξεληλυθότας ...] The priesthood gave a real preeminence, but still it did not alter the essential relationship of all Abraham's descendants. Nor did its claims extend beyond them. We might have expected naturally that the right of tithing (like the privilege of blessing) would have been exercised only by one

⁶ὁ δὲ μὴ γενεαλογούμενος ἐξ αὐτῶν δεδεκάτωκεν Ἀβραάμ, καὶ τὸν ἔχοντα τὰς ἐπαγγελίας εὐλόγηκεν. ⁷χωρὶς δὲ πάσης ἀντιλογίας τὸ ἔλαττον ὑπὸ τοῦ κρείττονος εὐλογεῖται. ⁸καὶ ὧδε μὲν δεκάτΑϹ ἀποθνήσκοντες ἄνθρωποι

6 ᾽Αβρ. ℵBCD₂*: +τὸν' ᾽Αβρ. ϚA.   εὐλόγηκεν ℵB, ηὐλόγηκεν D₂*: εὐλόγησεν C, ηὐλόγησεν A.

superior by birth. Here however the office itself established a difference among brethren. Thus the two clauses taken together indicate the dignity of the Levitical priesthood, and at the same time the narrow limits within which the exercise of its power was confined. This priesthood rested upon a definite and limited institution. For ἐκ τῆς ὀσφύος see Gen. xxxv. 11 (LXX.).

6. ὁ δὲ μὴ γενεαλ. ἐξ αὐ.] *he whose genealogy is not counted from them*, i.e. the sons of Levi (v. 5). Vulg. *cujus autem generatio non adnumeratur in eis;* O.L. *qui autem non enumeratur de his.* The claim of Melchizedek to the priesthood rested on no descent but on his inherent personal title.

Ἡρμήνευσε δὲ καὶ τὸ ἀγενεαλόγητος. ἐξ αὐτῶν γὰρ εἶπε τὸν Μελχισεδὲκ μὴ γενεαλογεῖσθαι. δῆλον τοίνυν ὡς ἐκεῖνος οὐκ ἀληθῶς ἀγενεαλόγητος ἀλλὰ κατὰ τύπον (Thdt.).

δεδεκάτωκεν...εὐλόγηκεν] *v.* 9 δεδεκάτωται. The fact is regarded as permanent in its abiding consequences. It stands written in Scripture as having a present force.

The use of the perfect in the Epistle is worthy of careful study. In every case its full force can be felt.

i. 4 κεκληρονόμηκεν.
— 13 εἴρηκεν, iv. 4.
ii. 14 κεκοινώνηκεν...μετέσχεν.
iii. 3 ἠξίωται.
— 14 γεγόναμεν.
iv. 2 ἐσμεν εὐηγγελισμένοι.
—14, 15 διεληλυθότα...πεπειρασμένον.
vii. 3 ἀφωμοιωμένος.
— 13 μετέσχηκεν.

vii. 14 ἀνατέταλκεν.
viii. 5 κεχρημάτισται.
— 6 τέτυχεν.
     νενομοθέτηται.
ix. 18 ἐνκεκαίνισται.
— 26 πεφανέρωται.
x. 14 τετελείωκεν.
xi. 5 μεμαρτύρηται.
— 17 προσενήνοχεν, *note.*
— 28 πεποίηκεν.
xii. 2 κεκάθικεν.
— 3 ὑπομεμενηκότα, *note.*
καὶ...εὐλόγηκεν...] Melchizedek received tithes: he gave a blessing. This exercise of the privilege of a superior is a second mark of preeminence; and he exercised it towards one who as *having the promises* might have seemed to be raised above the acceptance of any human blessing.

7. χωρὶς δὲ π. ἀντ....] *But without any gainsaying...* Vulg. *Sine ulla autem contradictione* (O. L. *controversia*).

τὸ ἐλ....τοῦ κρ....] The abstract form offers the principle in its widest application. Comp. xii. 13.

8—10. Melchizedek was superior to Abraham: he was superior also to the Levitical priests generally. This is shewn both by the nature of the priests themselves (*v.* 8); and by the position which the common ancestor occupied towards Abraham (9, 10).

8. καὶ ὧδε μέν...ἐκεῖ δέ...] *And, further, while here,* in this system which we see,...*there,* in that remote and solitary example...

The ὧδε refers to that Levitical priesthood which was nearer to the writer's experience than Melchizedek, though the latter is the immediately

λαμβάνουσιν, ἐκεῖ δὲ μαρτυρούμενος ὅτι ζῇ. ⁹καὶ ὡς
ἔπος εἰπεῖν, δι' Ἀβραὰμ καὶ Λευεὶς ὁ δεκάτας λαμβάνων
δεδεκάτωται, ¹⁰ἔτι γὰρ ἐν τῇ ὀσφύϊ τοῦ πατρὸς ἦν ὅτε

9 εἰπεῖν : εἶπεν C*D₂*.   Λευείς ℵ°BC*, Λευίς A: Λευεί ℵ*D₂*, Λευί ϛ.

preceding subject. So οὗτος is used: e.g. Acts iv. 11.

Under the Mosaic Law *dying men* (ἀποθνήσκοντες ἄνθρωποι), men who were not only liable to death, mortal, but men who were actually seen to die from generation to generation enjoyed the rights of priests. For such an order there is not only the contingency but the fact of succession. While Melchizedek was *one to whom witness is borne that he liveth.* (Euth. Zig. μαρτυρούμενος δὲ διὰ τοῦ σεσιγῆσθαι τὴν τελευτὴν αὐτοῦ.) The writer recurring to the exact form of the record in Genesis, on which he has dwelt before (*v.* 3), emphasises the fact that Melchizedek appears there simply in the power of life. So far he does not die ; the witness of Scripture is to his living. What he does is in virtue of what he is.

With μαρτυρούμενος ὅτι (Latt. *ibi autem contestatur quia...*Aug. *qui testificatur se vivere*) compare c. xi. 4 (ἐμαρτ. εἶναι δίκ.) ; *id.* 5 (μεμαρτ. εὐαρεστηκέναι). Philo, *Leg. Alleg.* iii. § 81 (i. 132 M.), Μωυσῆς ἄρχει μαρτυρούμενος ὅτι ἐστὶ πιστὸς ὅλῳ τῷ οἴκῳ.

δεκάτας] The plural is used here and *v.* 9, as distinguished from the singular in *vv.* 2, 4, to express the repeated and manifold tithings under the Mosaic system ; or perhaps the many objects which were tithed. The former interpretation is the more likely because in *vv.* 2, 4, the reference is to one special act.

9, 10. It might be said by a Jewish opponent : But Abraham was not a priest : the priesthood, with its peculiar prerogatives, was not instituted in his time. Τί πρὸς τοὺς ἱερέας ἡμῶν εἰ Ἀβραὰμ δεκάτην ἔδωκεν ; (Chrys.).

The answer is that Abraham included in himself, as the depositary of the divine promise and the divine blessing, all the forms, as yet undifferentiated, in which they were to be embodied.

9. καὶ... δι' Ἀβραάμ... δεδεκάτωται] *And through Abraham*, as the representative of the whole Jewish people, *Levi also...is tithed.* Vulg. *Et...per* (August. *propter) Abraham et Levi ...decimatus est.* The descendants of Abraham were included in him, not only as he was their forefather physically, but also because he was the recipient of the divine promises in which the fulness of the race in its manifold developments was included. And Levi includes his descendants in his own person just as he was himself included in Abraham.

It must be observed that Levi is not represented as sharing in the act (δεκάτην ἔδωκεν), but in the consequences of the act passively (δεδεκάτωται, Latt. *decimatus est*). The act of his father determined his relation to Melchizedek, just as if Abraham had made himself Melchizedek's vassal.

ὡς ἔπος εἰπεῖν] Vulg. *ut ita dictum sit.* V. L. *quemadmodum dicam* (Aug. *sicut oportet dicere*).

This classical phrase does not occur elsewhere in the N.T. or in LXX., but is found in Philo (*e.g. De plant. Noæ* i. 353 M.). It serves to introduce a statement which may startle a reader, and which requires to be guarded from misinterpretation.

10. ἔτι γὰρ ἐν τῇ ὀσφύϊ...] Comp. *v.* 5 ἐξελ. ἐκ τῆς ὀσφ. The repetition of the phrase, which occurs again in the N.T. only in Acts ii. 30, empha-

sises the idea of the real unity of Abraham's race in the conditions of their earthly existence. By this teaching a mystery is indicated to us into which we can see but a little way, a final antithesis in our being ; we feel at every turn that we are dependent on the past, and that the future will depend in a large degree upon ourselves. This is one aspect of life, and it is not overlooked in Scripture. At the same time it does not give a complete view of our position. On the one side our outward life is conditioned by our ancestry: on the other side we stand in virtue of our 'spirit' in immediate, personal connexion with God (c. xii. 9). Each man is at once an individual of a race and a new power in the evolution of the race. He is *born* (Traducianism), and also he is *created* (Creationism). Comp. Martensen *Dogm.* § 74. Additional Note on iv. 12.

τοῦ πατρός] The context in the absence of further definition, requires the sense 'his father' (not 'our father'). Abraham, who was the father of all Israel (Luke i. 73; John viii. 53, 56; Acts vii. 2; James ii. 21; Rom. iv. 1, 12, ὁ πατὴρ ἡμῶν), can be spoken of also as the father of Levi in particular, through Isaac and Jacob.

(c) The Levitical priesthood and the priesthood of Christ (11—25).

Having interpreted the type of an absolute priesthood, independent of descent and uninterrupted by death (*v.* 3) offered in the record of Melchizedek, and having pointed out the thoughts to which that history might guide a student of the O.T., in respect of the later priesthood of the Law, the writer goes on to consider in detail the characteristics of the Levitical priesthood and of the Law which it essentially represented in relation to the Priesthood of Christ. The Levitical priesthood (generally) was incapable of effecting that at which a priesthood aims, the 'perfecting' of the worshipper ; an end which the

Priesthood of Christ is fitted to secure. This is established by the fact that the Levitical priesthood was,

(a) Transitory : a new Priesthood was promised (11—14); and

(β) Temporal, as contrasted with that which is eternal, universal (15—19).

While on the other hand the new Priesthood is

(a) Immutable : confirmed by an oath (20—22); and

(β) Uninterrupted : embodied for ever in the One Priest (23—25).

Briefly, if we regard the argument in its bearing on the Gospel, the notes of Christ's Priesthood after the order of Melchizedek are that it is : (1) New, (2) effective, (3) sure, (4) one.

The argument turns mainly upon the nature of the Levitical priesthood, but the Law is involved in the Priesthood. The abrogation of the one carries with it the abrogation of the other. If the Hebrews came to feel that Christ had superseded the priests of the Old Covenant, they would soon learn that the whole Law had passed away.

Throughout it is implied that if Melchizedek was greater than Levi, then *a fortiori* Christ was, of Whom Melchizedek was a partial type.

¹¹ Now if there had been a bringing to perfection through the Levitical priesthood, for under it the people hath received the Law, what further need would there have been that another priest should arise after the order of Melchizedek and be styled not after the order of Aaron? ¹² For when the priesthood is changed, there is made also of necessity a change of law. ¹³ For He of whom these things are said belongeth to another tribe, from which no man hath given attendance at the altar. ¹⁴ For it is evident that our Lord hath risen out of Judah, as to which tribe Moses spake nothing of priests. ¹⁵ And what we say is yet more abundantly evident if after the likeness of Melchizedek

ϹΥΝΉΝΤΗϹΕΝ ΑΫ́Τῷ ΜΕΛΧΙϹΕΔΈΚ.   ¹¹ Εἰ μὲν οὖν τελείωσις

10 Μελχ. ℵBC*D₂*: +ὁ' Μελχ. ϛΑ.   11 εἰ: ἦ C.

there ariseth another priest, ¹⁶who hath been made not after the law of a carnal commandment but after the power of an indissoluble life; ¹⁷for it is witnessed of Him,

Thou art a priest for ever,
After the order of Melchizedek.

¹⁸ For there is a disannulling of a foregoing commandment, because of its weakness and unprofitableness— ¹⁹for the Law made nothing perfect— and a bringing in thereupon of a better hope, through which we draw nigh to God. ²⁰ And inasmuch as He hath not received His office without the taking of an oath—²¹for while they (the Levitical priests) have been made priests without any taking of an oath, He was made with taking of an oath, through Him that saith to Him,

The Lord sware and will not repent Himself,
Thou art a priest for ever—

²² by so much also hath Jesus become surety of a better covenant. ²³ And while they have been made priests many in number, because they are hindered by death from abiding with men, ²⁴He, because He abideth for ever, hath His priesthood inviolable. ²⁵ Whence also He is able to save to the uttermost them that come unto God through Him, seeing He ever liveth to make intercession for them.

11—14. The Levitical priesthood and the Law, which it represented, were alike transitional and transitory.

It is assumed that the object of the Law was to bring or to prepare for bringing the people to 'perfection': divine legislation can have no other end. The priesthood, on which the Law rested, embodied its ruling idea. And conversely in the Law as a complete system we can see the aim of the priesthood. The priesthood

therefore was designed to assist in bringing about this 'perfection.'

If then there had been a bringing to perfection through the Levitical priesthood—if in other words there had been a bringing to perfection through the Law—there would have been no need of another priesthood. If on the other hand the whole Law failed to accomplish that to which it pointed, then so far also the priesthood failed. Such a failure, not a failure but the fulfilment of the divine purpose, was indicated by the promise of another priesthood in a new line.

11. εἰ μὲν οὖν...ἦν...τίς ἔτι χρεία... λέγεσθαι;] Now if there had been a bringing to perfection...what further need would there have been...? Vulg. Si ergo consummatio...erat...quid adhuc necessarium...? The argument starts from the line of thought just laid down. Before the Levitical priesthood was organised another type of priesthood had been foreshewn. But if the utmost object of a priesthood—of a divine provision for man's progress to his true goal—had been capable of attainment under the Mosaic order, what need would there have been that another priest should arise and that this new priest should be styled after a different order? Experience however proved its necessity. The Levitical priesthood was, and was proved to be, only provisional. It could not effect that to which it pointed. This conviction was expressed by the Psalmist when he recalled the earlier type.

The conditional form (εἰ...ἦν...τίς ἔτι χρεία...;) may be rendered either 'if there had been (which was not the case) what further need would there have been (as in fact there was)?' or 'if there were (as is not the case) what further need would there be (as there

διὰ τῆς Λευειτικῆς ἱερωσύνης ἦν, ὁ λαὸς γὰρ ἐπ᾽ αὐτῆς
νενομοθέτηται, τίς ἔτι χρεία κατὰ τὴν τάξιν Μελχισεδὲκ
ἕτερον ἀνίστασθαι ἱερέα καὶ οὐ κατὰ τὴν τάξιν ᾽Ααρὼν
λέγεσθαι; ¹²μετατιθεμένης γὰρ τῆς ἱερωσύνης ἐξ ἀνάγκης

om. ἦν B.   ἐπ᾽ αὐτῆς ℵABCD₂*: ἐπ᾽ αὐτῇ ϛ.   νενομοθέτηται : -τητο ϛ.
τίς + γάρ D₂*.

is) ?' The former suits the context
best. Comp. c. iv. 8 Additional Note.
For the use of μὲν οὖν without any
δέ afterwards, see c. viii. 4; Acts i. 6;
ii. 41; xiii. 4; 1 Cor. vi. 4, 7; Phil.
iii. 8.

διὰ τῆς Λευειτικῆς ἱερ.] The word
Λευειτικός appears to have been formed
by the writer. It is not found in the
LXX., nor is it quoted from Josephus,
Philo or the Apostolic fathers. The
use of this title (as distinguished from
'Aaronic': κατὰ τὴν τάξιν ᾽Ααρών) illustrates the desire of the writer to
regard the priesthood as the concen-
tration (so to speak) of the hallowing
of the tribe (v. 5 note).

The word ἱερωσύνη occurs in the
N.T. only in this chapter (vv. 12, 24
[14 ἱερέων]). It is rare in the LXX.,
and found there only in the later
books. As distinguished from ἱερατία
(-εία) (v. 5 note) it expresses the abstract notion of the priestly office, as
distinguished from the priestly service.
The words are not distinguished in
the Versions.

ὁ λαὸς γάρ...νενομοθ.] Vulg. populus
enim sub ipso...legem accepit. The
efficacy of the Law may justly be
represented by the efficacy of the
priesthood, for the people, called to
be the people of God (v. 5), hath
received the Law, resting on it (the
priesthood) as its foundation. For
this use of ἐπί with gen. see Luke
iv. 29. The general sense is expressed
more naturally in English by 'under
it' as the forming, shaping power.
The temporal sense (Matt. i. 11) has
no force here.

For ὁ λαός comp. c. ii. 17 note.

This use of the passive (νενομοθέτηται comp. viii. 6) corresponds directly
with the active form νομοθετεῖν τινα
(Ps. xxiv. (xxv.) 8; cxviii. (cxix.) 33);
as it is found also in Plato, answering
to νομ. τινι. The Law is regarded as
still in force (x. 1; ix. 6).

τίς ἔτι χρεία...λέγεσθαι;] The explicit words of the Psalmist at once
separate the new priest from the
former line. He was styled 'not after
the order of Aaron.' The ἔτι marks
that the want was felt after the
Levitical priesthood had been established. The change was found by
experience to be required, and it was
described long before it came to pass
by one who lived under the Law and
enjoyed its privileges.

The negative (οὐ) belongs to the descriptive clause and not to λέγεσθαι.

For ἀνίστασθαι see Acts iii. 22; vii.
37. By the use of ἕτερον (not ἄλλον)
the two priesthoods are directly compared to the exclusion of all others.
Contrast iv. 8 (περὶ ἄλλης ἡμ.).

12. μετατιθ. γάρ...γίνεται] For when
the priesthood is changed...The γάρ
may refer to the main thought of v. 11
or to the parenthesis (ὁ λαὸς γάρ...).
The former connexion appears to be
the more natural. The change of
priesthood involves the change of
Law. Such a change must have been
called for by an overwhelming necessity.

The change of the priesthood is
presented as the transference, the
removal, of the priesthood from one
order, one line, to another : transla-
tum est sacerdotium de tribu in tribum,
de sacerdotali videlicet ad regalem

καὶ νόμου μετάθεσις γίνεται. ¹³ἐφ᾽ ὃν γὰρ λέγεται
ταῦτα φυλῆς ἑτέρας μετέσχηκεν, ἀφ᾽ ἧς οὐδεὶς προσέσχηκεν τῷ θυσιαστηρίῳ· ¹⁴πρόδηλον γὰρ ὅτι ἐξ Ἰούδα

12 om. καὶ νόμου B.   13 λέγεται : λέγει D₂*.   προσέσχηκεν אBD₂: προσέσχεν AC.

(Primasius). The 'removal' of the Law
is more complete : c. xii. 27. This
change is considered in the abstract
(νόμου μετάθεσις); and the use of the
pres. partic. (μετατιθεμένης) makes the
two processes absolutely coincident
(this thought is lost in the Vulg.
translato enim).

13. ἐφ᾽ ὃν γὰρ λ. τ.] Latt. *in quo
enim*...This clause goes back to *v.* 11,
the intervening verse 12 being treated as parenthetical. The necessity
there spoken of has been recognised
and met. The promise in the Psalm,
with all its consequences, has been
fulfilled ; *for He to whom these divine
words are directed*...For ἐφ᾽ ὅν comp.
Mark ix. 12 f. : εἰς ἥν *v.* 14 note.

μετέσχηκεν] Latt. (*de alia tribu*) *est*.
The choice of this word points to the
voluntary assumption of humanity by
the Lord. It is not said simply that
He was born of another tribe : He was
of His own will so born. Compare ii.
14 (μετέσχεν); and for the perfect *v.* 6
note.

The use of ἑτέρας appears to place
the royal and priestly tribes in significant connexion and contrast.

The *Glossa Ordin.* (following Chrysostom) draws a parallel between the
tribe of Judah and the Lord. Intuere
mysterium : primum fuit regalis [tri-
bus Iudæ], postea facta est sacerdo-
talis. Sic Christus rex erat semper ;
sacerdos autem factus est quando
carnem suscepit, quando sacrificium
obtulit.

It was not unnatural that some
endeavoured to claim for the Lord a
double descent from Levi as well as
from Judah. Comp. Lightfoot on
Clem. 1 *Cor.* 32.

προσέσχηκεν τῷ θυσιαστ.] *hath given
attendance at*...Latt. (*alt.*) *præsto fuit*.

For προσέχειν compare c, ii. 1 note.
From the sense of 'giving attention to,'
that of practical 'devotion' to an object follows naturally : 1 Tim. iv. 13 ; iii.
8 (τῷ οἴνῳ). The statement applies
only to the regular legitimate service
of the altar and does not take account
of any exceptional acts, as of the royal
sacrifices of David and Solomon.

14. πρόδηλον γάρ...]*For it is* openly,
obviously, *evident* to all...Comp. 1
Tim. v. 24 f. The word πρόδηλος
occurs several times in Clem. 1 *Cor.*
cc. 11, 12, 40, 51.

ἐξ Ἰούδα] *out of* the tribe of Judah.
Compare Apoc. v. 5 ὁ λέων ὁ ἐκ τῆς
φυλῆς Ἰούδα.

These are the only two passages in
the N.T. in which the Lord is definitely
connected with Judah except in the
record of the Nativity (Matt. ii. 6 ∥
Micah v. 2). The privilege of the tribe
is elsewhere concentrated in its representative, David (2 Sam. vii. 12 ; Jer.
xxiii. 5 ; Ps. cxxxii. 11 ; Luke i. 32 ;
Rom. i. 3). Comp. Gen. xlix. 8 ff.

Here the contrast with Levi makes
the mention of the tribe necessary.
The Lord traced His descent from the
royal and not from the priestly tribe.
There is no direct mention in this
Epistle of the relation of the Lord to
David.

It is important to observe that the
writer affirms here most plainly the
true manhood of the Lord (comp. v. 7
ff.). Like St John he combines the
most striking testimonies to His divine
and Human natures.

There is nothing to shew in what
exact form he held that the Lord's
descent from Judah through David
was reckoned : whether as the legal
representative of Joseph, or as the
Son of Mary, who was herself known

ἀνατέταλκεν ὁ κύριος ἡμῶν, εἰς ἣν φυλὴν περὶ ἱερέων
οὐδὲν Μωυσῆς ἐλάλησεν. ¹⁵Καὶ περισσότερον ἔτι κατά-
δηλόν ἐστιν, εἰ κατὰ τὴν ὁμοιότητα ΜελχιϲεΔὲκ ἀνίσταται

14 περὶ ἱερ. οὐδέν (א)ABC*D₂*: οὐδὲν περὶ ἱερωσύνης ϛ syrr.   οὐδ. M.: M. οὐδ.
א*.   15 om. τήν B.

to be of Davidic descent. The genealogies are in favour of the former view.
Compare Clem. R. xxxii. and Lightf.

ἀνατέταλκεν] *hath risen, sprung.*
Latt. *ortus est.* The image may be
taken from the rising of the sun or of
a star, or from the rising of a plant
from its hidden germ. For the former
image comp. Luke i. 78; 2 Pet. i. 19;
Num. xxiv. 17; Mal. iv. 2. For the
latter, Is. lxi. 11; Jer. xxiii. 5; Zech.
iii. 8; vi. 12. The usage of the N.T. is
in favour of the former interpretation;
and Theophylact, referring to Num.
xxiv. and Mal. iv., says well: δι' ὧν
δηλοῦται τὸ εἰς φωτισμὸν τοῦ κόσμου
τὴν παρουσίαν τοῦ κυρίου γενέσθαι.

ὁ κύριος ἡμῶν] Compare c. xiii. 20 ὁ
κύριος ἡ. Ἰησοῦς.
The title without any addition is
very rare and occurs (only) 1 Tim. i.
14; 2 Tim. i. 8; 2 Pet. iii. 15.
Comp. ὁ κύριος ii. 3 note.
In Apoc. xi. 15 the title is applied
to the Father; ὁ κύριος ἡμῶν καὶ ὁ
χριστὸς αὐτοῦ.

εἰς ἣν φ.] Latt. *in qua tribu.*
Comp. ἐφ ὅν v. 13; Luke xxii. 65;
Eph. v. 32; Acts ii. 25; and also
1 Pet. i. 11.

15—19. The Levitical priesthood
was transitory, and during its continuance it was stamped with the
conditions of limitation.

The incapacity of the Levitical
priesthood to bring to perfection was
shewn, as has been seen, by the fact
that the promise of another priesthood was made while it was still in
full activity (11—14). The conclusion
is established still more obviously from
the consideration that this promised
priesthood was after a wholly different
type, not legal but spiritual, not sacer-

dotal only, but royal, not transitory
but eternal.

15. καὶ περισσότερον ἔτι κατάδ....]
*And what we say is yet more abun-
dantly evident...*Vulg. *Et amplius adhuc manifestum est...*Doubt has been
felt as to the exact reference of this
statement. Is it the abrogation of
the Law which is more abundantly
proved by the language of the Psalm?
or the inefficacy of the Levitical priesthood? Both conclusions follow from
the special description of the new
priesthood. But the thought of the
abrogation of the Law is really secondary. This is involved in the inefficacy
of the priesthood which is the dominant thought in connexion with Christ's
work. Hence the new proof is directed to the former main argument.

This is the view given in the main
by patristic commentators: τί ἐστιν
κατάδηλον; τὸ μέσον τῆς ἱερωσύνης ἑκατέρας, τὸ διάφορον, ὅσον κρείττων ὃς οὐ
κατὰ νόμον ἐντολῆς σαρκικῆς γέγονε
(Chrys.).

ἢ ὅτι τὸ ἐναλλαγήσεσθαι καὶ τὴν ἱερωσύνην καὶ τὴν διαθήκην (Theophlct.).

*amplius manifestum est...*subaudi
destructum esse sacerdotium legis
(Primas.).

κατάδηλον] The word occurs here
only in the N. T. and it is not found in
LXX. (Hdt. Xen. Jos.). Compare for
the force of κατὰ, κατείδωλος (Acts xvii.
16), καταφιλεῖν.

εἰ κατὰ τὴν ὁμοιό. M.] *if,* as may be
most certainly laid down on the authority of Scripture, *it is after the
likeness of Melchizedek another priest
ariseth,* if this is to be the pattern of
the new priesthood. Rom. viii. 31 &c.
John vii. 23 &c.

The idea of 'order' is specialised

ἱερεὺς ἕτερος, ¹⁶ὃς οὐ κατὰ νόμον ἐντολῆς σαρκίνης γέγονεν

16 σαρκίνης : σαρκικῆς ς.

into that of likeness. Melchizedek furnishes, so to speak, the personal as well as the official type of the new High-priest. This 'likeness' brings out more clearly than before the difference between the new and the old priesthood.

For the use of εἰ, where the truth of the supposition is assumed, see Rom. viii. 31 ; John vii. 23 &c. Ὁμοιότης occurs again in c. iv. 15. The word is classical and is found in Gen. i. 11 f.; Wisd. xiv. 19.

ἀνίσταται] v. 11. The present describes the certain fulfilment of the divine purpose, which has indeed become a fact (v. 16, γέγονεν). Comp. Matt. ii. 4; xxvi. 2.

ἱερεὺς ἕτερος]v.11,i.e. Christ fulfilling the promise of the Psalm. Theodoret remarks (on v. 3) that while Melchizedek was only a type of Christ's Person and Nature, the Priesthood of Christ was after the fashion of Melchizedek. For the office of priest is the office of a man.

16. ὅς...γέγονεν...ἀκαταλύτου] who hath become priest not after a law expressed in a commandment of flesh, but after the power of an indissoluble life. There is a double contrast between 'law' and 'power,' and between the 'commandment of flesh' and the 'indissoluble life.' The 'law' is an outward restraint : the 'power' is an inward force. The 'commandment of flesh' carries with it of necessity the issue of change and succession : the 'indissoluble life' is above all change except a change of form.

A priesthood fashioned after the former type was essentially subject to the influence of death: a priesthood fashioned after the latter type must be eternal.

Each part also in the expression of the second contrast is contrasted, 'commandment' with 'life,' that which

is of external injunction with that which is of spontaneous energy : and 'flesh' with 'indissoluble,' that which carries with it the necessity of corruption with that which knows no change.

οὐ κατὰ νόμ. ἐντ. σαρκ.] Vulg. non secundum legem mandati carnalis. In the phrase κατὰ νόμον the writer necessarily thinks of the Jewish Law, but this is not directly referred to in its concrete form as 'the Law,' but indicated in its character as 'a law,' so that the words express a perfectly general idea : 'not according to a law of carnal commandment.' The gen. expresses that in which the law finds expression. Comp. John v. 29. See also v. 2 note.

In characterising the commandment (ἐντ. σαρκ.) the strong form which expresses the substance (σάρκινος) and not simply the character of flesh (σαρκικός) is used to mark the element with which the commandment dealt, in which it found its embodiment. It was not only fashioned after the nature of flesh: it had its expression in flesh (comp. ix. 10 δικαιώματα σαρκός). All the requirements, for example, to be satisfied by a Levitical priest were literally 'of flesh,' outward descent, outward perfectness, outward purity. No moral qualification was imposed.

The distinction between σάρκινος (carneus, of flesh, fleshy) and σαρκικός (carnalis, flesh-like, fleshly) is obvious. The former describes that of which the object is made (comp. λίθινος John ii. 6 ; 2 Cor. iii. 3 ; ξύλινος 2 Tim. ii. 20). The latter, which is a very rare and late word in non-Biblical Greek, and found only once as a false v. l. for σάρκινος in LXX. 2 Chron. xxxii. 8, is moulded on the type of πνευματικός, and expresses that of which the object bears the character.

There is considerable confusion in

ἀλλὰ κατὰ δύναμιν ζωῆς ἀκαταλύτου, 17 μαρτυρεῖται γὰρ

17 μαρτυρεῖται ℵ(-τε)ABD$_2$* syrr me the: μαρτυρεῖ ς C.

authorities as to the form used in some passages of the N. T. The following appears to be the true distribution of the words:

1. σάρκινος.

Rom. vii. 14 ἐγὼ δὲ σάρκινός εἰμι opposed to ὁ νόμος πνευματικός.

1 Cor. iii. 1 ὡς σαρκίνοις opposed to ὡς πνευματικοῖς.

2 Cor. iii. 3 πλάκες σάρκιναι opposed to πλάκες λίθιναι.

2. σαρκικός.

Rom. xv. 27 τὰ σαρκικά opposed to τὰ πνευματικά.

1 Cor. iii. 3 (*bis*) σαρκικοί ἐστε (in iii. 4 read ἄνθρωποι).

1 Cor. ix. 11 τὰ σαρκικά opposed to τὰ πνευματικά.

2 Cor. i. 12 ἐν σοφίᾳ σαρκικῇ.

x. 4 τὰ ὅπλα...οὐ σαρκικὰ ἀλλὰ δυνατὰ τῷ θεῷ.

1 Pet. ii. 11 αἱ σαρκικαὶ ἐπιθυμίαι.

The crucial passage for the use of the words is 1 Cor. iii. 1 ff. Here there can be no doubt as to the readings. In *v.* 1 we must read σαρκίνοις, in *v.* 3 (*bis*) σαρκικοί and in *v.* 4 ἄνθρωποι. The juxtaposition of the forms (though the difference is lost in the Latt.) seems to be conclusive as to the fact that there is a difference in their meaning.

The true reading in *v.* 4 throws light upon the other two. In *v.* 1 St Paul says that he was forced to address his readers as though they were merely 'men of flesh,' without the πνεῦμα. In *v.* 3, seeking to soften his judgment, he speaks of them as shewing traits which belong to the σάρξ. In *v.* 4 it seems to him enough to suggest, what was beyond all question, that they were swayed by simply human feelings.

In the present verse Chrysostom, following the later reading σαρκικῆς, gives part of the sense well: πάντα ὅσα διωρίζετο σαρκικὰ ἦν. τὸ γὰρ λέγειν περίτεμε τὴν σάρκα, χρῖσον τὴν σάρκα, λοῦσον τὴν σάρκα, περίκειρον τὴν σάρκα ...ταῦτα, εἰπέ μοι, οὐχὶ σαρκικά; εἰ δὲ θέλεις μαθεῖν καὶ τίνα ἃ ἐπηγγέλλετο ἀγαθά, ἄκουε· Πολλὴ ζωή, φησί, τῇ σαρκί, γάλα καὶ μέλι τῇ σαρκί, εἰρήνη τῇ σαρκί, τρυφὴ τῇ σαρκί.

ἀλλὰ κατὰ δύναμιν ζ. ἀκατ.] Latt. *sed secundum virtutem vitæ insolubilis* (*infatigabilis*).

The life of Christ was not endless or eternal only. It was essentially 'indissoluble' (ἀκατάλυτος). Although the form of its manifestation was changed and in the earthly sense He died, yet His life endured unchanged even through earthly dissolution. He died and yet He offered Himself as living in death by the eternal Spirit (c. ix. 14). Comp. John xi. 26; xix. 34 note.

This life found its complete expression after the Ascension, but it does not date from that consummation of glory (comp. vii. 3).

It must be further noticed that the possession of this indissoluble life is not only the characteristic of Christ's exercise of His priestly office: it is the ground on which He entered upon it. Other priests were made priests in virtue of a special ordinance: He was made priest in virtue of His inherent nature. He could be, as none other, victim at once and priest.

Yet again, the permanence of the personal life of the new Priest distinguishes Him essentially from the legal priests. To Phinehas 'the son of Eleazar the son of Aaron, and to his seed' was given 'the covenant of an everlasting priesthood' (Num. xxv. 13; Ex. xl. 15); but this was subject to the conditions of succession, and therefore to the possibility of change. A priesthood founded upon a covenant involves conditions on two sides: a priesthood founded on an oath to a

ὅτι Σὺ ἱερεὺς εἰς τὸν αἰῶνα κατὰ τὴν τάξιν Μελχισεδέκ.　¹⁸ ἀθέτησις
μὲν γὰρ γίνεται προαγούσης ἐντολῆς διὰ τὸ αὐτῆς ἀσθενὲς

σύ: σὺ + εἰ vg syrr me the (and v. 21).　　　18 προσαγούσης D₂*.

person for himself is absolute. Comp.
Gal. iii. 19 ff.

17. μαρτυρεῖται γὰρ ὅτι Σύ...] for it
is witnessed of him, Thou art...Vulg.
contestatur enim quoniam Tu......
Comp. v. 8. The quotation establishes
both the eternity and the character
of the new priesthood (εἰς τὸν αἰῶνα,
κατὰ τὴν τ. Μ.).
The ὅτι here is recitative (x. 8; xi.
18); and μαρτυρεῖται is used absolutely
(xi. 39).

The direct personal reference in
the Psalm (Σὺ ἱερεύς...) has not been
given since the first quotation: v. 6.
It occurs again in v. 21.

18, 19. ἀθέτησις μὲν γάρ...ἐπεισαγωγὴ
δέ...] For there is a disannulling...
and a bringing in thereupon...Vulg.
Reprobatio quidem fit...introductio
vero...The γὰρ goes back to v. 15.
The conclusion there pointed to is
confirmed by the decisive fact that the
promised priesthood is not only distinct from the Levitical but also irre-
concileable with it, exclusive of it; so
far, that is, that the Levitical priesthood has no longer any ground for
continuance when this has been established.

The whole sentence is divided by
μέν and δέ into two corresponding
parts. Γίνεται goes with both; and
οὐδὲν...νόμος is parenthetical. This
construction appears to be established
decisively by the correspondence of
ἀθέτησις...ἐπεισαγωγή, and of the general scope of the two clauses. The
'commandment' stands over against
the 'hope,' the 'weakness and unprofitableness' of the one over against
the power of the other, whereby 'we
draw nigh to God.' Παύεται, φησίν,
ὁ νόμος ἐπεισάγεται δὲ ἡ τῶν κρειττόνων
ἐλπίς (Thdt.).

18. ἀθέτησις...προαγ. ἐντ...] The
word ἀθέτησις occurs again c. ix. 26;

the verb ἀθετεῖν is found c. x. 28;
Gal. ii. 21; iii. 15; 1 Tim. v. 12; and
is common in the LXX.; but it is
generally used there of unfaithful,
rebellious action: Ex. xxi. 8; Jer. iii.
20 (ἀθεσία, ἀθέτημα).

This open, direct disannulling of
the previous system, which is, as it
were, set at nought, 'cometh to pass'
(γίνεται) in the fulfilment of the divine
order, as indicated by the mention
of an eternal priesthood on a new
type.

The indefinite form of the phrase
προαγούσης ἐντολῆς serves to express
the general thought of the character
of the foundation on which the Levitical priesthood rested as a 'preceding,'
a 'foregoing,' and so a preparatory
commandment.

The word προάγουσα (1 Tim. i. 18;
v. 24) expresses not only priority (an
earlier commandment) but connexion
(a foregoing commandment). The
divine commandment (ἐντολή), pointing to an earthly institution, stands
in contrast with the hope, rising above
earth.

The use of ἐντολή fixes the reference to the ordinance of the priesthood particularly (v. 16) in which, as
has been seen, the Law (οὐδὲν ἐτελ. ὁ
νόμος) was summed up, so far as it is
compared with the Gospel.

διὰ τὸ αὐτ. ἀσθ. καὶ ἀνωφ.] because of
its weakness and unprofitableness...
Vulg. propter infirmitatem ejus et
inutilitatem. A command, a law, is
essentially powerless to help. It cannot inspire with strength: it cannot
bring aid to the wounded conscience.
And the ritual priesthood was affected
by both these faults. It was external,
and it was formal. It did not deal
with the soul or with things eternal.

Infirmitatem habebat lex, quia oper-
antes se non valebat juvare: inutilita-

καὶ ἀνωφελές, ¹⁹οὐδὲν γὰρ ἐτελείωσεν ὁ νόμος, ἐπεισαγωγὴ δὲ κρείττονος ἐλπίδος, δι' ἧς ἐγγίζομεν τῷ θεῷ.

19 ἐπεισαγωγῆς D₂*.　　　　ἐγγίζωμεν A.

tem vero, quia nemini regnum cælorum valebat aperire (Primas.).

οὐδὲν οὖν ὠφέλησεν ὁ νόμος; ὠφέλησε
μὲν καὶ σφόδρα ὠφέλησεν ἀλλὰ τὸ
ποιῆσαι τελείους οὐκ ὠφέλησεν (Chrys.).
The use of the abstract forms τὸ
ἀσθ., τὸ ἀνωφ., marks the principle
and not only the fact. Comp. vi. 17.
For τὸ ἀσθενές comp. 1 Cor. i. 27; Gal.
iv. 9; Rom. viii. 3 (ἠσθένει).
ἐνταῦθα ἡμῖν ἐπιφύονται οἱ αἱρετικοί.
ἀλλ' ἄκουε ἀκριβῶς. οὐκ εἶπε διὰ τὸ
πονηρόν, οὐδὲ διὰ τὸ μοχθηρόν, ἀλλὰ διὰ
τὸ αὐτῆς ἀσθενὲς καὶ ἀνωφελές (Chrys.)
19. οὐδὲν γάρ...] The Law, of which
the institution of the Levitical priesthood (the special commandment just
noticed) was a part or indeed the
foundation (v. 11), brought nothing to
perfection. In every application (οὐδέν)
it was provisional and preparatory
(comp. ix. 21 ff.; Lev. xvi. 16). This
decisive parenthesis is explanatory of
'the weakness and unprofitableness'
of the commandment (for the Law...).
Man must strive towards the perfection, the accomplishment, of his destiny
on earth. The Law failed him in the
effort. He outgrew it. The very
scope of the Law indeed was to define
the requirements of life, and to shew
that man himself could not satisfy
them. Comp. Gal. ii. 15 f.; iii. 19;
Rom. iii. 19 f.; vii. 7 ff.

ἐτελείωσεν] v. 11 note. The tense
indicates the final view of the Law.
Contrast x. 14 τετελείωκεν.

ἐπεισαγωγὴ δὲ κρ. ἐλπ.] There was
on the one side the disannulling of a
preparatory commandment, and there
was on the other side the introduction
of a new (ἐπί) and better hope to
occupy the place which was held by
the commandment before.

This hope is described as better
than the commandment, and not
simply as better than the hope con-

veyed by the commandment. The
comparison is between the commandment characteristic of the Law and
the hope characteristic of the Gospel;
and not between the temporal hope
of the Law and the spiritual hope of
the Gospel. Though the Law had
(cf. viii. 6) a hope, the thought of it
seems to be out of place here.

For ἐπεισαγωγή compare ἐπεισέρχο-
μαι Luke xxi. 35 ; and for ἐλπίς c. iii.
6; vi. 19 notes.

δι' ἧς ἐγγ. τῷ θεῷ] through which
hope we draw nigh to God...Vulg. per
quam proximamus ad Deum. The
commandment was directed to the
fulfilment of ordinances on earth:
hope enters within the veil and carries
believers with it (c. vi. 19).

The phrase ἐγγίζειν τῷ θεῷ is used,
though rarely, in LXX. of the priests:
Ex. xix. 22 (יִגְּשׁוּ); Lev. x. 3 (קְרֹב); E-
zek. xlii. 13; xliii. 19.

But also more widely; Is. xxix. 13:
comp. Ex. xxiv. 2; Hos. xii. 6 (ἐγγ.
πρὸς τ. θ.).

It occurs again in the N.T., James
iv. 8.

All believers are, in virtue of their
Christian faith, priests: 1 Pet. ii. 5,9;
Apoc. i. 6; v. 10; xx. 6. That which
was before (in a figure) the privilege
of a class has become (in reality) the
privilege of all; and thus man is enabled to gain through fellowship with
God the attainment of his destiny
(τελείωσις). Comp. c. x. 19.

20—25. The Apostle goes on to
shew the superiority of Christ's Priesthood over the Levitical priesthood
from its essential characteristics.
Christ's Priesthood is immutable in
its foundation (20—22); and it is uninterrupted in its personal tenure (23
—25).

20—22. The And corresponds to

²⁰Καὶ καθ᾽ ὅσον οὐ χωρὶς ὁρκωμοσίας, (οἱ μὲν γὰρ χωρὶς
ὁρκωμοσίας εἰσὶν ἱερεῖς γεγονότες, ²¹ὁ δὲ μετὰ ὁρκωμοσίας διὰ τοῦ λέγοντος πρὸς αὐτόν Ὤμοϲεν Κύριοϲ, κὰι ογ

20 οἱ μὲν γὰρ χ. ὁρκ.: om. D₂* syr hl.

the *And* in *vv.* 15, 23, and introduces
a new moment in the argument.

The additional solemnity of the oath
gives an additional dignity to the covenant which is introduced by it (compare vi. 13 ff.). And yet further, by
this oath the purpose of God is declared
absolutely. Man's weakness no longer
enters as an element into the prospect
of its fulfilment. The permanence of
a covenant which rests upon an oath
is assured.

The introduction of the idea of a
'covenant' is sudden and unprepared.
It was probably suggested by the words
recorded in Matt. xxvi. 28. The
thought of Christ's Priesthood is necessarily connected with the history
of His Passion.

20 (22). καθ᾽ ὅσον...κατὰ τοσοῦτο
καί...] *And inasmuch...by so much
also*...Latt. *Quantum...in tantum...*
The sovereign validity of the divine
oath is the measure of the exceeding
authority of the dispensation which
rests upon it.

For the form of comparison see c.
i. 4 κρείττων...ὅσῳ διαφορώτερον. iii. 3
πλείονος...καθ᾽ ὅσον. ix. 27 καθ᾽ ὅσον
...οὕτως...; and for the introduction of
the parenthesis (οἱ μὲν γάρ...εἰς τὸν
αἰῶνα) compare c. xii. 18—24.

20. οὐ χωρὶς ὁρκ.] *not without the
taking of an oath* hath He received
His office. This addition is suggested
by *v.* 22, and by μετὰ ὁρκ. which follows.
The words however may be taken generally: 'the whole transaction doth not
take place without the taking of an
oath'...

The word ὁρκωμοσία, which occurs
again in *v.* 28; Ezek. xvii. 18 f.; 1
Esdr. viii. 90, expresses the whole action, and not simply the oath.

οἱ μὲν γάρ...ὁ δέ...εἰς τὸν αἰῶνα] *for*

*while they...He...*Vulg. *alii quidem
...hic autem...*This elaborate parenthesis is inserted to explain fully
the contrast implied in χωρὶς ὁρκωμοσίας.

'*For while the one class* of priests
(the Levitical priests) *have become
priests without any taking of an oath,
He* was made priest *with it*' (μετὰ
comp. Matt. xiv. 7). The stress laid
upon the oath suggests the contrast
between 'the promise' and 'the Law'
on which St Paul dwells (*e.g.* Gal. iii.
15 ff.). The Law is an expression of
the sovereign power of God Who requires specific obedience: the oath
implies a purpose of love not to be
disturbed by man's unworthiness.

εἰσὶν ἱερεῖς γεγον.] The periphrasis
marks the possession as well as the
impartment of the office: they have
been made priests and they act as
priests.

Comp. *v.* 27; iv. 2; x. 10 (ii. 13).
The construction is not uncommon
throughout the N.T., and is never
without force. Compare Moulton-
Winer, p. 438.

21. διὰ τοῦ λέγοντος] *through Him
that saith* (Latt. *per eum qui dixit*),
i.e. God through the mouth of the
Psalmist. The divine voice is not
regarded as an isolated utterance (διὰ
τοῦ εἰπόντος, c. x. 30; 2 Cor. iv. 6;
James ii. 11), but as one which is still
present and effective. Comp. xii. 25 (ὁ
λαλῶν); i. 6 note.

Though the words (ὤμοσεν...οὐ με-
ταμελ.) are not directly spoken by the
Lord, they are His by implication.
The oath is His.

πρὸς αὐτόν] The words have a
double meaning in relation to the two
parts of the verse quoted. The first
part has Christ for its object ('in

ΜΕΤΑΜΕΛΗΘΉΣΕΤΑΙ, Σὺ ἱερεὺς εἰς τὸν αἰῶνα,) ²²κατὰ τοσοῦτο καὶ κρείττονος διαθήκης γέγονεν ἔγγυος Ἰησοῦς. ²³Καὶ οἱ μὲν πλείονές εἰσιν γεγονότες ἱερεῖς διὰ τὸ θανάτῳ

21 om. εἰς τὸν αἰ. א*.   εἰς τὸν αἰ. BC vg the : + κατὰ τὴν τάξιν M. א°AD₂ syrr me.
22 τοσ. καὶ א*BC* : om. καὶ א°AD₂ vg me.   τοσοῦτον ϛ א° -τω D₂*.   23 γεγ.
ἱερ. אB vg syrr me : ἱερ. γεγ. ACD₂.

regard to Him': comp.ʳi. 7): in the second part He is directly addressed. For ὤμοσεν compare Luke i. 73; Acts ii. 30; and for οὐ μεταμεληθήσεται, Rom. xi. 29; Num. xxiii. 19; 1 Sam. xv. 29. The necessities of human thought require that sometimes, through man's failure or change, God, who is unchangeable, should be said to repent. The temporary interruption of the accomplishment of His counsel of love must appear in this light under the conditions of time to those 'who see but part': Gen. vi. 6: 1 Sam. xv. 10; 2 Sam. xxiv. 16; Jer. xviii. 8.

22. κρείττονος...Ἰησοῦς] *Jesus hath become surety of a better covenant* (Vulg. *melioris testamenti sponsor factus est Jesus*) in that He has shewn in His own Person the fact of the establishment of a New Covenant between God and man. This He has done by His Incarnation, issuing in His Life, His Death, His Resurrection, His eternal Priesthood. But inasmuch as the immediate subject here is Christ's Priesthood, the reference is especially to this, the consummation of the Incarnation. Jesus—the Son of man—having entered into the Presence of God for men is the sure pledge of the validity of the New Covenant.

In later passages of the Epistle (viii. 6 note) Christ is spoken of as the Mediator of the New Covenant. He Himself brought about the Covenant; and He is the adequate surety of its endurance.

Ἰησοῦς] The human name of the Lord stands emphatically at the end. (Comp. vi. 20; ii. 9 note.) Jesus,

the Son of man, has been exalted to the right hand of God, where He is seated as King and Priest. In His divine humanity He assures us that God has potentially accomplished the purpose of Creation, and will accomplish it.

The word ἔγγυος does not occur elsewhere in N.T. See Ecclus. xxix. 15 f.; 2 Macc. x. 28 ἔγγυον εὐημερίας καὶ νίκης.

A surety for the most part pledges himself that something will be: but here the Ascended Christ witnesses that something is: the assurance is not simply of the future but of that which is present though unseen.

It must be noticed that Christ is not said here to be a surety for man to God, but a surety of a covenant of God with man.

Theodoret interprets the phrase too narrowly : διὰ τῆς οἰκείας ἀναστάσεως ἐβεβαίωσε τῆς ἡμετέρας ἀναστάσεως τὴν ἐλπίδα.

For διαθήκη see Additional Note on ix. 16.

23—25. A second fact establishes the pre-eminence of Christ's Priesthood. It is held uninterruptedly by One Ever-living Priest.

23. καὶ οἱ μὲν πλ. εἰ. γεγ....ὁ δὲ...] *And while they*—the one class, the Levitical priests—*have been made priests many in number...He...hath His priesthood inviolable.* Vulg. *Et alii quidem plures facti sunt sacerdotes...hic autem....* The Levitical priests held the priesthood in succession, one after another. They were made priests many in number, not simultaneously but successively. The thought is of the line which repre-

κωλύεσθαι παραμένειν· ²⁴ὁ δὲ διὰ τὸ μένειν αὐτὸν εἰς τὸν
ἀιῶνα ἀπαράβατον ἔχει τὴν ἱερωσύνην· ²⁵ὅθεν καὶ σώζειν

24 ἱερατίαν D₂*.

sents the office. The covenant of an
everlasting priesthood was not with
Aaron personally, but with Aaron and
his sons 'throughout their generations'
(Ex. xl. 15; comp. Num. xxv. 13).
At the same time it is a true thought
that the perfect continuity of the
office could only be secured by the
existence of many priests at once
(comp. Ex. xxix.); but that is not the
point here.

The order in the words γεγονότες
ἱερεῖς as compared with v. 20 ἱερεῖς
γεγονότες is worthy of notice. In the
former passage ἱερεῖς was accentuated:
here the thought is of the number
who are 'made' priests.

διὰ τὸ θ. κωλ. παραμένειν] The multitude of the Levitical priests is a necessity, *because they are hindered by
death from abiding* as priests among
men. The statement is made generally
and not of the past only. The use of
the rare word παραμένειν (Phil. i. 25,
not 1 Cor. xvi. 6) implies the idea of
fellowship, service on the part of the
priests during their abiding (*i.e.* παραμένειν τοῖς ἀνθρώποις, not τῇ ἱερατείᾳ.
Hdt. i. 30 τέκνα...παραμείναντα). It
would be pointless to say that 'death
hindered them from living': it hindered them from discharging the
function which was necessary for man's
well-being.

24. ὁ δὲ διὰ τὸ μένειν...τὴν ἱερωσ.]
*He, because He abideth for ever, hath
His priesthood inviolable.* Vulg. *Hic
autem eo quod maneat in æternum
sempiternum habet sacerdotium.* In
both respects Christ offers a contrast
with the Levitical priests. He 'abides
for ever,' though in this sense it is
not said that He abides with us
(παραμένειν), while they were hindered
by death from so abiding. In this
respect Christ's eternal abiding as Son
(John viii. 35; xii. 34; comp. *v.* 28)

is contrasted with the transitory continuance of mortal men on earth. And
again the fact that He 'abides for ever'
in virtue of His Nature involves the
further fact that He will fulfil His
priestly office for ever.

Jesus quia immortalis est sempiternum habet sacerdotium; nec ullum
habere poterit subsequentem, eo quod
ipse maneat in æternum (Primas.).

ἀπαράβατον ἔχει τὴν ἱερ.] Literally
hath His priesthood inviolable, unimpaired, and so unchangeable. The
word ἀπαράβατος has caused difficulty
from early times (Ambr. *impræ-
varicabile,* Aug. *intransgressible:*
Theophlct. τουτέστιν ἀδιάκοπον, ἀδιά-
δοχον). There appears to be no independent authority for the sense 'un-
transmitted,' 'that does not pass to
another.' According to the analogy
of ἄβατος, ἐπίβατος, the form παράβατος
expresses that which is or may be
transgressed, invaded. Ἀπαράβατος
is therefore that which cannot be (or in
fact is not) overstepped, transgressed,
violated, that which is 'absolute.'
Thus Galen speaks of 'observing an
absolute law' (νόμον ἀπαράβατον φυλάττειν). Compare Epict. *Ench.* 50,
2 (νόμος ἀπαράβατος); Pseudo-Just.
Quæst. ad Orthod. § 27; Jos. *c. Ap.* ii.
41 (τί εὐσεβείας ἀπαραβάτου (*inviolate*)
κάλλιον; but in *Antt.* xviii. 9 (10), 2
he uses it of men ἀπαράβατοι μεμενη-
κότες in connexion with the phrase
οὐδ' ἂν αὐτοὶ παραβαίημεν). So the
word is used in connexion with θεωρία,
τάξις, εἱμαρμένη (comp. Wetst. *ad loc.*).
Christ's Priesthood is His alone, open
to no rival claim, liable to no invasion
of its functions.

25. ὅθεν καί] *whence* (c. ii. 17 note)
also, because His priesthood is absolute and final, He is able to fulfil completely the ideal office of the
priest.

εἰς τὸ παντελὲς δύναται τοὺς προσερχομένους δι᾽ αὐτοῦ
τῷ θεῷ, πάντοτε ζῶν εἰς τὸ ἐντυγχάνειν ὑπὲρ αὐτῶν.

If Christ's priesthood had failed in any respect then provision would have been made for some other. But, as it is, the salvation wrought by Christ reaches to the last element of man's nature and man's life. In relation to man fallen and sinful σώζειν expresses the same idea as τελειοῦν applied to man as he was made by God (comp. ii. 10), and it finds its fulfilment in the whole course of his existence. The thought here is not of 'the world' (John iii. 17) but of believers: not of salvation in its broadest sense, but of the working out of salvation to the uttermost in those who have received the Gospel.

Thus the present (σώζειν) as distinguished from the aorist (σῶσαι) has its full force. The support comes at each moment of trial.

The present occurs again 1 Cor. xv. 2; Jude 23; c. v. 7 (Acts xxvii. 20, contrasted with 31). For the aorist, see Rom. viii. 24; Tit. iii. 5; 1 Tim. i. 15.

εἰς τὸ παντελές] completely, wholly, to the uttermost. Comp. Lk. xiii. 11 (with neg.). The phrase does not occur elsewhere in the N.T. The old commentators strangely explain it as if it were εἰς τὸ διηνεκές (so Latt. in perpetuum).

τοὺς προσερχ. δι᾽ αὐτοῦ τῷ θ.] Compare John xiv. 6; x. 9; vi. 37. Something is required of men answering to the gift of Christ. They use the way of God, which He has opened and which He is.

The word προσέρχεσθαι (comp. ἐγγίζειν v. 19 note), is not used in this sense by St Paul nor elsewhere in N.T. except 1 Pet. ii. 4 (προσέρχ. πρός). Comp. c. iv. 16 note; x. 1, 22; xi. 6; xii. 18, 22. Theophylact expresses the thought very neatly: αὐτή ἐστι ἡ πρὸς τὸν πατέρα ὁδός, καὶ ὁ ταύτης δραξάμενος ἐκεῖ καταλύει.

A remarkable reading, accedens (for accedentes), which is not quoted from any existing MS., is noticed by Primasius (so also Sedul.): Quod vero quidam codices habent Accedens per semetipsum ad Deum, quidam vero plurali numero Accedentes, utrumque recipi potest.

πάντοτε ζῶν εἰς τὸ ἐντ.] seeing He ever liveth to make intercession, Vulg. semper vivens ad interpellandum (O. L. exorandum). The final clause εἰς τό... in connexion with ζῶν can only express the purpose (aimed at or attained). Comp. ii. 17 note. The very end of Christ's Life in heaven, as it is here presented, is that He may fulfil the object of the Incarnation, the perfecting of humanity.

The word πάντοτε belongs to later Greek and is said by the grammarians to represent the ἑκάστοτε of the classical writers. In the N.T. it has almost supplanted ἀεί (which occurs very rarely), yet so that the thought of each separate occasion on which the continual power is manifested is generally present (e.g. John vi. 34; Phil. i. 4). As often (speaking humanly) as Christ's help is needed He is ready to give it.

ἐντυγχάνειν] The word is of rare occurrence in the N.T. and is not found in the LXX. translation of the books of the Hebrew Canon; though it is not unfrequent in late Greek in the sense of 'meeting with' ('lighting upon') a person or thing. It is found in this sense 2 Macc. vi. 12 (τῇ βίβλῳ). Comp. 2 Macc. ii. 25; xv. 39.

From this sense comes the secondary sense of 'meeting with a person with a special object.' This purpose is sometimes definitely expressed: Wisd. viii. 21 ἐνέτυχον τῷ κυρίῳ καὶ ἐδεήθην αὐτοῦ. 3 Macc. vi. 37 ἐνέτυχον τῷ βασιλεῖ...αἰτούμενος. Sometimes it is only implied: Wisd. xvi. 28; 2 Macc. iv. 36 (ὑπὲρ τοῦ ἀπεκτάνθαι).

The purpose may be the invocation of action against another: 1 Macc. viii. 32 (ἐντ. κατά τινος); x. 61 ff.; xi. 25. This sense is implied in Acts xxv. 24 (ἐντυγχ. τινὶ περί τινος); and the exact phrase recurs, Rom. xi. 2 (ἐντυγχ. τινὶ κατά τινος).

Or again the invocation may be on behalf of another: Rom. viii. 27, 34 (ἐντυγχ. ὑπέρ), 26 (ὑπερεντ. ὑπέρ).

Compare ἔντευξις, 1 Tim. ii. 1; iv. 5. The object of supplication in this latter case may be either help or forgiveness. In the present passage (as in Rom. viii. 26 ff.) the idea is left in the most general form. Neither the Person who is approached nor the purpose of approaching Him is defined. Whatever man may need, as man or as sinful man, in each circumstance of effort and conflict, his want finds interpretation (if we may so speak) by the Spirit and effective advocacy by Christ our (High) Priest. In the glorified humanity of the Son of man every true human wish finds perfect and prevailing expression. He pleads our cause with the Father (1 John ii. 1 παράκλητος), and makes the prayers heard which we know not how to shape. In John xvii. we can find the substance of our own highest wants and of Christ's intercession.

ὑπὲρ αὐτῶν] The advocacy of Christ is both social and personal: for the Church and for each believer, for one because for the other. Comp. Rom. viii. 34; 1 John ii. 1, and Philo *de vit. Mos.* iii. § 24 (ii. 155 M.) ἀναγκαῖον ἦν τὸν ἱερώμενον τῷ κύσμου πατρὶ παρακλήτῳ χρῆσθαι τελειοτάτῳ τὴν ἀρετὴν υἱῷ, πρός τε ἀμνηστείαν ἁμαρτημάτων καὶ χορηγίαν ἀφθονεστάτων ἀγαθῶν.

The Fathers call attention to the contrasts which the verse includes between Christ's human and divine natures; and how His very presence before God in His humanity is in itself a prevailing intercession.

Interpellat autem pro nobis per hoc quod humanam naturam assumpsit pro nobis quam assidue ostendit vultui Dei pro nobis, et misereatur secundum utramque substantiam (Primas.).

Καὶ αὐτὸ δὲ τοῦτο τὸ σάρκα φοροῦντα τὸν υἱὸν συγκαθῆσθαι τῷ πατρὶ ἔντευξίς ἐστιν ὑπὲρ ἡμῶν· ὡσανεὶ τῆς σαρκὸς ὑπὲρ ἡμῶν δυσωπούσης τὸν πατέρα, ὡς δι' αὐτὸ τοῦτο προσληφθείσης πάντως, διὰ τὴν ἡμετέραν σωτηρίαν (Theophlct.). Αὐτὴ ἡ ἐνανθρώπησις αὐτοῦ παρακαλεῖ τὸν πατέρα ὑπὲρ ἡμῶν (Euth. Zig.).

In the Levitical ritual the truth was foreshadowed in the direction that 'Aaron shall bear the names of the children of Israel in the breastplate of judgment upon his heart when he goeth in unto the holy place...' (Ex. xxviii. 29).

(2) *Christ is High-priest for ever after the order of Melchizedek, that is the absolute High-priest* (26—28).

Up to this point the writer has developed the ideas lying in the phrase 'after the order of Melchizedek': he now shortly characterises Christ as High-priest after this order (vi. 20), before drawing out in detail the contrast between Christ and the Aaronic High-priest. Nothing is said in Scripture of the High-priesthood of Melchizedek, or of any sacrifices which he offered. In these respects the Aaronic High-priest (not Melchizedek) was the type of Christ.

The subject is laid open in a simple and natural order. First the personal traits of Christ are characterised (*v.* 26); and then His High-priestly work (*v.* 27); and lastly the contrast which He offers to the Levitical High-priests in regard to His appointment, nature and position (*v.* 28).

²⁶*For such a High-priest* [*in truth*] *became us, holy, guileless, undefiled, separated from sinners, and become higher than the heavens;* ²⁷*Who hath no need daily, as the high priests, to offer up sacrifices first for their own sins, then for the sins of the people, for this He did once for all in that He offered up Himself.* ²⁸*For the Law appointeth men high priests, having infirmity; but the*

²⁶ Τοιοῦτος γὰρ ἡμῖν [καὶ] ἔπρεπεν ἀρχιερεύς, ὅσιος,

26 ἡμῖν καὶ ABD₂ syrr : om καὶ אC vg me.

word of the oath-taking appointeth a Son perfected for ever.

26. The preceding verse furnishes a transition to the doctrine of Christ's High-priesthood. It is seen that something more is required for men than Melchizedek as priest could directly typify. He shewed the form of priesthood which Christ realised in its ideal perfection as High-priest.

τοιοῦτος γὰρ ἡμῖν] From the characteristics of Christ's priesthood foreshadowed in Melchizedek the writer deduces the general nature of His High-priesthood. The separation of τοιοῦτος from ἀρχιερεύς helps to lay stress upon the character which it summarises (comp. viii. 1). This the Vulgate translation *talis enim decebat ut nobis esset pontifex* endeavours to express, almost as if the translation were : 'Such an one became us as High-priest.'

τοιοῦτος] *Such a High-priest*, that is, one who is absolute in power (εἰς τὸ παντελές) and eternal in being (πάντοτε ζῶν). The word (τοιοῦτος) looks backwards, yet not exclusively. From the parallel (viii. 1 ; comp. 1 Cor. v. 1 ; Phlm. 9) it is seen that it looks forward also to ὃς οὐκ ἔχει (*v.* 27), which gives the most decisive feature of Christ's High-priesthood.

ἡμῖν [καὶ] ἔπρεπεν] Even our human sense of fitness is able to recognise the complete correspondence between the characteristics of Christ as High-priest and the believer's wants. Comp. c. ii. 10 note. And we shall observe that sympathy with temptation does not require the experience of sin. On the contrary his sympathy will be fullest who has known the extremest power of temptation because he has conquered. He who yields to temptation has not known its uttermost force. Comp. Hinton, *Life and Letters* p. 179.

The καὶ before ἔπρεπεν emphasises

this thought. 'Such a High-priest has been given us and also in very deed answers to our condition.' Comp. c. vi. 7 note ; and for ἔπρεπεν see c. ii. 10 note.

Primasius adds a thought beautiful in itself which may perhaps lie in the word (ἔπρεπεν): Judæi velut servi timore legis Deo servientes legales pontifices habuerunt, sibi conservos mortalesque ac peccatores...nos autem, quibus dictum est Jam non dico vos servos sed amicos meos, quia filii Dei sumus serviendo illi amore filiationis, decet ut habeamus pontificem immortalem, segregatum a peccatoribus.

ἡμῖν] '*us* Christians,' not generally ' us men.' The pronoun is apparently always used with this limitation in the Epistle.

The dominant thought is of the struggles of the Christian life, which are ever calling for divine succour. Christians have gained a view of the possibilities of life, of its divine meaning and issues, which gives an infinite solemnity to all its trials.

ὅσιος...] This detailed description characterises the fitness of the High Priest for the fulfilment of His work for man. Even in the highest exaltation He retains the perfection of His human nature. He is truly man and yet infinitely more than man. The three epithets (ὅσιος, ἄκακος, ἀμίαντος) describe absolute personal characteristics: the two descriptive clauses which follow express the issues of actual life. Christ is personally in Himself *holy*, in relation to men *guileless*, in spite of contact with a sinful world *undefiled*. By the issue of His life He has been *separated from sinners* in regard to the visible order, and, in regard to the invisible world, He has *risen above the heavens*.

ὅσιος] V. L. *justus*, Vulg. *sanctus*.

ἄκακος, ἀμίαντος, κεχωρισμένος ἀπὸ τῶν ἁμαρτωλῶν,

ἄκακος + καί A.

The word is of rare occurrence in the N. T. It is used of Christ (as quoted from Ps. xvi.) Acts ii. 27; xiii. 35: and again of 'the Lord' Apoc. xv. 4; xvi. 5; comp. Ps. cxlv. (cxliv.) 17; (Jer. iii. 12 Hebr.). It is used also of the 'bishop' Tit. i. 8; and of hands in prayer 1 Tim. ii. 8.

The word is found not very unfrequently in the LXX. and occurs especially in the Psalms (more than twenty times) as the regular equivalent of חָסִיד. Thus the people of God are characteristically described as οἱ ὅσιοι [τοῦ κυρίου] (οἱ ὅσιοι Ps. cxlix. 1, 5). The phrase οἱ ἅγιοι (קְדוֹשִׁים) is much rarer: Ps. xvi. (xv.) 2; xxxiv. (xxxiii.) 10; lxxxix. (lxxxviii.) 5, 7.

To speak broadly, ὅσιος refers to character and ἅγιος to destination. The former is used in Biblical Greek predominantly of persons (yet see Is. lv. 3 ‖ Acts xiii. 34; Deut. xxix. 19; Wisd. vi. 10; 1 Tim. ii. 8), the latter equally of persons and things.

As applied to God ἅγιος expresses that which He is absolutely: ὅσιος that which He shews Himself to be in a special relation to men.

Taken with regard to men in their relation to God ἅγιος describes their dedication to His service: ὅσιος their participation in His character, especially as shewn in His love towards them (חָסֵד). Comp. Hupfeld, Ps. iv. 4 note.

As applied to men in themselves ἅγιος marks consecration, devotion: ὅσιος marks a particular moral position.

Perhaps it is possible to see in this difference the cause of the remarkable difference of usage by which the people of God in the O. T. are οἱ ὅσιοι, and in the N. T. οἱ ἅγιοι. The outward relation of the people to God under the O. T., which was embodied in an outward system, included, or might

be taken to include, the corresponding character. Under the N. T. the relation of the believer to Christ emphasises an obligation.

The general opposite to ἅγιος is 'profane' (βέβηλος): the general opposite to ὅσιος is 'impious': the standard being the divine nature manifested under human conditions in the dealings of God with men. In this connexion ὅσιος is the complement of δίκαιος (Plat. Gorg. 507 B; comp. 1 Thess. ii. 10; Tit. i. 8; Luke i. 75; Eph. iv. 24) on the one side, and of ἱερός on the other (Thuc. ii. 52).

ἄκακος] Latt. innocens (sine malitia), guileless. Comp. Rom. xvi. 18: 1 Pet. ii. 22.

Ἄκακος τί ἐστίν; ἀπόνηρος, οὐχ ὕπουλος· καὶ ὅτι τοιοῦτος ἄκουε τοῦ προφήτου. Is. liii. 9. (Chrys.)

Ἄκακος and ἀκακία occur several times in the LXX., the former most often for פֶּתִי, the latter for תֹּם.

He who is ἄκακος embodies Christian love (1 Cor. xiii. 6 f.).

ἀμίαντος] V. L. immaculatus (incontaminatus), Vulg. impollutus, undefiled. 1 Pet. i. 4; James i. 27; (c. xiii. 4); Wisd. viii. 20.

No impurity ever hindered the fulfilment of His priestly office (Lev. xvi. 4).

Primasius tersely marks the application of the three words: Sanctus in interiore homine. Innocens manibus. Impolluto corpore.

Philo speaks of divine reason (ὁ ἱερώτατος λόγος) in man as ὁ ἀμίαντος ἀρχιερεύς (de prof. § 21; i. 563 M.), ἀμέτοχος γὰρ καὶ ἀπαράδεκτος παντὸς εἶναι πέφυκεν ἁμαρτήματος. Comp. de vict. § 10 (ii. 246 M.).

κεχωρισμένος…γενόμενος…] Latt. Segregatus a peccatoribus…excelsior factus.

The change of tense in the two participles (comp. i. 4) marks the

καὶ ὑψηλότερος τῶν οὐρανῶν γενόμενος· ²⁷ὃς οὐκ ἔχει
καθ᾽ ἡμέραν ἀνάγκην, ὥσπερ οἱ ἀρχιερεῖς, πρότερον ὑπὲρ

27 ὁ ἀρχιερεύς D₂*.

permanent issue of Christ's Life in
His exaltation, and the single fact
(to human apprehension) by which
it was realised. Contrast iv. 14 διεληλυθότα.

κεχωρ. ἀπὸ τῶν ἁμ.] The complete
separation of the Lord from sinners
(τῶν ἁμ.) which was realised through
His Life (John xiv. 30) was openly
established by His victory over death
at the resurrection (Acts ii. 24); and
that victory 'is the foundation of His
present work. (Syr vg *from sins*.)

This internal, moral, separation corresponded to the idea symbolised
by the legal purity of the Levitical
priests; and especially to the symbolic separation of the High Priest
who, according to the later ritual,
seven days before the great Day of
Atonement removed from his own
house to a chamber in the sanctuary
(Oehler, *O. T. Theol.* § 140).

ὑψηλ. τῶν οὐρ. γεν.] *having become*
(v. 9 note)...Both in His Person and
in the place of His ministry Christ
fulfilled in fact what the Jewish
priests presented in type.

Under different aspects Christ may
be said (1) to have been taken, or
to have entered, 'into heaven,' Mark
xvi. 19; Luke xxiv. 51; Acts i. 10 f.;
iii. 21; 1 Pet. iii. 22; c. ix. 24; and
to be 'in heaven,' Eph. vi. 9; and also
(2) 'to have passed beyond the heavens'
(Eph. iv. 10; c. iv. 14 note).

The former phrase expresses His
reception to the immediate presence
of God; the latter His elevation above
the limitations of sense.

27. ὃς οὐκ ἔχει καθ᾽ ἡμέραν...] The
comparison which is instituted here
is beset at first sight with a serious
difficulty. It seems to be stated that
the High-priests are under the daily
necessity of offering sacrifice for their
own sins and for the sins of the people.

This double sacrifice is elsewhere in
the Epistle (c. ix. 7) connected with
the great Day of Atonement and the
'yearly' work of the High-priest
(ix. 25); nor is it obvious how the
language can be properly used of any
daily function of the High-priest.

There can be no question that καθ᾽
ἡμέραν (Latt. *quotidie*) means only
'day by day,' 'daily' (c. x. 11). And
further 'to have necessity of sacrificing' cannot without violence be
limited to the meaning of 'feeling
daily the necessity of sacrificing' from
consciousness of sin, though the sacrifice is made only once a year.

Some interpretations therefore which
have found favour may be at once set
aside.

1. 'Who hath not necessity, as the
High Priests have on each Day of
Atonement (or 'on recurring days,'
'one day after another'), to offer sacrifices...'

This interpretation is ingeniously
represented by Biesenthal's conjecture
that the (assumed) Aramaic original
had אמוי, יומא, which the Greek translator misunderstood.

2. 'Who hath not necessity, as the
High Priests daily feel the necessity,
to offer...'

At the same time the order of the
words must be observed. The writer
says ὃς οὐκ ἔχει καθ᾽ ἡμ. ἀνάγκην...θυσίας
ἀναφέρειν, and not ὃς οὐκ ἔχει ἀνάγκην
καθ᾽ ἡμ. θ. ἀναφ. That is, the necessity
is connected with something which is
assumed to be done daily.

This peculiarity seems to suggest
the true solution of the difficulty.
The characteristic High-priestly office
of the Lord is fulfilled 'daily,' 'for
ever,' and not only, as that of the
Levitical High-priest, on one day
in the year. The continuity of His
office marks its superiority. But in

τῶν ἰδίων ἁμαρτιῶν θυσίας ἀναφέρειν, ἔπειτα τῶν τοῦ
λαοῦ· (τοῦτο γὰρ ἐποίησεν ἐφάπαξ ἑαυτὸν ἀνενέγκας·)

27 προσενέγκας

θυσίαν D₂.   ἀνενέγκας ⸂BD₂ : προσενέγκας ℵA.

this daily intercession He requires no
daily sacrifice, as those High-priests
require a sacrifice on each occasion of
their appearance before God in the
Holy of Holies.

Thus the καθ᾽ ἡμέραν belongs only to
the description of the Lord's work,
and nothing more than ἀνάγκην ἔχουσιν
is to be supplied with οἱ ἀρχιερεῖς, the
sense being : 'He hath not daily necessity [in the daily fulfilment of His
intercessory work], as the High-priests
[have necessity on each occasion when
they fulfil them], to offer sacrifices...'

This interpretation however does
not completely explain the use of καθ᾽
ἡμέραν. It might have seemed more
natural to say πολλάκις (x. 11). But
here a new thought comes in. The
daily work of the Priests was summed
up and interpreted by the special
High-priestly work of the Day of
Atonement. The two parts of the
daily sacrifice, the priestly (High-
priestly) Minchah (meal-offering) and
the lamb (the burnt-offering), were referred to the needs of the priests and
of the people respectively. See Philo,
Quis rer. div. hær. § 36 (i. p. 497 M.):
τὰς ἐνδελεχεῖς θυσίας ὁρᾶς εἰς ἴσα διη-
ρημένας, ἥν τε ὑπὲρ αὐτῶν ἀνάγουσιν οἱ
ἱερεῖς διὰ τῆς σεμιδάλεως καὶ τὴν ὑπὲρ
τοῦ ἔθνους τῶν δυοῖν ἀμνῶν οὓς ἀναφέρειν διείρηται.

And as the High-priests took part
in the daily sacrifices on special occasions, Jos. *B. J.* v. 5, 7, or at their
pleasure (Mishna, *Tamid* 7. 3), they
were said both by Philo (*de spec.
legg.* § 23, ii. 321 M.) and by the
Jewish Rabbis to offer daily : Delitzsch,
Ztschr. f. d. luther. Theol. 1860 ff.
593 f. The passage of Philo is of
considerable interest. He is dwelling
upon the representative character of

the High-priest. In this respect, he
says : τοῦ σύμπαντος ἔθνους συγγενὴς
καὶ ἀγχιστεὺς κοινὸς ὁ ἀρχιερεύς ἐστι...
εὐχάς...καὶ θυσίας τελῶν καθ᾽ ἑκάστην
ἡμέραν καὶ ἀγαθὰ αἰτούμενος ὡς ὑπὲρ
ἀδελφῶν καὶ γονέων καὶ τέκνων...

Comp. Eccles. xlv. 14 θυσίαι αὐτοῦ
('Ααρών) ὁλοκαρπωθήσονται καθ᾽ ἡμέραν
ἐνδελεχῶς δίς. *v.* 16. Ex. xxx. 7; Lev.
vi. 20 ff.; Jos. *Ant.* iii. 10, 7.

Under this aspect the daily sacrifices were a significant memorial of
the conditions of the High-priestly
intercession on the one Day of Atonement. It may be added that in this
connexion the variant ἀρχιερεύς in x.
11 is of considerable interest.

ὃς οὐκ ἔχει...] This, which is the
chief characteristic of the new High-
priest, is not given in a participial
clause, but as a substantive statement
(τοιοῦτος...ὃς οὐκ ἔχει).

ἔχ. ἀν. ... ἀναφέρειν] Lk. xiv. 18 ;
(xxiii. 17). The phrase is not in the
LXX.

οἱ ἀρχ.] the High-priests who belong
to the system under discussion.

(πρότερον)......ἔπειτα τῶν τοῦ λαοῦ]
Latt. *deinde pro populi.* This was
the order on the great Day of Atonement: Lev. xvi. 6 ff.

ἀναφέρειν] The Hellenistic use
of this verb for the offering of sacrifices occurs in N. T. in c. xiii. 15;
James ii. 21; 1 Pet. ii. 5. Comp. c. ix.
28; 1 Pet. ii. 24.

The full construction of the word
is ἀναφέρειν ἐπὶ τὸ θυσιαστήριον (James
ii. 21).

In the LXX. ἀναφέρειν is the habitual rendering of הֶעֱלָה in connexion
with the עֹלָה (ὁλοκαύτωμα); and of
הִקְטִיר in connexion with הַמִּזְבֵּחָה in
the Pentateuch.

²⁸ ὁ νόμος γὰρ ἀνθρώπους καθίστησιν ἀρχιερεῖς ἔχοντας

28 καθ. ἱερεῖς ἀνθρ. D₂.

It occurs very rarely in this sense for הֵבִיא (2 Chron. xxix. 31 f.).

On the other hand προσφέρειν is the habitual rendering of הֵבִיא and of הִקְרִיב.

It is not used in the Pentateuch as a rendering of הֶעֱלָה, though it does so occur in the later books: Jer. xiv. 12; and for הִקְטִיר 2 K. xvi. 15.

The full construction is προσφέρειν τῷ θεῷ (κυρίῳ).

From these usages it appears that in ἀναφέρειν (to offer up) we have mainly the notion of an offering made to God and placed upon His altar, in προσφέρειν (to offer) that of an offering brought to God. In the former the thought of the destination of the offering prevails: in the latter that of the offerer in his relation to God.

Ἀναφέρειν therefore properly describes the ministerial action of the priest, and προσφέρειν the action of the offerer (Lev. ii. 14, 16; vi. 33, 35); but the distinction is not observed universally; thus ἀναφέρειν is used of the people (Lev. xvii. 5), and προσφέρειν of the priests (Lev. xxi. 21).

τοῦτο γάρ...] It is generally supposed that the reference is to be limited to the latter clause, that is, to the making an offering for the sins of the people. It is of course true that for Himself Christ had no need to offer a sacrifice in any sense. But perhaps it is better to supply the ideal sense of the High-priest's offerings, and so to leave the statement in a general form. Whatever the Aaronic High-priest did in symbol, as a sinful man, that Christ did perfectly as sinless in His humanity for men.

ἐφάπαξ] c. ix. 12; x. 10. Comp. ἅπαξ vi. 4 note.

Contrary to the general usage of the Epistle ἐφάπαξ follows the word

with which it is connected instead of preceding it.

ἑαυτὸν ἀνενέγκας] in that He offered up Himself, Latt. se (seipsum) offerendo. Here first Christ is presented as at once the Priest and the victim. Comp. ix. 12, 14 (διὰ πν. αἰων.), 25 f., x. 10, 12; Eph. v. 2 (παρέδωκεν). Οὗτος δὲ τὸ ἑαυτοῦ προσενήνοχε σῶμα, αὐτὸς ἱερεὺς καὶ ἱερεῖον γενόμενος, καὶ ὡς θεὸς μετὰ τοῦ πατρὸς καὶ τοῦ πνεύματος τὸ δῶρον δεχόμενος (Thdt.).

Herveius calls attention to the uniqueness of Christ's sacrifice: ut quoniam quatuor considerantur in omni sacrificio, quid offeratur, cui offeratur, a quo offeratur, pro quibus offeratur, idem ipse unus verusque mediator per sacrificium pacis reconcilians nos Deo unum cum illo maneret cui offerebat, unum in se faceret pro quibus offerebat, unus ipse esset qui offerebat et quod offerebat.

The offering of Christ upon the Cross was a High-priestly act, though Christ did not become 'High-priest after the order of Melchizedek,' that is, royal High-priest, till the Ascension. Comp. vi. 20 note.

On the completeness of Christ's priestly work Chrysostom has a striking sentence: μὴ τοίνυν αὐτὸν ἱερέα ἀκούσας ἀεὶ ἱερᾶσθαι νόμιζε· ἅπαξ γὰρ ἱεράσατο καὶ λοιπὸν ἐκάθισεν. Comp. Euth. Zig. ὁ Χριστὸς ἅπαξ ἱεράτευσεν.

28. ὁ νόμος...ὁ λόγος τῆς ὁρκωμ....] The freedom of Christ from the necessity by which the Aaronic High-priests are bound follows from His nature, for the Law... The truth which has been laid open in the two preceding verses is here expressed summarily by recapitulation in its final form: the Levitical High-priests are weak men, the High-priest after the order of Melchizedek a Son eternally perfected.

ἀνθρώπους] in contrast with υἱόν:

ἀσθένειαν, ὁ λόγος δὲ τῆς ὁρκωμοσίας τῆς μετὰ τὸν
νόμον γιόν, εἰc τὸν ἀιῶνα *τετελειωμένον.*

many men (*v.* 23) are contrasted with the One Son. The plural also suggests the notion of death in contrast with εἰς τὸν αἰῶνα.

ἔχοντας ἀσθ.] cf. c. v. 2. For the force of ἔχων ἀσθένειαν as distinguished from ἀσθενής see 1 John i. 8 note. Compare v. 12; vii. 27; ix. 8; x. 36; xi. 25. This 'weakness' includes both the actual limitations of humanity as it is, and the personal imperfections and sins of the particular priest. The use of the sing. (ἀσθένεια) and the plur. (ἀσθένειαι) is always instructive.

For sing. in the Epistles see Rom. vi. 19; viii. 26; 1 Cor. ii. 3; xv. 43; 2 Cor. xi. 30.

For plur. c. iv. 15; 2 Cor. xii. 5, 10. The sing. and plur. occur together, 2 Cor. xii. 9. Compare Matt. viii. 17.

ὁ λ. τῆς ὁρκωμ. τῆς μ. τ. ν.] *the word of the oath,* spoken in Psalm cx. 4, *which was taken after the Law...* The 'oath-taking' and not the 'word' is the emphatic element (ὁρκ. τῆς μετὰ τ. ν. not ὁ μετὰ τ. ν.). The oath came after the Law, and must therefore have had respect to it, and so prospectively annulled it. In this respect the 'oath' takes up the 'promise.' Comp. Gal. iii. 17.

υἱόν, εἰς τ. αἰ. τετελ.] The idea of Son (i. 1 ff.; iii. 6; iv. 14 τὸν υἱὸν τοῦ θεοῦ) is now combined with that of High-priest. Our High-priest is not only a Son, but a Son who having become man has been raised above all the limitations of humanity. The complete idea of the Person of the High-priest of the new Dispensation is thus gained before His work is unfolded in detail.

Compare THEODORET: οὐ μὴν ἄλλον

υἱὸν νοητέον παρὰ τὸν φύσει υἱὸν ἀλλὰ τὸν αὐτὸν καὶ φύσει ὄντα υἱὸν ὡς θεὸν καὶ πάλιν δεχόμενον τὴν αὐτὴν προσηγορίαν ὡς ἄνθρωπον.

And PRIMASIUS: Ponit hic Apostolus Filii nomen ad distinctionem servorum qui fuerunt in lege; quia servi infirmi fuerunt sive quia peccatores sive quia mortales erant: Filium vero perfectum ostendit, quia semper vivit et sine peccato est.

τετελειωμένον] For the idea of τελείωσις see ii. 10 note. Hitherto the idea of Christ's consummation has been regarded in its historic realisation (ii. 10 τελειῶσαι, v. 9 τελειωθείς). Now it is regarded in its abiding issues. Comp. ii. 18 πέπονθεν note.

The participle, as contrasted with the adjective τέλειος, forms a complete antithesis to ἔχων ἀσθένειαν. The perfection is gained through the experience of a true human life (c. v. 7—9).

The realisation of the Priesthood of Christ necessarily carries with it the abrogation of the typical priesthood of the Law. The presence of 'weakness' in the Levitical priests was realised in the consequences of imperfection and death. Such a priesthood could not bring τελείωσις, and it was of necessity interrupted. On the other hand Christ took upon Himself human nature (iv. 15) subject to temptation and death, that so He might *taste death for all,* but as High-priest in His glory He is raised wholly above all infirmity and death, though still able to sympathise with those who are subject to them (cf. v 1 f.). Compare Additional Note.

Additional Note on vii. 1. *The significance of Melchizedek.*

The appearance of Melchizedek in the narrative of the Pentateuch is of deep interest, both (1) from the position which he occupies in the course of Revelation; and (2) from the manner in which the record of his appearance is treated in the Epistle.

1. Melchizedek appears at a crisis in the religious history of the world as the representative of primitive revelation, or of the primitive relation of God and man still preserved pure in some isolated tribe. If, as on the whole seems to be most likely, he was an Amorite, the fact that he had preserved a true faith becomes more impressive. On this point however Scripture is wholly silent. The lessons of his appearance lie in the appearance itself. Abraham marks a new departure, the beginning of a new discipline, in the divine history of mankind starting from a personal call. The normal development of the divine life has been interrupted. But before the fresh order is established we have a vision of the old in its superior majesty; and this, on the eve of disappearance, gives its blessing to the new. So the past and the future meet: the one bearing witness to an original communion of God and men which had been practically lost, the other pointing forward to a future fellowship to be established permanently. At the same time the names of the God of the former revelation and of the God of the later revelation are set side by side and identified (Gen. xiv. 22; comp. Deut. xxxii. 8 f.). *The position of Melchizedek in the course of Revelation.*

2. The writer of the Epistle interprets the Scriptural picture of Melchizedek, and does not attempt to realise the historical person of Melchizedek. He starts from the phrase in the Psalm *after the order of Melchizedek* (κατὰ τάξιν Μελχισεδέκ), and determines the ideas which such a description was fitted to convey from a study, not of the life of the king-priest, which was unknown, but of the single record of him which had been preserved. By the choice of the phrase the Psalmist had already broadly distinguished the priesthood of the divine king from the Levitical priesthood. It remained to work out the distinction. Therefore the writer of the Epistle insists upon the silence of Scripture. He draws lessons from the fact that in the narrative of the O. T. no mention is made of the parentage or genealogy of Melchizedek or of the commencement or close of his priestly office[1]. He seeks to set vividly before his readers the impression conveyed by the remarkable phenomena of his unique appearance in patriarchal life, and the thoughts which they might suggest. *The treatment of the Biblical record in the Epistle.*

[1] Philo uses the silence of Scripture in a similar way: *e.g.* the absence of any geographical details in the mention of the Euphrates (Gen. ii. 14), *Leg. Alleg.* i. 27 (i. 60 M.); the absence of the title 'son' in the record of the birth of Cain (Gen. iv. 1; contrast iv. 25), *de Cher.* §§ 16 f. (i. 149 M.); the absence of the personal name of the man who met Joseph, *Quod det. pot. insid.* § 8 (i. 195—6). Siegfried, *Philo v. Alex.* 179 f.

At the same time this mode of treatment leaves the actual human personality and history of Melchizedek quite untouched. The writer does not imply that that was true of him literally as a living man which is suggested in the ideal interpretation of his single appearance in the Bible. He does not answer the question Who and what was Melchizedek? but What is the characteristic conception which can be gained from Scripture of the Priesthood of Melchizedek?

The treatment typical not allegorical.
The treatment of the history of Melchizedek is typical and not allegorical. The Epistle in fact contains no allegorical interpretation. The difference between the two modes is clear and decisive. Between the type and the antitype there is a historical, a real, correspondence in the main idea of each event or institution. Between the allegory and the application the correspondence lies in special points arbitrarily taken to represent facts or thoughts of a different kind. A history, for example, is taken to illustrate the relation of abstract ideas (comp. Gal. iv.). The understanding of the type lies in the application of a rule of proportion. The law by which it is regulated lies in the record, which is taken to represent the life. The understanding of the allegory depends on the fancy of the composer. He determines which of many possible applications shall be given to the subject with which he deals.

A type presupposes a purpose in history wrought out from age to age. An allegory rests finally in the imagination, though the thoughts which it expresses may be justified by the harmonies which connect the many elements of life.

This consideration tends further to explain why the writer of the Epistle takes the Biblical record of Melchizedek, that is Melchizedek so far as he enters into the divine history, and not Melchizedek himself, as a type of Christ. The history of the Bible is the record of the divine life of humanity, of humanity as it was disciplined for the Christ. The importance of this limitation of the treatment of the subject is recognised by patristic writers; e.g. λέγει τὰ κατ᾽ ἐκεῖνον οὐ τὴν φύσιν ἐξηγούμενος ἀλλὰ τὴν κατ᾽ αὐτὸν διήγησιν ἀπὸ τῆς θείας τιθεὶς γραφῆς καὶ ἀπ᾽ ἐκείνης ἐμφαίνων τὸ ὅμοιον (Theodore ap. Cram. Cat. vii. p. 203).

The omission of the gift of bread and wine.
One omission in the Epistle cannot but strike the student. The writer takes no notice of the gifts of Melchizedek, who 'brought forth bread and wine' (Gen. xiv. 18) when he came to meet Abraham. This is the more remarkable as the incident is dwelt upon in the Midrash. The 'bread and wine' are regarded there as symbols of the shewbread and the drink-offering, or of the Torah itself (Beresh. R. xliii. 18 [Prov. ix. 5]; Wünsche p. 199). And stress was naturally laid upon this detail in later times. The Fathers from Clement of Alexandria (see below) and Cyprian (Ep. ad Caecil. 63, 4) downwards not unfrequently regard the bread and wine as the materials of a sacrifice offered by Melchizedek; and Jerome distinctly states that they were offered for Abraham (ad Matt. xxii. 41 ff.; comp. ad Matt. xxvi. 26 ff.)[1].

---

[1] Bellarmine (Controv. de Missa i. c. 6) dwells at considerable length on this aspect of the incident, and gives a long array of quotations in support. A still further collection is given by Petavius de Incarn. xii. 12. The true view is preserved by Josephus Antt. i. 10, 2; Philo (see below); Tertullian adv. Jud.

All this makes the silence of the Apostle the more significant. He presents, and we cannot but believe that he purposely presents, Melchizedek as priest, not in sacrificing but in blessing, that is, in communicating the fruits of an efficacious sacrifice already made. He only can bless who is in fellowship with God and speaks as His representative. And it is under this aspect that the writer of the Epistle brings before us characteristically the present work of Christ.

A similar lesson lies in the positive fact which stands out most signifi- *The com-* cantly in the words of the Epistle. Melchizedek is priest at once and king. *bination of* The combination of offices which meets us in the simplest forms of society *priestly* is seen to be realised also when humanity has attained its end. Philo in an *offices.* interesting passage points out the difficulty of combining the priesthood with kingly power (*de carit.* § 1 ; ii. p. 384 M.), and yet such a combination must exist in the ideal state. He who unites with the Unseen must direct action. He who commands the use of every endowment and faculty must be able to consecrate them. He who represents man to God with the efficacy of perfect sympathy must also represent God to man with the authority of absolute power.

It is remarkable that Melchizedek is not dwelt upon in early Jewish *Silence of* commentators. It does not appear that he was ever regarded as a type of *Jewish* Messiah (Schoettgen *ad loc.*). The only example of this interpretation is *writers as* quoted by Heinsius from Moses Hadarshan, whose person and writings are *zedek.* involved in great obscurity, but who seems to have lived in the 11th century (Heinsius, *Exercit. Sacrœ,* p. 517 ; and from him Deyling, *Exercit. Sacrœ,* ii. 73).

The writer of the Epistle, as we have seen, regards Melchizedek as a *Philo.* living type of a living and eternal King-priest. The old history, true in its literal reality, was, according to him, perfectly, ideally fulfilled in the facts of Christian history. Philo also deals with Melchizedek, but with characteristic differences. For Philo the history is a philosophic allegory and not a typical foreshadowing of a true human life. Melchizedek represents the power of rational persuasion which offers to the soul food of gladness and joy, and so in some sense answers to the priestly Logos : *Leg. Alleg.* iii. §§ 25 f. (i. p. 103 M.) : καλείσθω οὖν ὁ μὲν τύραννος ἄρχων πολέμου ὁ δὲ βασιλεὺς ἡγεμὼν εἰρήνης, Σαλήμ. καὶ προσφερέτω τῇ ψυχῇ τροφὰς εὐφροσύνης καὶ χαρᾶς πλήρεις· ἄρτους γὰρ καὶ οἶνον προσφέρει... Thus he recognises his position as a 'natural' priest, but his priesthood is a symbol of the action of 'right reason,' which brings to man righteousness and joy through thoughts of absolute truth. Compare *de congr. erud. grat.* § 18 (i. p. 533 M.) ὁ τὴν αὐτομαθῆ καὶ αὐτοδίδακτον λαχὼν ἱερωσύνην ; *de Abrahamo* § 40 (ii. 34 M.) ὁ μέγας ἀρχιερεὺς τοῦ μεγίστου θεοῦ.

Clement of Alexandria dwells on the combination of righteousness and *Clement of Alexandria.*

---

3 ; Epiph. *Hær.* lv. § 8, p. 475, nor can there be any doubt that the original narrative describes refreshment offered to Abraham and his company and not a sacrifice made on their behalf. Compare, in answer to

Bellarmine, Whitaker *Disputation,* pp. 167 f. (Park. Soc.) ; Jackson *On the Creed,* ix. 10 ; Waterland *App. to the Christian Sacrifice explained,* pp. 462 ff. (ed. 1868). Heidegger *Hist. Patr.* ii. Dissert. 2 § 21.

peace in Melchizedek and Christ, and sees in the offerings of bread and wine a figure of the Eucharist (εἰς τύπον εὐχαριστίας Strom. iv. 25 § 163, p. 637 P.; comp. Strom. ii. 5 § 21, p. 439 P.).

Jerome. Jerome gives in one of his letters (*Ep.* lxxiii. *ad Evangelum* ; comp. Vallarsius *ad loc.*) a summary of early opinions as to the person of Melchizedek in answer to a correspondent who had sent him an essay written with a view to shew that Melchizedek was a manifestation of the Holy Spirit.

Origen and Didymus, he says, regarded him as an Angel (compare Nagel *Stud. u. Krit.* 1849, ss. 332 ff.). Hippolytus, Irenæus, Eusebius of Cæsarea, Eusebius of Emesa, Apollinaris, and Eustathius of Antioch, as a man, a Canaanite prince, who exercised priestly functions, like 'Abel, Enoch, Noah, Job.'

The Jews, he adds (and so Primasius : 'tradunt Hebræi'), identified him with Shem, an opinion which finds expression in the Targums of Jonathan and Jerusalem : Melchizedek king of Jerusalem, he is Shem the son of Noah [*Jerus.* the High-priest (רבא כהן) of the Most High].

This last opinion has found much favour; but it is supported by no direct evidence (comp. Heidegger *Hist. Patriarch.* ii. Diss. 2). Epiphanius attributes it to the Samaritans (*Hær.* lv. 6 ; p. 471).

Some hold Melchizedek to be a divine manifestation. Two other strange opinions may be noticed. Some orthodox Christians supposed that Melchizedek was an Incarnation of the Son of God or perhaps simply a Christophany. How then, Epiphanius asks, could he be said to be made like to himself? (*Hær.* lv. 7 ; p. 474). Hierax (c. 280) in order to avoid this difficulty held, according to the view noticed by Jerome, that he was an Incarnation, or more probably an appearance, of the Holy Spirit (Epiph. *Hær.* lxvii. 7 ; p. 715). This opinion finds a very bold expression in the anonymous *Quæst. ex V. et N. Testamento* appended to the works of Augustine (Vol. iii. Ed. Bened.) : Similis Dei filio non potest esse nisi sit ejusdem naturæ. Et quid incredibile si Melchisedech ut homo apparuit cum intelligatur tertia esse persona ? Si enim Christus qui secunda persona est frequenter visus est in habitu hominis, quid ambigitur de iis quæ dicta sunt ? Summus sacerdos Christus est, Melchisedech secundus...Christus vicarius Patris est et antistes, ac per hoc dicitur et sacerdos. Similiter et Spiritus sanctus, quasi antistes, sacerdos appellatus est excelsi Dei, non summus, sicut nostri in oblatione præsumunt... (Aug. iii. App. § cix. Migne *P. L.* 35, p. 2329; comp. Hier. *Ep.* lxxiii. *ad Evang.* § 1).

The sect of the Melchizedechians. The sect of the 'Melchizedechians' described by Epiphanius (*Hær.* lv.) offers some points of interest. As an offshoot of the 'Theodotians' (Epiph. *l. c.* i.; p. 468) they started from humanitarian views of Christ, and naturally looked for some higher Mediator. Melchizedek, they argued, was higher than Christ, because Christ was appointed after his order. Christ was ordained by God to turn men from idols and shew them the way to the true knowledge of this eternal High-priest. They therefore 'made their offerings to the name of Melchizedek' (§ 8 εἰς ὄνομα τούτου τοῦ Μελχισεδὲκ ἡ...αἵρεσις καὶ τὰς προσφορὰς ἀναφέρει), in order that 'through him offerings might be made (προσενεχθῇ) for them and they might find life through him.' He was in their judgment the priest 'who brought men to God' (εἰσαγωγεὺς πρὸς τὸν θεόν)[1].

The tradition, or fiction, as to Melchizedek in 'the Book of Adam' is singularly picturesque. To him and Shem, it is said, the charge was given to bear the body of Adam to Calvary, and place it there where in after time the Incarnate Word should suffer, so that the blood of the Saviour might fall on the skull of the Protoplast. In the fulfilment of this mission Melchizedek built an altar of twelve stones, typical of the twelve apostles, by the spot where Adam was laid, and offered upon it, by the direction of an angel, bread and wine 'as a symbol of the sacrifice which Christ should make' in due time. When the mission was accomplished Shem returned to his old home, but Melchizedek, divinely appointed to this priesthood, continued to serve God with prayer and fasting at the holy place, arrayed in a robe of fire. So afterwards when Abraham came to the neighbourhood he communicated to him also 'the holy mysteries,' the symbolical Eucharist. (Dillmann, *Das Christl. Adambuch d. Morgenl.* ss. 111 ff., 1853.)

The legend of Melchizedek and Adam.

Additional Note on vii. 1. *The Biblical Idea of Blessing.*

The idea of 'blessing' in its simplest form, the solemn expression, that is, of goodwill towards another by one who occupies in this respect a position of superiority towards him, is a natural recognition of the spiritual influence of man upon man. The idea often becomes degraded, materialised, perverted : it gives rise to the opposite conception of 'cursing'; but in Scripture it assumes a characteristic form which throws light upon the Biblical teaching as to man's relation to God.

The general idea of Blessing.

The two words which are used in the Old and New Testaments for blessing בֵּרַךְ (בָּרַךְ) and εὐλογεῖν appear to convey two fundamental thoughts which are included in the act. The first (בָּרַךְ), from a root which describes 'kneeling,' 'prostration,' seems to express the feeling of reverent adoration which arises from the recognition of a spiritual presence by him who blesses[2]; and the second (εὐλογεῖν) marks the utterance of the good which is supposed to be prophetically seen or ideally anticipated and realised[3].

Biblical words for Blessing.

---

[1] The sect is noticed very briefly by Philastrius, *Hær.* 52; and by Augustine, *De hær.* 34. The writer whose fragment is attached to Tertull. *de præscr.* (§ 53) and Theodoret (*Hær. Fab.* ii. 6) assign its origin to another Theodotus, later than Theodotus of Byzantium. The former writer appears to have had some independent source of information. He grounds the superiority of Melchizedek on the fact 'eo quod agat Christus pro hominibus, deprecator eorum et advocatus factus, Melchizedek facere pro cælestibus angelis atque virtutibus'...(*l.c.*).

[2] The construction of בֵּרַךְ is normally with the simple accusative whether the object be God or man. In the later language it is construed with לְ : 1 Chron. xxix. 20; Neh. xi. 2; and Dan. ii. 19; iv. 31 (Chald.).

[3] Εὐλογεῖν in the LXX. generally takes an accusative of the object. In the later books it is rarely construed with the dative: Dan. iv. 31 (not ii. 19); Ecclus. l. 22; li. 12; 2 Macc. x. 38. Comp. Jer. iv. 2.

Thus the two words when taken together describe the conception of blessing in its loftiest sense as involving a true perception of what God is and what His will is, both generally and towards the person over whom it is pronounced, according as the blessing is addressed to God Himself or to man.

The Biblical idea of Blessing illustrated by the Blessings of the Patriarch.

The patriarchal blessings bring out this idea of blessing distinctly. This appears in the first exercise of the father's prophetic power (Gen. ix. 25 ff.). The curse and the blessing of Noah pronounced upon his sons is the unveiling of their future. The blessing of Shem lies in the recognition of the majesty of the Lord (Gen. ix. 26 *Blessed be (is) the LORD, the God of Shem*). The truth becomes plainer afterwards. The patriarch becomes the interpreter of the divine counsel to him through whom it is to be fulfilled. His own natural purpose is subordinated to the expression of the spiritual message which he delivers. The will of God found so clear a revelation in His direct dealings with Abraham and Isaac that no human voice was needed to enforce it. A new departure began with Jacob. Here a choice was made by God contrary to the wish of Isaac, but when once Isaac perceived what had been done he acknowledged that the will of God was his will also (Gen. xxvii. 33). Jacob himself, in his turn, consciously set aside the privilege of birth (Gen. xlviii. 14 ff.) and gave precedence to Ephraim the younger son in his blessing of Joseph (Gen. xlviii. 19). And so completely is the thought of the declaration of the divine counsel identified with the blessing of him to whom it is announced that in the prophetic outline of the fortunes of the twelve tribes (Gen. xlix.) even the outward disasters which were announced to Reuben, Simeon, and Levi are reckoned among blessings (Gen. xlix. 28) by him who saw beyond the human aspect of things (comp. Deut. xxxiii.).

Such an idea of blessing as the simple announcement of the counsel of God, which must in its essence be welcomed as a counsel of righteousness and love, is a fruit of revelation. It corresponds with the view of creation as destined to fulfil the purpose of the Creator in spite of the self-assertion of the creature. It embodies an absolute faith in human progress.

The ethnic idea of Blessing.

In sharp contrast with this divine idea of blessing is that which is expressed by Balak. For him blessings and curses are dispensed by the arbitrary will of one who is possessed of an exceptional power (Num. xxii. 6; comp. xxiv. 1). But the utter frustration of his hopes leaves in the record of Scripture the fullest possible affirmation of the fact that the prophet cannot do more than give utterance to that which is the mind of God (Num. xxii. 38; xxiii. 26; xxiv. 13. Comp. Josh. vi. 26; 2 K. ii. 24).

The ritual Blessing.

The prophetic blessing is necessarily exceptional, but the solemn declaration of God's purpose belongs to all time. Thus in the organisation of worship and life blessing is the voice of the authoritative minister of God, the priest or the head of the household, who acknowledges the love and power of God and prays that they may be effective for those on whose behalf they are invoked (comp. 2 Sam. vi. 18; 1 K. viii. 5 f., 55; 1 Chron. xvi. 2; 1 Sam. ii. 20; 2 Chron. xxx. 27). Blessings formed an important part of the public and of the private service of the Jews. When Aaron was solemnly invested with the priesthood '*he lifted up his hands towards the people and blessed them'* (Lev. ix. 22), and at this point of transition in the religious history of Israel Moses joined with him in repeating the action, *'and the glory of the LORD appeared to all the people'* (Lev. ix. 23). The first treatise in the Mishnah is on 'Blessings' (*Berachoth*); and the series of 'the Eighteen' Blessings is the most striking feature in the daily service of the Synagogue.

The form of sacerdotal blessing prescribed to 'Aaron and his sons' (Num. vi. 22 ff.) brings into a clear light the character and the foundation of the divine blessing:

The LORD bless thee and keep thee :

The LORD make His face to shine upon thee, and be gracious unto thee :

The LORD lift up His countenance upon thee, and give thee peace (comp. Ps. iv. 6; lxvii. 1).

So, it is added, *shall they put my Name upon the children of Israel, and I will bless them.* The blessing, that is, consists in the true fellowship of the people with God as He had made Himself known to them. Hence the act of blessing itself is said to be 'in the Name of the Lord' (1 Chron. xxiii. 13; Ecclus. xlv. 15). He who fulfils it does so in virtue of his own connexion with God (comp. John xiv. 13 note).

It appears from what has been already said that the idea of a true blessing lies in the vision and realisation of the divine will. This thought is applied in many different ways. Man 'blesses' God: God 'blesses' man: man 'blesses' man: and, much more rarely, both God and man 'bless' objects which are not personal. When man 'blesses' God he devoutly acknowledges some special feature in His nature or purpose or action which he regards as a ground of grateful praise: Deut. viii. 10; Jud. v. 2, 9; 1 K. x. 9; Neh. ix. 5. [*]*Blessing by God and by man.*

If God 'blesses' man, He makes known to him something as to His counsel which the man is able to appropriate for his spiritual good: Gen. i. 28; ix. 1; xii. 2 f. &c.; xvii. 16; xxv. 11; (Num. vi. 24).

If man 'blesses' man, he speaks as the representative of the Divine Voice declaring its message in the form of prayer or of interpretation: Gen. xxvii. 4 ff.; xlvii. 7; xlix. 28; Lev. ix. 23; Num. vi. 23; Deut. x. 8; xxi. 5.

When God blesses an impersonal object, He reveals His purpose to make known through it something of Himself: Gen. i. 22; ii. 3; Ex. xxiii. 25; Job i. 10; Ps. lxv. 10; cxxxii. 15; Prov. iii. 33.

When man 'blesses' an impersonal object he recognises in it the working of God: 1 Sam. ix. 13 (a unique example in the O. T.).

The last form of expression is specially liable to misunderstanding. In such a blessing there is nothing of the idea of a charm or of any magical working. The full phrase is 'to bless God for the thing'; and the early forms of blessing pronounced over various articles of food express the thought without any ambiguity. Mishna, *Berachoth,* vi. 1 'How do we bless for fruit? For fruit of a tree say "[Blessed art Thou, O Lord our God], who createst the fruit of the wood"... For fruits of the earth say "Who createst the fruit of the ground," excepting the bread. For the bread say "Who bringest forth bread from the earth"...' Compare De Sola's *Form of Prayers,* &c., Philadelphia, 5638 [1878], i. pp. 270* ff.

The Jewish idea of 'blessing' which passes from the thought of adoration to the thoughts of petition and thanksgiving, all lying in the central thought of God's revealed nature, finds a characteristic and most noble expression in the 'Eighteen' Benedictions which have formed a part of the Synagogue Service from the earliest times. The text has no doubt been revised; additions have been made to it: differences exist between the forms adopted in the congregations of the Spanish and German Jews: but substantially these 'Benedictions' seem to have been in use in the Apostolic age. The first three and the last three are probably some centuries older. The whole collection forms the most precious liturgical writing of the præ-Christian period, and it has exercised considerable influence upon Christian services. As the embodiment of Jewish devotion which the Apostles and the Lord Himself may have used it claims careful study. The Benedictions are given in the following form in the Spanish (Sephardic) recension:

1. Blessed art Thou, O LORD our God, and the God of our fathers, the God of Abraham, the God of Isaac, and the God of Jacob (Ex. iii. 15), the great God, the mighty, and the terrible (Deut. x. 17), God most High (Gen. xiv. 18), that bestowest gracious benefits (חֲסָדִים טוֹבִים), that possessest the universe, and rememberest the good deeds of the fathers (חַסְדֵי אָבוֹת), even He that bringeth a Redeemer unto their sons' sons for His Name's sake in love.

O King, Helper, and Saviour, and Shield, blessed art Thou, O LORD, the Shield of Abraham.

2. Thou art mighty for ever, O LORD. Thou causest the dead to live, plenteous to save, sustaining the living in Thy goodness, quickening the dead in Thy plenteous compassion, supporting the fallen, and healing the sick, and loosing them that are in bonds, and fulfilling Thy truth to them that sleep in the dust. Who is like unto Thee, O Lord of mighty deeds; and who can be compared unto Thee, O King, that bringest to death, and bringest to life, and causest salvation to spring forth? Yea, Thou art faithful to bring the dead to life.

Blessed art Thou, O LORD, that bringest the dead to life.

3. Thou art holy and Thy Name is holy. And the holy ones praise Thee every day. Selah.

Blessed art Thou, O LORD, the holy God.

4. Thou graciously givest to man (לְאָדָם) knowledge, and teachest mortal man (לֶאֱנוֹשׁ) understanding. So graciously give unto us knowledge and understanding and wisdom.

Blessed art Thou, O LORD, that graciously givest knowledge.

5. Turn us again, our Father, to Thy law; and make us draw near, our King, to Thy service; and bring us back with a perfect repentance to Thy presence.

Blessed art Thou, O LORD, that hast pleasure in repentance.

6. Pardon us, our Father, for we have sinned. Forgive us, our King,

for we have transgressed. For Thou, God, art good and ready to forgive.

Blessed art Thou, O LORD, most gracious, that dost abundantly pardon (Is. lv. 7).

7. Look, we beseech Thee, on our affliction; and plead our cause; and hasten to redeem us with a perfect redemption for Thy Name's sake. For Thou, God, art a strong Redeemer (Jer. l. 34).

Blessed art Thou, O LORD, the Redeemer of Israel.

8. Heal us, O LORD, and we shall be healed. Save us and we shall be saved (Jer. xvii. 14). For Thou art our praise. Yea, cure and heal all our diseases and all our pains and all our wounds. For Thou, God, art a compassionate and faithful Healer.

Blessed art Thou, O LORD; even He that healeth the diseases of His people Israel.

9. Bless us, our Father, in all the works of our hands; and bless our year with the dews of (Thy) favour, blessing and beneficence; and may its close be life and plenty and peace, as the good years that were for a blessing. For Thou, God, art good, and doest good, and blessest the years.

Blessed art Thou, O LORD, that blessest the years[1].

10. Sound the great trumpet for our freedom; and lift up a banner to gather our captives; and gather us together speedily from the four corners of the earth (land) to our own land (Deut. xxx. 4; Is. xxvii. 13).

Blessed art Thou, O LORD; even He that gathereth the outcasts of His people Israel.

11. Restore us our judges as at the first; and our counsellors as at the beginning (Is. i. 26); and turn from us sorrow and sighing; and reign over us speedily, Thou, O LORD, alone, in compassion, in righteousness and in judgment.

Blessed art Thou, O LORD, a king that lovest righteousness and judgment (Ps. xxxiii. 5).

12. To slanderers (traitors)[2] let there be no hope; and let all heretics (כָּל־הַמִּינִים) and all proud men perish in a moment. And let all thy enemies and all that hate Thee be speedily cut off. And let every one that doeth wickedness be speedily rooted up and broken in pieces and consumed. And bow them down speedily in our days.

Blessed art Thou, O LORD, that breakest the enemies in pieces, and bowest down the proud.

13. Upon the righteous, and upon the pious (הַחֲסִידִים), and upon the remnant of Thy people, the house of Israel, and upon the residue of the house of their scribes, and upon the proselytes of righteousness, and upon

---

[1] Two forms of this Benediction are given for use in Summer (given in the translation) and Winter respectively. Both texts differ considerably from that in the German service.

[2] For the history of this Section, which has been commonly applied to Christians, that is, Christian converts from Judaism, see Hamburger, *Real-Encycl. für Bibel u. Talmud* ii. s. v. *Schemone-Esre*; or Dr Ginsburg in Kitto-Alexander, *Cyclop. of Bibl. Literature*, s. v. *Synagogue*.

us let Thy compassions, we pray Thee, be moved, O Lord, our God, and give a good reward to all that trust in Thy Name in truth, and set our portion with them.   And let us not be put to shame for ever, for in Thee do we trust, and upon Thy great mercy are we stayed in truth.

Blessed art Thou, O Lord, that art a stay and confidence to the righteous.

14 *a.*   Dwell in the midst of Jerusalem, Thy city, as Thou hast said ; and establish in the midst of her speedily the throne of David ; and build her an eternal building speedily in our days.

Blessed art Thou, O Lord, that buildest Jerusalem.

14 *b.*   Cause the Shoot (צֶמַח) of David Thy servant speedily to spring forth ; and let his house be exalted in Thy Salvation; for we wait for Thy salvation day by day.

Blessed art Thou, O Lord, that causest the horn of salvation to spring forth.

15.   Hear our voice, O Lord, our God, merciful Father.   Have mercy and compassion upon us ; and receive in compassion and favour our prayer. For Thou, God, hearest prayers and supplications.   And send us not away, our King, empty from Thy presence.   Be gracious unto us, and answer us, and hear our prayer ; for Thou hearest the prayer of every mouth.

Blessed art Thou, O Lord, that hearest prayer.

16.   Look, O Lord our God, with favour on Thy people Israel ; and have regard to their prayer : and restore the service to the oracle (לִדְבִיר) of Thy house.   And mayest Thou receive with favour speedily the burnt offerings of Israel and their prayer in love.   And may the service of Israel be pleasing to Thee perpetually.   And do Thou in Thy plenteous compassion look kindly upon us and be favourable to us ; and may our eyes behold when Thou returnest with compassion to Zion.

Blessed art thou, O Lord, even He that restoreth His Shekinah to Zion.

17.   We confess unto Thee that Thou art He, the Lord our God, and the God of our Fathers, for ever and ever : our Rock, the Rock of our life, and the Shield of our salvation.   Thou art He.   From generation to generation we give thanks to Thee and declare Thy praise....

Blessed art Thou, O Lord; goodness is Thy Name, and to Thee it is meet to give thanks.

18.   Grant peace, goodness, and blessing, life, grace and mercy, righteousness and compassion unto us and unto all Israel Thy people; and bless us, our Father, all of us together, in the light of Thy countenance (Num. vi. 26).   For in the light of Thy countenance Thou hast given to us, O Lord our God, the Law and life, love and mercy, righteousness and compassion, blessing and peace.   And may it be good in Thine eyes to bless Thy people Israel with abundant strength and peace.

Blessed art Thou, O Lord ; even He that blesseth His people with peace.

Each section rests upon the Confession of some feature in the revealed character of God.   Prayer is only the application of that which He has made known of Himself to the circumstances of the worshipper. Even in judgment there is a manifestation of His righteousness which the believer welcomes with grateful reverence (compare Hamburger and Ginsburg in the articles quoted above).

When we pass from the Old Testament to the New we find that the use of εὐλογεῖν (εὐλογία, εὐλογητός, εὐλογημένος) in the N. T. closely corresponds with the use in the LXX. Εὐλογεῖν is used

Blessing in the N. T.
The use of Εὐλογεῖν.

1. Absolutely without any expressed object, but with the clear thought of Him to whom praise is due for every good : Mk. vi. 41 ‖ Matt. xiv. 19 ; Mk. xiv. 22 ‖ Matt. xxvi. 26 (all. εὐχαριστήσας) ; Lk. xxiv. 30. In these cases indeed it is possible to take τοὺς ἄρτους, τὸν ἄρτον, as the object from the context (see § 3), but the Jewish custom points very plainly in the other direction ; and this construction is decisively supported by the parallel use of εὐχαριστεῖν Mk. xiv. 23 ‖ Matt. xxvi. 27 ; Mk. viii. 6 ; Lk. xxii. 17, 19 ; John vi. 11. Both words describe the devout acknowledgment of God's power and love ; but while εὐλογεῖν regards these in relation to God as attributes of His glorious Majesty, εὐχαριστεῖν regards them in relation to man as the occasion of grateful thanksgiving.

In other connexions εὐλογεῖν is used absolutely in 1 Pet. iii. 9 ; 1 Cor. iv. 12 ; xiv. 16 ; (Rom. xii. 14).

In Mk. x. 16 αὐτά is probably to be supplied to κατευλόγει.

2. With a personal object ; either

(a) God : Lk. i. 64 ; ii. 28 ; xxiv. 53 ; James iii. 9 ; or

(b) Man : Lk. ii. 34 ; vi. 28 ; xxiv. 50 f. ; Acts iii. 26 ; Rom. xii. 14 ; Eph. i. 3 ; Hebr. vi. 14 (LXX.) ; vii. 1, 6, 7 ; xi. 20 f. (in these examples both man and God are the subjects).

3. With a material object : Mk. viii. 7 ; Lk. ix. 16 ; 1 Cor. x. 16.

In these cases 'blessing the bread' must be understood as 'blessing God the giver of the bread.' The formulas in use [at the Paschal meal] are given by Lightfoot on Matt. xxvi. 26. Compare p. 205.

The usage of εὐλογία answers to that of εὐλογεῖν. Εὐλογία is attributed (a) to Divine Beings ('the Lamb,' 'He that sitteth on the throne,' God) in Apoc. v. 12 f. ; vii. 12 ; (b) to men, whether it be given (a) by God (Christ) : Gal. iii. 14 ; Rom. xv. 29 ; Eph. i. 3 (comp. 1 Cor. x. 16 ; 1 Peter iii. 9) ; or (β) by man : Heb. xii. 17 ; and (c) to an impersonal object : Hebr. vi. 7. And 'the blessing' includes both the implied promise and that which is the substance of the promise, since from the divine side promise and fulfilment are one.

Εὐλογία.

The word occurs also in a wider sense of that generosity which realises the divine purpose of wealth : 2 Cor. ix. 5 f. ; Rom. xvi. 18 (comp. LXX. Gen. xxxiii. 11 ; Jos. xv. 19 ; Jud. i. 15 ; 1 Sam. xxv. 27) ; and again quite generally, James iii. 10.

Εὐλογητός is used (seven times) of God only, and ὁ εὐλογητός in Mk. xiv. 61 as the title of God (comp. Ign. *Eph.* 1 ; *Mart. Pol.* 14)[1]. By this limitation it is distinguished from εὐλογημένος which is used of 'Him that

Εὐλογητός.

---

[1] This is the general but not the exclusive use in the LXX. See Gen. xxiv. 31 ; Deut. vii. 14 ; 1 Sam. xxv. 33.

cometh' (Ps. cxviii. [cxvii.] 26; Matt. xxi. 9; xxiii. 39 and parallels [in John xii. 13 D reads εὐλογητός]), of the Mother of the Lord and her Son (Luke i. 42); of 'the nations on the King's right hand' (Matt. xxv. 34); and of 'the kingdom of David' (Mk. xi. 10).

Classical usage. In classical writers εὐλογεῖν, which is rare in early prose, is simply 'to speak well of,' 'to praise,' without any of the deeper thoughts which spring from the Jewish conception of the divine order and essence of things. Even in Philo and Josephus the full religious sense is comparatively rare; and Loesner remarks (on Eph. i. 3) that when the LXX. uses εὐλογία, Philo often introduces εὐχή or ἔπαινος.

Ecclesiastical usage. In the Christian Church the use of 'Benedictions' obtained a very wide extension, but these lie outside our present scope (see the article *Benedictions* in D. C. A. by Rev. R. Sinker). One detail in liturgical practice may be named. In the Eastern services the response to the call for a blessing is not unfrequently and characteristically an ascription of blessing to God, where in the Western it is a direct invocation of blessing on men (Sinker *l.c.* p. 197).

Additional Note on vii. 28. *The superiority of the High-priesthood of Christ to the Levitical High-priesthood.*

It is worth while to enumerate distinctly the points in which the writer of the Epistle marks the superiority of the High-priesthood of Christ over that of Aaron. He has already shewn that Christ possesses the qualifications of High-priesthood in ideal perfection, sympathy (ii. 17 f.; iv. 15; v. 8; vii. 26), and divine appointment (v. 5). And more than this he places His preeminence in a clear light by a detailed comparison as to

(*a*)   the form of His appointment (vii. 21), by an oath (promise) and not as dependent on the fulfilment of a covenant;

(*b*)   the rule of His priesthood (vii. 16), 'the power of an indissoluble life' and not 'a law of carnal commandment';

(*c*)   its duration (vii. 23 f.), unchangeable without succession;

(*d*)   its nature (vii. 28) as of a son made perfect, and not of a weak man;

(*e*)   the scene of His service (viii. 2; ix. 11), heaven not earth; and

(*f*)   the character (ix. 12) and

(*g*)   completeness (vii. 27·; x. 5 ff.) of His offering, consummated alike in life and death.

VIII.   ¹Κεφάλαιον δὲ ἐπὶ τοῖς λεγομένοις, τοιοῦτον

1 ἐπὶ τοῖς: ἐν τοῖς A.

IV. The Fulfilment of Christ's Priestly Work (viii. i.—x. 18).

The description of the great features of Christ's Priesthood which has been given in the last division of the Epistle is naturally followed by a view of the fulfilment of His office. This includes the final answer to the disappointments and doubts of the Hebrews. It has been shewn that Christ possesses completely the characteristics of a High-priest for men (c. v. 1—10): that the full apprehension of the dignity of His Person and Work requires effort and patience (c. v. 11—vi.): that under the Levitical system there existed an impressive type of a higher order of Priesthood which He has satisfied (c. vii.). The writer therefore goes on to indicate how He discharges the duties of this supreme and absolute Priesthood, and how it involves of necessity the abrogation of the Mosaic ritual.

To this end he first marks the scene and the conditions of Christ's Priestly work, the New Sanctuary and the New Covenant, a Sanctuary of heaven and not of earth, a Covenant of grace and not of works (c. viii.).

He then compares the High-priestly service under the Old and New Covenants in its most august forms, the service of the Day of Atonement under the Levitical system, and the Passion and Ascension of Christ; while he significantly suggests that we are still waiting for the Return of Christ from the Presence of God to announce the completion of His Work (c. ix.).

In conclusion he brings forward the consideration which is at once the foundation and the crown of his argument. The Levitical sacrifices could not have any value in themselves. The sacrifice of loyal service is that which God requires of men.

This has been rendered perfectly by the Incarnate Son of God; whose sacrifice of Himself in Life and Death avails for ever for that humanity which He has taken to Himself. Through His Work the Covenant of grace finds accomplishment (c. x. 1—18).

These three sections :

i. *A general view of the scene and the conditions of Christ's High-priestly work* (c. viii.),

ii. *The Old Service and the New: the Atonement of the Law and the Atonement of Christ* (c. ix.),

iii. *The Old Sacrifices and the New: the abiding efficacy of Christ's one Sacrifice* (c. x. 1—18),

complete the argument of the Epistle ; and shew that the Mosaic system, with its great memories and consoling institutions, has no value for the Christian.

i. *A general view of the scene and the conditions of Christ's High-priestly work* (viii. 1—13).

Before discussing in detail the High-priestly work of Christ, the writer gives a general view of its character in relation to (1) the new Sanctuary (viii. 1—6), and (2) the new Covenant (7—13).

(1) The new Sanctuary (1—6).

The eternal High-priest has a work to do corresponding with the spiritual dignity of His office in the heavenly sanctuary (1, 2). This work could not be fulfilled on earth, for there is already an earthly system of service (3, 4); but the earthly system is only a shadow of the divine archetype which is realised by Christ (5, 6).

The argument, it will be seen, meets indirectly difficulties which were felt as to the death of Christ (ἐζήτουν τινές, τίνος ἕνεκεν ἀπέθανεν ἱερεὺς ὤν; Chrys.); and as to the absence of Christ. The present work of Christ is the application of the virtue of His one Sacrifice of Himself. He is our High-priest who has entered into the Divine Presence, and we wait patiently for His Return (ix. 28). It was necessary therefore that He should have 'somewhat to offer,' and that could be nothing less than Himself. It was necessary that He should be withdrawn from us that He might make atonement, and enter on His Royal Priesthood. His Death and His absence are consequently an essential part of the fulfilment of our hope.

¹ *Now in the things which we are saying the chief point is this: We have such a High-priest as sat down on the right hand of the throne of the Majesty in the heavens,* ² *a minister of the sanctuary, and of the true tabernacle, which the Lord pitched, not man.* ³ *For every high-priest is appointed to offer both gifts and sacrifices; whence it was necessary that this high-priest also should have something to offer.* ⁴ *Now if he were still upon earth, he would not be a priest at all, seeing there are those who offer the gifts according to law,* ⁵ *such as serve a copy and shadow of the heavenly order, even as Moses is warned of God, when about to make the tabernacle, for See, saith he, thou shalt make all things according to the pattern that was shewed thee in the mount.* ⁶ *But, as it is, he hath obtained a ministry so much the more excellent, as also he is mediator of a better covenant, which hath been enacted upon better promises.*

1, 2. A general statement of Christ's High-priestly work, as He is King at once and Minister.

1. κεφάλαιον δὲ ἐπὶ τοῖς λεγ.] *Now in the things which we are saying the chief point is...* Latt. *capitulum autem super ea quæ dicuntur (dicimus).* The word κεφάλαιον admits of two different interpretations, which have both been adopted by some ancient and modern interpreters:

(1) *Summary, sum.* Ὅταν τις ἐν ὀλίγῳ τὰ κυριώτερα παραλαβεῖν μέλλῃ ἐν κεφαλαίῳ φησὶν ποιεῖσθαι τὸν λόγον, Theophlct. Comp. Ecclus. xxxv. (xxxii.) 8 κεφαλαίωσον λόγον, ἐν ὀλίγοις πολλά.

(2) *Chief point, main matter.* Κεφάλαιον ἀεὶ τὸ μέγιστον λέγεται, Chrys. Comp. Thucyd. iv. 50 πολλῶν ἄλλων γεγραμμένων κεφάλαιον ἦν, vi. 6. Plat. *Legg.* i. p. 643 ο κεφάλαιον δὲ παιδείας λέγομεν τὴν ὀρθὴν τροφήν.

It occurs again in Acts xxii. 28 for 'a sum of money'; and in the LXX. (*caput,* ראֹש) in a similar sense 'the capital sum': Lev. v. 24 ; (vi. 5); Num. v. 7 (comp. Num. iv. 2 ; xxxi. 26, 49).

The second sense falls in best with the context. What follows is not so much a summary of the Apostle's teaching, as an indication of the central thought by which it is inspired. If this sense be taken the question still remains whether κεφάλαιον refers to any new subject, as that of the spiritual sanctuary in which Christ fulfils His office, or to the whole sentence τοιοῦτον...ἄνθρωπος, in which the idea of the sanctuary is only one element in many.

The general construction of the sentence favours the latter view. The thought of a High-priest who has taken His seat on the right hand of God, who is King as well as Priest, is clearly the prominent thought in the sentence. It has not found distinct expression before; and it is the main point in the whole discussion on Christ's High-priestly work, from which the conviction of the efficacy of His one sacrifice follows. His Session on the divine throne shews that He is sovereign of the Kingdom which He has established by His Death; and at the same time this fact explains what seems to men His delay in the Sanctuary (x. 13).

The use of κεφάλαιον without the article in such a construction is strictly correct. It stands in apposition with the statement which follows. Comp. Rom. viii. 3.

ἔχομεν ἀρχιερέα, ὃς ἐκάθιϲεν ἐν Δεξιᾷ τοῦ θρόνου τῆς μεγα-

ἐπὶ τοῖς λεγομένοις] in the case of, in the consideration of, *the things which are now being said*, in the argument which we are now conducting. The reference is to the whole subject of Christ's High-priesthood which is still under discussion, and not to what has been advanced before (τοῖς εἰρημένοις). For ἐπί compare Lk. v. 5 ; (c. xi. 4).

τοιοῦτον...ὃς ἐκάθισεν...] The pronoun (τοιοῦτος) may be taken either as retrospective ('we have such a High-priest as has been already described, and He sat down...'), or as prospective ('we have such a High-priest...as sat down...'). The parallel in vii. 26 f. is not decisive either way (see note). The context however seems to require that Christ's kingly dignity in the exercise of His priestly office should be specially emphasised, so that the second sense is to be preferred: 'We have a High-priest who fulfils His office in royal dignity, not as priests on earth ; and the scene of His ministry is heaven.'

ὃς ἐκάθισεν...] Compare x. 12 ; xii. 2 (κεκάθικεν). The image is taken from Ps. cx. The writer of the Epistle is at length able to repeat, after gaining a full view of the significance of the statement, what he had said at the beginning c. i. 3 ἐκάθισεν ἐν δεξιᾷ τῆς μεγαλωσύνης ἐν ὑψηλοῖς (note).

Τοῦτο (the sitting down) οὐχὶ τοῦ ἱερέως ἀλλὰ τούτου ᾧ ἱεράσθαι ἐκεῖνον χρή (Chrys.). Θεὸν ἔχομεν ἀρχιερέα· τὸ γὰρ καθῆσθαι οὐδενὸς ἄλλου ἢ θεοῦ (Theophlct).

The idea of 'taking the seat' (ἐκάθισεν) is distinct from that of 'sitting' (κάθηται). Compare c. i. 13 note.

In this connexion the full meaning of passages like Apoc. iii. 21 becomes clear. Christ makes His people also kings and priests. A striking illustration is quoted from *Shemoth R.* § 8 (Wünsche, p. 74). 'A king of flesh and blood does not set his crown on

another, but God (Blessed be He) will set His crown on King Messiah : Cant. v. 11 ; Ps. xxi. 3.'

ἐν δεξ. τοῦ θρ. τῆς μεγαλ.] Latt. *in dextera sedis magnitudinis.* Comp. c. i. 3 ἐν δεξιᾷ τῆς μεγαλωσύνης and note. 'The power' (הַגְּבוּרָה) was a common Rabbinic name for God in His Majesty : 'we heard it from the mouth of the Power.' Comp. Buxtorf, Lex. *s. v.*; and Mark xiv. 62 ἐκ δεξιῶν τῆς Δυνάμεως.

The phrase '*the throne of the Divine Majesty*' is chosen with reference to the Glory which rested on the Mercy Seat in the Holy of Holies : Lev. xvi. 2 ; comp. Ex. xxv. 22.

The patristic interpretation of 'the Majesty' is uncertain (ἢ ὅτι καὶ ὁ πατὴρ λεχθείη ἂν αὐτῷ (αὐτὸς) μεγαλωσύνη ἢ ὅτι ἁπλῶς οὕτω θρόνος μεγαλωσύνης ὁ μέγιστος θρόνος, Theophlct), but the Fathers carefully avoid all 'puerile' anthropomorphism in their treatment of 'the right hand of God,' as for example : plenitudinem majestatis summamque gloriam beatitudinis et prosperitatis debemus per dexteram intelligere in qua filius sedet (Primas.). This Session declares under a natural figure that the Son of man has entered on the full and permanent participation of the divine glory and power. Compare a remarkable passage of Philo (*de Abr.* § 24, ii. p. 19 M.) πατὴρ μὲν τῶν ὅλων ὁ μέσος (the reference is to Gen. xviii. 1 ff.), ὅς... καλεῖται ὁ ὤν, αἱ δὲ παρ' ἑκάτερα πρεσβύταται καὶ ἐγγύταται τοῦ ὄντος δυνάμεις· ὧν ἡ μὲν ποιητικὴ ἡ δὲ αὖ βασιλικὴ προσαγορεύεται· καὶ ἡ μὲν ποιητικὴ θεός ...ἡ δὲ βασιλικὴ κύριος....And a little later (*id.* § 25) Philo speaks of 'the manifestation' (φαντασία) ἡ ἐπὶ δεξιὰ ἡ εὐεργέτις, ᾗ θεὸς ὄνομα.... Pearson (*On the Creed*, pp. 277 f.) has given a good collection of illustrative quotations. Contrast Acts vii. 55 (ἑστῶτα ἐκ δεξιῶν τοῦ θεοῦ).

λωσύνης ἐν* τοῖς οὐρανοῖς, ²τῶν ἁγίων λειτουργὸς καὶ
τῆς ϲκηνῆϲ τῆς ἀληθινῆς, ἣν ἔπηξεν ὁ κγριοϲ, οὐκ ἄνθρωποϲ.

2 οὐκ ἄνθρ. אBD₂*: + καὶ' οὐκ ἄνθρ. ς (A) vg me syrr.

ἐν τοῖς οὐρανοῖς] Compare c. ix. 24
note.

2. τῶν ἁγίων λειτ.] a minister of
the sanctuary, Latt. sanctorum
minister. The phrase τῶν ἁγίων is
unquestionably neuter: c. ix. 8, 12,
&c. It describes 'the Sanctuary,' and
specially what is elsewhere (c. ix. 3)
called 'the Holy of Holies' (ἅγια
ἁγίων).

The exact phrase occurs in Philo,
Leg. Alleg. iii. 46 (i. 114 M.), τοιοῦτος
ὁ θεραπευτὴς καὶ λειτουργὸς τῶν ἁγίων
(said of Aaron).

Some of the Fathers, both Greek
and Latin, treat τῶν ἁγίων as masc.
'of the Saints.' Thus Primasius:
sanctorum minister: quod duobus
modis potest accipi. Veniens quippe
dominus in mundum per incarnationis
exhibitionem ministravit sanctis aliis-
que fidelibus...et aliter: sanctorum
minister erit in futurum quando
semetipsum ministrabit illis ut cognoscant eum cum patre et spiritu
sancto sicuti est....Potest et altiori
sensu intelligi ut tabernaculum verum
accipiantur animæ justorum quibus
ipse filius Dei gaudia patriæ cælestis
administrat et in quibus ipse habi-
tare dignatur. Compare Œcumenius:
ἀρχιερεύς, φησίν, τῶν ἡγιασμένων παρ'
αὐτοῦ ἀνθρώπων, and so 'τινές' quoted
by Theophylact.

There is a significant contrast
between the Session of Christ and His
'serving': πῶς δὲ οἷόν τε αὐτὸν ὁμοῦ καὶ
συνεδρεύειν καὶ λειτουργεῖν; εἰ μή τις
ἄρα λειτουργίαν εἴποι τῶν ἀνθρώπων τὴν
σωτηρίαν ἣν δεσποτικῶς πραγματεύεται
(Theodt). The two words in fact
present the two complementary
aspects of Christ's Person and Work,
His divine Majesty and His infinite
love. Christ serves though He reigns
and reigns in serving. All that the
High-priest did in figure He does

absolutely. He makes atonement for
men with God: He makes God known
to men; and thus in both ways He
fulfils their destiny. For λειτουργός
and cognate words see Additional
Note.

τῆς σκ. τ. ἀλ....οὐκ ἄνθρ.] Comp. c. ix.
11 note. The action of Christ's Priesthood extends to all parts of the
divine Dwelling. Thus the more
general word σκηνή is added to τὰ
ἅγια, but no local distinction can be
pressed in regard to the heavenly
antitype (archetype). Comp. Apoc.
xv. 5; (xiii. 6). The general thought
is that of the immediate Presence
of God (τὰ ἅγια), and the scene of
His manifestation to His worshippers
(ἡ σκηνή). Christ in the High-priesthood of His glorified humanity represents man to God, and in His divine
Nature represents God to man.

This 'Tabernacle,' which Christ
serves and through which God is
made known to men, is the ideal
'Tabernacle' (ἡ σκ. ἡ ἀληθινή) of which
the earthly Tabernacle was a symbol.
For ἀληθινός compare c. ix. 24; x. 22
note (not ix. 14). The word is common in St John's writings (John i. 9;
iv. 23 note). Elsewhere in the N. T.
it occurs only in Luke xvi. 11;
1 Thess. i. 9. For the idea of the
Tabernacle see Additional Note on
v. 5. Compare Wisd. ix. 8.

ἣν ἔπηξεν] The verb is habitually
used by classical writers in this connexion (πηγνύναι σκηνήν). So it is used
of the heavens: Is. xlii. 5; (Ps. civ. 3).
Comp. Num. xxiv. 6 (LXX.).

ὁ κύριος] Comp. v. 11 (Jer. xxxi. 34
LXX.). Elsewhere in the Epistle 'the
Lord' (Jehovah) is always represented
by Κύριος (eleven times) while ὁ κύριος
is used of Christ: c. ii. 3 note. But
see Luke i. 6, 9, 28, 46; James iv. 15;
v. 15 &c.

³πᾶς γὰρ ἀρχιερεὺς εἰς τὸ προσφέρειν δῶρά τε καὶ θυσίας
καθίσταται· ὅθεν ἀναγκαῖον ἔχειν τι καὶ τοῦτον ὃ
προσενέγκῃ. ⁴εἰ μὲν οὖν ἦν ἐπὶ γῆς, οὐδ᾽ ἂν ἦν ἱερεύς,

3 τι καί : om. καί ℵ*?   4 οὖν ℵABD₂* vg me : γάρ ς syr hl.

οὐκ ἄνθρωπος] Compare c. ix. 11, 24
(οὐ χειροποίητα).

3, 4. The fact and the scene of
Christ's High-priestly work.

3. πᾶς γὰρ ἀρχ.] Compare c. v. 1.
The fact that the Lord is High-priest
—a minister of the sanctuary—involves of necessity and rests upon
His performance of High-priestly
functions ; *for every High-priest is
appointed to offer both gifts and
sacrifices.* He must therefore have
both an offering and a place of
approach to God: an offering that in
the virtue of the blood He might find
entrance to the Presence of God, as
the Aaronic High-priest on the Day of
Atonement ; a place of approach fulfilling the type of the Holy of Holies,
not on earth (*v.* 4) and consequently
in heaven.

εἰς τὸ προσφ. δ. καὶ θ.] Comp. c. v. 1
(ἵνα προσφέρῃ) note.

ὅθεν...ὁ προσενέγκῃ] *whence it was
necessary that this* High-priest *also
should have something to offer,* Vulg.
*unde necesse est et hunc habere
aliquid quod offerat.* This offering
is described as made once for all
(προσενέγκῃ contrasted with προσφέρῃ
ix. 25 ; comp. c. vii. 27). The one
sufficient offering was made by Christ
as the condition of entrance into the
sanctuary *through His own blood*
(c. ix. 12). On this His intercession
is based. That intercession knows no
end or interruption ; and therefore
no second offering is required, as in
the case of the Levitical High-priest,
who made a fresh offering every year
in order that he might again enter
and repeat the intercession which had
been made before.

The necessary condition of the
entrance of our High-priest into the

Presence of God throws light upon the
difficulty which the Hebrews felt as to
His death. Through no less an offering
than that of Himself could He come
before God for His people.

It has been debated whether ἦν or
ἐστίν should be supplied with ἀναγκαῖον. If the reference is to the
offering on the Cross, as seems to be
required by the type and the context,
then ἦν must be supplied.

ἔχειν τι] that is 'Himself' (vii. 27
ἀναφέρειν ; ix. 14, 25 προσφέρειν) or
His 'Body' (x. 10 προσφορά). It
seems necessary to supply that object
which is elsewhere used with προσφέρειν in the same connexion. Many
have interpreted the τι of 'the
Blood.' But the Blood was not
properly 'offered' in the Holy of
Holies on the Day of Atonement (yet
see c. ix. 7). It was used as the
means of entrance and purification.
Even so Christ entered into the
Divine Presence 'through (διά) His
own Blood' (c. ix. 12), and by that
purifies 'the heavenly things' (ix. 23)
and the people (c. xiii. 12) ; but we
do not read that He 'offered' it.
The indefinite pronoun, as contrasted
with δῶρα καὶ θυσίας, indicates the
mysteriousness of the offering.

ὁ προσενέγκῃ] For the construction,
which is rare in classical prose, see
Acts xxi. 16.

4. εἰ μὲν οὖν...ἱερεύς...] *Now if He
were* still *upon earth, He would not be
a priest at all,* and therefore still less
High-priest....The argument is directed to shew that, since Christ as High-
priest must do characteristic service,
the scene of His service must be
heaven and not earth. The wish
therefore which many entertained for
some priestly work of Christ on earth

ὄντων τῶν προσφερόντων κατὰ νόμον τὰ δῶρα· ⁵(οἵτινες
ὑποδείγματι καὶ σκιᾷ λατρεύουσιν τῶν ἐπουρανίων, καθὼς

ὄντων ℵABD₂* vg me : +τῶν ἱερέων ς syrr.   νόμον ℵ*AB : +τὸν' ν. ς ℵᶜD₂.
τὰ δ. κ. ν. syr vg me.

was really fatal to their noblest faith.
It is assumed that there cannot be
two divinely appointed orders of earthly priests. The actual existence and
service of one order therefore excludes the possibility of the coexist-
ence of another. The apodosis is in
v. 6 νῦν δέ. For εἰ ἦν...οὐδ' ἂν ἦν...
see c. iv. 8 Additional Note.

Theodoret (on v. 5) has an interesting note on the service of Christian
priests : τί δήποτε τῆς καινῆς διαθήκης
οἱ ἱερεῖς τὴν μυστικὴν λειτουργίαν ἐπι-
τελοῦσιν; ἀλλὰ δῆλον τοῖς τὰ θεῖα πε-
παιδευμένοις ὡς οὐκ ἄλλην τινὰ θυσίαν
προσφέρομεν ἀλλὰ τῆς μιᾶς ἐκείνης καὶ
σωτηρίου τὴν μνήμην ἐπιτελοῦμεν. τοῦτο
γὰρ ἡμῖν αὐτὸς ὁ δεσπότης προσέταξε
'τοῦτο ποιεῖτε εἰς τὴν ἐμὴν ἀνάμνησιν'
ἵνα τῇ θεωρίᾳ τὸν τύπον τῶν ὑπὲρ ἡμῶν
γεγενημένων ἀναμιμνησκώμεθα παθημάτων καὶ τὴν περὶ τὸν εὐεργέτην ἀγάπην
πυρσεύωμεν καὶ τῶν μελλόντων ἀγαθῶν
προσμένωμεν τὴν ἀπόλαυσιν.

ὄντων τ. προσφ.] seeing there are...
Vulg. cum essent qui offerrent, V. L.
aliis offerentibus. The tense of the
principal verb (λατρεύουσι) fixes the
translation of the participle to the
present. This offering is made κατὰ
νόμον, 'according to law,' not 'according to the Law.' The idea is that of
the authoritative character of the
institution generally, and not of the
specific form of the institution. Comp.
c. x. 8 (κατὰ νόμον) note.

τὰ δῶρα] not 'gifts' in the abstract,
but 'the gifts' which God requires.
The simple term is here used to include offerings of all kinds (c. xi. 4 ;
Matt. v. 23 f.; xxiii. 18 f.).

5, 6. The earthly Levitical service
points to that which corresponds with
a better covenant.

5. οἵτινες...] The qualitative relative (comp. c. ii. 3 note; v. 6 ἥτις)

emphasises the character of the Levitical priesthood : priests such as
serve that which is a copy and
shadow ... Latt. qui exemplari et
umbræ (serviunt) deserviunt. The
Mosaic system was not complete in
itself, original and independent: it
was a copy of an archetype. It had
no spiritual substance : it was only a
shadow. Comp. John i. 17.

Like our word 'copy' the word
ὑπόδειγμα expresses not only the
image which is made by imitation
(as here and c. ix. 23) but also the
model which is offered for imitation.
(John xiii. 15 ; James v. 10 ; 2 Pet. ii.
6 ; comp. 2 Macc. vi. 28, 31 ; Ecclus.
xliv. 16. Comp. c. iv. 11 note.)

For σκιᾷ compare c. x. 1 note ; Col.
ii. 17 (contrasted with σῶμα). The
word λατρεύουσι is not to be taken
absolutely ('serve God in, after, a
copy...'). The priest can rightly be
said to serve the system. Comp. c.
xiii. 10 οἱ τῇ σκηνῇ λατρεύοντες. Ezek.
xlv. 5 (οἴκῳ). Clem. R. i. 32. For
λατρεύειν see Additional Note on v. 2.

τῶν ἐπουρανίων] of the heavenly
order. The Tabernacle presented in
figures the ideas of the Divine Presence and the realities of heaven.

The phrase is to be taken generally
and not to be defined by the addition
of ἁγίων or the like.

The range of the occurrence of τὰ
ἐπουράνια in the N. T. is limited. It
is found in St John: iii. 12; in the
Ep. to Ephesians : i. 3, 20 ; ii. 6 ; iii.
10 ; vi. 12 ; and in this Epistle, here
and in ix. 23.

The general idea of the phrase is
that of 'the heavenly order,' the scene
of the spiritual life with the realities
which belong to it. The abstract
term is used here and in ix. 23 to
guard (as it seems) against the danger

κεχρημάτισται Μωυσῆς μέλλων ἐπιτελεῖν τὴν σκηνήν,
Ὅρα γάρ, φησίν, ποιήσεις πάντα κατὰ τὸν τύπον τὸν δειχθέντα coι

5 ποιήσεις ΧABD₂: ποιήσῃς Ϛ.

of transferring to another world the
local conditions which belong to the
earthly tabernacle.
The phrase is not found in the LXX.
For *ἐπουράνιος* generally see c. iii. 1
note. In one sense, as Theophylact,
following Chrysostom, points out, τὰ
ἐπουράνια are realised on earth by
faith : τὰ ἡμέτερα ἐπουράνια· ὅταν γὰρ
μηδὲν ἐπίγειον ἀλλὰ πάντα πνευματικὰ
ἐν τοῖς μυστηρίοις τελούμενα, ἔνθα
ὕμνοι ἀγγελικοὶ ἔνθα κλεῖδες τῆς βασιλείας τῶν οὐρανῶν καὶ ἄφεσις ἁμαρτιῶν
καὶ αὖ πάλιν δεσμά, ὅταν ἡμῶν τὸ πολίτευμα ἐν οὐρανοῖς ὑπάρχει, πῶς οὐκ
ἐπουράνια τὰ καθ᾽ ἡμᾶς; So Primasius
(on ix. 23): cælestia, *i.e.* spiritualia
quæ in veritate modo in ecclesia
celebrantur.

καθὼς κεχρημάτισται M.] *even as
Moses is warned of God*...Latt. *sicut
responsum est Moysi*... The verb χρη-
ματίζειν is used in the active of giving
a formal answer to an inquirer (as by
an oracle), and then of giving an authoritative (divine) direction generally:
Jer. xxvi. (xxxiii.) 2; c. xii. 25; so
χρηματισμός Rom. xi. 4. Hence the
passive is used of the person who
receives such a direction : Matt. ii. 12,
22; Luke ii. 26 (D) *κεχρηματισμένος
ἦν*; Acts x. 22; c. xi. 7. This use of
the *pass.* is very rare elsewhere: Jos.
Antt. iii. 8, 8 (a different usage is
found Acts xi. 26).
The direction is regarded as still
present in Scripture (comp. Gal. iv.
23 γεγέννηται). Comp. c. vii. 6 note.

μέλλων ἐπιτελεῖν] *when he is about*
(as destined by the divine counsel: c.
xi. 8) *to put into execution, to make*
(rather than *to complete*)...Vulg. *cum
consummaret* (O. L. *consummat*).
For *ἐπιτελεῖν* see c. ix. 6; 2 Cor. vii.
1; 1 Pet. v. 9.

ὅρα γάρ, φησίν, ποιήσεις...] *for See,
saith he* (i.e. God), *thou shalt make*...

Vulg. *Vide, inquit, omnia facito...*
Ex. xxv. 40 (comp. xxv. 9; xxvii. 8).
The quotation differs from the LXX. by
the addition of πάντα (which is not
found in the original) and the substitution of δειχθέντα for δεδειγμένον.
The former word really sums up the
specific directions given in regard to
the different objects in Ex. xxv. All
had a prescribed character and (it
is implied) a divine meaning.

The construction of ποιήσεις is uncertain. It may either go closely
with ῞Ορα : 'See that thou make...'; or
it may be a distinct command : 'See,
regard attentively, the pattern which
is shewn; thou shalt make'...as appears to be the sense of the original.
The γάρ belongs to the argument and
not to the quotation.

κατὰ τὸν τύπον] Latt. *secundum
exemplar.* Compare Acts vii. 44. It
is not to be supposed that even Moses
saw 'the heavenly things' as they are.
He saw them as he had power to see
them, *i.e.* according to human apprehension. So St Paul heard the divine
voice in 'Hebrew.' The heavenly
things on which Moses was allowed
to look took for him a shape, under
the divine guidance, which could be
reproduced on earth.
The command is applied to Solomon
in Wisd. ix. 8.
Philo dwells upon the subordinate
position of Bezaleel in regard to
Moses and finds in the interpretation
of his name ἐν σκιᾷ θεοῦ (בְּצֵל אֵל) an
indication of the position which his
work occupied : *Leg. Alleg.* iii. § 31
(i. p. 106 M.); *De Somn.* i. § 35 (i.
652 M.) τὸν τούτου τοῦ πλέγματος δη-
μιουργὸν ὁ ἱερὸς λόγος Βεσελεὴλ ἐκάλεσεν, ὅς ἑρμηνευθείς ἐστιν, ἐν σκιᾷ θεοῦ·
τὰ γὰρ μιμήματα οὗτος, τὰ δὲ παραδείγ-
ματα ἀρχιτεκτονεῖ Μωϋσῆς ὄνομα. *De*

έΝ τῷ ὄρει·) ⁶⌈νῦν⌉ δὲ διαφορωτέρας τέτυχεν λειτουργίας,
ὅσῳ καὶ κρείττονός ἐστιν διαθήκης μεσίτης, ἥτις ἐπὶ

6 νυνὶ

6 νῦν BD₂*: νυνὶ ⵏℵA.   τέτυχεν ℵ*AD₂*: τέτευχεν ℵᶜB.   καὶ κρ.: om. καὶ D₂*.
om. ἐστιν...κρειττο ℵ*.

Plant. Noœ § 6 (i. 333 M.). See Additional Note.

6. νῦν δὲ διαφ....] *But now, as it is,* as the case really stands, *he hath obtained* (ἱερουργῶν τὴν ὑπὲρ ἡμῶν πρὸς τὸν πατέρα μεσιτείαν, Euth. Zig.). ...For νῦν δέ see c. xi. 16 : so νυνὶ δέ c. ix. 26. The form τέτυχεν occurs, though rarely, in late writers.

διαφορωτέρας ... κρείττονος...] Latt. *melius...melioris...* The two words are used again together in close juxtaposition in c. i. 4. Perhaps κρείττων has regard to intrinsic superiority and διαφορώτερος to a superiority which is manifested directly. Moreover διαφ. recognises an exceptional excellence in that which is surpassed. The 'name' of angels and the ministry of the Levitical priests were both 'excellent.' The word λειτουργίας goes back to *v.* 2 λειτουργός.

διαφ. ὅσῳ καὶ κρ....] Compare c. vii. 20 ff. for the converse argument.

διαθ. μεσίτης] Latt. *testamenti mediator.* For διαθ. μεσίτης see c. ix. 15; xii. 24.

Elsewhere in N. T. μεσίτης is used with the genitive of the person : Gal. iii. 19 f. ὁ μεσίτης ἑνὸς οὐκ ἔστιν, 1 Tim. ii. 5 μεσίτης θεοῦ καὶ ἀνθρώπων. Comp. μεσιτεύω c. vi. 17. The word, which belongs to late Greek, answering to the Attic μεσέγγυος, is found once in the LXX., Job ix. 33; and it is found in Philo and Josephus.

A covenant generally, and obviously a covenant between God and man, requires a mediator, one who standing between the contracting parties shall bring them duly into fellowship. Μεσίτης describes the action of Christ at the establishment of the New Covenant, as ἔγγυος (c. vii. 22) describes the position which He holds towards

men by assuring them of its validity. The use of the term suggests a point of superiority in Christ over the Aaronic High-priests. Moses was the 'mediator' of the Law (Gal. iii. 19; Philo *de vit. Mos.* iii. § 19; ii. 160 M.), but Christ who is the High-priest is also the Mediator of the new 'Law.' He combines the offices of Moses and Aaron. Comp. c. iii. 1.

The limited office of 'the Mediator of a Covenant' suggests the thought of the wider work of a Mediator, which occupied the minds of early speculators on the relation of God to Creation. Philo, for example, gives a noble picture of the Word standing between the creature and the Father of all, the messenger of divine order and the inspirer of human hope : *Quis rer. div. hær.* § 42 (i. 502 M.) ὁ δὲ αὐτὸς ἱκέτης μέν ἐστι τοῦ θνητοῦ κηραίνοντος ἀεὶ πρὸς τὸ ἄφθαρτον· πρεσβευτὴς δὲ τοῦ ἡγεμόνος πρὸς τὸ ὑπήκοον· ἀγάλλεται δὲ ἐπὶ τῇ δωρεᾷ καὶ σεμνυνόμενος αὐτὴν ἐκδιηγεῖται φάσκων ' καὶ ἐγὼ εἱστήκειν ἀνὰ μέσον κυρίου καὶ ὑμῶν' (comp. Num. xvi. 48).... Perhaps there is no finer view of the relation of the world to its Maker possible apart from the Incarnation.

ἥτις...νενομοθέτηται] The superiority of the New Covenant is shewn by the superiority of the promises on which its conditions are founded (ἥτις, 'such that it is,' 'seeing that it is,' *v.* 5 note). A Covenant necessarily imposes conditions. And a Covenant (διαθήκη) made by God is 'enacted.' Thus the Gospel itself, though in one sense opposed to the Law, was not only the fulfilment of the Law; but in itself the 'perfect Law' (James i. 25). Freedom is the absolute consummation of Law.

κρείττοσιν ἐπαγγελίαις νενομοθέτηται. ⁷εἰ γὰρ ἡ πρώτη
ἐκείνη ἦν ἄμεμπτος, οὐκ ἂν δευτέρας ἐζητεῖτο τόπος·

7 δευτέρας: ἑτέρας B*.

ἐπὶ κρείττ. ἐπαγγ.] upon better promises, such as are contained in the
divine description which follows of
the spirituality and efficacy of the
new relation of man to God, based
upon complete forgiveness. For the
use of ἐπί with dat. to express the
conditions (accompaniments) see 2
Cor. ix. 6; 1 Thess. iv. 7; Phil. iii. 9;
(Luke xxiv. 47).

(2) The new Covenant (7—13).

The Levitical system corresponded
with a Covenant which was recognised
by the prophets as imperfect and
transitory, for they spoke of the
divine purpose to establish 'a new
Covenant.' The section consists of a
brief introduction (7, 8 a), the prophetic word (8 b—12), a general conclusion (13).

⁷ For if that first covenant had been
faultless, a place would not have been
sought for a second. ⁸ For finding
fault with them he saith
Behold the days come, saith the
Lord,
That I will make a new covenant
with the house of Israel and with
the house of Judah;
⁹ Not according to the covenant
that I made with their fathers,
In the day that I took them by the
hand to lead them forth out of the
land of Egypt;
¹⁰ Because they continued not in
my covenant,
And I regarded them not, saith
the Lord.
Because this is the covenant that
I will covenant with the house of
Israel
After those days, saith the Lord,
Even putting my laws into their
mind,
And upon their heart will I write
them:
And I will be to them a God,

And they shall be to me a people;
¹¹ And they shall not teach every
man his fellow-citizen,
And every man his brother, saying,
Know the Lord:
Because all shall know me,
From the least to the greatest of
them.
¹² Because I will be merciful to
their iniquities,
And their sins will I remember no
more.
¹³ In that he saith A new covenant,
he hath made the first old. But that
which becometh old and waxeth aged
is nigh unto vanishing away.

7. The teaching of the prophets
bears witness to the superiority of the
New order over the Old which has
been affirmed in the last verse, for if
the first Covenant had completely fulfilled the purpose to which a Covenant between God and man is directed, then there would have been no
room for another. The argument is
parallel to that in c. vii. 11 ff.

εἰ γὰρ...ἦν ἄμεμπτος] For if that
first covenant had been faultless, Latt.
nam si...culpa vacasset, fulfilling perfectly the purpose to which it pointed.
Comp. vii. 18.

The Law itself is not blamed: the
fault lay with those who received it
(v. 8). None the less the Covenant
did fail, so far as it brought no consummation of man's true destiny.

The Covenant is called first in contrast with δευτέρα by common Greek
usage. Comp. c. ix. 6 f.; x. 9; Acts
i. 1. The addition of the pronoun
(ἐκείνη) presents the Old Covenant as
occupying the mind of the readers.
Comp. 2 Cor. vii. 8; Matt. xviii. 32.

οὐκ ἂν δευτ. ἐζητ. τόπος] a place
would not have been sought for a
second, Vulg. non utique secundi
locus inquireretur. God made known

^{8} μεμφόμενος γὰρ ⌜αὐτοὺς⌝ λέγει

8 αὐτοῖς

8 αὐτούς א*AD$_2$* vg : αὐτοῖς א^{c}B.

His purpose to establish a second Covenant; but for this, in the order of His Providence, fitting conditions were required. Hence it was not the Covenant itself for which men sought, but the place for it, the circumstances under which it could be realised. The feeling of dissatisfaction, want, prompted to a diligent inquiry; and to this the words addressed to Jeremiah—the prophet of the national overthrow and exile—bear witness.

For the phrase ζητεῖν τόπον compare τόπον εὑρεῖν c. xii. 17 ; τ. διδόναι Rom. xii. 19; τ. λαβεῖν Acts xxv. 16.

The two imperfects εἰ ἦν...οὐκ ἂν ἐζητεῖτο mark a continuous state. While the first Covenant remained in force, there was yet searching for something more. This thought is expressed by: ‘If the first had been...a place would not have been sought’: and not by ‘If the first were...would not be sought.’ Comp. c. xi. 15 ; and Additional Note on iv. 8.

8 a. μεμφόμενος γὰρ αὐτούς] The existence of failure—fault—is established by the language of the Lord to Jeremiah: *for finding fault with them, he saith...*(Latt. *vituperans enim : si prius culpa vacasset* above). The people were not yet prepared to receive the revelation which God designed to give. The Law had not had its perfect work with them. They had not lived up to that which they had received.

The reference in *them* (*i.e.* the Israelites) is supplied from a knowledge of the circumstances. Comp. iv. 8; xi. 28. So Theophylact: τουτέστι τοῖς Ἰουδαίοις (reading αὐτοῖς) τοῖς μὴ δυναμένοις τελειωθῆναι διὰ τῶν νομικῶν προσταγμάτων. If αὐτοῖς is read the translation *finding fault with it he saith to them* is possible, but it appears to be very unlikely.

λέγει] Jer. xxxi. (xxxviii.) 31—34.

The speaker is the Lord Himself, not the prophet. The quotation (8 *b* —12) is taken, with some variations, from the LXX., which, in the main, agrees with the Hebrew. See Additional Note. Carpzov has pointed out that Philo in a remarkable passage places Jeremiah in connexion with Moses, γνοὺς ὅτι οὐ μόνον μύστης ἐστὶν ἀλλὰ καὶ ἱεροφάντης ἱκανός (*De Cher.* § 14 ; i. 148 M.).

The context of the quotation gives it a special force. Jeremiah at the crisis of national calamity pictures the final result of the discipline of the exile into which Judah was now going. The united people ‘Israel and Judah’ are to return to their land (xxx. 3). Ephraim is again recognised as firstborn (xxxi. 9). The sorrows of Rachel are consoled (xxxi. 15 ff.). The counsel of divine love finds certain accomplishment (xxxi. 37). This issue is summed up in the establishment of a New Covenant, by which the fulfilment of the whole of God’s purpose is assured, when trial has done its work. Under this Covenant, grace not law is the foundation of fellowship. God comes to man as giving and not as requiring.

The whole situation is Messianic no less than the special words. The time of national humiliation is the time of ardent hope. The fall of the Kingdom, which was of man’s will, is the occasion of a greater promise. And nowhere else in the O. T. is the contrast between the Law and the Gospel so definitely traced back to its essential principle.

The promises of the New Covenant are developed in due order.

1. The wide range of the Covenant:

It includes all the Old Covenant people:

Israel and Judah (8).

'Ιδογ ήμέραι ἔρχονται, λέγει Κγριος,
καὶ ϲγντελέϲω ἐπὶ τὸν οἶκον 'Ιϲραὴλ καὶ ἐπὶ τὸν οἶκον 'Ιογδα
διαθήκην καινήν,
9 ογ κατὰ τὴν διαθήκην ἣν ἐποίηϲα τοῖϲ πατράϲιν αγτῶν

ἐπὶ τόν (2): om. ἐπὶ D₂*.

2. Its character:
(a) Negatively:
Not after the type of that on which the people was first established (9).
(b) Positively:
Internal (10).
Uniformly efficacious (11).
Resting on complete forgiveness (12).

8 b. ἰδοὺ ἡμ. ἔρχ.] *Behold days come...*The phrase (הִנֵּה יָמִים בָּאִים) is singularly frequent in Jeremiah. Jer. vii. 32; ix. 25; xvi. 14; xix. 6; xxiii. 5, 7; xxx. 3; xxxi. 27; xlviii. (xxxi.) 12; xlix. (xxx.) 2; li. 47. Comp. Amos viii. 11; ix. 13; Is. xxxix. 6.

So Philo, as has been already noticed, dwells with special emphasis on the prophetic gifts of Jeremiah.

These 'last days' mark a period of trial and judgment. At the close of them the Divine Covenant is established in its glory.

For the construction ἡμ. ἔρχ....καὶ συντελέσω see Luke xix. 43.

συντελέσω] Vulg. *consummabo*, O. L. *disponam* (*confirmabo*). So LXX. Jer. xxxiv. 8, 15 (כָּרַתִּי...בְּרִית).

Perhaps, as Augustine suggests (*de spir. et lit.* 19 Quid est *Consummabo* nisi *Implebo*?), this rendering is chosen to emphasise the efficacy of the Covenant.

ἐπὶ τ. οἶ. 'Ισρ. καὶ ἐπὶ τ. ο. 'Ιού.] Once again the divided and exiled people shall be brought together (comp. *v.* 10). The schism which had brought ruin on the kingdom is to have no existence under the new order.

To this issue the other great prophets point: Is. xliii. ff.; Ezek. xvi. 60 ff.

διαθ. κ.] Latt. *testamentum novum.* The epithet (καινήν) is quoted specially in *v.* 13.

The phrase διαθήκη καινή occurs 1 Cor. xi. 25; 2 Cor. iii. 6; c. ix. 15. The reading in Lk. xxii. 20 is very doubtful; and the phrase is not found in the true text of Matt. xxvi. 28 and Mk. xiv. 24 (τὸ αἷμά μου, τὸ τῆς διαθήκης).

In c. xii. 24 we read διαθήκη νέα. The distinction between καινός and νέος is clearly marked in the N. T. usage. Καινός expresses that which is new in regard to what has preceded, as novel in character, or unused: νέος that which is new in regard to its own being, as having been in existence but a short time.

The words occur in close connexion in Matt. ix. 17 βάλλουσιν οἶνον νέον (which has been lately made) εἰς ἀσκοὺς καινούς (which have not been used before). Contrast Matt. xxvi. 29 ὅταν αὐτὸ πίνω μεθ᾽ ὑμῶν καινόν (such as has not been before).

See also Col. iii. 10 (τὸν νέον τὸν ἀνακαινούμενον) compared with Eph. iv. 24 (ii. 15) (τὸν καινὸν ἄνθρωπον τὸν κατὰ θεὸν κτισθέντα).

Hence καινός is used of the renovation of Creation: Apoc. xxi. 5; 2 Cor. v. 17 τὰ ἀρχαῖα παρῆλθεν, ἰδοὺ γέγονεν καινά.

The direct antithesis to καινός is ἀρχαῖος (that which has been from the beginning: 2 Cor. v. 17); but παλαιός (that which has been for a long time) forms a true opposite both to νέος and to καινός (Matt. ix. 17; 1 John ii. 7; Matt. xiii. 52; Mk. ii. 21; Lk. v. 39).

9. οὐ κατὰ τὴν διαθ.] The Lord having fixed the breadth of His New Covenant, as embracing the whole

ἐν ἡμέρᾳ ἐπιλαΒομένΟΥ ΜΟΥ τῆς χειρὸς ἀΥΤῶν ἐΖαγαγεῖν ἀΥΤΟΥς
ἐκ γῆς ΑἰγΥπτΟΥ,
ὅτι ἀΥΤΟὶ ΟΥΚ ἐνέμεινΑν ἐν τῇ ΔιαθήκΗ ΜΟΥ,
κἀγὼ ἠμέλΗςΑ ἀΥΤῶν, λέγει ΚΥριΟς.
¹⁰ὅτι ἀΥΤΗ ἡ ΔιαθήκΗ ἡν ΔιαθήςΟΜΑΙ τῷ οἴκῳ ᾽ΙςραΗλ

9 ἡμέρᾳ: ἡμέραις B.   ἐκ γῆς: ἐκ τῆς D₂.   10 ἡ διαθήκη אB vg me syrr : + μου AD₂.

people, goes on to describe its character, and first negatively (v. 9). It
is not *according to, after, the pattern*
of that which was made at the Exodus.
The Covenant was to be not only a
second one, but one of a different
type. For the use of κατά compare
1 Pet. i. 15; Eph. iv. 24.

ἣν ἐποίησα τοῖς πατρ.] The original
phrase is the same as that rendered
just above συντελέσω ἐπί...(comp. v. 10
διαθήσομαι τῷ οἴ.). These different
renderings bring out clearly the conception that the Covenant is a manifestation of the divine purpose of
love. He of His Goodness fixes the
terms. The Covenant is a διαθήκη
and not a συνθήκη.

ἐν ἡμ. ἐπιλαβομένου μου...] This is
an unusual rendering of the form
בְּיוֹם הֶחֱזִיקִי בְיָדָם. Comp. Barn. ii.
28 ἐν ἡμέρᾳ ἐντειλαμένου σου αὐτῷ
γράψαι τὸν νόμον.
The 'day' expresses vividly the
period which marked the fitting season for the action of God. Comp. 2
Cor. vi. 2 (LXX.); Jud. xviii. 30.

For ἐπιλαβομένου compare c. ii. 16
note.

More mulierum loquitur sermo divi-
nus, quæ apprehendere solent par-
vulorum manus et plerumque ad se
conducere, plerumque etiam huc illuc-
que sustentando ne labantur, utpote
firmos gressus non habentes adhuc
(Primas.).

ἐξαγ. ἐκ γῆς Αἰγ.] The Old Covenant
is connected with the first formation
of the nation and with that sovereign
display of God's power by which he
separated externally a people from
the world. This outward deliverance
and establishment of the chosen nation

stands in natural connexion with the
idea of the institution of a universal
Church. Compare Is. xi. 16; Hos.
xii. 9; xiii. 4.

The Covenant with Abraham still
remained (c. ii. 16 note). The Law
was a first step towards its fulfilment.

ὅτι αὐτοί...] *because they...and I...*
Both pronouns are emphatic. ὁρᾷς
πρῶτον παρ᾽ ἡμῶν ἀρχόμενα τὰ κακά;...
τὰ μέντοι ἀγαθὰ καὶ αἱ εὐεργεσίαι παρ᾽
αὐτοῦ ἄρχονται (Theophlct).

It is remarkable that ὅτι causal is
not found in the Epistle except in the
quotations in this Chapter. It occurs
in all the other writers of the N. T.

οὐκ ἐνέμειναν ἐν] Hebr. הֵפֵרוּ. The
same original word is used of the
Lord annulling His Covenant : Jer.
xiv. 21. The LXX. rendering expresses forcibly the idea of the constraining,
disciplining, power of the Law: Deut.
xxvii. 26 (Gal. iii. 10).

κἀγὼ ἠμέλησα αὐτῶν] Hebr. וְאָנֹכִי
בָּעַלְתִּי בָם. See Ges. *Thes.* s. v. בָּעַל,
and Additional Note.

10—12. The positive characteristics of the New Covenant, 'the better
promises' on which it rests, are to be
found in (1) its spirituality (v. 10),
(2) its universal efficacy (v. 11), (3) its
assurance of free forgiveness (v. 12).

10. *ὅτι αὕτη...ἐπιγράψω αὐτούς*]
*Because this is the covenant that I
will covenant with the house of Israel
...even putting my laws...and upon
their heart will I write them.* Under
the Mosaic system the law was fixed
and external: the new laws enter
into the understanding as active principles to be realised and embodied by
progressive thought. The old law

μετὰ τὰς ἡμέρας ἐκείνας, λέγει Κύριος,
διδοὺς νόμους μου εἰς τὴν διάνοιαν αὐτῶν,
καὶ ἐπὶ ⌐καρδίας⌐ αὐτῶν ἐπιγράψω αὐτούς,
καὶ ἔσομαι αὐτοῖς εἰς θεόν
καὶ αὐτοὶ ἔσονταί μοι εἰς λαόν.

10 καρδίαν

καρδίας αὐτῶν אcAD₂ (plur. me syrr) (καρΔιαεαγτωΝ B): καρδίαν αὐτῶν א*.   ἐπιγράψω: γράψω B.

was written on tables of stone: the
new laws are written on the heart
and become, so to speak, part of the
personality of the believer. The image
is universal. Comp. 2 Cor. iii. 3.

Philo speaks of the revelation of
God Himself as being the highest
form of Divine Covenant: δείξας ἑαυτὸν ὡς ἐνῆν δειχθῆναι τὸν ἄδεικτον διὰ
τοῦ φάναι 'καὶ ἐγώ' (Gen. xvii. 4), ἐπιλέγει
'ἰδοὺ ἡ διαθήκη μου,' ἡ πασῶν χαρίτων
ἀρχή τε καὶ πηγὴ αὐτός εἰμι ἐγώ (De
mut. nom. § 8; i. 587 M.).

The use of the simple dative (διαθ.
τῷ οἴκῳ Ἰσρ.) here as in v. 9 (ἐποίησα
τοῖς π.) presents God as the disposer,
framer, of the Covenant.

The people of God is now again
called by its one name 'the house of
Israel.' The division of Israel and
Judah (v. 8) has ceased to be. Compare Acts ii. 36; Rom. xi. 26; Gal.
vi. 16; c. iv. 9; xiii. 12 note.

μετὰ τὰς ἡμ. ἐκ.] 'Those days' from
the point of view of the prophet correspond with what the writer of the
Epistle has spoken of as 'the end of
these days' (i. 2). The phrase is used
peculiarly to mark the period of conflict which immediately precedes the
final triumph of Messiah. Comp.
Matt. xxiv. 19.

διδούς...αὐτῶν] The participle διδούς
may go with διαθήσομαι: 'I will make
a covenant even by putting (Latt.
dando)...and I will...'; or it may be
taken with καὶ ἐπιγράψω: 'I will make
a covenant even thus, putting my laws
...I will also write them....' On the
whole the former construction is the
more natural. For the transition from

the participle to the finite verb compare Moulton-Winer p. 717.

The rendering of אֶת־תּוֹרָתִי by the
plural νόμους is remarkable. It may
have been chosen to dissociate the
general idea of the divine 'instruction'
from the special Mosaic code with
which it had been identified.

The plural occurs again in the same
quotation c. x. 16, but not elsewhere
in the N. T.; nor does the plural
appear to be found in any other place
of the LXX. as a translation of תּוֹרָה.
It is found for the (Hebr.) plural in
Dan. ix. 10. Conversely ὁ νόμος is used
to express the plural; Ex. xviii. 20;
Lev. xxvi. 46 (הַתּוֹרֹת).

The construction διδούς...εἰς...is
found in classical writers, e.g. Xen.
Cyr. viii. 2, 20. Comp. Apoc. xvii. 17
(the usage in Acts xix. 31 is strange).

The result of διδόναι εἰς is marked
in the phrase διδόναι ἐν...2 Cor. i. 22;
viii. 16. Compare John iii. 35 with
John xiii. 3.

τὴν διάνοιαν...καρδίας] Διάνοια expresses the discursive faculty of
thought, while καρδία is the seat of
man's personal life, the moral character. Comp. Addit. Note on c. iv. 12.

Comp. Lk. i. 51 διανοίᾳ καρδίας.
1 Chron. xxix. 18. See also Eph. i.
18 (v. l.); 1 Pet. i. 13; Eph. iv. 18
(διάνοια, νοῦς); 1 John v. 20.

Καρδίας may be gen. sing. or acc.
pl. (Vulg. in corde. O. L. in cordibus).
Both constructions are good. The
corresponding word in the original is
singular, and so probably is καρδίας
here: Prov. vii. 3.

¹¹καὶ ΟΥ̓ ΜΗ ΔΙΔΑΞΩCΙΝ ἕκαστος τὸν πολίτην αὐτοῦ
καὶ ἕκαστος τὸν ἀδελφὸν αὐτοῦ, λέγων Γνῶθι τὸν κύριον,
ὅτι πάντες εἰδήCΟΥCΊΝ ΜΕ
ἀπὸ μικροῦ ἕως μεγάλου αὐτῶν.
¹²ὅτι ἵλεως ἔcομαι ταῖς ἀδικίαις αὐτῶν,

11 πολίτην אAB (πολείτην) D₂me syr vg syr hl txt: πλήσιον ς vg syr hl mg. αὐτοῦ (1):
ἑαυτοῦ D₂*.   αὐτοῦ (2): om. D₂*.   εἰδήσουσιν : εἰδουσιν B*.   ἀπὸ μικροῦ :
+ αὐτῶν ς me syrr.

καὶ ἔσομαι...λαόν] The end of the
new Covenant is the same as that of
the old. In both cases the purpose
of God was to form a people truly
His own: Ex. vi. 7.

This end was accomplished externally and typically by the separation
and training of the Jewish people;
but more than this was required.
The type had to find its fulfilment.
To this fulfilment the prophets looked;
and the apostles proclaimed it: Apoc.
xxi. 3 (λαοί v. λαός); 2 Cor. vi. 16.

Nothing is said directly in the
prophets or in the Epistle of the admission of the Gentiles into 'the
Commonwealth of Israel.' This fact
is included in the recognition of the
essential spirituality of the new Covenant. Compare Hos. i. 9; ii. 1; Is.
lxi. 9; Zech. xiii. 9; c. ii. 17 (τοῦ
λαοῦ); xiii. 12 notes.

For the construction εἶναι εἰς see
c. i. 5 note.

11. A second characteristic of the
new Covenant follows directly from
the first. The people are brought
into true fellowship with God, and
this involves an immediate knowledge
of Him. No privileged class is interposed between the mass of men and
God. All are true scribes (John
vi. 45) in virtue of the teaching within
them (1 John ii. 20, 27). All have immediate access to the divine Presence.

The description marks the absolute
relation, but does not define how the
universal privilege will be in fact
realised.

οὐ μὴ διδάξωσιν] v. 12; xiii. 5; x. 17
(fut.). See Moulton-Winer, p. 636.

τὸν πολ....τὸν ἀδ.] The more general
and the more special relations have
their respective obligations. Πολίτης
occurs a few times in the LXX. as a
rendering of רֵעַ e.g. Prov. xxiv. 43
(28); Jer. xxxvi. (xxix.) 23. Comp.
xi. 10 Additional Note.

γνῶθι...εἰδήσουσιν...] Latt. cognosce
...scient.... The Lord will not be a
stranger to be first recognised : all
will have an absolute, inborn, ac-
quaintance with Him from the least to
the greatest (Latt. a minore usque ad
majorem eorum). There will be no
distinction of age or station or endowments in respect of this fundamental
knowledge.

This end was gained by the Incarnation (John i. 18 ; xvii. 6): τοῦ θεοῦ
ἐπὶ τῆς γῆς ἐν σαρκὶ διατρίψαντος καὶ
τὴν φύσιν ἡμῶν τῇ προσλήψει θεώσαντος,
ἔλαμψεν ἐν ταῖς πάντων ψυχαῖς τὸ τῆς
ἀληθοῦς θεογνωσίας φῶς, καὶ οἷόν τις
ἐπιτηδειότης ἐνετέθη τῇ ἀνθρωπίνῃ φύσει
ὑπὸ τῆς χάριτος πρὸς τὸ τὸν ὄντως εἰδέναι
θεόν (Theophlct).

12. The third characteristic of
the New Covenant is that which
contains the pledge of its efficacy.
It rests upon forgiveness on the part
of God, not on performance on the
part of man. Its foundation is grace
and not works (John i. 17). In this
lies the assurance against such failure
as the Old Covenant brought to light.
Comp. Is. lix. 2.

ὅτι ἵλεως ἔσομαι] Vulg. quia pro-
pitius ero. The New Covenant will
be efficacious, for God Himself says
I will be merciful. The phrase
ἵλεως ἔσομαι (γενήσομαι) is found else-

καὶ τῶν ἁμαρτιῶν αγτῶν ογ μὴ μνηcθῶ ἔτι.

¹³ἐν τῷ λέγειν Καινήν πεπαλαίωκεν τὴν πρώτην, τὸ δὲ
παλαιούμενον καὶ γηράσκον ἐγγὺς ἀφανισμοῦ.

12 τῶν ἁμ. αὐτῶν ℵ*B vg me syr vg : +καὶ τῶν ἀνομιῶν αὐτῶν ℵᶜ(A)D₂ syr hl (see
x. 17).   13 τὸ δέ: τό τε D₂*.

where in the LXX. as a rendering of סָלַח
in reference to God's forgiveness of
sin : 1 K. viii. 34 ff.; and of men :
Num. xiv. 20 ; Jer. v. 1, 7.
In the N.T. ἵλεως occurs again only
in the phrase ἵλεώς σοι Κύριε (Matt.
xvi. 22 absit a te domine), a form
which is found in the LXX. (for
חָלִילָה לְ): 2 Sam. xx. 20; xxiii. 17;
1 Chron. xi. 19 ἵλεώς μοι ὁ θεός.
For the sense and usage of the
cognate words see note on 1 John
ii. 2 ; c. ii. 17 note.

ταῖς ἀδικίαις] The plural is found
here only in N.T., though it occurs
often in the LXX., and in combination
with ἐξιλάσασθαι Dan. ix. 24; comp.
Ps. lxiv. 4 ; Ecclus. iii. 30; c. ii. 17.

In connexion with this promise of
forgiveness the prophetic disparagement of sacrifices and ritual as
spiritually inefficacious must be
noticed. The development of this
inward religion begins with 1 Sam.
xv. 22 f.; compare Psalm l. 8 ff.;
li. 15 ff.; Hos. vi. 4 ff.; Amos v. 21 ff.;
Micah vi. 6 ff.; Is. i. 11 ff.

In the writings of Jeremiah, on the
eve of the long exile, when the
sacrificial ritual became impossible,
it was natural in the order of divine
Providence that the realities symbolised by sacrifices should be brought
into prominence. Comp. Jer. vii.
21 ff.

Sacrifice, however, had its place in
restored Israel: Jer. xxxiii. 11. Compare Is. lvi. 7 ; lxvi. 20 ff.; Mal.
i. 10 f.; Hebr. xiii. 15 note. See
Oehler, Theol. of O.T., § 201.

13. The conclusion goes beyond
that which the prophetic passage was
quoted to establish. The New Cove-

nant is not only better, and founded
upon better promises than the Old ;
but, yet more, it supersedes the Old.
The characteristics of the New Covenant, and the very name which it
bears, point to the abrogation of that
which has now become 'the old.'

ἐν τῷ λέγειν] In that he saith
(Latt. dicendo). Comp. c. ii. 8 ;
iii. 15.

πεπαλαίωκεν] Latt. veteravit. By
the use of the term 'new' in reference to another Covenant God
has necessarily placed the other
Covenant in the position of 'old'
relatively. Even in the days of
Jeremiah this sentence stands already
written (perf.). Comp. v. 5 κεχρημάτισται.

The active use of παλαιόω, which is
generally found in the middle form
(i. 11 note) in the sense of 'growing
old,' is rare. It occurs in the LXX.:
Lam. iii. 4 ἐπαλαίωσε σάρκα.   Is.
lxv. 22 τὰ ἔργα παλαιώσουσι (יְבַלּוּ)
i.e. continue long, use to the full);
comp. Job xxi. 13 ; Job ix. 5 ὁ παλαιῶν
ὄρη ; xxxii. 15 ἐπαλαίωσαν λόγους (they
spoke no more).

τὸ παλαιούμενον καὶ γηρ.] Vulg. quod
autem antiquatur (O.L. veteratur)
et senescit. The use of the present
as distinguished from πεπαλαιωμένον
and παλαιωθέν is significant. The
divine words spoken to the prophet
were accomplished slowly on the scene
of life. The addition of γηράσκον adds
a new thought. When that which is
temporal has existed a long time it
draws to its natural end. So Theophylact : οὐκ ἀκαίρως κατέπαυσεν ἡ νέα
τὴν παλαιὰν ἀλλὰ διὰ τὸ γῆρας...

ἐγγ. ἀφανισμοῦ] nigh unto vanish-

ing away, Latt. *prope interitum.* The word ἀφανισμός is singularly frequent in the LXX. of Jeremiah as the representative of שַׁמָּה and שְׁמָמָה. It is used, for example, of Babylon li. (xxviii.) 26 ff. The verb ἀφανίζειν occurs in several interesting con-nexions: Matt. vi. 16, 19 f.; James iv. 14; Acts xiii. 41 (LXX). For ἐγγύς see c. vi. 8.

For a time the continuance of the Temple services gave to the Old Order an outward semblance of en-during reality even after it was es-sentially abrogated by fulfilment.

Additional Note on viii. 1. *Christ the High-priest and the Highpriest-King.*

The student will find it of deep interest to trace through the Epistle the gradual unfolding of the thought of Christ's two offices, concentrated in one Person, and to consider the view which is given of the twofold relation in which He is shewn to stand to His people as High-priest and as King. Compare Additional Note on ii. 17. The double thought is indicated plainly in the Introduction : i. 3 καθαρισμὸν τῶν ἁμαρτιῶν ποιησάμενος ἐκάθισεν ἐν δεξιᾷ τῆς μεγαλωσύνης ἐν ὑψηλοῖς: the completed Atonement is followed by the assumption of the Royal throne. The idea of priesthood and high-priesthood is then developed ; and in vii. 1 ff. the type of Melchizedek is brought forward to make it clear that God had designed for man something beyond that which was realised in Abraham, and still more beyond that which was realised in the Levitical order. {Christ High-priest and King.}

This type of Melchizedek is declared to be fulfilled in the ascended Christ, viii. 1 τοιοῦτον ἔχομεν ἀρχιερέα, ὃς ἐκάθισεν ἐν δεξιᾷ τῆς μεγαλωσύνης ἐν τοῖς οὐρανοῖς (comp. vii. 16 f.; 27).

And Christ as King, *having offered one sacrifice for sins for ever,* waits upon His throne for the complete establishment of the sovereignty which He has finally won (comp. John xvi. 33 νενίκηκα): x. 11—14.

In these passages the two offices are placed in the closest connexion; and the Session of Christ on the right hand of God is, with one exception (i. 13), always connected with the fulfilment of priestly work (i. 3 ; viii. 1 ; x. 12 ; xii. 2).

Thus it is plainly shewn that as High-priest Christ fulfilled two types ; and we must therefore distinguish two aspects of His High-priestly work : (1) as the fulfilment of the Levitical High-priesthood; and (2) as the fulfilment of the royal High-priesthood of Melchizedek, the first before His Session (as High-priest), and the second after His Session (as High-priest-King). {A twofold High-priesthood.}

As High-priest before His Session, fulfilling the type of Aaron, Christ (1) 'offered Himself' (vii. 27 ἑαυτὸν ἀνενέγκας; viii. 3; ix. 14 ἑαυτὸν προσήνεγκεν ; ix. 26 διὰ τῆς θυσίας αὐτοῦ ; x. 10—12 διὰ τῆς προσφορᾶς τοῦ σώματος 'Ι. Χ....μίαν προσενέγκας θυσίαν); and (2) He entered into the Presence of God [iv. 14 διεληλυθότα τοὺς οὐρανούς; vi. 20 ὅπου (εἰς τὸ ἐσώτερον τοῦ καταπετάσματος)...εἰσῆλθεν...; viii. 12, 16; ix. 12, 24 εἰσῆλθεν εἰς τὰ ἅγια...]; ix. 23 f. {Fulfilment of the type of Aaron.}

The whole discipline of earthly life was the preparation for the final High-priestly service. When the word Τετέλεσται (John xix. 30) had declared the fulfilment of every condition, the Lord made the offering of Himself, and so entered into the Presence of God *through His own Blood.* Thus He fulfilled the type of the Aaronic High-priesthood (comp. Addit. Note on ix. 7, *s. f.*).

The passages which deal with Christ's offering of Himself bring before us successively the fact of His sacrifice (vii. 27); its necessity (viii. 3); its possibility (ix. 14); its absolute efficacy (ix. 25, 26, 28); its fulness (x. 10); and its continuous personal validity (x. 12—14).

So again the passages which deal with Christ's entrance into the Presence of God declare the fact (iv. 14); the purpose for man (vi. 20); the corresponding work (viii. 1, 2, 6); the single entrance made once for all (ix. 12); and the purification of the Sanctuary of redeemed humanity (ix. 23 f.).

The 'offering' and the 'entrance' together present the accomplishment of the work typified in the Aaronic priesthood. This was gathered up into the service of the great Day of Atonement, which was marked by two chief acts, the double sacrifice, and the restoration of the covenant fellowship between the people and God by the application of the blood (the life) of the sacrifice to the chosen place of God's Presence. So Christ offered Himself upon the Cross and humanity in Himself, and entering before God, through His own blood, realised the abiding fellowship of man and God in His glorified humanity, openly seen before the face of God (ix. 24). By this appearance the ascended Lord perfectly fulfilled that which was typified by the bringing of the blood of the victim as a hallowing power to the Mercy-seat, the crowning service of the Aaronic priest. In Him, Priest at once and people, the Life which was offered was present in a nobler and eternal form.

Assumption of the Royal Highpriesthood after the type of Melchizedek.

Thereupon the Lord entered on the fulness of His work as Highpriest-King; and the ideas connected with His Session gain their full interpretation in its connexion with His one Divine-human Person (i. 3): His twofold office (viii. 1 f.); the gathering the fruits of His victory (x. 12; i. 13); the efficacy of His present help (xii. 2).

After His Session—if we may use words of time of that which is beyond time—He still fulfils his work as 'High-priest after the order of Melchizedek,' which we regard under two aspects, as the work of our King and the work of our High-priest: see xiii. 15 and Additional Notes on vv. 1, 2; xi. 10.

Silence as to the Resurrection.

The aspect under which the writer of the Epistle thus regards the work of the Risen Christ explains his silence as to the fact of the Resurrection. The fact itself underlies all his argument. He assumes the permanence of Christ's perfect humanity through death of which the Resurrection is the pledge; and dwells on the continued activity of Christ in His glorified humanity; but he refers to the Resurrection directly only once: xiii. 20. He thinks, so to speak, as St John in his Epistles, not so much of Christ's victory as of His triumph.

Yet more, this treatment was necessarily suggested by the comparison of Christ's priestly work with the typical service of the High-priest. Christ occupied the place both of the victim and of the priest, in regard both to the people and to God; and in that symbolic service the death of the victim was subordinated to the unbroken ministry of the priest; and there was nothing in the type which answered to the Resurrection.

Additional Note on viii. 1, 2.   *The present work of Christ as High-priest.*

The present work of the Glorified and Ascended Son of man for men is indicated to us in the Epistle, in accordance with what has been already said, under two aspects, as the work of a High-priest and as the work of a King. As High-priest He represents man to God: as King He represents God to man. In the latter relation He is even now the Sovereign of the new Commonwealth, hereafter to be realised in its completeness (compare Additional Note on xi. 10). But in the present passage the thought is mainly of His High-priestly work. To understand this we must recall the type. The sacrifices on the Day of Atonement provided the means of entrance to the Divine Presence. The application of the blood removed every impurity which hindered the approach to God of him in whom the people were summed up. So cleansed the representative of Israel was able to sustain that awful fellowship for which man was made. And simply standing before the Lord he fulfilled his work. No words were spoken: no uttered intercession was made. It was enough that man was there according to divine appointment, to witness in the most emphatic manner to the continued preservation of the established relation of man to God. Comp. Philo, *de Monarch.* ii. 6 (ii. 227 M.); *de vit. Mos.* iii. § 14. {.marginnote} Two aspects of the present work of Christ.

{.marginnote} The type of the Levitical High-priest.

Thus we read in a figure the High-priestly Work of Christ. By His offering of Himself He has *made purification of sins* (i. 3); He has applied the virtue of His Blood, to speak in earthly language, to the scene of the worship of redeemed humanity (ix. 23); He has taken His seat upon the throne, entering in His humanity upon the full enjoyment of every privilege won by His perfect fulfilment of the will of God. Henceforth He applies for the benefit of men the fruits of the Atonement which He has completed. {.marginnote} The type fulfilled by Christ

This work is shewn to us in the Epistle in three distinct forms, and we have no authority to go beyond its teaching. {.marginnote} in three forms.

i. Christ intercedes for men as their present representative before God: vii. 25, 27; ix. 24.

ii. Christ brings the prayers and praises of His people to God, embodying their true spiritual desires, so that at each moment they become articulate through His Spirit and are brought through Him to the Throne: xiii. 15.

iii. Christ secures access for His people in their present state to 'the holy place,' where He Himself is, *in His Blood*—the virtue of His earthly life lived and offered: iv. 16; x. 19—22.

These three forms of Christ's work shew under the conditions of human experience what He does for humanity eternally. Our fellowship with God will grow closer, more perfect, more conscious, but still our approach to God, our worship, our spiritual harmony, must always be 'in Him' in Whom we have been incorporated.

The modern conception of Christ pleading in heaven His Passion, 'offering His blood,' on behalf of men, has no foundation in the Epistle. His glorified humanity is the eternal pledge of the absolute efficacy of His accomplished work. He pleads, as older writers truly expressed the thought, by His Presence on the Father's Throne.

Meanwhile men on earth in union with Him enjoy continually through His Blood what was before the privilege of one man on one day in the year.

So far the thought of the priestly work of the Ascended Christ is expressed under the images of the Levitical covenant, as He works for 'the people' (ἡ ἐκκλησία); but He has yet another work, as 'priest after the order of Melchizedek,' for humanity. He does not lay aside this wider relation in completely fulfilling the narrower. Rather it is through the fulfilment of His work for the Church—the firstfruits—that He moves towards the fulfilment of His work for the world. We have no powers to pursue the development of the truth, but it is necessary to remember it.

In illustration of this conception of an universal priesthood it is interesting to compare Philo's conception of the priesthood of the righteous man: *Leg. Alleg.* iii. 87 (i. 135 M.); *de post. Cain.* 54 (i. 261 M.); *de Monarch.* i. 8 (ii. 220 M.).

Additional Note on viii. 2. *On the words* λειτουργεῖν, λατρεύειν *&c.*

The groups of words connected with λειτουργεῖν and λατρεύειν are naturally of frequent occurrence in this Epistle. Thus we find λειτουργός i. 7; λειτουργεῖν x. 11; λειτουργία viii. 6; ix. 21; λειτουργικός i. 14; and λατρεία ix. 1, 6; λατρεύειν viii. 5; ix. 9, 14; x. 2; xii. 28; xiii. 10. The former group of words is found elsewhere in the N. T. only in the writings of St Luke and St Paul: the latter group is found also in St Matthew (LXX.) and St John (Gosp. Apoc.). The ideas which they express require to be distinguished.

1. Λειτουργεῖν, &c.

1. The group λειτουργός, λειτουργεῖν, λειτουργία, is of common occurrence in the LXX. Λειτουργός in every place represents מְשָׁרֵת, which is less often rendered by διάκονος and θεράπων. Λειτουργεῖν is the general translation of שֵׁרֵת (more than sixty times), and in a very limited range it is used also for עָבַד. Λειτουργία is nearly always a rendering of עֲבֹדָה. The words are used habitually of the service of priests (Ex. xxviii. 31, 39) and Levites (1 Chron. xvi. 4, 6). But they have also a wider application, of the service of Samuel to God (1 Sam. ii. 18; iii. 1); of service to the people (Ezek. xliv. 11 f.); of service to men (Num. iii. 6; xviii. 2; 1 Kings i. 4, 15; Ecclus. x. 25).

There is however one common feature in the different applications of the words. The λειτουργία is the fulfilment of an office: it has a definite representative character, and corresponds with a function to be discharged. This appears to be true even when the office is most personal. The classical usage of the term accentuated this thought of public service which lies in the word by its derivation (λαός, λήϊτος, λεῖτος). The Athenian 'Liturgies'

(Dict. of Ant. *s. v.*) expressed vividly the idea of a necessary service rendered to the state by a citizen who had the means of rendering it. And the usage of the word in the N.T. reflects something of the colour thus given to it.

The words λειτουργός, -εῖν, -ία, are used in the apostolic writings of services rendered to God and to man, and that in the widest relations of social life.

(*a*) Thus the officers of civil government are spoken of as λειτουργοὶ θεοῦ (Rom. xiii. 6). St Paul describes himself as λειτουργὸς Χριστοῦ Ἰησοῦ εἰς τὰ ἔθνη (Rom. xv. 16) in the discharge of his debt to mankind in virtue of his commission to proclaim the Gospel (Rom. i. 5, 14). The priestly office of Zachariah was a λειτουργία (Lk. i. 23). 'Prophets and teachers' performed a public service for the Church to the Lord (λειτουργούντων αὐτῶν τῷ κυρίῳ Acts xiii. 2[1]). In the widest sense the whole life of a Christian society becomes a sacrifice and ministry of faith (εἰ καὶ σπένδομαι ἐπὶ τῇ θυσίᾳ καὶ λειτουργίᾳ τῆς πίστεως ὑμῶν Phil. ii. 17), to which the life-blood of their teacher is as the accompanying libation. And in a narrower sense the vessels of the Tabernacle were 'vessels of the ministry' (τὰ σκεύη τῆς λειτουργίας Hebr. ix. 21). The Levitical priests serve (λειτουργεῖν *absol.* Hebr. x. 11). And Christ Himself 'has obtained a more excellent ministry' (διαφορωτέρας τέτυχε λειτουργίας Hebr. viii. 6), being 'a minister of the sanctuary and of the true tabernacle' (τῶν ἁγίων λειτουργὸς καὶ τῆς σκηνῆς τῆς ἀληθινῆς Hebr. viii. 2).

The ministry to God is in a most true sense a ministry to men and for men. This λειτουργία is the accomplishment of an office necessary for human well-being.

(*b*) The λειτουργία directly rendered to men has an equally broad character. It is a service which answers to deep relations of social life. The wealthy have a ministry to fulfil towards the poor which belongs to the health of the body (ὀφείλουσιν καὶ ἐν τοῖς σαρκικοῖς λειτουργῆσαι αὐτοῖς Rom. xv. 27); the due accomplishment of which brings wider blessings to the society (ἡ διακονία τῆς λειτουργίας ταύτης...ἐστί...περισσεύουσα διὰ πολλῶν εὐχαριστιῶν τῷ θεῷ 2 Cor. ix. 12). In the closer relations of the Christian life a corresponding ministry has its place which cannot be disregarded without loss (λειτουργὸν τῆς χρείας μου Phil. ii. 25; ἵνα ἀναπληρώσῃ τὸ ὑμῶν ὑστέρημα τῆς πρός με λειτουργίας *id. v.* 30).

In Ecclesiastical usage the word λειτουργία was used specially of the stated services of public worship, of 'the evening service' (ἡ ἑσπερινὴ λειτουργία), of 'the service of Baptism' (ἡ τοῦ θείου βαπτίσματος λειτ.), and specially of the service of Holy Communion (ἡ τῶν θείων μυστηρίων λειτ. and simply ἡ λειτουργία[2]). See exx. in Sophocles *Lex.* s. v.

The words are common in Clement: 1 *Cor.* 8, 9, 20, 32, 34, 40, 41, 43 f.

---

[1] The words find a remarkable parallel in *Doctr. Apost.* § 15 χειροτονήσατε οὖν ἑαυτοῖς ἐπισκόπους καὶ διακόνους... ὑμῖν γὰρ λειτουργοῦσι καὶ αὐτοὶ τὴν λειτουργίαν τῶν προφητῶν καὶ διδασκάλων. The ministry to the Lord is also a ministry to His people.

[2] There is an interesting discussion of the use of the word in this connexion by Melanchthon in the *Apology for the Augsburg Confession* (c. xii. §§ 80 ff.) in answer to the assertion that 'Λειτουργία signifies sacrifice.'

They are found also in Hermas: *Mand.* v. 1, 2, 3: *Sim.* v. 3, 3, 8; vii. 6; ix. 27, 3: but they are not noted from Ignatius, Polycarp or Barnabas. Comp. *Test. Lev.* 2, 3, 4.

2. Λατρεύ-
ειν, &c.

2. The usage of λατρεύειν and λατρεία is more limited. The verb λατρεύειν is common in the LXX. and is almost always a rendering of עָבַד (*Pent. Josh. Jud.*: twice of שֵׁרֵת). The noun λατρεία is rare and in each case represents עֲבֹדָה. The words always describe a divine service, a service to God or to gods. This idea appears to spring from the conception of complete devotion of powers to a master which lies in the root of the word (λάτρις, *latro, a hired servant*). In classical writers the word λατρεία is used of an absolute service, personal (Æsch. *P. V.* 966), or moral (Plut. *Consol. ad Apoll.* 107 c and Wyttenbach's note), or religious (Plat. *Apol.* § 9 p. 23 B).

The usage of the N.T. agrees with that of the LXX. Λατρεύειν and λατρεία uniformly express a divine service. This sense Augustine gives very well: ad societatem [civitatis cælestis] pietas vera perducit, quæ non exhibet *servitutem relligionis*, quam λατρείαν Græci vocant, nisi vero Deo. The noun λατρεία is rare. It describes the whole religious ritual of the Law: ἡ λατρεία (Vulg. *obsequium*) καὶ αἱ ἐπαγγελίαι (Rom. ix. 4); δικαιώματα λατρείας (Hebr. ix. 1); and also the spiritual antitype in the Christian order: τὴν λογικὴν λατρείαν (Rom. xii. 1). The plural, αἱ λατρείαι (Hebr. ix. 6), marks the different elements of service. In John xvi. 2 the spiritual blindness of the persecutors of the Faith is shewn in its most extreme form where it is said that he who kills Christians will think λατρείαν προσφέρειν τῷ θεῷ, that in that sacrifice he offers the service of complete devotion to God. The verb λατρεύειν is much more frequent. It is commonly used with an object (*e.g.* τῷ θεῷ); but it is used also absolutely (Lk. ii. 37; Acts xxvi. 7; Phil. iii. 3 οἱ πνεύματι θεοῦ λατρ.; Hebr. ix. 9; x. 2).

The words (λατρεύειν, λατρεία) occur in the same sense in Clement (1 *Cor.* 45), Ignatius (*Smyrn.* 9 τῷ διαβόλῳ λατρεύει); *Mart. Ign.* 2 εἰ μὴ τὴν τῶν δαιμόνων ἔλοιτο λατρείαν. *Doctr. Apost.* 6 ἀπὸ τοῦ εἰδωλοθύτου λίαν πρόσεχε· λατρεία γάρ ἐστι θεῶν νεκρῶν. The word λατρεία is also applied to the Service of Holy Communion (*Const. Apost.* viii. 15 ἡ μυστικὴ λατρεία, and Cotelier's note).

As far as the actual position is concerned λατρεύειν is closely akin to δουλεύειν, but the position is accepted voluntarily by the λάτρις (λατρεύει· ἐλεύθερος ὢν δουλεύει *Hesych.*), while it belongs to the state of the δοῦλος. Λειτουργεῖν and λατρεύειν occur together Ecclus. iv. 14.

3. Διακο-
νεῖν, &c.

3. Both groups of words are clearly distinguished from διακονεῖν, διακονία, which describe definite acts of service rendered to another, and that specially in obedience to express direction. So the Christian becomes a διάκονος of God and Christ (John xii. 26; Rom. xiii. 4; Col. i. 7; 1 Tim. iv. 6 &c.), waiting for the least expression of the divine will that he may obey it in deed. The word διακονεῖν is not found in the LXX. and διάκονος occurs only in Esther (three times; διακονία in 1 Macc. xi. 58). See Hebr. i. 14; vi. 10. Comp. 2 Cor. ix. 12.

Speaking generally then λειτουργία marks the fulfilment of function in regard to the claims of a larger life: λατρεία, the service of perfect subjection to a sovereign power: διακονία, the ministry of appointed action. Or, to express the thought in another form, he who fulfils a λειτουργία acts for the body, of which he is a part: he who renders a λατρεία recognises a supreme claim in rendering it: he who offers a διακονία looks to the discharge of a personal service.

Additional Note on viii. 5. The general significance of the Tabernacle.

It is characteristic of the Epistle that all the arguments from the divine worship of Judaism which it contains are drawn from the institutions of the Tabernacle. These, which are treated as the direct embodiment of the heavenly archetype, are supposed to be still preserved in the later forms and to give force to them. They were never superseded even when they were practically modified. The Temple indeed no less than the Kingdom, with which it corresponded, was the sign of a spiritual declension. *The Tabernacle, not the Temple, gives the ideal of Jewish worship.* Both were endeavours to give a fixed and permanent shape, according to the conditions of earthly life, to ideas which in their essential nature led the thoughts of men forward to the future and the unseen. God was pleased to use, in this as in other cases, the changes which were brought about by the exigences of national life for the fulfilment of His own counsel, but the divine interpreter of the Old Testament necessarily looked, beyond the splendours of the sacred buildings (Matt. xxiv. 1 ff.), and the triumphs of the monarchy of David, to the sacred tent of the pilgrim people and the heavenly sovereignty[1].

The usage of the Epistle in this respect (viii. 2, 5: ix. 11) is felt to be more significant when we take account of the usage of the other Books of the New Testament. *References to the Tabernacle and Temple in the N. T.* The only other references to the Tabernacle (earthly or heavenly) are in Acts vii. 44 (ἡ σκηνὴ τοῦ μαρτυρίου), and in the Apocalypse (xiii. 6 βλασφημῆσαι τὸ ὄνομα αὐτοῦ καὶ τὴν σκηνὴν αὐτοῦ, τοὺς ἐν τῷ οὐρανῷ σκηνοῦντας, xv. 5 ὁ ναὸς τῆς σκηνῆς τοῦ μαρτυρίου, xxi. 3 ἡ σκηνὴ τοῦ θεοῦ μετὰ τῶν ἀνθρώπων). In the passage of the Acts St Stephen appears to draw a contrast between the 'tent' and the 'house' (vv. 47 ff.); and the language of the Apocalypse illustrates in several points the wider views of the Tabernacle which are opened in the Epistle. The term τὸ ἱερόν (the Temple with its courts and subordinate buildings) is found outside the Gospels and Acts only in 1 Cor. ix. 13, where the reference to the Jewish Temple is fixed by θυσιαστήριον (c. x. 18). Ναός (the Sanctuary) is used in a spiritual sense in John ii. 21; 1 Cor. iii. 16 f.; vi. 19; 2 Cor. vi. 16; Eph. ii. 21 (comp. Apoc. xxi. 22), and again literally in 2 Thess. ii. 4. The word οἶκος is used of the material building in the Gospels and Acts,

---

[1] It does not in any way belong to the present subject to discuss critical questions as to the account of the Tabernacle in the Pentateuch. That narrative unquestionably expressed and fashioned the faith of the Jews from the Return to the Apostolic Age, and it is with that faith that we are concerned. Yet it must be added that it seems to be an incredible inversion of history to suppose that the Tabernacle was an imaginary ideal constructed either from the Temple of the Monarchy or from the Temple of the Return.

and of the human antitype in 1 Pet. iv. 17; 1 Tim. iii. 15, as in Hebr. iii. 2 ff.; x. 21 (from Num. xii. 7 LXX.). Thus the actual reference to the Mosaic Tabernacle as a lesson in the divine revelation is peculiar to the Epistle. What then was its general teaching?

Original names of the Tabernacle.
(a) The Dwelling.

The names of the Tabernacle offer an instructive answer to the question.

(a) The commonest single name is that which expresses generally 'a habitation,' מִשְׁכָּן. The root שָׁכַן is used of 'settling,' 'resting,' 'dwelling,' and that both of man and beasts (so of the glory of God—the *Shekinah* in later language—Ex. xxiv. 16 &c.). The word מִשְׁכָּן suggests then nothing more than 'dwelling-place' (of men, Num. xvi. 24, 27; Ps. lxxxvii. 2, &c.; of the Temple in the pl., Ps. xliii. 3; xlvi. 5, &c.), and, as it is expressed definitely, 'the dwelling-place of Jehovah' (מִשְׁכַּן י'''): Lev. xvii. 4; Num. xvi. 9; xvii. 13 (28); xix. 13; xxxi. 30, 47 [Josh. xxii. 19; 1 Chron. xxi. 29] (LXX. ἡ σκηνὴ Κυρίου, Vulg. *tabernaculum Domini*). Comp. Ex. xxix. 45 f. It is generally rendered in the LXX. by σκηνή (106 times [Trommius]) and less frequently by σκήνωμα (17 times); and in the Vulg.

The Tent.

by *tabernaculum*. A second name 'tent,' אֹהֶל, is more definite, and describes the characteristic dwelling of the wilderness, though it was used also in later times (Ps. xv. 1; xxvii. 4). This name is used sometimes alone (Ex. xxvi. 9, 11 ff., 36; xxxiii. 7 ff.; xxxvi. 18 f., 37; xxxix. 33, 38; Num. ix. 17; xviii. 3; Deut. xxxi. 15), but more frequently in combination with other words ('the tent of meeting,' 'the tent of the witness' [testimony]). The 'habitation' ('dwelling') and the 'tent' are clearly distinguished (Ex. xxvi. 7; xxxv. 11; xxxvi. 14; Num. ix. 15). The 'tent' was over the 'dwelling,' as its 'covering' (Num. iii. 25), so that we find the phrase 'the tabernacle (dwelling) of the tent of meeting' (Ex. xxxix. 32; xl. 2, 6, 29 מִשְׁכַּן אֹהֶל מוֹעֵד: comp. Apoc. xv. 5 ὁ ναὸς τῆς σκηνῆς τοῦ μαρτυρίου). Unhappily the LXX. rendered אֹהֶל in the same way as מִשְׁכָּן (σκηνή nearly 140 times, and by σκήνωμα 44 times); and in this it was followed by the Vulgate which gives for the most part *tabernaculum* for both. The word *tentorium*, which is elsewhere used for 'tent,' and not unfrequently for the tents of the people in the narrative of the Exodus (Num. i. 53; ii. 3, 27, &c.), is used in the Vulgate in connexion with the Tabernacle for the 'curtains' (Ex. xxvi. 2), for the 'screen' at the entrance of the Tent (Ex. xxvi. 36 f.; xxxv. 15; xxxvi. 37; xxxix. 38, &c.), for the 'hangings' and the 'screen' of the court (Ex. xxvii. 9 ff., 16; xxxv. 17; xxxviii. 9 ff.; xxxix. 39 f., &c.). Once only it is used for the sacred אֹהֶל (Ex. xxxiii. 8), and once for the sacred מִשְׁכָּן (Num. ix. 15). The name 'palace' (הֵיכָל) belongs to a later time (1 Sam. i. 9; iii. 3); but 'house' (בַּיִת) is used of the Tabernacle (Ex. xxiii. 19), as it is used of the tents of the patriarchs (Gen. xxvii. 15; xxxiii. 17; בֵּית הָאֱלֹהִים 1 Chron. vi. 33).

More commonly, however, the Tabernacle is described by a compound title. The simple terms 'habitation' and 'tent' are defined by the addition of some other word as 'witness' (testimony) or 'meeting'; and these two designations express two distinct aspects of the Tabernacle.

(b) The title 'the tent of witness', אֹהֶל הָעֵדֻת, is rare. It occurs Num. ix. 15 (LXX. τὸν οἶκον τοῦ μαρτυρίου); xvii. 7 f. (22 f.) (ἡ σκηνὴ τοῦ μαρτ.); xviii. 2 (ἡ σκ. τ. μ.). We find also 'the habitation (tabernacle) of witness,' מִשְׁכַּן הָעֵדֻת, Ex. xxxviii. 21; Num. i. 50, 53; x. 11 (ἡ σκ. τ. μ.). The Vulgate rendering of both phrases, except in the last place (which has *tabernaculum fœderis*), is *tabern. testimonii.* The sense of the titles is fixed by the use of עֵדֻת in other connexions; 'the ark of the witness' (אֲרוֹן הָעֵדֻת) Ex. xxv. 22; xxvi. 33 f.; xxx. 6, 26 (LXX. ἡ κιβωτὸς τοῦ μαρτυρίου, Vulg. *arca testimonii* [*testamenti* xxx. 26]); the 'tables of the witness' (לֻחוֹת הָעֵדֻת) Ex. xxxi. 18; xxxiv. 29 (LXX. αἱ πλάκες [τοῦ μαρτυρίου], Vulg. *tabulæ testimonii*); and 'the veil of the witness' (פָּרֹכֶת הָעֵדֻת) Lev. xxiv. 3 (Vulg. *velum testimonii*). The 'witness' was the revelation which God had made of His will expressed in 'the ten words' (Ex. xxv. 16, 21). Comp. Ex. xvi. 34; xxvii. 21; xl. 20; Lev. xvi. 13; Num. xvii. 4—10. This 'witness' was the solemn declaration of the claims and nature of God, who took up His dwelling in the midst of Israel (Lev. xix. 2). The Tent under which He dwelt had this enshrined in it to determine its character. So it was that this Tabernacle was specially called a 'holy place,' a 'sanctuary' (מִקְדָּשׁ LXX. ἁγίασμα, τὸ ἁγιαστήριον, τὸ ἡγιασμένον, τὰ ἅγια, Vulg. *sanctuarium*. Ex. xxv. 8; Lev. xii. 4; xxi. 12; Num. x. 21; xviii. 1).

(c) But the usual name of the Tabernacle is 'the tent of meeting,' אֹהֶל מוֹעֵד. This title occurs constantly in Exodus, Leviticus and Numbers (from Ex. xxvii. 21 onwards), but once only in Deuteronomy (xxxi. 14). It is translated in the LXX. by the same phrase as 'the tent of witness,' ἡ σκηνὴ τοῦ μαρτυρίου, and in the Vulg. (following the Old Latin) by *tabernaculum testimonii* (Ex. xxvii. 21; xxxv. 31 &c.; Num. ii. 17; iii. 7; xvii. 7, 10), and, habitually in Numbers, by *tabern. fœderis* (Ex. xxxi. 7; xxxiii. 7; Lev. xxiv. 3; Num. i. 1 &c.). Two interpretations have been given of it: 'the tent of the congregation,' the place where the congregation of Israel was gathered together (A. V. *the tabernacle of the congregation*), and 'the tent of meeting,' the place where God revealed Himself to His people (so R. V.). Both senses are defensible on linguistic grounds; but the second is clearly required by the narrative itself. The Tabernacle was the place where God made Himself known (Ex. xxv. 8, 22), speaking to the representatives of the nation (Ex. xxix. 42 f.; Num. xvii. 4 [19]); and it could not truly be said that the people were assembled in 'the tent' (yet see Matt. xxiii. 38). The 'tent of meeting' was so completely identified with the revealed Presence of the Lord that it is said to 'dwell with the people in the midst of their uncleannesses' (Lev. xvi. 16).

Taking then these three general titles of the Tabernacle we see that the structure was held to represent provisionally in a sensible form three truths, (a) the Presence of God with men, (b) His righteousness, (c) His 'conversableness[1].' It is scarcely necessary to add that the idea of a

(b) The tent and of witness.

(c) The tent of Meeting.

General result of these titles.

---

[1] I venture to use this most significant word of Howe. 'Such a sort of Deity as should shut up itself and be reclused from all converse with men,

'dwelling' of the Lord in no way tended to confine His Presence to one spot: it simply gave a distinct reality to the fact of His Presence. So again the conditions of the 'witness' and the 'meeting' were not absolute. They emphasised the truths that God Himself determines the terms and mode under which He offers Himself to men conformably to His own Nature.

The building and fabric of the Tabernacle.　　If now we consider the account of the building and arrangement of the Tabernacle we shall recognise that it was fitted to convey most impressively the three lessons which it embodied. It was held to be wholly of divine design. No part was originated by human invention. It was reared after the pattern in which God prescribed the details of the way in which He should be approached (Ex. xxv. 9, 40; Hebr. viii. 5). So the people confessed that if God is to be known, He must reveal Himself.

Again: it was framed substantially out of free-will offerings (Ex. xxv. 2). There was indeed ransom-money, equal in amount for every one, which was used in the structure (Ex. xxxviii. 25 ff.), but this was employed for definite purposes; and the narrative emphasises the willingness with which the people contributed to 'the work of the tent, and all the service thereof' (Ex. xxxv. 20 ff.; xxxvi. 5 ff.). A revelation comes from God only, but it is for man to embrace it from the heart and give form to it.

The threefold division.　　The general plan of the Tabernacle suggested, even to the simplest worshipper, the Majesty of God, Who hides Himself even when He comes among men. The three divisions of the whole fabric, the sacred inclosure (הֶחָצֵר, LXX. ἡ αὐλή, Vulg. atrium, Ex. xxvii. 12 ff.; xxxv. 17 f. &c.) and the twofold Tabernacle, 'the Holy Place,' and 'the Holy of Holies' (הַקֹּדֶשׁ, LXX. τὸ ἅγιον, Vulg. sanctuarium; and קֹדֶשׁ הַקֳּדָשִׁים, τὸ ἅγιον [τὰ ἅγια] τῶν ἁγίων, sanctuarium sanctuarii [sanctum, -ta, sanctorum], Ex. xxvi. 33 f.; Num. iv. 4, 19; but the simple term הַקֹּדֶשׁ is also used of the innermost sanctuary, Lev. xvi. 3, and perhaps קֹדֶשׁ הַקֳּדָשִׁים of the whole sanctuary, Num. xviii. 10), marked stages in human approach to Him; and the increasing richness of the material in the successive parts suggested thoughts of His immeasurable dignity. The chamber—the perfect cube (comp. Apoc. xxi. 16)—which expressed His most immediate manifestation, was in itself wholly dark. For man perfect darkness and perfect light (1 Tim. vi. 16) are in effect the same. We, in our weakness, can see objects only when the two are mixed. Comp. Ps. xviii. 11; xcvii. 2; 1 K. viii. 12. So also the limitations in the right of entrance to each part shewed that as yet God could not be fully known by men even with the

would leave us as disfurnished of an object of religion, and would render a temple on earth as vain a thing, as if there were none at all...We might, with as rational design, worship for a God what were scarce worthy to be called a shadow of a man, as dedicate temples to a wholly unconversable Deity...For that measure and latitude of sense must be allowed unto the expression 'conversableness with men,' as that it signify both capacity and propension to such converse; that God is both by His nature capable of it and hath a gracious inclination of will thereunto' (The Living Temple, i, ch. vi. § 1).

knowledge to which they could attain. The way to His presence was not yet open (Hebr. ix. 8). None but the members of the chosen race could enter the Court: none but the members of the representative tribe could enter the Holy Place: none but the one representative of the priestly body could enter, and that only on one day in the year, to the innermost sanctuary where God shewed His glory.

The furniture of the different parts still further illustrated by intelligible symbols the conditions and the limits of the approach to God. The Court contained two objects which could not fail to speak to the hearts of the worshippers, the Laver, and the Altar of burnt-offering. The first requirements for drawing near to God were seen to be purity and sacrifice. In the Holy Place there was fuller teaching. The Table of the Shewbread and the Seven-branched Candlestick exhibited human service in a higher form, as the light of men, and the food of God. The Altar of Incense, placed against the inner veil, so as to be in face of the Ark and in closest connexion with the Holy of Holies, expressed yet another thought, the thought of human aspiration, prayer and not action. *The furniture of the Tabernacle.*

So far the vessels of the Tabernacle represented the relations of man to God. The vessels of the most Holy Place represented the relations of God to man, His holiness, His grace, His sovereignty. The Law—the 'witness' —was set as the foundation of all. Over that was spread the Mercy seat; out of which rose the two Cherubim—the representatives of creation— bending over it, as if eager to look into the mysteries of redeeming love, while between and above them was the sign of the Divine Presence on which man could look only through the atmosphere of adoring aspiration (Lev. xvi. 13)[1].

But when all was thus ordered according to the heavenly pattern, by men in whom God put His Spirit, and out of materials which were gifts of devotion, the structure was not yet complete. It was as a fair body not quickened by life. So when everything was ready, the Tabernacle itself with all its furniture was solemnly anointed, like the High-priest, or the King, or the Prophet; and then at last it was fit for the fulfilment of its office (Ex. xl. 9 ff.; Num. vii. 1 ff.). *The consecration.*

So far, it appears, there can be no reasonable doubt as to the symbolism of the Tabernacle. It conveyed of necessity deep religious thoughts to those who reverently worshipped in it. It was however a natural, and indeed a justifiable belief, that the spiritual teaching of the fabric was not confined to its ruling features but extended also to every detail. There are correspondences between all the works of God which deeper knowledge and reflection make clear. The significance attached to the numbers which continually recur in the relations of the several parts cannot be questioned. Many therefore in all times have endeavoured to read the meaning of the parts, either as symbols of a divine order in creation, or as types of the divine counsel fulfilled by the coming of Christ. Into these ingenious speculations we cannot enter at length ; but the Jewish opinion current in *The details possibly all significant.*

---

[1] The general view of the Tabernacle and its Furniture is given admirably by Hengstenberg, *Beiträge zur Einl. ins A. T.* iii. 628 ff.

the apostolic age must be noticed, if only to place the originality of the Epistle in a true light.

Views of Philo and Josephus on the Tabernacle. Both Josephus and Philo, representing at no great interval of time the complementary teaching of Jerusalem and Alexandria, agree in regarding the Tabernacle as being in some sense a symbol of the universe. There is a characteristic difference in their treatment of the subject. Josephus is definite and literal in his interpretation: Philo plays, as it were, with many thoughts, and is not always consistent in the meanings which he indicates. But both alike follow a naturalistic symbolism. The Tabernacle is not for either of them the sign of another order.

Josephus. The interpretation of Josephus is contained in a single chapter which may be quoted entire as illustrating a dominant type of thought at the time when the Epistle was written. After describing the Tabernacle and its furniture, he continues: 'One might marvel at the hatred which men persistently shew towards us as though we made light of the Divinity (τὸ θεῖον) which they are minded to worship. For if any one will consider the structure of the Tabernacle, and regard the dress of the priest and the vessels which we use in the divine service, he will find that the lawgiver was a godlike (θεῖον) man and that we are visited with evil reproaches by the world without any good ground. For he will find that the several parts have been framed to imitate and represent the universe (τὰ ὅλα), if he takes the trouble to observe them with impartiality and intelligence. The Tabernacle for example, which was thirty cubits long, the Lawgiver divided into three parts[1]: two of these he left open to all the priests, as an ordinary and common place, and so indicated the earth and the sea, for these are accessible to all: the third portion he confined to God alone, because the heaven is also inaccessible to men. Again by setting the twelve loaves upon the Table he indicated the year, divided into so many months. By making the Candlestick a combination of seventy members he expressed darkly the influences of the planets exercised over definite portions of the zodiac, each of ten degrees[2], and by setting seven lamps upon it, he shews the course of the planets, for they are so many in number. The veils being woven of four fabrics signify the nature of the elements: that is to say, the fine linen seems to indicate the earth because flax springs from the earth; and the purple the sea, from the fact that it is dyed with the blood of fish; the blue is designed to signify the air, and the scarlet is a natural emblem of fire. Further the High-priest's robe being

---

[1] Josephus (unlike Philo) neglects the Symbolism of the Court, and thus is driven to regard the Porch of the Sanctuary as a separate part.

[2] τὰς τῶν πλανητῶν δεκαμοιρίας ἠνίξατο. The allusion is not to the number seventy, but to the combination of *seven* with *ten* (10 × 7), the number of the planets with the number which measured the extent of their active influence. The thirty degrees of the whole circle of the heavens (360°) which was occupied by each sign of the Zodiac, was divided into three parts of ten degrees each (δεκαμοιρίαι). Each part was assigned to a particular planet, which thus 'exercised its dominion and power over spaces of ten degrees.' The planet which so presided over the space was called 'decanus' a ruler of ten; and each sign had three 'decani.' Jul. Firmicus Maternus, *Astron.* ii. 4.

of linen indicates the earth, and the blue, the sky, having a resemblance to lightning given by the pomegranates and to thunder by the sound of the bells. The Ephod [he wished to represent] the nature of the world which it was the pleasure of God should be formed of four elements, inwoven with gold, I fancy, to suggest the splendour which attaches to all things. And he set the Breastplate in the middle of the Ephod to serve as the earth, for the earth occupies the midmost place. Yet more by investing the High-priest with a Girdle, he indicates the ocean, for this embraces the world. Furthermore the two sardonyx-stones by which he fastened the dress of the High-priest signify severally the sun and the moon; and whether we please to understand by the twelve jewels the twelve months or the twelve groups of stars which Greeks call the Zodiac, we shall not go far from the meaning which they convey. The mitre again seems to me to be emblematic of heaven, since it is made of blue, for otherwise the name of God would not have been placed upon it, set conspicuously upon the fillet, and that a fillet of gold, for the sake of its splendour in which the Divinity especially delights[1].'

Philo's earlier exposition is much more elaborate. He supposes that PHILO. the Court represented the objects of sense (τὰ αἰσθητά), the Sanctuary, the objects of thought (τὰ νοητά). On this view the five pillars of the porch indicate the senses, which have relations both outwards and inwards. The fourfold fabric of the veil he interprets exactly as Josephus of the four elements, and so also the seven lamps of the Candlestick, of the planets, with the Sun in the midst. He sees in the High-priest's robes a clear image of the world, but he differs in many parts from Josephus in his explanation of the parts. The words with which he closes his account of the dress exhibit favourably his general method: ' Thus is the High-priest arrayed when he undertakes his sacred service, in order that when he enters the Sanctuary, to make the prayers and sacrifices of our fathers, all the world may enter with him, through the symbols which he wears; for the long robe is a symbol of the air, the pomegranate, of water, the flower-border, of earth, the scarlet, of fire, the Ephod, of heaven; and, more particularly, the round emeralds on his shoulders, on which severally are six carvings representing six signs of the Zodiac, are symbols of the two hemispheres; and the twelve stones upon his breast in four rows of three, the ' Rational' (Logeion), as it is called (τὸ λόγειον), is the symbol of the Logos who holds together and administers the whole. For it was necessary that he who performs priestly service to the Father of the world should use as Advocate (παράκλητον) a Son most perfect in virtue, both to secure oblivion of sins and a supply of most bounteous blessings[2].'

[1] Antt. III. 7, 7. Comp. Bell. Jud. v. 5, 4—7. Weber (Altsynag. Theol. s. 191) has some interesting references to the Rabbinic ideas on the relation of the Tabernacle to creation. See particularly Bammidbar R. § xii. (Wünsche, 295). Compare also Bähr, Symb. i. 109 f.
[2] Philo Vit. Mos. iii. § 14 (ii. 155 M.). Comp. De epist. § 34 (i. 378 M.). This

naturalistic, symbolic form of interpretation found acceptance among some of the early Greek Fathers, and it has found considerable support in recent times (Bähr, Symb. d. Mos. Cult. 1837—9). See Clem. Alex. Strom. v. 6, §§ 32 ff.: Theod. Mops. and Theodoret on Hebr. ix. 1. Origen (Hom. in Ex. ix.) interpreted the Tabernacle

The teach-
ing of the
Epistle.

If now we turn from these material and intellectual analogies to the teaching of the Epistle, it will be evident that we have passed into another region. The Tabernacle is indeed regarded by the writer as formed after a heavenly pattern (c. viii. 5; comp. Wisd. ix. 8): it has its divine correlative (c. viii. 2, 5; ix. 11): it served as a figure (c. ix. 9) up to the time when Christ's apostles were able to declare the fulfilment of its signs; and its furniture was charged with a meaning which he could not discuss from due regard to proportion (ix. 2—5). But it was not simply an epitome of that which is presented on a larger scale in the world of finite being: the archetype to which it answered belonged to another order: the lessons which it conveyed were given in the fulness of time (c. i. 1) in a form which is final for man.

The Hu-
manity of
Christ the
archetypal
Taber-
nacle.

The Tabernacle, as we have seen, presented three main ideas, the ideas of the dwelling of God among men, of His holiness, of His 'conversableness.' It was that through which He was pleased to make His Presence and His Nature known under the conditions of earth to His people Israel. The antitype of the Tabernacle, whether on earth or in heaven, must fulfil the same office, and fulfil it perfectly. Such an antitype we find in the humanity of Christ, realised in different modes and degrees during His life on earth, in His Body, the Church, and in the consummation in 'heaven.' In each stage, if we may so speak, of the 'fulfilment' (Eph. i. 23), Christ satisfies in actual life more and more completely, according to our apprehension, that which the Tabernacle suggested by figures. His earthly Body was a Sanctuary (John ii. 19 ff.). In Him it was the Father's pleasure that 'all the fulness should dwell' (Col. i. 19 κατοικῆσαι), and so 'in Him dwelleth all the fulness of the Godhead bodily' (Col. ii. 9). Even now 'His Body' is that in which God is, and through which He reveals Himself (John xiv. 16 ff.; 1 John ii. 20; Apoc. xxi. 3). And so it shall be in the end. The saints 'who dwell in heaven' are His 'tabernacle' (Apoc. xiii. 6 om. καί); and when they are revealed in glory, in fellowship with Christ (1 John iii. 2), the goal of creation will be reached (Rom. viii. 19). Comp. c. ix. 11 note.

Additional Note on viii. 8 ff.

The quotation (Jer. xxxviii. (xxxi.) 31 ff.) offers an instructive example of variations in N. T. quotations from the LXX., from the Hebrew, and from a repetition of part of the quotation in the same book.

The following are variations from the LXX.:

v. 8. λέγει] LXX. φησίν with *v. l.* λέγει.

in a religious and moral sense. Different schemes of interpretation are discussed briefly by Fairbairn, *Typology of Scripture*, ii. 253 ff. Abundant references to modern works are given in the various Dictionaries of the Bible.

There are several mediæval discussions of the Tabernacle which deal chiefly with its moral and religious, as distinguished from its cosmical, import; Bede, *De Tabernaculo…*(Migne, *P. L.* xci. 393 ff.); Adamus Scotus (†1180), *De tripartito Tabernaculo* (*P. L.* cxcviii. 609 ff.); Petrus Callensis (†1187), *Tab. Mos. mystica et moralis expositio* (*P. L.* ccii. 1047 ff.).

THE EPISTLE TO THE HEBREWS. 241

v. 8. συντελέσω ἐπὶ τὸν οἶ...καὶ ἐπὶ τὸν οἶ.] διαθήσομαι τῷ οἴκ....καὶ τῷ
οἴκ. Συντελεῖν διαθ. occurs in LXX., *c.* xli. (xxxiv.) 8, 15.

9. ἐποίησα] διεθέμην.
— λέγει] φησίν.
10. διαθ.] some add μου.
— λέγει] φησίν.
— διδούς] some add δώσω.
— ἐπιγράψω] some read γράψω. Α ἐπιγράψω αὐτοὺς ἐπὶ τὰς κ. αὐ.
— αὐτούς] א Α insert καὶ ὄψομαι αὐτούς before καὶ ἔσομαι. Comp.
c. xxiii. 24 LXX.

11. πολίτην...ἀδελφόν...] ἀδελφόν...πλησίον...
— μικροῦ] add αὐτῶν.
The LXX. follows the Hebrew closely except
9. οὐκ ἐνέμειναν ἐν τῇ δ. 'הֵפֵרוּ אֶת־בְּ.
10. διδούς...εἰς τὴν δ. αὐ. בְּקִרְבָּם ... נָתַתִּי אֶת־תּוֹרָתִי.
11. om. עוֹד.
— γνῶθι דְּעוּ.
— om. נְאֻם יְהוָֹה.

To these certain differences must be added the rendering κἀγὼ ἠμέλησα
αὐτῶν for וְאָנֹכִי בָּעַלְתִּי בָם, which is generally rendered *although I was a
lord (a husband) to them.* In this sense בָּעַל is used with a simple *acc.*
(Is. lxii. 5). In Jer. iii. 14 and xxxi. 32 it is construed with בְּ, and
Gesenius (so appy. Delitzsch), following the LXX. and Syriac versions and
Arabic usage, is inclined to adopt in these places the sense 'I rejected, I
was displeased with, grew weary of them.' This interpretation appears to
fall in best with the context, though the common rendering can be
explained.

The differences between the quotation here and in c. x. 16 f. are
remarkable :

10. τῷ οἴκῳ Ἰσρ.   16. πρὸς αὐτούς.
     εἰς τὴν διάν. αὐτ.   ἐπὶ καρδίας αὐτ.
     ἐπὶ καρδίας.   ἐπὶ τὴν διάνοιαν.

12. καὶ τῶν ἁμ. αὐτ.   17. καὶ τῶν ἁμ. αὐτ.   καὶ τῶν ἀνομιῶν αὐτῶν.
     μνησθῶ.   μνησθήσομαι.

The quotation in x. 16 f. seems to be made from memory.

IX. ¹ Εἶχε μὲν οὖν [καὶ] ἡ πρώτη δικαιώματα

1 [καὶ] ἡ πρ.: om. καί B syr vg me : om. ἡ D₂*: +σκηνή ϛ me.   +καὶ' λατρ. D₂*.

ii. *The Old Service and the New: the Atonement of the Law and the Atonement of Christ* (c. ix.).

Having pointed out generally the new scene and the new conditions of Christ's High-priestly work, the writer goes on to consider it in detail in comparison with that of the Levitical system. He (1) describes with affectionate reverence the ordered arrangements of the Old Sanctuary and its furniture, and the limited privileges of the Old Priesthood (ix. 1—10); and then (2) he places in contrast with these the High-priestly Atonement of Christ resting upon a New Covenant, of which the issue will yet be revealed in glory (ix. 11—28).

(i) ix. 1—10. The Sanctuary and Priests under the Old Covenant.

This section falls into three subdivisions.

(*a*) The Tabernacle; its parts and furniture : (1—5).

(*b*) The priestly Service of the Tabernacle : (6, 7).

(*c*) The lesson of the restrictions of the service : (8—10).

¹*Now even the first* covenant *had ordinances of divine service and its sanctuary,* a sanctuary *of this world.* ²*For a tabernacle was prepared, the first, wherein were the candlestick and the table and the shew-bread, that which is called the Holy place.* ³*And after the second veil a tabernacle which is called the Holy of Holies,* ⁴*having a golden altar of incense, and the ark of the covenant overlaid all round about with gold, wherein* was *a golden pot holding the manna, and the rod of Aaron that budded, and the tables of the covenant;* ⁵*and above it Cherubim of glory overshadowing the mercy-seat; whereof we cannot now speak severally.* ⁶*But when these things have been thus prepared, the priests enter into*

the first tabernacle continually, accomplishing the divine services; ⁷*but into the second, once in the year, the High-priest alone, not without blood, which he offereth for himself and for the ignorances of the people,* ⁸*the Holy Ghost thus signifying that the way into the Holy place hath not yet been made manifest, while the first tabernacle hath still an* appointed *place;* ⁹*which is a parable for the season now present, and according to this* (parable) *gifts and sacrifices are offered, such as cannot make the worshipper perfect in conscience,* ¹⁰*being only ordinances of flesh, resting upon* (accompanied by) *meats and drinks and divers washings, imposed until a season of reformation.*

(*a*) 1—5. The writer begins his account of the High-priestly service of Christ with a retrospective view of the Levitical Service; and in doing this he first describes the Tabernacle —the divinely appointed scene of its performance—and not the Temple, with its parts and its characteristic furniture. As he had spoken at the close of the last chapter of the imminent disappearance of the old system, he now pauses for a moment to dwell upon the glories of that Old Covenant before he contrasts them with the supreme glory of the Christian order. He seems indeed to linger over the sacred treasures of the past ; and there is a singular pathos in the passage, which is unique in the N. T. There was, he says, something majestic and attractive in the Mosaic ordinances of worship. Christians do not question the fact; nay rather when they acknowledge the beauty and meaning of the Law they can understand the Gospel better.

So Œcumenius gives the connexion rightly : ἐπεὶ κατέβαλεν αὐτὴν [τὴν παλαιὰν διαθήκην] τῇ πρὸς τὴν νέαν παραθέσει ἵνα μή τις εἴπῃ ὅτι οὐκοῦν ἀεὶ ἀπόβλητος ἦν, προλαβὰν φησὶν ὅτι εἶχε κἀκείνη δικαιώματα λατρείας, νόμους, φησίν, καὶ τάξιν καὶ ἀκολουθίαν ἐμπρέπουσαν λατρείᾳ θεοῦ. Philo discusses the meaning of the arrangements of the Tabernacle : *de vit. Mos.* iii. §§ 3 ff. (ii. 146 ff. M.).

1. εἶχε μὲν οὖν [καὶ] ἡ πρώτη...] *Now even the first covenant had...* Vulg. *Habuit quidem et prius* (O.L. *Habebat autem)...*The past tense (εἶχε) can be explained in different ways. The writer may regard the original institution of the Mosaic ritual (*v.* 2 κατεσκευάσθη); or he may regard the system as essentially abrogated by the fulfilment of Christ's work.

The latter is the view commonly taken from early times : δείκνυσιν ἤδη τούτῳ αὐτὴν ἐκκεχωρηκυῖαν· τότε γὰρ εἶχε, φησίν· ὥστε νῦν, εἰ καὶ ἔστηκεν, οὐκ ἔστι (leg. ἔχει) (Chrys.). τὸ εἶχε δηλοῖ ὅτι νῦν οὐκ ἔχει· ὥστε εἰ καὶ μὴ παντελῶς ἐπαύσατο διὰ τὸ τινὰς αὐτῇ ἔτι στοιχεῖν, τὰ μέντοι δικαιώματα οὐκ ἔχει (Œcum.).

But it seems more likely that the writer is considering the Mosaic system in its divine constitution.

The particles μὲν οὖν correspond with the δέ in *v.* 6. There were divine and significant elements in the service which corresponded with the first Covenant, but they were subject to particular limitations in use. The Christian Order (*v.* 11 Χριστὸς δέ) offers a contrast to both parts of this description : its institutions are spiritual, and its blessings are for all. The combination does not occur again in the Epistle ; and it is found in St Paul only in 1 Cor. ix. 25 ἐκεῖνοι μὲν οὖν...ἡμεῖς δέ... ; Phil. ii. 23 τοῦτον μὲν οὖν...πέποιθα δέ...ὅτι καὶ αὐτός...It is frequent in the Acts (viii. 4, 25; &c.).

There can be no doubt that διαθήκη (not σκηνή) is to be supplied with ἡ πρώτη. This interpretation, which is supported by the ancient Versions (except *Memph.*) and Fathers, is re-

quired by the context : c. viii. 13. Ἡ πρώτη τίς; Chrysostom asks, and answers Ἡ διαθήκη.

If the καὶ is retained (καὶ ἡ πρώτη) it emphasises the parallel of the Covenants. Thotgh the first was destined to pass away, it had, no less than the second, ordinances of divine institution.

δικαιώματα λατρ.] *ordinances of divine service*...Vulg. *justificationes* (O. L. *constitutiones*) *culturæ.* The word δικαίωμα occurs again in a similar sense in *v.* 10. Δικαίωμα expresses the result, as δικαίωσις expresses the process (Rom. iv. 25 ; v. 18), corresponding to δικαιοῦν, to make right (righteous) in the widest sense. Two main meanings at once arise as the object of the verb is a word or a deed. The δικαίωμα may be 'that which is declared right,' an ordinance or a sentence pronounced by an authoritative power; or 'that which is rightly done,' righteousness realised in act. There is the same twofold meaning in the word 'judgment' (מִשְׁפָּט) in the O. T. which is constantly rendered by δικαίωμα in the LXX. It may be further noticed that an obligatory 'ordinance' viewed from another point of sight often becomes a 'claim.' For the use of the word δικαίωμα in the N. T. see (1) τὸ δικαίωμα the ordinance, regarded as requirement : Rom. i. 32 ; viii. 4. (2) τὰ δικαιώματα of special ordinances : Luke i. 6 ; Rom. ii. 26 ; Hebr. ix. 1, 10. (3) δικαίωμα a sentence or act fulfilling the claims of righteousness : Rom. v. 16, 18. (4) τὰ δικαιώματα of special acts of righteousness : Apoc. xv. 4 ; xix. 8.

The gen. which is connected with δικαίωμα may either express the authority from which it springs (Lk. i. 6 δικ. τοῦ Κυρίου : Rom. viii. 4) ; or the object to which it is directed, as here : comp. Ex. xxi. 9 τὸ δ. τῶν θυγατέρων ; 1 Sam. ii. 12 τὸ δ. τοῦ ἱερέως ; viii. 9 ; x. 25 τὸ δ. τοῦ βασιλέως.

λατρείας τό τε ἅγιον κοσμικόν.   ²σκηνὴ γὰρ κατεσκευ-

τό τε : τὸ δέ D₂*.

For λατρεία compare Additional
Note on c. viii. 2.

τό τε ἅγ. κοσμ.] *and its sanctuary,
a sanctuary of this world*...Vulg.
et sanctum sæculare. Euthymius reads
and interprets τότε ἅγιον κοσμικόν (so
arm.): 'τότε' δὲ ἀντὶ τοῦ πάλαι, ὅτε
ἐκράτει, νῦν γὰρ οὐκ ἔχει. The peculiar
form of expression is chosen in order
to recognise the familiar and characteristic place of the Mosaic worship—
the Holy place—and at the same time
to distinguish it from its antitype
(comp. vii. 24; 1 Pet. iv. 8). The
conjunction τε is rarely used by itself
in the Epistles : c. i. 3 note; vi. 5 ;
xii. 2; Rom. ii. 19; xvi. 26; 1 Cor.
iv. 21; Eph. iii. 19. It marks something which is not regarded as distinct
from and coordinate with that with
which it is connected, but which serves
to complete the fulness of one main
idea.

The singular τὸ ἅγιον in the sense
of *the sanctuary* is not found elsewhere in the N. T. It occurs not
unfrequently in the LXX. for מִקְדָּשׁ
(Num. iii. 38; Ezek. xlv. 4, 18; xlviii.
8) and for קֹדֶשׁ (Ex. xxvi. 33 &c.)
without any obvious law. Here it
appears to give naturally the general
notion of the sanctuary without regard to its different parts.

It is not unlikely that the predicative force of κοσμικόν reaches back
to δικ. λατρ.—'had ordinances of
divine service and its sanctuary, both
of this world.'

The word κοσμικός occurs elsewhere
in the N. T. only in Tit. ii. 12 (comp.
Didaché xi. 11).

The thought which it conveys here
is otherwise expressed under a different aspect by χειροποίητος (*vv.* 11, 24 ;
comp. viii. 2). The opposite is given
in *v.* 11 οὐ ταύτης τῆς κτίσεως.

The Mosaic sanctuary was not only
'on earth' (ἐπίγειος), as opposed to
'in heaven' (ἐπουράνιος *v.* 23; viii. 5 ;
xi. 16), but it partook of the nature
of the world, and was therefore essentially transitory.

There does not appear to be any
reference to the familiar thought that
the Tabernacle was a symbol of the
world, though this interpretation has
patristic support : τὴν σκηνὴν οὕτως
ἐκάλεσε τύπον ἐπέχουσαν τοῦ κόσμου
παντός (Theodt.).

But in connexion with this thought
it is to be remarked that both Josephus and Philo speak of the Jewish
service as having a universal, a 'cosmical,' destination : Philo *De Monarch.* ii. 6 (ii. p. 227 M.) βούλεται τὸν
ἀρχιερέα πρῶτον μὲν εἰκόνα τοῦ παντὸς
ἔχειν ἐμφανῆ περὶ ἑαυτὸν ἵνα ἐκ τῆς
συνεχοῦς θέας ἄξιον παρέχῃ τὸν ἴδιον
βίον τῆς τῶν ὅλων φύσεως, ἔπειτα ὅπως
ἐν ταῖς ἱερουργίαις συλλειτουργῇ πᾶς ὁ
κόσμος αὐτῷ. Joseph. *B. J.* iv. 5, 2
τῆς κοσμικῆς θρησκείας κατάρχοντες.
And this thought was adopted by
Chrysostom and many later fathers
in various forms : ἐπεὶ καὶ Ἕλλησι
βατὸν ἦν κοσμικὸν αὐτὸ καλεῖ, οὐ γὰρ
δὴ οἱ Ἰουδαῖοι ὁ κόσμος ἦσαν (Chrys.).
Sanctum sæculare i.e. quo sæculi
homines, hoc est, gentiles, ad Judais-
mum transeuntes recipiebat; patebat
enim non solum Judæis sed etiam
talibus gentilibus (Primas.).

Such an interpretation however
belongs to the later development of
Judaism and not prominently to its
first institution, though indeed it had
from the first a universal element.

2. σκηνὴ γάρ...ἡ πρώτη] *For a
tabernacle (tent) was prepared, the
first*...the outermost as approached
by the worshipper. The writer explains and justifies the general statement in *v.* 1. For this construction,

ἀσθη ἡ πρώτη ἐν ᾗ ἥ τε λυχνία καὶ ἡ τράπεζα καὶ ἡ
πρόθεσις τῶν ἄρτων, ἥτις λέγεται ᾿῾Αγια· ³μετὰ δὲ τὸ

2, 3 Τὰ ἅγια......λεγομένη Τὰ ἅγια τῶν ἁγίων.

2 ἡ λυχν. : D₂*.
θυμ. καί in v. 4].

ἄρτων : +καὶ τὸ χρυσοῦν θυμιατήριον B (æg) [omitting χρυσοῦν
ἅγια : +τὰ' ἅγια B : +ἁγίων AD₂* : om. אB vg syrr ægg.

by which a noun first regarded indefinitely ('a tabernacle') is afterwards
defined ('the first'), see c. vi. 7 ; 2
John 7 ; Acts x. 41 ; Phil. iii. 6, &c.
and especially with a *partic.* 1 Pet. i.
7 ; Moulton-Winer, pp. 174 f.
The two parts of the Tabernacle
are regarded as two Tabernacles.
κατεσκευάσθη] *was prepared...fac-
tum est* V. Comp. c. iii. 3 note. The
tense points to the first construction
of the Tabernacle. Contrast *v.* 6
κατεσκευασμένων.
ἐν ᾗ...] The substantive verb appears
to be omitted purposely. The whole
description (*v.* 4) will not apply to the
existing Temple; and yet the writer
will not exclude the Temple (λέγεται,
v. 6 εἰσίασιν). He says therefore
neither 'was' nor 'is,' but uses, as in *v.*
4 ἔχουσα, a neutral form of expression.
ἡ λυχνία]—*candelabra* V. (-*brum*
O. L.); literally *the lampstand* (מְנוֹרָה)
on which the lamp (נֵר) was placed
(Ex. xxv. 37; Zech. iv. 2; Matt. v.
15 and parallels ; comp. Apoc. i. 12 ;
ii. 5 ; xi. 4). See Ex. xxv. 31—40 ;
xxxv. 16 ; xxxvii. 17—24 (xxxviii.
13—17) ; Zech. iv. 2 f. ; 11 ff. ; Jos.
B. J. v. 5. 5 ; vii. 5. 5.
In the account of Solomon's Temple
ten candlesticks are mentioned : 1 K.
vii. 49 (35) ; 2 Chron. iv. 7 ; comp. 1
Chron. xxviii. 15 ; Jer. lii. 19.
So also in 2 Chron. iv. 8 Solomon is
said to have made ten tables ; but in
1 K. vii. 48 (34) only one table is mentioned. Comp. Jos. *Antt.* viii. 3, 7.
Primasius, following the plural of the
Vulgate, supposes that the allusion is
to the Temple : non de illo tabernaculo disputaturus est hic apostolus
quod Moyses fecit in eremo ubi tan-

tummodo unum candelabrum fuit, sed
de templo quod postea Salomon ædi-
ficavit in Hierusalem ubi fuerunt plura
candelabra.
ἡ τράπεζα] *the table...mensa* V. Ex.
xxv. 23—30 (הַשֻּׁלְחָן, הַפָּנִים שֻׁלְחַן,
(הש' הטָהֹר 'ש' הַמַּעֲרָכֶת); xxxvii. 10—
16.
ἡ πρόθεσις τῶν ἄρτων] Vulg. *propo-
sitio panum, the shewbread,* literally
'the setting out of the bread (loaves)'
that is 'the bread set forth in two
rows.' The later Hebrew term for
the 'shewbread' (לֶחֶם פָּנִים Ex. xxv. 30;
comp. Lev. xxiv. 5 ff.) is לֶחֶם הַמַּעֲרָכֶת
'bread of the row' (*e.g.* 1 Chron. ix.
32 οἱ ἄρτοι τῆς προθέσεως LXX.) or
simply 'the row' (2 Chron. ii. 4 πρόθεσις ; xiii. 11 πρόθεσις ἄρτων ; xxix.
18 τὴν τράπεζαν τῆς προθέσεως) in
which the N. T. phrases (Matt. xii. 4
οἱ ἄρτοι τῆς προθ. and ἡ πρόθ. τ. ἄ.) find
their origin.
ἥτις λέγ. ῞Αγια] *which is called the
Holy place*...Vulg. *quæ dicitur Sancta.*
The qualitative relative (ἥτις) directs
attention to the features of the place
which determines its name as 'Holy.'
The anarthrous form ῞Αγια (literally
Holies) in this sense appears to be
unique, as also ῞Αγια ἁγίων below, if
indeed the reading is correct. Perhaps it is chosen to fix attention on
the character of the sanctuary, as in
other cases. The plural suggests the
idea of the sanctuary with all its
parts : comp. Moulton-Winer, p. 220.
Philo (*Quis rer. div. hær.* § 46 ;
i. p. 504) interprets the three things
in the Holy Place (ἐν τοῖς ἁγίοις), the
Candlestick, the Table and the Golden
Altar of Incense (τὸ θυμιατήριον), as

δεύτερον καταπέτασμα σκηνὴ ἡ λεγομένη ʽʹΑγια ʽΑγίων¹,
⁴χρυσοῦν ἔχουσα θυμιατήριον καὶ τὴν κιβωτὸν τῆς δια-

3 ἅγια ἁγίων 5א*AD₂*: τὰ ἅγ. τῶν ἁγ. אᶜB me (æg).   4 χρ. ἔχ. θυμ. καί :
ἔχουσα B [see v. 2].

symbolic of thanksgiving from all parts of creation heavenly, human, elemental. Comp. de vita Mos. iii. §§ 9 f. (ii. pp. 150 f. M.). For a general interpretation of their meaning see Oehler, Old Test. Theology, § 117.

3. μετὰ δὲ τὸ δ. κ.] and after the second veil...Vulg. post velamentum autem secundum. This is the only place in which μετά is used in this local sense in the N. T. For καταπέτασμα see c. vi. 19 note. Ex. xxvi. 31 f.

σκηνὴ ἡ λεγ. ʽʹΑγια ʽΑγίων] a tabernacle (tent) was prepared (κατεσκευάσθη, v. 2) which is called the Holies of Holies. The form σκ. ἡ λεγομένη corresponds with σκ. ἡ πρώτη of v. 2. In the LXX. two translations of קָדָשׁ קָדָשִׁים the Holy of Holies, the most holy place, are found, τὸ ἅγιον τῶν ἁγ. (e.g. Ex. xxvi. 33), and τὰ ἅγια τῶν ἁγ. (e.g. 1 K. viii. 6). This innermost sanctuary is also called simply τὸ ἅγιον in Lev. xvi. 2. On the name דְּבִיר which was applied to it in later times (1 K. viii. 8) see Hupfeld on Ps. xxviii. 2. The Holy of Holies was a cube, like the New Jerusalem in the imagery of the Apocalypse: Apoc. xxi. 16.

For the general idea of the Tabernacle, as figuring the residence of God with His covenant people, see Oehler, l.c. § 116; and Additional Note on viii. 5. Chrysostom says of the two parts: τὰ μὲν οὖν ἅγια τοῦ προτέρου καιροῦ σύμβολά ἐστιν· ἐκεῖ γὰρ διὰ θυσιῶν πάντα γίνεται· τὰ δὲ ἅγια τῶν ἁγίων τούτου τοῦ νῦν ἐνεστῶτος. And so Theodoret: ἐμιμεῖτο τὰ μὲν ἅγια τὴν ἐν τῇ γῇ πολίτειαν, τὰ δὲ ἅγια τῶν ἁγίων τὸ τῶν οὐρανῶν

ἐνδιαίτημα· αὐτὸ δὲ τὸ καταπέτασμα τοῦ στερεώματος ʽἐπλήρου τὴν χρείαν. Œcumenius follows out the parallel at length.

4. χρ. ἔχ. θυμ.] having a golden altar of incense...Vulg. aureum habens turibulum (altare O. L.). The word θυμιατήριον has two distinct meanings, (1) Altar of incense, (2) Censer, and from very early times each has been adopted here.

Philo (Quis rer. div. hær. § 46, i. p. 504; de vit. Moysis, iii. § 9, ii. p. 150); and Josephus (Antt. iii. 6, 8 μεταξὺ δὲ αὐτῆς καὶ τῆς τραπέζης ἔνδον, ὡς προεῖπον, θυμιατήριον...B. J. v. (vi.) 5, 5 τὸ θυμιατήριον δὲ διὰ τῶν τρισκαίδεκα θυμιαμάτων οἷς ἐκ θαλάσσης ἀνεπίμπλατο τῆς τʼ ἀοικήτου καὶ οἰκουμένης ἐσήμαινεν ὅτι τοῦ θεοῦ πάντα καὶ τῷ θεῷ) use θυμιατήριον for the altar of incense in their accounts of the furniture of the Temple. And so also Clement of Alexandria (Strom. v. 6, § 33, p. 665 P. ἀνὰ μέσον δὲ τοῦ καλύμματος (the outer veil) καὶ τοῦ παραπετάσματος (the inner veil)...θυμιατήριον ἔκειτο...); and Origen, probably on the authority of this passage, places the Altar of incense in the Holy of Holies: Hom. in Ex. ix. 3 ibi collocatur...propitiatorium sed et altare aureum incensi.

But it is urged on the other hand that in the LXX. the altar of incense is never called by this name, but (τὸ) θυσιαστήριον (τοῦ) θυμιάματος (Ex. xxx. 1, 27; Lev. iv. 7; 1 Chron. vi. 49; comp. Luke i. 11) and τὸ θυσ. τῶν θυμιαμάτων (1 Chron. xxviii. 18 : 2 Chron. xxvi. 16, 19), while θυμιατήριον is twice used in the LXX. for a censer (מִקְטֶרֶת): 2 Chron. xxvi. 19; Ezek. viii. 11; and in Jer. lii. 19 by

Aquila and Symmachus for מַחְתָּה (fire-pan).

It must however be remarked that the translation of the LXX. was practically inevitable. The use of מִזְבֵּחַ in the original required to be represented by θυσιαστήριον. The only other rendering βωμός was inapplicable. And further in Ex. xxx. 1 where the full phrase מִזְבֵּחַ מִקְטַר קְטֹרֶת is found, Symmachus and Theodotion read θυσιαστήριον θυμιατήριον θυμιάματος, a reading which Origen introduced with an asterisk into his Greek text. Nor does the use of θυμιατήριον for 'censer' fix this single meaning to the word, for Josephus, who calls the altar of incense θυμιατήριον, uses the same word for 'censer' in his narrative of the rebellion of Korah (*Antt.* iv. 2, 6) where the LXX. has πυρεῖον (מַחְתָּה).

It cannot therefore be urged that the usage of the LXX. offers a valid argument against adopting here the sense which is unquestionably justified by the contemporary evidence of Philo and Josephus. External evidence then, it may be fairly said, is in favour of the rendering *Altar of incense*.

If now we turn to internal evidence it appears to be most unlikely that the 'golden altar' (Ex. xxx. 1 ff.; xxxvii. 25 ff.; xl. 5, 26), one of the most conspicuous and significant of the contents of the Tabernacle, on which other writers dwell with particular emphasis, should be omitted from the enumeration here; and no less unlikely that a golden censer should be mentioned in its place, while no such vessel is mentioned in the O. T. as part of the furniture of the Holy of Holies, or even in special connexion with the service of the Day of Atonement. The mention in the Mishna (*Joma*, iv. 4) of the use of a golden censer on the Day of Atonement, instead of the silver censer used on other days, does not furnish sufficient explanation for the place which

it would hold here in the Holy of Holies of the Tabernacle. Nor indeed is there any evidence that the censer so used was in any sense part of the furniture of the Holy of Holies: on the contrary it was removed after the service (*Joma*, vii. 4).

At first sight however it is difficult to understand how the Altar of incense could be described as part of the furniture of the Holy of Holies; or, to speak more exactly, as properly belonging to it (ἔχουσα θυμιατήριον). But this phrase probably suggests the true explanation. The Altar of incense bore the same relation to the Holy of Holies as the Altar of burnt offering to the Holy place. It furnished in some sense the means of approach to it. Indeed the substitution of ἔχουσα for ἐν ᾗ (*v.* 2) itself points clearly to something different from mere position. The Ark and the Altar of incense typified the two innermost conceptions of the heavenly Sanctuary, the Manifestation of God and the spiritual worship of man. And thus they are placed in significant connexion in the Pentateuch: Ex. xxx. 6; xl. 5; comp. Lev. iv. 7; xvi. 12, 18 (before the Lord).

In one passage indeed (1 K. vi. 22) the Altar of incense is described in language closely resembling that which is used here as 'belonging to the shrine' (אֲשֶׁר־לַדְּבִיר).

It is further to be observed that the word θυμιατήριον is left indefinite. While the writer says ἡ λυχνία, ἡ τράπεζα (ἡ πρόθεσις τῶν ἄρτων), ἡ κιβωτὸς τῆς διαθήκης, τὸ ἱλαστήριον, he says simply χρυσοῦν θυμιατήριον, 'a golden incense (altar).' The word is descriptive and not the technical name of a special object.

On the whole therefore it appears that both the evidence of language and the evidence of the symbolism of the passage are in favour of the sense 'Altar of incense.' This sense is given by the O.L. The Syriac is ambiguous

θήκης περικεκαλυμμένην πάντοθεν χρυσίῳ, ἐν ᾗ στάμνος
χρυσῆ ἔχουσα τὸ μάννα καὶ ἡ ῥάβδος Ἀαρὼν ἡ βλαστή-

ἡ βλαστ.: om. ἡ B.

‎ܒܝܬ ܒܣܡܐ‎ incense-vessel (lit. house of perfumes).

In Apoc. viii. 3, 5 the word for 'censer' is λιβανωτός which is not found in LXX. (elsewhere λιβανωτίς).

It may be added that in the service of the Day of Atonement the Golden Altar was treated in the same manner as the Holy of Holies by the sprinkling of blood: Ex. xxx. 10.

In prophetic imagery also there is an altar in heaven (Is. vi. 6; Apoc. viii. 3). The type of heaven therefore could not be without its proper altar; though it was not placed locally within it.

Perhaps it is worthy of notice that in the legend mentioned in 2 Macc. ii. 5 Jeremiah hides the Ark and the Altar of incense in the cave.

τὴν κιβωτὸν τῆς διαθ.] the ark of the covenant...Vulg. arcam testamenti. Ex. xxv. 10 ff.: xxxvii. 1 ff. (Deut. x. 3). The writer of the Epistle, as has been noticed before, fixes attention on the Mosaic type, the Tabernacle. The Ark, which had belonged to the Tabernacle, was placed in Solomon's Temple (1 K. viii. 1 ff.); but in the later Temple the Holy of Holies was entirely empty (Jos. B. J. v. 6, 5 ἔκειτο δὲ οὐδὲν ὅλως ἐν αὐτῷ; Tac. Hist. v. 9). The site which the Ark should have occupied was marked by 'the stone of foundation' (אֶבֶן שְׁתִיָּה), a raised platform on which, according to a late tradition, the sacred Tetragrammaton was inscribed. Comp. Buxtorf, Lex. s. v. שְׁתִיָּה.

On the traditional later history of the Ark see Grimm on 2 Macc. ii. 1—5; and Wetstein on Apoc. ii. 17.

περικεκ. π. χρυσίῳ] This clause is added predicatively: 'the Ark of the covenant, an Ark overlaid all round about with gold.' Χρυσίον as dis-

tinguished from χρυσός has the secondary idea of gold wrought for a particular use, as jewels 1 Pet. iii. 3, or coin, Acts iii. 6. For πάντοθεν compare Ex. xxv. 10 ἔσωθεν καὶ ἔξωθεν.

στάμνος] Vulg. urna. Ex. xvi. 32 ff. The epithet, 'a golden pot,' is an addition to the Hebrew text which is found in the LXX. (Ex. xvi. 33). In the Pentateuch the pot of manna and Aaron's rod are said to be laid up 'before the Testimony' (Ex. xvi. 34; Num. xvii. 10; comp. Ex. xxv. 16, 21) and not definitely in the Ark. The significance of the Manna is indicated in Apoc. ii. 17 τὸ μ. τὸ κεκρυμμένον.

χρυσοῦν...χρυσίῳ...χρυσῆ...] The solemn repetition of the word emphasises the splendour of this typical sanctuary (comp. Æn. iv. 138 f.). Gold was the characteristic metal of the Holy of Holies. Comp. 1 K. vii. 48 ff. It is remarkable that Ezekiel in describing the Temple of his vision makes no mention of the materials of which it was constructed.

ἡ ῥάβδος] Num. xvii. 10 ff. The pot of manna and Aaron's rod are not mentioned in Scripture except in the places of the Pentateuch referred to, and here.

When the Ark was removed to the Temple it contained only the Tables of the Law (1 K. viii. 9; comp. Jos. Ant. iii. 6, 5).

αἱ πλάκες τῆς διαθ.] Vulg. tabulæ testamenti. These are called in the LXX. αἱ πλάκες τοῦ μαρτυρίου (לֻחֹת הָעֵדֻת) Ex. xxxi. 18; xxxii. 15, and (αἱ) πλάκες (τῆς) διαθήκης (לוּחֹת הַבְּרִית) Deut. ix. 9, 11, 15. In 1 K. viii. 9 πλάκες τῆς διαθήκης is added as a gloss to πλάκες λίθιναι.

Chrysostom remarks that these memorials in the Ark were monu-

σασα καὶ αἱ πλάκες τῆς διαθήκης, ⁵ὑπεράνω δὲ αὐτῆς
Χερουβεὶν δόξης κατασκιάζοντα τὸ ἱλαστήριον· περὶ ὧν

5 ὑπεράνω...αὐτῆς: ὑπέρ...αὐτήν D₂*.
κατασκιάζοντα: -ζον A.

χερουβεὶν (-ιν) אBD₂: -βείμ (-βίμ) ς A me.

ments of the rebellious spirit of Israel: πάντα ταῦτα σεμνὰ ἦν καὶ λαμπρὰ τῆς Ἰουδαϊκῆς ἀγνωμοσύνης ὑπομνήματα. καὶ αἱ πλάκες τῆς διαθήκης· κατέαξε γὰρ αὐτάς· καὶ τὸ μάννα· ἐγόγγυσαν γάρ... καὶ ἡ ῥάβδος Ἀαρὼν ἡ βλαστήσασα· ἐπανέστησαν γάρ.

5. ὑπεράνω δὲ αὐτῆς...] and above it, i.e. the Ark (superque eam V.), Cherubim of glory (Ex. xxv. 18 ff.), not simply 'glorious Cherubim,' as if the epithet characterised their nature, but 'Cherubim of glory' ministering to the divine revelation. The divine glory, the revelation of God's majesty, was in a peculiar sense connected with them. God revealed Himself 'from between them': Ex. xxv. 22; Num. vii. 89; 1 Sam. iv. 4; 2 Sam. vi. 2; 2 K. xix. 15 || Is. xxxvii. 16; Ps. lxxx. 1; xcix. 1. Comp. Lev. xvi. 2; Ecclus. xlix. 8.

κατασκιάζοντα] The Cherubim are treated as ζῷα (Apoc. iv. 6). Compare Ex. xxv. 20 συσκιάζοντες.

τὸ ἱλαστήριον] Vulg. propitiatorium, O.L expiationem. Lev. xvi.14f.(כַּפֹּרֶת).

The literal meaning of כַּפֹּרֶת is simply covering, but the 'covering' is distinct from the Ark which is complete without it (comp. Dillm. Ex. xxv. 17). It is possible that at a later time the idea of the 'covering,' atonement, for sin may have been added to the material sense (1 Chron. xxviii. 11 בֵּית הַכַּפֹּרֶת). In itself the 'covering' of the Ark had a natural symbolic meaning. It was interposed between the Ark containing the Tables of the Law and the Divine glory.

On its first occurrence כַּפֹּרֶת is translated in the LXX. ἱλαστήριον ἐπίθεμα (Ex. xxv. 15); but generally it is rendered by ἱλαστήριον only. The rendering θυσιαστήριον in Lev.

xvi. 14 seems to be an error, though there is a trace of this rendering in one of the Greek Versions in Ex. xxxvii. 6 (ἄλλος· θυσιαστήριον). The word ἱλαστήριον is used as technical by Philo: de vit. Mos. iii. § 8, ii. p. 150 M.; de prof. § 19, i. 561 M.

This rendering was taken from the use made of the 'covering' on the Day of Atonement when it was sprinkled with the atoning blood: Lev. xvi. 15.

In Ezekiel ἱλαστήριον is used as the rendering of עֲזָרָה (xliii. 14: Aqu. κρηπίδωμα; Sym. περιδρομή; 17, 20), the 'settle' or 'ledge' of the altar.

περὶ ὧν...κατὰ μέρος] Vulg. de quibus modo non est dicendum per singula. There is, it is implied, a typical significance in the details, but the writer notices only the lesson of the two great divisions of the Sanctuary, determined by the ordinances of service. For οὐκ ἔστιν comp. 1 Cor. xi. 20.

6—10. After speaking of the material arrangements of the Sanctuary, the writer goes on to shew the significant limitations which determined the use of it. The priests entered day by day into the Holy place: the High-priest once in the year, with special ceremonies, into the Holy of Holies (vv. 6, 7). As yet, under the Mosaic order, it was clearly taught that there was no free access to God (8—10). The people could only approach him through their representatives; and these had only a partial right of drawing near to Him.

Though there was an august array of typical instruments and means of service, the access to the Divine Presence was not yet open. Part of the Sanctuary was open to the priests: part to the High-priest only on a single day in each year.

οὐκ ἔστιν νῦν λέγειν κατὰ μέρος. ⁶Τούτων δὲ οὕτως
κατεσκευασμένων, εἰς μὲν τὴν πρώτην σκηνὴν διὰ παντὸς
εἰσίασιν οἱ ἱερεῖς τὰς λατρείας ἐπιτελοῦντες, ⁷εἰς δὲ τὴν

ἔστιν : ἔνεστιν א*.

It must be kept in mind throughout that the Holy place was the scene of man's worship, and the way by which he approached God; while the Holy of Holies symbolised the Divine Presence itself.

Thus the Tabernacle witnessed constantly to the aim of man and to the fact that he could not as yet attain it. He could not penetrate to that innermost sanctuary to which he necessarily looked, and from which blessing flowed. The same institutions which brought forcibly to the soul of the Israelite the thought of Divine Communion made him feel that he could not yet enjoy it as it might be enjoyed.

Compare Chrysostom: τουτέστιν, ἦν μὲν ταῦτα, οὐκ ἀπέλαυον δὲ τούτων αὐτῶν οἱ Ἰουδαῖοι, οὐ γὰρ ἑώρων αὐτά· ὥστε οὐκ ἐκείνοις μᾶλλον ἦν ἢ οἷς προετυποῦτο.

(b) 6, 7. The priestly service of the Sanctuary.

6. τούτων δέ...] But when these things have been thus prepared.... Vulg. His vero (O. L. autem) ita compositis (O. L. aptatis). The perf. (κατεσκ.) expresses that the historical foundation (v. 2 κατεσκευάσθη) issued in an abiding system (comp. v. 8 πεφανερῶσθαι, v. 18 ἐνκεκαίνισται).

εἰς μὲν τὴν πρ. σκ....εἰσίασιν...ἐπιτελοῦντες] into the first (v. 2) tabernacle, the Holy place, the scene of spiritual, symbolic worship, the priests enter continually accomplishing the services....Vulg. in priori quidem tabernaculo semper introibant sacerdotes, sacrificiorum officia consummantes.

The present (εἰσίασιν) expresses the ideal fulfilment of ·the original Mosaic institution. The writer here deals only with the original conception realised in the Tabernacle, though elsewhere (c. viii. 4) he recognises the perpetuation of the Levitical ritual; and the existing Temple system was naturally present to his mind as the representation of it. The Latin rendering is an accommodation to εἶχε in v. 1.

διὰ παντός] The word is used peculiarly in the N. T. of Divine Service which knows essentially no formal limits: c. xiii. 15; Lk. xxiv 53; Acts x. 2. Comp. Matt. xviii. 10 Acts xxiv. 16.

As distinguished from πάντοτε (c vii. 25 note) it seems to express th continuous, unbroken permanence o a characteristic habit, while πάντοτ marks that which is realised ou each several occasion.

τὰς λατρείας ἐπιτελ.] accomplishing the divine services, such as the placing and removal of the shewbread on the Sabbath (Lev. xxiv. 5 ff.), the offering of incense every morning and evening, and the dressing of the lamps (Ex. xxx. 7 ff.). The Vulgate rendering (O.L. ministeria consummare) leads the thought away from the purely symbolic service of the Holy place to the animal sacrifices of the Temple Court.

The word ἐπιτελεῖν is used frequently of sacred observances in Herodotus (ii. 37; iv. 186) and in other classical writers. Comp. c. viii. 5 ἐπιτελεῖν τὴν σκηνήν. Philo, de somn. i. § 37 (i. 653 M.) τὰς νόμῳ προστεταγμένας ἐπιτελεῖν λειτουργίας.

7. εἰς δὲ τὴν δ....ἀρχιερεύς] but into the second tabernacle, the tabernacle beyond 'the second veil' (v. 3), the symbol of the immediate Divine Presence, the High-priest alone, once in the year, that is, on one day in the year, though on that day he entered twice (Lev. xvi. 12 ff.), or, according to the later tradition, four times (Mishnah

δευτέραν ἅπαξ τοῦ ἐνιαυτοῦ μόνος ὁ ἀρχιερεύς, οὐ χωρὶς
αἵματος, ὃ προσφέρει ὑπὲρ ἑαυτοῦ καὶ τῶν τοῦ λαοῦ
ἀγνοημάτων, [8]τοῦτο δηλοῦντος τοῦ πνεύματος τοῦ ἁγίου,

Joma v. 1, 7, 4). But see Philo, *Leg. ad Cai.* § 39 (ii. 591 M.) καὶ ἂν αὐτὸς ὁ ἀρχιερεὺς δυσὶν ἡμέραις τοῦ ἔτους ἢ καὶ τῇ αὐτῇ τρὶς ἢ καὶ τετράκις ἐπιφοιτήσῃ θάνατον ἀπαραίτητον ὑπομένει.

The words, ἅπαξ μόνος ὁ ἀρχιερεύς, emphasise the restrictions with which the approach was beset. There was only one occasion of entrance, and the entrance was allowed to one representative of the people only. And even he entered only in the power of another life (comp. c. x. 19 ἐν τῷ αἵματι).

Philo insists on the peculiar privilege in the same words: *Leg. ad Cai.* l. c. (εἰς τὰ ἄδυτα) ἅπαξ τοῦ ἐνιαυτοῦ ὁ μέγας ἱερεὺς εἰσέρχεται. See also *de monarch.* ii. § 2 (i. 223 M.) τούτῳ δι᾽ ἔτους ἐπιτετραμμένον ἅπαξ εἰσιέναι. *de ebriet.* § 34 (i. 378 M.) δι᾽ ἔτους ἅπαξ εἰσιόντα. And he applies the limitation even to the Logos: ὁρᾷς ὅτι οὐδὲ ὁ ἀρχιερεὺς λόγος, ἐνδιατρίβειν ἀεὶ καὶ σχολάζειν ἐν τοῖς ἁγίοις δώμασι δυνάμενος, ἄδειαν ἔσχηκε κατὰ πάντα καιρὸν πρὸς αὐτὰ φοιτᾶν ἀλλ᾽ ἅπαξ δι᾽ ἐνιαυτοῦ μόλις; (*de gig.* § 11; i. 269 M.).

οὐ χωρὶς αἵματος...ἀγνοημάτων] The High-priest first took the blood of the bullock, which was a sin-offering for himself, within the veil, and sprinkled it seven times before the Mercy seat (Lev. xvi. 11 ff.).

After this he offered the goat which was a sin-offering for the people, and brought the blood of this within the veil, and did with it as with the blood of the bullock (Lev. xvi. 15).

This sprinkling of the blood is regarded in a wider sense as an 'offering' (Lev. i. 5) which he makes *for himself and for the ignorances of the people.* The most general phrase is used in regard to the High-priest (ὑπὲρ ἑαυτοῦ, O.L. *pro se*

et populi delictis). The absence of the article before ἑαυτοῦ excludes the repetition of ἀγνοημάτων (as Vulg. *pro sua et populi ignorantia*). Compare Lev. xvi. 11, with Lev. xvi. 16.

For οὐ χωρίς see c. vii. 20.

The word ἀγνόημα (sin of ignorance) occurs here only in the N.T., but the thought is included in τοῖς ἀγνοοῦσιν c. v. 2. Comp. 1 Macc. xiii. 39; Ecclus. xxiii. 2; Num. xv. 22 ff., 30 f. Theophylact notices that some thought that there is a reference here to the superior efficacy of the Christian covenant: αἱ μὲν γὰρ νομικαὶ [θυσίαι] τὰ ἐν ἀγνοίᾳ συνεχώρουν πλημμελήματα, ἡ δὲ τοῦ Χριστοῦ καὶ τὰ ἐν εἰδήσει ἁμαρτήματα ἀφίησι.

In connexion with the idea of ἀγνόημα Chrysostom expresses a striking thought: ὅρα, οὐκ εἶπεν ἁμαρτημάτων ἀλλ᾽ ἀγνοημάτων ἵνα μὴ μέγα φρονήσωσιν· εἰ γὰρ καὶ μὴ ἑκὼν ἥμαρτες, φησίν, ἀλλ᾽ ἄκων ἠγνόησας, καὶ τούτου οὐδείς ἐστι καθαρός.

(*c*) 8—10. The restrictions which limited the approach of priests and High-priest to God contained an obvious lesson. There was no way to God opened by the Law. The Law had a symbolical, disciplinary, value and looked forward to a more perfect system.

8. τοῦτο δηλ. τοῦ πν. τ. ἁγ.] Vulg. *hoc significante spiritu sancto.* There is a divine meaning both in the words of Scripture and in the ordinances of worship. The Spirit which inspired the teaching and fixed the ritual Himself discloses it, and this He does continuously (δηλοῦντος not δηλώσαντος) as long as the veil rests over any part of the record. For δηλοῦν see c. xii. 27; 1 Pet. i. 11; 2 Pet. i. 14.

Compare the words of Theophylact: ...ἐδηλοῦτο συμβολικῶς ὅτι ἕως

μήπω πεφανερῶσθαι τὴν τῶν ἁγίων ὁδὸν ἔτι τῆς πρώτης

οὗ ἵσταται ἡ σκηνὴ αὕτη, τουτέστιν ἕως
οὗ κρατεῖ ὁ νόμος καὶ αἱ κατ᾽ αὐτὸν
λατρεῖαι τελοῦνται, οὐκ ἐστὶ βάσιμος ἡ
τῶν ἁγίων ὁδός, τουτέστιν, ἡ εἰς τὸν
οὐρανὸν εἴσοδος.

μήπω πεφαν....] that the way into
the Holy place hath not yet been made
manifest while the first tabernacle
hath still an appointed place; Vulg.
nondum propalatam esse sanctorum
viam adhuc priore tabernaculo ha-
bente statum (O.L. virtutem). It is
evident that this phrase 'the Holy
place' must include 'the Holy of
holies,' the symbolic Presence of
God (v. 12; 24 f.; x. 19), even if it
does not mean this exclusively. Perhaps however a general phrase is
chosen by the Apostle to include
both the scene of worship and the
scene of the Divine revelation. The
people had no way into the Holy
place which was open to the priests
only: the priests had no way into the
Holy of holies which was open to the
High-priest alone.

For the construction ἡ τῶν ἁγίων
ὁδός compare c. x. 19; Matt. x. 5;
Gen. iii. 24.

The comprehensive sense which has
been given to τὰ ἅγια, as including
both the Holy and the Most Holy
place, explains the use of ἡ πρώτη
σκηνή. This phrase has been used
just before (v. 6; comp. v. 2) of the
Holy place as the vestibule, so to
speak, of the Divine presence-cham-
ber; and it is very difficult to suppose
that it should be suddenly used in
another sense for 'the first (the
Mosaic) tabernacle' as opposed to
'the heavenly archetypal tabernacle'
(v. 11). 'The first, the outer, tabernacle,' the sanctuary of habitual
worship, did in a most impressive
way shew the limits which were
placed upon the worshipper. While
this held a recognised place among
divine institutions the people were
separated from the object of their

devotion. All had not as yet the
privilege of priests: all priests had
not the right of approach to the
Divine throne. Thus the outer sanctuary was the representative symbol
of the whole Tabernacle as the place
of service.

The phrase ἐχούσης στάσιν must,
it is reasonable to suppose, express
something more than simply standing
(ἑστηκυίας, ἑστώσης) as the Latin
Versions indicate. The periphrasis
with ἔχω (comp. 1 John i. 8 note)
marks the general position and not
only the isolated fact: 'while the
first tabernacle still has an appointed
place answering to a Divine order'
(c. x. 9). The phrase is used of the
prevalence of periodic winds: Polyb.
v. 5, 3 τῶν ἐτησιῶν ἤδη στάσιν ἐχόντων.

9. ἥτις παραβ....ἐνεστηκότα] Vulg.
quae parabola est temporis instan-
tis, which is (seeing it is) a parable,
a figure, and nothing more, for the
season now present, 'the present
age,' that period of preparation which
will be followed by 'the age to come'
for which we look. This sense of ὁ
καιρὸς ὁ ἐνεστώς is established beyond
all doubt. In technical language all
time was divided into 'the past, the
present (ἐνεστώς), and the future'
(Sext. Emp. Pyrrh. Hypot. iii. 17,
144 ὁ χρόνος λέγεται τριμερὴς εἶναι· καὶ
τὸ μὲν παρῳχηκώς, τὸ δὲ ἐνεστώς, τὸ δὲ
μέλλων); and the use of the word
ἐνέστηκα in the N. T. is decisive in
favour of the sense the season that
is present (not the season that is at
hand): see 2 Thess. ii. 2; Gal. i. 4;
1 Cor. vii. 26. Things 'present' (ἐνε-
στῶτα) are contrasted with things
'future' (μέλλοντα): 1 Cor. iii. 22;
Rom. viii. 38.

It may therefore be reasonably laid
down that ὁ καιρὸς ὁ ἐνεστώς must be
taken in connexion with that which
the writer of the Epistle speaks of
as 'future,' 'the future world' (ii. 5),
'the future age' (vi. 5), 'the future

σκηνῆς ἐχούσης στάσιν, ⁹ἥτις παραβολὴ εἰς τὸν καιρὸν
τὸν ἐνεστηκότα, καθ᾽ ἣν δῶρά τε καὶ θυσίαι προσφέρονται μὴ δυνάμεναι κατὰ συνείδησιν τελειῶσαι τὸν λα-

9 ἥτις : +πρώτη D₂*.   καθ᾽ ἥν ℵABD₂*: καθ᾽ ὅν ς.

blessings' (x. 1). If then, as is beyond doubt, 'the future,' in the vision of the writer, is that which is characteristic of the Christian order, 'the present' must be that which is characteristic of the preparatory order, not yet outwardly abolished (comp. Gal. i. 4), that which is commonly called in other writings, 'this age,' or 'the present age'; and in the present context ὁ καιρὸς ὁ ἐνεστώς stands in opposition to καιρὸς διορθώσεως (v. 10), and parallel with 'these days' in c. i. 1 (note).

It will be noticed also that καιρός is chosen (in place of αἰών) as suggesting the idea of a present crisis : comp. Rom. iii. 26; xi. 5 (2 Cor. viii. 13).

Thus 'the present season' must be carefully distinguished from the fulness of the Christian time, though in one sense the blessings of Christianity were already realised essentially. So far Primasius, while he gives a wrong sense to 'present,' says truly : Quod enim agebatur in templo tunc temporis figura erat et similitudo istius veritatis quæ jam in ecclesia completur.

The Levitical system then, represented by 'the first Tabernacle,' is described here as a parable 'to serve for' or, perhaps 'to last as long as' the present season. It conveyed its lessons while the preparatory age continued up to the time of change. It did indeed foreshadow that which is offered in the Gospel, but that is not the aspect of it which is here brought forward. As a parable (c. xi. 19) it is regarded not so much in relation to a definite future which is directly prefigured ('type') as in regard to its own power of teaching. The parable suggests thoughts : the type points to a direct fulfilment.

9, 10.   καθ᾽ ἣν δῶρα...μόνον ἐπὶ βρ. ...βαπτισμοῖς, δικαιώματα... ἐπικείμενα] in accordance with which (and after this parable, or teaching by figure) gifts and sacrifices are offered such as cannot make the worshipper perfect as touching the conscience (in conscience), being only ordinances of flesh, resting upon meats and drinks and divers washings, imposed until a season of reformation. If the καί is retained (καὶ δικαιώματα) then two things are stated of the Levitical sacrifices, 'that they cannot bring perfection, as resting only on meats'...and 'that they are ordinances of flesh...'.

This sense is given in a rude form by the Old Latin version : quæ [munera et bestiæ] non possunt conscientia consummare servientes, solum in cibis et potu et variis baptismis, justitia carnis usque ad tempus restitutionis imposita.

The Vulgate renders καὶ δικαιώμασιν...ἐπικειμένοις quæ non possunt ...in cibis...et variis baptismatibus et justitiis carnis usque ad tempus correctionis impositis.

Three points in this complicated sentence require consideration, the weakness of the Levitical offerings (μὴ δυν. κατὰ συν. τελ. τὸν λατρ.), the ground of their weakness (μόνον ἐπὶ βρώμασιν...δικαιώματα σαρκός), the purpose of their enactment (μέχρι καιροῦ διορθ. ἐπικ.).

μὴ δυν....τελ. τὸν λατρ.] For the idea of τελείωσις 'a bringing to perfection' according to some assumed standard, see c. vii. 11 note. Here that standard is said to be 'according to' 'as touching the conscience.' The Levitical offerings were able to secure an outward perfecting, the admission of each worshipper to a full partici-

τρεύοντα, ¹⁰μόνον ἐπὶ βρώμασιν καὶ πόμασιν καὶ δια-
φόροις βαπτισμοῖς, ᵀ δικαιώματα σαρκὸς μέχρι καιροῦ

10 καὶ

10 βαπτισμοῖς ℵ*AD₂* syr vg me the : + καί ℵᶜB vg syr hl the.   δικαιώματα
ℵAB syr vg me : δικαίωμα D₂* the : δικαιώμασιν ς vg syr hl.

pation in the privileges of the ancient commonwealth of God, which depended on the satisfaction of ceremonial conditions. But they could not bring a spiritual perfecting. They could not, to notice one aspect, 'cleanse the conscience from dead works to serve a living God' (c. 14).

For συνείδησις see Additional Note.

τὸν λατρεύοντα expresses each worshipper who approached God through the appointed minister. Compare c. x. 2 τοὺς λατρεύοντας (of the whole body); xiii. 10. For the absolute use of λατρεύω see x. 2 note.

10. μόνον ἐπὶ βρώμ....δικ. σ.] These offerings were unable to satisfy man's destiny *being only ordinances of flesh* combined with, *resting upon, meats and drinks and divers washings.*

The μόνον and the ἐπὶ βρώμ. both serve to limit and explain the character of the Mosaic institutions. These institutions were only ordinances of flesh, ordinances which dealt with that which is external (comp. c. vii. 16 κατὰ νόμον ἐντολῆς σαρκίνης); and the accompaniments of the sacrifices, the personal requirements with which they were connected, indicated their purely outward significance.

For the use of the preposition ἐπί to express the accompanying circumstances or conditions see 1 Thess. iv. 7; 1 Cor. ix. 10; 2 Cor. ix. 6; Gal. v. 13; Eph. ii. 10; 2 Tim. ii. 14. Compare also vv. 15, 17; c. viii. 6; x. 28.

The reference in βρώμ. καὶ πόμ. καὶ διαφ. βαπτ. is general, and must be taken to include the various Levitical regulations positive and negative as to meats and drinks, developed by tradition. The mention of 'drinks'

has caused difficulty, for the Law gave no universal directions in this respect: so Theophylact asks : πῶς δὲ εἶπε πόμασι; καίτοι περὶ πομάτων διαφορᾶς οὐ διελάμβανεν ὁ νόμος; He suggests that the reference may be to the conditions of the Nazarite vow (Num. vi. 3), or to the injunctions laid upon the ministering priests (Lev. x. 9). Comp. Col. ii. 16.

For the 'different washings' see Mark vii. 4. Comp. Ex. xxix. 4; Lev. xi. 25, 28 ff.; xvi. 4, 24 ff.; Num. viii. 7; xix. 17, &c.

μέχρι κ. διορθ. ἐπικείμενα] The provisional character of the Levitical institutions illustrates their enactment. They were *imposed until a season of reformation.* The word διόρθωσις is not found elsewhere in biblical Greek. It is used in late Greek writers for the reformation of laws, institutions, states. Comp. Acts xxiv. 3 διόρθωμα. The verb διορθοῦν is used in the LXX. of 'amending ways': Jer. vii. 3, 5 (הֵיטִב דְּרָכָי); comp. Wisd. ix. 18; and also of 'setting up,' 'establishing': Is. xvi. 5; lxii. 7 (כּוֹנֵן). The thought of 'making straight, erect' passes naturally into that of 'making stable.'

Under different aspects this 'reformation' is spoken of as a 'restitution' (Acts iii. 21 ἀποκατάστασις), and a 'regeneration' (Matt. xix. 28 παλιγγενεσία).

The anarthrous form of the phrase (καιρὸς διορθώσεως) marks the character of the coming change. The very nature of the Law shewed that it was transitory, if it did not shew the definite issue to which it led.

The Greek commentators call at-

διορθώσεως ἐπικείμενα.

tention to the force of the word ἐπικείμενα. Thus Theodoret: καλῶς τὸ ἐπέκειτο, βάρος γὰρ ἦν μόνον τὰ ἐν τῷ νόμῳ (Acts xv. 10, 28).

(2) ix. 11—28. The High-priestly Atonement under the New Covenant.

The work of the Jewish High-priest has been indicated as the climax of the old system (v. 7); and the High-priestly work of Christ is now considered in contrast with it. The comparison is instituted in respect of that which was the unique and supreme privilege of the Levitical High-priest, the access to God on the Day of Atonement. Thus two main points come into consideration: the entrance of the High-priest into the Divine Presence, and the fact that the entrance was through blood.

Under this aspect the work of Christ is first (a) described generally in vv. 11, 12; and then the truths suggested (b) by the shedding of His Blood (vv. 13—22), and (c) by His entrance into the Presence of God whence He has not yet returned (23—28), are followed out in detail.

(a) A summary description of Christ's High-priestly work (11, 12).

The work of Christ as High-priest of the new order now established stands in sovereign superiority over that of the Levitical type in regard to scene, and offering, and efficacy. The tabernacle through which He ministered was not of this creation but heavenly (11 b). The blood through which He entered before God was not that of sacrificed animals but His own (12 a). The redemption which He obtained was not for a brief season but for ever (12 b).

¹¹ *But Christ, having come a High-priest of the good things realised, through the greater and more perfect tabernacle, not made by hands, that is, not of this creation, ¹²nor yet through blood of goats and calves, but through His*

¹¹ Χριστὸς δὲ παραγε-

own blood, entered in once for all into the Holy place, having obtained eternal redemption.

11, 12. In contrast (Χριστὸς δέ) with the repeated entrance of the Jewish High-priest into the Holy of Holies through the blood of appointed victims Christ once for all entered into the true Sanctuary, the actual Presence of God, through His own blood, and obtained not a temporary but an eternal deliverance. Thus the contrast extends to the system (τὰ γενόμενα ἀγαθά), the place and mode of the Atonement (διὰ τῆς μ. καὶ τελ. σκ., διὰ τοῦ ἰδ. αἷ.), the issue (αἰών λύτρ.). In all these points the 'parable' finds fulfilment.

11. Χριστὸς δέ...] *But Christ having come a High-priest of good things realised...*O. L. *Christus autem, sacerdos quando advenit bonorum factorum.* Vulg. *Christus autem adsistens pontifex futurorum bonorum.* For the simple Χριστός (contrast ὁ χριστός iii. 14 note) see v. 24; iii. 6.

παραγενόμενος] Christ has not only become (γενόμενος) High-priest as one of an appointed line, He has made His presence as High-priest felt among His people as sent from another realm to fulfil the office in part on earth.

So Chrysostom says: οὐκ εἶπε γενόμενος ἀλλὰ παραγενόμενος, τουτέστιν, εἰς αὐτὸ τοῦτο ἐλθών, οὐχ ἕτερον διαδεξάμενος· οὐ πρότερον παρεγένετο καὶ τότε ἐγένετο ἀλλ᾽ ἅμα ἦλθε.

The idea of παραγενέσθαι is that of coming to, reaching, being present at, some marked place or company. Compare Matt. iii. 1 παραγίνεται Ἰωάνης. Luke xii. 51 δοκεῖτε ὅτι εἰρήνην παρεγενόμην δοῦναι ἐν τῇ γῇ; Acts v. 21 (and often in that book).

ἀρχ. τῶν γενομένων ἀγ.] The title of Christ at once marks His absolute supremacy. He is a High-priest whose work deals with blessings which have been gained and which do not

νόμενος ἀρχιερεὺς τῶν ⌜γενομένων⌝ ἀγαθῶν διὰ τῆς μεί-

11 μελλόντων

11 γενομένων BD₂* syrr: μελλόντων ℵA vg syr hl mg me (æg) [comp. c. x. 1].

exist only in hope and prophecy. He is High-priest of the good things which are already realised by the fulfilment of the divine conditions, and which are not promised only and future. The same blessings can be spoken of as 'realised' in respect of Christ's work, and as 'future' in respect of the preparatory discipline of the law (c. x. 1), or the actual position of Christians (comp. c. xiii. 14). In this place it seems natural that 'the good things' should be spoken of as realised from the divine side. Even if men have not entered upon their inheritance, it is already gained. In c. x. 1 the case is different and there the reading (τῶν μελλ. ἀγ.) is undisturbed.

For the *gen.* τῶν γεν. ἀγ. compare c. iii. 1 ἀρχ. τῆς ὁμολογίας (dealing with and belonging to).

11 *b*, 12. The Majesty of Christ's title ('High-priest of the good things realised') is justified by a description of His Work. In the circumstances and the effects of His High-priestly service He offers the heavenly counterpart of that which was exhibited under an earthly figure in the Mosaic system. This is shewn first in respect of the Tabernacle 'through which' Christ fulfils His work.

διὰ τῆς μ....οὐδὲ δι' αἵμ....διὰ δέ...] *through the greater...nor yet through blood...but through his own...*Vulg. *per...tabernaculum...neque per sanguinem...sed per...sanguinem....*It seems to be best to take the preposition in each case in the same general sense and to join both διὰ τῆς μ. καὶ τ. σκ. and διὰ τοῦ ἰδ. αἵ. with εἰσῆλθε. Christ employed in the fulfilment of His office 'the greater Tabernacle' and 'His own Blood' (compare the corresponding though not parallel use of διά in 1 John v. 6).

The local sense which has been given to διά in the first clause ('*passing through the greater...tabernacle* into the Presence of God') does not give a very clear thought. It is true indeed that the High-priest passed through 'the first tabernacle' to the Holy of Holies, but no such stress is laid on this 'passage through' as to make it the one thing noticeable in the Sanctuary. The outer Sanctuary was not merely a portal to the Holy of Holies but the appointed place of priestly service. And on the other hand the idea conveyed by this limited (local) sense of 'through' is included in the wider (instrumental) sense of 'through' which describes that which Christ used in His work.

In this work it must be observed that Christ is said to make use not of '*a* greater tabernacle' but of '*the* greater tabernacle,' 'the true, ideal, tabernacle' (c. viii. 2). The thought of the reader is thus carried back to the heavenly pattern which Moses followed (c. viii. 5 note; Ex. xxv. 9). The earthly Tabernacle witnessed not only to some nobler revelation of God's Presence, but definitely to the archetype after which it was fashioned.

What then is this heavenly Tabernacle? Some preparation will be made for the answer if we call to mind the two main purposes of the transitory Tabernacle. It was designed on the one hand to symbolise the Presence of God among His people; and on the other to afford under certain restrictions a means of approach to Him. The heavenly Tabernacle must then satisfy these two ends in the highest possible degree. It must represent the Presence of God, and offer a way of approach to God, being in both

ζονος καὶ τελειοτέρας σκηνῆς οὐ χειροποιήτου, τοῦτ᾽

respects eternal, spiritual, ideal (ἀλη-θινή c. viii. 2).

In seeking for some conception which shall satisfy these conditions it is obvious that all images of local circumscription must be laid aside, or, at least, used only by way of accommodation. The spiritual Tabernacle must not be defined by the limitations which belong to 'this creation.' We may then at once set aside all such interpretations as those which suppose that the lower heavens, through which Christ passed, or the supra-mundane realm, or the like, are 'the greater tabernacle.' We must look for some spiritual antitype to the local sanctuary.

And here we are brought to the patristic interpretation which it requires some effort to grasp. The Fathers both Greek and Latin commonly understood the greater Tabernacle to be the Lord's 'flesh,' or 'humanity.' Thus Chrysostom: τὴν σάρκα ἐνταῦθα λέγει. καλῶς δὲ καὶ μείζονα καὶ τελειοτέραν εἶπεν, εἴ γε ὁ θεὸς λόγος καὶ πᾶσα ἡ τοῦ πνεύματος ἐνέργεια ἐνοικεῖ ἐν αὐτῇ.

And Theodoret, followed by Œcumenius: σκηνὴν ἀχειροποίητον τὴν ἀνθρωπείαν φύσιν ἐκάλεσεν ἣν ἀνέλαβεν ὁ δεσπότης Χριστὸς...οὐ κατὰ νόμον φύσεως τῆς ἐν τῇ κτίσει πολιτευομένης. Compare also Euthymius: διὰ τοῦ ἰδίου φημὶ σώματος ἐν ᾧ ᾤκησεν ἡ τούτου θεότης, ὃ μεῖζον ὡς ἡνωμένον τῇ θεότητι τούτου πάντοτε.

And Primasius: Tabernaculum per quod assistit deo patri humanitas illius est.

In this connexion Chrysostom and Theophylact notice how the Lord's 'Body' and 'heaven' are each spoken of as 'a veil' and as 'a tabernacle.' The text of Chrysostom is confused, but Theophylact has preserved his meaning: καλεῖ τὸ σῶμα τοῦ Κυρίου καὶ σκηνήν, ὡς ἐνταῦθα, διὰ τὸ τὸν Μονογενῆ σκηνῶσαι ἐν αὐτῇ· καὶ κατα-

πέτασμα, ὡς ἀποκρύπτουσαν τὴν θεότητα. καλεῖ καὶ τὸν οὐρανὸν τοῖς αὐτοῖς τούτοις ὀνόμασι, σκηνήν, ὡς ἐκεῖ ὄντος τοῦ ἀρχιερέως· καταπέτασμα, ὡς ἀποτειχιζομένων τῶν ἁγίων δι᾽ αὐτοῦ.

This interpretation was met by one interesting objection in early times: How could the Lord's Body be said to be 'not of this creation'? Was not this assertion, it was asked, a denial of His true humanity? ἐνταῦθα, Theophylact says, ἐπιπηδῶσιν οἱ αἱρετικοὶ λέγοντες οὐράνιον εἶναι τὸ σῶμα καὶ αἰθέριον. He replies that 'heaven' and 'sky' are themselves 'of this creation.' But Œcumenius meets the difficulty more satisfactorily by saying that under different aspects the Lord's Body was and was not 'of this creation': τὸ σῶμα Χριστοῦ καὶ ταύτης ἦν τῆς κτίσεως καὶ οὐ ταύτης, ταύτης μέν, κατὰ τὸ ἴσον εἶναι καὶ διὰ πάντων ὅμοιον τῷ ἡμετέρῳ σώματι, οὐ ταύτης δέ, κατὰ τὸ ἔχειν ἀσυγχύτως καὶ ἀδιαιρέτως τὴν θεότητα.

As far as the Lord's historical work on earth is concerned this interpretation is adequate. He was the perfect revelation of the Father and the way to Him. But in considering the ideal antitype, or rather archetype, of the Tabernacle we must take account of the Lord's ministry in heaven. In this (c. viii. 1 f.) the heavenly High-priest and the heavenly Tabernacle are in some sense distinguished; and the Lord acts as High-priest in His human Nature (c. iv. 14 ff.). Bearing this in mind we may perhaps extend the patristic conception so as to meet the difficulty, though, with our present powers of conceiving of divine things we must speak with the most reverent reserve. In this relation then it may be said that 'the greater and more perfect Tabernacle' of which Christ is minister, and (as we must add) in which the Saints worship, gathers up the various means under which God

ἔστιν οὐ ταύτης τῆς κτίσεως, ¹²οὐδὲ δι᾽ αἵματος τράγων
καὶ μόσχων διὰ δὲ τοῦ ἰδίου αἵματος, εἰσῆλθεν ἐφάπαξ

reveals Himself in the spiritual order, and through which men approach to Him. Under one aspect these are represented by the union of the redeemed and perfected hosts made one in Christ as His Body. Through this glorified Church answering to the complete humanity which Christ assumed, God is made known, and in and through this each believer comes nigh to God. In this Body, as a spiritual Temple, Christ ministers. As members in this Body believers severally enjoy the Divine Presence. Thought fails us under the bondage of local limitations, and still we can dimly apprehend how we have opened to us in this vision the prospect of a spiritual reality corresponding to that which was material and earthly in the old ordinances of worship. It enables us to connect redeemed humanity with the glorified human Nature of the Lord, and to consider how it is that humanity, the summing-up of Creation, may become in Him the highest manifestation of God to finite being, and in its fulness that through which each part is brought near to God.

This heavenly Tabernacle is spoken of as *greater and more perfect* (Vulg. *amplius et perfectius*), *greater* in comparison with the narrow limits of the earthly Tabernacle, *more perfect* as answering to the complete development of the Divine plan. And in its essential character it is *not made by hands, that is, not of this creation* (Vulg. *non manu factum, id est, non hujus creationis*). Human skill had nothing to do with its structure, for man's work finds its expression in the visible order of earth, to which this does not belong.

For οὐ χειροποίητον see *v.* 24 ; Mk. xiv. 58 (ἀχειροποίητος); 2 Cor. v. 1 (οἰκίαν ἀχειροποίητον αἰώνιον ἐν τοῖς

οὐρανοῖς). Compare Acts vii. 48 ; xvii. 24. For οὐ ταύτης τῆς κτίσεως compare 2 Cor. iv. 18 τὰ γὰρ βλεπό-μενα πρόσκαιρα, τὰ δὲ μὴ βλεπόμενα αἰώνια ; c. viii. 2 ἡ σκηνὴ ἡ ἀληθινὴ ἣν ἔπηξεν ὁ Κύριος ; and for κτίσις, Rom. viii. 19 ff.

Philo, in a striking passage, speaks of the world as 'the house and city' of the first man μηδεμιᾶς χειροποιήτου κατασκευῆς δεδημιουργημένης ἐκ λίθων καὶ ξύλων ὕλης.

12 *a.* A second point which marks the heavenly character of Christ's work is seen in the nature of His offering. He made not a twofold offering but one only. He entered into the Holy place through His own Blood, and that once for all.

οὐδὲ δι᾽ αἵμ. τράγ. καὶ μόσχ.] *nor yet through blood of goats and bulls....* The οὐδέ seems to be due to the preceding οὐ χειρ. as if the sentence had run οὐ διὰ χειροπ....οὐδὲ δι᾽ αἵμα-τος.... The goat was the offering for the people (Lev. xvi. 15): the bullock for the High-priest himself (Lev. xvi. 11). The plural generalises the thought. The words used in the LXX. version of Leviticus are μόσχος and χίμαρος. Symmachus and Aquila seem to have used τράγος for χίμαρος. The phrase τράγοι καὶ ταῦροι (*v.* 13) gives the form in which the reference to animal victims would be popularly expressed. Compare Ps. xlix. 13 ; Is. i. 11 (elsewhere μόσχος seems to be always used in the LXX.).

διὰ δὲ τοῦ ἰδ. αἵμ....τὰ ἅγια] *but through His own blood (He) entered once for all into the Holy place,* the immediate Presence of God in heaven (see *v.* 8 note).

The use of διά as marking the means but not defining the mode (μετά) is significant when taken in connexion with *v.* 7 (οὐ χωρίς). The earthly High-priest took with him

εἰς τὰ ἅγια, αἰωνίαν λύτρωσιν εὑράμενος.   ¹³ εἰ γὰρ τὸ

the material blood: Christ 'through His own blood' entered into the Presence of God, but we are not justified in introducing any material interpretations of the manner in which He made it efficacious. Comp. c. xiii. 12 διὰ τοῦ ἰδίου αἵματος: Acts xx. 28 ἣν περιεποιήσατο διὰ τοῦ αἵματος τοῦ ἰδίου.

ἐφάπαξ] See vii. 27 note. Christ did not need (like the Jewish High-priest) a double entrance, even as He did not need to repeat His entrance. One entrance left the way open for ever. The 'veil was rent' (Matt. xxvii. 51). There was no longer any obstacle interposed between the worshipper—for all are now priests (Apoc. i. 6)—and the Object of his worship.

12 b. A third element in the absolute supremacy of Christ's High-priesthood lies in the abiding efficacy of His One priestly act. He obtained an eternal Redemption in contrast with the limited, recurrent, redemption of the yearly Atonement.

αἰων. λύτρ. εὑρ.] *having obtained eternal redemption*, Vulg. *æterna inventa redemptione*, O. L. *æterna expiatione reperta*. In combination with εἰσῆλθεν, εὑράμενος may express a coincident (comp. c. ii. 10 note), or a precedent fact: 'Christ entered... therein obtaining' or 'Christ entered ...having already obtain̊ed.' The choice between these senses will be decided by the meaning given to 'redemption.' If 'redemption' is the initial work, the conquest of death (c. ii. 14 f.), then this was completed in the Passion and Resurrection; but it seems more natural to find the fulness of the word satisfied in the Triumph of the Ascension. Compare Additional Note on λύτρωσις.

The form εὑράμενος is found here only in the N. T. The force of the middle voice (compare c. i. 3 ποιησά-

μενος) is that of 'having obtained as the issue of personal labour' directed to this end.

Chrysostom sees an emphatic sense in the word: σφόδρα τῶν ἀπόρων ἦν καὶ τῶν παρὰ προσδοκίαν πῶς διὰ μιᾶς εἰσόδου αἰωνίαν λύτρωσιν εὕρατο.

And so Theophylact: ὅρα δὲ καὶ τὸ εὑρόμενος, ὡς παρὰ προσδοκίαν γενομένου τοῦ πράγματος οὕτω ταύτῃ τῇ λέξει ἐχρήσατο. ἄπορον γὰρ ἦν τὸ τῆς ἐλευθερίας ἡμῖν, ἀλλ᾽ αὐτὸς εὗρε τοῦτο.

Œcumenius also touches upon the voice: εὑράμενος...οὐχ ἑαυτῷ, πῶς γὰρ ὁ ἀναμάρτητος; ἀλλὰ τῷ λαῷ αὐτοῦ· ἡ ἐπειδὴ κεφαλὴ τῆς ἀνθρωπότητος ἠξίωσεν εἶναι, τὰ ἡμῖν κατορθωθέντα αὐτῷ κατωρθῶσθαι λέγει ὁ ἀπόστολος.

(b) The truths taught by the shedding of Christ's Blood (vv. 13—22).

The thoughts springing out of the fulfilment of Christ's High-priestly work which have found a summary expression in vv. 11, 12 are developed in the remainder of the chapter. The efficacy of Christ's Blood is (a) first contrasted with that of the Jewish victims as a purifying power (13, 14); and then a new thought is introduced, which arises from the extension of the virtue of Christ's Blood to His people. The Blood is (β) the ratification of a new Covenant, as comprehensive in its application as the blood 'of the calves and the goats' by which the Old Covenant was ratified (15—22).

¹³ *For if the blood of goats and bulls and the ashes of a heifer, sprinkling them that have been defiled, sanctifieth unto the cleanness of the flesh,* ¹⁴*how much more shall the blood of Christ, who through His eternal spirit offered Himself without blemish to God, cleanse our conscience from dead works, to the end that we may serve a living God?* ¹⁵*And for this reason He is mediator of a new covenant, in order that a death having taken place for redemption*

αἷμα τράγων καὶ ταύρων καὶ σποδὸς δαμάλεως ῥαντίζουσα τοὺς κεκοινωμένους ἁγιάζει πρὸς τὴν τῆς σαρκὸς

13 τρ. καὶ ταύρ. אABD₂ vg syr vg me (æg): ταύρ. καὶ τρ. ς syr hl.   κεκοιν. :
κεκοιμημένους D₂*.

*from the transgressions that were
under the first covenant, they that
have been called may receive the
promise of the eternal inheritance.
¹⁶ For where there is a covenant, the
death of him that made it must
needs be presented. ¹⁷ For a covenant
is sure where there hath been death ;
since it doth not ever have force
when he that made it liveth.
¹⁸ Whence not even hath the first
covenant been inaugurated without
blood. ¹⁹ For when every commandment had been spoken according to
the Law by Moses to all the people,
taking the blood of the calves and the
goats, with water and scarlet wool
and hyssop, he sprinkled both the
book itself and all the people, ²⁰ saying
This is the blood of the covenant
which God commanded to youward.
²¹ And the tabernacle also and all
the vessels of the ministry he sprinkled
in like manner with the blood.
²² And I may almost say, it is in
blood all things are cleansed according to the Law, and apart from outpouring of blood there cometh no
remission.*

(a) vv. 13, 14. A sense of difficulty
might arise at the prospect of the
vast claim which has been made for
Christ's work. How, it might be
asked, can it avail for ever? The
Mosaic institutions furnish the answer.

The ritual purification of the Jewish
system had a limited validity. It was
directed to that which was outward.
In this respect it removed outward
defilement, and gave outward cleanness. If then it availed within its
proper sphere, much more (we may
confidently conclude) the blood of
Christ will avail within its proper
sphere, which is spiritual. The con-

sequence which follows in the one
case is (so to speak) due to an arbitrary enactment : the consequence in
the other case lies in the very nature
of things. The conclusion rests upon
the comparison of a twofold relation,
the relation of the blood of Christ to
the blood of animals, and the relation
of the inward sphere of religion to the
outward.

13.   Two typical examples of the
purificatory Levitical sacrifices are
taken in illustration : the yearly sacrifices 'of goats and bulls' on the day
of Atonement (Lev. xvi.), and the
occasional sacrifice of the red heifer
(Num. xix.). The first regarded the
impurity contracted from daily action,
the second the impurity contracted
from contact with death.

τράγων καὶ ταύρων] Comp. v. 12 note.

σποδὸς δαμάλεως] In this case the
blood of the sacrifice was also burnt :
Num. xix. 5.

ῥαντίζουσα τοὺς κεκοιν. ἁγ...] *sprinkling them that have been defiled*, who
by a definite act have contracted some
stain, *sanctifieth unto the cleanness
of the flesh*...Vulg. *adspersus* (O.L.
sparsus) *inquinatos sanctificat ad
emundationem carnis* (O.L. *ad emun-
dandam carnem*). For the use of
the word κεκοινωμένους, which is not
found in the LXX., see Matt. xv. 11 ff. ;
Acts xxi. 28.   The accus. depends on
ῥαντίζουσα: Ps. l. (li.) 9 ῥαντιεῖς με
ὑσσώπῳ.   The verb ῥαντίζειν occurs in
the N.T. only in this Epistle : vv. 19,
21 ; x. 22 note.   In the LXX. the form
ῥαίνειν is more common.   The 'water
of separation (impurity)' is called in
the LXX. ὕδωρ ῥαντισμοῦ, Num. xix.
9, 13, 20 f.

Theophylact calls attention to the
distinction between ἁγιάζει, 'sancti-

καθαρότητα, ¹⁴πόσῳ μᾶλλον τὸ αἷμα τοῦ χριστοῦ, ὃς
διὰ πνεύματος αἰωνίου ἑαυτὸν προσήνεγκεν ἄμωμον τῷ

14 αἰωνίου ℵ*AB syrr : ἀγίου ℵᶜD₂* vg me (æg).

fieth,' 'halloweth,' in regard to destination, and καθαρίζει (v. 14 καθαριεῖ),
'cleanseth' in regard to character:
ὅρα δὲ σύνεσιν, οὐκ εἶπεν ὅτι ἐκαθάρισε
τὸ αἷμα τῶν τράγων, ἀλλ᾿ ἡγίαζεν...ἐκεῖ
μὲν εἶπε τὸ ἁγιάζει...ἐνταῦθα δὲ καθαριεῖ
εἰπὼν ἔδειξεν εὐθὺς τὴν ὑπεροχήν.

The idea is that of the ceremonial
purity which enabled the Jew to
enjoy the full privileges of his covenant worship and fellowship with the
external Church of God. The force of
the words καθαρός, ἅγιος—moral, external: ideal, personal—is determined
by the context.

14. πόσῳ μᾶλλον] The superior
efficacy of Christ's Blood is based
generally on the considerations that
His Sacrifice was

1. Voluntary, not by constraint as
in the case of the animal sacrifices of
the Law.

2. Rational, and not animal.

3. Spontaneous, not in obedience
to a direct commandment.

4. Moral, an offering of Himself
by the action of the highest power in
Himself, whereby He stood in connexion with God, and not a mere mechanical performance of a prescribed rite.
Comp. John x. 17 f.

τὸ αἷμα τοῦ χριστοῦ] The blood of
Christ stands parallel both to the blood
of goats and bulls and to the ashes
of the heifer, as the means (1) of atonement for sins, and (2) of purification
from contact with death: of access to
God and of life in His Church.

It will be observed that it is not
the death of the victim as suffering,
but the use of the Blood (that is, the
Life) which is presented here as the
source of purification.

The efficacy of Blood—the life, Lev.
xvii. 11—is regarded in different aspects in this passage. Now one aspect

predominates and now another. It is a
means of atonement, and it is a means
of purification: it has a power retro-
spectively and prospectively. Death
again, which makes the blood available,
is the seal of the validity of a covenant. But no one view exhausts the
meaning of that which is the fulness
of a life made available for others.
Compare Additional Note on 1 John
i. 7.

ὃς...ἑαυτ. προσ. ἄμωμον τ. θ.] who
through His eternal spirit offered
Himself without blemish to God,
Vulg. qui per spiritum sanctum semetipsum obtulit immaculatum Deo.
The sacrifice upon the altar of the
Cross preceded the presentation of
the blood. The phrase ἑαυτὸν προσήνεγκεν clearly fixes the reference to
this initial act of Christ's High-priestly
sacrifice. This act He accomplished
διὰ πνεύματος αἰωνίου. In virtue of
His inseparable and unchangeable
Divine Nature Christ was Priest
while He was victim also. He offered
Himself, living through death and in
death. Epiphanius puts together the
different aspects of Christ's work in
His sacrifice of Himself in a striking
passage: αὐτὸς ἱερεῖον, αὐτὸς θῦμα,
αὐτὸς ἱερεύς, αὐτὸς θυσιαστήριον, αὐτὸς
θεός, αὐτὸς ἄνθρωπος, αὐτὸς βασιλεύς,
αὐτὸς ἀρχιερεύς, αὐτὸς πρόβατον, αὐτὸς
ἀρνίον, τὰ πάντα ἐν πᾶσιν ὑπὲρ ἡμῶν
γενόμενος, ἵνα ἡμῖν ζωὴ κατὰ πάντα τρόπον γένηται...(Hær. lv. § 4, 471 f.).

The absence of the article from
πνεῦμα αἰώνιον marks the spirit here
as a power possessed by Christ, His
'Spirit.' It could not be said of any
man absolutely that his spirit is eternal; but Christ's Spirit is in virtue
of His Divine Personality eternal.
By this, while truly man, He remained in unbroken connexion with God.

θεῷ, καθαριεῖ τὴν συνείδησιν ⌜ἡμῶν⌝ ἀπὸ νεκρῶν ἔργων

14 ὑμῶν

καθαρ.: +δs′ καθαρ. D₂* [B ends with καθα].   ἡμῶν AD₂* (vg) syr vg me : ὑμῶν
א (vg) syr hl.

Through this He had 'the power of an indissoluble life' (c. vii. 16).

The truth will become clearer if we go yet a step further. In men the 'spirit' is, as has been said, that by which they are capable of connexion with God. But in Christ, who did not cease to be the Son of God by becoming man, the 'spirit' is to be regarded as the seat of His Divine Personality in His human Nature. So far the πνεῦμα αἰώνιον included the limited πνεῦμα of the Lord's humanity. This πνεῦμα, having its own proper existence, was in perfect harmony with the πνεῦμα αἰώνιον. (Comp. ep. Barn. vii. 3 ὑπὲρ τῶν ἡμετέρων ἁμαρτιῶν ἔμελλεν τὸ σκεῦος τοῦ πνεύματος προσφέρειν θυσίαν.)

This 'eternal spirit' obtained complete sovereignty at the Resurrection (1 Cor. xv. 45); and it is probably by reference to this fact that the difficult passage 2 Cor. iii. 17 ff. is to be explained. See also 1 Pet. iii. 18.

Another more obvious thought lies in the phrase.

Other sacrifices were wrought by the hand, being outward acts of flesh, but this was wrought by that which is highest in man's nature whereby he holds fellowship with God, being a truly spiritual act. Chrysostom indicates this thought under another aspect : τὸ διὰ πνεύματος ἁγίου (so he reads) δηλοῖ ὅτι οὐ διὰ πυρὸς προσήνεκται οὐδὲ δι' ἄλλων τινῶν, though this is but a small part of the meaning. Comp. Euthymius : διά τινος πυρὸς ὡλοκαύτωσεν ἑαυτὸν τῷ θεῷ καὶ πατρὶ ἄμωμον καλλιέρημα.

For ἑαυτ. προσ. τῷ θεῷ, compare c. vii. 27 note, vv. 25, 28 (προσενεχθείς). See also c. xi. 4; John xvi. 2.

The epithet ἄμωμον describes Christ as a perfect victim. That which was required outwardly in the Levitical victims was satisfied absolutely by Christ.

The word ἄμωμος is used technically in this sense in the LXX. (e.g. Ex. xxix. 1 תָּמִים). Comp. Philo de agric. § 29 (i. 320 M.); de merc. mer. § 1 (ii. 265 M.) Δεῖ δὴ τὸν μέλλοντα θύειν σκέπτεσθαι μὴ εἰ τὸ ἱερεῖον ἄμωμον, ἀλλ' εἰ ἡ διάνοια ὁλόκληρος αὐτῷ καὶ παντελὴς καθέστηκε. The connexion in which it stands shews that it refers here to the conditions and issue of the Lord's earthly life.

καθαριεῖ…θεῷ ζῶντι] (shall) cleanse our (your) conscience from dead works to the end that we (ye) may serve a living God. Vulg. emundabit conscientiam vestram ab operibus mortuis ad serviendum Deo viventi. The action of the blood of Christ is not to work any outward change but to communicate a vital force. It removes the defilement and the defiling power of 'dead works,' works which are done apart from Him who is 'the life' (comp. c. vi. 1 note). These stain the conscience and communicate that pollution of death which outwardly 'the water of separation' was designed to remove. The Levitical ritual contemplated a death external to the man himself : here the effects of a death within him are taken away.

For καθαρίζειν compare Acts xv. 9; Eph. v. 26 ; Tit. ii. 14; 1 John i. 7, 9; c. x. 2; c. i. 3 (καθαρισμὸν ποιησάμενος).

Καθαρός as distinguished from ἅγιος marks what the object is itself ('clean' ceremonially or morally), while ἅγιος marks its destination.

τὴν συνείδησιν] Comp. v. 9 note.

Chrysostom says on 'dead works': καλῶς εἶπεν ἀπὸ νεκρῶν ἔργων, εἴ τις γὰρ ἥψατο τότε νεκροῦ ἐμιαίνετο· καὶ ἐνταῦθα εἴ τις ἅψαιτο νεκροῦ ἔργου

εἰς τὸ λατρεύειν θεῷ ζῶντι.　¹⁵ Καὶ διὰ τοῦτο διαθήκης
καινῆς μεσίτης ἐστίν, ὅπως θανάτου γενομένου εἰς ἀπολύτρωσιν τῶν ἐπὶ τῇ πρώτῃ διαθήκῃ παραβάσεων τὴν
ἐπαγγελίαν λάβωσιν οἱ κεκλημένοι τῆς αἰωνίου κληρο-

θ. ϛ.: τῷ θ. τῷ ϛ. D₂*: +καὶ ἀληθινῷ A me (1 Thess. i. 9).

μολύνεται διὰ τῆς συνειδήσεως, and
again τὰ παρ᾽ ἡμῖν καὶ ζῶντα καὶ ἀληθινά,
ἐκεῖνα δὲ τὰ παρὰ Ἰουδαίοις καὶ νεκρὰ καὶ
ψευδῆ.

εἰς τὸ λατρ. θ. ζ.] Purity is not the
end but the means of the new life.
The end of the restored fellowship is
energetic service to Him Who alone
lives and gives life. The thought of
performing certain actions is replaced
by that of fulfilling a personal relation.
This service is specifically the service of a sacred ministry of complete
surrender (λατρεύειν). Compare Apoc.
xxii. 3 οἱ δοῦλοι αὐτοῦ λατρεύσουσιν
αὐτῷ, and contrast 1 Thess. i. 9 δουλεύειν θ. ζ. καὶ ἀληθινῷ. Acts xx. 19
δουλεύων τῷ Κυρίῳ. Rom. xiv. 18 δουλεύων τῷ χριστῷ. xvi. 18 τῷ Κυρίῳ
ἡμῶν Χριστῷ οὐ δουλεύουσιν. Col. iii.
24 τῷ Κυρίῳ Χριστῷ δουλεύετε.

For θεὸς ζῶν see c. iii. 12 note.

(β) vv. 15—22. From the thought
of the efficacy of Christ's Blood as
the means through which He entered
into the Divine Presence and cleanses
the individual conscience the writer
of the Epistle goes on to shew that
through the shedding of His Blood
came the inauguration of a new Covenant. The idea of death gives validity
to the compact which it seals (15—
17); and the communication of the
blood of the victim to those with
whom God forms a covenant unites
them to Him with a power of life, a
principle which was recognised in the
ritual ordinances of the Mosaic system
(18—22).

15. καὶ διὰ τ....μεσ. ἐ.] And for
this reason, even that the Blood of
Christ purifies the soul with a view
to a divine service, He is mediator

of a new covenant... Vulg. Et ideo
novi testamenti mediator (O. L. arbiter) est. The transition from the
thought of the one all-efficacious
atonement to that of the corresponding covenant is natural. The new
internal and spiritual relation of man
to God established by Christ involved
of necessity a New Covenant. The
Blood —the Life— of Christ, which
was the source and support of the
life, was the seal of the Covenant.

The words διαθήκης μεσίτης go back
to the prophetic promise c. viii. 8,
which found its fulfilment in Christ.
The emphasis lies on the phrase new
covenant and specially upon the word
covenant. It is of interest to notice
the variation of emphasis in 2 Cor.
iii. 6 διακόνους καινῆς διαθήκης and
here διαθήκης καινῆς μεσίτης. For
διαθήκη compare c. vii. 22; vii. 6
note, and xii. 24; and for μεσίτης c.
viii. 6 note; xii. 24; Gal. iii. 19 f.;
1 Tim. ii. 5.

ὅπως θαν. γεν....τὴν ἐπαγγ. λάβ....]
that a death having taken place for
redemption from the transgressions
that were under the first covenant
they that have been called may receive... Vulg. ut morte intercedente
in redemptionem earum prævari-
cationum quæ erant... The Old Covenant had been proved incapable of
bringing men to perfection. God
therefore provided them with fresh
and more powerful help. At the same
time He opened to them a nobler
view of their end. In place of a material inheritance He shewed them an
eternal inheritance. And the aim of
the New Covenant was the attainment
of the spiritual realities shadowed

forth in the temporal blessings of Israel.

But the establishment of a New Covenant, a new and permanent relation between God and man, required as its preliminary condition the discharge of man's existing obligations. The sins which the Law had set in a clear light could not be ignored. The atonements provided for sin under the Law could not but be felt to be inadequate. They were limited in their application and so to speak arbitrary. Christ at last offered the sacrifice, perfect in efficacy and moral value, to which they pointed. This sacrifice was the characteristic basis of the New Covenant (c. viii. 12).

Thus the death of Christ appears under a twofold aspect. His Blood is the means of atonement and the ratification of the Covenant which followed upon it.

For γενέσθαι εἰς compare Mk. xiv. 4 εἰς τί...γέγονεν; and with different shades of meaning Lk. xiii. 19; Matt. xxi. 42 (LXX.); Rom. xi. 9 (LXX.); 1 Cor. xv. 45 (LXX.); Apoc. viii. 11; xvi. 19; Acts v. 36; 1 Thess. iii. 5; i. 5; 2 Cor. viii. 14; Gal. iii. 14; Eph. iv. 32. Γεν. πρός occurs 1 Pet. iv. 12.

The phrase εἰς ἀπολ. τῶν...παραβάσεων is remarkable : for redemption from the transgressions...from their consequences and their power. The genitive expresses in a wide sense the object on which the redemption is exercised ('redemption in the matter of the transgressions,' 'transgression-redemption'). So it is that elsewhere the genitive is used for that which is delivered : Rom. viii. 23 τὴν ἀπολύτρωσιν τοῦ σώματος. Eph. i. 14 εἰς ἀπολ. τῆς περιποιήσεως.

The transgressions are spoken of as 'the transgressions that were under the first covenant.' The phrase is general in its application. It includes all transgressions committed on the basis of Law, all transgressions against the revealed will of God made known as Law. Ἐπί expresses the condi-

tions, the accompanying circumstances, under which anything takes place, see v. 10.

In this connexion the covenant with Abraham (Acts iii. 25) does not come into consideration. It was of the nature of a universal promise. The 'first covenant' was that between God and the Jewish people represented by Moses: the 'new covenant' that between God and men represented by Christ.

When the necessary condition has been satisfied (θανάτου γενομένου εἰς ἀπ. τῶν...παραβάσεων) scope is given for the positive fulfilment of the Covenant, that they that have been called may receive in fact what had been promised before. Compare vi. 12 κληρονομούντων τὰς ἐπαγγ. vi. 15; x. 36; xi. 13, 39; Gal. iii. 14.

The blessing is no longer limited to a particular people. It is for all to whom the invitation has been sent (Acts ii. 39; comp. iii. 1).

The phrase οἱ κεκλημένοι, which occurs nowhere else in the epistles, is an echo of the Parables: Matt. xxii. 3, 4, 8; Luke xiv. 17, 24; comp. Apoc. xix. 9. The word κλητοί, though not very common, has a wide range (Rom., 1 Cor., Jude, Apoc.).

τὴν ἐπαγγ....τῆς αἰ. κληρ.] The position of the gen. dependent on τὴν ἐπ. is due to the fact that it is added as a further definition of the promise (comp. xii. 11 note). The sentence stands essentially complete without it : that they that have been called may receive the promise (comp. c. vi. 15). But the explanation is naturally suggested by the thought of the contrast of the Old and the New. Moses secured to the people an 'inheritance,' which was however only a figure of that which was prepared (comp. Ex. xxxii. 13).

16, 17. The mention of a 'new covenant' and of 'death' in close connexion suggests a fresh thought. The Death of Christ fulfilled two distinct purposes. It provided an

νομίας. ¹⁶ὅπου γὰρ διαθήκη, θάνατον ἀνάγκη φέρεσθαι
τοῦ διαθεμένου· ¹⁷διαθήκη γὰρ ἐπὶ νεκροῖς βεβαία, ἐπεὶ

atonement for past sins; and, besides
this, it provided an absolute ratification of the Covenant with which it
was connected.

The Death set man free : the Covenant gave him the support which he
required. The Death removed the
burden of the past : the Covenant
provided for the service of the future.

In any case a covenant is ratified
by the death of a representative
victim. But here Christ died in His
own Person ; and by thus dying He
gave absolute validity to the covenant
which He mediated : the preceding
thought of the atonement shews how
such a covenant was possible.

The Death of Christ was a chief
difficulty of the Hebrews, and therefore the writer presents it under different aspects in order to shew its
full significance in the Christian dispensation.

For a justification of the interpretation of the following verses see the
Additional Note.

16. ὅπου γάρ ... διαθεμένου] *For
where there is a covenant the death
of him that made it must needs be
presented.* Vulg. *Ubi enim testamentum mors necesse est intercedat tes-
tatoris.* The circumstances under
which the New Covenant was made,
however unlooked for in man's anticipation of the Christ (τοῦτο τὸ ταράσσον
αὐτοὺς τὸ τοῦ θανάτου τοῦ Χριστοῦ
Œcum.), are to deeper thought most
intelligible, for an unchangeable covenant implies death. It is not said that
he who makes the covenant 'must die,'
but that his death must be 'brought
forward,' 'presented,' 'introduced upon
the scene,' 'set in evidence,' so to speak.
This sense of φέρεσθαι appears to be
perfectly natural, and to be more
simple than the sense commonly attributed to the word, either 'to be
alleged' as a fact, or to be pleaded in
the course of an argument, or to be

'current' as a matter of common
notoriety.

He who makes the covenant (ὁ
διαθέμενος) is, for the purposes of the
covenant, identified with the victim
by whose representative death the
covenant is ordinarily ratified. In
the death of the victim his death is
presented symbolically.

In the case of the New Covenant
Christ in His Divine-human Person
represented God who reveals through
and in Him the unfailing greatness of
the divine love, and at the same time
He represented the complete self-
surrender of humanity. A covenant
so made could not fail. The weakness and instability of men had no
longer any place. The thought expressed by the representative victim
had become an eternal fact.

17. διαθήκη γάρ...διαθέμενος] *For
a covenant is sure where there hath
been death, since it doth not ever have
force when he that made it liveth.*
Vulg. *Testamentum enim in mortuis
confirmatum est ; alioquin nondum
valet dum vivit qui testatus est.* The
statement which has been made is
supported by an explanation which is
borrowed from ancient usage and
language. A solemn covenant was
made upon the basis of a sacrifice.
The death of the victim was supposed
to give validity to it. The idea which
is involved in the symbolic act is
intelligible and important. The unchangeableness of a covenant is
seen in the fact that he who has
made it has deprived himself of all
further power of movement in this
respect : while the ratification by
death is still incomplete, while the
victim, the representative of him who
makes it, still lives, that is, while he
who makes it still possesses the full
power of action and freedom to change,
the covenant is not of force.

The sense here given to the death

266   THE EPISTLE TO THE HEBREWS.   [IX. 18, 19]

⌈μή ποτε⌉ ἰσχύει ὅτε ζῇ ὁ ⌈διαθέμενος.⌉   ¹⁸ʲΟθεν οὐδὲ ἡ
πρώτη χωρὶς αἵματος ἐνκεκαίνισται· ¹⁹λαληθείσης γὰρ

17 μὴ τότε id. διαθέμενος ;

17 μή ποτε №ᶜA : μὴ τότε №*D₂* [the verss. are free].   18 ἡ πρ. : +διαθήκη D₂*.

of the victim appears more natural than to suppose that it indicates the penalty for the violation of the covenant.

For the sense of ἐπί (ἐπὶ νεκροῖς), as giving the accompanying conditions, see v. 10 note, and compare also Lev. xxi. 5 (LXX.); Eurip. *Ion*, 228 f.

The subjective negative may be explained on the principle that the reason alleged is regarded as a thought (John iii. 18) and not as a fact. The clause may be taken interrogatively (*for is it ever of force...?* John vii. 26); so Œcumenius : κατ᾽ ἐρώτησιν ἀνάγνωθι. Perhaps this best suits the rhetorical form of the passage.

If the reading μὴ τότε is adopted, and it has high claims on consideration, the rendering will necessarily be : *since hath it then force when...?*

18—22. The great, inaugurating, sacrifice of the Old Covenant embodied the same thought that death marks the immutability of the terms laid down (Ex. xxiv.); and yet more : this death also was employed to convey the thought of atonement, of life surrendered that it may be given back. The blood was sprinkled on the altar and on the people. Thus the law which was enacted for the yearly access of the High-priest to the Divine Presence (v. 7 οὐ χωρὶς αἵματος) was observed when the people entered into the Divine Covenant.

In relation to the use which is made of this thought, it is important to observe, that it is not said of the first covenant that it was inaugurated 'not without death' but 'not without blood.' By the use of the words 'not without blood' the writer of the Epistle suggests the two ideas of atonement and quickening by the

impartment of a new life which have been already connected with Christ's work (vv. 14, 15).

18. ὅθεν...ἐνκεκαίνισται] (Vulg. *dedicatum est) whence,* since every absolute, inviolable, covenant is based upon a death, and, further, since every covenant of God with man requires complete self-surrender on the part of man, *not even hath the first covenant,* though it failed in its issue, *been inaugurated without blood.*

The word ἐγκαινίζω occurs again in the N. T. in c. x. 20, note. It is used several times in the LXX. to render חִדֵּשׁ (*to renew, e.g.* 1 Sam. xi. 14) and חָנַךְ (*to dedicate, e.g.* 1 K. viii. 63). Compare 1 Macc. iv. 36, 54, 57 ; and τὰ ἐνκαίνια John x. 22.

19. λαληθείσης γάρ...] Vulg. *lecto enim omni mandato legis....* The ceremonies connected with the establishment of the Law-Covenant emphasise the ideas already seen to be involved in 'blood'; *for when every commandment had been spoken according to the Law by Moses...taking the blood....*The terms of the divine covenant were declared fully to the people (Ex. xxiv. 3) and they expressed their acceptance of them (*id.*). Then an altar was built 'and twelve pillars.' Burnt-offerings were offered and peace-offerings were sacrificed (*vv.* 4, 5). Half the blood was sprinkled upon the altar: half was sprinkled over the people (*vv.* 6, 8).

These sacrifices were offered by young men of the children of Israel, representatives of the fulness of the people's life (Ex. xxiv. 5). The ordinances of the Levitical priesthood were not yet given (Ex. xxviii.); though some form of priesthood still

πάσης ἐντολῆς κατὰ τὸν νόμον ὑπὸ Μωυσέως παντὶ τῷ
λαῷ, λαβὼν τὸ αἷμα τῶν μόσχων καὶ τῶν τράγων μετὰ
ὕδατος καὶ ἐρίου κοκκίνου καὶ ὑσσώπου αὐτό τε τὸ

19 π. ἐντ.: π. τῆς ἐντ. D₂*.   τὸν ν. ℵᶜACD₂*: om. τὸν ς ℵ*.   ὑπὸ M. :
om. ὑπὸ D₂*.   τῶν μ. καὶ τῶν τράγων ℵ*AC : τῶν τρ. καὶ τῶν μόσχων D₂: om.
καὶ τῶν τρ. ℵᶜ syrr : om. τῶν 2° ς.

remained (Ex. xix. 22). Compare Ex.
xix. 6.

In this connexion Philo speaks of
Moses as ἀρχιερεύς : Quis r. d. hær.
§ 38 (i. 498 M.) θαυμαστὴ μέντοι καὶ ἡ
τῶν θυσιῶν αἵματος ἴση διανομή, ἦν ὁ
ἀρχιερεὺς Μωϋσῆς φύσει διδασκάλῳ χρη-
σάμενος διένειμε.

It is of interest to notice that
'sprinkling of persons with blood' is
noticed in the O. T. only on one other
occasion : Ex. xxix. 21 (the consecration of Aaron).

The words according to the law
go with spoken. Every commandment
was spoken by Moses 'according to
the tenor of the Law' in which they
were included. The Law represented
the sum of the whole revelation made
to Moses. The separate fundamental
commandments which preceded the
conclusion of the covenant were
fashioned (so to speak) after its
scope.

The word λαλεῖν is used frequently
in the Epistle of divine communications: i. 1 f.; ii. 2 f.; iii. 5; iv. 8; v. 5;
vii. 14 ; xi. 18; xii. 25.

λ. τὸ αἷμα τῶν μ. καὶ τῶν τ....] taking
the blood of the calves and the goats...
Goats are not directly spoken of in
the Mosaic narrative (Ex. xxiv. 5) and
Philo notices the fact : Non autem
agni neque hædi (offeruntur) ; quia
hæ bestiæ vitulo debiliores sunt ; sacrificium vero ex fortioribus videtur
(velle) facere (Quæst. in Ex. l. c.).

The addition is the more remarkable
because the offering of a goat (i.e.
τράγος, see Dillmann on Lev. i. 10) is
never prescribed in the Law except
as a sin-offering ; while the sacrifices
in Ex. xxiv. are described as 'burnt-

offerings' and 'peace-offerings.' Yet
see Num. vii. 17, 23, 29, 35, &c.

At the same time the use of the
definite article (τῶν μ. καὶ τῶν τρ.)
points distinctly to the sacrifices
offered at the inauguration of the
Law.

The explanation of the difficulty is
probably to be found in the fact that
these sacrifices were not made according to the Mosaic ritual. They were
initiatory sacrifices offered not by
priests but by the 'young men,'
representing the people, and so partook of the patriarchal type. Under
this aspect it is noticeable that in the
record of the original covenant-sacrifice of Abraham 'a heifer of three
years old and a she goat of three
years old' are specially mentioned
(Gen. xv. 9).

τὸ αἷμα] He used half the blood for
the sprinkling : Ex. xxiv. 6.

μετὰ ὕδ....καὶ ὑσσ.] These details
are not given in Exodus. Water is
mentioned in connexion with blood
Lev. xiv. 5 f. (comp. Num. xix. 9) in
the purification of the leper, when
also a sprinkler of 'cedar wood and
scarlet and hyssop' was used (Lev.
xiv. 4: comp. Num. xix. 18).

Compare Philo de vict. offer. § 3,
ii. 252 f. Barn. Ep. c. 8.

For κόκκινος compare Clem. 1 Cor.
c. 12 (in reference to Josh. ii. 18 τὸ
σπαρτίον τὸ κόκκινον), πρόδηλον ποιοῦντες ὅτι διὰ τοῦ αἵματος τοῦ κυρίου
λύτρωσις ἔσται....See also Barn. Ep. c.
7. The significance of blood and water
is marked 1 John v. 6 ; John xix. 34.

αὐτό τε τὸ βιβλ.] i.e. the Book of
the Covenant (Ex. xxiv. 7). This detail
also is an addition to the Mosaic

βιβλίον καὶ πάντα τὸν λαὸν ἐράντισεν, ²⁰λέγων Τοῦτο
τὸ αῖΜα τῆς Διαθήκης ῆς ἐνετείλατο πρὸς ὙΜᾶϲ ὁ θεόϲ· ²¹καὶ τὴν
σκηνὴν δὲ καὶ πάντα τὰ σκεύη τῆς λειτουργίας τῷ αἵματι
ὁμοίως ἐράντισεν. ²²καὶ σχεδὸν ἐν αἵματι πάντα καθα-

20 ἐνετείλατο : διέθετο C (Ex. xxiv. 8 LXX.).

narrative. Though 'the Book' was
the record of the words of God it was
outwardly the work of man, and so
required the application of the purifying, vivifying, blood. Thus in a
figure the 'letter' received a power
of life.

πάντα τὸν λαόν] all the people : not
of course literally ('every individual
of the people') but representatively.
All were present, and the act of
sprinkling was directed to all.

For ἐράντισεν see v. 13 note.

20. τοῦτο τὸ αῖμα τ. δ.] The words
in Ex. xxiv. 8 are Ἰδοὺ (so Hebr.)
τὸ αῖμα τῆς διαθήκης ῆς διέθετο Κύριος
πρὸς ὑμᾶς περὶ πάντων τῶν λόγων τούτων. It is possible that the corresponding phrase at the institution of
the New Covenant (Matt. xxvi. 28)
may have influenced the quotation.

The force of the words is : 'This
Blood shed, offered, sprinkled upon
you, shews the validity and the power
of the purpose of God.' So Primasius :
ac si diceret : Hæc est confirmatio
hujus testamenti quod mandavit ad
vos Deus.

ἐνετ. πρὸς ὑμᾶς] commanded to youward,...Vulg. mandavit ad vos, to be
brought to you ; you were the people
to whom the Lord looked in the commandments which He gave me. The
full construction appears in Ecclus.
xlv. 3 ἐνετείλατο αὐτῷ [Μωυσεῖ] πρὸς
λαὸν αὐτοῦ. Yet comp. Acts iii. 25
διαθ. ῆς ὁ θεὸς διέθετο πρὸς τοὺς πατέρας....

The sprinkling of the Tabernacle
and its vessels took place at a later
time. They were not yet made when
the Sacrifice of the Covenant was
offered. Moreover it is not recorded
in the Pentateuch that the Tabernacle

was sprinkled with blood, though it
'and all that was therein' was anointed
with oil (Ex. xl. 9; comp. Philo, Vit.
Mos. iii. § 18; ii. 158 M.). But Josephus,
like the writer of the Epistle, regards
the Tabernacle as having been consecrated with blood : τήν τε σκηνήν, καὶ
τὰ περὶ αὐτὴν σκεύη ἐλαίῳ τε προθυ-
μιωμένῳ καθὼς εῖπον καὶ τῷ αἵματι τῶν
ταύρων καὶ κριῶν σφαγέντων καθ᾽ ἑκάστην ἡμέραν ἑνὸς κατὰ γένος [ἐθεράπευε]
(Antt. iii. 8, 6).

21. καί...δέ...] And the tabernacle
also....Vulg. Etiam (tabernaculum).
The combination is found here only
in the Epistle. It occurs in the Epistles of St Paul, Rom. xi. 23 κἀκεῖνοι
δέ; 1 Tim. iii. 10 καὶ οῦτοι δέ ; 2 Tim.
iii. 12 καὶ πάντες δέ. Comp. 1 John i.
3 note.

τῷ αἵματι] with the blood. The definite form (contrast v. 22 ἐν αἵματι,
xii. 24 αἵματι ῥαντισμοῦ) is used to
bring out the thought that this was
not the ordinary blood of purification,
but the blood of the covenant, the
blood of inauguration.

22. καὶ σχ. ἐν αῖμ. π.] The position
of σχεδόν, separated from πάντα by ἐν
αἵματι, shews that it qualifies the whole
of the following clause : And, I may
almost say, it is in blood all things...
The position of ἐν αῖμ. is significant.
Blood was the characteristic mean for
cleansing, though fire and water were
also used. It is the power of a pure
life which purifies. Under this aspect
the Blood becomes, as it were, the
enveloping medium in which (ἐν), and
not simply the means or instrument
through or by which, the complete
purification is effected.

The main reference is naturally to
the service of the Day of Atonement.

THE EPISTLE TO THE HEBREWS.

ῥίζεται κατὰ τὸν νόμον, καὶ χωρὶς αἱματεκχυσίας οὐ

The word σχεδόν occurs again in the N.T. in Acts xiii. 44; xix. 26. It is found in the LXX. only in 2 Macc. v. 2.

πάντα] all things, things and men alike. The reference is probably to the dress of the priests, the attendants of the Temple, the offerers of sacrifice.

κατὰ τὸν νόμον] according to the law which was itself thus inaugurated by blood.

καὶ χωρὶς αἱματ. οὐ γ. ἄφ.] and apart from outpouring of blood there cometh no remission. The former statement was general (σχεδόν): this is universal (yet there is an exception Lev. v. 11).

The principle which is here affirmed belongs to the Law; and finds expression in the Pentateuch (Lev. xvii. 11). It occurs in identical terms in a later legal maxim (אֵין כַּפָּרָה אֶלָּא בְּדָם).

The 'outpouring' of blood may be understood in two ways; either of the actual slaughter of the victim, or of the pouring out of the blood upon the altar. Neither idea is in itself complete. The provision of the blood and the application of the blood are both necessary. Maimonides, in speaking of the Passover, lays down that 'the sprinkling of the blood is the main point (עִיקָּר) in sacrifice' (de Sacr. i. 2, § 6).

The word αἱματεκχυσία, Vulg. sanguinis effusio (fusio), is found elsewhere only in patristic writings.

ἄφεσις] The absolute use of ἄφεσις is remarkable. Elsewhere in the N. T., except Luke iv. 18 (from LXX.), the word is always used with a gen. (usually ἁμαρτιῶν). The absence of further definition here (contrast x. 18) leaves it with the broad sense of 'release,' 'deliverance,' not so much from special sins as from the bondage of which wrong-doing is a result. In this sense 'cleansing' is to a certain degree opposed to 'release.' The one marks the removal of the stain, the other the enabling for action.

At the same time the choice of γίνεται, in place of ἐστίν, presents the release as the issue of the operation of a divine law. Comp. vii. 12, 18; xi. 6.

Chrysostom in comparing the use of Blood under the Old and New Covenants writes of Christ and His disciples: ποῦ τοίνυν τὸ βιβλίον ἐ- κάθηρε; τὰς διανοίας αὐτῶν· αὐτοὶ γὰρ ἦσαν βιβλία τῆς καινῆς διαθήκης. ποῦ δὲ τὰ σκεύη τῆς λειτουργίας; αὐτοί εἰσι· ποῦ δὲ ἡ σκηνή; αὐτοί εἰσι πάλιν· ἐνοι- κήσω γὰρ ἐν αὐτοῖς καὶ ἐμπεριπατήσω, φησί.

23—28. The writer of the Epistle goes back now to the consideration of the fulfilment of the work of Christ. The exposition of the full meaning of 'blood' as the means of atonement and ratification came in as a necessary parenthesis. The last illustration— the use of the blood in cleansing all human means of approach to God under the Old Covenant—supplies the transition to the thought of Christ's cleansing the heavenly sanctuary 'through His own Blood' (v. 23); so He entered once for all into heaven itself to fulfil His atoning work (24— 26). And that single entrance suggests the thought of a corresponding return (27 f.).

The paragraph offers an additional feature in the preeminence of the new order over the old. The sacrifice on which it rests is better (12 f.): the covenant in which it is embodied is better (15—22): the service also—one sovereign and all-sufficing act—is better (23—28).

(c) vv. 23—28. The truths taught by Christ's Entrance into the Presence of God.

The Blood of Christ by which the New Covenant was inaugurated was available also for the cleansing of the heavenly archetype of the earthly sanctuary (23). For Christ has entered once for all into the Presence

γίνεται ἄφεσις. ²³ Ἀνάγκη οὖν τὰ μὲν ὑποδείγ-

23 (ἀνάγκη)...καθαρίζεσθαι : (ἀνάγκη)...καθαρίζεται D₂* me.

of God for us, having overcome sin for ever (24—26); and men now await the Return of the great High-priest to announce the accomplishment of His work (27, 28).

²³ *It was necessary therefore that the copies of the things in the heavens should be cleansed with these, but the heavenly things themselves with better sacrifices than these.* ²⁴ *For Christ entered not into a Holy place made with hands, like to the pattern of the true, but into the heaven itself, now to appear openly before the face of God on our behalf;* ²⁵ *nor yet did He enter in order that He may often offer Himself, as the High-priest entereth into the Holy place year by year with blood not his own;* ²⁶ *since in that case He must often have suffered since the foundation of the world; but now once for all, at the close of the ages, hath He been manifested to disannul sin by the sacrifice of Himself.* ²⁷ *And inasmuch as it is appointed for men once to die, and after this* cometh *judgment;* ²⁸ *even so Christ also, having been once offered to carry the sins of many, shall appear a second time, apart from sin, to them that wait for Him, unto salvation.*

23. This verse serves for the return from the line of thought in *vv.* 13—22 to that indicated generally in *vv.* 11, 12. The consideration of the use of blood for cleansing and for remission under the Law throws light upon the significance of Christ's Blood in connexion with His heavenly ministry. That which was done in symbol on earth required to be done truly in the spiritual order. In regard to the individual conscience, the Blood of Christ has absolute eternal validity (*v.* 14): in regard to the scene—if we may so speak—of the future service of the Church, the Living Christ fulfils

that which was represented by the blood of victims.

ἀνάγκη οὖν...] *It was necessary therefore,* since blood is the means of purification for all that is connected with man's service of God, that the typical sanctuary, *the copies of the things in the heavens, should be cleansed with these, but the heavenly things themselves with better sacrifices than these.* The fact that such a mode of purifying by blood was enjoined for the material instruments of worship carried with it the inevitable consequence that some analogous and therefore some nobler purification should be provided for the divine archetypes.

In an external system the purification might be external, but in the spiritual order it was requisite that the purification should be of corresponding efficacy, spiritual and not material only.

The whole structure of the sentence requires that 'cleansed' should be supplied in the second clause from the first, and not any more general term as 'inaugurated.' In what sense then can it be said that 'the heavenly things' needed cleansing?

The necessity for the purification of the earthly sanctuary and its vessels came from the fact that they were to be used by man and shared in his impurity (comp. Lev. xvi. 16).

Agreeably with this view it may be said that even 'heavenly things,' so far as they embody the conditions of man's future life, contracted by the Fall something which required cleansing (comp. 1 Tim. iv. 4 f. καλόν, ἁγιάζεται). Man is, according to the revelation in Scripture, so bound up with the whole finite order that the consequences of his actions extend through creation in some way which we are unable to define (compare Gen. iii.

ματα τῶν ἐν τοῖς οὐρανοῖς τούτοις καθαρίζεσθαι, αὐτὰ
δὲ τὰ ἐπουράνια κρείττοσι θυσίαις παρὰ ταύτας. ²⁴οὐ
γὰρ εἰς χειροποίητα εἰσῆλθεν ἄγια Χριστός, ἀντίτυπα
τῶν ἀληθινῶν, ἀλλ᾽ εἰς αὐτὸν τὸν οὐρανόν, νῦν ἐμφανι-

ταύτας: ταύτης D₂*.　　24 εἰσ. ἄγια אA : ἄγια εἰσ. CD₂.　　Χριστός: ὁ χρ. ς.

17 ff.; Is. xxiv. 5, 6; Jer. xxiii. 10;
Rom. viii. 18 ff.). And conversely
the effect of Christ's work extends
throughout creation with reconcil-
ing, harmonising power: Eph. i. 10;
Col. i. 20.

ἀνάγκη] It was necessary. The reference is definite, to the purification of
the earthly sanctuary on the one hand
by the High-priest, and of the heavenly
sanctuary by Christ. For ἀνάγκη see
v. 16; Matt. xviii. 7; and for ὑποδείγ-
ματα (Vulg. exemplaria) c. viii. 5 note.

τούτοις καθ.] with these ceremonial
observances, that is, the blood of bulls
and goats, applied according to the
directions of the Law. The Mosaic
system was external: the means of
purification were external also.

αὐτὰ τὰ ἐπουράνια] This phrase, as
distinguished from τὰ ἐν τοῖς οὐρανοῖς,
expresses those things, answering to
the sanctuary with all its furniture,
which have their proper sphere in the
heavenly order (comp. c. iii. 1; viii. 5
notes; John iii. 12), and not simply
those things which are there.

κρείττοσι θυσίαις] The plural is used
for the expression of the general idea
(κρ. θ. παρὰ ταύτας). And in point of
fact the single sacrifice of Christ fulfilled perfectly the ideas presented by
the different forms of the Levitical
sacrifices, the sacrifices of service
(burnt-offering and peace-offering), and
the sacrifices for atonement (sin-offering and trespass-offering).

24—26. The writer shews that
Christ has satisfied the requirement
which he has described in v. 23. He
has entered heaven itself to make ready
a place for us (v. 24); and that not by
providing for the accomplishment of a

recurrent atonement (vv. 25, 26 a);
but by vanquishing sin for ever (26 b).

24. οὐ γὰρ εἰς χειρ.] The clause
justifies the reference to the purification of the heavenly things. If we
consider what was needed for the due
preparation of that spiritual Tabernacle for man's service and God's
revelation of Himself we shall feel the
greatness of the requirements. For
it was no Holy place made by hands
Christ entered, and entered once for
all, but heaven itself. He has fulfilled therefore, necessarily fulfilled,
all those requirements to which the
symbols pointed.

The epithet χειροποίητα stands emphatically first: 'for it was not into
a hand-made sanctuary Christ entered.'

The title Χριστός has become a
proper name: v. 11; c. iii. 6. It
stands emphatically at the end of the
sentence as χειροποίητα at the beginning.

ἀντίτυπα τῶν ἀλ.] like to the pattern
(τύπος c. viii. 5) of the true....Vulg.
exemplaria verorum, O.L. exempla-
rium veritatis (allegoria verorum).

In the two passages in which the
word ἀντίτυπον is used in the N.T. the
sense corresponds with the two fundamentally different ideas of τύπος. The
τύπος may be the archetype (comp.
Acts vii. 44) of which the ἀντίτυπον is
the provisional copy, as here; or the
τύπος may be the provisional ad-
umbration (comp. Acts vii. 43) of
that which the ἀντίτυπον more completely expresses. So the water of
baptism answered as ἀντίτυπον to the
water of the flood which bore in safety
the tenants of the ark (1 Pet. iii. 21).

σθῆναι τῷ προσώπῳ τοῦ θεοῦ ὑπὲρ ἡμῶν· ²⁵ οὐδ᾽ ἵνα

ἡμῶν: ὑμῶν C.

Comp. *Const. Apost.* v. 14, 4 παραδοὺς τὰ ἀντίτυπα μυστήρια τοῦ τιμίου σώματος καὶ αἵματος...vi. 30, 1 τὴν ἀντίτυπον τοῦ βασιλείου σώματος Χριστοῦ δεκτὴν εὐχαριστίαν προσφέρετε....2 Clem. c. xiv. and Bp Lightfoot's Note. εἰς αὐτὸν τὸν οὐρ.] The sing. (οὐρανός) occurs again xi. 12; xii. 26. The plural marks the whole heavenly order: the singular that which we conceive of as locally definite. 'The heaven itself,' 'the very heaven,' is regarded as the absolute truth which the Holy of Holies symbolised, 'quo nihil ulterius.'

νῦν ἐμφανισθ. τῷ προσ. τ. θ.] *now to appear openly before the face of God.* Vulg. *ut appareat nunc vultui Dei.* (The Old Latin rendering *modo apparuit personæ Dei* implies a reading ἐνεφανίσθη.) The open evident appearance of Christ before the face of God is contrasted with the appearance of the High-priest in the dark sanctuary veiled by the cloud of incense (Lev. xvi. 12 f.).

So too the 'face of God' suggests the idea of a vision direct and absolute, not like that of 'the glory of the Lord' (Ex. xl. 34 ff.), or even that granted to Moses (Ex. xxxiii. 18 ff.).

The word ἐμφανίζεσθαι (Matt. xxvii. 53; comp. Rom. x. 20), as distinguished in such a connexion from φανεροῦσθαι (2 Cor. v. 11 f.), conveys the thought of that being made a clear object of sight, which under ordinary circumstances is not so (comp. Wisd. i. 2; xvi. 21; xvii. 4 φάσματα ἐνεφανίζετο; John xiv. 21 f.). Ἐμφανής is the general opposite to 'invisible,' as φανερός is to 'indistinct.' In Christ humanity becomes the object of the regard of God. In the glorified Son the words used at critical revelations during His earthly work find absolute fulfilment: ἐν σοὶ εὐδόκησα (Lk. iii. 22; Matt. xvii. 5 : [xii. 18]).

The phrase 'the face of God (of the Father)' occurs in the N. T. only Matt. xviii. 10; Apoc. xxii. 4; and in quotations from the LXX.: Acts ii. 28; 1 Pet. iii. 12; in addition to the occurrence of the phrase πρὸ προσώπου κυρίου (Matt. xi. 10 &c.). In the O. T. the thought of 'the face' (פָּנִים) of God occupies an important place, as expressing the revelation of His Presence (Ex. xxxiii. 14; Deut. iv. 37, R. V.); and that either in judgment (Ps. xxi. 10 Hebr.); or, as the defence (Ps. xxxi. 20) and crowning joy of the faithful (Ps. iv. 7; xvii. 15). The significance of the phrase is seen specially in the priestly blessing : Num. vi. 25 ; comp. Ps. iv. 6.

In this connexion it appears strange at first that Christ should be said to have entered the heavenly sanctuary 'to appear openly' before the face of God and not to look on the face of God : that he should be described as the object of the vision of God and not that God should be spoken of as seen perfectly by Him. The explanation of the form of thought seems to lie in this, that everything finally must be referred to God: that which bears His regard is accepted by Him. Comp. Gal. iv. 9 γνόντες θεὸν μᾶλλον δὲ γνωσθέντες ὑπὸ θεοῦ : 1 Cor. xiii. 12 τότε ἐπιγνώσομαι καθὼς καὶ ἐπεγνώσθην : 1 Cor. viii. 2, 3 εἴ τις ἀγαπᾷ τὸν θεὸν, οὗτος ἔγνωσται ὑπ᾽ αὐτοῦ.

Nor must we limit the conception of the appearance of Christ before the face of God to one part of His work. It is commonly regarded only as the effective manifestation of His redeeming Passion (e.g. apparet vultui, id est præsentiæ et benevolentiæ Dei Patris, intercedens apud eum pro nobis ostendendo cicatrices vulnerum quæ pro nostra redemptione pertulit. Herv.); but it is necessary to include in it also the thought of the revelation of

πολλάκις προσφέρῃ ἑαυτόν, ὥσπερ ὁ ἀρχιερεὺς εἰσέρχεται εἰς τὰ ἅγια κατ᾽ ἐνιαυτὸν ἐν αἵματι ἀλλοτρίῳ,

25 τὰ ἅγια: +τῶν ἁγίων ℵ° the (æg).

humanity consummated by the fulfilment of the will of God (x. 9 ff.). The
'appearance' of Christ alone is, to our
conception, the adequate presentment
of the whole work of the Son to the
Father (comp. c. vii. 25 note).

There is another peculiarity in the
form of expression which requires to
be noticed, the combination of νῦν
with the *aor.* ἐμφανισθῆναι. This
combination appears to affirm two
complementary truths and to exclude
two opposite errors. The manifestation of Christ, in whom humanity is
shewn in its perfect ideal before the
face of God, is 'one act at once'
(ἐμφανισθῆναι); and still for us who
work in time it is in the case of each
believer a present act (νῦν). There is,
to look at the subject from the opposite side, no succession in the fulfilment of His work ; and, on the other
hand, it cannot in any sense grow old.

Such epexegetical infinitives as
ἐμφανισθῆναι are generally in the aorist
as expressing the abstract thought
(*v.* 9; Matt. xi. 7 ; xx. 28; Luke i. 17);
but the present is also used when the
idea of continuance or repetition predominates: John iv. 15; Lu. viii. 8 ;
Mk. iii. 14; vii. 4; 1 Cor. i. 17. Both
tenses are combined 1 Cor. x. 7.

The manifestation of Christ before
God is 'on our behalf' (ὑπὲρ ἡμῶν).
In Him humanity obtains its true
harmony with God, and in Him it
can bear the full light of God. He
can be therefore, in virtue of His
perfect manhood, our Advocate (1
John ii. 2 Ἰησοῦν Χριστὸν δίκαιον).
Νῦν γὰρ πρῶτον, as Theodoret says,
εἰς τὸν οὐρανὸν φύσις ἀνελήλυθεν ἀνθρω-
πεία ; and each Christian *in Christ*,
as well as *through Him*, has access to
God: Eph. iii. 12 (ἐν ᾧ ἔχομεν τὴν...
προσαγωγήν). Comp. c. vii. 25.

25. The writer of the Epistle goes

on to meet another difficulty of his
Jewish readers while he unfolds the
absolute uniqueness of Christ's Death.
They found it hard to understand
how Christ should die, and how
one death could have never-ending
virtue. It is shewn from the very
nature of the case that He could only
die once, and that by this Death He
satisfied completely the wants of
humanity.

οὐδ᾽ ἵνα...] *Nor yet* did He enter
(εἰσῆλθεν) *in order that He may again
offer Himself,* and so enter afresh
as the High-priest from time to time.
The main idea of the writer seems to
be : 'Christ did not enter in order to
secure an access to God which might
be available on repeated occasions.'
Then for such a phrase as 'in order
to repeat His entrance' he substitutes 'in order to offer Himself,' and
thus by bringing into preeminence the
preliminary condition of entrance he
shews the impossibility of repetition.

πολλάκις] The parallel is between
Christ's offering and entrance and the
High-priest's offering and entrance as
a whole repeated year by year. The
idea that the parallel is between
Christ's work and the repeated entrances of the High-priest into the
Holy of Holies on each day of Atonement, which involved the two sacrifices of the bullock and goat, is against
the whole form of the argument in
the Epistle. The ceremony of the
Day of Atonement is treated as one
great act. The thought of the High-
priest's offering for himself is necessarily excluded in the case of Christ
(vii. 27); but this consideration does
not come into account here.

προσφέρῃ ἑαυτόν] Two different interpretations of this offering have
been proposed. It has been supposed
to correspond with the bringing of

²⁶ἐπεὶ ἔδει αὐτὸν πολλάκις παθεῖν ἀπὸ καταβολῆς κόσμου·
νυνὶ δὲ ἅπαξ ἐπὶ συντελείᾳ τῶν αἰώνων εἰς ἀθέτησιν τῆς

26 πολλάκις: πολλά D₂*.　　παθεῖν: ἀποθανεῖν the (æg).　　νυνὶ ℵAC: νῦν ς D₂.

the blood into the Holy of Holies, and again with the offering of the victim upon the altar. The general usage of the writer, apart from other considerations, is decisive in favour of the second view. It is unreasonable to give a different sense to the words from that which they bear in *v.* 14 ἑαυτὸν προσήνεγκεν ἄμωμον τῷ θεῷ (comp. *v.* 28), where the reference is to the Passion of Christ. See also xi. 17; vii. 27 *v. l.*; viii. 3 note.

It was only by the offering upon the Cross that the Blood 'through which' the divine High-priest entered into the heavenly sanctuary was made available. This sense of the phrase is confirmed by the words which follow, where προσενεχθείς stands parallel to ἀποθανεῖν. Compare also c. x. 10 διὰ τῆς προσφορᾶς τοῦ σώματος Ἰησοῦ Χριστοῦ, which can only refer to the offering on the Cross.

The contrast of tenses in προσφέρῃ here and προσενέγκῃ c. viii. 3 is clearly marked.

ὥσπερ...] An annually repeated sacrifice was the necessary means for obtaining the atoning blood in virtue of which the Levitical High-priest entered the Sanctuary year by year.

ἐν αἵματι ἀλλοτρίῳ] The use of different prepositions in this connexion will repay study: *v.* 7 οὐ χωρὶς αἵματος, *v.* 12 δι᾽ αἵματος. For the use of ἐν compare *v.* 22 ἐν αἵματι καθ.: x. 19 ἐν τῷ αἵμ. Ἰησοῦ : xiii. 20 ἐν αἵμ. διαθήκης αἰωνίου: and in other Books: Rom. iii. 25 ὃν προέθ. ἱλαστ...ἐν τῷ αἵμ.: v. 9 δικαιωθέντες ἐν τῷ αἵμ.: Eph. ii. 13 ἐγενήθητε ἐγγὺς ἐν τῷ αἵμ. τοῦ χρ. (i. 7 ἐν ᾧ...διὰ τοῦ αἵματος): Apoc. i. 5 λύσαντι...ἐν τῷ αἵμ.: v. 9 ἠγόρασας...ἐν τῷ αἵμ.: vii. 14 ἐλεύκαναν...ἐν τῷ αἵμ.

The High-priest was, as it were, surrounded, enveloped, in the life sacrificed and symbolically communi-

cated. Christ Himself living through death came before God.

26. If the one offering of Christ is (as has been shewn from its nature) sufficient to atone for the sins of the whole world, then it is evident that its efficacy reaches through all time past and future. If it had not been sufficient, then it must have been repeated. It is assumed that it is God's will that complete atonement should be made for sin; and if He had willed that this should be made in detail and by successive acts, occasion must have arisen in earlier ages for Christ's sufferings, a thought in itself inconceivable. The virtue of Christ's work for the past in the eternal counsel of God is taken for granted.

ἐπεί] Vulg. *alioquin, since in that case, else.* See *v.* 17, c. x. 2; Rom. iii. 6; 1 Cor. v. 10, &c.

ἔδει] For the force of δεῖ see c. ii. 1; and for the absence of ἄν 1 Cor. v. 10 ἐπεὶ ὠφείλετε. Wine·, pp. 353 f.

παθεῖν] See c. xiii. 12 note; ii. 9. The word is not used in the Epistles of St Paul for the Death ('the Passion') of Christ. Comp. Acts i. 3; (iii. 18); xvii. 3.

ἀπὸ καταβολῆς κόσμου] Vulg. *ab origine mundi.* Compare c. iv. 3 note. A prospect is opened beyond the beginning of the Mosaic system. The divine counsel had a universal scope.

νυνὶ δέ] but now, as things actually are, *once for all, at the close of the ages, hath He been manifested to disannul* (set at naught) *sin by the sacrifice of Himself,* Vulg. *nunc autem semel in consummatione sæculorum ad destitutionem peccati per hostiam suam apparuit.* Each element in this sentence brings out some contrast between the work of Christ and that

ἁμαρτίας διὰ τῆς θυσίας αὐτοῦ πεφανέρωται.   ²⁷ καὶ καθ'

τῆς ἀμ. אA ægg : om. τῆς C : ἁμαρτιῶν D₂*.

of the Levitical High-priests. Their sacrifices were repeated year by year during a long period of preparation : His sacrifice was offered once for all at the close of the succession of ages. They by their action called sins to mind (c. x. 3): He annulled sin. They provided typical atonement through the blood of victims : He provided an absolute atonement by the sacrifice of Himself. With them the most impressive fact was the entrance into the darkness in which the Divine Presence was shrouded : with Him the manifestation on earth, still realised as an abiding reality, brought the Divine Presence near to men.

Generally it is made plain that Christ accomplished all that the Levitical Service pointed to.

ἅπαξ] The absolute oneness of Christ's offering has been touched upon before, v. 12 ; c. vii. 27. In proportion as this truth was felt, the weakness of the Levitical offerings, shewn by their repetition, became evident.

It is assumed that the repetition of Christ's suffering in the future is inconceivable.

ἐπὶ συντελείᾳ τῶν αἰ.] at the close of the ages, of a long and complex course of finite development. The exact phrase is not found elsewhere in the N.T.

Compare Matt. xiii. 39 συντέλεια αἰῶνος : vv. 40, 49 ἐν τῇ συντ. τοῦ αἰῶνος : xxiv. 3 ἡ σὴ παρουσία καὶ συντ. τοῦ αἰ.: xxviii. 20 ἕως τῆς συντ. τοῦ αἰ. For ἐπὶ (as distinguished from ἐν) see vv. 10, 15 notes ; Phil. i. 3.

Similar phrases occur in the Greek translations of Daniel : ix. 7 συντ. καιρῶν ; xii. 13 συντ. ἡμερῶν.

Ἐπὶ συντελείᾳ τῶν αἰώνων has a somewhat different meaning from ἐπ' ἐσχάτου τῶν ἡμ. τούτων (c. i. 2). This latter phrase describes the last period of 'the present age' (see note) ; while

ἐπὶ συντελείᾳ τῶν αἰ. marks a point of termination of a series (so to speak) of preparatory ages. The Death of the Lord, including His Resurrection and Ascension, is essentially the beginning of a new development in the life of man and in the life of the world. It was needful, as we speak, that the 'natural' development of man should have had fullest scope before Christ came.

Διὰ τί ἐπὶ συντελείᾳ τῶν αἰώνων; Chrysostom asks, and answers μετὰ τὰ πολλὰ ἁμαρτήματα· εἰ μὲν οὖν παρὰ τὴν ἀρχὴν ἐγένοντο (leg. ἐγένετο) εἶτα οὐδεὶς ἐπίστευσεν, ἦν ἂν τὸ τῆς οἰκονομίας ἀνόνητον.

The word συντέλεια occurs in the N.T. only in the passages which have been quoted. It occurs frequently in the LXX. A characteristic use is found in Ex. xxiii. 16 ἑορτὴ συντελείας ('of ingathering'). As distinguished from τέλος, the end as one definite fact, συντέλεια expresses a consummation, an end involving many parts. Compare συντελεῖν Luke iv. 2 ; Acts xxi. 27 ; c. viii. 8 ; Luke iv. 13.

The plural αἰῶνες occurs again in the Epistle ; xiii. 8, 21 ; and, in a different connexion, i. 2 (note) ; xi. 3.

In each case it preserves its full meaning. The whole discipline and growth of creation in time is made up of manifold periods of discipline, each having its proper unity and completeness. Per sæcula debemus intellegere omnia quæ facta sunt in tempore (Primas. ad c. i. 2).

εἰς ἀθέτησιν τῆς ἁμαρτ.] This thought goes beyond 'the redemption from transgressions' (v. 15). It is literally 'for the disannulling of sin' (vii. 18 ἀθέτησις προαγ. ἐντ.). Sin is vanquished, shewn in its weakness, 'set at naught' (Mk. vii. 9 ; Gal. iii. 15).

The comment of Theodoret deserves notice : παντελῶς τῆς ἁμαρτίας κατέ-

ὅσον ἀπόκειται τοῖς ἀνθρώποις ἅπαξ ἀποθανεῖν, μετὰ δὲ

λῦσε τὴν ἰσχὺν ἀθανασίαν ἡμῖν ὑποσχό-
μενος· ἐνοχλεῖν γὰρ αὕτη τοῖς ἀθανάτοις
οὐ δύναται σώμασι.

The use of the singular τῆς ἁμαρτίας
brings out this general, abstract conception (comp. x. 18 προσφορὰ περὶ
ἁμαρτίας). Elsewhere in the Epistle
the work of Christ is regarded in its
action on the many actual sins in
which sin shews itself. Comp. p. 32.
In this connexion different phrases
are used which present different aspects of its efficacy.

[The Son] sat down on the right
hand of the Majesty καθαρισμὸν τῶν
ἁμαρτιῶν ποιησάμενος (i. 3). He is a
merciful and faithful High-priest εἰς
τὸ ἱλάσκεσθαι τὰς ἁμαρτίας τοῦ λαοῦ
(ii. 17). (Compare ix. 15 ἀπολύτρωσιν τῶν ἐπὶ τῇ πρώτῃ διαθήκῃ παραβάσεων.)

It is further said that the 'blood of
bulls and goats is unable ἀφαιρεῖν
ἁμαρτίας (x. 4),' and that the Levitical
sacrifices cannot περιελεῖν ἁμαρτίας
(x. 11); where it is implied that the
Blood and Sacrifice of Christ have
this efficacy.

So sins are presented as a defilement which clings to man, a force
which separates him from God, a
burden which he bears, a robe of
custom in which he is arrayed.

διὰ τῆς θυσίας αὐτοῦ] The phrase,
referring as it does to ἐν αἵματι ἀλλοτρίῳ v. 25, cannot mean anything less
than 'the sacrifice of Himself.' The
word θυσία is used again of Christ c.
x. 12; and in connexion with προσφορά in Eph. v. 2.

πεφανέρωται] He, who is our High-
priest, hath been manifested, hath
entered the visible life of men as
man. On the scene of earth, before
the eyes of men, He has overcome
death (comp. 1 Cor. xv. 54—57). And
more than this: the fact of the Incarnation is regarded in its abiding
consequences. The manifestation of
Christ continues in its effects.

In this relation the 'manifestation'
of Christ offers a contrast to the veil-
ing of the High-priest in darkness when
he was engaged in fulfilling his atoning
service. Christ is withdrawn and yet
present: hidden and yet seen.

Contrast 1 John iii. 5, 8; i. 2 (ἐφα-
νερώθη); 1 Pet. i. 20 (φανερωθέντος).
The perfect occurs again v. 8; 2
Cor. v. 11 ; Rom. iii. 21.

27, 28. The fulfilment of the work
of the Levitical High-priest suggests
another thought. When the atonement was completed the High-priest
came again among the people (Lev.
xvi. 24). So too Christ shall return.
He shall in this respect also satisfy
the conditions of humanity. His
Death shall be followed by the manifestation of His righteousness in the
judgment of God.

27. The conditions of human life
are regarded as furnishing a measure
by analogy of the conditions of Christ's
work as man. He fulfilled the part
of man perfectly in fact and not in
figure (as by the Mosaic sacrifices).
For Him therefore Death, necessarily
one, must be followed by a Divine
Judgment.

καθ᾽ ὅσον...οὕτως καί...] inasmuch
as...even so also...Vulg. quemadmodum...sic et...Καθ᾽ ὅσον is found in
the N.T. only in this Epistle (iii. 3 ;
vii. 20); ἐφ᾽ ὅσον occurs Matt. ix. 15 ;
xxv. 40, 45; Rom. xi. 13; 2 Pet. i. 13.

Καθ᾽ ὅσον...οὕτως καί expresses a
conclusion drawn from an identity
between two objects in some particular respects (comp. καθώς...οὕτω v. 3),
while ὥσπερ...οὕτως...(not found in
this Epistle) describes a complete
correspondence so far as the objects
are compared (Rom. v. 12, 19, 21).

ἀπόκειται] Vulg. statutum est. Death
lies stored in the future, 'laid up' for
each man: 2 Tim. iv. 8; Col. i. 5.

μετὰ δὲ τοῦτο...] and after this
cometh judgment, not in immediate
sequence of time, but in the develop-

τοῦτο κρίσις, ²⁸οὕτως καὶ ὁ χριστός, ἅπαξ προσενεχθεὶς

εἰς τὸ πολλῶν ἀνενεγκεῖν ἁμαρτίας, ἐκ δευτέρου χωρὶς ἁμαρ-

28 οὕτως καί ℵACD₂ vg syrr ægg: om. καί ϛ.

ment of personal being. The writer
appears to connect the Judgment with
the Return of Christ on 'the Day':
c. x. 25, 37 f.

For the distinction of κρίσις, the
act, the process, of judgment, from
κρίμα, the issue of judgment, the
sentence, compare c. vi. 2 with x. 27;
see also John ix. 39; 1 John iv. 17 note.

28. οὕτως καί...] Death finally closes
man's earthly work, and is followed
by the judgment which reveals its
issue. So too Christ as man died
once only; and that which answers to
judgment in His case is the revelation
of His glory, the revelation of Himself as He is.

Sicut enim unusquisque nostrum
post mortem recipit juxta opera sua,
ita Christus devicta morte et adepto
regno secundo apparebit expectanti-
bus se in salutem ut juste vindicet
suos qui injuste passus est ab alienis
(Primas.).

For the force of ὁ χριστός, 'the
Christ,' see Addit. Note i. 4.

ἅπαξ προσενεχθείς] Vulg. semel oblatus. The passive form (contrast v.
25 ἵνα προσφέρῃ ἑαυτόν) completes the
conception of the Lord's offering. It
is on the one side voluntary and on
the other side it is the result of outward force. How this outward force
was exerted and by whom is not
made known. It cannot be said directly that Christ was 'offered up' by God,
nor yet that He was 'offered up' by
men; nor would such a form be used
to express the offering of Christ by
Himself (ὑπὸ τίνος προσενεχθείς; ὑφ'
ἑαυτοῦ δηλονότι· ἐνταῦθα οὐδὲ ἱερέα
δείκνυσιν αὐτὸν μόνον ἀλλὰ καὶ θῦμα
καὶ ἱερεῖον. Chrys.). There is a divine
law which men unconsciously and even
involuntarily fulfil. This embodies the
divine will of love and right. The Jews
were instruments in carrying it out.

εἰς τὸ πολλ.ἀνεν.ἁμ.] to carry the sins
of many, Vulg. ad multorum exhau-
rienda peccata. This most remarkable phrase appears to be taken from
Is. liii. 12 (6) LXX., where the sense is
'to take upon himself and bear the
burden of sin.' But φέρειν as distinguished from βαστάζειν (comp. c. i.
3 note) involves the notion of carrying
to some end; and so in 1 Pet. ii. 24
(the nearest parallel in the N. T.) we
read τὰς ἁμαρτίας ἀνήνεγκεν ἐπὶ τὸ
ξύλον ('carried up to'). Hence comes
the sense of 'offering,' 'carrying up to
the altar' (vii. 27; xiii. 15; James ii.
21); and it is difficult to suppose that
this idea is not present in the phrase
here. Christ 'carried to the cross'
and there did away with sin and sins.
Compare Chrysostom: τί δέ ἐστιν ἀνενεγκεῖν ἁμαρτίας; ὥσπερ ἐπὶ τῆς προσφορᾶς ἧς ἀναφέρομεν, προφέρομεν καὶ
τὰ ἁμαρτήματα λέγοντες Εἴτε ἑκόντες
εἴτε ἄκοντες ἡμάρτομεν συγχώρησον·
τουτέστι μεμνήμεθα αὐτῶν πρῶτον καὶ
τότε τὴν συγχώρησιν αἰτοῦμεν, οὕτω δὴ
καὶ ἐνταῦθα γέγονε. πού τοῦτο πεποίηκεν
ὁ Χριστός; ἄκουσον αὐτοῦ λέγοντος· Καὶ
ὑπὲρ αὐτῶν ἁγιάζω ἐμαυτόν. ἰδοὺ ἀνήνεγκε τὰ ἁμαρτήματα, ἦρεν αὐτὰ ἀπὸ τῶν
ἀνθρώπων καὶ ἀνήνεγκε τῷ πατρὶ οὐχ
ἵνα τι ὁρίσῃ κατ' αὐτῶν ἀλλ' ἵνα αὐτὰ
ἄρῃ.

In any case it is essential to the
understanding of the passage to keep
strictly to the literal statement. The
burden which Christ took upon Him
and bore to the cross was 'the sins of
many,' not, primarily or separately
from the sins, the punishment of sins.
'Punishment' may be a blessing to the
child conscious of his sonship.

In the LXX. ἀναφέρειν is used with
ἁμαρτία in Is. liii. 12 (נָשָׂא); comp.
Num. xiv. 33; and Is. liii. 11 (סָבַל).
Commonly נָשָׂא in connexion with Sin

τίας ὀφθήσεται τοῖς αὐτὸν ἀπεκδεχομένοις εἰς σωτηρίαν.

ἀπεκδεχ.: ἐκδεχ. D₂*.   εἰς σωτ. ℵCD₂ vg syr vg ægg: + διὰ πίστεως A syr hl.

is rendered in LXX. (Pent. Ezek.) by λαμβάνειν: Lev. v. I, 17; vii. 8 (18) &c. Num. ix. 13; xviii. 22 ff. &c. Ezek. iv. 5; xxiii. 49; comp. Ezek. xviii. 19 f.

The word 'many' does not (of course) imply 'many out of the whole number of men'; but 'many' is simply contrasted with Christ's single person, and His single entrance. Compare ii. 10 note; Matt. xx. 28; xxvi. 28.

Chrysostom's note is strangely wide of the meaning: διὰ τί δὲ πολλῶν εἶπε καὶ μὴ πάντων; ἐπειδὴ μὴ πάντες ἐπίστευσαν. ὑπὲρ ἁπάντων μὲν γὰρ ἀπέθανεν εἰς τὸ σῶσαι πάντας, τὸ αὐτοῦ μέρος, ἀντίρροπος γὰρ ἦν ὁ θάνατος ἐκείνος τῆς πάντων ἀπωλείας, οὐ πάντων δὲ τὰς ἁμαρτίας ἀνήνεγκε διὰ τὸ μὴ θελῆσαι πάντας.

ἐκ δευτέρου...σωτηρίαν] The 'appearance' of Christ corresponds in the parallel to the judgment of men. In this case the complete acceptance of Christ's work by the Father, testified by the Return in glory, is the correlative to the sentence given on human life. He rises above judgment, and yet His absolute righteousness receives this testimony. For Him what is judgment in the case of men is seen in the Return to bear the final message of salvation.

The fulness of this thought finds more complete expression by the description of Christ's Return as a return 'for salvation' and not (under another aspect) as a return 'for judgment,' which might have seemed superficially more natural. 'Salvation' emphasises the actual efficacy of His work, while 'judgment' declares its present partial failure.

Nothing indeed is said of the effect of Christ's Return upon the unbelieving. This aspect of its working does not fall within the scope of the writer; and it is characteristic of the Epistle that judgment is not directly referred to Christ, whom the writer regards

peculiarly as the Royal High-priest. Compare c. x. 27 note.

ἐκ δευτέρου] in comparison with His first manifestation on earth: Acts i. 11.

χωρὶς ἁμαρτίας] c. iv. 15. Here the words stands in contrast with εἰς τὸ πολλῶν ἀνενεγκεῖν ἁμαρτίας. At His first manifestation Christ took on Him the sins of humanity, and, though Himself sinless, endured the consequences of sin. At His second coming this burden will exist no longer. Sin then will have no place. (χώραν οὐκέτι ἐχούσης κατὰ τῶν ἀνθρώπων τῆς ἁμαρτίας. Theodt.)

ὀφθήσεται] Apoc. i. 7; I John iii. 2. The vision is regarded from the side of man who sees, and not (v. 26 πεφανέρωται) from that of God who reveals.

By the use of the word ὀφθήσεται the Return of Christ is presented as a historical fact (comp. Acts i. 10 f.). But it is to be noticed that the writer does not use the word παρουσία, which is found in St Matthew, 2 Peter, St James, St Paul, St John. Nor does he use the word ἐπιφάνεια which has a more limited range: 2 Thess. (ii. 8 ἡ ἐπιφ. τῆς παρουσίας αὐτοῦ), I, 2 Tim., Tit.

This revelation will be the completion of the transitory revelations after the Resurrection (1 Cor. xv. 5 ff. ὤφθη). But, like those, it will be for *such as wait for Him*, even as the people of Israel waited for the return of the High-priest from the Holy of Holies after the atonement had been made.

The word ἀπεκδέχεσθαι appears to be always used in the N. T. with reference to a future manifestation of the glory of Christ (1 Cor. i. 7; Phil. iii. 20), or of His people (Rom. viii. 19, 23, 25). Comp. 2 Tim. iv. 8.

εἰς σωτηρίαν] to accomplish, consummate salvation, which includes not only the removal of sin but also the attainment of the ideal of humanity.

Additional Note on ix. 7. *The service of the Day of Atonement.*

The ritual of the Day of Atonement, 'the Day' (*Joma*), is present to the mind of the writer throughout this section of the Epistle, and it will be convenient to set out the Levitical ordinances in a clear form, that the relation of their typical teaching to the work of Christ may be distinctly seen (Lev. xvi.; xxiii. 26—32; comp. Lev. xxv. 9; Num. xxix. 11; Ezek. xlv. 18 ff.).

The Mishnaic treatise *Joma*, of which there is a convenient edition by Sheringham, gives some additional details as to later usage; and Delitzsch has given a translation of the full account of the service by Maimonides. To the edition of Sheringham's *Joma* of 1696 is added a very elaborate comparison of the work of the High-priest with that of Christ by J. Rhenferd.

The Service of the Day summed up and interpreted the whole conception of Sacrifices, which were designed by divine appointment to gain for man access to God.

In the same way the High-priest summed up the idea of consecration and religious service, represented in different stages by the people, the Levites, the priests.

The occasion of the institution of the Service illustrates its central thought. It followed on the death of the eldest sons of Aaron, Nadab and Abihu, for 'offering strange fire' (Lev. x. 6 f.; xvi. 1; comp. Num. iii. 4; xxvi. 61). The way of access to God was not yet freely open: even the most privileged servants could only draw near as God provided a way.

The day was the one Fast of the Law: Acts xxvii. 9 (ἡ νηστεία).

All the ordinary priestly duties of the day were done by the High-priest in his 'golden robes,' and according to custom he prepared for his work by a retirement of seven days.

On the day itself, after bathing, the High-priest put on his [white] linen robes (Lev. xvi. 4; comp. Lk. ix. 29) as representing the people before God, while 'the golden robes' were appropriate to the messenger of God to the people.

Then the victims for the congregation and for the High-priest were prepared and presented (for sin offerings, a bullock for the High-priest, and two goats for the people; for burnt-offerings, a ram for each: Lev. xvi. 3, 5, 6), and one of the two goats was assigned by lot 'to the Lord' and the other 'to Azazel' (*v.* 8 ff.).

All being thus made ready, the High-priest killed the bullock, and made atonement 'for himself and for his house' (the priesthood), entering within the veil, under cover of a cloud of incense that 'he might not die' (*vv.* 11 ff.; comp. *v.* 2).

After this (and according to the later ritual he returned meanwhile from the Holy of Holies and re-entered it with the blood) he took of the blood and sprinkled it with his finger 'upon the mercy seat eastward,' and 'before the mercy seat seven times' (v. 14).

So the High-priest and the scene of the manifestation of God were duly atoned, and the High-priest was able to act for the people. He then killed the goat, the sin-offering for the people, and dealt with its blood as with the blood of the bullock (v. 15). As in the ordinary sacrifices the blood was applied in some cases to the altar of burnt-offering and in other cases to the altar of incense, so now it was brought to the mercy seat. Afterwards the High-priest 'made atonement' for the Holy place, being there alone (Ex. xxx. 10), and for the altar of burnt-offering (vv. 16 ff.).

Atonement having been thus made for priests and people and the whole place of service (the sanctuary in its three parts), the High-priest 'laid both his hands upon the head of the live goat, and confessed over it all the iniquities of the children of Israel [with which the Law dealt]...putting them upon the head of the goat, and sent it away...into the wilderness' (vv. 20 ff.).

Thus the special service was ended. The High-priest put off his linen garments in the Holy place, washed himself, put on his robes and offered the burnt-offerings for himself and the people, 'and made an atonement for himself and the people' (vv. 23 ff.).

Last of all the bodies of the sin-offerings were carried without the camp and wholly consumed (v. 27).

Thus in a figure year by year the people had access to the Presence of God in the person of the High-priest. The fellowship between God and the people, established by the Covenant but marred by sins against its conditions, was restored. By the virtue of an offered life communion became possible.

To this end there was a double sacrifice for the High-priest and for the people, and a double representation of the people by the High-priest and by the sin-offering; and till the atonement was made for the High-priest he could only enter the Holy of Holies under the cloud of incense. It is needless to point out the general fulfilment of the type by Christ. One point only, which appears to have been left unnoticed, may be suggested for consideration. The High-priest entered 'the unseen' twice, once for himself, once for the people. May we not see in this a foreshadowing of the two entrances of Christ into 'the unseen'? Once He entered, and came back victorious over death, ready in His glorified humanity to fulfil His work for His people. Again He entered the unseen 'to appear (ἐμφανισθῆναι) before the face of God for us,' and hereafter returning thence 'He shall appear (ὀφθήσεται) a second time to them that wait for Him.'

Additional Note on ix. 9.   *The præ-Christian idea of Sacrifice.*

There is no reason to think that Sacrifice was instituted in obedience to a direct revelation[1].

Sacrifice universal.

It is mentioned in Scripture at first as natural and known.

It was practically universal in præ-Christian times [Kalisch's reference to Strabo xi. 11, 8 is in error (οὐδὲν θῆλυ θύουσι)]. Compare Hes. *Op.* 134 ff.; Porph. *de abst.* ii. 8 [Theophrastus].

In due time the popular practice of Sacrifice was regulated by revelation as disciplinary, and also used as a vehicle for typical teaching.

Sacrifice, in fact, in the most general form, belongs to the life of man, and, in the truest sense, expresses the life of man. It is essentially the response of love to love, of the son to the Father, the rendering to GOD in grateful use of that which has been received from Him. Language cannot offer a more impressive example of moral degeneration in words, than the popular connexion of thoughts of loss and suffering with that which is a divine service.

In considering the Biblical teaching on Sacrifice we must take account of

I. NATURAL CONCEPTIONS.

II. BIBLICAL TEACHING.

I. NATURAL CONCEPTIONS.

1. *The general idea.*

The natural idea of sacrifices in each case is shaped by the view which is entertained by men of their relation to the unseen.

(1) Sacrifices as a tribute;

(1) They recognise, to speak generally, a relation of dependence on unseen powers, conceived after their own likeness. Hence they bring

A royal tribute, as to some earthly king, either

(*a*) Regular offerings, from a common sense of obligation; or

(*β*) Special offerings, in respect of particular occasions.

---

[1] As in the case of the præ-Christian Priesthood I had hoped to write an Essay on præ-Christian Sacrifice, but I can do no more than set down a few notes which may be useful in marking some main points in the inquiry. Those who have dealt with the Scriptural ordinances and teaching on Sacrifice have too commonly neglected ethnic institutions. Even now more illustrations may be expected from Egypt and from Assyria. The articles in the different Encyclopædias give references to the Literature, but I am not acquainted with any book which deals with the subject in its full range and significance. Kalisch has accumulated a great mass of material in his Essay attached to his edition of Leviticus, but it requires sifting; and Dillmann's notes in the *Kurzgef. Exeg. Handb.* are extremely useful. The books of Lippert and Tylor already referred to (p. 137 note) contain much that is valuable.

(2) as gifts on special occasions.

(2) More particularly they necessarily connect joy and suffering with the unseen. Hence follow

> (a) Eucharistic offerings in acknowledgment of benefits.
>
> (β) Deprecatory offerings to obtain relief.
>
> (γ) Impetratory offerings to obtain blessings. These are connected with prayer as a gift with a request. Comp. Tylor, ii. 340.

Express different purposes and

Such offerings are of two kinds :

> (a) To gratify : the offering of that which is valued, as presents in homage ; self-abnegation in fasting.
>
> (β) To benefit: the offering of that which is thought useful as food, of which the spiritual element is supposed to be consumed. Comp. Monier Williams, *Indian Wisdom*, p. 428.

different feelings.

And they embody two kinds of feeling (love or fear) according as the power is conceived to be

> (a) Good and righteous ; or
>
> (β) Malevolent or capricious.

The difference is shewn in the most extreme case. Thus there are two aspects of human sacrifices.

> (a) To prove the complete devotion of the worshipper.
>
> (β) To propitiate the cruelty of the power to which the sacrifice is made.

Classification.

So far, with the partial exception of the Eucharistic offerings, the sacrifices have a personal end (thank-offerings : fear-offerings : prayer-offerings).

In accordance with this general view Theophrastus (quoted and adopted by Porphyry, *de abst.* ii. 24 ; comp. 44) classes Sacrifices as ἢ διὰ τιμὴν ἢ διὰ χάριν ἢ διὰ χρείαν τῶν ἀγαθῶν. Moreover they are concerned with material things. The feeling by which they are prompted may be that of the slave, the subject, the friend, the son.

But one signal omission will be observed. There are so far no expiatory offerings.

The idea of expiatory offerings, answering to the consciousness of sin, does not belong to the early religion of Greece. Expiation was the work of special ministers.

Comp. Plat. *Resp.* ii. p. 364 B. J. Bernays' *Theophrastos üb. Frömmigkeit*, pp. 106 f.

It is not possible to determine absolutely in what order the different kinds of sacrifice came into use. The order probably depended in a great degree upon physical conditions, as the ordinary phenomena of life suggested terror or gratitude. This is the teaching of present experience.

(1) Produce of the earth.
(2) Prepared produce.

2. *Materials of sacrifice.*

> (1) Simple produce of the earth.

Comp. Ovid, *Fast.* i. 337 ff.; Porphyr. [Theophr.] *de Abst.* ii. 5 ff. ; iv. 22.

> (2) Prepared produce of the earth : first-fruits of food : juice of *soma*.

Comp. Porphyr. [Theophr.] ii. 6.

(3) Animals.

Comp. Porphyr. ii. 9. These were generally limited to those used for food : Porphyr. *l.c.* ii. 24, 25 ; offered to 'demons' : *id.* ii. 36, 38.

(4) Human beings.

Comp. Porphyr. ii. 27 ff. ; 54 ff. ; Just. M. *Ap.* ii. 12 ; Tertull. *Ap.* 9 ; *C. Quest.* 7 ; Aug. *de Civ.* vii. 19.

The custom of offering human sacrifices was not unfrequently signified by representative offerings : Herod. ii. 47 ; Ovid, *Fasti*, v. 621 ff. ; Tylor, ii. 366 f.

See E. v. Lasaulx, *D. Sühnopfer der Gr. u. Röm.*

Here again it is impossible to determine what materials were first used in sacrifice. General tradition points to the offering of the fruits of the earth as the earliest form of worship. Comp. Plato, *Legg.* vi. p. 782 c ; Plut. *Quaest. Conv.* viii. 8. 3.

3. *Modes of Sacrifice.*

The primitive manner of sacrifice was determined by the thought that the Divine Power received the gifts, and shared the feast. Hence the use of

(1) The altar.

The gifts were symbolically brought near to God.

(2) Fire.

The etherealised essence of the gift was borne aloft (Hom. *Il.* i. 317).

For descriptions of sacrifices compare Hom. *Il.* i. 458 ff. ; *Od.* iii. 439 ff. ; xiv. 414 ff. ; Eur. *Electr.* 792 ff. ; Ar. *Pax*, 940 ff. : Apoll. Rhod. i. 425 ff.

The adorning, &c. of the victims preserved the fiction that they met death willingly.

4. *Effect of sacrifice.*

The effect of sacrifices was conceived of either as

(1) Relative,

When the offering was welcomed as an expression of a real harmony of spirit and fellowship between the worshipper and the object of his worship ; or

(2) Absolute,

When the sacrifice had in itself a positive virtue. This view finds the most complete expression in Hindu theology. Comp. Monier Williams, *Indian Wisdom*, p. 31 note. In its popular form it became a subject for Classical Satirists : *e.g.* Luc. *de sacr.* 2.

In addition to the sacrifices which formed part of common worship, account must be taken of those which were made by vows (*e.g. Spolia opima*), and by voluntary devotion (legends of *Macaria, Curtius*, the *Decii*).

Meanwhile the true idea of sacrifice found not infrequent expression : *e.g.* Porphyr. ii. 34, 46.

Nowhere, as far as I know, is the ethnic conception of sacrifice, as the means of a fellowship of men with spirits, and of the one representative of the nation—the Emperor—with God, given more fully or impressively than in the Sacred Books of China. See *Li Ki* (*Sacred Books of the East*, xxvii, xxviii.) Books xx, xxi.   Comp. Book vii. § 4.

II.   Biblical teaching.

1.   *Præ-Mosaic Sacrifices.*

Præ-Mosaic sacrifice is presented to us in two forms :

(1) Primitive Sacrifice.

(1)   Primitive.

(a)   Gen. iv. 4 (Cain and Abel) (i).

Both offerings are called מִנְחָה (*gift* : comp. Gen. xxxii. 14 ; xliii. 11 ; Num. xvi. 15 ; 1 Sam. ii. 17 ; xxvi. 19).

No altar is mentioned.

The narrative implies that

(*a*)   The material is indifferent.

(*b*)   The spirit of the offerer is that to which God looks ('*Abel* and his offering,' '*Cain* and his...').

Comp. Heb. xi. 4.

(β)   Gen. viii. 20 (Noah) (ii).

An Altar is now first mentioned.

The offerings are 'of every clean beast and every clean fowl.' Thus we have the widest offering : a universal consecration in worship of all that is for man's support.

(2) Patriarchal Sacrifice.

(2)   Patriarchal Sacrifice.

(a)   Abraham.

Gen. xii. 6, 7, 8 (iii) ; xiii. 4 (iv).

An altar at Shechem : Josh. xxiv. 1, 26.

Gen. xiii. 18 (v).

An altar at Hebron : 2 Sam. xv. 7.

Gen. xv. 9 ff. (vi).

The Covenant offerings.   Animals allowed by the Levitical Law.   For the birds see Lev. i. 14—17.

Gen. xxii. 1 ff. (vii).

At Moriah.   The practice of sacrifice familiar (*v.* 7).

The offering of Isaac is a critical point in the history of the Biblical teaching on Sacrifice.   It is shewn that the most absolute faith and devotion exists without the material exhibition of it.   The human sacrifices of Canaan were most effectively condemned by the clear proof that the element of good to which they witnessed was wholly independent of their horrors.

It was plainly declared what God would and what He would not have.

Isaac, the child of promise, was a second time given to faith.   Faith received him at his birth, as a divine gift, and again from death.   He became the sign of the power of God and of human self-surrender : Hebr. xi. 19.

Under the Law the first-born were given representatively : Ex. xxii. 29.

Comp. Euseb. *Præp. Ev.* i. 10, p. 37.

(β)   Isaac.

Gen. xxvi. 25 (viii).

An altar at Beer-sheba (the altar first, then the tent).   Comp. c. xxi. 33.

(γ) Jacob.

Gen. xxviii. 18 ff. (ix).

A 'pillar' at Beth-el. Comp. c. xxxi. 45; xxxv. 14; Ex. xxiv. 4;
Is. xix. 19: 'pillars' forbidden, Deut. xvi. 22. Comp. Gen. xxxv. 7 (an altar:
El-beth-el).

Gen. xxxi. 54 (x).

A sacrifice and feast at Mizpah: a 'pillar' and 'heap' set up. Comp.
c. xxvi. 30; Ex. xxiv. 11; 2 Sam. iii. 20.

Gen. xxxiii. 20 (xi).

An altar at Shalem: El-elohe-Israel (comp. xxxv. 7; Ex. xvii. 15).

Gen. xxxv. 1 ff. (xii), 7 (xiii).

An altar at Beth-el (El-beth-el). Comp. c. xxviii. 18 ff.

Gen. xxxv. 14 (xiv).

A pillar at Beth-el (comp. xxviii. 18). A drink-offering first mentioned.

Gen. xlvi. 1 (xv).

Sacrifices at Beer-sheba (c. xxvi. 25).

The student will notice the wide range of details in these incidents. *Wide range of details.*

(a) There is mention of
Minchah (i); Olâh (ii) (vii); Zebach (x) (xv); Nesek (xiv).
Anointing with oil (ix).

(b) The altar is said to be
' built ' (ii) (iii) (v) (vii) (xiii); 'made' (iv) (xii); 'set up' (xiv).

(c) A pillar is
'placed' (ix); 'set up' (xiv).

(d) In other cases no altar or pillar mentioned: (i) (vi) (x).

Compare also Gen. xxi. 33. Abraham planted 'a tamarisk-tree' in
Beer-sheba (R. V., אֵשֶׁל) and called there on the name of the Lord...
(Amos v. 5; viii. 14).

To these references may be added: Job i. 5; xlii. 8; Ex. x. 25.

On the other hand there is no trace of the idea of *Idea represented.*

(a) a vicarious substitution of the victim for the offer (not Gen.
xxii. 13; comp. Mic. vi. 7 f.); or of

(b) propitiation.

The thoughts of (a) gratitude and (b) tribute are dominant.

There is no application of the blood before the Law.

The perfect ' naturalness' of the record is most impressive.

God is invited to share in the common feast: fellowship with God is
realised by the worshipper.

In Ex. xviii. 12 (Jethro) we have the transition to the new order.
Here the primitive conception of sacrifice is fully recognised when it was
about to be replaced by a more definite typical teaching. The sacrifice
of Jethro bears the same relation to the Levitical Law of sacrifice as the
appearance of Melchisedek to the Levitical Law of Priesthood.

In Ex. xxiv. 4—11 (the Covenant sacrifice) specific mention is made of
' burnt-offerings,' 'peace-offerings,' and of the sprinkling of the blood.

NOTE. On human sacrifices in Palestine. The following references will be useful in investigating how far human sacrifices were offered in Palestine :

(1)   Among the non-Jewish peoples :

Lev. xviii. 21; xx. 2 ff.

Deut. xii. 30 ff.; xviii. 10.

2 K. iii. 26 f. (the King of Moab).

— xvii. 31 (the Sepharvites).

The passages in the Pentateuch shew how great the temptation would be to the Jew to try whether his own faith could rival the devotion of the neighbouring nations.

(2)   Among the Jews :

Jud. xi. 30 ff. (v. 31 distinctly suggests a human offering; so LXX. ὁ ἐκπορευόμενος, Vulg. quicunque primus fuerit egressus. Comp. v. 2).

[The incident in 2 Sam. xxi. 1—14 is in no sense a sacrifice. See also 2 Sam. xii. 31.]

2 K. xvi. 3 (Ahaz): 2 Chron. xxviii. 3.

— xvii. 17 (the children of Israel).

— xxi. 6 (Manasseh): 2 Chron. xxxiii. 6.

— xxiii. 10.

Is. lvii. 5 (the people).

Jer. vii. 31 (the children of Judah).

— xix. 5 (—).

— xxxii. 35 (—).

Ezek. xvi. 20 f. (Jerusalem).

— xx. 25 f., 31 (the house of Israel).

Ps. cvi. 37 f.

Comp. Mic. vi. 7.

2.   The Levitical Sacrifices[1].

The Levitical Sacrifices were based upon existing customs (Lev. xvii. 1—7). They were in some sense a concession to the spiritual immaturity of the people (Jer. vii. 22 f.); but at the same time the legislation by which they were regulated guarded them from superstitious excesses, and preserved the different true ideas to which natural sacrifice bore witness, and completed this instructive expression of devotion by fresh lessons corresponding with deeper knowledge of God and man.

The Levitical Sacrifices include the true ethnic thoughts.

(1)   The general idea.

The Levitical offerings express the main thoughts which are expressed by the Gentile offerings though they express much more. They are in a true sense a tribute brought by a people to its Sovereign (Ex. xxiii. 15; xxxiv. 20; Deut. xvi. 16 f.); and they represent what man, in human fashion, conceives of as 'the bread—the food—of God' (Lev. iii. 11, 16; xxi. 6, 8, 17, 21; xxii. 25; Num. xxviii. 2, 24; Ezek. xliv. 7).

This conception was embodied specially in 'the Shew-bread'; and in

---

[1] The most general term for an offering, sacrifice, is קָרְבָּן (הִקְרִיב to offer, προσφέρειν). This includes all sacred gifts, even those which are not brought to the altar: Lev. i. 3; ii. 1; iii. 1; iv. 23; vii. 13; Num. ix. 7.

those sacrifices which are described as 'of a sweet savour' (Lev. i. 9, 13, 17; ii. 2, 9, 12; iii. 5; iv. 31; vi. 15; viii. 21; xxvi. 31; Num. xv. 7, 10, 13 f.; xxviii. 6, 13; xxix. 2, 6. Comp. Gen. viii. 21; Ex. xxix. 18; 1 Sam. xxvi. 19; Phil. iv. 18; Eph. v. 2).

The idea is naturally connected with idolatrous services (Deut. xxxii. 38; Is. lxv. 11; Jer. vii. 18; Ezek. xvi. 19; xxiii. 41; Bel and Dr.); but it admits of a true spiritual interpretation. In this sense it has been most justly remarked that God says to us, 'Give Me my daily bread' (Hengstenberg); and under one aspect the Jewish sacrifices were a type of this 'reasonable service' (comp. Jos. B. J. vi. 2, 1 ἡ καθ' ἡμέραν τροφὴ [τοῦ θεοῦ]).

At the same time while God is represented as accepting these gifts from men, it is carefully laid down that He does not need them (Is. xl. 16 f.; Ps. l. 8 ff.).

Another thought contained in the Gentile sacrifices was recognised in the Law. He to whom the sacrifice was offered admitted His worshippers (with certain limitations) to His table. They 'had communion with the altar' (1 Cor. x. 18 οἱ ἐσθίοντες τὰς θυσίας κοινωνοὶ τοῦ θυσιαστηρίου εἰσί). They shared with the Lord in a common feast.

But all these thoughts of homage, service, fellowship, were shewn to rest, as men are, upon the thought of a foregoing atonement, cleansing, consecration. This thought was brought out into fullest relief in the Levitical ritual by the characteristic use which was made of the blood—the virtue of the offered life.

The foundation of the Levitical law of sacrifice is laid in the Covenant Sacrifice (Ex. xxiv.). '*Young men of the children of Israel*'—the representatives of the people in the fulness of their vigour—'*offered burnt-offerings and sacrificed peace-offerings of oxen unto the Lord*' (v. 5). Such was the spontaneous expression of human worship. But it was not enough. '*Moses took half of the blood and put it in basons, and half of the blood he sprinkled on the altar*' (v. 6). Then followed the pledge of obedience; '*and Moses took the blood and sprinkled it on the people and said, Behold the blood of the covenant, which the Lord hath made with you...*' (v. 8). '*Then went up Moses and Aaron, Nadab and Abihu, and seventy of the elders of Israel; and they saw the God of Israel...they saw God and did eat and drink*' (vv. 9 ff.). So the human desire was justified and fulfilled. The blood of the Covenant, the power of a new life made available for the people of God, enabled men to hold communion with God (v. 11 *upon the nobles of the children of Israel He laid not His hand:* contrast c. xix. 21). The lessons of sacrifice were completed: service, cleansing, consecration, fellowship.

The teaching thus broadly given in the consecration of the people to God found a more detailed exposition in the consecration of the priests, the representatives of the people in the divine service (Ex. xxix.; Lev. viii.). Here, as was natural, the acknowledgment of personal sin was more prominent. The bathing, robing, anointing, were followed by the sacrifice of a sin-offering (Ex. xxix. 10 ff.). Then one of two rams was offered as a whole burnt-offering, 'a sweet savour,' and of the other, after the blood had been duly applied to the altar and the candidates for the

[margin] The Law of Sacrifices founded in the Covenant Sacrifice.

The ideas enforced in the consecration of the priests.

priesthood, part, together with a portion of the prepared bread, was burnt for a 'sweet savour before the Lord,' and part with the remainder of the bread was eaten by Aaron and his sons by the door of the tent of meeting (*v.* 32): they ate *those things wherewith the atonement was made, to consecrate, to sanctify them* (*v.* 33).

It follows from the general idea of the Jewish sacrifices that they were ruled by the conception of the Covenant. In part they embodied the devout action of those for whom the full privileges of the Covenant were in force; and in part they made provision for the restoration of the privileges which had been temporarily forfeited.

Two main groups of sacrifices.

Thus the customary sacrifices fall into two groups[1]:

(*a*)   Sacrifices made while the covenant relation is valid.

(*a*) The Covenant valid.

    (*a*)   The burnt-offering (עֹלָה).

        Lev. i. 3 ff.

    (β)   The peace-offerings (שְׁלָמִים, of three kinds: (1) תּוֹדָה thanks-giving: (2) נֶדֶר vow: (3) נְדָבָה free-will offering: Lev. vii. 12, 16).

        Lev. iii. 1 ff.

With these must be combined

    (γ)   The meal-offering (מִנְחָה).

        Lev. ii. 1 ff.

    (δ)   The Shew-bread (לֶחֶם פָּנִים and later הַמַּעֲרֶכֶת ל׳).

    (ε)   First-fruits.

(*b*) The Covenant violated.

(*b*)   Sacrifices made in regard to violations of the Covenant.

    (*a*)   The sin-offering (חַטָּאה).

        Lev. iv. 1 ff.

    (β)   The guilt- (trespass-) offering (אָשָׁם).

        Lev. v. 15 ff.

To these must be added the various sacrifices for Purification : Lev. xiv. (lepers); xv. (uncleanness); Num. xix. (contact with dead).

The Peace-offering, through which man entered in a peculiar sense into fellowship with God, was offered after the Sin-offering and the Burnt-offering: Lev. ix. 18; Num. vi. 16 f.

The narrow range of sacrificial atonements.

It is necessary to observe that the range of the Levitical atonements was very narrow. They were confined to

    (*a*)   Bodily impurity.

    (β)   Ceremonial offences.

    (γ)   Sins of ignorance.

    (δ)   Certain specified offences: Lev. vi. 1, 7; xix. 20.

They did not deal with moral offences as such: they had no relief for

---

[1] The student will find it a most instructive exercise to set down in a tabular form the details of the ritual given in Lev. i—vii, marking clearly the elements which are peculiar to or absent from each type of sacrifice. There is no other way in which the meaning of the Service can be apprehended with equal force.

'high-handed sins.' Here the voice of Psalmist and Prophet met the heart-broken penitent with promises which the Law could not give.

To the other Sacrifices the Passover must be added, which stood by itself and renewed the foundation of the Covenant.

(2) Materials of Sacrifice.

The distinction of Sacrifices as 'bleeding' and 'unbloody' is not expressly noticed in the O. T.; but there were occasions when they were made separately according to the Levitical ritual. Thus we have to notice offerings of

(a) The produce of the earth.

Wine: oil: meal.

Simple fruits (grapes, olives, &c.[1]) or flowers were not accepted.

(a) The produce of the earth.

It was required that man's life and labour should have entered into that which he offered to God (Gen. iii. 17—19).

These kinds were mixed in the Meal- (and Drink-) offering (*Minchah, Nesek*) and offered separately in the Holy Place: Bread: Oil (the lamps): with Incense, but not with Wine.

Incense was not offered by itself.

No details are given as to the Wine: it is once spoken of as שֵׁכָר (Num. xxviii. 7).

The Meal was of 'corn': not less than one-tenth of an ephah (a day's food: Ex. xvi. 16). Barley, which was half the value (2 K. vii. 1), was admitted only in the offering of jealousy: Num. v. 15 ff.

The sheaf of first-fruits was of barley, because that is ripe earliest: Lev. xxiii. 10 (comp. Ruth ii. 23; 2 Sam. xxi. 9).

Oil is a natural symbol of refreshment, light, life, spirit. So it was used for consecration. Comp. Gen. xxviii. 18; xxxv. 14.

The Incense was given wholly to God: of this the priest had no part. It was a symbol of prayer offered to God only (comp. Apoc. viii. 3 f.; v. 8).

It was not used with the sin-offering (Lev. v. 11); or with the jealousy-offering (Num. v. 15).

Leaven was not admitted except Lev. vii. 13; xxiii. 17; nor honey (except as an oblation of first-fruits) which was especially used in offerings to the dead: Porphyr. *de antr. Nymph.* 18.

The use of water as 'poured out before the Lord' (1 Sam. vii. 6; 2 Sam. xxiii. 16) is obviously exceptional.

For the Meal-offering, see Lev. ii. 1 ff.: for the Drink-offering, Lev. xxiii. 13, 18, 37; Ex. xxix. 40 f.; xxx. 9; Num. xv. 1 ff.; for Incense, Ex. xxx. 22 ff.

(b) Animals.

(b) Animals.

Clean domestic (not wild) animals: oxen; sheep; goats; pigeons: representing different types of service (comp. Jukes, *The Law of the Offerings*, pp. 77 ff.).

These served as the support of man's own life, and were nearest to him in labour, and as food.

[1] The nearest approach to the offering of the simple grain is Lev. ii. 14; yet here the grains are 'roasted.' The offering of the sheaf of the firstfruits is different: Lev. xxiii. 10. Comp. Ex. xxii. 29; Lev. ii. 12.

They were required to be perfect (תְּמִים, ἄμωμοι): Deut. xvii. 1 ; and, in detail: Lev. xxii. 18 ff.; comp. Mal. i. 8.   There was relaxation only in the case of the 'free-will offering': Lev. xxii. 23.   The victims were always male in a public offering for the people; and generally a year old: in no case less than seven days: Lev. xxii. 27.

As compared with the requirements of other rituals, the Levitical rules are singularly simple and significant.   They contain no restrictions as to colour, &c.

Salt was used with all sacrifices: Lev. ii. 13; Ex. xxx. 35 R.V.; comp. Ezek. xliii. 24; Mk. ix. 49 *v. l.;* and see also LXX. Lev. xxiv. 7 (add. καὶ ἅλα).

Salt keeps off corruption; removes impurity; acts internally like fire; sustains peace (by withdrawing elements of disorder): Mk. ix. 50; and so it came to be regarded as a symbol of an indissoluble covenant: Num. xviii. 19.

Compare Philo *de vict.* § 3 (ii. 240 M.) οἱ ἅλες [σύμβολον] διαμονῆς τῆς τῶν συμπάντων, οἷς γὰρ ἂν περιπασθῶσι διατηροῦσι, καὶ ἱκανοῦ προσοψή- ματος.

The 'meal-offering' made alone was represented by the 'Shew-bread.' The offering in Lev. v. 11 was not a true *Minchah;* and the offerings of first-fruits were of a different order.

Animal sacrifices alone were made in the sin and guilt offerings (yet notice Lev. v. 11).

The burnt and peace offerings included meal and drink offerings.

(3) Characteristics of ritual.

The sacrifices were to be made at an appointed place: Lev. xvii. 3—5. The access to God was not yet freely open (comp. John iv. 21).

The structure of the Altar was prescribed: Ex. xx. 24 f.; xxvii. 1 ff.

In the Sacrifice itself notice must be taken of (*a*) the imposition of hands, (*b*) the killing, (*c*) the exception of the blood, (*d*) the application of the blood, (*e*) the disposition of the victim, (*f*) the sacrificial meal.

(*a*) The *Semicah.*   The imposition of hands (Rabb. סְמִיכָה χειρο- θεσία).   The offerer laid his hands on all offerings except the Paschal offering (and birds).   Lev. i. 4; iii. 2; iv. 4, 15.

Compare Num. viii. 10 (Num. xxvii. 20; Deut. xxxiv. 9) (hands laid on the Levites); Lev. xvi. 21 (the High-priest laid both hands on the scape-goat); Lev. xxiv. 14 (the hands of the witnesses laid on the blasphemer before he was stoned).

The action expressed an intimate connexion between the offerer and the victim: in some sense a connexion of life : a dedication to a repre-sentative office.

The interpretation in each case depended upon the particular office or act to be fulfilled by the offering.

The killing.

(*b*) The killing (שְׁחִיטָה : זָבַח and שָׁחַט to be distinguished).   As a general rule the killing of the victim (unless it was a bird) was not the work of the priest but of the offerer in the case of private sacrifices : Lev. i. 5; iii. 2; iv. 24, 29, 33; though the priests might kill them.   Compare Oehler, § 126.

In sacrifices for the whole nation the victims were killed by the priests who here represented the offerers ; and so on the Great Day of Atonement they were killed by the High-priest: Lev. xvi. 15.

In the cleansing of the leper the victims were necessarily killed by the priest: the leper was outside the Congregation: Lev. xiv. 13, 25.

The victim was killed with the least possible pain : no stress was laid on death as suffering.

(c) The exception of the blood.

The blood of the victim was the appointed means of atonement: Lev. xvii. 11.

(c) The exception of the blood.

It was received by the priests (2 Chron. xxix. 22; comp. 2 Chron. xxx. 16).

In certain cases it was mixed with water: Lev. xiv. 5 f. ; but nothing is said in the O. T. of the mixture noticed in Hebr. ix. 19.

(d) The application of the blood.

This was the most significant part of the sacrifice. The rules in their solemn variety of detail are characteristic of the Levitical ritual. Elsewhere we read generally of the blood being poured upon the altars. In some cases (*e.g.* in Arabia) idols were smeared with blood. But there is apparently no parallel to the minute distinctions as to the use of the blood observed in Judaism.

(d) The application of the blood.

The blood was applied by the priests only, and in four different wa s.

i. It was 'sprinkled' (זָרַק *to asperse*), *i.e.* probably it was all thrown about from the bowl directly or by the hand from the bowl 'on the altar [of burnt-offering] round about': Lev. i. 5 ; iii. 2; vii. 2, &c. This was done in the case of burnt-, peace- and guilt-offerings.

ii. It was 'applied' (נָתַן *to give*) to the horns of the altar of burnt-offering, and the remainder poured out at the base of the altar: Lev. iv. 30. This was done in the case of a sin-offering for 'one of the common people.'

iii. It was carried into the Holy place, and some of it was applied to the horns of the altar of incense and sprinkled (הִזָּה) with the finger upon the veil seven times: the remainder was poured out at the base of the altar of burnt-offering: Lev. iv. 6, 17 f. This was done in the case of a sin-offering for a priest or for the congregation.

iv. It was carried into the Holy of holies and sprinkled with the finger 'upon the mercy-seat, and before the mercy-seat seven times': afterwards it was applied to the horns of the altar of burnt-offering, and sprinkled upon it with the finger seven times: Lev. xvi. 14, 15, 18, 19. [Nothing is said of the disposition of the remainder of the blood.] This was done on the Day of Atonement.

(e) The disposition of the victim.

The gift to God by fire followed on the completion of the atonement by the use of the blood.

(e) The disposition of the victim.

In this connection the word for 'burning' was not שָׂרַף (used of consuming the remains of offerings outside the camp), but הִקְטִיר 'to cause to [ascend as] smoke.'

The fire was kept perpetually burning: Lev. vi. 13.

The burnt-offerings, and the offerings whose blood was carried into the Holy or most Holy place (sin offerings for the priest or the congregation) were wholly consumed: Lev. iv. 11, 21; xvi. 27; Hebr. xiii. 11. So also were the unbloody offerings for priests.

Other offerings, under special limitations, were consumed by the priests or made the materials of a feast by the offerer.

Two rites, apparently peculiar to the Jews, have to be noticed in this connexion, the 'waving' (תְּנוּפָה) and the 'heaving' (תְּרוּמָה) of parts of the offering which were so presented to God and then in some cases resigned by Him to the priests: Ex. xxix. 23 ff.; Lev. vii. 34; viii. 27 ff.; xxiii. 11, 20; Num. v. 25; xv. 19 ff.; xviii. 26 ff.; comp. Num. viii. 9 ff.; xviii. 6 f.

The absence of all inspection of the entrails of the victims, which was usual in Phœnicia, Egypt, &c., is specially to be noticed.

(f) The Sacrificial meal.

(f) The Sacrificial meal.

The parts of the offerings which were not consumed by fire were disposed of in different ways.

i. The unbloody offerings of the people except the part burnt as a 'memorial' (אַזְכָּרָה) were eaten by the priests alone in the court of the sanctuary: Lev. vii. 9 f.; x. 12 ff.

ii. The flesh of the guilt-offerings and of the sin-offerings for one of the people were eaten by the priests in the Holy place: Lev. vi. 25 ff.; vii. 6 ff.; x. 16 ff.

iii. In the case of the peace- (thank-) offerings (שְׁלָמִים), after the disposal of the assigned parts, the offerer made a feast of the remainder within a fixed time and at a fixed place, to which he invited his household, his friends and the poor: Lev. vii. 15 ff.; xix. 5 ff.; xxii. 29 f.; Deut. xii. 6 ff.

In this last case we have the completest view of the sacrifice offered in virtue of a covenant relation with God. The offering is made to God, and He returns part to His worshipper through whom it is made a common blessing. Thus, as Philo pointed out, God received the faithful offerer to His own table: *de vict.* § 8 (ii. 245 M.).

The student will not fail to notice the representative completeness of the references to the Levitical Sacrifices in the Epistle. Thus we have the general description *gifts and sacrifices* (v. 1; viii. 3 f.); and, more particularly *sacrifices and offerings and whole burnt-offerings and sacrifices for sin* (x. 8). Mention is made of the daily (x. 11) and of the yearly sacrifices (ix. 6 ff.; x. 1); of the Covenant Sacrifice (ix. 18 ff.); and of the sacrifices which were provided for removing the legal impurities which impaired the validity of the Covenant, through contact with death (ix. 13), or in the common conduct of life, on the Day of Atonement (v. 3; vii. 27 ff.; ix. 7 f.).

Additional Note on ix. 9. *The idea of* συνείδησις.

The conception of 'the conscience' (ἡ συνείδησις), which is not developed in the O. T. (comp. Ecclus. x. 20; Wisd. xvii. 11), comes into clear prominence in the N. T. It presents man as his own judge. Man does not stand alone. He has direct knowledge of a law—a law of God—which claims his obedience, and he has direct knowledge also of his own conduct. He cannot then but compare them and give sentence His 'conscience,' as the power directing this process, is regarded apart from himself (Rom. ix. 1; ii. 15). The conscience may be imperfectly disciplined and informed (1 Cor. x. 25 ff.; viii. 7 ff.; contrast Acts xxiii. 1; 1 Tim. iii. 9; 2 Tim. i. 3; 1 Pet. iii. 16, 21). It may again be modified (1 Cor. viii. 10, 12), and defiled (Tit. i. 15); and finally it may be seared and become insensible (1 Tim. iv. 2). The man is responsible for the character which it assumes.

The distribution of the word in the Books of the N. T. is interesting. It is not found in the Gospels (notice the occurrence in some copies in [John] viii. 9). It occurs in Acts, the central group of St Paul's Epistles (1, 2 Cor., Rom.), the Pastoral Epistles (1, 2 Tim., Tit.), the Epistle to the Hebrews and 1 Peter.

The simplest use is that for direct, personal, knowledge with the *gen.* of the object (1 Cor. viii. 7 εἰδώλου, 1 Pet. ii. 19 θεοῦ, Hebr. x. 2 ἁμαρτιῶν), corresponding to συνειδέναι τι (1 Cor. iv. 4).

The absolute use of the word presents various functions which the conscience fulfils. It is a witness (2 Cor. i. 12; Rom. ii. 15); a judge (2 Cor. iv. 2; v. 11); a motive (1 Pet. ii. 19 διὰ σ.; 1 Cor. x. 25 ff. διὰ τὴν σ.; Rom. xiii. 5). It is turned to God (Acts xxiii. 1 τῷ θεῷ; xxiv. 16 πρὸς τὸν θεόν); and it becomes an object of consideration to men (1 Cor. x. 28 f.).

In one passage it is placed in a most significant relation with 'the heart' and 'faith' (1 Tim. i. 5). The end of the Apostolic charge is love 'out of a pure heart, and a good conscience, and faith unfeigned.' Purity of personal character, rectitude of moral judgment, sincerity of trust in the unseen, form the triple foundation of active Christian work.

For the manifold description of the conscience see c. x. 22 note; and for references to general discussions see Thayer-Grimm, *s.v.* ʃNowhere have the claims of conscience been more nobly set out than in the 'writings of Mencius: Legge's *Chinese Classics* ii, Prolegg. 61 ff.

Additional Note on ix. 12. *On the use of the term 'Blood' in the Epistle.*

I have endeavoured to shew elsewhere (Addit. Note on 1 John i. 7) that the Scriptural idea of Blood is essentially an idea of life and not of death. This idea is widely spread among primitive races, and finds a striking illustration in the familiar passage of the Odyssey, where the

The Blood the energy of physical life.

ghosts of the dead are represented as receiving strength for a time from the blood which they eagerly drink: *Od.* xi. 36 ff.; 95 ff.; 152; 231.

The Blood, in other words, represents the energy of the physical, earthly, life as it is. The use of the term in the Epistle to the Hebrews becomes first fully intelligible by taking account of this truth. The Blood poured out is the energy of present human life made available for others.

1. 'Blood' in relation to the Incarnation.

1. The first mention of Blood prepares for all that follows from the conception : *Since the children are sharers in blood and flesh, He also Himself in like manner partook of the same...*(ii. 14). Christ became true man under such conditions that He could die even as men die, and in dying make the virtue of His life accessible to the race. For it must be remembered that in Scripture death under its present form is not regarded as a natural necessity, but as a consequence of sin. By this perfect assumption of humanity, the sacrifice of absolute obedience became possible. In life and in death Christ was able 'to do the will of God,' both as Son of man and under the circumstances of the Fall (x. 4 ff.).

2. Christ enters 'through His Blood' into the Divine Presence.

2. The next mention of Christ's Blood brings before us the accomplishment of this work: *Through His own Blood [Christ] entered once for all into the Holy place, having obtained eternal redemption* (ix. 12). As, in the type, the Jewish High-priest came before God through and in (*v.* 25) the power of the life of victims offered up, Christ came before Him 'through His own Blood[1].' Through a life lived and a death willingly borne according to the mind of God, He could rightly approach God in His glorified humanity; and at the same time He provided for men also the means of approach 'in His Blood.'

3. The Blood of Christ gives access to God to the believer.

3. This thought comes next. The Life of Christ offered in its purity and fulness to God cleanses men, and enables them also to serve Him Who is a living God (ix. 14). Just as the blood of the appointed victims was efficacious by Divine promise for the representative of the people, the Blood of Christ in its essential nature is efficacious for those to whom it is applied. *In the Blood of Jesus*—not simply 'through' it—*we have boldness to enter into the Holy place* (x. 19). In this respect the Blood has a twofold action, personal and social. It is the 'blood of sprinkling' (xii. 24), touching with its quickening power each believer; and it is also a force of consecration through which 'Jesus sanctified the people' (xiii. 12).

4. The Blood of Christ the ratification of an eternal Covenant.

4. This last passage brings into prominence yet another thought. The Blood of Christ is not only available for individual men. It has established for the race a new relation to God. The offered Life in which Christ found the glorified Life of the Resurrection (xiii. 20 ὁ ἀναγαγὼν ἐκ νεκρῶν... ἐν αἵματι...), is, in virtue of His Nature, the *blood of an eternal covenant* (*l. c.*). In this the Christian is sanctified (x. 29) when he is admitted into the Christian Society. And, however little we may be able to give distinctness to the truth, its hallowing, cleansing, power reaches to all finite things with which man has contact.

The mere indication of the passages, as they follow one after the other

---

[1] In connexion with the thought in ix. 23 it is interesting to notice that according to the primitive Chinese ritual temples and their vessels were consecrated by blood: *Li Ki* xviii. § 2, pp. 2, 33 (S. B. E. xxviii. 169 f.).

and reveal the harmonious completeness of the apostolic teaching, will be enough to encourage the student to examine them in detail in their mutual relations.

Additional Note on ix. 12. The idea of λυτροῦσθαι, λύτρωσις, &c.

The use in the N. T. of the group of words connected with λύτρον is The use of based upon their use in the LXX. All the simple forms (λύτρον, λυτρόω, λύτρον &c. λύτρωσις, λυτρωτής) are found there together with the compound ἀπολυτροῦν in the LXX. (Ex. xxi. 8 for פָּדָה; Zeph. iii. 1 for גָּאַל).

The word λύτρον, in relation to men, represents כֹּפֶר, as a ransom for a life: Ex. xxi. 30; xxx. 12; Num. xxxv. 31 f.; Prov. xiii. 8 (ἐξίλασμα Aq. Sym. Th.) comp. Prov. vi. 35; מְחִיר, as the price of a captive: Is. xlv. 13; הַפְּדֻה (פָּדָה), and גְּאֻלָּה as the price of redemption of a slave: Lev. xix. 20, and xxv. 51 f. (comp. Num. iii. 46 ff.; xviii. 15); and more widely גְּאֻלָּה, as the price of redemption of land: Lev. xxv. 24.

The verb λυτροῦσθαι is very frequent as the translation of גָּאַל and פָּדָה (of each more than forty times). It is used literally of the 'redemption' of that which has been alienated: Lev. xxv. 25 ff. (λυτρώσεται τὴν πρᾶσιν τοῦ ἀδελφοῦ); xxvii. 13 ff.; and in a more general sense of deliverance from the power of outward enemies: Ps. cvi. [cvii.] 2, &c.; from the power of sin: Ps. cxxix. [cxxx.] 8; Dan. iv. 24; and from the power of death: Hos. xiii. 14. It was specially used of the 'redemption' of Israel from Egypt: Ex. vi. 6 (λυτρώσομαι ὑμᾶς ἐν βραχίονι ὑψηλῷ καὶ κρίσει μεγάλῃ); xv. 13; Deut. vii. 8; ix. 26; xiii. 5; 2 Sam. vii. 23; Ps. lxxvi. [lxxvii.] 16; Mic. vi. 4; and of that future 'redemption' of which this was a type: Is. xxxv. 9; xli. 14; xliii. 1, 14).

Λύτρωσις occurs with the full breadth of the meaning of the verb: of the redemption of a slave (Lev. xxv. 48), of the firstborn (Num. xviii. 16), of the people (Ps. cx. [cxi.] 8), of the penitent (Ps. cxxix. [cxxx.] 7). Comp. Jud. i. 15 (a false reading of the Hebr.).

Λυτρωτής, which is not quoted from classical authors, is found in Ps. xviii. [xix.] 15; lxxvii. [lxxviii.] 35 (for גֹּאֵל). [The form λυτρωταί in Lev. xxv. 31, 32 is wrongly referred to the noun; it is evidently from the verbal λυτρωτός.]

In the N. T. λύτρον occurs only in Matt. xx. 28 ‖ Mk. x. 45 δοῦναι τὴν The use in ψυχὴν αὐτοῦ λύτρον ἀντὶ πολλῶν. The compound ἀντίλυτρον is found in the N. T. 1 Tim. ii. 6 X. 'Ι. ὁ δοὺς ἑαυτὸν ἀντίλυτρον ὑπὲρ πάντων.

The verb λυτροῦσθαι is comparatively rare. It occurs only three times, Lk. xxiv. 21 ὅτι αὐτός ἐστιν ὁ μέλλων λυτροῦσθαι τὸν Ἰσραήλ. Tit. ii. 14 ἵνα λυτρώσηται ἡμᾶς ἀπὸ πάσης ἀνομίας. 1 Pet. i. 18 οὐ φθαρτοῖς...ἐλυτρώθητε ἐκ τῆς ματαίας ὑμῶν ἀναστροφῆς...ἀλλὰ τιμίῳ αἵματι.... The variety of construction in these three passages is strikingly representative, (1) absolutely, (2) with ἀπό, (3) with ἐκ and the addition of dat. instr. Ἀπολυτροῦσθαι is not found in N.T.

Λύτρωσις occurs Lk. i. 68 ἐποίησεν λύτρωσιν τῷ λαῷ αὐτοῦ. ii. 38 τοῖς προσδεχομένοις λύτρωσιν Ἰερουσαλήμ. Hebr. ix. 12 αἰωνίαν λύτρωσιν εὑράμενος. Ἀπολύτρωσις is much more common : Lk. xxi. 28 ἐγγίζει ἡ ἀπολύτρωσις ὑμῶν. Rom. iii. 24 διὰ τῆς ἀπ. τῆς ἐν Χ. Ἰ. viii. 23 τὴν ἀπ. τοῦ σώματος. 1 Cor. i. 30 ὅς (Ἰησοῦς) ἐγενήθη...ἡμῖν...ἀπ. Eph. i. 7 ‖ Col. i. 14 ἐν ᾧ ἔχομεν τὴν ἀπολύτρωσιν. id. i. 14 εἰς ἀπ. τῆς περιποιήσεως. iv. 30 εἰς ἡμέραν ἀπ. Hebr. ix. 15 εἰς ἀπ. τῶν ἐπὶ τῇ πρώτῃ διαθήκῃ παραβάσεων. xi. 35 οὐ προσδεξάμενοι τὴν ἀπ.

Λυτρωτής is found only in Acts vii. 35 τοῦτον (Μωυσῆν) ὁ θεὸς καὶ ἄρχοντα καὶ λυτρωτὴν ἀπέσταλκεν.

The whole group of words, it will be seen, with the exception of the single occurrence of λύτρον in the Synoptic narrative, is confined to the Epistles of St Paul and writings (including 1 Peter) which are strongly coloured by his language. They are entirely absent from the writings of St John.

The general idea of the image. The conception of 'redemption' lies in the history of Israel. The deliverance from Egypt furnished the imagery of hope. To this the work of Christ offered the perfect spiritual antitype. This parallel is of importance, for it will be obvious from the usage of the LXX. that the idea of a ransom received by the power from which the captive is delivered is practically lost in λυτροῦσθαι, &c. It cannot be said that God paid to the Egyptian oppressor any price for the redemption of His people. On the other hand the idea of the exertion of a mighty force, the idea that the 'redemption' costs much, is everywhere present. The force may be represented by Divine might, or love, or self-sacrifice, which become finally identical. But there is no thought of any power which can claim from God what is not according to the original ordinance of His righteous compassion.

No thought of the power which receives the ransom. It follows that the discussions which have been raised on the question 'To whom was the ransom for man's redemption paid' are apt to be misleading. The deliverance of man from the debt, the captivity, the bondage of sin—however we express the image—could only be through the satisfaction of the claims of a violated law. These claims regarded under the light of punishment present a twofold aspect. To him who rebels against the divine law, they are simply pain: to him who humbly submits himself to it, they are a salutary discipline. The first aspect includes the truth which was expressed by the patristic conception that Christ paid the ransom of man to the devil: the second includes the truth expressed by the later view that the ransom was paid to God. Each view however is essentially incomplete, and it is perilous to attempt to draw conclusions from limited interpretations of Scripture.

The idea of 're-demption' completed by the idea of 'pur-chase.' The idea of 'redemption,' 'deliverance,' in the spiritual order requires to be supplemented by the idea of 'purchase.' Man has no power of standing by himself. His freedom lies in his complete acceptance of the will of God. When therefore he is 'redeemed' from the power of evil he is also 'purchased,' so as to become wholly in the hands of God. The idea of 'purchase,' though of less frequent occurrence in the N. T. than the idea of 'redemption,' is more widely spread. It occurs in St Paul, 2 Peter, and the Apocalypse (ἀγοράζειν, ἐξαγοράζειν).

1 Cor. vi. 20 οὐκ ἐστὲ ἑαυτῶν, ἠγοράσθητε γὰρ τιμῆς.

1 Cor. vii. 22 f. ὁ ἐλεύθερος κληθεὶς δοῦλός ἐστι Χριστοῦ. τιμῆς ἠγοράσθητε
μὴ γίνεσθε δοῦλοι ἀνθρώπων.
2 Pet. ii. 1 τὸν ἀγοράσαντα αὐτοὺς δεσπότην ἀρνούμενοι.
Apoc. v. 9 ἐσφάγης καὶ ἠγόρασας τῷ θεῷ ἐν τῷ αἵματί σου ἐκ πάσης φυλῆς
καὶ γλώσσης καὶ λαοῦ καὶ ἔθνους....
— xiv. 3 f. (ᾄδουσιν ὡς ᾠδὴν καινὴν) οἱ ἠγορασμένοι ἀπὸ τῆς γῆς...
οὗτοι ἠγοράσθησαν ἀπὸ τῶν ἀνθρώπων, ἀπαρχὴ τῷ θεῷ καὶ
τῷ ἀρνίῳ.

The compound ἐξαγοράζειν combines the thought of redemption with that
of purchase :
Gal. iii. 13 Χριστὸς ἡμᾶς ἐξηγόρασεν ἐκ τῆς κατάρας τοῦ νόμου γενόμενος
ὑπὲρ ἡμῶν κατάρα.
— iv. 4 f. ἐξαπέστειλεν ὁ θεὸς τὸν υἱὸν αὐτοῦ...ἵνα τοὺς ὑπὸ νόμον
ἐξαγοράσῃ, ἵνα τὴν υἱοθεσίαν ἀπολάβωμεν.

The Christian, it appears, is bought at the price of Christ's Blood for
God. He is Christ's bond-servant, and at the same time God's son by
adoption. They that have been purchased have a work for others : they
are first-fruits to God and the Lamb.

Additional Note on ix. 14. Aspects of Christ's Sacrifice.

The Levitical Sacrifices expressed, as we have seen, several great ideas,
the ideas of atonement and fellowship resting upon the idea of a covenant.
They brought before the people in vivid types thoughts of cleansing and
divine communion through which God realised the gracious purpose which
He made known when He took them to Himself. Under outward forms
and limitations they shewed how man might yet reach the destiny for
which he was created.

The self-sacrifice of Christ upon the Cross fulfilled absolutely all that
was thus shadowed forth. That Sacrifice is presented to us in the Epistle
under three distinct aspects :

(1) As a Sacrifice of Atonement (ix. 14, 15);
(2) As a Covenant Sacrifice (ix. 15—17); and
(3) As a Sacrifice which is the groundwork of a Feast (xiii. 10, 11).

In each respect it had a spiritual, an eternal, a universal validity, where
the type had been necessarily external and confined.

These several aspects are considered in detail in the notes on the
passages which deal with them, but there is one common feature which
may be more conveniently noticed here. In the animal sacrifices of the
Law two points are carefully distinguished which our own habits of thought
lead us more or less to confuse, the killing of the victim and the application
of the blood. The killing was properly the act of the person on whose
behalf the victim was presented, or, in the case of a public sacrifice, of the
representative of the people. The application of the blood was the office
of the priests only. Christ was Offerer at once and Offering. In Him the
victim and the people and the priest were one. He therefore performed
both acts, He *offered Himself through the eternal Spirit* (ix. 14), and so

by the surrender of life He fulfilled the work of the people, of the humanity which He had assumed. Through His Blood He entered into the Divine Presence and cleansed the heavenly archetypes of the earthly sanctuary (ix. 12, 23), and so by the impartment of a new life He fulfils the work of the priest, having realised in His divine-human nature the end of man's existence.

The direct references to Christ's Death are naturally less frequent than the references to His Blood. Death, with its unnatural agony, was the condition, under the actual circumstances of fallen man, whereby alone the Life of the Son of man could be made available for the race (ii. 9, 14; comp. 1 Cor. xi. 26; Rom. v. 10; vi. 3 f.; Phil. ii. 8; iii. 10; Col. i. 22). The Blood was the energy of Christ's true human life, under the circumstances of earth, whereby alone man's life receives the pledge and the power of a divine glory (see Addit. Note on *v.* 12).

Thus the two—the Blood and the Death—correspond generally with the two sides of Christ's work, the fulfilment of the destiny of man as created and the fulfilment of this destiny though man has fallen. The first would have been necessary even though sin had not interrupted the due course of man's progress and relation to God. It becomes necessary therefore, in order to gain a complete view of the Sacrifice of Christ, to combine with the crowning act upon the Cross His fulfilment of the will of God from first to last (x. 5 ff.), the Sacrifice of Life with the Sacrifice of Death. And when we look back over the facts of Christ's Sacrifice brought forward in the Epistle we notice two series of blessings gained for men by Him, the one series answering to the restoration of man's right relation to God which has been violated by sin, and the other answering to the fulfilment of the purpose of creation, the attainment by man of the Divine likeness: on the one side we recognise a re-opened entrance into the Holiest closed against fallen man and fresh access to God, on the other side sovereignty over 'the house' and free intercourse with God.

Additional Note on ix. 16. *The meaning of* διαθήκη *in* ix. 15 ff.

1. The meaning of διαθήκη in the N. T. must be determined in the first instance by the use of the word in the LXX. In the LXX. διαθήκη and διατίθεμαι are the regular representatives of בְּרִית and כָּרַת בּ "(with two exceptions: Deut. ix. 15 αἱ δύο πλάκες τῶν μαρτυρίων. 1 K. xi. 11 τὰς ἐντολάς). In one place (Zech. xi. 14) διαθήκη represents the more specific idea of 'brotherhood' (אַחֲוָה) (comp. *Ed.* 5, Ps. ii. 7). Elsewhere it has uniformly the meaning of *Covenant* in the translation of the books of the Hebrew Canon (so in the three other places where it represents other words than בְּרִית: Ex. xxxi. 7 [עֵדוּה]; Deut. ix. 5 [דָּבָר]; Jer. xli. (xxxiv.) 18 [דִּבְרֵי הַבְּרִית]; compare also Lev. xxvi. 11; Ezek. xvi. 29); and, as representing בְּרִית, it is applied to a covenant between peoples (Josh. ix. 6;

Jud. ii. 2) and between persons (1 Sam. xxiii. 18; 2 Sam. iii. 12 f. &c.;
Mal. ii. 14). The same sense is preserved in the Apocrypha except in
Ecclus. xxxviii. 33 διαθήκην κρίματος οὐ διανοηθήσονται, and xlv. 17 ἐν
διαθήκαις κριμάτων, where it appears to have the original and wider sense
of 'disposition,' 'arrangement.' There is not the least trace of the meaning
'testament' in the Greek Old Scriptures, and the idea of a 'testament'
was indeed foreign to the Jews till the time of the Herods: comp. Jos. *Ant.*
xiii. 1, 16, 1; xvii. 3, 2; *B. J.* ii. 2, 3.

Συνθήκη, the ordinary word for *covenant*, is very rare in the LXX., though
it is used several times by the later translators (Aqu. Symm. Theod.) as the
rendering of בְּרִית. The choice of διαθήκη to express the notion of a divine
covenant is easily intelligible. In a divine 'covenant' the parties do not
stand in the remotest degree as equal contractors (συνθήκη). God in His
good pleasure makes the arrangement which man receives, though he is
not passive (2 K. xi. 17). Such a covenant is a 'disposition,' an 'ordain-
ment,' an expression of the divine will which they to whom it is made
reverently welcome.

2. In classical writers, on the other hand, from the time of Plato,
διαθήκη generally means 'a testament,' 'a will,' a 'disposition' (of property,
&c.) to take effect after death; though the more general sense of 'arrangement,' 'agreement,' is also found (Arist. *Av.* 440).

3. PHILO (*de nom. mut.* §§ 6 ff.; i. 586 f. M.) refers to a treatise of his on
'Covenants' (διαθήκαι), which has unfortunately been lost. But in the same
context he states the general idea which he attached to a Divine διαθήκη.
'Covenants' he says 'are written for the benefit of those who are worthy of
bounty. So a Covenant is a symbol of grace, which God sets between Himself
Who extends the boon and man who receives it' (*l. c.*). And directly after
he presents God Himself as 'the highest kind of Covenant, the beginning
and source of all graces.' In another phrase of the passage he shews how
easy it was to pass from the sense of 'covenant' to 'will': '[God] acknowledges that He will leave to the sinless and blameless an inheritance by
terms of a covenant (κατὰ διαθήκας), which it is fitting for God to give and
for a wise man to receive. For He says: I will place My Covenant between
Me and thee' (Gen. xvii. 2). Comp. *de sacr. Ab.* § 14 (i. 172 f. M.).

JOSEPHUS uses the word several times for 'will' (*Ant.* xvii. 3, 2; 9, 7;
B. J. ii. 2, 3), and he appears to avoid the phrases of the LXX. ἡ κιβωτὸς τῆς
διαθήκης and the like, using κιβωτός only.

4. In the N. T. the sense of 'covenant' is unquestionable, except in two
passages: Gal. iii. 15; and the passage under consideration (Heb. ix. 15 f.).
For the former passage see Bp. Lightfoot's note, who defends the sense
'covenant.' Compare Matt. xxvi. 28 and parallels; Acts iii. 25; vii. 8;
and notice the plural: Rom. ix. 4; Gal. iv. 24; Eph. ii. 12 (Wisd. xviii. 22;
Ecclus. xliv. 11; 2 Macc. viii. 15).

5. The Latin renderings of διαθήκη are instructive. In the N. T. the
rendering is uniformly *testamentum*, even where the sense of *covenant* is
unquestionable (Lk. i. 72; Acts iii. 25 (d. *dispositionis*); vii. 8 (d. *dispo-
sitionem*); Rom. xi. 27) and in quotations from the O. T. where *fœdus*
stands in the Vulgate rendering of the O. T. itself: Jer. xxxi. 31 (c. viii. 8).

The rendering is undoubtedly due to the Old Latin translation which Jerome in his cursory revision left untouched. The first translators naturally gave the ordinary equivalent of διαθήκη. It is, however, not unlikely that in the common language *testamentum* was not restricted to the classical sense of *will* but had the wider meaning of *charta testium subscriptionibus firmata*, which is not uncommon in later ecclesiastical documents. See Du Cange *s. v.*

Even in the O. T. the Old Latin rendering had such authority that the phrase *arca testamenti* occurs four times (Ex. xxx. 26; Num. xiv. 44; 2 Regg. vi. 15; Jer. iii. 16) for the common rendering *arca fœderis*; and so in Mal. iii. 1 we have *angelus testamenti*; comp. Zech. ix. 11 and Dan. iii. 34 (Vulg.); xi. 28, 30, 32; Is. xiv. 13.

Elsewhere (except in the version of the Psalms taken from O. L. where Jerome has *pactum*), the rendering of בְּרִית by *fœdus* appears to be universal.

The Syriac Versions transliterate the Greek word.

6. The Biblical evidence then, so far as it is clear, is wholly in favour of the sense of 'covenant,' with the necessary limitation of the sense of the word in connexion with a Divine covenant. When we pass to the consideration of the sense of διαθήκη in c. ix. 15 ff. one preliminary remark offers itself. The connexion of *vv.* 15—18 is most close: *v.* 16 ὅπου γάρ... : *v.* 18 ὅθεν οὐδέ....

This connexion makes it most difficult to suppose that the key-word (διαθήκη) is used in different senses in the course of the verses, and especially that the characteristic of a particular kind of διαθήκη, essentially different from the πρώτη διαθήκη of *vv.* 15, 18, should be brought forward in *v.* 16. For it is impossible to maintain that the sacrifices with which the Old Covenant was inaugurated could be explained on the supposition that it was a 'Testament.' Nor does it appear that it could be called a 'Testament' in any sense.

It is then most reasonable to conclude that διαθήκη has the same sense throughout, and that the sense is the otherwise universal one of 'covenant,' unless there are overwhelming arguments against such a view.

7. But it is said that there are such arguments: that the mention of an 'inheritance' suggests the thought of 'a will,' and that the phrases θάνατον φέρεσθαι τοῦ διαθεμένου, ἐπὶ νεκροῖς, ὅτε ζῇ ὁ διαθέμενος require it; and further it is asked how can it be said that a covenant requires 'death' to give it validity?

8. In answer to these contentions it must be replied that the mention of the 'inheritance' in *v.* 15 does not appear to furnish any adequate explanation of a transition from the idea of 'Covenant' to that of 'Testament.' It is true that Christ has obtained an inheritance (i. 4); and it is also true that He entered on the possession of it through death; but it cannot be said that He 'bequeathed' it to His people. He 'made a disposition' in favour of His people (Luke xxii. 29). By union with Him they enjoy together with Him what is His. But He does not give them anything apart from Himself. It is also of importance in this respect to notice that the thought of the bequeathal of an inheritance by Christ to

His people is not supported by any other passage of Scripture (not by Luke xxii. 29).

Again there can be no question that in *v.* 15 Christ is spoken of as 'the mediator of a new covenant' (comp. vii. 22 ἔγγυος). Now the conceptions of Christ as the 'Mediator of a Covenant' and as a 'Testator,' the 'framer of a will,' are essentially distinct. A Covenant is a disposition of things determined by God for man and brought about through Christ: a Testament would be the expression of Christ's own will as to what should be after His death. The thoughts are wholly different; and the idea of death is unable in itself to combine them. The Covenant might include the necessity of the Mediator's Death, but the admission of that necessity does not convert the Covenant into a Testament, or place the Mediator in a position of a Testator. He who fulfils the Covenant may indeed by the Covenant secure rights which He can communicate to others after death, but such a communication is not a testamentary disposition.

Yet further: if the writer had had in his mind the simple fact of the death of a testator it is unintelligible that he should have used language so strange as ἐπὶ νεκροῖς and φέρεσθαι. Nor is the use of ἐπὶ νεκροῖς explained by the supposed choice of the words to meet the case of the Old Covenant, to which the idea of a Testament does not apply (yet comp. Lact. *Inst.* iv. 20).

9. It does not therefore appear that the sense of 'testament' clears away the difficulties of the passage in itself, or in relation to the context. Is it possible then, on the other hand, to give an intelligible meaning to the passage if the sense 'covenant' is retained throughout? To meet this question fairly it is necessary to recal what has been already said by the Apostle.

The course of thought appears to be this. In *v.* 15 the two notions of a 'covenant' and a 'death' have been introduced. The death, as it is first presented, is presented as a means for redemption from past obligations. But when it has once been brought forward the question arises: Had it no further meaning in this connexion? The answer is found in a reference to the rites by which covenants were solemnly ratified. A sacrifice was a constituent part of the ratification; and it must be remembered that the sacrifices of the Old Covenant included not only death but also the sprinkling of blood, already touched on in the reference to the Sacrifice of the New Covenant. The early phrases used for making a covenant shew that the idea of death actually entered into the conception of a covenant: בָּרַת בְּרִית, ὅρκια τέμνειν, *icere fœdus.*

In some way or other the victim which was slain and, in some cases at least, divided (Gen. xv. 10, comp. *v.* 18; Jer. xxxiv. 18 f.), represented the parties to the covenant.

Probably the fundamental idea was that so far as this special arrangement was concerned they had no longer will or life. The arrangement was final and unchangeable.

In ordinary covenants the death of the persons who made the covenant was represented of necessity in symbol only, and both parties were alike liable to change. In the Covenant of the Gospel, Christ, being Himself truly man, represented humanity, as the victims represented the Jewish people at the founding of the Mosaic Covenant; and by His death He fulfilled the Covenant for men eternally, and satisfied the conditions on which forgiveness rests. He shewed that the promise of God was inviolable, and He shewed also how man could avail himself of its provisions. The redemption which was accomplished was the pledge of the fulfilment of the promise in the Covenant still to be realised.

For here fresh considerations offer themselves which underlie the argument of the passage. The Covenant to which the writer looks is, as has been seen, not one between man and man, who meet as equal parties, but between man and God. The death of the covenant-victim therefore assumes a new character. It figures not only the unchangeableness of death but also the self-surrender of death.

10. If then the view be adopted that the sense of διαθήκη remains unchanged throughout as 'Covenant,' the general force of the argument will be this :

The system, the dispensation, established by Christ corresponds in the truest sense to a New Covenant, and rests upon a Covenant. A Covenant indeed requires for absolute validity the ratification by death, as is conspicuously illustrated by the fundamental covenant-sacrifice in Gen. xv. and by the Covenant with Israel.

And this condition was satisfied by Christ. He was Himself the Covenant-Victim. In this aspect He attested the inviolable force of the Covenant which He established. Not in a figure only, but in reality, He shewed how the Covenant was valid and must be valid. He made the new relation of man to God possible and sure. His Death was an atonement for sin, and it was a perfect ratification of the Covenant which He made 'in His blood,' in His life offered and communicated. In Him humanity fulfilled its part. For here we are considering not a Covenant between man and man, but between man and God. And that man may enter into such a relation he must yield up life, that he may receive it again. This Christ has done once for all for men, and in Him, in virtue of His Life, all men can draw nigh to God.

Hence the ceremonies connected with the inauguration of the Old Covenant become fully intelligible. In that case also the life offered was imparted to the people in a symbol. The blood of the victims whose death marked the ratification of the Covenant was sprinkled on the people and on the sanctuary.

It can cause no surprise that the patristic interpretations rest on the sense of 'will.'

It was natural that the Greek Commentators (from Chrysostom downwards) should take the familiar sense of διαθήκη, and Latin Commentators found it given (apparently) by the text which they used. Yet there are traces of the other idea being still remembered, as in an interesting note of Isidore of Pelusium : τὴν συνθήκην, τουτέστι τὴν ἐπαγγελίαν, διαθήκην ἡ θεία καλεῖ γραφή, διὰ τὸ βέβαιον καὶ ἀπαράβατον· συνθῆκαι μὲν γὰρ πολλάκις ἀνατρέπονται, διαθῆκαι δὲ νόμιμοι οὐδαμῶς (Epp. ii. 196).

X. ¹ Σκιὰν γὰρ ἔχων ὁ νόμος τῶν μελλόντων

iii. *The Old Sacrifices and the New: the abiding efficacy of Christ's One Sacrifice* (c. x. 1—18).

In the preceding section the writer of the Epistle has pointed out the completeness of the one single High-priestly work of Christ in comparison with the crowning service of the Old Covenant on the Day of Atonement. He once for all was offered (c. ix. 28); and in due time, coming forth from the Divine Presence, He will proclaim the consummation of His work. Thus He stands in sharp contrast to the Levitical High-priests. Their work was repeated because it was essentially imperfect. In other words, that which seemed to give it special attractiveness and power, as appealing sensibly to the worshipper year by year by a visible and impressive service, was a sign of its inefficacy and transitoriness to those who looked deeper. Because the Law witnessed to something which it did not include or convey, its message was given again and again. This thought is now extended from the general representative sacrifice to the Levitical sacrifices generally. The Apostle points out (1) the inherent weakness and the provisional office of these sacrifices (x. 1—4); and, in contrast with these, (2) the true nature of the Sacrifice of Christ (5—10). He then shews (3) the perpetual efficacy of Christ's Sacrifice from His present position of Kingly Majesty (11—14); and (4) the consequent fulfilment in Him of the prophetic description of the New Covenant (15—18).

(1) *vv.* 1—4. The essential inadequacy of the Legal sacrifices to remove sin.

The sacrifices of the Mosaic system could not bring τελείωσις, for just what they did once they did afresh when the time came round (*v.* 1); and such repetition could not have been required if they had been spiritually efficacious (*v.* 2). Viewed in their real

character they were designed to declare a need which they did not satisfy (*v.* 3); and which essentially they could not satisfy (*v.* 4).

¹ *For as having a shadow only of the good things to come, not the very image of the objects, the Law can never, by the same sacrifices which they offer year by year, make perfect for ever those who come to worship.* ² *Since in that case would they not have ceased to be offered because the worshippers would have had no more conscience of sins, when they had been cleansed once for all ?* ³ *But in them sins are called to remembrance year by year;* ⁴ *for it is impossible that blood of bulls and goats should take away sins.*

1. σκιάν... τελειῶσαι] The sentence is complicated, and the natural order of the words is modified by the desire of the writer to emphasise the main ideas of his statement. If we adopt the reading δύναται the rendering appears to be fairly clear: *For as having a shadow only of the good things to come, not the very image of the objects, the Law can never, by the same sacrifices which they*—the appointed ministers of the system—*offer year by year,* in a continually recurring cycle, *make perfect for ever those who come to* God on the way which it opens.

In this rendering it is assumed that the two phrases κατ' ἐνιαυτόν and εἰς τὸ διηνεκές are placed (irregularly) at the head of the clauses to which they belong in order to bring out the conceptions of 'yearly repetition' and 'perpetuity' of effect, which respectively characterise the Old and New Covenants.

The same purpose of emphasis explains the fact that εἰς τὸ διηνεκές precedes the verb to which it belongs, while elsewhere it follows it: *vv.* 12, 14; vii. 3.

The connexion of εἰς τὸ διηνεκές with

ἀγαθῶν, οὐκ αὐτὴν τὴν εἰκόνα τῶν πραγμάτων, κατ'

τελειῶσαι is further supported by the parallel in v. 11 where the words καθ' ἡμέραν, τὰς αὐτὰς προσφ. θ., exactly correspond with κατ' ἐνιαυτόν, ταῖς αὐταῖς θ. ἃς προσφ., and περιελεῖν ἁμαρτίας with εἰς τὸ διην. τελ. It also agrees better with the sense of εἰς τὸ διηνεκές.

If εἰς τὸ διηνεκές is joined with προσφέρειν in the sense of the Vulgate *indesinenter*, 'without cessation,' 'as long as the Law lasts,' it loses the peculiar force which it has elsewhere of marking an act which issues in a permanent result, permanent in continuous duration and not only in successive repetition; and it is specially difficult to suppose that the same combination of words should be used differently in the same chapter.

σκιὰν γὰρ ἔχων...οὐκ αὐτὴν τὴν εἰκ.] *For as having a shadow of the good things to come the Law*...Vulg. *Umbram enim habens...non ipsam imaginem rerum*...The emphatic position of the participle (as opposed to ὁ γὰρ νόμος σκιὰν ἔχων) contrasts forcibly the nature of the Law with the nature of Christ's work which has been just set forth. The iteration, the inefficacy, the transitoriness of the services of the Law which culminated in that on the Day of Atonement, followed from the fact that it 'had a shadow only of the good things to come.' It could provide nothing more than symbolic, and therefore recurrent, offerings, which in different ways witnessed to an idea that they were inadequate to fulfil.

The words contain one of the very few illustrations which are taken from art in the N.T. The 'shadow' is the dark outlined figure cast by the object—as in the legend of the origin of the bas-relief—contrasted with the complete representation (εἰκών) produced by the help of colour and solid mass. The εἰκών brings before us under the conditions of space, as we can understand it, that which is spiri-

tual: Rom. viii. 29; Col. i. 19 (with Lightfoot's note); iii. 10.

Compare Cic. *De Offic.* iii. 17. 69 Nos veri juris *germanæque justitiæ* solidam et expressam effigiem nullam tenemus, umbra et imaginibus utimur. *Pro Clælio*, c. v. 12.

The figure is common in Philo. See *de migr. Abr.* § 2 (i. 438 M.); *de conf. ling.* § 37 (i. 434 M.).

See c. viii. 5 note.

Chrysostom explains the language (inadequately) of the outline in contrast with the finished picture. ἕως μὲν γὰρ ἂν ὡς ἐν γραφῇ περιάγῃ τις τὰ χρώματα σκιά τις ἐστίν, ὅταν δὲ τὸ ἄνθος ἐπαλείψῃ τις καὶ ἐπιχρίσῃ τὰ χρώματα, τότε εἰκὼν γίνεται (so Alcuin).

Comp. Euthym. Zig. τῆς σκιᾶς τελείωσις ὁ διὰ τῶν χρωμάτων ἀπαρτισμός, ἡγοῦν ἡ εἰκών.

The difference between the 'shadow' and the 'image' is well illustrated by the difference between a 'type' and a 'sacrament,' in which the characteristic differences of the Old and New Covenants are gathered up. The one witnesses to grace and truth beyond and outside itself: the other is the pledge and the means through which grace and truth are brought home to us.

Hence many saw in 'the good things to come' the sacraments of the Christian Church; and Theophylact, accepting this interpretation, carries our thoughts still further. As the image is better than the shadow, so, he argues, will the archetype be better than the image, the realities of the unseen world than 'the mysteries' which now represent them.

One other point is to be noticed. Things visible and sensible are the shadows: things unseen and spiritual are the substance. The whole world is made for us a shadow of some unimaginable glory.

τῶν μελλ. ἀγ.] *of the good things to come*, the blessings which belonged to

ἐνιαυτὸν ταῖς αὐταῖς θυσίαις ᵀ ἃς προσφέρουσιν εἰς τὸ
διηνεκὲς οὐδέποτε δύναται τοὺς προσερχομένους τελει-

1 αὐτῶν

1 ταῖς αὐταῖς...δύναται. See Additional Note.   τελειῶσαι: καθαρίσαι D₂*.

the 'coming age' (c. vi. 5), 'the coming order' (c. ii. 5). These are here
spoken of as future from the stand-
point of the Law. And, though they
were essentially realised by the accomplishment of Christ's work (c. ix. 11
τῶν γενομένων ἀγ.), they still remain
in part yet future in regard to man's
full enjoyment of them (c. xiii. 14).

τῶν πραγμάτων] 'the real objects.'
The word is unusual in this sense. It
expresses τὰ μέλλοντα ἀγαθά so far as
they were embodied. Comp. c. vi. 18;
xi. 1.

κατ' ἐνιαυτόν] The words go with the
whole clause. The reference is not
exclusively to the services of the Day
of Atonement, but to the whole sacrificial system of the Law, completed in
a yearly cycle, which started (so to
speak) from the 'continual' burnt-
offering and was crowned on the Day
of Atonement 'once in the year' (c. ix.
7). Year by year, when all had been
done only to be repeated, the powerlessness of the legal atonements was
vividly set forth. And on the other
hand (this thought lies behind) all the
Levitical sacrifices, the daily sacrifices
habitually offered by the priests (v.
11), and the single yearly sacrifice of
the High-priest, found their fulfilment
in Christ.

ταῖς αὐταῖς...] The identical repetition was a sign of the powerlessness
of the system. It could provide
nothing fresh. And yet further, what
it had once done it did again. Evidently therefore the effect was as
inadequate as it was unalterable.

ἃς προσφέρουσιν] which they, the
appointed ministers of the system,
offer. For this impersonal use of the
plural, compare John xv. 6; xx. 2;
Apoc. xii. 6; Matt. vii. 16; Mk. x.
13; Lk. xvii. 23. It is far less natural

to take the subject from τοὺς προσερχομένους.

εἰς τὸ διην....τοὺς προσερχ. τελειῶσαι]
make perfect for ever—so that the
effect once obtained lasts onwards
without break—those worshippers who
come to God through the High-priest
or priests. The whole congregation
is included in the title, which cannot
be limited either to the priests or to
special offerers. The daily sacrifices
and the sacrifices on the Day of Atonement were for all.

τελειῶσαι] See Additional Note on
ii. 10.

εἰς τὸ διηνεκές] Vulg. indesinenter,
O. L. in frequentiam. The phrase is
found in the N. T. only in this Epistle:
vv. 12, 14 (Vulg. in sempiternum);
vii. 3 (Vulg. in perpetuum) note. As
distinguished from εἰς τὸν αἰῶνα it
expresses the thought of a continuously abiding result. The former
phrase looks to the implied absence
of limit while εἰς τὸ διηνεκές affirms
uninterrupted duration in regard to
some ruling thought.

οὐδέποτε] v. 11. The use of this
temporal negative in place of the simple negative emphasises the thought
of the many occasions, of the long
experience, by which the inefficacy of
the sacrifices was shewn.

The word οὐδέποτε is rare in N.T.
(in Epp. only here and 1 Cor. xiii. 8
οὐδέποτε πίπτει). The use in Matt.
xxi. 16, 42 (οὐδέποτε ἀνέγνωτε) is instructive.

τοὺς προσερχομένους] See c. vii. 25
note.

2. The inefficacy of the sacrifices
is proved by their repetition. If it be
said that the repeated sacrifice dealt
only with the later sins; the answer
is that we have to deal with sin and
not with sins only: to be assured that

ὦσαι· ²ἐπεὶ οὐκ ἂν ἐπαύσαντο προσφερόμεναι, διὰ τὸ
μηδεμίαν ἔχειν ἔτι συνείδησιν ἁμαρτιῶν τοὺς λατρεύοντας
ἅπαξ κεκαθαρισμένους ; ³ἀλλ᾽ ἐν αὐταῖς ἀνάμνησις ἁμαρ-

2 om. οὐκ H* syrvg (lat.).   om. ἔτι D₂*.   τούς: +δέ D₂*.

our true relation with God has been
re-established. A sacrifice which
effects this for humanity, and we need
no less, cannot be repeated.

ἐπεὶ οὐκ ἄν...] Vulg. *alioquin cessassent*...O.L. *nam nec cessassent*... The
words are a question which is followed
up by ἀλλά *v.* 3. '*Since in that case
(Else), would they not...? but* in fact...'
For ἐπεί see c. ix. 26 note.

ἐπαύσ. προσφερόμεναι] So frequently
with an active participle: Acts v. 42 ;
vi. 13 &c.

συνείδησιν ἁμ.] Vulg. *conscientiam
peccati.* Compare 1 Pet. ii. 19 (συνείδησις θεοῦ), (in 1 Cor. viii. 7 συνηθείᾳ
τοῦ εἰδώλου not συνειδήσει τοῦ εἰδ.).
For συνείδησις see c. ix. 9 Additional Note.

τοὺς λατρεύοντας] Vulg. *cultores.*
The worship would still continue
though the necessity for atoning sacrifices had ceased to exist. Comp.
Apoc. xxii. 3 f.; c. ix. 9.

Λατρεύειν is used absolutely for
divine worship c. ix. 9; Lk. ii. 37 ;
Acts xxvi. 7 ; Phil. iii. 3 (οἱ πν. θεοῦ
λατρ.).

ἅπαξ κεκαθαρισμένους] *when they had
once for all been cleansed.* The effect
of the cleansing is regarded in its
continuance, and not in its actual
accomplishment (Eph. v. 26 καθαρί-
σας). Compare *v.* 10 ἡγιασμένοι. Such
permanent cleansing would have involved τελείωσις (*v.* 1). The application of the virtue of the one effectual
sacrifice would have met the wants of
every true worshipper. The case of a
single body of worshippers is taken,
but the principle holds true of all.
For καθαρίζειν see c. ix. 14, 23 ;
Tit. ii. 14 ; and for ἅπαξ c. vi. 4 note,
ἐφάπαξ vii. 27.

3, 4. The Levitical sacrifices had

however an important function to fulfil in the discipline of men. The repetition, which shewed their inefficacy,
kept alive the sense of sin. They
were, in the words of Primasius :
Accusatio infirmitatis, non virtutis
ostensio. In eo enim quod offerebatur,
redargutio peccatorum ; in eo quod
semper offerebatur, redargutio infirmitatis ejusdem sacrificii.

Comp. Euth. Zig. τὸ μὲν θύειν ἔλεγχος ἁμαρτημάτων, τὸ δὲ ἀεὶ ἀπόδειξις
ἀσθενείας.

3. ἀλλ᾽ ἐν αὐτ.] *But in them sins are
called to remembrance...* That is :
'so far from the sacrifices being dis-
continued because they have fulfilled
their work, they serve in fact to keep
alive the recollection of sin as a present burden.' This seems to be on
the whole the simplest and most
natural explanation of ἀλλά. It is however possible to take ἐπεί...κεκαθαρι-
σμένους as parenthetical, and to take
ἀλλά as introducing a direct continuation of *v.* 1, οὐδέποτε δύναται...ἀλλά...

ἀνάμνησις ἁμ.] not simply 'a remembrance' or 'a record made' of sins
(Vulg. *commemoratio peccatorum*),
but *a calling to mind of sins,* whereby
men are put in remembrance of them
by a divine institution. This is more
than a public acknowledgment and
confession of sins, such as at present
(and by immemorial usage) forms an
important part of the synagogue service for the Day of Atonement.

So Philo speaks of sacrifices as a
ὑπόμνησις of sins (*De plant. Noe,* § 25 ;
De vit. Mos. iii. § 10), but when they
are rightly offered he assigns to them
real efficacy (*de vict.* § 7). Compare
Num. v. 15 (LXX.) θυσία μνημοσύνου
ἀναμιμνήσκουσα ἁμαρτίαν, of which the
opposite is expressed in *v.* 17 (τῶν

τιῶν κατ᾽ ἐνιαυτόν, ⁴ἀδύνατον γὰρ αἷμα ⌜ταύρων καὶ

4 τράγων καὶ ταύρων

3 κατ᾽ ἐν.: +γίνεται D₂* vg.   4 ταύρ. καὶ τρ. ACD₂ vg syrr me: τρ. καὶ ταύρ. ℵ æg.

ἁμαρτιῶν...οὐ μὴ μνησθήσομαι ἔτι).
Under the new Covenant God Himself
does not remember the sins of His
people, still less does He bring them
solemnly to their remembrance.

The use of the word ἀνάμνησις suggests a contrast between the Jewish
sacrifices and the Christian Eucharist.
In them there was ἀνάμνησις ἁμαρτιῶν.
They were instituted to keep fresh the
thought of responsibility: that was
instituted, in Christ's words, εἰς τὴν
ἐμὴν ἀνάμνησιν (Luke xxii. 19; 1 Cor.
xi. 24 f.), to bring to men's minds the
recollection of the redemption which
He has accomplished. The word is
not found elsewhere in the N. T.
Ἀναμιμνήσκειν (act.) occurs 1 Cor. iv.
17; 2 Tim. i. 6.

In the LXX. ἀνάμνησις is found Lev.
xxiv. 7 (comp. ii. 2); Num. x. 10;
Wisd. xvi. 6. Comp. [Sym.] Ps. vi. 6;
cxxxiv. 13.

κατ᾽ ἐνιαυτόν] The words are repeated
from v. 1. The thought of sin is
brought home in various aspects by
the whole system of sacrifice *year by
year.*

4. ἀδύνατον...ἀφαιρεῖν] Vulg. *impossibile est...sanguine...auferri* V.;
O.L. *difficile...est...*

The spiritual inefficacy of the Levitical sacrifices, which was indicated
by their repetition, is patent also
from their very nature. The physical
suffering and death of an irrational
creature—unwilling and unconscious
—can make no atonement for man's
sin. Man can have no true fellowship
with such beings. Such a sacrifice
cannot be more than a symbol, a
sign.

ταύρων καὶ τράγων] c. ix. 12 f.; 19.
The sacrifices of the Day of Atonement still suggest the general language. Comp. Ps. l. 13.

ἀφαιρεῖν ἁμ.] Is. i. 16 ἀφέλετε τὰς
πονηρίας ἀπὸ τῶν ψυχῶν (הָסִירוּ). Ex.
xxxiv. 7, 9 ἀφελεῖς σὺ τὰς ἁμαρτίας
ἡμῶν (סָלַח). Lev. x. 17 ἵνα ἀφέλητε
τὴν ἁμαρτίαν. Num. xiv. 18 ἀφαιρῶν
ἀνομίας καὶ ἀδικίας καὶ ἁμαρτίας. Ecclus. xlvii. 11 κύρ. ἀφεῖλε τὰς ἁμ.
αὐτοῦ.

The phrase does not occur elsewhere
in the N. T. except in a quotation :
Rom. xi. 27 ὅταν ἀφέλωμαι ἁμαρτίας
(Is. xxvii. 9 LXX.). It is not unfrequent in the LXX. The image appears
to be that of the removal of a load
bound upon the sinner. Compare
Jer. xi. 15; Zech. iii. 4.

Contrast v. 11 περιελεῖν, both in form
and tense.

The limited yet real power of the
Levitical sacrifices has been recognised in c. ix. 13.

(2) 5—10. The one valid sacrifice
of the perfect fulfilment of the Will
of God offered by Christ.

In the last paragraph the inefficacy of the Levitical sacrifices has
been brought out. In this paragraph Christ's efficacious sacrifice of
Himself is placed in contrast with
them.

The argument is expressed in the
language of a Davidic Psalm.

The Christ coming into the world
gives utterance to the conviction of
man that the only sacrifice which he
can offer to God is perfect obedience
(*vv.* 5—7). In doing this He contrasts
the fulfilment of the will of God with
the Levitical sacrifices so as to abolish
the latter by the former (*vv.* 8, 9).
He obeys perfectly; and of the fruits
of His obedience men are made partakers (*v.* 10).

Psalm xl. is regarded with probability as an expression of David's feeling

towards the close of his persecution by Saul, when the promised kingdom was now in near view. The present text of the Psalm consists of two parts which differ widely in general tone. The second part (*vv.* 13—18) cannot be applied to the Messiah (*v.* 13); and most of it (*vv.* 14—18) occurs again in the Psalter, with slight variations, as Ps. lxx.

The first part (*vv.* 1—12) stands out from the writings of the Old Testament as giving not only a view of the essential inadequacy of external sacrifices but also a clear indication of that which they represent and of that which fulfils the idea to which they bear witness. In the contemplation of God's mercies, and in the declaration of God's righteousness, the Psalmist feels that no offering of that which is without the worshipper can rightly convey the return of gratitude or make atonement (*sin-offering*). Nothing but perfect self-devotion answers to the claims of God and man's desire.

Such a confession, which embodies the aspiration of man, and rises above his power of fulfilment, describes what Christ has done as the Son of man, through whom man's ideal has been realised (c. ii. 6 ff.; Ps. viii.). Thus the words are rightly applied to Him. His power to do the will of God corresponded with His purpose to do it. That will being once accomplished for humanity by its perfect representative, the use of sacrifices was done away.

The words in their original context gain fresh force from a comparison with I Sam. xv. 22. David, the true divine type of a king, spontaneously embodied the principle which Saul, the human type of a king, violated to his own overthrow.

The writer of the Epistle follows the rendering of the LXX. with some slight differences, ὁλοκαυτώματα (LXX., Hebr. ὁλοκαύτωμα): εὐδόκησας (LXX.,

Hebr. ᾔτησας), compressing also the last verse (τοῦ ποιῆσαι, ὁ θεός, τὸ θέλημά σου : LXX. τοῦ ποιῆσαι τὸ θέλημά σου, ὁ θεός μου, ἠβουλήθην...). The LXX., as is well known, differs from the Hebrew in one remarkable clause: for לִי כָּרִיתָ אָזְנַיִם *ears hast thou opened* (*dug*) *for me*, it gives σῶμα δὲ κατηρτίσω μοι. There can be no question that this is the true reading of the Greek. The conjecture that ϲⲱⲙⲁ is an early blunder for ⲱⲧⲓⲁ (the reading of the other Greek versions) cannot be maintained in the face of the evidence. The rendering must therefore be considered to be a free interpretation of the original text. In this respect it extends and emphasises the fundamental idea. The ' body ' is the instrument for fulfilling the divine command, just as the ' ear ' is the instrument for receiving it. God originally fashioned for man in his frame the organ for hearing His voice, and by this He plainly shewed that he was made to obey it.

5 *Wherefore when He entereth into the world, He saith*

> *Sacrifice and offering Thou wouldest not,*
> *But a body didst Thou prepare for me;*
> 6 *In whole burnt-offerings and sacrifices for sin Thou hadst no pleasure :*
> 7 *Then said I, Lo, I am come (in the roll of the book it is written of me) to do, O God, Thy will.*

8 *Saying above, Sacrifices and offerings and whole burnt-offerings and offerings for sin Thou wouldest not (the which are offered according to the Law),* 9 *then hath He said, Lo, I am come to do Thy will. He removeth the first that He may establish the second.* 10 *In which will we have been sanctified through the offering of the body of Jesus Christ once for all.*

τράγων¹ ἀφαιρεῖν ἁμαρτίας.   ⁵ Διὸ εἰσερχόμενος εἰς τὸν κόσμον λέγει

Θυςίαν καὶ προσφορὰν οὐκ ἠθέλησας, σῶμα δὲ κατηρτίσω μοι·

ἀφαιρεῖν: ἀφελεῖν (ἀφερεῖν) ℵ*.

5 σῶμα: ears syr hl mg.

5. διὸ εἰσερχ. εἰς τὸν κόσμον] *Wherefore....* Because the Levitical sacrifices were essentially ineffective the Christ speaking through the Psalmist or, to express the same idea otherwise, the Psalmist giving utterance to the highest thought of man which Christ alone can realise, recognised the fact, and offered the reality of rational self-surrender which they represented.

The words *when He entereth into the world* (Vulg. *ingrediens mundum;* O. L. *incedens in orbem*) are not to be confined to the moment of the Incarnation though they found their complete fulfilment then. They apply to each manifestation of Christ in the realm of human life (John i. 9; comp. vi. 14; xi. 27). The entrance of the divinely chosen King upon His earthly Kingdom corresponds with the entrance of the Son of man upon the inheritance of the world.

The words, it will be observed, assume the preexistence of the Christ. It is worthy of notice that Philo especially affirms of the Logos that 'he came not in visible form': *de prof.* § 19 (i. 561 M.); comp. *Quis rer. div. hær.* § 9 (i. 479 M.).

On the thought of Christ 'entering into the world' Primasius says: Quando, qui ubique præsens erat sed tamen invisibilis, factus postea homo visibilis mundo apparuit, quodammodo ubi erat illuc ingressus.

λέγει] The words of the Psalmist are ideally the words of the Christ; and they are not past only but present. Compare c. i. 6 f.; iii. 7; v. 6; viii. 8. No person is named. The thought of the true speaker is present to the mind of every reader.

θυσ. καὶ προσφ....ὁλοκ. καὶ περὶ ἁμ.]

The two pairs of words give a complete view of the Jewish sacrifices. The first pair describe them according to their material, the animal-offering (זֶבַח) and the meal-offering (מִנְחָה). The second pair give in the burnt-offering (עוֹלָה) and the sin-offering (חַטָּאָה), representative types of the two great classes of offerings, eucharistic offerings, which belonged to the life of the Covenant, and expiatory offerings, which were provided for the restoration of the life of the Covenant.

In themselves, this is laid down generally, the sacrifices gave no pleasure to God. Their value was in what they represented. Under this aspect that which corresponds to the first pair is distinctly stated (σῶμα κατηρτίσω μοι). The aspirations and wants expressed by the second pair find their complete satisfaction in the fulfilment of the will of God by the Son of man through suffering and death (*v.* 7).

Several passages in the O. T. recognise the powerlessness of sacrifices in themselves: 1 Sam. xv. 22; Ps. l. 8 ff.; li. 16 ff.; Hos. vi. 6; Is. i. 10 ff.; Jer. vii. 21 f. But these words of Ps. xl. go further: they point to a perfect service, and perhaps to the sacrifice (death) of one who has served perfectly.

σῶμα κατηρτίσω μοι] *a body didst thou prepare for me,* Vulg. *corpus aptasti mihi.* The King, the representative of men, recognises in the manifold organs of His personal power—His body—the one fitting means for rendering service to God. Through this, in its fulness, He can do God's will.   Not by anything outside

⁶ὁλοκαυτώματα καὶ περὶ ἀμαρτίας οὐκ εὐδόκησας.
⁷τότε εἶπον Ἰδοὺ ἥκω, ἐν κεφαλίδι βιβλίου γέγραπται περὶ ἐμοῦ,

6 ὁλοκαυτώματα⸴: -τωμα D₂*.   7 Ἰδού: +ἐγώ D₂* syr vg.   om. ἥκω א*.
γέγρ.: +γάρ D₂*.

Himself, not by animals in *sacrifices*, not by the fruits of the earth in *offerings*, but by the use of His own endowments, as He is enabled to use them, He will accomplish that which God designed for Him to do.

It will be seen that the idea in this clause is that of a perfect life irrespective of any thought of sin. Man as created had for his end this perfect exercise and perfect development of every human faculty that so he might bring all to God, fulfilling in this way the conception of sacrifice. And sin has not altered the obligation: Rom. xii. 1 f.

Some ancient thinkers regarded the humanity of Christ as the final cause of all created things (comp. *Epp. of St John*, pp. 291 f.). The thought throws light upon the gradual progress of the world throughout the ages, the humanity of Christ holding out the promise of the unity of men and of Creation in man.

The tense of κατηρτίσω does not mark any point in time. The divine act is supratemporal (comp. c. i. 2 ἔθηκεν). The words are the confession of the Christ at each moment of His entrance on a fresh stage of His historic work.

The verb καταρτίζειν suggests the thought of the 'many members' fitly framed together for varied and harmonious service. The body of man, like 'the world' itself (c. xi. 3 κατηρτίσθαι τοὺς αἰῶνας), consists of parts which fulfil different functions and contribute in their measure to the effect of the whole. These require to be brought into due relation in the individual by discipline and help (1 Thess. iii. 10; Gal. vi. 1; c. xiii. 21; 1 Pet. v. 10); even as the individuals

have to be duly brought together in the Christian society (1 Cor. i. 10; 2 Cor. xiii. 9, 11), through the work of the appointed ministry (Eph. iv. 12).

6. ὁλοκαυτώματα...οὐκ εὐδόκ.] For the construction with *acc.* compare Matt. xii. 18 ὅν (not εἰς ὅν) εὐδ. (from LXX.); and so not unfrequently in LXX.

In N. T. εὐδοκεῖν is commonly found with ἐν: v. 38 (LXX.); Lk. iii. 22; 2 Cor. xii. 10: and it is also found with *inf.*: Lk. xii. 32.

Ὁλοκαύτωμα, which occurs again in Mk. xii. 33, is the habitual rendering in LXX. of עוֹלָה, 'that which ascends,' *i.e.* in the flame to heaven, rather than to the altar.

The phrase περὶ ἀμαρτίας is used as a compound indeclinable noun: *e.g.* Lev. vii. 27 οὗτος ὁ νόμος τῶν ὁλοκ. ...καὶ περὶ ἀμαρτίας....

7. τότε εἶπον...] *then said I...* at the time when the Divine Will was made clear: when it was seen that no eucharistic offerings could satisfy the divine claim to grateful service; and no expiatory offerings do away with sin.

ἥκω] *I am come*, not 'I will come' or 'I come.' Obedience is immediate and complete. This sense of the will of God was, as it were, the Master's call in the heart, and the servant's answer was in the new connexion: '*Here am I*' (Is. vi. 8).

For ἥκω compare John viii. 42; 1 John v. 20; *v.* 37.

ἐν κεφ. β. γ.] Vulg. *in capite volumine*) *libri*. The interpretation of the original (בִּמְגִלַּת־סֵפֶר כָּתוּב עָלָי ἐν εἰλήματι β. Aqu.) is uncertain. Per-

τοῦ ποιῆϲαι, ὁ θεόϲ, τὸ θέλημά ϲογ.

⁸ ἀνώτερον λέγων ὅτι   Θγϲίαϲ καὶ προϲφορὰϲ καὶ ὁλοκαγτώματα

8 θυσίας καὶ προσφοράς ℵ*ACD₂* vg syr vg me the: -ίαν καὶ -άν 5ℵ° syr hl.

haps the simplest rendering is : *in the book-roll* (the roll of the Law) *a law is written for me*, which lays down perfectly my duty. The King acknowledges a definite standard of the will of God, before He undertakes to aim at fulfilling it. The περὶ ἐμοῦ of the LXX. is not inconsistent with this sense. The Law which foreshadowed the duties of a King of Israel (περὶ ἐμοῦ) was the rule of the King's life. Here the reference appears to be quite general : John v. 39. The word κεφαλίς is of difficult interpretation. It is generally supposed that the word, which was used for the capital of a shaft, was applied to the little knobs (*cornua*) at the ends of the stick round which the roll was wound, and then to the roll itself. But it does not appear that any example of this sense of the word is found. Others think that the sense of 'roll' was derived from the Rabbinic usage of קָפַל 'to roll,' 'to fold' Buxtorf, *Lex. Rabb.* p. 2090) ; but no instance of the application of the word to a manuscript roll is quoted. The general meaning of 'roll,' however derived, is found elsewhere in LXX. : Ezek. ii. 9 ; iii. 1 f. ; Esdr. vi. 2 ; and in Aquila Is. viii. 1 where the LXX. has τόμος. Comp. Euth. Zig.: οἱ Ἑβραῖοι βιβλία μὲν καλοῦσι τὰ συγγράμματα, κεφαλίδας δὲ τὰ εἰλητάρια (*volumina*)...εἰλητραρίοις γὰρ ἐνέγραφον καὶ οὐ τεύχεσι τετραγώνοις ὡς ἡμεῖς.

The Latin fathers, taking the translation *in capite*, were inclined to explain it of some special passage of Scripture, as Gen. i. 1 ; or Ps. i.; or of Lev. i. 3, as interpreted of Christ. Quidam intelligunt hic initium Genesis, ubi scriptum est *In principio*, id est in Filio, *fecit Deus cœlum et terram*. Quidam primum Psalmum

...Sed quia in his nihil de morte Christi præfiguratur...melius videtur intelligi de initio libri Levitici dictum...(Primas.).

τοῦ ποιῆσαι...] The shortening of the verse brings the purpose of the speaker into closer connexion with His coming. At the same time the Greek of the LXX. places that which God willed (τὸ θέλημα) in sharp contrast with that which did not represent His will (οὐκ ἠθέλησας). The words in the original are different (לֹא־חָפַצְתָּ, רְצוֹנֶךָ).

τὸ θέλημά σου] The will of God answers to the fulfilment of man's true destiny ; and this, as things actually are, in spite of the Fall. Christ, as Son of man, made this will His own and accomplished it. The utterance of the King of Israel expressed man's true aim, which was beyond human reach, and so rightly belongs to the Messiah who attained it. Compare John iv. 34 ; viii. 29.

It is of interest to notice how constantly 'the will of God' is connected with the redemption and consummation of man : John iv. 34 ; v. 30 ; vi. 38 ff.; Eph. i. 5, 9, 11 ; 1 Tim. ii. 4 ; and in one special aspect : 1 Thess. iv. 3. Compare Apoc. iv. 11. On the construction τοῦ ποιῆσαι see Additional Note.

8, 9. ἀνώτερον λέγων...τότε εἴρηκεν] *saying above...then hath he said...;* Vulg. *superius dicens...tunc dixit....* The continuous expression of the divine will is contrasted with the one abiding declaration of its fulfilment by Christ.

8. θυσίας καὶ προσφοράς] The plurals seem to be accommodated to ὁλοκαυτώματα, which itself generalises the singular (עוֹלָה) of the original.

καὶ περὶ ἁμαρτίας ογκ ΗθέλΗσας ογδὲ εγδόκΗσας, *αἵτινες κατὰ νόμον προσφέρονται,* ⁹τότε εἴρηκεν Ἰδογ Ηκω τογ ποιΗϲαι τὸ θέλΗμά ϲογ· *ἀναιρεῖ τὸ πρῶτον ἵνα τὸ δεύτερον στήσῃ.* ¹⁰*ἐν ᾧ* θελΗματι *ἡγιασμένοι ἐσμὲν διὰ τῆς* προϲφορᾶϲ *τογ*

ἁμαρτίας: -ιῶν D₂.   οὐδὲ εὐδ.: om. syr vg.   κατὰ ν. אAC: κατὰ τὸν ν. ϛD₂.
9 ποιῆσαι א*ACD₂ syr hl txt ægg: +ὁ θεός ϛ א° vg syr vg.   10 ἐσμὲν οἱ ϛ (i.e. μενοιεϲμενοι).

αἵτινες...] such as are offered..., compare v. 11 ; c. ii. 3 note.

κατὰ νόμον] The absence of the article directs attention to the general character of the sacrifices as *legal*, and not to their specific character as *Mosaic*. Compare viii. 4; and contrast vii. 5 ; ix. 19, 22.

9. εἴρηκεν] Compare c. i. 13; iv. 3 f., 7 ; xiii. 5; (Luke iv. 12); John xv. 15 ; Acts xiii. 34; 2 Cor. xii. 9; Apoc. vii. 14; xix. 3.

ἀναιρεῖ] *He (i.e. the Christ) removeth, doeth away with* (Vulg. *aufert*). This is the only occurrence of the word in the Epistles except the doubtful reading in 2 Thess. ii. 8. In the sense of 'kill' it is frequent in the Acts. It is not found elsewhere in the N. T. or in the LXX. in the sense of 'removing.' In Classical Greek it is used of laws (to abrogate : Æsch. *in Ctes.* §§ 16, 39), of wills (to revoke: Is. *de Cleon. hær.* § 14), of propositions (to deny: Sext. *Pyrrh. Hyp.* i. 20 § 192; iii. 16 § 119 οἱ μὲν ἔθεσαν, οἱ δὲ ἀνεῖλον, οἱ δὲ ἐπέσχον περὶ αὐτοῦ), of appetites (to extinguish : Epict. *Enchir.* ii. 2 ; comp. *Diss.* i. 8, 15 ; ii. 20, 6).

τὸ πρῶτον...τὸ δεύτερον (Vulg. *sequens*)] *the first*—the offering outward sacrifices: *the second*—the fulfilment of the divine will by rational self-devotion.

στήσῃ] Vulg. *statuat.* Compare Rom. iii. 31 (νόμον ἱστάνομεν); x. 3; xiv. 4; Gen. vi. 18, &c.

10. ἐν ᾧ θελ. ἡγιασμ. ἐσμέν] *In which will,* Vulg. *in qua voluntate...* perfectly accomplished by Christ for

all time, according to His abiding declaration (εἴρηκεν), *we have been sanctified,* as included in its scope. The will of God fulfilled by Christ is regarded not as that through (διά) which, nor as that according to which (κατά) men are sanctified. They are included in it, even in that purpose of love which Christ has realised (Eph. i. 7). Compare v. 19 ; 29 ; xiii. 20.

The thought of Christians as included in the Father's will, which Christ fulfilled, corresponds with St Paul's thought of Christians being 'in Christ,' an expression which is not found in the Epistle.

For the resolved form ἡγιασμ. ἐσμέν see c. vii. 20 note ; and for the use of the perfect John xvii. 19; Acts xx. 32; xxvi. 18; 1 Cor. i. 2; vii. 14 ; (Rom. xv. 16).

For the connexion of the redemption of men with the will of God see v. 7 note.

διὰ τῆς προσφ. τοῦ σώματος] *through the offering of the body* divinely prepared, which offering, slowly matured through life, was consummated on the cross. The clause contains an answer to the question which naturally arises 'How are we sanctified in the will of God?' That will was realised in the perfect life of the Son of man, in which each man as a member of humanity finds the realisation of his own destiny.

The use of προσφορά (used of Christ's offering only in this chapter and Eph. v. 2) connects the self-sacrifice of Christ with the typical

cώματος Ἰησοῦ Χριστοῦ ἐφάπαξ.   ¹¹ Καὶ πᾶς μὲν ⌈ἱερεὺς⌉

11 ἀρχιερεὺς

σώματος: αἵματος D₂*.   Ἰησοῦ: +τοῦ' Ἰ. ς.   11 ἱερεύς ℵD₂ vg syr hl txt me:
ἀρχιερεύς AC syr vg æg.

sacrifices (comp. c. v. 1 note). And
the compound name *Jesus Christ*
(c. xiii. 8, 21 only) characterises the
completeness of the sacrifice under
the divine and human aspects of the
Lord's Person. At the same time
the specific reference to 'the body,'
the appointed organ for doing God's
will under particular conditions, emphasises the reference to the totality
of Christ's earthly work. Elsewhere
in the Epistle He is said to 'offer
Himself' (vii. 27; ix. 14, 25 f.). The
Western reading αἵματος, *sanguinis*,
expresses only one side of the whole
thought.
   Compare Additional Note.
   ἐφάπαξ] The word (c. vii. 27; ix. 12)
goes with the whole sentence. The
sanctification of all believers is completed on the divine side. Comp.
v. 14.
   (3) 11—14. The efficacy of Christ's
sacrifice shewn by His present Majesty.
   A view of the efficacy of Christ's
present work follows on the general
description of His historic sacrifice in
Life and Death. This is given by
presenting the contrast between the
continuous service of the Levitical
priests and Christ's position of Royal
assurance (11—13); and then shewing
the ground of Christ's preeminence
in the abiding sufficiency of His one
offering for the needs of every member of His Church (14).
   ¹¹*And while every priest (high-
priest) standeth day by day ministering and offering oftentimes the same
sacrifices which can never take away
sins,* ¹²*He, when He had offered one
sacrifice for sins for ever, sat down
on the right hand of God,* ¹³*henceforward waiting till His enemies be*

made the footstool of His feet. ¹⁴*For
by one offering He hath perfected for
ever them that are sanctified.*
   11—13. The eleventh verse takes
up the three thoughts of *v.* 1. The
Levitical service consists of repeated
acts (καθ' ἡμέραν, κατ' ἐνιαυτόν), and
these the same (αἱ αὐταὶ θυσίαι), and
essentially ineffective (οὐδέποτε δ.
περιελ. ἁμ., οὐδέποτε δ. τ. προσερχ.
τελ.). On the other hand Christ
having offered one sacrifice efficacious
for ever took His place on the divine
throne in certain expectation of final
victory (12, 13).
   11. καὶ πᾶς μὲν ἱερεύς] *And* further,
there is another characteristic of
Christ's priestly work which marks
its infinite superiority, *while every
Levitical priest standeth...He...sat
down....* Christ's sacrifice is not only
pleasing to God, but it has an absolute
power: it issues in perfect sovereignty for the Son of man, the representative of men (ii. 9).
   For the opposition of the clauses
(πᾶς μέν—οὗτος δέ) compare i. 7;
iii. 5; vii. 8; ix. 23; xii. 10.
   The general term 'priest' (ἱερεύς,
Latt. *sacerdos*) suits the argument
better than the specific term 'high-
priest.' The work of Christ is considered in relation to the whole
hierarchical and sacrificial system of
Judaism. The Jewish priests 'stand'
in their service (Deut. x. 8; xviii. 7).
   ἔστηκεν] standeth, Latt. *præsto est.*
The idea of 'standing' is that of a
work still to be done, of service still
to be rendered, of homage still to be
paid. So the angels stand before
God: Is. vi. 2; Lu. i. 19; Apoc. vii.
11. Comp. i. 3 note.
   The attitude of the Lord in Acts
vii. 56 is explained in the *Apostolical*

ἕστηκεν καθ᾽ ἡμέραν λειτουργῶν καὶ τὰς αὐτὰς πολλάκις
προσφέρων θυσίας, αἵτινες οὐδέποτε δύνανται περιελεῖν
ἁμαρτίας. ¹² οὗτος δὲ μίαν ὑπὲρ ἁμαρτιῶν προσενέγκας
θυσίαν εἰς τὸ διηνεκὲς ἐκάθισεν ἐν δεξιᾷ τοῦ θεοῦ, ¹³τὸ λοιπὸν

λειτ. καθ᾽ ἡμ. ℵ*.   καὶ τὰς αὐ.: om. καί D₂*.   12 οὗτος: αὐτός ς.
ἐν (ἐκ ℵ*) δεξιᾷ (ℵᶜ) CD₂: ἐκ δεξιῶν A.

Constitutions on the supposition that He appears ὡς ἀρχιερεὺς πάντων τῶν λογικῶν ταγμάτων (vi. 30, 5). See also John iii. 29.

'They also serve who only stand and wait.'

καθ᾽ ἡμέραν...θυσίας] The divine service and the sacrifices of the Tabernacle and Temple are repeated day by day. This could be said even of the duties of the High-priest: see c. vii. 27 note. The verb λειτουργεῖν is found in the N. T. elsewhere only Acts xiii. 2; Rom. xv. 27. For the meaning see c. viii. 2 Addit. Note. The order of the original, by which the thoughts of the identity and frequency of the Levitical sacrifices are brought together (τὰς αὐτὰς πολ. προσφ. θυσ.), is expressive.

αἵτινες] 'which are such that...'. Comp. c. ii. 3 note.

περιελεῖν ἁμαρτίας] Latt. *auferre peccata*. Contrast περίκειται, c. v. 2. Man is, so to speak, wrapped in sins. He weaves, as it were, in action (ἁμαρτίαι not ἁμαρτία) a terrible robe for himself (comp. Ps. xxxv. 26; cix. 18 notes). This enveloping shroud, no part of his true self, has to be stripped off (2 Cor. iii. 16; Judith x. 3). For περιελεῖν compare Zeph. iii. 11 περιελῶ τὰ φαυλίσματα, 15 περιεῖλε κύριος τὰ ἀδικήμ. (הֵסִיר). The image is found also in Classical writers.

12. οὗτος δὲ μίαν...εἰς τὸ διηνεκές, ἐκάθισεν...] *He, when He had offered one sacrifice for sins for ever, sat down...;* O.L. *una oblata hostia in sempiterno sedit;* Vulg. *hic autem unam offerens hostiam in sempiternum....* The sacrifice was efficacious for ever, through all time, being appropriated by each believer (v. 14). The con-

nexion of εἰς τὸ διηνεκές with the following ἐκάθισεν (*for ever sat down*) is contrary to the usage of the Epistle; it obscures the idea of the perpetual efficacy of Christ's one sacrifice; it weakens the contrast with ἕστηκεν; and it imports a foreign idea into the image of the assumption (ἐκάθισεν) of royal dignity by Christ.

For οὗτος see iii. 3; vii. 4; and for ἐκάθισεν, c. i. 3 note. The word ἐκάθισεν is in sharp opposition to ἕστηκεν λειτουργῶν (v. 11). Throughout the Epistle (except i. 13 καθοῦ from the LXX.) the reference is uniformly to the act of taking the royal seat (καθίζειν as contrasted with καθῆσθαι: i. 3; viii. 1; xii. 2). Compare Eph. i. 20: Apoc. iii. 21; and contrast the phrase of the Apocalypse ὁ καθήμενος ἐπὶ τ. θρόνου (iv. 9 ff.). On the general thought Chrysostom says tersely: τὸ ἑστάναι τοῦ λειτουργεῖν ἐστι σημεῖον, οὐκοῦν τὸ καθῆσθαι τοῦ λειτουργεῖσθαι.

13. τὸ λοιπὸν ἐκδεχ.] *henceforward waiting.* Christ Himself in His royal majesty 'waits' as the husbandman for the processes of nature (James v. 7) and the patriarchs for the divine promise (c. xi. 10). There is an aspect in which the time of the triumphant Return of Christ is known only to the Father (Matt. xxiv. 36; Mark xiii. 32; Acts i. 7), and is in some sense contingent on the action of men (Acts iii. 19 ὅπως ἄν...ἀποστείλῃ...; 2 Pet. iii. 12).

Elsewhere in the N. T. the word (ἐκδέχεσθαι) is used only of one man waiting for another (Acts xvii. 16; 1 Cor. xi. 33; xvi. 11: not John v. 3; 1 Pet. iii. 20).

τὸ λοιπὸν] Vulg. *de cetero,* O. L.

ἐκδεχόμενος ἕως τεθῶϲιν οἱ ἐχθροὶ ἀγτοῦ ϒποπόΔιον τῶν ποΔῶν
ἀγτοῦ, ¹⁴μιᾷ γὰρ προσφορᾷ τετελείωκεν εἰς τὸ διηνεκὲς

postea. 2 Thess. iii. 1; Phil. iii. 1;
iv. 8; 1 Cor. vii. 29. (Mk. xiv. 41.)
Eph. vi. 10 (τοῦ λοιποῦ).

ἕως τεθῶσιν] The Return of Christ
appears to be placed after the conquest of His enemies. Compare 1
Cor. xv. 22 ff.

The reference to Ps. cx. carries
back the thoughts of the reader to
the portraiture of the majesty of the
Son in c. i. 13. His victory is won
(John xvi. 33 νενίκηκα): only the
fruits of it remain to be gathered.

14. μιᾷ γὰρ προσφορᾷ] *For by one
offering...*, so that no fresh duty can
interrupt the continuance of His royal
Majesty.

The word προσφορά goes back to
v. 10 (note). It extends more widely
than θυσία (*v.* 12; ix. 16). St Paul
combines both words in Eph. v. 2
which, as was noticed, is the only
passage besides this chapter (*vv.* 5, 8,
10, 18) in which the word is used in
connexion with Christ's work; nor
indeed does it occur elsewhere in the
Epistles at all except Rom. xv. 16.

The 'offering' of Christ, His perfect
life crowned by a willing death, in
which He fulfilled the destiny of man
and bore the punishment of human
sin, is that by and in which every
human life finds its consummation.

It is significant that Christ Himself
is said to perfect 'by the offering': it
is not said that 'the offering' perfects.
His action is personal in the application of His own work. The importance of this form of expression appears
from the language used of the Law:
vii. 19 οὐδὲν ἐτελείωσεν ὁ νόμος. Comp.
ix. 9; x. 1. In the case of the Levitical institutions the action of the appointed ministers fell into the background.

τετελ. εἰς τὸ διην.] *He hath perfected
for ever...*Latt. *consummavit in sempiternum.* For the perfect see xi. 17

note; vii. 6 note, 28; ix. 6, 8, 18; and
contrast ἐτελείωσεν c. vii. 19.

For εἰς τὸ διην. see c. vii. 3; x. 1
notes. The virtue of Christ's work
remains ever available as long as the
need of man exists.

τοὺς ἁγιαζομένους] Vulg. *sanctifica-
tos;* O. L. *nos sanctificans:* all who
from time to time realise progressively
in fact that which has been potentially
obtained for them. Compare c. ii. 11;
and contrast *v.* 10 ἡγιασμένοι.

The endeavour of the Old Latin to
express the continuous form of the
present is interesting (see for the converse i. 3).

There is a similar contrast between
οἱ σωζόμενοι (comp. 1 Cor. xv. 2); Luke
xiii. 23; Acts ii. 47; 1 Cor. i. 18; 2
Cor. ii. 15; and σεσωσμένοι Eph. ii. 5,
8. Compare ἔσωσεν 2 Tim. i. 9;
Tit. iii. 5.

(4)   15—18.   The fulfilment in
Christ of the prophetic description of
the New Covenant.

The Apostle goes back in conclusion
to the testimony of the prophet from
which he commenced his exposition
of the high-priestly and sacrificial
service of the new Covenant. A
characteristic of that Covenant, which
has been established by Christ, was
the forgiveness of sins. Under it,
therefore, offerings for sin were necessarily done away; and the Temple
services could no longer have any
value for the Christian.

¹⁵ *And the Holy Spirit also beareth
witness to us; for after that He hath
said,*

¹⁶ *This is the covenant that I will
covenant with them
After those days, saith the Lord,
Even putting my laws upon their
heart,
And upon their mind will I write
them;*
then saith He

τοὺς ἁγιαζομένους.	¹⁵ Μαρτυρεῖ δὲ ἡμῖν καὶ τὸ πνεῦμα
τὸ ἅγιον, μετὰ γὰρ τὸ εἰρηκέναι

¹⁶Αὗτη ἡ Διαθήκη ἡΝ Διαθήϲομαι πρὸς αὐτούϲ

μετὰ τὰϲ ἡμέραϲ ἐκείναϲ, λέγει Κύριοϲ,

Διδούϲ νόμουϲ μου ἐπὶ καρδίαϲ αὐτῶν,

καὶ ἐπὶ τὴν Διάνοιαν αὐτῶν ἐπιγράψω αὐτούϲ,—

¹⁷Καὶ τῶν ἁμαρτιῶν αὐτῶν καὶ τῶν ἀνομιῶν αὐτῶν οὐ μὴ μνηϲθῆ-

15 μετὰ δέ D₂*.   εἰρηκέναι: προειρ. Ϛ.   16 αὕτη δέ D₂* vg.
τὴν διάν. אACD₂* (vg): τῶν διαν. Ϛ (vg) syrr me æg.   17 τῶν ἁμ. αὐ.: om. αὐτῶν
D₂* vg.   μνησθήσομαι: μνησθῶ Ϛ א°.

¹⁷And their sins and their iniquities will I remember no more.
¹⁸Now where there is remission of
these, there is no more offering for
sin.

15.	μαρτυρεῖ δὲ ἡμῖν καὶ τὸ π. τὸ ἅ.]
Vulg. contestatur nos (O.L. nobis). And
the Holy Spirit also beareth witness
to us Christians and confirms our common faith. Ἡμῖν can also be taken as
a dat. comm. 'for us,' 'in our favour,'
in which case μαρτυρεῖ is used absolutely. The general sense is the same
in both cases. The witness of the
Holy Spirit in the promise of the New
Covenant is added to the witness of
Christ contained in the Psalm. The
emphatic position of μαρτυρεῖ seems
to mark the anxiety of the writer to
convince his readers of the perfect validity of Christ's claim. The words of
the Christ in the Psalm are supported
by an independent divine testimony.

15—17. μετὰ τὸ εἰρηκέναι...καὶ τῶν...]
It is difficult to determine the construction of the whole passage. Some
have supposed that the writer uses
λέγει Κύριος as part of his own statement: 'For after that he hath said...'
the Lord saith 'I will give...and their
sins...will I remember no more.'
But the point of the apodosis lies in
the declaration of the forgiveness of
sins, and the force of this declaration
is weakened by the addition of the
two preceding lines, which describe
the human conditions of the covenant

that have been fulfilled by Christ. It
is better therefore to suppose that
the construction is broken, and that
the apodosis begins with v. 17. 'For
after that He hath said...write them;
then saith He, Their sins...' So Primasius: In sequentibus verbis de-
fectus est sententiæ satis necessarius,
quapropter dicatur ita: Postquam
enim dixit Omnipotens Deus per pro-
phetam...statim subintulit: Et peccatum eorum non memorabor amplius....

16.	Comp. c. viii. 8 ff. note. (Jer.
xxxi. (xxxviii.) 31 ff.)

For the special phrase τῷ οἴκῳ
Ἰσραήλ here the writer substitutes
πρὸς αὐτούς; and καρδία and διάνοια
are transposed, and the clause καὶ τῶν
ἀνομιῶν αὐτῶν is added.

17.	οὐ μὴ μνησθήσομαι] Contrast v.
3 ἀνάμνησις ἁμαρτιῶν.

18.	ὅπου δὲ ἄφεσις τούτων] Now
where there is remission of these sins.
For ἄφεσις see c. ix. 22 note. The
consequences of sin are threefold:
debt which requires forgiveness, bondage which requires redemption, alienation which requires reconciliation.
See note on 1 John i. 9. The words
ἄφεσις, ἀφιέναι express the first idea:
comp. Matt. xviii. 27, 32, 35.

These words are rare in the Epistles,
more frequent in the Synoptic Gospels
and (ἄφεσις ἁμ.) Acts. The 'remission' of sins is essentially a creative act:
compare Matt. ix. 2 ff. and parallels.

COMAI ἔτι· ¹⁸ ὅπου δὲ ἄφεσις τούτων, οὐκέτι προσφορὰ περὶ ἁμαρτίας.

18 ἄφεσις: ἄφεις א*.   om. τούτων א*.

Comp. c. ix. 22.

The only other places where ἄφεσις occurs in the Epistles are Eph. i. 7 ἐν ᾧ ἔχομεν τὴν ἀπολύτρωσιν διὰ τοῦ αἵματος αὐτοῦ, τὴν ἄφεσιν τῶν παραπτωμάτων. Col. i. 14 ἐν ᾧ ἔχομεν τὴν ἀπολύτρωσιν, τὴν ἄφεσιν τῶν ἁμαρτιῶν. Contrast πάρεσις Rom. iii. 25. The prophetic words shew that under the New Covenant no place is left for the Levitical sacrifices. The Christian can therefore dispense with them without any loss. To be forced to give up their shadowy consolation is to be led to realise more practically the work of Christ. This is the last—the decisive—word of the argument.

V. THE APPROPRIATION AND VITAL APPLICATION OF THE TRUTHS LAID DOWN (x. 19—xiii. 25).

Having established his theoretical view of the relation of Christianity to Judaism, as its complete fulfilment, the substance answering to the shadow, the writer of the Epistle at once goes on to enforce the practical consequences of his conclusions. The privileges must be used : the duties must be discharged. The faith is not for speculation but for life. All the consolations of the Levitical system can be surrendered without loss ; and they must be surrendered at once if they come in any way into competition with Christian obligation.

This main line of thought is developed under four sections. The writer first makes a direct application of his teaching to his readers, defining sharply their privileges and perils and encouragements (x. 19—39). Having thus insisted on the necessity of faith as an element in that patient endurance which God requires in the discipline of His Pro-

vidence, he next shews that it was by faith the spiritual heroes of earlier times wrought their victories (c. xi). Such examples had an immediate application to the circumstances of the crisis in which the Hebrews were placed ; and they were sufficient to enable them to realise the grandeur of the responsibilities and hopes which were given to them (c. xii). The last chapter (c. xiii) is a kind of appendix to the Epistle in which detailed instructions and personal notices find a place.

Thus we have :

i. *The privileges, perils, encouragements of the Hebrews* (x. 19—39).

ii. *The past triumphs of Faith* (xi. 1—40).

iii. *The general application of the lessons of the past to the present season of trial* (xii. 1—29).

iv. *Last words* (xiii. 1—25).

i. *The privileges, perils, encouragements of the Hebrews* (x. 19—39).

The application of the lessons to be drawn from the view which the Apostle has given of the absolute supremacy of the Christian Faith over the preparatory system of Judaism begins with a vivid picture of the position of the Hebrews, (1) of their privileges and duties (19—25), (2) of their perils (26—31), and (3) of their encouragements (32—39). Each section has traits taken directly from scenes of persecution, from the isolation of proud or timid believers (*v.* 25), the abjuration of apostates (*v.* 29), the triumph of confessors (*v.* 34).

(1) *vv.* 19—25. The privileges and duties of Christians.

The section deals first with the personal privileges (19—22), and then with the social duties of believers (23—25).

The privilege of direct access to

¹⁹Ἔχοντες οὖν, ἀδελφοί, παρρησίαν εἰς τὴν εἴσοδον
τῶν ἁγίων ἐν τῷ αἵματι Ἰησοῦ, ²⁰ἣν ἐνεκαίνισεν ἡμῖν ὁδὸν

God is confirmed by general and personal considerations. We have a way of approach and an effective Mediator (19—21). And on our part certain conditions have to be fulfilled personally. These are both subjective (*with a true heart, in fulness of faith*), and objective (*sprinkled in our hearts, washed in our body*) (22).

¹⁹*Having therefore, brethren, boldness to use the entrance into the Holy place in the blood of Jesus, the* entrance *which He inaugurated for us,* ²⁰*even a fresh and living way through the veil, that is to say a way of His flesh,* ²¹*and a great priest over the house of God,* ²²*let us come to God with a true heart in fulness of faith, having our hearts sprinkled from an evil conscience, and our body bathed with pure water.* ²³*Let us hold fast the confession of our hope that it waver not, for He is faithful that promised.* ²⁴*And let us consider one another to provoke unto love and good works,* ²⁵*not forsaking the gathering of ourselves together, as the custom of some is, but exhorting one another; and so much the more as ye see the day drawing nigh.*

19—21. The writer sums up briefly the blessings which he has shewn to belong to Christians. They have an entrance to the Divine Presence in virtue of Christ's Blood, a way made by the Incarnation, and an availing personal Advocate, a Priest over the house of God.

19. ἔχοντες οὖν, ἀδελφοί...] *Having therefore, brethren...*That which was under the Law a privilege of one only, once a year, is now the privilege of all Christians at all times. The form of the sentence is closely parallel to c. iv. 13 ff.

The title ἀδελφοί (compare c. iii. 1 note) is an impressive recognition of the new fellowship established in

Christ. By using it the writer appeals to his readers to consider what they have received as Christians.

παρρησίαν] *boldness* in spite of the frankest recognition of our sins. Comp. iii. 6 note; iv. 16.

Παρρησίαν πόθεν; ἀπὸ τῆς ἀφέσεως ...οὐ μόνον δὲ τοῦτο, ἀλλὰ καὶ τὸ συγκληρονόμους γενέσθαι καὶ τοσαύτης ἀπολαῦσαι ἀγάπης (Chrys.).

εἰς τὴν εἴσ. τ. ἁ.] *to use the entrance into the Holy place,* Vulg. *in introitu (-um) sanctorum.* Each Christian in virtue of his fellowship with Christ is now a high-priest, and is able to come to the very presence of God. The 'entrance' expresses primarily the way itself, and then also the use of the way. Elsewhere in the N. T. εἴσοδος is used generally of 'the act of entering': 1 Thess. i. 9; ii. 1; Acts xiii. 24; but in 2 Pet. i. 11 it has rather the sense of 'the means of entering,' and the parallel with ὁδός (v. 20) seems to fix this as the dominant sense here.

The use of the phrase 'boldness for (to use) the entrance' instead of the simpler 'boldness to enter' (παρρησίαν τοῦ εἰσιέναι) calls up distinctly both the characteristic act of the High-priest, and the provision made by Christ. For the gen. τῶν ἁγίων see c. ix. 8.

For εἰς, describing the end, compare v. 24; Acts ii. 38; Rom. viii. 15; 2 Cor. vii. 9; 2 Pet. ii. 12; and for παρρησία εἰς c. xi. 11; Rom. i. 16 (δύναμις εἰς); 2 Cor. vii. 10; Phil. i. 23.

ἐν τῷ αἵματι] Vulg. *in sanguine.* The entrance of Christians into the divine presence is 'in the blood of Jesus'—even as the Levitical High-priest entered into the Holy of holies 'in blood,' though it was the blood of 'bulls and goats': c. ix. 25 ἐν αἵματι ἀλλοτρίῳ—in the power, that is, of the human life of the Lord offered up and made available for them : His life is

πρόσφατον καὶ ζῶσαν διὰ τοῦ καταπετάσματος, τοῦτ'

20 om. καί D₂*.

their way ('vita Tua via nostra'). The human name of the Lord in every place where it occurs in the Epistle emphasises His true humanity and rests the point of the argument upon that. Compare ii. 9 note. For ἐν αἵματι compare c. ix. 25 note.

ἣν ἐνεκαίνισεν] the entrance *which He inaugurated for us, even a fresh and living way*... Vulg. *quam* (O. L. in *qua*) *initiavit* (Vigil. *dedicavit*) *viam* ...Christ has made available for others the road by which He Himself travelled. He not only made the way, but He also used it (ἐνεκαίνισεν...ἣν κατεσκεύασε, φησί, καὶ δι' ἧς αὐτὸς ἐβάδισεν, Chrys.). Compare c. vi. 20 (πρόδρομος); ix. 12 (διὰ τοῦ ἰδίου αἵματος εἰσῆλθεν). The word ἐγκαινίζειν (c. ix. 18 note) is used in the LXX. of the inauguration (dedication) of the altar, the temple, the kingdom (1 Sam. xi. 14), a house (Deut. xx. 5)[1].

The ἣν is the direct object of ἐνεκαίνισεν. Comp. Rom. ix. 24. It has been taken (less naturally) predicatively : 'for to be this—as which—He inaugurated a fresh and living way...'

Thus ὁδὸν πρ. καὶ ζῶσαν are in apposition with εἴσοδον and descriptive of it. The way, however the words which follow may be interpreted, must finally be Christ Himself (John xiv. 6; x. 7) ; and it is therefore 'fresh' not only in the sense that it is a way which was before unknown, but also as one that retains its freshness and cannot grow old (c. viii. 13) ; and it is 'living' as a way which consists in fellowship with a Person (οὐκ εἶπε ζωῆς, ἀλλὰ ζῶσαν αὐτὴν ἐκάλεσε, τὴν μένουσαν οὕτω δηλῶν Chrys.).

The word πρόσφατος is found here

only in the N. T. (προσφάτως Acts xviii. 2). It occurs in the LXX. (e.g. Ps. lxxx. (lxxxi.) 10; Eccles. i. 9) and in Classical writers from Homer downwards. The current derivations from σφάω (σφάζω), φάω (φένω), φάω (φημί), are all unsatisfactory.

The language of the Apostle finds a remarkable parallel in the words with which Florus (i. 9, 14) describes the self-devotion of Decius Mus, who 'quasi monitu deorum capite velato primam ante aciem Dis Manibus se [devovit], ut in confertissima se hostium tela jaculatus novum ad victoriam iter sanguinis sui limite aperiret.'

διὰ τοῦ καταπετάσματος]...There can be no doubt that the 'veil' is here regarded as excluding from the Divine Presence and not (as some Fathers took it) as the door by which the Divine Presence was approached. Comp. c. vi. 8; ix. 8.

The way into the holiest place can now be traversed. The veil is not indeed removed so long as we live on earth, but we can pass through it in Christ. Comp. Matt. xxvii. 51 and parallels.

How then are we to understand the words which follow, τῆς σαρκὸς αὐτοῦ ?

These words are by common consent taken either as dependent on τοῦ καταπετάσματος, 'the veil, that is the veil of His flesh' (*i.e.* consisting in His flesh), or as in apposition with it, 'the veil, that is, His flesh.' In both cases 'the flesh' of Christ is presented as that through which He passed, a veil which for a time shut off access to God. Such a thought is strange and difficult ; but it becomes in some degree

---

[1] The clause παρρησίαν...σαρκός is transferred to the Prayer of the Veil in the Greek Liturgy of St James, where the printed texts give ἀνεκαίνισας, but the reading of the MSS. is ἐνεκαίνισας (Swainson, *Greek Liturgies*, pp. 262, 3). The argument which has been built on the difference of the verb to establish the originality of the clause in the Liturgy is therefore wholly unfounded.

intelligible if 'the flesh' of Christ is used in a strictly limited sense to describe His humanity under the limitations of earthly existence, of temptation and suffering, as in St Paul's phrase γινώσκειν κατὰ σάρκα Χριστόν (2 Cor. v. 16). In favour of such a sense the words in c. v. 7 may be quoted ἐν ταῖς ἡμέραις τῆς σαρκὸς αὐτοῦ and (with less point) ii. 14 κεκοινώνηκε αἵματος καὶ σαρκός. The word ('flesh') being thus understood, it can be said that Christ passed through 'the flesh' which He assumed, which did actually to common eyes hide God from men, into the presence of God; but the greatest care must be taken to guard against the error of supposing that in 'passing through,' and thus leaving behind, His 'flesh,' Christ parted with anything which belongs to the full perfection of His humanity.

It must also be observed that, if this interpretation be adopted, it seems to be necessary to connect διὰ τοῦ καταπ...τ. σαρκὸς αὐτοῦ closely with ἐνεκαίνισεν, and to confine the expression to the action of Christ. For it is most unlikely that the Apostle would describe Christ's 'flesh' as a veil hiding God from men, through which they too must pass, though it is true that His humanity did, during His historic Presence, veil His Godhead, and that, in one sense, 'the flesh profiteth nothing.'

Still even with these restrictions this interpretation is hardly satisfactory. It remains surprising that 'the flesh' of Christ should be treated in any way as a veil, an obstacle, to the vision of God in a place where stress is laid on His humanity (ἐν τῷ αἵματι Ἰησοῦ). And we should certainly expect to find a complete parallelism between the description of the approach of Christ to God and the approach of the believer to God.

These difficulties point to a different view of the construction by which the clause τοῦτ᾽ ἔστιν τῆς σαρκὸς αὐτοῦ is connected with ὁδόν (and not with τοῦ καταπετάσματος), 'a way through the veil, that is, a way consisting in His flesh, His true human nature.' The whole clause ὁδόν...καταπετάσματος will thus become a compound noun, 'a fresh and living way through the veil.'

This construction appears to be followed by our Early English translations : 'by the new and living way which He hath prepared for us through the veil, that is to say (Gen. om. to say) by His flesh' (Tynd., Cov., G.B., Gen.). The 'by' is omitted in the Bishops' Bible. Perhaps Vigilius Tapsensis (c. Varim. i. c. 27 ; Migne P. L. lxii. 371) gives the same construction : qui dedicavit nobis viam recentem et viam per velamen, id est, carnem suam, offerens seipsum pro nobis.

The Greek certainly admits this construction : τουτέστιν does not necessarily refer to the words which immediately precede : c. vii. 5. And the sense agrees perfectly with the argument.

At first sight indeed the connexion of τῆς σαρκὸς with ὁδόν seems to be less natural than the connexion with τοῦ καταπετάσματος only ; but the thought which is thus expressed of 'a way consisting in Christ's flesh' falls in perfectly with the scope of the passage. It was by the 'way of His flesh,' by a way which lay in His humanity, that Christ entered through the veil after the offering of Himself as a High-priest able to sympathise with men. And it is by the 'way of His flesh,' as sharing in the virtue of His humanity, and sprinkled with His blood, that Christians come before God. Comp. John vi. 53 ff.; xiv. 19; Col. i. 22 ἀποκατήλλαξεν (v. ἀποκατηλλάγητε) ἐν τῷ σώματι τῆς σαρκὸς αὐτοῦ διὰ τοῦ θανάτου.

Chrysostom says with singular want of clearness : ἡ σὰρξ αὕτη ἔτεμε πρώτη τὴν ὁδὸν αὐτῷ ἐκείνην, ἣν καὶ ἐγκαινίσαι λέγει, τῷ καὶ αὐτὸς ἀξιῶσαι διὰ ταύτης βαδίσαι. καταπέτασμα δὲ εἰκότως ἐκάλεσε τὴν σάρκα, ὅτε γὰρ ἤρθη εἰς ὕψος τότε ἐφάνη τὰ ἐν τοῖς οὐρανοῖς.

ἔστιν τῆς σαρκὸς αὐτοῦ, ²¹καὶ ἱερέα μέγαν ἐπὶ τὸν οἶκον
+ διὰ' τῆς σ. D₂*.

Theophylact repeats the last idea:
τοῦτο γὰρ ἴδιον τοῦ καταπετάσματος τὸ
ὅταν ἄρθῃ ἀνακαλύπτειν τὰ ἔνδον.

Theodoret regards the veil as the
appointed means of approach, and not
as the obstacle which hindered access:
καταπέτασμα τὴν δεσποτικὴν ὠνόμασε
σάρκα· διὰ ταύτης γὰρ ἀπολαύομεν τῆς
εἰς τὰ ἅγια τῶν ἁγίων εἰσόδου. ὥσπερ
γὰρ ὁ κατὰ νόμον ἀρχιερεὺς διὰ τοῦ
καταπετάσματος εἰς τὰ ἅγια τῶν ἁγίων
εἰσῄει, ἑτέρως δὲ αὐτὸν εἰσελθεῖν ἀδύνατον ἦν, οὕτως οἱ εἰς τὸν Κύριον πεπι-
στευκότες διὰ τῆς τοῦ παναγίου σώματος
μεταλήψεως τῆς ἐν οὐρανοῖς ἀπολαύσουσι
πολιτείας. But this view, though it
has found wider acceptance (e.g. Primasius: Sicut per velamen pervenie-
batur ad interiora, ita per humanita-
tem pervenitur ad divinitatis cogni-
tionem), is wholly at variance with
the imagery of the Epistle, and with
the symbolism of the Old Testament.
On the other hand it witnesses to the
truth that Christ's 'flesh' is 'the way.'

21. καὶ ἱερέα μέγαν] Christians have
open access to the Divine Presence;
and in the court of the Divine Majesty
they have an effectual Intercessor.

The epithet great describes the
sovereign power of our Priest (a great
High-priest c. iv. 14), and does not
simply serve in combination with ἱερεύς
as an equivalent for ἀρχιερεύς (Lev.
xxi. 10 ὁ ἱερεὺς ὁ μέγας).

ἐπὶ τὸν οἶκον τ. θ.] Vulg. super do-
mum (O. L. in domo) Dei. The House
of God includes the whole Christian
economy both in its earthly and in its
heavenly elements; in its organisation
and in its members. The Church on
earth, so far as it has a true existence,
lives by its embodiment of the heavenly
idea. Under other aspects this 'house'
is spoken of as 'the order to come'
(ἡ οἰκουμένη ἡ μέλλουσα c. ii. 5) and
'the city to come' ([ἡ πόλις] ἡ μέλλουσα c. xiii. 14).

See c. iii. 4; 6 (ἐπί); and compare

c. xii. 22; Phil. iii. 20; Zech. vi. 11 ff.
Philo speaks of the righteous soul,
and again, by a remarkable image, of
the Word itself, as 'the house of God':
τίς γὰρ οἶκος παρὰ γενέσει (in things
created) δύναιτ' ἂν ἀξιοπρεπέστερος
εὑρεθῆναι θεῷ πλὴν ψυχῆς τελείας κεκα-
θαρμένης...; (de sobr. § 13; i. 402 M.);
σπούδασον οὖν, ὦ ψυχή, θεοῦ οἶκος γενέσθαι, ἱερὸν ἅγιον...(de somn. i. § 23; i.
643 M.);...τὸν τῶν ὅλων νοῦν, τὸν θεόν,
οἶκον ἔχειν φησὶ τὸν ἑαυτοῦ λόγον (de
migr. Abr. § i.; i. 437 M.).

22. These privileges of Christians
are to be used. They must personally exercise their right of access to
God. And this they must do in
sincerity and faith, even as they have
received the fulness of divine blessing
in preparation for the fulfilment of
their priestly work.

The connexion of the clauses in vv.
22—24 is uncertain. It is possible to
begin each main sentence with the
verb: προσερχώμεθα...κατέχωμεν...καὶ
κατανοῶμεν; or to regard the καί as
giving the new beginning: προσερχώμεθα...καὶλελουσμένοι...κατέχωμεν...καὶ
κατανοῶμεν...; or to make the break
after πίστεως. The last arrangement
may be dismissed at once. In favour
of the second, it may be urged that it
gives a natural succession of conditions; internal and external, both
personal and social: and further
that the separation of Baptism (λελ.
τὸ σῶμα) from the confession naturally
included in it is harsh; while the
accumulation of fresh thoughts by καί
is in the style of the writer (let us
come to God...; and having our body
bathed...let us hold fast...; and let us
consider...).

But on the other hand it seems
most likely that the writer would
complete the description of the conditions of personal approach, corresponding with the priestly preparations
in the Levitical code, and then pass

τοῦ θεοῦ, ²²προσερχώμεθα μετὰ ἀληθινῆς καρδίας ἐν
πληροφορίᾳ πίστεως, ῥεραντισμένοι τὰς καρδίας ἀπὸ
συνειδήσεως πονηρᾶς καὶ λελουσμένοι τὸ σῶμα ὕδατι

22 προσερχόμεθα D₂.

on to the social obligations of Christians. So that on the whole it seems
best to make the break at the end of
v. 22 (*let us come to God...bathed with
pure water. Let us hold fast.... And
let us consider...*).
The fourfold characterisation of
worshippers in *v.* 22 ((1) μετὰ ἀληθινῆς
καρδίας, (2) ἐν πληροφορίᾳ πίστεως,
(3) ῥεραντισμένοι, (4) λελουσμένοι) deals
with what they are and with what
they have received, with their disposition and with their divine endowment. In themselves there is required
sincerity and faith; in regard to the
gift of God, the participation in the
spiritual reality and in the outward
sacramental sign of cleansing.
προσερχώμεθα]The word in this sense
of the approach of the worshipper to
God is found in the N. T. only in this
Epistle and in 1 Pet. ii. 4. The usage
is not unfrequent in the LXX. Comp.
iv. 16 note.
This approach is characterised by
two personal qualities, real devotion
and ripe faith.
μετὰ ἀληθινῆς καρδίας] *with a true
heart*—Vulg. *cum vero* (O. L. *certo
v. puro) corde*—a heart which fulfils
the ideal office of the heart, the seat
of the individual character, towards
God—a heart which expresses completely the devotion of the whole
person to God. There is no divided
allegiance: no reserve of feeling.
The phrase ἀληθινὴ καρδία is found
in Is. xxxviii. 3 (LXX.) ἐπορεύθην ἐνώ
πιόν σου μετὰ ἀληθείας ἐν ἀληθινῇ
καρδίᾳ (בְּלֵבָב שָׁלֵם, *a whole heart*).

Test. xii Patr. Dan § 5 ἀγαπᾶτε...
ἀλλήλους ἐν ἀληθινῇ καρδίᾳ.
For ἀληθινός see c. viii. 2; ix. 24.
(Deut. xxv. 15; Is. lxv. 2 A.). Comp. c.

viii. 2 note. For καρδία see Additional
Note on c. iv.
ἐν πληροφ. πίστ.] *in fulness of faith*,
Vulg. *in plenitudine* (O. L. *confirmatione* al. *satisfactione) fidei*, in faith
which has reached its mature vigour.
Compare c. vi. 11 πρὸς τὴν πληροφορίαν
τῆς ἐλπίδος. The sense of perfect self-
surrender must be completed by sure
reliance on One Who is ready to help.
The three members of the Christian
triad of earthly discipline are forcibly
recognised in the familiar order of
St Paul (1 Cor. xiii. 13) ἐν πληροφορίᾳ
πίστεως, κατέχωμεν τὴν ὁμολογίαν ἐλ
πίδος (*v.* 23), εἰς παροξυσμὸν ἀγάπης
(*v.* 24).
For the possible origin of the Christian triad in a saying of the Lord
(Ἐπιμελεῖσθε πίστεως καὶ ἐλπίδος δι᾽
ὧν γεννᾶται ἡ φιλόθεος καὶ φιλάνθρωπος
ἀγάπη, ἡ τὴν αἰώνιον ζωὴν παρέχουσα
Macar. Alex. *Hom.* xxxvii.; Migne,
P. G. xxxiv. p. 749), compare Resch,
l.c. 179 ff.
ῥεραντισμένοι...λελουσμένοι]There are
also Divine blessings corresponding to
human character. The heart is touched
with the cleansing power of the Divine
life: faith rests on the pledge of a
historic fact. In each case there is a
reference to Levitical ceremonies. So
it is said that *we have our hearts*—
the seat of personal character—and
not our outward persons and garments
(Ex. xxix. 21; Lev. viii. 30. Chrys.
ἐκεῖνοι τὸ σῶμα ἐρραντίζοντο, ἡμεῖς δὲ
τὴν συνείδησιν)—*sprinkled,* that is with
Christ's Blood and not with any water
of purification, and so cleansed *from
an evil conscience;* and *our body is
bathed with pure water.* In the latter
clause there is a reference both to the
consecration of priests (Ex. xxix. 4),
and to the bathing of the High-priest

καθαρῷ· ²³κατέχωμεν τὴν ὁμολογίαν τῆς ἐλπίδος ἀκλινῆ,

23 τῆς ἐλπ. τὴν ὁμολ. D₂ vg.　　　τῆς ἐλπ. ἡμῶν ℵ*.

on the day of Atonement (Lev. xvi. 4). With these symbolic bathings the sacramental 'bathing' of Christians is contrasted.

For ῥαντίζειν see c. ix. 13 note; Lev. xiv. 5 ff.; Num. xix. 9 ff. Twice only is the sprinkling of men with blood noticed in the Levitical ritual, and in each case the symbolism is most expressive: Ex. xxiv. 8 (c. ix. 19); xxix. 21. For the construction ῥαντίζειν ἀπό compare 2 Cor. xi. 3; Rom. ix. 3; Luke xviii. 3.

συνειδ. πονηρ.] The conscience takes its character from the actions of the man: c. xiii. 18 (καλὴν συν.); Acts xxiii. 1 (συν. ἀγαθή, and often); 1 Tim. iii. 9; 2 Tim. i. 3 (καθαρὰ συν.). See also Acts xxiv. 16 (ἀπρόσκοπος συν.): and c. ix. 9 Additional Note p. 293.

For the phrase and thought compare Barn. *Ep.* xix. 12 οὐ προσήξεις ἐπὶ προσευχὴν ἐν συνειδήσει πονηρᾷ. *Did.* § xiv.

λελουσμ. τὸ σῶμα ὕ. κ.] *having our body bathed with pure water* (Vulg. *abluti corpus...*). For λούεσθαι see Eph. v. 26; Tit. iii. 5; and especially John xiii. 10. For ὕδωρ καθαρόν see Num. v. 17 (מַיִם קְדֹשִׁים); Ezek. xxxvi. 25.

The two phrases appear to contain allusions to the Christian sacraments. That to the Eucharist is veiled: that to Baptism is unquestionable. In the one case the reference is primarily to the spiritual efficacy of the divine working, of which the Holy Eucharist is the appointed but not the sole means: in the other to the outward act, the decisive, sensible, rite in which the believer recognised the foundation of his assurance outside himself. The change in number from τὰς καρδίας to τὸ σῶμα is not to be overlooked.

23—25. The exhortation to the use of the personal privilege of approach to God is followed by the charge to fulfil the social duties of believers. Christians are required to maintain the open confession of their hope (*v.* 23); to regard one another with a view to bringing the influence of example to bear upon the development of life (*v.* 24); and to use occasions of meeting together in the prospect of a near crisis (*v.* 25).

The reference to Baptism in the last clause furnishes a direct transition. The confession then publicly and gladly made must be firmly held:

23. κατέχωμεν τὴν ὁμολ.] *Let us hold fast the confession of our hope that it waver not.* Compare c. iv. 14 κρατῶμεν τῆς ὁμολογίας.

For κατέχειν see c. iii. 6, 14.

For ὁμολογία see c. iii. 1; iv. 14. The word was used specially of the confession at Baptism: ἔθος γέγονεν ἐκ τούτου [the Lord's questions to St Peter] τρεῖς ὁμολογίας ἀπαιτεῖσθαι τοὺς μέλλοντας βαπτισθῆναι (Ammon. *Cat. in Joh.* xxi.). ὡμολογήσαμεν ὅτε τὰς συνθήκας τῆς πίστεως ἐποιούμεθα εἰς ἀνάστασιν νεκρῶν πιστεύειν καὶ εἰς ζωὴν αἰώνιον (Theophlct.). The illustrations given by Suicer (*Thes. s. v.* ἀποτάσσομαι) are worthy of study.

The phrase 'confession of hope' is remarkable. The Apostle substitutes for the more general word 'faith,' that word which gives distinctness to special objects of faith to be realised in the future. Hope gives a definite shape to the absolute confidence of Faith. Faith reposes completely in the love of God: Hope vividly anticipates that God will fulfil His promises in a particular way.

The conception of Hope naturally occupies a prominent place in an Epistle directed to meet despondency.

iii. 6 οὗ οἶκός ἐσμεν ἡμεῖς ἐὰν τὴν

πιστὸς γὰρ ὁ ἐπαγγειλάμενος· ²⁴καὶ κατανοῶμεν ἀλλήλους εἰς παροξυσμὸν ἀγάπης καὶ καλῶν ἔργων, ²⁵μὴ

παρρησίαν καὶ τὸ καύχημα τῆς ἐλπίδος
μέχρι τέλους βεβαίαν κατάσχωμεν.

vi. 11 ἐπιθυμοῦμεν......ἐνδείκνυσθαι
σπουδὴν πρὸς τὴν πληροφορίαν τῆς
ἐλπίδος ἄχρι τέλους.

vi. 18,19 οἱ καταφυγόντες κρατῆσαι τῆς
προκειμένης ἐλπίδος ἦν...ἔχομεν...ἀσφα-
λῆ τε καὶ βεβαίαν, καὶ εἰσερχομένην εἰς
τὸ ἐσώτερον τοῦ καταπετάσματος.

vii. 19 κρείττονος ἐλπίδος, δι' ἧς ἐγγίζομεν τῷ θεῷ.

The hope in each case appears to
be fixed upon the realisation of a
complete divine fellowship under new
conditions, as it was laid down by the
schoolmen: proprium ac principale
spei objectum est ipsa æterna beatitudo (Th. Aq. *Sum. Th.* ii. 2 qu. 17,
art. 2). To this the Christian looks
forward with a vivid anticipation. In
it he sees the assurance of the transfiguration of the conditions of earthly
being (1 John iii. 2, 3). The resurrection of Christ is the pledge of its
fulfilment (1 Pet. i. 3, 21). Hence
'Christ Jesus' Himself is 'our hope'
(1 Tim. i. 1; Col. i. 27).

In the presence of such a hope the
visible glories of the Temple fade
away. Those who can realise it will
feel no loss when they are withdrawn.

Comp. Acts ii. 26 (LXX.); xxiii. 6;
xxiv. 15; 2 Cor. iii. 12; Rom. v. 2;
viii. 20 ff.; Col. i. 5.

Ἐλπίς is not found in the Gospels.
The translation 'faith' in A. V. is
an innovation: 'hope' is found in the
earlier versions (Tynd. Cov. GB. Gen.
Bps. Rh.).

ἀκλινῆ] Vulg. *indeclinabilem*, O.L.
inprævaricabilem, *so that it waver
not*: or, according to the image, *so
that it remain erect and firm.* The
word is not found elsewhere in N. T.
Comp. Luc. *Dem. Enc.* § 32 (p. 514)
Δημοσθένην ὑπερηγάμην...ἀκλινῆ τὴν
ψυχὴν ἐπ' ὀρθῆς ἐν ἁπάσαις φυλάττοντα

τρικυμίαις τῆς τύχης καὶ πρὸς μηδὲν τῶν
δεινῶν ἐνδιδόντα.

For the form of the sentence see c.
v. 14; vii. 24.

πιστὸς γὰρ ὁ ἐπαγγ.] The fidelity
of God is not only the sure ground of
our confidence but (as men speak) it
challenges our fidelity. Compare 1
Cor. i. 9; x. 13; 1 Thess. v. 24.

Sicut enim fidelis et verus remune-
rator est Christus in promissionibus
suis, ita fideles nos esse vult in pro-
missis nostris quæ vovimus tempore
baptismatis, diabolo videlicet contra-
dicere Christoque servire (Primas.).

24. καὶ κατανοῶμεν ἀλλήλους] *And
let us consider one another*, Vulg.
et consideremus (O. L. *aspiciamus*)
invicem. It is our duty to declare
what we are and what we look for: it
is our duty also to consider what
others are. The well-being of each
believer is bound up with the well-
being of the whole body. He is therefore constrained to give careful heed
to others in the hope that he may
rouse them to nobler action; and
again that he may himself draw encouragement and inspiration from
noble examples. Comp. c. xii. 15.
Consideremus nos invicem, scilicet
perfecti minores eos hortando, et
minores perfectos imitando eos (Ambr.
ap. Pet. Lomb.).

For κατανοεῖν see c. iii. 1 note.

παροξ. ἀγάπης] Vulg. *in provocatio-
nem caritatis* (O. L. *amoris*). The
combination has a startling sound.
Christians are to be roused, provoked,
but to love. Compare 1 Thess. iv. 11
φιλοτιμεῖσθαι ἡσυχάζειν. Xen. *Mem.*
iii. 3, 13 ἥπερ [φιλοτιμία] μάλιστα πα-
ροξύνει πρὸς τὰ καλὰ καὶ ἔντιμα.

[Isocr.] *ad Demon.* § 46 (p. 12 B)
μάλιστα δ' ἂν παροξυνθείης ὀρέγεσθαι
τῶν καλῶν ἔργων.

Euthym. Zig. λίθος μὲν πρὸς λίθον
τριβόμενος πῦρ ἀφίησιν, ἄνθρωπος δὲ

ἐγκαταλείποντες τὴν ἐπισυναγωγὴν ἑαυτῶν, καθὼς ἔθος

25 ἐγκαταλείποντες A -λιπόντες ℵ: καταλιπόντες D₂*.   τὴν ἐπισ. αὐτῶν (αὑ.) ℵ*.
ἔθος+ἐστίν D₂*.

πρὸς ἄνθρωπον ἁμιλλώμενος θερμότερος
γίγνεται. The noun occurs in a different
sense Acts xv. 39; and the verb
Acts xvii. 16; 1 Cor. xiii. 5.

καλῶν ἔργων] good deeds, or rather,
noble works, works which by their
generous and attractive character win
the natural admiration of men. For
καλός see c. v. 14; vi. 5.

It is a misfortune that we cannot
distinguish καλὰ ἔργα and ἀγαθὰ ἔργα
in translation : we are constrained to
render both phrases by 'good works.'
Yet the ideas suggested by the two
phrases are distinct. In ἀγαθὰ ἔργα
we mark only the intrinsic character
of the works : they are essentially
good. In καλὰ ἔργα we emphasise the
notion of their effect upon others, of
their nobility which attracts. The
same work may be regarded both as
ἀγαθόν and as καλόν, but so far as it is
καλόν it is looked at under the aspect
of moral beauty.

Compare Matt. v. 16 ὅπως ἴδωσιν
ὑμῶν τὰ καλὰ ἔργα; xxvi. 10 ἔργον
καλὸν ἠργάσατο (you fail to see its
beauty); ‖ Mk. xiv. 6; John x. 32
πολλὰ ἔργα ἔδειξα ὑμῖν καλά; 1 Tim.
iii. 1 καλοῦ ἔργου ἐπιθυμεῖ; v. 10 ἐν
ἔργοις κ. μαρτυρουμένη; v. 25; vi. 18;
Tit. ii. 7 τύπον καλῶν ἔργων; 14; iii.
8, 14; 1 Pet. ii. 12 ἐκ τῶν καλῶν ἔργων.
See also Rom. xii. 17; 2 Cor. viii. 21.

On the other hand, for ἔργα ἀγαθά,
ἀγαθὸν ἔργον see Rom. ii. 7; xiii. 3; 2
Cor. ix. 8; Eph. ii. 10; Col. i. 10; 2
Thess. ii. 17; 1 Tim. ii. 10; v. 10; 2
Tim. ii. 21; iii. 17; Tit. i. 16; iii. 1;
Hebr. xiii. 21.

25. μὴ ἐγκαταλ. τὴν ἐπισ. ἑ.] not for-
saking the gathering of our own
selves together for fellowship in divine
worship. Vulg. non deserentes collectionem nostram. The fulfilment of
this social duty is presented under a

twofold aspect, negatively and positively : Christians are not to abandon
the opportunities of meeting; and
they are to use the power of mutual
influence.

The word ἐγκαταλείποντες conveys
the notion not simply of leaving, as
no longer taking part in the assembly,
but of abandoning, leaving the assembly exposed to peril in the conflict.
Compare c. xiii. 5 note; 2 Tim. iv.
10, 16 (Δ. με ἐγκατέλιπεν); 2 Cor. iv. 9
(διωκόμενοι ἀλλ᾽ οὐκ ἐγκαταλειπόμενοι);
Matt. xxvii. 46 ἵνα τί με ἐγκατέλιπες;
Ἐπισυναγωγή, which expresses the
assembly formed and not only the act
of assembling (compare σύναξις Suicer, Thes. s. v.), occurs again in a
different connexion in 2 Thess. ii. 1,
where the force of the ἐπί is seen, as
marking a definite centre to which the
gathering is directed, that is, Christ.
Comp. Matt. xviii. 20 συνηγμένοι εἰς
τὸ ἐμὸν ὄνομα. The verb is found in
significant passages : Matt. xxiii. 37;
xxiv. 31; Luke xvii. 37; compare 2
Macc. ii. 7.

The use of ἑαυτῶν (i.e. ἡμῶν αὐτῶν)
for the simple ἡμῶν fixes attention
on the meeting as characteristically
Christian. For the use of ἑαυτῶν
see c. iii. 13 note.

Wetstein quotes from Augustine
(Conf. viii. 2, 4) the striking account
of the conversion of the rhetorician
Victorinus : dicebat Simpliciano [his
Christian friend] non palam sed secre-
tius et familiarius : Noveris me jam
esse Christianum. Et respondebat
ille : Non credam, nec deputabo te
inter Christianos, nisi in ecclesia Christi
te videro. Ille autem irridebat dicens :
Ergo parietes faciunt Christianos?
Et hoc sæpe dicebat jam se esse
Christianum; et Simplicianus illud
sæpe respondebat, et sæpe ab illo
parietum irrisio repetebatur.

τισίν, ἀλλὰ παρακαλοῦντες, καὶ τοσούτῳ μᾶλλον ὅσῳ
βλέπετε ἐγγίζουσαν τὴν ἡμέραν.   ²⁶ Ἑκουσίως

The account of his public profession
(§ 5) illustrates the ὁμολογία.
Chrysostom notices the twofold
blessing of the Christian gatherings :
οἶδεν ἀπὸ τῆς συνουσίας καὶ τῆς ἐπισυναγωγῆς πολλὴν οὖσαν τὴν ἰσχύν (Matt.
xviii. 20)...οὐ διὰ τοῦτο δὲ μόνον, ἀλλ᾽
ἐπειδὴ καὶ τὰ τῆς ἀγάπης αὐξάνεται διὰ
τῆς ἐπισυναγωγῆς.

καθὼς ἔθος τισίν] Vulg. sicut est
consuetudinis (—ni V. L.) quibusdam.
Such conduct on the side of Christians
would arise partly from fear lest they
should provoke the active hostility of
the Jewish authorities; partly from
self-confidence, as though they no
longer needed the assistance of ordinary common worship where the general average of spiritual life might be
counted too low to aid more mature
believers. And yet more than this,
the Christian assemblies must have
appeared insignificant when compared with those to which the Hebrews were accustomed. Other traces
of the practice are found : Jude 19
οἱ ἀποδιορίζοντες (perhaps, though
ἑαυτοὺς must be omitted). Barn. Ep.
iv. 10 μὴ καθ᾽ ἑαυτοὺς ἐνδύνοντες μονά-
ζετε ὡς ἤδη δεδικαιωμένοι. Herm. Sim.
ix. 26 μονάζοντες ἀπολλύασι τὰς ἑαυτῶν
ψυχάς. Comp. Ign. ad Ephes. 5, 13 ;
Did. 16.

And Primasius gives the same explanation of the evil habit: deserebant
collectionem habitantes soli, ut deo
liberius viderentur vacare.

ἀλλὰ παρακαλοῦντες] But on the
contrary cheer (Vulg. consolantes) the
timid, and stimulate the backward,
by your example. Comp. c. iii. 13 ;
xii. 5 ; xiii. 22 τοῦ λόγου τῆς παρακλήσεως.

Such 'exhortation' would have regard both to dangers from without
and to dangers from within. Christians
had need of courage and they had
need of progress. [Hortatur] consolari

simpliciores et suo exemplo confortare
(Primas.). Sublevatio laboris est visio
collaborantis ut in itinere fit (Ambr.
ap. Pet. Lomb.).

καὶ τοσ. μᾶλλον ὅσῳ...τὴν ἡμέραν]
The actual position of the things, the
nearness of the great crisis of the
Lord's coming, made the obligation
of mutual support among Christians
urgently pressing. The danger was
great and the time was short. Those
who deserted the Christian Faith
would be swept away in the ruin soon
to follow, without the opportunity of
return.

The change to the direct address
(βλέπετε in contrast with κατανοῶμεν)
adds force to the appeal. The beginning of the Jewish war was already
visible to the Hebrews.

This absolute use of 'the day' (τὴν
ἡμέραν) is peculiar. The nearest parallels are 1 Thess. v. 4; Rom. xiii. 12;
in both of which passages the contrast
with 'night' is brought out. Compare
1 John ii. 8.

'The day' is elsewhere spoken of,
according to the phrase of the O. T.,
as 'the day of the Lord' (ἡμέρα Κυρίου,
ἡ ἡμέρα τοῦ Κυρίου) Acts ii. 20 (LXX.);
1 Thess. v. 2; 2 Thess. ii. 2; 2 Pet.
iii. 10; or, more generally, as 'that
day' (ἐκείνη ἡ ἡμέρα) Matt. vii. 22;
xxiv. 36 ‖ Mk. xiii. 32; Lk. x. 12 (xvii.
31); xxi. 34; 2 Thess. i. 10; 2 Tim. i.
12, 18; iv. 8.

Elsewhere it is called 'the day of
God' (2 Pet. iii. 12); 'the day (days)
of the Son of man'; Lk. xvii. 26 (30);
comp. John viii. 56; 'the day of
Christ,' 'of Jesus Christ,' 'of our Lord
Jesus' [Christ] Eph. i. 6, 10; ii. 16;
1 Cor. i. 8 (v. 5); 2 Cor. i. 14; Phil. i.
6, 10; ii. 16.

It is also called 'the great day':
Jude 6; Apoc. vi. 17; xvi. 14; 'a
day of judgment': Matt. x. 15; xi.
22, 24; xii. 36; (Rom. ii. 16); 2 Pet.

γὰρ ἁμαρτανόντων ἡμῶν μετὰ τὸ λαβεῖν τὴν ἐπίγνωσιν

26 τῆς ἐπιγνωσίαν ℵ* (sic).

ii. 9; iii. 7; 1 John iv. 17; and, in regard to its contrasted issues, 'a day of redemption': Eph. iv. 30; 'a day of wrath': Rom. ii. 5. Comp. 'the last day' in St John (vi. 39 note).

In working out these various thoughts it will be seen that each day of Christ's coming is at once a fulfilment and a prophecy: a judgment and a promise. Such was the final overthrow of the Jewish system at the fall of Jerusalem.

The expectation of the Lord's speedy coming, which then had accomplishment, is found expressed in each group of writings of the N.T., and under the same term παρουσία.

'The day' is spoken of as 'drawing nigh' (ἐγγίζουσαν), as in other apostolic writings: Rom. xiii. 12 (ἡ ἡμ. ἤγγικεν); Phil. iv. 5 (ὁ Κύριος ἐγγύς); James v. 8 (ἡ παρουσία τοῦ Κυρίου ἤγγικεν); 1 Pet. iv. 7 (πάντων τὸ τέλος ἤγγικεν). Compare c. viii. 13 (ἐγγὺς ἀφανισμοῦ); and John xxi. 21 ff.

(2) vv. 26—31. The perils of apostasy.

The charge which has been given in the last section to fulfil the personal and social claims of the Faith is enforced by a consideration of the perils of apostasy. There is, the writer shews, no sacrifice available for apostates from Christ (26, 27).

Death was the punishment of the corresponding offence under the Old Covenant (28); and the same principle must find application to Christians (29); who serve the same God (30, 31).

It must be observed that the argument assumes that the sacrifice of Christ is finally rejected, and sin persisted in (ἁμαρτανόντων). The writer does not set limits to the efficacy of Christ's work for the penitent.

The whole section must be compared with c. vi. 4—8.

The Fathers commonly interpret the passage as laying down that there can be no repetition of Baptism: so, for example, Chrysostom: [οὗ] τὴν μετάνοιαν ἀναιρεῖ ἢ τὸν διὰ μετανοίας ἐξιλασμόν, οὐδὲ ὠθεῖ καὶ καταβάλλει διὰ τῆς ἀπογνώσεως τὸν ἐπταικότα... ἀλλὰ τί; τὸ δεύτερον ἀναιρεῖ βάπτισμα· οὐ γὰρ εἶπεν, Οὐκέτι ἐστὶ μετάνοια, οὐδέ, Οὐκέτι ἐστὶν ἄφεσις, ἀλλὰ Θυσία οὐκέτι ἐστί, τουτέστι σταυρὸς δεύτερος οὐκέτι ἐστί: and, following him, Primasius: [non dicit] non est ultra pœnitentia, neque peccatorum remissio, sed hostia, inquit, ultra non est, hoc est crux ultra non est secunda, ut iterum Christus crucifigatur, iterumque nos baptizemur.

[26] *For if we wilfully sin after that we have received the knowledge of the truth, there is no longer left a sacrifice for sins, [27]but a certain fearful expectation of judgment, and a jealousy of fire ready to devour the adversaries. [28]One that setteth at naught Moses' law dieth without compassion on the word of two or three witnesses; [29]of how much sorer punishment, think ye, shall he be judged worthy who trampleth under foot the Son of God, and counteth the blood of the covenant a common thing, the blood wherein he was sanctified, and doth outrage to the Spirit of grace? [30]For we know Him that said Vengeance is mine, I will recompense; and again The Lord will judge His people. [31]It is a fearful thing to fall into the hands of a living God.*

26, 27. The mention of 'the day' in v. 25 calls out the sad severity of the warning which follows. We must use the help which God has provided and in His way; for if we set this at naught nothing remains for our relief.

26. ἑκουσίως ἁμαρτανόντων ἡμῶν] Vulg. *voluntarie* (O. L. *ultro*) *peccantibus nobis*. The phrase includes two

τῆς ἀληθείας, οὐκέτι περὶ ἁμαρτιῶν ἀπολείπεται θυσία,
²⁷φοβερὰ δέ τις ἐκδοχὴ κρίσεως καὶ πυρὸϲ ζῆλοϲ ἐϲθίειν

περὶ...θυσία: περιλείπεται θυσίαν περὶ ἁμαρτίας προσενενκῖν D₂*.

distinct elements, the voluntariness, that is the realised consciousness, of the sin, and the habitual indulgence in the sin. Such sin involves apostasy from Christ (*v.* 29 καταπατήσας). The adverb ἑκουσίως stands first with emphasis: ix. 25. For ἑκουσίως compare 1 Pet. v. 2 μὴ ἀναγκαστῶς ἀλλὰ ἑκουσίως, and Philem. 14 μὴ κατὰ ἀνάγκην...ἀλλὰ κατὰ ἑκούσιον. Philo *de post. Cain.* § 3 (i. 228 M.) τὸ ἑκούσιον, ἅτε βουλῇ καὶ προμηθείᾳ γενόμενον, ἀνιάτους εἰς ἀεὶ κῆρας ἐνδέξεται. Contrast Philo, *quod Deus immut.* § 28 (i. 292 M.).

For the opposite ἀκουσίως ἁμαρτάνειν (בִּשְׁגָגָה) see Lev. iv. 2; v. 15; Num. xv. 25 ff. Comp. Philo *de vit. Mos.* i. § 49 (ii. 123) Balaam sought forgiveness of the angel συγγνῶναι δεόμενος ὑπ᾽ ἀγνοίας ἀλλ᾽ οὐ καθ᾽ ἑκούσιον γνώμην ἁμαρτόντι. *de Prof.* § 14.

On ἁμαρτανόντων Theophylact says justly: ὅρα δὲ πῶς οὐκ εἶπεν ἁμαρτόντων ἀλλ᾽ ἁμαρτανόντων, τουτέστιν ἐμμενόντων τῇ ἁμαρτίᾳ ἀμετανοήτως. Compare 1 John iii. 6, 9; v. 18; and contrast c. iii. 17 (τοῖς ἁμαρτήσασιν).

By the addition of ἡμῶν the writer softens the severity of his words with a touch of deep sympathy. No one of us, he implies, can set aside the warning as needless. If he dwells on the danger of others he does not forget his own. Comp. 1 John ii. 1 note.

μετὰ τὸ λαβεῖν τὴν ἐπίγν. τῆς ἀλ.] Vulg. *post acceptam notitiam veritatis.* Compare 1 Tim. iv. 3 ἐπεγνωκόσιν τὴν ἀλήθειαν. The use of the compound phrase (λαβεῖν τὴν ἐπίγν.) for the simple verb (Col. i. 6; 1 Pet. ii. 21) brings out the double aspect of the knowledge as God's gift and man's acquisition (λαβεῖν). In gaining it

man is active and yet it is not from him. For similar uses of λαβεῖν see c. ii. 3; xi. 29; 2 Pet. i. 9 (λήθην λαβ.) ; 2 Tim. i. 5 (ὑπόμνησιν λαβ.).

The knowledge thus received is treated as complete (τὴν ἐπίγ. τῆς ἀλ.: contrast Tit. i. 1 ; 1 Tim. ii. 4 ἐπίγ. ἀλ.); and the use of the emphatic ἐπίγνωσις in place of the simple γνῶσις marks the greatness of the fall which is contemplated. Those whose case is taken into account have vigorously applied themselves to pursue the study of Christian truth. Ἐπίγνωσις is a characteristic word of St Paul's later Epistles (from Romans onwards). It occurs here only in this Epistle. Comp. 2 Pet. ii. 21 ; Rom. i. 28; x. 2; and Lightfoot on Phil. i. 9 ; Col. i. 9.

τῆς ἀληθείας] 'The Truth' absolutely is coincident with the revelation of Christ. This use of the term is characteristic of St John (i. 17; iii. 21 ; xvi. 13, &c.; 1 John ii. 21, &c.); but is found also in each group of the Epistles: James iii. 14; v. 19; 1 Peter i. 22; 2 Thess. ii. 12; Gal. v. 7; Eph. i. 13; 2 Tim. ii. 15.

οὐκέτι...ἀπολείπεται] The sacrifice of Christ has been rejected; and there is no other sacrifice which can be effectual. The order of the words is remarkable. The words περὶ ἁμαρτιῶν and θυσία are separated so that the fact of sin stands out prominently : 'for sins there is left no sacrifice.' So too the writer appeals to individual experience when he says 'for sins' and not generally 'for sin.' Contrast *v.* 18 προσφορὰ περὶ ἁμαρτίας. ix. 26 εἰς ἀθέτησιν ἁμαρτίας. xii. 4 πρὸς τὴν ἁμαρτίαν ἀνταγωνιζόμενοι. xiii. 11.

Non reservatur nobis ultra hostia pro peccato quæ pro nobis offeratur, sicut in veteri lege donatum est

μέλλοντος τοὺς ὑπεναντίους. ²⁸ἀθετήσας τις νόμον Μωυσέως χωρὶς οἰκτιρμῶν ἐπὶ Δυσὶν ἢ τρισὶν μάρτυσιν ἀποθνήσκει·

28 οἰκτιρμῶν: +καὶ δακρύων D₂* syr hl.

hostias sæpe offerre pro peccatis (Primas.).

27. φοβερὰ δέ τις...] but there is ...there abideth... (comp. John iii. 36). This issue is represented on its two sides, as man's expectation (ἐκδοχὴ κρ.), and God's provision (πυρὸς ζῆλος).

The rhetorical use of the indefinite τις gives a solemn awe to the statement. The fact that the expectation cannot be exactly defined necessarily makes it more impressive. Comp. Acts viii. 9; v. 36.

ἐκδοχὴ κρίσεως] The noun ἐκδοχή occurs here only in the N.T. Compare v. 13 ἐκδεχόμενος, c. xi. 10.

Such a judgment (c. ix. 27) would be, for those whom the Apostle describes, condemnation. Comp. John v. 24, 29.

πυρὸς ζῆλος] Latt. ignis æmulatio, a jealousy (fierceness) of fire. The words are adapted from Is. xxvi. 11 (LXX.) ζῆλος λήψεται λαὸν ἀπαίδευτον καὶ νῦν πῦρ τοὺς ὑπεναντίους κατέδεται. The word ζῆλος suggests the thought of love which has been wronged, just as πῦρ describes one aspect of the Divine Nature: c. xii. 29 ὁ θεὸς ἡμῶν πῦρ καταναλίσκον.

Ὅρα says Theophylact πῶς οἷον ἐψύχωσε τὸ πῦρ. It is the fire which consumes.

The word ὑπεναντίος, which is not unfrequent in the LXX., occurs again Col. ii. 14.

For the thought of vv. 26—7 compare a striking passage of Philo, quod Deus immut. § 37 (i. 299 M.).

28, 29. The anticipation of fatal punishment for apostasy is confirmed by the consideration of the enactment for a similar offence under the Old Covenant. The same form of argument from the less to the greater occurs c. ii. 2 f.; ix. 13 f.; xii. 25.

The thought finds a striking illustration in Philo de Prof. § 16, i. p. 558 M.: εἰ οἱ τοὺς θνητοὺς κακηγορήσαντες γονεῖς ἀπάγονται τὴν ἐπὶ θανάτῳ (Ex. xxi. 15) τίνος ἀξίους χρὴ νομίζειν τιμωρίας τοὺς [τὸν] τῶν ὅλων πατέρα καὶ ποιητὴν βλασφημεῖν ὑπομένοντας;

28. ἀθετήσας τις ν. Μ.] One that setteth at naught Moses' law... Vulg. Irritam quis faciens legem... O.L. Cum enim quidam relinqueret legem... The offence like the correlatives (καταπατήσας, ἡγησάμενος, ἐνυβρίσας) is regarded in its isolated completeness; the culprit 'set the law at naught.' His act was final and decisive; and it is not presented in its present fulfilment (ἀθετῶν τις) or in its abiding permanence (ἠθετηκώς τις).

The verb ἀθετεῖν occurs here only in the Epistle (comp. ἀθέτησις vii. 18; ix. 26 note). It describes not only the violation of an ordinance or authority in details, but the denial of the validity of the ordinance or the authority altogether. Comp. Gal. iii. 15; 1 Tim. v. 12; Jude 8; John xii. 18.

The unique absence of the article here in νόμον Μωυσέως (elsewhere ὁ νόμ. M. Luke ii. 22; xxiv. 44; John vii. 23; Acts xiii. 39; xv. 5; xxviii. 23 (1 Cor. ix. 9)) gives the sense of 'that which was a prescription of Moses.' The reference, as marked by the clause ἐπὶ δυσὶν ἢ τρισὶν μ. ἀποθ. (Deut. xvii. 6), appears to be to the specific warning against idolatry (Deut. xvii. 2 ff.). Not every offence against the Law was visited with death, but specially, among others, this offence to which the apostasy from Christ corresponded. In the case of the Old Covenant the sanction lay in the declaration of the Lawgiver: in the case of the New Covenant the believer

²⁹ πόσῳ δοκεῖτε χείρονος ἀξιωθήσεται τιμωρίας ὁ τὸν υἱὸν
τοῦ θεοῦ καταπατήσας, καὶ τὸ ἀῖΜΑ τᾶ̂ς ΔιαθΉκΗς κοινὸν

29 δοκεῖδε D₂*.

had direct experience of the power
of the Divine Presence.

χωρὶς οἰκτιρμῶν] All the people
shared in the infliction of the punishment (Deut. xiii. 9; xvii. 7 ; Acts vii.
58).

The word οἰκτιρμός (compassion) appears to be very rare in classical Gk.
(Pind. Pyth. i. 85 [164]) and the plural
(LXX. רַחֲמִים) is peculiar to ecclesiastical writers. The word expresses the
feeling which witnesses to fellowship
and natural sympathy, while ἔλεος
(pity) describes the feeling which is
called out by the sight of misery.
Comp. Rom. xii. 1 ; 2 Cor. i. 3; Phil.
ii. 1; Col. iii. 12; Luke vi. 36; James
v. 11.

ἀποθνήσκει] The Law is valid and
effective. For ἐπί see ix. 10.

29. πόσῳ δοκεῖτε…] Vulg. quanto
magis putatis deteriora mereri sup-
plicia (O. L. deteriora deprecabitur
vindictæ). The parenthetical δοκεῖτε
makes the appeal to the readers more
direct and pointed : τὴν κρίσιν αὐτοῖς
ἐπιτρέπει· ὅπερ εἰώθαμεν ποιεῖν ἐπὶ
τῶν σφόδρα ὁμολογουμένων, τοὺς ἀκρο-
ατὰς δικαστὰς ποιοῦντες (Theophl ct

The verb ἀξιωθήσεται, which is commonly used in connexion with words
of reward (c. iii. 3; 1 Tim. v. 17), is
used also of meet punishment, like
ἄξιος Acts xxiii. 29.

τιμωρίας] The noun occurs nowhere
else in the N. T. (the verb τιμωρεῖν is
found Acts xxii. 5; xxvi. 11). It
expresses simply the notion of retri-
butive punishment in regard of the
offence. It will be seen that in the
case of the perfect fulfilment of a
perfect law the ends of retribution
and correction absolutely coincide.

ὁ… καταπατήσας…ἡγησάμενος… ἐνυ-
βρίσας] There is a triple indict-
ment. The manifestation of the apos-

tasy of the offender is described under
three distinct aspects, as an act (καταπατήσας), as an opinion (ἡγησάμενος),
as a personal and wilful assault (ἐνυβρίσας). His conduct shews that he
has already abandoned his faith, and
that too after he had made trial of
its blessings. His decision, expressed
in deed, is regarded as complete and
final.

The language used suggests the
open repudiation of the baptismal
confession and covenant: 1 Cor. xii. 3.
Pliny reports to Trajan that those
who were brought away from the
Faith imaginem tuam deorumque
simulacra venerati sunt et Christo
male dixerunt (Epp. x. 96).

The strangeness of the metaphor in
καταπατεῖν as applied to a person is
enhanced by the use of the title 'the
Son of God' (comp. vi. 6 note). The
word καταπατεῖν occurs Matt. v. 13 ;
vii. 6 in connexions which illustrate
the image. That which claims to be
precious is not only regarded as
having no value: it is also treated
with utter contempt.

Καταπατεῖν is not unfrequent in the
LXX. in a similar connexion for different Hebrew words : Ps. lvi. (lv.)
2, 3; lvii. (lvi.) 4 (שָׁאַף); Is. lxiii. 6,
18 (בּוּס).

The act of contemptuous rejection
of Christ is joined with or rests upon
a deliberate judgment. The apostate
held the blood of the covenant to be
a common thing. The word ἡγεῖσθαι
occurs again in this sense : xi. 11, 26.

τὸ αἷμα τῆς διαθήκης] The phrase
suggests the contrast on which the
writer has already dwelt between the
inaugurations of the Old and New
Covenants: Ex. xxiv. 8 (c. ix. 20).
Comp. c. xiii. 20; Matt. xxvi. 28 ;
Mk. xiv. 24 (τὸ αἷμά μου τῆς διαθήκης);

ἡγησάμενος ἐν ᾧ ἡγιάσθη, καὶ τὸ πνεῦμα τῆς χάριτος

om. ἐν ᾧ ἡγιάσθη A.

Luke xxii. 20 (τοῦτο τὸ ποτήριον ἡ κ. διαθ. ἐν τῷ αἵμ. μου).

κοινὸν ἡγησάμενος] Vulg. *pollutum duxerit.* O. L. *communem æstimaverit.* Syr. vg. *as that of any man.* The two senses given by the Latin have each found support in later times. Some have taken κοινός as 'common' in the sense of 'undistinguished from the blood of any other man'; others as (positively) 'impure,' 'unholy,' as if Christ had suffered justly as an evildoer. This sense is supposed to be suggested by the clause ἐν ᾧ ἡγιάσθη which follows. In either case the clause, added after the structure of the sentence was complete, brings in a new thought which places the greatness of the offence in a clearer light: 'holding that *common* wherein he was made *holy*.'

The usage of the N. T. uniformly places κοινός in contrast with ἅγιος or καθαρός. Comp. c. ix. 13 note.

For the sense 'like that of other men,' 'ordinary,' see Just. M. *Apol.* i. 66 κοινὸς ἄρτος. Perhaps it is simplest here to take the word as negatively opposed to ἅγιος in the sense of 'having no divine virtue.'

ἐν ᾧ...] *wherein he was sanctified (hallowed).* Vulg. *in quo sanctificatus est.* Compare Rom. v. 9 (δικαιωθέντες ἐν τῷ αἵμ. αὐτοῦ); Eph. ii. 13 (ἐγενήθητε ἐγγὺς ἐν τῷ αἵμ. Χριστοῦ); Apoc. i. 5 (λύσαντι...ἐν τῷ αἵμ.); and c. ix. 25; x. 19 notes.

The blood of Christ is as 'the fountain' in which the sinner is 'plunged' for cleansing (βαπτίζειν ἐν Matt. iii. 11).

In connexion with ἁγιάζειν the preposition (ἐν) expresses in various forms the idea of the complete introduction (immersion) of that which is hallowed into that element which by embracing hallows. Compare John xvii. 17 (ἁγ. ἐν τῇ ἀληθείᾳ); Rom. xv.

16 (ἡγιασμ. ἐν πν. ἁγ.); 1 Cor. i. 2 (ἡγιασμ. ἐν Χ. 'Ι.); vii. 14 (ἡγ. ὁ ἀνὴρ (ἡ γυνὴ) ἐν...); Jude 1 (τοῖς ἐν θ. πατρὶ ἡγιασμένοις).

The 'hallowing' of the Christian is spoken of as one definite act (ἡγιάσθη). By incorporation into Christ he was once for all devoted to God. Comp. 1 Cor. vi. 11.

τὸ πν. τῆς χάρ. ἐνυβρ.] Vulg. *et (qui) spiritui gratiæ contumeliam fecerit, and (who) doth outrage to the Spirit of grace.* There is still a third element in the apostasy. The apostate offers insult and outrage to that Power through Whom the highest divine influences flow to man. This act of open rebellion against the present power of God, active through the Body of the Church, crowns the personal hostility to Christ and the violation of the allegiance which had been pledged.

The word ἐνυβρίζειν is not found elsewhere in the N. T. or LXX. Ὕβρις is that insolent self-assertion which disregards what is due to others. It combines arrogance with wanton injury. Comp. Rom. i. 30; 1 Tim. i. 13.

This outrage is directed against One Who is spoken of by the unique title 'the Spirit of grace.' Comp. *Const. Apost.* vi. 18 οἱ βλασφημήσαντες τὸ πνεῦμα τῆς χάριτος καὶ ἀποπτύσαντες τὴν παρ' αὐτοῦ δωρεὰν μετὰ τὴν χάριν.

Other corresponding phrases are: τὸ πνεῦμα τῆς ἀληθείας (John xv. 26; xvi. 13; 1 John iv. 6); τὸ αὐτὸ πν. τῆς πίστεως (2 Cor. iv. 13); τὸ πν. τῆς ἐπαγγελίας τὸ ἅγ. (Eph. i. 13).

In these cases the *gen.* expresses that which finds expression through the spirit, as in the commoner forms πνεῦμα δουλείας (Rom. viii. 15), πνεῦμα σοφίας (Eph. i. 17, &c.). Here then 'the Spirit of grace' is the Spirit through whom the grace of God is

ἐνυβρίσας. ³⁰οἴδαμεν γὰρ τὸν εἰπόντα Ἐμοὶ ἐκδίκηϲιϲ,
ἐγὼ ἀνταποδώϲω· καὶ πάλιν Κρινεῖ Κύριοϲ τὸν λαὸν αὐτοῦ.
³¹φοβερὸν τὸ ἐμπεσεῖν εἰς χεῖρας θεοῦ ζῶντος.   ³²'Ανα-

30 ἀνταποδώσω א* D₂* vg syr vg me : +λέγει κύριος 5 א°A syr hl.   + ὅτι´ κρ.
κύρ. D₂ vg.   κρ. κύρ. א*AD₂ vg syrr: κύρ. κρ. 5 א° me.

manifested. The apostate wilfully
wrongs the Power whose action he
has felt.

It will be observed that the action
of the Holy Spirit falls into the background in the Epistle from the
characteristic view which is given of
the priestly work of Christ. Comp.
c. vi. 4 note.

30. The certainty of the retribution to which the writer has pointed
lies in the knowledge of the divine
character.

οἴδαμεν γάρ...] *For we know Him
that said.* We know not only who
He is that said, but we know His
character who said.... We know that
He is a 'living God,' and that His
words will find fulfilment to the uttermost. Comp. John iv. 22 ; vii.
28 f.; 1 Thess. iv. 5; 2 Thess. i. 8;
Tit. i. 16; c. viii. 11 note.

The two quotations establish two
facts with regard to the divine judgment. It will carry with it strict requital ; and it will extend to all those
who stand to God as His people.

The first quotation is an adaptation
of Deut. xxxii. 35, which differs from
the Hebrew (*To me* belongeth *vengeance and recompense*) and the LXX.
(ἐν ἡμέρᾳ ἐκδικήσεως ἀνταποδώσω). It
occurs in the same form in Rom. xii.
19, and had probably taken this shape
in popular use. The clause is rendered
very nearly in the same way in the
Targum of Onkelos (*Vengeance is
before me, and I will repay*). Philo
quotes the words differently : *Leg.
Alleg.* iii. § 34 (i. 108 M.).

The second quotation is also taken
from the same passage of Deuteronomy (xxxii. 36 ; comp. Ps. cxxxv. 14).
In the original context the idea of

judgment is that of just vindication.
But the character of God requires
that the same act which upholds the
righteous should punish the wicked.
The point of this quotation is that
God's people will be judged, that
they from their peculiar position will
be specially objects of His care.
What the judgment will be for them
lies in themselves (*v.* 27).

31. φοβερόν] The word takes up
the φοβερά of *v.* 27. The adjective is
found in the N. T. only in these
passages and in c. xii. 21.

ἐμπ. εἰς χ.] The phrase occurs in the
LXX. in a different connexion, 2 Sam.
xxiv. 14; 1 Chron. xxi. 13 ; Ecclus.
ii. 18.

θεοῦ ζῶντος] See c. iii. 12 note.

(3) *vv.* 32—39. Encouragements
from past experience.

Words of encouragement follow
upon the words of warning, just as
the warnings in c. vi. 4-8, were followed
by the expression of joyful confidence.
The Hebrews are reminded of their
former courageous faith (32—34); and
they are exhorted not to peril its
fruit at· the last moment (35—39).
They had fought their battle : all that
was required was that they should
endure to wait for their crown : ἄρα
ἐνὸς ὑμῖν δεῖ μόνου, ἵνα ἀναμείνητε τὴν
μέλλησιν οὐχ ἵνα ἀθλήσητε πάλιν...πρὸς
τὸ στεφανωθῆναι ἑστήκατε λοιπόν· τοῦτο
μόνον φέρετε, τὴν μέλλησιν τοῦ στε-
φάνου (Chrys.).

³² *But call to mind the days of
former time wherein after ye were
enlightened ye endured a great struggle of sufferings,* ³³*partly being made
a gazing-stock both by reproaches
and afflictions, and partly claiming
fellowship with those who so lived.*

μιμνήσκεσθε δὲ τὰς πρότερον ἡμέρας, ἐν αἷς φωτισθέντες
πολλὴν ἄθλησιν ὑπεμείνατε παθημάτων, ³³τοῦτο μὲν

32 ταῖς προτέραις ἡμέραις D₂*.

³⁴*For ye both had compassion on
them that were in bonds and accepted
with joy the spoiling of your possessions, knowing that ye had your own
selves for a better possession and an
abiding one.* ³⁵*Cast not away therefore your boldness seeing it hath great
recompense of reward.* ³⁶*For ye have
need of patience, that having done
the will of God ye may receive His
promise.*

³⁷*For, yet a very little while,*
*He that cometh shall come, and
shall not tarry.*

³⁸*But my righteous one shall live
by faith;*
*And if he shrink back, my soul
hath no pleasure in him.*

³⁹*But we are not of shrinking back
unto destruction, but of faith unto
gaining of the soul.*

32—34. The retrospect of their
own history was sufficient to inspire
the Hebrews with patience. They
had borne sufferings themselves and
shared the sufferings of others. They
had experienced in all this the assurance of a better possession than any
that they could lose by persecution.
And, as Chrysostom says: πολλὴ ἡ
διὰ τῶν ἔργων παράκλησις. τὸν γὰρ
ἀρχόμενον πράγματος προϊόντα ἐπιδι-
δόναι χρή.

32. ἀναμιμνήσκεσθε δέ...] *Call a-
gain to remembrance...Call to mind*
...Latt. *Rememoramini autem* (*igitur*). 2 Cor. vii. 15 ; 2 Tim. i. 6 (ἀνα-
μιμνήσκω σε ἀναζωπυρεῖν). The word
is used of recalling specific subjects to
the mind. Contrast c. xiii. 2 μιμνήσκεσθε τῶν δεσμίων.

The phrase τὰς πρότερον ἡμέρας does
not so much express 'the former
days' (τὰς προτέρας ἡμ.) as a definite
period, as 'the days at a former time,'
at an earlier stage of your faith
(Thuc. vi. 9 ἐν τῷ πρότερον χρόνῳ).

ἡμέρας : ἀμαρτίας ὑμῶν ℵ*.

Compare 1 Pet. i. 14 ταῖς πρότερον ἐν
τῇ ἀγνοίᾳ ὑμῶν ἐπιθυμίαις. 2 Pet. i. 9
(τῶν πάλαι αὐτοῦ ἁμαρτημάτων); iii. 6
(ὁ τότε κόσμος); iii. 7 (οἱ νῦν οὐρανοί);
Rom. iii. 26 (ἐν τῷ νῦν καιρῷ); c. viii.
18; xi. 5 ; 1 Cor. iv. 11 (ἄχρι τῆς ἄρτι
ὥρας); 2 Cor. viii. 14; Gal. iv. 25 (τῇ
νῦν Ἱερουσαλήμ); 1 Tim. iv. 8 (ζωῆς
τῆς νῦν καὶ τῆς μελλούσης); vi. 14 (ἐν
τῷ νῦν αἰῶνι); 2 Tim. iv. 10; Tit. ii.
12.

ἐν αἷς...πολ. ἄθλησιν ὑπεμ. παθημά-
των] *wherein...ye endured a great
struggle of sufferings*, that is, consisting in sufferings, Lat. *in quibus
illuminati ... certamen sustinuistis
passionum.* The use of the word
ἄθλησις (here only in N. T., and not
in LXX.: comp. 2 Tim. ii. 5) adds to
the picture the image of the resolute
combatant. The Hebrews not only
suffered, but bore themselves as those
who were contending for a crown.

Πολύς is frequently used (like 'much,'
multus) of that which is great in degree and not only frequent in repetition: Acts xxiv. 3 π. εἰρήνη ; xxvii.
10 π. ζημία; *id.* 27 π. ἀσιτία &c. Here
the notions of intensity and repetition
are both applicable to the struggle of
the Hebrews.

Chrysostom notices the force of
ἄθλησις: οὐκ εἶπε πειρασμοὺς ἀλλὰ
ἄθλησιν, ὅπερ ἐστὶν ἐγκωμίου ὄνομα καὶ
ἐπαίνων μεγίστων.

For φωτισθέντες (Syrr. *having received baptism*) see c. vi. 4 note : for
ὑπομένειν comp. c. xii. 2, 3, 7 ; *v.* 36.

33. τοῦτο μέν...τοῦτο δέ...] Vulg.
*et in altero quidem...in altero au-
tem.* The courage of the Hebrews
was shewn both in what they bore
personally, and (which is often more
difficult) in their readiness to shew
sympathy to those who were in affliction. The contrast in the tenses of
the participles, θεατριζόμενοι, γενη-

ὀνειδισμοῖς τε καὶ θλίψεσιν θεατριζόμενοι, τοῦτο δὲ
κοινωνοὶ τῶν οὕτως ἀναστρεφομένων γενηθέντες· ³⁴καὶ
γὰρ τοῖς δεσμίοις συνεπαθήσατε, καὶ τὴν ἁρπαγὴν τῶν

33 θεατριζόμενοι: ὀνιδιζόμενοι D₂*.   34 δεσμίοις AD₂* vg syrr me: δεσμοῖς μου ℵ*.

θέντες, which is necessarily lost in translation (as in the Latin), suggests that upon some special occasion the persons addressed had in a signal manner identified themselves with fellow-Christians in an outbreak of persecution (συνεπαθήσατε, προσεδέξασθε); while they were habitually exposed to public reproach.

The combination τοῦτο μέν...τοῦτο δέ..., which is frequent in Greek writers from Demosthenes downwards, is found here only in N.T.

ὀνειδισμοῖς τε καὶ θλίψεσιν] The personal sufferings of the Hebrews were twofold. They had endured reproaches, which contrast a man's conduct with what might have been expected from him (Matt. xi. 20; Mk. xvi. 14; James i. 5): and afflictions, in which force is the expression of ill-will. Reproaches affect the character: afflictions affect material prosperity. (Syr. vg. connects these words with the preceding verse.)

For ὀνειδισμός see c. xi. 26; xiii. 13. Comp. 1 Pet. iv. 14. The word is common in the LXX. in the prophetic and later books.

θεατριζόμενοι] Vulg. spectaculum facti, made a gazing stock. Comp. 1 Cor. iv. 9. The simple verb θεατρί-ζειν appears to be found here only and in derived passages. The compound ἐκθεατρίζειν is not uncommon in late Greek in the same sense: to expose as a spectacle for derision. See Schweigh. Polyb. Ind. s. v.

κοιν. τῶν οὕτως ἀναστρεφ. γεν.] avowing your fellowship with those who were so facing reproaches and afflictions in their daily life. The Hebrews, so far from abandoning their fellow-Christians, courageously claimed connexion with them, sharing their perils

by the active avowal of sympathy. The οὕτως applies more naturally to the description which immediately precedes than to the more remote πολλ. ἄ. ὑπεμ. παθ.; and this latter reference is excluded by the form of the sentence (ὑπεμ....τοῦτο μέν...τοῦτο δέ...).

For κοινωνοὶ γενηθέντες (in place of κοινωνήσαντες) see c. iii. 14; and for ἀναστρέφεσθαι c. xiii. 18 (ἀναστροφή c. xiii. 7).

For the difference between κοινωνός and μέτοχος see c. iii. 1. Κοινωνός, even when it is used in connexion with material things, includes the idea of a personal fellowship: 1 Cor. x. 18; 2 Cor. i. 7; 1 Pet. v. 1 (2 Pet. i. 4).

34. The statements of the former verse are defined in inverse order by reference to specific facts. The Hebrews had shewn sympathy when it could not but be perilous to do so: and they had welcomed material loss.

καὶ γάρ...] Constant usage suggests that the καί emphasises the general statement and does not simply correspond with the καί which follows: For in fact ye... Comp. c. iv. 2; v. 12; xii. 29; xiii. 22; and so constantly in the epistles of St Paul: 1 Thess. iv. 10; Rom. xi. 1 &c.

τοῖς δεσμίοις συνεπαθήσατε] ye had compassion on them that were in bonds, Vulg. vinctis compassi estis (O. L. consensistis). The definite article points to some familiar fact. Comp. c. xiii. 3. Elsewhere the word δέσμιος is used in the epistles of the N.T. only by St Paul of himself: Eph. iii. 1 &c.

For συνεπαθήσατε see c. iv. 15, note (Job ii. 11 Symm.).

καὶ τὴν ἁρπ....προσεδέξασθε] and

ὑπαρχόντων ὑμῶν μετὰ χαρᾶς προσεδέξασθε, γινώσκοντες ἔχειν ἑαυτοὺς κρείσσονα ὕπαρξιν καὶ μένουσαν.
35 Μὴ ἀποβάλητε οὖν τὴν παρρησίαν ὑμῶν, ἥτις ἔχει
μεγάλην μισθαποδοσίαν, 36 ὑπομονῆς γὰρ ἔχετε χρείαν

γινωσκον ℵ.   ἑαυτούς ℵAH₃ vg me: ἑαυτοῖς D₂: ἐν ἑαυτοῖς ς.   ὕπαρξιν
ℵ*AD₂*H₃* vg me: +ἐν οὐρανοῖς ς ℵ° syrr.   35 ἀποβάλητε: ἀπολύητε (i.e.
ἀπολλύ.) D₂*.   μισθ. μεγ. ς.   36 χρ. ἔχ. ℵ*.

accepted (welcomed) with joy the spoiling of your possessions... You gladly
accepted loss as if it were gain. For
προσδέχομαι see c. xi. 35 οὐ προσδεξάμενοι τὴν ἀπολύτρωσιν. Phil. ii. 29
προσδέχεσθε αὐτὸν ἐν Κυρίῳ μετὰ πάσης
χαρᾶς; for ἁρπαγή, Matt. xxiii. 25;
Luke xi. 39; and for τὰ ὑπάρχοντα 1
Cor. xiii. 3; Matt. xxiv. 17 &c.

γινώσκοντες ἔχειν ἑαυτούς...μένου-
σαν] knowing that ye had your own
selves for a better possession and an
abiding one. Stripped of their goods
the Christians learned better than
before that their true self remained
unchangeable. That was not marred
but purified: they had 'won their
souls in patience' (Luke xxi. 19).
This possession they had so that they
could never lose it. By the use of
the word γινώσκοντες, as distinguished
from εἰδότες (Eph. vi. 8 f.; Rom. v. 3;
vi. 9 &c.), the writer implies that the
knowledge was realised through the
trial: through that the confessors came
to know the value of their faith. Comp.
James i. 3.

The order in the words κρείσσονα
ὕπαρξιν καὶ μένουσαν gives distinctness
to the two thoughts: 'a better possession and that too an abiding one.'
Comp. 1 Pet. i. 23. The word ὕπαρξις
(Latt. substantia) occurs again Acts
ii. 45, and several times in the later
books of the LXX.

35—39. The sacrifices which the
Hebrews once made proved their confidence — confidence in an unseen
future—which they boldly proclaimed;
and at the same time they confirmed
it. The lesson of the past therefore

encouraged them to still further endurance. And such endurance God
claims from His people.

35. μὴ ἀποβάλητε οὖν] Vulg. Nolite
itaque amittere.... The Latin rendering can be justified, but the context
evidently requires the stronger sense
Do not therefore cast (fling) away
(Mark x. 50), as though it were of no
value, the boldness which you once
made you own. The opposite is
expressed c. iii. 6 τὴν παρρησίαν κατα-
σχεῖν. The exact phrase occurs in
Dion Chrys. xxxiv. p. 425; and a fragment of Nicostratus gives the image
with singular force: ταύτην [τὴν παρ-
ρησίαν] ἐάν τις ἀπολέσῃ, τὴν ἀσπίδ' ἀπο-
βέβληκεν οὗτος τοῦ βίου (Fragm. Inc. 5).
Chrysostom remarks on the encouraging form of the address: οὐκ
εἶπεν ... ἀνακτήσασθε ... ἀλλὰ ... μὴ ἀποβάλητε, ὁ μᾶλλον αὐτοὺς ἐψυχαγώγει
καὶ ἐποίει ῥωσθῆναι.

τὴν παρρησίαν] The Apostle first
chooses the term which describes
endurance under its most command-
ing aspect, as ready to proclaim the
hope on which it rests and as secure
of victory; and then afterwards (v.
36) he presents the idea of simple
endurance. Comp. c. iii. 6 note.

ἥτις ἔχει] seeing that it hath great
recompense. The recompense is included even now in the spirit of the
believer who has learnt to rate outward afflictions at their true value
(Rom. viii. 37).

For μισθαποδοσία compare c. ii. 2
note; and for one aspect of the
thought c. vi. 10.

36. ὑπομ. γὰρ ἔ. χ.] for of patience

ἵνα τὸ θέλημα τοῦ θεοῦ ποιήσαντες κομίσησθε τὴν
ἐπαγγελίαν·
³⁷ἔτι γὰρ μικρὸν ὅσον ὅσον,

κομίσασθαι ℵ.   37 ὅσον...ὁ: ὅθεν D₂*.

ye have need.... The force of the
reason lies in the moral efficacy of
endurance. 'Do not cast away your
confidence, for you have need of it.
The trials to which you are subjected
belong to the perfect discipline of
the faith which you hold. You have
need of patience therefore that you
may obtain what you expect.'
The word ὑπομονή occurs again xii.
1 ; contrast μακροθυμία c. vi. 12 note.
ἔχετε χρείαν] See c. v. 12 note.
Primasius works out the thought
of the athlete who has completed his
struggles asking impatiently for his
prize: Sustine parumper usque dum
veniat arbiter aut etiam rex, qui tibi
bravium referat pro victoria tua.
Ἐκάμετε, φησίν, ἠθλήσατε, κἀγὼ τοῦτό
φημι· ἀλλὰ ἀναμείνατε· τοῦτο γάρ ἐστι
πίστις· μὴ ἐνταῦθα ζητεῖτε τὸ πᾶν (Chrys.
on c. xi. 1).
ἵνα τὸ θ. τ. θ. ποι....τὴν ἐπ.] *that,
having done the will of God, ye may
receive the promise...* This general
term 'the will of God,' which occurs
throughout the N. T., takes its colour
from the context. Not unfrequently
the mention of 'the will of God'
suggests a contrast to man's will
through the discipline of suffering
(Matt. xxvi. 42 ; Eph. vi. 6 ; 1 Pet. ii.
15 ; iii. 17 ; iv. 19), as is the case
here.
The phrase also necessarily recals
what was said of Christ's work (c. x.
5 ff.) as a fulfilment of the will of
God. Man in his little field must
follow the example of his Lord (1
Pet. ii. 21), which is always set before
us as an example of suffering.
The aor. part. (ποιήσαντες, Vulg. *fa-
cientes* inadequately : O. L. *voluntate
Dei consummata*) marks that which
precedes the fulness of reward ('after

doing'), and not (as it does in some
places) that which is coincident with
it (c. ii. 10 note). From the point of
sight here the work is seen to be
completed before the prize is received.
By *receiving the promise*, we must
understand 'receiving all that was
expressed in the promise.' The exact
phrase occurs again c. xi. 39 (comp.
vi. 15 ἐπέτυχεν τῆς ἐπαγγ.) ; and with
the plural noun c. xi. 13 (μὴ κομισ.
τὰς ἐπαγγ.). There is a difference between ἐπιτυχεῖν ἐπαγγ. and κομίσασθαι
ἐπαγγ. which is at once felt. Ἐπιτυχεῖν describes the simple fact of obtaining : κομίσασθαι adds the thought
of personal appropriation and enjoyment, of taking as one's own for use :
Matt. xxv. 27. So the word κομίσασθαι is used specially with regard
to future retribution : 2 Cor. v. 10 ;
Eph. vi. 8 ; Col. iii. 25 ; 1 Pet. i. 9 ; v.
4 ; [2 Pet. ii. 13 *v.l.*].
'The promise' in this connexion is
defined by St John as 'eternal life'
(1 John ii. 25), which is the complete
expression of 'the promise made to
the fathers' (Acts xiii. 32 ; xxvi. 6).
Of this the gift of the Spirit (Luke
xxiv. 49 ; Acts i. 4 ; ii. 33 ff. ; Gal. iii.
14 ; Eph. i. 13) and 'the presence of
the Lord' (2 Pet. iii. 4, 9) were pledges.
Compare c. vi. 12 note.
37 f. The writer of the Epistle
uses freely the language of ancient
prophecy to express the general truth
which he wishes to enforce, that the
purpose of God will be fulfilled in its
due time even if it seems to linger.
So it was when Isaiah charged the
people to withdraw for a space and
wait till the divine wrath was spent.
So it was when the Chaldæans threat-
ened Israel with utter destruction.

ὁ ἐρχόμενος ἥξει καὶ οὐ χρονίσει

38 ὁ δὲ δίκαιός [μου] ἐκ πίστεως ζήσεται,

καὶ ἐὰν ὑποστείληται, οὐκ εὐδοκεῖ ἡ ψυχή μου ἐν αὐτῷ.

38 ὁ δὲ δίκ. μου ἐκ πίστ. אA vg : ὁ δὲ δίκ. ἐκ πίστ. μου D₂* syrr me (so LXX. אB) :
ὁ δὲ δίκ. ἐκ πίστ. ς (no varr. in Gal. iii. 11).   om. καὶ ἐὰν ὑποστείληται D₂*.
μου ἡ ψ. D₂*.

In old times the faithful had to wait for the manifestation of the salvation of God. It must be so always; and past experience furnishes a sufficient support for hope.

37. ἔτι γὰρ…ὅσον] *For, yet a very little while… (modicum [ali]quantulum, V.)*. These words with which the quotation from Habakkuk is prefaced by the writer of the Epistle occur in Is. xxvi. 20 (LXX.), where the prophet charges the people to hide themselves 'for a little moment until the indignation should be overpast.' The thought of the purposes of God wrought through the discipline of Israel thus serves as a preparation for the understanding of His counsel for the Church.

For ἔτι μικρόν compare John xiv. 19; xvi. 16 ff. (μικρόν).

Ὅσον ὅσον, which appears to be a colloquial form, occurs in Arist. *Vesp.* 213 and Leon. Tarent. LXX. 4 (*Anthol.* i. 238).

37 b, 38. ὁ ἐρχόμενος…ἐν αὐτῷ] These words are taken with modifications and transpositions from the LXX. version of Hab. ii. 3 f. (see Additional Note). In the original context that which is expected is the fulfilment of the prophetic vision of the destruction of the Chaldæans, the enemies of God's people, to be followed by the revelation of His glory. The judgment was executed and the promise was accomplished in due time, but not as men had hoped. The lesson had a significant application to the condition of the early Church.

ἥξει] *v.* 7 note; 2 Pet. iii. 10; Apoc. iii. 3, 9; xv. 4; xviii. 8. He will make His coming felt as a present fact.

38. The original text gives the sense: 'His soul is puffed up with pride: it is not right within him; but the righteous shall live by his faithfulness,' where the reference is to the vain confidence of the Chaldæan invader as contrasted with the trust of the people upon God. The LXX. represents a different text in the first clause; and the author of the Epistle has transposed the two clauses of the LXX. in order to bring out more clearly the idea which he wishes to enforce, the necessity of endurance in the righteous.

38. ὁ δὲ δίκ.…ζήσεται] *but my righteous one shall live by faith…*Vulg. *justus autem meus ex fide vivit* (sic). The argument requires that the words ἐκ πίστεως ζήσεται should be taken together. The just—the true believer —requires faith, trust in the unseen, for life. Such faith is the support of endurance (ὑπομονή) and the seal of confidence (παρρησία).

It is said that the phrase was held in Rabbinic teaching to declare the essence of the Law: Delitzsch, *Römerbrief* s. 75. Compare Gal. iii. 11 ; Rom. i. 17.

καὶ ἐὰν ὑποστ.] *and if he,* who has been spoken of as 'the just,' *draw* (shrink) *back,* Vulg. *quod si subtraxerit se.* The insertion of 'any man,' so as to avoid the thought of the falling away of 'the just one,' is wholly unwarranted, and it is precisely this contingency which gives the point to the words (comp. *v.* 32 φωτισθέντες). Thus Theophylact says expressly ἐὰν ὑποστείληται ὁ δίκαιος.

The word ὑποστέλλεσθαι implies a shrinking away from fear of or regard

³⁹ἡμεῖς δὲ οὐκ ἐσμὲν ὑποστολῆς εἰς ἀπώλειαν, ἀλλὰ πίστεως εἰς περιποίησιν ψυχῆς.

39 ἀπωλίας ℵ*.

for another. Compare Wisd. vi. 8 οὐ γὰρ ὑποστελεῖται πρόσωπον ὁ πάντων δεσπότης. Job xiii. 8 (פָּנָיו אִשָּׂ֑א); Deut. i. 17; Ex. xxiii. 21; Gal. ii. 12 (ὑπέστελλεν καὶ ἀφώριζεν ἑαυτόν); Acts xx. 27, (20).

οὐκ εὐδ. ἡ ψ. μ. ἐν αὐ.] *my soul hath no pleasure in him*, Vulg. *non place-bit animæ meæ.* The construction εὐδ. ἐν is a reproduction of the Hebrew בְּ חָפֵץ. Compare Matt. iii. 17 and parallel; xvii. 5; 1 Cor.x. 5; 2 Cor. xii. 10. Εὐδοκεῖν εἰς is also found: [Matt. xii. 18]; 2 Pet. i. 17.

For ἡ ψυχή μου compare Is. i. 14.

39. ἡμεῖς δὲ...ὑποστ.] *But we are not of shrinking back (of them that shrink back)*... Vulg. *nos autem non sumus subtractionis* [all. add. *filii*). The thought of shrinking back is at once put aside.

The writer here identifies his readers with himself, as before he has identified himself with them (vi. 1; v. 26 f.).

The genitives ὑποστολῆς, πίστεως, express that which marks the two classes. Our character is not expressed by 'shrinking back' but by 'faith.' Compare c. xii. 11 (οὐ δοκεῖ χαρᾶς εἶναι); 1 Thess. v. 5 (οὐκ ἐσμὲν νυκτός, v. 8 ἡμέρας ὄντες); 1 Cor. xiv. 33 (οὐκ ἔστιν ἀκαταστασίας ὁ θεός); Luke ix. 55 (οἵου πνεύματός ἐστε); Acts ix. 2 (τῆς ὁδοῦ ὄντας).

Primasius dwells on the 'filii' of his Latin text: non sumus ego et vos filii eorum paganorum et gentilium qui se subtrahunt a vita fidei...sed sumus filii patriarcharum...

Ἀπώλεια, which occurs here only in the Epistle, is the opposite of σωτηρία, which is represented vividly under one aspect as περιποίησις ψυχῆς (Vulg. *acquisitio* (O. L. *renascentia*) *animæ*). This phrase exactly expresses the Lord's promise Luke xxi. 19 ἐν τῇ ὑπομονῇ ὑμῶν κτήσεσθε τὰς ψυχὰς ὑμῶν. Compare also Luke xvii. 33 (ζωογονήσει); Matt. x. 39.

For περιποίησις see 1 Thess. v. 9; 2 Thess. ii. 14.

Additional Note on the reading of x. 1.

The clause κατ᾽ ἐνιαυτὸν ταῖς αὐταῖς...δύναται is given with unusual variations of form by the most ancient authorities.

(1) ταῖς αὐταῖς θυσίαις   ἃς προσφέρουσιν...   οὐδέποτε δύνανται...C.

(2) ταῖς αὐταῖς θυσίαις αὐτῶν ἃς προσφέρουσιν...   οὐδέποτε δύνανται...אP₂.

(3) ταῖς αὐταῖς θυσίαις   προσφέρουσιν...[αἱ]οὐδέποτε δύνανται...A syr. hl. arm.

(4) ταῖς αὐταῖς θυσίαις   αἷς προσφέρουσιν...   οὐδέποτε δύναται...D₂H₃ me vg.

The later manuscripts are divided between δύναται and δύνανται, a few read αἷς for ἃς, and a few omit the relative, one adding αἱ before οὐδέποτε. The Latin and Egyptian versions read δύναται. The Syriac Versions represent δύνανται, and translate the first clause as a finite sentence ('For there was in the Law...,' 'For since the Law had...'), but there is no reason to suppose that this fact points to any further variation of the text not now preserved in the Greek copies. The translators treated σκιὰν γὰρ ἔχων ὁ νόμος... as an 'absolute clause' (so Theophylact expressly); and, if δύνανται is read, this appears to be the only way of dealing with the passage. It must be supposed that the construction of the sentence is suddenly broken after πραγμάτων, and the subject changed from the Law to the priests. In this case two explanations of the second clause are possible, represented by (3) and by (1), (2).

If (3) is adopted the sense will be that given by the Harklean Syriac: 'For since the Law has a shadow...they [the priests, the appointed ministers,] make offering year by year with the same sacrifices continually, which can never make perfect...' This is the general view of Theodoret, but such a sense of θυσίαις προσφέρειν is most strange, and the whole construction is singularly harsh, for there is nothing to lead to a sudden break.

If the general form of (1) and (2) be taken, for the addition of αὐτῶν appears to be simply an emphasising of the action of the Levitical ministers, we must translate: 'For since the Law has a shadow...they[the priests] can never with the same sacrifices year by year, which they offer continually, make perfect...' So Theophylact: but the harshness of the construction is still essentially the same as before, though it is hidden in the rendering; and, according to the teaching of the Epistle, the Law, and not the priest, is the instrument of the divine action. 'The Law made nothing perfect.'

Hence it is best to adopt (as in the notes) the reading δύναται, and to regard the construction as continuous throughout. The change from δύναται to δύνανται (ΔΥΝΑΤΑΙ) is of a type which occurs constantly and it was suggested by προσφέρουσιν. It seems right also to adopt the αἷς of the same authorities (comp. vi. 10), though it may be thought that such an attraction would be more likely to be introduced than changed. The preceding -αις cannot be urged confidently on either side, yet it explains naturally the omission of the relative in the form αἷς.

Additional Note on x. 5. *The Body of Christ.*

The idea of 'the Body.'

The idea of 'the Body of Christ' has a very wide and important bearing upon the apprehension of the truth of the Incarnation. The 'body' is the one complete organism through which the life is realised under special conditions. The body, if we may so speak, is the expression of the life in terms of the environment. Thus the one life of the Son of man is equally manifested under different circumstances by 'the body of humiliation' and by 'the body of glory.'

The conception of 'the body' is fundamentally different from that of 'flesh and blood,' the symbolic (representative) elements, which go to form our present bodies. Of these 'the blood' is taken to symbolise the principle of the earthly life. That in us which is represented by 'the blood' has no place in the body of the Resurrection (Luke xxiv. 39 σάρκα καὶ ὀστέα. Compare the early addition to Eph. v. 30).

We have then to consider the relation of the Lord's 'body of humiliation,' and of His 'body of glory,' to humanity and to men.

The work of Christ in His Body of humiliation.

The writer of the Epistle in treating finally of the Lord's redemptive and consummative work finds the lesson which he desires to convey in the words of the Psalmist spoken in the person of the Christ: *Lo I am come to do Thy will, O Lord: a body didst Thou prepare for me.*

This earthly body became the organ of a perfect, a universal, human life. By the offering of His body (x. 10) in the absolute service of life, in the voluntary endurance of death, the Lord fulfilled the destiny of man as created, and bore the penalty which fallen man had brought upon himself. In the offering of Himself He offered to God the humanity which He had taken. The effect of this offering is both individual and social. Each believer finds himself in Christ, and in Him realises the fulfilment of his own destiny. He was potentially included in Him, so that the death of Christ was his death, and the life of Christ through death is his own life. At the same time the separated fragments of creation are brought together, and the barriers by which men are kept apart are removed.

These thoughts find clear expression in the Apostolic writings:

He Himself bore (ἀνήνεγκεν carried up and laid as upon an altar) *our sins* IN HIS BODY *upon the tree, that we having died unto sin might live unto righteousness* (1 Pet. ii. 24).

Ye were made dead to the law through THE BODY OF CHRIST (Rom. vii. 4; comp. vi. 3 ff.).

By the offering of THE BODY OF JESUS CHRIST *we have been sanctified* (Hebr. x. 10).

So far the personal effects accomplished through 'the Body of Christ'— 'the Body of His humiliation'—are affirmed. The wider effects are described no less distinctly.

It was the good pleasure [*of the Father*]...*through Him to reconcile all things unto Himself, having made peace through the blood of His cross ...and you did he reconcile* (ἀποκατήλλαξεν) *in* THE BODY OF HIS FLESH *through death*...(Col. i. 19—22).

He is our peace, who made both one (τὰ ἀμφότερα ἕν)...that He might create in Himself of the twain one new man (τοὺς δύο...εἰς ἕνα καινὸν ἄνθρωπον); and might reconcile them both in ONE BODY *unto God through the cross*...(Eph. ii. 14—16).

What is thus begun has to be fulfilled. This fellowship with the ascended Christ finds a realisation on earth. There is still an organism of the life of the Son of man, a Body through which He works, and to which men may minister.

The work of Christ in His Body, the Church.

I...fill up on my part (ἀνταναπληρῶ) that which is lacking of the afflictions of Christ in my flesh for HIS BODY'S *sake, which is the Church* (Col. i. 24).

Of this Body He is even now the Head:

The Father...gave Him to be head over all things to the Church, which is HIS BODY...(Eph. i. 23; comp. iv. 15; v. 23).

He is the head of THE BODY, *the Church*...(Col. i. 18).

This Body is necessarily one, even as Christ is one:

In one Spirit were we all baptized into ONE BODY, *whether Jews or Greeks, whether bond or free* (1 Cor. xii. 13).

There is ONE BODY *and one Spirit...one Lord, one faith, one baptism, one God and Father of all*...(Eph. iv. 4, 5).

Let the peace of Christ rule in your hearts, to the which also ye were called in ONE BODY (Col. iii. 15).

At the same time, like the natural body, it 'grows' by the action of its own vital law through the ministry of its constituent parts, and it is 'built up' by the introduction of new members; but 'growth' and 'building up' are alike manifestations of the informing power of Christ, the Head:

...the Head, from Whom all THE BODY, *being supplied and knit together through the joints and bands, increaseth with the increase of God (αὔξει τὴν αὔξησιν τοῦ θεοῦ)* (Col. ii. 19).

He gave some to be apostles, and some prophets,...for (πρός) the perfecting of the saints, unto (εἰς) the work of ministering, unto the building up (οἰκοδομή) of THE BODY OF CHRIST (Eph. iv. 11, 12).

From Whom ALL THE BODY...*maketh the increase of* THE BODY *unto the building up of itself in love* (Eph. iv. 16).

Into this Body Christians are incorporated by Baptism:

We are members of HIS BODY (Eph. v. 30; comp. *v.* 26); 1 Cor. xii. 13.

And they are sustained in their vital union with Christ by the fellowship of His body and blood (1 Cor. x. 16 f.).

So it is that Christians themselves are *one body in Christ* (Rom. xii. 5); and severally *members one of another* (Eph. iv. 25; Rom. xii. 5), sharing in a common life but charged with different offices (Rom. xii. 4, 6 ff.; 1 Cor. xii. 27 ὑμεῖς ἐστε σῶμα Χριστοῦ καὶ μέλη ἐκ μέρους); and under this aspect our bodies are *members of Christ* (1 Cor. vi. 15).

It is obvious that the view which is thus opened to us of the Body of Christ as the one organism, if the word may be allowed, through which His life is fulfilled, throws light upon the 'words of Institution' at the Last Supper. Christ does not say 'This is my flesh': He does say 'This is my blood.' He offers us part in the one organisation of the One Life which transcends earth (*This is* MY BODY, 1 Cor. xi. 24; Matt. xxvi. 26; Mk. xiv.

22 ; Lk. xxii. 19): He offers us the virtue of His life on earth through which we may now fulfil our work. Compare Additional Note on St John vi.

The discernment and appropriation of this spiritual reality is at once the great trial and the highest blessing of the Christian life (...*if he discern not* THE BODY. 1 Cor. xi. 27—29).

Additional Note on x. 7. *The expression of an end or purpose.*

The purpose, end, expressed by

The purpose or end of an action is expressed in the Greek of the N. T. by many different forms of construction which are found also in classical language, though the relative frequency of their occurrence varies in different periods : each form presents the thought under a distinct aspect; and it will be interesting to the student to consider in connexion the examples which are offered in the Epistle. The purpose or end—if we use the words in a very wide sense—is expressed in the Epistle by (1) the infinitive, (2) the preposition εἰς, (3) the final particles ὅπως, ἵνα, (4) the conjunction ὥστε.

(1) The Infinitive.

(1) *The infinitive.*

The *infin.* is used to mark the end in two forms :

(*a*) The simple *infin.* :

v.   5 ὁ χριστὸς οὐχ ἑαυτὸν ἐδόξασεν γενηθῆναι ἀρχιερέα...

vi. 10 οὐ γὰρ ἄδικος ὁ θεὸς ἐπιλαθέσθαι τοῦ ἔργου ὑμῶν...

vi. 18 οἱ καταφυγόντες κρατῆσαι...

ix. 24 (εἰσῆλθεν) νῦν ἐμφανισθῆναι...οὐδ᾽ ἵνα πολλάκις προσφέρῃ ἑαυτόν...

xi. 8 Ἀβραὰμ ὑπήκουσεν ἐξελθεῖν...

In these cases the *infin.* is the complement of the direct verbal statement, defining how that was fulfilled.

Compare also vii. 5, 11, 27.

(*b*) The *infin.* with *gen.* τοῦ :

x. 7, 9 ἰδού, ἥκω τοῦ ποιῆσαι τὸ θέλημά σου (LXX.).

xi. 5 Ἐνὼχ μετετέθη τοῦ μὴ ἰδεῖν θάνατον.

Here the *gen.* seems to express that which is closely connected with the action as its motive (or cause).

The *gen.* in v. 12 is probably to be explained differently.

This construction is characteristic of St Luke. It is not found in St John (? Apoc. xii. 7) or St Mark (not iv. 3). For the use in the LXX. see Moulton-Winer, pp. 410 f.

In St Luke ii. 22, 24 the two uses of the *infin.* occur together.

(2) *The preposition* εἰς.

(a) Εἰς with nouns :

    i. 14 εἰς διακονίαν ἀποστελλόμενα.

    iii. 5 εἰς μαρτύριον τῶν λαληθησομένων.

    ix. 15 θανάτου γενομένου εἰς ἀπολύτρωσιν τῶν...παραβάσεων...

    ix. 26 εἰς ἀθέτησιν τῆς ἁμαρτίας...πεφανέρωται.

    x. 19 ἔχοντες...παρρησίαν εἰς τὴν εἴσοδον...

The preposition corresponds with the English '*for*,' '*unto*,' and in combination with the noun describes the direct purpose of the action. Compare the use of πρός, v. 14 ; vi. 11 ; ix. 13.

(b) Εἰς with *infin.* and *art.* :

    ii. 17 ὤφειλεν...ὁμοιωθῆναι...ἵνα ἐλ. γένηται...εἰς τὸ ἱλάσκεσθαι...

    vii. 25 ζῶν εἰς τὸ ἐντυγχάνειν.

    viii. 3 πᾶς ἀρχιερεὺς εἰς τὸ προσφέρειν...καθίσταται...

    ix. 14 καθαριεῖ...εἰς τὸ λατρεύειν...

    ix. 28 ...προσενεχθεὶς εἰς τὸ πολλῶν ἀνενεγκεῖν ἁμαρτίας...

    xi. 3 νοοῦμεν κατηρτίσθαι...εἰς τὸ μή...γεγονέναι.

    xii. 10 ὁ δὲ (ἐπαίδευεν)...εἰς τὸ μεταλαβεῖν...

    xiii. 21 ...καταρτίσαι ὑμᾶς...εἰς τὸ ποιῆσαι...

Here the end appears, in the light of a result which is (at least potentially) secured by the foregoing action rather than as a purpose aimed at. The difference will be realised by substituting in vii. 25 ἵνα ἐντυγχάνῃ for εἰς τὸ ἐντυγχάνειν. See also ii. 17 ; v. 1 (notes). This construction is very rare in St Luke : v. 17 ; Acts vii. 19.

(3) *The final particles* ὅπως, ἵνα.

  (a) Ὅπως is rare in the Epistles generally. It occurs :

    ii. 9 ...βλέπομεν...ἐστεφανωμένον, ὅπως χάριτι θεοῦ...γεύσηται...

    ix. 15 μεσίτης ἐστίν, ὅπως...τὴν ἐπαγγελίαν λάβωσιν οἱ κεκλημένοι...

  (b) Ἵνα and ἵνα μή are frequent.

    (a) Ἵνα.

      ii. 14 ...μετέσχεν...ἵνα καταργήσῃ...

      ii. 17 ...ὤφειλεν...ὁμοιωθῆναι ἵνα ἐλεήμων γένηται...

      iv. 16 προσερχώμεθα...ἵνα λάβωμεν...

      v. 1 ...καθίσταται...ἵνα προσφέρῃ...

      vi. 18 ...ἐμεσίτευσεν...ἵνα...παράκλησιν ἔχωμεν...

      ix. 25 οὐδ' (εἰσῆλθεν) ἵνα πολλάκις προσφέρῃ ἑαυτόν.

      x. 9 ἀναιρεῖ...ἵνα...στήσῃ.

      x. 36 ...ἔχετε χρείαν...ἵνα...κομίσησθε...

      xi. 35 ...οὐ προσδεξάμενοι...ἵνα...τύχωσιν...

      xii. 27 ...δηλοῖ...μετάθεσιν...ἵνα μείνῃ...

      xiii. 12 ...ἵνα ἁγιάσῃ...ἔπαθεν.

      xiii. 17 πείθεσθε...ἵνα...ποιῶσιν...

      xiii. 19 παρακαλῶ...ἵνα...ἀποκατασταθῶ ὑμῖν.

(β) Ἵνα μή.

iii. 13 παρακαλεῖτε...ἵνα μὴ σκληρυνθῇ τις...

iv. 11 σπουδάσωμεν...ἵνα μή...τις...πέσῃ...

vi. 12 ἐπιθυμοῦμεν...ἐνδείκνυσθαι σπουδήν...ἵνα μή...γένησθε...

xi. 28 πεποίηκεν τὸ πάσχα...ἵνα μή...θίγῃ.

xi. 40 ...τοῦ θεοῦ...προβλεψαμένου, ἵνα μή...τελειωθῶσιν.

xii. 3 ἀναλυγίσασθε...ἵνα μὴ κάμητε...

xii. 13 τροχιὰς ὀρθὰς ποιεῖτε...ἵνα μή...ἐκτραπῇ.

In all these cases there is the thought of a definite end aimed at in the foregoing action.

(4) ὥστε.   (4) Ὥστε.

xiii. 6 εἴρηκεν...ὥστε...λέγειν...

The particle gives the natural sequence of that which has been stated.

Additional Note on x. 10. The effects of Christ's Sacrifice.

Christ has gained for man the end of his creation.

The effect of Christ's Sacrifice of Himself is presented in different places of the Epistle under various aspects in relation to man's position and needs. In consequence of sinfulness and sin man is spiritually in bondage, in debt, alienated from God. He requires redemption, forgiveness, atonement, reconciliation. All these blessings Christ has brought to humanity by His Incarnation, His Life, His Passion, His Ascension. By His perfect fulfilment of the destiny of man under the conditions of the Fall, He has brought again within man's reach the end of his creation (Ps. viii.; c. ii. 5 ff.).

The general teaching of the Epistle upon the subject can be summarised most conveniently into two heads :

i. The effect of Christ's Sacrifice on the general relation of man to spiritual powers.

ii. The effect of Christ's Sacrifice on man's personal state.

i. In relation to spiritual powers ; and

i. *The relation of man to spiritual powers.*

(1) The might of the devil is brought to naught. Christ was Incarnate ἵνα διὰ τοῦ θανάτου καταργήσῃ τὸν τὸ κράτος ἔχοντα τοῦ θανάτου τοῦτ᾽ ἔστι τὸν διάβολον (ii. 14). Comp. Apoc. i. 18.

(2) As a consequence of this men are delivered from

(a) a present tyranny : καὶ ἀπαλλάξῃ τούτους ὅσοι φόβῳ θανάτου διὰ παντὸς τοῦ ζῆν ἔνοχοι ἦσαν δουλείας (ii. 15); and

(b) an obligation contracted in the past : θανάτου γενομένου εἰς ἀπολύτρωσιν τῶν ἐπὶ τῇ πρώτῃ διαθήκῃ παραβάσεων (ix. 15). Comp. ix. 22, x. 18 (ἄφεσις) ; ix. 12 αἰωνία λύτρωσις.

(3) At the same time a propitiation is offered for the sins of the people, so that they can come before God : ii. 17, 18.

These blessings are made permanent because the dominion of sin is set at naught, shewn in its essential impotence : εἰς ἀθέτησιν τῆς ἁμαρτίας διὰ τῆς θυσίας αὐτοῦ πεφανέρωται (ix. 26).

ii. *Man's personal state.*　　　　　　　　　　　　　　　　　　　　　ii. man's

Man was created to gain the divine likeness: he needs therefore perfect hallowing.　　personal state.

He is sin-stained : he needs cleansing.

He has powers capable of exercise, cultivation, development: he needs perfecting.

These three, hallowing, cleansing, perfecting, are connected in the Epistle with Christ's Sacrifice in Life and Death.

(1) Hallowing :

(a) The purpose of Christ : Ἰησοῦς ἵνα ἁγιάσῃ διὰ τοῦ ἰδίου αἵματος τὸν λαόν, ἔξω τῆς πύλης ἔπαθεν (xiii. 12).

(b) The fact : τὸ αἷμα τῆς διαθήκης ἐν ᾧ ἡγιάσθη (x. 29).

(c) The realisation : ἐν ᾧ θελήματι ἡγιασμένοι ἐσμὲν διὰ τῆς προσφορᾶς τοῦ σώματος Ἰησοῦ Χριστοῦ ἐφάπαξ (x. 10). μιᾷ προσφορᾷ τετελείωκεν εἰς τὸ διηνεκὲς τοὺς ἁγιαζομένους (x. 14). The work is complete on the divine side (ἡγιασμένοι, τετελείωκεν) and gradually appropriated on man's side (ἁγιαζομένους).

(d) The ground: ὅ τε ἁγιάζων καὶ οἱ ἁγιαζόμενοι ἐξ ἑνὸς πάντες (ii. 11). The Redemption completes and crowns the purpose of Creation, which included the possibility of it.

(e) An object of human effort: διώκετε...τὸν ἁγιασμόν, οὗ χωρὶς οὐδεὶς ὄψεται τὸν κύριον (xii. 14).

(2) Cleansing :

Consecration requires as the beginning of its actual fulfilment cleansing. This is presented

(a) Generally : καθαρισμὸν τῶν ἁμαρτιῶν ποιησάμενος (i. 3).

(b) Individually: τὸ αἷμα τοῦ χριστοῦ...καθαριεῖ τὴν συνείδησιν ἡμῶν ἀπὸ νεκρῶν ἔργων εἰς τὸ λατρεύειν θεῷ ζῶντι (ix. 14).

(c) As complete on the divine part: διὰ τὸ μηδεμίαν ἔχειν ἔτι συνείδησιν ἁμαρτιῶν τοὺς ἅπαξ κεκαθαρισμένους (x. 2).

(d) As extending to the scene of man's heavenly service : αὐτὰ τὰ ἐπουράνια κρείττοσι θυσίαις παρὰ ταύτας (καθαρίζεται) (ix. 23).

(3) Perfecting.

The perfecting of men is wholly dependent on Christ's own perfecting (comp. Addit. Note on ii. 10). Of this perfecting we see

(a) The ground, in Christ's work : τετελείωκεν εἰς τὸ διηνεκὲς τοὺς ἁγιαζομένους (x. 14).

(b) The accomplishment, according to a purpose of God slowly fulfilled to our eyes: τοῦ θεοῦ περὶ ἡμῶν κρεῖττόν τι προβλεψαμένου, ἵνα μὴ χωρὶς ἡμῶν τελειωθῶσιν (xi. 40).

(c) The partial fulfilment in a vision of the heavenly city: προσε-ληλύθατε...πνεύμασι δικαίων τετελειωμένων (xii. 23).

Different forms in which the work is presented.

In this connexion it is desirable to study together the four verbs which present typical views of Christ's work, καθαρίζειν, τελειοῦν, ἱλάσκεσθαι, ἁγιάζειν. The two former deal with man in himself in his present and final state: the two latter with man in his relation to God as devoted to and in fellowship with Him. Of these τελειοῦν and ἱλάσκεσθαι have been discussed elsewhere (Additional Notes on c. ii. 10; 1 John ii. 2): ἁγιάζειν and καθαρίζειν still require notice.

i. Ἁγιά-ζειν.

The sense of 'holy' (ἅγιος) is derived from the highest application of the word to God Himself. God is spoken of as 'holy' under the aspect of His inviolable purity, majesty, awe-inspiring glory. Those who are devoted to Him that they may reflect His character are 'holy' (ἅγιοι). That is hallowed which is made to minister to the manifestation of His glory: Matt. vi. 9 (ἁγιασθήτω τὸ ὄνομά σου); comp. 1 Pet. iii. 15.

Hence generally ἁγιάζειν, קָדַשׁ, הִקְדִּישׁ (unclassical, partly represented by ἁγίζειν), has two man's senses.

(1) To set apart for God: to separate from 'the world.'

(2) To make conformable in character to such a dedication. Compare Lev. xx. 26.

As applied to Christians there are therefore two distinct aspects of the words 'holy,' 'hallowed': the initial consecration which marks the destiny for which as Christians they are set apart—the 'indelible character,' in theological language, which is given by Baptism—and the progressive hallowing by which the divine likeness is slowly formed (comp. John x. 36; xvii. 19). The different tenses in which the verb is used place the different aspects of 'hallowing' in a clear light.

Thus the *aorist* marks the historic fact: x. 29 (ἐν ᾧ ἡγιάσθη) (xiii. 12); John x. 36.

The *present* shews the continuous process by which the divine gift is slowly realised from stage to stage in the individual life or in successive generations: x. 14 (τοὺς ἁγιαζομένους); ii. 11.

The *perfect* expresses a state abiding in its divine stability: Acts xx. 32 (LXX.); xxvi. 18; 1 Cor. i. 2; vii. 14; Rom. xv. 16; 2 Tim. ii. 21.

The use of the *pres.* and *perf.* together in John xvii. 19 is instructive.

ii. Καθαρί-ζειν.

ii. The idea of 'purity' (καθαρότης, καθαρός) expresses primarily the satisfaction of external conditions. In the first instance it marks ceremonial cleanness. The leper as unclean was excluded from the outward commonwealth of Israel. He was restored by cleansing (Matt. viii. 2 f.).

Hence καθαρίζειν (טָהַר very rarely חָטָּא, the corresponding classical form is καθαίρειν) is

(1) To remove outward defilement; and so to make ceremonially fit to draw near to God.

(2) To remove spiritual defilement; and so to make morally fit to come before God. Comp. Acts xv. 9; Eph. v. 26; Tit. ii. 14; 1 John i. 7.

The difference between ἁγιάζειν, καθαρίζειν, and ἱλάσκεσθαι may be pre- Relation sented in another light by the consideration of the parallel forms ἁγιασμός, of ἁγιάζειν, καθαρισμός, ἱλασμός. Of these ἁγιασμός is prospective, and points forward καθαρίζειν, ἱλάσκεσθαι. to a future state not yet attained (xii. 14); καθαρισμός is retrospective and points to a past which has been done away (i. 3; 2 Pet. i. 9); ἱλασμός marks the present restoration of fellowship with God, by the removal of that which stays the outflow of His love (1 John ii. 2).

The use of the words in the LXX. is of considerable interest (see Lev. viii. Use in the 15; xvi. 19 f.); and each of them is used to represent כִּפֶּר: ἁγιάζειν, Ex. LXX. xxix. 33; καθαρίζειν, Ex. xxix. 36 f.; xxx. 10; ἱλάσκεσθαι, Ps. lxiv. (lxv.) 4; lxxvii. (lxxviii.) 38; lxxviii. (lxxix.) 9. Comp. Eph. v. 26.

It may be added that both ἁγιάζειν and καθαρίζειν are used in certain connexions of divine and of human action.

i.   Of divine action: ἁγιάζειν, John xvii. 17; 1 Thess. v. 23: καθαρίζειν, Acts xv. 9; Tit. ii. 14; 1 John i. 7.

ii. Of human action: ἁγιάζειν, 1 Pet. iii. 15: καθαρίζειν, James iv. 8; 2 Cor. vii. 1.

The verb δικαιοῦν is not found in the Epistle.

Additional Note on x. 37 f.   On the quotation from Hab. ii. 3 f.

The quotation in c. x. 37 f. consists of an introductory clause [ἔτι γὰρ] μικρὸν ὅσον ὅσον from Is. xxvi. 20, and an adaptation of the LXX. version of Hab. ii. 3, 4.

The text of the LXX. is

[διότι ἔτι ὅρασις εἰς καιρόν......
ἐὰν ὑστερήσῃ, ὑπόμεινον αὐτόν,]
ὅτι ἐρχόμενος ἥξει καὶ οὐ μὴ χρονίσῃ·
ἐὰν ὑποστείληται, οὐκ εὐδοκεῖ ἡ ψυχή μου ἐν αὐτῷ·
ὁ δὲ δίκαιος ἐκ πίστεώς μου (Α μου ἐκ π.) ζήσεται.

The Hebrew is rendered (R.V.)

[For the vision is yet for the appointed time...
Though it tarry, wait for it;]
Because it will surely come, it will not delay.
Behold, his soul is puffed up, it is not upright in him:
But the just shall live by his faith.

In contrast with both the writer of the Epistle gives :

ὁ ἐρχόμενος ἥξει καὶ οὐ χρονίσει·
ὁ δὲ δίκαιός [μου] ἐκ πίστεως ζήσεται,
καὶ ἐὰν ὑποστείληται οὐκ εὐδοκεῖ ἡ ψυχή μου ἐν αὐτῷ.

He that cometh shall come, and shall not tarry.
But my righteous (just) one shall live by faith;
And if he shrink back, my soul hath no pleasure in him.

A comparison of these words with those of the LXX., taken in connexion with the introductory clause, shews that the writer is freely using familiar language to convey his own thought. The LXX. had given a personal interpretation to the Vision which embodied the divine promise : *wait for Him* (*i.e.* the Lord, or His representative); and the writer of the Epistle, in the light of his Christian faith, defines the Person 'He that cometh,' even the Ascended Christ, adding the article and so separating ἐρχόμενος from ἥξει. It was natural therefore that he should at once connect with this assurance of the coming of the Saviour the reward of faith, and transpose to the end the clause which reveals the peril of slackened zeal. By this adaptation prophetic words conveyed the lesson which he desired to enforce, and the associations which they carried with them gave a solemn colouring to the thought of necessary endurance. The deliverance from Chaldæa, however real, was not such as Israel looked for.

The text of the Epistle has influenced some MSS. of the LXX. (which give some ὁ ἐρχόμενος and others οὐ χρονίσει -ιεῖ) and patristic quotations : Euseb. *Dem. Ev.* vi. 14 (p. 276); Cyr. Alex. *In Is.* c. viii. 3 (ii. 134); Theophlct. *ad loc.*

It is interesting to notice that the words of the same passage are combined with words of Malachi (iii. 1) in Clem. 1 *ad Cor.* 23...συμμαρτυρούσης καὶ τῆς γραφῆς ὅτι

ταχὺ ἥξει καὶ οὐ χρονιεῖ,

καὶ ἐξαίφνης ἥξει ὁ κύριος εἰς τὸν ναὸν αὐτοῦ,

καὶ ὁ ἅγιος ὃν ὑμεῖς προσδοκᾶτε (LXX. ὁ ἄγγελος τῆς διαθήκης ὃν ὑμεῖς θελετε).

XI. ¹Ἔστιν δὲ πίστις ἐλπιζομένων ὑπόστασις, πραγμάτων ἔλεγχος οὐ βλεπομένων· ²ἐν ταύτῃ γὰρ ἐμαρ-

1 ὑπόστασιν D₂*.   βλεπ.: βουλομένων A.

ii. *The past triumphs of Faith* (c. xi. 1—40).

The reference to Faith, as the characteristic of the true people of God, leads the writer of the Epistle to develop at length the lesson of Faith given in the records of the Old Covenant. From the first the divine revelation has called out Faith. The elementary presuppositions of religion, the existence and moral attributes of God and the creation of the world, rest on Faith. Hence it is to be expected that Faith should still find its appropriate trial. Thus the appeal to the past experience of the readers, and to the general law of God's dealings, is confirmed in detail by the manifold experience of the saints.

The development of the work of Faith appears to follow an intelligible and natural plan. The writer first marks the characteristics of Faith generally (*v*. 1) and its application to the elementary conceptions of religion (*v*. 3; comp. *v*. 6). He then shews that the spiritual history of the world is a history of the victories of Faith. This is indicated by the fragmentary records of the old world (4—7), and more particularly by the records of the growth of the Divine Society (ἡ ἐκκλησία). This was founded in the Faith of obedience and patience of the patriarchs (8—16); and built up in the Faith of sacrifice, sustained against natural judgment (17—22); and carried to victory by the Faith of conquest (23—31). The later action of Faith in the work of the people of God is indicated up to the last national conflict under the Maccabees (32—38); and it is then declared that all these preliminary victories of Faith await their consummation from the Faith of Christians (39, 40).

The contents of the chapter may therefore be thus arranged:

(1) *vv*. 1—2. Preliminary view of the characteristics and work of Faith.

(2) *vv*. 3—7. Faith as seen in the prophetic records of the old world.

(3) *vv*. 8—22. The Faith of the Patriarchs:
   (*a*) The Faith of Obedience and Patience.
   (*b*) The Faith of Sacrifice.

(4) *vv*. 23—31. The Faith of Conflict and Conquest.

(5) *vv*. 32—38. Faith active in national life.

(6) *vv*. 39, 40. Conclusion.

(1) 1—2. General view of the characteristics and work of Faith.

The reality, the sphere, and the power of Faith are affirmed (*v*. 1); and the religious history of mankind is appealed to generally in support of its claims (*v*. 2).

¹*Now faith is the substance of things hoped for, the test of things (objects) not seen;* ²*for herein the elders had witness borne to them.*

1. ἔ. δὲ π. ἐλπ....οὐ βλεπ.] *Now faith is the substance of things hoped for, the test of objects not seen.* Vulg. *est autem fides sperandorum substantia, rerum argumentum non parentum* (Later texts give *sperandarum* and *apparentium*): Aug. *sperantium substantia, convictio rerum quæ non videntur.*

The order (ἔστιν δὲ πίστις) shews that the object of the writer is not to give a formal definition of Faith but to bring out characteristics of Faith which bear upon his argument. It seems to suggest the affirmation of the reality of faith as well as the nature of faith, as if it were 'Now faith is, and it is this....' This fulness of meaning explains the γάρ which follows.

The copula stands similarly at the beginning of the sentence: Lk. viii. 11; 2 Cor. xi. 10; 1 Tim. vi. 6; 1 John i. 5. (Dan. iii. 17; Wisd. xv. 9.)

The noun (πίστις) has no article as indicating faith in its abstract conception, and not specially the Christian faith. Comp. Rom. i. 5; iii. 28 (Moulton-Winer, p. 149).

In the characterisation of Faith which is given we have to consider (a) its object and (β) its office. Its object is ἐλπιζόμενα and πράγματα οὐ βλεπόμενα: its office is to be the ὑπόστασις of the former, the ἔλεγχος of the latter.

(a) The object of Faith is distinctly intelligible. Faith essentially deals with the future and with the unseen, the regions not entered by direct physical experience. The statement is perfectly general ('things hoped for,' 'objects not seen'), and not specific in regard to the contents of the revelation given by God. Faith deals with everything which comes under these two categories. By Faith we attach the idea of permanence to the law which represents the results of past observation. By Faith we discern the love which is offered to our notice by outward signs.

In considering things 'future' and 'unseen' it will be felt that hope has a wider range than sight. Hope includes that which is internal as well as that which is external. Hence ἐλπιζόμενα is left indefinite as extending to the whole field of mental and spiritual activity, while πράγματα οὐ βλεπόμενα suggest a definite order of objects and events outside the believer, which are conceived of as realities which may fall under man's senses. Under another aspect 'things hoped for' are more limited than 'objects not seen,' for the latter embrace all that belongs to the requital and purification of the

guilty, and the present government of God.

(β) In regard to the office of Faith it may be laid down that the interpretations of the two words ὑπόστασις ...ἔλεγχος... must be coordinate: that they must describe Faith under the same general aspect. Now, as far as the description of Faith here is concerned, it may be presented to us in regard to what it *is*, as a particular frame of mind, or in regard to what it *does*, as producing particular results. Senses have been given to ὑπόστασις and ἔλεγχος which correspond with both views. Thus ὑπόστασις has been translated 'assurance,' a meaning which it has in c. iii. 14. And again 'essence' (substance), that is, that which gives real existence to a thing, a sense closely akin to the sense in i. 3. So too ἔλεγχος has been translated 'conviction,' that is, the feeling of certainty, and 'proof,' that is, the means by which certainty is gained.

The two senses of ὑπόστασις are well established; but it is difficult to suppose that ἔλεγχος can express a state.

If then ἔλεγχος must be understood of the 'proof,' the 'test,' by which the reality of the unseen is established; it seems to follow necessarily that the parallel meaning must be given to ὑπόστασις, 'that which gives true existence' to an object.

This meaning is that which is uniformly followed by the Greek Fathers in commenting on the passage: ἐπειδὴ τὰ ἐν ἐλπίδι ἀνυπόστατα εἶναι δοκεῖ, ἡ πίστις ὑπόστασιν αὐτοῖς χαρίζεται· μᾶλλον δὲ οὐ χαρίζεται ἀλλ' αὐτό ἐστιν οὐσία αὐτῶν· οἷον ἡ ἀνάστασις οὐ παραγέγονεν οὐδέ ἐστιν ἐν ὑποστάσει, ἀλλ' ἡ ἐλπὶς ὑφίστησιν αὐτὴν ἐν τῇ ἡμετέρᾳ ψυχῇ (Chrys.). So Theophylact: οὐσίωσίς ἐστι τῶν μήπω ὄντων καὶ ὑπόστασις τῶν μὴ ὑφεστώτων; and Theodoret: πρὸς τὴν τῶν ἐλπιζομένων θεωρίαν ὀφθαλμὸς ἡμῖν γίνεται, καὶ δείκνυσιν ὡς ὑφεστῶτα τὰ μηδέπω γεγενημένα.

τυρήθησαν οἱ πρεσβύτεροι.

The Latin renderings also follow this interpretation without variation (*substantia*), though they present many differences in other parts of the sentence; and the Latin Fathers reproduce the ideas already quoted from the Greek Fathers.

Nor is it a valid objection that ὑπόστασις is not in this case strictly 'essence' as applied to the several objects of hope, but (generally) that which gives reality to them. For it is in virtue of Faith that things hoped for *are* now, so that Faith is their essence in regard to the actual experience of the believer.

Thus the general scope of the statement is to shew that the future and the unseen can be made real for men by Faith.

Things which in the succession of time are still 'hoped for' as future have a true existence in the eternal order; and this existence Faith brings home to the believer as a real fact. So also things unseen are not mere arbitrary fancies : Faith tries them, tests them, brings conviction as to their being.

For ὑπόστασις compare i. 3 note; iii. 14 note (2 Cor. ix. 4; xi. 17); and Philo *de migr. Abr.* § 9 (i. 442 M.); and for τὰ ἐλπιζόμενα compare 1 Pet. i. 13; 1 Cor. xv. 19; Rom. viii. 24 f.; 1 Tim. iv. 10.

The word ἔλεγχος is found here only in N. T. (in 2 Tim. iii. 16 l. ἐλεγμόν). The verb ἐλέγχειν is not unfrequent (c. xii. 5). Compare especially John xvi. 8 note.

The sense of 'proof' is found in classical writers from Euripides downwards. In the LXX. ἔλεγχος is frequent in the sense of 'reproof.' (Job xxiii. 4, 7 do not seem to form exceptions.)

For πραγμάτων compare vi. 18 note; x. 1 ; and for οὐ βλεπομένων Rom. viii. 24.

Primasius gives a good illustration

3 Πίστει νοοῦμεν κατηρ-

of the thought : Quæ apparent jam fidem non habent...sed agnitionem. Dum ergo vidit Thomas dum palpavit, cur ei dicitur Quia vidisti me credidisti ?—Sed aliud vidit, aliud credidit. A mortali enim homine divinitas videri non potest. Videndo ergo credidit, qui considerando hominem verum Deum, quem videre non poterat, exclamavit.

2. ἐν ταύτῃ γάρ...] *for herein*, as living and acting in this atmosphere of Faith, of Faith by which the future is realised and the unseen apprehended, *the elders had witness borne to them*. The religious history of man is taken as the proof of the power which Faith possesses to test and realise the unseen.

With ἐν ταύτῃ ἐμαρτ. compare *vv.* 4 δι' ἧς ἐμαρτ., 39 μαρτυρηθέντες διὰ τῆς π.; and for the thought Ign. *ad Philad.* 11 ; *ad Ephes.* 12 ; Just. M. *Dial.* 29 *s. f.* οἱ τοσοῦτοι δίκαιοι... μεμαρτύρηνται ὑπὸ τοῦ θεοῦ αὐτοῦ. Μαρτυρεῖσθαι is used absolutely in the passages of Ignatius just quoted and in Clem. 1 *ad Cor.* 17, 18 f. &c.

Faith is indeed the characteristic of all the Jewish heroes, though Faith, as such, is very little noticed in the O. T. The witness is borne to the life which was inspired by Faith.

οἱ πρεσβύτεροι] Comp. c. i. 1 οἱ πατέρες.

(2) 3—7. Faith as seen in the prophetic records of the old world.

The first view of Faith is taken from the brief records of the old world given in Gen. i.—ix. It is first laid down that our fundamental view of the origin (and so of the course) of the world rests on Faith (*v.* 3); and then in Abel, Enoch, Noah, the writer considers three types of Faith under different circumstances, as answering to man's constitution, to the development of life, to special revelation. Abel recognised the natural obligations of man to God generally, and

τίσθαι τοὺς αἰῶνας ῥήματι θεοῦ, εἰς τὸ μὴ ἐκ φαινομένων

fulfilled them unto death, through which he still lives (v. 4). Enoch realised fellowship with God in action till it was crowned in an eternal fellowship (5 f.). Noah obeyed a specific direction of God and was saved through suffering (7). Theophylact comparing the examples of Abel and Enoch says well: ὅρα δὲ πῶς διὰ μὲν τοῦ Ἄβελ ἔδειξεν ὁ θεὸς τὴν ἀπόφασιν τὴν περὶ τοῦ θανάτου ἀληθῆ, διὰ δὲ τοῦ Ἐνὼχ πάλιν ἔδειξεν ὅτι πρόσκαιρος ἡ ἀπόφασις καὶ ἀναιρεθήσεται. And it may be added that, as in Abel and Enoch there were revelations of death and life, so in Noah there was a revelation of judgment.

3 *By faith we perceive that the world hath been framed by God's word, to the end that that which is seen be known to have arisen not from things which appear.*

4 *By faith Abel offered to God a more abundant sacrifice than Cain, through which he had witness borne to him that he was righteous, God bearing witness on occasion of his gifts; and through it he being dead yet speaketh.*

5 *By faith Enoch was translated so as not to see death; and he was not found, because God translated him; for before his translation the witness is recorded that he had been well-pleasing to God;* 6 *and without faith it is impossible to be well-pleasing to Him; for he that cometh to God must have faith (believe) that He is, and that He shews Himself a rewarder to them that diligently seek Him.*

7 *By faith Noah being warned by God concerning the things not yet seen, moved with pious care, prepared an ark for the saving of his house, through which he condemned the world and became heir of the righteousness which is according to faith.*

3 The belief in creation—the belief

in a divine will manifested in the existence of the world—is the necessary foundation for the life of faith in all its manifestations. Hence this primary action of faith is declared first. By faith we attain to the assurance that the world—history—is not the result of blind fate but answers to an expression of the will of God; and so we can attain to fresh victories corresponding to our position, even as in the past the heroes of faith triumphed.

The verse presents two distinct thoughts. It declares the fundamental act of faith by which we apprehend the fact of creation, and then points out the consequence which ought to follow from it in our view of the world, as it lies before us. The conception of creation by God's word rightly leads to a present belief in the power of God as Preserver and Governor of that which He created.

πίστει...ῥήμ. θεοῦ] *By faith we perceive that the world hath been framed by God's word...* Vulg. *Fide intellegimus aptata esse sæcula verbo Dei...* The conclusion, which we are so constituted as to form, is an interpretation of the external phenomena which are presented to us made by the highest rational faculty in man (νοῦς), to which Faith gives validity.

For νοοῦμεν compare Rom. i. 20; Wisd. xiii. 4. It expresses a mental as distinguished from a sensuous perception (Mk. viii. 17). The term νοῦς, which is not found in this Epistle, is characteristic of St Paul: 1 Cor. ii. 16; Rom. xii. 2; Col. ii. 18; 1 Tim. v. 5.

Κατηρτίσθαι expresses the manifoldness and the unity of all creation; and by the tense marks that the original lesson of creation remains for abiding use and application. Comp. Herm. *Mand.* i. 1. For καταρτίζειν compare c. x. 5; xiii. 21; 1 Thess. iii.

τὸ βλεπόμενον γεγονέναι.   ⁴Πίστει πλείονα θυσίαν

3 τὸ βλεπόμενον אAD₂* me : τὰ -να ς vg syrr.

10; Gal. vi. 1 ; Ps. lxvii. (lxviii.) 10; lxxiii. (lxxiv.) 16 ; lxxxviii. (lxxxix.) 38; xxviii. (xxix.) 9 &c. For τοὺς αἰῶνας see c. i. 2 note; ix. 26; 1 Cor. ii. 7 ; 1 Tim. i. 17; Eph. iii. 21. This conception of creation as unfolded in time, the many ' ages ' going to form one ' world,' is taken up into Christian literature. Thus Clem. R. i. c. 35 (ὁ δημιουργὸς καὶ πατὴρ τῶν αἰ.); 55 (θεὸς τῶν αἰ.); 61 (βασιλεὺς τῶν αἰ.).

πίστει] By the direct exercise of faith, by an act of faith.... The (instrumental) dative is used by St Paul : 2 Cor. i. 24; Rom. xi. 20 (τῇ π. ἑστηκέναι); iii. 28 (δικαιοῦσθαι πίστει) ; [iv. 20]; Col. i. 23; [Tit. ii. 2]. The simple dative is used throughout the chapter, except v. 33 διὰ πίστεως (comp. vi. 12) and v. 13 κατὰ πίστιν (διὰ τῆς πίστεως v. 39 is different). With πίστει contrast τῇ πίστει c. iv. 2.

ῥήματι θεοῦ] Comp. Gen. i. ; Ps. xxxiii. 6, 9 (LXX. τῷ λόγῳ). Philo de sacrif. Abel. § 18 (i. 175 M.): ὁ γὰρ θεὸς λέγων ἅμα ἐποίει. The term ῥῆμα retains its full meaning: a single expression of the divine will. Comp. c. vi. 5. For creation see i. 2 note.

The 'world' was conceived to exist archetypally in the 'mind' of God before it was brought under the limitations of time and space. Invisibiliter mundus antequam formaretur in dei sapientia erat, qui tamen per expletionem operis factus est visibilis... (Primas.). Comp. Apoc. iv. 11 (ἦσαν, ἐκτίσθησαν) ; John i. 3 f. note.

εἰς τὸ μὴ...τὸ βλεπ. γεγονέναι] to the end that that which is seen be known to have arisen not from things which appear. Vulg. ut ex invisibilibus visibilia fierent. The purpose and end of the knowledge gained by faith as to the creation of the world is the conviction that the visible order as we observe it, as a whole (τὸ βλεπ.),

has not come into being by simple material causation. We learn to recognise that there is a divine power behind. Such a conclusion is the fundamental triumph of Faith. Creation can best be conceived of by us as the limitation of that which is, and not as the addition of anything to the sum of being.

The phrase εἰς τό... can, according to usage, have no other sense than that of expressing the end. Comp. c. x. 7 note. It occurs eight times in the Epistle, and uniformly in this meaning.

By a not unnatural brevity of expression 'the becoming of the world' is used for ' our conception of the becoming of the world.'

The negative in the phrase μὴ ἐκ φαιν. was transposed in interpretation (as if it were ἐκ μὴ φαινομένων) from early times (from things which do not appear). Thus Chrysostom, having quoted the Greek as it stands in the text, goes on at once to say : δῆλον, φησίν, ἐστὶν ὅτι ἐξ οὐκ ὄντων τὰ ὄντα ἐποίησεν ὁ θεός, ἐκ τῶν μὴ φαινομένων τὰ φαινόμενα, ἐκ τῶν οὐχ ὑφεστώτων τὰ ὑφεστῶτα. So Theodoret: ἐξ ὄντων δημιουργοῦσιν οἱ ἄνθρωποι· ὁ δὲ τῶν ὅλων θεὸς ἐκ μὴ ὄντων τὰ ὄντα παρήγαγε.

Such a transposition is wholly unsupported. The passage quoted from Arist. de Phys. ausc. v. 1 has, in the true text ἡ γὰρ οὐκ ἐξ ὑποκειμένου.

On the dogma of creation ἐξ οὐκ ὄντων see Herm. Vis. i. 1. 6 and Harnack's note; Hatch, Hibbert Lectures p. 197 note. The apostolic phrase expresses whatever truth is conveyed by it. No purely physical explanation of the origin of the world is possible. Things that appear cannot give an explanation of the origin of the universe which we see. So Philo speaks of ὁ ἀσώματος καὶ νοητὸς...κόσ-

'Άβελ παρὰ Καὶν προσήνεγκεν τῷ θεῷ, δι' ἧς ἐμαρτυρήθη
εἶναι δίκαιος, μαρτυροῦντος ἐπὶ τοῖc Δώροιc ⌈αγτογ τογ θεογ⌉,

4 αὐτοῦ τῷ θεῷ v. αὐτῷ τοῦ θεοῦ.   See Addit. Note.

4 ἐπὶ τ. δ. αὐ. τοῦ θεοῦ ϛ᾽ Ν° (vg) syrr me : ἐπὶ τ. δ. αὐ. τῷ θεῷ Ν* AD₂*.

μος, τὸ τοῦ φαινομένου τοῦδε ἀρχέτυπον,
ἰδέαις ἀοράτοις συσταθεὶς ὥσπερ οὗτος
σώμασιν ὁρατοῖς (De conf. ling. § 34;
i. 431 M.).

φαινομένων τὸ βλεπόμενον] The
visible order, as one whole, is contrasted with the many elements which
fall under the senses.

For γεγονέναι see John i. 3 note.

4. πίστει πλ. θ....τῷ θεῷ] Gen. iv.
2 ff. By faith Abel offered to God a
more abundant sacrifice than Cain...
Vulg. Fide plurimam hostiam Abel
quam Cain....

The use of πλείων in c. iii. 3; Matt.
vi. 25 (ἡ ψυχὴ πλεῖόν ἐστι τῆς τροφῆς,
xii. 41 πλεῖον Ἰωνᾶ, id. 42) has been
supposed to justify the general sense
of 'more excellent,' 'better' quali-
tatively only. But the narrative in
Genesis suggests that the deeper
gratitude of Abel found an outward
expression in a more abundant offering. He brought of the 'firstlings'
and did not offer like Cain at 'the
end of time,' while he also brought
'of the fat' of his flock. Comp. Philo,
de conf. ling. § 25 (i. 423).

It is impossible to determine certainly in what Abel's Faith consisted.
The fact that he offered 'a more
abundant' sacrifice shews a fuller
sense of the claims of God. It has
been reasonably suggested that the
sacrifice of animals, which were not
yet given for food, indicates a general
sense that life was due to the Living
One alone.

For πλείονα παρά K. see c. iii. 3; i.
4 note.

δι' ἧς ἐμαρτ.] i.e. θυσίας, through
which sacrifice. The sacrifice was
the sign of the righteousness—the
true relation to God by faith—which
he had inwardly. Through this the

witness came, as God bore witness on
occasion of his gifts. Comp. v. 7.
The express title of 'righteous' is not
given to Abel in the O. T. narrative,
but to Noah first (v. 7). The character
however is given to him, and the title
in later times: Matt. xxiii. 35; 1 John
iii. 12.   For ἐπί see c. ix. 10 note.

There is nothing in Scripture to
shew in what way the divine witness
was given to Abel (LXX. ἐπεῖδεν Gen.
iv. 4). A widespread legend current
still among Mohammedans (Korân,
v. § 30 notes), related that fire came
down and consumed his sacrifice :

Λέγεται πῦρ κατελθὸν ἀναλαβεῖν τὰς
θυσίας, ἀντὶ γὰρ τοῦ ἐπὶ "Αβελ ἐπέβλεψε
καὶ ἐπὶ τὰς θυσίας αὐτοῦ ὁ Κύριος [ὁ
Σύρος] καὶ ἐνεπύρισεν εἶπεν (Chrys. ad
loc.: comp. Field Hex. ad Gen. iv. 7).
So Theophylact : ἐπέβλεπεν ἐπὶ τὰς
θυσίας "Αβελ ὁ Κύριος καὶ ἐνέπρησε.

In the Gelasian and Gregorian
Canon the three sacrifices of Abel,
Abraham and Melchizedek are placed
in significant connexion : ...digneris
...accepta habere sicuti accepta habere dignatus es munera pueri tui
justi Abel et sacrificium patriarchæ
nostri Abrahæ et quod tibi obtulit
summus sacerdos Melchisedech sanctum sacrificium, immaculatam hostiam.

According to an Eastern tradition
the ram which Abraham offered was
the ram of Abel's offering which was
sent down from Paradise (Sale on
Korân xxxvii. 107). A similar thought
finds expression in the Jewish legend
(Pirke R. Eliez. 31 ap. Biesenthal
p. 297 n.) that the altar of Abraham's
sacrifice was that on which Adam,
Abel and Noah had sacrificed (Gen.
xxii. 9 אֶת־הַמִּזְבֵּחַ not מִזְבֵּחַ).

On the fitness of the reference to

καὶ δι᾽ αὐτῆς ἀποθανὼν ἔτι λαλεῖ.　⁵ Πίστει ᾽Ενὼχ
μετετέθη τοῦ μὴ ἰδεῖν θάνατον, καὶ οὐχ ηὑρίσκετο διότι μετέθηκεν αὐτὸν ὁ θεός· πρὸ γὰρ τῆς μεταθέσεως μεμαρτύρηται

διὰ ταύτης D₂*.　λαλεῖ אA vg syrr me : λαλεῖται 5 D₂.　5 μετέθηκεν : μετετεθ.
א*.　μεταθ. א*AD₂* vg me :+αὐτοῦ 5 אᶜ (syrr).

Abel to the position of the Hebrews
Primasius says (after Chrysostom):
Ponit primum eum qui mala passus
est et hoc a fratre, proprium illorum
ponens exemplum: etenim eadem
passi fuerant illi a contribulibus suis
et fratribus.

δι᾽ αὐτῆς...ἔτι λαλεῖ] *through it, i.e.*
faith. Abel's faith was the ground of
his living activity after death. Qui
enim alios suo exemplo admonet ut
justi sint, quomodo non loquitur?
(Primas.)
᾽Ανεῖλεν αὐτὸν ἀλλὰ οὐ συνανεῖλεν
αὐτῷ τὴν δόξαν καὶ τὴν τιμήν· οὐ
τέθνηκεν ἐκεῖνος, οὐκοῦν, οὐδὲ ὑμεῖς
τεθνήξεσθε...ὥσπερ οὖν ὁ οὐρανὸς φαι-
νόμενος μόνον λαλεῖ, οὕτω καὶ ἐκεῖνος
μνημονευόμενος (Chrys.).

Philo argues that Cain truly died
and Abel lived: ὥσθ᾽ οὕτως ἀναγνωστέον
᾽Ανέστη Κάϊν καὶ ἀπέκτεινεν ἑαυτὸν ἀλλ᾽
οὐχ ἕτερον...ὥσθ᾽ ὁ ῎Αβελ, τὸ παραδοξό-
τατον, ἀνῄρηταί τε καὶ ζῇ...πῶς γὰρ ὁ
μηκέτ᾽ ὢν διαλέγεσθαι δυνατός; (*quod
det. pot. insid.* § 14 ; i. 200 M.).

῎Ετι may refer historically to ἀπο-
θανών, 'after death he still (in the
record of Scripture Gen. iv. 10, comp.
c. xii. 24) speaketh as indeed not
dead.' Or it may be fully temporal
and describe the present voice of the
first righteous martyr. It seems most
in accordance with the language of
Scripture on the unseen world not
to exclude the second view: Apoc. vi. 9.

δι᾽ ἧς...δι᾽ αὐτῆς...] *through which*
(sacrifice or faith?)...*through it* (faith
or sacrifice?).... The reference of the
pronouns is ambiguous. Each may
refer either to 'faith' or to 'the
sacrifice'; and every combination has
found advocates. On the whole it
appears to be most natural to see in

the sacrifice the means through which
the testimony was borne, and in the
faith which prompted the sacrifice
that whereby Abel still speaks. The
decision must be made by consideration of the general thought of the
passage. The words themselves admit equally all interpretations. Yet
comp. *v.* 7 δι᾽ ἧς.

5. ᾽Ενώχ] Gen. v. 21—24. Compare Ecclus. xliv. 16; xlix. 14; Wisd.
iv. 10. In Enoch the view of the
true destiny of man was again revealed, fellowship with God. Side
by side with advancing material
civilisation the revelation of the
spiritual life was also given.

μετετέθη τοῦ μὴ ἰδ. θάν.] (*Enoch*)
was translated so as not to see death.
Vulg. *translatus est ne videret mortem.* For the construction see c. x.
7, 9 (LXX. τοῦ ποιῆσαι) note.

The legendary interpretation in
Primasius is worth noticing: translatus est in paradisum terrenum unde
quondam Adam ejectus est.

οὐχ ηὑρ....διότι μετέθ. ὁ θ.] The
writer follows the interpretative rendering of the LXX. while the Hebrew
has simply: *he was not, for God took
him,* a phrase which leaves the mode
of Enoch's departure from life quite
open. Comp. Wisd. iv. 10 f.

πρὸ γὰρ τῆς μετ.] Faith was the
ground of the translation because his
pleasing God is specially mentioned
before this took place; and such
pleasing implies faith. The circumstances under which Enoch lived
gave prominence to his Faith. In a
corrupt age he is said to have maintained that fellowship with God which
is identical with pleasing Him.

μεμαρτύρηται] The witness stands

εγΔρεστηκέΝΔι τῷ θεῷ, ⁶χωρὶς δὲ πίστεως ἀδύνατον εγΔρεςτῆςΔι, πιστεῦσαι γὰρ δεῖ τὸν προσερχόμενον [τῷ] θεῷ ὅτι ἔστιν καὶ τοῖς ἐκζητοῦσιν αὐτὸν μισθαποδότης γίνεται. ⁷Πίστει χρηματισθεὶς Νῶε περὶ τῶν μηδέπω βλεπομένων εὐλαβηθεὶς κατεσκεύασεν κιβωτὸν εἰς σωτηρίαν τοῦ οἴκου αὐτοῦ, δι' ἧς κατέκρινεν τὸν κόσμον, καὶ τῆς κατὰ

6 τῷ θεῷ ℵ°AD₂* : θεῷ ℵ*.

recorded. For the use of the perfect see c. vii. 6 note.

εὐαρεστηκέναι] The LXX. use the word εὐηρέστησε to render הִתְהַלֵּךְ אֶת־הָאֱלֹהִים (walked with God Gen. v. 22; Aqu. περιεπάτει (Sym. ἀνεστρέφετο)...σὺν τῷ θεῷ).

6. The simple notice that Enoch 'pleased God' (or 'walked with God') is a sufficient proof of his Faith. For Faith is an essential condition of 'pleasing' (or of 'fellowship'). The aorists εὐαρεστῆσαι, πιστεῦσαι express the absolute idea.

πιστεῦσαι δεῖ...] The Faith which is thus declared to be necessary for everyone who approaches God as a worshipper (τὸν προσερχόμενον c. vii. 25 note), includes two elements, the belief (a) that God is, and (β) that He is morally active; in other words it is a Faith in the existence and in the moral government of God.

ὅτι ἔστιν καὶ...γίνεται] that He is—that there is One Who answers to the intuition—and that He shews Himself a rewarder.... Vulg. quia est et ...fit. For μισθαποδότης see c. ii. 2 note. In connexion with this statement Chrysostom asks πόθεν; οὔπω γὰρ οὐδὲ τῷ Ἀβὲλ ἀπέδωκεν. ὥστε ὁ λογισμὸς ἕτερα ὑπέβαλλεν ἡ δὲ πίστις τὰ ἐναντία τῶν ὁρωμένων.

The word ἐκζητεῖν, which is common in the LXX., wherever it occurs in the N. T. in the sense of 'searching' suggests the notion of strenuous endeavour: c. xii. 17; Acts xv. 17 (LXX.); Rom. iii. 11 (LXX.); 1 Pet. i. 10.

7. Νῶε] Gen. vi. The Faith of Noah was directed to a special revelation which was made known to others also. In this respect it differed from the Faith of Abel and Enoch. Thus Chrysostom τὸ μὲν ὑπόδειγμα τοῦ Ἐνὼχ πίστεως ἦν ὑπόδειγμα μόνον, τὸ δὲ τοῦ Νῶε καὶ ἀπιστίας.

For χρηματισθεὶς (Vulg. responso accepto) see c. viii. 5 note. 'The things not yet seen' (not indefinitely 'things'), the judgment which was to come upon the world with all its attendant circumstances, were the subject of the divine communication. Contrast περὶ μελλ. v. 20.

εὐλαβηθεὶς κατεσκ.] moved with pious care (he) prepared... Vulg. metuens aptavit... Compare c. v. 7 (ἀπὸ τῆς εὐλαβείας); xii. 28 (μετὰ αἰδοῦς καὶ εὐλαβείας); Acts xxiii. 10.

This characteristic was at once called out by the divine warning. Χρηματισθεὶς and εὐλαβηθεὶς appear to be coincident in time.

The word κατεσκεύασεν (1 Pet. iii. 20) includes both the construction and the fitting up of the ark: comp. c. iii. 3 note.

δι' ἧς] through which ark (comp. v. 4). His Faith was visibly presented to the eyes of his contemporaries by the construction of the ark. Through this then he condemned the unbelieving world, as witnessing to the divine destruction which was to come upon them in just recompense for their deeds.

Both here and in v. 4 δι' ἧς may be referred to Faith, but in both cases

πίστιν δικαιοσύνης ἐγένετο κληρονόμος. ⁸Πίστει καλού-

8 ὁ καλούμ. AD₂* vg: καλούμ. ⲥ ℵ.

the form of the argument seems to require a reference to the outward expression of the Faith. The sacrifice of Abel and the ark of Noah were, so to speak, the Faith of each made visible. And so it can rightly be said that Noah through the ark—the embodiment of his Faith in deed— *became heir of the righteousness according to Faith.*

κατέκρινεν...ἐγένετο] The first verb though the form is ambiguous, is probably an imperfect and describes the constant significance of his action, comparatione scilicet melioris fidei et facti (Primas.).

τὸν κόσμον] Compare *v.* 38.

τῆς κατὰ πίστ. δικαιοσ. κληρ.] Noah is the first man who receives the title of 'righteous' in the O. T. (Gen. vi. 9 צַדִּיק), as was remarked by Philo, *de congr. erud. gr.* § 17 (i. p. 532 M.). Comp. Ezek. xiv. 14, 20; Ecclus. xliv. 17; Wisd. x. 4, 6; 2 Pet. ii. 5.

'Faith' and 'righteousness' are placed in different connexions one with the other, which will repay study.

(a) ἡ δικ. τῆς πίστεως (δικ. πίστ.) Rom. iv. 11, 13.

(β) δικ. ἡ ἐκ π. (ἡ ἐκ π. δικ.) Rom. ix. 30; x. 6.

(γ) ἡ ἐκ θεοῦ δικ. ἐπὶ τῇ π. Phil. iii. 9.

(δ) ἡ κατὰ π. δικ.

' *The righteousness according to faith,*' the righteousness which ' answers to,' 'corresponds with' faith, is that righteousness which God alone can give, which answers to, corresponds with, that spiritual order which faith alone enters.

For κατὰ πίστιν see *v.* 13 note.

κληρονόμος] The righteousness was something which came to him as having its source without, and yet according to a certain law. It was his by an unquestionable right: it corresponded with the position of a

son; and this position Noah shewed by his conduct to be his. Compare c. i. 14 (κληρονομεῖν σωτηρίαν); xii. 17 (κληρ. τὴν εὐλογίαν). The righteousness was not a hope for the future but a real possession by the gift of God. Compare Addit. Note on vi. 12.

(3) 8—22. The Faith of the Patriarchs.

With the call of Abraham the records of Faith enter on a new phase. Faith is treated henceforth in relation to a society, a people of God, through whom the divine blessings were to be extended to mankind. Under this wider aspect Faith is regarded in two forms as shewn by the representative founders of the ancient people in (a) the Faith of patient Obedience which is the foundation of the Kingdom of God, and in (b) the Faith of Sacrifice which is the principle of its development.

(a) The patriarchal Faith of Obedience and Patience (8—16).

The Faith of patient Obedience is traced mainly in the life of Abraham who impressed his own character upon his descendants (8—12) (a). In him and in them it was openly shewn that the societies of earth have a spiritual archetype which is the true object of human endeavour (13—16) (β).

(a) The Faith of patient Obedience seen in the Faith of Abraham (8—12).

The Faith of the patriarchs, represented by the Faith of Abraham, is presented under three different aspects :

(i) As Abraham trusted God wholly, going forth he knew not whither (v. 8). (The Faith of self-surrender.)

(ii) As he waited on the scene of his hope looking for God's work (vv. 9 f.). (The Faith of patience.)

(iii) As he communicated his faith to Sarah, so that through them ('one flesh') the innumerable offspring

μενος 'Αβραὰμ ὑπήκουσεν ἐξελθεῖν εἰς τόπον ὃν ἤμελλεν

εἰς τ. ἐξελ. D₂.   τόπον ℵ*AD₂*: τὸν τ. ς ℵᶜ.

of faith were born (vv. 11 f.). (The Faith of influence.)

In each case Abraham cast himself upon the unseen and realised the future.

The promise was thus carried to its first typical fulfilment (vi. 15).

The Faith of Abraham is no less conspicuous in later Jewish teaching than in Christian teaching. He is said (Mechilta on Ex. xiv. 31, ap. Delitzsch l.c.) to have gained this world and the world to come by Faith. In this respect he is spoken of as a father of the Gentiles (Delitzsch, Brief an d. Römer p. 80). His experience was reflected in the experience of Israel (Beresh. R. § 40, on Gen. xii. 16). Israel also fulfilled a work for the nations.

On the trials of Abraham see Dr Taylor on Aboth, v. 4.

In this place the Faith of Abraham is not connected directly with personal righteousness, as in St Paul's Epistles, but is presented as the power through which the patriarch was enabled to work towards the fulfilment of God's counsel for the nations by his trust in the unseen.

⁸ By faith Abraham, when called, obeyed, to go forth into a place which he was to receive as an inheritance; and he went forth, while he knew not whither he was coming (going).

⁹ By faith he entered as a sojourner into the land of promise, as into a land not his own, dwelling in tents with Isaac and Jacob, the heirs with him of the same promise; ¹⁰for he looked for the city that hath the foundations, whose designer and maker is God.

¹¹ By faith even Sarah herself received power to conceive seed, and that when she was past age, since she counted Him faithful who had promised. ¹² Wherefore also children

were born from one, and him as good as dead, as many as the stars in heaven for multitude, and as the sand that is by the seashore that cannot be counted.

8. (i) The Faith of self-surrender.

The beginning of the Messianic nation was a call, a separation. The founder had a promise of an inheritance. This promise he could trust though he knew not how it would be fulfilled.

πίστει καλούμ....κληρονομίαν] By faith Abraham when called obeyed, to go forth into a place which he was to receive as an inheritance. Vulg. Fide qui vocatur Abraham (ὁ καλ. 'Αβρ.) obedivit exire in locum...

The present participle (καλούμενος not κληθείς) serves to emphasise the immediate act of obedience (ὑπήκουσεν). He obeyed the call while (so to say) it was still sounding in his ears.

If the reading ὁ καλούμενος is adopted the sense will be: 'he that in a unique sense received the new name Abraham': τὸ ὁ καλούμενος 'Αβραὰμ διὰ τὴν τοῦ ὀνόματος ἐναλλαγὴν εἴρηκεν (Theod.). Fide qui vocatur nunc Abraham tunc vocabatur Abram (Primas.).

ἐξελθεῖν] The point in this 'going forth' was that Abraham gave up all in faith upon the invisible God (Gen. xii. 1; Acts vii. 3: comp. xiii. 13); and in doing this he knew not what he was to receive. The future was safe in God's counsel. In this supreme act, by which he became 'the father of the faithful,' Abraham had no example to follow. Τίνα γὰρ εἶδεν ἵνα ζηλώσῃ; ὁ πατὴρ αὐτῷ εἰδωλολάτρης ἦν, προφητῶν οὐκ ἤκουσεν· ὥστε πίστεως ἦν τὸ ὑπακοῦσαι ὡς ἀληθεύοντι τῷ θεῷ περὶ ὧν ὑπισχνεῖτο καὶ ἀφεῖναι τὰ ἐν χερσίν (Theophlct. after Chrys.). He went forth to 'a place' (not 'the place') of

λαμβάνειν εἰς κληρονομίαν, καὶ ἐξῆλθεν μὴ ἐπιστάμενος ποῦ ἔρχεται. ⁹ Πίστει παρῴκησεν εἰς γῆν τῆς ἐπαγγελίας ὡς ἀλλοτρίαν, ἐν σκηναῖς κατοικήσας μετὰ Ἰσαὰκ καὶ Ἰακὼβ τῶν συνκληρονόμων τῆς ἐπαγγελίας τῆς αὐτῆς·

κληρ. λαμβ. ℵ*: εἰς κληρ. λαμβ. ℵᵃ: λαμβ. εἰς κληρ. ℵᶜ.　9 πίστει: +καί′ π. D₂*.　γῆν ℵA: +τὴν′ γ. ⸌ D₂*.　τῆς ἐπ. τῆς αὐτῆς ℵᶜA: τῆς ἐπ. αὐτῆς ℵ*: τῆς αὐτῆς ἐπ. ℵᵃ: τῆς ἐπ. αὐτοῦ D₂*.

which all that he knew was that in the end it should be his.

καὶ ἐξῆλθεν...ἔρχεται] *and he went forth while he knew not whither he was coming (going)*. It was not revealed to Abraham till he had left Haran what was to be his abode: Gen. xii. 7; comp. Acts vii. 2 f. Hence Philo says truly: τὸν μέλλοντα τῇ ὑποσχέσει χρόνον προδιώρισται, εἰπὼν οὐχ ἣν δείκνυμι ἀλλ᾽ ἥν σοι δείξω, εἰς μαρτυρίαν πίστεως ἣν ἐπίστευσεν ἡ ψυχὴ θεῷ (*de migr. Abr.* § 9; i. 442 M.).

The use of ἔρχεται presents the patriarch as already on his journey; and the writer seems to regard his end as the promised land in which he himself is ideally (ἔρχεται not πορεύεται).

9, 10. (ii) The Faith of patience. The Faith of self-surrender was submitted to a longer proof. When Abraham reached the land which was to be his, he occupied it only as a sojourner. He had to learn that the promise of God would not be fulfilled by any material possession.

9. πίστει παρῴκησεν εἰς...] *By faith he entered as a sojourner (peregrinatus est* Hier.) *into the land of promise* ...For παρῴκ. εἰς compare Acts xii. 19; and for παρῴκησεν see Luke xxiv. 18; compare Acts vii. 6, 29 (πάροικος); xiii. 17 (παροικία); Eph. ii. 19(πάροικος); 1 Pet. ii. 11 (πάροικος); i. 17 (παροικία). The word is common in the LXX. *e.g.* Gen. xxi. 23; xxiii. 4.

The phrase γῆ τῆς ἐπαγγελίας (Vulg. *terra repromissionum*) occurs here only in the N. T. There is no corresponding Hebrew phrase in the O. T., nor is there any exact parallel. It

describes the land which was attached to the promises; to which they pointed; which was assured to Abraham by God. Comp. Gen. xii. 7; xiii. 15 &c. For the use of ἐπαγγελίας compare Eph. i. 13. And for ἀλλοτρίαν see Acts vii. 6; Gen. xv. 13 (LXX. οὐκ ἰδίᾳ); comp. Matt. xvii. 25 f.

ἐν σκ. κατοικήσας...τῆς αὐτῆς] Abraham dwelt throughout the time of his sojourn (κατοικήσας) in tents, so declaring that that which was to be permanent was not yet attained. And Isaac and Jacob, who shared his hope, shewed the same patience of faith. The premature settlement of Lot and its disastrous issue point the lesson of Abraham's discipline.

The paradox in ἐν σκηναῖς κατοικήσας is to be noticed. On the contrast of κατοικεῖν and παροικεῖν see Philo *de agric.* § 14 (i. p. 310 M.); *de conf. ling.* § 17 (i. p. 416 M.); *quis rer. div. hær.* § 54 (i. p. 511 M.).

Isaac and Jacob are specially mentioned because these three, Abraham, Isaac, and Jacob, cover the whole period of disciplinary sojourning in Canaan; and to these three the foundation promise was repeated (Gen. xii. 2 f.; xxvi. 3 ff.; xxviii. 13 f.; comp. Ex. vi. 3, 8). For συνκληρ. τῆς ἐπαγγ., compare vi. 12, 17.

Biesenthal quotes a striking passage from Sanh. f. iii. *a* in which the patient faith of the patriarchs is illustrated by the fact that while they were heirs of the land they bore without complaint the trial of gaining with difficulty what they needed there for the

¹⁰ἐξεδέχετο γὰρ τὴν τοὺς θεμελίους ἔχουσαν πόλιν, ἧς
τεχνίτης καὶ δημιουργὸς ὁ θεός. ¹¹Πίστει καὶ αὐτὴ
Σάρρα δύναμιν εἰς καταβολὴν σπέρματος ἔλαβεν καὶ

11 Σάρρα ϛ ℵA: +στεῖρα D₂ vg syrr me the.   ἔλ.: +εἰς τὸ τεκνῶσαι D₂* syr hl.
om. καὶ (παρά) D₂*.

simplest wants (Gen. xxiii. 4 ff.; xxvi.
17 ff.; xxxiii. 19).

10. The ground of this patient
waiting was the growing sense of
the greatness of the divine purpose.
Abraham felt, under the teaching of
his pilgrim life, that no earthly resting-place could satisfy the wants and
the powers of which he was conscious.
He looked beyond the first fulfilment
of the promise which was only a step
in the accomplishment of the purpose
of God.

ἐξεδέχετο γὰρ...ὁ θεός] for he looked
for the city that hath the foundations
... For ἐξεδέχετο compare c. x. 13;
James v. 7; and ἀπεκδέχομαι c. ix. 28
note. The object of his desire was
social and not personal only. 'He
looked for the city that hath the
foundations'—the divine ideal of
which every earthly institution is but
a transitory image. The visible Jerusalem, the visible Temple, were farther
from this spiritual archetype than the
tents of the patriarch and the Tabernacle of the wilderness. They were
in large measure of human design and
wholly of human construction. But
God Himself frames and constructs
the heavenly city (v. 16) no less than
the heavenly sanctuary: c. viii. 2.
Comp. c. xii. 22 f.; xiii. 14; Apoc.
xxi. 2; Gal. iv. 26 (and Lightfoot's
note); (Is. xxxiii. 20; Ps. lxxxiv.). See
Additional Note.

The idea of τοὺς θεμ. ἔχ. is that of
the one 'city' which has 'the eternal
foundations.' To this outwardly the
tents of the patriarchs offered the
most striking contrast. Comp. Apoc.
xxi. 14.

ἧς τεχν. καὶ δημ. ὁ θεός] whose designer and maker is God. Vulg. cujus
artifex et conditor Deus. The word
τεχνίτης in this connexion refers to
the plan and δημιουργός to the execution of it. Τεχνίτης occurs in the more
general sense of 'craftsman' Acts xix.
24, 38; Apoc. xviii. 22: δημιουργός is
not found again in N. T.

For τεχνίτης compare Wisd. xiii. 1;
Philo Leg. Alleg. i. 7 (i. 47 M.) οὐ
τεχνίτης μόνον ἀλλὰ καὶ πατὴρ ὢν τῶν
γιγνομένων: De mut. nom. § 4 (i. 583
M.) ὁ γεννήσας καὶ τεχνιτεύσας πατήρ:
and for δημιουργός Clem. R. i. 20, 26,
33, 35; Philo de incorr. mundi § 4
(ii. 490 M.).

11, 12. (iii) The Faith of influence.
Abraham had to sustain yet a third
trial before the promise received an
initial fulfilment. The son through
whom the blessing was to come was
not born while his birth was naturally
to be expected and according to man's
reckoning possible. But Sarah, who
was at first unbelieving, was at last inspired with her husband's Faith by his
example and influence; and the promise found amplest accomplishment.

11. πίστει καὶ αὐτὴ Σάρρα...] By
faith even Sarah herself...though she
more than doubted. Sarah is evidently
regarded in the closest union with
Abraham (v. 12 ἀφ' ἑνός). She was
'one with him.' Her faith was a condition for the fruitfulness of his faith.
Ἐγέλασε τὸ πρῶτον οὐκ εἰδυῖα τοῦ
ὑπισχνουμένου τὴν φύσιν καὶ τῆς ἀνθρω-
πείας φύσεως τοὺς ὅρους ἐπισταμένη...
ὕστερον μέντοι μαθοῦσα τὸν ὑποσχόμε-
νον καὶ ἐπίστευσε καὶ ἐγέννησεν ὡς
ἐπίστευσε (Theodt.).

παρὰ καιρὸν ἡλικίας, ἐπεὶ πιστὸν ἡγήσατο τὸν ἐπαγγει-
λάμενον· ¹²διὸ καὶ ἀφ᾽ ἑνὸς ⌜ἐγεννήθησαν⌝, καὶ ταῦτα
νενεκρωμένου, καθὼς τὰ ἄϲτρα τοῦ οὐρανοῦ τῷ πλήθει καὶ ὡϲ ἡ

12 ἐγενήθησαν

ἡλικίας א*AD₂* vg me the: + ἔτεκεν ϛ אᶜ syrr.   12 ἐγεννήθ. א: ἐγενήθ. AD₂*.
ὡς ἡ אA: καθὼς ἡ D₂* : ὡσεί ϛ.

εἰς καταβ. σπ.] Vulg. *in conceptio-
nem seminis.* The translation 'for
the founding of a race' is altogether
unnatural. The thought here extends
no farther than to the direct personal
issue of Sarah's Faith. She was
enabled to become the mother of
Abraham's son. She co-operated on
her part with Abraham towards the
fulfilment of the promise. The promise was to Abraham, and the work of
faith was primarily his (hence εἰς καταβολὴν σπ. [*e.g.* Chrys. *Ad illum.* ii. § 1
ἐν ἡμέρᾳ μιᾷ δυνατὸν ὁμοῦ καὶ σπέρματα
καταβαλεῖν καὶ ἀμητὸν ποιήσασθαι] and
not εἰς σύλληψιν σπ. or the like), but
it was needful that Sarah should join
by faith with him. Ἐνεδυναμώθη εἰς
τὸ ὑποδέξασθαι καὶ κρατῆσαι τὸ κατα-
βληθὲν εἰς αὐτὴν σπέρμα τοῦ Ἀβραάμ
(Theophlct.).

καὶ παρὰ κ. ἡλ.] Even against the
natural expectation of the age which
she had reached, ὥστε διπλῆν εἶχε
πήρωσιν, τήν τε ἀπὸ φύσεως ὅτι στεῖρα
ἦν καὶ τὴν ἀπὸ τοῦ γήρως (Theophlct.).
Comp. Plat. *Theæt.* 149 c ταῖς...δι᾽
ἡλικίαν ἀτόκοις.

For πιστὸν ἡγ. τὸν ἐπαγγ., compare
c. x. 23.

12. διὸ καὶ ἀφ᾽ ἑνός] *Wherefore
also* children *were born* through her
*from one, and that from one as good
as dead...* Though Sarah is lost, so
to speak, in Abraham with whom she
was united (ἀφ᾽ ἑνός), yet her act of
Faith completing his Faith is made
the reason of the fulfilment of the
promise (διό).

For διὸ καί see Lk. i. 35; Acts x.
29; (xiii. 35;) xxiv. 26; Rom. iv. 22?;
xv. 22; 2 Cor. i. 20; iv. 13; v. 9;
Phil. ii. 9.

Ἀφ᾽ ἑνὸς τοῦ Ἀβραάμ. εἰ δὲ καὶ
ἀμφοτέρους ἕνα νοήσαιμεν οὐχ ἁμαρτη-
σόμεθα· ἔσονται γάρ, φησίν, οἱ δύο εἰς
σάρκα μίαν (Theodt.).

The classical phrase καὶ ταῦτα is
found here only in N. T.; καὶ τοῦτο
occurs Rom. xiii. 11 ; 1 Cor. vi. 6, 8 ;
3 John 5. For νενεκρωμένου compare
Rom. iv. 19.

καθὼς τὰ ἄστρα...] Gen. xxii. 17;
xxxii. 12. At first the promise is of
an heir, and then of a countless pro-
geny. Comp. vi. 13 note.

The references in the O. T. to
Abraham as 'the one' are significant:
Mal. ii. 15; Is. li. 1 f.; Ezek. xxxiii.
24.

(β) Characteristics of the patriarchal life of faith (13—16).

The life of the patriarchs was a life
of faith to the last, supported by trust
in the invisible which they had realised,
resting on complete surrender, directed
beyond earth (13). They shewed that
the true satisfaction of human powers,
the 'city' which answers to man's
social instincts, must be 'heavenly'
(14—16).

¹³*These all died in faith, not having
received the promises, but having
seen them and greeted them afar,
and having confessed that they are
strangers and sojourners on the earth.*
¹⁴*For they that say such things make
it plain that they are seeking after a
fatherland (a country of their own).*
¹⁵*And if indeed they had thought of
that from which they went out, they
would have had opportunity to return.* ¹⁶*But now they desire a better,
that is a heavenly* fatherland; *wherefore God is not ashamed of them,
not ashamed to be called their God;*

362   THE EPISTLE TO THE HEBREWS.   [XI. 13

ἄμμος ἡ παρὰ τὸ χεῖλος τῆς θαλάσσης ἡ ἀναρίθμητος. ¹³Κατὰ
πίστιν ἀπέθανον οὗτοι πάντες, μὴ κομισάμενοι τὰς
ἐπαγγελίας, ἀλλὰ πόρρωθεν αὐτὰς ἰδόντες καὶ ἀσπασάμενοι, καὶ ὁμολογήσαντες ὅτι ξένοι καὶ παρεπίδημοί εἰσιν

om. ἡ π. τ. χ. D₂*.   13 κομισάμενοι א*: λαβόντες ϛ א°D₂: προσδεξάμενοι A.
ἰδόντες אAD₂ vg syrr me the: +καὶ πεισθέντες ϛ.   ξένοι: +καὶ πάροικοι D₂*.

for He (hath) prepared for them a
city.
   13. Having described the victories
of faith gained by the patriarchs the
writer marks the great lessons of
their death and of their life. 'These
all'—the three to whom the promises
were given, Abraham, Isaac and Jacob, with Sarah, the representative of
faithful womanhood—'died in faith';
and in life they had realised the promises which they had not outwardly
received in a threefold order of growing power. They had seen them: they
had welcomed them: they had acknowledged that earth could not fulfil them.
   κατὰ π. ἀπέθανον] they died in faith,
literally 'according to faith' (Vulg.
juxta fidem), that is, under the influence and according to the spirit of
Faith, inspired, sustained, guided by
Faith. Faith was the rule of their
lives, the measure of their growth,
even to the end. They faced death
as men who retained their hold on the
invisible, which was offered to them in
the promises of God, though earth
'gave them no pledge.' So their departure was transformed into 'a going
home.' For κατὰ πίστιν compare
Matt. ix. 29 κατὰ τὴν π. γενηθήτω σοι:
Tit. i. 1, 4; v. 7.
   By οὗτοι πάντες we must understand
the first representatives of the patriarchs and not (as Primasius and others)
the whole array of their descendants
(v. 12).
   μὴ κομ....ἀλλά] The clause does not
simply state a fact (οὐ κομισ....ἀλλὰ),
but gives this fact as the explanation
of the assertion that the patriarchs

'died in faith': 'They died in faith
inasmuch as they had not received the
outward fulness of the promises—the
possession of Canaan, the growth of
the nation, universal blessing through
their race—but had realised them
while they were still unseen and
future.'
   For κομισάμενοι see c. x. 36 note;
v. 39.
   πόρρωθεν αὐ. ἰδόντες...ἀσπασάμενοι...
ὁμολογήσαντες...] The three thoughts
rise in a natural succession. They
saw the promises in their actual fulfilment: they welcomed the vision with
joy though it was far off: they confessed what must be the true end of
God's counsel. For ἰδόντες compare
John viii. 56. Πόρρωθεν occurs again
in N. T. Luke xvii. 12.
   On ἀσπασάμενοι Chrysostom says
well: ἀπὸ μεταφορᾶς εἶπε τῶν πλεόντων
καὶ πόρρωθεν ὁρώντων τὰς πόλεις τὰς
ποθουμένας, ἃς πρὶν ἢ εἰσελθεῖν εἰς
αὐτὰς τῇ προσρήσει λαβόντες αὐτὰς
οἰκειοῦνται. Compare Æn. iii. 522.
   Italiam primus conclamat Achates,
   Italiam læto socii clamore salutant.
   καὶ ὁμολογήσαντες] The language of
Abraham (Gen. xxiii. 4 LXX.; comp.
Gen. xlvii. 9; xxiv. 37; xxviii. 4) is
used as expressing the view which the
patriarchs took of their life. Compare
Ps. xxxix. (xxxviii.) 12; cxix. (cxviii.)
19, 54.
   Philo places a similar interpretation
on the 'sojourning' of the fathers: de
conf. ling. § 17, i. p. 416 M. Not
only was the 'land' of Palestine
'strange' to them (v. 9), but the
'earth' itself.

ἐπὶ τῆς γῆς· ¹⁴οἱ γὰρ τοιαῦτα λέγοντες ἐμφανίζουσιν ὅτι πατρίδα ἐπιζητοῦσιν. ¹⁵καὶ εἰ μὲν ἐκείνης ἐμνημόνευον ἀφ᾽ ἧς ἐξέβησαν, εἶχον ἂν καιρὸν ἀνακάμψαι· ¹⁶νῦν δὲ

14 ζητοῦσιν D₂*.   15 ἐμνημόνευον א°A vg: μνημονεύουσιν א* (D₂*?).   ἐξέβησαν
א*AD₂*: ἐξῆλθον ϛ א°.   om. ἄν D₂*.   16 νῦν: νυνί ϛ.

ξένοι καὶ παρεπίδημοι] Vulg. peregrini et hospites. Things seen were not their true home, and they remained among them only for a short space. For ξένοι compare Eph. ii. 12, 19; and for παρεπίδημοι, 1 Pet. i. 1; ii. 11 (Gen. xxiii. 4); Ps. xxxix. (xxxviii.) 12 (LXX.); Lev. xxv. 23. Comp. Addit. Note on v. 10.
For the thought compare a striking passage of the Letter to Diognetus, c. 5.

14—16. These verses develop the last clause of v. 13, and define the grounds of the statement which has been made that the patriarchs 'died in Faith.' Their language shewed that they continued to the last to look for that which they had not attained. As 'strangers' they acknowledged that they were in a foreign land: as 'sojourners' that they had no permanent possession, no rights of citizenship. At the same time they kept their trust in God. Their natural fatherland had lost its hold upon them. They waited for a 'city' of God's preparing.

14. οἱ γὰρ τοιαῦτα...] The language of the patriarchs makes clear that they sought for a country, which should be naturally and essentially their own, not simply the fruit of gift or conquest, but a true 'fatherland.' They had no fatherland on earth. The word πατρίς, which is rare in the LXX. (Jer. xlvi. 16 אֶרֶץ מוֹלֶדֶת), is found here only in the Epistles (John iv. 41 and parallels).
For ἐμφανίζουσιν (Vulg. significant) comp. c. ix. 24 note; and for ἐπιζητοῦσιν, c. xiii. 14. Compare Is. lxii. 12 σὺ (Zion) κληθήσῃ ἐπιζητουμένη πόλις.

15. καὶ εἰ μέν...] They spoke of a home not yet reached; and in so speaking they could not have referred to that home which they had left in Mesopotamia, the seat of primitive civilisation; for return thither was easy. Nor again could Palestine, even when occupied at last, have satisfied their hopes; this remained the Lord's land: Lev. xxv. 23.
ἐμνημόνευον] Vulg. meminissent. The verb μνημονεύω has commonly in the N. T., as in this Epistle c. xiii. 7, the sense of 'remember'; but in v. 22, and perhaps in 1 Thess. i. 3, it has the second sense of 'make mention.' It seems on the whole more natural to take that sense here and to suppose that the reference is to the language just quoted rather than to a general feeling: 'and if their words, when they so spoke, had been directed to the country from which they went...' 'if they had meant that....' The imperfect is used rather than the aorist (ὁμολογήσαντες) since the words were the expression of a continuous state of mind.
ἀφ᾽ ἧς ἐξέβησαν] The word ἐκβαίνειν occurs here only in N. T. (βαίνειν does not occur at all). It gives a more personal colour to the act than the general word ἐξῆλθον used before. Compare v. 29 διέβησαν.
εἶχον ἂν καιρόν...] Vulg. habebant utique tempus revertendi. Comp. Acts xxiv. 25 καιρὸν μεταλαβών. Gal. vi. 10 ὡς καιρὸν ἔχομεν. For ἀνακάμψαι see Matt. ii. 12; Lk. x. 6; Acts xviii. 21.

16. νῦν δέ...] But now, as the case is,...see 1 Cor. vii. 14; xii. 20; c. viii. 6 note.

κρείττονος ὀρέγονται, τοῦτ᾽ ἔστιν ἐπουρανίου. διὸ οὐκ
ἐπαισχύνεται αὐτοὺς ὁ θεὸς θεὸς ἐπικαλεῖσθαι αὐτῶν,
ἡτοίμασεν γὰρ αὐτοῖς πόλιν. ¹⁷ Πίστει προσενήνοχεν

ἐπικ. αὐ. θεός D₂*.

Though their expectation received no definite fulfilment, the desire remained still fresh; and all partial fulfilments led them to look forward, and to look beyond the transitory.

For ὀρέγονται (Vulg. adpetunt), which is not in the LXX., see 1 Tim. iii. 1; vi. 10; and for ἐπουρανίου, see c. iii. 1 note.

διό...] wherefore..., because their thoughts were directed to spiritual realities, God, Who is spirit, acknowledged them as His own, revealing Himself as 'the God of Abraham, the God of Isaac and the God of Jacob' (Ex. iii. 6, 15 f.; Matt. xxii. 32). Compare Chrysostom: ἱ τῆς οἰκουμένης θεὸς οὐκ ἐπαισχύνεται τριῶν καλεῖσθαι θεός· εἰκότως· οὐ γὰρ τῆς οἰκουμένης ἀλλὰ μυρίων τοιούτων εἰσὶν ἀντίρροποι οἱ ἅγιοι.

οὐκ ἐπαισχ. αὐτούς...θεὸς ἐπικ....] God is not ashamed of them, not ashamed to be called their God. Vulg. non confunditur deus vocari deus eorum.

The second clause is added in explanation: 'is not ashamed of them, is not ashamed, that is, to be called'—named by a peculiar title (Acts iv. 36; x. 5, 18, 32 &c.)—'their God.'

The title 'the God of Abraham and the God of Isaac and the God of Jacob' is the characteristic name of God at the Exodus: Ex. iii. 6. For ἐπαισχ. αὐτούς see Mk. viii. 28; Rom. i. 16; 2 Tim. i. 8, 16; and for (ἐπαισχ.) ἐπικαλεῖσθαι c. ii. 11.

ἡτοίμ. γὰρ αὐ. π.] The proof of God's acceptance of the patriarchs lies in what He did for them. Their faith truly corresponded with His purpose. They entered into His design and He acknowledged their devotion and trust. He was pleased to establish a

personal relation with them, and to fulfil His spiritual promise; for 'He prepared for them a city.' He made provision for their abiding continuance with Him in the fulness of human life. The statement is made in the most absolute form without any definition of time ('He had prepared,' or 'thereupon He prepared').

The fulfilment of the promise in its highest form is set before us as social and not simply as personal. God prepared for His chosen not a home but a 'city,' a Divine Commonwealth (Vulg. paravit illis civitatem). Ps. cvii. 36.

For the idea of πόλις see Additional Note on v. 10; and for ἐτοιμάζειν compare John xiv. 2; Apoc. xxi. 2.

(b) The patriarchal Faith of sacrifice (against natural judgment) (18—22).

From the general description of the life of faith in the patriarchs, to whom the promise was first committed, the writer goes on to give special illustrations of the power of faith, as the promise was seen to advance towards fulfilment through trial. Thus he notices

(a) The primary trial (vv. 17—19). That through which God works is first wholly surrendered to Him.

(β) The patriarchal blessings. The natural order reversed: Isaac, Jacob (vv. 20, 21).

(γ) The world abandoned (v. 22).

In the former paragraph the personal triumph of faith over death has been described: here faith is seen to look through death to the later issue for others.

¹⁷ By faith Abraham, being tried, offered up (hath offered up) Isaac; yea, he that had gladly received the

Ἀβραὰμ τὸν Ἰσαὰκ πειραζόμενος, καὶ τὸν μονογενῆ προσέφερεν

17 τὸν Ἰ. πειρ. Ἀβρ. D₂*.

promises prepared to offer up his only son; ¹⁸he to whom it was said In Isaac shall thy seed be called; ¹⁹accounting that God is able to raise up even from the dead, whence he also in a figure received him. ²⁰By faith Isaac blessed Jacob and Esau and that concerning things to come. ²¹By faith Jacob, when he was dying, blessed each of the sons of Joseph; and he worshipped, leaning upon the top of his staff. ²²By faith Joseph, when his end was nigh, made mention of the departure of the children of Israel; and gave commandment concerning his bones.

(a) The trial of Abraham (17—19).
The references to Abraham in the O. T. are fewer than might have been expected. There appears to be no mention of his sacrifice unless it is implied in Is. xli. 8 (Abraham that loved me). It is referred to in Ecclus. xliv. 20 ἐν πειρασμῷ εὑρέθη πιστός; and the same words are found in 1 Macc. ii. 52. Compare Wisd. x. 5; James ii. 21.

The trial of Abraham was not so much in the conflict of his natural affection with his obedience to God, as in the apparent inconsistency of the revelations of the will of God which were made to him.

Thus the greatness of Abraham's Faith was shewn by the fact that he was ready to sacrifice his only son, though it had been before declared that the fulfilment of the promise which he had received was to come through him. His obedience therefore included the conviction of some signal and incomprehensible work of God whose promise could not fail. At the same time the nature of the trial left an opportunity for the right exercise of Faith. The specific command could

be fulfilled only in one way: the promise might be fulfilled in more ways than one. So Faith triumphed.

Chrysostom calls attention to this feature in Abraham's trial as involving an apparent conflict in the divine will towards him: τὰ γὰρ τοῦ θεοῦ ἐδόκει τοῖς τοῦ θεοῦ μάχεσθαι, καὶ πίστις ἐμάχετο πίστει, καὶ πρόσταγμα ἐπαγγελίᾳ... ἐναντία ταῖς ὑποσχέσεσι προσετέτακτο ποιεῖν καὶ οὐδὲ οὕτως ἐθορυβήθη οὐδὲ ἰλιγγίασεν οὐδὲ ἠπατῆσθαι ἐνόμισεν. And so Theophylact more tersely: ἐνταῦθα οὐ μόνον φύσις ἐμάχετο ἀλλὰ καὶ λόγος θεοῦ θείῳ προστάγματι.

17. πίστει...πειραζόμενος] By faith Abraham, being tried, offered up (literally hath offered up) Isaac. The contrast between προσενήνοχεν and προσέφερεν which follows (Vulg. obtulit, offerebat, Syr. vg. offered, lifted on the altar) is easily felt, but it is difficult to represent it in translation. The first verb expresses the permanent result of the offering completed by Abraham in will: the second his actual readiness in preparing the sacrifice which was not literally carried into effect. As far as the trial went (πειραζόμενος) the work was at once completed. Comp. James ii. 21 ἐδικαιώθη ἀνενέγκας.

For the perfect προσενήνοχεν compare v. 28 πεποίηκεν, and c. vii. 6 note.

The use of the word πειραζόμενος (Gen. xxii. 1 ff.) marks the decisive severity of the trial. The tense (as distinguished from πειρασθείς (comp. c. ii. 18) marks the immediate coincidence of the act of obedience with the call for it. Comp. v. 8 καλούμενος.

On the trial Theophylact observes [ὁ θεὸς] αὐτὸς πειράζει ἵνα δοκιμωτέρους δείξῃ. Comp. James i. 12.

καὶ τὸν μονογ....ἀναδεξάμενος] yea, he that had gladly received the promises prepared to offer up his only son. Vulg. et unigenitum offerebat qui

ὁ τὰς ἐπαγγελίας ἀναδεξάμενος, ¹⁸πρὸς ὃν ἐλαλήθη ὅτι
Ἐν Ἰσαὰκ κληθήσεταί σοι σπέρμα, ¹⁹λογισάμενος ὅτι καὶ ἐκ
νεκρῶν ἐγείρειν δυνατὸς ὁ θεός· ὅθεν αὐτὸν καὶ ἐν
παραβολῇ ἐκομίσατο. ²⁰Πίστει καὶ περὶ μελλόντων

18 om. ὅτι D₂*.   19 ἐγείρειν אD₂: ἐγεῖραι (-ε) A.   δυνατός אD₂* vg: δύναται A.
20 πίστει καί AD₂* vg: om. καί ϛ א syrr me the.

susceperat repromissiones. The 'only
son' is placed in significant parallelism
with the 'promise.' In regard to the
promise Isaac was 'the only son' of
Abraham (Gen. xvii. 19). So Theophylact (and others): πῶς δὲ μονογενὴς
ἦν Ἰσαὰκ ὅπουγε καὶ τὸν Ἰσμαὴλ εἶχε;
ἀλλ' ὅσον κατὰ τὸν ἐπαγγελίας λόγον
μονογενής. Comp. Gen. xv. 2 f.; xvi.
15; xvii. 16 ff. The LXX. in Gen. xxii.
2 gives τὸν υἱόν σου τὸν ἀγαπητὸν ὃν
ἠγάπησας, but Aquila has τὸν μονογενῆ
(or μοναχόν) and Symmachus τὸν μόνον
σου.

Μονογενής occurs in St Luke vii. 12;
viii. 42; ix. 38. Compare John i. 14, 18,
and ὁ υἱὸς ὁ μονογενής of Christ in
John iii. 16, 18; 1 John iv. 9.

The word ἀναδέχεσθαι is unusual.
It occurs again in N. T. only in Acts
xxviii. 7. The idea which it suggests
here seems to be that of welcoming
and cherishing a divine charge which
involved a noble responsibility. The
word is used frequently of undertak-
ing that which calls out effort and
endurance (e.g. πόλεμον, πολιορκίαν
Polyb., Plut. *Indd.*). Clement says of
Adam τέλειος κατὰ τὴν κατασκευὴν οὐκ
ἐγένετο πρὸς δὲ τὸ ἀναδέξασθαι τὴν
ἀρετὴν ἐπιτήδειος (*Strom.* vi. 12).

18. πρὸς ὃν ἐλαλ.] *he to whom it
was said* (*i.e.* Abraham). Vulg. *ad
quem dictum est,*...not '*him in reference to whom*' (Isaac)...; Luke ii.
18, 20. The latter rendering is against
the structure of the sentence; though
it is in itself possible: comp. i. 7, 8.

ἐν Ἰσαάκ...] Gen. xxi. 12. The
words ἐν Ἰσαάκ stand emphatically
first: *In Isaac,* and in no other, a

seed shall bear thy name, shall be
called thine. Comp. Rom. ix. 7.

Sedulius sums up well the elements
in Abraham's act of faith: Triplex
bonum fecit, quod filium, et quod
unigenitum, et repromissionem in quo
accepit, offerebat.

19. The obedience of Abraham
rested on his faith in the creative
power of God. His conclusion was
made at once and finally (λογισάμενος
not λογιζόμενος) that God could
raise from the dead. That this was
his judgment follows of necessity from
the fact that he was ready to surrender Isaac without giving up his faith
in the fulfilment of the divine promise.

For λογίζομαι ὅτι compare John xi.
50; 2 Cor. x. 11; Rom. ii. 3; viii. 18.

καὶ ἐκ νεκρῶν ἐγ....] The belief is
expressed quite generally that God
'is able even from the dead to raise'
(Vulg. *quia et a mortuis suscitare
potens est Deus*). The order of the
sentence is telling in every word, as
also is its absolute form (not ἐγ.
αὐτόν); and the choice of δυνατός in
place of δύναται extends the idea of
the power of God beyond this particular act which would reveal it.
Comp. 2 Tim. i. 12. Δυνατός is practically equivalent to δυνατεῖ (Rom.
xiv. 4; 2 Cor. ix. 8: opposed to
ἀσθενεῖ) as contrasted with δύναται.

ὅθεν...ἐκομίσατο] *whence* (i.e. from
the dead) *he also in a figure received
him.* Elsewhere in the Epistle (see
ii. 17 n.) the word has the sense of
'wherefore'; but such a connexion of
the clauses here (*pro hoc etiam* Aug.),

whether the words which follow are supposed to express the reward or the circumstances of his Faith, is altogether unnatural, and the local sense is common (Luke xi. 24, &c.). But it is doubted whether the reference is to the birth of Isaac or to his deliverance from the altar. The latter explanation, which is adopted by the great majority of commentators from early times, and is perfectly justified by the original words, adds nothing to the thought of the passage. It seems to be pointless to complete the description of Abraham's faith by saying that something really came to pass far less than he was able to look forward to. On the other hand there is great meaning in the clause if it reveals the grounds of the patriarch's expectation. The circumstances of Isaac's birth (v. 12 νενεκρωμένου) were such as to lead him to look beyond the mere fact. It evidently contained a divine lesson and had a spiritual meaning. That giving of a son beyond nature included a larger hope. Comp. Aug. Serm. ii. § 1 Cogitavit Abraham Deum qui dedit ut ille de senibus nasceretur qui non erat posse etiam de morte reparare.

If this sense be adopted then the interpretation of ἐν παραβολῇ follows from it. Abraham received the gift of his son not literally from the dead but figuratively, in such a way that the gift suggested a further lesson. This appears to be the force of the order of the phrase (καὶ ἐν παρ. ἐκομίσατο) in which the καὶ goes with the compound verb ‘ ἐν παρ. ἐκομίσατο.’ Thus the exact sense is not ‘whence in figure he also received him’ (ἐν παρ. καὶ ἐκομ.), but ‘whence he also received him in figure.’ The manner in which the birth took place was, so to speak, part of the divine gift. It constrained the father to see in it a type of other quickening.

If, however, ἐκομίσατο be referred to the deliverance of Isaac, then ἐν παραβολῇ will mark the significance

of the sacrifice and restoration of Isaac as typical of the death and resurrection of Christ. His restoration was not only such that it might be called figuratively a resurrection, but it pointed forward.

In either case we seem to have here the explanation of St John viii. 56.

The patristic interpretations of ἐν παραβολῇ are various and wavering. Chrysostom is singularly obscure, if the text is correct : ἐν παραβολῇ τουτέστιν ὡς ἐν αἰνίγματι· ὥσπερ γὰρ παραβολὴ ἦν ὁ κριὸς τοῦ Ἰσαάκ· ἢ ὡς ἐν τῷ τύπῳ· ἐπειδὴ γὰρ ἀπήρτιστο ἡ θυσία καὶ ἔσφακτο ὁ Ἰσαάκ τῇ προαιρέσει, διὰ τοῦτο αὐτὸν χαρίζεται τῷ πατριάρχῃ.

Theodoret is at least more definite : ἐν παραβολῇ τουτέστιν ὡς ἐν συμβόλῳ καὶ τύπῳ τῆς ἀναστάσεως...ἐν αὐτῷ δὲ προεγράφη καὶ τοῦ σωτηρίου πάθους ὁ τύπος (John viii. 56).

Theophylact, like Chrysostom, gives alternative explanations: ἀντὶ τοῦ ἐν τύπῳ, εἰς ἔνδειξιν μυστηρίου τοῦ κατὰ Χριστόν...ἢ ἀντὶ τοῦ ἐν τῷ κριῷ ἐκομίσατο αὐτὸν ὁ Ἀβραάμ, τουτέστιν ἐν τῇ ἀντιδόσει τοῦ κριοῦ.

Œcumenius offers confusedly several interpretations, but prefers that which represents the whole action of Abraham and Isaac as typical of the gift of the Son by the Father.

Primasius gives the sense which became current in the West, that the ram represented the manhood of Christ in which He was not only offered but slain : Occisus est Isaac quantum ad voluntatem patris pertinet. Deinde redonavit illum Deus patriarchæ in parabola, id est, in figura et similitudine passionis Christi ...Aries significabat carnem Christi. Isaac oblatus est et non est interfectus sed aries tantum: quia Christus in passione oblatus est sed divinitas illius impassibilis mansit.

The word παραβολή occurs again c. ix. 9. Besides, it occurs only in the Synoptic Gospels.

THE EPISTLE TO THE HEBREWS.

εὐλόγησεν Ἰσαὰκ τὸν Ἰακὼβ καὶ τὸν Ἠσαῦ. ²¹ Πίστει
Ἰακὼβ ἀποθνήσκων ἕκαστον τῶν υἱῶν Ἰωσὴφ εὐλόγησεν,

om. Ἰσαάκ א*.

(β) The patriarchal blessings : the
reversal of natural expectations (20,
21).

The Faith of the patriarchs in
looking towards the fulfilment of the
promise was able to set aside the
expectations which were based on
the rules of human succession, whether,
as in the case of Isaac, they accepted
the divine will when it was contrary
to their own purpose (v. 20), or, as in
the case of Jacob, they interpreted
it (v. 21).

An element beyond human calculation entered into the gradual accomplishment of the promise as into its
initial foundation.

20. The blessing of Isaac forms
a crisis in the fulfilment of the divine
counsel. A choice is made between
those through whom the promise
might equally have been fulfilled.
The choice was not, as in the case of
Ishmael and Isaac, between the son
of the bondwoman and the son of
the free, but between twin brothers.
And the will of God inverted the
purely human order. Both sons were
blessed, but the younger had the
precedence and became heir of the
promise (τὸν Ἰακὼβ καὶ τὸν Ἠσαῦ).
Compare Mal. i. 2, 3 (Rom. ix. 13);
c. xii. 16.

Isaac acknowledged the overruling
of his own purpose (Gen. xxvii. 33).

καὶ περὶ μελλ. εὐλόγ.] Isaac blessed
Jacob and Esau and that concerning
things to come (Gen. xxvii), concerning things to come as well as
(καὶ) in regard to their immediate
position. (Syr. vg. by faith in that
which was to come.)

The blessing of Isaac reached beyond the immediate future which
could be realised by his sons in their
own life-time. His words pointed
onward to a distant order (μελλόντων

not τῶν μελλ.). The faith of Isaac
was shewn by his acceptance of the
destination of his highest blessing,
'the blessing,' to the younger son
which was against his own will; and
by his later blessing of Esau. In
itself the supreme value attached to
'the blessing' (xii. 17) with its unseen
consequences was a sign of faith.

Throughout the later history of the
O. T. the fortunes of the children of
Israel and of the children of Esau are
in constant connexion and conflict.

With the indefinite μέλλοντα contrast τὰ ἐρχόμενα John xvi. 13.

21. The blessing of Jacob, like that
of Isaac, marked a fresh stage in the
fulfilment of the promise. The providential office was then entrusted not to
one but to a whole family the members
of which had separate parts to perform.
But the writer of the Epistle does
not refer to the general foreshadowing
of the future of the several patriarchs.
He confines himself to the peculiar
blessing given to Joseph through his
sons, in whom the service of Egypt was,
so to speak, received for divine use.
Here again one point seems to be
the freedom of God's choice. In this
case also, as in the case of Jacob, the
younger is preferred to the elder.
But at the same time the practical
exaltation of Joseph to the privilege
of the firstborn in place of Reuben
indicates the fulfilment of a righteous
judgment in the providence of God.

The blessing itself is remarkable :
Gen. xlviii. 16 The angel which redeemed me from all evil bless the
lads... Compare the prophetic words
to Joseph : Gen. xlix. 25.

π. Ἰ. ἀποθν. ἕ. τ. υἱ. Ἰ. εὐλ.] By faith
Jacob when he was dying blessed
each of the sons of Joseph, Gen. xlviii.
At the close of life (Gen. xlviii. 21
ἰδοὺ ἐγὼ ἀποθνήσκω) Jacob's faith was

καὶ προσεκýνΗCΕΝ ἐπὶ τὸ ἄκρον τΗc ῥάΒΔΟΥ αÝτοΫ.   ²²Πίστει Ἰωσὴφ

still fresh; and he blessed each of the two sons born to Joseph before he himself came to Egypt (Gen. xlviii. 5).

Such a blessing was exceptional. Joseph received in his two sons a double share of the divine inheritance, the privilege of the firstborn. And, as it was given, the younger was again preferred to the elder. But while Isaac would have followed, had he been able, the natural order of birth in assigning privilege, Jacob deliberately inverted the order. It was not however till a late date that the superiority of Ephraim was established (Num. xxvi. 34, 37).

A further point must also be noticed. In blessing the sons of Joseph, who were also the sons of Asenath, Jacob recognised that the gifts of Egypt, a fresh element, were consecrated to God. So Joseph became, as it were, head of a new line. Comp. Ps. lxxvii. 15; (lxxviii. 67). It would be interesting to inquire how far the failure of Ephraim answered to the misuse of powers corresponding to Egyptian parentage.

καὶ προσεκ....τ. ῥ. αὐ.] and he worshipped leaning upon the top of his staff. Vulg. et adoravit fastigium virgæ ejus. These words are not taken from the narrative of the blessing of Joseph's sons, but from an earlier passage (Gen. xlvii. 31) in which Jacob pledged Joseph to provide for the removal of his bones to the burial-place of his fathers (comp. v. 22). The quotation is probably designed to direct thought to this act of Faith, while at the same time it stamps the closing scenes of Jacob's life with a religious character. The blessing was given in the presence of God which the patriarch distinctly recognised. The infirmity of age had not dulled his devotion.

The quotation follows the text of the LXX. which renders a different pointing of the original from that adopted by the Masoretes and by the other Greek translations (עַל־רֹאשׁ הַמִּטָּה upon the head of his staff for עַל־רֹאשׁ הַמִּטָּה upon the head of his bed: ἐπὶ κεφαλὴν τῆς κλίνης Aqu., ἐπὶ τὸ ἄκρον τῆς κλίνης Symm.).

But at the same time the Masoretic text describes an act of adoration, and not simply a sinking back in exhaustion. A close parallel occurs in 1 K. i. 47 προσεκύνησεν ὁ βασιλεὺς ἐπὶ τὴν κοίτην. Προσκυνεῖν is to be taken absolutely, 'bowed himself in worship, i.e. to God': compare Apoc. v. 14; John iv. 20; xii. 20; Acts viii. 27; xxiv. 11.

The connexion of προσκυνεῖν with ἐπὶ τὸ ἄκρον τῆς ῥάβδου αὐτοῦ as the object of the adoration (Vulg. virgæ ejus, i.e. the staff of Joseph) is against usage. When προσκυνεῖν is used with ἐπί it appears to be always in a local connexion (ἐπὶ τὴν γῆν, ἐπὶ πρόσωπον, ἐπὶ τὰ δώματα, Zeph. i. 5).

Not less unnatural is the notion that Joseph was the object of this 'worship,' being so marked out as the head of the family; though this view is very commonly held by patristic writers. So Chrysostom: ἐπειδὴ ἔμελλεν ἀπὸ τοῦ Ἐφραῒμ ἀνίστασθαι βασιλεὺς ἕτερος διὰ τοῦτό φησι· καὶ προσεκύνησεν ἐπὶ τὸ ἄκρον τῆς ῥάβδου αὐτοῦ· τουτέστι καὶ γέρων ὢν ἤδη προσεκύνει τῷ Ἰωσήφ, τὴν παντὸς τοῦ λαοῦ προσκύνησιν δηλῶν τὴν ἐσομένην αὐτῷ (so also Theodoret, Œcumenius, Theophylact). Primasius follows out the thought more in detail, giving at the same time an alternative interpretation: Spiritu siquidem prophetico afflatus Jacob cognovit designari per illam virgam Joseph regnum Christi, per fastigium vero, id est, summitatem virgæ, potentiam et honorem Christi regni, de qua Psalmista dicit: Virga recta est virga regni tui.... Quantum vero ad litteram pertinet, fortassis...adoravit virgam

τελευτῶν περὶ τῆς ἐξόδου τῶν υἱῶν Ἰσραὴλ ἐμνημόνευσεν,
καὶ περὶ τῶν ὀστέων αὐτοῦ ἐνετείλατο.   ²³ Πίστει

Joseph, quem videbat dominum esse totius regni terræ Ægypti; ea scilicet ratione Esther legitur adorasse virgam Assueri.

Such an application of the image of 'the staff' to the Messiah is found also in Rabbinic writers: *Beresh. R.* Gen. xxxviii. 18 with references to Is. xi. 1; Ps. cx. 2.

It may be added that Jerome distinctly condemns this use which was made of the Latin rendering: in hoc loco (Gen. xlvii. 31) quidam frustra simulant adorasse Jacob summitatem sceptri Joseph, quod videlicet honorans filium potestatem ejus adoraverit, cum in Hebræo multo aliter legatur: *et adoravit*, inquit, *Israel ad caput lectuli;* quod scilicet postquam ei juraverat filius securus de petitione quam rogaverat, adoraverit Deum contra caput lectuli sui, *Quæst. Hebr. in Gen.* ad loc. (Vulg. *adoravit Israel Deum conversus ad lectuli caput*).

The 'staff,' 'rod,' played an important part in Jewish tradition. It was one of the ten things created 'between the Suns,' before the first Sabbath (*Aboth*, v. 9 with Dr Taylor's note). It was given to Adam, and transmitted through Enoch, Noah, Shem, Abraham,...Joseph to Moses, and is still reserved for Messiah. Comp. Wetstein *ad loc.*

(γ) The world abandoned (23).

The death of Joseph marked a third stage in the history of the promise. He made clear in the fulness of his prosperity that those whom he had invited to Egypt were not to find there an abiding home. Neither rest nor misery was to bring forgetfulness of their destiny.

22. π. Ἰ. τελ. περὶ τῆς ἐξ....καὶ περὶ τ. ὀ....] Gen. l. The Faith of Joseph was national at once and personal. He looked forward to the independence of his kindred; and he claimed

for himself a share in their future. His prosperity in Egypt had not led him to forget ·the promise to Abraham. The personal charge was fulfilled: Ex. xiii. 19; Josh. xxiv. 32.

The word τελευτῶν (*when his end was nigh*) is taken from the LXX. Gen. l. 26. For ἐμνημόνευσεν (*made mention of*...Gen. l. 24) see *v.* 15 note.

Ἔξοδος occurs again Lk. ix. 31 (of Christ); 2 Pet. i. 15 (of St Peter).

The phrase οἱ υἱοὶ Ἰσραήλ is not of frequent occurrence in the N. T. In addition to the places where it occurs in references to the LXX. (Matt. xxvii. 9; Acts vii. 23; Rom. ix. 27) it is found in Lk. i. 16; Acts v. 21; vii. 37; ix. 15; x. 36; 2 Cor. iii. 7, 13; Apoc. ii. 14; vii. 4; xxi. 12.

(4) 23—31. The Faith of Conflict and Conquest.

The Faith which has been hitherto regarded under the discipline of patience and sacrifice is now considered in action. Under this aspect it is traced both (*a*) in the great leader, Moses (23—28), and (*b*) in the people whom he led (29—31).

(*a*) The Faith of Moses the leader of Israel (23—28).

Moses 'the first Redeemer,' like Abraham 'the father of the faithful,' is treated at some length. His Faith is shewn (*a*) in its personal (23—26) and (β) in its public working (27, 28).

²³ *By faith Moses, when he was born, was hidden for three months by his parents, because they saw the child was goodly* to look on; *and they feared not the king's order.*

²⁴ *By faith Moses, when he was grown up, refused to be called son of Pharaoh's daughter,* ²⁵ *choosing rather to be evil entreated with the people of God than to have enjoyment of sin for a season,* ²⁶ *since he counted*

Μωυσῆς γεννηθεὶς ἐκρύβη τρίμηνον ὑπὸ τῶν πατέρων
αὐτοῦ, διότι εἶδον ἀστεῖον τὸ παιδίον καὶ οὐκ ἐφοβήθησαν
τὸ διάταγμα τοῦ βασιλέως. ²⁴Πίστει Μωυσῆς μέγας
γενόμενος ἠρνήσατο λέγεσθαι υἱὸς θυγατρὸς Φαραώ,
²⁵ μᾶλλον ἑλόμενος συνκακουχεῖσθαι τῷ λαῷ τοῦ θεοῦ ἢ

23 διάταγμα: δόγμα Α (?). βασιλέως: +πίστι μέγας γενόμενος Μωυσῆς
ἀνἵλεν τὸν Αἰγύπτιον κατανοῶν τὴν ταπίνωσιν τῶν ἀδελφῶν αὐτοῦ D₂* (latt).

the reproach of the Christ greater
riches than the treasures of Egypt;
for he looked unto the recompense
of reward.

²⁷ By faith he left Egypt, not fearing
the wrath of the king; for he endured
as seeing Him who is invisible.

²⁸ By faith he kept (he hath kept)
the Passover and the sprinkling of
the blood, that he who destroyed the
firstborn should not touch them.

(a) 23—26. The Faith of Moses
was prepared, as it were, by the
Faith which he called out in his
parents (23). When the time came
his choice shewed his own Faith (24
—26).

23. π. Μ....ὑπὸ τῶν πατέρων αὐτοῦ]
In Ex. ii. 2 (Hebr.) the mother of
Moses only is mentioned as concealing
the child; but the LXX. renders the
text ἰδόντες αὐτὸ ἀστεῖον ἐσκέπασαν.
There is no ground for supposing
that the reference is to Kohath and
Amram to the exclusion of Jochebed.
The general term (Vulg. a parentibus
suis) marks, so to speak, the social
character of the faith; and οἱ πατέρες
(like patres) is used in the same
sense as οἱ γονεῖς (Lk. ii. 27, 41 ff.;
John ix. 2 ff.).

διότι...τοῦ βασιλέως] Faith under
two forms moved the parents of
Moses to preserve him. Something
in his appearance kindled hope as to
his destiny; and then looking to God
for the fulfilment of His promise they
had no fear of the king's orders.

The word ἀστεῖος (Vulg. elegans)
occurs in this connexion Ex. ii. 2

(LXX.); Acts vii. 20; (Jud. iii. 17;
Judith xi. 23). Compare Philo, de
vit. Mos. i. § 3 (ii. 82) γεννηθεὶς οὖν ὁ
παῖς εὐθὺς ὄψιν ἐνέφηνεν ἀστειοτέραν ἢ
κατ᾽ ἰδιώτην ὡς καὶ τῶν τοῦ τυράννου
κηρυγμάτων ἐφ᾽ ὅσον οἷόν τ᾽ ἦν τοὺς
γονεῖς ἀλογῆσαι. De conf. ling. § 22
(i. p. 420 M.).

The word διάταγμα occurs here only
in the N. T.

24. μέγας γενόμενος] when he was
grown up (Ex. ii. 11), in contrast with
γεννηθείς (Vulg. grandis factus). As
an infant he had quickened faith: as
a man he shewed it.

ἠρνήσατο...] The tenses ἠρνήσατο...
ἑλόμενος...ἡγησάμενος... point to a
crisis when the choice was made, as
distinct from Moses' habitual spirit
(ἀπέβλεπεν).

On ἠρνήσατο Œcumenius says, τὸ
μετὰ σπουδῆς ἀλλοτριῶσαι ἑαυτὸν δηλοῖ.
The use of λέγεσθαι (as distinguished
from καλεῖσθαι, κληθῆναι) marks the
habitual language of familiar intercourse.

υἱὸς θυγ. Φαρ.] The anarthrous form
is significant (not τῆς θυγ.): son of
a royal princess, of one who was
Pharaoh's daughter. Comp. Euseb.
Præp. Ev. ix. 27.

25. μᾶλλον ἑλόμενος...ἀπόλαυσιν]
choosing rather to be evil entreated...
than to have enjoyment of sin for a
season. Vulg. magis eligens adfligi...
quam temporalis peccati habere ju-
cunditatem. Moses was called to
devote himself to his people. He
knew the source of the call: to have
disobeyed it therefore by seeking to

πρόσκαιρον ἔχειν ἁμαρτίας ἀπόλαυσιν, ²⁶μείζονα πλοῦ-
τον ἡγησάμενος τῶν Αἰγύπτου θησαυρῶν τὸν ὀνειδιϲμὸν
τοῦ χριϲτοῦ, ἀπέβλεπεν γὰρ εἰς τὴν μισθαποδοσίαν.

26 Αἰγύπτου אD₂ syrr me: ἐν Αἰγύπτου A: ἐν Αἰγύπτῳ ϛ.

retain his place in the Egyptian court
would have been 'sin,' though such
disloyalty would have given him the
opportunity for a transitory enjoyment of the resources of princely
state.

The word συνκακουχεῖσθαι, which is
classical, is found here only in the
N. T. Compare κακουχεῖσθαι v. 37;
c. xiii. 3.

τῷ λαῷ τοῦ θεοῦ] Compare iv. 9
note. Moses was able to recognise
in a host of bondsmen a divine nation.
By faith he saw what they were called
to be.

ἁμαρτ. ἀπόλαυσιν] enjoyment of sin,
that is of that life which was sin.
The gen. ἁμαρτίας is the direct object
of ἀπόλαυσις, though ἀπόλαυσις may
be used absolutely, and ἁμαρτίας characterise it ('sinful enjoyment'). 'Από-
λαυσις, which is not found in LXX.,
occurs again in 1 Tim. vi. 17. Comp.
2 Clem. x. προῃρημένοι μᾶλλον τὴν ἐν-
θάδε ἀπόλαυσιν ἢ τὴν μέλλουσαν ἐπαγγελίαν.

For the order πρόσκ. ἔχειν ἁμαρτ.
ἀπ. compare c. vi. 5 καλὸν γευσ. θ. ῥ.;
and for πρόσκαιρος see Mt. xiii. 21;
2 Cor. iv. 18.

Ὅρα δὲ πῶς ἁμαρτίαν ὀνομάζει τὸ μὴ
συγκακουχεῖσθαι τοῖς ἀδελφοῖς...εἰ δὲ
οἱ μὴ συγκακουχούμενοι ἑκόντες τοῖς
κακοπαθοῦσιν ἁμαρτάνουσι, τί λογιστέον
περὶ τῶν κακουχούντων καὶ κακοποιούν-
των; (Theophlct).

26. μ. π. ἡγησ....τοῦ χριστοῦ] since
he counted the reproach of the
Christ..., Vulg. majores divitias œsti-
mans...inproperium Christi. This
clause is commonly taken as parallel
with that which precedes: μᾶλλον
ἑλόμενος...μείζ. πλ. ἡγησ. (choosing...
accounting...), but it seems rather to

give the ground of the choice: 'choosing rather...since he accounted...'

The reproach of the Christ is the
reproach which belongs to Him who
is the appointed envoy of God to a
rebellious world. This reproach which
was endured in the highest degree
by Christ Jesus (Rom. xv. 3) was
endured also by those who in any
degree prefigured or represented Him,
those, that is, in whom He partially
manifested and manifests Himself,
those who live in Him and in whom
He lives. Comp. Bern. Ep. xcviii. § 4.

In this wider sense the people of
Israel was 'an anointed one,' 'a
Christ,' even as Christians are 'Christs'
(comp. Ps. cv. 15; 1 John ii. 20). 'The
Christ' is the support and the spring
of all revelation to men (1 Cor. x. 4).
For the general thought compare
Ps. lxxxix. 50 f.; lxix. 9; 2 Cor. i. 5;
Col. i. 24; c. xiii. 13.

Chrysostom takes the τοῦ χριστοῦ
as defining the nature of the sufferings: τοῦτό ἐστιν [ὁ] ὀνειδισμὸς τοῦ
χριστοῦ, τὸ μέχρι τέλους καὶ ἐσχάτης
ἀναπνοῆς πάσχειν κακῶς...ὅταν τις παρὰ
οἰκείων, ὅταν τις παρ' ὧν εὐεργετεῖ
ὀνειδίζηται...

ἀπέβλεπεν γάρ...] Vulg. aspiciebat
enim in remunerationem, for he
continued to look away from the
things of earth unto the (divine)
recompense for suffering (συνκακουχεῖσθαι) and reproach (ὀνειδισμός).

The nature of this recompense,
though it is definite, is left undefined (v. 6). It must not be limited
to the future occupation of Canaan
by the people. The fulfilment of
God's counsel includes blessings which
man cannot anticipate: 1 Cor. ii. 9
(Is. lxiv. 4).

²⁷ Πίστει κατέλιπεν Αἴγυπτον, μὴ φοβηθεὶς τὸν θυμὸν
τοῦ βασιλέως, τὸν γὰρ ἀόρατον ὡς ὁρῶν ἐκαρτέρησεν.

27 κατέλιπεν אD₂: -έλειπεν A.

For μισθαποδοσία see c. ii. 2 note.
'Αποβλέπειν occurs here only in
N. T. Compare ἀφορᾶν c. xii. 2. The
word occurs in the same sense of
'looking away from one object to
another' in classical writers (Plato,
Xen., Dem.). Philo, de mund. opif.
§ 4 (i. p. 4 M.) ἀποβλέπων εἰς τὸ
παράδειγμα (of the builder).
For the choice of Moses compare
Philo de vit. Mos. i. § 7 (ii. 85 f. M.).
(β) 27, 28. The work of Moses.
27. π. κατέλιπεν Αἴγυπτον...] It is
doubtful to what event reference is
made. From the order in which the
fact is mentioned, and from the manner in which it is described (κατέλιπεν
as contrasted with διέβησαν) it has
been concluded that the reference is
to the flight of Moses to Midian,
which could be rightly spoken of as a
'leaving' since it involved the temporary abandonment of the work to
which Moses had felt himself called.
Nor is it a fatal objection to this view
that in the narrative of Exodus it is
said that 'Moses was afraid' (Ex. ii.
14), though the superficial contradiction has occasioned some difficulty.
If this interpretation be adopted
the exact thought will be that Moses
was not afraid of the anger of the
king in itself. For the sake of his
people he could have braved death;
but, though he was so far fearless, yet
the lack of faith in those whom he
would have delivered (Acts vii. 23 ff.)
forced him to retire: 'He left Egypt
though he feared not the wrath of
the king.' This he did 'by faith,' for
even at the moment when he gave up
his work he felt the divine presence
with him. 'He endured (ἐκαρτέρησεν
not ἐκαρτέρει) as seeing Him who is
invisible.'
Philo gives this general interpreta-

tion of the flight to Midian: οὐ φεύγει
Μωυσῆς ἀπὸ τοῦ Φαραώ, ἀνεπιστρεπτὶ
γὰρ ἂν ἀπεδίδρασκεν, ἀλλὰ ἀναχωρεῖ,
τουτέστιν ἀνακωχὴν ποιεῖται τοῦ πολέμου ἀθλητοῦ τρόπον διαπνέοντος καὶ
συλλεγομένου τὸ πνεῦμα (Leg. Alleg.
iii. § 4; i. p. 90 M.).
Theodoret gives a different explanation of μὴ φοβηθείς: τὴν μὲν
Αἴγυπτον φοβηθεὶς κατέλιπε, θαρσαλέως
δὲ τὸν Αἰγύπτιον κατηκόντισε. τὴν
φυγὴν τοίνυν ἀντὶ τῆς αἰτίας τέθεικε τῆς
φυγῆς.
It is however more likely that the
words refer to the Exodus. Moses,
the leader of the people, left the safe
though servile shelter and support of
Egypt, casting himself on the protection of the unseen God against the
certain vengeance of the king in the
fulfilment of his arduous and self-
sacrificing work. Comp. Philo, de
vit. M. i. § 27 (ii. p. 104 M.). τὴν
Αἴγυπτον κατέλιπεν ἡγεμονίαν, θυγα-
τριδοῦς τοῦ τότε βασιλεύοντος ὤν...
Jos. Antt. ii. 15, 2. The change of
tenses, κατέλιπεν, πεποίηκεν, helps to
explain the historical transposition.
τὸν γὰρ ἀόρ....ἐκαρτέρησεν] The most
characteristic trait in the life of Moses
is that he spoke with God face to
face, Ex. xxxiii.; Num. xii. 7, 8. The
'vision of God' is that which distinguishes him from the other prophets.
Compare Philo de mut. nom. § 2 (i. p.
579 M.) Μωυσῆς οὖν ὁ τῆς ἀειδοῦς
φύσεως θεατὴς καὶ θεόπτης, εἰς γὰρ τὸν
γνόφον (Ex. xx. 21) φασὶν αὐτὸν οἱ
χρησμοὶ εἰσελθεῖν, τὴν ἀόρατον οὐσίαν
αἰνιττόμενοι...; de vit. M. i. § 28 (ii. p.
106 M.).
The words ὡς ὁρῶν are in themselves
ambiguous. They may mean either
'as though he saw,' or 'inasmuch as
he saw.' The peculiar gift of Moses
determines that the latter is the

²⁸ Πίστει πεποίηκεν τὸ πάϲχα καὶ τὴν πρόϲχυϲιν τοῦ αἵματοϲ, ἵνα μὴ ὁ ὀλοθρεγων τὰ πρωτότοκα θίγῃ αὐτῶν.   ²⁹ Πίστει

28 ὀλοθρεύων ℵ: ὀλεθρεύων AD₂.

sense here. The irregular position of the ὡς is due to the emphasis laid on τὸν ἀόρατον.

For ὁ ἀόρατος compare Col. i. 15 (ὁ θεὸς ὁ ἀόρατος); 1 Tim. i. 17 (ἀόρατος μόνος θεός); 1 John iv. 20; John i. 18; 1 Tim. vi. 16.

The word καρτερεῖν occurs here only in N. T. Comp. Jos. *Antt.* ii. 11, 1; Ecclus. ii. 2; xii. 15.

The idea of καρτερεῖν is complementary to the ideas of ὑπομένειν (c. x. 32) and μακροθυμεῖν (c. vi. 15). The Christian has not only to bear his burden in the conflict of life, and to wait for the fulfilment of the promise which seems to be strangely delayed: he must also bear himself valiantly and do his work with might through the Spirit (1 Cor. xvi. 13; Eph. iii. 16).

Augustine in striking words extends to the people the gift of the leader: Errabant quidem adhuc et patriam quærebant; sed duce Christo errare non poterant. Via illis fuit visio Dei (ad 1 Joh. *Tract.* 7).

28. π. πεποί. τὸ π....αἶμ.] *By faith he kept (he hath kept) the Passover and the sprinkling of the blood....* The first celebration of the Passover was not only a single act. The Passover then instituted and kept remained as a perpetual witness of the great deliverance. For the *perf.* see c. vii. 6 note. The sacrifice of the lamb and the open sprinkling of the blood was a signal act of faith challenging the superstition of the Egyptians (Ex. viii. 22). Compare *Midr. Shemoth R. l. c.* (Wünsche, p. 132).

The phrase ποιεῖν τὸ πάσχα (Matt. xxvi. 18) is not unfrequent in the LXX. for the observance of the Passover (Ex. xii. 48; Num. ix. 2 ff.; 2 K. xxiii. 21 &c.). It does not appear to be used of the institution.

The special ceremony of 'the sprinkling of the blood' (Ex. xii. 7, 22 f.) is mentioned as foreshadowing the deeper mystery involved in the deliverance from Egypt (c. ix. 22).

The word πρόσχυσις is not found in the LXX. and occurs here only in N. T. (πρ. αἷμ. ἐκάλεσε τὴν κατὰ τῶν φλιῶν τῶν θυρῶν χρίσιν Œcum.). But the verb προσχέω is commonly used in the LXX. of the sprinkling of blood upon the altar (זָרַק).

ἵνα μὴ ὁ ὀλ....αὐτῶν] The phrase ὁ ὀλοθρεύων (Vulg. *qui vastabat [primitiva]*) is used in Ex. xii. 23 by the LXX. for הַמַּשְׁחִית according to the strict participial sense. The translators realised the action of God through a destroying angel: 1 Cor. x. 10 (ὁ ὀλοθρευτής); and this seems to be the most natural sense of the original text. Compare 1 Chron. xxi. 12, 15; 2 Chron. xxxii. 21; Ecclus. xlviii. 21; Ps. lxxviii. 49.

θίγῃ αὐτῶν] The object is naturally supplied by the reader.

Primasius sees a foreshadowing of Christian practice in the detail: Sanguine agni illinuntur Israelitarum postes ne vastator angelus audeat inferre mortem: signantur dominicæ mortis signo fideles populi in frontibus ad tutelam salutis ut ab interitu liberentur.

(*b*) The Faith of the people (29—31).

The great leader, like Abraham, communicated to others the Faith by which he was inspired. Just as the Faith of Abraham was united with that of his wife and of his children, so the Faith of Moses was bound up with that of Israel. By Faith they overcame difficulties of nature (29), and the force of enemies (30); and

διέβησαν τὴν Ἐρυθρὰν Θάλασσαν ὡς διὰ ξηρᾶς γῆς, ἧς πεῖραν λαβόντες οἱ Αἰγύπτιοι κατεπόθησαν. ³⁰ Πίστει τὰ τείχη Ἱερειχὼ ἔπεσαν κυκλωθέντα ἐπὶ ἑπτὰ ἡμέρας. ³¹ Πίστει Ῥαὰβ ἡ πόρνη οὐ συναπώλετο τοῖς ἀπειθή-

29 διὰ ξηρᾶς γῆς ℵAD₂* vg syr vg me: om. γῆς ⸝ (LXX.).   30 ἔπεσαν : -εν ⸝.   31 ἡ πόρνη : ἡ ἐπιλεγομένη π. ℵ*.

called out responsive Faith even in aliens, so that a remnant of them was saved (31).

²⁹ *By faith they passed over the Red Sea as by dry land, which the Egyptians essaying to do were swallowed up.*
³⁰ *By faith the walls of Jericho fell, after they had been compassed for seven days.*
³¹ *By faith Rahab the harlot perished not with them that were disobedient, having received the spies with peace.*

29. διέβησαν] The subject has already been suggested by αὐτῶν (v. 28). The Faith of the people met the Faith of the leader. Theophylact rightly marks the importance of the transition : ἵνα μὴ λέγωσι Τί φέρεις εἰς μέσον ἀμιμήτους ἄνδρας; ἤγαγε καὶ λαὸν εἰς ὑπόδειγμα.

Compare Ps. cvi. 9 ff.; cxiv. 5; Is. xliii. 16; li. 10.

The word διαβαίνειν is found in N. T. also in Lk. xvi. 26; Acts xvi. 9. Ἡ ἐρ. θάλ., the LXX. rendering of יַם סוּף 'the sea of weed,' occurs again Acts vii. 36.

ἧς π. λαβόντες] Vulg. *quod experti, which essaying to do,* literally 'of which (*i.e.* sea) making trial.' Κατεπόθησαν Ex. xv. 12 (LXX.) : Num. xvi. 30. Καταπίνω is found not unfrequently in N. T. in a metaphorical sense: *e.g.* 1 Cor. xv. 54; 1 Pet. v. 8.

30. πίστει...ἔπεσαν] Josh. vi. The walls fell overthrown by faith which was shewn through a long trial by leader, priests and people.

The fall of the walls of Jericho is

the symbol of the victory of the Church : Matt. xvi. 18.

31. πίστει Ῥαάβ...] The record of the separation of the people of God from Egypt is closed by the incorporation of a stranger.

Rahab at once looked forward with confidence to the triumph of Israel : Josh. ii. 9. Comp. James ii. 25; Clem. R. i. 12 (διὰ πίστιν καὶ φιλοξενίαν ἐσώθη). Midr. Bemidbar R. 8 (on Num. v. 9; Wünsche, p. 136), (the ancestress of priests and prophets).

The addition of the title ἡ πόρνη places in a fuller light the triumph of Faith.

The list of the champions of Faith whose victories are specially noticed is closed by a woman and a gentile and an outcast. In this there is a significant foreshadowing of its essential universality. So Theodoret : θαυμάσαι δὲ ἄξιον τὴν ἀποστολικὴν σοφίαν, μᾶλλον δὲ ὑμνῆσαι προσήκει τοῦ θείου πνεύματος τὴν ἐνέργειαν, ὅτι τῷ Μωϋσεῖ...καὶ τοῖς ἄλλοις ἁγίοις ἀλλόφυλον γυναῖκα καὶ πόρνην συνέταξεν, ἵνα καὶ τῆς πίστεως ἐπιδείξῃ τὴν δύναμιν καὶ καταστείλῃ τὴν Ἰουδαίων ὀφρύν.

οὐ συναπ. τ. ἀπειθ.] *perished not with them that were disobedient,* Vulg. *non periit cum incredulis.* The form of expression places in relief the punishment of the disobedient; and the ground of their destruction. They too had heard of the wonders which God had wrought for His people and were not moved by them to submission.

For ἀπειθεῖν (of which the force is lost by the Latin Vulgate) see John iii. 36; Rom. ii. 8; c. iii. 18 note.

σασιν, δεξαμένη τοὺς κατασκόπους μετ᾽ εἰρήνης. ³²Καὶ
τί ἔτι λέγω; ἐπιλείψει με γὰρ διηγούμενον ὁ χρόνος
περὶ Γεδεών, Βαράκ, Σαμψών, Ἰεφθάε, Δαυεὶδ τε καὶ

32 om. ἔτι D₂*.   ἐπιλ. με γὰρ אAD₂*: ἐπιλ. γάρ με ς.   περὶ δὲ
Γεδεών D₂*.   Βαράκ אA vg me: καὶ B. D₂* syr vg: B. τε ς.   Σαμψών
Ἰεφθάε אA vg me : καὶ Σ. καὶ Ἰ. ς D₂ syr vg.

(5) 32—38. Faith in national life.
The entrance to Canaan and the
representative victory at Jericho
forms a close to a complete cycle of
divine discipline. The history of
Israel from the Call of Abraham to
the occupation of the Promised Land
offers a type of the religious history
of man. So far then the writer of
the Epistle has given examples of
faith in detail. From this point he
simply recites in a summary form the
names and exploits of later heroes of
Faith. In part (a) they wrought
great things (32—35 a): in part (b)
they suffered great things (35 b—38).
The enumeration extends to the
time of the Maccabees, the last decisive national struggle of the Jews
before the coming of Christ.

(a) The victorious successes of
Faith : the great things which it has
wrought (32—35 a).

³²And what can I (why do I) say
more? For the time will fail me as
I tell of Gideon, Barak, Samson,
Jephthah ; of David and Samuel
and of the prophets : ³³who through
faith subdued kingdoms, wrought
righteousness, obtained promises,
stopped the mouths of lions, ³⁴quench-
ed the power of fire, escaped the edge
of the sword, from weakness were
made strong, proved mighty in war,
turned to flight armies of aliens.
³⁵Women received their dead by a
resurrection.

The summary recital of these outward successes of Faith consists first
(a) of two groups of names, which
represent the theocracy and the kingdom (v. 32); and then (β) of a descrip-

tion of the chief types of victory (33—
35 a).

(a) Representative heroes of the
theocracy and the kingdom (32).

32. καὶ τί...] Vulg. et quid adhuc
dicam (dico d)? The verb may be
conj. And what shall I more say ? or
indic. And why (or what) say I more?
The sense seems to be 'Why do I go
on farther ?' 'What can I say more ?'
as if the writer saw already stretching
before him the long record on which
he is entering. The pres. indic. occurs Matt. xxvi. 65, and in John xi.
47 with τί as the object ; and the
pres. conj. occurs John vi. 28 : the
aor. conj. is common: Acts ii. 37 ;
vi. 16 &c.

ἐπιλ. διηγ. ὁ χρ....] time will (I see)
fail me as I tell of... Vulg. deficiet
me tempus enarrantem.... Ποῖος ;
ἢ ὁ πᾶς· εἴρηται δὲ τοῦτο ὡς σύνηθες
ἡμῖν ὑπερβολικῶς· ἢ ὁ τῇ ἐπιστολῇ
σύμμετρος (Theophlct).

The phrase is common in classical
literature: ἐπιλείποι δ᾽ ἄν με πᾶς χρόνος
εἰ ἐκτίθεσθαι βουληθείην τὰς σεμνὰς τῶν
φιλοσόφων μέμψεις (Athenæ. v. § 63,
p. 220 F): tempus hercule te citius
quam oratio deficeret (Cic. pro Sext.
Rosc. 32 § 89). Philo de somn. § 9 (ii.
667) ἐπιλείψει με ἡ ἡμέρα τὰς διαφορὰς
τοῦ ἀνθρωπείου βίου διεξιόντα. καίτοι
τί δεῖ μακρηγορεῖν ; τίς γὰρ αὐτῶν ἀνή-
κοός ἐστι ;

The persons are named first, and
then types of achievement. The persons fall into two groups, the representatives of the theocracy and the
representatives of the monarchy.

Γεδ. Βαρ. Σαμψ. Ἰεφθ.] These representative heroes of the theocracy are

Σαμουὴλ καὶ τῶν προφητῶν, ³³ οἳ διὰ πίστεως κατηγωνίσαντο βασιλείας, ἠργάσαντο δικαιοσύνην, ἐπέτυχον

33 δικαιοσύνη D₂*.

not given in the order of the Book of
Judges, but apparently according to
their popular fame. Records of their
exploits are preserved : Judg. vi.—
viii. (Gideon); iv. v. (Barak); xiii.—
xvi. (Samson); xi. xii. (Jephthah).

It may be noticed that they overcame different enemies, Midianites,
Canaanites, Philistines, Ammonites;
and in referring to them the writer
passes no judgment on character : οὐ
βίων ἐξέτασιν ποιεῖται ἀλλὰ πίστεως
ἔνδειξιν (Theophlct).

Δαυ. τε κ. Σαμ. κ. τ. πρ.] The great
king and the great statesman-prophet
sum up all that was noblest in the
second stage of the divine history of
Israel. With them are joined the
spiritual leaders of the people through
whom the growing counsel of God
was interpreted through apparent
failure and loss. David and Samuel
appear to be closely connected (τε,
καί) and the prophets are added as
a second element.

(β) Characteristic achievements of
Faith (33—35 a).

The Judges, the Kings, and the
Prophets represent adequately the
chief types of believers under the
theocracy and the kingdom. Having
signalised these, the writer goes on to
mark the characteristic manifestations
of the power of Faith. These are
described with remarkable symmetry :

(i) κατηγωνίσαντο βασιλείας,
 ἠργάσαντο δικαιοσύνην,
 ἐπέτυχον ἐπαγγελιῶν.

(ii) ἔφραξαν στόματα λεόντων,
 ἔσβεσαν δύναμιν πυρός,
 ἔφυγον στόματα μαχαίρης.

(iii) ἐδυναμώθησαν ἀπὸ ἀσθενείας,
 ἐγενήθησαν ἰσχυροὶ ἐν πολέμῳ,
 παρεμβολὰς ἔκλιναν ἀλλοτρίων.

In each group there is a progress,

and there is a progress in the succession of groups in the direction of that
which is more personal.

33. The first triplet describes the
broad results which believers obtained:
 Material victory.
 Moral success in government.
 Spiritual reward.
The second triplet notices forms of
personal deliverance from :
 Wild beasts.
 Physical forces.
 Human tyranny.
The third triplet marks the attain-
ment of personal gifts :
 Strength.
 The exercise of strength.
 The triumph of strength (the be-
liever against the alien).

οἱ διὰ πίστεως...] The form πίστει
which has been used before is now
changed. The writer speaks of the
general inspiring power of faith: c. vi.
12. Compare v. 39 διὰ τῆς πίστεως.

κατηγωνίσαντο βασιλείας] For example Gideon (Midianites), Jud. vii.;
Barak (Canaanites), Jud. iv.; Samson
(Philistines), Jud. xiv. f.; Jephthah
(Ammonites), Jud. xi. ; Jonathan (Philistines), 1 Sam. xiy. 6 ff.; David (Philistines), 2 Sam. v. 17 ; (Moabites &c.)
2 Sam. viii. 2 ; (Ammonites) 2 Sam. x.
12 ; in each case with weaker forces
than their enemies.

ἠργάσαντο δικαιοσ.] The phrase is to
be understood not only of purely individual virtues, but of the virtues of
leaders : 1 Sam. xii. 4 ; 2 Sam. viii.
15 ; Ps. xiv. [xv.] 2 ; Zephan. ii. 3.
Conquerors used their success for the
furtherance of right. Righteousness
was shewn to be the solid foundation
of enduring power : Is. ix. 7 ; liv. 14 ;
1 K. x. 9.

For the phrase ἐργάζ. δικαιοσύνην

ἐπαγγελιῶν, ἔφραξαν στόματα λεόντων, ³⁴ἔσβεσαν δύναμιν πυρός, ἔφυγον στόματα μαχαίρης, ἐδυναμώθησαν
ἀπὸ ἀσθενείας, ἐγενήθησαν ἰσχυροὶ ἐν πολέμῳ, παρεμβολὰς ἔκλιναν ἀλλοτρίων· ³⁵ἔλαβον γυναῖκες ἐξ ἀνα-

33 στόμα D₂*.   34 ἐδυναμώθησαν א*AD₂*: ἐνεδ. ϛ אᶜ.   35 γυναῖκες אᶜ:
γυναῖκας א*AD₂* me.

compare Acts x. 35; (James i. 20);
Matt. vii. 23 (ἀνομίαν); James ii. 9
(ἁμαρτίαν).

ἐπέτυχον ἐπαγγελιῶν] Victory was
gained and rightly used in just government, and so it was followed by a
deeper apprehension of the will of
God. The phrase ἐπιτυχεῖν ἐπαγγελιῶν has been noticed before, c. vi. 15
note.

It appears to be used here in the
most general sense, which includes
both the attainment of that which
had been already promised, and the
quickened expectation of something
yet to come. Each partial fulfilment
of a divine word is itself a prophecy.
A promise gained is also a promise
interpreted in a larger meaning. Here
the truth is set out in its fulness. The
many 'promises' successively realised
in many parts and many fashions led
up to the one 'promise' (v. 39) which
is still held before the eye of faith.

33 b, 34 a. The notice of public,
general, successes is followed by the
notice of personal deliverances.

ἔφραξαν στ. λ.] Dan. vi. 22 ἐνέφραξε
τὰ στόματα τῶν λεόντων Theod. (Daniel); 1 Macc. ii. 60. There may also
be a reference to Jud. xiv. 6 (Samson);
1 Sam. xvii. 34 (David).

ἔσβεσαν δύν. π.] Dan. iii.; 1 Macc. ii.
59. The natural force of the elements
was overpowered (comp. Wisd. xix.
6). οὐκ εἶπεν ἔσβεσαν πῦρ, ἀλλὰ Δύναμιν πυρός, ὃ καὶ μεῖζον (Theophlct).

ἔφυγον στ. μαχ.] Ex. xviii. 4 (Moses).
1 Sam. xviii. 11; xix. 10 ff.; xxi. 10;
Ps. cxliv. 10 (David); 1 K. xix. 1 ff.
(Elijah); 2 K. vi. (Elisha).

The phrase ἐν στόματι μαχαίρας (ῥομ-

φαίας, ξίφους) (לְפִי־חָרֶב) is not uncommon in the LXX. (Gen. xxxiv. 26).
The plural (στόματα), which does not
appear to occur elsewhere, expresses
the many assaults of human violence
answering in part to στόματα λεόντων.

34 b. Examples of deliverance from
external perils are followed by examples of personal strengthening.

ἐδυναμ. ἀπὸ ἀσθ.] This general
phrase may be interpreted of various
forms of physical weakness as in the
case of Samson (Jud. xvi. 28 ff.); Hezekiah (Is. xxxviii.); and of moral distress (Ps. vi. 3, 8; Ps. xxii. 21 f.). For
ἀπὸ ἀσθενείας compare Luke v. 15;
viii. 2; and contrast 2 Cor. xiii. 4
ἐξ ἀσθενείας.

ἐγεν. ἰσχ. ἐν π.] waxed mighty in
war, not only in the moment of battle,
but in the whole conduct of the conflict. Ps. xviii. 34 ff.; cxliv. 1 f. For
ἰσχυροί compare Luke xi. 21 f.

παρεμβ. ἔκλ. ἀλλ.] The addition of
ἀλλοτρίων distinguishes this clause
from κατηγωνίσαντο βασιλείας and fixes
the thought here on the religious contrast between the children of the
kingdom and strangers (Matt. xvii. 25
f.). This sense of κλίνειν (inclinare
aciem), which is found in classical
Greek from Homer downwards, does
not occur elsewhere in the N. T. or
LXX.

The word παρεμβολή (like מַחֲנֶה,
which it represents in the LXX.) is
used for an armed force as well as for
a camp, the position which it occupies:
Jud. iv. 16; viii. 10; Ezek. i. 24 (A);
1 Macc. v. 28.

35 a. The triple triplet of victorious
faith is followed by a single, abrupt

στάσεως τοὺς νεκροὺς αὐτῶν· ἄλλοι δὲ ἐτυμπανίσθησαν,

ἀπετυνπ. D₂*.

clause which presents the highest conquest of faith, 'women received from
resurrection their dead.' In this
case faith appears under a twofold
aspect. There is a silent, waiting,
passive faith of love, which works with
the active faith. Women, in whom the
instinct of natural affection is strongest,
cooperated with the prophets through
whom the restoration was effected.
They received their dead. The word
λαβεῖν occurs in the narrative of the
Shunamite : 2 K. iv. 36.

It cannot be without significance
that the recorded raisings from the
dead are predominantly for women :
1 K. xvii. 17 ff.; 2 K. iv. 17 ff.; Luke
vii. 11 ff.; John xi.; Acts ix. 36 ff.

In the phrase ἐξ ἀναστάσεως the
Resurrection, which is the transition
from death to life, is that out of
which the departed were received.

(b) The victorious sufferings of
Faith : the great things which it has
borne (35 b—38).

The record of the open triumphs of
Faith is followed by the record of its
inward victories in unconquered and
outwardly unrewarded endurance.
Theophylact remarks on the contrast : ὅρα πῶς οἱ μὲν ἀπὸ πίστεως
στόματα μαχαίρας ἔφυγον οἱ δὲ ἐν φόνῳ
μαχαίρας ἀπέθανον· τοιοῦτον γὰρ ἡ
πίστις καὶ ἀνύει μεγάλα καὶ πάσχει
μεγάλα καὶ οὐδὲν οἴεται πάσχειν.

*And others were tortured to death,
not accepting their deliverance, that
they might obtain a better resurrection;* ³⁶*and others had trial of mock-
ings and scourgings, yea moreover
of bonds and imprisonment:* ³⁷*they
were stoned, they were sawn asunder,
they were tempted, they were slain
with the sword: they went about in
sheepskins, in goatskins; being destitute, afflicted, evil-entreated,* ³⁸*men
of whom the world was not worthy,*

*wandering in deserts and mountains
and caves and the holes of the earth.*

The order of arrangement is not
obvious. The enumeration appears
to consist of two great groups (35 b,
36, and 37, 38) each consisting of two
members, the first of suffering to
death, the second of sufferings short of
death. It is difficult to define the
relation in which the two main groups
stand to each other.

Perhaps the first group describes
constancy in the face of release offered
in the moment of trial, on the supposition that οὐ προσδεξάμενοι τὴν ἀπολ.
extends in idea to ἕτεροι, while the
second group gives generally forms of
suffering.

35 b. ἄλλοι δέ...] But others in a
new class triumphed 'in that they
seemed to fail.' The restoration
from death, the highest victory of
active faith, is surpassed by a nobler
triumph, the victory over death.

ἐτυμπανίσθησαν] Vulg. *distenti sunt.*
The reference is to the martyrdom of
the seven brethren related in 2 Macc.
vi. 18 ff.; vii.

The word τυμπανίζειν is used very
vaguely of the infliction of heavy
blows; and the Greek commentators
were at a loss as to its exact meaning. Chrysostom says : ἀποτυμπανισ-
μὸς λέγεται ὁ ἀποκεφαλισμός, referring
to John the Baptist and St James.
So also Theophylact : τουτέστιν ἀπε-
τμήθησαν...τινὲς δὲ τὸ τυμπανισθῆναι
ῥοπάλοις τυφθῆναι εἶπον. Œcumenius
adds : ἄλλοι δὲ τὸ τυμπανίζεσθαι τὸ
ἐκδέρεσθαι φασίν. Hesychius gives
ἐτυμπ. ἐσφαιρίσθησαν, i.e. beaten with
leaded scourges. It appears to describe a punishment like breaking
on the wheel. The extremities of
the sufferer were fastened to a frame,
and his limbs then broken by heavy
clubs. The original reading of D₂

οὐ προσδεξάμενοι τὴν ἀπολύτρωσιν, ἵνα κρείττονος ἀναστάσεως τύχωσιν· ³⁶ἕτεροι δὲ ἐμπαιγμῶν καὶ μαστίγων
πεῖραν ἔλαβον, ἔτι δὲ δεσμῶν καὶ φυλακῆς· ³⁷ἐλιθάσθησαν,
⌜ἐπειράσθησαν, ἐπρίσθησαν⌝, ἐν φόνῳ μαχαίρης ἀπέθανον,

37 ἐπρίσθησαν, ἐπειράσθησαν

36 ἐμπ.: ἐνπεγμάτων D₂*.   37 ἐπειράσθησαν ἐπρίσθησαν ‭א‬: ἐπρίσθ. ἐπειρ.
ς A vg me: ἐπιράσθησαν ἐπιράσθησαν D₂*: om. ἐπειρ. syr vg.

(ἀπετυμπανίσθησαν) expresses more
distinctly 'beaten to death.'

Philo speaks of the spectacles of
the early part of festival days as consisting in Ἰουδαῖοι μαστιγούμενοι, κρε-
μάμενοι, τροχιζόμενοι, καταδικαζόμενοι,
διὰ μέσης τῆς ὀρχήστρας ἀπαγόμενοι τὴν
ἐπὶ θανάτῳ (in Flacc. § 10, ii. p. 529).
The whole description which he
gives of the sufferings of the Jews
should be compared with this passage
(l. c., cc. 10, 20).

οὐ προσδεξ. τὴν ἀπολ.] when they
did not in fact accept the deliverance
which was placed within their reach :
2 Macc. vi. 21; vii. 27. For προσδέ-
ξασθαι see c. x. 34 note.

ἵνα κρείττ. ἀναστ. τύχ.] a resurrection
better than the mere restoration to
the remnant of an earthly life gained
by the acceptance of the offered deliverance. Comp. vii. 19. For ἀν.
τύχ. see Lk. xx. 35.

The comparison between the resurrection to eternal life and the resurrection to an earthly life, though it is
not made directly, lies implicitly in
κρείττονος, as interpreted by the Mac-
cabean history: 2 Macc. vii. 9, 14.
The patristic commentators generally
dwell on this: κρείττονος, οὐ τοιαύτης
οἵας τὰ παιδία τῶν γυναικῶν, ἢ κρείττονος
παρὰ τὴν τῶν λοιπῶν ἀνθρώπων (ἐξανάστασις Phil. iii. 11)...καὶ ἄλλως ὅτι εἰς
ζωὴν αἰώνιον (Theophlct).

36. ἕτεροι δέ] The apostle goes on
to notice a second class among those
(ἄλλοι) who shewed their faith not in
conquering but in bearing. Some
endured death, some endured afflic-

tions less in immediate extent, yet no
less terrible as trials of endurance.
For ἄλλοι, ἕτεροι see 1 Cor. xii. 8 ff.;
Gal. i. 6 f. with Lightfoot's note.

πεῖραν ἔλαβον] v. 29. They experienced sufferings which were sharp
and direct (ἐμπ. καὶ μάστ....2 Macc.
vii. 7, 1), strokes on soul and body;
and sufferings also which were dull
and long (δεσμ. καὶ φυλ.): 1 K.
xxii. 27; Jerem. xxxvii.; xxix. 26; 1
Macc. xiii. 12; 2 Macc. vii. 7, 10.
The ἔτι δέ marks a climax (Acts ii. 26
[Luke xiv. 26, ἔτι τε]). The sharp,
short trial is easier to bear.

The phrase πεῖρ. ἔλαβεν occurs in
LXX. Deut. xxviii. 56 (Aqu. ἐπείρασεν).

37, 38. A fresh summary is given
of sufferings to death (if ἐπειράσθησαν
be corrupt) (v. 37); and of sufferings
short of death (v. 38).

ἐλιθάσθησαν] Stoning was a characteristic Jewish punishment: 2 Chron.
xxiv. 20f. (Zechariah son of Jehoiada);
(Lk. xi. 51); Matt. xxi. 35; xxiii. 37.

Ut Naboth; Jeremias in Ægypto
a reliquiis transmigratorum (comp.
Tertull. Scorp. i. 8); Ezechiel in Baby-
lone; aliique quamplures in Novo
Testamento (Primas.).

ἐπειράσθησαν] This word seems to
be foreign to the context. The reference to Job (Primas., Œcum.) is not
satisfactory. Of the many conjectures
which have been suggested the most
plausible are, ἐπρήσθησαν or ἐνεπρήσθησαν (Philo ad Flacc. § 20; ii. p. 542
M., ζῶντες οἱ μὲν ἐνεπρήσθησαν οἱ δὲ διὰ
μέσης κατεσύρησαν ἀγορᾶς ἕως ὅλα τὰ
σώματα αὐτῶν ἐδαπανήθη).

περιῆλθον ἐν μηλωταῖς, ἐν αἰγίοις δέρμασιν, ὑστερούμενοι,
θλιβόμενοι, κακουχούμενοι, ³⁸ ὧν οὐκ ἦν ἄξιος ὁ κόσμος
⌜ἐπὶ⌝ ἐρημίαις πλανώμενοι καὶ ὄρεσι καὶ σπηλαίοις καὶ
ταῖς ὀπαῖς τῆς γῆς· ³⁹ Καὶ οὗτοι πάντες μαρτυρη-

38 ἐν

38 ἐπὶ ἐρ. אA: ἐν ἐρ. ς D₂*.

ἐπρίσθησαν] So Isaiah suffered according to tradition : Just. M. *Dial.*
120; Orig. *Ep. ad Afric.* § 9, and
Wetstein's note.
For the punishment itself see 2
Sam. xii. 31; 1 Chron. xx. 3; Amos
i. 3 (LXX.).
ἐν φόν. μ. ἀπέθ.] Comp. 1 K. xix. 10
τοὺς προφήτας σου ἀπέκτειναν ἐν ῥομ-
φαίᾳ. Jerem. xxvi. (xxxiii.) 23 (Uri-
jah).
The exact phrase ἐν φόνῳ μαχαίρας
occurs in the LXX. as a rendering of
לְפִי חֶרֶב, Ex. xvii. 13 &c.
The enumeration of sufferings of
death is followed by references to
sufferings in life.
περιῆλθον ἐν μηλ....] *They went
about* from place to place with no sure
abode. Compare Clem. R. i. 17.
(Clem. Alex. *Strom.* iv. 17 § 107 ὁ
ἀπόστολος Κλήμης.) Μηλωτή is used
in the LXX. for אַדֶּרֶת, the characteristic prophet's dress: 1 K. xix. 13, 19;
2 K. ii. 8, 13, 14. This was of sheep
(or goat) skin (compare אַדֶּרֶת שֵׂעָר
Zech. xiii. 4; Gen. xxv. 25); and was
afterwards adopted as a monastic
dress. See Suicer *s. v.*
ὑστ. θλιβ. κακουχ.] in want of the
ordinary means of life (Ecclus. xi. 11;
Luke xv. 14; Phil. iv. 12; 2 Cor. xi.
9), afflicted by pressure (Vulg. *angus-
tiati*) from without (2 Thess. i. 6 f.),
in evil plight generally (xiii. 3; *v.* 25).
38. ὧν οὐκ ἦν ἄξ. ὁ κ.] They were
men worth more than the whole world,
and they lacked all. This appears to
be the meaning, and not that 'the
world in all its beauty was not fit to
be their home.' Comp. Prov. viii. 11

39 πάντ. μαρτ. οὗτοι D₂.

κρείσσων γὰρ σοφία λίθων πολυτελῶν,
πᾶν δὲ τίμιον οὐκ ἄξιον αὐτῆς ἐστι.
Εἰ πᾶς ὁ κόσμος, Theophylact asks,
οὐκ ἔστιν ἄξιος ἑνὸς ἁγίου, τί μέρος
ζητεῖς ;
From this thought the last clause
follows naturally. The best thing men
can give is the sympathy of fellowship :
the last thing which they withdraw
is simple intercourse. But the prophets had no place among their fel-
low-men; and 'even the deserts offered them no safe resting-place'
(Theophlct).
ἐπὶ ἐρημίαις πλανώμ....] Compare 1 K.
xviii. 4, 13 (ἐν σπηλαίῳ); xix. 9 (εἰς τὸ
σπήλαιον) ; 1 Macc. ii. 31; 2 Macc. v.
27 ; vi. 11 ; x. 6.
The clause ταῖς ὀπαῖς τῆς γῆς—*the
holes of the land*—seems to be a
quotation from some familiar description. The word ὀπή occurs again
James iii. 11 with a reference to another feature of the limestone rocks
of Palestine.
(6) 39, 40. General conclusion.
The whole record of past divine
history shews us that the trial of faith
depended on the will of God, who
looked forward to the end. Here
then lies our patience.
³⁹ *And these all, having had witness
borne to them through. their faith,
received not the promise,* ⁴⁰ *God having foreseen some better thing in our
case, that they, apart from us, should
not be made perfect.*
39. οὗτοι πάντες] These all from
the beginning of human discipline to
the fulfilment of man's destiny in
Christ.
μαρτυρηθέντες διὰ τῆς π....] Latt.

θέντες διὰ τῆς πίστεως οὐκ ἐκομίσαντο τὴν ἐπαγγελίαν,
⁴⁰τοῦ θεοῦ περὶ ἡμῶν κρεῖττόν τι προβλεψαμένου, ἵνα
μὴ χωρὶς ἡμῶν τελειωθῶσιν.

τὴν ἐπαγγ. אD₂: τὰς ἐπαγγ. A.   40 κρ. τι π. ημ. D₂*.

testimonio fidei probati... These old
heroes, though they received the witness of divine approval given in what
they were enabled to do and to suffer
through their faith, died before the
end was reached to which they looked
from first to last.

διὰ τῆς πίστεως] *through their faith.*
The faith by which they welcomed
the divine promises became the power
through which the fellowship of God
with them was made evident. For
διά compare *v.* 33 διὰ πίστεως.

With οὐκ ἐκομίσ. τὴν ἐπαγγ. compare *v.* 13 μὴ κομισ. τὰς ἐπαγγ. c. x.
36; 1 Pet. i. 9; v. 4; and for the
relation of ἡ ἐπαγγ. and αἱ ἐπαγγ. see
v. 33.

40. The reason of this failure of
the fathers to 'receive the promise,'
which men might think strange, lay in
the far-reaching Providence—Fore-
sight—of God. It was His purpose
that the final consummation should be
for all together, as indeed it is of all,
in Christ; so that no one part of the
Body can, if we realise the meaning of
the figure, gain its fulfilment independently. The cônsummation of all the
Saints therefore followed upon the
completion of Christ's work, the accomplishment by Him of the destiny
of man, though fallen. So far then
God foresaw in the order of His great
counsel in our case (περὶ ἡμῶν) something better than the fathers experienced: for we have actually seen
in part that towards which they
strained: Matt. xiii. 17; 1 Pet. i. 12.
The fathers with a true faith looked
for a fulfilment of the promises which
was not granted to them. To us the
fulfilment has been granted, without
the trial of deferred hope, if only we

regard the essence of things. Christ
has already opened the way to the
Divine Presence on which we can
enter, and He offers to us now a
kingdom which cannot be shaken (xii.
28). At the same time there is the
thought that God has looked further,
even beyond our age of trial, to the
end.

κρεῖττόν τι] Hoc melius est, promissæ
salutis revelatio clarior, confirmatio
testatior, expectatio propior, per
Christum exhibitum, et tandem ipsa
salus et gloria (Bengel). Chrysostom
has some striking words on this prospect of the consummation: ἐννοήσατε
καὶ ὑμεῖς τί ἐστι καὶ ὅσον ἐστὶ τὸν
Ἀβραὰμ καθῆσθαι καὶ τὸν ἀπόστολον
Παῦλον περιμένοντας πότε σὺ τελειωθῇς
ἵνα δυνηθῶσι τότε λαβεῖν τὸν μισθόν....
εἰ σῶμα ἕν οἱ πάντες ἐσμέν, μείζων
γίνεται τῷ σώματι τούτῳ ἡ ἡδονὴ ὅταν
κοινῇ στεφανῶται καὶ μὴ κατὰ μέρος.
καὶ γὰρ οἱ δίκαιοι καὶ ἐν τούτῳ εἰσὶ
θαυμαστοὶ ὅτι χαίρουσιν ὡς ἐπὶ οἰκείοις
ἀγαθοῖς τοῖς τῶν ἀδελφῶν.

The perfection (τελείωσις) of the
individual Christian must in its fullest
sense involve the perfection of the
Christian society. The 'perfection'
which Christ has gained for humanity
in His Person (ii. 10; v. 9; vii. 28; x.
1, 14) must be appropriated by every
member of Christ. In part this end
has been reached by the old saints in
some degree, in virtue of Christ's exaltation (c. xii. 23), but in part it
waits for the final triumph of the
Saviour, when all that we sum up in
confessing the truth of 'the resurrection of the body' is fulfilled.

Primasius interprets the gift of the
'white robe' in Apoc. vi. 11 (*ad loc.*)
of that endowment of love whereby

the waiting souls gladly accept the postponement of their own consummation : acceperunt singuli stolas albas, id est, ut per caritatis perfectionem, quæ per Spiritum Sanctum infunditur in corda credentium, hac consolatione contenti ipsi mallent pro ceterorum numero fratrum supplendo differri...And Herveius notes in remarkable words the unity of the resurrection-life : Propter hoc etiam mysterium illud in ultimum diem dilati judicii custoditur, quia unum corpus est quod justificari expectatur, unum corpus est quod resurgere in judicium dicitur.

ἵνα μὴ χ. ἠ.] *that they apart from us should not be perfected*....The words seem to depend directly on οὐκ ἐκομ. τὴν ἐπαγγ., though the parenthesis which comes between makes the connexion more intelligible.

For χωρίς see John xv. 5 note.

Additional Note on the reading of xi. 4.

The division of authorities and the strange reading of the most ancient Greek MSS. suggest the existence of a primitive corruption in the clause μαρτυροῦντος ἐπὶ τοῖς δώροις αὐτοῦ τοῦ θεοῦ (τῷ θεῷ). In such a case the loss of B is keenly felt. The best attested reading (μαρτ. ἐπὶ τ. δ. αὐτοῦ τῷ θεῷ) gives a sense which, though it is at first sight foreign to the argument, becomes intelligible if we suppose that a parallel is suggested between the witness of God to Abel and the witness of Abel to God: *he had witness borne to him that he was righteous, while he* on his part, *on occasion of his gifts,* by the faith which inspired them, *bore witness to God.* But such a parallel seems to be artificial, and it is more natural to suppose that the character of the divine witness to the righteousness of Abel should be more distinctly defined. Thus the sense given by the later Greek MSS. is satisfactory; but that reading leaves τῷ θεῷ unexplained. Clement of Alexandria (*Strom.* ii. 4, p. 434) quotes the clause, in a continuous citation, in the form μαρτ. ἐπὶ τοῖς δώροις αὐτῷ τοῦ θεοῦ. If this was the original text a mechanical change would account for both the current readings. It may be added that Clement also omits τῷ θεῷ after προσήνεγκε.

Additional Note on xi. 10. On the social imagery in the Epistle.

Political terms applied to the Christian Society.

No words are more liable to be misunderstood than those which describe forms of social organisation. They survive the state of things to which they were originally applied, and are transferred to a new order, more or less analogous to the past yet widely distinguished from it. For this reason the language which is used in the N. T. to describe the Christian Society is exposed to many difficulties of interpretation. Believers are represented in the apostolic writings as united in a 'congregation' (ἐκκλησία), a 'state,' or 'city' (πόλις), a 'kingdom,' and it is important to endeavour to realise the thoughts associated with these terms in the first age, if we wish to realise the primitive conception of Christianity as a social power. In this connexion the teaching of the Epistle to the Hebrews is of the greatest moment. It offers a view of the organisation of the Gospel in most respects singularly comprehensive; and it is not unlikely that the imminent over-throw of the Jewish state gave occasion for dwelling upon this aspect of the Gospel. There is however one striking omission. The Epistle is almost silent as to ecclesiastical organisation. No one of the words which have come to represent the main ideas of Church government is used in it with its limited technical sense. The title 'Apostle' is used only of Christ Himself (iii. 1 τὸν ἀπόστολον καὶ ἀρχιερέα τῆς ὁμολογίας ἡμῶν Ἰησοῦν). The verb ἐπισκοπεῖν, in the one place where it occurs, suggests no thought of official oversight (xii. 15). 'The elders' are simply the heroes of the Old

Dispensation (xi. 2). The word διάκονος is not found in the book; nor is the term ἐκκλησία used in the sense of 'a particular church' or of 'the universal church' (ii. 12 ἐν μέσῳ ἐκκλησίας LXX.; xii. 23 ἐκκλησίᾳ πρωτοτόκων). The single term which indicates the existence of ordered discipline in the body is the most general, 'those that have rule,' 'that lead' (οἱ ἡγούμενοι, xiii. 7, 17, 24).

With this exception the view given in the Epistle of the social embodi- Variety of ment of the Gospel is most varied. Eight passages present it under five social distinct aspects: imagery in the

1. ii. 5 ἡ οἰκουμένη ἡ μέλλουσα. The Divine Order in its fullest extent Epistle and realisation. to the Hebrews.

2. iii. 2 f.; x. 21 ὁ οἶκος τοῦ θεοῦ. The relation of the Order to God, as its Head and Indweller.

3. xi. 10, 16; xiii. 14 ἡ τοὺς θεμελίους ἔχουσα πόλις, ἡ μέλλουσα (πόλις). Comp. viii. 11. The social constitution of the Order.

4. xii. 22 ff. The vision of the fulness of the Order.

5. xii. 28 βασιλεία ἀσάλευτος. Comp. Col. i. 13. A present kingdom.

Each of these aspects of the Christian Society must be considered separately.

1. *The Christian Society as the Society of the 'age to come'* (ii. 5). The Christian The far-reaching phrase ἡ οἰκουμένη ἡ μέλλουσα, which is inadequately Society is rendered by 'the world to come,' suggests the thought of the Order towards (1) The which the earlier discipline of the world had been directed. It has been embodi-all along foreseen. It is the true fulfilment of the destiny of humanity: ment of the initial stage of the consummation which answers to creation. It is 'the order essentially comprehensive. It includes men as men, and places them in their due connexion with Nature. This inherent universality of the Order, as contemplated under this aspect, explains the silence of the Epistle on the call of the Gentiles. Old divisions, which had their place in the times of preparation, could not continue when man was seen to have reached the divine end in Christ. Henceforth 'the people' and 'the nations' were united in a larger fellowship. The spiritual Order was revealed in Him, of which Greek civilisation and Roman government were partial types.

2. *The Christian Society as the House of God* (iii. 2 ff.; x. 21). (2) The House of Under the image of 'the House of God' the Christian Society is regarded God. in a different light. It is the organised system in which God dwells, and of which He is the Master. The sense of the dwelling-place, which is dominant, passes into that of the family, and then the dwelling-place consists of human hearts. The image is derived directly from Num. xii. 7. The earliest and simplest expression of the thought of 'the House of God' is in Gen. xxviii. 17. The phrase is rarely applied to the Tabernacle: Ex. xxiii. 19; xxxiv. 26; Josh. vi. 24; Judg. xviii. 31. It is used of the Temple in 2 Sam. vii. 5; 1 K. viii. 17 and later writings.

The passage from the thought of a material to that of a spiritual 'House' is natural: Jer. vii. 4; John ii. 16, 19 (comp. Matt. xxiii. 38).

In its widest meaning the 'House' includes Nature no less than Humanity; but it is through man that all other things reach their end. Hence while Christ is 'a great Priest over the House of God' (x. 21), Christians are in a peculiar sense 'His House' (iii. 6). As St Paul writes to the Ephesians: *Each several building*—each chamber in the whole fabric of the universe—*fitly framed together, groweth into a holy sanctuary in the Lord; in Whom ye also are builded together for a habitation of God in the Spirit* (Eph. ii. 21 f.). Compare 1 Tim. iii. 15; 1 Pet. ii. 5; iv. 17.

(3) The abiding πόλις.

3. *The Christian Society as the abiding City* (xi. 10, 16; xiii. 14).

It is however under the idea of the 'city,' the 'state' (πόλις), that the Christian Society enters most fully upon the inheritance of earlier life. Three distinct elements contribute to the fulness of the conception of the Christian πόλις, (*a*) the Jewish, (*b*) the Greek, and (*c*) the Stoic.

(a) The Jewish πόλις.

(*a*) The Jewish idea of the πόλις is centred in the thought of a divine sovereignty, of privileges answering to complete devotion to a Heavenly King. From the first the blessings which were assured to a chosen family were held to be capable of extension to those who accepted the obligations of the Covenant. The natural principle of birth was recognised, but it was subordinated to the principle of a common faith. Stated gatherings of the whole race were enjoined, but they were designed to keep fresh the vigour of institutions which were fixed once for all.

'The city of the Great King' (Ps. xlviii. 2; comp. Matt. v. 35) was ideally the home of every member of the commonwealth of Israel, and by the necessity of the case it tended to create a sense of spiritual fellowship offering the hope of an indefinite enlargement (Ps. lxxxvii.). If slavery found a modified acceptance, it was treated as a transitory condition, and not allowed to destroy the spiritual rights of the slave.

The prophets looked forward to a time when Zion should be the seat of a holy kingdom, of which the Davidic kingdom was a symbol; when the restoration of 'the people' should be the prelude to the gathering of 'the nations' to the mountain of the LORD; when the Redeemer of Israel should be 'the God of the whole earth': when Jerusalem should become a universal centre of worship (Joel iii.; Amos ix. 11 ff.; Is. liv.; lxvi. 20 [LXX.]; Ezek. xl. ff.; Zech. xii. xiv.). In this larger view of the divine πόλις nothing was lost of the original conception of a community of worshippers, ideally citizen-priests; but it was recognised that the privileges which belonged to Israel corresponded with the destiny of humanity and must therefore be at last presented in a form which was able to bring them within the reach of all men (comp. Tob. xiii. 9 ff.).

(b) The Greek πόλις.

(*b*) The πόλις of Judaism was in its conception the most comprehensive in the old world. So far from the Jews deserving the reproach of illiberal narrowness, as long as they remained true to their Scriptures, they offered a unique example of a nation most definite in its organisation, which admitted freely the incorporation of new members and looked forward to a world-wide religious communion in one faith. The Greek conception of the πόλις was sharply contrasted with the Jewish. The Jewish was essentially universal because it was the embodiment of the One Divine will: the Greek was limited, because it was the affirmation of personal rights. It was designed to realise as fully as possible the powers of man in the best and not in all. It rested on a community of blood, religion, law. It assumed the inherent superiority of the Greek race, and was founded upon slavery (Arist. *Pol.* iii. 5). It tended to develop in the privileged few the immediate sense of privilege, of responsibility, of individual freedom, in the highest degree; but it excluded the possibility of wide extension. Each citizen exercised his power directly. The power therefore could not be extended to more than might be supposed to be able to meet for counsel. Thus while it has been maintained that the πόλις was anterior to the citizen, it was also maintained that the πόλις could be no greater than sufficed for the fullest development of the citizen. In the face of facts Plato admitted that the end of civic life was not reached in existing states, but he added in remarkable words: ἐν οὐρανῷ ἴσως παράδειγμα ἀνάκειται τῷ βουλομένῳ ὁρᾶν, καὶ ὁρῶντι ἑαυτὸν κατοικίζειν (*Resp.* ix. *s. f.* p. 592).

(c) The Greek conception of the πόλις emphasised as strongly as possible the rights and the duties of the citizen, the privileged man; but his position of advantage was purchased at a high price. It required for its attainment the subjection of all others. Those who looked at the capacities of men as men could not rest in such a state of things. The great Stoic leaders, who came at many points into contact with Jewish teaching, proclaimed a universal πόλις, a city co-extensive with the world. 'What is man?' Epictetus asks. 'A member of a state' (μέρος πόλεως, comp. Sen. *Ep.* xcv. 52) he replies, 'of that primarily which consists of Gods and men (comp. Cic. *de fin.* iii. 19, 64; Sen. *de otio* iv. 1), and next of that which bears the name and is most near to us, a state which is a small copy of the universal state' (*Dissert.* ii. 5, 26; comp. iii. 22, 4; 85; 24, 10). 'Man,' Marcus Aurelius says, 'is a citizen of that sublimest state of which all other states are (as it were) houses' (*Medit.* iii. 11). 'The end of a rational being is to follow the principle and law of the state and constitution which is anterior to all beside' (*id.* ii. 16; comp. iv. 4; 23; vi. 44).

This conception was adopted by Philo. 'The supreme state (ἡ μεγαλόπολις),' he writes, 'is this world, and it obeys one constitution and one law' (*de Jos.* § 6; ii. 46 M.). 'The soul of the wise accounts in very truth heaven as its fatherland, and earth as a strange country' (*de agric.* § 14; i. 310 M.). Such souls after a time 'go back again thither whence they first started, holding that the heavenly region, in which they live their true life (ἐν ᾧ πολιτεύονται), is their fatherland, and the earthly, in which they sojourn, a strange place' (*de conf. ling.* § 17; i. 416 M.).

These three distinct conceptions of the πόλις, which were widely influential in the Apostolic age, are combined in the conception of the Christian commonwealth. It is the seat of a Divine Presence which carries with it the promise of the fulfilment of a divine counsel in the fellowship of man with God. It is a community in which each citizen is endowed with the completest privileges and charged with the fullest responsibility for the general welfare. It is a world-wide organisation embracing in a communion of the largest hope 'all thinking things, all objects of all thought.'

(marginal notes: (c) The Stoic πόλις. These three conceptions fulfilled in the Christian Society.)

In the Apocalypse the Jewish conception finds its most striking application. In the Epistles of St Paul the Greek conception is dominant. But
in each case the idea of universality raises the particular conception to its
loftiest form.

The
teaching
of the
Apoca-
lypse.

The real significance of the imagery of the Apocalypse is liable to
be mistaken. This is largely derived from Ezekiel. 'The holy city, new
Jerusalem' (xxi. 2), is in fact not a city, made up of human dwellings, but
one building, a Temple, a House of God (comp. Ezek. xl. 2), which has
hitherto been in heaven (cc. iv. v; xi. 19; xiv. 15, 17; viii. 3; xvi. 7;
comp. Hebr. viii. 5). It is a perfect cube (xxi. 16), 'four-square to all the
elements,' of absolute symmetry and strength. Angel-watches guard its
gates (xxi. 12). A single 'street,' as in the earthly Temple, gives an
approach to that manifestation of God which takes the place of the Sanctuary (xxi. 21 ff.). The people live in a Paradise around it, and have free
access to the divine throne (xxii. 1 ff.; 14, 19); and at the same time,
under another aspect, some at least among them are themselves part of the
spiritual Sanctuary (iii. 12). 'The name of God, and the name of the city
of God, and the new name of Christ' is the signature of believers (id.).
The revelation of this new Society, no less than the revelation of God
Himself, in other words, gives to the Christian his abiding character. As a
citizen of this new city, a priest doing service (xxii. 3) to a present Lord, a
servant and yet a king (xxii. 5), he reaches the goal of his creation. Meanwhile a wider work is accomplished. The leaves of 'the tree' by 'the river
of the water of life' are 'for the healing of the nations' (xxii. 2). So it is
that 'the nations shall walk amidst the light' of the city—which is 'the
glory of God'—and 'the kings of the earth do bring their glory into it'
(xxi. 24).

In such a vision, given as the consummation of the work of the
Incarnate Lord, the most far-reaching words of the prophets find their
accomplishment. The new πόλις is seen to be a Temple. The centre, the
light, the law, of its constitution is the revelation of God through the Lamb
(xxi. 23, ὁ λύχνος); and those who first enter upon its privileges are
allowed to see the extension of their own privileges to 'the nations,' and
to fulfil a work for these later fellow-citizens.

The teach-
ing of
St Paul.

St Paul recognised this spiritual city, 'the Jerusalem which is above,'
which is 'free and our mother' (Gal. iv. 26); but he dwelt more upon the
individual privileges which belong to its citizens (comp. 2 Cor. v. 1 f.) than
upon their social fellowship. As one who knew and used the rights of
Roman citizenship, he felt keenly how those who enjoyed a divine citizenship were raised above all who were not spiritually enfranchised. The
Christian 'citizenship' or 'commonwealth' (Phil. iii. 20, πολίτευμα) was for
him a great and present reality, the full power of which would be shewn in
due time (Phil. iii. 21). Those who before were 'alienated from the
commonwealth (πολιτείας) of Israel and strangers to the covenants of the
promise' were 'made near in the blood of Christ' (Eph. ii. 12 f.). The
boundary wall (חֵל) which had hindered their approach to the Sanctuary
was broken down (Eph. ii. 14). They were therefore 'no longer strangers
(ξένοι without any civic rights) or sojourners (πάροικοι, licensed dwellers,

enjoying a defined status), but fellow-citizens with the Saints and of the household of God' (Eph. ii. 19). Their life was necessarily an endeavour to realise under the conditions of earth the privileges of the new State of which the Gospel of Christ was the charter (Phil. i. 27 ἀξίως τοῦ εὐαγγελίου τοῦ Χριστοῦ πολιτεύεσθε), even as the true Jew had enjoyed the rights and duties of the commonwealth of Israel (Acts xxiii. 1)[1].

In the Epistle to the Hebrews the idea of the Christian πόλις is con- The teach-nected with the whole course of Revelation. The Call of Abraham pointed ing of the to this abiding issue of the counsel of God. The patriarch recognised that to the Epistle he was but a 'sojourner' in the land of promise: for 'he waited for the city Hebrews. that hath the foundations' (c. xi. 10), the one definite organisation of the people of God, already existing in the divine idea. For if men, for the fulfilment of preparatory discipline, 'waited,' God had already provided that towards which they reached forth : ' He had prepared them a city' (c. xi. 16). On His side all has been eternally ready, but even now Chris-tians, conscious of the transitoriness of the things amidst which they move, 'seek after the city which is to come' (c. xiii. 14 τὴν μέλλουσαν [πόλιν] ἐπιζητοῦμεν). This city has not still to be founded: it is, and the believer as he is able uses the high prerogatives which belong to its members[2].

The thought of the Christian πόλις, πολιτεία, which must be regarded on the one side as opposed to all earthly states and institutions, and on the other as absorbing and transforming them, finds frequent expression in early writers: Clem. ad Cor. i. 2, 54; Polyc. 5; Herm. Sim. i. 1; Ep. ad Diogn. 5; Clem. Al. Strom. iv. 174.

4. The vision of the fulness of the Christian Society (xii. 22 f.).

The full realisation of the Christian πόλις lies still in the future, but meanwhile the believer is allowed to contemplate its glories in contrast with the terrors of the legislation from Sinai. See notes on the passage.

5. The Christian Society as a present kingdom (xii. 28).

One further image is used of the Christian Society, which is not derived from Greek or Roman thought, but from the monarchies of the East. Believers receive from the hands of God 'a kingdom which cannot be shaken' (xii. 28). The figure appears to include a twofold idea. They are under a sovereignty of infinite wisdom, and they are also themselves kings (comp. Rev. i. 6; v. 10 βασιλείαν). The Society which is established has an office towards the nations. The kingdom of Christ is a kingdom of kings, who in turn ruling in His name, bring all people under His sway.

The thought lies in the first proclamation of the Gospel (Matt. iii. 2; iv. 17). It was the topic of the teaching of the Risen Lord (Acts i. 3); and it forms the substance of the latest apostolic teaching recorded in the Acts

---

[1] Comp. E. L. Hicks, Classical Re-view, i. pp. 4 ff.; 41 ff.

[2] In contrast with the πολίτης stands the πάροικος (Hebr. xi. 9; 1 Pet. i. 17; ii. 11) who has a defined position as a recognised sojourner, the παρεπίδημος (Hebr. xi. 13; 1 Pet. i. 1; ii. 11) who resides in the city but has no status, the ξένος (Hebr. xi. 13) who is simply a foreigner.

(Acts xxviii. 31). Its present symbol is the Cross (John xii. 32), which points to the way of true dominion, when the single ruler gives himself for his people and does not use his people for selfish ends. ‘He who bears the reproach of his country shall be called the lord of the land, and he who bears the calamities of his country shall be called the king of the world[1].’ The unconscious prophecy of the Chinese teacher has found its fulfilment; and the truth is committed to Christians that it may be embodied.

[1] *Lao-tzu*, § lxxviii. (Chalmers' translation).

XII.   ¹ Τοιγαροῦν καὶ ἡμεῖς, τοσοῦτον ἔχοντες περι-

1 τοσ.: τηλικοῦτον א*.

(iii.) *The general application of the lessons of the past to the present season of trial* (c. xii.).

The consideration of the past victories of Faith suggests three main lines of thought which are pursued in this chapter.

(1) 1—13. The virtue of discipline.
(2) 14—17. The necessity of peace and purity.
(3) 18—29. The character and obligations of the New Covenant.

(1) 1—13. The virtue of discipline.

The teaching on the virtue of discipline falls into two parts, (*a*) The motive to endurance in suffering (1, 2); and (*b*) The measure and end of suffering (3—13).

(*a*) The motive to endurance in suffering (1, 2).

Christians in one sense had entered on the inheritance of the promises for which the fathers had waited (xi. 39); but the full enjoyment of possession was still delayed. In such a case the example of the earlier heroes of faith was of prevailing power. With less encouragement than the Hebrew Christians enjoyed they had conquered. They had looked to a Christ imaged in prophecy: the Hebrews could look to a Christ Who had 'come in the flesh' (Jesus). Thus the writer marks (*a*) the position, (β) the preparation, (γ) the effort, (δ) the aim, of Christians looking to One Who had Himself conquered through suffering.

(*a*) *The position of Christians.*

The writer regards himself and his fellow Christians as placed in an arena and contending for a great prize. The image of the amphitheatre with the rising rows of spectators seems to suggest the thought of an encircling cloud. The witnesses of whom the cloud is composed are unquestionably the countless heroes of faith whose deeds have been sum-

marised in c. xi. The testimony which they bear can only be the testimony which they bear to God, either by victorious achievements or by courageous sufferings, answering to that which He has wrought for and in them. In both respects, as conquerors and as sufferers, they witness to His power and faithfulness; and those who regard them cannot but be strengthened by their testimony.

There is apparently no evidence that μάρτυς is ever used simply in the sense of a 'spectator.' Even in such a passage as Wisd. i. 6 τῶν νεφρῶν αὐτοῦ μάρτυς ὁ θεὸς καὶ τῆς καρδίας αὐτοῦ ἐπίσκοπος ἀληθὴς καὶ τῆς γλώσσης ἀκουστής there is the thought of the open testimony to be given: comp. 1 Tim. vi. 12; 2 Tim. ii. 2; Acts x. 41.

At the same time it is impossible to exclude the thought of the spectators in the amphitheatre. The passage would not lose in vividness though it would lose in power if θεατῶν were substituted for μαρτύρων. These champions of old time occupy the place of spectators, but they are more than spectators. They are spectators who interpret to us the meaning of our struggle, and who bear testimony to the certainty of our success if we strive lawfully (2 Tim. ii. 5).

There is no confusion in this fulness of sense. The word περικείμενον gives the thought of the great company to whom the Christian athlete is made a spectacle (1 Cor. iv. 9 θέατρον ἐγενήθημεν: c. x. 33 θεατριζόμενοι); and μαρτύρων explains what the true nature of this host is, widely different from the pitiless throng visible to the bodily eye at the heathen games.

Tertullian describes the scene which actually met the eye (*ad Martyras*, c. 1): nec tantus ego sum ut vos alloquar, verumtamen et gladiatores

κείμενον ἡμῖν νέφος μαρτύρων, ὄγκον ἀποθέμενοι πάντα

perfectissimos non tantum magistri et præpositi sui sed etiam idiotæ et supervacue (-cui?) quique adhortantur de longinquo, ut sæpe de ipso populo dictata suggesta profuerint. In a cognate passage of Longinus (*de sublim.* § xiv.), quoted by Wetstein, the 'witnesses' are regarded as those who will bear testimony of what they see in the trial: τῷ γὰρ ὄντι μέγα τὸ ἀγώνισμα...ἐν τηλικούτοις ἥρωσι κριταῖς τε καὶ μάρτυσι ὑπέχειν τῶν γραφομένων εὐθύνας.

The true idea of the 'witnesses' is given by the Fathers, as by Chrysostom: Μάρτυρας δὲ οὐχὶ τοὺς ἐν τῇ καινῇ λέγει μόνον ἀλλὰ καὶ τοὺς ἐν τῇ παλαιᾷ· καὶ γὰρ καὶ αὐτοὶ ἐμαρτύρησαν τῇ τοῦ θεοῦ μεγαλειότητι· and Primasius: Nubem testium appellat multitudinem patriarcharum ac prophetarum reliquorumque fidelium qui testes fuerunt perfectæ fidei.

Epictetus uses the image of the games to support a spirit of effort and endurance: *Dissert.* iii. 25 ; *Enchir.* li. 2.

¹ *Therefore let us also, seeing we have so great a cloud of witnesses encompassing us, lay aside every encumbrance and the sin which doth so easily beset us, and with patience run the race that is set before us,* ²*looking unto Him Who is the leader and finisher of Faith, even Jesus, Who, for the joy that was set before Him, endured the cross, despising shame, and hath sat down on the right hand of the throne of God.*

1. τοιγαροῦν καὶ ἡμεῖς...] Vulg. *Ideoque et nos...Therefore assuredly let us also,* who are under the New Covenant in the time of our trial... The writer identifies himself with those whose courage he desires to animate : c. x. 39.

Τοιγαροῦν occurs again 1 Thess. iv. 8 (τοίνυν, c. xiii. 13); elsewhere the writer introduces his conclusion with διὰ τοῦτο or ὅθεν.

ἔχ. περικείμενον ἡμῖν] Vulg. *habentes impositam,* literally 'having spread about us.' The competitors feel the crowd towering about and above them. Hence the Apostle does not say simply περικείμενοι νέφος (comp. c. v. 2) or περικειμένου νέφους, but ἔχοντες περικείμενον. Believers are conscious of the surrounding host. For ἔχοντες περικ. comp. v. 14 note.

The words occur in a very different connexion in 2 Clem. i. 6 ἀποθέμενοι ἐκεῖνο ὃ περικείμεθα νέφος.

νέφος μαρτύρων] Vulg. *nubem* (d *imbrem*) *testium.* A 'cloud' is used in all languages for a dense mass of living beings from the time of Homer downwards : *Il.* iv. 274 ἅμα δὲ νέφος εἵπετο πεζῶν. *Æn.* vii. 793 Insequitur nimbus peditum. Priscill. iii. p. 63 testimoniorum nube.

Chrysostom (followed by others) finds in the 'cloud' the idea of shelter from the scorching heat : ἡ μνήμη τῶν ἁγίων ἐκείνων ὥσπερ νέφος τὸν φλεγόμενον ὑπὸ ἀκτῖνος θερμοτέρας σκιάζει... ἀνίστησι καὶ ἀνακτᾶται ψυχήν.

(β) *The preparation of Christians.*

The solemnity of the position of the Christian naturally leads to the consideration of the preparation which he is bound to make for the fulfilment of his arduous duty. This is twofold. He must lay aside natural encumbrances (ὄγκον πάντα), and also the positive sin by which he is hindered.

ὄγκον ἀποθέμενοι π.] *(let us)...lay aside every encumbrance...*Vulg. *deponentes omne pondus.* The word ὄγκος, which does not occur elsewhere in N. T. or LXX., is used for bulk of body (Galen, *in Hippocr. Aphor.* 1 (xvii. (2) p. 363, Kühn) τῆς τῶν ἀθλητῶν εὐεξίας οὐ μικρὸν τοῦτό ἐστιν ἔγκλημα τὸ περιβάλλεσθαι πειρᾶσθαι μέγεθος ὄγκου κατὰ τὸ σῶμα...), for an arrogant bearing, and for a burdensome load. These several senses have been applied to the interpretation of the word here. The competitor in

καὶ τὴν εὐπερίστατον ἁμαρτίαν, δι᾽ ὑπομονῆς τρέχωμεν

a race seeks by training to reduce all superfluity of flesh, and in the contest lays aside all undue confidence and every encumbrance of dress. There can be little doubt that the image is taken from the immediate preparation for the decisive effort, so that the first sense is inapplicable, and it is hardly possible that ἀποθέσθαι ὄγκον could be used of the effects of training. The last interpretation is in every way the most appropriate. The writer seems to have in his mind the manifold encumbrances of society and business which would be likely to hinder a Christian convert. The duty of the convert would be to free himself from associations and engagements which, however innocent in themselves, hindered the freedom of his action.

It may however be noticed that Philo says that the soul which would seek God must not remain ἐν τοῖς σωματικοῖς ὄγκοις (Leg. Alleg. iii. § 15; i. 96 M.).

Compare Chrysostom: πάντα τίνα; τουτέστι τὸν ὕπνον, τὴν ὀλιγωρίαν, τοὺς λογισμοὺς τοὺς εὐτελεῖς, πάντα τὰ ἀνθρώπινα.

Theodoret: τὸν τῶν περιττῶν φροντίδων ἀπορρίψωμεν ὄγκον.

Theophylact: τουτέστι τὸ βάρος τῶν γηΐνων πραγμάτων καὶ τῶν ἐπ᾽ αὐτοῖς φροντίδων.

For the image in ἀποθέμενοι, 'putting off from one's self' as a robe, see Acts vii. 58; comp. c. x. 11 (περιελεῖν); Rom. xiii. 12; Col. iii. 8, &c.

τὴν εὐπερίστατον ἁμαρτίαν] The Christian must put off not only encumbrances but, that which is the source of all failure, sin (ἁμαρτία not ἁμαρτίαι). This sin is described as εὐπερίστατος. The word εὐπερίστατος is not found except in places where it has been derived from this passage. The sense is doubtful. Three meanings have support either from analogy or from early Greek interpreters.

(1) 'easy to be put off,' 'avoided,' 'removed,' from the sense of περιίστασθαι in 2 Tim. ii. 16; Tit. iii. 9. This sense is adopted by Chrysostom in treating of the passage: εὐπερίστατον ἤτοι τὴν εὐκόλως περισταμένην ἡμᾶς ἢ τὴν εὐκόλως περίστασιν δυναμένην παθεῖν λέγει· μᾶλλον δὲ τοῦτο· ῥᾴδιον γὰρ ἐὰν θέλωμεν περιγενέσθαι τῆς ἁμαρτίας: and d gives fragile. But the form is decisive against the derivation on which it rests. The compound could not lose the -ι-: it must be formed from στατός.

(2) 'well-befriended,' 'popularly supported,' 'admired of many.' This interpretation is derived from the corresponding sense of περίστατος (from Isocrates downward), and ἀπερίστατος 'unsupported,' 'desolate' (Phocyl., Arrian). The form of the word is favourable to this sense.

(3) 'readily besetting' (Vulg. circumstans). There is no exact parallel for such an active sense in compounds of ἵστασθαι, but this interpretation has been most generally adopted; and it is given by Chrysostom as an alternative on the passage, and by other Greek writers.

Theodoret gives a different explanation, 'easily contracted': εὐπερίστατον τὴν ἁμαρτίαν ἐκάλεσεν ὡς εὐκόλως συνισταμένην τε καὶ γινομένην: and Theophylact adds to the two explanations given by Chrysostom yet another: ἢ δι᾽ ἣν εὐκόλως τις εἰς περιστάσεις ἐμπίπτει· οὐδὲν γὰρ οὕτω κινδυνῶδες ὡς ἁμαρτία.

Of these interpretations (1) and (2) do not seem to fall in well with the scope of the passage, or with the imagery. It does not seem likely that the writer would choose an epithet for sin which should describe it from the side of its impotence. Nor again is the common estimate or regard of sin that with which the Christian is concerned. It is rather the personal relation of sin to the believer in his

τὸν προκείμενον ἡμῖν ἀγῶνα, ²ἀφορῶντες εἰς τὸν τῆς

work that we expect to find noticed. In this connexion the sense of 'readily encircling, besetting, entangling' is singularly appropriate. Nor is there anything contrary to analogy in such a sense. The simple verbal στατός, from which the compound is formed, is used of anything 'standing' (a house, a stone, water): περίστατος would then naturally bear the sense of 'placed, standing round,' as enclosing, confining; and εὖ would express the fatal facility with which this fence of evil custom hems us in. The sin by which we are practically encircled answers to the cloud of witnesses with which God surrounds us for our encouragement.

Περίστατος is found in a sense not unlike this in a fragment of Theopompus (*Pamph.* fr. 2) περίστατον βοῶσα τὴν κώμην ποιεῖ ('causes the village to stand round her').

(γ) *The effort of Christians.*

Having marked our position and preparation as Christians, the writer bids us begin and continue the effort to which we are called with patient endurance.

δι᾿ ὑπομονῆς...ἀγῶνα] For ὑπομονή see c. x. 36 note. The thought of this 'patient endurance' is prominent in the context (*v.* 2 ὑπέμεινεν, *v.* 3 ὑπομεμενηκότα, *v.* 7 εἰς παιδείαν ὑπομένετε).

For διά see 2 Cor. v. 7; Rom. viii. 25. The δι᾿ ὑπομονῆς stands first as colouring τρέχωμεν.

The construction of τρέχειν ἀγῶνα (Lat. strangely, *curramus ad propositum nobis certamen*) is formed on τρέχειν δρόμον: *miserabile currunt certamen*, Stat. *Theb.* iii. 116.

τὸν προκ. ἡμῖν ἀγῶνα] The image of the race is common in St Paul: 1 Cor. ix. 24 ff.; Gal. ii. 2; Phil. ii. 16; iii. 12; 2 Tim. iv. 7. Compare Acts xiii. 25; xx. 24; Rom. ix. 16.

It is found in classical writers : *e.g.* Eur. *Orest.* 847 ψυχῆς ἀγῶνα τὸν προ-

κείμενον πέρι δώσων; and in Philo, *de agric.* §§ 25 ff. (i. 317 ff. M.).

The 'race' is spoken of by the more general title of 'a contest' in regard to the strain and peril which it involves. Comp. Herod. viii. 102 πολλοὺς πολλάκις ἀγῶνας δραμέονται περὶ σφέων αὐτέων οἱ Ἕλληνες. Eur. *Or.* 877 ὁρᾷς...ἀγῶνα θανάσιμον δραμούμενον. And still, as Chrysostom remarks, the Apostle chooses the image of athletic effort, which is least repellent : οὐκ εἶπε Πυκτεύωμεν, οὐδὲ Παλαίωμεν, οὐδὲ Πολεμῶμεν, ἀλλ᾿ ὃ πάντων κουφότερον ἦν, τὸ τοῦ δρόμου, τοῦτο εἰς μέσον τέθεικεν.

Προκεῖσθαι (*proponi*) is the usual word in this connexion. God Himself has set our work and our prize before us as ἀγωνοθέτης. Comp. c. vi. 18.

(δ) *The aim of Christians.*

2. The encouragement to be drawn from earthly witnesses passes into the supreme encouragement which springs from the contemplation of Christ. Above the 'cloud of witnesses,' who encompass us, is our King, no Roman Emperor dispensing by his arbitrary will life or death to the stricken combatant, but One Who has Himself sustained the struggle which we bear. He Who is 'the captain (author) of our salvation,' 'the righteous Judge' (2 Tim. iv. 8), is also the example and the inspiration of our faith. He in His humanity endured suffering and shame beyond all others and received compensating joy and glory. We therefore may hope by sharing His sufferings to share His glory (Rom. viii. 17 εἴπερ συνπάσχομεν ἵνα καὶ συνδοξασθῶμεν). Compare Thomas a Kempis *De imit.* iii. 18, 3 Vita tua vita nostra : et per sanctam patientiam ambulamus ad te qui es corona nostra. Nisi tu nos praecessisses et docuisses, quis sequi curaret ?

ἀφορῶντες εἰς] Vulg. *aspicientes in, looking* away from all that distracts on earth *into*...not only at the first

πίστεως ἀρχηγὸν καὶ τελειωτὴν Ἰησοῦν, ὃς ἀντὶ τῆς
προκειμένης αὐτῷ χαρᾶς ὑπέμεινεν σταυρὸν αἰσχύνης

2 +τὸν' στ. D₂*.

moment, but constantly during the whole struggle. Contrast *v.* I ἀποθέ-μενοι. Christ is always near and in sight. The word does not occur elsewhere in the N. T. or in the LXX. (4 Macc. xvii. 10); but see ἀπέβλεπεν c. xi. 26; and compare Arrian, *Epict.* ii. 19, 29 εἰς τὸν θεὸν ἀφορῶντες ἐν παντὶ μικρῷ καὶ μεγάλῳ; and *id.* iii. 24, 16. Clement uses ἀτενίζειν εἰς frequently: I *Cor.* 7, 9; 19 &c.

Theophylact expresses the thought tersely: ἐὰν θέλωμεν μαθεῖν τὸ τρέχειν δι᾽ ὑπομονῆς, πρὸς τὸν Χριστὸν ἀφορῶμεν, ὥσπερ οἱ τέχνας μανθάνοντες πρὸς τοὺς διδασκάλους.

In one form or other the hope of the vision of God has been the support of the saints in all ages: Job xix. 26 f.; Ps. xvii. 15.

τὸν τῆς πίστεως...Ἰησοῦν] Christ in His humanity—*Jesus*—is 'the leader and consummator of faith.' To Him our eyes are to be turned while we look away from every rival attraction. From Him we learn Faith. The 'faith' of which the Apostle speaks is faith in its absolute type, of which he has traced the action under the Old Covenant. The particular interpretations, by which it is referred to the faith of each individual Christian, as finding its beginning and final development in Christ; or to the substance of the Christian Creed; are foreign to the whole scope of the passage, which is to shew that in Jesus Christ Himself we have the perfect example —perfect in realisation and in effect —of that faith which we are to imitate, trusting in Him. He too looked through the present and the visible to the future and the unseen. In His human Nature He exhibited Faith in its highest form, from first to last, and placing Himself as it were at the head

of the great army of heroes of Faith, He carried faith, the source of their strength, to its most complete perfection and to its loftiest triumph.

This ascription of 'faith' to the Lord is of the highest importance for the realisation of His perfect humanity. Comp. c. v. 8; ii. 13; iii. 2; John v. 19; xi. 41.

Chrysostom (with the Greek Fathers generally) limits the word to our faith: αὐτὸς ἐν ἡμῖν τὴν πίστιν ἐνέθηκεν, αὐτὸς τὴν ἀρχὴν δέδωκεν. The Latin Vulgate translation necessarily led the Western Fathers to the same interpretation.

ἀρχ. καὶ τελειωτήν] Vulg. *auctorem et consummatorem* (O. L. *principem et perfectorem*). As 'leader' of Faith, Christ supported unparalleled sufferings in every stage of human life, and as 'finisher,' 'consummator,' He brought Faith to its sovereign power. The phrase has been compared with the Rabbinic מתחיל וגומר.

For ἀρχηγός see c. ii. 10 note. Christ is 'leader' and not 'beginner' only.

The word τελειωτής is not found elsewhere in the N. T. or in the LXX. or classical writers. It occurs in Greg. Naz. *Orat.* xl. *in bapt.* § 44 of the minister who baptizes; and in Methodius *de Sim. et Anna* 5, of God Who admits those who are initiated into the Christian mysteries.

For the emphatic position of Ἰησοῦν at the end of the clause compare ii. 9 note.

ὃς ἀντὶ τ. πρ....καταφρ.] The nature of Christ's example is indicated. The joy that was set before Him was accepted as an equivalent (and more than an equivalent) for the sufferings which He endured. The joy was that of the work of redemption accom-

καταφρονήσας, ἐν δεξιᾷ τε τοῦ θρόνου τοῦ θεοῦ κεκάθικεν.

om. τοῦ θεοῦ ℵ.   κεκάθικεν ℵAD₂: ἐκάθισεν ς.

plished through self-sacrifice. The suffering was that of the cross, a death at once most painful and most humiliating.

For the correspondence between the sufferings and the glory of Christ compare ii. 9; Phil. ii. 9 (διό); Is. liii. 11; and for ἀντί v. 16; Matt. xvii. 27; xx. 28. Προκειμένης points to προκείμενον ἀγῶνα (v. 1). For χαρά (not a Pauline idea) see John xv. 11 note.

Σταυρός, which occurs here only in the Epistle, is used without the article, as in Phil. ii. 8, in order to fix attention on the nature of the Death. Elsewhere ὁ σταυρός (Col. i. 20; ii. 14 &c.) expresses the actual fact as well as the specific character of the Passion.

Σταυρόν, Theophylact says, τουτέστιν οὐχ ἁπλῶς θάνατον ἀλλὰ τὸν ἐπονείδιστον, a punishment which Cicero spoke of as 'crudelissimum teterrimumque' (adv. Verr. v. 64). Comp. 1 Cor. i. 18, 23. But what men count shame was seen by Christ in another light. From His position, raised infinitely above them, He could disregard their judgment.

ἐν δεξιᾷ τε...κεκάθικεν] The contrast of tenses is significant. He endured ...and hath sat down...The fact of suffering is wholly past but the issue of it abides for evermore. Contrast ἐκάθισεν c. viii. 1 note. For the perfect see v. 3 note.

Chrysostom says: ὁρᾷς τὸ ἔπαθλον; ὅπερ καὶ ὁ Παῦλος γράφων φησί (Phil. ii. 9 f.).

Œcumenius sees in the words Christ's power to requite His servants: ἱκανὸς οὖν καὶ ἀμείψασθαι ὑμᾶς ὑπὲρ τῶν δι' αὐτὸν θλίψεων.

It is impossible not to feel the progress of thought in the phrases ἐν δεξιᾷ τῆς μεγαλωσύνης (i. 3), ἐν δ. τοῦ θρόνου τῆς μεγαλ. (viii. 1), ἐν δ. τοῦ

θεοῦ (x. 12), and here ἐν δ. τ. θρ. τοῦ θεοῦ.

(b) The measure and the end of suffering (3—13).

The example of the triumph of Christ through suffering leads to a further consideration of the work of suffering for the Christian. Suffering is essentially a divine discipline. Under this aspect the author shews that the contemplation of Christ's victory through suffering brings sovereign support in affliction.

(a) The sufferings of the Hebrews were not more than simple chastisements (3—6); and

(β) Chastisement is the discipline of sons (7, 8).

(γ) He then characterises earthly and heavenly discipline (8, 9, 10), in the beginning and the end (11), and

(δ) draws a practical conclusion for the Hebrews in their trial (12, 13).

(a) Sufferings as chastisements (3—6).

Two thoughts are suggested by the consideration of Christ's sufferings (3). The sufferings of the Hebrews were relatively slight (4); and all sufferings which come from God are the wise discipline of a Father (5, 6). So it was (the thought is implied though not expressed here) in some sense which we hardly grasp even in the case of Christ, the Son (v. 7 f.).

At this point the image is changed. The thought is no longer of effort but of endurance; of the assault of a powerful adversary which must be met, and not of a struggle voluntarily sought.

Chrysostom notices the use of different forms of consolation: ἔστιν εἴδη παρακλήσεως δύο, ἐναντία ἀλλήλοις εἶναι δοκοῦντα...τὸ μὲν γὰρ ὅταν πολλὰ λέγωμεν πεπονθέναι τινάς...τὸ δὲ ὅταν λέγωμεν ὅτι οὐ μέγα τι πέπονθας...καὶ τὸ μὲν

³ἀναλογίσασθε γὰρ τὸν τοιαύτην ὑπομεμενηκότα ὑπὸ

3 om. τὸν′ (τοι. ὑπ.) D₂*.　　　ὑπό: ἀπό D₂*.

τετρυχωμένην τὴν ψυχὴν διαναπαύει...τὸ δὲ ῥαθυμοῦσαν αὐτὴν καὶ ὑπτίαν γενομένην ἐπιστρέφει....

³For consider Him that hath endured such gainsaying by sinners against their own selves, that ye fail not through weariness, fainting in your souls: ⁴ye have not yet resisted unto blood, contending against sin; ⁵and have ye forgotten the exhortation that discourseth with you as sons,

My son, regard not lightly the Lord's chastening,
Nor faint when thou art reproved by Him;
⁶For whom the Lord loveth He chasteneth,
And scourgeth every son whom He receiveth?

3. ἀναλογίσασθε γάρ...] Vulg. Recogitate enim...For consider Him that hath endured...Be patient, the writer says, look to Christ; for I charge you to consider His sufferings. If the eyes are steadfastly turned to Him (ἀφορῶντες) the believer cannot fail to ponder the vision and to estimate the power of His work in relation to Life. That is sufficient in order that Christians may support their afflictions. If the leader bears the brunt of the battle the soldier can follow.

The use of γάρ with imp. implies the result of the comparison.

The word ἀναλογίζομαι does not occur elsewhere in the LXX. or N. T. It is common in classical Greek, and expresses in particular the careful estimate of one object with regard to another. Plat. Theæt. p. 186 A (ἀναλ. τὰ γεγονότα...πρὸς τὰ μέλλοντα); Resp. x. 618 c. The use here is in respect of a person and not of a thing is remarkable. The writer seems to say ' Consider Christ, reckoning up His suffer-

ings point by point, going over them again and again, not the sufferings on the Cross only, but all that led up to it.' This is to be done once for all (ἀναλογίσασθε not ἀναλογίζεσθε).

τὸν τοιαύτ. ὑπομεμ....ἀντιλογίαν] Him that hath endured such gainsaying, such opposition as shewed itself in the infliction of the most cruel shame and death, in comparison with which your sufferings are insignificant.

For the use of the perfect (ὑπομεμενηκότα) in connexion with the abiding results of Christ's work the following passages should be carefully studied:

v. 2 (κεκάθικεν): i. 4 (κεκληρονόμηκεν); ii. 9 (ἠλαττωμένον...ἐστεφανωμένον); 18 (πέπονθεν); iv. 14 (διεληλυθότα); 15 (πεπειρασμένον); vii. 26 (κεχωρισμένος); 28 (τετελειωμένον); ix. 26 (πεφανέρωται).

Compare c. vii. 6 (note) for the use of the perfect generally.

The remarkable reading ὑπὸ τῶν ἀμ. εἰς ἑαυτ. gives the idea expressed in Num. xvi. 38, ' sinners against their own selves.' The definite form (ὑπὸ τῶν ἁμαρτ. not ὑφ. ἁμαρτ.) describes the representative class in the great crisis of the nation's history. Ἀμαρτάνειν εἰς is the common construction (Luke xv. 28 &c.).

Theodoret strangely joins εἰς αὐτούς with ἀναλογίσασθε : τὶ εἰς αὐτοὺς ἀντὶ τοῦ εἰς ἑαυτούς. λογίσασθε, φησί, παρ' ὑμῖν αὐτοῖς...

For the word ἀντιλογία, which corresponds to רִיב in Pss. xvii. (xviii.) 44; xxx.(xxxi.) 21, compare Jude 11; John xix. 12; Luke ii. 34; Acts xxviii. 19; Tit. i. 9; ii. 9.

The opposition in words is the beginning of every form and act of opposition.

τῶν ἁμαρτωλῶν εἰς ⌐ἑαυτοὺς⌐ ἀντιλογίαν, ἵνα μὴ κάμητε ταῖς ψυχαῖς ὑμῶν ἐκλυόμενοι. ⁴ Οὔπω μέχρις αἵματος ἀντικατέστητε πρὸς τὴν ἁμαρτίαν ἀνταγωνιζόμενοι,

3 ἑαυτὸν

ἑαυτούς אּ*D₂* (vg) syr vg (αυτους אᶜ): ἑαυτόν A: αὐτόν ς.   ἐκλυ.: ἐκλελυμένοι
D₂*.   4 οὔπω: +γάρ D₂* (vg) me the.

ἵνα μὴ κάμητε … ἐκλυόμενοι] The final failure comes from continuous weakening. The moral strength is enfeebled little by little (ἐκλυόμενοι as contrasted with ἐκλυθέντες). So it may be that those who, like the Hebrews, had begun well are unable to sustain the long stress of the conflict.

For the use of ἐκλύεσθαι see v. 5 ; Gal. vi. 9; Matt. xv. 32.

The rhythm of the sentence seems to be decisive for the connexion of ταῖς ψ. ὑ. with ἐκλυόμενοι. Comp. Polyb. xx. 4 ἀνέπεσον ταῖς ψ. Κάμνειν is used absolutely James v. 15.

Theophylact gives the general sense very happily : τὸ ἀναλογίσασθαι τὸν Χριστὸν τονώσει ἡμῶν τὰς ψυχὰς καὶ νευρώσει καὶ οὐκ ἐάσει ἐκλελύσθαι καὶ ἀπαγορεῦσαι πρὸς τὰς θλίψεις.

4. οὔπω…ἀντικατέστητε…] The sufferings of the Hebrews are contrasted with those of Christ. Their struggle had not yet been to death. At the same time it is implied (οὔπω) that they must be prepared for a deadly encounter.

The statement is in no way opposed to the view that the Epistle was addressed to a Palestinian Church out of which St Stephen and St James had suffered martyrdom. The recollection of what these early witnesses had borne would in fact add point to this exhortation to the second generation of the Church.

πρὸς τὴν ἁμ. ἀνταγων.] The conflict of the Hebrews is spoken of as a conflict with sin rather than sinners (v. 3), in order to emphasise its essential character (even believers are 'sinners') and to include its various forms. Christians had to contend primarily with open enemies whose assaults seem to be contemplated here in μέχρις αἵματος. At the same time there is an inward struggle which cannot be wholly overlooked, though this did not involve literally ' a resistance to blood.'

There is no authority for giving a metaphorical sense to μέχρις αἵματος (' to the uttermost '), and such a sense would be pointless here. Comp. 2 Macc. xiii. 14. The words of Phil. ii. 1 μέχρι θανάτου seem to be present to the thoughts of the writer.

Both the words ἀντικαταστῆναι and ἀνταγωνίζεσθαι are classical, but the latter does not occur elsewhere in the Greek Scriptures. The balance of the sentence requires πρὸς τὴν ἁμ. to be taken with ἀνταγωνιζόμενοι. The imagery of the arena still floats before the writer's mind. For the simple ἀγωνίζεσθαι see 1 Tim. vi. 12 ; 2 Tim. iv. 7 (1 Cor. ix. 25) ; ἐπαγωνίζεσθαι Jude 5.

The personification of sin (ἀνταγωνιζ. πρὸς ἁμ.) is natural and common : James i. 15 ; Rom. vi. 12 ff. Ἀντικατέστητε οἷον εἰς παράταξιν, εἰς πόλεμον, ὡς καὶ τῆς ἁμαρτίας ἀνθεστώσης (Œcum.). Sin is one whether it shew itself within, in the Christian himself (v. 1), or without, as here, in his adversaries.

For the difference between ἡ ἁμαρτία and ἁμαρτία see iii. 13 ; v. 1 (ἡ ἁμ.) and iv. 15 ; ix. 26 note, 28 ; x. 6, 8, 18 ; xi. 25 ; xiii. 11 (ἁμ.). See also Additional Note on i. 3.

⁵καὶ ἐκλέλησθε τῆς παρακλήσεως, ἥτις ὑμῖν ὡς υἱοῖς διαλέγεται,

Υἱέ μογ, μὴ ὀλιγώρει παιΔείας Κγρίογ,
μηΔὲ ἐκλγογ ὑπ' αὐτοῦ ἐλεγχόμενος·
⁶ὅν Γὰρ ἀγαπᾷ Κγριος παιΔεγει,
μαστιΓοῖ Δὲ πάντα γίον ὅν παραΔέχεται.

5 εκλελΗсθαιπαρατΗсπαρακλΗсεωс D₂*.   om. μου D₂*.   ἐλ. ὑ. αὐ. D₂.

---

5. καὶ ἐκλέλησθε τῆς παρακλ....] *and have ye forgotten the exhortation* (Vulg. *consolationis*)..? It is doubtful whether the sentence is to be taken interrogatively or affirmatively (*and ye have forgotten*). The former interpretation gives the most forcible sense. The question pleads against the forgetfulness which it implies; and still it is in form less severe than a statement.

The idea of παράκλησις (as of παράκλητος) goes beyond any single rendering. The divine word, to which appeal is made, is at once an encouragement and a consolation. Sufferings are tempered by the providence of God, and they are a sign of sonship.

ʼΕκλανθάνεσθαι occurs here only in the Greek Scriptures. It is in classical writers from Homer downwards.

ἥτις...διαλέγεται] *that discourseth with you as sons.* The utterance of Scripture is treated as the voice of God conversing with men. Through the written word the Wisdom of God addresses us.

This peculiar use of διαλέγεσθαι does not occur elsewhere in N. T., but the personification in Gal. iii. 8 (προϊ-δοῦσα ἡ γραφή) is even bolder.

For ἥτις see ii. 3 note.

υἱέ μου...] Prov. iii. 11 f. Comp. Job v. 17. Philo quotes the words *de congr. erud. grat.* § 31 (i. 544 M.) οὕτω τοίνυν ἡ ποιὰ κάκωσις (Deut. viii. 2) ὠφέλιμόν ἐστιν...ἔνθεν δ' ἐμοὶ δοκεῖ τις τῶν φοιτητῶν Μωϋσέως, ὄνομα Εἰρηνικός,

ὅς πατρίῳ γλώσσῃ Σαλομῶν καλεῖται, φάναι, Παιδείας θεοῦ, υἱέ, μὴ ὀλιγώρει... οὕτως ἄρα ἡ ἐπίπληξις καὶ νουθεσία καλὸν νενόμισται, ὥστε δι' αὐτῆς ἡ πρὸς θεὸν ὁμολογία συγγένεια γίγνεται. τί γὰρ οἰκειότερον υἱῷ πατρὸς ἢ υἱοῦ πατρί;

In a remarkable passage Epictetus claims for man a divine sonship : διατί μὴ εἴπῃ τις αὐτὸν Κόσμιον (a citizen of the Universe); διατί μὴ υἱὸν τοῦ θεοῦ; διατί δὲ φοβηθήσεταί τι τῶν γινομένων ἐν ἀνθρώποις; ...τὸ δὲ τὸν θεὸν ποιητὴν ἔχειν καὶ πατέρα καὶ κηδεμόνα οὐκέτι ἡμᾶς ἐξαιρήσεται λυπῶν καὶ φόβων; (*Dissert.* i. 9, 6 f.).

μὴ ὀλιγώρει] Vulg. Hebr. אַל־תָּמְאָס *regard not lightly.* Do not make it of little account ; do not neglect to consider its real scope and end.

The verb ὀλιγωρεῖν does not occur again in the Greek Scriptures. For ἐκλύου see *v.* 3.

6. μαστιγοῖ] The LXX. read כְּאָב, which the Masoretic text points כְּאָב (*as a father*), as if it were some form from כָּאַב 'he was pained.'

For παιδεύειν compare 1 Tim. i. 20.

(β) *Chastisement is the discipline of sons* (7, 8).

⁷*It is for chastening ye endure; it is as with sons God dealeth with you. For what son is there whom his father chasteneth not?* ⁸*But if ye are without chastening, whereof all have become partakers, then are ye bastards and not sons.*

⁷εἰς παιδείαν ὑπομένετε· ὡς υἱοῖς ὑμῖν προσφέρεται ὁ
θεός· τίς γὰρ υἱὸς ὃν οὐ παιδεύει πατήρ ; ⁸εἰ δὲ χωρίς
ἐστε παιδείας ἧς μέτοχοι γεγόνασι πάντες, ἄρα νόθοι

7 εἰς παιδείαν ὑπομένετε ℵA vg syr vg me the: (παραδ.) εἰς παιδ. | ὑπομείνατε | D₂
(recepit in disciplinam | perseverare d -ate e): εἰ παιδ. ὑπομ. ϛ.   τίς γάρ ℵ*A vg
the: +ἐστίν ℵᶜD₂ syr vg me.   8 νόθροι A.

7. εἰς π. ὑπομ.] Vulg. in disciplina
perseverate. The clause may be either
imperative or indicative. The absence
of a connecting particle in the next
clause favours the latter view. It is
for chastening ye endure : it is as
with sons God dealeth with you. The
divine purpose is unquestionable, but
at the same time the efficacy of the
discipline depends on the spirit with
which it is received. Patient endurance alone converts suffering into a
beneficent lesson. 'Επειδὴ τοσαῦτα
ἐπάθετε κακά, νομίζετε ὅτι ἀφῆκεν ὑμᾶς ὁ
θεὸς καὶ μισεῖ; εἰ μὴ ἐπάθετε, τότε ἔδει
τοῦτο ὑποπτεύειν (Chrys.). Compare
Priscill. x. p. 133 ecce Deus dum cor-
ripit diligit, et erudit potius peccati
agnitione quam plectit. Comp. 2
Macc. vi. 12.

The difference between παιδεύειν
and διδάσκειν is always clearly marked.
Παιδεύειν, the habitual rendering of
יָסַר in the LXX. (about 40 times),
suggests moral training, disciplining
of the powers of man, while διδάσκειν
expresses the communication of a
particular lesson. This force of παιδεύειν is to be taken account of in
Acts vii. 22 ; xxii. 3. The training
given by a great master is something
far more than his teaching.

The word παιδεία is used differently
in this verse and the next. Discipline is here regarded as the end,
and in the following verse as the
means. The corresponding word מוּסָר
is used with like variation of meaning:
e.g. Prov. xxiii. 12, 13. For εἰς of the
end see c. iv. 16; vi. 16. 'Υπομένειν is
used absolutely 2 Tim. ii. 12; 1 Pet.
ii. 20 ; James v. 11; Rom. xii. 12.

ὡς υἱ. ὑ. προσφ.] The very fact that
you suffer is, if you rightly regard it,
an assurance of your sonship. You
can recognise in it the dealing of a
Father. The clause is independent.
The title of privilege (υἱός) is naturally
used : comp. ii. 10. The title τέκνον
(-να) does not occur in the Epistle.

The use of προσφέρεσθαι in ὑμῖν
προσφ. (Vulg. vobis offert se) is not
found again in the Greek Scriptures ;
but it is common in classical writers
and in Philo.

It is worth observing again in this
connexion that the absolute title of
πατήρ is not given to God in the
Epistle, except in the quotation i. 5.
It is found in all the other groups of
Books in the N. T.

τίς γὰρ υἱ. ὃν οὐ παιδ.] The words
can be rendered either For who is
a son whom his father...; or For
what son is there whom... The latter
construction is more simple and expresses more distinctly the thought
of suffering on the part of sons.
Apoc. iii. 19 ὅσους ἐὰν φιλῶ ἐλέγχω
καὶ παιδεύω.

Comp. Philo de Joseph. § 14 (ii. p.
52 M. τέκνα γνήσια); de vit. Mos. i.
§ 60 (ii. p. 132 M. υἱοὶ γνήσιοι).

8. εἰ δὲ χωρίς ἐστε παιδείας...πάντες]
The order of the words throws the
emphasis on χωρίς. All true sons, all
who have ever realised this relation,
have been made partakers in chastening. The reference is apparently to
divine sonship and not to human.

The use of the compound perfect
form μέτοχοι γεγόνασιν (comp. c. iii.
14 note) shews that the chastisement
was personally accepted and perma-

καὶ οὐχ υἱοί ἐστε. ⁹εἶτα τοὺς μὲν τῆς σαρκὸς ἡμῶν
πατέρας εἴχομεν παιδευτὰς καὶ ἐνετρεπόμεθα· οὐ πολὺ
μᾶλλον ὑποταγησόμεθα τῷ πατρὶ τῶν πνευμάτων καὶ

καὶ οὐχ υἱ. ἐ. אAD₂* vg: ἐ. καὶ οὐχ υἱ. ς syr vg.   9 εἶτα: εἰ δέ syr vg.
πολύ אAD₂*: πολλῷ ς.   ϛολὺ+δέ א°D₂*.

nent in its effects, and not simply a
transitory pain (μετέσχον, μέτ. ἐγένοντο). Compare v. 11 (γεγυμνασμένοις);
iv. 15 πεπειρασμένον: Matt. v. 10 δε-
διωγμένοι.

πάντες] Notandum autem quia non
omnis qui flagellatur filius est, sed
omnis qui filius est flagellatur (Primas.
after Chrys.).

ἄρα νόθοι ἐστέ] Vulg. ergo adulteri
...then are ye bastards who stand in
no recognised position towards their
father as heirs to his name and for-
tune : for their character he has no
anxiety as for that of sons : they are
without the range of his discipline.
῞Ωσπερ ἐν ταῖς οἰκίαις τῶν νόθων κατα-
φρονοῦσιν οἱ πατέρες κἂν μηδὲν μανθά-
νωσι, κἂν μὴ ἔνδοξοι γίνωνται, τῶν δὲ
γνησίων ἕνεκεν υἱῶν δεδοίκασι μήποτε
ῥαθυμήσωσι, τοῦτο καὶ ἐπὶ τοῦ παρόν-
τος (Chrys.). For ἄρα see c. iv. 9
note.

(γ) Characteristics of earthly and
heavenly discipline (9—11).

The thought of filial discipline on
earth, which has been already introduced (v. 8), is followed out in some
detail in order to illustrate the obligations and issues of the discipline of
God. The discipline of God answers
to greater claims (v. 9), and is directed by higher wisdom to a nobler end
(v. 10), than belong to natural parents.
And while all discipline alike is painful to bear we are taught by experience to look to its issue (v. 11).

⁹Furthermore we had the fathers
of our flesh to chasten us, and we
gave them regard : shall we not
much rather be in subjection to the
Father of spirits and live ?   ¹⁰For
while they chastened us as it pleased

them for a few days, He chastens us
for our profit that we may receive
of His holiness.   ¹¹All chastening for
the present seemeth to be not joyous
but grievous; but afterward it yieldeth peaceable fruit to them that have
been exercised thereby, even the fruit
of righteousness.

9. εἶτα ... ἐνετρεπόμεθα] Furthermore we had the fathers of our flesh
to chasten us, and we gave them regard
...This particle εἶτα has been taken as an
interrogative : 'Is it so then that we
had...,' according to common classical
use, but in this case the following
sentence would naturally begin with
καί (καὶ οὐ πολὺ μᾶλλον).   It is better
therefore to regard it as introducing
a second argument : further, yet a-
gain.   In v. 8 the Apostle has shewn
the universality of filial discipline :
he now shews in what spirit it should
be borne, drawing his conclusion from
natural experience.   There is no exact parallel in the N. T. to this use of
εἶτα, which is used in enumerations
(e.g. 1 Cor. xii. 28 ; xv. 5, 7) as well as
in sequences (e.g. Mk. iv. 28).

The word παιδευτής (Vulg. erudi-
tores) is found again in Rom. ii. 20 ;
Hos. v. 2 ; Ecclus. xxxvii. 19. It expresses not only the fact of the discipline, but the parental office to exercise it.

Ἐντρέπομαι (Vulg. reverebamur) is
found in Luke xviii. 2, 4 ; xx. 13 (and
parallels).

τοὺς τ. σ. ἡ. πατ....τῷ πατ. τ. πν.]
The fathers of our earthly, corporeal,
being are contrasted with the Father
of spirits, the Author not only of our
spiritual being but of all spiritual
beings (τῶν πνευμ. not τοῦ πν. ἡμῶν).

ζήσομεν; ¹⁰οἱ μὲν γὰρ πρὸς ὀλίγας ἡμέρας κατὰ τὸ

10 οἱ : ὁ ℵ*.

Their limited relation to us (τῆς σ. ἡμῶν) is contrasted with His universal power. By our spirit (v. 23) we have connexion with Him and with a higher order. We owe to Him therefore a more absolute subjection than to those from whom we derive the transitory limitations of our nature. The language is perhaps based upon Num. xvi. 22, xxvii. 16 (LXX.) (ὁ) θεὸς τῶν πνευμάτων καὶ πάσης σαρκός (τῶν ἀνθρώπων). Comp. Clem. R. i. 58 ὁ πανεπόπτης θεὸς καὶ δεσπότης τῶν πνευμάτων καὶ Κύριος πάσης σαρκός. id. 59 τὸν παντὸς πνεύματος κτίστην καὶ ἐπίσκοπον (and Lightfoot's note); and Apoc. xxii. 6 ὁ Κύριος, ὁ θεὸς τῶν πνευμάτων τῶν προφητῶν.

οὐ πολὺ μ....καὶ ζήσομεν;] The form of this clause is different from that of the clause to which it corresponds. Instead of saying τῷ δὲ π. τ. πν. οὐχ ὑποταγ.; the writer brings forward the overwhelming superiority of the obligation (οὐ πολὺ μᾶλλον). So also the careful regard (ἐνετρεπόμεθα) due to an earthly parent is contrasted with the complete submission due to God (ὑποταγησόμεθα).

For the use of μέν without δέ following compare Luke xxii. 22; Col. ii. 23.

Such absolute subjection is crowned by the highest blessing (καὶ ζήσομεν). True life comes from complete self-surrender. As the One Son fulfilled His Father's will and lives through Him, so the many sons live through His life in obedience to Him: John vi. 57 (διά), xiv. 15, 19. This life is given on the part of God, but it has to be realised by the individual: 1 John v. 16.

Compare the striking words of Theophylact: καὶ ζήσομεν προσέθηκεν ἵνα δείξῃ ὅτι ὁ ἀνυπότακτος οὐδὲ ζῇ. ἔξω γάρ ἐστι τοῦ θεοῦ ὅς ἐστι ζωή: and

Œcumenius: τοῦτο γὰρ ζωὴ τὸ ὑποτετάχθαι θεῷ.

The phrase ὁ πατὴρ τῶν πνευμάτων is quite general, the Father of spirits embodied, disembodied, unembodied. The context, which regards disobedience as possible, seems to exclude the idea that τὰ πνεύματα means only the spirits in conscious, willing, fellowship with God.

The πνεῦμα corresponds with the σάρξ, in the narrower sense, as an integral element in man's nature. By the latter he is bound to the line of ancestors who determine the conditions of his earthly life (vii. 5, 10 note): by the former he stands in immediate connexion with God.

The Greek Fathers are vague in their interpretation of the phrase, as Chrysostom: τῷ πατρὶ τῶν πνευμάτων. ἤτοι τῶν χαρισμάτων λέγει ἤτοι τῶν εὐχῶν (leg. ψυχῶν) ἤτοι τῶν ἀσωμάτων δυνάμεων. Theophylact adds to χαρισμάτων and ἀσωμάτων δυνάμεων, ἤ, ὅπερ καὶ οἰκειότερον, τῶν ψυχῶν. Theodoret: πατέρα πνευμάτων τὸν πνευματικὸν πατέρα κέκληκεν ὡς τῶν πνευματικῶν χαρισμάτων πηγήν.

The later Latin Fathers speak more decidedly: Pater spirituum, id est creator animarum, Deus omnipotens est, qui bona creavit, primum ex nihilo, deinde vero ex elementis, corpora hominum aliorumque animalium. Animam vero hominis ex nihilo creavit et creat adhuc; non est enim probandum quod anima pars deitatis sit; quoniam deitas increata est, anima autem creatura est. Idcirco autem omnipotentem Deum creatorem animarum appellat, non corporum, cum omnium creator sit quia...anima ...semper a Deo ex nihilo creatur (Primas.).

10. The method of human discipline is as inferior to the method of

δοκοῦν αὐτοῖς ἐπαίδευον, ὁ δὲ ἐπὶ τὸ συμφέρον εἰς τὸ
μεταλαβεῖν τῆς ἁγιότητος αὐτοῦ. ¹¹πᾶσα ⌜μὲν⌝ παιδεία
πρὸς μὲν τὸ παρὸν οὐ δοκεῖ χαρᾶς εἶναι ἀλλὰ λύπης,
ὕστερον δὲ καρπὸν εἰρηνικὸν τοῖς δι᾽ αὐτῆς γεγυμνασ-

11 δὲ

ἐπαίδευεν ἡμᾶς καὶ τὰ δοκοῦντα αὐτοῖς D₂*.   συμφέρων A.   om. εἰς τό א*.
11 δέ א°A vg syr vg me: μέν א*: om. D₂*.   αὐτῆς: αὐτοῖς D₂*.

the divine discipline as the claims of
the one are inferior to the claims of
the other.

The clauses in the verse are related
inversely :

πρὸς ὀλίγας ἡμέρας
κατὰ τὸ δοκοῦν
ἐπὶ τὸ συμφέρον
εἰς τὸ μεταλαβεῖν τῆς ἁγιότητος αὐτοῦ.

The discipline of the human father
is regulated 'according to his pleasure.' Even when his purpose is best,
he may fail as to the method, and his
purpose may be selfish. But with
God, for His part, purpose and accomplishment are identical; and His aim
is the advantage of His children.
The spiritual son then may be sure
both as to the will and as to the
wisdom of his Father.

Again the discipline of the earthly
father is directed characteristically
to the circumstances of a transitory
life : (πρὸς ὀλ. ἡμ. 'with a view to a
few days,' 'for a few days,' in the
final sense of 'for'): that of the
heavenly Father has in view the participation of His son in His own eternal nature (comp. 2 Pet. i. 4), 'after
His likeness.'

The interpretation of πρὸς ὀλ. ἡμ.
(Vulg. in tempore paucorum dierum)
simply of the short period of life
during which the paternal discipline
both of man and God lasts ('for a
few days' in the temporal sense of
'for') seems to introduce a thought
foreign to the context. To insist
on the brevity of human discipline
would be to weaken the argument,

which rests on general relations.
The discipline of the earthly parent
is for a short time, and that which
the discipline directly regards is short
also.

For the use of πρός compare v. 11
(πρὸς τὸ παρόν); 1 Tim. iv. 8 (πρὸς
ὀλίγον). Notantur dies non solum ii
quos durat ipsa disciplina sed ad quos
disciplinæ fructus pertinet (Bengel).

With ἐπὶ τὸ συμφέρον compare 1
Cor. xii. 7 πρὸς τὸ συμφέρον. The word
ἁγιότης occurs again 2 Cor. i. 12 ; μεταλαβεῖν, c. vi. 7. With the general
idea compare Philo, Leg. Alleg. i. § 13
(i. 50) φιλόδωρος ὢν ὁ θεὸς χαρίζεται
τὰ ἀγαθὰ πᾶσι καὶ τοῖς μὴ τελείοις,
προκαλούμενος αὐτοὺς εἰς μετουσίαν καὶ
ζῆλον ἀρετῆς.

So Chrysostom says of our relation
to God: φιλούμεθα οὐχ ἵνα λάβῃ ἀλλ᾽
ἵνα δῷ. And God gives that which
He is : 1 Pet. i. 15 f. (Lev. xi. 44);
Matt. v. 48.

11. πᾶσα μὲν παιδ....λύπης] Yet the
fruit of discipline is not gained at
once. All chastening, the divine no
less than the human, seemeth, even
though it is not so in its essence, for
the present, looking at that only, to
be not joyous but grievous. It might
have been supposed that divine discipline would be free from sorrow.
But this also is first brought under
the general law and then considered
in itself.

For χαρᾶς (λύπης) εἶναι, see x. 39,
note.

ὕστερον δὲ...δικαι.] yet, afterward it
yieldeth, as its proper return (ἀποδί-

μένοις ἀποδίδωσιν δικαιοσύνης. ¹²Διὸ τὰς παρειμένας χεῖρας
καὶ τὰ παραλελυμένα γόνατα ἀνορθώσατε, ¹³καὶ τροχιὰς ὀρθὰς ⌜ποιεῖτε⌝

13 ποιήσατε

13 ποιεῖτε ℵ* : ποιήσατε ⸏ ℵᶜAD₂.

δωσιν, comp. Apoc. xxii. 2), *peaceable fruit to them that have been exercised thereby*, even the fruit *of righteousness*.

The conflict of discipline issues in that perfect peace which answers to the fulfilment of law. Castigator demonstrat se fideliter fecisse : castigatus id agnoscit et gratiam habet : inde pax (Bengel).

In the LXX. ἀποδιδόναι most commonly represents הֵשִׁיב (over 50 times), less frequently שִׁלֵּם (over 20 times), and נָתַן (21 times). It suggests that there is a claim in response to which something is given. Comp. Acts iv. 33.

For the singular καρπόν see Matt. iii. 8, 10 ; εἰρηνικός (Vulg. *pacatissimum*), which is common in the LXX. occurs again James iii. 17. For the perfect γεγυμνασμένοις see *v.* 8 note ; and for the image Chrysostom's note : ὁρᾷς πῶς καὶ εὐφήμῳ ὀνόματι κέχρηται ; ἄρα γυμνασία ἐστὶν ἡ παιδεία, τὸν ἀθλητὴν ἰσχυρὸν ἐργαζομένη καὶ ἀκαταγώνιστον ἐν τοῖς ἀγῶσι καὶ ἄμαχον ἐν τοῖς πολέμοις.

The word δικαιοσύνης stands impressively at the end (James ii. 1, τῆς δόξης), explaining and summing up what has been said generally : *peaceful fruit —even the fruit of righteousness,* that is, consisting in righteousness. Comp. James iii. 18 ; 2 Tim. iv. 8 ; c. ix. 15 ; x. 20. Peace and righteousness both in different ways correspond to the issue of perfect discipline, through which all action becomes the expression of obedience to the divine will. Compare Is. xxxii. 17.

There is a striking parallel to the thought in a saying of Aristotle preserved by Diogenes Laert.: τῆς παι-

δείας τὰς μὲν ῥίζας εἶναι πικρὰς, γλυκεῖς δὲ τοὺς καρποὺς (Diog. Laert. v. 18).

(δ) *Practical conclusion for the Hebrews in their trial* (12, 13).

¹² *Wherefore set right the hands that hang down and the palsied knees;* ¹³ *and make straight paths for your feet, that the limb which is lame be not put out of joint, but rather be healed.*

12. διό...] *Wherefore* since discipline is necessary, painful, and salutary, provide, as you can, that it may be effectual. Strengthen where it is possible those who are called to endure it ; and remove from their way stumbling-blocks which can be removed.

The Apostle urges those who were themselves in danger to help others in like peril. Such efforts are the surest support of the tempted.

The figurative language which he borrows from various parts of the O. T. suggests the manifold strengthening of powers for conflict ('hands') and for progress ('knees'); and also the removal of external difficulties. Αἱ μὲν χεῖρες ἐνεργείας, οἱ δὲ πόδες κινήσεως σύμβολον (Theophylact).

The images are found Is. xxxv. 3 ; Ecclus. xxv. 23. For παρειμένας and παραλελυμένα compare Deut. xxxii. 36 ; 2 Sam. iv. 1 (LXX.); for ἀνορθώσατε (Vulg. *erigite*) Ps. xx. (xix.) 9 ; Lk. xiii. 13 ; Acts xv. 16 (Amos ix. 11).

13. καὶ τροχ....] Vulg. *et gressus rectos facite pedibus vestris.* The phrase is taken from Prov. iv. 26 ὀρθὰς τροχιὰς ποίει σοῖς ποσὶ καὶ τὰς ὁδούς σου κατεύθυνε (פַּלֵּס מַעְגַּל רַגְלֶךָ) i.e. make plain (straight) the path of thy foot). The words may be rendered 'make straight paths *for* your feet,'

τοῖς ποσὶν ὑμῶν, ἵνα μὴ τὸ χωλὸν ἐκτραπῇ, ἰαθῇ δὲ
μᾶλλον.   ¹⁴Εἰρήνην διώκετε μετὰ πάντων, καὶ τὸν

i.e. for the feet of the whole society
to tread in ; or '*with* your feet,' as
giving a good example to others.
Chrysostom says apparently in the
latter sense: ὀρθά, φησί, βαδίζετε ὥστε
μὴ ἐπιταθῆναι τὴν χωλείαν; and this
is the meaning given by the Latin
Vulgate. But the context favours
the first rendering. The thought
seems to be that of a road prepared
to walk in without windings or stumbling-blocks: Matt. iii. 3.
For the image generally compare
Philo, *de migrat. Abr.* § 26 (i. p. 458
M.).
The word τροχιά (*orbita, wheel-track*)
is found in LXX. only in the book of
Proverbs as the translation of מַעְגָּל
(ii. 15; iv. 11; v. 6, 21).
The common reading (ποιήσατε)
gives an accidental hexameter.

ἵνα μὴ τὸ χ.] *that the* limb which is
lame be not put out of joint. The
more exact form would be ἵνα τὸ χ.
μὴ ἐκτρ., but the negative is attracted
(as it were) to the final particle.
Comp. 1 Tim. vi. 1. By τὸ χωλόν
(Vulg. *claudicans*) the Apostle describes the lame member in the Church,
who is unable to stand or walk firmly
on his way. Compare 1 K. xviii. 21.
The 'halting' of the Hebrews 'between
two opinions' is the characteristic type
of their weakness.
The word ἐκτρέπεσθαι is elsewhere
found in the Greek Scriptures in the
sense of 'being turned out of the way';
and it is commonly so interpreted here
(Vulg. *erret*); but there is no obvious
fitness in adding to 'lameness' the
idea of 'straying,' and the sense 'put
out of joint' has adequate support,
and the addition of ἰαθῇ, which has
no connexion with 'straying,' seems
to require it.   Hippocr. *de offic. med.*
vi. p. 745 H. (in discussing the treatment of injured limbs) θέσις δὲ μαλ-

θακή, ὁμαλή, ἀνάρροπος τοῖσιν ἐξέχουσι
τοῦ σώματος, οἷον πτέρνῃ καὶ ἰσχίῳ, ὡς
μήτε ἀνακλᾶται μήτε ἐκτρέπεται (ἢ-ηται).
(2) 14—17. The necessity of peace
and purity.
The special exhortations which arose
directly from circumstances of trial
and discipline lead on to directions
of a general character. The duty of
mutual help (*v.* 13) naturally suggests
the consideration of the power of
mutual influence (*vv.* 14—18); and
this, in the actual state of society,
gives occasion to a solemn warning
as to the irremediable consequences
of faithlessness (*v.* 17).

¹⁴*Follow after peace with all men,
and the sanctification without which
no man shall see the Lord;* ¹⁵*looking
carefully lest* there be *any man that
falleth back from the grace of God;
lest any root of bitterness springing
up trouble you, and through this the
many be defiled;* ¹⁶*lest there be any
fornicator, or profane person as
Esau, who for one mess of meat sold
his own birthright.* ¹⁷*For ye know
that even afterward, when he wished
to inherit the blessing, he was rejected
—for he found no place for repentance—though he sought it diligently
with tears.*

14. εἰρ. διώκ....καὶ τὸν ἀγ....] Ps.
xxxiv. 14; 1 Pet. iii. 11; Rom. xii. 18.
The writer extends his view to the
wider relations of life; and the two
commands which he gives express the
aim and the necessary limitation of
the Christian's intercourse with 'the
world.' The Christian seeks peace
with all alike, but he seeks holiness
also, and this cannot be sacrificed for
that.
The parallel with Rom. xii. 18 suggests that πάντων must not be limited
in any way. On the other hand the
next verse takes account of members of the Christian society. But

ἁγιασμόν, οὗ χωρὶς οὐδεὶς ὄψεται τὸν κύριον, ¹⁵ἐπισκο-
ποῦντες μή τις ὑστερῶν ἀπὸ τῆς χάριτος τοῦ θεοῦ,

14 κύριον: θεόν d (vg). 　　　　　 15 +ἵνα´ μήτις D₂*.

the thought of ἁγιασμός supplies a
natural transition from a wider to a
narrower view. The graces of purity
and peacemaking are the subjects of
two successive beatitudes : Matt. v.
8, 9.
The use of διώκετε marks the eager-
ness and constancy of the pursuit.
Compare 1 Pet. iii. 11 (Ps. xxxiv. 15)
ζητησάτω εἰρήνην καὶ διωξάτω αὐτήν
(וְרָדְפֵהוּ). Elsewhere the metaphorical use of the word in the N. T. is
confined to St Paul. Διώκετε, τουτέστι
καὶ πόρρω οὖσαν τὴν εἰρήνην σπουδάζετε
καταλαβεῖν (Theophlct.).
For τὸν ἁγιασμόν (Vulg. sanctimo-
niam) compare v. 10; Rom. vi. 16, 22.
The definite article (again only 1
Thess. iv. 3) marks the familiar Christian embodiment of the virtue. (Contrast the anarthrous εἰρήνην.)
The word ἁγιασμός is peculiar to
Biblical and Ecclesiastical Greek. It
occurs rarely in the LXX. (not in Lev.
xxiii. 27 according to the true reading). On the idea see c. ix. 13, note.
Perhaps it may be most simply described as the preparation for the
presence of God. *Without it no man
shall see the Lord*, that is, Christ, for
whose return in glory believers wait:
c. ix. 28. For ὄψεται see Matt. v. 8;
1 John iii. 2 ; 1 Cor. xiii. 12 ; Ex.
xxxiii. 19 ff. (Judg. xiii. 22); and for
τὸν κύριον, c. viii. 2 note.

15, 16. The conditions of social
intercourse impose upon Christians
the obligation of constant watchful-
ness lest the unchristian element
should communicate its evil to the
Church.
The three clauses μή τις ὑστ. ἀπό...,
μή τις ῥίζα..., μή τις πόρνος... are in
some sense bound together by the
use of a finite verb in the second
only. At the same time the element

of evil is presented in successive stages
of development. At first it is want of
progress : this defect spreads as a
source of positive infidelity : at last
there is open contempt of duties and
privileges.
The first and third clauses may be
treated as parallel with the second,
so that ἐνοχλῇ is taken with all three ;
or (which seems a simpler construction) ᾖ may be supplied in them, so
that they become independent clauses :
'lest there be any among you falling
short...lest there be among you any
fornicator...' In Deut. xxix. 18 the
verb expressed is ἐστίν: 'whether
there be...'; but ἐνοχλῇ more naturally
suggests ᾖ here.

15. ἐπισκοποῦντες μή τις ὑστ....]
(1 Pet. v. 2 ; not in LXX. Vulg. *con-
templantes*.)
The word ἐπισκοποῦντες expresses
the careful regard of those who occupy
a position of responsibility (as a physician, or a superintendent). Each
Christian shares this in due degree.
Μὴ τοίνυν πάντα ἐπὶ τοὺς διδασκάλους
ἐπιρρίπετε· μὴ πάντα ἐπὶ τοὺς ἡγου-
μένους· δύνασθε καὶ ὑμεῖς, φησίν, ἀλλήλους οἰκοδομεῖν (Chrys.). Μὴ μόνον
δὲ ἑαυτῶν ἀλλὰ καὶ ἀλλήλων ἐπιμελεῖσθε, καὶ τὸν κλονούμενον ὑπερείδετε καὶ
τὸν χειραγωγίας δεόμενον ἰατρεύσατε
(Theodt.).
In ὑστερεῖν ἀπὸ τῆς χ. τ. θ. the idea
seems to be that of falling behind,
not keeping pace with the movement
of divine grace which meets and stirs
the progress of the Christian (c. v.
11). The present participle describes
a continuous state and not a single
defection.
The construction ὑστερεῖν ἀπὸ τινος
marks a 'falling back' from that with
which some connexion exists, implying
a moral separation, while ὑστερεῖν

ΜΗ ΤΙC ῥίΖΑ ΠΙΚΡίΑC ἄΝω ΦΥΟΥϲΑ ἐΝΟΧΛΗ καὶ ⌜δι᾽ αὐτῆς⌝ μιαν-
θῶσιν οἱ πολλοί, ¹⁶μή τις πόρνος ἢ βέβηλος ὡς Ἠcaῦ,

15 διὰ ταύτης

δι᾽ αὐτῆς A: διὰ ταύτης ℵD₂.

οἱ πολλοί ℵA: πολλοί ⌣ D₂.

τινος expresses actual defect only, a falling short of. Compare Eccles. vi. 2 (LXX.) οὐκ ἔστι ὑστερῶν τῇ ψυχῇ αὐτοῦ ἀπὸ παντὸς οὗ ἐπιθυμεῖ. Compare Ecclus. vii. 34 μὴ ὑστέρει ἀπὸ κλαιόντων.

Theophylact applies the words to Christians as fellow-travellers on a long journey: καθάπερ ὁδόν τινα μακρὰν ὁδευόντων αὐτῶν ἐν συνοδίᾳ πολλῇ, φησί, Βλέπετε μή (whether) τις ἀπέμεινεν.

μή τις ῥ. π....ἐνοχλῇ] The image is taken from Deut. xxix. 17 f. The original connexion points to the perils of allurements to serve strange gods. The 'root' is personal (1 Macc. i. 10 ῥίζα ἁμαρτωλὸς 'Αντ. 'Επιφ.) and not doctrinal : a pernicious man and not a pernicious opinion. Compare Acts viii. 23.

The phrase 'root of bitterness' (as distinguished from 'bitter root') expresses the product and not simply the quality of the root itself. Οὐκ εἶπε πικρὰ ἀλλὰ πικρίας, τὴν μὲν γὰρ πικρὰν ῥίζαν ἔστι καρποὺς ἐνεγκεῖν γλυκεῖς, τὴν δὲ πικρίας ῥίζαν...οὐκ ἔστι πῃ γλυκὺν ἐνεγκεῖν καρπόν (Chrys.).

The clause ἄνω φύουσα adds a vivid touch to the picture. The seed, the root, lies hidden and reveals its power slowly (φύειν Lk. viii. 6, 8).

For the image compare Ign. Eph. 10 ἵνα μὴ τοῦ διαβόλου βοτάνη τις εὑρεθῇ ἐν ὑμῖν. id. Trall. 6; Philad. 1.

The word ἐνοχλεῖν occurs again in N. T. in Luke vi. 18. The pres. conj. ἐνοχλῇ leaves it uncertain whether the fear of such a present evil is actually realised. [The strange coincidence of letters between ΕΝΟΧΛΗ and ΕΝΧΟΛΗ of Deut. xxix. 18 cannot escape notice.]

μιανθ. οἱ πολλοί] the many be defiled. The poisonous influence spreads corruption through the society. For μιαίνειν see Tit. i. 15 (2 Pet. ii. 10, 20); and for οἱ πολλοί—the many, the mass of men, the body considered in its members—Matt. xxiv. 12; Rom. v. 15, 19; xii. 5; 1 Cor. x. 17, 33; 2 Cor. ii. 17.

16. μή τις πόρνος ἢ βέβ. ὡς Ἠσαῦ...] A question has been raised whether both πόρνος and βέβηλος are connected with 'Ησαῦ, or the latter only. The second view seems unquestionably to be right. Esau is presented in Scripture as the type of a 'profane' man, but he does not appear as πόρνος either literally or metaphorically. The later Jewish traditions can hardly have a place here. And, yet again, the words of explanation which follow justify the epithet βέβηλος, but they do not extend further. They imply therefore that πόρνος does not refer to him.

Another question arises whether πόρνος is to be taken literally or metaphorically, of moral or religious impurity. The word occurs again c. xiii. 4 in the literal sense, and it is found only in this sense elsewhere in the N. T., though it naturally occurs in close connexion with idolatry: 1 Cor. vi. 9; Apoc. xxi. 8; xxii. 15. The literal sense therefore is to be kept here as following out the thought of ἁγιασμός (v. 14). The obstacles to holiness are gathered up under two heads, those which centre in the man himself, and those which concern his view of the divine gifts. A man may fail by personal impurity : he may fail also by disregard of the blessings of God. Esau is a characteristic

ὃς ἀντὶ βρώσεως μιᾶς ἀπέδετο τὰ πρωτοτόκιᾰ ἑαυτοῦ. ¹⁷ἴστε
γὰρ ὅτι καὶ μετέπειτα θέλων κληρονομῆσαι τὴν εὐλογίαν
ἀπεδοκιμάσθη, μετανοίας γὰρ τόπον οὐχ εὗρεν, καίπερ

16 om. ὅς D₂*.   ἑαυτοῦ א*AC: αγτογ אᶜD₂*.   17 θέλων: λέγων D₂*.

example of the latter form of sin, as one who by birth occupied a position of prerogative which he recklessly sacrificed for an immediate and sensuous pleasure. The Hebrews, on their part, might also barter their blessings as firstborn in the Church for the present outward consolations of the material Temple service. Peace with Judaism might be bought at the price of Christian holiness.

The use of βέβηλος in the N. T. is limited: 1 Tim. i. 9; iv. 7; vi. 20; 2 Tim. ii. 16; comp. Matt. xii. 5; Acts xxiv. 6. The word describes a character which recognises nothing as higher than earth: for whom there is nothing sacred: no divine reverence for the unseen.

Esau appears in Scripture as the embodiment of this character. *For one mess of meat* (Vulg. *propter unam escam*), not only for a transitory and material price, but that the smallest, *he sold his own birthright* (τὰ πρωτοτόκια ἑαυτοῦ).

The language of the original narrative (Gen. xxv. 33 f.) is singularly expressive of the thoughtlessness of Esau, 'וַיֹּאכַל וַיֵּשְׁתְּ וַיָּקָם וַיֵּלֶךְ וג, καὶ ἔφαγε καὶ ἔπιε καὶ ἀναστὰς ᾤχετο καὶ ἐφαύλισεν Ἡσαῦ τὰ πρωτοτόκια.

For the double portion of the first-born see Deut. xxi. 17 (1 Chron. v. 1).

17. The neglect of privileges and responsibilities brings irreparable consequences.

ἴστε γὰρ...ἀπεδοκιμάσθη] *For ye know that even afterward, when he wished to inherit the blessing, he was rejected*, Vulg. *Scitote enim quoniam et postea...reprobatus est.* The form ἴστε, which is very rare in the N. T. (Eph. v. 5; James i. 9) is ambiguous.

It may be (as Vulg.) imperative; but the indicative makes an impressive appeal to the history with which the Hebrews were familiar.

The consequences of Esau's act reached farther than he had cared to look (*even afterward*). In spite of his impulsive disregard of divine things he retained still some sense of God's promise, and sought to secure what had naturally belonged to him. Thus his profane irreverence was seen in a new form. He paid no heed to his own act, but wished to occupy the position which he had voluntarily abandoned. He had sold the right of the first-born and yet, as if that were a trivial thing, he claimed to inherit the blessing which belonged to it. The use of κληρονομῆσαι emphasises his sin. He asserted the prerogative of birth, a gift of God, when he had himself recklessly surrendered it.

ἀπεδοκιμάσθη] *he was rejected* by his father who confirmed the blessing which he had unknowingly given to Jacob. Isaac spoke what was indeed the judgment of God (Gen. xxvii. 33, 37): δῆλον γὰρ ὅτι καὶ ὁ πατὴρ κατὰ θεὸν ἀπεδοκίμασεν αὐτόν (Theophlct.).

For ἀποδοκιμάζειν see 1 Pet. ii. 4; Luke xix. 22.

μετ. γὰρ τ. οὐχ εὗρεν] *for he found no place of repentance.* The son who had sacrificed his right could not undo the past, and it is this only which is in question. No energy of sorrow or self-condemnation, however sincere, could restore to him the prerogative of the first-born. The consideration of the forgiveness of his sin against God, as distinct from the reversal of the temporal consequences of his sin, lies wholly without the argument.

The clause is to be taken parenthetically: Esau *was rejected*—his claim to the blessing was disallowed —*for he found no place of repentance—though he sought* the blessing *earnestly with tears.* Equally abrupt parentheses are found *v.* 21; xiii. 17.

'A place of repentance' is an opportunity for changing a former decision so that the consequences which would have followed from it if persisted in follow no longer. The repentance in such a case corresponds with the particular effects under consideration. It would be equally true to say that in respect of the privileges of the first-born which Esau had sold, he found no place for repentance, and that in respect of his spiritual relation to God, if his sorrow was sincere, he did find a place for repentance.

The phrase *locus pœnitentiœ* is so used by the Roman jurists. A passage quoted by Wetstein (Ulpian ap. *Corp. J. C. Dig.* XL. Tit. vii. 3 § 13) is instructive, and offers a close parallel. A slave is to have his freedom if he pays ten *aurei* to his master's heir on three several days. He offers them the first day and they are refused; and again on the second and third days with the same result. The heir has no power of refusing to receive the payment, and therefore the slave, having done his part, is free. But a case is proposed where the slave has only ten *aurei* in all. They have been refused on the first and second days : will they avail for the third payment? The answer is in the affirmative : puto sufficere hæc eadem et pœnitentiæ heredi locum non esse : quod et Pomponius probat.

The last words of Pliny's letter to Trajan on the Christians are: ex quo facile est opinari quæ turba hominum emendari possit, si sit locus pœnitentiæ (*Epp.* x. 97). Comp. Liv. xliv. 10.

Μετανοίας τόπος is found Wisd. xii. 10 κρίνων κατὰ βραχὺ ἐδίδους τόπον

μετανοίας. Clem. *ad Cor.* i. 7 μετανοίας τόπον ἔδωκεν ὁ δεσπότης τοῖς βουλομένοις ἐπιστραφῆναι ἐπ' αὐτόν. Tat. *c. Grœc.* 15 ἡ τῶν δαιμόνων ὑπόστασις οὐκ ἔχει μετανοίας τόπον· τῆς γὰρ ὕλης καὶ τῆς πονηρίας εἰσὶν ἀπαυγάσματα *Constit. Apost.* ii. 38; v. 19. Comp. Acts xxv. 1 τόπος ἀπολογίας.

The rendering '*he* (Esau) *found* in Isaac *no place for change of mind,* though he sought it (the change of mind) earnestly—that is, he found his father firmly resolved to maintain what he had said,—is equally against the language and the argument.

The αὐτήν in the last clause can only be referred to εὐλογίαν. The phrase ἐκζητεῖν μετάνοιαν would be very strange, and if the writer had wished to express this form of thought, he would have said αὐτόν with reference to μετανοίας τόπον, so that the object of ἐκζητεῖν and εὑρίσκειν might be the same. The reference to εὐλογίαν on the other hand seems to be pointed by μετὰ δακρύων ἐκζ. Gen. xxvii. 38 ἀνεβόησεν φωνῇ Ἡσαῦ καὶ ἔκλαυσεν.

(3) 18—29. The character and obligations of the New Covenant.

This section forms a solemn close to the main argument of the Epistle. It offers a striking picture of the characteristics of the two Covenants summed up in the words 'terror' and 'grace'; and at the same time, in harmony with the whole current of thought, it emphasises the truth that greater privileges bring greater responsibility. The section falls into two parts:

(*a*) The contrast of the position of Christians with that of the Israelites at the giving of the Law (18—24); and

(*b*) The duties of Christians which flow from their position (25—29).

(*a*) The contrast of the position of Christians with that of the Israelites at the giving of the Law (18—24).

The writer first describes (*a*) the scene at Sinai; and then he describes

μετὰ δακρύων ἐκζητήσας αὐτήν.   ¹⁸ Οὐ γὰρ
προσεληλύθατε ψηλαφωμένῳ καὶ κεκαυμένῳ πυρὶ καὶ γνόφῳ

18 ψηλαφ. אAC vg syr vg me the: +ὄρει ς D₂ (om. d).   καὶ κεκαυμένῳ:
κεκαλυμμένῳ D₂*.

(β) the position of Christians (22—24).

¹⁸ For ye are not come to a material and kindled fire, and to blackness, and darkness, and tempest, ¹⁹ and the sound of a trumpet, and the voice of words; which voice they that heard intreated that no word more should be spoken to them: ²⁰ for they could not bear that which was enjoined, If even a beast touch the mountain it shall be stoned; ²¹ and, so fearful was the appearance, Moses said, I exceedingly fear and quake.

²² But ye are come to mount Zion, and to the city of the Living God, a heavenly Jerusalem, and to innumerable hosts of angels ²³ in festal assembly, and to the church of the firstborn, enrolled in heaven, and to the God of all as Judge, and to spirits of just men made perfect, ²⁴ and to the Mediator of a new Covenant even Jesus, and to the blood of sprinkling that speaketh better than Abel.

(a) The scene at Sinai (18—21).

The description is designed to bring out the awfulness of the whole revelation which attended the making of the Old Covenant. Step by step the writer advances from the physical terrors by which it was accompanied (18—20) to the confession of the Lawgiver himself (21), who alone of all prophets was allowed to speak to God face to face.

18 ff. The peril of disregarding the Christian privileges, which have been indicated in the last section, is proportioned to their greatness. Therefore the Apostle says, 'Endure, advance, aim at the highest purity, cherish the loftiest view of divine things, for ye are not come to a vision of outward awfulness, but ye are come to mount

Zion. You stand in view of heavenly glories immeasurably nobler than the terrors of Sinai. If then the people who were admitted to that revelation were charged to make every external preparation (Ex. xix. 14 f.), much more must you prepare yourselves spiritually.

18. οὐ γὰρ προσελ. ψηλ. καὶ κεκ. π.] For ye are not come to a material (palpable) and kindled fire... Vulg. Non enim accessistis ad tractabilem et accensibilem (d ardentem et tractabilem) ignem. The position once taken (προσήλθετε Deut. iv. 11) is presented as still retained. In this respect Christians were differently circumstanced from those who heard the Law at Sinai. The Jews were forbidden to draw near: Christians shrank back when they were invited to approach. For the word προσελθεῖν see iv. 16 note.

The scene of the old legislation is described simply as 'a palpable and kindled fire and blackness...' The earthly, local, associations of the divine epiphany fall wholly into the background. That which the writer describes is the form of the revelation, fire and darkness and thunder, material signs of the nature of God (v. 29). Thus every element is one which outwardly moves fear; and in this connexion the mention of Sinai itself may well be omitted. The mountain is lost in the fire and smoke. It was, so to speak, no longer a mountain. It becomes a manifestation of terrible majesty, a symbol of the Divine Presence.

The fire is outward, material, derivative. It is palpable, to be 'felt,' like the darkness of Egypt (Ex. x. 21 γενηθήτω σκότος...ψηλαφητὸν σκότος),

καὶ ζόφῳ καὶ θυέλλῃ ¹⁹καὶ cάλπιγγος ἤχῳ καὶ φωνῇ ῥημάτων,
ἧς οἱ ἀκούσαντες παρῃτήσαντο ᵀ προστεθῆναι αὐτοῖς
λόγον· ²⁰οὐκ ἔφερον γὰρ τὸ διαστελλόμενον   Κἂν θηρίον

19 μή

ζόφῳ א*ACD₂* : σκότῳ אᶜ.   19 om. μή א*.   προσθεῖναι A.

and has been kindled from some other source. So Philo speaks of πυρὸς οὐρανίου φορᾷ καπνῷ βαθεῖ τὰ ἐν κύκλῳ συσκιάζοντος (de decal. § 11, ii. 187). The use of the partic. ψηλαφώμενος brings out that which was felt in actual experience as distinguished from the abstract nature of the object.

Chrysostom says τί τὸ ψηλαφώμενον πῦρ πρὸς τὸν ἀψηλάφητον θεόν; ὁ θεὸς γὰρ ἡμῶν, φησίν, πῦρ καταναλίσκον (v. 29).

Primasius expands this thought well: Non enim accessistis ad tractabilem et accessibilem (l. accensibilem) ignem, id est, non accessistis ad visibile et palpabile lumen ignis, quod visu corporeo tractari possit, sicut de veteri Judaico populo legimus; sed ad invisibilem et incomprehensibilem Deum.

καὶ γνόφῳ...] The several features of the awful manifestation are taken from Deut. iv. 11; v. 22; Ex. xix. 16 ff. The 'blackness' 'thick darkness' (ὁ γνόφος, הָעֲרָפֶל) was that into which Moses entered 'where God was' (Ex. xx. 21). Comp. Philo, de mut. nom. § 2, i. 579; de vit. Moys. i. § 28, ii. 106.

19. καὶ σάλπ. ἤχῳ...] The 'sound of a trumpet' is mentioned in Ex. xix. 16; xx. 18; αἱ δὲ σάλπιγγες ὡς βασιλέως παρόντος· τοῦτο γὰρ καὶ ἐν τῇ δευτέρᾳ παρουσίᾳ ἔσται (Œcum.). Comp. Matt. xxiv. 31; 1 Thess. iv. 16. Ἦχος occurs again Lk. iv. 37; Acts ii. 2. The 'voice of words' is mentioned in Deut. iv. 12.

ἧς (sc. φωνῆς) οἱ ἀκούσαντες] Even that which was most intelligible, most human, the articulate voice, inspired the hearers with overwhelming dread:

which voice they that heard intreated that no word more should be spoken to them, that is by God Himself, but only through Moses (Ex. xx. 19).

For παρῃτήσαντο see v. 25; Acts xxv. 11; 1 Tim. iv. 7; 2 Tim. ii. 23. The word admits the construction with and without a negative particle (παραιτεῖσθαι προστεθῆναι and παραιτ. μὴ προστεθῆναι). For the former compare Lk. xxiii. 2; Rom. xv. 22; and for the latter 1 John ii. 22; Gal. v. 7. By αὐτοῖς must be understood τοῖς ἀκούσασιν not τοῖς ἀκουσθεῖσιν, the hearers not the words.

20. οὐκ ἔφερον...] for they could not bear that which was enjoined.... Vulg. non enim portabant quod dicebatur. Ex. xix. 12 f. The most impressive part of the whole command is taken to convey its effect: If even a beast...

The form in which the command is conveyed (τὸ διαστελλόμενον) presents it as ringing constantly in their ears (quod dicebatur). The word διαστέλλεσθαι does not occur again in the Epistles; elsewhere in the N. T. it is only used in the midd. sense: Mk. vii. 36; viii. 15 &c.

21. The fear which was felt by the people was felt also by the Lawgiver himself.

And—so fearful was the appearance—Moses said...The parenthesis (see v. 17) is in the style of the writer. The variety and living fulness of the vision presented to Moses is expressed by the form τὸ φανταζόμενον. The word φαντάζεσθαι occurs nowhere else in the N. T. Comp. Wisd. vi. 17 (Matt. xiv. 26 φάντασμα).

θίγη τοῦ ὄρους, λιθοβοληθήσεται· ²¹καί, οὕτω φοβερὸν ἦν
τὸ φανταζόμενον, Μωυσῆς εἶπεν   Ἔκφοβός εἰμι καὶ
⌜ἔντρομος⌝. ²²ἀλλὰ προσεληλύθατε Σιὼν ὄρει καὶ

21 ἔκτρομος

20 λιθοβ.: +ἢ βολίδι κατατοξευθήσεται ς.   21 οὕτω: ου D₂*.   ἦν: η א*.
om. εἰμι א*.   ἔντρομος ACM₂: ἔκτρομος אD₂*.   22 ἀλλά: οὐ γάρ A.

ἔκφοβός εἰμι...] Similar words were
used by Moses in connexion with the
worshipping of the golden calf Deut.
ix. 19; but it is hardly possible that the
writer of the Epistle transferred these
directly to the scene at the giving of
the Law, when the fear was due to
circumstances essentially different.
It is more likely that he refers to
some familiar tradition in which the
feelings of Moses were described in
these terms.

(β) The position of Christians (22
—24).

The view which the Apostle gives
of the position is marvellously full.
The arrangement of the details is
beset with great difficulties; but, on
the whole, that which is most symmetrical appears to be the best. Thus
the clauses are grouped in pairs
προσεληλύθατε
Σιὼν ὄρει, καὶ
 πόλει θεοῦ ζῶντος, Ἰερουσαλὴμ ἐπου-
  ρανίῳ·
καὶ μυριάσιν ἀγγέλων πανηγύρει, καὶ
 ἐκκλησίᾳ πρωτοτόκων, ἀπογεγραμμένων ἐν οὐρανοῖς·
καὶ κριτῇ, θεῷ πάντων, καὶ
 πνεύμασι δικαίων τετελειωμένων,
καὶ διαθήκης νέας μεσίτῃ, Ἰησοῦ, καὶ
 αἵματι ῥαντισμοῦ, κρεῖττον λαλοῦντι
  παρὰ τὸν Ἄβελ.

According to this arrangement the
development of thought may be presented in the following form:
I. The Christian Revelation seen
in its fulfilment: from the divine
side (22, 23 a).
 (a) The scene.
  (a) The Foundation.
  (b) The Structure.

 (β) The persons.
  (a) Angels.
  (b) Men.
II. The Christian Revelation seen
in its efficacy: from the human side
(23 b, 24).
 (a) The judgment: earthly life
over.
  (a) The Judge.
  (b) Those who have been perfected.
 (β) The gift of grace: earthly life
still lasting.
  (a) The Covenant.
  (b) The Atonement.
There is, it will be noticed, a complete absence of articles. The thoughts
are presented in their most abstract
form.

Theodoret sums up admirably the
contrasts between the Old and the
New; ἐκεῖ, φησί, δέος, ἐνταῦθα δὲ ἑορτὴ
καὶ πανήγυρις· καὶ ἐκεῖνα μὲν ἐν τῇ γῇ,
ταῦτα δὲ ἐν τοῖς οὐρανοῖς· ἐκεῖ χιλιάδες
ἀνθρώπων, ἐνταῦθα δὲ μυριάδες ἀγγέλων·
ἐκεῖ ἄπιστοι καὶ παράνομοι, ἐνταῦθα ἐκκλησία πρωτοτόκων ἀπογεγραμμένων ἐν τοῖς
οὐρανοῖς καὶ πνεύματα δικαίων τετελειω-
μένων· ἐκεῖ διαθήκη παλαιά, ἐνταῦθα
καινή· ἐκεῖ δοῦλος μεσίτης, ἐνταῦθα
υἱός· ἐκεῖ αἷμα ἀλόγων, ἐνταῦθα αἷμα
ἀμνοῦ λογικοῦ.

22 ff. ἀλλὰ προσελ....] Ye are not
brought face to face with any repetition of the terrors of Sinai; but ye
are even now still standing in a heavenly presence, not material but spiritual, not manifested in elemental
powers but in living hosts, not finding
expression in threatening commands
but in means of reconciliation, inspiring not fear but hope. Yet, it is im-

πόλει θεοῦ ζῶντος, Ἰερουσαλὴμ ἐπουρανίῳ, καὶ μυριάσιν ἀγγέλων ²³πανηγύρει καὶ ἐκκλησίᾳ πρωτοτόκων

καὶ πόλει: πόλει D₂* (d). ἐπουρ. Ἱερ. D₂*. ἐπουρανίων A*. μυριάσιν:
μυρίων ἁγίων D₂*: μυριάδων vg.

plied, that the awfulness of the position is not less but greater than that
of the Israelites.

For προσεληλύθατε see v. 18.
Ἐκεῖνοι οὐ προσῆλθον ἀλλὰ πόρρωθεν
εἰστήκεισαν· ὑμεῖς δὲ προσεληλύθατε.
ὁρᾷς τὴν ὑπεροχήν; (Theophlct.). In
one sense the heavenly Jerusalem
is already reached : in another sense
it is still sought for : xiii. 14.

(a) The scene to which Christians
are come (22 a).

22 a. Σιὼν ὄρει...ἐπουρ.] Over against
'the material and kindled fire' of Sinai
is set the mountain and city of God,
His palace and the home of His people, shewn by images in the earthly
Zion and Jerusalem. In this heavenly,
archetypal, spiritual mountain and
city, God is seen to dwell with His
own. He is not revealed in one passing vision of terrible Majesty as at
the giving of the Law, but in His
proper 'dwelling-place.' Zion is dis-
tinctively the 'acropolis,' the seat of
God's throne, and Jerusalem the city.
Sometimes Zion alone is spoken of as
the place where God exercises sovereignty and from which He sends
deliverance. Ps. ii. 6; xlviii. 2; l. 2;
lxxviii. 68; cx. 2; (iii. 4; xv. 1); Is.
xviii. 7; sometimes Zion and Jerusalem are joined together: Mic. iv.
1 ff.; Joel ii. 32; Amos i. 2.
In the spiritual reality Mount Zion
represents the strong divine foundation of the new Order, while the City
of the Living God represents the
social structure in which the Order is
embodied. God—Who is a Living
God (c. iii. 12 note)—does not dwell
alone, but surrounded by His people.
His Majesty and His Love are equally
represented in the New Jerusalem.
For the idea of the Heavenly Jeru-

salem, compare Apoc. xxi. 2, 10 (ἡ
ἁγία Ἰερουσαλήμ. Is. lii. 1); iii. 12
(ἡ καινὴ Ἱερ.); Gal. iv. 26 (ἡ ἄνω Ἱερ.).
This is 'the city which hath the foundations' (xi. 10), for which Abraham
looked; and for which we still seek
(c. xiii. 14). It is like 'the good things'
of the Gospel, in different aspects
future and present. For ἐπουράνιος
see c. iii. 1 note.
Compare Philo de somn. ii. § 38 (ii.
691) ἡ δὲ τοῦ θεοῦ πόλις ὑπὸ Ἑβραίων
Ἰερουσαλὴμ καλεῖται, ἧς μεταληφθὲν τὸ
ὄνομα ὅρασίς ἐστιν εἰρήνης (Clem. Al.
Strom. i. 5, 29; Orig. Hom. in Jos.
xxi. 2).
Chrysostom suggestively contrasts
the city with the desert of Sinai
(ἐκεῖ ἔρημος ἦν, ἐνταῦθα πόλις). So
Theophylact, a little more fully : ἀντὶ
τοῦ Σινᾶ ἔχομεν Σιὼν ὄρος νοητόν, καὶ
πόλιν νοητὴν Ἰερουσαλήμ· τουτέστιν
αὐτὸν τὸν οὐρανόν, οὐκ ἔρημον ὡς ἐκεῖνοι.
See also Additional Note on xi. 10.

(β) The persons to whom Christians are come (22 b, 23 a).

22 b. καὶ μυρ....καὶ ἐκκλησίᾳ] The
description of the scene of the Divine
Kingdom to which Christians are
come is followed by a description of
the representative persons who are
included in it, with whom believers
are brought into fellowship. These
are angels and men, no longer separated, as at Sinai, by signs of great
terror, but united in one vast assembly.
The exact construction of the words
which describe the two bodies who
constitute the population of the heavenly city is disputed and uncertain.
They have been arranged :
(1) μυριάσιν ἀγγέλων πανηγύρει, καὶ
ἐκκλησίᾳ...
(2) μυριάσιν ἀγγέλων, πανηγύρει καὶ
ἐκκλησίᾳ...

(3) μυριάσιν, ἀγγέλων πανηγύρει καὶ ἐκκλησίᾳ...

The main difference lies in the connexion of πανήγυρις. Is this to be taken with that which precedes, or with that which follows? Ancient authority is uniformly in favour of the first view. The Greek MSS., which indicate the connexion of words (including AC), uniformly (as far as they are recorded) separate πανηγύρει from καὶ ἐκκλ. πρωτοτ. So also the Syriac and Latin Versions; and by implication Origen, Eusebius, Basil (d *multitudinem angelorum frequentem*, Vulg. *multorum millium angelorum frequentiam*).

This construction is favoured also by the general symmetry of the arrangement, which seems to be decidedly unfavourable to the combination of πανηγύρει καὶ ἐκκλησίᾳ.

But if this general division be adopted, a further question arises. Is ἀγγέλων to be taken with μυριάσιν or with πανηγύρει? The decision is not without difficulty. The rhythm of the sentence appears to require that μυριάσιν ἀγγέλων should go together, though πανηγύρει sounds harsh by itself. Still, in spite of this harshness, this construction seems to be the best upon the whole. Thus πανηγύρει colours the whole clause: 'and countless hosts of angels in festal assembly.' The Syriac and Latin translations and the variant of D are probably endeavours to express the thought simply. If indeed there were more authority for μυριάδων, which would most naturally be changed, this reading would deserve great consideration.

If μυριάσιν be taken absolutely, it may be explained either by ἀγγέλων πανηγύρει ('innumerable hosts, even a festal assembly of angels') or by ἀγγέλων πανηγύρει......ἐν οὐρανοῖς ('innumerable hosts, even a festal assembly of angels and church of firstborn...'). But it seems that the special thought of πανήγυρις accords

better with the angelic company alone.

The phrase μυριάσιν ἀγγέλων is probably used with direct reference to the ministration of the angels at the giving of the Law (Deut. xxxiii. 2), and in the manifestations of the Lord for judgment (Dan. vii. 10; Jude 14). Such associations give force to the addition πανηγύρει. These countless hosts are not now messengers of awe, as then, but of rejoicing. At the consummation of Creation, as at the Creation itself (Job xxxviii. 7), 'they shout for joy.'

The word πανήγυρις, which was used specially of the great national assemblies and sacred games of the Greeks (Thuc. i. 25; v. 50) occurs here only in N. T. It is used rarely in the LXX. version of the prophets for מוֹעֵד (commonly ἑορτή) (Ezech. xlvi. 11; Hos. ii. 13 (11); ix. 5); and for עֲצָרָה (Amos v. 21). It is also used by Symmachus for חַג. The suggestion is that of the common joy of a great race.

Philo uses the word in connexion with the thought of the reward of victorious self-control: κάλλιστον ἀγῶνα τοῦτον διάθλησον καὶ σπούδασον στεφανωθῆναι κατὰ τῆς τοὺς ἄλλους ἅπαντας νικώσης ἡδονῆς καλὸν καὶ εὔκλεᾶ στέφανον, ὃν οὐδεμία πανήγυρις ἀνθρώπων ἐχώρησε (*Leg. Alleg.* ii. § 26; i. 86 M.).

The notes of the Greek Commentators are worth quoting (comp. Theodt. *supr.*):

καὶ μυριάσιν ἀγγέλων πανηγύρει· ἐνταῦθα τὴν χαρὰν δείκνυσι καὶ τὴν εὐφροσύνην ἀντὶ τοῦ γνόφου καὶ τοῦ σκότους καὶ τῆς θυέλλης (Chrys.).

καὶ μυριάσιν ἀγγέλων· ἀντὶ τοῦ Ἰουδαϊκοῦ λαοῦ ἄγγελοι πάρεισι. καὶ πανηγύρει, φησίν, ἐν μυριάσιν ἀγγέλων ὑπαρχούσῃ (Œcumen.).

καὶ μυριάσιν ἀγγέλων πανηγύρει. ἀντὶ τοῦ λαοῦ ἔχομεν ἡμεῖς ἀγγέλων μυριάδας· ἀντὶ τοῦ φόβου χαράν, τοῦτο γὰρ δηλοῦται διὰ τοῦ πανηγύρει· ἔνθα γὰρ πανήγυρις ἐκεῖ χαρά. ἡ πανήγυρις οὖν αὕτη ἐν μυριάσιν ἀγγέλων συνίσταται (Theophlct.).

ἐκκλησίᾳ...ἐν οὐρανοῖς] The second constituent body in the divine commonwealth is the 'church of the firstborn.' This represents the earthly element (men) as the former the heavenly element (angels). Men are described as a 'church,' a 'congregation,' gathered for the enjoyment of special rights, even as the angels are assembled for a great festival; and they are spoken of as 'firstborn,' enjoying the privileges not only of sons but of firstborn sons.

The word ἐκκλησία occurs again in the Epistle in c. ii. 12 (LXX.). The thought in each case is that of the people of God assembled to exercise their privileges and to enjoy their rights.

It is worthy of notice that while the word occurs only in two places in the Gospels (Matt. xvi. 18; xviii. 17), it is used in the former place in the sense of the universal church and in the latter of a special church. Both senses are found in the Acts (e.g. ix. 31; viii. 1) and in the Epistles of St Paul (e.g. Eph. i. 22; Col. iv. 16). In the Apocalypse, St James (v. 14) and 3 John the word is used only in the special sense.

πρωτοτόκων] Vulg. primitivorum. In the divine order not one son only but many enjoy the rights of primogeniture, the kingdom and the priesthood (Apoc. i. 6). Perhaps there is still some faint reminiscence of the reckless sacrifice of his birthright (v. 16 πρωτοτόκια) by Esau.

The term 'firstborn' here appears to describe a common privilege and is not used in relation to the circumstances of earth, as of the dead compared with the living. Christian believers in Christ, alike living and dead, are united in the Body of Christ. In that Body we have fellowship with a society of 'eldest sons' of God, who share the highest glory of the divine order. Thus the idea of the Communion of Saints gains distinctness. The word suggests still another thought. The 'firstborn' in Israel were the representatives of the consecrated nation. We may then be justified in regarding these, the firstborn in the Christian Church, the firstborn of humanity, as preparing the way, in Him Who is 'the Firstborn' (c. i. 6), for many brethren. Through them Creation enters on the beginning of its consummation (comp. Apoc. i. 5; Col. i. 15; Rom. viii. 29).

The Greek Commentators are vague in their interpretation of the word.

Τίνας δὲ πρωτοτόκους καλεῖ λέγων καὶ ἐκκλησίᾳ πρωτοτόκων; πάντας τοὺς χοροὺς τῶν πιστῶν. τοὺς αὐτοὺς δὲ καὶ πνεύματα δικαίων τετελειωμένων καλεῖ (Chrys.).

ἐπειδὴ κοινός ἐστι πατὴρ πάντων ὁ θεός, πάντες μὲν ἄνθρωποι υἱοί εἰσιν αὐτοῦ κοινῶς, πρωτότοκοι δὲ τούτων οἱ πιστεύσαντες καὶ ἄξιοι τῆς κατὰ πρόθεσιν (al. προαίρεσιν) υἱοθεσίας. ἢ καὶ πάντες μὲν ἁπλῶς οἱ πιστεύσαντες υἱοί, πρωτότοκοι δὲ οἱ εὐάρεστοι καὶ τῶν πρεσβείων ἐν λόγῳ καὶ πολιτείᾳ ἠξιωμένοι παρὰ θεῷ (Theophlct.).

These 'firstborn' are described as enrolled in heaven (Vulg. qui conscripti (d professi) sunt in cœlis). The same image of the enrolment of citizens on the register of the city, as possessed of the full privileges of the position, is found in the O. T.: Ex. xxxii. 32 f.; Ps. lxix. 28; Is. iv. 3; Dan. xii. 1. Compare Luke x. 20 (ἐνγέγραπται); Apoc. xiii. 8; xvii. 8 (γέγραπται); iii. 5; Phil. iii. 20 (τὸ πολίτευμα ἐν οὐρ. ὑπάρχει); Ps. lxxxvii. 4 ff. Herm. Vis. i. 3 (with Gebhardt and Harnack's note); Sim. ii. 9. For the word ἀπογράφεσθαι see Luke ii. 1 ff.

Herveius has a striking remark: cum pluribus major erit beatitudo, ubi unusquisque de alio gaudebit sicut de seipso.

The word πρωτότοκοι appears to be wholly inapplicable to angels, nor could they be described as 'enrolled in heaven.'

ἀπογεγραμμένων ἐν οὐρανοῖς, καὶ κριτῇ θεῷ πάντων, καὶ
πνεύμασι δικαίων τετελειωμένων, ²⁴καὶ διαθήκης νέας

23 ἀπογεγρ. ἐν οὐρ.: ἐν οὐρ. ἀπογεγρ. ϛ.   πνεύματι D₂* (d).   δικαίων
τετελειωμένων אᶜACM₂: δικ. τεθεμελιωμένων D₂* (d): τελίων δεδικαιωμένοις א*.

23 b, 24. From the contemplation
of the divine order in its ideal glory
the Apostle goes on to describe it in
relation to men and the conflicts of
life, (a) when the struggle is over,
and (β) while it is yet being maintained. Thus the point of sight now
becomes human, and the two great
ideas of judgment and redemption
come into prominence. The Judge is
the universal sovereign, and spirits of
just men made perfect witness to His
mercy. The Mediator is one truly
man, Jesus, and His blood calls not
for vengeance but for pardon.

(a) The judgment when life is
over.

23 b. κριτῇ θεῷ πάντων] to the God
of all as Judge. The order appears
to be decisive against the common
rendering 'God the Judge of all'
though the Greek Commentators take
the words so; and on the other hand
the simple phrase θεὸς πάντων is
unusual in place of ὁ ὢν ἐπὶ πάντων, or
παντοκράτωρ. But there is a certain
parallelism between κριτής, διαθήκης
νέας μεσίτης, and θεὸς πάντων, Ἰησοῦς.
He to Whom we draw near as Judge
is God of all. His judgment is universal, not of one race only or of one
order of being. It seems best to
take πάντων as neuter.

The word κριτής retains something
of its widest meaning (Acts xiii. 20).
The action of the Judge is not to be
limited to punishment only. The
Divine Judgment is the manifestation
of right, the vindication of truth, an
object of desire for believers, though
the light in which it is revealed (John
iii. 19) is fire also (comp. v. 29).
Δικαστής strictly has reference to a
legal and technical process: Acts vii.
27, 35 (not Lk. xii. 14); 1 Sam. viii.

1; Wisd. ix. 7. Christians 'in Christ'
can draw near to the Judge.

καὶ πνεύμασι δικ. τετελ.] The judgment—the revelation of that which
is—has been in part triumphantly
accomplished. We realise the presence of the Judge, and also of those
for whom His work has been fulfilled
in righteousness. These are spoken
of as 'spirits,' for in this passage the
thought is no longer, as in the former
clauses, of the complete glory of the
divine commonwealth, but of spiritual
relations only; not of the assembly in
its august array, but of the several
members of it in their essential
being.

The departed saints are therefore
spoken of now as 'spirits,' not yet
'clothed upon' (2 Cor. v. 4). Comp.
1 Pet. iii. 19 τοῖς ἐν φυλακῇ πνεύμασιν.
The word ψυχή—the principle of human life—is used in a similar manner:
Wisd. iii. 1 (δικαίων ψυχαὶ ἐν χειρὶ
θεοῦ); Apoc. vi. 9 ff. We have no
warrant to draw any deductions from
these glimpses of disembodied humanity, nor indeed can we apprehend
them distinctly. We can feel however
that something is yet wanting to the
blessedness of the blessed.

But while the work of Christ is as
yet uncompleted in humanity, though
'the righteous' are spoken of as
spirits only, yet they are essentially
'made perfect.' They have realised
the end for which they were created
in virtue of the completed work of
Christ. When the Son bore humanity
to the throne of God—the Father—
those who were in fellowship with
Him were (in this sense) perfected,
but not till then: c. xi. 40. In this
connexion reference may be made to
the impressive picture of 'the har-

μεσίτη Ἰησοῦ, καὶ αἵματι ῥαντισμοῦ κρεῖττον λαλοῦντι

24 μεσίτης D₂*.　　　　　κρεῖττον : κρείττονα ς.

rowing of hell' by Christ in the Gospel of Nicodemus : cc. xxi. ff. For the general idea of τελειοῦσθαι see ii. 10; vii. 11; x. 14 (notes).

With this conception of the righteous man gaining his perfection in Christ contrast the Rabbinic conception of 'the perfect righteous man' who fulfils all the Law: Weber *Altsynag. Theol.* 278 f. For δίκαιος see x. 38 (LXX.); xi. 4. The verb δικαιοῦν is not found in the Epistle.

Primasius reading *ad spiritum* (πνεύματι) explains it of the Holy Spirit: per quem justi creantur omnes in baptismate, accipientes ab illo remissionem omnium peccatorum.

(β) The support while the struggle lasts.

24. καὶ διαθ. ν. μεσ. Ἰ. καὶ...Ἄβελ] For some the struggle of life is over: by some it has still to be borne. In these last two clauses the spiritual covenant is shewn in relation to those whose work has yet to be completed.

Their assurance lies in the facts that He through Whom the covenant is established has perfect sympathy with them as true man; and that the blood through which it was ratified is an energetic power of purifying life.

The work of *Jesus, the author and perfecter of faith* (v. 2), is placed in these respects in significant connexion with that of Moses, the mediator of the first covenant, the deliverer from Egyptian bondage, and that of Abel the first martyr of faith (xi. 4).

διαθ. νέας μεσίτη Ἰ.] This is the only place in which διαθήκη νέα occurs in N. T.; compare διαθήκη καινή c. viii. 8, 13 (LXX.); ix. 15.

For the contrast of νέος and καινός see Col. iii. 10 (and Lightfoot's note). The Covenant is spoken of as νέα in regard of its recent establishment, and not as καινή in regard of its character.

The Covenant was in relation to the Hebrews 'new' in time and not only 'new' in substance. Christians had just entered on the possession of privileges which the elder Church had not enjoyed.

For μεσίτης compare c. viii. 6 note; and for the force of the human name Ἰησοῦς see c. iii. 1 note; and for the order c. ii. 9 note; v. 2.

καὶ αἵμ. ῥαντ....λαλοῦντι] Vulg. *et sanguinis sparsionem loquentem.* There is a voice to be heard here also as at Sinai (v. 19), but not terrible like that.

The blood—'the life'—is regarded as still living. This thought finds expression in the first record of death (Gen. iv. 10), but the voice 'of the blood of Jesus' is doubly contrasted with the voice of the blood of Abel. That, appealing to God, called for vengeance, and making itself heard in the heart of Cain, brought despair; but the blood of Christ pleads with God for forgiveness and speaks peace to man.

For ῥαντισμός compare c. ix. 19 f.; x. 22 (ῥεραντισμένοι τὰς καρδίας); 1 Pet. i. 2 ῥαντισμὸν αἵματος Ἰησοῦ. Barn. v. 1 ἵνα τῇ ἀφέσει τῶν ἁμαρτιῶν ἁγνισθῶμεν ὅ ἐστιν ἐν τῷ αἵματι τοῦ ῥαντίσματος αὐτοῦ. For the idea of Blood in Scripture see Addit. Note on 1 John i. 7.

παρὰ τὸν Ἄ.] *better than Abel.* Comp. c. xi. 4 ἀποθανὼν ἔτι λαλεῖ. It seems more natural to take the words thus quite simply than to render them '*better than that* (the blood) *of Abel*' (παρὰ τὸ Ἄ. L and some mss.).

Κρεῖττον is an adverb as in 1 Cor. vii. 38 (Winer, p. 580). For κρ. παρά see c. ix. 23; i. 4 note.

(b) The duties of Christians which flow from their position (25—29).

The picture of the position of Christians has been drawn. Its dan-

παρὰ τὸν ῎Αβελ. ²⁵ Βλέπετε μὴ παραιτήσησθε τὸν
λαλοῦντα· εἰ γὰρ ἐκεῖνοι οὐκ ἐξέφυγον ἐπὶ γῆς παραι-

25 λαλοῦντα+ὑμῖν D₂ the.　　ἐξέφυγον א*AC: ἔφυγον אᶜM₂.　　ἐπὶ γ. παρ.
τόν א*ACD₂M₂: τὸν ἐπὶ γ. παρ. ϛ אᶜ.　　γῆς: +τῆς´ γῆς ϛ.

gers and glories have been set forth.
The last application now follows.

The section consists of two parts.
In the first (a) the writer emphasises
the responsibility of Christians in
respect of their position towards a
final revelation (25—27); and then (β)
he makes a practical appeal (28, 29).

²⁵*See that ye refuse not him that
speaketh. For if they escaped not,
when on earth they refused him
that dealt with them, much less* shall
*we escape who turn away from him
that dealeth with us from heaven.*
²⁶ *Whose voice shook the earth then,
but now he hath promised saying
Yet once more will I make to tremble
not only the earth but also the heaven.*
²⁷ *And the* word, *Yet once more,*
signifieth the removal of the things
which are shaken, as of things that
have been made, that the things
may abide which are not shaken.*
²⁸ *Wherefore let us, as receiving a
kingdom that cannot be shaken, feel
thankfulness* (or *have grace*), *whereby
we may offer service to God, as is
well-pleasing, with reverence and
awe;* ²⁹ *for our God is a consuming
fire.*

(a) 25—27. The punishment of the
Israelites may remind Christians of
their responsibility. They rejected
an earthly dispensation. He who
speaks to us is 'from heaven' (25).
The shaking of the earth then was
but a symbol of the shaking of earth
and heaven now (26), which is final,
as introducing an order which cannot
be shaken (27).

25. βλέπετε μὴ παραιτ. τὸν λαλ.]
See that ye refuse not him that even
now *is speaking.* The warning springs
directly from the contemplation of the
picture which the Apostle has drawn.

The absence of a connecting particle
gives greater force to the appeal :
'you know what lies before us : see
that you do not disregard it.'

For βλέπετε compare c. iii. 12 ; and
for παραιτήσησθε v. 19 note.

The words which follow (εἰ γὰρ...
ἀποστρεφόμενοι) are really a parenthesis; so that τὸν λαλοῦντα goes
closely with οὗ ἡ φωνή (v. 26). However the intervening words may be
interpreted, the speaker, through
whatever agency, is God. He Who
'spake in a Son' (c. i. 2) still speaks
in Him.

εἰ γὰρ...ἐπὶ γῆς...τὸν χρημ....ἀποστρ.]
For if they—the people of the Exodus
whose history has just been recalled
to us—*escaped not* the consequences
of their want of faith *when on earth
they refused him that dealt with
them, much less* shall *we* escape *who
are turning away from him* that
dealeth with us *from heaven.* The
long sufferings in the wilderness witnessed to the punishment of that
unbelief which made the people
rescued from Egypt unfit and unwilling to hold converse with God.
Their sin was not in the request that
Moses only should speak to them
(Deut. v. 28), but in the temper
which made the request necessary
(Deut. v. 29).

The position of ἐπὶ γῆς, when τόν
is transferred according to the true
reading, makes it impossible to take
the words exclusively with τὸν χρηματίζοντα (as in τὸν ἐπὶ γῆς χρηματίζοντα). They qualify the whole clause
which follows : *If they escaped not
when on earth* (having their position
on earth) *they refused* (begged no
longer to hear) *him that dealt with
them....* The scene and the conditions

τησάμενοι τὸν χρηματίζοντα, πολὺ μᾶλλον ἡμεῖς οἱ
τὸν ἀπ᾽ ⌈οὐρανῶν⌉ ἀποστρεφόμενοι· ²⁶οὗ ἡ φωνὴ τὴν

25 οὐρανοῦ

πολύ ℵACD₂*: πολλῷ ς.   ἡμεῖς: ὑμεῖς C.   οὐρανῶν ℵACD₂: οὐρανοῦ M₂.
26 ἡ φ.: φ. M₂.

of the revelation, the trial and the failure, were earthly, on earth.

The corresponding phrase ἀπ᾽ οὐρανῶν expresses only the position of the revealer and not that of those to whom the revelation is given. Hence it is limited by its place to Him (τὸν ἀπ᾽ οὐρ.).

For ἐκεῖνοι see c. iv. 2.

The word παραιτησάμενοι (when they refused...) takes up παρῃτήσαντο in v. 19. The object then was not the voice of Moses but the voice of God. It seems to follow necessarily therefore that the object here (τὸν χρηματίζοντα) must be God and not the minister of God. Thus the contrast is not between the two mediators Moses and Christ, but between the character of these two revelations which God made, 'on earth' and 'from heaven.'

For χρηματίζοντα compare c. viii. 5 (κεχρ. Μωυσῆς); xi. 7. The word appears to be specially chosen to describe the manifold circumstances connected with the giving of the Law.

π. μ. ἡμεῖς (sc. οὐκ ἐκφευξούμεθα) οἱ τὸν ἀπ᾽ οὐρ. ἀποστρ.] The form in which this supposition is expressed is remarkable. The writer does not say 'if we turn away from him' (τὸν ἀπ᾽ οὐρ. ἀποστρ.), nor yet 'after turning away from' (ἀποστραφέντες 2 Tim. i. 15). He looks upon the action as already going on, and does not shrink from including himself among those who share in it: 'we who are turning away,' if indeed we persevere in the spirit of unfaithfulness.

The phrase τὸν ἀπ᾽ οὐρανῶν (him that dealt and dealeth with us from heaven) is left in an undefined and general form as including the work of the Son on earth and after He was glorified, through Whom the Father speaks. His revelation was 'from heaven' in both cases.

In one sense God 'spake from heaven' when He gave the Law (Ex. xx. 22; Deut. iv. 36), but His voice even then was 'of earth.'

For ἀποστρεφόμενοι compare Tit. i. 14; Matt. v. 42; 2 Tim. i. 15.

The tense stands in marked contrast with that used in the former clause (παραιτησάμενοι, ἀποστρεφόμενοι). The action if commenced was not yet completed.

26. οὗ ἡ φωνή...] The words go back to v. 25 τὸν λαλοῦντα Ex. xix. 18 f. (Hebr.). Ὁρᾷς ὅτι τότε ὁ λαλῶν αὐτὸς ἦν ὁ νῦν ἀπ᾽ οὐρανοῦ χρηματίζων ἡμῖν (Theophlct.).

For ἐσάλευσεν compare Ex. xix. 18 (Hebr.); Judges v. 4 f. γῆ ἐσείσθη... ὄρη ἐσαλεύθησαν. Ps. cxiv. 7 (LXX.) ἀπὸ προσώπου κυρίου ἐσαλεύθη ἡ γῆ. The word is used of violent elemental convulsions (e.g. Matt. xxiv. 29).

νῦν δὲ ἐπήγγ.] Hagg. ii. 6. But now, in relation to the Christian order as distinguished from that of Sinai (τότε), He hath promised, whose voice then shook the earth....

The former outward 'shaking' was the symbol of a second 'shaking' far more extensive and effective. Heaven and earth will at last be moved that men may contribute to the fulfilment of the divine purpose. And the announcement of this final catastrophe of the world, however awful in itself, is a 'promise,' because it is for the triumph of the cause of God that believers look.

The prophecy of Haggai (ii. 6 ff.,

γῆν ἐσάλευσεν τότε, νῦν δὲ ἐπήγγελται λέγων Ἔτι
ἅπαξ ἐγὼ ϲείϲω οὐ μόνον τὴν ΓῆΝ ἀλλὰ καὶ τὸν ογρανόν.
²⁷τὸ δέ Ἔτι ἅπαξ δηλοῖ [τὴν] τῶν σαλευομένων μετά-
θεσιν ὡς πεποιημένων, ἵνα μείνῃ τὰ μὴ σαλευόμενα.

ἔτι: ὅτι ἔτι M₂.   ἐγὼ ἅπαξ D₂.   σείσω ℵACM₂ vg syr vg me the:
σείω ϛ D₂.   +λέγει D₂*.   27 τὴν τῶν σαλ. ℵ*AC: τῶν σαλ. τήν ϛ ℵ°:
om. D₂*M₂.   om. ἵνα...σαλ. A.

21 ff.) deals with two main subjects, the superior glory of the second temple in spite of its apparent poverty: the permanent sovereignty of the house of David in spite of its apparent weakness. The prophet looks forward from the feeble beginnings of the new spiritual and national life to that final manifestation of the majesty and kingdom of God in which the discipline begun on Sinai is to have an end. He naturally recals in thought the phenomena which accompanied the giving of the Law; and foreshadows a correspondence between the circumstances of the first and the last scenes in the divine revelation. That which was local and preparatory at Sinai is seen in the consummation to be universal.

The quotation is adapted from the LXX. ἔτι ἅπαξ ἐγὼ σείσω τὸν οὐρανὸν καὶ τὴν γῆν καὶ τὴν θάλασσαν καὶ τὴν ξηράν. The interpretation of the words עוֹד אַחַת מְעַט הִיא ו rendered by ἔτι ἅπαξ is doubtful; but in any case the LXX. gives the main thought. The character of this 'shaking' compared with that which foreshadowed it marks it as final.

For ἐπήγγελται compare Rom. iv. 21; Gal. iii. 19 (to whom He hath given the promise).

27. τὸ δέ Ἔτι ἅπαξ] And the word Yet once more.... Vulg. Quod autem...dicit. The use of this phrase shews that the second 'shaking' will be final. No other is to follow. All then that admits of being shaken must be for ever removed.

For ἅπαξ see c. vi. 4 n.; ix. 26 ff.; and for δηλοῖ, c. ix. 8 note.

τὴν τῶν σαλευομένων...πεπ.] the removal of the things which are being shaken as of things that have been made. The convulsion is represented as in accomplishment. It is not simply possible. This vivid feature is lost in the Latin mobilium (Vulg.).

ὡς πεποιημένων] The visible earth and heaven are treated as transitory forms, which only represent in time the heavenly and eternal. As the material types of spiritual realities they are spoken of characteristically as 'made' and so as being liable to perish. The 'invisible' archetypes are also, as all things, 'made' by God: Is. lxvi. 22. They are not imperishable in themselves, but they abide in virtue of the divine will, which they are fitted peculiarly to express as being spiritual.

For μετάθεσις compare vii. 12 (xi. 5). The word only occurs in this Epistle in the N. T. In the LXX. it is found only in 2 Macc. xi. 24. The verb occurs Acts vii. 16; Gal. i. 6; Jude 4; c. vii. 12; xi. 5.

A similar idea is expressed by St John and St Paul. 1 John ii. 8; 17 (παράγεσθαι); 1 Cor. vii. 31 (παράγει).

ἵνα μείνῃ] The abiding of the eternal is naturally presented as the object of the removal of the temporal. By this the eternal is shewn as it is. The veils in which it was shrouded are withdrawn.

τὰ μὴ σαλ.] Vulg. quæ sunt immobilia (ἀσάλευτον v. 28, immobile),

²⁸ Διὸ βασιλείαν ἀσάλευτον παραλαμβάνοντες ἔχωμεν

28 ἔχωμεν ACD₂M₂ syr vg me: ἔχομεν ℵ d vg (comp. *v.* 1 Tischdf.).

all that stands undisturbed in the present trial. The 'shaking' is looked upon as already taking place. For μείνῃ see c. x. 34; xiii. 14.

The crisis to which the writer of the Epistle looks forward is, speaking generally, the establishment of the 'heavenly,' Christian, order when the 'earthly' order of the Law was removed. He makes no distinction between the beginning and the consummation of the age then to be inaugurated, between the catastrophe of the fall of Jerusalem and the final return of Christ: the whole course of the history of the Christian Church is included in the fact of its first establishment. It is impossible to say how far he anticipated great physical changes to coincide with this event. That which is essential to his view is the inauguration of a new order, answering to the 'new heavens and the new earth' (Is. lxv. 17; Apoc. xxi. 1).

Signs in nature however did accompany the Birth and Death of Christ.

The representation of great spiritual changes under physical imagery occurs elsewhere both in the Old and New Testaments: Is. lxv.; Matt. xxiv.; 2 Peter iii.; Apoc. xx.; xxi.

Many recent writers have connected πεποιημένων with ἵνα: 'so made that...,' 'made to the end that....' According to this view the transitory is treated as the preparation for the continuance of that which abides. The thought itself is important; but it does not seem to lie in the context, which does not deal directly with the purpose of that which passes away.

(β) 28, 29. The consideration of the position in which the Hebrews were placed issues in a practical appeal.

28. διὸ βασ....] *Wherefore*, seeing

that this great catastrophe, this revelation of the eternal, is imminent, *let us as receiving a kingdom that cannot be shaken*...The thought of the 'kingdom' lies in the second part of Haggai's prophecy, which the quotation naturally suggested to the readers. The 'shaking' of which the prophet spoke, and which was now being fulfilled, was designed to issue in an eternal sovereignty of the house of faith.

The mention of the Divine Kingdom is comparatively rare in the Epistles. In the Gospels and Acts the phrase is always definite, 'the kingdom,' 'the kingdom of heaven,' 'the kingdom of God,' 'the Father's kingdom' (ἡ βασιλεία, ἡ β. τῶν οὐρανῶν, ἡ β. τοῦ θεοῦ, ἡ β. τοῦ πατρός), and by implication 'the kingdom of the Son of man' (comp. Lk. xxii. 29 διέθετό μοι βασιλείαν). The phrase 'the kingdom of God' (ἡ β. τοῦ θ.) occurs: 2 Thess. i. 5; 1 Cor. iv. 20; Rom. xiv. 17; Col. iv. 11: comp. 1 Thess. ii. 12. Elsewhere we have 'the kingdom of Christ and God' (Eph. v. 5 ἐν τῇ β. τοῦ Χριστοῦ καὶ θεοῦ); and 'the eternal kingdom of our Lord and Saviour Jesus Christ' (2 Pet. i. 11 ἡ αἰώνιος β. τοῦ κυρίου ἡμῶν καὶ σωτῆρος Ἰ. Χρ.; comp. 1 Cor. xv. 24; Col. i. 13; 2 Tim. iv. 1, 18); and 'the kingdom which was promised' (James ii. 5). In other places the anarthrous form βασιλεία θεοῦ is used in the phrase, κληρονομεῖν β. θ.: 1 Cor. vi. 9 f.; xv. 50; Gal. v. 21, where it is natural that emphasis should be laid on the character of that which men looked to receive.

παραλαμβάνοντες] *receiving* from the hands of God as His gift. Believers are already entering upon the kingdom (c. iv. 3); and this kingdom is described as 'immovable'(ἀσάλευτον) and not simply as 'not moved' in the crisis which the Apostle pictures.

χάριν, δι' ἧς λατρεύωμεν εὐαρέστως τῷ θεῷ μετὰ εὐλαβείας καὶ δέους, ²⁹καὶ γὰρ ὁ θεὸς ἡμῶν πῦρ κΑΤΑΝΑΛίσκον.

λατρεύωμεν ACD₂ vg: λατρεύομεν אM₂.   εὐαρέστως: εὐχαρίστως D₂*.
εὐλαβείας καὶ δέους א*ACD₂* syr vg me the: εὐλ. καὶ αἰδοῦς אᶜM₂: αἰδοῦς καὶ εὐλ. ϛ vg.
29 καί: κύριος D₂ (d).

Comp. Dan. vii. 18 παραλήψονται τὴν βασιλείαν ἅγιοι ὑψίστου, after the four kingdoms of force had been removed; Col. iv. 17 π. διακονίαν.

ἔχωμεν χάριν] Vulg. habemus (ἔχομεν) gratiam. The use of the phrase χάριν ἔχειν elsewhere in the N. T. is strongly in favour of the sense 'let us feel and shew thankfulness to God': Luke xvii. 9; 1 Tim. i. 12; 2 Tim. i. 3. This sense is supported by Chrysostom (οὐ μόνον οὐκ ὀφείλωμεν ἀποδυσπετεῖν ἐπὶ τοῖς παροῦσιν ἀλλὰ καὶ χάριν αὐτῷ μεγίστην εἰδέναι ἐπὶ τοῖς μέλλουσι), Œcumenius and Theophylact. And, though at first sight there is something strange in the idea that thankfulness is the means whereby we may serve God, we are perhaps inclined to forget the weight which is attached in Scripture to gratitude and praise. It is the perception and acknowledgement of the divine glory which is the strength of man. The sense of love is the motive for proclaiming love. Ps. li. 14 f.

At the same time in 3 John 4, ἔχειν χάριν is used in the sense of 'having a gracious favour.' Thus there is nothing absolute in usage against giving to the words here the sense 'let us have (i.e. realise) grace.' The gift of God is certain, but we must make it our own. Comp. iv. 16 ἵνα...χ. εὕρωμεν, xiii. 9 καλὸν γὰρ χάριτι βεβαιοῦσθαι. This sense is given by the Peshito and by the Latin Fathers. Gratiam dicit fidem rectam, spem certam, caritatem perfectam, cum operatione sancta, per quæ debemus Deo servire cum metu, timentes illum ut Deum et judicem omnium, et cum reverentia diligentes eum ut patrem (Primas.).

For the sense of ἔχωμεν in this case see Rom. v. 1.

δι' ἧς λατρεύωμεν] The verb λατρεύωμεν is attracted to ἔχωμεν, 'let us thank God, and by that gratitude let us serve Him' (λατρ. τῷ θεῷ); ἐὰν γὰρ ὦμεν εὐχάριστοι τότε καὶ λατρεύομεν εὐαρέστως καὶ ὡς εἰδότες ποῖον δεσπότην ἔχομεν (Theophlct.). The saints, though kings, shall serve: Apoc. vii. 15; xxii. 3.

εὐαρέστως] c. xiii. 21 (τὸ εὐάρεστον). Elsewhere εὐάρεστος occurs in the N. T. only in St Paul (eight times), and except in Tit. ii. 9 (δούλους δεσπόταις εὐαρέστους) always of divine relations.

μετὰ εὐλαβ. καὶ δέους] Vulg. cum metu et reverentia (O. L. verecundia). The mention of δέος here, a word which does not occur again in the N. T., arises out of the context. Comp. Phil. ii. 12; 1 Pet. i. 17.

The common reading μετὰ αἰδ. καὶ εὐλ. occurs in Philo, Leg. ad Cai. § 44 (ii. 597 M.). For εὐλάβεια, see c. v. 7 note.

29. καὶ γὰρ...] for indeed.... See iv. 2 note.

ὁ θεὸς ἡμῶν] The significant addition of ἡμῶν extends the description of the God of the revelation from Sinai to the God of the new revelation. In other respects there may be a wide chasm between the Law and the Gospel; but the One God of both is in His very nature in relation to man as He is, and not in one manifestation only, 'a consuming fire.' He purifies by burning up all that is base in those who serve Him, and all that is unfit to abide in His Presence: Mal. iii. 2 f. (Is. iv. 4); Mal. iv. 1.   Comp. Matt. iii. 12.

With ὁ θεὸς ἡμῶν contrast ὁ θεός (Additional Note on 1 John iv. 8).

The image occurs several times in the O. T.; Deut. iv. 24; Is. xxxiii. 14. Comp. Deut. ix. 3; Ex. xxiv. 17.

The Latin Fathers develop the thought:

Deus omnipotens ignis appellatur non ut materiam quam fecit con-

sumat, sed quam exterius homo attrahit, rubiginem scilicet peccatorum; non enim illud consumit quod ipse fecit sed quod malitia hominum intulit (Primas.).

Ignis quatuor sunt officia, id est quoniam purgat et urit et illuminat et calefacit, sicque Spiritus sanctus purgat sordes vitiorum, et urit renes et cor ab humore libidinum, illuminat mentem notitia veritatis, et calefacit incendio caritatis (Herv.).

Additional Note on xii. 2.   *The Christology of the Epistle.*

The
breadth of
the Christ-
ology of
the
Epistle.

The view of the Person and Work of Christ which is given in the Epistle
to the Hebrews is in many respects more comprehensive and far-reaching
than that which is given in any other Book of the New Testament. The
writer does not indeed, like St John, trace back the conception of the
Personality of the Lord to immanent relations in the Being of a Living
God. He does not, like St Paul, distinctly represent each believer as
finding his life 'in Him' and so disclose the divine foundation of the
solidarity of the human race. But both thoughts are implicitly included in
his characteristic teaching on the High-priestly office of Christ through
which humanity reaches the end of creation.

Plan of
the Note.

In the following note I wish to offer for connected study the passages of
the Epistle in which the author deals with *The Divine Being of the Son*
(i), and with *The work of the Incarnate Christ* (ii); but before doing this
it is necessary to observe that he recognises one unchanged Personality
throughout in Him through Whom finite things were called into existence
and under Whom they find their final peace.

Christ is
One Per-
son in and
beyond
time (1—
4).

This fundamental truth finds complete expression in the opening paragraph (comp. pp. 17, 18). From first to last, through time to that eternity
beyond time which we have no powers to realise, One Person fulfils the will
of God :

> ὁ θεὸς ἐλάλησεν ἡμῖν ἐν υἱῷ
> ὃν ἔθηκεν κληρονόμον πάντων
> δι' οὗ καὶ ἐποίησεν τοὺς αἰῶνας.

And when we contemplate Him in His Nature and His Work there is
the same unbroken continuity through changes which to our eyes interrupt
or limit His activity :

> ὃς ὢν
>   ἀπαύγασμα τῆς δόξης καὶ
>   χαρακτὴρ τῆς ὑποστάσεως αὐτοῦ
>   φέρων τε τὰ πάντα τῷ ῥήματι τῆς δυνάμεως αὐτοῦ
>   καθαρισμὸν τῶν ἁμαρτιῶν ποιησάμενος
> ἐκάθισεν ἐν δεξιᾷ τῆς μεγαλωσύνης.

One Person is the agent in creation, the medium of revelation, the heir
of the world. One Person makes God known to us in terms of human
life, and bears all things unceasingly to their proper goal, and 'having made
purification of sins' waits for that issue which man's self-assertion has
delayed.

Other
forms in
which the
truth is
conveyed.

The same thought is traced in the O. T. where the Son is spoken of as
King and Creator (i. 8—12). And it appears in its simplest form in the
combination of the two contrasted Names 'Jesus' and 'the Son of God'
(iv. 14 note; compare xiii. 20 τὸν κύριον ἡμῶν Ἰησοῦν with 1 Cor. xii. 3;
Rom. x. 9); and again in the abrupt and unique phrase, c. xiii. 8, Ἰησοῦς
Χριστὸς ἐχθὲς καὶ σήμερον ὁ αὐτὸς καὶ εἰς τοὺς αἰῶνας.

i. *The Divine Being (Nature and Personality) of the Son.*

(1) In relation to God.

The Divine Being of the Son in relation to God is presented (a) by the
use of the general titles 'Son,' 'the Son,' 'the Firstborn'; and (b) by the
definite description of His nature and work.

(a) The use of the anarthrous title 'Son,' which emphasises the
essential nature of the relation which it expresses, is characteristic of the
Epistle (i. 2 note, 5 [comp. v. 5]; iii. 6; v. 8; vii. 28 note; comp. p. 34).
The form occurs elsewhere in the Epistles only in Rom. i. 4 ὁρισθέντος υἱοῦ
θεοῦ (comp. John xix. 7 υἱὸν θεοῦ).

This title is defined by the personal titles 'the Son' (i. 8), 'the Son of
God' (vi. 6; vii. 3; x. 29), 'the Firstborn' (i. 6 note); and 'the Son of God'
is identified with 'Jesus' (iv. 14 note).

The title 'Son' is used in the Epistle only in reference to the Incarnate
Lord. This follows from the scope of the teaching. But the title expresses
not merely a moral relation, but a relation of being; and defines in
human language that which 'was' beyond time immanent in the Godhead (x. 5; vii. 3 notes). There was (so to speak) a congruity in the
Incarnation of the Second Person of the Holy Trinity (comp. p. 18).

In this connexion it must be noticed that the writer represents the
Father as the Source (μία πηγὴ θεότητος) from which the Son derived all
that He has (i. 2 ἔθηκεν; v. 5 οὐχ ἑαυτὸν ἐδόξασεν).   Comp. St John v. 26.

It is remarkable that God is spoken of as 'Father' only in i. 5 (from the
LXX.; comp. xii. 9, 7). The title is used by St Paul in all his Epistles.

(b) The definite description of the Divine Personality given in i. 3 has
been examined in detail in the notes upon the passage. The use of the
absolute, timeless, term 'being' (ὤν) guards against the thought that the
Lord's 'Sonship' was by adoption and not by nature. In Him the 'glory'
of God finds manifestation, as its 'effulgence' (ἀπαύγασμα), and the
'essence' (ὑπόστασις) of God finds expression, as its embodiment, type
(χαρακτήρ). The two ideas are complementary and neither is to be pressed
to consequences. In ἀπαύγασμα the thought of 'personality' finds no
place (ἐνυπόστατον οὐκ ἐστίν); and in χαρακτήρ the thought of 'coessen-
tiality' finds no place. The two words are related exactly as ὁμοούσιος and
μονογενής, and like those must be combined to give the fulness of the
Truth. The Truth expressed thus antithetically holds good absolutely; and
it is offered to us under the conditions of human life in the Incarnation.
In Christ the essence of God is made distinct: in Christ the revelation of
God's character is seen (comp. John v. 19, 30; xiv. 9).

(2) In relation to the World.

In relation to the World the Son is presented to us as (a) the Creator,
(b) the Preserver, and (c) the Heir of all things. From the divine side
indeed these three offices are one.

(a) The Creative work of the Son is affirmed both in the writer's own
words (i. 2 δι' οὗ καὶ ἐποίησεν τοὺς αἰῶνας), and by an application of the
language of the Psalms (i. 10). At the same time the creation is finally

i. The
Divine
Being of
the Son.
(1) In
relation
to God.
(a) The
titles
'Son,'
'the Son,'
'the First-
born.'

(b) The
nature and
work of
the Son.

(2) In
relation to
the World.

(a) Crea-
tor.

referred to God (xi. 3 πίστει νοοῦμεν κατηρτίσθαι τοὺς αἰῶνας ῥήματι θεοῦ). Thus the teaching of the Epistle exactly corresponds with the Nicene phrases: πιστεύομεν εἰς ἕνα θεόν, πατέρα...πάντων...ποιητήν· καὶ εἰς ἕνα κύριον Ἰησοῦν Χριστόν...δι᾽ οὗ τὰ πάντα ἐγένετο....

(b) Pre-
server.

(b) The thought of creation passes into that of the preservation, government, consummation of created things. The Son by 'the word of His power' (i. 3 φέρων note; comp. xi. 3) bears all things to their true end. He is over the whole house of God in virtue of what He is (iii. 6 υἱός) and of what He has done (x. 21 ἱερεύς). This work was in no way interrupted by the Incarnation. St Paul also combines the creative and sustaining power of Christ:. Col. i. 16, 17 (ἐκτίσθη, ἔκτισται, συνέστηκεν).

(c) Heir.

(c) The idea of the 'heirship' of Christ, though in a limited sense, finds a place in the Synoptic Gospels (Matt. xxi. 38 and parr.). It is connected by St Paul with the work of creation: Col. i. 16 τὰ πάντα δι᾽ αὐτοῦ καὶ εἰς αὐτὸν ἔκτισται. This conception is emphasised by the true order of the words in i. 2 δι᾽ οὗ καὶ ἐποίησεν τ. αἰ. The fact that He created suggests the fitness that He should inherit. Comp. Addit. Note on vi. 12.

The Sovereignty of Christ over 'the order to come' (ii. 5) presents His 'heirship' under one special aspect; and in part this Sovereignty is exercised even now (iii. 6; x. 21). In part however it awaits accomplishment (i. 13; x. 13).

ii. The
work of
the Incar-
nate
Christ.
(1) The
Incarna-
tion.

ii. *The Work of the Incarnate Christ.*

The Work of the Incarnate Christ is presented under the aspect, (1) of His earthly life, and (2) of His Work in His glorified humanity in heaven.

(1) The Incarnation.

The Incarnation requires to be considered (a) in relation to the assumption of human nature (σαρκωθῆναι), and (b) in relation to human life (ἐνανθρωπῆσαι). Both views are required for a full view of the Truth.

(a)
Christ's
human
nature.

(a) The Lord's humanity is declared to be real (ii. 14; comp. v. 10; vii. 14), perfect (ii. 17 κατὰ πάντα), and representative (ii. 9 ὑπὲρ παντός). At the same time, as has been seen, the Divine Personality was unchanged by the assumption of manhood. We must not however suppose that the body with its powers was simply an instrument which was directed by a divine 'principle.' The body prepared for Him by God (x. 5) is not, any more than 'flesh' in John i. 14, to be interpreted in a partial sense. The use of the human name (Ἰησοῦς, see p. 33) guards the fulness of His humanity (comp. ii. 6 LXX.). At the same time His perfect humanity was in absolute harmony with His Divine Nature, and so He could work through it using all men's powers; but it did not limit His Divine Nature in any way in itself: it limited only its manifestation.

(b)
Christ's
human
life.

(b) Thus the perfect human nature of Christ found expression in a perfect human life. By the discipline of suffering the Lord was 'made perfect,' bearing without the least failure every temptation to which we are exposed (iv. 15; v. 7 ff.; vii. 26). Comp. Addit. Note on ii. 10. His growth was not only negatively sinless, but a victorious development of every human power. Nor can it be without deep interest to notice how the writer recognises in Christ separate human virtues: trust in God (ii. 13 ἔσομαι πεποιθώς...); faithfulness (ii. 17; iii. 2); mercy and sympathy (ii. 17; iv. 15); dependence on God (v. 7 f.); faith (xii. 2). For the connexion of the discipline of Christ with the discipline of men, compare ii. 10 f. with xii. 7.

Christ did not however cease at any time to be the Son of God. He lived through death, offering Himself through His eternal spirit (ix. 14 note); and He exercises His priesthood in virtue of 'the power of an indissoluble life' (vii. 16).

In this union of two Natures in the one Person of Christ, Whose Personality is Divine, to use the technical language of Theology, we recognise the foundation-fact of a true fellowship of God and man. There would be no true fellowship, no sure hope for men, if the Person of Christ were simply a manifestation of Deity, or a divine principle working through human nature as its material.

As it is we can see how in virtue of His humanity and human life the Lord was able to fulfil His twofold office for men, as 'Apostle and High-priest' (iii. 1), declaring the will of God and preparing men to appear before Him.

(2) The Exaltation.

(2) The Exaltation.

The exaltation of Christ is placed in this Epistle, as by St Paul (Phil. ii. 9 ff. διό), in close connexion with His sufferings (ii. 9; xii. 2). But the writer differs from St Paul in his mode of presenting it. While St Paul dwells on the Resurrection in each group of his Epistles, the writer of the Epistle to the Hebrews refers to it once only (xiii. 20; comp. v. 7), fixing his attention on the Ascension (iv. 14; vi. 20; vii. 26; ix. 11 f.; 24), and the Session on the right hand of God (i. 3; viii. 1; x. 12; xii. 2). This difference follows from the unique teaching of the Epistle on the work of Christ as King-priest. Comp. Addit. Notes on viii. 1 and viii. 1, 2.

From what has been said it will be seen that there is a very close connexion between the Christology of the writer to the Hebrews and the Christology of St Paul. Both Apostles fix the minds of their readers upon what Christ is and what He did and does, and not upon what He taught: with both His prophetic work falls into the background. Both again rise to the thought of the glorified Christ through the work of Christ on earth. But in this respect the writer to the Hebrews forms a link between St Paul and St John. He dwells upon the eternal nature and unchangeable work of the Son before he treats of His historic work; while for St John even the sufferings of Christ are a form of His glory.

But though there is a remarkable agreement in idea between the teaching of the Epistle on the Person of Christ and that of St Paul's (later) Epistles (Phil. ii. 5—11; Eph. i. 3—14; Col. i. 15—20), even where the thoughts approach most nearly to coincidence, there still remain significant differences of phraseology: e.g.

i. 3 ἀπαύγασμα χαρακτήρ.	Col. i. 15 (2 Cor. iv. 4) εἰκών.
id. φέρων τὰ πάντα τῷ ῥήμ. τῆς δυν. αὐτοῦ.	Col. i. 17 τὰ π. ἐν αὐτῷ συνέστηκεν.
i. 2 κληρονόμον πάντων.	Col. i. 16 τὰ πάντα εἰς αὐτὸν ἔκτισται.

i. 6 ὁ πρωτότοκος.

ii. 17 ὤφειλεν κατὰ πάντα τοῖς ἀδελφοῖς ὁμοιωθῆναι.

Col. i. 15 πρωτότοκος πάσης κτίσεως.

Col. i. 18 πρωτότοκος ἐκ τῶν νεκρῶν.

Phil. ii. 7 ἐν ὁμοιώματι ἀνθρώπων
γενόμενος. Comp. Rom. viii. 3.

Compare also the use of Ps. viii. in ii. 6 ff. with the use of it in 1 Cor. xv.
27; Phil. iii. 21 (Eph. i. 22).

It is also of importance to observe that the writer of the Epistle does
not use St Paul's images of Christ as 'the Second Adam' (1 Cor. xv. 22, 45),
and 'the Head' of the Church (Eph. i. 22; iv. 15 f.; Col. i. 18), though he
does dwell on the fellowship between the One Son and the 'many sons' (ii.
10 ff.; comp. x. 5 ff.); nor does he offer the thought of the Christian as
dead and risen with Christ. On the other hand St Paul does not speak of
Christ's work as High-priest, nor does he set forth the discipline of His
human life as bringing to men the assurance of prevailing sympathy.

It follows also from the prominence which the writer gives to the
priestly work of Christ that he represents the Lord as more active in His
Passion than St Paul does. Even on the Cross he shews Christ as working
rather than as suffering. Christ in St Paul is regarded predominantly as
the Victim, in the Epistle to the Hebrews as the Priest even more than
the Victim. In this point again the Epistle comes near to the gospel of
St John, in which Christ on the Cross is seen in sovereign majesty.

There is, it may be added, no trace in the Epistle of the Dualistic views
which find a place in the Pastoral Epistles (1 Tim. iv. 3 ff.; Tit. i. 15);
nor of the Docetism which is met by St John (1 John iv. 2 f.; 2 John 7).

Compare Additional Note on i. 4, *On the Divine Names in the
Epistle.*

XIII.   ''Η φιλαδελφία μενέτω.   ²τῆς φιλοξενίας

2 τὴν φιλοξενίαν ℵ*.

The thirteenth chapter is a kind of appendix to the Epistle, like Rom. xv., xvi. The first twelve chapters form a complete treatise; and now for the first time distinct personal traits appear. A difference of style corresponds with the difference of subject; but the central portion brings back with fresh power some of the main thoughts on which the writer has before insisted.

The chapter falls into three divisions:

(1)   *Social duties* (1—6).
(2)   *Religious duties* (7—17).
(3)   *Personal instructions of the writer* (18—25).

(1)   *Social duties* (1—6).

The character of the precepts suggests that the society to which they were addressed consisted of wealthy and influential members. The two special illustrations of the practical exhibition of 'love to the brethren' point to services which such persons especially could render; and the warnings which follow regard the temptations of a similar class to luxury and love of money.

The succession of thought is perfectly natural. Particular duties spring out of the recognition of the new relation to God and men established in Christ. Sympathy (1, 2), self-respect and self-control (4, 5), confidence in spiritual support (6), express the application of the one truth to different spheres.

¹ *Let love of the brethren continue.* ² *Forget not to entertain strangers, for thereby some entertained angels unawares.* ³ *Remember them that are in bonds, as bound with them: them that are evil entreated, as being yourselves also in the body.* ⁴ *Let marriage be had in honour in all things; and let the bed be undefiled; for fornicators and adulterers God*

will judge. ⁵ *Let your character be free from the love of money.* *Be content with the things ye have; for Himself hath said, I will in no wise fail thee, nor will I in any wise forsake thee.* ⁶ *So that with good courage we say, The Lord is my helper: I will not fear.* *What shall man do to me?*

1.   ἡ φιλαδελφία] *love of the brethren*, Vulg. *caritas fraternitatis.* The relation of Christians one to another in virtue of their common Lord (ii. 11 f.) led necessarily to the extension of the term for the affection of natural kinsmanship to all the members of the one 'brotherhood' (ἀδελφότης 1 Pet. ii. 17; v. 9). Comp. 2 Pet. i. 7 (1 Pet. iii. 8); Rom. xii. 10; 1 Thess. iv. 9; 1 Pet. i. 22.

The love of the Jew for his fellow Jew, his 'brother' (Deut. xxiii. 19; comp. Philo, *de carit.* § 6, ii. 388 M.), was national: the Christian's love for his fellow-Christian is catholic. The tie of the common faith is universal, and in proportion as the ill-will of those without increased, it became necessary to deepen the feeling of affection within.

The use of μενέτω suggests that the bond had been in danger of being severed. Compare vi. 10; x. 33.

Jugiter *maneat in vobis caritas fraternitatis,* id est semper diligatis fraternitatem, hoc est, fratres qui sunt aqua et spiritu renati sicut et vos (Herv.).

῞Ορα πῶς τὰ παρόντα προστάττει φυλάττειν αὐτοὺς καὶ οὐχὶ προστίθησιν ἕτερα· οὐ γὰρ εἶπε, Γίνεσθε φιλάδελφοι ἀλλά, Μενέτω ἡ φιλαδελφία (Chrys.).

2.   τῆς φιλοξ. μὴ ἐπιλ.] The circumstances of the time made private hospitality almost a necessity for travellers.   In writing to the Corinthians Clement mentions among their former glories τὸ μεγαλοπρεπὲς τῆς φιλοξενίας

μὴ ἐπιλανθάνεσθε, διὰ ταύτης γὰρ ἔλαθόν τινες ξενίσαντες ἀγγέλους. ³μιμνήσκεσθε τῶν δεσμίων ὡς συνδεδεμένοι, τῶν κακουχουμένων ὡς καὶ αὐτοὶ

ἐπιλανθάνεσθαι D₂* (so v. 18 προσεύχεσθαι, v. 22 ἀνέχεσθαι, v. 24 ἀσπάσασθαι). ἔλαθον: didicerunt d (ἔμαθον). 3 δεσμίων: δεδεμένων D₂*. κακουχουμένων: κακωχ. C: κακοχ. M₂.

ὑμῶν ἦθος (ad Cor. i. 17), and dwells on the 'hospitality' of Abraham, Lot, Rahab (cc. 10—12). Comp. 1 Tim. v. 10; 3 John 5 ff.; 1 Pet. iv. 9; 1 Tim. iii. 2; Tit. i. 8 (φιλόξενος). Φιλοξενία occurs again Rom. xii. 13. See also Herm. Mand. viii. ἄκουε... τῶν ἀγαθῶν τὰ ἔργα ἅ γε δεῖ ἐργάζεσθαι ...χήραις ὑπηρετεῖν, ὀρφανοὺς καὶ ὑστερουμένους ἐπισκέπτεσθαι, ἐξ ἀναγκῶν λυτροῦσθαι τοὺς δούλους τοῦ θεοῦ, φιλόξενον εἶναι, ἐν γὰρ τῇ φιλοξενίᾳ εὑρίσκεται ἀγαθοποίησις... Lucian mocks at the liberality of Christians to strangers: ἐξῄει (Peregrinus) τὸ δεύτερον πλανησόμενος, ἱκανὰ ἐφόδια τοὺς χριστιανοὺς ἔχων, ὑφ' ὧν δορυφορούμενος ἐν ἅπασιν ἀφθόνοις ἦν (de morte Peregr. § 16; comp. §§ 12 f.).

The use of the phrase μὴ ἐπιλανθάνεσθε, compared with μιμνήσκεσθε, implies that the virtue was now being neglected: τοῦτο γὰρ εἰκὸς ἀπὸ τῶν θλίψεων γίνεσθαι (Chrys.).

There is a marked correspondence between φιλαδελφία and φιλοξενία. Compare Rom. xii. 10, 13.

διὰ ταύτης γὰρ...] Comp. Gen. xviii. xix.; Philo, de Abr. § 22, i. pp. 16 f. M. The form of the illustration seems to be that we only observe the outside surface of those whom we receive. More lies beneath than we can see. Christ indeed comes in the least of those who are welcomed in His name (Matt. xxv. 40, 45 ; John xiii. 20).

The idiomatic form of expression, ἔλαθον ξενίσαντες (Vulg. latuerunt quidam angelis hospitio recepti) does not occur again in the N. T. or in the LXX. Compare the use of λανθ. in the corresponding passage of Philo: οἱ

δὲ (sc. ὁδοιποροῦντες ἄνδρες) θειοτέρας ὄντες φύσεως ἐλελήθεισαν (l. c. § 22).

Primasius and Gregory (Hom. xxiii. in Ev. § 2) (with some Latin copies) read placuerunt quidam [sc. Deo].

3. Hospitality is the answer to a direct appeal. We must also seek for those who need our help, and whose circumstances withdraw their claims from our sight. Such sufferers may owe their distress either to direct persecution (τῶν δεσμίων), or to the 'changes and chances of this mortal life' (τῶν κακουχουμένων). In both cases Christians must acknowledge the obligation of fellowship.

μιμνήσκεσθε] Remember 'in precibus, in beneficiis' (Bengel). Compare c. x. 32 ἀναμιμνήσκεσθε. Elsewhere μνημονεύειν, v. 7; Gal. ii. 10.

For τῶν δεσμίων compare c. x. 34.

ὡς συνδεδεμένοι] as bound with them, rather than as if you were bound with them. The participle appears to give the reason in this as in the following clause (ὡς...ὄντες...). The members of the Christian body are so closely united that the suffering of one is really, though it may be unconsciously, shared by all. This is the ideal which each believer must strive to realise.

Compare 2 Cor. xi. 29 τίς ἀσθενεῖ καὶ οὐκ ἀσθενῶ; τίς σκανδαλίζεται καὶ οὐκ ἐγὼ πυροῦμαι;

Non sint vobis oblivioni quamvis teneantur in abditis reclusi (Herv.).

Public intercession for 'prisoners' has formed part of the Church service from the earliest times down to our own Litany.

The petition is found in the prayer

ὄντες ἐν σώματι.　⁴ Τίμιος ὁ γάμος ἐν πᾶσιν καὶ

which closes the Epistle of Clement: λύτρωσαι τοὺς δεσμίους ἡμῶν· ἐξανάστησον τοὺς ἀσθενοῦντας· παρακάλεσον τοὺς ὀλιγοψυχοῦντας (c. lix.). So in the Apostolical Constitutions (viii. 10) the direction is given ὑπὲρ τῶν ἐν μετάλλοις καὶ ἐξορίαις καὶ φυλακαῖς καὶ δεσμοῖς ὄντων διὰ τὸ ὄνομα τοῦ κυρίου δεηθῶμεν. ὑπὲρ τῶν ἐν πικρᾷ δουλείᾳ καταπονουμένων δεηθῶμεν. And petitions to this effect are found in early liturgies:

Liturgy of Alexandria, p. 32 (Swainson); *Liturgy of St Basil*, p. 84; *St James* (Cod. Rossan.), p. 250; *Coptic*, p. 371.

A similar petition is found in the daily Synagogue Morning Service, p. 19 (Artom).

Ignatius in describing false Christians says περὶ ἀγάπης οὐ μέλει αὐτοῖς, οὐ περὶ χήρας, οὐ περὶ ὀρφανοῦ, οὐ περὶ θλιβομένου, οὐ περὶ δεδεμένου ἢ λελυμένου, οὐ περὶ πεινῶντος ἢ διψῶντος (*ad Smyrn.* 6).

τῶν κακουχουμένων] them that are evil entreated, Vulg. *laborantium*, c. xi. 37 (only in N. T.), comp. xi. 25. The word is used in late Greek authors (twice in LXX.), but κακουχία is found in Æschylus. The meaning appears to be quite general.

ὡς καὶ αὐτοὶ ὄ. ἐν σ.] as being yourselves also in the body and so exposed to the same sufferings, Vulg. *tanquam et ipsi in corpore morantes*. The former injunction had been enforced by the consideration of the true nature of the Christian body; this one is enforced by the actual outward circumstances of life: Cuivis potest accidere quod cuiquam potest.

Per hoc enim quia in corpore mortali manetis, sicut et illi, experimento probatis quia militia est vita hominis super terram, et homo ad laborem nascitur et (ut?) avis ad volatum (Primas.).

For the phrase ὄντες ἐν σώμ. com-

pare 2 Cor. v. 6 (1). It occurs in Porphyr. *de abstin.* i. 38 εἰ γὰρ μὴ ἐνεπόδιζε τὰ αἰσθήματα τῇ τῆς ψυχῆς ἐνεργείᾳ, τί δεινὸν ἦν ἐν σώματι εἶναι. The thought is that of the body as being the home (or the prison) of the soul.

The interpretation 'as being yourselves also members in the one body of Christ'—beautiful as the thought is—is inadmissible. This would require a more definite phrase than ἐν σώματι (at least ἐν τῷ σώματι).

4. From the widest duties of the social life of Christians the epistle passes to the closest. Warnings on the sacredness of marriage were the more necessary from the license of divorce among the Jews which had been sanctioned by the teaching of the school of Hillel. Comp. Matt. xix. 3 ff. (κατὰ πᾶσαν αἰτίαν).

It is questioned whether the sentence contains a precept (*Let marriage be...*) or a declaration (*Marriage is...*), whether, that is, ἔστω or ἐστί is to be supplied.

The Syriac version gives the indicative: *Marriage is honourable...* So also Chrysostom (πῶς τίμιος ὁ γάμος; ὅτι ἐν σωφροσύνῃ, φησί, διατηρεῖ τὸν πιστόν) reading δέ, and by implication Theodoret and Œcumenius (but not Theophylact: see below).

The Latin leaves the construction ambiguous: *Honorabile connubium in omnibus et torus immaculatus*, while in the corresponding phrase below it inserts the substantive verb, *sint mores sine avaritia*. The Latin Fathers generally take the words as declaratory. Primasius adds: sit vobis sive placet Deo; but goes on to explain the words as declaratory. *Connubium est honorabile*, id est legales nuptiæ sunt honorabiles *in omnibus*, nihil est in eis quod honore careat, et *torus* talium conjugum est *imma-*

ἡ κοίτη ἀμίαντος, πόρνους γὰρ καὶ μοιχοὺς κρινεῖ ὁ
θεός.   ⁵Ἀφιλάργυρος ὁ τρόπος· ἀρκούμενοι τοῖς

4 γὰρ אAD₂*M₂ vg me: δέ C syr vg.   5 ἀρκούμενοι: ἀρκούμενος M₂.

culatus, id est sine macula criminis (Herv.).

In spite of the concurrence of ancient opinion towards the other view, the general structure of the passage and the unquestionable sense of ἀφιλ. ὁ τρόπος are sufficient to decide in favour of regarding the clauses as hortatory and not indicative. This interpretation is confirmed if not required by the γάρ which follows in the true text (*Let marriage be had in honour..,for...*). It may be added that ὁ γάμος is used here only in the N. T. in the sense of 'marriage.'

ἐν πᾶσιν] in all respects, and in all circumstances, so as to be guarded not only from graver violations but from everything which lowers its dignity. Πᾶσιν is neuter as in *v.* 18; 1 Tim. iii. 11; 2 Tim. iv. 5; Tit. ii. 9.

Μὴ ἐν θλίψει μὲν [ἐν] ἀνέσει δὲ οὔ· μὴ ἐν τούτῳ μὲν τῷ μέρει τίμιος ἐν ἄλλῳ δὲ οὔ· ἀλλ' ὅλος δι' ὅλου τίμιος ἔστω (Theophlct.).

For τίμιος compare Acts v. 34.

The masc. interpretation (*among all*) gives a better sense with the *indic.* than with the *imper.* construction.

πόρνους γάρ...] Compare 1 Thess. iv. 6. The words ὁ θεός stand emphatically at the end. Whatever the opinion of man be from ignorance or indifference, God will judge.

5. ἀφιλάργυρος ὁ τρ.] *Let your character be free from the love of money*, Vulg. *Sint mores sine avaritia*. Sins of impurity and of covetousness go together. Both are typical examples of πλεονεξία (self-seeking, selfishness). Eph. v. 3 ff.

Ὁ τρόπος describes the general character. It is not found elsewhere in N. T. in this sense. Compare *Didache*

xi. 9. For ἀφιλάργυρος see 1 Tim. iii. 3; *Didache* xv. 1 (comp. iii. 5); 2 Clem. iv. 3.

ἀρκ. τοῖς παρ.] The form of words had passed into a moral commonplace. Comp. [Phocyl.] 6 ἀρκεῖσθαι παρέουσι καὶ [al. παρ' ἑοῖς τῶν δ'] ἀλλοτρίων ἀπέχεσθαι. Teles. *ap.* Stob. *Floril.* 97 (95) § 31 τί οὖν μοί ἐστι φιλοσοφήσαντι; ...βιώσῃ ἀρκούμενος τοῖς παροῦσι, τῶν ἀπόντων οὐκ ἐπιθυμῶν... Comp. Clem. 1 Cor. 2 τοῖς ἐφοδίοις τοῦ θεοῦ ἀρκούμενοι.

For the construction see Rom. xii. 9.

Οὐκ εἶπεν Μηδὲν κέκτησθε ἀλλὰ Κἂν ἔχητε μὴ ἦτε δεδουλωμένοι ἀλλ' ἐλευθέρως ταῦτα ἔχετε... (Theophlct.).

The patristic commentators suggest that the losses of the Hebrews (x. 32 ff.) had checked their liberality and given occasion to the desire of accumulating fresh wealth.

αὐτὸς γὰρ εἴρ.] *for He Himself*, God our Father, *hath said*...—the phrase sounds like an echo of the Pythagorean αὐτὸς ἔφα, *Ipse dixit*, 'the Master said'—*I will in no wise fail thee, nor will I in any wise forsake thee.*

The exact source of the quotation is not certain. Similar words occur in several places: Gen. xxviii. 15; Jos. i. 5; Deut. xxxi. 6 ff.; and a quotation in exactly the same form occurs in Philo, *de conf. ling.* § 32 (i. p. 430 M.). There seems however to be no sufficient reason for supposing that the quotation was taken from him. The words had probably been moulded to this shape by common use.

ἀνῶ...ἐγκαταλίπω] Vulg. *deseram... derelinquam*. The idea of ἀνίημι is that of loosing hold so as to withdraw the support rendered by the sustaining grasp: that of ἐγκαταλείπω

παροῦσιν· αὐτὸς γὰρ εἴρηκεν   Οὐ μή ϲε ἀνῶ ογΔ' ογ μή
ϲε ἐγκαταλίπω·   ⁶ὥστε θαρροῦντας ἡμᾶς λέγειν

Κύριοϲ ἐμοὶ Βοηθόϲ, ογ φοΒηθήϲομαι·
τί ποιήϲει μοι ἄνθρωποϲ;

ἐγκαταλίπω 5 D₂ (ενκ.): -λείπω ℵACM₂.   6 λέγειν ἡμᾶς D₂: om. ἡμᾶς M₂.
οὐ ℵ*C* vg syr vg me: +καί' οὐ ℵᶜAD₂M₂.

of deserting or leaving alone in the field of contest, or in a position of suffering.

'Ανίημι does not occur elsewhere in the N. T. in this sense; for ἐγκαταλείπω see 2 Cor. iv. 9; 2 Tim. iv. 10, 16; Matt. xxvii. 46 (LXX.); Acts ii. 27 (LXX.); comp. c. x. 25. The use of the word in Matt. xxvii. 46 is a clue to the true meaning of the passage. It was the Father's good pleasure to leave the Son exposed to the assaults of His enemies 'in their hour' (Luke xxii. 53).

Biesenthal most truly points out the fitness of an allusion to the encouragement given to Joshua at such a crisis as the Hebrews were passing through. The position of Jewish Christians corresponded spiritually with that of their fathers on the verge of Canaan.

For εἴρηκεν see c. x. 8 note.

6. ὥστε θαρρ. ἡ. λ.] Ps. cxviii. 6 (comp. Ps. cvi. 12). The LXX. by inserting καί has led to an alteration in the original division of the words. There can be no doubt that the last clause should be taken as an independent question.

We Christians—such is the writer's meaning—can use with confidence the most joyful expression of thanksgiving used in the Church of old times. Ps. cxviii. formed an important part of the Jewish Festival services, and is quoted several times in the N. T. The key-word given here would call up at once to the mind of the readers the thought of 'the chief corner-stone' (Matt. xxi. 42) and of Him 'that came in the name of the Lord' (Matt. xxi.

9). In the triumph of the Lord through suffering they would see the image of the triumph of His people.

The word θαρρεῖν occurs elsewhere in the N. T. only 2 Cor. (v. 6, 8; &c.). The imperative θάρσει (-εῖτε) is found only as a divine voice (Gospp., Acts).

(2) *Personal religious duties* (7—17).

The mode in which religious duties are presented indicates the presence of a separatist spirit among those who are addressed. They are charged to remember (a) the example of their first rulers (7); and, following on this, they are (b) bidden to render complete devotion to Christ, and to men in and through Him (8—16); and practically (c) to obey their present rulers (17).

⁷ *Remember them that had the rule over you, which spake unto you the word of God; and considering the issue of their life, imitate their faith.*

⁸ *Jesus Christ is the same yesterday and to-day, yea and for ever.* ⁹ *Be not carried away by manifold and strange teachings; for it is good that the heart be stablished by grace, not by meats; for they that occupied themselves therein were not profited.* ¹⁰ *We have an altar whereof they have no right to eat who serve the tabernacle.* ¹¹ *For the bodies of those animals whose blood is brought into the Holy place by the High-priest as an offering for sin, are burned without the camp.* ¹² *Wherefore Jesus also, that He might sanctify the people through His own blood, suffered without the gate.* ¹³ *Let us therefore go forth unto Him without the camp,*

⁷ Μνημονεύετε τῶν ἡγουμένων ὑμῶν, οἵτινες ἐλάλησαν ὑμῖν τὸν λόγον τοῦ θεοῦ, ὧν ἀναθεωροῦντες τὴν ἔκβασιν

7 τ. ἡγουμένων ὑμῶν : τ. προηγουμένων D₂* (sic).   ἀναθεωροῦντες: -ρήσαντες C.

carrying His reproach. ¹⁴For we have not here an abiding city, but we seek after that which is to come. ¹⁵Through Him let us offer up a sacrifice of praise to God continually, that is, the fruit of lips which make confession to His Name. ¹⁶But to do good and to communicate forget not; for with such sacrifices God is well pleased.

¹⁷Obey them that have the rule over you, and submit to them, for they watch in behalf of your souls, as men that shall give account, that they may do this with joy and not with grief; for this were unprofitable for you.

(a) The writer has spoken of the help of God generally. He now appeals to examples in which it had been conspicuously shewn before he passes on to enforce religious duties.

7. μνημονεύετε τῶν ἡγ.] Remember, though they have now passed away, them that had the rule over you. Scripture everywhere recognises the living power of a great example. Comp. c. vi. 12. The word μνημονεύειν is used of our relation to Christ 2 Tim. ii. 8 (μνημ. 'Ι. Χ. ἐγηγερμένον).

The term οἱ ἡγούμενοι (Vulg. præpositi) occurs again vv. 17, 24; Clem. 1 ad Cor. 1 (in c. 7 of civil rulers); 21 τοὺς προηγουμένους ἡμῶν. Compare Acts xv. 22 (ἄνδρας ἡγουμένους ἐν τοῖς ἀδελφοῖς). The word occurs frequently in the LXX. of various forms of authority; and in later Greek of bishops and abbots. Compare pp. 384 f.

οἵτινες ἐλάλ....] men that spake to you.... Comp. ii. 3 note. The phrase ὁ λόγος τοῦ θεοῦ is used from Luke v. 1 throughout the N. T. both of the revelation in the O. T. and of the revelation through Christ.

For the thought compare 1 Thess.

v. 12 f.; Didache iv. 1 τέκνον μου, τοῦ λαλοῦντός σοι τὸν λόγον τοῦ θεοῦ μνησθήσῃ νυκτὸς καὶ ἡμέρας, τιμήσεις δὲ αὐτὸν ὡς κύριον.... Barn. Ep. xix. 9 ἀγαπήσεις ὡς κόρην ὀφθαλμοῦ σου πάντα τὸν λαλοῦντά σοι τὸν λόγον κυρίου.

ὧν ἀναθ. τὴν ἔκβ. τῆς ἀναστρ.] and considering with attentive survey again and again the issue of their life... Vulg. quorum intuentes exitum conversationis. This last scene revealed the character of their 'conversation' before. Perhaps the writer had in his mind the words of the persecutors of the righteous man : Wisd. ii. 17, ἴδωμεν εἰ οἱ λόγοι αὐτοῦ ἀληθεῖς, καὶ πειράσωμεν τὰ ἐν ἐκβάσει αὐτοῦ. The word ἔκβασις occurs in a different connexion 1 Cor. x. 13 : compare ἔξοδος Lk. ix. 31; 2 Pet. i. 15. Ἀναστροφή describes life under its moral aspect (comp. v. 18; x. 33) wrought out in intercourse with men. The image occurs in St Paul, St James, St Peter; compare περιπατεῖν in St John: 1 John i. 7 note.

For ἀναθεωρεῖν see Acts xvii. 23 (not in LXX.); c. vii. 4 (θεωρεῖτε).

The reference here seems to be to some scene of martyrdom in which the triumph of faith was plainly shewn. Theodoret refers to St Stephen, St James the son of Zebedee, and St James the Just.

μιμεῖσθε τ. π.] imitate their faith. The spirit and not the form of their lives is proposed for imitation : the faith by which they were supported and not the special actions which the faith inspired in their circumstances.

Δείκνυσιν ὅτι πιστεύσαντες βεβαίως τοῖς μέλλουσι τὴν ἀρίστην πολιτείαν κατώρθωσαν· οὐ γὰρ ἂν ἐπεδείξαντο βίον καθαρὸν εἴ γε ἡμφισβήτουν περὶ τῶν μελλόντων, εἴ γε ἀμφέβαλλον (Chrys.).

τῆς ἀναστροφῆς μιμεῖσθε τὴν πίστιν.   ⁸Ἰησοῦς
Χριστὸς ἐχθὲς καὶ σήμερον ὁ αὐτός, καὶ εἰς τοὺς αἰῶνας.
⁹διδαχαῖς ποικίλαις καὶ ξέναις μὴ παραφέρεσθε· καλὸν

8 ἐχθές אAC*D₂*M₂: χθές ς.   αἰῶνας: +ἀμήν D₂*.   9 παραφέρεσθε
אACD₂M₂ vg syr vg me: περιφέρεσθε ς.

(b) The rule and strength of Christian devotion (8—16).

Having glanced at the former leaders of the Hebrew Church the Apostle goes on to shew that

(a) Christ Himself is the sum of our religion : which is eternal, spiritual (8, 9); and that

(β) He who is our sin-offering is also our continuous support (10—12); and that

(γ) He claims our devotion and our service (13—16).

(a) 8, 9. The thought of the triumph of faith leads to the thought of Him in whom faith triumphs. He is unchangeable, and therefore the victory of the believer is at all times assured.

The absence of a connecting particle places the thought as a reflection following the last sentence after a pause.

Ad superiora pertinent ista, ubi testatus est dixisse Dominum Non te deseram neque derelinquam : poterant illi respondere Hoc non pertinet ad nostrum auxilium, quia non nobis est promissum, sed potius Josue promisit hoc Deus. Ad hoc Apostolus Nolite deficere...Nolite putare quasi qui tunc fuit non sit modo : idem enim qui fuit heri, idem erit et in sæculum (Primas.).

8. Ἰ. Χ....αἰῶνας] *Jesus Christ is the same yesterday and to-day, yea and for ever*, Vulg. *J. Ch. heri et hodie ipse est, et in sæcula*.

The statement is true universally, but the immediate thought appears to be that as Christ had but just now brought victory to His disciples so He would do in the present trials.

Ac si dicatur : Idem Christus qui

cum illis fuit vobiscum est, et erit cum eis qui futuri sunt usque ad consummationem sæculi. Heri fuit cum patribus, hodie est vobiscum, ipse erit et cum posteris vestris usque in sæcula (Herv.).

Ceterum divinitas ejus interminabilis plenitudinem totam pariter comprehendit ac possidet, cui neque futuri quidquam absit nec præteriti fluxerit, quoniam esse ejus totum est et semper est nescitque mutabilitatem (*id.*).

The full title Ἰησοῦς Χριστός occurs again in the Epistle in *v.* 21; c. x. 10. The words ἐχθὲς καὶ σήμερον express generally ' in the past and in the present' (comp. Ecclus. xxxviii. 22 ἐμοὶ χθὲς καὶ σοὶ σήμερον) ; and the clause καὶ εἰς τοὺς αἰῶνας is added to the sentence which is already complete to express the absolute confidence of the Apostle : ' Jesus Christ is the same yesterday and to-day : yea, such a confession falls wholly below the truth : He is the same for ever.'

The phrase εἰς τοὺς αἰῶνας occurs here only in the Epistle (Rom. i. 25 ; ix. 5 ; xi. 36 ; xvi. 27 ; 2 Cor. xi. 31).

Compare *v.* 21 (εἰς τοὺς αἰ. τῶν αἰώνων); vi. 20; vii. 17 ff. (εἰς τὸν αἰῶνα); i. 8, LXX. (εἰς τὸν αἰῶνα τοῦ αἰῶνος).

For ὁ αὐτός compare i. 12. The usage is common in classical writers, *e.g.* Thucyd. ii. 61 ἐγὼ μὲν (Pericles in the face of Athenian discontent) ὁ αὐτός εἰμι καὶ οὐκ ἐξίσταμαι.

9. The unchangeableness of Christ calls up in contrast the variety of human doctrines. The faith of the Christian is in a Person and not in doctrines about Him.

διδ. π. καὶ ξ. μὴ παρ.] *Be not carried*

γὰρ χάριτι βεβαιοῦσθαι τὴν καρδίαν, οὐ βρώμασιν, ἐν

away by manifold and strange teach-ings, Vulg. *Doctr. variis et peregri-nis (novis* d) *abduci nolite.* These 'manifold and strange teachings' seem to have been various adaptations of Jewish thoughts and practices to Christianity. There was a danger lest the Hebrews should be carried by these away from the straight course of the Christian life. The phrase shews that the activity of religious speculation had by this time produced large results. For the plural διδαχαί compare διδασκαλίαι Col. ii. 22; 1 Tim. iv. 1.

Œcumenius takes the image of παραφέρεσθαι (Jude 12 ; comp. 1 Sam. xxi. 13) to be derived from the move-ments of those beside themselves, τῶν τῇδε κἀκεῖσε παραφερομένων. Wetstein gives examples of the word being used of objects swept out of their right course by the violence of a current. Comp. ii. 1 (παραρρυῶμεν).

The tense (μὴ παραφέρεσθε) marks the danger as actually present. Com-pare *vv.* 2, 16, μὴ ἐπιλανθάνεσθε, and contrast c. x. 35 μὴ ἀποβάλητε.

These doctrines are characterised as 'manifold' (c. ii. 4) in contrast with the unity of Christian teaching (Eph. iv. 5), and 'strange' (1 Pet. iv. 12) in contrast with its permanence (comp. Col. ii. 8 and Bp Lightfoot's note).

There is indeed a sense in which the wisdom of God is 'most manifold' (πολυποίκιλος Eph. iii. 10).

For διδαχαὶ ξέναι compare Herm. *Sim.* viii. 5.

καλὸν γὰρ...βρώμασιν] *for it is good that by grace the heart* (c. iii. 8 note) *be stablished* (βεβαιοῦσθαι 1 Cor. i. 8; 2 Cor. i. 21; Col. ii. 7). Vulg. *opti-mum enim....* The attractiveness of the novel views which endangered the faith of the Hebrews lay in their promise of security and progress; but such promises in the case before the Apostle were obviously vain. For

no true stability can be gained by outward observances to which Ju-daizing and Jewish teachings lead. This must come from a spiritual, divine influence. The position of χάριτι throws a strong emphasis upon the idea of 'grace.' Our strength must come from without. And 'grace' is the free outflow of divine love for the quickening and support of man (c. ii. 9), though, in one sense, man 'finds' it (c. iv. 16).

The opposition χάριτι...οὐ βρώμα-σιν..., shews that here the βρώματα represent something to be enjoyed ; and therefore that the reference is not, at least in the first instance, to any ascetical abstention from 'meats.' And again the next verse suggests the contrast of some sacrificial meal, so that the term 'meats' does not simply point to such as were pure according to the provisions of the Levitical Law. It appears to point primarily to 'meats' consecrated by sacrifice, and then used for food; though other senses of the word are not necessarily excluded. No doubt the Passover was present to the writer's mind, but with it would be included all the sacrificial feasts, which were the chief element in the social life of the Jews.

The context seems to justify and to require this sense of βρώματα, which is used in the Gospels for 'food' generally (Matt. xiv. 15 ; Luke iii. 11). Elsewhere in the Epistles the word is used with reference to ritual or ascetic distinctions of 'meats' (Rom. xiv. 15 ff.; 1 Cor. vi. 13; viii. 8; 1 Tim. iv. 3). But this usage does not super-sede the wider one, and it is natural that the Apostle should describe the privileges which were over-valued by a term which set them in a truer light as simply outward things. Comp. Ign. *ad Trall.* 2 οὐ γὰρ βρω-μάτων καὶ ποτῶν εἰσιν διάκονοι ἀλλ' ἐκκλησίας θεοῦ ὑπηρέται.

οἷς οὐκ ὠφελήθησαν οἱ ⌈περιπατοῦντες⌉.   ¹⁰ἔχομεν θυσι-

9 περιπατήσαντες

9 περιπατοῦντες א*AD₂* vg: περιπατήσαντες ⸃ אᶜCM₂.

It is said of bread literally that καρδίαν ἀνθρώπου στηρίζει (Ps. ciii. [civ.] 15). So Jud. xix. 5. There is a somewhat similar contrast of the material and spiritual in Eph. v. 18. Compare also 'the notes of the kingdom of heaven' Rom. xiv. 17.

The remarks of Herveius, which are interesting in themselves, leave out of account the circumstances of the Hebrews: Datur intelligi quosdam inter eos fuisse qui dogmatizarent non esse peccatum escis vacare. Nam quia per gratiam licitum est omnibus cibis uti, prædicabant non esse culpam cibis affluere sed bonum esse. So also Chrysostom appears to miss the point: μονονουχὶ τὸ τοῦ Χριστοῦ λέγει ἐν οἷς ἔλεγεν οὐ τὸ εἰσερχόμενον κοινοῖ τὸν ἄνθρωπον ἀλλὰ τὸ ἐξερχόμενον, καὶ δείκνυσιν ὅτι τὸ πᾶν πίστις ἐστίν. ἂν αὕτη βεβαιώσῃ ἡ καρδία ἐν ἀσφαλείᾳ ἕστηκεν.

For the use of καλόν compare Rom. xiv. 21; 1 Cor. vii. 1, 8, 26; Gal. iv. 18; Matt. xvii. 4 &c. In each case the idea of the observable effect of that which is described appears to be dominant. Comp. c. x. 24, note.

ἐν οἷς...οἱ περιπ.] Vulg. (non profuerunt) inambulantibus in eis, for they that occupied themselves (walked) therein were not profited, that is, they did not gain the end of human effort, fellowship with God. There is no thought here of the disciplinary value of the Law.

For the image of περιπατεῖν [ἐν βρώμασιν] compare Eph. ii. 10 (ἐν [ἔργοις ἀγαθοῖς] περιπ.); Col. iii. 7; and the more general phrases Rom. vi. 4 (ἐν καινότητι ζωῆς π.); 2 Cor. x. 3 (ἐν σαρκὶ π.); Col. iv. 5 (ἐν σοφίᾳ π.). The ἐν expresses the defined sphere of action and thought.

For οὐκ ὠφελήθησαν see Herm. Vis. ii. 2 προδόντες οὐκ ὠφελήθησαν.

(β) 10—12. The strength of the Christian comes from God's gift, but He uses the natural influences of life for the fulfilment of His purpose. Provision is made in the Christian society for the enjoyment of the benefits of Christ's Life and Death in social fellowship. In this respect Christians have that which more than compensates for any apparent loss which they may incur in their exclusion from the Jewish services.

10. ἔχομεν θυσιαστήριον] Vulg. habemus altare (hostiam d). The position of ἔχομεν and the absence of the personal pronoun indicate that the statement presents a contrast to some supposed deficiency. Christians, as such, so it appears to have been urged, are in a position of disadvantage: they have not something which others have. The reply is 'We have an altar....' 'We have that which furnishes us also with a feast upon a sacrifice.'

There is not a sharp opposition between Christians and Jews at first: that difference comes out later. The main contention is that the exclusion from the sacrificial services of the Temple is compensated by something which answers to them and is of a nobler kind. At the same time the writer, as he develops the thought, goes further. Hitherto he has shewn that the Christian can dispense with the consolations of the Jewish ritual: he now prepares to draw the conclusion that if he is a Christian he ought to give them up (v. 13 Let us go forth...).

From the connexion which has been pointed out it seems clear that the 'altar' (θυσιαστήριον) must correspond with the Temple altar as including

ἀστήριον ἐξ οὗ φαγεῖν οὐκ ἔχουσιν [ἐξουσίαν] οἱ τῇ

10 ἐξουσίαν ℵAC: om. D₂*M₂.

both the idea of sacrifice and the idea of food from the sacrifice (1 Cor. ix. 13). Primarily there is but one sacrifice for the Christian and one means of support, the sacrifice of Christ upon the Cross and the participating in Him (John vi. 53 ff.). In this first and highest sense, into which each secondary sense must be resolved, the only earthly 'altar' is the Cross on which Christ offered Himself: Christ is the offering: He is Himself the feast of the believer. The altar is not regarded at any time apart from the victim. It is the source of the support which the Christian partakes. When the idea of the one act of sacrifice predominates, the image of the Cross rises before us: when the idea of our continuous support, then the image of Christ living through death prevails.

So it is that as our thoughts pass from the historic scene of the Passion to its abiding fruit, Christ Himself, Christ crucified, is necessarily regarded as 'the altar' from which we draw our sustenance, and on (in) which (to go on to a later idea) we offer ourselves.

There is no confusion therefore when Thomas Aquinas says : Istud altare vel est crux Christi in qua Christus pro nobis immolatus est, vel ipse Christus in quo et per quem preces nostras offerimus; et hoc est altare aureum de quo dicitur Apoc. viii.

The latter thought is recognised also in the Glossa Ordinaria which is enlarged by Lanfranc : quod [corpus Christi] et in aliis divinarum locis Scripturarum altare vocatur, pro eo videlicet quod in ipso, id est, in fide ipsius, quasi in quodam altari oblatæ preces et operationes nostræ acceptabiles fiunt Deo (Migne, *P. L.* cl. p. 405).

Compare Rupert of Deutz *in Amos* iv. c. ix. (Migne, *P. L.* clxviii. 366) : Vidi, inquit, Dominum stantem super altare...Quærentibus autem in toto Christi Evangelio ... nihil tam magnum, nihil tam evidens secundum hujus visionis proprietatem nobis occurrit quam schema vel habitus Domini nostri Jesu Christi crucifixi. Crucifixus namque et sacrificium pro nobis factus super altare crucis stetit, statione difficili, statione laboriosa sibi.... Taliter stans ipse hostia, crux vero altare erat.

The universality of this altar is finely expressed by Leo the Great with a reference to this passage : extra castra crucifixus est ut, veterum victimarum cessante mysterio, nova hostia novo imponeretur altari, et crux Christi non templi esset ara sed mundi (*Serm.* lx. (lvii.) § 5).

For the history of the word θυσιαστήριον see Additional Note.

The sacrifice is one, the altar is one. But, just as in the discourse at Capernaum, the absolute idea points towards or even passes into the outward form in which it was embodied. The fact of that Death was visibly set forth, and the reality of that participation pledged, in the Eucharist. The 'Table' of the Lord (1 Cor. x. 21), the Bread and the Wine, enabled the believer 'to shew forth Christ's Death,' to realise the sacrifice upon the Cross and to appropriate Christ's 'flesh and blood.' In this sacrament then, where Christ gives Himself as the support of His faithful and rejoicing people, the Christian has that which more than fulfils the types of the Jewish ritual.

ἐξ οὗ φαγεῖν] *whereof*, as denoting the class of sacrifice and not the particular sacrifice, *they have no right to eat*.... Vulg. *de quo edere*.... The phrase occurs again in the com-

σκηνῇ λατρεύοντες.   ¹¹ὧν γὰρ εἰϲφέρεται ζῴων τὸ αἶμα

11 ζῶον D₂*.

mon text of 1 Cor. ix. 13, but the true reading is τὰ ἐκ τοῦ ἱεροῦ ἐσθίουσιν and not ἐκ τοῦ ἱ. ἐσθ.

οἱ τῇ σκ. λατρ.] Vulg. *qui taber-naculo deserviunt*, the priests whose office it is to fulfil the duties of the legal ritual (c. viii. 5 ; comp. Clem. 1 *ad Cor*. 32 οἱ λειτουργοῦντες τῷ θυσιαστηρίῳ τοῦ θεοῦ), rather than the whole assembly of Israel (c. x. 2). These, the most highly privileged of the people of Israel, who were allowed to eat of sacrifices of which none other could partake (Lev. vi. 26; vii. 6; x. 17), were not allowed to partake of that sacrifice which represented the sacrifice of Christ under the aspect of an atonement for sin.

The superiority which the Christian enjoyed over the Jew became most conspicuous when the highest point in each order was reached. The great sacrifice for sin on the Day of Atonement was wholly consumed. Though they 'who served the taber-nacle' 'were partakers with the altar,' even those who were most privileged had no right to eat of this offering. But Christ who is our sacrifice for sin, the perfect antitype of that sym-bol, is our food also. He is our atonement; and He is our support. He died as the sin-offering 'outside the gate,' and He lives to be our life by the communication of Himself. By His blood He entered into the archetypal Sanctuary and made a way for us, and He waits to guide us thither. Meanwhile 'we have become partakers of the Christ' (c. iii. 14), and live with the power of His life which in His own appointed way He brings to us.

Thus the point of the passage is not simply that those who continue Jews, and cling to the worship of the Temple, are excluded from the highest advantages of the Gospel; but that in itself absolutely the Gospel as com-pared with the Law offers not less but more to believers under that aspect of social worship in which the believer felt his loss most keenly. The Christian enjoys in substance that which the Jew did not enjoy even in shadow. If the Christian was now called upon to sacrifice all the consolations of the old ritual, he had what was far beyond them. It does not however appear that the writer of the Epistle implies that Jews by birth who still observed the Law could not enjoy the privileges of Christianity.

Briefly the argument is this: We Christians *have* an altar, from which we draw the material for our feast. In respect of this, our privilege is greater than that of priest or high-priest under the Levitical system. Our great sin-offering, consumed in one sense outside the gate, is given to us as our food. The Christian therefore who can partake of Christ, offered for his sins, is admitted to a privilege unknown under the old Cove-nant.

The phrase τῇ σκηνῇ λατρεύειν is remarkable : comp. c. viii. 5 ὑπο-δείγματι καὶ σκιᾷ λατρεύουσιν. The Tabernacle itself—the outward form —is represented as the object of service. Christians also serve the Antitype of the Tabernacle, but that is Christ Himself. The use of λα-τρεύειν (the divine service) as con-trasted with λειτουργεῖν (the official service) is to be noticed. Contrast Clem. 1 *ad Cor*. 32 (quoted above).

11. ὧν γὰρ εἰσφέρ.] The proof of the reality of this surpassing privilege of Christians lies in the familiar ordi-nances in regard to the sacrifice on the Day of Atonement: Lev. xvi. 27. Of these victims only was the blood brought into the Holy of Holies. In two other cases the blood was brought into the Holy place; and here also the

περὶ ἀμαρτίας εἰc τὰ ἅγια διὰ τοῦ ἀρχιερέως, τούτων τὰ σώματα κατακαίεται ἔξω τῆc παρεμβολῆc· ¹²διὸ καὶ Ἰησοῦς, ἵνα ἁγιάσῃ

11 περὶ ἀμ. εἰς τ. ἅγ. אD₂M₂ vg: om. περὶ ἀμ. A: εἰς τὰ ἅγ. περὶ ἀμ. C* syr vg me.
κατακαίεται: καταναλίσκονται D₂*.

bodies were consumed outside: Lev.
iv. 11 f. (the sin-offering for a priest);
id. 21 (the sin-offering for the congregation).

ζῴων] Vulg. animalium. The use
of this word is apparently unique.
Elsewhere the victims are spoken of
by their special names — 'bulls and
goats,'—and I am not aware of any
place in the Greek Scriptures in
which a victim is spoken of by the
general term ζῷον. In the N. T. the
word is used of 'irrational animals'
(ἄλογα ζῷα: 2 Pet. ii. 12; Jude 10),
and of the four 'living creatures' of
the apocalyptic vision (Apoc. iv. 6 ff.;
comp. Ezek. i. 5 ff. LXX.). Perhaps
the word is chosen here to mark the
contrast between the sacrifices which
were of nature only and the sacrifice
of 'Jesus,' who was truly man and yet
more than man.

περὶ ἀμαρτίας] See Additional Note
on i. 3.

εἰς τὰ ἅγια] The phrase may describe 'the Holy of Holies' (c. ix. 8
note), so that the reference is to the
ceremonial of the Day of Atonement
only; or it may include 'the Holy
place,' and take account of the victims
whose blood was brought there.

The use of the preposition διά
'through' (per pontificem Vulg.,
sacerdotem d), where we might have
expected ὑπό 'by,' is of interest. The
High-priest is the agent through
whom the act of the people is accomplished. Compare v. 15 δι' αὐτοῦ
ἀναφέρωμεν.

ὧν...τούτων] The emphatic insertion of the demonstrative is not
uncommon: Phil. iv. 9; 2 Tim. ii.
2; Gal. ii. 18. Compare Rom. ix. 8
οὐ τὰ τέκνα...ταῦτα...; James i. 25,
23 εἴ τις...οὗτος....

ἔξω τῆς παρεμβολῆς] Vulg. extra

castra, compare Ex. xxix. 14 (at the
consecration of the priests); Lev. iv.
11 (sin-offering for the priest); id. 21
(sin-offering for the congregation); xvi.
27 (sin-offering on the Day of Atonement). See also Lev. vii. 17; ix. 11.

The life is taken to the presence of
God: that which has been the transitory organ of life is taken beyond the
limits of the ordered Society to be
wholly removed.

12.   διὸ καὶ Ἰησοῦς] Wherefore
Jesus also—the Lord truly man—the
sin-offering for humanity—in order
that He might so fulfil the symbolism
of the Law and sanctify the people
by His Blood, suffered without the
gate. Even as the Levitical High-
priest entered into the Sanctuary
through the blood of the atoning
victims while their bodies were burnt
without, Jesus as our High-priest
entered through His own Blood into
heaven; and His mortal Body, laid in
the grave, was glorified, consumed, so
to speak, by the divine fire which
transfigured it. In both respects He
satisfied completely the thoughts suggested by the type.

ἵνα ἁγ....τὸν λαόν] that He might
sanctify the people, those who are
truly Israel (c. ii. 17 note), through
His own blood as contrasted with the
blood of victims: c. ix. 12. By His
death on the Cross Christ not only
'made purification of sins' (i. 3), but
He also 'sanctified' His people. In
the offering of Himself, He offered
them also, as wholly devoted to God.
His blood became the blood of a New
Covenant (x. 29) by which the privilege of sonship was restored to men
in the Son through His offered life
(x. 10); and the Covenant sacrifice
became the groundwork of a feast
(comp. Ex. xxiv. 8, 11).

δια τοῦ ἰδίου αἵματος τὸν λαόν, ἔξω τῆς πύλης ἔπαθεν.

12 τῆς πόλεως syr vg.   om. ἔπαθεν א*.

For the idea of ἁγιάζειν, see c. ix. 13. With διὰ τοῦ αἵματος compare c. ix. 12; Acts xx. 28; Eph. i. 7; Col. i. 20; and contrast ἐν τῷ αἵματι c. x. 19, 29; (ix. 22, 25; v. 20); Rom. iii. 25; v. 9; (1 Cor. xi. 25); Eph. ii. 13; Apoc. i. 5; v. 9; vii. 14; and διὰ τὸ αἷμα Apoc. xii. 11.

(γ) 13—16. The relation in which the Christian stands to Christ—the perfect sin-offering and the continuous support of the believer—carries with it two consequences. Believers must claim fellowship with Him both in His external humiliation and in His divine glory, both as the Victim consumed (v. 11) and as the Priest who has entered within the veil. Hence follows the fulfilment of two duties, to go out to Christ (13, 14), and to offer through Him the sacrifice of praise and well-doing (15, 16).

ἔπαθεν] The Fathers commonly think of the Passion as a 'consuming of Christ by the fire of love,' so that the effect of the Passion is made to answer directly to κατακαίεται. But the Passion is never to be separated from the Resurrection. Here indeed the writer of the Epistle, though he goes on at once to speak of Christ as living, naturally dwells on the painful condition by which the triumph was prepared, because he wishes to encourage his readers to endurance in suffering. But the thought of victory lies behind. And there are traces in early writers of the truer view which sees in the transfiguration of the Risen Lord the correlative to the burning of the victim.

Extra castra sunt carnes ejus crematæ, id est extra Jerusalem igne passionis consumptæ. Vel concrematio ad signum pertinet resurrectionis, quia natura ignis est ut in superna moveatur...(Herv.).

The use of the verb πάσχειν of

Christ is characteristic of this Epistle, of 1 Peter, and of the Acts. It is found again c. ii. 18; v. 8; ix. 26; in 1 Peter ii. 21, 23; (iii. 18;) iv. 1; and in Acts i. 3; iii. 18; xvii. 3. It does not occur in this connexion in the epistles of St Paul, though he speaks of the παθήματα of Christ: 2 Cor. i. 5, 7; Phil. iii. 10.

It is found in the Synoptic Gospels, Matt. xvi. 21; xvii. 12 and parallels: Luke xxii. 15; xxiv. 26, 46.

See c. ii. 10 note.

ἔξω τῆς πύλης] Vulg. extra portam. The change from ἔξω τῆς παρεμβολῆς, which occurs immediately before and after, is remarkable. Πύλη suggests the idea of 'the city,' rather than that of the camp, and so points to the fatal error of later Judaism, which by seeking to give permanence to that which was designed to be transitory marred the conception of the Law. In this aspect the variant πόλεως (comp. Tert. adv. Jud. 14) is of interest.

The fact that the Lord suffered 'without the gate' (Lev. xxiv. 14; Num. xv. 35) is implied in John xix. 17, but it is not expressly stated.

The work of Christ, so far as it was wrought on earth, found its consummation outside the limits of the symbolical dwelling-place of the chosen people. It had a meaning confined within no such boundaries. The whole earth was the scene of its efficacy. So also in the new Jerusalem there is no sanctuary (Apoc. xxi. 22). The whole city is a Temple and God Himself is present there.

13, 14. Christ—not a dead victim merely but the living leader—is represented as 'outside the camp,' outside the old limits of Israel, waiting to receive His people, consumed and yet unconsumed. Therefore, the Apostle concludes, even now let us be on our way to Him, carrying His reproach,

^{13}τοίνυν ἐξερχώμεθα πρὸς αὐτὸν ἔξω τῆς παρεμβολῆς, τὸν ὀνειδισμὸν αὐτοῦ φέροντες, ^{14}οὐ γὰρ ἔχομεν ὧδε μένουσαν

13 ἐξερχόμεθα D₂.

and abandoning not only the 'city,' which men made as the permanent home for God, but also moving to something better than ' the camp,' in which Israel was organised. No Jew could partake of that typical sacrifice which Christ fulfilled: and Christians therefore must abandon Judaism to realise the full power of His work. In this sense 'it is expedient' that they also ' should go away,' in order to realise the fulness of their spiritual heritage.

It is worthy of notice that the first tabernacle which Moses set up was 'outside the camp' (Ex. xxxiii. 7): 'and it came to pass that every one which sought the Lord went out unto the tabernacle of the congregation which was without the camp.' The history is obscure, but as it stands it is significant in connexion with the language of the Epistle.

13. τοίνυν] The word occurs in the same position in Luke xx. 25 (v. l.) and in the LXX. Is. iii. 10 &c., like τοιγαροῦν c. xii. 1; 1 Thess. iv. 8.

ἐξερχώμεθα] The present expresses vividly the immediate effort. Comp. c. iv. 16; Matt. xxv. 6; John i. 47; vi. 37.

The words necessarily recal the voice said to have been heard from the Sanctuary before the destruction of the Temple, Μεταβαίνωμεν ἐντεῦθεν (Jos. B. J. vi. 5, 3).

Compare also the Lord's prophecy: Matt. xxiv. 15 ff.

The Fathers commonly understand the phrase of ' leaving the world' and the like. This may be a legitimate application of the command, but it is wholly foreign to the original meaning.

One example may be quoted: Qui enim vult corpus et sanguinem ejus

accipere debet ad locum passionis ejus accedere, ut honores et opes tabernaculi relinquens improperia et paupertatem pro nomine ejus ferre non respuat...(Herv.).

τὸν ὀνειδ. αὐ. φέρ.] carrying His reproach, Vulg. improperium ejus portantes. Comp. xi. 26 (τὸν ὀνειδισμὸν τοῦ Χριστοῦ); Luke xxiii. 26 (ἐπέθηκαν αὐτῷ τὸν σταυρόν, φέρειν...). The thought is not only of a burden to be supported (βαστάζειν Gal. vi. 2, 5); but of a burden to be carried to a fresh scene. Comp. i. 3 note.

ἔξω τῆς παρ.] 'outside the camp,' and not only 'outside the gate.' Ἔξω τῆς παρεμβολῆς ἀντὶ τοῦ ἔξω τῆς κατὰ νόμον γενώμεθα πολιτείας (Theodt.). Christians are now called upon to withdraw from Judaism even in its first and purest shape. It had been designed by God as a provisional system, and its work was done.

The exhortation is one signal application of the Lord's own command, Lk. ix. 23.

14. οὐ γὰρ ἔχομεν ὧδε] The necessity for the abandonment of the old, however dear, lies in the general fact that we have no abiding system, no unchanging organisation, in the present transitory order (ὧδε here on earth). That which 'abides' belongs to the spiritual and eternal order. And such an 'abiding city' lies before us. For we are seeking, not with a vague search for ' one to come,' but ' that which is to come,' ' that which hath the foundations,' of which the organisation and the stability are already clearly realised.

For μένουσαν compare c. x. 34; xii. 27; 1 Pet. i. 23.

The inadequate and misleading translation 'one (a city) to come' is due to the Latin futuram inquirimus.

πόλιν, ἀλλὰ τὴν μέλλουσαν ἐπιζητοῦμεν· ¹⁵δι᾽ αὐτοῦ
ᵀἈΝΑΦΈΡΩΜΕΝ ΘΥCΊΑΝ ἈΙΝΈCΕΩC διὰ παντὸς τῷ θεῷ, τοῦτ᾽ ἔστιν

15 οὖν

15 δι᾽ αὐτοῦ ℵ*D₂* syr vg: δι᾽ αὐτοῦ + οὖν ℵᶜACM₂ vg me.

But the object of Christian hope and effort is definite (τὴν μέλλ. ἐπιζ.). All earthly institutions are imperfect adumbrations of the spiritual archetype. Compare c. xi. 10 (τὴν τοὺς θεμελίους ἔχουσαν πόλιν); 16 (ἡτοίμασεν αὐτοῖς πόλιν); xii. 22 (πόλει θεοῦ ζῶντος). Herm. *Sim.* i. 1 ἡ πόλις ὑμῶν μακράν ἐστιν ἀπὸ τῆς πόλεως ταύτης.

For ἐπιζητοῦμεν compare c. xi. 14 note; and contrast *v.* 10 ἔχομεν.

15, 16. There is another side to our duty to Christ. Our sacrifice, our participation in Him, involves more than suffering for His sake: it is also an expression of thanksgiving, of praise to God (15), and of service to man (16), for Christ has made possible for us this side also of sacrificial service.

15. δι᾽ αὐτοῦ...] *Through Him—and through no other—let us offer up a sacrifice of praise.* The emphatic position of δι᾽ αὐτοῦ brings out the peculiar privilege of the believer. He has One through Whom he can fulfil the twofold duty of grateful worship: through Whom (c. vii. 25) as High-priest every sacrifice for God and for man must be brought and placed upon the altar of God. Compare 1 Pet. ii. 5 (ἀνενέγκαι...διὰ ᾽Ι. Χ.); iv. 11 (ἵνα...δοξάζηται ὁ θεὸς διὰ ᾽Ι. Χ.); Rom. i. 8 (εὐχαριστῶ...διὰ ᾽Ι. Χ.); xvi. 27 (θεῷ διὰ ᾽Ι. Χ....ἡ δόξα); Col. iii. 17; Clem. 1 *ad Cor.* 36, 44 and Bp Lightfoot's note. Thus we gain the significance of petitions made 'through Jesus Christ.' The passage is illustrated by the adaptation made of it to Melchizedek by the sect which regarded him as the divine 'priest for ever': εἰς ὄνομα τούτου τοῦ Μελχισεδὲκ ἡ προειρημένη αἵρεσις καὶ τὰς προσφορὰς ἀναφέρει καὶ αὐτὸν εἶναι εἰσαγωγέα πρὸς τὸν θεόν, καὶ δι᾽ αὐτοῦ, φησί, δεῖ τῷ θεῷ

προσφέρειν, ὅτι ἄρχων ἐστὶ δικαιοσύνης...καὶ δεῖ ἡμᾶς αὐτῷ προσφέρειν, φασίν, ἵνα δι᾽ αὐτοῦ προσενεχθῇ ὑπὲρ ἡμῶν καὶ εὕρωμεν δι᾽ αὐτοῦ ζωήν (Epiph. *Hær.* lv. § 8, p. 474). Compare also Iren. *Hær.* iv. 17, 5.

For the full meaning of ἀναφέρειν comp. c. vii. 27 note. Men in the fulfilment of their priestly work still act through their great High-priest.

θυσίαν αἰνέσ.] Vulg. *hostiam laudis.* The phrase occurs in Lev. vii. 12 (זֶבַח תּוֹדָה: comp. xxii. 29; Ps. cvii. 22; cxvi. 17; [l. 14, 23]), of the highest form of peace-offering. The thank-offering was made not in fulfilment of a vow (נֶדֶר), nor in general acknowledgment of God's goodness (נְדָבָה), but for a favour graciously bestowed. Comp. Oehler *O. T. Theology* ii. 2 f.

In this connexion διὰ παντός *continually* has a peculiar force. That which was an exceptional service under the Old Dispensation is the normal service under the New.

The Jewish teachers gave expression to the thought: R. Pinchas, R. Levi, and R. Jochanan said in the name of R. Menachem of Galilee: One day all offerings will cease, only the Thank-offering will not cease: all prayers will cease, only the Thanksgiving-prayer will not cease (Jer. xxxiii. 11; Ps. lvi. 13). *Vajikra R.* ix. (Lev. vii. 12); and xxvii. (Lev. xxii. 29) (Wünsche, pp. 58, 193). Comp. Philo, *de vit. offer.* § 3 (ii. 253 M.), on the offering of the true worshipper.

The word θυσία in Mal. i. 11 (θυσία καθαρά) appears to have been understood in the early Church of the prayers and thanksgivings connected with the Eucharist. Thus *Doctr. Apost.* xiv. 2 ἵνα μὴ κοινωθῇ ἡ θυσία

καρπὸν χειλέων ὁμολογούντων τῷ ὀνόματι αὐτοῦ. ¹⁶τῆς δὲ εὐποιίας καὶ κοινωνίας μὴ ἐπιλανθάνεσθε, τοιαύταις γὰρ θυσίαις εὐαρεστεῖται ὁ θεός. ¹⁷Πείθεσθε τοῖς ἡγουμένοις ὑμῶν καὶ ὑπείκετε, αὐτοὶ γὰρ ἀγρυπ-

16 +τῆς´ κοιν. D₂.   ΤΟΙΑΥΤΑΙ...ΘΥΣΙΑΙ M₂.   εὐαρεστεῖται: εὐεργετεῖται M₂.

ὑμῶν is represented in the Latin by 'ne inquinetur et impediatur oratio vestra.' Comp. Apoc. v. 8.

At the same time the 'first-fruits of God's creation' were offered (Iren. iv. 17, 5 f.), and this outward expression of gratitude was also called θυσία. Comp. Just. M. *Dial.* 117. Immediately below acts of benevolence are included under the term 'sacrifices.'

καρπὸν χειλέων] The phrase is borrowed from the LXX. (paraphrase?) of Hos. xiv. 3 (פָּרִים שְׂפָתֵינוּ, 'as bullocks, our lips'). Another example of the image occurs in Is. lvii. 19 (נִיב שְׂפָתָיִם). Comp. 2 Macc. x. 7 ὕμνους ἀνέφερον.

ὁμολ. τῷ ὀν. αὐ.] The revelation of God in Christ (*His Name*) is the source of all thanksgiving (1 Pet. i. 13). This illuminates, and is illuminated by, every object of joy.

The phrase ὁμολογεῖν τῷ ὀνόματι does not occur again in the N. T. nor in the LXX. (not Jer. xliv. (li.) 26).

ἐξομολογεῖσθαι (τῷ θεῷ) (הוֹדָה לְ) 'to make confession to, in honour,' 'to celebrate, praise,' is common in the LXX. Comp. Matt. xi. 25; Rom. xiv. 11.

16. At the same time spiritual sacrifice must find an outward expression. Praise to God is service to men.

τῆς εὐπ. καὶ κοιν.] Vulg. *beneficentiæ et communionis*, Syr. vg. *compassion and communication to the poor*. The general word for kindly service (εὐποιία) is followed by that which expresses specially the help of alms. The two nouns form a compound idea (not τῆς εὐπ. καὶ τῆς κοιν.). The word εὐποιία is not found elsewhere in N. T. nor in LXX. For κοινωνία compare 2 Cor. ix. 13 (ἁπλότητι τῆς κοινωνίας εἰς

αὐτούς); Rom. xv. 26 (κοινωνίαν τινὰ ποιήσασθαι εἰς τοὺς πτωχούς); *Did.* iv. 8 συγκοινωνήσεις πάντα τῷ ἀδελφῷ σου. μὴ ἐπιλ.] See v. 2 note.

τοιαύταις γὰρ θ.] The direct reference appears to be to εὐποιία καὶ κοινωνία, but 'praise' has been already spoken of as a 'sacrifice,' and is naturally included in the thought.

The construction εὐαρεστεῖται ὁ θεός, Vulg. *promeretur (placetur) Deus* (*placetur Deo* Aug.), is found in late Greek, but not again in N. T. or LXX.

(c) The obligation to loyal obedience.

The section began with a reference to leaders of the Church, and so it closes. The Hebrews have been charged to remember and imitate those who have passed away (v. 7); now they are charged to obey and yield themselves to those who are still over them. This duty rests upon the most solemn nature of the relation in which they stand to them.

17. πείθεσθε...καὶ ὑπείκετε] Vulg. *obedite...et subjacete*. Obedience to express injunctions is crowned by submission to a wish. The word ὑπείκειν is not found elsewhere in N. T. or LXX. For τοῖς ἡγ. see v. 7 note.

αὐτοὶ γάρ...] Vulg. *ipsi enim pervigilant*...The emphatic pronoun serves to bring out the personal obligation of the rulers with which the loyal obedience of the ruled corresponded; *for they*, and no other...Comp. James ii. 6 f.; 1 Thess. i. 9; Matt. v. 3 ff. The image in ἀγρυπνοῦσιν ὑ. τ. ψ. is that of the 'watchmen' in the O. T.: Is. lxii. 6; Ezek. iii. 17.

For the word ἀγρυπνεῖν compare Eph. vi. 18; Ps. cxxvii. (cxxvi.) 1 ἐὰν μὴ ὁ κύριος φυλάξη πόλιν, εἰς μάτην ἠγρύπνησεν ὁ φυλάσσων. Wisd. vi. 15.

νοῦσιν ὑπὲρ τῶν ψυχῶν ὑμῶν ὡς λόγον ἀποδώσοντες,
ἵνα μετὰ χαρᾶς τοῦτο ποιῶσιν καὶ μὴ στενάζοντες,
ἀλυσιτελὲς γὰρ ὑμῖν τοῦτο.

17 ὑπείκετε: +αὐτοῖς **ℵ°**.   ὑπὲρ τ. ψ. ὑμ. ὡς λ. ἀποδ. **ℵ**CM₂ syr vg me: ὑπὲρ
τ. ψ. ὑμ. ὡς λ. ἀποδώσονται περὶ ὑμῶν D₂*: ὡς λ. ἀποδ. ὑπὲρ τ. ψ. ὑμ. A vg.

ὑπὲρ τῶν ψυχῶν] The writer chooses
this fuller phrase in place of the simple
ὑπὲρ ὑμῶν to suggest the manifold
sum of vital powers which the Christian has to make his own: Lk. xxi. 19.
Comp. 1 Pet. i. 9; ii. 25; c. x. 39.
The Vulg. joins the clause with λόγ.
ἀποδ. *quasi rationem pro animabus
vestris reddituri.*

ἵνα μετὰ χαρᾶς...] *that they may do
this* (*i.e.* watch) *with joy*....The clause
depends on π. καὶ ὑπ., the intervening
words being parenthetical: xii. 17
note.

Tunc vigilant præpositi cum gaudio
quando vident subjectos suos proficere
in Dei verbo, quia et agricola tunc
cum gaudio laborat quando attendit
arborem et fructum videt, quando attendit segetem et fructificare prospicit
ubertatem (Herv.). Compare Herm.
Vis. iii. 9, 10.

For στενάζοντες see James v. 9;
(Rom. viii. 23 ; 2 Cor. v. 2, 4). Ἀλυσιτελής does not occur again in N. T. or
in LXX. Λυσιτελεῖ is found Lk. xvii. 2.
The Greek Fathers gave a stern
meaning to the words :

Ὁρᾷς ὅση ἡ φιλοσοφία. στενάζειν δεῖ
τὸν καταφρονούμενον, τὸν καταπατούμε-
νον, τὸν διαπτυόμενον, μὴ θαρρήσῃς ὅτι
σε οὐκ ἀμύνεται· ὁ γὰρ στεναγμὸς πάσης
ἀμύνης χείρων· ὅταν γὰρ αὐτὸς μηδὲν
ὀνήσῃ στενάζων καλεῖ τὸν δεσπότην
(Chrys.).

Ὥστε μὴ ἐπειδὴ στεναγμός ἐστι κατα-
φρονήσῃς ὁ τῷ ἡγουμένῳ ἀπειθῶν, ἀλλὰ
πλέον φοβήθητι, ὅτι τῷ θεῷ σε παραδί-
δωσι (Theophlct.).

Herveius says with a wider view :
expedit illis ipsa tristitia et prodest
illis, sed non expedit vobis.

(3) *Personal instructions of the
writer* (18—25).

The Epistle closes with wide-reach-
ing words of personal solicitude and
tenderness. The writer asks for the
prayers of his readers (18, 19) and
offers a prayer for them (20, 21). He
then adds one or two details which
shew the closeness of the connexion
by which they were bound to him,
(22, 23) and completes his salutations
(24) with a final blessing (25).

¹⁸*Pray for us ; for we are persuaded
that we have an honest conscience, desiring to live honestly in all things.*
¹⁹*And the more exceedingly do I exhort you to do this, that I may be
restored to you the sooner.*
²⁰*Now the God of peace, who brought
up from the dead the Shepherd of His
sheep, the great* Shepherd, *in the blood
of an eternal covenant, even our
Lord Jesus,* ²¹*make you perfect in
every good thing, to the end that you
do His will, doing in us that which
is well-pleasing in His sight, through
Jesus Christ; to whom be the glory
for ever and ever. Amen.*
²²*But I exhort you, brethren, bear
with the word of exhortation ; for I
have written unto you in few words.*
²³*Know ye that our brother Timothy
hath been discharged, with whom, if
he come shortly, I will see you.*
²⁴*Salute all them that have the rule
over you, and all the saints. They of
Italy salute you.*
²⁵*Grace be with you all. Amen.*

18, 19. The thought of the duty
which the Hebrews owed to their
own leaders leads the writer naturally
to think of their wider duties, of
what they owed to him and his fellow-
workers. The same spirit which led
to wilful self-assertion at home was
likely to cherish distrust towards

¹⁸ Προσεύχεσθε περὶ ἡμῶν, πειθόμεθα γὰρ ὅτι καλὴν
συνείδησιν ἔχομεν, ἐν πᾶσιν καλῶς θέλοντες ἀναστρέφε-

18 + καὶ περὶ D₂*.   πειθόμεθα AC*D₂*M₂ syr vg : πεποίθαμεν ς Ν°.   ἡμῶν
ὅτι καλὴν|θα γὰρ ὅτι καλήν Ν* (i.e. ὅτι καλὴν written for πειθόμε).

teachers at a distance who sought
to restrain its evil tendencies. The
Apostle therefore asks for the prayers
of those to whom he writes. He
awakens their deepest sympathy by
thus assuring them that he himself
desires what they would beg for him.

Hic superbiam elationemque mentis
quorundam pontificum destruit qui
typo (typho) superbiæ inflati dedig-
nantur deprecari suos subjectos
quatenus pro eis orationes fundant
(Primas.).

18. προσεύχ. π. ἡμῶν...παρακαλῶ...]
Pray for us...I exhort you.... The
passage from the plural to the singular is like Col. iv. 3 προσευχόμενοι...
περὶ ἡμῶν...δι' ὃ καὶ δέδεμαι...Gal. i. 8 f.
ἐὰν ἡμεῖς...ὡς προειρήκαμεν καὶ ἄρτι
πάλιν λέγω...Rom. i. 1 Παῦλος δοῦλος...
δι' οὗ ἐλάβομεν χάριν... In all these
cases the plural appears to denote the
Apostle and those who were immediately connected with him. The force
of a true plural is evident in 1 Thess.
iii. 1 ; v. 25 ; 2 Thess. iii. 1. The
separate expression of personal feeling in connexion with the general
statement is easily intelligible.

πειθόμεθα γάρ...] *for we are persuaded...* Vulg. *confidimus* (*suade-
mur* d) *enim*. The ground of the
Apostle's request lies in the consciousness of the perfect uprightness of
those with whom he identifies himself. However they might be represented so as to be in danger of losing
the affection of some, he could say
upon a candid review that their
endeavours were pure. Such a conviction must underlie the request
for efficacious intercession. The
prayers of others will not avail for
our neglect of duty. They help, when
we have done our utmost, to supply

what we have failed to do, and to correct what we have done amiss.

πειθόμεθα] Acts xxvi. 26 λανθάνειν
αὐτὸν τούτων οὐ πείθομαι οὐθέν. The
perfect is more common : πέπεισμαι
c. vi. 9 ; Rom. viii. 38 ; xv. 14, &c.
The present seems to express a conclusion drawn from the immediate
survey of the facts.

καλ. συν. ἔχ.] Comp. ἀγαθὴν συν.
ἔχειν 1 Tim. i. 19 ; 1 Pet. iii. 16 ;
ἀπρόσκοπον συν. ἔχ. Acts xxiv. 16.
The phrase καλὴ συν. occurs here
only : συν. ἀγαθή is found (in addition
to the places quoted) in Acts xxiii. 1 ;
1 Tim. i. 5 ; 1 Pet. iii. 21. See also
καθαρὰ συνείδησις 1 Tim. iii. 9 ; 2 Tim.
i. 3. Comp. c. x. 22, συν. πονηρά.

For συνείδησις see ix. 9 Additional
Note ; and p. 116.

The adj. καλός seems to retain its
characteristic sense of that which
commands the respect and admiration of others. So far the word
appeals to the judgment of the
readers.

ἐν πᾶσιν κ. θ. ἀναστρ.] This clause
may go either with πειθόμεθα or with
ἔχομεν, expressing the ground of the
conviction : 'since we wish to live
honestly' ; or describing the character
of that to which the conscience testified : 'as wishing to live honestly.'
The latter connexion appears to be
the more natural and simpler.

ἐν πᾶσιν] *in all respects, in all things,*
in the points which cause misgivings,
as in others. The word is neuter and
not masculine. Comp. *v.* 4 note.

Hoc est, non ex parte sed ex toto
studemus bene vivere (Herv.). The
Greek Fathers take it as masculine :
ἄρα οὐκ ἐν ἐθνικοῖς μόνον ἀλλὰ καὶ ἐν
ὑμῖν (Chrys., Œcum., Theophlct.).

καλὴν...καλῶς...] *an honest con-*

σθαι. ¹⁹περισσοτέρως δὲ παρακαλῶ τοῦτο ποιῆσαι ἵνα
τάχειον ἀποκατασταθῶ ὑμῖν.   ²⁰῾Ο δὲ θεὸς τῆς

science...to live honestly..., in the old
sense of the word. Comp. v. 22 (παρακαλῶ...παρακλήσεως); Matt. xxi. 41.
θέλοντες] desiring and not merely
being willing: c. xii. 17. Whatever
the issue might be this was the
Apostle's earnest wish. Compare 1
Thess. ii. 18; 2 Tim. iii. 12.
ἀναστρέφεσθαι] Vulg. conversari, to
enter into the vicissitudes and activi-
ties of social life. See v. 7 note.
19. περισσ. δὲ...] Amplius autem
deprecor vos hoc facere (hoc peto
faciatis d). The writer enforces the
common request by a personal consideration, And the more exceedingly
do I exhort you to do this... The
transition from the plural to the singular, no less than the order, points to
the connexion of περισσ. with παρακαλῶ
and not with ποιῆσαι.
ἵνα τάχ. ἀποκατ. ὑ.] that I may be
restored to you the sooner, Vulg. quo
(ut quo am.) celerius restituar vobis.
The expression does not necessarily
imply a state of imprisonment, which
is in fact excluded by the language of
v. 23, since the purpose thus declared
presupposes, so far, freedom of action.
All that the word requires is that the
writer should have been kept from
the Hebrews (in one sense) against his
will. It may have been by illness.
For the word see Matt. xii. 13;
xvii. 11; Acts i. 6. Comp. Acts iii.
21. It is not unfrequent in Polybius:
iii. 5, 4; 98, 9; viii. 29, 6 &c.
By the use of it the writer suggests
the idea of service which he had rendered and could render to his readers.
He was in some sense required for
their completeness; and by his presence he could remove the causes of
present anxiety. Δείκνυσιν ὅτι θαρρεῖ
τῷ συνειδότι καὶ διὰ τοῦτο προστρέχει
αὐτοῖς (Theophlct.).
Quo celerius restituar vobis, hoc est,
amplius pro vestra quam pro mea

salute deprecor vos ut oretis pro
me...ut...restituar non mihi sed vobis
(Herv.).
20, 21. The Apostle has first asked
for the prayers of his readers, and
then he anticipates their answer by
the outpouring of his own petitions
in their behalf.
Notandum quod primo postulat
ab eis orationis suffragium ac deinde
non simpliciter sed tota intentione et
omni prorsus studio suam orationem
pro eis ad Dominum fundit (Primas.).
Comp. 1 Thess. v. 23; 1 Pet. v. 10 f.
20. The aspects under which God
is described as 'the God of peace'
and the author of the exaltation of
Christ, correspond with the trials of
the Hebrews. They were in a crisis
of conflict within and without. They
were tempted to separate themselves
from those who were their true
leaders under the presence of unexpected afflictions (comp. xii. 11); and
they were tempted also to question
the power of Christ and the efficacy
of the Covenant made through Him.
The title 'the God of peace' is not
uncommon in St Paul's Epistles: Rom.
xv. 33; xvi. 20; 2 Cor. xiii. 11 (ὁ θεὸς
τῆς ἀγάπης καὶ εἰρ.); 1 Thess. v. 23.
Comp. 1 Cor. xiv. 33.
It is through God, as the author
and giver of peace, that man is able
to find the harmony which he seeks
in the conflicting elements of his own
nature, in his relations with the world,
in his relations to God Himself. Τοῦτο
εἶπε διὰ τὸ στασιάζειν αὐτούς (Chrys.).
Ἐπειδὴ θεὸς εἰρήνης ἐστὶ οὐ δεῖ ὑμᾶς
διαστασιάζειν πρὸς ἐμὲ καὶ ταῦτα ἀπὸ
ἀκοῆς ψιλῆς (Theophlct.).
The thoughts which spring from the
contemplation of the general character of God are deepened by the contemplation of His work for 'our Lord
Jesus.' In the Resurrection of Christ
we have the decisive revelation of

εἰρήνης, ὁ ἀναγαγὼν ἐκ νεκρῶν τὸν ποιμένα τῶν προβάτων τὸν
μέγαν ἐν αἵματι διαθήκης αἰωνίου, τὸν κύριον ἡμῶν Ἰησοῦν,

20 Ἰησοῦν ℵACM₂: +Χριστόν D₂* syr vg me.

victory over all evil, in the victory over death. Christ's Resurrection is the perfect assurance of the support of those who in any degree fulfil in part that pastoral office which He fulfilled perfectly.

This is the only direct reference to the Resurrection in the Epistle, just as c. xii. 2 is the only direct reference to the Cross. The writer regards the work of Christ in its eternal aspects. Compare Additional Note.

ὁ ἀναγ. ἐκ ν.] Vulg. *qui eduxit de mortuis (suscitat ex mortuis* d). The phrase occurs again in Rom. x. 7. Compare Wisd. xvi. 13 κατάγεις εἰς πύλας ᾅδου καὶ ἀνάγεις. The usage of the verb ἀνάγειν generally in the N. T., as well as the contrast in which it stands in these two passages to κατάγειν, shews that ἀναγαγών must be taken in the sense of 'brought up' and not of 'brought again.' The thought of restoration is made more emphatic by the addition of the thought of the depth of apparent defeat out of which Christ was raised.

τὸν ποιμένα...] *the Shepherd of the sheep, the great* Shepherd. Pastor est quia totum gregem conservat et pascit. Pascit autem non solum verbo doctrinæ sed corpore et sanguine suo (Herv.).

The image is common from Homer downwards. Philo in commenting on the application of the title of Shepherd to God in Ps. xxiii. says that as Shepherd and King He leads in justice and law the harmonious courses of the heavenly bodies 'having placed His right Word, His first-born Son, as their leader, to succeed to the care of this sacred flock, as a viceroy of a great king' (*de Agric.* § 12; i. 308 M.); and elsewhere he speaks of 'the divine Word' as a 'Shepherd-king' (*de mut.*

nom. § 20; i. p. 596 M.). Comp. John x. 11 note; and for the addition τὸν μέγαν c. iv. 14; x. 21. Πολλοὶ προφῆται διδάσκαλοι ἀλλ' εἰς καθηγητὴς ὁ Χριστός (Theophlct.).

The old commentators saw rightly in the words here a reference to Is. lxiii. 11 (LXX.) ποῦ ὁ ἀναβιβάσας ἐκ τῆς θαλάσσης τὸν ποιμένα τῶν προβάτων; The work of Moses was a shadow of that of Christ: the leading up of him with his people out of the sea was a shadow of Christ's ascent from the grave: the covenant with Israel a shadow of the eternal covenant.

ἐν αἵμ. διαθ. αἰ.] This clause, based on Zech. ix. 11, goes with all that precedes, ὁ ἀναγ....ἐν αἵ. δ. αἰ. The raising of Christ was indissolubly united with the establishment of the Covenant made by His blood and effective in virtue of it. His 'blood' is the vital energy by which He fulfils His work. So, when He was brought up from the dead, the power of His life offered for the world was, as it were, the atmosphere which surrounded Him as He entered on His triumphant work. Comp. x. 19 note. Εἰ μὴ ἐγήγερτο, οὐκ ἂν ἦν ἡμῖν τὸ αἷμα αὐτοῦ εἰς διαθήκην (Theophlct.). For αἵμ. διαθ. compare *Test. xii. Patr.* Benj. 3 ὑπὲρ ἀσεβῶν ἀποθανεῖται [ὁ ἀμνὸς τοῦ θεοῦ] ἐν αἵματι διαθήκης.

The covenant is described in its character (ἐν αἵ. δ. αἰ.). The new covenant is 'an eternal covenant': Jerem. xxxii.; Is. lv., lxi. Comp. c. viii. 8 ff. Αἰωνίαν τὴν καινὴν κέκληκε διαθήκην ὡς ἑτέρας μετὰ ταύτην οὐκ ἐσομένης (Theodt.).

τὸν κύρ. ἡ. Ἰ.] The phrase expresses the sum of the earliest Creed: Rom. x. 9; 1 Cor. xii. 3.

The title 'the Lord Jesus' is common in the book of the Acts (i. 21; iv.

²¹καταρτίσαι ὑμᾶς ἐν παντὶ ἀγαθῷ εἰς τὸ ποιῆσαι τὸ
θέλημα αὐτοῦ, ᵀ ποιῶν ἐν ἡμῖν τὸ εὐάρεστον ἐνώπιον
αὐτοῦ διὰ 'Ιησοῦ Χριστοῦ, ᾧ ἡ δόξα εἰς τοὺς αἰῶνας τῶν

21 αὐτῷ.   ? αὐτός

21 ὑμᾶς: ἡμᾶς D₂*.	ἐν παντί אD₂* vg : + ἔργῳ CM₂: + ἔργῳ καὶ λόγῳ A
(2 Thess. ii. 17).	ποιῆσαι: + ἡμᾶς D₂*. ποιῶν א°D₂M₂ vg syr vg me :
+ αὐτῷ' ποιῶν א*(A)C*.	ἐν ὑμῖν C vg me : ἐν ἡμῖν אAD₂M₂ syr vg. om. τῶν αἰ. D₂.

33; [vii. 59;] viii. 16; xi. 20; xv. 11;
xix. 13, 17 ; xx. 24, 35; xxi. 13). In
other books it is much more rare (1
Cor. v. 5 (?); xi. 23; xvi. 23; 2 Cor.
iv. 14 (?); xiii. 13 (?); Eph. i. 15; 2
Thess. i. 7 ; Phm. 5) and the fuller title
'the Lord Jesus Christ' is generally
used. ' Our Lord Jesus' occurs 2 Cor.
i. 14; viii. 9 (?); 'Jesus our Lord'
Rom. iv. 24 ; 2 Pet. i. 2.

Here it is natural that the writer of
the Epistle should desire to emphasise the simple thoughts of the Lord's
sovereignty and humanity as 'the
Great Shepherd.' For the contrast of
Moses and 'Jesus' see c. iii. 1 note.

21.   καταρτίσαι ὑ. ἐν π. ἀγ.] make
you perfect in every good thing. Vulg.
aptet vos in omni bono.

Comp. 1 Pet. v. 10. The word
καταρτίζειν, to make perfect, includes
the thoughts of the harmonious combination of different powers (comp.
Eph. iv. 12 καταρτισμός, 2 Cor. xiii. 9
κατάρτισις), of the supply of that which
is defective (1 Thess. iii. 10), and of
the amendment of that which is faulty
(Gal. vi. 1 ; comp. Mk. i. 19). Comp.
Ign. Eph. 2; Phil. 8; Smyrn. 1; Mart.
Ign. 4.

Chrysostom remarks wisely on the
choice of the word, πάλιν μαρτυρεῖ
αὐτοῖς μεγάλα· τὸ γὰρ καταρτιζόμενόν
ἐστι τὸ ἀρχὴν ἔχον εἶτα πληρούμενον.

The general phrase ἐν παντὶ ἀγαθῷ
conveys the thoughts expressed by
the explanatory glosses ἔργῳ and
ἔργῳ καὶ λόγῳ.

εἰς τὸ ποιῆσαι...] to the end that
you do.... Action is the true object
of the harmonious perfection of our

powers. And each deed is at once
the deed of man and the deed of God
(ποιῆσαι, ποιῶν). The work of God
makes man's work possible. He Himself does (αὐτὸς ποιῶν), as the one
source of all good, that which in
another sense man does as freely
accepting His grace. And all is
wrought in man 'through Jesus
Christ.' Comp. Acts iii. 16.

τὸ εὐάρ. ἐνώπ. αὐτοῦ] Compare 1 John
iii. 22 τὰ ἀρεστὰ ἐνώπιον αὐτοῦ; and
for ἐνώπιον αὐτοῦ Acts iv. 19 ; 1 Pet.
iii. 4; 1 Tim. ii. 3; v. 4.

διὰ 'Ιησοῦ Χριστοῦ] Εἰ μεσίτης γενέσθαι θεοῦ καὶ ἡμῶν ἠθέλησεν εἰκότως
δι' αὐτοῦ ὁ πατὴρ τὶ εὐάρεστον αὐτῷ εἰς
ἡμᾶς ἐπιτελέσει (Œcum.).

ᾧ ἡ δόξα...] The doxology may be
addressed to Christ as in 2 Tim. iv.
18; 2 Pet. iii. 18; Apoc. i. 6. The
Greek, however, admits the reference
of the relative to the main subject of
the sentence, ὁ θεός (cf. c. v. 7 ; 2 Thess.
ii. 9), and this is the most likely interpretation. Primasius combines both
persons : Cui est gloria, id est, Deo
Patri et Jesu Christo. Compare Additional Note.

εἰς τοὺς αἰ. τῶν αἰ.] Comp. v. 8 note.
The phrase occurs here only in the
Epistle. It is common in the Apocalypse (twelve times, with the varied
phrase εἰς αἰῶνας αἰώνων in xiv. 11),
and is found also in Phil. iv. 20;
1 Tim. i. 17; 2 Tim. iv. 18; 1 Pet. iv.
11 (all doxologies).

The language of the Apostle's
prayer has given occasion to an instructive expression of the characteristic differences of Greek and Latin

αἰώνων· ἀμήν.   ²²Παρακαλῶ δὲ ὑμᾶς, ἀδελφοί,
⌈ἀνέχεσθε⌉ τοῦ λόγου τῆς παρακλήσεως, καὶ γὰρ διὰ

22 ἀνέχεσθαι

22 ἀνέχεσθε ℵ(A)CM₂ me : ἀνέχεσθαι D₂* vg.   om. γάρ ℵ*.

theology in regard to man's share in good works. The Greek Commentators find in the word καταρτίζειν the recognition of the free activity of man : the Latin Commentators see in the prayer itself a testimony to man's complete dependence upon God.

Thus Chrysostom writes: ὁρᾷς πῶς δείκνυσι τὴν ἀρετὴν οὔτε ἐκ τοῦ θεοῦ τὸ ὅλον οὔτε ἐξ ἡμῶν μόνον κατορθουμένην· τῷ γὰρ εἰπεῖν καταρτίσαι....ὡσεὶ ἔλεγεν Ἔχετε μὲν ἀρετὴν δεῖσθε δὲ πληρώσεως. Theophylact goes farther: ὅρα ὅτι δεῖ ἡμᾶς πρότερον ἄρχεσθαι καὶ τότε αἰτεῖσθαι τὸ τέλος παρὰ τοῦ θεοῦ. And so Œcumenius ἡμᾶς δεῖ ἐνάρξασθαι τὸν δὲ πληροῦντα ἱκετεύειν.

On the other hand Primasius writes: A vobis nihil boni habere potestis nisi illo præveniente et subsequente.... Per illum facti et redempti sumus, et per illum quidquid boni habemus nobis subministratur. And this thought is forcibly expressed by Herveius in a note on *v.* 25 : Hæc est gratia quæ mentem prævenit et adjuvat ut homo suæ voluntatis et operationis obsequium subjungat; et dictum ex hoc ne de liberi arbitrii sui viribus præsumerent et quasi ex seipsis hæc posse bene agere putarent (Herv.).

It is obvious that the two views are capable of being reconciled in that larger view of man's constitution and destiny which acknowledges that the Fall has not destroyed the image of God in which he was created. Every act of man, so far as it is good, is wrought in fellowship with God.

22. *παρακαλῶ δέ...] But I exhort you, brethren, bear with the word of exhortation....* The words come as a postscript after the close of the letter,

when the writer has reviewed what he has said. As he looks back he feels that the very brevity of his argument on such themes as he has touched upon pleads for consideration. *παρακαλῶ...παρακλήσεως*] Comp. *v.* 19 ; iii. 13 ; x. 25 ; vi. 18 note; xii. 5.

ἀνέχεσθε] *bear with* that which makes demands on your self-control and your endurance. 2 Tim. iv. 3 ὑγιαινούσης διδασκαλίας οὐκ ἀνέξονται. The word is frequently used in regard to persons: Matt. xvii. 17 ; 2 Cor. xi. 1 ; &c.

τ. λόγ. τ. παρακλ.] the word of exhortation (Vulg. *verbum solacii*) with which the writer had encouraged them to face their trials. Acts xiii. 15 εἰ ἔστιν λόγος ἐν ὑμῖν παρακλήσεως, λέγετε.

Οὐ λέγει παρακαλῶ ὑμᾶς ἀνέχεσθε τοῦ λόγου τῆς παραινέσεως, ἀλλὰ τοῦ λόγου τῆς παρακλήσεως· τουτέστι, τῆς παραμυθίας, τῆς προτροπῆς (Chrys.).

καὶ γάρ...] c. iv. 2 note. 'I ask for patient attention, for in fact (Vulg. *etenim...*) I have written little when I might have extended my arguments to far greater length if I had not feared to weary you.' This appears to be the natural sense of the words. It is less likely that the writer wishes to apologise for any obscurity or harshness in what he has written on the ground of his brevity.

ἐπέστειλα] I have written, Vulg. *scripsi.* The word ἐπιστέλλειν is used in a similar connexion in Clem. 1 *ad Cor.* 62 περὶ τῶν ἀνηκόντων τῇ θρησκείᾳ ἡμῶν...ἱκανῶς ἐπεστείλαμεν ὑμῖν, ἄνδρες ἀδελφοί. Compare also cc. 7 ; 47 ; *Ign. Mart.* c. 4. Iren. iii. 3, 3 ἐπέστειλεν ἡ ἐν Ῥώμῃ ἐκκλησία ἱκανωτάτην γραφὴν τοῖς Κορινθίοις.

βραχέων ἐπέστειλα ὑμῖν.   ²³Γινώσκετε τὸν
ἀδελφὸν ἡμῶν Τιμόθεον ἀπολελυμένον, μεθ᾽ οὗ ἐὰν
τάχειον ἔρχηται ὄψομαι ὑμᾶς.
²⁴Ἀσπάσασθε πάντας τοὺς ἡγουμένους ὑμῶν καὶ
πάντας τοὺς ἁγίους. Ἀσπάζονται ὑμᾶς οἱ ἀπὸ τῆς
Ἰταλίας.

ἐπέστειλα: ἀπέστειλα D₂.   23 ἀδ. ἡμῶν ℵ*(Α)CD₂*M₂ vg syr vg me: om.
ἡμῶν ς ℵᶜ.   ἔρχηται: ἔρχητε D₂*: ἔρχησθε ℵ*.

The verb occurs again Acts xv. 20 (and *v. l.* in xxi. 25) where the sense is somewhat uncertain (*write* or *enjoin*). For the aor. comp. 1 John ii. 12 ff. (γράφω, ἔγραψα) note.

διὰ βραχέων] *in few words* (Vulg. *perpaucis*), that is, relatively to the vastness of the subject. Compare 1 Pet. v. 12 δι᾽ ὀλίγων ἔγραψα.

23.   γινώσκετε] The order, no less than the general scope of the verse, seems to shew that the verb is imperative: *Know ye, that our brother Timothy has been discharged* (ἀπολελυμένον, Vulg. *dimissum*), that is discharged from confinement (Acts xvi. 35 f.), or more generally set free from the charge laid against him (Acts iii. 13; xxvi. 32). It can cause no surprise that the details of this fact are wholly unknown.

τὸν ἀδ. ἡμ. Τιμ.] The order which St Paul adopts invariably is [Τιμ.] ὁ ἀδελφός. Rom. xvi. 23; (1 Cor. i. 1); 1 Cor. xvi. 12; (2 Cor. i. 1); ii. 13; Phil. ii. 25; (Col. i. 1); iv. 7; 1 Thess. iii. 2; (Philem. 1).

ἐὰν τάχειον...] Vulg. *si celerius*.... The comparative suggests the occurrence of hindrances which the Apostle could not distinctly foresee. Compare *v.* 19.

ὄψομαι ὑμᾶς] Rom. i. 11; 1 Thess. ii. 17; iii. 6, 10; 2 Tim. i. 4; 3 John 14.

24.   ἀσπάσασθε...] A general salutation of this kind is found in most of the Epistles of the N. T. (Rom., 1, 2 Cor., Phil., Col., 1 Thess., Tit., 1 Pet.,

3 Joh.); but the form of this is unique; and there appears to be an emphasis in the repetition πάντας... πάντας...all...all... which probably points to the peculiar circumstances of the Church. Comp. Phil. iv. 21 ἀσπ. πάντα ἅγιον ἐν Χριστῷ. The special salutation of 'all that have the rule' implies that the letter was not addressed officially to the Church, but to some section of it. The patristic commentators notice the significance of the clause:

Αἰνίττεται ὁ λόγος ὡς οἱ προστατεύοντες αὐτῶν τοιαύτης διδασκαλίας οὐκ ἐχρῆζον· οὗ δὴ χάριν οὐκ ἐκείνοις ἐπέστειλεν ἀλλὰ τοῖς μαθηταῖς (Theodt.).

Ὅρα πῶς αὐτοὺς τιμᾷ εἴγε δι᾽ αὐτῶν τοὺς ἡγουμένους προσαγορεύει (Theophlct.).

ἀσπ. ὑ. οἱ ἀπὸ τῆς Ἰτ.] *They of Italy salute you*, Vulg. *Salutant vos de Italia.* The phrase may mean either (1) 'those who are in Italy send greeting from Italy,' or (2) 'those of Italy,' that is Italian Christians who were with the writer at the time, 'send greeting.' The former rendering is adequately illustrated by Matt. xxiv. 17; Luke xi. 13; Col. iv. 16; and it is adopted by the Fathers: οἱ ἀπὸ τῆς Ἰταλίας· ἔδειξε πόθεν γέγραφε τὴν ἐπιστολήν (Theodt.); apertissime his verbis nobis innuit quod Romæ hanc epistolam scripserit quæ in regione Italiæ sita est (Primas.).

The choice between the two renderings will be determined by the view

²⁵'Η χάρις μετὰ πάντων ὑμῶν.ᵀ

25 ἀμήν.

25 ὑμῶν : τῶν ἀγίων D₂*.   ἀμήν : om. ℵ*.

which is taken of the place from which the Letter was written. The words themselves contribute nothing to the solution of the question.

25. The same greeting is found Tit. iii. 15. Every Epistle of St Paul includes in its final greeting the wish for 'grace' to those who receive it. 'Η χάρις is used absolutely in Eph. vi. 24 ἡ χάρις μετὰ πάντων τῶν ἀγαπώντων.... Col. iv. 18 ; 1 Tim. vi. 21 ; 2 Tim. iv. 22 ἡ χάρις μεθ' ὑμῶν.

Generally 'the grace' is defined as 'the grace of our Lord [Jesus Christ]' (Rom., 1, 2 Cor., Gal., Phil., 1, 2 Thess., Phm.).

In 1 Cor. xvi. 23 and 2 Cor. xiii. 13 significant additions are made to the prayer for grace ('my love, 'the love of God, and the fellowship of the Holy Spirit'). In 1 Pet., 3 John the prayer is for 'love,' not for 'grace.' There is no corresponding greeting in James, 2 Pet., 1, 2 John, Jude.

The simplicity of the final greeting when compared with the ordinary forms of salutation in the Epistles is remarkable.

μετὰ π. ὑμ.] 2 Thess. iii. 18 ; 1 Cor. xvi. 24 ; 2 Cor. xiii. 13; Rom. xv. 33.

On the sense of χάρις Theophylact writes: τίς δέ ἐστιν ἡ χάρις; ἡ ἄφεσις τῶν ἁμαρτιῶν, ἡ κάθαρσις, ἡ τοῦ πνεύματος μετάληψις. And Primasius, more in detail: Gratiæ nomine debemus hic accipere fidem perfectam cum exsecutione bonorum operum, remissionem quoque peccatorum quam percipiunt fideles tempore baptismatis, donum etiam Spiritus Sancti quod datur in baptismate per impositionem manus episcoporum, quæ omnia gratis a Deo dantur. The changes in the revised texts of Haymo and Atto are worth notice.

Additional Note on xiii. 10.   *On the history of the word*
θυσιαστήριον.

The word θυσιαστήριον is found first in the LXX.   From the LXX. it A word of
passed into the vocabulary of Philo, of the N.T., and of Christian writers. the LXX.
It is not quoted from classical authors, who have (though rarely) the corresponding form θυτήριον: Arat. *Phœn.* 402 &c. [*ara* Cic.]; Hyginus, xxxix.;
comp. Eurip. *Iph. Taur.* 243; Hesych. Suid. θυτηρίοις· θυμιατηρίοις.

The word is an adjectival form derived from θυσιάζω (LXX. Ex. xxii. 20, Form and
&c.), like θυμιατήριον, περιρραντήριον, ἱλαστήριον, χαριστήριον &c., and, general
expressing generally 'that which is connected with the act of sacrifice,' meaning.
it is used specially in a local sense to describe 'the place of sacrifice'
(compare δειπνητήριον, ὁρμητήριον, φυλακτήριον, &c.).

The usage of the word in the LXX. is of considerable interest.   It is the Use in
habitual rendering of מִזְבֵּחַ, as applied to the altar of the true God, from LXX.
Gen. viii. 20 onwards, in all the groups of books (more than 300 times).
It occurs once as a variant for ἱλαστήριον (כַּפֹּרֶת) in Lev. xvi. 14; once
again as a rendering of בָּמָה in 2 Chron. xiv. 5; and once in a clause
which varies widely from the Hebrew text (Ex. xxvii. 3; comp. xxxviii. 3).

On the other hand מִזְבֵּחַ is rendered also by βωμός (more than twenty θυσιαστή-
times), and once by στήλη, 2 Chron. xxxiii. 3 (θυσιαστήριον Compl.).   There ριον and
is however a general difference of usage between θυσιαστήριον and βωμός. βωμός.
Θυσιαστήριον is characteristically the altar of God, and βωμός the altar of
idolatrous or false worship.   Thus βωμός is used of idol altars, Ex. xxxiv.
13 (*ara*); Deut. vii. 5 (*ara*); Is. xvii. 8 (*altare*), &c., and in the Apocrypha,
1 Macc. i. 54, 59; ii. 23; 2 Macc. x. 2.   It is used also of the altar of
Balaam, Num. xxiii. 1 ff., and of the altar of the Reubenites, Josh. xxii.
10 ff. (contrast *vv.* 28 f. θυσιαστήριον, and in *v.* 19 βωμός and θυσιαστήριον
are opposed).   In accordance with this usage it is found seven times as a
rendering of בָּמָה (high place).   It is never used, I believe, of the altar
of God in the translation of the Books of the Hebrew Canon.   In some of
the later Books it is so used: Ecclus. l. 12, 14; 2 Macc. ii. 19; xiii. 8 (not
x. 2); but 1 Macc. follows the earlier precedent (1 Macc. i. 47, 59; ii. 23 ff.
45 ; v. 68).

It must, however, be added that θυσιαστήριον is not unfrequently used of
idol altars: Jud. ii. 2; vi. 25, 28, 31 f.; 1 K. xvi. 32; xviii. 26; 2 K. xi. 18;
xxi. 5; xxiii. 12; Ezek. vi. 4 ff.; Hos. x. 1, &c.

As a general rule, but by no means uniformly, βωμός was represented in
the Old Latin by *ara* and θυσιαστήριον by *altare*, and traces of the distinction remain in the Vulgate[1].

---

[1] Durandus (*Rationale*, i. 2, 2)
gives a distinction between *altare* and
ara which, although it is utterly inconsistent with the usage of the
O. T., suggests an important thought
as to the different conceptions of an

altar: altare quasi alta res vel alta ara
dicitur, in quo sacerdotes incensum
adolebant: ara quasi area, id est
platea, vel ab ardore dicitur, quia in
ea sacrificia ardebant.

The exact relation of βωμός to θυσιαστήριον in 1 Macc. i. 59 (comp. Jos. *Antt.* xii. 5, 4), Ecclus. l. 11 f. is not easy to determine. Perhaps θυσιαστήριον is (see below) the altar-court.

Use in the N. T. Gospels and Epistles.

In the Gospels and Epistles of the N. T. θυσιαστήριον is used of

(1) The brazen altar of burnt-offering, Matt. v. 23 f. (*altare*).

—— xxiii. 35 &c. (*altare*).

(2) The golden altar of incense, Luke i. 11, τὸ θυσιαστήριον τοῦ θυμιάματος.

(3) And generally of the altar

(*a*) for the worship of Jehovah: James ii. 21 (O. L. and Vulg. *altare*); Rom. xi. 3 (LXX.) (*altare*).

(*b*) for the Levitical service: 1 Cor. ix. 13 (O. L. *altarium*, Vulg. *altare*); x. 18 (*altare*)[1].

In the Apocalypse it is used, according to the general interpretation, of

Apocalypse.

(1) The altar of sacrifice: vi. 9 (O. L. *ara*, Vulg. *altare*); viii. 3 a (O. L. *altarium*, Vulg. *altare*), which proclaims the justice of God's judgments: xvi. 7 (Vulg. *altare*).

(2) The golden altar which is before the throne, viii. 3 b (O. L. *ara*, Vulg. *altare*), 5; before God, ix. 13 (O. L. *ara*, Vulg. *altare*).

(3) The place of the altar (the altar-court): xi. 1 (O. L. *ara*, Vulg. *altare*). Compare xiv. 17 f.; and see also Clem. xli. with Bp Lightfoot's note[2].

Use in Philo.

Philo appears to use βωμός commonly of the altar of God (*de vict. off.* § 4; ii. 253 M.: προστάξας δύο κατασκευασθῆναι βωμούς), but he recognises θυσιαστήριον as the characteristic name of the altar of sacrifice: *de vit. Mos.* iii. § 10 (ii. 151 M.) τὸν ἐν ὑπαίθρῳ βωμὸν εἴωθε καλεῖν θυσιαστήριον: and elsewhere he speaks of this as 'a peculiar and special name': *de vict. off.* § 6 (ii. 255 M.) κέκληκε θυσιαστήριον, ἴδιον καὶ ἐξαίρετον ὄνομα θέμενος αὐτῷ παρὰ τὸ διατηρεῖν ὡς ἔοικε τὰς θυσίας. It is consonant with his manner of thought that he should regard 'the thankful soul' as the θυσιαστήριον of God (*de vict. offer.* § 5; ii. 255 M.) τοῦ θεοῦ θυσιαστήριόν ἐστιν ἡ τοῦ σοφοῦ ψυχή, παγεῖσα ἐκ τελείων ἀριθμῶν ἀτμήτων καὶ ἀδιαιρέτων.

---

[1] The variation in the language in *vv.* 18, 21 deserves careful study: οὐχ οἱ ἐσθίοντες τὰς θυσίας, κοινωνοὶ τοῦ θυσιαστηρίου εἰσί;...οὐ δύνασθε τραπέζης Κυρίου μετέχειν καὶ τραπέζης δαιμονίων. When the offering is regarded as the material of a feast the 'altar' becomes a 'table.' Not only was the Table of Shewbread so called, but the Altar of incense (Ezek. xli. 22), and perhaps the Altar of burnt-offering (Ezek. xliv. 16; Mal. i. 12).

[2] It is however by no means clear that the imagery is that of the Jewish Temple with its two altars, and not rather a foreshadowing of the arrangements of the Christian Basilican Church with its single altar, and sanctuary, and nave and narthex. It is indeed difficult to agree with Mr G. G. Scott in thinking that the picture is directly drawn from any existing Christian building, but the general view which he gives of its agreement with Christian as distinguished from Jewish ritual deserves careful consideration: *Essay on English Church Architecture,* pp. 27 ff.

Josephus does not seem to make any distinction between the two Josephus. words. He speaks of the altar of burnt-offering (*Antt.* iii. 6, 8), and of the golden altar (xii. 5, 4), no less than of the altar of Balaam (iv. 6, 4) by the name βωμός. And again he calls the altar of burnt-offering θυσιαστήριον (*Antt.* viii. 3, 7).

The early Christian writers follow the custom of the LXX. Clement. Clement. (1 *ad Cor.* 32 οἱ λειτουργοῦντες τῷ θυσιαστηρίῳ τοῦ θεοῦ) uses θυσιαστήριον as the general term for the divine altar, and perhaps, though this seems to be uncertain, for 'the court of the altar' (c. 41 οὐ πανταχοῦ προσφέρονται θυσίαι...ἀλλ' ἔμπροσθεν τοῦ ναοῦ πρὸς τὸ θυσιαστήριον...Lightfoot *ad loc.*). On the other hand he calls the altar of the Sun βωμός (c. 25).

Barnabas uses θυσιαστήριον for the altar of Abraham's sacrifice on Barnabas. Moriah (vii. 3), and for the Levitical altar (vii. 9). The Latin rendering *ad aram illius* (i. 7), which suggests τῷ βωμῷ αὐτοῦ, for 'the altar of God,' cannot be maintained against the reading of both the Greek MSS. τῷ φόβῳ αὐτοῦ.

The usage of θυσιαστήριον in the Epistles of Ignatius is very remark- Ignatius. able. In one place it occurs by a natural image for the arena in which Ignatius expected to die (*ad Rom.* 2 πλέον μοι μὴ παράσχησθε τοῦ σπονδισθῆναι θεῷ, ὡς ἔτι θυσιαστήριον ἕτοιμόν ἐστιν). In three other passages the word expresses that which represents the unity of the Christian Society.

Eph. 5. Μηδεὶς πλανάσθω· ἐὰν μή τις ᾖ ἐντὸς τοῦ θυσιαστηρίου ὑστερεῖται τοῦ ἄρτου [τοῦ θεοῦ]. εἰ γὰρ ἑνὸς καὶ δευτέρου προσευχὴ τοσαύτην ἰσχὺν ἔχει, πόσῳ μᾶλλον ἥ τε τοῦ ἐπισκόπου καὶ πάσης τῆς ἐκκλησίας.

Here the θυσιαστήριον—the place of sacrifice—is evidently the place of assembly of the spiritual Israel, where the faithful meet God in worship, like the altar-court of the old Temple, the court of the congregation. He who has no place within this sacred precinct is necessarily excluded from the privileges which belong to the Divine Society. He is not a member of the Body of Christ, and therefore cannot share in the sacrifices which are offered there, the common prayer of the Church, or in 'the bread of God' which is given to believers (comp. Bp Lightfoot *ad loc.*).

The same general thought is expressed in a second passage :

Trall. 7. ὁ ἐντὸς θυσιαστηρίου ὢν καθαρός ἐστιν· ὁ δὲ ἐκτὸς θυσιαστηρίου ὢν οὐ καθαρός ἐστιν· τουτέστιν, ὁ χωρὶς ἐπισκόπου καὶ πρεσβυτερίου καὶ διακόνων πράσσων τι, οὗτος οὐ καθαρός ἐστιν τῇ συνειδήσει.

The idea of the Christian θυσιαστήριον is here more exactly defined. To be included in the holy precinct, is to be in fellowship with the lawfully organised society.

In a third passage the thought is different and yet closely connected :

Magn. 7. πάντες οὖν ὡς εἰς ἕνα ναὸν συντρέχετε θεοῦ (Ltft. conj. θεόν), ὡς ἐπὶ ἓν θυσιαστήριον ἐπὶ ἕνα Ἰησοῦν Χριστόν, τὸν ἀφ' ἑνὸς πατρὸς προελθόντα καὶ εἰς ἕνα ὄντα καὶ χωρήσαντα.

Here the Father is Himself the Sanctuary, and Christ the means through Whom and in Whom we have access to the Father. He is Himself the living source of unity, just as the altar-court was the symbol of unity for the people of God. To be 'in Him' is to be within the θυσιαστήριον.

These passages serve to determine the meaning of the word in the last place in which it occurs :

Philad. 4. σπουδάσατε οὖν μιᾷ εὐχαριστίᾳ χρῆσθαι· μία γὰρ σάρξ τοῦ Κυρίου ἡμῶν Ἰησοῦ Χριστοῦ, καὶ ἓν ποτήριον εἰς ἕνωσιν τοῦ αἵματος αὐτοῦ· ἓν θυσιαστήριον, ὡς εἷς ἐπίσκοπος, ἅμα τῷ πρεσβυτερίῳ καὶ διακόνοις τοῖς συνδούλοις μου· ἵνα ὃ ἐὰν πράσσητε, κατὰ θεὸν πράσσητε.

There is one organised congregation, which is the Body of Christ, in which the blessings of communion with God are realised.

Polycarp.

In the Epistle of Polycarp the image of the 'altar' finds still another application in the narrower sense. Just as Christ Himself can be spoken of as the θυσιαστήριον, and the whole Christian body which is 'in Him,' so also a part of the Body may receive the name.

Philipp. 4. διδάξωμεν...τὰς χήρας...γινωσκούσας ὅτι εἰσὶ θυσιαστήριον θεοῦ, καὶ ὅτι πάντα μωμοσκοπεῖται, καὶ λέληθεν αὐτὸν οὐδέν....

The widows are an altar in a double sense, both because on them the alms of the faithful are offered to God, and also because they themselves offer to God sacrifices of service and prayer (comp. *Const. Apost.* ii. 26; iii. 6; 14; iv. 3). The last passage is instructive : ὁ δὲ ἡλικίαν...ἢ τέκνων πολυτροφίαν λαμβάνων, ὁ τοιοῦτος οὐ μόνον οὐ μεμφθήσεται ἀλλὰ καὶ ἐπαινεθήσεται· θυσιαστήριον γὰρ τῷ θεῷ λελογισμένος ὑπὸ τοῦ θεοῦ τιμηθήσεται.... οὐκ ἀργῶς λαμβάνων ἀλλὰ τῆς δόσεως αὐτοῦ, ὅση δύναμις, τὸν μισθὸν διδοὺς διὰ τῆς προσευχῆς[1].

Hermas.

Hermas uses θυσιαστήριον twice in a purely spiritual sense. For him the altar is, after the imagery of the Apocalypse, that whereon the offerings of men are placed that they may be brought before God.

Mand. x. 3, 2 f. λυπηροῦ ἀνδρὸς ἡ ἔντευξις οὐκ ἔχει δύναμιν τοῦ ἀναβῆναι ἐπὶ τὸ θυσιαστήριον τοῦ θεοῦ.

Whatever sacrifice man makes must be made with joy.

Sim. viii. 2, 5. ἐὰν δέ τίς σε παρέλθῃ, ἐγὼ αὐτοὺς ἐπὶ τὸ θυσιαστήριον δοκιμάσω.

So the angel speaks to the Shepherd. If a penitent passes human scrutiny unworthily, a severer trial awaits him. The angel himself will test him (comp. μωμοσκοπεῖσθαι Clem. i. 41; Polyc. 4 quoted above) before he is laid on the altar of God.

No material θυσιαστήριον of Christians in this first period.

In this first stage of Christian literature there is not only no example of the application of the word θυσιαστήριον to any concrete, material, object, as the Holy Table, but there is no room for such an application. As applied to the New Order the word expresses the spiritual correlatives of the altar and altar-court of the Old Order. Two of these in which it was referred to Christians and to Christ Himself continued current in later times.

Later examples of the spiritual senses.

Thus Clement of Alexandria speaks of 'our altar here, our altar on earth' as being the assembly of those devoted to prayer: ἔστι γοῦν τὸ παρ' ἡμῖν θυσιαστήριον ἐνταῦθα τὸ ἐπίγειον τὸ ἄθροισμα τῶν ταῖς εὐχαῖς ἀνακειμένων μίαν ὥσπερ ἔχον φωνὴν τὴν κοινὴν καὶ μίαν γνώμην (*Strom.* vii. § 31, p. 848). And in the following section he extends the image to the single soul, using, however, the word βωμός....βωμὸν ἀληθῶς ἅγιον τὴν δικαίαν ψυχὴν καὶ τὸ ἀπ'

---

[1] The word is not, I believe, used literally of the Christian Holy Table in the Constitutions.

αὐτῆς θυμίαμα τὴν ὁσίαν εὐχὴν λέγουσιν ἡμῖν ἀπιστήσουσιν (id. § 32; comp. Philo de vict. offer. § 5 quoted above).

So Origen, in reply to the charge that Christians βωμοὺς καὶ ἀγάλματα καὶ νεὼς ἱδρύσθαι φεύγειν, answers that 'the sovereign principle of the righteous is an altar': βωμοὶ μέν εἰσιν ἡμῖν τὸ ἑκάστου τῶν δικαίων ἡγεμονικόν, ἀφ' οὗ ἀναπέμπεται ἀληθῶς καὶ νοητῶς εὐώδη θυμιάματα, αἱ προσευχαὶ ἀπὸ συνειδήσεως καθαρᾶς (c. Cels. viii. 17); and Methodius speaks of the social interpretation of the word as traditional: θυσιαστήριον ἀναίμακτον εἶναι παρεδόθη τὸ ἄθροισμα τῶν ἁγνῶν (Symp. v. 6).

Chrysostom uses the image somewhat differently, and speaks of the Christian poor as 'the living altar' on which the alms of the faithful are offered. Such offerings are not consumed like the burnt sacrifices but pass into 'praise and thanksgiving': ἐκεῖνο μὲν γὰρ ἄψυχον τὸ θυσιαστήριον τοῦτο δὲ ἔμψυχον· κἀκεῖ μὲν τὸ ἐπικείμενον ἅπαν τοῦ πυρὸς γίνεται δαπάνη καὶ τελευτᾷ εἰς κόνιν...ἐνταῦθα δὲ οὐδὲν τοιοῦτον ἀλλ' ἑτέρους φέρει τοὺς καρπούς...ὁρᾷς εἰς εὐχαριστίαν ἀναλυομένην αὐτὴν (τὴν λειτουργίαν 2 Cor. ix. 12 ff.) καὶ αἶνον τοῦ θεοῦ...· θύωμεν τοίνυν, ἀγαπητοί, θύωμεν εἰς ταῦτα τὰ θυσιαστήρια καθ' ἑκάστην ἡμέραν (Hom. xiii. in Joh. § 4: Migne, P. G. lix. 90).

Cyril of Alexandria again speaks of Christians as 'living stones,' who are framed together into an altar as well as into a temple: οὐδὲν ἧττόν ἐσμεν καὶ οἱονεί τι θυσιαστήριον, συναγηγερμένοι μὲν καθ' ἕνωσιν τὴν πνευματικὴν καὶ τὴν ἐν Χριστῷ πίστιν εὐωδιάζοντες, προσκομίζοντες δι' αὐτοῦ τῷ θεῷ καὶ πατρὶ καθάπερ ἐν τάξει τῶν εὐοσμοτάτων θυμιαμάτων τὰ ἐξ ἀρετῶν αὐχήματα (Glaph. in Deut. p. 427; P. G. lxix. p. 668). So the altar which Moses erected at the making of the Covenant (Ex. xxiv. 4 f.) was a type of the Church of Christ: τὸ μὲν οὖν θυσιαστήριον τύπος ἂν εἴη καὶ μάλα σαφῶς τῆς ἐκκλησίας τοῦ Χριστοῦ, τῆς οἱονεί πως ἐπὶ τὸ ὄρος κειμένης (Glaph. in Ex. iii. p. 330: P. G. id. 517).

Not Christians only, however, but Christ Himself is spoken of as an altar by later Fathers. Cyril of Alexandria uses the phrase several times. Thus, in commenting on the command to make an altar of earth (Ex. xx. 24 f.), he says: γήϊνον ὀνομάζει θυσιαστήριον τὸν Ἐμμανουήλ, γέγονε γὰρ σάρξ ὁ λόγος· γῆ δὲ ἐκ γῆς ἡ σαρκός ἐστι φύσις. ἐν Χριστῷ δὴ οὖν ἡ πᾶσα καρποφορία καὶ πᾶσα προσαγωγή, φησὶ γὰρ αὐτὸς Χωρὶς ἐμοῦ οὐ δύνασθε ποιεῖν οὐδέν...ἐπαγγέλλεται δὲ τοῖς τὸ ἐκ γῆς ἱστᾶσι θυσιαστήριον ἀφιξίν τε καὶ εὐλογίαν, Ἥξω γάρ, φησί, πρός σε καὶ εὐλογήσω σε (de ador. in sp. et ver. ix. p. 290: P. G. lxviii. 592). In another place of the same treatise he speaks of Christ as being the altar of incense and the incense itself: μεμνησόμεθα δὲ καὶ τὸ θυσιαστήριον τὸ χρυσοῦν καὶ αὐτὸ δὲ τὸ σύνθετον καὶ λεπτὸν θυμίαμα Χριστὸν εἰρηκότες καὶ αὐτὸν ἡμῖν τὸν Ἐμμανουὴλ δι' ἀμφοῖν σημαίνεσθαι (id. ix. p. 324: P. G. lxviii. 648; comp. x. p. 335: P. G. id. p. 664).

Epiphanius, in a striking passage, points to Christ as fulfilling in Himself all the elements of a perfect sacrifice: μένει...τὴν ἐντελεστέραν ζῶσαν [θυσίαν] ὑπὲρ παντὸς κόσμου ἱερουργήσας, αὐτὸς ἱερεῖον, αὐτὸς θῦμα, αὐτὸς ἱερεύς, αὐτὸς θυσιαστήριον, αὐτὸς θεός, αὐτὸς ἄνθρωπος, αὐτὸς βασιλεύς, αὐτὸς ἀρχιερεύς, αὐτὸς πρόβατον, αὐτὸς ἀρνίον τὰ πάντα ἐν πᾶσιν ὑπὲρ ἡμῶν γενόμενος....(Hær. lv. 4)[1].

Christ an altar.

---

[1] Origen gives another suggestive interpretation of the two altars of

Jewish worship: Altaria duo, id est interius et exterius, quoniam altare

A transition to the concrete meaning in Irenæus, and

In Irenæus there appears to be a transition from the spiritual sense of θυσιαστήριον to that of an earthly Christian altar. Such a use of the word followed naturally from the habitual thought of material offerings. Thus, in a passage preserved only in the Latin translation, after dwelling on the material offerings in the Eucharist, he adds, ideo nos quoque offerre vult [Verbum Dei] munus ad altare frequenter sine intermissione. Est ergo altare in cælis (illuc enim preces nostræ et oblationes diriguntur) et templum, quemadmodum Ioannes in Apocalypsi, xi. 19; xxi. 3 (adv. hær. iv. 18, 6). The words are obscure, but the heavenly altar seems to be made to correspond with an earthly altar. In the first clause munus is material and it appears that altare must correspond with it. The heavenly counterpart answers to the spiritual element in prayers and oblations.

Tertullian.

Tertullian repeats the figure of Polycarp (see p. 456), and, arguing against the second marriage of widows, says: aram enim Dei mundam proponi oportet (ad ux. i. 7). But in another place he uses the word ara in connexion with the Eucharist: Ergo devotum Deo obsequium Eucharistia resolvit an magis Deo obligat? Nonne solemnior erit statio tua si et ad aram Dei steteris? (de orat. 14 [19])[1].

Cyprian marks a new stage.

The writings of Cyprian mark a new stage in the development of ecclesiastical thought and language. In them the phraseology of the Levitical law is transferred to Christian institutions. The correspondence between the Old system and the New is no longer generally that of the external and material to the inward and spiritual, but of one outward order to another. Thus he writes: oportet enim sacerdotes et ministros qui altari et sacrificiis deserviunt integros atque immaculatos esse, cum Dominus Deus in Levitico loquatur et dicat: homo in quo fuerit macula et vitium non accedit offerre dona Deo (Lev. xxi. 21); item in Exodo hæc eadem præcipiat et dicat: et sacerdotes qui accedunt ad Dominum Deum sanctificentur ne forte derelinquat illos Dominus (Ex. xix. 22); et iterum: et cum accedunt ministrare ad altare sancti, non adducent in se delictum ne moriantur (Ex. xxviii. 43) (Ep. lxxii. 2). As a necessary consequence the Christian minister is said to serve at a material 'altar,' which becomes the habitual name for the Holy Table, Ep. lxix. (lxxvi.) 1 falsa altaria, et illicita sacerdotia, et sacrificia sacrilega; comp. Ep. xliii. (xl.) 5; xlv. (xlii.) 2; de eccles. unit. 17[2].

---

orationis indicium est, illud puto significare quod dicit Apostolus, orabo spiritu, orabo et mente. Cum enim corde oravero, ad altare interius ingredior...cum autem quis clara voce et verbis cum sono prolatis...orationem fundit ad Deum, hic spiritu orat, et ,offerre videtur hostiam in altare quod foris est ad holocaustomata populi constitutum (Hom. x. in Num. § 3).

[1] The words de orat. 10 (11) ad Dei altare, and de pat. 12 apud altare, refer to Matt. v. 23 f., and cannot be

pressed to give decisive evidence as to Christian usage.

[2] Cyprian seems to feel the difference between altare and ara though he does not rigidly observe it: e.g. Ep. lix. (lv.) 18 Domini altare...idola cum aris suis...; Ep. lxv. (lxiv.) 1 quasi post aras diaboli accedere ad altare Dei fas sit...(comp. Ep. lv. (lii.) 14 aræ diaboli; de lapsis 15); and on the other hand he writes de lapsis 8 diaboli altare (with ara in the context); Ep. lix. [lv.] 12 diaboli altaria.

From this time there can be no doubt that the names θυσιαστήριον and altare were applied habitually though not exclusively to the Holy Table. The custom had grown up from intelligible causes. No conclusion to the contrary can be drawn from the common statements of the Apologists, that Christians had no shrines or altars (Orig. c. Cels. viii.; Minuc. Fel. Oct. xxxii.; Arnob. adv. gentes, vi. 1). Their language in its context shews that they had before them all the associations of the heathen ritual. In a similar sense Julian accused the Christians of neglecting to sacrifice in spite of the injunctions of the Law, at a time when beyond all question sacrificial language was everywhere current among them (Cyril Alex. adv. Jul. ix.; P. G. lxxvi. 970 ff.).

We read of altars as soon as we read in detail of churches. Eusebius, in his description of the great Church at Tyre, mentions especially τὸ τῶν ἁγίων ἅγιον θυσιαστήριον as placed in the middle of the sanctuary (H. E. x. 4, 43). Elsewhere, speaking of the abolition of heathen worship, he says ἐπὶ τῆς καθ' ὅλης ἀνθρώπων οἰκουμένης θυσιαστήρια συνέστη ἐκκλησιῶν τε ἀφιερώματα, νοερῶν τε καὶ λογικῶν θυσιῶν ἱεροπρεπεῖς λειτουργίαι (de laud. Const. xvi.). See also Can. Apost. 3 εἴ τις ἐπίσκοπος...προσενέγκῃ ἕτερά τινα ἐπὶ τὸ θυσιαστήριον ἢ μέλι ἢ γάλα...(comp. Conc. Carthag. iii. can. 24). Cyr. Hier. Cat. xxiii. (Myst. v.) § 2 ἑωράκατε τοίνυν τὸν διάκονον τὸν νίψασθαι διδόντα τῷ ἱερεῖ καὶ τοῖς κυκλοῦσι τὸ θυσιαστήριον τοῦ θεοῦ πρεσβυτέροις. Chrys. c. Jud. et Gent. § 12: P. G. xlviii. 830 αἱ βρεταννικαὶ νῆσοι...τῆς δυνάμεως τοῦ ῥήματος ᾔσθοντο· καὶ γὰρ κἀκεῖ ἐκκλησίαι καὶ θυσιαστήρια πεπήγασι. And Chrysostom points to the old distinction between θυσιασ- τήριον and βωμός in a passage in which the spiritual and material are strangely mixed : εἰ αἵματος ἐπιθυμεῖς, φησί (in 1 Cor. x. 16), μὴ τὸν τῶν εἰδώλων βωμὸν τῷ τῶν ἀλόγων φόνῳ ἀλλὰ τὸ θυσιαστήριον τὸ ἐμὸν τῷ ἐμῷ φοίνισσε αἵματι (Hom. xxiv. in 1 Cor. § 1 : P. G. lxi. 200). Synesius, as is not unnatural, uses the two words convertibly: κυκλώσομαι τὸ θυσιασ- τήριον...οὐ μὴν ὅ γε θεὸς περιόψεται τὸν βωμὸν τὸν ἀναίμακτον ἱερέως αἵματι μιαινόμενον (Catast. p. 303 : P. G. lxvi. 1572 f.).

Gregory of Nyssa places θυσιαστήριον in an interesting connexion with τράπεζα: τὸ θυσιαστήριον τοῦτο τὸ ἅγιον ᾧ παραστήκαμεν λίθος ἐστὶ κατὰ τὴν φύσιν κοινός...ἐπειδὴ δὲ καθιερώθη τῇ τοῦ θεοῦ θεραπείᾳ...ἐστι τράπεζα ἁγία, θυσιαστήριον ἄχραντον, οὐκέτι παρὰ πάντων ψηλαφώμενον...(in Bapt. Christi, P. G. xlvi. p. 581).

It was seen that in regard to the Jewish Temple θυσιαστήριον was used not only for the altar itself, but also for the altar-court. A corresponding application of the word in the larger sense was made in Christian Churches. The Sanctuary itself (Βῆμα, Ἁγίασμα, Euseb. H. E. vii. 15) was called θυσιαστήριον as well as the Holy Table. Thus Procopius speaking of the Church of Sancta Sophia writes : ὁ τοῦ ἱεροῦ τὰ μάλιστα χῶρος ἀβέβηλος καὶ μόνοις ἱερεῦσι βατός, ὅνπερ καλοῦσι θυσιαστήριον, λιτρῶν ἀργύρου μυριάδας ἐπιφέρεται τέτταρας (de Sancta Soph., Migne, P. G. lxxxvii. 3, p. 2336 c). The sense occurs in earlier writings : Conc. Laod., Can. xix. μόνοις ἐξὸν εἶναι τοῖς ἱερατικοῖς εἰσιέναι εἰς τὸ θυσιαστήριον καὶ κοινωνεῖν. xliv. ὅτι οὐ δεῖ γυναῖκας ἐν τῷ θυσιαστηρίῳ εἰσέρχεσθαι. Socr. H. E. i. 37 (comp. Soz. ii. 39) [Ἀλέξανδρος] ἐν τῇ ἐκκλησίᾳ ᾗ ἐπώνυμον Εἰρήνη μόνον ἑαυτὸν κατάκλειστον ποιήσας καὶ εἰς τὸ θυσιαστήριον εἰσελθὼν ὑπὸ τὴν ἱερὰν τράπεζαν ἑαυτὸν ἐπὶ στόμα ἐκτείνας εὔχεται δακρύων. And the word is so used still in the Greek Church (Leo Allatius, *de rec. Gr. templ.* p. 153). In rare cases *altarium* is also found in the sense of the altar-place, the Sanctuary: Hieron. *Ep.* lxix. (*ad Ocean.*) § 9, Heri catechumenus, hodie pontifex: heri in amphitheatro, hodie in ecclesia: vespere in circo, mane in altario. Greg. Turon. *Hist. Franc.* ii. 14 Habet (the original church of St Martin at Tours) fenestras in altario triginta duas, in capso [the nave] viginti, columnas quadraginta unam.

Use in the Liturgies.   In the Greek Liturgies, as might have been expected, the word θυσιαστήριον is used in different meanings. It will be enough to take illustrations from the Liturgy of St James (Swainson, pp. 213—332). Commonly the word is used for the Holy Table (pp. 216, 222—6, 246, 254—6, 260—2, 282—8). In one place it occurs in a rubric as a various reading for τράπεζα (p. 238, Rot. Mess. ἐν τῷ θυσιαστηρίῳ, Cod. Rossan. ἐν τῇ ἁγίᾳ τραπέζῃ· comp. pp. 318, 319). In two rubrics it is used for the Sanctuary (p. 222 ἀπὸ τῶν θυρῶν τῆς ἐκκλησίας ἕως τοῦ θυσιαστηρίου, p. 223 μετὰ τὸ εἰσελθεῖν εἰς τὸ θυσιαστήριον, Cod. Par. 2509). Elsewhere it is used for the heavenly, spiritual, altar (p. 229 ἀναληφθήτω...εἰς τὸ ἅγιον καὶ ὑπερουράνιόν σου θυσιαστήριον, εἰς ὀσμὴν εὐωδίας...p. 260 εἰς τὸ ἅγιον καὶ ὑπερουράνιον καὶ νοερόν σου θυσιαστήριον, εἰς ὀσμὴν εὐωδίας...p. 304 εἰς τὸ ἅγιον καὶ ὑπερουράνιον, νοερὸν καὶ πνευματικὸν αὐτοῦ θυσιαστήριον, εἰς ὀσμὴν εὐωδίας[1]). Once, it may be added, ἡ τράπεζα is used for the heavenly food upon it: p. 322...καταξιώσας ἡμᾶς μετασχεῖν τῆς ἐπουρανίου τραπέζης.

θυσιαστήριον and τράπεζα.   The Liturgies bring out plainly the parallel use of θυσιαστήριον and τράπεζα. The earlier word τράπεζα still held its place, and with it the central thought of a divine feast to which it bore witness. Early writers found the foreshadowing of the heavenly table in Prov. ix. 1 ff. (Cypr. *Testim.* ii. 2; *Ep.* lxiii. 5; comp. the spurious *Disp. c. Ar.* § 17, printed in the works of Athanasius). Sometimes this Holy Table was made at an early date of wood (Athan. *Hist. Ar. ad Mon.* § 56 ἁρπάσαντες τὰ συμψέλλια [subsellia] καὶ τὸν θρόνον καὶ τὴν τράπεζαν, ξυλίνη γὰρ ἦν, καὶ τὰ βῆλα [vela] τῆς ἐκκλησίας...ἔκαυσαν), but afterwards it was of stone (Greg. Nyss. *in Bapt. Chr.*, *P. G.* xlvi. p. 581 τὸ θυσιαστήριον τοῦτο...λίθος ἐστὶ κατὰ τὴν φύσιν κοινός...ἐπειδὴ δὲ καθιερώθη τῇ τοῦ θεοῦ θεραπείᾳ...ἔστι τράπεζα ἁγία, θυσιαστήριον ἄχραντον...The words are translated by Nicholas 1., *Ep.* ii.; comp. Sozom. *H. E.* ix. 2 τὸ ἐπίθεμα τῆς θήκης ὥσπερ εἰς ἱερὰν ἐξηρσκεῖτο τράπεζαν). Basil appears to use the two words θυσιαστήριον and τράπεζα as interchangeable (*Ep.* ccxxvi. 2; *P. G.* xxxii. 485 εἰ ὀρθόδοξος νῦν Βασιλείδης ὁ κοινωνικὸς Ἐκδικίου, διὰ τί...τὰ θυσιαστήρια ἐκείνου...κατέστρεφον καὶ ἑαυτῶν τράπεζας ἐτίθεσαν;) for it is difficult to see any contrast between them as they are used. Comp. Cyr. Hier. *Cat.* xxii. (*Myst.* iv.) § 7. The corresponding word *mensa* is common in Latin writers (see *e.g.* Index to Augustine); and it came to be used as a technical term for the altar-slab (*tabula*)[2].

---

[1] Compare the petition in the Roman and Ambrosian Liturgies: Supplices Te rogamus, omnipotens Deus, jube hæc proferri per manus sancti Angeli Tui in sublime altare Tuum in conspectu divinæ Majestatis Tuæ, ut quotquot ex hac altaris participatione sacrosanctum Filii Tui corpus et sanguinem sumpserimus, omni benedictione cælesti et gratia repleamur.

[2] Postea vero lapis, qui mensa altaris dicitur, super altare adaptatur, per

The history of the word offers an instructive illustration of the way in which spiritual thoughts connected with material imagery clothe themselves in material forms, till at last the material form dominates the thought. The three notes of the three chief Greek Commentators who expound the passage shew the action of this natural influence.

CHRYSOSTOM. οὐχ οἷα τὰ Ἰουδαϊκά, φησί, τοιαῦτα τὰ παρ' ἡμῖν, ὡς μηδὲ ἀρχιερεῖ θέμις εἶναι μετέχειν αὐτῶν· ὥστε ἐπειδὴ εἶπε Μὴ παρατηρεῖσθε, ἐδόκει δὲ τοῦτο καταβάλλοντος εἶναι τὰ ἴδια, πάλιν αὐτὸ περιστρέφει. Μὴ γὰρ καὶ ἡμεῖς οὐ παρατηροῦμεν; φησί, καὶ παρατηροῦμεν καὶ σφοδρότερον, οὐδὲ αὐτοῖς τοῖς ἱερεῦσι μεταδίδοντες αὐτῶν.

Patristic interpretations.

ŒCUMENIUS. ἐπειδὴ εἶπεν ὅτι οὐ χρὴ παρατηρεῖσθαι βρώματα...φησί, Μὴ γὰρ καὶ ἡμεῖς οὐκ ἔχομεν παρατηρήσεις; ἀλλ' οὐ βρωμάτων, ἀλλὰ τοῦ θυσιαστηρίου ἡμῶν· τῶν γὰρ ἐκεῖ κειμένων οὐδὲ αὐτοῖς τοῖς ἀρχιερεῦσιν ἔξεστι μετασχεῖν. Then he adds shortly afterwards : τοῦτο δὴ οὖν τὸ αἷμα [τὸ τοῦ Χριστοῦ] διὰ τοῦ παρ' ἡμῖν ἀρχιερέως εἰσφέρεται εἰς τὸ παρ' ἡμῖν θυσιαστήριον, where the θυσιαστήριον in the Christian order is made parallel with τὰ ἅγια in the Jewish order.

THEOPHYLACT. καὶ ἡμεῖς ἔχομεν παρατήρησιν, ἀλλ' οὐκ ἐπὶ βρώμασι τοιούτοις ἀλλ' ἐπὶ τῷ θυσιαστηρίῳ ἤτοι τῇ ἀναιμάκτῳ θυσίᾳ τοῦ ζωοποιοῦ σώματος, ταύτης γὰρ οὐδὲ τοῖς νομικοῖς ἀρχιερεῦσι μεταλαβεῖν ἔξεστιν ἕως ἂν λατρεύωσι τῇ σκηνῇ, τουτέστι τοῖς νομικοῖς τύποις...ὁ Χριστός, ὑπὲρ τῶν ἁμαρτιῶν τοῦ κόσμου παθών, τὸ μὲν αἷμα αὐτοῦ εἰς τὰ ἅγια εἰσεκόμισε τῷ πατρὶ ὡς ἀρχιερεύς...ἀνάμνησιν οὖν τῆς θυσίας ἐκείνης τελοῦντες οἱ παρ' ἡμῖν ἀρχιερεῖς τὸ αἷμα τοῦ Κυρίου εἰς τὰ παρ' ἡμῖν ἅγια καὶ εἰς τὸ θυσιαστήριον εἰσκομίζουσιν ὡς εἰς οὐρανόν.

Additional Note on xiii. 10.

The main thoughts of the verse can be presented clearly in the following propositions.

1. A sacrifice (according to the Levitical usage) may be regarded generally under two distinct aspects: as something offered to God and as something, by divine appointment, partaken of, enjoyed by man. Christ, as the perfect sacrifice for the whole world, offered Himself once for all to God, and, as He offered Himself, so He gives Himself to us, His flesh and blood, and this gift, in respect of its source, comes to us from the Cross on which the offering was made. Comp. Aug. *in Psalm.* xxxiii. *Enarr.* i. § 6...ut jam de cruce commendaretur nobis caro et sanguis Domini, novum sacrificium (commenting on Ps. lxxviii. 25 and Phil. 6 ff.).

quam perfectionem et soliditatem notitiæ Dei possumus, intelligere, quæ non propter duritiam sed propter soliditatem fidei lapidea esse debet. Alex. III. quoted by Durandus, *Rationale*, i. 7, 25. The chapters of Duran-

dus on the Altar (c. 2) and the consecration of the Altar (c. 7) give a most interesting summary of mediæval thought upon the ideas of the Altar.

2. The context shews that in this passage the main conception is of a sacrifice to be enjoyed ('eaten') and not of a sacrifice to be offered. There is for Christians a feast following upon a sacrifice accomplished, whereby the sacrifice is made the support of the believer.

3. The ideas of the Passover and of the sacrifices on the Day of Atonement were both fulfilled in the sacrifice of Christ. Christ—'our Passover' (1 Cor. v. 7)—is both our covenant sacrifice and our sin-offering. The Passover indeed itself recalled the thoughts of redemption and covenant; but the service of the Day of Atonement emphasised the conception of sin, and so made a separation between the sin-offering and the material of the common feast. In Christ that which was presented in distinct parts in the types has been brought together: He was and is the sacrifice of the New Covenant: the sacrifice of Atonement: the substance of the Feast.

4. This sacrifice of the New Covenant and of effectual Atonement is, in respect of Christ, in each case one eternal act. He once offered Himself (vii. 27; ix. 25 f.; x. 10), and once entered into the Presence of God in His own Blood (ix. 12). There is no repetition in any way of these acts. But the Feast which was thus provided continues for man's sustenance while the world lasts. Christ communicates to His people, in His appointed way, the virtue of His life and death.

5. The earthly altar is the Cross, from which, as including the Crucified Christ, we draw our life and the support of life[1]. The heavenly altar is Christ Himself, on and in Whom we offer all that we are and have, and through Whom we bring all to God.

Regarded in the light of this passage the Holy Eucharist is seen under two aspects as a μετοχή (a participation) and a κοινωνία (a fellowship). The thought of the participation has been adequately guarded, the thought of fellowship is not unfrequently lost sight of. In early writers the fellowship is justly presented as a fellowship of man with man, and as a fellowship of man with God, both realised in and through the Son of man. The first fellowship is represented by 'the one loaf' (ἄρτος), by sharing which we 'the many are one body' (1 Cor. x. 17). For those thus united in Christ the second fellowship becomes possible, and Christians can offer themselves to God and hold converse with Him. The symbolism of 'the loaf' finds a striking illustration in the earliest liturgical prayer which has been preserved to us: Εὐχαριστοῦμέν σοι Πάτερ ἡμῶν ὑπὲρ τῆς ζωῆς καὶ γνώσεως ἧς ἐγνώρισας ἡμῖν διὰ Ἰησοῦ τοῦ παιδός σου (Is. liii.)· σοὶ ἡ δόξα εἰς τοὺς αἰῶνας. Ὥσπερ ἦν τοῦτο τὸ κλάσμα διεσκορπισμένον ἐπάνω τῶν ὀρέων καὶ συναχθὲν ἐγένετο ἕν, οὕτω συναχθήτω σου ἡ ἐκκλησία ἀπὸ τῶν περάτων τῆς γῆς εἰς τὴν σὴν βασιλείαν· ὅτι σοῦ ἐστιν ἡ δόξα καὶ ἡ δύναμις διὰ Ἰησοῦ Χριστοῦ εἰς τοὺς αἰῶνας. The thought of the bringing of man to God in the Holy Communion is expressed by the characteristic Dionysian conception of Σύναξις, which in the Dionysian writings is not the gathering of Christians together, but the gathering of Christians to God: σύναξιν νοητέον οὐ τὴν τοῦ λαοῦ, καθὼς τὴν λέξιν τινὲς σήμερον ἐκλαμβάνονται, ἀλλὰ τὴν πρὸς θεὸν συναγωγὴν καὶ κοινωνίαν

---

[1] The thought is preserved in the words of the prayer before Holy Communion attributed to Ambrose: Summe Sacerdos...qui Te obtulisti Deo Patri hostiam puram et immaculatam in ara crucis pro nobis....

(Pachym. *Paraph. Hier. Eccles.* c. 3). The Father Himself is the Συναγωγός (*Hier. cœl.* c. 1).

In this connexion the words of the Lord gain a fresh force,

κἀγὼ ἐὰν ὑψωθῶ ἐκ τῆς γῆς πάντας ἑλκύσω πρὸς ἐμαυτόν.

Additional Note on xiii. 20. *On the references in the Epistle to the Gospel History.*

The direct references in the Epistle to the facts of the Gospel History are not very numerous, but it can be seen that the record, such as it has been handed down to us in the (Synoptic) Gospels, was constantly present to the mind of the writer.

The Incarnation, as it is described in the Synoptic Gospels and summarily presented by St John, is implied in ii. 14 (μετέσχεν τῶν αὐτῶν) compared with i. 2, 5 (see p. 426); and it is definitely said that the Lord sprang 'out of the tribe Judah' (vii. 14 note). Nothing is said in detail of the Lord's life of silent preparation. On the other hand the general account of the completeness of His experience, as corresponding to that of man 'in all things, sin apart' (iv. 15), necessarily involves the recognition of His perfect growth from stage to stage, and this truth of a complete human development is made clear by the conception of His τελείωσις (see Addit. Note on ii. 10). The Epistle contains no certain reference to the Baptism, but the form in which the quotation from Ps. ii. 7 is given in c. v. 5 suggests the thought that the writer may have had in mind the divine voice at that time (comp. i. 5 note; v. 5). The emphatic assertion of the fact that the Lord was tempted and suffered (ii. 18; iv. 15) probably presupposes a knowledge of the critical Temptation before His public ministry. The proclamation of the Gospel 'through the Lord in whom God spake' (i. 2) is specially noticed (ii. 3), but nothing is said of His works. There can be no doubt that the description of the 'prayers and supplications with strong crying and tears' (v. 7) includes a reference to the Agony, though it may point also to other moments of peculiar trial. The reality (ii. 14) and the voluntariness (ix. 14; comp. *v.* 26) of the Lord's death are marked. He endured a cross (xii. 2; comp. vi. 6). He suffered 'without the gate' (xiii. 12; comp. John xix. 17); and perhaps from among the details of the Passion, there is an allusion to the rending of the veil of the Temple in x. 20. Afterwards God 'brought Him back from the dead' (xiii. 20); and He has ascended (vi. 20; comp. ix. 12, 24), and passed through the heavens (iv. 14; comp. vi. 20), and taken His seat on the Right hand of God (i. 3; iv. 14; viii. 1; x. 12); and now believers look for His Return (ix. 28; comp. i. 6). The mention of 'the Spirit of grace' after the 'Blood of the Covenant' in x. 29 may point to the gift at Pentecost. From first to last through every vicissitude of life the Lord remained absolutely faithful to God in the administration of the Divine Economy (iii. 2 ff.), and sinless (vii. 26).

Additional Note on xiii. 21. *On the Apostolic Doxologies.*

The Doxologies in the N. T. form an interesting study. They are found in each group of the Epistles and in the Apocalypse, and corresponding forms occur in the Synoptic Gospels.

The following table shews the general symmetry of their form:

1. Gal. i. 5   ᾧ [τῷ θεῷ καὶ πατρὶ ἡμῶν]
ἡ δόξα
εἰς τοὺς αἰῶνας τῶν αἰώνων· ἀμήν.

2. Rom. xi. 36   αὐτῷ [τίς ἔγνω νοῦν κυρίου......ὅτι ἐξ αὐτοῦ καὶ δι'
αὐτοῦ καὶ εἰς αὐτὸν τὰ πάντα]
ἡ δόξα
εἰς τοὺς αἰῶνας· ἀμήν.

3. Rom. xvi. 27   μόνῳ σοφῷ θεῷ
διὰ Ἰησοῦ Χριστοῦ [ᾧ]
ἡ δόξα
εἰς τοὺς αἰῶνας· ἀμήν.

4. Phil. iv. 20   τῷ θεῷ καὶ πατρὶ ἡμῶν
ἡ δόξα
εἰς τοὺς αἰῶνας τῶν αἰώνων· ἀμήν.

5. Eph. iii. 21   αὐτῷ [τῷ δυναμένῳ ὑπὲρ πάντα ποιῆσαι...]
ἡ δόξα
ἐν τῇ ἐκκλησίᾳ καὶ ἐν Χριστῷ Ἰησοῦ
εἰς πάσας τὰς γενεὰς τοῦ αἰῶνος τῶν αἰώνων· ἀμήν.

6. 1 Tim. i. 17   τῷ βασιλεῖ τῶν αἰώνων...μόνῳ θεῷ
τιμὴ καὶ δόξα
εἰς τοὺς αἰῶνας τῶν αἰώνων· ἀμήν.

7. 1 Tim. vi. 16   ᾧ [τῷ μακαρίῳ καὶ μόνῳ δυνάστῃ...]
τιμὴ καὶ κράτος
αἰώνιον· ἀμήν.

8. 2 Tim. iv. 18   ᾧ [τῷ κυρίῳ]
ἡ δόξα
εἰς τοὺς αἰῶνας τῶν αἰώνων· ἀμήν.

9. Hebr. xiii. 21   ᾧ [τῷ θεῷ τῆς εἰρήνης or possibly Ἰησοῦ Χριστῷ]
ἡ δόξα
εἰς τοὺς αἰῶνας τῶν αἰώνων· ἀμήν.

10. 1 Pet. iv. 11   ᾧ [τῷ θεῷ, or possibly Ἰησοῦ Χριστῷ]
ἐστὶν
ἡ δόξα καὶ τὸ κράτος
εἰς τοὺς αἰῶνας τῶν αἰώνων· ἀμήν.

11. 1 Pet. v. 11   αὐτῷ [τῷ θεῷ]
τὸ κράτος
εἰς τοὺς αἰῶνας· ἀμήν.

12. 2 Pet. iii. 18   αὐτῷ [τῷ κυρίῳ ἡμῶν καὶ σωτῆρι Ἰησοῦ Χριστῷ]
ἡ δόξα
καὶ νῦν καὶ εἰς ἡμέραν αἰῶνος.

13. Jude 25   μόνῳ θεῷ σωτῆρι ἡμῶν
διὰ Ἰησοῦ Χριστοῦ τοῦ κυρίου ἡμῶν
δόξα μεγαλωσύνη κράτος καὶ ἐξουσία
πρὸ παντὸς τοῦ αἰῶνος καὶ νῦν καὶ εἰς πάντας τοὺς
αἰῶνας· ἀμήν.

14. Apoc. i. 6,   αὐτῷ [τῷ ἀγαπῶντι ἡμᾶς καὶ λύσαντι ἡμᾶς...]
ἡ δόξα καὶ τὸ κράτος
εἰς τοὺς αἰῶνας· ἀμήν.

15. Apoc. v. 13   τῷ καθημένῳ ἐπὶ τοῦ θρόνου καὶ τῷ ἀρνίῳ
ἡ εὐλογία καὶ ἡ τιμὴ καὶ ἡ δόξα καὶ τὸ κράτος
εἰς τοὺς αἰῶνας τῶν αἰώνων.
καὶ τὰ τέσσαρα ζῷα ἔλεγον· Ἀμήν.
Compare iv. 11; v. 12; xii. 10 ff.

16. Apoc. vii. 12   Ἀμήν·
ἡ εὐλογία καὶ ἡ δόξα καὶ ἡ σοφία καὶ ἡ εὐχαριστία καὶ
ἡ τιμὴ καὶ ἡ δύναμις καὶ ἡ ἰσχὺς
τῷ θεῷ ἡμῶν
εἰς τοὺς αἰῶνας τῶν αἰώνων [· ἀμήν].
Compare v. 10.

Compare Lk. ii. 14; xix. 38; [Matt. vi. 13]. Rom. i. 25; ix. 5.

Several points at once offer themselves for notice.

(1) All the Doxologies except (12) and perhaps (16) are closed by Ἀμήν. Notice (15), (16).

(2) They exhibit singular variety in detail. Two only are substantially identical in form ; (1), (4). Compare also (2), (8).

(3) Three are directly addressed to Christ ; (8), (12), (14), and possibly also (9), (10).

(4) In one case the verb is expressed in the indicative (10). In some cases the phrase appears to be affirmative; (7), (11), (12): in others it appears to be precatory ; (3), (5), (13). In most cases it is difficult to determine which interpretation is most natural.

(5) In two cases the ascription of glory to God is made through Christ ; (3), (13).

The (first) Epistle of Clement offers a remarkable series of Doxologies, which reproduce the three chief types: (1) ᾧ [*i.e.* τῷ θεῷ] ἡ δόξα εἰς τοὺς αἰῶνας τῶν αἰώνων· ἀμήν (38, 43, 50 ; comp. 45); (2) ᾧ [τῷ δεσπότῃ τῶν ἁπάντων or possibly Ἰησοῦ Χριστῷ] ἡ δόξα καὶ ἡ μεγαλωσύνη... (20 ; comp. 58, 61); (3) δι' οὗ [Ἰησοῦ Χριστοῦ] ἐστὶν αὐτῷ ἡ δόξα...(58).

ON THE USE OF THE OLD TESTAMENT
IN THE EPISTLE.

ὅϲΑ προεγράφη, πάντΑ εἰϲ τὴν ἡμετέρΑν διδΑϲκΑλίΑν ἐγράφη, ἵνΑ διὰ τῆϲ ὑπομονῆϲ κΑὶ διὰ τῆϲ πΑρΑκλήϲεωϲ τῶν γρΑφῶν τὴν ἐλπίδΑ ἔχωμεν.

Rom. xv. 4.

ON THE USE OF THE OLD TESTAMENT
IN THE EPISTLE.

A study of the quotations from the O. T. in the Epistle brings The quotations a clue to the understanding of Revelation. light upon the whole relation of the Old Testament to the New, and upon the manner of the divine education of the world. Taken in connexion with their contexts they suggest a general outline of prophetic interpretation, and indicate the steps by which the chosen people were led onwards to prepare the birthplace of the Christ and the first home of the Gospel. At the same time they offer a clue to the understanding of the present and eternal revelation of God through the Spirit sent to us in Christ's name (John xiv. 26).

In order to realise more thoroughly these general lessons of the quotations, it is desirable to notice some external features of interest which they offer in regard to (i) their range, (ii) the mode of citation, and (iii) their text, before considering the principles of interpretation (iv) which they involve.

i. Range of the Quotations.

The quotations in the order of the Books of the Old Testament The quotations in the Epistle. are the following:

1. Gen. ii. 2 : c. iv. 4 ff. εἴρηκεν γάρ που.
2. — xxi. 12 : c. xi. 18, πρὸς ὃν ἐλαλήθη. Comp. Rom. ix. 7.
3. — xxii. 16 f. : c. vi. 13 f. ὁ θεός...ὤμοσεν...λέγων.
4. Ex. xix. 12 f. : c. xii. 20 τὸ διαστελλόμενον.
5. — xxv. 40 : c. viii. 5, φησίν. Comp. Acts vii. 44.
6. Deut. xxxi. 6, 8 : c. xiii. 5 αὐτὸς γὰρ εἴρηκεν.

7. Deut. xxxii. 35 : c. x. 30 οἴδαμεν τὸν εἰπόντα. Comp. Rom. xii. 19.

8. —   xxxii. 36 : c. x. 30.

9. —   xxxii. 43 (LXX.); comp. Ps. xcvii. 7 : c. i. 6 λέγει.

10. 2 Sam. vii. 14 : c. i. 5 καὶ πάλιν [εἶπεν]. Comp. 2 Cor. vi. 18; Apoc. xxi. 7.

11. Is.   viii. 17 f. : c. ii. 13 καὶ πάλιν [λέγων].

12. Jer.   xxxi. 31 f. : c. viii. 8 ff. μεμφόμενος λέγει [ὁ κύριος]. c. x. 15 μαρτυρεῖ τὸ πνεῦμα τὸ ἅγιον.

13. Hagg. ii. 6 : c. xii. 26 ff. ἐπήγγελται λέγων.

14. Ps.   ii. 7 : c. i. 5 τίνι εἶπεν...; c. v. 5 ὁ λαλήσας πρὸς αὐτόν (comp. vii. 28). Comp. Acts iv. 25 ff. ; Apoc. ii. 27; xii. 5; xiv. 1; xix. 15.

15. —   viii. 5 ff. : c. ii. 6 ff. διεμαρτύρατο δέ πού τις. Comp. Eph. i. 22.

16. —   xxii. 22 : c. ii. 11 f. οὐκ ἐπαισχύνεται [ὁ ἁγιάζων] ἀδελφοὺς αὐτοὺς καλεῖν.

17. —   xl. 6 ff. : c. x. 5 ff. εἰσερχόμενος εἰς τὸν κόσμον λέγει.

18. —   xlv. 6 f. : c. i. 8 f. πρὸς δὲ τὸν υἱὸν [λέγει].

19. —   xcv. 7 ff. : c. iii. 7 ff. λέγει τὸ πνεῦμα τὸ ἅγιον. c. iv. 1 ff. καθὼς εἴρηκεν [ὁ θεός].

20. —   cii. 25 ff. : c. i. 10 ff. καὶ [πρὸς τὸν υἱὸν λέγει].

21. —   civ. 4 : c. i. 7 λέγει.

22. —   cx. 1 : c. i. 13 πρὸς τίνα...εἴρηκεν; (comp. i. 3; viii. 1; x. 12 f.; xii. 2). Comp. Matt. xxii. 44 and parr.; Acts ii. 34.

23. —   cx. 4 : c. v. 6, 10 λέγει [ὁ θεός]; (vi. 20); c. vii. 11 ff., 21 διὰ τοῦ λέγοντος.

24. Prov. iii. 11 f. : c. xii. 5 f. ἥτις (ἡ παράκλησις) διαλέγεται. Comp. Apoc. iii. 19.

To these must be added the following passages which are used verbally though not formally quoted:

25. Gen. xiv. 17 ff. : c. vii. 1 ff.

26. Ex.   xxiv. 8 : c. ix. 20.

27. Num. xii. 7 : c. iii. 1 ff.

28. Hab. ii. 3 f. : c. x. 37. Comp. Gal. iii. 11; Rom. i. 17.

29. Ps.   cxviii. 6 : c. xiii. 6.

Besides these quotations there are man, passages with clear Allusions. reminiscences of the language of the LXX. and references to the contents of the Old Testament.

Gen. i. 11 f. :	c. vi. 7
— iii. 17 f. :	c. vi. 8
[— iv. 4 :	c. xi. 4]
— iv. 10 :	... c. xii. 24
— v. 24 :	c. xi. 5 f.
— vi.	c. xi. 7
— xii. 1 ; xxiii. 4 :	c. xi. 8, 9
— xiv. 17 ff. :	c. vii. 1 ff.
— xviii., xix. :	... c. xiii. 2
— xxii. 1 f. :	... c. xi. 17
— xxii. 17 :	... c. xi. 12
— xxiii. 4 :	... c. xi. 13
— xxv. 33 :	c. xii. 16
— xxvii.	... c. xi. 20
— xlvii. 31 (differs from Hebr.) : ...	... c. xi. 21
— xlviii. 16, 20	... c. xi. 21
— l. 24 f. :	... c. xi. 22
[Ex. ii. 2, 11 :	... c. xi. 23]
— xii. 21 ff. :	... c. xi. 28
— xvi. 33 :	... c. ix. 4
[— xix. 10 :	... c. ix. 13]
— xix. 16 ; Deut. v. 23, 25 f. : ...	c. xii. 19
— xxvi. 33 :	c. ix. 2 f.
[— xxx. 10 :	... c. ix. 7]
Lev. vii. 12 ; Ps. cxv. (cxvi.) 17 : ...	c. xiii. 15
— xvi. 2, 12 :	... c. vi. 19
— xvi. 18 :	c. ix. 12 f.
— xvi. 27 :	c. xiii. 11, 13
Num. xii. 7 :	c. iii. 1 ff.
— xiv. 32 :	... c. iii. 17
— xvi. 38 :	... c. xii. 3
[— xvii. 8 ; xix. 9 :	c. ix. 4, 13]
— xxiv. 6 (differs from Hebr.) : ...	... c. viii. 2
Deut. iv. 11 f. :	c. xii. 18 f.

Deut. iv. 24 :	...	...	...	...	c. xii. 29
— ix. 19 :	...	...	...	...	c. xii. 21
— xvii. 6 :	...	...	...	...	... c. x. 28
— xxix. 18 :	...	...	...	...	... c. xii. 15
Is. xxvi. 11 :	...	...	...	...	... c. x. 27
— — 20 :	...	...	...	...	... c. x. 37
— xxxv. 3 (comp. Prov. iv. 26) :		...		...	... c. xii. 12
— xli. 8 f. :	...	...	...	...	... c. ii. 16
— xlv. 17 :	...	...	...	...	... c. v. 9
— liii. 12 :	...	...	...	...	... c. ix. 28
— lxiii. 11; lv. 3 :	...	...	...		c. xiii. 20
Dan. vi. 22 :	...	...	...	...	... c. xi. 33
Hos. xiv. 2 (comp. Is. lvii. 19 Hebr.) :					... c. xiii. 15
Zech. vi. 11 ff. : ...		...	...	...	... c. x. 21
— ix. 11 :	...	...	...	...	c. xiii. 20
Ps. lxix. 9 (lxxxix. 50) :		...	...	...	... c. xi. 26
— xxxiv. 14 : ...		...	...	...	... c. xii. 14
Prov. iv. 26 :	...	...	...	...	... c. xii. 13

Distribution.

Reckoning direct quotations and allusions there are

	Quotations	Allusions
Pentateuch	12	39
Historical Books	1	—
Prophets		
Isaiah	1	7
Jeremiah	1	—
Daniel	—	1
Hosea	—	1
Habakkuk	1	—
Zechariah	—	2
Haggai	1	—
In all	4	11
Psalms	11	2
Proverbs	1	1
	29	53

General remarks.

Several reflections at once arise from this enumeration.

1. Of the twenty-nine passages quoted twenty-three are taken from the Pentateuch and the Psalms; the fundamental Law, and the Book of common devotion.

The absence of detailed illustrations from the history of the kingdom, and the fewness of the references to the teaching of the prophets, are both striking facts.

2. On the other hand no difference is stated or implied as to the authority of the Books which are quoted. All are placed upon the same level. All are, so to speak, 'Law.' Compare 1 Cor. xiv. 21 ἐν τῷ νόμῳ (Isaiah); John x. 34; xv. 25 ἐν τῷ νόμῳ (Psalms); John xii. 34; Rom. iii. 19.

3. It is yet more remarkable that, with two exceptions (2 Sam. vii. 14; Is. viii. 17 f.), all the primary passages which are quoted to illustrate the true nature of the Person and Work of Christ are taken from the Psalms. No direct prophetic word is quoted. Nor again is anything quoted from the Prophets on the inefficiency of ritual sacrifices. The use made of the symbolism of the Mosaic worship is essentially distinct.

4. The large proportion of passages taken verbally from the Greek Psalter points to the familiar use of the Book both by the writer and by the readers. Under this aspect the absence of verbal coincidences with the Psalms apart from quotations from them is remarkable.

5. Of the *twenty-nine* passages which are reckoned as direct quotations *twenty-one* are peculiar to the writer of the Epistle. Of the remaining eight one is quoted also in the Synoptic Gospels and in St Paul (Ps. cx. 1): one by St Stephen (Ex. xxv. 40): two by St Paul (Acts, Eph.), and in the Apocalypse (2 Sam. vii. 14; Ps. ii. 7): four by St Paul in the Acts and in his Epistles (Gen. xxi. 12; Deut. xxxii. 35; Ps. viii. 5 ff.; Hab. ii. 3 f.).

There are no quotations from the Apocryphal Books of the Greek Bible, though the incidents described in 2 Macc. vi., vii. are referred to (Hebr. xi. 35).

It would be of great interest to determine, if there were adequate evidence, how far the quotations are connected with the Lessons or Psalms of particular days. None of the quotations from the Psalms are taken from the Psalms known to have been appointed for use on the successive days of the week in the Temple (Pss. xxiv., xlviii., lxxxii., xciv., lxxxi., xcii.), nor from the Lesser (Pss. cxiii.—cxviii.) or Greater (cxx.—cxxxvi.) or Daily Hallel (cxlvi.—cl.). Comp. Grätz, *Monatschrift f. Gesch. u. Wissenschaft d. Judenthums* 1878, 217 ff.; 1879, 193 ff.

ii. *The Mode of Citation.*

The human author never named.

The quotations are without exception made anonymously. There is no mention anywhere of the name of the writer (iv. 7 is no exception to the rule).

The Speaker is God.

God is presented as the speaker through the person of the prophet, except in the one place where He is directly addressed (ii 6 ff. διεμαρτύρατο δέ πού τις); e.g.

i. 5 τίνι γὰρ εἶπεν (sc. ὁ θεός) (Ps. ii. 7); i. 7 λέγει (Ps. civ. 4); 13 εἴρηκεν (Ps. cx. 1); v. 5 ὁ λαλήσας πρὸς αὐτόν (Ps. ii. 7).

Christ.

In two places the words are attributed to Christ.

ii. 11, 13 οὐκ ἐπαισχύνεται ἀδελφοὺς αὐτοὺς καλεῖν λέγων (Ps. xxii. 22); x. 5 ff. εἰσερχόμενος εἰς τὸν κόσμον λέγει...τότε εἴρηκεν (Ps. xl. 6 ff.).

The Holy Spirit.

In two other places the Holy Spirit specially is named as the speaker:

iii. 7 ff. καθὼς λέγει τὸ πνεῦμα τὸ ἅγιον (Ps. xcv. 7 ff.); x. 15 μαρτυρεῖ ἡμῖν καὶ τὸ πνεῦμα τὸ ἅγιον (Jer. xxxi. 31 ff.). Comp. ix. 8 τοῦτο δηλοῦντος τοῦ πνεύματος τοῦ ἁγίου.

But it is worthy of notice that in each of these two cases the words are also quoted as the words of God (iv. 7; viii. 8).

Even where the prophet speaks in his own person.

This assignment of the written word to God, as the Inspirer of the message, is most remarkable when the words spoken by the prophet in his own person are treated as divine words, as words spoken by Moses:

i. 6 (Deut. xxxii. 43); iv. 4; comp. *vv.* 5, 7, 8 (Gen. ii. 2); x. 30 (Deut. xxxii. 36); and by Isaiah:

ii. 13 (Is. viii. 17 f.).

Compare also xiii. 5 (Deut. xxxi. 6).

Generally it must be observed that no difference is made between the word spoken and the word written. For us and for all ages the record is the voice of God.

The record is the voice of God; and as a necessary consequence the record is itself living. It is not a book merely. It has a vital connexion with our circumstances and must be considered in connexion with them. The constant use of the present tense in quotations emphasises this truth:

No difference between the word spoken and written.

ii. 11 οὐκ ἐπαισχύνεται...καλεῖν, λέγων.

iii. 7 καθὼς λέγει τὸ πνεῦμα τὸ ἅγιον.

xii. 5 ἥτις ὑμῖν...διαλέγεται.

Comp. xii. 26 ἐπήγγελται λέγων.

There is nothing really parallel to this general mode of quotation in the other books of the N.T. Where the word λέγει occurs elsewhere, it is for the most part combined either with the name of the prophet or with 'Scripture': e.g.

No parallel to this usage in other parts of the N. T.

Rom. x. 16 Ἡσαίας λέγει.

— x. 19 Μωυσῆς λέγει.

— xi. 9 Δαυεὶδ λέγει.

— iv. 3 ἡ γραφὴ λέγει.

— ix. 17 λέγει ἡ γραφή &c.

When God is the subject, as is rarely the case, the reference is to words directly spoken by God:

2 Cor. vi. 2 λέγει γὰρ (ὁ θεός).

Rom. ix. 15 τῷ Μωυσεῖ λέγει.

——— 25 ἐν τῷ Ὡσηὲ λέγει.

Compare Rom. xv. 9—12 (γέγραπται...λέγει...Ἡσαίας λέγει). The two passages in the Epistle to the Ephesians (iv. 8; v. 14 διὸ λέγει) appear to be different in kind.

This 'personal' character of citation is the more significant when it is remembered how frequent elsewhere (in St Paul for example) are the forms (καθὼς) γέγραπται (16 times in the Epistle to the Romans),

Absence of the phrase 'it is written.'

ἡ γραφὴ λέγει, and the like, which never occur in the Epistle to the Hebrews; and whereas St Paul not unfrequently quotes the words of God as 'Scripture' simply (*e.g.* Rom. ix. 17), it has been seen that in this Epistle prophetic words recorded in Scripture are treated as 'words of God.'

Nor can it be maintained that the difference of usage is to be explained by the difference of readers, as being Jews, for in the Gospels γέγραπται is the common formula (nine times in St Matthew).

No anticipation of a N. T.   In connexion with this belief in the present, personal, voice of God in the O.T. it may be noticed that there is no indication of any anticipation of a written N.T. The record of Christ's Coming is spoken of as traditional: ii. 3 f., though the authority of the Apostles is implied (ἐβεβαιώθη), as that which had been justified by the experience of life.

A partial parallel in the Epistles of Clement and Barnabas.   The method of citation on which we have dwelt is peculiar to the Epistle among the writings of the New Testament; but it is interesting to notice that there is in the Epistle of Clement a partial correspondence with it. Clement generally quotes the LXX. anonymously. He attributes the prophetic words to God (15, 21, 46); to Christ (16, 22); to the Holy Word (13, 56); to the Holy Spirit (13, 16). But he also, though rarely, refers to the writers (26 Job; 52 David), and to Books (57 Proverbs, 'the all-virtuous Wisdom'); and not unfrequently uses the familiar form γέγραπται (14, 39 &c.). The quotations in the Epistle of Barnabas are also commonly anonymous, but Barnabas mentions several names of the sacred writers, and gives passages from the Law, the Prophets and the Psalms with the formula 'the Prophet saith' (vi. 8; 2; 4, 6).

iii. *The Text of the Quotations.*

The quotations taken mainly from the LXX.   The text of the quotations agrees in the main with some form of the present text of the LXX. This will be seen from a brief review of those quotations which seem to be more than passing allusions to phrases and details of the Old Testament. In two cases however it is possible that adaptations of Scriptural language used by the writer (9, 10) were taken from a written source. Compare Dr Hatch, *Essays on Biblical Greek*, Essay v., pp. 203 ff.

1. Gen. ii. 2: Hebr. iv. 4 (εἴρηκεν γάρ που). The subject (ὁ θεός) is added and ἐν (before τῇ ἡμέρᾳ) as in many MSS. of LXX. Otherwise the words agree with LXX. text. Ἔργων answers to a sing. noun in the original.

2. — xiv. 17 f.: Hebr. vii. 1 ff. Not expressly quoted. The text agrees with LXX., which agrees with Hebr.

3. — xxi. 12: Hebr. xi. 18 (ἐλαλήθη). Agrees verbally with LXX., which agrees with Hebr.

4. — xxii. 16 f.: Hebr. vi. 13 f. (ὁ θεὸς...ὤμοσε...λέγων). LXX. and Hebr. (πληθυνῶ) τὸ σπέρμα σου for σε.

5. Ex. xix. 13: Hebr. xii. 20 (τὸ διαστελλόμενον). A free quotation.

6. — xxiv. 8: Hebr. ix. 20 (λέγων). The text gives ἐνετείλατο for διέθετο, θεός for κύριος, τοῦτο for ἰδού against LXX. and Hebr.

7. — xxv. 40: Hebr. viii. 5 (φησίν). The text gives δειχθέντα, as in some MSS. of LXX. for δεδειγμένον. The LXX. agrees with the Hebr.

8. Num. xii. 7: Hebr. iii. 2, 5, 6. Not expressly quoted. The text agrees with the LXX., which agrees with Hebr.

9. Deut. xxxi. 6, 8: Hebr. xiii. 5 (εἴρηκεν). Ἀνῶ an unusual word in the text and in the LXX. Comp. Gen. xxviii. 15; Josh. i. 5.

10. — xxxii. 35: Hebr. x. 30 (τὸν εἰπόντα). The quotation, which occurs again verbally in Rom. xii. 19, differs from LXX., and is nearer to Hebr.

11. — xxxii. 36: Hebr. x. 30 (τὸν εἰπόντα). Agrees with LXX. and Hebr.

12. — xxxii. 43: Hebr. i. 6 (λέγει). Not in Hebr. Comp. Ps. xcvi. (xcvii.) 7.

13. 2 Sam. vii. 14: Hebr. i. 5 (εἶπεν). Agrees with LXX. and Hebr.

14. Ps. ii. 7: Hebr. i. 5 (εἶπεν); v. 5 (ὁ λαλήσας). Agrees with LXX. and Hebr.

15. — viii. 5 ff.: Hebr. ii. 5 ff. (διεμαρτύρατο δέ πού τις λέγων). Text agrees with LXX., omitting first clause of v. 7, and this agrees with Hebr.

16. — xxii. (xxi.) 22: Hebr. ii. 12 (λέγων). Text gives ἀπαγγελῶ for διηγήσομαι of LXX. The LXX. agrees with Hebr.

17. — xl. (xxxix.) 6—8: Hebr. x. 5—10 (λέγει). Differs considerably from Hebr., agreeing with LXX. verbally except in reading οὐκ εὐδόκησας for οὐκ ἤτησας.

18. — xlv. (xliv.) 6 f.: Hebr. i. 8 f. (λέγει). Agrees with LXX. and Hebr.

19. — xcv. (xciv.) 7—11: Hebr. iii. 7 ff. (λέγει τὸ πνεῦμα τὸ ἅγιον). The connexion in v. 10 is altered. Otherwise the text agrees substantially with Alex. text of LXX. and differs in v. 10 from Hebr.

19*. — xcvii. (xcvi.) 7. See Deut. xxxii. 43.

20. — cii. (ci.) 25 ff.: Hebr. i. 10 ff. (λέγει). Agrees with LXX., differing in several slight points from Hebr. (κατ᾽ ἀρχάς, καὶ (ὡσεί), ἑλίξεις, ἐκλείψουσιν).

21. — civ. (ciii.) 4: Hebr. i. 7 (λέγει). Cod. A reads with text πυρὸς φλόγα. Agrees with LXX. and Hebr.

22. — cx. (cix.) 1: Hebr. i. 13 (εἴρηκε). Agrees with LXX. and Hebr.

23. — cx. (cix.) 4: Hebr. v. 6 (λέγει); vii. 7, 21 (μαρτυρεῖ, ὁ λέγων). Agrees with LXX. and Hebr.

24. — cxviii. (cxvii.) 6. Hebr. xiii. 6. Not expressly quoted. Agrees with LXX. and Hebr.

25. Prov. iii. 11 f.: Hebr. xii. 5 f. (ἥτις διαλέγεται). Text gives παιδεύει for ἐλέγχει and so A. Differs from Hebr.

26. Is. viii. 17 f. : Hebr. ii. 13 (λέγων). Agrees with LXX. and Hebr.

27. Jerem. xxxi. (xxxviii.) 31 ff. : Hebr. viii. 8 ff. (λέγει). Comp. c. x. 15 ff. The text agrees very closely with LXX. and differs greatly from Hebr. in v. 32. See Note.

28. Hab. ii. 3, 4 : Hebr. x. 37 f. Not expressly quoted. The text agrees with LXX., differing from Hebr.

29. Hagg. ii. 6 : Hebr. xii. 26 ff. (λέγων) The quotation is somewhat free, differing from Hebr.

Summarising the results of this enumeration we find that of the General results. quotations

1. Fifteen quotations agree with the LXX. where the LXX. agrees with the Hebrew: 2, 3, 7, 8, 11, 13, 14, 15, 16, 18, 21, 22, 23, 24, 26.

2. Eight quotations agree with the LXX. where it differs from the Hebrew: (1), 17, 19, (20), 25, 27, 28, (29).

3. Three quotations differ from the LXX. and from the Hebrew: 4, 6, 10.

4. Three passages are free renderings of the sense of the words referred to: 5, (9), (12).

Nothing need be said on the quotations in the first group. The quotations in the second group offer several points of interest, for use is made of peculiarities of the LXX. rendering in (17) Ps. xl. (xxxix.) 6—8 σῶμα δὲ κατηρτίσω μοι, (28) Hab. ii. 3 f. ἐὰν ὑποστείληται, (29), Hagg. ii. 6 ἔτι ἅπαξ and (25) Prov. iii. 11 f. μαστιγοῖ.

In the third group one quotation, (10) Deut. xxxii. 35, is found in exactly the same form in Rom. xii. 19; and so also (9) Deut. xxxi. 6, 8 occurs in the same form in Philo, de confus. ling. § 32 (i. p. 430 M.).

Two conclusions appear to follow from the facts :

1. The writer regarded the Greek Version as authoritative; and, it may be added, he nowhere shews any immediate knowledge of the Hebrew text.

2. Certain adaptations and combinations of Scriptural language passed into currency, and came to be treated as phrases of Scripture. The two phrases used in the Epistle may have already found a place in some popular manual.

Compare Matt. xv. 8 (true text) with Clem. R. i. 15 (Is. xxix. 13); Barn. ii. with Just. M. *Dial.* 114 (a combination of Jer. ii. 13 and Is. xvi. 1). The quotation in 1 Cor. ii. 9 (Is. lxiv. 4) is to be thus explained.

For (12) Deut. xxxii. 43 (LXX.) see note on i. 6.

iv. *Interpretation.*

General view.

It has been already observed in the course of the notes that the writer of the Epistle everywhere assumes that there is a spiritual meaning in the whole record of the Old Testament. This deeper sense is recognised in the history both personal (vii. 1 ff.) and national (iv. 1 ff.): in the Mosaic ritual (ix. 8): in the experience of typical characters (ii. 13 note); and in the general teaching (ii. 6 ff.). Every detail in the record is treated as significant; and even the silence of the narrative suggests important thoughts (vii. 3).

Generally it may be said that Christ and the Christian dispensation are regarded as the one end to which the Old Testament points and in which it finds its complete accomplishment, not as though the Gospel were the answer to the riddle of the Law (as is taught in the Letter of Barnabas: see *Introd.* § XIII.), but as being the consummation in life of that which was prepared in life. Those therefore who acknowledged Jesus as the Christ, when they realised His Nature, could not fail to see that He had abrogated the outward system of Judaism by fulfilling it.

It follows that the historical truth of the Scriptural records is everywhere guarded, but the recorded facts are treated as 'signs,' and the believer is led to see in them a fuller meaning as the course of life is unfolded. The records are not changed, but men are changed by gaining deeper insight into nature and history.

The use which the author makes of Holy Scripture is, in other words, not dialectic or rhetorical, but interpretative. The quotations are not brought forward in order to prove anything, but to indicate the correspondences which exist between the several stages in the fulfilment of the divine purpose from age to age. The Christian faith is assumed, and on this assumption the Hebrews are taught to recognise in the Old Testament the foreshadowings of that growing purpose which the Gospel completes and crowns. This being so, the object of the writer is not to shew that Jesus fulfils the idea of the Christ, and that the Christian Church fulfils the idea of Israel, but, taking this for granted, to mark the relation in which the Gospel stands to the Mosaic system, as part of one divine whole. Looking back therefore over the course of the divine discipline of humanity, outlined in the Old Testament, he indicates how Christ, Lawgiver and Priest, fulfilled perfectly the offices which Moses (c. iii.), Aaron (c. v.) and Melchizedek (c. vii.) held in typical and transitory forms; and yet more than this, how as Man He fulfilled the destiny of fallen man through suffering (c. ii.). In regard to God, the whole history of the Bible is, according to the teaching of the Apostle, a revelation of the progress of the unchanging method of salvation through which creation is carried to its issue. In regard to man, it is a revelation of the necessity and the power of faith, by which he attains to a realisation of the eternal and the unseen, through suffering and failure, in fellowship with the Christ (c. xi. 26).

These general remarks require to be justified in somewhat fuller detail. The affirmation of the correspondence of the many stages of life according to that which we speak of as the divine plan contains, as has been already said, the principle which regulates the whole interpretation of Scripture in the Epistle. This principle is plainly laid down in the opening words which announce that there is a divine education of the world. Little by little men are brought to the end for which they were designed, now in one way and now in another. The final revelation in Him Who is Son was preceded by other revelations *in many parts and in many modes*. From the first, in our language of time, there was an end answering to the beginning : a consummation answering to creation : a destiny of humanity answering to its nature.   God *appointed* His Son *heir of all things, through Whom He also made the world.*   In Scripture then we are taught to see how the Son—Son of God and Son of man—reached His heritage in spite of the self-assertion of man whose nature He took to Himself.

1. The Divine purpose for man.

1. The significant connexion in which the writer of the Epistle places the fulfilment of man's destiny with the record of creation suggests a most pregnant figure of the purpose of God for the being whom He made in His own image (Gen. i. 27).   God promised to man 'to enter into His (own) rest' (Ps. xcv. 11).   The rest of God is symbolised by that 'Sabbath' which followed the Hexaemeron (Gen. ii. 1—3).   Nothing therefore less than such a rest of communion with God can satisfy the capacity of man.   Each partial and limited rest points forward to that which is more complete and more far-reaching.   Each promise fulfilled brings the sense of a larger promise.   The promises connected with the possession of Canaan (for example) quickened a hope of far greater blessings than the actual possession gave (Gen. xvii. 8; Lev. xxvi. 4—12; comp. 1 Cor. x. 1 ff.). And we are constrained still to say, whatever may have been attained : *there remaineth a Sabbath-rest for the people of God* (Hebr. iv. 9)   But this 'Sabbath-rest,' the 'rest of God,' can only be enjoyed by those who, as the issue of their discipline, have gained the divine 'likeness' (Gen. i. 26).   In this condition therefore is involved the necessity for the long education of the world, of which the Old Testament is the comprehensive summary[1].

The 'inheritance.'

Meanwhile, during the time of growth, of education, of training, of discipline, there remain for the support and for the guidance of men the two thoughts of 'the inheritance,' and of 'the promise.' The idea of 'inheritance' is that of possession marked by the fulness of right which rests upon the personal position of the heir.

---

[1] Little is said in the Epistle of the relation of Nature to man in regard to the fulness of his hope (Rom. viii. 18 f.), but the 'parables of nature' in c. vi. 7 f., pointing to Gen. i. 11 f., iii. 17 f., indicate the connexion between man and his realm.

Because the heir is what he is, he vindicates his right to that which he claims or holds (compare Additional Note on vi. 12).

The heirship of man to the divine blessing answering to his nature is founded on God's purpose in creation, on the gift of His image with the power of attaining to His likeness. But we are conscious of disorder and corruption. We shrink from that holy Presence in which alone is perfect rest. We lack the qualification of heirs. The normal growth of man into the divine likeness has been interrupted. Hence, lest it should seem that the divine destiny of man had been made void by man's self-will, it has been confirmed by the promise in which God has repeated His counsel of love (iv. 1 ; vi. 13 ff. ; vii. 6 ; viii. 6 ; ix. 15 ; x. 23, 36 ; xi. 9, 11, 17 ; xii. 26).

The 'promise.'

This promise confirming the heirship carries with it the certainty of final victory (i. 13 ; x. 13, 36 f.).

2.   The fulfilment of the divine purpose for man necessarily required a long preparation. Even if he had not fallen he would have needed the discipline of life to reach the divine likeness through a free moral growth. The sinless Son of man 'learnt obedience' (v. 8). As it is, the necessity of discipline is twofold. Divine gifts have to be exercised: and human failures have to be repaired. The capacities and needs of man have to be revealed and satisfied. Thus the purpose of God for man indicated in creation is wrought out in two ways, by that which we may speak of as a natural growth through the unfolding of the life of the nations, and by a special discipline. Both elements are recognised in the Epistle. Melchizedek is set forth as the representative of the natural growth of man in fellowship with the Divine Spirit. The revelation to Israel (the 'Law') is interpreted as the special preparation and foreshadowing of a fellowship of man with God, in spite of sin and death.

2. The course of its fulfilment.

(a)   The appearance of Melchizedek is of deep interest from the point which he occupies in the religious history of the world.   'The King of Salem,' 'the Priest of the Most High God' comes forward suddenly at a time of decisive change (Gen. xiv. 17 ff.), and then he passes away from the record of Scripture. His name does not occur again in the O. T. except in the phrase of the Psalm which is quoted

(a) The natural growth. Melchizedek.

by the writer of the Epistle (Ps. cx. 4); and he is mentioned in the
New Testament only in this Epistle. But the significance of his
single appearance is unmistakeable. He stands out as the representative of the original revelation, of the primitive and normal
relation of God and man, still preserved pure in some isolated tribe.
He is a high-priest, so to speak, of men, of humanity, and not of a
chosen race. He does not derive his office, so far as the record
shews, from any special appointment. He is, as he appears in the
history of revelation, 'without father, without mother, without
genealogy' (vii. 3). In him also civil and religious life appear in
their true unity, as they must be finally united (comp. Zech. vi. 13).
Abraham marks a new departure, the beginning of a new discipline
resting on a personal call (Gen. xii. 1). Experience had shewn
(Gen. xi.) that the natural development of the divine life had been
fatally interrupted. 'But before the fresh order is established we
'have a vision of the old in its superior majesty; and this on the eve
'of disappearance gives its blessing to the new. So the past and
'the future meet, the one bearing witness to an original communion
'of God and man which had been practically lost, the other pointing
'forward to a future fellowship to be established permanently
'without the possibility of loss. At the same time the name of the
'God of the former revelation and of the God of the later revelation
'are set side by side, and identified (Gen. xiv. 22; comp. Deut. xxxii.
'8 f.).' (p. 199; Additional Note on vii. 1.)

(b) The special discipline through Israel and the Christ,

(b) But it is on the special revelation of God through Israel and
the Christ that the writer of the Epistle chiefly dwells. This falls
into two great divisions, corresponding essentially with the two
'ages' which sum up for us the divine history of the world, 'this
age' ('these days') and 'the age to come' (vi. 5). God spake 'in the
prophets' and then 'at the end of these days,' at the close of the
first age, He spake in Him who is Son (i. 1, 2 a).

(a) in the Old Dispensation, and

(a) The special preparatory revelation of God is described in
words which cannot be quoted too often: πολυμερῶς καὶ πολυτρόπως
πάλαι ὁ θεὸς λαλήσας τοῖς πατράσιν ἐν τοῖς προφήταις...(ἐλάλησεν
ἡμῖν...); and it is of interest to notice that in his main argument the

writer dwells by name on the three men who mark the three great epochs in the divine history, Abraham (vi. 13; vii. 1 ff.), Moses (iii. 2 ff.; vii. 14; viii. 5; ix. 19; x. 28; xii. 21), and David (iv. 7); while in his outline of the victories of faith he continues the record through the primitive fathers of mankind, the Patriarchs, the Law-giver and the Conqueror, the Judges, the Prophets, to the heroes of a later age in the last great struggle against heathen tyranny (xi. 35).

Thus the Epistle brings out clearly step by step that the advance towards the realisation of the inheritance of the promises is made through long-suffering and faith (vi. 12). Or, to put the truth in another light, the teaching of the O. T. as a whole is a perpetual looking forward. Under the symbols of earth spiritual thoughts are indicated. Canaan becomes as it were, a sacrament of the Divine Presence and Indwelling (c. iv. 8 f.; Lev. xxvi. 4—12): the Kingdom, a Sacrament of a Divine Sovereignty. Compare c. xi. 13, 26, 39 f.; Matt. v. 5; xxv. 34; James ii. 5; 1 Pet. iii. 9.

(β) The final revelation ἐν υἱῷ—in Him who is not prophet only but Son—is recognised at once in its essential completeness and in its progressive unfolding to men according to their power of apprehension. God 'spake' (ἐλάλησεν) with one absolute message on the verge of the New Order (i. 2), and He speaks still from heaven (xii. 25), not to give any new gospel but to guide men to the fuller understanding of that which they have received. In this sense the old words 'to-day if ye will hear His voice' have a direct application to Christians in every age (iii. 15), especially if it be a period of outward change. There is danger still lest a natural reverence for the Old should deprive believers of sympathetic sensibility for fresh visions of the one Truth. *(β) in the New.*

In this comprehensive view of the whole course of revelation the writer necessarily dwells almost exclusively upon the past. He does not attempt to trace the future action of *the powers of the world to come* which he has realised: it is enough to point out how the divine end, the coming of the new age, was reached. This history offers a figure of that which, as we may expect, still awaits us. Looking *The outlines of the revelation through Israel.*

back we can see, written for our instruction, how God was pleased to use for the fulfilment of His will both the society and the individual, and how He endowed both in due measure with the gifts of the Spirit.   We recognise in the revelation which is recorded in the Old Testament the work of the Messianic nation, 'the people of God, 'the Church' (Ex. xix. 5 f.), and the work of the personal Messiah, typified on the one side by the Davidic king and on the other side by the afflicted and faithful servant of the Lord (comp. Jer. xxxii. 16; xxiii. 6).   Both factors in the accomplishment of the counsel of God must be taken into account.   Both are marked in their main outlines in the Epistle.

(*a*) The work of the Messianic nation.

(*a*)   In dealing with the work of the Messianic nation the writer of the Epistle emphasises the three great stages in the determination of their privileges and their office : i. The original promise; ii. The discipline of the Law; iii. The new promise.   These three crises mark three special forms of the Divine Covenant (Dispensation), by which God has been pleased to enter into a living fellowship with His people, the Covenant of grace, the Covenant of works, and the final Covenant of divine fellowship based on perfect knowledge and sympathy (for διαθήκη see vii. 22 note).

i. The original promise.

i.   The promise to Abraham is given in its final form, when it was repeated 'with an oath' after the surrender of Isaac (c. vi. 13). Only the first clause is quoted, but the whole is necessarily carried with it.   In xi. 8 ff. the salient points in Abraham's life of faith are noticed, and the great end for which he looked: *the city that hath the foundations*.   It was for this the nation was to be disciplined.

ii. The discipline of the Law.

ii.   But it is natural that the writer should speak chiefly of the Law, as moulding day by day the religious life of the Israelite ; and specially, in view of the failures of men, he seeks to interpret the Levitical ritual as a provisional system for atonement.   The Tabernacle with its characteristic institutions, divisions, limited approaches to God, was *a parable* he says *for the time now present* (ix. 9).   It had lessons to teach.   It witnessed to the needs of men ; and yet the whole ritual which it embodied could not reach beyond the outward and visible (ix. 10, 13).   Thus we see in the Epistle that the

Levitical system discharged a two-fold office. It had an educational value, as enforcing the great thoughts of Judaism; and it had also an immediate value, as dealing under the conditions of the Mosaic Covenant with the sins and weaknesses of the people of God.

The latter function of the Law has been already touched upon in considering the provision which was made by the Levitical sacrifices for maintaining and restoring the outward divine fellowship with which it corresponded (p. 288).

The puri-ficatory power of the Levitical ordi-nances.

The educational value of the Levitical system is affirmed in the Epistle both in respect of its general character (viii. 5; ix. 24), and even in details (ix. 21, 23). As a 'copy' (ὑπόδειγμα) it could not but carry the thoughts of the devout worshipper to the archetype: as 'a shadow' it suggested the reality to which it bore witness. The ordinances testified with eloquent insistence to the two central facts of man's inner life, that he is constrained to draw near to God, and that he has no free access to Him. In other words they kept before the faithful Israelite the essential conceptions of man's destiny and man's sin.

Their edu-cational value.

These thoughts were brought out especially by the institutions of the priesthood and the offerings. In both there was a recognition at once of a fundamental need of human life, and of the inadequacy of the manner in which it was met. The priests themselves had no inherent right to the privilege which they were allowed to exercise. They had no personal fitness for approach to the Divine Presence (vii. 27); and they had no continuance in the exercise of their office (vii. 23). The living offerings again were both irrational and involuntary (x. 4), and alien in nature ·from those whom they represented. At the same time priests and offerings were fitted to keep alive the sense of an ideal Son of man who should 'walk with God' according to the purpose of creation, and of a perfect sacrifice rendered in the glad obedience of life and death under the actual circumstances of humanity (vii. 16; x. 5 ff.).

Especially in the priesthood and the offerings.

The 'Law' is thus presented, according to St Paul's image, as the 'tutor' (παιδαγωγός) appointed to lead men to Christ (Gal. iii. 24; comp. 1 Cor. iv. 15) unto the freedom of mature life;

to deepen the feeling of God's righteousness and man's sin, and at the same time to suggest the thought of forgiveness, through which that which was 'naturally' impossible was to be reached in due time, when a new Melchizedek once more in the dignity of a true manhood united for ever the elements of the fulness of life in one Person, as Priest and King.

iii. This consummation was brought emphatically before Israel in a second promise when their first hopes had failed most signally. Looking out on national disruption, overthrow, captivity, the prophet declared that the purpose of God had not failed; that a new Covenant would be established on grace and not on law, spiritual and not external, uniformly efficacious, bringing a complete forgiveness (viii. 7 ff.). So at last Israel was to fulfil its priestly work for the nations to which it was called (Lev. xix. 2), and which for a time it could not face (Ex. xx. 19; Deut. v. 28).

The comprehensiveness of the references to the record of the revelation in the Old Testament will appear in a tabular arrangement.

i. The original promise. The Covenant of grace. Abraham: the Patriarchs.

(a) Abraham. Gen. xxii. 16 f. (comp. xii. 3; xiii. 15 ff.; xvii. 4 ff.): Hebr. vi. 13 ff.; xi. 8 ff.: Gen. xxi. 12: Hebr. xi. 18. Comp. Gen. xxiii. 4: Hebr. xi. 13. Abraham offers an example of faith in self-surrender (xi. 8), patience (9 f.), influence (11 ff.), looking beyond the outward (9 ff.) and through death (17 ff.).

(β) The patriarchs, to whom the promise was repeated, shewed Abraham's faith (xi. 9; 20 ff.).
More was implied in the promise than Abraham obtained (vi. 17, 15).
Hence the full force of 'a seed of Abraham' (ii. 16 note).

ii. The Law. The Covenant of works. Moses: Joshua.

(a) The circumstances of the history.

(1) The lessons of the Exodus. Ps. xcv. 7 ff.; Hebr. iii. 7 ff.; iv. 1 ff.
A continuous revelation bringing with it a continuous trial ('to-day').

(2) The giving of the Law. Ex. xix. 12 f.; Deut. iv. 11 f.; Hebr. xii. 18 ff.
The awfulness of revelation. Physical terrors symbols of the spiritual. Comp. Deut. xxxii. 35 f.; Hebr. x. 30.

(3) The Covenant. Ex. xxiv. 8; Hebr. ix. 19 f.; x. 29. Comp.
       Matt. xxvi. 28.
       A Covenant ratified by death.

(4) The Conquest. Hebr. xi. 30 f.; iv. 8.
       A sign of a truer rest. Gen. ii. 2.

(β) The characteristics of the institutions.

   (1) The Tabernacle. Ex. xvi. 33; xxv. 40; xxvi. 33; xxx. 10;
          Hebr. viii. 5 f.; ix. 1 ff.
          A copy and a shadow.

   (2) The Service. The Day of Atonement. 'The Day.' Lev. xvi.;
          Hebr. vi. 19; ix. 12 f.; 28; x. 4; xiii. 11, 13.
          Essentially provisional, representative, transitory.

iii. The later promise. The Covenant of Divine Fellowship.

   (a) The promise. Jer. xxxi. 31 ff.; Hebr. viii. 8 ff.; x. 15.
          Forgiveness. Personal knowledge of God.

   (β) The conditions. Hagg. ii. 6; Hebr. xii. 26 ff.
          The eternal revealed through the removal of the temporal.

All the quotations are peculiar to the Epistle except those referring to
the promise to Abraham.

Throughout it will be noticed that the words quoted are hints sufficient
to recal to the reader the main thoughts of the passages referred to.

(b) The fulfilment of the great prophetic promise of a dispensa- (b) The
tion of divine fellowship leads to the thought of the work of the personal Messiah.
personal Messiah. The nation is gathered up in its perfect representative: the 'seed' (many *pl.*) in the one 'seed' (*sing.*) (Gal. iii.
16 and Bp Lightfoot's note; 28 f. εἰς; Matt. ii. 15; for the history
of the word 'Christ' see Addit. Note on 1 John v. 1).

The personal Messiah is presented in the Epistle with singular
completeness of portraiture. In no other Book of the New Testament
is He shewn with equal fulness of delineation; and each trait is
connected with some preparatory sign in the Old Testament. In
Him, as has been already indicated in part (Additional Note on ii.
13), i. The Divine Son, ii. The Divine King, iii. The manifestation of
God, iv. The Priest-King, v. The true Man, are perfectly united. He
is all, satisfying every hope and every claim, without change or loss.

i. The Divine Sonship of Christ is proclaimed at the beginning Different
of the Epistle. By this He is distinguished from all earlier Messiah's
messengers of the will of God, and that in respect of His work for Person and Work.

man and of His work for God (ii. 2), of His priesthood and of His sovereignty.

ii.   As Son in this unique sense Christ satisfies all the expectations which were stirred by the glory of the Davidic kingdom (i. 8 f.).

iii.   And yet more than this.   He 'through whom the world was made' (v. 2) is identified with the 'LORD' of the O. T.   The Covenant with Israel finds its issue in the Incarnation (i. 10 ff.).

iv.   But the office of Christ goes beyond Israel.   He fulfils as Priest-King the ethnic type of Melchizedek, in whom the highest authority in civil and religious life is seen united (i. 13; v. 6, 10; vi. 20; vii. 11 ff.; x. 12 f.).

v.   And thus Christ, without the least derogation from His dignity, is recognised as a true man, who reaches through suffering the destiny of fallen humanity (ii. 6 ff.).   In the accomplishment of this work, He fulfilled three marked types of different service, (a) the type of the king rising through sorest tribulation to his throne (ii. 11 f.), (b) the type of the prophet who kept his faith unshaken in the midst of judgments (ii. 13), and (c) the type of the servant who is able to do with perfect obedience the will of God which he knows with perfect understanding (x. 5 f.).

By distinguishing and combining these different aspects of the work of Christ we can see how the manifold teachings of the past in life and in institutions were concentrated on the final revelation of the Gospel.   They had their fulfilment at the Coming of the Christ; and no less the spiritual experiences of those to whom they were first given have an application to Christians still.   Whatever of encouragement was written for Israel on the entrance into Canaan (c. xiii. 5), on the approach to the sanctuary (c. xiii. 6), in the prophetic delineation of the Messianic age (c. xii. 12 f.), and in the words of the wise (c. xii. 5 f.), was of force for the Hebrews in their crisis of trial and is of force for the Church in all time. Counsels of patience (c. x. 37 f.) and warnings of judgment (c. x. 27) from the Prophets and the Law are still addressed to those who are under a divine discipline.   In one sense the revelation given through the Son is final and unchanging (c. x. 26), but its meaning is brought home to believers by a living voice, and we also must listen heedfully if haply the voice may sound in our ears 'To-day' with a fresh message for us (c. iii. 7 &c.).

It is unnecessary to add any comments on this general summary of the lessons which are based upon the quotations in the Epistle. It amply justifies the conclusions which were drawn from a fuller examination of the quotations in the first two chapters (pp. 69 f.). It enables us to feel, as was said there, that the O. T. does not simply contain prophecies, but that it is one vast prophecy, in the record of national fortunes, in the ordinances of a national Law, in the expression of a national hope. Israel in its history, in its ritual, in its ideal, is a unique enigma among the peoples of the world, of which the Christ is the complete solution.

The different aspects of the Christ which have been distinguished above are traced in a wide range of quotations.

Quotations illustrating the Person and Work of the Christ.

i. The Divine Sonship of the Christ. Ps. ii. 7 : Hebr. i. 5 ; v. 5 ; 2 Sam. vii. 14 : Hebr. i. 5 ; Deut. xxxii. 43 (LXX): comp. Ps. xcvii. 7 : Hebr. i. 6.
    His work for man and for God, and His final victory. Comp. Hab. ii. 3 f. : Hebr. x. 37.

ii. The Christ the Sovereign of the Divine Kingdom. Ps. xlv. 6 f. : Hebr. i. 8 f.
    The King with His people. Comp. xii. 28.

iii. The Christ, the revelation of 'the Father' (the Lord). Ps. cii. 25 ff. : Hebr. i. 10 ff.
    The Son the Creator. Comp. i. 2 (xi. 3).

iv. The Christ the Priest-King of humanity. Ps. cx. 1 : Hebr. i. 13 ; x. 12 f.; Ps. cx. 4 : Hebr. v. 6, 10 ; vi. 20 ; vii. 11 ff.
    The work of the Christ for the world. Comp. i. 2 κληρονόμος πάντων.

v. The Christ the Son of man : true, perfect, representative man. Ps. viii. 5 ff. : Hebr. ii. 6 ff. ; Ps. xxii. 22 : Hebr. ii 11 f.; Ps. viii. 17 f. : Hebr. ii. 13 ; Num. xii. 7 : Hebr. iii. 1 ff.; Ps. ii. 7 : Hebr. v. 5 ; Ps. xl. 6 ff. : Hebr. x. 5 ff.
    The Christ fulfils the destiny of man though fallen, and realises the types of king, prophet, lawgiver, high-priest, servant.

The absence of references to Is. liii. is remarkable.

Im-
portance
of the
teaching
on the
O. T. for
ourselves.
The broad principles of the interpretation of Scripture, and the view of the gradual unfolding of the counsel of God through the education of the nations and of the people, which are contained in the Epistle to the Hebrews, are of present importance to ourselves. The lessons of the Old Testament to the Church—the lessons of the Law and the Prophets and the Psalms,—have not as yet been completely learnt. Each age must find in the divine record new teaching. Our fathers were not in a position to learn the social lessons which the Old Testament contains for us. They could not distinguish the many sources from which precious fragments were brought together to contribute to its representative fulness. They could not compare the Sacred Books of Israel, either as to their contents or as to their history, with the Sacred Books of other nations. Fresh materials, fresh methods of inquiry, bring fresh problems and fresh trials. Difficulties of criticism press upon us now. It is well then to be reminded that there have been times of trial at least as sharp as our own. When the Epistle to the Hebrews was written, it might have seemed that there was nothing for the Christian to do but either to cling to the letter of the Jewish Bible or to reject it altogether. But the Church was more truly instructed by the voice of the Spirit; and the answer to the anxious questionings of the first age which the Epistle contains has become part of our inheritance. We know now, with an assurance which cannot be shaken, that the Old Testament is an essential part of our Christian Bible. We know that the Law is neither a vehicle and a veil for spiritual mysteries, as Philo thought, nor a delusive riddle, as is taught in the Epistle of Barnabas (comp. Introd. § XII.). We know this through the trials of other men.

New
lessons
come
through
seeming
loss.
For that new 'voice' on which the Apostle dwells in the Letter was not heard without distressing doubts and fears and sad expectations of loss. Such indeed is the method of the discipline of God at all times. Many must feel the truth by their own experience in the present day, when, as it seems, He is leading His people towards a fuller apprehension of the character of the written word than has hitherto been gained. New voices of God are heard 'to-

day' as in old time, and there is still the same danger of neglecting to hear them. The Hebrews had determined in their own minds the meaning which the divine message should bear: they had given a literal and outward permanence to the institutions of the Old Covenant; and when the voice came to them to leave that which they had identified with their noblest hopes, they were in danger of apostasy.

It may still be so with us, and that too in respect to our view of the Old Testament. It is likely that study will be concentrated on the Old Testament in the coming generation. The subject is one of great obscurity and difficulty where the sources of information are scanty. Perhaps the result of the most careful inquiry will be to bring the conviction that many problems of the highest interest as to the origin and relation of the constituent Books are insoluble. But the student, in any case, must not approach the inquiry with the assumption—sanctioned though it may have been by traditional use—that God must have taught His people, and us through His people, in one particular way. He must not presumptuously stake the inspiration and the divine authority of the Old Testament on any foregone conclusion as to the method and shape in which the records have come down to us. We have made many grievous mistakes in the past as to the character and the teaching of the Bible. The experience may stand us in good stead now. The Bible is the record, the inspired, authoritative record, of the divine education of the world. The Old Testament, as we receive it, is the record of the way in which God trained a people for the Christ *in many parts and in many modes*, the record which the Christ Himself and His Apostles received and sanctioned. How the record was brought together, out of what materials, at what times, under what conditions, are questions of secondary importance. We shall spare no effort in the endeavour to answer them. Every result which can be surely established will teach us something of the manner of God's working, and of the manner in which He provides for our knowledge of it. At the same time we must remember that, here as elsewhere, His ways in the fulfilment of His counsel are, for the most part, not as

The study of the O.T. beset by difficulties which call for patience.

our ways, but infinitely wider, larger, and more varied.   And when
we strive to realise them on the field of life, we must bear ourselves
with infinite patience and reverence as scholars in Christ's School,
scholars of a Holy Spirit, Who is speaking to us as He spoke in old
time.

The history of Judaism a type of divine action.
Whatever else may be obscure, the main outlines of the history
of Israel appear to be unquestionable ; and it is of the greatest
moment for us as Christians to strive, as we may, to enter into the
spirit of Judaism ; to study it not as a stereotyped system but as an
advancing manifestation of the Living God; to see in it examples and
types of the various modes in which God deals with His people ; to
recognise from the manifold fortunes of His kingdom in old time that
He applies, enforces, interprets, in new and unexpected ways, what He
has once given ; to learn somewhat better, from an apprehension of
the prophetic work, that He chooses His own instruments freely, that
He speaks through the conflicts of social and political life, that the
organisation which He has established for the due fulfilment of His
service does not limit the manner of His operation, that He provides
for progress as well as for order, or (may we not say?) that He
provides for progress because He provides for order.

If we regard Judaism in this way, the history of Christianity itself
will be quickened for us with a new life.   We shall have before our
eyes what is really by anticipation a divine commentary upon its
most perplexing passages.   Acts of faithlessness and apostasy in the
history of the Church, self-willed divisions, premature settlements of
practice or doctrine, will appear at once more significant and, for
those who inherit the burden which they impose, more endurable.
The record of the history of Israel is a concrete philosophy of history.
If we read its meaning we shall be better enabled, and then only
truly enabled, to look with hope upon the chequered annals of
Christendom without extenuating the sins and issues of sin by
which they are defaced.

The social aspect of the Gospel.
In this respect the Epistle to the Hebrews brings before us a forgotten aspect of the divine working.   It marks, as we have seen, the
office of the Messianic nation no less than the office of a personal

Messiah. By doing so its teaching falls in with the tendency of modern thought. Once again the social, the corporate view of life is gaining power if not predominance. By the help of this Book we can see how the view was recognised in the apostolic outline of the Faith, and gain encouragement for studying it with confidence and hope.

In the pursuit of this inquiry the Epistle reminds us that there is a correspondence between the Word of God in the heart, and the written Word: that both deal with the fulness of hope in man and in nature (iv. 11, 13). Trusting to this living Word therefore we must gladly allow ourselves to be 'borne forward' to further knowledge, leaving that which we have already gained, or rather regarding it as our starting-point (vi. 1). Our highest joy is to recognise the divine law that each fulfilment opens a vision of something yet beyond. The Wilderness, Jordan, Canaan, necessarily take a new meaning as the experience of man extends. The outward ritual, the earthly kingdom, suggested hopes which they could not satisfy. So perhaps it is still. At least the words of the Psalmist as they fall on our ears every morning have an application which is never exhausted : *To-day if ye will hear His voice* (iii. 14, 15). As yet we do not see the end.

INDEX